Third Edition

HUMAN DEVELOPMENT
ACROSS THE LIFESPAN

John S. Dacey
Boston College

John F. Travers
Boston College

Boston, Massachusetts   Burr Ridge, Illinois   Dubuque, Iowa
Madison, Wisconsin   New York, New York   San Francisco, California   St. Louis, Missouri

Book Team

Executive Publisher *Edgar J. Laube*
Acquisitions Editor *Steven Yetter*
Developmental Editor *Ted Underhill*
Production Editor *Kristine Queck*
Proofreading Coordinator *Carrie Barker*
Designer *K. Wayne Harms*
Art Editor *Rachel Imsland*
Photo Editor *Rose Deluhery*
Production Manager *Beth Kundert*
Production/Costing Manager *Sherry Padden*
Marketing Manager *Carla Aspelmeier*
Copywriter *Jennifer Smith*

Basal Text *10/12 Garamond*
Display Type *Garamond Book*
Typesetting System *Macintosh/QuarkXPress*
Paper Stock *50# Mirror Matte*

McGraw-Hill

A Division of The **McGraw·Hill** *Companies*

President and Chief Executive Officer *Thomas E. Doran*
Vice President of Production and Business Development *Vickie Putman*
Vice President of Sales and Marketing *Bob McLaughlin*
Director of Marketing *John Finn*

The credits section for this book begins on page 595 and is considered an extension of the copyright page.

Cover image © Tony Stone Images/Chicago Inc.; Cover background from Digital Stock

Copyedited by Laurie McGee; proofread by Rose R. Kramer

Permissions research by Karen Dorman

Library of Congress Catalog Card Number: 95–75268

ISBN 0–697–21004–9

Printed in the United States of America

10 9 8 7 6 5 4 3

This book is dedicated with deep affection to the two people who have helped us the most—Linda Schulman and Barbara Travers, our wives.

Brief Contents

Contents

🌳 Part Three

Infancy

🌳 Part Four

Early Childhood

🌳 **Part Five**

Middle Childhood

🌳 **Part Six**

Adolescence

An Applied View

A Multicultural View

What's Your View?

Preface

As we move toward the twenty-first century, our society has clearly adopted a belief that all individuals should have the opportunity to develop their potential to the fullest. One way of achieving this goal is to know as much as possible about human development—how we change from the helplessness of infancy to the competence of adulthood to the wisdom of old age.

Perhaps the human saga is not written as clearly as we would like. As Thomas Jefferson once noted, although the human condition is not open to complete scrutiny, it is, nevertheless, susceptible to considerable improvement. Clues providing insights into the riddle of human development are beginning to multiply. Genetic discoveries are occurring at a rate that can only be described as breathtaking: The gene that causes cystic fibrosis has been identified; genetic markers that point to a family disposition for breast cancer are known; the march to identify all the human genes (the Human Genome Project) continues unabated.

As the population of our nation continues to change, we have become more sensitive to the influence that culture exerts on development. We recognize that all children do not learn in the same manner; all cultures do not view adolescence from the same perspective; not all cultures place the same value on work. Never before has it been so clear that development results from the interaction of heredity and environment and that neglect of either side of our equation can only lead to damaging misinterpretations.

Basic Themes of Human Development Across the Lifespan

Reflecting the exciting changes that are taking place in our knowledge of human development, we have woven our narrative around several integrating themes: the biopsychosocial model, the cultural context of development, the role of gender, and applications to daily living. We return to these themes in each chapter as a means of making more meaningful the basic knowledge of human development.

The Biopsychosocial Model

The biopsychosocial model will help you to integrate the wealth of information that you will find in the pages to come. If you think of lifespan development as the product of the interaction of biological, psychological, and social forces, you will better appreciate the complexity of development. For example, biological influences on development range from the role of genes in development to adult health concerns; psychological influences include all aspects of cognitive and personality development; social influences refer to such powerful forces as family, school, peers, and the media. The biopsychosocial model helps to explain how the interaction of these forces is the key to understanding human development.

Cultural Influences on Development

Our goal in urging you to adopt a multicultural perspective is to help you develop a greater understanding of those who seem "different." If you adopt this perspective, you will come to realize that different people have different worldviews that decisively influence their thinking. In this way, you can work, play, or study more congenially with others, thus fostering more positive relations in our society. People from different cultures do *not* all think alike and, as we will stress, these differences are not deficits. Recognizing how diverse people are in their thinking and behavior will help you to identify and comprehend variations in how individuals are raised, how they think, and how they become functioning members of their culture. Since we feel so strongly about this matter, you will find a discussion of multicultural issues in each chapter; we also open several sections of the book with a multicultural perspective on the issues to be discussed.

The Role of Gender

As concern about gender equity has received more publicity, the stereotypes about males and females are slowly eroding. If, however, people are treated according to stereotypical characteristics, then their potential is immediately limited. Although gender stereotyping is only one part of the gender story, it illustrates the importance of the relationship between gender and development. For example, children at an early age construct social categories from the world around them, attach certain characteristics to these categories, and then label the categories. This process may be positive because it helps to organize the world; it may also be negative if the characteristics associated with the category are limiting—"girls just can't do math." We'll examine how this theme plays out, both positively and negatively, throughout the lifespan.

Applications to Daily Living

The study of lifespan development is an exciting, rapidly changing, and highly relevant subject that can shed light on the developmental changes you witness in yourself and see in your friends and family members of all ages. To help you put the theories and research of this book into a meaningful framework, we have written several *An Applied View* boxes for each chapter. These range from the appeal of street gangs for some children to the role of television in a child's life to an adolescent's search for identity to problems that the adult children of alcoholics encounter.

We have also included boxes that ask you to interact with the text's material. Called *What's Your View?*, these boxes are intended to have you think about and act on topics you have just read about and discussed. What does *your* knowledge and *your* experience tell you about these matters? We are not presenting answers in these boxes. Rather we hope you apply your best judgment to the questions raised.

Major Changes in the Third Edition

Thanks to suggestions from students who used the second edition of our text and the insightful comments of reviewers, we have made the following substantial changes in the second edition.

- A major change in this edition is the incorporation of a student study guide throughout the text. After each major section of a chapter, we have provided a set of between four and seven fill-in-the-blank questions, together with the correct answers. These are meant to offer immediate review of material as you read through the chapter. At the end of each chapter, we have provided a set of 15 to 20 multiple-choice questions and their answers so that you may review your knowledge of the entire chapter. Professors may well use some of each type of questions on their tests, so the questions are not only reviews, but also may be previews of "coming attractions."

- Another major change involves the chapter on "troubled adolescents" in the previous edition of this book. A number of reviewers have suggested that this chapter, which addresses problems that are serious for only about 10 percent of the teen population, is an overemphasis on the difficulties of adolescence, which has an unwarranted reputation as a particularly troubled period of life. In addition, it must be admitted that adolescent problems are often the result of circumstances of the times, and as such, are not strictly developmental. Therefore, coverage of adolescent problems has been moved to appropriate sections of several other chapters. Special care has been taken to be sure that discussion of these topics is as up-to-date as possible.

- We have decided to incorporate research on cultural diversity as a regular part of the text but also continue to highlight some of this material in our *A Multicultural View* boxes. We have done this because we feel that in a society where diversity is playing a greater and greater role, this material deserves special attention. Furthermore, we have replaced some of these boxes and added new ones with what we consider to be information of particularly high quality.

- Given the importance of education in a modern society, we have completely revised the section on schools and development.

- We have integrated and referred to the biopsychosocial model even more in this edition. Because the data relating to developmental psychology are so extensive, we believe that this model helps you to better organize developmental data, and it also serves as an effective memory aid. We are likewise aware that it is impossible to understand development from a single perspective. That is, biological development has both psychological and social consequences; social development has both biological and psychological effects; and psychological development has both biological and social influences.

- Earlier in this preface we mentioned that development is a lifelong process, which implies that lifespan psychology books must constantly change to accommodate fresh insights into the developmental process. To meet this challenge, we have incorporated such current topics as the exciting new genetic research, the role of early education programs in development, and the impact of poverty on learning and development.

- Because we believe that the vignettes that open each chapter in our book set the tone for that chapter, we have continued our efforts to improve these vignettes or to replace them with better ones.

Teaching–Learning Features of the Third Edition

You will enjoy and learn from this book to the extent that its topics, organization, and clarity make its contents meaningful to you. Helping you to master the book's contents in as uncomplicated a manner as possible has been the most important pedagogical goal of our work. To accomplish this task, we have built a number of features into each chapter:

- *Chapter Outlines.* The major topics of each chapter are presented initially so that you may quickly find the subject you need. An outline helps you to retain material (a memory aid) and is an efficient method for reviewing content.

- *Opening Vignette.* Each chapter opens with a vignette that illustrates the chapter's content. These vignettes are intended to demonstrate how the topics described in the chapter actually "work" in the daily lives of human beings, young and old.

- *List of Objectives.* Following the introductory section of each chapter, we present a carefully formulated list of objectives to guide your reading. When you finish reading the chapter, return to the objectives and test yourself to see if you can respond to their intent; that is, can you analyze, can you apply, can you identify, can you define, can you describe?

- *View Boxes.* We have designed our boxes to expand on the material under discussion and to do so in a manner calculated to aid student retention. The view boxes are of three types:

  - *What's Your View?* Here we present controversial issues and you are asked to give your opinion after you have studied the facts.

  - *An Applied View.* Here you will see how the topics under discussion apply to an actual situation, in settings such as a classroom or a medical facility.

  - *A Multicultural View.* Here we analyze the contributions of different cultures to individual development.

- *Conclusion.* At the end of each chapter you will find a brief concluding statement that summarizes the main themes of the chapter. This statement provides you with a quick check of the purpose of the chapter and the content covered.

- *Chapter Highlights.* Following the brief concluding section is a more detailed number of summary statements that are grouped according to the major topics of the chapter. This section should help you to review the chapter quickly and thoroughly. Turn to the chapter's table of contents and then check against the chapter highlights to determine how successful you are in recalling the pertinent material of the chapter.

- *Key Terms.* You will find at the end of each chapter a list of those terms that are essential to understanding the ideas and suggestions of that chapter. These terms are highlighted and explained in the context of the chapter. They also appear in the margins and the book's glossary. We urge you to spend time mastering the meaning of each of these terms and relate them to the context in which they appear.

- *What Do You Think?* Following the Key Terms, you will find a series of questions intended to have you demonstrate your knowledge of the chapter's content, not only by applying the material to different situations but also by asking you to be creative in answering the question or solving the problem.

- *Suggested Readings.* At the end of each chapter, you will find an annotated list of four or five books or journal articles that we think are particularly well suited to supplement the contents of the chapter. These references are not necessarily textbooks; they may not deal specifically with either education or psychology. We believe, however, that they shed an illuminating light upon the chapter's material.

- *Student Study Guide.* As we mentioned earlier, we have decided to include the student study guide in the body of the text as one means of making the material as meaningful as possible and to aid retention.

- *Questions in the Margins.* We have written several questions in the margins of the text. These questions are intended to encourage reader interaction with the material; they can also be used as the basis of discussion and as a means of relating the material to other pertinent topics.

Supplementary Materials

Brown & Benchmark Publishers has gathered a group of talented individuals with many years of experience in teaching lifespan development to create supplementary materials that will assist instructors and students who use this text. The supplements are designed to make it as easy as possible to customize the entire package for the unique needs of professors and their students.

An **Instructor's Manual** has been prepared by Lynne Blesz Vestal. Each chapter of the manual includes a chapter overview, learning objectives, key terms (page referenced to the text), lecture suggestions, classroom/student activities, and questions for review and discussion. The instructor's manual is conveniently housed within an attractive 11″ × 13″ × 9″ carrying case. This case is designed to accommodate the complete ancillary package. It contains the material for each chapter within a separate handling file, allowing you to keep all your class materials organized and at your fingertips.

The Instructor's Manual includes a comprehensive **Test Item File** consisting of more than 1,000 items. Each test item is referenced to its related learning objective and text page and is classified as factual, conceptual, or applied, based on the first three levels of Benjamin Bloom's taxonomy.

The questions in the Test Item File are available on **MicroTest III,** a powerful but easy-to-use test-generating program by Chariot Software Group. MicroTest is available for DOS, Windows, and Macintosh. With MicroTest, you can easily select questions from the Test Item File and print a test and an answer key. You can customize questions, headings, and instructions, you can add or import questions of your own, and you can print your test in a choice of fonts if your printer supports them. You can obtain a copy of MicroTest III by contacting your local Brown & Benchmark Sales Representative or by phoning Educational Resources at 800–338–5371.

The *Brown & Benchmark Developmental Psychology Transparency/Slide Set* consists of 100 newly developed acetate transparencies or slides. These full-color illustrations include graphics from various outside sources. Created by Lynne Blesz Vestal, these transparencies were expressly designed to provide comprehensive coverage of all major topic areas generally covered in developmental psychology. A comprehensive annotated guide provides a brief description for each transparency and helpful suggestions for use in the classroom.

A large selection of **Videotapes,** including *Seasons of Life,* and *Childhood,* is also available to instructors, based upon the number of textbooks ordered from Brown & Benchmark Publishers by your bookstore.

The AIDS Booklet, 3e by Frank D. Cox of Santa Barbara City College, is a brief but comprehensive introduction to the Acquired Immune Deficiency Syndrome which is caused by HIV (Human Immunodeficiency Virus) and related viruses.

The Critical Thinker, written by Richard Mayer and Fiona Goodchild of the University of California, Santa Barbara, uses excerpts from introductory psychology textbooks to show students how to think critically about psychology. Either this or the AIDS booklet are available at no charge to first-year adopters of our textbook or can be purchased separately.

A **Customized Transparency Program** is available to adopters for *Human Development Across the Lifespan,* third edition, based on the number of textbooks ordered. Consult your Brown & Benchmark Representative for ordering policies.

The **Human Development Interactive Videodisc Set** produced by Roger Ray of Rollins College, brings lifespan development to life with instant access to over 30 brief video segments from the highly acclaimed *Seasons of Life* series. The 2-disc set can be used alone for selecting and sequencing excerpts, or in tandem with a Macintosh computer to add interactive commentary capability, as well as extra video and search options. Consult your Brown & Benchmark Sales Representative for details.

B&B CourseKits™

B&B CourseKits™ are course-specific collections of for-sale educational materials custom packaged for maximum convenience and value. CourseKits offer you the flexibility of customizing and combining Brown & Benchmark course materials (B&B CourseKits™, Annual Editions®, Taking Sides® etc.) with your own or other material. Each CourseKit contains two or more instructor-selected items conveniently packaged and priced for your students. For more information on B&B CourseKits™, please contact your local Brown & Benchmark Representative.

Annual Editions®. Magazines, newspapers, and journals of the public press play an important role in providing current, first-rate, relevant educational information. If in your lifespan development course you are interested in exposing your students to a wide range of current, well-balanced, carefully selected articles from some of the most important magazines, newspapers, and journals published today, you may want to consider *Annual Editions: Human Development, Annual Editions: Aging,* or *Annual Editions: Death, Dying, & Bereavement,* published by the Dushkin Publishing Group, a unit of Brown & Benchmark Publishers. Each *Annual Editions* contains articles on topics related to the latest research and thinking in lifespan development. *Annual Editions* is updated on an annual basis, and there are a number of features designed to make it particularly useful, including a topic guide, an annotated table of contents, and unit overviews. For the professor using *Annual Editions* in the classroom, an Instructor's Resource Guide with Test Questions is available. Consult your Brown & Benchmark Sales Representative for more details.

CourseMedia™. As educational needs and methods change, Brown & Benchmark adds innovative, contemporary student materials for the computer, audio, and video devices of the 1990s and beyond. These include:

- Stand-alone materials

- Study guides

- Software simulations

- Tutorials

- And exercises

CourseMedia™ also includes instructional aids you can use to enhance lectures and discussions, such as:

- Videos
- Level I and III videodiscs
- CD ROMs

CourseWorks. CourseWorks (formerly Kinko's CourseWorks in the U.S.) is the Brown & Benchmark custom publishing service. With its own printing and distribution facility, CourseWorks gives you the flexibility to add current material to your course at any time. CourseWorks provides you with a unique set of options, including:

- Customizing Brown & Benchmark CourseBooks
- Publishing your own material
- Including any previously published material for which we can secure permissions
- Adding photos
- Performing copy-editing
- And, creating custom covers

Acknowledgments

This book was produced through the cooperation of many individuals at Brown & Benchmark Publishers. Steven Yetter, acquisitions editor, provided gentle guidance and Ted Underhill, developmental editor, was always there when we needed him. We were extremely fortunate to have Kris Queck as our production editor and Laurie McGee as our copy editor. Their suggestions and hard work helped us with the difficult moments all authors experience.

Several graduate research assistants also contributed their ideas, research skills, and criticisms to this edition. We are most grateful to Susan Chamberlin, Mary Hackenson, Jacqueline Scarbrough, and Judy Robinson.

In addition, several colleagues contributed to our work. We are grateful to the following individuals for their helpful suggestions:

- Roger Baumgarte, Winthrop University
- Steven Fulks, University of Tennessee
- Stephanie M. Clancy-Dollinger, Southern Illinois University
- Mary Mindess, Lesley College
- Marilyn Walker, Incarnate Word College
- Joan McDowd, Pomona College
- Beverly Slichta, Buffalo Area Community College
- Leonard Abbeduto, University of Wisconsin–Madison
- Chris J. Boyatzis, California State University–Fullerton
- JoAnn Farver, University of Southern California

To the Student

Owner's Manual: A Guide to Content Features

Chapter Outline
Outlines at the beginning of each chapter show what material will be covered.

List of Objectives
A carefully formulated list of objectives is presented after each chapter introduction to help guide your reading. After reading each chapter, you can use the objectives as a way to test your knowledge and to review the material.

The Biological Basis of Development 51

When you finish reading this chapter, you should be able to

- Recall that development results from the interaction of heredity and environment.
- Identify the essential elements in the reproductive process.
- Distinguish between internal and external fertilization.
- List the steps that lead to ovulation.
- Describe how the genetic process functions.
- Formulate questions relating to the sensitive nature of the new reproductive technology.

Internal fertilization
A natural process in which fertilization occurs within the woman.

External fertilization
Fertilization occurs outside of the woman's body.

In vitro fertilization
Fertilization that occurs "in the dish"; an external fertilization technique.

The Fertilization Process
The fusion of two specialized cells, the sperm and the egg (or ovum), mark the beginning of development and the zygote (the fertilized ovum) immediately begins to divide. This fertilized ovum contains all of the genetic material that the organism will ever possess. During the initial phase of development following fertilization, distinguishing the male from the female is almost impossible.

The Beginnings
Any discussion of fertilization today must account for the advances that both research and technology have made available. Consequently, our discussion will be broken into two parts:

- **Internal**, or natural, **fertilization**
- **External fertilization** techniques, such as **in vitro fertilization** (the famous "test-tube" babies)

Table 3.1 contains a glossary of many of the terms you will find in this discussion. Be sure to refer to it when you meet an unfamiliar term. Otherwise, the amazing richness of the genetic world can escape you.

In our analysis of genetic material and its impact on our lives, we'll attempt to follow the manner in which we receive genes from our parents. (Even this fundamental fact today requires further explanation. Genes may come from surprising sources, thanks to our technology [Grobstein, 1988]—more about this later.) But our story begins with the male's sperm and the female's egg.

The Sperm
Certain cells are destined to become the sperm and eggs. The chief characteristics of the sperm are its tightly packed tip (the acrosome), containing 23 chromosomes, a short neck region, and a tail to propel it in its search for the egg (Wolpert, 1991). Sperm are so tiny that estimates are that the number of sperm equal to the world's population could fit in a thimble. Sperm remain capable of fertilizing an egg for about 24 to 48 hours after ejaculation. Of the 200 million sperm that enter the vagina, only about 200 survive the journey to the woman's fallopian tubes, where fertilization occurs.

The major purpose of a male's reproductive organs is to manufacture, store, and deliver sperm. The sperm has as its sole objective the delivery of its DNA to the egg. Males, at birth, have in their testes those cells that will eventually produce sperm. At puberty, a meiotic division occurs in which the number of chromosomes is halved and actual sperm are formed. Simultaneously, the pituitary gland stimulates the hormonal production that results in the male secondary sex characteristics: pubic hair, a beard, and a deep voice.

(a)

(b)

The sperm (a), in its search for the egg (b), carries the 23 chromosomes from the male.

CHAPTER 1   Lifespan Psychology: An Introduction

Chapter Outline
The Meaning of Lifespan Psychology 6
   A Multicultural Perspective 6
History of Lifespan Studies 7
   Childhood 8
   Adolescence 9
   Adulthood 11
Issues in Lifespan
   Development 12
   Culture and Development 12
   Gender and Development 13
   Continuity versus
     Discontinuity 14
   Stability versus Resiliency 14
   Sensitive Periods versus Equal
     Potential 15
Developmental Research 15
   Data Collection Techniques 17
   Time Variable Designs 18

Conclusion 22
Chapter Highlights 22
Key Terms 23
What Do You Think? 23
Suggested Readings 23
Chapter Review Test 23

This is a book about lifespan psychology, that is, those changes in life that occur from conception to death. If you think about changes in your own life—beginning school, perhaps going off to college, beginning a job, getting married, having a child—you begin to appreciate the complexity of development. It's usually difficult, however, to look at ourselves objectively, so let's examine the life of an outstanding individual—Colin Powell—whose rise to fame and power offers an insightful view into what is meant by lifespan development.

Powell, whom America came to know quite well as chairman of the Joint Chiefs of Staff, was born in Harlem on April 5, 1937, the son of Jamaican immigrant parents. He gained confidence and self-esteem from the care, love, and attention that he received from his family. His parents valued education and he quickly realized the importance of learning. As a young African American, Powell decided that opportunities were greater in the army than in the corporate world.

A product of the ROTC program at the City College of New York, Powell soon demonstrated those leadership qualities that would mark him as an outstanding soldier. In 1963, as a second lieutenant and newly married, Powell was sent to Vietnam. Wounded in action there, he showed the bravery and the compassion for his colleagues that have been constant themes in his career. Returning to the United States, he obtained a master's degree in business administration and in 1972 was selected as a White House Fellow.

During the following years, Powell served in various parts of the world, gradually attaining the rank of Major General. He was recalled to the White House to be military adviser to the Secretary of Defense in 1982, then in 1986 returned to the army. In 1987 he was asked to be National Security Adviser to the president, and in 1989 he became chairman of the Joint Chiefs of Staff. During these years, he became the first African American to attain the rank of a four-star general.

Powell's rise to the top military post in the United States confounded many who thought that only West Point graduates could ascend to such heights. His courage in Vietnam, however, resulted in six medals (including the Purple Heart and a Bronze Star) and earned him the respect and admiration of President George Bush, who recommended his appointment. During the Gulf War, Powell played a pivotal role in determining strategy and in advising the president.

As you examine the paths that Colin Powell followed in his life, you can begin to identify those themes that make studying the human lifespan so fascinating. You can see how his family was a powerful and positive influence throughout his early years. Later, his wife, Alma Johnson, and their three children provided additional support. His decision to make the army a career led to international experiences and a network of friends who would help shape his future. These developmental milestones in Colin Powell's life served to make him the person he is today, but at the same time it is possible to discern behaviors that have been remarkably persistent throughout his lifespan: courage, compassion for others, and devotion to family and country. ♣

In Colin Powell's life we see the impact of those forces that so powerfully affect development: family, peers, and experiences.

3

Opening Vignette
Each chapter opens with a vignette or quotation that illustrates the chapter's content and demonstrates how chapter material actually works in our daily lives.

Key Terms

Because key terms are essential to your ability to understand material, they are highlighted and explained in the context of each chapter, and are briefly defined in the text's margins. The key terms are also listed and page referenced at the end of each chapter, and are defined again in a glossary at the end of the book.

A Multicultural View

Research on cultural diversity has been integrated throughout the third edition of *Human Development Across the Lifespan*. Highlights of this material are featured in the Multicultural View boxes.

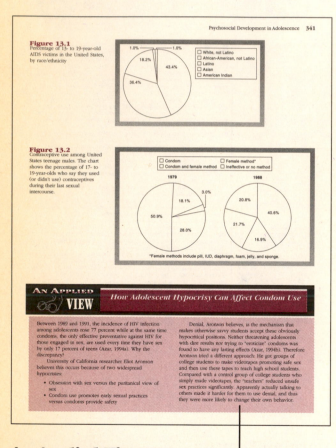

Figure 13.1
Percentage of 13- to 19-year-old AIDS victims in the United States, by race/ethnicity

Psychosocial Development in Adolescence   341

- White, not Latino — 43.4%
- African-American, not Latino — 36.4%
- Latino — 18.2%
- Asian — 1.0%
- American Indian — 1.0%

Figure 13.2
Contraceptive use among United States teenage males. The chart shows the percentage of 17- to 19-year-olds who say they used (or didn't use) contraceptives during their last sexual intercourse.

- Condom
- Condom and female method
- Female method*
- Ineffective or no method

1979: 50.9%, 28.0%, 18.1%, 3.0%
1988: 40.6%, 16.9%, 21.7%, 20.8%

*Female methods include pill, IUD, diaphragm, foam, jelly, and sponge.

AN APPLIED VIEW
How Adolescent Hypocrisy Can Affect Condom Use

Between 1989 and 1991, the incidence of HIV infection among adolescents rose 77 percent while at the same time condoms, the only effective preventative against HIV for those engaged in sex, are used every time they have sex by only 17 percent of teens (Azar, 1994a). Why the discrepancy?

University of California researcher Eliot Aronson believes this occurs because of two widespread hypocrisies:

- Obsession with sex versus the puritanical view of sex
- Condom use promotes early sexual practices versus condoms provide safety

Denial, Aronson believes, is the mechanism that makes otherwise savvy students accept these obviously hypocritical positions. Neither threatening adolescents with dire results nor trying to "eroticize" condoms was found to have any lasting effects (Azar, 1994b). Therefore Aronson tried a different approach: He got groups of college students to make videotapes promoting safe sex and then use these tapes to teach high school students. Compared with a control group of college students who simply made videotapes, the "teachers" reduced unsafe sex practices significantly. Apparently actually talking to others made it harder for them to use denial, and thus they were more likely to change their own behavior.

An Applied View

These boxed features give examples to show how the material you are learning can be applied to real life situations, such as in a classroom or medical facility.

What's Your View?

Controversial issues related to developmental psychology are presented in these boxes for you to read and think over.

Marginal Questions

Questions that encourage you to think about pertinent issues and promote discussion are placed in the margins of the text.

Background and Context in Adolescence   289

Negative identity
Persons with a negative identity adopt one pattern of behavior because they are rebelling against demands that they do the opposite.

Erikson suggests that the young Martin Luther was an excellent example of his concept of negative identity. Because of what happened in his youth, he spent his adulthood rebelling against what he had been taught. Here Frau Cotta, the woman who cared for him when he was 11 (in 1494) introduces the shy boy to her family.

suggest to youths that the adult community now has more confidence in their ability to make decisions. The effect depends on the explanation of the goals of the ceremony.

Although some youths tend to be overly idealistic, Erikson believed that idealism is essential for a strong identity. In young people's search for a person or an idea to be true to, they are building a commitment to an ideology that will help them unify their personal values. They need ideals to avoid the disintegration of personality that is the basis of most forms of mental illness.

Negative Identity

Although most adolescents do not go through changes as great as Erikson did in his youth, many do take on what he calls a **negative identity.** People with negative identities adopt one pattern of behavior because they are rebelling against demands that they do the opposite. An example is the boy who joins a gang of shoplifters, not because he wants to steal, but because he doubts his masculinity and seeks to prove, through the dangerous act of theft, that he is not a coward. Another example is the sexually permissive girl who is punishing her mother for trying to keep unreasonably strict control over her. Sex is not her goal; proving that she is no longer her mother's baby is.

In his psychohistorical biography of German religious leader Martin Luther (1483–1546), called *Young Man Luther* (1958), Erikson painted a somber picture of negative identity. Luther's greatness as a leader, says Erikson, was partly built on the enormous anger and unresolved conflict he experienced in his late teens. Luther's decision to become a monk and enter the monastery was the assumption of a negative identity. The choice expressed his rejection of fifteenth-century society rather than his devotion to Catholicism. Luther indulged in further contrariness by trying to be a better monk than anyone else. Luther's strong internal conflict is illustrated by the story of his falling into a faint while performing in the choir. As he fell to the ground, he is said to have cried out, "It isn't me!" Many other incidents also indicate that he couldn't accept being who he was.

A MULTICULTURAL VIEW
Ethnic Self-Concept

One African American male recalls, "Much of my junior and high school years were difficult because, on top of the typical problems of this time period, I had to combine the struggle of being Black and having my race always looked down upon, expected to fail, expected to cause trouble, and expected to be unproductive. During this time, I had to fight to maintain my confidence. I did not know who I was . . . I was confused." He went on to describe how he was kicked off the football team for a failing grade, but when his parents spoke to the teacher, it was discovered that he actually had a C+. "He had given me an F not because I earned it, but because he expected me to deserve it" (John B. Diamond in Schoem, 1991).

A Mexican American male stated, "As I moved to junior high, the issue of my ethnicity became a problem. I remember thinking that I would be a great deal more popular if only I had Bobby's face and body and brains. I would look in the mirror and imagine what I would look like. The mythical Bobby was, of course, always white and popular with girls. This fantasy ate away at my self-esteem, and I found myself bitterly questioning why I had been born a brown-faced Mexican. . . . From this point on, all my energies were spent on the elusive quest for acceptance by my peers—and unconsciously, by myself" (Carlos Manharrez in Schoem, 1991).

Do you think ethnic prejudice can make the development of self-concept and positive self-esteem difficult? Do you think the African American teen felt that he mattered to his teacher? What are the social expectations for him and how might they influence self-concept? What values of American society make the development of self-concept and positive self-esteem challenging for adolescents of color?

---

58   Beginnings

WHAT'S YOUR VIEW?
ADOPTION: CLOSED OR OPEN?

For many couples who remain childless in spite of several attempts at external fertilization, adoption (to take a child of other parents voluntarily as one's own) offers a viable option. The process of adoption has changed radically in the past few years because of a limited number of children and an increase in the number of couples who wish to adopt. This statement is not quite as simple as it appears. More children are available for adoption than is commonly thought, but they fall into several categories.

- Older children
- Minority children
- Handicapped children

While these children are available for immediate adoption, the waiting period for healthy white infants may run into years.

Adoption procedures were formerly *closed,* that is, the biological parents were completely removed from the life of their child once the child was surrendered for adoption. The bonds between birth parent(s) and child were legally and permanently severed; the child's history was sealed by the court. The child was effectively cut off from its genetic past (Gilman, 1987). Supposedly this prevented the natural parents and the adoptive couple from emotional upset. Many biological mothers, however, reported in later interviews that they never recovered from the grieving process.

Today, however, if a pregnant woman approaches an adoption agency, she gets what she wants. She can insist that her child be raised by a couple with specific characteristics: nationality, religion, income, number in family. She can ask to see her child several times a year,

perhaps take the youngster on a vacation, and telephone the child frequently. The adoption agency will try to meet these demands. This process is called *open* adoption, and although many adoptive couples dislike the arrangement, they really have no choice. Thus we see a new definition of adoption: the process of accepting the responsibility of raising an individual who has two sets of parents (Gilman, 1987).

Open adoption is a radical departure from the days when a woman who had decided to give up her baby for adoption had to wear a blindfold and earplugs during delivery so she wouldn't see or hear her baby. Today the natural mother may actually select the adoptive couple from several profiles that are given to her. (These profiles contain information about the adoptive couple: food preferences, television, politics, how the couple deals with stress, how they would handle a 2-year-old with a temper tantrum.) Most officials at adoption agencies agree that biological mothers rarely select a couple solely on the basis of income. Religion, lifestyle, and family stability seem much more important. Face-to-face meetings between the couples are becoming more common and often are decisive in the natural mother's decision.

Although problems occur with open adoption—for example, frequently the adoptive parents resent the continuing presence of the biological mother—most experts agree that a change was needed. Too many adopted children have shown emotional difficulties on learning that they were relinquished, and a large number of biological mothers have prolonged difficulty as a result of relinquishing their babies. Only time can tell how successful this new procedure will be.

What's your view—closed or open adoption?

Could you be an adopting parent under open adoption conditions?

Guided Review

1. _____ is the process uniting sperm and egg.
2. A fertilized egg is known as a _____.
3. The _____ gland secretes hormones that stimulate the ovaries to ripen and release an egg each month.
4. The most well known example of an external fertilization technique is _____ fertilization.
5. The most popular external fertilization technique is _____.
6. Estimates are that _____ in _____ American couples are infertile.
7. A form of adoption that today is becoming more popular is _____ adoption.

Answers

1. Fertilization 2. zygote 3. pituitary 4. in vitro 5. AID 6. one, five 7. open

Chapter Highlights

Each chapter conclusion is followed by a series of summary statements. These highlights are grouped according to chapter topic and help you review the chapter quickly and thoroughly.

What Do You Think?

Following the Key Terms, you will find a series of questions challenging you to demonstrate your knowledge of the chapter's content.

Suggested Readings

An annotated list of four or five books or journal articles to supplement the chapter reading can be found at the end of each chapter.

Student Study Guide

To help you fully learn the material, the third edition of this text includes a built-in student study guide. (Students need not buy a separate study guide—it is part of the book!) The student study guide is composed of:

- Chapter opening learning objectives

- In-chapter guided reviews featuring fill-in-the-blank questions

- End of chapter multiple-choice sample tests

Sample page 212 (Early Childhood):

CONCLUSION

At the beginning of the early childhood years, most children meet other youngsters. By the end of the period, almost all children enter formal schooling. Their symbolic ability enriches all of their activities, although limitations still exist. Given their boundless energy and enthusiasm, early childhood youngsters require consistent and reasonable discipline. Yet they should be permitted to do as many things for themselves as possible to help them gain mastery over themselves and their surroundings.

By the end of the early childhood period, children have learned much about their world and are prepared to enter the more complex, competitive, yet exciting world of middle childhood.

CHAPTER HIGHLIGHTS

The Family in Development
- The meaning of "family" in our society has changed radically.
- How parents treat their children has a decisive influence on developmental outcomes.
- Baumrind's types of parenting behavior help to clarify the role of parents in children's development.
- Research has demonstrated how divorce can affect children of different ages.

- Divorce plus remarriage produces a series of transitions to which children must adjust.
- Many children attend some form of day care, and the developmental outcomes of these experiences are still in question.

The Self Emerges
- The emergence of the self follows a clearly defined path.
- Self-esteem plays a crucial role in a child's development.

- Youngsters acquire their gender identity during the early childhood years.
- Children initially seem to acquire an understanding of gender before they manifest sex-typed behavior.

The Importance of Play
- Play affects all aspects of development: physical, cognitive, social, and emotional.
- The nature of a child's play changes over the years, gradually becoming more symbolic.

KEY TERMS

Authoritarian parents 190	Intimidated parents 191	Reconciliation fantasies 197
Authoritative parents 190	Overinterpretive parents 191	Secure parents 191
Day care 197	Pathological parents 192	Sex cleavage 205
Individuation 188	Permissive parents 190	Socialization 188
Insecure parents 191	Play 208	Victimized parents 191

WHAT DO YOU THINK?

1. With today's accepted changes in the gender roles of males and females, do you think that a boy or girl growing up in these times could become confused about gender identity? Does your answer also apply to gender roles? Why?
2. Think back on your days as a child. Can you put your parents' behavior in any of Baumrind's categories? Do you think it affected your behavior? Explain your answer by linking your parents' behavior to some of your personal characteristics.
3. In this chapter you read about the "sleeper" effect of divorce (effects show up quite a bit later). Do you agree with these findings? Can you explain them by the child's age at the time of the divorce? (Consider all aspects of a child's development at that age.)
4. You probably have read about child abuse in some day-care centers. Do you think there should be stricter supervision? Why? By whom?

Sample page 213 (Psychosocial Development in Early Childhood):

SUGGESTED READINGS

Ambrose, S. (1983). *Eisenhower.* (Vol. I). New York: Simon & Schuster. Includes the boyhood days of the man who would become soldier, general, and president. A revealing account of the family and community forces that helped to shape his destiny.

Brazelton, T. B. (1981). *On becoming a family: The growth of attachment.* New York: Delacorte. An engrossing account of the development of family relationships by one of America's most renowned pediatricians.

Garvey, C. (1990). *Play.* Cambridge, MA: Harvard Univ. Press. A brief, thorough examination of what we mean by play and how children play with objects, language, and rules, among others.

Wallerstein, J. & Blakeslee, S. (1989). *Second chances.* New York: Simon & Schuster. This book is must reading for anyone interested in the effect of divorce on children. It summarizes Wallerstein's 10-year follow-up of the children of divorced parents and furnishes insights into the entire spectrum of divorce in our society today.

CHAPTER REVIEW TEST

1. The National Commission on Children has identified several characteristics of a strong family. Which of the following is *not* included?
   a. open and frequent communication among members
   b. respect for individual members
   c. an ability to cope with stressful events
   d. extended generational membership

2. A child who is aggressive and demonstrates a lack of responsibility is associated with _____ parenting behavior.
   a. authoritative
   b. permissive
   c. indifferent
   d. doting

3. Conditions associated with homelessness can produce hardships on children. Which of the following conditions is *not* necessarily associated with homelessness?
   a. health problems
   b. hunger and poor nutrition
   c. lower intelligence
   d. developmental delays

4. _____ percent of divorced mothers remarry.
   a. Seventy-five
   b. Eighty
   c. Fifty
   d. Twenty-five

5. Almost _____ percent of today's marriages will end in divorce.
   a. 25
   b. 50
   c. 10
   d. 75

6. Which one of the following is *not* a commonly reported reaction of early childhood youngsters to divorce?
   a. lowered cognitive competence
   b. shock
   c. depression
   d. loyalty conflict

7. Wallerstein discovered that even after 10 years following a divorce, children wished their parents would get together again. This phenomenon is called
   a. reconciliation fantasy.
   b. divorce related depression.
   c. cognitive incompetence.
   d. separation anxiety.

8. Almost _____ of women with children under age 14 are in the labor force.
   a. 1/2
   b. 3/4
   c. 2/3
   d. 1/3

9. Most children in day care are being cared for
   a. by a father at home.
   b. by a grandparent in another home.
   c. by a nonrelative in another home.
   d. in a nursery/preschool.

10. A long-term developmental consequence of day care is
   a. insecurity.
   b. adaptability.
   c. self-sufficiency.
   d. No definite conclusion is possible.

11. There are about _____ places providing day-care services.
   a. 20,000–25,000
   b. 25,000–30,000
   c. 30,000–35,000
   d. 35,000–40,000

12. Probably the best type of day care is found in the _____ center, which may not provide an accurate picture of all centers.
   a. research
   b. company
   c. commercial
   d. family run

13. _____ is how children feel about themselves and how they value themselves.
   a. Self-identity
   b. Self-esteem
   c. Sense of belonging
   d. Sense of competence

14. Social learning theory states that parents _____ appropriate gender-role behavior.
   a. discuss
   b. analyze
   c. reinforce
   d. ignore

15. In cognitive development theory, children first acquire their
   a. gender identity.
   b. appropriate gender behavior.
   c. psychic stability.
   d. conditioned behavior.

16. Social learning theory depends on the concept of _____ to explain the acquisition of appropriate gender behavior.
   a. schema
   b. assimilation
   c. reinforcement
   d. adaptation

PART I

Introduction

Life is like playing a violin in public
and learning the instrument as one
goes on.

Samuel Butler

Lifespan Psychology: An Introduction

In Colin Powell's life we see the impact of those forces that so powerfully affect development: family, peers, and experiences.

This is a book about lifespan psychology, that is, those changes in life that occur from conception to death. If you think about changes in your own life—beginning school, perhaps going off to college, beginning a job, getting married, having a child—you begin to appreciate the complexity of development. It's usually difficult, however, to look at ourselves objectively, so let's examine the life of an outstanding individual—Colin Powell—whose rise to fame and power offers an insightful view into what is meant by lifespan development.

Powell, whom America came to know quite well as chairman of the Joint Chiefs of Staff, was born in Harlem on April 5, 1937, the son of Jamaican immigrant parents. He gained confidence and self-esteem from the care, love, and attention that he received from his family. His parents valued education and he quickly realized the importance of learning. As a young African American, Powell decided that opportunities were greater in the army than in the corporate world.

A product of the ROTC program at the City College of New York, Powell soon demonstrated those leadership qualities that would mark him as an outstanding soldier. In 1963, as a second lieutenant and newly married, Powell was sent to Vietnam. Wounded in action there, he showed the bravery and the compassion for his colleagues that have been constant themes in his career. Returning to the United States, he obtained a master's degree in business administration and in 1972 was selected as a White House Fellow.

During the following years, Powell served in various parts of the world, gradually attaining the rank of Major General. He was recalled to the White House to be military adviser to the Secretary of Defense in 1982, then in 1986 returned to the army. In 1987 he was asked to be National Security Adviser to the president, and in 1989 he became chairman of the Joint Chiefs of Staff. During these years, he became the first African American to attain the rank of a four-star general.

Powell's rise to the top military post in the United States confounded many who thought that only West Point graduates could ascend to such heights. His courage in Vietnam, however, resulted in six medals (including the Purple Heart and a Bronze Star) and earned him the respect and admiration of President George Bush, who recommended his appointment. During the Gulf War, Powell played a pivotal role in determining strategy and in advising the president.

As you examine the paths that Colin Powell followed in his life, you can begin to identify those themes that make studying the human lifespan so fascinating. You can see how his family was a powerful and positive influence throughout his early years. Later, his wife, Alma Johnson, and their three children provided additional support. His decision to make the army a career led to international experiences and a network of friends who would help shape his future. These developmental milestones in Colin Powell's life served to make him the person he is today, but at the same time it is possible to discern behaviors that have been remarkably persistent throughout his lifespan: courage, compassion for others, and devotion to family and country. 🌳

Figure 1.1
The interactive nature of development

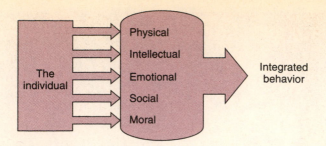

Biopsychosocial model
A framework that views development as the interaction of biological, psychological, and social forces.

In our work, we'll trace the significant changes that occur at various times in the lifespan, emphasizing that the potential for development is constant throughout our lives—from youth to old age. Although these changes in our lives may not be as dramatic as those we have just traced in Colin Powell's life, they are important to us as individuals making our own progress throughout our lifespans.

Before beginning our work on analyzing the lifespan in this chapter, however, we'll first present a model—the **biopsychosocial model**—that helps to explain human development. If you think of lifespan development as the product of the interaction of biological, psychological, and social forces, you can better understand and appreciate the complexity of development. Biological elements range from the role of our genes in development to adult health issues; psychological elements include all aspects of cognitive and personality development; social elements refer to such influences as family, school, and peers. We believe the biopsychosocial model illustrates the constant interaction of heredity and environment that explains the complexity of development. (See figure 1.1.)

For example, let's consider Lindsey, a 5-year-old who entered first grade in September. Lindsey is unhappy, and most mornings she pleads that she is too sick to go to school. She is having difficulty with her school work and her teacher reports that she disrupts the class by interrupting others and wandering around the room. Because of Lindsey's classroom behavior, she is unpopular with the other children in the class. After complaining of headaches, Lindsey is examined by the school nurse, who finds that she needs glasses. Here is an example of how a physical problem can affect psychological development (learning and reading) as well as social development (popularity with classmates).

We believe that by analyzing lifespan development with the biopsychosocial model, you will have a tool that better enables you to understand and remember the material of any chapter. This model also helps to emphasize those social-cultural features that so powerfully influence development through the lifespan.

With the biopsychosocial model in mind, then, we'll first explore the meaning of lifespan development in this chapter and attempt to indicate its importance to you by illustrating how peaks and valleys come into all of our lives. Although we all chart our own course, we can still identify many similarities in our lives. We walk, we talk, we attend school, and we search for a satisfying career. Yet within this sameness, we all have different experiences that shine a unique light on our journey through the lifespan.

Following this discussion, we'll briefly trace the role that different disciplines have played in the emergence of lifespan studies. Then we turn to several issues that are crucial in any analysis of a person's passage through the lifespan. Finally, we'll examine those research techniques that will help you to assess and interpret the issues, theories, and studies you will meet in the coming pages.

When you complete your reading of this chapter, you should be able to

- Use the biopsychosocial model as a means of interpreting and recalling developmental data.

- Define lifespan development.

- Describe the antecedents of lifespan developmental studies.

(a)

(b)

(c)

(d)

(e)

These photos (a–e) show Bill Clinton at various stages of his lifespan.

- Identify major developmental issues.

- Apply your knowledge of lifespan techniques to the studies you read.

The Meaning of Lifespan Psychology

Lifespan development is the study of human development from conception to death. As such, it is important to you personally because it helps you to understand your own behavior once you have grasped its main ideas. Studying lifespan development should also provide you with insights into the behavior of others and, because of this, you should achieve better relationships with those around you. To help you fulfill this objective, we have included *What's Your View?, A Multicultural View,* and *Applied View* boxes.

As you can tell from the brief discussion at the chapter's opening, development is a lifelong process. Psychologists now realize that development, once thought to end at childhood, or possibly adolescence, is a process that continues from conception to death. Today we realize that the changes of adulthood—maturity and aging—are as developmental as those of any other period. By analyzing the various developmental periods—infancy, early childhood, middle childhood, adolescence, and adulthood—researchers are trying to discover the features of each period and to uncover the mechanisms by which we move from one stage of life to the next.

As you continue your reading, remember that development does not proceed randomly. It is tightly linked to what psychologists call context; that is, the circumstances in which an individual develops. Context is such an important feature of development that we will return to it frequently throughout this book because to understand development as fully as possible, you must also understand its context.

A Multicultural Perspective

As our nation changes, we all will interact with others from quite different backgrounds. How we respond to others who seem different can have a serious impact on success in school, work, and harmonious relationships with others.

We begin our discussion in this section by defining several terms that will guide our analysis of how multiculturalism has become a critical component of our lives. **Culture** refers to those values, beliefs, and behaviors characteristic of a large group of people, for example, those of Hispanic origin. **Ethnic,** however, usually applies to national or linguistic backgrounds and can be included within the larger culture, for example, Mexican Americans, Italian Americans. **Race,** on the other hand, does not refer to nationality, culture, or language but is identified by blood type, such as African. Anthropologists have identified nine major groups: African, American Indian, Asian, Australian, European, Indian, Melanesian, Micronesian, and Polynesian (Tiedt & Tiedt, 1990).

The purpose of this discussion as we begin our work of studying lifespan development is to impress on you the need to be aware that "different does not mean deficient." Few would challenge the view that the Japanese place great value on formal education. Japanese children, through their experiences, internalize this value. For example, they will remember their educational programs that they attended at the end of their regular school day. British children will be aware of the class differences attributed to either public or private schools. These, and countless other socialization experiences, once internalized, help children to become accepted members of their adult society (Brislin, 1990).

Merging Cultures

If you now think of how we defined *ethnic,* you realize how members of one group—Irish American, Italian American, African American—can use standards

Culture
Those values, beliefs, and behaviors characteristic of a large group of people, for example, those of Hispanic origin.

Ethnic
Refers to national or linguistic backgrounds included within the larger culture, for example Mexican Americans.

Race
Usually identification by blood type.

Have you ever been in a group when someone makes a derogatory remark about another person's race, sex, or ethnicity? How did you react? What did you do?

from their own cultural backgrounds to form opinions about those from other cultures. If people can understand *why* those from other groups behave as they do, they are less inclined to conclude that "different means deficient." For example, meeting someone from another culture, we are initially struck by differences: behavior, speech, clothing, food. If these differences aren't too sharp, we accept them; if the differences are quite distinct, we judge them unfavorably. Remember, however, if you were a member of some other group, you would probably behave just as they do (Triandis, 1990).

Taking the time and making the effort to understand these differences can move our relationships with others to a level of mutual understanding in all settings. As an illustration, think of the changing American classrooms, where children and teachers from many different cultures are now coming together. Many minority children have had to make major adjustments to the dominant culture in the classroom. Teachers who are aware of the differences between the home culture and that of the school can do much to ensure that these children succeed academically and personally to achieve their potential.

A good example of this kind of endeavor can be seen in Kim's (1990) description of Hawaiian children's school experiences. Many Hawaiian children achieve at the lowest academic level and are labeled as lazy and disruptive by some teachers. Yet these same children are remarkably responsible at home—cooking, cleaning, taking care of their brothers and sisters. They demonstrate considerable initiative and a high performance level. When something needs to be done, they get together and make a group effort to do whatever is necessary. When they find themselves in an individualistic, competitive classroom, however, their performance suffers.

In a series of experiments, teachers were encouraged to model desired behaviors and not assign specific tasks to students. By the end of the academic year, the students would begin the day by examining the schedules of their learning centers and then divide themselves into groups that assigned tasks to individual members, obtained materials, and used worksheets. Although their achievement scores improved significantly, once the students were returned to regular classrooms for the fourth grade, a familiar pattern of problems appeared (Kim, 1990).

The classroom is not the only location in which cultures merge. The business world now has people of various cultures working side by side and also has those designated as minorities—women, African Americans, Asian Americans, Hispanic Americans—assuming leadership positions in which members of the dominant culture report to them. As companies become more global and as the number of international markets increases steadily, the workplace is beginning to resemble the classroom as a meeting place of cultures (Brislin, 1990).

Our goal in urging you to adopt a multicultural perspective is to help you develop a greater understanding of those who seem different. If you adopt this perspective, you will come to realize that different people have different worldviews that decisively influence their thinking (Shweder, 1991). People from different cultures do *not* all think alike. Recognizing how diverse people are in their thinking and behavior will help you to identify and comprehend variations in how children are raised and become functioning members of their culture. In this way, you can work, play, or study more congenially with others, thus fostering more positive relations in our society.

History of Lifespan Studies

The impetus for lifespan studies, as we mentioned earlier, came with the recognition that changes occur in adulthood as well as infancy and early childhood. Now that you understand the meaning of lifespan development, you may be interested in learning about the roots of lifespan studies. These roots have led developmental psychologists to interesting and, in some cases, surprising discoveries. What seems

Chart Your Own Lifespan

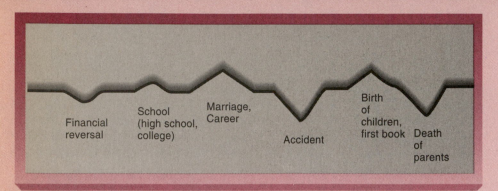

Financial reversal · School (high school, college) · Marriage, Career · Accident · Birth of children, first book · Death of parents

valley was a serious accident followed by years of recuperation and then the birth of children and the publication of a first book. You can see that it looks like a temperature chart. Try it for yourself.

Sugarman (1986) suggested that when you finish, sit back and ask yourself these questions:

Endeavoring to illustrate how important knowledge of the lifespan is to each of us, Sugarman (1986) has devised a simple exercise that you can do quickly. Using a blank sheet of paper, assume that the left edge of the page represents the beginning of your life and the right edge where you are today. Now draw a line across the page that indicates the peaks and valleys that you have experienced so far.

For example, the chart for one of the authors is shown above.

In this chart, the first valley was a financial reversal for the author's parents. The first peak represents happy and productive high school years, followed by entry into teaching, and then marriage a few years later. The deep

- Are there more peaks than valleys?
- Is there a definite shape to my chart?
- Would I identify my peaks and valleys as major or minor?
- What caused the peaks and valleys?
- Could I have done anything to make the peaks higher and the valleys more shallow?
- What happened during the plateaus?
- What's my view of these highs and lows in my life?

You have drawn a picture of your lifespan and the questions that you have just answered are actually the subject matter of lifespan development.

Guided Review

1. The biopsychosocial model illustrates the interaction of _____ and _____ in development.
2. The values, beliefs, and behaviors that characterize a large group of people refer to that group's _____ .
3. Ethnic refers to _____ or _____ background.
4. _____ refers to identification by blood-type.
5. People use the standards of their _____ to judge other people.
6. Kim's study of Hawaiian schoolchildren indicated that classroom _____ negatively affected their performance.

to have happened is that each developmental epoch—infancy, early childhood, middle childhood, adolescence, and early, middle, and late adulthood—has in its turn become a primary focus of research and speculation.

Childhood

Children and childhood are relatively new concepts; for example, celebrating a child's birthday did not begin until the end of the eighteenth century. In the twentieth century, our attitudes toward children have changed and have been accompanied by remarkable advances in our knowledge of children. From a belief that

Answers

1. heredity, environment 2. culture 3. national, linguistic 4. Race 5. culture 6. competition

children passively accept what is done to them, we now think that children actively shape their surroundings: people, events, and situations. Children change as a result of what is done to them, and the changes in the children produce changes in those around them, which is the meaning of **reciprocal interaction.**

Reciprocal interaction
Similar to transactional model; recognizes the child's active role in its development; I do something to the child, the child changes; as a result of the changes in the child, I change.

Action theory
A belief that proposes people influence the paths of their own development throughout the lifespan.

In explaining typical development and individual differences in normal development, Scarr (1992) notes that during the past decade European psychologists have argued that children participate in their own development. This belief, called **action theory,** proposes that people influence, in important ways, the paths of their development through the lifespan. Children construct reality from the opportunities that their environments present. This constructed reality emerges from the interaction among children's heredity, the behavior of others, and the environments children select because of their interests, talent, and personality (Scarr, 1992).

Thus, from seeing children as the objects of adult actions, we now view them as active, creative individuals who help to shape their environments. Fussy babies, for example, elicit a much different response from those around them than happy, cheerful babies. Both types of children have shaped their environments and tend to see their worlds differently. Once you realize that children process and interpret information from their environments, and then change their behaviors because of it, you can understand how their reactions affect those around them.

As the twentieth century comes to a close, the agenda for children has taken on a decidedly different look. Although developmental psychologists still wrestle with the relative importance of heredity and environment, new problems, especially those involving the context of development, have captured their attention. For example, how can we best understand the rich multicultural backgrounds of our changing population (Konner, 1991)? What will be the long-term impact of day care on children who are placed in centers soon after birth (Belsky & Braungart, 1991)? How does homelessness affect children's development (Rafferty & Shinn, 1991)? We address these questions in the pages to come. Before we do, however, it is interesting to identify some pioneers in the field.

Children were not always prized as they are by most parents today. This photo shows children in a typical nineteenth-century sweatshop, reflecting an attitude in which children as young as 5 or 6 were valued for their economic work.

Great Names in the History of Child Development

You may well recognize some of these famous figures who have been associated with the study of child development over the years. They are but a few of the well-known individuals who have contributed so much to the child development movement.

- *G. Stanley Hall* is often referred to as the founder of the child development movement in the United States. He became famous for using questionnaires to discover what children were thinking about.

- *Sigmund Freud* startled the world with his psychoanalytic theory (see chap. 2) and stressed the importance of the early years in a child's life, a belief that remains strong today.

- *John Watson's* views on child rearing, especially his belief that children should be conditioned early in life, were extremely popular in the 1920s and the 1930s.

- *Arnold Gesell* pioneered the use of creative methods—such as one-way mirrors and motion pictures—to record development in child development research.

- *Jean Piaget* has dominated our thinking about the cognitive development of children since the 1930s. His views are presented in detail throughout this book.

Adolescence

After recounting the picture of adolescence as described by a psychiatrist with a sense of humor—"think of your children as poisoned by hormones for five to ten

Adolescent girls come to their growth spurt earlier than boys, which creates some interesting social situations.

years"—Konner (1991) stated that we can do better than this definition. For most parents of adolescents, tears, trouble, and turbulence *never materialize*. In fact, most adolescents display noteworthy responsibility and even idealism.

G. Stanley Hall's book, *Adolescence,* published in 1904, signaled the beginning of intense and continuing study of adolescence as a distinct developmental period. Hall's views of adolescence (including that of storm and stress) greatly influenced those writing about adolescence for the next 50 years. Gradually, however, researchers began to concentrate less on the problems of adolescence and more on the developmental characteristics of the period, which produced a great deal of basic data about adolescents. Three topics have received considerable attention.

Adolescent Adjustment or Adolescent Turmoil

Research has seriously questioned the early belief of Hall and others that for adolescents turmoil is natural, a phenomenon they outgrow with continued development. For example, Petersen (1988) stated that those adolescents demonstrating severe turmoil frequently exhibit later serious problems. In fact, it is becoming clear that those adolescents who have stormy lives belong to the relatively small group who suffer from two or more of three linked problems: substance abuse, mental disorders, and juvenile delinquency (Elliot & others, 1989).

If not all adolescents experience problems, how can we identify those at risk? One marker seems to be gender. For example, adolescent boys with psychological difficulties usually have a history of childhood problems; anxiety seems to play a key role in the appearance of adolescent difficulties (achievement situations—tests, games—are more likely to arouse anxiety in males, whereas interpersonal relations are more likely to cause anxiety in females).

Another issue relates to part-time employment. Studies have shown that work in excess of 15 to 20 hours per week leads to numerous problems. For example, working more than 20 hours can lead to disengagement from school, greater rates of delinquency, and drug use (Steinberg & others, 1993).

Puberty and Its Effects

The mechanisms that control pubertal change develop prenatally. For most children, pubertal hormonal levels begin increasing at about 7 years of age, with bodily changes appearing about four or five years later. Girls begin these changes about a year or two earlier than boys.

You probably remember how intensely aware you were of these changes within yourself. Also, the timing of puberty is crucial in relation to others because of the psychological and social processes involved. The well-developed, physically mature girl can only wonder about male classmates still running around in baseball caps and chewing bubble gum.

Changes in adolescence— physical, social, cognitive— require teenagers to develop different methods of coping. Still searching for identity and susceptible to peer pressure, adolescents can engage in thrill-seeking and dangerous behavior. It is a time when the adults around teenagers need to respond sensitively and treat adolescents as "almost adults."

Here are some of the major findings that have resulted from studies of the relationship between puberty and psychological functioning:

- Little evidence indicates that puberty is linked to psychological problems; its effects may be positive as well as negative.

- Although puberty may affect psychological variables, its impact is specific—on depression, aggression, or self-concept, for example.

- Puberty affects boys and girls differently.

Adolescent-Family Interactions

Recent research into adolescent-family relations has focused on the reciprocal effects of the family on the adolescent. Studies suggest that most adolescents' reactions to their families are based on their perceptions of the affective quality of family relations (Newman & others, 1993), which reflects the current interpretation of development as one of reciprocal interactions.

Is there a generational gap between adolescents and their families? As you can see, this question is an extension of the belief that "adolescence is an age of turmoil" for all adolescents. Again, research has shown that such beliefs are incorrect; parents and their adolescents have more similar attitudes and values than adolescents and their friends. (Adolescent peer similarities such as dress and music are more common in the adolescent culture.)

Adolescent-parent conflict, when it exists, results not only from adolescent difficulties but also from parental factors, such as divorce, excessive parental control, or a parental midlife crisis. Today's research into adolescent-family interactions looks at the family as a system, particularly the developmental status of its members. If an adolescent does indeed face a problem, are the parents sufficiently mature to adjust?

WHAT'S YOUR VIEW?

THE EFFECTS OF EARLY EXPERIENCE: LASTING OR TEMPORARY?

As an example of a youth who got off to a rocky start but selected his own environments, consider the early school problems of Winston Churchill. Coming from a family environment in which he was emotionally neglected, Churchill constructed a reality that enabled him to overcome these early disadvantages. Beginning school at 7 years of age, he immediately set his own agenda: He refused to learn anything he wasn't interested in; he was rebellious and troublesome; he waged a constant battle with authority.

At the bottom of his class, Churchill maintained this pattern through his years at Harrow, the famous British prep school. As one of his biographers, William Manchester, writes:

Churchillian stubborness, which would become the bane of Britain's enemies, was the despair of his teachers. He refused to learn unless it suited him. He was placed in what today would be called a remedial reading class, where slow boys were taught English. He stared out the window. Math, Greek, and French were beneath his contempt. (Manchester, 1983, p. 157)

These words describe one of the world's greatest leaders, a statesman who led the English people through the darkest days of World War II and ultimately triumphed. Yet by today's standards he probably would be labeled a difficult child "with a behavior disorder." Do you think other children can overcome the effects of an early negative environment? What's your view? (Remember your answer to this question, because we'll return to it later in this chapter.)

Adulthood

Adulthood is that time of our lives when we begin a career, form long-lasting relationships, assume personal and civic responsibilities, care for aging parents, and adjust to the aging process. Is it any wonder that this period has captured the interest of scholars and become a discipline in itself, much as we have seen happen in childhood and adolescence?

One only has to read the daily newspaper to be reminded of the growing number and contributions of senior citizens. Given the accomplishments of many individuals in their later years and the crucial developmental tasks of adulthood, we can understand why these years have attracted so much scholarly attention. Evidence of the growing interest in adulthood may be seen in the number of studies of this period of life (U.S. Department of Health and Social Services, 1991). One of the topics most heavily researched is intellectual ability: What is the reality and extent of intellectual decline with age? This is an important question when we consider America's aging population—"the graying of America."

As each of these age periods assumed its place in the developmental mainstream, psychologists felt a growing need to integrate findings, to devise some mechanism that would renew focus on the totality of human development. Consequently lifespan development was born, a study committed to the view that development is not confined to any period or periods but is a lifelong process encompassing the time from conception to death.

Guided Review

7. G. Stanley Hall is remembered for his work with _____ .

8. Sigmund Freud is associated with the belief that the _____ _____ are crucial in human development.

9. Jean Piaget is credited for his insights into _____ _____ .

10. Lifespan psychology is distinguished because of its acceptance of change in _____ .

As with any discipline, lifespan studies must address several controversial issues. These topics engage the time and energy of developmental psychologists and help to give direction to the field.

Issues in Lifespan Development

Here we'll discuss several issues that appear repeatedly throughout the book and then examine the positions of several developmental theorists, each of whom has taken a position on these issues.

Culture and Development

We pride ourselves on being a nation of immigrants, a country that welcomes newcomers with the promise of unrestricted opportunity. To achieve this objective during a time of increasing immigration demands consideration and tolerance for those of different color, nationality, and beliefs.

Americans pride themselves on living in a culturally diverse nation that encourages newcomers to share their way of life. Even under the best of conditions, however, immigrants can experience difficulties: language, customs, acceptance, job opportunities. The receiving country also must adapt. Schools, churches, markets, and politics all must change accordingly. We explore these ideas in later chapters but first, what do we know about immigration today that illustrates changing cultural conditions?

The United States is now experiencing its *third* great immigration wave. The federal government began keeping immigration records in 1820, which was the peak of the first significant immigration movement. Most of these immigrants arrived from Great Britain, Ireland, Germany, and Scandinavia, with a smaller number of Chinese entering California (Kellogg, 1988).

The second major wave, mainly immigrants from Italy, Hungary, Poland, and Russia, occurred between 1900 and 1920. In 1907 more than 1.3 million immigrants entered the United States; during the years 1900 to 1910, 8.8 million newcomers, representing more than 40 countries, arrived. It wasn't until the economy collapsed in the late 1920s that immigration slowed.

The third significant wave began in the late 1960s and still continues. If we count the three categories of immigrants—legal immigrants, refugees, and undocumented immigrants—today's migration is the largest in our history. More than two-thirds of this latest migration are Asian and Latino (Kellogg, 1988).

Children from different cultures bring their differences with them; thus, their different customs may influence the relationships they form. Certainly their diets are different. Learning styles vary, which can affect their classroom achievement. Many immigrant children, who frequently are fleeing war and poverty, carry emotional scars. As you can well imagine, all of these conditions have developmental consequences.

For example, a white female elementary school teacher in the United States recently gave her students a math problem: If there are four blackbirds sitting in a

Answers

tree and you shoot one of them with a slingshot, how many are left? A white student quickly answers, "Three." An African immigrant student answered with equal confidence, "Zero." The teacher was puzzled, thinking that the new student either had misunderstood the wording or had a math problem. Actually the immigrant student reasoned that if you shoot one bird, the others will fly away (Wing, 1992). Here is a good example of the need to understand the backgrounds of our changing population.

Gender and Development

Another issue that has attracted the attention of developmental psychologists is that of gender development, which raises a basic question: Are females receiving the support they need to fulfill their potential? Or is their development being frustrated by a form of discrimination so subtle and sophisticated that it has become part of our daily lives?

Let's begin by defining terms that we can use in a consistent manner. For several years developmental psychologists, responding to Unger's plea (1979), have urged that we use the terms *sex* and *gender* more carefully. In this new context, sex would refer to *biological* maleness or femaleness (for example, the sex chromosomes), whereas gender would suggest *psychosocial* aspects of maleness and femaleness (for example, changing gender roles).

Although no absolute distinction is possible—we can't completely separate our ideas about gender from a person's body—this distinction will help us to focus on the major forces contributing to the acquisition of gender identity while preserving the integrity of the biopsychosocial model. Within this framework, we can now distinguish among gender identity, gender stereotypes, and gender roles.

Gender identity
The conviction that one belongs to the sex of birth.

Gender stereotypes
Beliefs about the characteristics associated with male or female.

Gender role
Culturally acceptable sexual behavior.

- **Gender identity** is a conviction that one belongs to the sex of birth.
- **Gender stereotypes** reflect those beliefs about the characteristics associated with male or female.
- **Gender role** refers to culturally acceptable sexual behavior.

Studies of gender development have focused on theoretical explanations, research into gender similarities and differences, and gender stereotypes. We'll analyze these topics throughout our work, but here it is instructive to mention a few signs that indicate the changing status of women in our society.

Recent census figures (U.S. Bureau of the Census, 1992) reveal that 18.7 percent of females 25 years or older had four or more years of college compared with 24.3 percent of males. For women, this is a substantial increase from the 3.8 percent who completed four or more college years in 1940. During the 1980s the number of women on campus increased by 17 percent until today estimates are that women constitute about 53 percent of the post–high school population (Sadker & Sadker, 1994).

Given the changing conditions in society—family, school, workplace—the role that women play, and can play, has serious developmental implications. As one example, the issue of gender stereotyping deserves our consideration. Try this. Fill in several characteristics that you think apply to males and females.

Male   **Female**

_____   _____
_____   _____
_____   _____
_____   _____

Now compare your responses with those of college students in the 1980s (Ruble, 1983).

Male	Female
aggressive	kind
forceful	gentle
confident	understanding
strong	people-oriented
career-oriented	thoughtful
independent	emotional
dynamic	nurturing

Has gender stereotyping, either male or female, had any impact on you in school or in work or in your relationships with others?

Your answers are probably quite different. As concern about gender equity has received more publicity, the stereotypes about males and females are steadily eroding. If, however, people are treated according to stereotypical characteristics, then their developmental potential is immediately limited. Although gender stereotyping is only one part of gender development, it illustrates the importance of the relationship between gender and development.

Continuity versus Discontinuity

Continuity
The lasting quality of experiences; development proceeds steadily and sequentially.

Discontinuity
Behaviors that are apparently unrelated to earlier aspects of development.

We can summarize the issue of continuity versus discontinuity as follows: Do developmental changes appear as the result of a slow but steady progression (**continuity**) or as the result of abrupt changes and stages (**discontinuity**) (Rutter, 1989)? As a rather dramatic illustration, consider the phenomenon known as attachment in infancy. Sometime after 6 months of age, babies begin to show a decided preference for a particular adult, usually the mother. We then say that the infant has attached to the mother. During any time of stress—anxiety, illness, appearance of strangers—the child will move to the preferred adult. With regard to *continuity* or *discontinuity,* does attachment appear suddenly as completely new and different behavior, or do subtle clues signal its arrival? (For an excellent overview of this topic, see Robins & Rutter, 1990.)

Continuities and discontinuities appear in all our lives because the term *development* implies change. Puberty, leaving home, marriage, and career all serve to shape psychological functioning. Continuities will occur, however, because our initial experiences, our early learning, our temperaments remain with us. The form of the behavior may change over the years but the underlying processes may remain the same. For example, the conduct disorders of childhood (stealing, fighting, truancy) may become the violence of adulthood (theft, wife abuse, child abuse, murder, personality disorders). Surface dissimilarities may be evident in the types of behavior, but the processes that cause both kinds of behavior may be identical, which has caused some developmental psychologists to argue for continuity in development (Rutter, 1989).

Have the transitions you have experienced affected you in any way? How? Give specific examples.

We must explain, however, those periods in our lives that seem to be quite different from those that preceded them; for example, walking and talking. We also negotiate *transitions* at appropriate times in our lives, such as leaving home, beginning a career, getting married, adjusting to the birth of children. It's not just a matter of "doing these things," because the circumstances surrounding them also have important developmental effects. What is the "right" age to get married? Is it a positive occasion and not something that "should" be done? The reality of these events has caused other developmental psychologists to see development as mainly discontinuous. Most developmental psychologists now believe that both continuity and discontinuity characterize development.

Stability versus Resiliency

Whether children's early experiences (either positive or negative) affect them throughout their lifespan is a question that today intrigues most developmental

Stability
A belief that children's early experiences affect them for life.

Resiliency
The ability to recover from either physiological or psychological trauma and return to a normal developmental path.

Have you had any personal experiences (in your life or in the lives of those close to you) that would explain how you feel about stability or resiliency?

Sensitive periods
Certain times in the lifespan when a particular experience has a greater and more lasting impact than at another time.

Equal potential
Experiences have the same capacity to be meaningful at all times in our lives.

psychologists. If a child suffers emotional or physical neglect, abuse, or malnutrition, does it mean the child is scarred for life? If you answer yes, you believe in **stability;** if your answer is no, then you accept the likelihood of change. We know, for example, that human beings show amazing resiliency; recovery from damage (both physical and psychological) has been a well-documented fact of biological and psychological research (Robins & Rutter, 1990). Yet **resiliency** has its limits, which brings us to a critical question: Under what conditions will children and adults recover from damage?

Human growth seems to have considerable flexibility, especially during the early months. For example, the human infant who is swaddled during the first year of life still walks normally in the second year. The stand you take on this issue has serious implications. Consider, for example, those who believe that whatever happens to a child in the early years leaves an indelible mark; that is, early damage remains with the child for life. Proponents of stability believe that, since the damage will remain with the child for life, rehabilitation efforts are useless. Adherents of flexibility take exactly the opposite view: Since human beings demonstrate tremendous recuperative powers, refusal to offer help borders on the criminal in their minds.

Sensitive Periods versus Equal Potential

The *timing* of experiences and an individual's reactions to them are crucial in development. At different times in our lives, are certain experiences more meaningful than similar events at other times **(sensitive periods)?** Or does each experience have the same chance to be meaningful **(equal potential)?** Was going off to school for the first time more intense than walking into a class in developmental psychology?

Many developmental psychologists believe that at certain times in the lifespan, a particular experience has a greater and more lasting impact than at other times (Rutter, 1989; Sroufe & others, 1992). These are called *sensitive periods*. For example, the care and attention of a loving adult during the first months of life seems obviously to be linked to the appearance of attachment. If such an experience is lacking during these early days but comes at a later age (say 5 years), does it produce the same results? Or was the sensitive period missed? Here we have another explosive question that cuts across many of society's activities—socially, politically, economically.

Let's assume for the sake of argument (and we don't agree with this conclusion) that once a sensitive period is missed, the damage can never be repaired. Why, then, should we bother to pour hundreds of millions of dollars into intervention programs (such as Head Start) in the hope of "making up" for lost experiences? Politicians who vote on the use of public monies must take a stand on this question; voters either agree or disagree with their decisions. Most developmental psychologists don't agree that "once missed, never catch up." But they also believe that nobody, child or adult, can withstand severe deprivation, either physical or psychological, indefinitely. We all have our limits.

These issues help to identify lifespan psychology as a dynamic discipline, one that has great theoretical and practical implications. But, as fascinating as these issues are, we can't forget the integrated nature of development. With these ideas in mind to help you interpret developmental data, we turn now to those research techniques that developmental psychologists use in resolving questions about the lifespan.

Developmental Research

Having identified several key developmental issues and theoretical viewpoints, we must now ask: How can we obtain reliable data about these topics so that we may better understand them?

11. Although newcomers to any society must adapt to that country, those in the _____ country must also adjust.

12. In the latest wave of immigration, almost two-thirds are of _____ and _____ descent.

13. The term *gender* implies _____ aspects of maleness and femaleness.

14. When children believe they belong to the sex of their birth, this is called _____ _____ .

15. _____ _____ refers to culturally acceptable sexual behavior.

16. A belief in _____ is to hold the opinion that early experiences in a child's life continue to exert influence throughout the lifespan.

17. When a particular experience has a more lasting effect on an individual at one time rather than at other times, it is referred to as _____ _____ .

AN APPLIED VIEW

When Are Research References Too Old?

Probably for the rest of your career, you will be reading research—articles, chapters in books, monographs, and so on. When should you decide that a reference is too old to be credited any longer? As with so many aspects of social science, the answer is "It all depends." Guidelines exist, however, so let's try to understand them by looking at several references. Before reading our decision, you might try to guess what a good judgment would be.

■ As many as one-third of adolescents receive less than 70 percent of their minimum daily requirement for the most common minerals such as calcium and iron (U.S. Department of Health, Education, and Welfare, 1972).

Since eating habits of adolescents are likely to change with the times (depending, among other things, on the economic condition of the country), this statistic is unreliable because more than 20 years have passed since the data were collected.

■ Although the average number of homosexuals who are contracting AIDS each year is decreasing, they are still the most vulnerable group (U.S. National Center for Health Statistics, 1990).

This study is much more recent, but it too is suspect because we know that the AIDS epidemic is changing very rapidly. In fact, heterosexual females are now experiencing the greatest rate of increase per capita.

■ Noise-induced hearing loss is recognized as the second most common cause of irreversible hearing loss in older persons (Surjan & others, 1973).

Here is another study that is quite dated, but because there is no known reason to believe that aging factors have changed much over the years, if the study was well designed, we may still accept the results.

■ The major crisis in the first year and one-half of human life is the establishment of basic trust (Erikson, 1963).

This statement is not a research finding but rather represents Erikson's belief as reflected in his psychosocial theory of human development. As such, it is accurate because that is exactly what Erikson said.

Can you think of other factors that influence the timeliness of research references? Can you think of other criteria for judging them?

Descriptive studies
Studies in which information is gathered on subjects without manipulating them in any way.

Manipulative experiments
Studies in which attempts are made to keep all variables (all the factors that can affect a particular outcome) constant except one, which is carefully manipulated.

Today we use many approaches to understanding human behavior. Each has its strengths and weaknesses; none is completely reliable. Most developmental psychologists employ one of three data collection methods: **descriptive studies, manipulative experiments,** and **naturalistic experiments.** In the first type, information is gathered on subjects without manipulating them in any way. In the second two, an experiment is performed before the information is gathered.

Developmental psychologists also use one of four time variable designs: **one-time, one-group studies; longitudinal studies; cross-sectional studies;** and a combination of the last two, called **sequential studies.** Each type of study varies according to the effect of time on the results.

Answers

11. receiving 12. Asian, Latino 13. psychological 14. gender identity 15. Gender role 16. stability 17. sensitive periods

Figure 1.2
The classic experiment

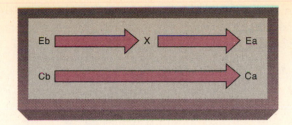

Naturalistic experiments
Studies in which the researcher acts solely as an observer and does as little as possible to disturb the environment.

One-time, one-group studies
Studies carried out only once on one group of studies.

Longitudinal studies
Studies in which the same individuals are observed at two or more times in their lives.

Cross-sectional studies
Studies in which groups of individuals of various ages are compared at the same time to investigate the effects of aging.

Sequential studies
A cross-sectional study done at several times with the same groups of individuals.

Treatment
The variable that the experimenter manipulates.

Data Collection Techniques

The three data collection techniques are described in the following sections.

Descriptive Studies

Descriptive studies are quite common. Most are numerically descriptive; for example, how many 12-year-olds versus 17-year-olds think the government is doing a good job? How much money does the average 40-year-old woman have to spend per week? How many pregnant teenage girls were or were not using birth control? How happily or unhappily does the average 66-year-old man view his sex life? Some studies ask people their opinions about themselves (called *self-report studies*) or other people. These studies may use interviews or questionnaires. Other studies describe people simply by counting the number and types of their behaviors (called *observational studies*). A third type of study, *case studies,* presents data on an individual or individuals in great detail, in order to make generalizations about a particular age group.

An example of the case study approach is Mack and Hickler's *Vivienne: The Life and Suicide of an Adolescent Girl* (1982). After Vivienne's death, the researchers obtained the family's permission to read her diary, poems, and letters. They also interviewed her relatives, friends, and teachers to shed light on her thinking as she came closer and closer to committing this tragic act. Although their findings may explain the suicide of only this one person, the researchers' hope was to discover the variables that caused such a decision. Many of the best theories about development have been based on detailed case studies of small numbers of individuals.

Descriptive studies have the advantage of generating a great deal of data. Because the sequence of events is not under the observer's control, however, causes and effects cannot be determined.

Manipulative Experiments

In the quest for the causes of behavior, psychologists have designed many manipulative experiments. In these, the investigators attempt to keep all variables (all the factors that can affect a particular outcome) constant except one, which they carefully manipulate; this is called a **treatment.** If differences occur in the results of the experiment, they can be attributed to the variable that was manipulated in the treatment. The experimental subjects must respond to some test the investigator selects to determine the effect of the treatment. Figure 1.2 illustrates this procedure.

In the figure, E is the experimental group and C is the control group, which receives no special treatment; x stands for the treatment; and the lowercase b and a refer to measurements done before and after the experiment. The two groups must have no differences between them, either before or during the experiment (except the treatment). Otherwise, the results remain questionable.

An example would be Dacey's study (1993) in which two similar groups of eighth graders were randomly selected from all those in two inner-city middle schools. The experimental group was given the treatment (a series of 16 lessons in self-control), whereas a second group studied the traditional curriculum. Two years after the end of this experiment, researchers checked to see whether any decrease in dropping out of school had occurred in either group. Forty percent more of the experimental group was still in school, as compared with those who did not get the lessons.

Though manipulative experiments often can lead us to discover what causes what in life, they have some problems. How do you know your results are reliable? Was the treatment similar to normal conditions? Do subjects see themselves as special because you picked them and thus react atypically? For these reasons, researchers may turn to naturalistic experiments.

Naturalistic Experiments

In naturalistic experiments, the researcher acts solely as an observer and does as little as possible to disturb the environment. "Nature" performs the experiment, and the researcher acts as a recorder of the results. (Note: Do not confuse these experiments with descriptive studies that are done in a natural setting, such as a park; those are not experiments.) An example is the study of the effects of the Northeast blizzard of 1978 by Nuttall and Nuttall (1980). These researchers compared the reactions of those people whose homes were destroyed with the reactions of people whose homes suffered only minor damage.

Only with a naturalistic experiment do we have any chance of discovering causes and effects in real-life settings. The main problems with this technique are that it requires great patience and objectivity, and it is impossible to meet the strict requirements of a true scientific experiment.

Time Variable Designs

In the following sections, we'll describe the four time variable designs.

One-Time, One-Group Studies

As the name implies, one-time, one-group studies are those that are carried out only once on one group of subjects. Thus investigating causes and effects is impossible because the *sequence* of events cannot be known.

Longitudinal Studies

Would you ever volunteer to be a participant in a longitudinal study? Why? Why not?

The longitudinal study, which makes several observations of the same individuals at two or more times in their lives, can answer important questions. Examples are determining the long-term effects of learning on behavior; the stability of habits and intelligence; and the factors involved in memory.

Although much of childhood behavior disappears by adulthood, a suspicion has long existed that some adult traits develop steadily from childhood and remain for life. In his search for such stable characteristics, Benjamin Bloom, in his classic work *Stability and Change in Human Characteristics* (1964), noted that the development of some human characteristics appears visible and obvious, whereas that of others remains obscure. The following are three growth studies in which more than 300 persons have participated for more than 30 years.

1. *The Berkeley Growth Study,* begun in 1928, was designed to study the mental, motor, and physical development of a sample of full-term healthy babies.

2. *The Guidance Study* took youngsters born in 1928 and 1929 and began to study them at 21 months of age. The aim was to study physical, mental, and personality development in a normal group.

3. *The Oakland Growth Study* of 200 fifth and sixth graders, begun in the early 1930s, was designed to study many interrelations between developmental changes and behavior. The investigators tried to discover whether developmental changes affect a child's potential.

Figure 1.3

Comparison of the longitudinal and cross-sectional approaches

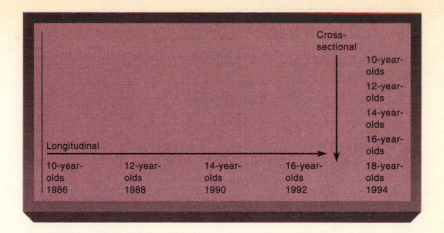

One of the longitudinal growth studies most often quoted is that of the Fels Research Institute (Kagan & Moss, 1962). The subjects were 45 girls and 44 boys, all white, whose personality development was traced from birth through early adulthood. The investigators conducted extensive interviews with both the children and their parents.

The chief advantage of the longitudinal method is that it permits the discovery of lasting habits and of the periods in which they appear. A second advantage is the possibility of tracing those adult behaviors that have changed since early childhood. Longitudinal research, however, has many problems. It is expensive and often hard to maintain because of changes in availability of researchers and subjects. Changes in the environment can also distort the results. For example, if you began in 1960 to study changes in political attitudes of youths from 10 to 20 years of age, you would probably have concluded that adolescents become more and more radical as they grow older. But the war in Vietnam would surely have had much to do with this finding. The results of the same study done between 1970 and 1980 would probably not show this trend toward the radical.

Cross-Sectional Studies

The cross-sectional method compares groups of individuals of various ages at the same time to investigate the effects of aging. For example, if you want to know how creative thinking changes or grows during adolescence, you could administer creativity tests to groups of 10-, 12-, 14-, 16-, and 18-year-olds and check on the differences of the average scores of the five groups. Jaquish and Ripple (1980) did just this, but their subjects ranged in age from 10 to 84!

As with each of the other research designs, a problem occurs with this method. Although careful selection can minimize the effects of cultural change, it is possible that the differences you may find may be due to differences in *age cohort,* rather than maturation. Age cohorts are groups of people born at about the same time. Each cohort has had different experiences throughout its history, and this can affect the results as well as the actual differences in age. Figure 1.3 compares the longitudinal and cross-sectional approaches.

Sequential (Longitudinal/Cross-Sectional) Studies

When a cross-sectional study is done at several times with the same groups of individuals (such as administering creativity tests to the same five groups of youth, but at three different points in their lives), the problems mentioned before can be alleviated. Table 1.1 illustrates such a study. Although this type of research is complicated and expensive, it may be the only type that is capable of answering important questions in the complex and fast-changing times in which we live.

Table 1.1	Illustration of a Longitudinal/Cross-Sectional Study		
Creativity Test			
Test 1 *March 4, 1970*	*Test 2* *March 4, 1980*	*Test 3* *March 4, 1990*	
Group A (12 years old)	Group A (14 years old)	Group A (16 years old)	Mean Score Group A
Group B (14 years old)	Group B (16 years old)	Group B (18 years old)	Mean Score Group B
Group C (16 years old)	Group C (18 years old)	Group C (20 years old)	Mean Score Group C
Mean Score 1970	Mean Score 1980	Mean Score 1990	

Table 1.2	Relationships of Data Collection Techniques and Time Variable Designs		
	Data Collection Techniques		
Time Variable Designs	*Descriptive*	*Manipulated*	*Naturalistic*
One-time, one-group			
Longitudinal			
Cross-sectional			
Sequential			

Figure 1.4
A comparison of research techniques

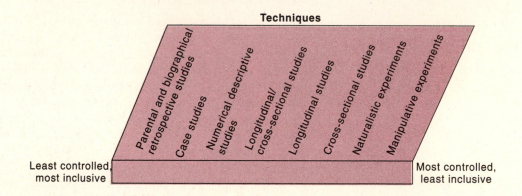

Table 1.2 shows how each of the data collection methods may be combined with each of the time variable designs. For each of the cells in this table, a number of actual studies could serve as examples. Can you see where each study mentioned in this section would go?

To conclude this section, figure 1.4 compares the various research techniques. By *controlled,* we mean the degree to which the investigator can control the relevant variables. By *inclusive,* we mean the degree to which all relevant information is included in the data.

AN APPLIED VIEW

Understanding the Research Article

As you continue your reading and work in lifespan development, your instructor will undoubtedly ask you to review pertinent articles that shed light on the topic you're studying. Many of these articles present the results of an experiment that reflects the scientific method.

The typical research article contains four sections: the *Introduction,* the *Method* section, the *Results* section, and *Discussion* (Moore, 1983). We'll review each of these sections using a well-designed study—*The Effects of Early Education on Children's Competence in Elementary School,* published in *Evaluation Review* (Bronson & others, 1984)—to illustrate each of the four parts.

1. The Introduction

The introductory section states the purpose of the article (usually as an attempt to solve a problem) and predicts the outcome of the study (usually in the form of hypotheses). The introduction section also contains a review of the literature. In the introductory section of the article by Bronson and associates, the researchers state that their intent is to coordinate the effects of early education programs on the performance of pupils in elementary school. They concisely review the pertinent research and suggest a means of evaluating competence.

2. The Method Section

The method section informs the reader about the subjects in the experiment (Who were they? How many? How were they chosen?), describes any tests that were used, and summarizes the steps taken to carry out the study. In the study by Bronson and her associates, the subjects were 169 second-grade children who had been in an early education program and 169 other children who had not been in the preschool program. The outcome measure was a classroom observation instrument. The authors then explained in considerable detail how they observed the pupils.

3. The Results Section

In the results section the information gathered on the subjects is presented, together with the statistics that help us to interpret the data. In the article we are using, the authors present their data in several clear tables and present differences between the two groups using appropriate statistics.

4. Discussion

Finally, the authors of any research article will discuss the importance of what they found (or did not find) and relate their findings to theory and previous research. In the Bronson article, the authors report that the pupils who had experienced any early education program showed significantly greater competence in the second grade. The authors conclude by noting the value of these programs in reducing classroom behavior problems and improving pupils' competence.

Do not be intimidated by research articles. Look for the important features and determine how the results could help you to understand people's behavior at a particular age.

Guided Review

18. In a manipulative experiment, the experimenter attempts to keep all the variables constant except one, which is called the _____ .

19. A study that observes the same individuals two or more times in their lives is known as a _____ study.

20. Comparing groups of individuals of various ages at the same time is an example of _____ research.

21. The typical research article contains four sections: _____ , _____ , _____ , and _____ .

Answers

18. treatment   19. longitudinal   20. cross-sectional   21. introduction, method, results, discussion

🌳 CONCLUSION

In this chapter we have presented a model of development—the biopsychosocial model—that forms the structure of the book. We urge you to use this model to help you grasp and retain the material and meaning of the various chapters. We have also identified the various age groups that constitute the lifespan and that are the focus of this book. Lifespan study can aid us in adjusting to a society in which rapid change seems to be an inevitable process. By acquiring insights into your own development and recognizing the developmental characteristics of people of differing ages, you can hope to have more harmonious relationships with others. Also, as a result of reading about the strengths and weaknesses of different research methods, you should be more analytical and critical of the studies that are presented.

With these basic ideas firmly in place, we now turn to a closer look at those theorists who have made lasting contributions to the field of developmental psychology. As you read their explanations of development, keep in mind the purposes they were trying to achieve: Freud's search for the causes of behavior in the unconscious; Piaget's endeavors to identify the cognitive structures that underlie cognitive development; Vygotsky's emphasis on the context of development; Erikson's efforts to describe the psychosocial crises of life; the behaviorists' attempt to explain the role that the environment plays in development.

🌳 CHAPTER HIGHLIGHTS

The Meaning of Lifespan Psychology

- As psychologists realized that development did not cease at adolescence but continued into adulthood and old age, lifespan psychology assumed an important place in developmental psychology.
- Reciprocal interactions is a valuable concept in understanding development.
- The timing of experiences as well as the transitions during the lifespan help us to gain insights into developmental processes.
- Today we are aware of the significance of context in development.

History of Lifespan Studies

- The concept of childhood is relatively new.
- Children are now seen as active participants in their development.
- Most adolescents are not so troubled as the individuals we read about frequently.
- Today's adolescent research places greater emphasis on the family's role.

- Studies of adulthood have indicated that individuals continue to grow and change during these years.

Issues in Lifespan Development

- Any analysis of lifespan development must address key developmental issues, such as the importance of culture and development, if it is to present a complete picture of development.
- A growing concern today is opportunity for girls in our classrooms.
- Many psychologists believe that development occurs as a steady progression of small accomplishments (for example, most infants begin to move on the floor by pulling themselves on their stomachs; they then move to a position on their hands and knees and move much more quickly, which is an example of continuous development); other psychologists believe that development occurs in spurts or stages, such as the marked

difference between crawling and walking, which is an example of discontinuity.
- The controversy over stability versus resiliency continues to divide developmental psychologists.
- Sensitive periods seem to exist; that is, there are times in our lives when we acquire new behaviors more easily than at other times.

Developmental Research

- To explain the various ages and stages of development, we must use the best data available to enrich our insights and to provide a thoughtful perspective on the lifespan.
- Good data demand careful research methods, otherwise we would be constantly suspicious of our conclusions.
- The most widely used research techniques include: descriptive studies, manipulative experiments, and naturalistic experiments.
- Developmental psychologists also use four time variable designs: one-time, one-group; longitudinal studies; cross-sectional studies; and sequential studies.

🌳 KEY TERMS

Action theory 9
Biopsychosocial model 4
Continuity 14
Cross-sectional studies 16
Culture 6
Discontinuity 14
Descriptive studies 16
Equal potential 15

Ethnic 6
Gender identity 13
Gender role 13
Gender stereotypes 13
Longitudinal studies 16
Manipulative experiments 16
Naturalistic experiments 16
One-time, one-group studies 16

Race 6
Reciprocal interaction 9
Resiliency 15
Sensitive periods 15
Sequential studies 16
Stability 15
Treatment 17

🌳 WHAT DO YOU THINK?

1. We urged you to refer to the biopsychosocial model as you continue your reading of the text. Can you explain its potential value? Now think of an example in your own life, or in the life of a family member, and describe how biological, psychological, and social factors interacted to produce a particular effect. Do you think the model helped you to explain that person's behavior?

2. We presented several issues that thread their way through lifespan studies; for example, culture and development, gender and development, the role of sensitive periods, continuity versus discontinuity, stability versus resiliency. Why do you think these are issues? Examine each one separately and defend your reasons for stating that they have strong developmental implications.

3. Throughout the chapter, we have stressed the important role that context plays in development. What do you think of this emphasis? Although this is only the first chapter of your reading, recall your own life and think about the influence (both positive and negative) that those around you have had. Use these personal experiences in your answer.

🌳 SUGGESTED READINGS

Banks, J. & Banks, C. (1993). *Multicultural education*. Needham Heights, MA: Allyn and Bacon. An excellent introduction to issues of race, culture, ethnicity, and gender applied to a particular setting. If you would like a well-written, interesting analysis of many of the critical issues facing our society, this would be a good beginning.

Lips, H. (1993). *Sex & gender: An introduction*. Mountain View, CA: Mayfield. An interesting and thorough investigation into current perspectives on how sex and gender influence lifespan development; a good source of information on gender differences and similarities.

Woodward, B. (1991). *The commanders*. New York: Simon & Schuster. A fascinating look at the Gulf War in which Colin Powell played such a key role. Woodward's analysis of Powell's behavior during these tense days provides telling insights into Powell's development and character.

🌳 CHAPTER REVIEW TEST

1. A model that uses the interaction of biological, psychological, and social influences to explain development is the
   a. psychoanalytic.
   b. cognitive.
   c. biopsychosocial.
   d. behavioral.

2. When one person's reactions bring about change in the behavior of another person, this is called
   a. transfer.
   b. reciprocal interactions.
   c. accommodation.
   d. psychosocial crisis.

3. Tracing children's cognitive development was the work of
   a. Freud.
   b. Hall.
   c. Skinner.
   d. Piaget.

4. Who believed that children should be conditioned early in life?
   a. Watson
   b. Piaget
   c. Freud
   d. Hall

5. When we refer to the values, beliefs, and characteristics of a people, we are referring to
   a. culture.
   b. race.
   c. ethnicity.
   d. customs.

6. One of the first investigators of adolescence was
   a. Watson.
   b. Hall.
   c. Piaget.
   d. Skinner.

7. What wave of immigration is the United States now experiencing?
   a. first
   b. second
   c. third
   d. fourth

8. If you believe that a child carries the scars of childhood abuse for life, you believe in
   a. equal potential.
   b. stability.
   c. continuity.
   d. resiliency.

9. When you refer to the national or linguistic origins of a person, you are referring to
   a. race.
   b. culture.
   c. ethnicity.
   d. blood type.

10. When you believe that you belong to the sex of your birth, you have acquired
    a. gender identity.
    b. gender stereotypes.
    c. gender role.
    d. equality.

11. Beliefs about the characteristics associated with males and females is called
    a. gender identity.
    b. gender stereotype.
    c. gender role.
    d. equality.

12. Descriptive studies
    a. determine cause and effect.
    b. manipulate variables.
    c. require experimenter control.
    d. generate considerable data.

13. When an experimenter keeps all variables constant but one, that one is called
    a. determined.
    b. predicted.
    c. descriptive.
    d. treatment.

14. An example of a cross-sectional study is
    a. comparing individuals of various ages at the same time.
    b. continued observations of the same individuals.
    c. careful description by the researcher.
    d. one that requires no manipulation.

15. The typical research article contains four sections. Which item is not included in a research article?
    a. introduction
    b. method
    c. results
    d. author biography

Answers

1. c 2. b 3. d 4. a 5. a 6. b 7. c 8. b 9. c 10. a 11. b 12. d 13. d 14. a 15. d

Theoretical Viewpoints

Chapter Outline

Ellen Marie Cotter was born on February 17, 1931, in Boston. The daughter of middle-class parents, she seemed a normal, healthy, and happy baby. It was not until she was 5 years old that she began to exhibit behavior that bothered her parents. From having an outgoing, cheerful personality, Ellen slowly started to withdraw until she refused to speak to anyone but her parents. She also had a disturbing tendency to sit and stare out the window.

Deeply bothered, her parents decided to do everything they could to help their child, no matter what the financial sacrifice might be. Their family doctor, Dr. John Patterson, finding no physical causes of her problem, mentioned that he had heard of a new technique for treating psychological problems, called psychoanalysis. The leader of the psychoanalytic movement, an individual by the name of Sigmund Freud, believed that a person's behavior was a clue to inner thoughts and feelings. Ellen's parents seized on this and wanted to know more about it: What was involved in psychoanalysis? Who were the leading proponents of the movement? Where was the movement located?

Their doctor, a well-read man of his times, told them as much as he knew about Freud. When Ellen's parents said they were willing to take her to Vienna, regardless of the expense, Dr. Patterson said that Freud was almost 80 years old and in poor health but that he had a very kind habit of writing thoughtful replies to the letters of strangers, especially if the problem interested him.

The Cotters decided to contact Freud and sent him a detailed description of their daughter's condition. Dr. Patterson also suggested that they tell Freud as much as possible about the early years of Ellen's life because Freud was particularly fascinated by the effect of early experiences. After sending off their lengthy letter, the Cotters anxiously awaited each day's mail. Much to their amazement and delight, about three months later an envelope postmarked *Vienna* arrived at their home.

In his reply, Freud, although declaring his inability to conduct therapy under the circumstances, wrote that the Cotters should examine certain conditions in their daughter's life very carefully. He told them to search for any signs of anxiety, which can be extremely painful for a child and could actually produce some of the symptoms they had described. He pointed out that small children suffered from many anxieties that can radically affect their behavior.

Pleased with this professional and caring reply, Ellen's parents spent hours trying to identify anything that might have caused her any anxiety. They could only think of one episode: The previous summer while on a train trip Ellen had become separated from them while they were storing their luggage. She had stepped from the train thinking she had seen her father standing on the platform and then thought the train was leaving without her. The Cotters decided they would redouble their efforts to provide a sense of security for their daughter.

Six years passed, and in the summer of 1937, Ellen's father, an excellent salesman, was asked by his company to travel to Switzerland to train the staff of the company's newly opened office. Both parents thought the trip, especially the ocean voyage, would be enjoyable for Ellen. They were to be in Switzerland for only four weeks, but soon after their arrival they heard stories about a remarkable Swiss psychologist, Jean Piaget. A relatively young man of 41, Piaget was then at the peak of his experimental career. Through their Swiss contacts, the Cotters arranged to meet Piaget and discuss their daughter's problem with him. Arriving at Piaget's hotel overlooking beautiful Lake Geneva, the Cotters were immediately taken with him. As the father of three daughters, Piaget was quite sympathetic about Ellen's problems. Although Piaget emphasized that his focus on children's cognitive development had left him little time to study emotional development, after hearing the Cotters' story, he made some insightful comments.

He told them that children of Ellen's age had a natural tendency to relate everything to themselves (e.g. "The moon follows me around"). No matter what happened, children believed it was about them; they felt responsible. The term he used to describe this phase of development was *egocentric*. Piaget said that something might have happened—he didn't know what—for which Ellen blamed herself. The Cotters deeply appreciated the window into cognitive development Piaget had opened for them and thanked him profusely. Piaget, with his customary courtesy, asked them to keep him informed of Ellen's progress.

On the boat trip home, the parents discussed what Piaget had said and decided that both Freud's and Piaget's ideas were helpful. But they wondered whether they themselves could do anything specific. Ellen's father rather casually remarked that he had read recently about a young psychologist by the name of B. F. Skinner who believed that behavior was powerfully influenced by carefully planned reinforcements. That is, if people selected the behaviors they think are appropriate, and reinforced those behaviors, they will continue to appear. Ellen's parents decided they would reinforce those behaviors that were directed toward social development in an effort to encourage Ellen to interact with others.

Both parents agreed that although it had been a lengthy journey from the United States to Vienna to Switzerland and then back to the United States, they had learned much about human behavior and could now offer some realistic help to their daughter. 🌳

Dr. Sigmund Freud was a medical doctor before he invented psychiatry.

In the scenario just described, three historical figures were introduced to illustrate several leading developmental theories: psychoanalytic, cognitive developmental, and behavioral. Each of the six theorists you will read about in this chapter represents a major developmental theory. For many people, the word *theory* means someone's guess about why something happens the way it does. In this book, we use the word differently. We believe that theories do not stand alone; they are related to other aspects of science. Although we cannot give you the one final answer on how humans develop—no one can do that—we can, however, introduce you to the best current thinking in the study of human development.

In this chapter, you will begin to understand how theories help to explain human development by examining six important developmental theorists: Sigmund Freud, Erik Erikson, Abraham Maslow, Jean Piaget, B. F. Skinner, and Albert Bandura. As a result of your reading in this chapter, you should be able to

- Describe the purposes of theory making and the relationships of theory to other aspects of science.

- Itemize Freud's stages of development, together with his concepts of the functions and constructs of the human psyche.

- Compare and contrast Erik Erikson's eight stages of psychosocial crisis.

- Identify and apply the basic needs in Abraham Maslow's hierarchy of needs.

- Define Piaget's four stages of cognitive development, as well as explain the roles played by the two central processes of organization and adaptation.

- Explain the role of reinforcement, punishment, and extinction in Skinner's behavioral theory.

- Apply Bandura's theory of observational learning to specific situations.

- Discuss these issues from an applied, a multicultural, and your own point of view.

The Psychoanalytic Approach

In more than 100 years of psychological research, it is impossible to think of anyone who has played a larger role than Sigmund Freud. Even his most severe critics admit that his theory on the development of personality is a milestone in the social sciences. In fact, many people mistakenly think **psychoanalytic theory,** the name he gave to his theory, is the same as psychology.

Probably due to his experiences as a medical doctor, Freud doubted the reliability of people's testimony about themselves. He also distrusted behavior as a source of the truth. For him, the unconscious was the key to understanding the human being. The most important motives and values reside there. Because many of the ideas in the unconscious are primitive, they are not acceptable to the conscious mind. For example, if a child is furious with her mother, she may not be able to acknowledge it because she is not supposed to hate her mother. Only bad people do that. Here it would be helpful to examine Freud's idea of mind (or *psyche*).

Structures of the Psyche

Freud divided the mind into three structures: the **id,** the **ego,** and the **superego.** These structures appear at different stages of the young child's development. They are empowered by the *libido,* Freud's term for psychic energy, which is similar to the physical energy that fuels bodily functions. Freud argued that the libido is motivated mainly by sexual and aggressive instincts. The characteristics of the three structures of the mind are as follows:

- *The id.* This structure, the only one present at birth, contains all of our basic instincts, such as our need for food, drink, dry clothes, and nurturance. It is the simplest of the structures, operating only in the pursuit of bodily pleasures. The id is not realistic; its needs can be satisfied merely by imagining that we have gotten what we wanted. The id has no clear notion of time, space, or any other aspect of reality. Think about your dreams; they are a good example of the id in operation.

- *The ego.* The ego is the central part of our personality, the (usually) rational part that does all the planning and keeps us in touch with reality. It begins to develop from the moment of birth.

    Imagining that you get what you want does not work very well, or for very long. Consider a baby who awakens from a nap and starts to cry. Soon it stops and drifts back into a doze. Before long it awakens again and cries longer this time. If the baby is left unattended, the dozing periods get shorter and the crying periods longer. Freud suggested that the awakening baby probably is hungry (or thirsty or wet). At first, the baby imagines that the problem is solved and is comforted, but this works less and less well as it becomes hungrier. Over time, the baby learns to cry loudly if it wants its caregiver, and not to stop until she or he comes. This is the beginning of an ego. The ego is necessary so that we can learn to live in the real world. The stronger the ego becomes, the more realistic, and usually the more successful, the person is likely to be.

- *The superego.* Throughout infancy, we gain an increasingly clearer conception of what the world is like. Toward the end of the first year our parents and others begin to teach us what they believe it should be like. They instruct us in right and wrong and expect us to begin to behave according to the principles they espouse. This is the beginning of the superego. Freud disagreed with the religious idea of an inborn conscience. He argued that all morality is learned as a function of the superego.

Psychoanalytic theory
Freud's theory of the development of personality.

Have you ever been angry with a person (mother, father) and felt you could do little about it? What were the circumstances? How did you resolve it?

Id
One of the three structures of the psyche according to Freud; the source of our instinctive desires.

Ego
One of the three structures of the psyche according to Freud; mediates between the id and the superego

Superego
One of the three structures of the psyche according to Freud; acts as a conscience.

Sigmund Freud suggested that babies react to needful feelings such as hunger in several steps. First they become aware of the need, then they cry; next they imagine that the need has been met, and then they fall back to sleep. Slowly they learn that imagination is no substitute for real satisfaction of a need.

Table 2.1	Some Common Defense Mechanisms
Repression	Unconsciously forgetting experiences that are painful to remember. Example: sexual abuse
Compensation	Attempting to make up for an unconsciously perceived inadequacy by excelling at something else. Example: learning to play the guitar if unable to make the soccer team
Rationalization	Coming to believe that a condition that was contrary to your desires is actually what you had wanted all along. Example: being glad a trip was canceled, because "it would have been boring anyway"
Introjection	Adopting the standards and values of someone you are afraid to disagree with. Example: joining a gang
Regression	Reverting to behaviors that were previously successful when current behavior is unsuccessful. Example: crying about getting a low grade in school with the unconscious hope that the teacher will change the grade
Displacement	When afraid to express your feelings toward one person (e.g., anger at your teacher), expressing them to someone less powerful, such as your sister

Now starts the never-ending battle between the desires of the id and the demands of the superego. The main job of the ego is to strive unceasingly for compromises between these two "bullies."

Defending the Unconscious Mind

Freud believed that an array of defense mechanisms keeps important information in the unconscious mind from awareness (Gay, 1988). These mechanisms are unconscious attempts to prevent awareness of unpleasant or unacceptable ideas. The psychic censor, a function of the mind, stands guard over these unconscious thoughts by using defense mechanisms to block awareness. Table 2.1 describes some of the most common defense mechanisms.

WHAT'S YOUR VIEW?

DEFENSE MECHANISMS: POSITIVE OR NEGATIVE?

Defense mechanisms function to protect the conscious mind from the truth. They distort the realities that we find too painful to face. Because they mislead us, and because their maintenance requires spending a lot of energy that could better be spent elsewhere, many psychologists feel we should try to eliminate them if possible.

Others argue that some truths are just too painful to face and, therefore, at least in the short run, defense mechanisms are useful. Those who believe defense mechanisms are useful say that most people go through difficult periods (e.g., breaking up with your first love) and that during these periods defense mechanisms can provide a beneficial buffer for a vulnerable self-image. There will be time enough later to "face the music" of reality. What do you think?

The Developing Personality

For Freud, development means moving through five instinctive stages of life, each of which he assigns to a specific age range. Each stage is discrete from the others and has a major function, which is based on a pleasure center. Unless this pleasure center is stimulated appropriately (not too much, not too little), the person becomes fixated (stuck at that stage) and is unable to become a fully mature person. Here are the five stages.

Oral stage

Freud's belief that the mouth is the main source of pleasure from 0 to 1 1/2 years.

Anal stage

Freud's belief that the anus is the main source of pleasure during the years 1 1/2 to 3 years.

Phallic stage

Freud's belief that the sex organs become the main source of pleasure from 3 to 5 years.

Latency stage

Freud's belief that the sex drive becomes dormant from 5 to 12 years.

Genital stage

Freud's belief in a resurgence of a strong sex drive from 12 years and beyond.

- The **oral stage** (0 to 1 1/2 years old). The oral cavity (mouth, lips, tongue, gums) is the pleasure center. Its function is to obtain an appropriate amount of sucking, eating, biting, and talking.

- The **anal stage** (1 1/2 to 3 years old). The anus is the pleasure center. The function here is successful toilet training.

- The **phallic stage** (3 to 5 years old). The glans of the penis and the clitoris are the pleasure centers in this stage and in the two remaining stages. The major function of this stage is the healthy development of sexual interest. This is achieved through masturbation and unconscious sexual desire for the parent of the opposite sex. Resolution of the conflicts caused by this desire (called the Oedipal conflict in males and the Electra conflict in females) is the goal.

- The **latency stage** (5 to 12 years old). During this stage, sexual desire becomes dormant. This is especially true for males, through the defense mechanism of introjection (see table 2.1). Boys refuse to kiss or hug their mothers and treat female age-mates with disdain. Because our society is more tolerant of the daughter's attraction to her father, the Electra complex is less resolved and girls' sexual feelings are less repressed during this stage.

- The **genital stage** (12 years old and older). At this stage a surge of sexual hormones occurs in both genders, which brings about an unconscious recurrence of the phallic stage. Normally, however, youths have learned that desire for one's parents is taboo, and so they set about establishing relationships with members of the opposite sex who are their own age. Freud believed that if these five stages are not negotiated successfully, homosexuality or an aversion to sexuality itself results. (It should be noted that this concept is not popular among homosexuals, many of whom believe that their sexual orientation goes much deeper than this.) If fixation occurs at any stage, anxiety results, and defense mechanisms will be used to deal with it.

Guided Review

1. For Freud, the best way to understand the human being was through the
_____ .

2. Unconscious attempts to avoid awareness of unpleasant ideas are called
_____ .

3. The structure of the mind containing our basic instincts is called _____ .

4. When a person attempts to excel at one thing because of feeling inadequate in another, this is called _____ .

5. Reverting to behaviors of an earlier age is called _____ .

6. In the developing personality, when pleasure is derived from such behaviors as sucking, this is the _____ stage.

Answers

1. unconscious 2. repression 3. id 4. compensation 5. regression 6. oral

Table 2.2		Erik Erikson's Psychosocial Theory of Development
Stage	**Age**	**Psychosocial Crisis**
1	Infancy (0 to 1 1/2)	Basic trust vs. mistrust
2	Early childhood (1 1/2 to 3)	Autonomy vs. shame and doubt
3	Play age (3 to 5)	Initiative vs. guilt
4	School age (5 to 12)	Industry vs. inferiority
5	Adolescence (12 to 18)	Identity and repudiation vs. identity confusion
6	Young adult (18 to 25)	Intimacy and solidarity vs. isolation
7	Adulthood (26 to 65)	Generativity vs. stagnation
8	Maturity (65+)	Integrity vs. despair

Adapted from *Childhood and Society* by Erik H. Erikson, with the permission of W. W. Norton & Company, Inc. Copyright 1950, © 1963 by W. W. Norton & Company, Inc., renewed © 1978, 1991 by Erik H. Erikson.

Psychologist Erik Erikson is best known for his theory of psychosocial crises.

The Psychosocial Crises Approach

The chief proponent of the psychosocial theory of development is Erik Erikson. Among other important books, Erikson wrote *Childhood and Society* (1963). It is an amazingly perceptive and at times poetically beautiful description of human life. Erikson's view of human development derives from his extensive study of people living in an impressive variety of cultures: Germans, East Indians, the Sioux of South Dakota, the Yuroks of California, and wealthy adolescents in the northeastern United States (Erikson, 1959, 1968). His ideas also stem from intensive studies of historical figures such as Martin Luther (1959) and Mahatma Gandhi (1969), which led him to see human development as the interaction between genes and the environment.

According to Erikson, human life progresses through a series of eight stages. Each of these stages is marked by a crisis that needs to be resolved so that the individual can move on. Erikson used the term *crisis* in a medical sense; that is, it is like an acute period during illness, at the end of which the patient takes a turn for the worse or better. At each life stage, the individual is pressured, by internal needs and the external demands of society, to make a major change in a new direction.

The ages at which people go through each of the stages vary somewhat, but the sequence of the stages is fixed. The ages of the first five stages are exactly the same as in Freud's theory (Erikson was an ardent student of Freud). Unlike Freud and Piaget, however, Erikson believed that the stages overlap.

Each of the crises involves a conflict between two opposing characteristics. Erikson suggested that successful resolution of each crisis should favor the first of the two characteristics, although its opposite must also exist to some degree. Table 2.2 gives an overview of his psychosocial theory.

According to Erikson, people must experience each crisis before proceeding to the next. Inadequate resolution of the crisis at any stage hinders development at all succeeding stages, unless special help is received. When a person is unable to resolve a crisis at one of the stages, Erikson suggested that "a deep rage is aroused comparable to that of an animal driven into a corner" (1963, p. 68). This is not to say that anyone ever resolves a crisis completely. Erikson's description of the eight stages of life is a picture of the ideal; no one ever completes the stages perfectly.

Erikson's Eight Psychosocial Stages

Let us look at each stage more closely.

1. *Basic trust versus mistrust* (birth to 1 1/2 years old). In the first stage, which is by far the most important, a sense of basic trust should develop. For Erikson, trust has an unusually broad meaning. To the trusting infant, it is not so much that the world is a safe and happy place but rather that it is an orderly, *predictable* place. There are causes and effects that one can learn to anticipate. For Erikson, then, trust flourishes with warmth and care, but trust also might well include knowledge that one will be spanked regularly for disobeying rules.

   If the infant is to grow into a person who is trusting and trustworthy, a great deal of regularity must exist in the infant's early environment. The child needs variation, but this variation should occur in a regular order that the child can learn to anticipate. For example, the soft music of an FM radio can provide regular changes in sound level. So does the movement of the colorful toy birds hanging over a child's crib.

   Some children begin life with irregular and inadequate care. Anxiety and insecurity have a negative effect on family and other relationships so important to the development of trust. When a child's world is unreliable, we can expect mistrust and hostility, which under certain circumstances can develop into antisocial, even criminal, behavior. Of course, not all such people become criminals. It is also possible to gain basic trust in infancy and then lose it later. Sometimes people who have not suffered an injurious childhood can lose their basic sense of trust because of damaging experiences later in life.

2. *Autonomy versus shame and doubt* (1 1/2 to 3 years old). When children are about 1 1/2 years old, they should move into the second stage, characterized by the crisis of autonomy versus shame and doubt. This is the time when children begin to gain control over their bodies and is the usual age at which toilet training is begun. Erikson agreed with other psychoanalysts that toilet training has far more important consequences in one's life than control of one's bowels. The sources of generosity and creativity lie in this experience. If children are encouraged to explore their bodies and environment, a level of self-confidence develops. If they are regularly reprimanded for their inability to control excretion, they come to doubt themselves. They become ashamed and afraid to test themselves.

   Of course, excretion is not the only target for regulation in this stage. Children of this age usually start learning to be self-governing in all of their behaviors. Although some self-doubt is appropriate, general self-control should be fostered at this stage.

3. *Initiative versus guilt* (3 to 5 years old). The third crisis, initiative versus guilt, begins when children are about 3 years old. Building on the ability to control themselves, children now learn to have some influence over others in the family and to successfully manipulate their surroundings. They should not merely react, they should initiate. If parents and others make children feel incompetent, however, they develop a generalized feeling of guilt about themselves. In the autonomy stage they can be made to feel ashamed by others; in this stage, they learn to make themselves feel ashamed.

4. *Industry versus inferiority* (5 to 12 years old). The fourth stage corresponds closely to the child's elementary school years. Now the task is to go beyond imitating ideal models and to learn the elementary technology of the culture. Children expand their horizons beyond the family and begin to explore the neighborhood. Their play becomes more

purposeful, and they seek knowledge to complete the tasks that they set for themselves. A sense of accomplishment in making and building should prevail. If it does not, children may develop a lasting sense of inferiority. Here we begin to see clearly the effects of inadequate resolution of earlier crises. As Erikson put it, the child may not be able to be industrious because he may "still want his mother more than he wants knowledge." Erikson suggested that the typical American elementary school, staffed almost entirely by women, can make it difficult for children (especially boys) to make the break from home and mother. Under these circumstances, children may learn to view their productivity merely as a way to please their teacher (the mother substitute) and not as something good for its own sake. Children may perform to be "good little workers" and "good little helpers" and fail to develop the satisfaction of pleasing themselves with their own industry.

5. *Identity and repudiation versus identity confusion* (12 to 18 years old). The main task of the adolescent is to achieve a state of identity. Erikson, who originated the term **identity crisis,** used the word in a special way. In addition to thinking of identity as the general picture one has of oneself, Erikson referred to it as a state toward which one strives. If one were in a state of identity, the various aspects of one's self-image would be in agreement with each other; they would be identical. Ideally, a person in the state of identity has no internal conflicts whatsoever.

   Repudiation of choices is another essential aspect of reaching personal identity. In any choice of identity, the selection we make means that we have repudiated (turned down) all the other possibilities, at least for the present. When youths cannot achieve identity, when identity confusion ensues, it is usually because they are unable to make choices. As Biff, the son in Arthur Miller's *Death of a Salesman,* says, "I just can't take hold, Mom, I can't take hold of some kind of life!" Biff sees himself as many different people; he acts one way in one situation and the opposite way in another—a hypocrite. Because he refuses to make choices and shies away from commitments, his personality has no cohesiveness. He is aware of this lack but is unable to do anything about it. (We will have much more to say about this stage in chap. 12.)

6. *Intimacy and solidarity versus isolation* (18 to 25 years old). In the sixth stage, intimacy with others should develop. Erikson is speaking here of far more than sexual intimacy. He is talking about the essential ability to relate one's deepest hopes and fears to another person, and to accept in turn another person's need for intimacy.

Identity crisis

Erikson's term for those situations, usually in adolescence, that cause us to make major decisions about our identity.

Could you improve any of the relationships in your life? How would you bring about change?

According to Erikson, a sense of intimacy with another person of the opposite gender should develop between the ages of 18 and 25. If it does not, a sense of isolation results.

Each of us is entirely alone in the sense that no one else can ever experience life exactly the way we do. We are imprisoned in our own bodies and can never be certain that our senses experience the same events in the same way as another person's senses. Only if we become intimate with another are we able to understand and have confidence in ourselves. During this time of life, our identity may be fulfilled through the loving validation of the person with whom we have dared to be intimate.

7. *Generativity versus stagnation* (25 to 65 years old). Generativity means the ability to be useful to ourselves and to society. As in the industry stage, the goal here is to be productive and creative. However, productivity in the industry stage is a means of obtaining recognition and material reward. In the generativity stage, one's productivity is aimed at generating a sense of personal fulfillment. Thus, the act of being productive is itself rewarding, regardless of whether recognition or reward results. Furthermore, a sense of trying to make the world a better place for the young in general, and for one's own children in particular, emerges. In this stage many people become mentors to younger individuals, sharing their knowledge and philosophy of life. When people fail in generativity, they begin to stagnate, to become bored and self-indulgent, unable to contribute to society's welfare. Such adults often act as if they are their own child.

8. *Integrity versus despair* (65 years old and older). When people look back over their lives and feel they have made the wrong decisions, or more commonly, that they have too frequently failed to make any decision at all, they see life as lacking integration. They feel despair at the impossibility of "having just one more chance to make things right." They often hide their terror of death by appearing contemptuous of humanity in general, and of those of their own religion or race in particular. They feel disgust for themselves.

   To the extent that individuals have been successful in resolving the first seven crises, they achieve a sense of personal integrity. Adults who have a sense of integrity accept their lives as having been well spent. They feel a kinship with people of other cultures and of previous and future generations. They have a sense of having helped to create a more dignified life for humankind. They have gained wisdom.

🌳 Guided Review 🌳

7. Each of Erikson's stages is highlighted by a _____ that must be resolved before passage to the next stage.

8. At each stage the individual is pressured by _____ needs and the demands of _____ .

9. In Erikson's first stage, it is critical for infants to learn that their world is a _____ place.

10. During Erikson's fifth stage, which occurs during or after adolescence, it is frequently necessary to resolve an _____ _____ .

Answers

7. crisis   8. internal, society   9. predictable   10. identity crisis

Figure 2.1
Maslow's hierarchy of needs

The Humanistic Approach

Another way to understand lifespan changes is to identify those needs that must be satisfied if personal goals are to be achieved. To help you recognize the role that needs play in our lives, we'll turn to the work of Abraham Maslow and his needs hierarchy.

Maslow and Needs Satisfaction

Self-actualization

Maslow's term that means that we use our abilities to the limit of our potentialities.

Are there needs in your life that you believe are unmet? Has this affected your behavior? What are you doing about it?

One of Maslow's most famous concepts is that of **self-actualization,** which means that we use our abilities to the limit of our potentialities (Maslow et al., 1987). If people are convinced that they should—and can—fulfill their promise, they are then on the path to self-actualization. *Self-actualization is a growth concept,* and individuals move toward this goal (physical and psychological health) as they satisfy their basic needs. Growth toward self-actualization requires the satisfaction of a hierarchy of needs. Maslow's theory identifies five basic needs: physiological, safety, love and belonging, esteem, and self-actualization. (See figure 2.1.)

The Hierarchy of Needs

In the hierarchy of needs, those needs at the base of the hierarchy are assumed to be more basic relative to the needs above them in the hierarchy.

Physiological needs

Maslow's term to indicate the importance of satisfying basic needs such as hunger, thirst, and sleep.

- **Physiological needs,** such as hunger and sleep, are dominant and are the basis of motivation. Unless they are satisfied, everything else recedes. For example, students who frequently do not eat breakfast or suffer from poor nutrition generally become lethargic and withdrawn; their learning potential is severely lowered. This is particularly true of adolescents, who can be extremely sensitive to their weight.

Safety needs

Maslow's term to represent the importance of security, protection, stability, freedom from fear and anxiety, and the need for structure and limits.

- **Safety needs** represent the importance of security, protection, stability, freedom from fear and anxiety, and the need for structure and limits. For example, individuals who are afraid of school, of peers, of a superior, or of a parent's reaction have their safety needs threatened and their well-being can be affected.

Love and belongingness needs

Maslow's term that refers to the need for family and friends.

- **Love and belongingness needs** refers to the need for family and friends. Healthy, motivated people wish to avoid feelings of loneliness and isolation. People who feel alone, not part of the group, or who lack any sense of belongingness usually have poor relationships with others, which can then affect their achievement in life.

Esteem needs

Maslow's term that refers to the reactions of others to us as individuals; it also refers to our opinion of ourselves.

Self-actualization needs

Maslow's term that refers to the need to use our abilities to the fullest extent.

- **Esteem needs** refer to the reactions of others to us as individuals and also to our opinion of ourselves. We want a favorable judgment from others, which should be based on honest achievement. Our own sense of competence combines with the reactions of others to produce a sense of self-esteem. Consequently, we must acquire competence and find the opportunities that permit us to achieve and to secure reinforcement, both from others and our own sense of satisfaction in what we have done.

- By **self-actualization needs,** Maslow was referring to that tendency, in spite of the lower needs being satisfied, to feel restless unless we are doing what we think we are capable of doing. As Maslow noted (Maslow et al., 1987), musicians must make music, artists must paint, and writers must write. The form that needs take isn't important: One person may desire to be a great parent; another may desire to be an outstanding athlete. Regardless of professions, *"what human beings can be, they must be"* (Maslow et al., 1987, p. 22).

Closely allied to these basic needs are cognitive needs (the desire to know and understand) and aesthetic needs. But as Maslow noted, we must be careful not to make too sharp a distinction between these and the basic needs; they are tightly interrelated (Maslow et al., 1987). As you can see, Maslow's remarkably perceptive analysis furnishes us with rich general insights into human behavior, especially those needs that lead to developmental changes during the lifespan.

AN APPLIED VIEW

Maslow and Street Gangs

Maslow's hierarchy of needs has widespread application to all members of society, including those youth who find themselves in a dangerous environment. In his analysis of Chicago's African American street gangs, Perkins (1987) identified several features of street gangs that many youths find appealing:

- *A sense of identity*. Gang membership provides recognition for those youths who have not received it elsewhere, thus compensating for low self-esteem.
- *A sense of belonging*. Belongingness gives gang members a feeling of acceptance by those who face similar problems and hardships. These youths find a sharing of common values and needs to be personally rewarding (Perkins, 1987).
- *A sense of power*. Many African American youths think power is crucial for their survival. The gang affords such youths a buffer to feelings of alienation and low self-esteem.

- *A sense of security*. Youths who live in high-risk settings often need protection; for many of them, gang membership is their only means of obtaining security.
- *A sense of discipline*. Gangs demand a strict adherence to structure that appeals to many African American youths.

Interpreting these five features as needs, Perkins (1987) then related them to Maslow's needs hierarchy in an attempt to explain why a street gang appeals to some youth. For example, the gang member's need for security and power can be found at Maslow's levels of physiological and safety needs; identity, belonging, and discipline are needs found at the love and belongingness level; identity, belonging, and power appear as esteem needs. Perkins believed that satisfaction of self-actualizing needs probably can never be achieved through membership in a street gang.

Guided Review

11. Using our potential as fully as possible is an example of _____ .
12. Basic to Maslow's theory is the satisfaction of basic _____ .
13. When Maslow referred to safety needs, he meant _____ as well as physical security.
14. The satisfaction of esteem needs depends on honest _____ .
15. Human beings have a need for _____ and _____ .

Jean Piaget was among the first to study normal intellectual development.

The Cognitive Developmental Approach

Two of the most highly regarded theorists of cognitive development are Swiss biologist Jean Piaget and Russian psychologist Lev Vygotsky. Although both theorists concentrated on cognitive development, they emphasized different developmental influences: Piaget placed the development of cognitive structures at the heart of his theory, whereas Vygotsky placed greater emphasis on the role of social forces.

Jean Piaget's Theory

Whereas Freud was concerned with the structures of the personality, Jean Piaget (1896–1980) sought to understand the cognitive structures of the intellect (1953, 1966; Flavell, 1963). Beginning his scholarly career at the age of 11(!), Piaget published numerous papers on birds, shellfish, and other topics of natural history. As a result, the diligent Swiss was offered the curator's position at the Geneva Natural History Museum. He was only 15 at the time and turned the offer down to finish high school. He received his Ph.D. in biology at the age of 21 and wrote more than 50 books during his lifetime.

Piaget began his research on cognitive development in 1920, when he took a position in the Binet Laboratory in Paris. He was given the task of standardizing a French version of an English-language test of reasoning ability, which enabled him to observe how children responded to the questions. He discovered that similarities were evident in the wrong answers given by each age group. Five-year-olds would give a wrong answer for one reason, whereas older age groups gave the same wrong answer for other reasons. This discovery led Piaget to the idea that children of different age groups have different thinking patterns. Prior to 1920 little research had been done on the nature of intelligence, and children were viewed as miniature adults who used adult thinking methods but used them poorly. Scientists felt that as information was poured into the child, mental maturity gradually developed. Piaget discovered that specific abilities must be acquired before the child's intellect could fully mature; information alone is not enough. Furthermore, he observed that these mental abilities develop in stages, each one preparing the way for the development of the next.

Piaget believed that intelligence matures through the growth of increasingly effective **cognitive structures.** These structures can best be defined as the blueprints that equip us to affect our environment. They are the tools of adaptation. At birth, all babies simply reflect the environment. When a specific event (a stimulus) occurs, infants react automatically to it. Sucking and crying are examples of these reflexes.

Soon after birth, reflexes are transformed into **schemes.** Schemes are patterns of behavior that infants use to interact with the environment. Figure 2.2 depicts this relationship. Infants develop schemes for looking, for grasping, for placing objects in their mouths. As infants grow older and begin to encounter more elements of

Cognitive structures

Piaget's term to describe the basic tools of cognitive development.

Schemes

Piaget's term to describe the patterns of behavior that infants use to interact with their environment.

Answers

11. self-actualization 12. needs 13. psychological 14. achievement 15. love, belongingness

Figure 2.2

Piaget's concept of the schema. Mental structures are held in the mind direct and control our behaviors.

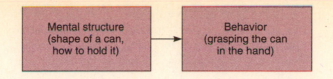

Mental structure (shape of a can, how to hold it) → Behavior (grasping the can in the hand)

their world, schemes are combined and rearranged into more efficient means of adapting. (See the discussion to follow under "Schemes.")

According to Piaget, adult thinking is composed of numerous operations that enable the individual to manipulate the environment. *Operations* are mental, internalized actions. They are similar to programs in a computer. Programs enable the computer to manipulate the data fed into it in various ways. Mental operations do the same. In fact, mental operations allow people to take things apart and reassemble them without actually touching the object. To continue the metaphor, schemes are like files used in computer programs. How did Piaget explain these accomplishments?

Key Concepts in Piaget's Theory

Stages.   After many years of observing children of all ages, Piaget deduced that cognitive development has four stages, each of which builds on the previous one. They are the *sensorimotor stage* (birth to 2 years old); the *preoperational stage* (2 to 7 years old); the *concrete operational stage* (7 to 11 years old); and the *formal operational stage* (11 years old and up). The change from one stage is quite clear, and regression from later to earlier stages does not happen. Thus, Piaget believed that cognitive functioning begins as responses to concrete phenomena—babies know only what they can touch, taste, or see. Our ability to use symbols and to think abstractly increases with each subsequent stage until we are able to manipulate abstract concepts and consider hypothetical alternatives. We'll carefully analyze Piaget's stages of cognitive development in later chapters.

Functional Invariants.   Piaget stated that we inherit a method of intellectual functioning that enables us to respond to our environment by forming cognitive structures. He suggested that two psychological mechanisms, **adaptation** and **organization,** are responsible for the development of our cognitive structures. Because we use these same two mechanisms constantly throughout our lives, Piaget named them *functional invariants.*

Piaget believed that adaptation consists of **assimilation** and **accommodation.** When we assimilate something we incorporate it; we take it in. Think of eating. We take food into the structure of our mouths and change it to fit the shape of our mouths, throats, and digestive tract. We take objects, concepts, and events into our minds similarly: We incorporate them into our mental structures, changing them to fit the structures as we change the food to fit our physical structures. For example, you are now studying Piaget's views on cognitive development. These ideas are unique and will require effort to understand them. You are attempting to comprehend them by using the cognitive structures you now possess. You are assimilating Piaget's ideas; that is, you are mentally taking them in and shaping them to fit your cognitive structures.

But we also change as a result of assimilation; that is, we accommodate to what we have taken in. The food we eat produces biochemical changes; the stimuli we incorporate into our minds produce mental changes. *We change because of what we take in; we are also changed by it*. For example, not only are you taking in Piaget's ideas, but they are also changing your views on intelligence and cognitive development. The change in your cognitive structures will produce corresponding behavioral changes; this is the process of accommodation.

Adaptation

One of the two functional invariants in Piaget's theory.

Organization

One of the two functional invariants in Piaget's theory.

Functional invariants

In Piaget's theory, the psychological mechanisms of adaptation and organization.

Assimilation

Piaget's term to describe the manner in which we incorporate data into our cognitive structures.

Accommodation

Piaget's term to describe the manner by which cognitive structures change.

Equilibration
Piaget's term to describe the balance between assimilation and accommodation.

Thus, the adaptive process is the heart of Piaget's explanation of learning. As we try to "fit" new material into existing cognitive structures, we try to strike a balance between assimilation and accommodation, a process that is called **equilibration.** For example, we all make mistakes but by continued interaction with the environment, we correct these mistakes and change our cognitive structures (we have accommodated).

But our mental life doesn't consist of random activities; it is organized. The cognitive structures that we form enable us to engage in ever more complex thinking. Physical structures can again provide an analogy for Piaget's ideas on organization. To read this text you are balancing it, turning the pages, and moving your eyes. All of these physical structures are organized so that you can read. Likewise, for you to understand this material, your appropriate cognitive structures are organized so that they can assimilate and accommodate.

Schemes.   Organization and adaptation are inseparable; they are two complementary processes of a single mechanism. Every intellectual act is related to other similar acts, which introduces Piaget's notion of schemes. *Schemes* are organized patterns of thought and action, that is, they are the cognitive structures *and* behavior that make up an organized unit. Schemes help us to adapt to our environment and may be best thought of as the inner representation of our activities and experiences. A scheme is named by its activity: the grasping scheme, the sucking scheme, the kicking or throwing scheme.

To give you an idea of how schemes develop, consider a baby reaching out and touching something, say a blanket. The child immediately begins to learn about the material (e.g., its heaviness, its size); the child is forming a cognitive structure about the blanket. When the child combines knowledge about the blanket with the act of reaching for it, Piaget called this behavior a scheme—in this case, the grasping scheme.

How do these schemes "work" in Piaget's theory? If you think of his theory in this way it may help: Stimuli come from the environment and are filtered through the functional invariants. The functional invariants, adaptation and organization, use the stimuli to form new structures or change existing structures. For example, you may have had your own idea of what intelligence is, but now you change your structures relating to intelligence because of your new knowledge about Piaget. Your content or behavior now changes because of the changes in your cognitive structures. The process is as follows.

Environment

(filtered through)

the Functional Invariants

(produce)

Cognitive Structures

(which combine with behavior to form)

Schemes

One of Piaget's classic experiments illustrates the process. To replicate this experiment, you'll need a 5-year-old child (in Piaget's preoperational stage), a 7-year-old child (in Piaget's concrete operational stage), six black tokens, and six orange tokens. Make a row of the black tokens. If you give the 5-year-old child the orange tokens with instructions to match them with the black tokens, the child can easily do it. When the tokens are in a one-to-one position, a 5-year-old can tell us that both rows have the same number.

But if we spread the six black tokens to make a longer row, the 5-year-old will tell us that the longer row has more tokens!

Even when Piaget put the tokens on tracks and let the child move and match them, the child still believed the longer row had more tokens.

Present the 7-year-old with the same problem. The child will think it is a trick—both rows obviously still have the same number.

Conducting Your Own Cognitive Experiment

Most readers of this text are in Piaget's formal operational stage. This means that they already have the ability to make reasonable hypotheses. If you would like to test yourself on this ability, try the following experiment (you may want to do it with several friends/classmates). To do it, you need two sheets of paper 10 by 10 inches in size, both ruled off in 1-inch squares, with each of the 100 squares numbered consecutively. You also need three crayons: one yellow, one orange, and one red. Now follow these instructions:

1. Hypothesize which part or parts of the squared sheet most people will point to, and say why.

2. Make a second hypothesis, explaining why you think that part or parts will be chosen second most often.

3. Show one of the ruled sheets to at least 50 people (the more, the better), and ask them to point to one square, any square, at random.

4. Make a note of how many times each of the squares is chosen, and whether the chooser is left- or right-handed.

5. Color the squares on one of the sheets, using your data for right-handers only. Leave those squares with no choices white. Color those with one choice yellow, those with two choices orange, and those with three or more choices red.

6. Do the same thing on the second sheet for the data for left-handers.

Do the data support your hypotheses? If not, can you think of reasons why? Can you think of better ways to go about hypothesizing in general?

Lev Vygotsky's Theory

Think about your home, school, friends, and neighborhood. Have they influenced the way you think and the way you think about people and events? Does this make Vygotsky seem more meaningful?

Piaget was criticized for not adequately considering the role of social interactions in cognitive development. The work of Russian psychologist Lev Vygotsky (1896–1934) has attracted considerable attention because of his emphasis on social processes. For Vygotsky (1962, 1978), the clues to understanding mental development are in children's social processes; that is, cognitive growth depends on children's interactions with those around them. The adults around children interact with them in a way that emphasizes those things that a culture values. For example, a child points to an object; those around the child respond in a way that not only conveys information about the object but also how the child should behave. To understand cognitive growth, we need to concentrate on the social processes by which these higher mental forms are established.

Vygotsky's (1978, 1981) emphasis on the role of culture and society in cognitive development was in sharp contrast with Piaget's concept of a child struggling to understand a problem on its own. Development of higher mental processes such as memory, attention, and reasoning often occur as children acquire language, mathematics, and memory techniques. Speech, for example, continues to help them in their efforts at mastery, producing new, verbal relationships with the environment. An interesting question here is, How does learning facilitate development?

The Zone of Proximal Development

Commenting on the relationship between learning and development, Vygotsky (1978) noted that learning, in some way, must be matched with a pupil's developmental level, which is too frequently identified by an intelligence test score. Vygotsky believed, however, that we cannot be content with the results of intelligence testing, which only provides a student's present developmental level. For example, after administering a Stanford-Binet intelligence test, we find that a pupil's intelligence quotient (IQ) on this test is 110, which would be that student's current level of mental development. We then assume that the pupil can only work at this level. Vygotsky argued, however, that with a little help, pupils might be able to do work that they could not do on their own.

We know that pupils who have the same IQ are quite different in other respects. Motivation, interest, health, and a host of other conditions produce different achievement levels. For example, our student with an IQ of 110 may be able to deal effectively with materials of various levels of difficulty. That is, when working alone, this student may be able to do addition problems but can solve subtraction problems only with the teacher's help.

To explain this phenomenon, Vygotsky introduced his notion of the **zone of proximal development.** He defined the zone of proximal development as the distance between a child's actual developmental level as determined by independent problem solving and the higher level of potential development as determined by problem solving under adult guidance or in collaboration with more capable peers (Vygotsky, 1978). It is the difference between what pupils can do independently and what they can do with help.

As Vygotsky noted (1978), instruction is good only when it proceeds ahead of development. That is, teaching awakens those functions that are maturing and that are in the zone of proximal development. Although teaching and learning are not development, they can act to stimulate developmental processes.

Zone of proximal development

The distance between a child's actual developmental level and a higher level of potential development with adult guidance.

🌳 Guided Review 🌳

16. Piaget's major concern was with the development of _____
    _____ .

17. Vygotsky differed from Piaget in that he was more interested in the role that _____ _____ played in cognitive development.

18. Piaget believed that cognitive development occurred by passage through cognitive _____ .

19. _____ are mental, internalized actions.

20. Vygotsky believed that for learning to be effective, it must be matched with a pupil's _____ level.

21. The difference between a child's actual developmental level and the level of potential developmental is what Vygotsky called the _____ _____ _____ _____ .

Answers

16. cognitive structures 17. social interactions 18. stages 19. Operations 20. developmental 21. zone of proximal development

The Behavioral Approach

We turn now to a third approach to human development, behavioral theory. Two of its best-known proponents are B. F. Skinner and Albert Bandura.

Skinner and Operant Conditioning

B. F. Skinner (1904–1990) received his doctorate from Harvard and after teaching for several years at the Universities of Minnesota and Indiana, he returned to Harvard. Convinced of the importance of **reinforcement,** Skinner developed an explanation of learning that stressed the consequences of behavior. What happens after we do something is all-important. Reinforcement has proven to be a powerful tool in the developing, shaping, and control of behavior, both in and out of the classroom.

Skinner's Views

Skinner has been in the forefront of psychological and educational endeavors for the past several decades. Innovative, practical, tellingly prophetic, and witty, Skinner's work has had a lasting impact. In several major publications—*The Behavior of Organisms* (1938), *Science and Human Behavior,* (1953), *Verbal Behavior* (1957), *The Technology of Teaching* (1968), *Beyond Freedom and Dignity* (1971), *About Behaviorism* (1974)—and in a steady flow of articles, Skinner reported his experiments and developed and clarified his theory. He never avoided the challenge of applying his findings to practical affairs. Psychology, education, religion, psychotherapy, and other subjects have all felt the force of Skinner's thought.

In his theory, called **operant conditioning** (also sometimes called **instrumental conditioning**), Skinner demonstrated that the environment has a much greater influence on learning and behavior than previously realized. Skinner argued that the environment (parents, teachers, peers) reacts to our behavior and either reinforces or eliminates that behavior. Consequently, the environment holds the key to understanding behavior.

For Skinner, behavior is a causal chain of three links:

1. Something in the environment (a *stimulus*) acts on the child—a teacher asks a question of the class

2. Some inner condition causes the child to respond (a *response*) in the presence of the stimulus—the pupil answers the question, either correctly or incorrectly

3. One of three things happens in reaction to the pupil's response: The response is *reinforced,* the response is *punished,* or the response is *ignored*.

Skinner argued that if the response is reinforced, it is more likely to result the next time that stimulus occurs. Thus, if the teacher asks that question again, the student is more likely to give the right answer, because that response was reinforced. If the response is punished, the response is less likely in the future. If the response is simply ignored, it also becomes less likely in the future. Each of these three concepts—reinforcement, **punishment,** and no response (which Skinner calls **extinction**)—needs further explanation.

Notice that Skinner did not use the word *reward*. He felt that reward is distinct from reinforcement. A reward is something you give a person because you think it will make that person feel good for having made a response. The problem with this definition is that it assumes that we know what is going on in the mind of another person. We know what is rewarding to us, but we can only guess what is rewarding to someone else. Skinner preferred to define reinforcement as anything that makes a response more likely to happen in the future, without making any reference to how it makes the individual feel inside.

Harvard psychologist B.F. Skinner is known as the father of American behaviorism.

Reinforcement
Usually refers to an increase in the frequency of a response when certain pleasant consequences immediately follow it.

Operant conditioning
Skinner's form of conditioning in which a reinforcement follows the desired response; also known as instrumental conditioning.

Instrumental conditioning
Skinner's form of conditioning in which a reinforcement follows the desired response; also known as operant conditioning.

Punishment
Usually refers to a decrease in the frequency of a response when certain unpleasant consequences immediately follow it.

Extinction
Refers to the process by which conditioned responses are lost.

Positive reinforcement
Refers to those stimuli whose presentation as a consequence of a response strengthens or increases the rate of the response.

Negative reinforcement
Refers to those stimuli whose withdrawal strengthens behavior.

There are two kinds of reinforcement, and the difference between them is important. **Positive reinforcement** refers to any event that, when it occurs after a response, makes that response more likely to happen in the future. **Negative reinforcement** is any event that, when it ceases to occur after a response, makes that response more likely to happen in the future. Notice that both types of reinforcement make a response more likely to happen. Giving your daughter candy for doing the right thing would be positive reinforcement. Ceasing to twist your brother's arm when he gives you back your pen would be negative reinforcement.

What does operant conditioning have to do with development? In Skinner's opinion, human development is the result of the continuous flow of learning that comes about from the operant conditioning we receive from the environment every day. For Skinner, development is a continuous, incremental sequence of conditioned acts that fulfill children's needs as quickly and completely as possible. Ideally, then, the demands of normal living are introduced at a controlled rate that helps a child to master them without acquiring negative feelings (Thomas, 1992).

AN APPLIED VIEW

Who Can Find the Raisin?

Probably the best way to understand Skinner's view of behaviorism is to apply its principles to teaching someone. For this suggested activity, you need two cups, a raisin, and two squares of paper of different colors, big enough to cover the cups.

For 1- to 2-year-olds, you must start very simply. Follow these steps:

1. Place a raisin in one of the cups and cover that cup with a large square of either color.

2. Cover the empty cup with the large square of the other color. Do this so that the child cannot see what you are doing.

3. Ask the child to guess which cup the raisin is in by pointing to one of the squares. If the child gets the right one, he or she wins the prize. If not, say, "Too bad. Maybe you'll get it next time. Let's try again."

4. Now, out of the child's sight, switch the positions of the cups, but cover the cup with the raisin with the same square. Do this until the child regularly guesses correctly. This is called *continuous reinforcement*. Generally speaking, the older the child, the quicker the learning.

5. Now cut out two large circles, each a different color, and repeat steps 1 through 4 using circles instead of squares. Does the child learn more quickly this time?

For older children, the game can be made more and more complex. Use a greater variety of shape combinations, and use three or even four cups. Finally, try to get the child to verbalize what he or she thinks is the principle behind this activity. Perhaps the child could even invent another way of doing it! As you perform this experiment, you will gain insights into the behaviorist ideas of reinforcement and extinction.

These concepts of change in human behavior have been enhanced by the ideas of Albert Bandura and his associates. They extend the behaviorist view to cover social behavior.

Modeling
Bandura's term for observational learning.

Social (cognitive) learning theory
Bandura's theory that refers to the process whereby the information we glean from observing others influences our behavior.

Bandura and Social Cognitive Learning

Albert Bandura, one of the chief architects of social learning theory, has stressed the potent influence of **modeling** on personality development. He called this *observational learning*. In a famous statement on **social (cognitive) learning theory,** Bandura and Walters (1963) cited evidence to show that learning occurs through observing others, even when the observers do not imitate the model's responses at that time and get no reinforcement. For Bandura, observational learning means that the information we get from observing other people, things, and events influences the way we act.

Social learning theory has particular relevance for development. As Bandura and Walters noted, children often do not do what adults tell them to do but rather what they see adults do. If Bandura's assumptions are correct, adults can be a potent force in shaping the behavior of children because of what they do.

The importance of models is seen in Bandura's interpretation of what happens as a result of observing others:

Have you ever modeled your behavior on that of someone else? Did you change as a result? Give some specific examples.

- The observer may acquire new responses, including socially appropriate behaviors.

- Observation of models may strengthen or weaken existing responses.

- Observation of a model may cause the reappearance of responses that were apparently forgotten.

- If children witness undesirable behavior that is either rewarded or goes unpunished, undesirable pupil behavior may result. The reverse is also true.

Bandura, Ross, and Ross (1963) studied the relative effects of live models, filmed human aggression, and filmed cartoon aggression on preschool children's aggressive behavior. The filmed human adult models displayed aggression toward an inflated doll; in the filmed cartoon aggression, a cartoon character displayed the same aggression.

Later, all the children who observed the aggression were more aggressive than youngsters in a control group. Filmed models were as effective as live models in transmitting aggression. The research suggests that powerful, competent models are more readily imitated than models who lack these qualities (Bandura & Walters, 1963).

 A Multicultural View

Modeling Among Latino Youth

For most teens the family plays an important role, but for Latino adolescents this is especially true. This quotation shows how a Latino teenage girl chose her mother as her model of behavior and values:

> As far as I can remember, my mother was strong and independent. She loved us so much that she protected us from the dangers of the barrio. She kept the family together as long as she could, and the traditions were a big part of her life. She is a very pretty woman with strong Mexican Indian features: high cheek-bones and a tired clear face. She is short, heavyset, and has a physically tired body. She always wore a little makeup and red lipstick. . . . "Mi madre" is the pride and joy of my life, and she is not only my mother but my closest friend. (Kunjifu, 1985, p. 29)

In summary, the behaviorist position holds that human development does not happen in predictable stages but as the result of stimuli from the environment. Since millions of stimuli occur in a person's lifetime, behaviorists see development as continuous, something that usually happens in small steps every day.

🌳 Guided Review 🌳

22. Skinner's view of learning is referred to as _____ or _____ conditioning.

23. This explanation of learning depends heavily on the role of the _____ .

24. When a response is _____ , it is more likely to reoccur.

25. Bandura's social learning theory, also called observational learning, stresses the place of _____ in learning.

Answers

22. operant, instrumental 23. environment 24. reinforced 25. modeling

A Multicultural View

Enrichment Through Diversity

As research on human beings includes more and more diverse groups, our understanding of how different we are from each other grows. For instance, as more women conduct research, our view of what it means to be human is changing. Psychology now takes a lifespan perspective, which means we must examine not only each stage of life, but the relationships between them. More research is looking at diverse ethnic, cultural, and racial groups. It is increasingly important that we learn about all these differences as our society becomes more diversified.

However, this new emphasis on difference can lead to the conclusion that one group must be somehow inferior to another. In the past, assumptions that non-whites are more likely to be unmarried parents or to commit criminal acts were accepted stereotypes. Women were either considered as imperfect men or assumed to develop exactly like men. Latinos or Native Americans were totally missing from our research. In using the white middle-class male point of view as the norm, the rest of society is either ignored or becomes abnormal by comparison. Rather than treating women or other cultural or racial groups as needing more appreciation or help, recent research is seeking to understand diversity as a valuable contribution to expanding knowledge.

Psychological research has become increasingly attuned to the importance of context. No one lives in a social vacuum. Each theory is embedded in a time and place, just as each person is. Throughout this book, we will continue to explore the diversity of human development, in part through the regular sections of the book, and in part through separate "A Multicultural View" boxes like this one. In addition, you should ask yourself, as you read various research reports, "Does this study reflect nearly all people of this group, or is it only relevant to the kinds of people under study?"

Conclusion

In this chapter, we covered a great deal of important ground. We introduced you to the framework on which, in many ways, the rest of the book depends. Although we might have chosen many theories to include in this chapter (some of which we will discuss later), the ones we have presented here have played or are playing major roles in our understanding of human development.

You have a lot to remember, but we will be coming back again and again to these seminal ideas to help you to gain a firm understanding of them. In these first two chapters, you have received an overview of the fascinating study of human development. Now we begin to take a much closer look at each of the major aspects of life, using the powerful insights of theory and research.

Chapter Highlights

The Psychoanalytic Approach

- The unconscious mind is the key to understanding human beings.
- Important information in the unconscious mind is kept hidden through an array of defense mechanisms.
- The mind is divided into three constructs: the id, the ego, and the superego, each of which appears at different stages of a child's development.
- Personality development is divided into five instinctive stages of life—oral, anal, phallic, latency, and genital—each stage serving a major function.
- Failure to pass through a stage of development results in fixation, which halts a person from becoming fully mature.

The Psychosocial Crises Approach

- Human life progresses through eight "psychosocial" stages, each one marked by a crisis and its resolution.
- Although the ages at which one goes through each stage vary, the sequence of stages is fixed. Stages may overlap, however.
- A human being must experience each crisis before proceeding to the next stage. Inadequate resolution of the crisis at any stage hinders development.

The Humanistic Approach

- Maslow believed that progress toward fulfillment of an individual's potential depended on needs satisfaction.

- Maslow identified five basic needs in his needs hierarchy.

The Cognitive Developmental Approach

- Piaget focused on the development of the cognitive structures of the intellect during childhood and adolescence.
- Organization and adaptation play key roles in the formation of structures.
- Piaget believed that cognitive growth occurred in four discrete stages: sensorimotor, preoperational, concrete operational, and formal operational.
- Vygotsky believed that the capacity to learn depends on abilities of the child's teachers as well as on the child's abilities.

- The difference between the child's ability to learn independently and to learn with help is called the zone of proximal development.

The Behavioral Approach

- Skinner believed that the consequences of behavior are critical.

- Skinner's paradigm involves three steps: a stimulus occurs in the environment; a response is made in the presence of that stimulus; and the response is reinforced, punished, or extinguished.

- Bandura has extended Skinner's work to the area of social learning, which he calls observational learning.

🌳 KEY TERMS

Accommodation 37
Adaptation 37
Anal stage 29
Assimilation 37
Cognitive structures 36
Ego 27
Equilibration 38
Esteem needs 35
Extinction 41
Functional invariants 37
Genital stage 29
Id 27

Identity crisis 32
Instrumental conditioning 41
Latency stage 29
Love and belongingness needs 34
Modeling 42
Negative reinforcement 42
Operant conditioning 41
Oral stage 29
Organization 37
Phallic stage 29
Physiological needs 34

Positive reinforcement 42
Psychoanalytic theory 27
Punishment 41
Reinforcement 41
Safety needs 34
Schemes 36
Self-actualization 34
Self-actualization needs 35
Social (cognitive) learning theory 42
Superego 27
Zone of proximal development 40

🌳 WHAT DO YOU THINK?

1. What is your reaction to the statement, "The truth or falseness of a theory has little to do with its usefulness"?
2. Some people say that in his concept of human development, Freud emphasizes sexuality too much. What do you think?

3. Which is better, assimilation or accommodation? If you could do only one, which would it be? Why?
4. Skinner criticized the other theorists in this chapter for believing they can describe what goes on in the human mind. After all, he said, no one has ever looked inside one. What's your position?

5. Is it possible for a person to be deeply intimate with another person and still be in a state of identity confusion?

🌳 SUGGESTED READINGS

Clark, Ronald W. (1980). *Freud: The man and the cause*. New York: Random House. This is one of the most judicious and even-handed books written about the father of psychoanalysis.

Erikson, Erik. (1958). *Young man Luther*. New York: Norton. Martin Luther was the main force behind the Protestant Reformation. In Erikson's penetrating analysis of the causes behind Luther's actions,

we have a wonderfully clear example of his ideas about adolescence in general and negative identity in particular.

Skinner, B. F. (1948). *Walden two*. New York: Macmillan. Many students find it hard to see how Skinner's behaviorism would function in everyday life. In this novel, we see how a community based on his principles would operate. In fact,

for a while at least, several such communities really existed. This is a good way to understand this theory.

Tyler, Anne. (1986). *The accidental tourist*. New York: Knopf. This story of a man who tries desperately to avoid the bumps of life offers a fine example for you to use in analyzing each of the theories presented in this chapter.

🌳 CHAPTER REVIEW TEST

1. Freud's structure of the mind included
   a. cognitive structures.
   b. safety needs.
   c. ego.
   d. reinforcing elements.

2. The id is that structure of the mind that is present
   a. at birth.
   b. through experience.
   c. by internal representations.
   d. through crisis resolution.

3. Freud believed that development entailed moving through psychosexual stages. Difficulty at any stage can cause a person to become
   a. fixated.
   b. operational.
   c. negatively reinforced.
   d. displaced.

4. Ideas that are rejected by the conscious mind are kept from consciousness by
   a. the ego.
   b. fear reactions.
   c. the superego.
   d. defense mechanisms.

5. Jimmy was told by his teacher that he could not go on a field trip with the class because of his misbehavior. Jimmy said he was glad; the trips are "no fun any way." Jimmy's defense mechanism is called
   a. regression.
   b. compensation.
   c. rationalization.
   d. displacement.

6. One-year-old Jane has already learned that her mother will be there when Jane needs her. This predictable world helps a child to develop
   a. creativity.
   b. intimacy.
   c. generativity.
   d. trust.

7. The psychosocial crisis of industry versus inferiority must be resolved during
   a. the school years.
   b. early childhood.
   c. adolescence.
   d. adulthood.

8. When we analyze our personal sense of competence and combine it with the opinion of others, we are attempting to satisfy our need for
   a. belongingness.
   b. self-actualization.
   c. esteem.
   d. security.

9. Maslow has arranged his theory of needs satisfaction in the form of a
   a. spiral.
   b. hierarchy.
   c. stage sequence.
   d. plateau.

10. Piaget's theory of cognitive development focused on the formation and development of
    a. zones of proximal development.
    b. reinforcement schedules.
    c. cognitive structures.
    d. modeling strategies.

11. Piaget placed considerable emphasis on operations, which he viewed as
    a. reflexes.
    b. age-appropriate responses.
    c. internalized actions.
    d. interactions.

12. Although both Piaget and Vygotsky devoted their lives to studying cognitive development, Vygotsky placed greater emphasis on
    a. cognitive structures.
    b. social interactions.
    c. sensitive periods.
    d. observational learning.

13. Skinner carefully analyzed the role of reinforcement in development and distinguished it from
    a. cognitive structures.
    b. reward.
    c. operations.
    d. needs.

14. In operant conditioning, the environment acts as the major source of
    a. operations.
    b. cognitive structures.
    c. defense mechanisms.
    d. reinforcement.

15. The great value of observational learning is that a person need not overtly react to learn
    a. mental operations.
    b. new responses.
    c. ego identity.
    d. schedule of reinforcements.

Answers

1. c 2. a 3. a 4. d 5. c 6. d 7. a 8. c 9. b 10. c 11. c 12. b 13. b 14. d 15. b

PART II

Beginnings

My mother groan'd!
My father wept.
Into the dangerous world I leapt.

William Blake

The Biological Basis of Development

On October 6, 1992, Frank and Ellen Smith arrived at Dr. James Otis's office a few minutes early for their appointment. Married for seven years, they had been unable to conceive and had found that their problem was caused by male infertility, in this case, a low sperm count. As they attempted to learn more about their problem, they discovered that they were not alone; estimates are that one in six heterosexual couples has a fertility problem.

Other couples whom they had met in their search for a solution had recommended Dr. Otis as a physician who was sympathetic, knowledgeable, and successful in using DI—donor insemination. (Currently, close to 100,000 women in the United States will use DI each year.) Frank and Ellen chose this procedure because the screening process in accepting sperm for freezing lowers the risk of sexually transmitted diseases (STDs) and also provides detailed information about the donor: race, ethnic background, blood type, hair and eye color, physical characteristics, and personal background information.

The Smiths found that Dr. Otis was exactly as he had been described. Unhurried and calm, he told the couple just what would be expected of them. He also stressed that he received sperm from a large, nationally known, respected sperm bank. He explained that freezing techniques had improved in the last few years. Cryobiology, the study of how best to freeze living tissue, had made great strides by adding chemicals such as glycerol to liquid nitrogen at a temperature of –190° C. This technique protects cells and tissues by preventing any damage that could be caused by the formation of ice crystals.

Frank and Ellen felt reassured by their discussion with Dr. Otis. They couldn't afford the time and money required for adoption, but from their reading they had decided their chances of conceiving through donor insemination were high. Healthy couples with no other problems have a 70 to 80 percent success rate within one year. This figure compares with a natural conception rate of 85 to 90 percent for fertile couples.

The Smiths were also pleased that the procedure was relatively simple. After carefully tracking a woman's menstrual cycle and searching for accurate clues to the time of ovulation by examining her vaginal mucus and urine, the physician injects the semen through the cervix with a needleless syringe.

Their hopes and expectations were justified. Ellen conceived on the couple's fourth attempt and later gave birth to a healthy baby boy.

Any journey begins with the first step. For students of the lifespan, this means the time that development begins when sperm joins with egg, uniting the mother's genetic endowment with that of the father. As you can tell from the chapter's opening, today's technology gives couples a bewildering array of reproductive choices. In this chapter, you will explore a world so tiny that it is almost impossible to imagine. You will read about some great biological discoveries of the past century and about recent breakthroughs that have led scientists to the origins of life itself.

At this point, identify those influences that you think make you unique. List them in two columns, heredity and environment. What does your answer tell you about your interpretation of the influence of heredity and environment on development?

Think for a moment about yourself. You probably think of yourself as an individual—and you are right! Thanks to your genetic inheritance, no one in the world is quite like you. You may not be impressed by this fact, but you must occasionally have wondered what made you what you are. How much of what you are came from your parents, and how much came from your contacts with your environment? Remember, however, that heredity and environment are so interrelated that we really can't divide them; they must be considered together. We'll remind you of this at key points in the chapter.

In this chapter you'll read about the fertilization process, during which the sperm and egg unite. Today, however, we can no longer refer to "the union of sperm and egg." We must ask additional questions: Whose sperm? Whose egg? Where did the union occur? Was it in the woman's body? Was it in a test tube? Which woman will carry the fertilized egg? You can see, then, that fertilization is a process filled with the potential for conflict and controversy because of new techniques that enable fertilization to occur outside of a woman's body.

Sometime in your life you probably have said, "Oh, I've inherited that trait." That's the easy answer. How did you inherit that characteristic? Do you remember that DNA you heard about in your science classes? Here you'll learn that the discovery of DNA involved some of the world's greatest biologists in a race to be the first to find the "secret of life." Today scientists are engaged in a struggle to "map the human genome" in *The Human Genome Project,* which is an endeavor to identify our genetic endowment—the 50,000 to 100,000 genes that lie in the nucleus of every cell (Bishop & Waldholz, 1990). Once this is accomplished, we will be able to eliminate more than 3,000 genetic diseases! Perhaps equally as exciting is the attempt to identify "susceptibility" genes, which do not of themselves cause disease but make certain individuals susceptible to such diseases as breast cancer, colon cancer, and Alzheimer's.

The strong resemblance of these family members to each other is testimony to the role of heredity in our makeup.

Humans' characteristics, however, don't just appear; they're passed on from generation to generation. Following our discussion of genes, we'll trace the manner in which hereditary traits are transmitted. Unfortunately, we are all too well aware that occasionally the transmission of traits produces abnormalities, which we also discuss. Finally, no discussion of human heredity is complete without acknowledging the ethical issues that have arisen because of these new developments. Answers still elude us, but at least we can ask several critical questions: Should scientists be allowed to implant specific genes to satisfy a couple's preferences? Should society determine that certain types of genes be implanted to ensure "desirable" products? No easy questions, these, but you can be sure that they will arise in the future.

Genotype

An individual's genetic composition.

Phenotype

The observable expression of gene action.

Any discussion of the biological basis of development must place considerable emphasis on our genetic makeup. To avoid any misunderstanding, however, remember that development results from the interaction of heredity and development. It is the process by which our **genotype** (the genetic contribution of our parents) is expressed as a **phenotype** (our observable characteristics). Genes always function in an environment, and environmental circumstances affect the way that genes express themselves. For example, a child may be born with great intellectual potential, but because of a lack of opportunity and education the child's intellectual capacity may never reach fulfillment. These ideas help to explain why we have turned to a biopsychosocial model of development that encompasses both heredity and environment.

When you finish reading this chapter, you should be able to

- Recall that development results from the interaction of heredity and environment.

- Identify the essential elements in the reproductive process.

- Distinguish between internal and external fertilization.

- List the steps that lead to ovulation.

- Describe how the genetic process functions.

- Formulate questions relating to the sensitive nature of the new reproductive technology.

Internal fertilization

A natural process in which fertilization occurs within the woman.

External fertilization

Fertilization occurs outside of the woman's body.

In vitro fertilization

Fertilization that occurs "in the dish"; an external fertilization technique.

The Fertilization Process

The fusion of two specialized cells, the sperm and the egg (or ovum), mark the beginning of development and the zygote (the fertilized ovum) immediately begins to divide. This fertilized ovum contains all of the genetic material that the organism will ever possess. During the initial phase of development following fertilization, distinguishing the male from the female is almost impossible.

The Beginnings

Any discussion of fertilization today must account for the advances that both research and technology have made available. Consequently, our discussion will be broken into two parts:

- **Internal,** or natural, **fertilization**

- **External fertilization** techniques, such as **in vitro fertilization** (the famous "test-tube" babies)

Table 3.1 contains a glossary of many of the terms you will find in this discussion. Be sure to refer to it when you meet an unfamiliar term. Otherwise, the amazing richness of the genetic world can escape you.

In our analysis of genetic material and its impact on our lives, we'll attempt to follow the manner in which we receive genes from our parents. (Even this fundamental fact today requires further explanation. Genes may come from surprising sources, thanks to our technology [Grobstein, 1988]—more about this later.) But our story begins with the male's sperm and the female's egg.

The Sperm

Certain cells are destined to become the sperm and eggs. The chief characteristics of the sperm are its tightly packed tip (the acrosome), containing 23 chromosomes, a short neck region, and a tail to propel it in its search for the egg (Wolpert, 1991). Sperm are so tiny that estimates are that the number of sperm equal to the world's population could fit in a thimble. Sperm remain capable of fertilizing an egg for about 24 to 48 hours after ejaculation. Of the 200 million sperm that enter the vagina, only about 200 survive the journey to the woman's fallopian tubes, where fertilization occurs.

The major purpose of a male's reproductive organs is to manufacture, store, and deliver sperm. The sperm has as its sole objective the delivery of its DNA to the egg. Males, at birth, have in their testes those cells that will eventually produce sperm. At puberty, a meiotic division occurs in which the number of chromosomes is halved and actual sperm are formed. Simultaneously, the pituitary gland stimulates the hormonal production that results in the male secondary sex characteristics: pubic hair, a beard, and a deep voice.

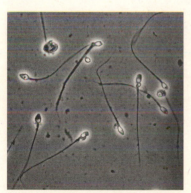

(a)

(b)

The sperm (a), in its search for the egg (b), carries the 23 chromosomes from the male.

Table 3.1	**A Genetic Glossary**

Acrosome: Area at the tip of the sperm.

Allele: Alternate forms of a specific gene; there are genes for blue eyes and brown eyes.

Autosome: Chromosomes other than the sex chromosomes.

Chromosome: Stringlike bodies that carry the genes; they are present in all of the body's cells.

DNA: Deoxyribonucleic acid, the chemical structure of the gene.

Dominance: The tendency of a gene to be expressed in a trait, even when joined with a gene whose expression differs; brown eyes will appear when genes for blue and brown eyes are paired.

Fertilization: The union of sperm and egg to form the fertilized ovum or zygote.

Gametes: The mature sex cells, either sperms or eggs.

Genes: The ultimate hereditary determiners; they are composed of the chemical molecule deoxyribonucleic acid (DNA).

Gene locus: The specific location of a gene on the chromosome.

Genotype: The genetic composition of an individual.

Heterozygous: The gene pairs for a trait differ; a person who is heterozygous for eye color has a gene for brown eyes and one for blue eyes.

Homozygous: The gene pairs for a trait are similar; the eye color genes are the same.

Meiosis: Cell division in which each daughter cell receives one-half of the chromosomes of the parent cell. For humans this maintains the number of chromosomes (46) at fertilization.

Mitosis: Cell division in which each daughter cell receives the same number of chromosomes as the parent cell.

Mutation: A change in the structure of a gene.

Phenotype: The observable expression of a gene.

Recessive: A gene whose trait is not expressed unless paired with another recessive gene; both parents contribute genes for blue eyes.

Sex chromosome: Those chromosomes that determine sex; in humans they are the 23d pair, with an XX combination producing a female, and an XY combination producing a male.

Sex-linkage: Genes on the sex chromosome that produce traits other than sex.

Trisomy: Three chromosomes are present rather than the customary pair; Down syndrome (mongolism) is caused by three chromosomes at the 21st pairing.

Zygote: The fertilized egg.

The Ovum (Egg)

The egg is larger than the sperm, about the size of the period at the end of this sentence. The egg is round and its surface is about the consistency of stiff jelly. You may find it hard to believe, but a whale and a mouse come from eggs of about the same size. In fact, the eggs of all mammals are about the same size and appearance (Guttmacher & Kaiser, 1986). When females are born, they already have primal eggs. From 1 to 2 million eggs have been formed in the ovaries. Since only one mature egg is required each month for about 35 years, the number present far exceeds the need.

Many of these primal eggs succumb before puberty. They simply shrivel up and disappear. At puberty the pituitary gland stimulates the hormonal production that results in the female secondary sex characteristics: pubic hair, breasts, wider hips, and a higher voice.

The Menstrual Cycle

The pituitary gland secretes another hormone that stimulates the ripening of eggs, and after two weeks one egg, which has ripened more than the others, is discharged from the ovary's surface. (Figure 3.1 illustrates the relationship of the ovum

Figure 3.1

The relationship of ovary, egg, fallopian tube, and uterus.

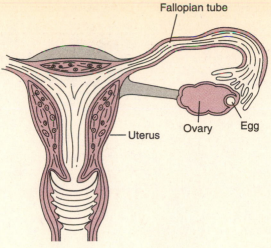

Figure 3.2

Fertilization of the egg. The sperm, carrying its 23 chromosomes, penetrates the egg, with its 23 chromosomes. The nuclei of sperm and egg fuse, resulting in 46 chromosomes.

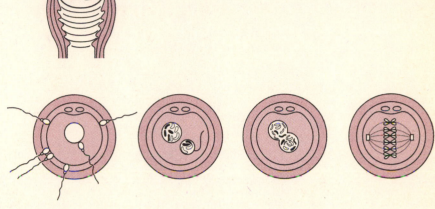

to the ovary, the fallopian tubes, and the uterus.) This process, called *ovulation,* triggers a chemical reaction that inhibits the ripening of further eggs. It also prepares the uterine lining for a potential fertilized ovum.

If fertilization does not occur, the prepared uterine lining is shed in menstruation. When the menstrual bleeding ceases, the entire process begins again. During each menstrual cycle many eggs are discarded. As a woman approaches the end of her egg-producing years, these last ova have been present for as many as 40 years. This may explain why the children of older women are more susceptible to genetic defects. The eggs have been exposed to environmental hazards (such as radiation) too long to escape damage (Singer, 1985).

Implantation

When the egg is discharged from the ovary's surface, it is enveloped by one of the **fallopian tubes.** The diameter of each fallopian tube is about that of a human hair, but it almost unfailingly ensnares the egg and provides a passageway to the uterus. If fertilization occurs, it takes place soon after the egg enters the fallopian tube. Figure 3.2 illustrates the fertilization process.

Fusion of the two cells is quickly followed by the first cell division. As the fertilized egg, now called the **zygote,** travels toward **implantation** within the uterus, cell division continues. The cells multiply rapidly and after about seven days reach the uterine wall. The fertilized egg is now called a **blastocyst.** The journey is pictured in figure 3.3.

Although individuals may change in the course of their lives, their hereditary properties do not change. The zygote (the fertilized egg), containing all 46 chromosomes, represents the "blueprint" for our physical and mental makeup. Under ordinary circumstances, environmental conditions leave the 46 chromosomes unaltered. (We know today that environmental agents such as drugs, viruses, or radiation may cause genetic damage.)

Fallopian tubes

Passageway for the egg once it is discharged from the ovary's surface.

Zygote

The fertilized egg.

Implantation

Fertilized egg attaches and secures itself to uterine wall.

Blastocyst

Name of the fertilized egg after initial divisions.

Figure 3.3
From ovulation to implantation.

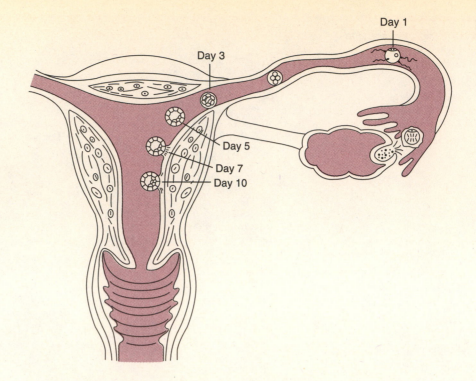

Once fertilization occurs, the zygote is not yet free from risk. Let's use a figure easy to work with and assume that 100 eggs are exposed to sperm. Here is the estimated mortality rate from fertilization to birth:

84 are fertilized
69 are implanted
42 survive one week
37 survive seven weeks
31 survive to birth

Thus, nature's toll results in about a 70 percent mortality rate.

Infertility

Although the fertilization process just described is the normal process for most women, there are exceptions. For some couples, **infertility,** for whatever reason, is an inescapable problem. Today hundreds of thousands of childless couples desperately desire children. These couples share a growing problem in our society: infertility.

Causes of Infertility

Estimates are that one in five American couples meet the criteria for infertility: an inability to achieve pregnancy after two years. Here are some reasons for this increased rate:

- **Sexually transmitted diseases (STDs)** show a marked increase. These can lead to **pelvic inflammatory disease (PID),** which in turn can cause infertility.

- A growing number of women are delaying child bearing until their thirties or later. Older women are more likely to become infertile because they may have used **intrauterine devices (IUDs),** had more abdominal surgery, and may be subject to **endometriosis,** which increases with age. (Endometriosis, typically found in the lining of the uterus, is the growth of endometrial tissue outside of the uterus.)

Infertility
An inability to achieve pregnancy after two years.

Sexually transmitted diseases (STDs)
A major cause of infertility.

Pelvic inflammatory disease (PID)
A disease that results from a STD that can cause infertility.

Intrauterine devices (IUDs)
Usually a plastic loop inserted into the uterus as a contraceptive device.

Endometriosis
A condition in which tissue normally found in the uterus grows in other areas, such as the fallopian tubes.

WHAT'S YOUR VIEW?

WHAT MAKES TWINS ALIKE?

Occasionally, and for reasons that still elude us, twins are born. Most twins occur when a woman's ovaries release two ripened eggs (rather than one) and both are fertilized by separate sperm. These twins are called **nonidentical,** or **dizygotic.** Their genes are no more alike than those of siblings born of the same parents but at different times.

Less frequently, twins develop from a single fertilized egg that divided after conception. Interestingly, identical twins usually do not result when the fertilized egg initially divides into two cells; separation occurs later when the dividing egg consists of several hundred cells (Wolpert, 1991). This process leads to **identical,** or **monozygotic,** twins whose genes are identical; that is, they share the same genotype.

There are an estimated 50 million pairs of twins around the world, with about 2 million pairs in this country. Regardless of country, the incidence of identical twins is about the same—3 in every 1,000 live births. In the United States, two-thirds of all twin births are dizygotic (Alexander, 1987). The rate of nonidentical (dizygotic) twin births, however, varies considerably from country to country. For example:

- In the United States about 11 or 12 pairs of dizygotic twins are born per 1,000 live births (once in 90 white births, once in 73 black births). The rate is about the same in Great Britain and other European countries.

- In Japan about 2 or 3 pairs of dizygotic twins are born per 1,000 live births.
- In Nigeria 40 pairs of dizygotic twins are born per 1,000 live births (Alexander, 1987).

Although it is difficult to explain these different figures, certain facts about twin births are now clear. For example, a mother's chances of giving birth to dizygotic twins increases with age, peaking at about the age of 37. The chances of a mother of twins giving birth to twins again is one in twenty. Birth control pills also seem to be linked to an increase in twin births. Twins likewise seem to appear more frequently in some families. With regard to sex, almost one-third of all twins are boy-girl. The remaining two-thirds (same-sex twins) are equally divided between boys and girls (Alexander, 1987).

As you can well imagine, twins, especially identical twins that have been separated at birth, have long fascinated psychologists. By comparing these twins who have grown up in different environments, researchers can estimate the influence of heredity and environment on behavior. For example, studies have consistently shown that the IQs of monozygotic (identical) twins are quite similar, whereas those of dizygotic (nonidentical) are much less so (Berndt, 1992). Yet Riese (1990), while studying differences in temperament between monozygotic and dizygotic twins, found little evidence of genetic influence during the neonatal period. How do you explain these differences? Is it heredity or environment? What's your view?

Do you think monozygotic twins should be kept in as similar environments as possible or should they be separated whenever possible? Why?

Nonidentical
Refers to twins conceived by the union of two different eggs with two different sperm cells within a brief time.

Dizygotic
Derived from two cells.

Identical
Refers to twins resulting from the division of a single zygote after fertilization.

Monozygotic
Derived from a single cell.

Artificial insemination by donor (AID)
A procedure that infertile couples may use to achieve pregnancy.

- Males are responsible in 35 percent of the cases.

- No cause is identified in 10 percent of the cases.

- In about 30 percent of all cases, both partners have fertility difficulties. For example, a male may have problems with either a low sperm count or defective sperm; a female may have ovarian or uterine problems; either the man or woman may have some type of genital disease such as gonorrhea (Tapley & Todd, 1988).

Simply because a woman does not become pregnant within a specific time does not necessarily indicate infertility. The best advice given to couples is to wait for two years before suspecting infertility if a woman is in her twenties, one year if she is between 30 and 35, and six months if she is over 35. Even if a couple finds that they are indeed infertile, they needn't abandon their hopes of parenthood. Many external fertilization techniques are available today. The new technologies we are about to discuss offer couples new hope. Hundreds of in vitro fertilization centers and sperm banks now exist around the country.

Although you are probably most familiar with in vitro fertilization, another process, **artificial insemination by donor (AID),** is by far the most widely used procedure. Here are some techniques now available (Grobstein, 1988):

- Artificial insemination

- In vitro fertilization (fertilization of egg and sperm occurs in dish)

"Let me get this straight. One bouquet goes to the mother who donated the egg. A second goes to the mother who housed the egg for insemination. A third goes to the mother who hosted the embryo and gave birth to the child. A fourth goes to the mother who raised it and a fifth goes to the mother with legal custody."

© 1992 by Nick Downes.

- Embryo transfer (an embryo from one woman's womb is transferred to that of another woman)

- Women sell their eggs

- Human embryos are frozen for long-term storage

- Surrogate motherhood (a woman agrees to be inseminated by the sperm of a man whose wife is infertile and returns the child to the couple after birth)

Consequently, today a child may have as many as five parents:

- A sperm donor (father or other male)

- An egg donor (mother or other female)

- A surrogate mother

- The couple who raises the child

WHAT'S YOUR VIEW?

SPERM BANKS: SCIENTIFIC PROGRESS OR BIG BUSINESS?

Closely allied to the new external fertilization techniques has been the development of sperm banks. Many couples have also opted for donor insemination (DI). In 1987 the Office of Technology Assessment announced that 80,000 American women had attempted artificial insemination using anonymous donor sperm, resulting in 30,000 live births. (Single women make up about 15 percent of this group.) Since 1960 about 400,000 babies have been born through this process.

Today about 135 sperm banks operate in the United States. Sixteen cryobanks store and sell frozen sperm, which are frozen in liquid nitrogen at −190° C and remain potent for years. As we mentioned in the chapter's opening, much of the appeal of this technique lies in the screening processes used, which are intended to reduce the possibility of sexually transmitted diseases.

The donors' traits are carefully recorded, since many couples want to match the male's characteristics as closely as possible. Donors usually receive a fee of about $100 or less and are not told about the use of their sperm. They must sign a form waiving all parental rights to any children conceived with their sperm (Tapley & Todd, 1988).

Although donor insemination has undoubtedly been in practice for most of this century, it came to public notice in the 1950s with the founding of the Repository for Germinal Choice. The repository originally was intended to accept and freeze the sperm of Nobel Prize winners, but due to the few who volunteered and their age (most were in their seventies and had less vigorous sperm), the repository's acceptance standards were relaxed to include scientists and mathematicians.

Many people have eagerly accepted the idea of sperm banks. On Madison Avenue in New York City sits the largest sperm bank in the world, holding more than 35,000 samples of frozen sperm. Do you think this practice should be encouraged or discouraged? What's your view?

In Vitro Fertilization (IVF)

In vitro fertilization (IVF) is the external fertilization technique you are probably most familiar with. The steps in IVF are as follows:

1. The woman is usually treated with hormones to stimulate maturation of eggs in the ovary, and she is observed closely to determine the timing of ovulation (i.e., the time at which the egg leaves the surface of the ovary).

2. The physician makes an incision in the abdomen and inserts a laparoscope (a thin tubular lens through which the physician can see the ovary) to remove mature eggs.

3. The egg is placed in a solution containing blood serum and nutrients.

4. Capacitation takes place—this is a process in which a layer surrounding the sperm is removed so that it may penetrate the egg.

5. Sperm are added to the solution; fertilization occurs.

6. The fertilized egg is transferred to a fresh supporting solution.

7. Fertilized eggs (usually three) are inserted into the uterus.

8. The fertilized egg is implanted in the uterine lining.

Do you have any doubts about the use of external fertilization techniques? For example, a daughter asks her mother to carry her baby to birth. Are there issues here that society must explore in much greater depth?

Zygote intrafallopian transfer (ZIFT)

The fertilized egg (the zygote) is transferred to the fallopian tube.

Gamete intrafallopian transfer (GIFT)

The sperm and the egg are placed in the fallopian tube to achieve fertilization in a more natural environment.

During this period, the woman is being treated to prepare her body to receive the fertilized egg. For example, the lining of the uterus must be spongy or porous enough to hold the zygote. The fertilized egg must be inserted at the time it would normally reach the uterine cavity. Variations on this procedure include **zygote intrafallopian transfer (ZIFT),** in which the fertilized egg is transferred to the fallopian tube, and **gamete intrafallopian transfer (GIFT),** in which sperm and egg are placed in the fallopian tube with the intent of achieving fertilization in a more natural environment.

A recent interesting development relates to the success rate that IVF centers have claimed. Noting that some advertising seemed inflated, the Society for Assisted Reproductive Technology (SART), a division of the American Fertility Society representing most of the IVF centers in this country, reported that it would disclose success rates for its member clinics. This action was in response to congressional criticism of centers that were advertising a success rate of up to 40 percent. Federal investigations had shown that nationally a woman has a 9 to 10 percent chance of success from any single treatment attempt.

Many centers resisted the disclosure of results because an apparently low success rate would damage their reputation, resulting in a loss of potential patients. This would be unfair to those centers that report their results honestly but work with a wide range of patients. Some centers work with an older population and make no restrictions about the male's sperm count. Consequently, their success rate is lower than that for centers accepting a more limited group of patients.

YOUR VIEW?

ADOPTION: CLOSED OR OPEN?

For many couples who remain childless in spite of several attempts at external fertilization, adoption (to take a child of other parents voluntarily as one's own) offers a viable option. The process of adoption has changed radically in the past few years because of a limited number of children and an increase in the number of couples who wish to adopt. This statement is not quite as simple as it appears. More children are available for adoption than is commonly thought, but they fall into several categories.

- Older children
- Minority children
- Handicapped children

While these children are available for immediate adoption, the waiting period for healthy white infants may run into years.

Adoption procedures were formerly *closed;* that is, the biological parents were completely removed from the life of their child once the child was surrendered for adoption. The bonds between birth parent(s) and child were legally and permanently severed; the child's history was sealed by the court. The child was effectively cut off from its genetic past (Gilman, 1987). Supposedly this prevented the natural parents and the adoptive couple from emotional upset. Many biological mothers, however, reported in later interviews that they never recovered from the grieving process.

Today, however, if a pregnant woman approaches an adoption agency, she gets what she wants. She can insist that her child be raised by a couple with specific characteristics: nationality, religion, income, number in family. She can ask to see her child several times a year,

perhaps take the youngster on a vacation, and telephone the child frequently. The adoption agency will try to meet these demands. This process is called *open* adoption, and although many adoptive couples dislike the arrangement, they really have no choice. Thus we see a new definition of adoption: the process of accepting the responsibility of raising an individual who has two sets of parents (Gilman, 1987).

Open adoption is a radical departure from the days when a woman who had decided to give up her baby for adoption had to wear a blindfold and earplugs during delivery so she wouldn't see or hear her baby. Today the natural mother may actually select the adoptive couple from several profiles that are given to her. (These profiles contain information about the adoptive couple: food preferences, television, politics, how the couple deals with stress, how they would handle a 2-year-old with a temper tantrum.) Most officials at adoption agencies agree that biological mothers rarely select a couple solely on the basis of income. Religion, lifestyle, and family stability seem much more important. Face-to-face meetings between the couples are becoming more common and often are decisive in the natural mother's decision.

Although problems occur with open adoption—for example, frequently the adoptive parents resent the continuing presence of the biological mother—most experts agree that a change was needed. Too many adopted children have shown emotional difficulties on learning that they were relinquished, and a large number of biological mothers have prolonged difficulty as a result of relinquishing their babies. Only time can tell how successful this new procedure will be.

What's your view—closed or open adoption?

Could you be an adopting parent under open adoption conditions?

Guided Review

1. _____ is the process uniting sperm and egg.

2. A fertilized egg is known as a _____ .

3. The _____ gland secretes hormones that stimulate the ovaries to ripen and release an egg each month.

4. The most well known example of an external fertilization technique is _____ fertilization.

5. The most popular external fertilization technique is _____ .

6. Estimates are that _____ in _____ American couples are infertile.

7. A form of adoption that today is becoming more popular is _____ adoption.

Answers

1. Fertilization 2. zygote 3. pituitary 4. in vitro 5. AID 6. one, five 7. open

Heredity at Work

The original cell, the possessor of 46 chromosomes, begins to divide rapidly after fertilization, until the infant has billions of cells at birth. The cells soon begin to specialize: some become muscle, some bone, some skin, some blood, and some nerve cells. These are the somatic, or body, cells. The process of division by which these cells multiply is called **mitosis** (see figure 3.4). In a mitotic division, the number of chromosomes in each cell remains the same.

A second type of cell is also differentiated: the germ, or sex, cell that ultimately becomes either sperm or egg. These reproductive cells likewise divide by the process of mitosis until the age of puberty. But then a remarkable phenomenon occurs—another type of division called **meiosis,** or reduction division (see figure 3.5). Each sex cell, instead of receiving 46 chromosomes upon division, now receives 23.

Mitosis is basically a division of cells in which each chromosome is duplicated so that each cell receives a copy of each chromosome of the parent cell. What is doubled in mitotic division is the amount of deoxyribonucleic acid (DNA), the chief component of the genes. Meiosis, which occurs only in germ cell reproduction, is responsible both for the shuffling of hereditary characteristics received from each parent and for their random appearance in offspring. During the reduction division, the chromosomes separate longitudinally so that 23 go to one cell and 23 to another.

For the male, reduction division begins to occur just before puberty. For the female, the process differs slightly. Since she is required to produce only one mature egg a month, there is no provision for an indefinitely large number of eggs, as there is for sperm. A woman normally sheds only 300 to 400 mature ova in her lifetime, whereas the normal male in a single ejaculation emits hundreds of millions of sperm.

At birth the female's ovaries contain tiny clusters of all the eggs that will mature in later years. Just before puberty, the final phases of the reduction division occur, and mature eggs are formed. It is as if there is a lengthy waiting period, from birth until about the age of 12 or 13, before the process is finally completed. The 23 chromosomes with their hereditary content are present at birth but must await the passage of time before biological maturity occurs in the female.

Now that we have traced the process by which fertilization occurs and discovered what is passed from parents to child, we still need to know "why I am who I am." This brings us to the discovery of DNA, one of this century's greatest achievements.

DNA: Structure and Function

We know that each chromosome contains thousands of genes and that each of these thousands of genes has a role in the growth and development of each human being. The amazing chemical compound **DNA** is the chemical key to the life force in humans, animals, and plants. It constitutes about 40 percent of the chromosomes and is the molecular basis of the genes (Singer, 1985). Genes not only perform certain duties within the cell but also join with other genes to reproduce both themselves and the whole chromosome (see figure 3.6).

Each gene follows the instructions encoded in its DNA and sends these instructions, as chemical messages, into the surrounding cell. The cell then produces certain substances or performs certain functions according to instructions. These new products then interact with the genes to form new substances. The process continues to build the millions of cells needed for various bodily structures.

Examine figure 3.6 and note how the strands intertwine. The strands, similar to the sides of a ladder, are connected by chemical rings: adenine (A), guanine (G), cytosine (C), and thymine (T). The letters are not randomly connected: A joins with T, G with C. If a code were written as AGCTTGA, it must appear as:

A G C T T G A
T C G A A C T

Thus, one sequence determines the other.

Mitosis

Cell division in which the number of chromosomes remains the same.

Meiosis

Cell division in which the number of chromosomes is halved.

DNA

Deoxyribonucleic acid; the chemical structure of the gene that accounts for our inherited characteristics.

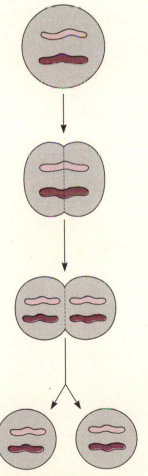

Figure 3.4

A mitotic division is a cell division in which each daughter cell receives the same number of chromosomes as the parent cell—46.

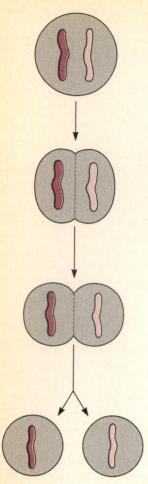

Figure 3.5

A meiotic division is a cell division in which each daughter cell receives one half of the chromosomes of the parent cell—23.

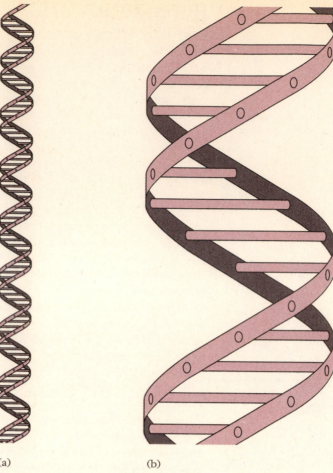

(a)   (b)

Figure 3.6

The DNA double helix. (a) The overall structure that gave DNA its famous name. (b) A closer examination reveals that the sides of the spiral are connected by chemicals similar to the rungs of a ladder.

A remarkable feature of DNA is its ability to reproduce itself and ensure that each daughter cell receives identical information. During mitosis the DNA splits as readily as a person unzips a jacket. Each single strand grows a new mate, A to T and G to C, until the double-helix model is reproduced in each daughter cell.

The four letter possibilities, AT, TA, GC, and CG, seem to limit genetic variation. But when we consider that each DNA molecule is quite lengthy, involving thousands, perhaps millions of chemical steps (TA, GC, AT, CG, AT, CG, TA), the possible combinations seem limitless. The differences in the DNA patterns account for the individual genetic differences among humans and for differences between species.

How Are Traits Transmitted?

One intriguing question is how the encoded information contained in DNA is transmitted to the surrounding cell. The process is essentially as follows: RNA (ribonucleic acid) forms within the nucleus of the cell, acts as a messenger for DNA, and moves into the cell body to direct the building of the body's substances.

What color are your eyes? Do your brothers and sisters have the same color eyes? Theirs could be different from yours; the mother and father who produced a brown-eyed child can also have a youngster with blue eyes. For centuries, guesses, myths, and speculation were used to explain the bewildering and mysterious happenings of heredity.

Table 3.2	Mendel's Round and Wrinkled Peas

I. First Pairing—R × W

		W	W
R		RW	RW
R		RW	RW

II. Second Pairing—RW × RW

		R	W
R		RR	RW
W		RW	WW

Hemophilia is an example of sex-linked inheritance, which affected several of the royal families of Europe (such as the Romanovs, pictured here).

Dominant

The tendency of a gene to be expressed in a trait.

Recessive

A gene whose trait is not expressed unless paired with another recessive gene; for example, both parents contribute genes for blue eyes.

It was not until the end of the nineteenth century that Gregor Mendel offered a scientific explanation. (Note the relatively recent emergence of genetic facts: the transmission of traits by Mendel in the 1860s, the Watson-Crick double-helix model of DNA in 1953, and the number of human chromosomes in 1956.)

Gregor Mendel, an Austrian monk who studied plants as a hobby, attempted to crossbreed pure strains of pea plants. He used pure sets of plants, that is, peas that were either round or wrinkled, yellow or green, tall or dwarf. He discovered that the first generation of offspring all had the same trait: After crossbreeding round and unwrinkled peas, Mendel noted that the offspring were all round. Did the offspring inherit the trait from only one parent?

Mendel quickly eliminated this explanation, since the missing trait (wrinkled) reappeared in the second generation. But the trait that was exclusively expressed in the first generation (roundness) was the majority trait in the second generation. That is, the ratio of round peas to wrinkled peas consistently remained at 3 to 1 in the second generation.

Thus roundness is the **dominant** trait and wrinkled is the **recessive** trait. These two genes, round (R) and wrinkled (W), yield four possible peas: RR, WW, RW, and WR. Peas RR and WW are pure strains and breed true; RW and WR contain both the dominant and recessive trait.

A genetic grid based on Mendel's first pairing (round and wrinkled) is shown in table 3.2. Note how the 3 to 1 ratio appears in the second generation.

What Is Transmitted?

Is it a boy or a girl? Is it healthy? These are the two questions asked most frequently by parents following the birth of a child. The 23d pair of chromosomes determines the sex of a child: XY = boy; XX = girl. (See the discussion to follow under "Chromosomes and Genes.") Thus, it is the male who determines the baby's sex, since the egg always carries the X chromosome; the sperm may contain either an X or a Y.

Sperm X + egg X = female
Sperm Y + egg X = male

Prospective parents also usually speculate about the color of their child's eyes. What is the genetic explanation for the presence of different eye colors? One gene is responsible for blue eyes and another is responsible for brown eyes. The gene for brown eyes is dominant and the gene for blue eyes is recessive. For example, a child receiving two "brown" genes will have brown eyes; a child receiving two "blue" genes will have blue eyes. Finally, the youngster who receives one of each will have brown eyes, because the gene for brown eyes is dominant.

The basic principle is that genes producing dark eye colors (brown, black) dominate over those producing light eye colors (blue, green, gray). If the mother,

Table 3.3   **Predicting Eye Color**

		Father			B = brown gene
		b	b		b = blue gene
Mother	B		Bb	Bb	
	b		bb	bb	

		Father		
		b	b	
Mother	B		Bb	Bb
	B		Bb	Bb

for instance, has brown eyes, she may carry only those genes for brown eyes (if her family is mostly brown-eyed) or a brown and a blue (if there are blue-eyed relatives somewhere in the family tree). Let's assume that we don't know anything about the mother's family. If the father has blue eyes, he most certainly has two "blue" genes. Table 3.3 reports the chances of blue-eyed children. With this in mind, let's turn to a more detailed examination of chromosomes and genes.

🌳 Guided Review 🌳

8. Cell division in which each daughter cell receives the same number of chromosomes as the parent cell is called _____ .

9. A reduction division, in which the number of chromosomes is halved is called

    _____ .

10. The chemical key to life is _____ .

11. Of the two sexes, the _____ is the more vulnerable at conception.

12. Information in DNA is transmitted to the surrounding cell by the chemical messenger

    _____ .

13. If a dominant and recessive gene appear together, the _____ trait is expressed.

Chromosomes and Genes

After the sperm and egg unite, the new cell (the potential individual) possesses 23 pairs of chromosomes, or 46 chromosomes, which represents the individual's total biological heritage. One member of each pair of chromosomes has been contributed by the father and one by the mother. Each pair, except the 23d, is remarkably alike. The 23d pair defines the individual's sex: an XX combination indicates a female; XY indicates a male. The sperm actually determines sex, since it alone can carry a Y chromosome. Thus there are two kinds of sperm: the X chromosome carrier and the Y chromosome carrier. Figure 3.7 illustrates the chromosomal arrangement of a typical male and female.

How much information is contained in this biological heritage? Each chromosome contains the equivalent of about 3 billion letters. Since the average word contains six letters, each chromosome incorporates information equal to about 500 million words. At about 300 words per typical printed page, this translates into the equivalent of about 2 million pages. The average book consists of about 500 pages. Thus the information in one human chromosome corresponds to that in 4,000 books.

Answers

8. mitosis 9. meiosis 10. DNA 11. male 12. RNA 13. dominant

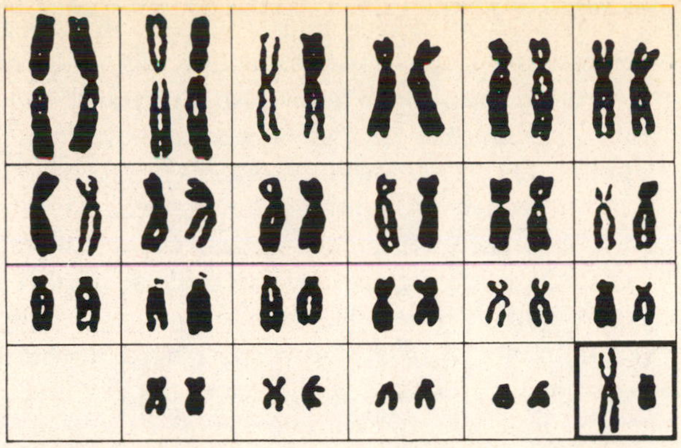

Figure 3.7
(a) At the top is the chromosome structure of a male, and (b) at the bottom is the chromosome structure of a female. The 23d pair is shown in the bottom right box of each figure; notice that the Y chromosome of the male is smaller. To obtain this chromosomal picture, a cell is removed from the individual's body, usually from the inside of the mouth. The chromosomes are magnified extensively and then photographed.

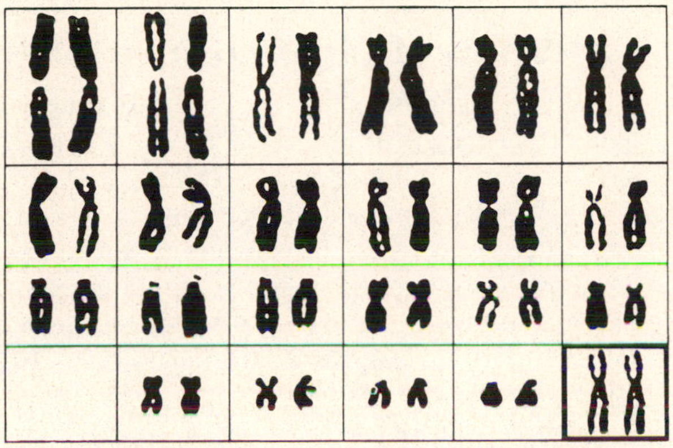

(a)

(b)

By a process of division, each cell in the body will have a replica of all 46 chromosomes. The size of the elements involved is almost bewildering. We have commented on the size of the sperm—so small that it can only be seen microscopically. The head of the sperm, which is about one-twelfth of its total length, contains the 23 chromosomes. The Y carrier is smaller than the X, which contains more genetic material. The Y carrier is also lighter and speedier and can reach the egg more quickly. But it is also more vulnerable.

Consequently, the male, from conception, is the more fragile of the two sexes. Estimates are that 160 males are conceived for every 100 females. However, so many males are spontaneously aborted that only 105 males are born for every 100 females. A similar pattern appears in neonatal life and continues throughout development, until women finally outnumber men, reversing the original ratio. Certain conclusions follow:

- Structurally and functionally, females resist disease better than males.

- The male is more subject to hereditary disease and defect.

- Environmental elements expose the male to greater hazards.

- Females are born with and retain a biological superiority over males (Singer, 1985).

The significance of the chromosomes lies in the material they contain—the genes. Each gene is located at a particular spot on the chromosome, called the *gene locus*. The genes, whose chemical structure is DNA, account for all inherited characteristics, from hair and eye color to skin shade, even the tendency toward baldness.

Aside from performing their cellular duties, the genes also reproduce themselves. Each gene constructs an exact duplicate of itself, so that when a cell divides, the chromosomes and genes also divide and each cell retains identical genetic material. As the cells divide, however, they do not remain identical. Specialization appears and different kinds of cells are formed at different locations.

The genes, then, are continuously active in directing life's processes according to their prescribed genetic codes. The action of the genes is remarkable not only because of complexity but also because of an elegant simplicity. For example, the genes initially form the body's basic materials. Although this activity continues throughout our lives, more specialized functions gradually appear and begin to form a circulatory system, a skeletal system, and a nervous system. The process continues until a highly complex human being results (Grobstein, 1988). (Remember the distinction between genotypes and phenotypes that you read about in the genetic glossary.)

Examples of Chromosomal Disorders

Cytogenetics
The study of chromosomes.

Down syndrome
Genetic abnormality caused by a deviation on the 21st pair of chromosomes.

Klinefelter syndrome
A chromosomal disorder in which males possess an XXY chromosomal pattern.

The study of chromosomes is called **cytogenetics** and thanks to new research techniques that enlarge prints of the chromosomes 2,000 to 3,000 times, our knowledge has increased tremendously. (During the process of in vitro fertilization—see p. 57—it is now possible to detect genetic and chromosomal abnormalities a few days after conception; researchers removed one cell from the first eight cells to develop!) Although the chance of a chromosomal error in pregnancy is small, the risk increases with the age of the woman. Increasing age of the father may also be a factor, though less significant (Feinbloom, 1993). A discussion of chromosomal disorders follows.

Down syndrome is caused by a deviation on the 21st pair of chromosomes; the individual may have 47 chromosomes. This defect was discovered in 1866 by a British doctor, Langdon Down, and produces distinctive facial features, small hands, a large tongue, and possible functional difficulties such as mental retardation, heart defects, and an added risk of leukemia.

The appearance of Down syndrome is closely related to the mother's age: Chances of giving birth to a child with Down syndrome are about 1 in 750 between the ages of 30 and 35; 1 in 300 between 35 and 39; and 1 in 80 between 40 and 45. After 45 years the incidence jumps to 1 in 40 births. Under age 30 the ratio is only 1 in 1,500 births.

Although the exact cause of Down syndrome remains a mystery, the answer may lie in the female egg production mechanism, which results in eggs remaining in the ovary for 40 or 50 years. The longer they are in the ovary, the greater the possibility of damage. No treatment exists for Down syndrome other than good medical supervision and special education. These individuals usually are cheerful, perhaps slightly stubborn, with a good sense of mimicry and rhythm. Since the severity of the defect varies, institutionalization of the child is no longer immediately recommended. Some youngsters develop better in the home, especially if the parents believe they can cope successfully.

Other disorders relate to the sex chromosomes. If you recall, the 23d pair of chromosomes are the sex chromosomes, XX for females, XY for males. Estimates are that 1 in every 1,200 females and 1 in every 400 males has some disorder in the sex chromosomes. Occasionally a male will possess an XXY pattern rather than the normal XY. This is called **Klinefelter syndrome** (named after Dr. Harry Klinefelter in 1942), a disorder that may cause small testicles, reduced body hair, possible infertility, and language impairment. Klinefelter's occurs in about 1 in 1,000 male births; the condition may be helped by injections of testosterone. Another pattern that appears in males is XYY, which may cause larger size and increased aggression (about 1 in 1,000 male births). Heated controversy and inconclusive results have surrounded the study of the "super male."

Down syndrome is caused by a deviation on the 21st pair of chromosomes. These children have distinctive facial features and are usually motorically and mentally retarded.

Turner syndrome

A chromosomal disorder in which females possess an XO chromosomal pattern.

Females occasionally possess an XO pattern (lack of a chromosome) rather than XX. This is called **Turner syndrome** and is characterized by short stature, poorly developed secondary sex features (such as breast size), and usually sterility (about 1 in 2,500 female births).

Examples of Genetic Disorders

This section discusses the incidence and characteristics of several specific genetic disorders. Even as this is being written, thanks to the Human Genome Project, new genetic discoveries are being announced daily.

Tay-Sachs disease

A genetic disorder that primarily afflicts Jewish children of Eastern European origin.

Jews of Eastern European origin are struck hardest by **Tay-Sachs disease,** which causes death by the age of 4 or 5. At birth the afflicted children appear normal, but development slows by the age of 6 months, and mental and motor deterioration begin. About 1 in every 25 to 30 Jews of Eastern European origin carries the defective gene, which is recessive; thus danger arises when two carriers marry. The disease results from a gene failing to produce an enzyme that breaks down fatty materials in the brain and nervous system. The result is that fat accumulates and destroys nerve cells, causing loss of coordination, blindness, and finally death. Today there are reliable genetic tests to identify carriers, and amniocentesis can detect the genetic status of a fetus of carrier parents (Cherry, 1992).

Sickle-cell anemia

A genetic disorder resulting in abnormal hemoglobin.

Sickle-cell anemia, which mainly afflicts those of African descent, appeared thousands of years ago in equatorial Africa and increased resistance to malaria. Estimates are that 10 percent of the African American population in the United States carry the sickle-cell trait. Thus, two carriers of the defective gene who marry have a one in four chance of producing a child with sickle-cell anemia.

The problem is that the red blood cells of the afflicted person are distorted and pointed. Because of the cells' shape, they encounter difficulty in passing through the blood vessels. They tend to pile up and clump, producing oxygen starvation accompanied by considerable pain. The body then acts to eliminate these cells, and anemia results.

Cystic fibrosis (CF)

A genetic disorder producing a malfunction of the exocrine glands.

In the population of the United States, **cystic fibrosis (CF)** is the most severe genetic disease of childhood, affecting about 1 in 1,200 children. About 1 in 30 individuals is a carrier. The disease causes a malfunction of the exocrine glands, the glands that secrete tears, sweat, mucus, and saliva. Breathing is difficult because of the thickness of the mucus. The secreted sweat is extremely salty, often producing heat exhaustion. Cystic fibrosis kills more children than any other genetic disease.

Cystic fibrosis has been deadly for several reasons: Its causes remained unknown, and carriers could not be detected. Thus until a child manifested the breathing and digestive problems characteristic of the disease, identification was impossible. The CF gene now has been identified, however, and new research offers hope. For example, researchers are placing healthy copies of the CF gene into the genetic material of cold viruses and then spraying the virus into the patient's air passages in the hope of supplying the person with a healthy CF gene. Discovery of the CF gene has made possible the detection of carriers, a tremendous legacy of the Human Genome Project.

Phenylketonuria (PKU)

A genetic disorder resulting in a failure of the body to break down the amino acid phenylalanine.

Phenylketonuria (PKU) results from the body's failure to break down the amino acid phenylalanine, which then accumulates, affects the nervous system, and causes mental retardation. Most states now require infants to be tested at birth. If PKU is present, the infants are placed on a special diet that has been remarkably successful.

But this success has produced future problems. Women treated successfully as infants may give birth to retarded children because of a toxic uterine environment. Thus at the first signs of pregnancy, these women must return to a special diet. The "cured" phenylketonuric still carries the faulty genes.

Spina bifida
A genetic disorder resulting in the failure of the neural tube to close.

Spina bifida (failure of the spinal column to close completely) is an example of a genetic defect caused by the interaction of several genes. During the first few weeks following fertilization, the mesoderm sends a chemical signal to the ectoderm that causes the beginnings of the nervous system. The process is as follows:

1. The chemical signal is sent from the mesoderm to the ectoderm.

2. A tube (the neural tube) begins to form, from which the brain and spinal cord develop.

3. Nerve cells are formed within the tube and begin to move to other parts of the developing brain.

4. These neurons now begin to form connections with other neurons.

5. Some of the neurons that don't connect with other neurons die.

If the neural tube does not close, spina bifida results, which can cause mental retardation.

Sex-linked inheritance
Since the female carries more genes on the 23d chromosome than the male (some of which can cause a defect), the lack of an equivalent gene on the mate's 23d chromosome can result in problems such as hemophilia and color blindness.

Disorders also occur because of what is known as **sex-linked inheritance.** If you recall, the X chromosome is substantially larger than the Y (about three times as large). Therefore the female carries more genes on the 23d chromosome than the male. This difference helps to explain sex linkage. Think back now to the difference between dominant and recessive traits. If a dominant and recessive gene appear together, the dominant trait is expressed. An individual must have two recessive genes for the recessive trait (say, blue eyes) to appear.

But on the 23d set of chromosomes, nothing on the Y chromosome offsets the effects of a gene on the X chromosome. As far as we know today, the Y chromosome almost completely lacks genes except for the one that determines maleness—with the possible exception of a condition producing exceptionally hairy ears (Singer, 1985).

Hemophilia
A genetic condition causing incorrect blood clotting; called the "bleeder's disease."

Color blindness
A sex-linked condition attributed to the X chromosome.

Perhaps the most widely known of these sex-linked characteristics is **hemophilia** (the bleeder's disease). The blood of hemophiliacs does not clot properly. Several of the royal families of Europe were particularly prone to this condition. Another sex-linked trait attributed to the X chromosome is **color blindness.** The X chromosome contains the gene for color vision and if it is faulty, nothing on the Y chromosome counterbalances the defect.

Fragile X syndrome
A sex-linked inheritance disorder in which the bottom half of the X chromosome looks as if it is ready to fall off; causes mental retardation in 80 percent of the cases.

In 1970 a condition called **fragile X syndrome** was discovered. In this disorder, the end of the X chromosome looks ready to break off. Recent research points to a genetic abnormality as the cause, which offers promise of greater insights into symptoms of the problem (Feinbloom, 1993). Although fragile X seems to cause no physical problems, about 80 percent of these boys are mentally retarded. Fragile X appears in about 1 in 2,000 live births.

Although these are the more frequent chromosomal and genetic diseases, other diseases also have, or are suspected of having, a strong genetic origin: diabetes, epilepsy, heart disorders, cancer, arthritis, and some mental illnesses. (See table 3.4 for a summary of this discussion.)

To end this part of our work on a more optimistic note, let's turn our attention to the promising and exciting discoveries of the Human Genome Project.

The Human Genome Project

Human Genome Project
The attempt to identify and map the 50,000 to 100,000 genes that constitute the human genetic endowment.

On August 24, 1989, Pete Rose was banished from baseball. For baseball fans, that was the news of the day. In fact, it was headline news around the country. That same day, another announcement far more important for human health appeared in most news outlets, but with far less fanfare. Researchers had found the gene that caused cystic fibrosis (CF).

The CF gene discovery came as part of the **Human Genome Project,** an undertaking comparable to the Manhattan Project that resulted in the atomic bomb and the Apollo Project that produced the first moon landings. The Human Genome

Table 3.4	Chromosomal and Genetic Disorders	
Chromosomal Disorders		
Name	*Effects*	*Incidence*
Down syndrome	47 chromosomes; distinctive facial features, mental retardation, possible physical problems	Varies with age; older women more susceptible (under 30—1 in 1,500 births, 35–39—1 in 300 births)
Klinefelter syndrome	XXY chromosomal pattern in males; possible infertility, possible psychological problems	About 1 in 1,000 male births
Turner syndrome	One X chromosome missing in female; lack of secondary sex characteristics, infertile	About 1 in 2,500 female births
XYY syndrome	XYY chromosomal pattern in males; tend to be large, normal intelligence and behavior	About 1 in 1,000 male births
Genetic Disorders		
Tay-Sachs disease	Failure to break down fatty material in central nervous system; results in blindness, mental retardation, and death (usually by 4 or 5 years of age)	One in 25 Jews of Eastern European origin is a carrier
Sickle-cell anemia	Blood disorder producing anemia and considerable pain; caused by sickle shape of red blood cells	About 1 in 10 African-Americans is a carrier
Cystic fibrosis	Body produces excessive mucus, causing problems in the lungs and digestive tract; may be fatal, suspect gene recently identified	About 1 in 2,000 births
Phenylketonuria (PKU)	Body fails to break down amino acid (phenylalanine); results in mental retardation, treated by special diet	About 1 in 15,000 births
Spina bifida	Neural tube problem in which the developing spinal column does not close properly; may cause partial paralysis and mental retardation	About 1 in 1,000 births (depending on geographical area)

Project is nothing less than an attempt to identify and map the 50,000 to 100,000 genes that constitute our genetic makeup. It is a project, international in scope, that will take about 15 years and cost at least 3 billion dollars!

Several exciting discoveries have already been made: The first preliminary, comprehensive map of all human chromosomes has been accomplished (Angier, 1993); the genes responsible for cystic fibrosis and Huntington's disease have been identified; scientists are confident that they are close to detecting the defective gene that can trigger breast cancer (Waldholz, 1992); genetic defects have been identified only days after fertilization.

To give you an idea of the potential uses of a gene map, Bishop and Waldholz (1990) estimate that as many as 2.4 million women each year will undergo prenatal tests for chromosomal abnormalities. Almost 2.8 million women will try to discover if they are carriers of any of the genes of the four major inherited diseases: cystic fibrosis, sickle-cell anemia, hemophilia, and muscular dystrophy.

Studies of genetic susceptibility will undoubtedly follow the same pattern. The genes that make people susceptible to certain diseases do not, of themselves, cause disease. It is the combination of a particular environment with a particular gene. For example, a person may be born with a susceptibility to lung cancer and never develop any malignancy. If that same person is a heavy smoker, however, the chances of developing cancer are much greater.

Once the mechanisms that cause a susceptibility gene to spring into action are more fully understood, such preventative measures as screening techniques and drug therapy will save many lives.

🌳 Guided Review 🌳

14. The genetic composition of an individual is referred to as the _____ , whereas the observed expression of a gene is called the _____ .

15. In assessing action, it is necessary to recall that there are _____ types of sperm, the _____ _____ carrier and the _____ _____ carrier.

16. The genetic information contained in one chromosome is equal to that in _____ books.

17. Down syndrome is perhaps the best-known _____ disorder.

18. _____ anemia and _____ disease are examples of genetic disorders.

Heredity and Environment

As you have read this chapter, the amazing biological advances in studies of human development probably fascinated you. You may be tempted to believe that biology holds clues to most of the secrets of development. Remember, however, the environmental role in development. As a pertinent reminder, consider the longitudinal study conducted by Emmy Werner (1991) that began in 1954. Studying all of the infants born on the Hawaiian island of Kauai in 1955 (698 infants), Werner and her colleagues analyzed their development at 1, 2, 10, 18, and 31 or 32 years of age. Of the 698 infants, 276 were identified as "at risk"; that is, they had experienced reproductive stress, lived in dysfunctional families, or had mentally disturbed or alcoholic parents. The study involved remarkable cultural diversity, including children of Hawaiian, Japanese, Philipino, Portuguese, Chinese, and Korean descent. The population studied also was stable: 88 percent of the group were available for the 18-year follow-up. (Recall the strengths and weaknesses of longitudinal studies that we described in chap. 1.)

Gathering a vast array of data on the children, Werner was able to identify various high-risk categories:

- Prenatal or perinatal stress (complications during pregnancy, labor, or delivery) was found in 69 children.

- Severe prenatal or perinatal stress was diagnosed in 23 children. Only 14 of these children lived until the age of 2 years.

- One of every six children had physical or intellectual complications of perinatal or neonatal origin that required long-term care.

Answers

14. genotype, phenotype 15. two, X chromosome, Y chromosome 16. 4,000 17. chromosomal 18. Sickle-cell, Tay-Sachs

- One of five children developed serious learning or behavior problems.

- By the time the children were 10 years of age, twice as many needed mental health services as required medical care.

As they followed these children from birth to 18 years of age, Werner and her research team found that the impact of reproductive stress lessened with time and that the outcome of every biological problem depended on the child's environment. Family dysfunction, parental mental illness, or generally poor home conditions were consistently related to long-term biological complications.

One in three of the high-risk children who grew up in troubled environments turned out to be competent young adults. Using several of these children as case studies, Werner discovered several predictive factors that helped the children to overcome their difficulties: a child's temperament (active, low excitability), a high degree of sociability, alertness, and concentration. Families of competent children had four or fewer children, with at least two years between each child. The competent children also established a bond with someone who gave them positive attention (a grandparent, uncle, or older sibling). These relationships helped the children to find meaning in their lives and gave them a belief that they could control their destinies. In their thirties, these individuals were leading satisfactory adult lives.

Biological–Cultural Interactions

As you can tell from our discussion of the role of genetics in development, biology exercises a powerful impact on the nature and direction of development. Assessing the influence of a gene or genes, however, is difficult because a gene is expressed in an environment. Phenylketonuria (PKU) is a good example of how the environment can dramatically alter the expression of a gene: Eliminating the amino acid phenylalanine from the diet of an affected person prevents retardation (Horgan, 1993).

As Plomin and his colleagues (1993) have noted, several major obstacles limit analysis of the gene–environment interaction. One is a lack of environmental measures that permit direct assessment of how shared and nonshared environments interact with a gene(s) and affect a child's growth. Another problem is our inability to capture the dynamics of the genetic–environmental interactions that occur within individuals. Still another issue is that genetically similar children usually share similar environments, which further clouds attempts to weigh genetic and environmental influences. Further complicating this issue is, as Baumrind (1993) noted, families may differ markedly in the extent to which they provide a shared environment. Families also differ in how they endeavor to offer specific environmental experiences for each of their children.

A good way to conclude our work in this chapter is to return to Werner's study and examine her findings in light of the need to accept the conclusion that the outcome of genetic action can only result from its interaction with environmental experiences. If you recall, the ultimate outcome of a newborn's difficulties was determined by the environment into which the child was born—heredity interacting with environment.

At this point, reassess your position on the importance of heredity (your answer to Personal Question # 1). Is it the same? Why? Why not?

Guided Review

19. Werner's study is a sharp reminder that development is explained by the _____ of genes and the environment.

20. Mapping the human genes is the goal of the _____ _____ _____ .

Answers

19. interaction   20. Human Genome Project

CONCLUSION

In this chapter we explored the biological basis of our uniqueness. We considered not only the power and beauty of nature in establishing our genetic endowment but also the growing influence of technology. The genes the mother and father provide unite to produce a new and different human being. Yet this new life still shows many of the characteristics of both parents. We saw how this newness and sameness has challenged researchers for decades.

Beginning with the discoveries of Mendel and still continuing, the secrets of hereditary transmission remain at the forefront of scientific endeavor, especially given the impetus of the Human Genome Project. Today's work, building on our knowledge of DNA, provides hope for the future while simultaneously raising legal and ethical questions that have yet to be resolved.

Following fertilization—either by natural or external methods—there begins a nine-month period (at least for most children) that concludes with expulsion into the waiting world. It is this period that occupies us in chapter 4.

CHAPTER HIGHLIGHTS

The Fertilization Process
- Knowledge of hormonal control of the menstrual cycle is crucial for understanding fertilization.
- The study of twins, especially monozygotic twins, has long fascinated psychologists.
- The increasing number of infertile couples has led to a growing demand for external fertilization.
- The most widely used external fertilization technique is AID (artificial insemination by donor).
- The success rate of external fertilization procedures has improved with increasing knowledge.
- Today's adoption procedures include both closed and open adoption.

Heredity at Work
- Mitosis and meiosis are the means of cell division.
- DNA is the chemical key to life.
- Understanding how traits are transmitted requires a knowledge of the workings of dominant and recessive genes.

Chromosomes and Genes
- The Human Genome Project is an endeavor to map all of the genes.
- Chromosomal defects include: Down syndrome, Klinefelter syndrome, and Turner syndrome.
- Genetic defects include: Tay-Sachs, sickle-cell anemia, cystic fibrosis, phenylketonuria, and spina bifida.

Heredity and Environment
- Development can only be explained in light of the interactions between genes and the environment.
- The exact nature of the dynamic interactions between genes and the environment still eludes us.

KEY TERMS

Artificial insemination by donor (AID) 55
Blastocyst 53
Color blindness 66
Cystic fibrosis (CF) 65
Cytogenetics 64
Dizygotic 55
DNA 59
Dominant 61
Down syndrome 64
Endometriosis 54
External fertilization 51
Fallopian tubes 53
Fragile X syndrome 66
Gamete intrafallopian transfer (GIFT) 57
Genotype 50
Hemophilia 66
Human Genome Project 66
Identical 55
Implantation 53
Infertility 54
Internal fertilization 51
Intrauterine devices (IUDs) 54
In vitro fertilization (IVF) 51
Klinefelter syndrome 64
Meiosis 59
Mitosis 59
Monozygotic 55
Nonidentical 55
Pelvic inflammatory disease (PID) 54
Phenotype 50
Phenylketonuria (PKU) 65
Recessive 61
Sex-linked inheritance 66
Sexually transmitted diseases (STDs) 54
Sickle-cell anemia 65
Spina bifida 66
Tay-Sachs disease 65
Turner syndrome 65
Zygote 53
Zygote intrafallopian transfer (ZIFT) 57

🌳 WHAT DO YOU THINK?

1. You may have begun your work in lifespan psychology with the idea that either heredity or environment was all-important. Do you still think that way? Or do you believe that one may be somewhat more important than the other? Does the biopsychosocial model help you to answer these questions?

2. Several controversies have occurred lately about surrogate mothers and the children they bear. Do you have any strong feelings about surrogacy? Can you defend it? Regardless of your personal feelings, can you present what you see as the pros and cons of surrogacy?

3. In your reading, perhaps you noticed that the process of in vitro fertilization depended on research findings from studies of the menstrual cycle. Can you explain this, paying particular attention to the administering of hormones and the timing of their administration?

4. James Watson and Francis Crick received a Nobel Prize for their discovery of the double-helix structure of DNA. Why is the discovery of DNA so important in our lives? Can you think of anything you have read about in the newspapers or seen on television that derives from this discovery?

5. Given what you know about the role of heredity in development, how would you evaluate the importance of genetic counseling? If you were thinking of having children, and you were concerned about the genetic background of yourself or your partner, would you seek genetic counseling?

🌳 SUGGESTED READINGS

Bishop, J. & Waldholz, M. (1990). *Genome*. New York: Simon & Schuster. An excellent, readable account of the Human Genome Project. The personal histories are especially appealing.

Watson, J. (1968). *The double helix*. Boston: Atheneum. A classic, Watson's personal, colorful look at the discovery of DNA is guaranteed to hold your attention. If you are the least bit intimidated by the thought of reading about your genetic heritage, this book should eliminate your concerns. (Available in paperback.)

Wingerson, L. (1990). *Mapping our genes*. New York: Plume. An enlightening and human look at the field of genetics; a well-written and fascinating account of a rapidly changing world.

🌳 CHAPTER REVIEW TEST

1. From ovulation to implantation takes about
   a. seven days.
   b. two weeks.
   c. one month.
   d. nine months.

2. The union of sperm and egg is a process known as
   a. mitosis.
   b. fertilization.
   c. meiosis.
   d. mutation.

3. In vitro fertilization takes place
   a. in the fallopian tube.
   b. in the uterus.
   c. outside the woman's body.
   d. in the ovary.

4. Which of the following is *not* a female secondary sex characteristic?
   a. higher voice
   b. wider hips
   c. breasts
   d. thick hair

5. The process by which eggs are ripened and released is called
   a. ovulation.
   b. mitosis.
   c. fertilization.
   d. implantation.

6. Each sex cell carries a total of _____ chromosomes.
   a. 23
   b. 24
   c. 47
   d. 46

7. _____ twins are likely to occur when a woman's ovaries release two ripened eggs that are fertilized by separate sperm.
   a. Nonidentical
   b. Identical
   c. Siamese
   d. Monozygotic

8. Which factor is *not* thought to be a cause of infertility in men?
   a. influenza
   b. low sperm count
   c. defective sperm
   d. genetic disease

9. Which of the following statements is true?
   a. XX indicates male.
   b. XY indicates male.
   c. XO indicates male.
   d. X—indicates male.

10. Which of the following is an example of a genetic disorder?
    a. sickle-cell anemia
    b. Turner syndrome
    c. Klinefelter syndrome
    d. Down syndrome

11. If a mother carries only genes for brown eyes (and she has no blue-eyed relatives) and the father has blue eyes, which statement is most likely?
    a. Their children will all be blue-eyed.
    b. Twenty-five percent of their children will be blue-eyed.
    c. Twenty-five percent of their children will be brown-eyed.
    d. Their children will all be brown-eyed.

12. Which of the following is an example of a chromosomal disorder?
    a. spina bifida
    b. chronic disease syndrome
    c. phenylketonuria
    d. Turner syndrome

13. _____ is the most widely used external fertilization technique.
    a. IVF
    b. AID
    c. SART
    d. PID

14. Which combination is *not* possible?
    a. AT
    b. TA
    c. GT
    d. GC

15. _____ was an early scientist in the field of genetics.
    a. Freud
    b. Mendel
    c. Watson
    d. Vygotsky

16. Which of the following populations is more likely than others to be afflicted with sickle-cell anemia?
    a. Eastern Europeans
    b. African Americans
    c. Asians
    d. Hispanics

17. Down syndrome is caused by
    a. the body's failure to break down amino acids.
    b. the fragile X syndrome.
    c. a deviation on the 21st pair of chromosomes.
    d. an XO pattern.

18. An example of sex-linked inheritance includes
    a. PKU.
    b. neural tube defects.
    c. Tay-Sachs disease.
    d. hemophilia.

19. The Human Genome Project is an endeavor to identify and map
    a. certain substances within cells.
    b. all human genes.
    c. cell divisions.
    d. nucleotides within DNA.

20. Which of the following is *not* suspected of having a strong genetic origin?
    a. polio
    b. epilepsy
    c. diabetes
    d. cancer

Answers

1.a 2.b 3.c 4.d 5.a 6.a 7.a 8.a 9.b 10.a 11.d 12.d 13.b 14.c 15.b 16.b 17.c 18.d 19.b 20.a

Pregnancy and Birth

Ellen and Kevin were delighted. The parents of a 3-year-old boy, they were now looking forward to their second child. Kevin, having shared in the birth of their first child, was calmer but even more excited as he looked forward to the events of this pregnancy and birth. Ellen, a healthy 31-year-old, was experiencing all the signs of a normal pregnancy. The morning sickness abated at 12 weeks. She felt movement at 17 weeks, and an ultrasound at 20 weeks showed normal development. Weight gain, blood glucose levels, blood pressure, and AFP (alpha-fetoprotein) test results were all within acceptable ranges.

Since this was Ellen's second pregnancy, she felt more comfortable with her changing body. Visits to the obstetrician were pleasant and uneventful. At 28 weeks, loosening ligaments caused her pelvis to irritate the sciatic nerve at the base of the spine. Her obstetrician recommended Tylenol, a heating pad, and rest. He also recommended a visit to an orthopedist to confirm the treatment. Ellen refused to take any medication and decided not to bother with a second opinion. Since she felt she could tolerate the pain for the 12 weeks until delivery, she would not be X-rayed or take even a mild painkiller. She rationalized that the back pain was acceptable because it accompanied a normal pregnancy.

At 31 weeks, Ellen noticed episodes of unusual movement and became concerned. A week later, fearing that the baby might be in distress, she called the obstetrician to describe the jabs, pokes, and excessive movements she was experiencing. The doctor immediately scheduled a biophysical profile: an eight-point check of the internal organs and another ultrasound.

Ellen nervously gulped the required 32 ounces of water an hour before the examination. Arriving at a glistening new medical center, she was quickly escorted to an examining room. The technician was both professional and serious as he looked for a problem (increasing Ellen's anxiety). The examination included a thorough check of the baby's heart chambers, a type of EKG (electrocardiogram) measurement, and an assessment of blood flow—all displayed in vibrant colors. The cord, internal organs, position of the baby, and body weight were all evaluated. Ellen was able to listen to the baby's heartbeat while watching the heart chambers function.

Later that day, Ellen's obstetrician called to tell her the results: no apparent medical problems, just an unusually active baby. Ellen and Kevin sagged with relief. They also received a bonus: a reassuring ultrasound image of their unborn child's face—in living color.

Ellen's journey through the nine months of her pregnancy is quite typical: normal prenatal development accompanied by occasional worrisome moments. As you read about her journey in this chapter, you'll discover that a myth is being destroyed. In fact, several myths are on the road to extinction. The notion that babies at birth know nothing and are passive sponges has been totally disproved. We now know that newborns are amazingly competent. After all, they have been flourishing in a highly protected environment, sometimes humorously called "the prenatal university," for nine months. Researchers, however, are asking serious questions about the potential of prenatal life. The basic issue is this: Can fetal enrichment (a fancy name for fetal education) produce a better baby? 🌳

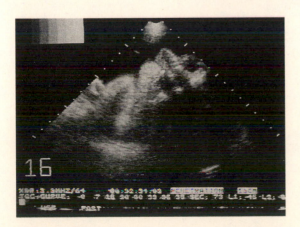

Ultrasound is frequently used when questions arise about a pregnancy. Soundwaves directed onto the uterus bounce off the bones and tissues of the fetus and are formed into an image.

Even if prenatal learning is possible, do you think it should be attempted? Why? Why not?

Is it fact or fancy to think that prenatal learning is a possibility? Although we cannot as yet answer this question with certainty, several clues can help us. First, little doubt exists that the senses (hearing, taste, smell, touch, vision) develop during pregnancy; they do not appear instantly at birth. Taste and smell are present by 20 weeks; touch appears at about 25 weeks; fetuses respond to sound by about 27 or 28 weeks; brain life begins by the seventh month. EEGs (electroencephalograms) taken just before birth show brain waves similar to those of infants.

One of the leading centers of research into fetal life is at the University of North Carolina. Here, Anthony DeCasper and his colleagues are attempting to piece together the puzzle of fetal learning. For example, they had infants suck on a nipple attached to a tape recorder. Fast sucking activated a recording of their mothers' voices, and slower sucking produced another woman's voice. The babies showed a preference for their mothers' voices, as indicated by fast sucking.

Taking these results one step further, DeCasper asked a group of pregnant women to read a children's story aloud twice a day for six weeks prior to their expected delivery day. At birth the infants' patterns showed that they preferred the familiar story to one they had never heard (DeCasper & Fifer, 1980). Obviously, some fetal "learning" had occurred. Results are sufficiently promising to stimulate continued research.

In this chapter, we'll first explore the prenatal world, that nine-month period that provides nourishment and protection and serves as a springboard for birth. Next we'll turn to those agents that can influence prenatal development. These are both physical and psychological and can be either positive or negative. We'll then look at birth itself, the completion of a journey that has involved remarkable development. For various reasons, some fetuses can't endure this nine-month journey, so our final focus in this chapter will be the special case of these early, or premature, births. In the past few years, great advances—technological, medical, and psychological—have resulted in an increasing number of premature babies surviving.

When you complete your reading of this chapter you should be able to

- Describe the periods of prenatal development.

- Analyze the major features of each period.

- Indicate the times of greatest sensitivity to insult.

- Identify dangerous maternal diseases.

- Distinguish those drugs that can cause permanent damage during prenatal development.

- Assess the potential of fetal surgery.

- Discriminate the various stages of the birth process.

- Designate the possible causes of prematurity.

The Prenatal World

Although it may be difficult to imagine, you are the product of one cell, the zygote, or fertilized egg. Once the union of sperm and egg took place, in only a matter of hours (about 24–30) that one cell began to divide rapidly. The initial phase of the event occurred in a very protected world—the prenatal environment.

Once the egg is released from the ovary, it passes into the fallopian tube. Fertilization occurs in the first part of the fallopian tube, about three days after the egg has entered the tube. The fertilized egg must now pass through the remainder of the fallopian tube to reach the uterus, a journey of about three to four days to travel five or six inches. Hormones released by the ovary stimulate the muscles of the fallopian tube wall so that it gently pushes the zygote toward the uterus. During its passage through the fallopian tube, the zygote receives all of its nourishment from the tube. Figure 4.1 illustrates passage into the uterus and **implantation**.

Implantation
The time when the fertilized egg attaches and secures itself to the uterine wall.

Figure 4.1

Passage of the zygote into the uterus

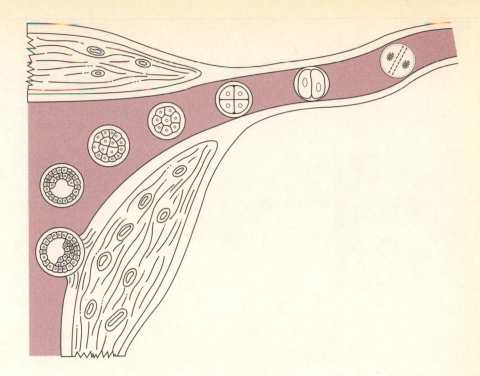

Apposition

The time when the fertilized egg, now called a blastocyst, comes to rest against the uterine wall.

Adhesion

The time during which the prepared surface of the uterus and the outer surface of the fertilized egg, now called the trophoblast, touch and actually "stick together."

Trophoblast

The outer surface of the fertilized egg

Invasion

Period during which the trophoblast digs in and begins to bury itself in the uterine lining.

Germinal period

The first two weeks following fertilization.

Placenta

The organ that supplies the embryo with all its needs, carries off all its wastes, and protects it from danger.

Umbilical cord

A cord that contains blood vessels that go to and from the mother through the arteries and veins supplying the placenta.

Amniotic sac

A thin membrane that surrounds the embryo.

Implantation seems to occur in three phases:

1. **Apposition,** during which the fertilized egg, now called a blastocyst, comes to rest against the uterine wall.

2. **Adhesion,** during which the prepared surface of the uterus and the outer surface of the fertilized egg, now called the **trophoblast,** touch and actually "stick together."

3. **Invasion,** during which the trophoblast digs in and begins to bury itself in the uterine lining (Beaconsfield & others, 1983).

Two events in this process are particularly remarkable:

- During the invasion phase, the trophoblast penetrates the uterine lining only so far and then stops. The distance varies depending on the species. Why? As yet, we have no answers to this question.

- The mother's uterine lining doesn't reject this invasive tissue. Why? Again, there are no answers to this question.

We can identify three fairly distinct stages of prenatal development: germinal, embryonic, and fetal.

The Germinal Period

The **germinal period** extends through the first two weeks. Since the passage through the fallopian tube takes seven days, the zygote is now 1 week old and called a blastocyst. During the second week, the blastocyst becomes firmly implanted in the wall of the uterus. From its outer layer of cells, the **placenta,** an **umbilical cord,** and the **amniotic sac** begin to develop. The inner cell layer develops into the embryo itself. Figure 4.2 illustrates the developmental significance of the blastocyst.

The placenta and the umbilical cord serve critical functions during development. The placenta supplies the embryo with all its needs, carries off all its wastes, and protects it from danger. The placenta has two separate sets of blood vessels, one going to and from the baby through the umbilical cord, the other going to and from the mother through the arteries and veins supplying the placenta.

Figure 4.2

During the second week, the blastocyst becomes firmly implanted in the wall of the uterus and the placenta, umbilical cord, and embryo itself begin to form from its outer layer of cells.

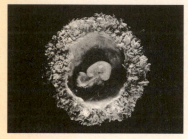

Fertilization through the embryonic period: The moment of fertilization

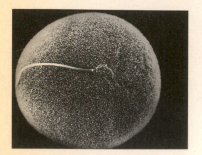

This 4-week-old embryo now has a beating heart, body buds are beginning to emerge, and the eye region is becoming discernible.

Embryonic period

Third through the eighth week following fertilization.

Ectoderm

The outer layer of the embryo that will give rise to the nervous system, among other developmental features.

Mesoderm

The middle layer of the embryo that gives rise to muscles, the skeleton, and the excretory system.

Endoderm

The inner layer of the embryo that will give rise to the lungs, liver, and pancreas, among other developmental features.

Organogenesis

The formation of organs during the embryonic period.

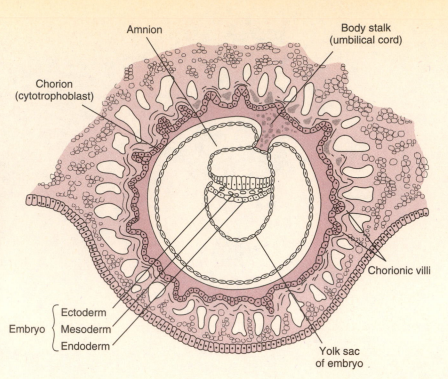

We can summarize the first two weeks following conception as follows:

Week 1: The zygote moves through the fallopian tube to the uterus with continued cell division.

Week 2: The blastocyst adheres to the uterine wall and begins to form the placenta, umbilical cord, and amniotic sac.

The Embryonic Period

When the second week ends, the germinal period is complete. In the **embryonic period,** from the third through the eighth week, development of a recognizable human being begins. The nervous system develops rapidly, which suggests that the embryo at this time is quite sensitive to any obstructions to its growth. Our earlier discussion of sensitive periods as a time when certain experiences have a significant impact on the developing organism is clearly supported during the embryonic period. With the rapid formation of many different organ systems, any negative agent (drugs, disease) can have long-lasting effects.

Perhaps the most remarkable change in the embryo is cellular differentiation. Three distinct layers are being formed: the **ectoderm,** which will give rise to skin, hair, nails, teeth, and nervous system; the **mesoderm,** which will give rise to muscles, skeleton, and the circulatory and excretory systems; and the **endoderm,** which will give rise to lungs, liver, and pancreas. (See figure 4.3 for details.)

Usually by the completion of the fourth week, the heart begins to beat—the embryo's first movement. The accompanying photographs show that during the fifth week eyes and ears begin to emerge, body buds give clear evidence of becoming arms and legs, and the head area is the largest part of the rapidly growing embryo.

During the sixth and seventh weeks, fingers begin to appear on the hands, the outline of toes is seen, and the beginnings of the spinal cord are visible. During the germinal period, the number and differentiation of cells rapidly increase; in the embryonic period, the organs are formed, a process called **organogenesis** (Sadler, 1985).

After eight weeks, 95 percent of the body parts are formed and general body movements are detected. During these weeks embryonic tissue is particularly sensitive to any foreign agents during differentiation, especially beginning at the third or fourth week of the pregnancy.

Figure 4.3
Development from the three
layers of the blastocyst

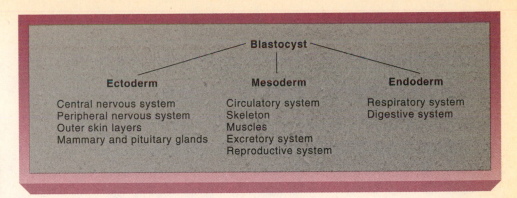

Blastocyst		
Ectoderm	**Mesoderm**	**Endoderm**
Central nervous system	Circulatory system	Respiratory system
Peripheral nervous system	Skeleton	Digestive system
Outer skin layers	Muscles	
Mammary and pituitary glands	Excretory system	
	Reproductive system	

We can summarize the embryonic period as follows:

Weeks 3+: Rapid development of nervous system
Week 4: Heart beats
Week 5: Eyes and ears begin to emerge, body buds for arms and legs
Week 6 and 7: Fingers and toes, beginning of spinal cord
Week 8: About 95 percent of body parts differentiated—arms, legs, beating
heart, nervous system

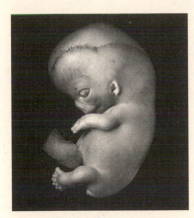

This 45-day-old embryo has
visible arms and legs, with the
beginnings of toes and fingers. It
is possible to detect eyes and
ears in the rapidly growing head
area.

The embryonic period can be hazardous for the newly formed organism.
Estimates are that about 30 percent of all embryos are aborted at this time without
the mother's knowledge; about 90 percent of all embryos with chromosomal abnormalities are spontaneously aborted.

At the end of this period, a discernible human being with arms, legs, a beating
heart, and a nervous system exists. It is receiving nourishment and discharging
waste through the umbilical cord, which leads to the placenta. The placenta itself
never actually joins with the uterus but exchanges nourishment and waste products
through the walls of the blood vessels (Guttmacher & Kaiser, 1986). The future
mother begins to experience some of the noticeable effects of pregnancy: the need
to urinate more frequently, morning sickness, and increasing fullness of the breasts.

Fetal period
The period extending from the
beginning of the third month to
birth.

The Fetal Period

The **fetal period** extends from the beginning of the third month to birth. During
this time, the fetus grows rapidly both in height and weight. The sex organs appear
during the third month, and it is possible to determine the baby's sex. Visible sexual differentiation begins, and the nervous system continues to increase in size and
complexity.

By the fourth month, the fetus is about 8 to 10 inches in length and weighs
about 6 to 8 ounces. The fourth to the fifth month is usually the peak growth
period. During this time, the mother begins to feel movement. The fetus now swallows, digests, and discharges urine. Growth is rapid during the fourth month to
accommodate an increasing oxygen demand (Nilsson & others, 1987). The fetus
produces specialized cells: red blood cells to transport oxygen and white blood
cells to combat disease.

The fetus is now active—sucking, turning its head, and pushing with hands and
feet—and the mother is acutely aware of the life within her. Figure 4.4 represents
the fetus in the fourth month.

By the end of the fifth month, the baby is 10 to 12 inches long and weighs
about a pound. The fetus sleeps and wakes like the newborn does, even manifest-
ing a favorite sleep position. Rapid growth continues in the sixth month, with the
fetus gaining another 2 inches and 1 pound, but slows during the seventh month.
Viability, the ability to survive if born, is attained. After six months very few new
nerve and muscle cells appear, since at birth the nervous system must be fully functioning to ensure automatic breathing.

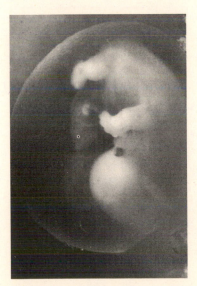

Coming to the end of the
embryonic period, this 7-week-
old embryo has begun to assume
a more human appearance. It is
now about 1 inch in length with
discernible eyes, ears, nose,
mouth, arms, and legs.

Table 4.1	Prenatal Development
Name	**Development**
Zygote	Fertilization (union of sperm and egg)
	Cleavage (about 30 hr)
Blastocyst	Rapid cell division (about four days)
	Implantation (about sixth or seventh day)
Embryo	Begins at third week
	Central nervous system grows rapidly
	Heart begins to beat at about 28 days
	Digestive organs form during the second month
	Muscular system appears during the second month
	Sex differentiation at about seven weeks
	95% of body parts differentiated at the end of the eighth week
Fetus	Organs begin to function from 8–12 weeks
	Rapid growth during fourth month
	Viability at about 27 weeks
	Exercises functioning systems until birth

Figure 4.4

The fetus at 4 1/2 months—a time of rapid growth and considerable activity

During the two final fetal months, organ development prepares the fetus for the shock of leaving the sheltered uterine world. The senses are ready to function; some, in fact, are already functioning. For example, the fetus is able to hear sound—the silent world of the fetus is a myth—and responds to auditory stimuli. The fetus hears many environmental sounds—voices, stomach rumblings, and the pulsing of the mother's blood.

The sense of touch becomes functional by the beginning of the third month (Blass & Ciaramitaro, 1994). Taste buds appear during the third month; the visual system continues to develop throughout pregnancy and structural changes occur as late as nine months.

We can summarize these developments as follows:

Third month: Sex organs appear
Fourth month: Rapid growth, red blood cells, white blood cells; active sucking
Fifth month: Hears sound, sleeps, 10 to 12 inches long, 1 pound
Sixth month: Rapid growth, 12 to 14 inches, 2 pounds
Seventh month: Growth slows, viability attained
Eighth and ninth months: Preparation for birth; senses ready to function, brain is 25 percent of adult weight

At the end of the ninth month, the fetus (just before birth) is about 20 inches long, weighs about 7 pounds, 6 ounces, and its brain at birth is 20 to 25 percent of its adult weight.

Few babies (about 1 in 20) are born on the day predicted. Several reasons account for this discrepancy. The varying length of the menstrual cycles can affect estimates of the time of ovulation. Also, conception occurs at different times. Finally, fetuses mature at different rates, which affects fetal size and the onset of labor.

Most women begin to experience some discomfort as the time of birth approaches. The extra weight, body changes, and sheer effort of movement all contribute to this discomfort. During this period of preparation, the major influence on the growing child is its mother. If the mother is healthy, happy, and reasonably cautious, both she and her child will be the beneficiaries. Table 4.1 summarizes the course of prenatal development.

This summary of fetal life leads to an inevitable conclusion: Given adequate conditions, the fetus at birth is equipped to deal effectively with the transition from its sheltered environment to the extrauterine world.

FETAL SURGERY: BRIGHT FUTURE OR FUTURE PROBLEMS?

The first meeting of the Fetal Medicine and Surgery Society took place in 1982. In slightly more than a decade, we have seen the emergence of several new surgical techniques (Kolata, 1990). As amazing as it may sound, surgeons can operate on a fetus. Fetal surgery has saved several lives and with continued refinement promises a healthy future for many babies. Three types of fetal surgery have received considerable attention:

- To cure a condition in which the brain ventricles fill with fluid and expand (called *fetal hydrocephalus*), surgeons now operate within the womb. They must pierce the woman's abdomen and uterine wall and penetrate the fetal skull. They then insert a tube (catheter) into the brain to drain this region until birth. Unless this condition is treated, fluid presses against the walls (membranes) of the fetal brain ventricles and can cause mental retardation or even death.
- To correct a blocked urinary tract in the fetus (called *fetal hydronephosis*), the surgeon removes the fetus from the womb, operates, and then returns the fetus to the uterus. The surgeon then adds either saline solution (salt water) or amniotic fluid that has been saved and warmed and, finally, sews the uterus. This surgery could not be accomplished unless drugs preventing labor were available. If the condition is not corrected, the lungs of the fetus cannot develop. The blocked urinary tract causes urine to stay in the bladder, which can actually burst. Or urine can back up into the kidneys, causing serious damage. The major problem is that the fetus stops producing amniotic fluid, which is mainly fetal urine. The fetus swallows amniotic fluid, which causes the lungs to grow. Without

the amniotic fluid, the lungs don't grow; and at birth, the fetus simply can't breathe.
- To correct a condition in which the fetus has a hole in its diaphragm (the muscle separating the abdomen from the chest cavity), surgeons make an incision across the uterus and cut into the fetal chest and abdomen. (This condition is called *diaphragmatic hernia*.) Surgeons push back into the abdomen any abdominal organs that might have moved through the hole in the diaphragm into the chest cavity. They then close the hole. Without this surgery, the abdominal organs that have pushed into the chest cavity restrict the growth of the lungs and eventually the fetus cannot breathe.

These three procedures are merely examples of what the future holds: lung and liver transplants using adult tissue. Another intriguing finding of fetal surgery is that cutting fetal tissue leaves no scars. The implications of this discovery for surgery treating such problems as cleft lips and palates are enormous.

These advances, however, have not occurred without giving rise to new ethical questions. Here are a few examples:

- Who decides which fetuses will benefit from surgery and which will not?
- Are the outcomes of fetal surgery sufficiently known to undertake the risk?
- Does this mean that the fetus is an actual patient?
- What are the implications of the growing ability to perform pregnancy reductions? (A woman finds that she has four fetuses, not all of which can survive under these conditions. Who decides which fetuses will be eliminated?)

These are not easy questions. Do you think fetal surgery should continue until these questions are answered? What's your view?

Influences on Prenatal Development

When we speak of "environmental influences" on children, we usually think of the time beginning at birth. But remember: At birth an infant has already had nine months of prenatal living, with all of this period's positive and negative features. Many women today experience the benefits of the latest research about prenatal care. Diet, exercise, and rest are all carefully programmed to the needs of the individual woman. Where women, especially pregnant teenagers (see chap. 13), lack such treatment, the rates of prenatal loss, stillbirths, and neonatal (just after birth) mortality are substantially higher.

In spite of this care, some children still experience problems, which introduces the concept of **developmental risk.** Developmental risk is a term used to identify those children whose well-being is in jeopardy. Such risks incorporate a continuum of biological and environmental conditions. These range from the very serious (genetic defects) to the less serious (mild oxygen deprivation at birth). What now seems clear is that the earlier the damage (a toxic drug or maternal infection), the greater the chance of negative long-term effects.

If you recall our earlier discussion of sensitive periods (see chap. 1), times of rapid growth (especially during the embryonic period with the accelerated development of the central nervous system) are also times of particular susceptibility. Risks, however, that arise just before, during, and after birth show the most serious consequences during infancy and early childhood and gradually recede during the school years. Specifically, what causes a child to be developmentally at risk?

Teratogens

With regard to developmental risk, our major concern here is with those substances that exercise their influence in the prenatal environment, a time of increased sensitivity. Teratogenic agents, which are any agents that cause abnormalities, especially demand our attention. **Teratogens** that can cause birth defects are drugs, chemicals, infections, pollutants, or a mother's physical state, such as diabetes. Table 4.2 summarizes several of the more common teratogenic agents and the times of greatest potential risk. By examining table 4.2, you can see that these teratogenic agents fall into two classes: infectious diseases and different types of chemicals.

Developmental risk

A term used to describe children who may be susceptible to problems because of some physical or psychological difficulty ("at-risk" children).

Teratogens

Any agents that can cause abnormalities, including drugs, chemicals, infections, pollutants, and the mother's physical state.

Answers

1. fallopian tube 2. implantation 3. third, eighth 4. ectoderm, mesoderm, endoderm 5. fetal 6. fourth, fifth 7. mother, fetus

Table 4.2	Teratogens, Their Effects, and Time of Risk	
Agent	**Possible Effects**	**Time of Risk**
Alcohol	Fetal alcohol syndrome (FAS), growth retardation, cognitive deficits	Throughout pregnancy
Aspirin	Bleeding problems	Last month, at birth
Cigarettes	Prematurity, lung problems	After 20 weeks
DES	Cancer of female reproductive system	From 3–20 weeks
LSD	Isolated abnormalities	Before conception
Lead	Death, anemia, mental retardation	Throughout pregnancy
Marijuana	Unknown long-term effects, early neurological problems	Throughout pregnancy
Thalidomide	Fetal death, physical and mental abnormalities	The first month
Cocaine	Spontaneous abortion, neurological problems	Throughout pregnancy
AIDS	Growth failure, low birth weight, developmental delay, death from infection	Before conception, throughout pregnancy, during delivery and breast feeding
Rubella	Mental retardation, physical problems, possible death	First three months, may have effects during later months
Syphilis	Death, congenital syphilis, prematurity	From five months on
CMV	Retardation, blindness, deafness	Uncertain, perhaps 4–24 weeks
Herpes simplex	Central nervous system (CNS) damage, prematurity	Potential risk throughout pregnancy and at birth

Infectious Diseases

Some diseases that are potentially harmful to the developing fetus and that are acquired either before or during birth are grouped together as the STORCH diseases (Blackman, 1984):

Syphilis
Toxoplasmosis
Other infections
Rubella
Cytomegalovirus
Herpes

Syphilis

A sexually transmitted disease that, if untreated, may affect the fetus.

Syphilis. **Syphilis** is sexually transmitted and, if untreated, may affect the fetus. It makes no difference whether the mother contracted the disease during pregnancy or many years before. If the condition remains untreated, about 50 percent of the infected fetuses will die any time during or after the second trimester. Of those who survive, serious problems such as blindness, mental retardation, and deafness may affect them. Given the advances in antibiotic treatments, the incidence of congenital syphilis has steadily decreased.

Toxoplasmosis

A disease caused by a protozoan that may cause damage to the nervous system; transmitted by animals, especially cats.

Toxoplasmosis. **Toxoplasmosis** is caused by a protozoan (a single-celled microorganism) that is transmitted by many animals, especially cats. Because the infection is usually undetected, the woman may pass the organism to the fetus. The results include both spontaneous abortions and premature deliveries. Low birth weight, a large liver and spleen, and anemia characterize the disease.

Serious long-term consequences include mental retardation, blindness, and cerebral palsy. The incidence of toxoplasmosis is about 1 or 2 per 1,000 live births.

Other Infections. This category includes such diseases as influenza, chicken pox, and several rare viruses.

German measles (rubella)
A typically mild childhood disease caused by a virus that, when contracted by pregnant women, may cause defects in a baby: congenital heart disorder, cataracts, deafness, or mental retardation.

Rubella (German measles). When pregnant women hear the name ***German measles*** (the technical term is ***rubella***), warning signals are raised, and with good reason. German measles is typically a mild childhood disease caused by a virus. Children who become infected develop a slight fever and perhaps swollen glands behind the ears. A rash usually appears at about the second or third day. By the fourth or fifth day, all the symptoms have usually disappeared.

For pregnant women, however, the story is quite different. Women who contract this disease may give birth to a baby with a serious defect: congenital heart disorder, cataracts, deafness, or mental retardation. The risk is especially high if the disease appears early in the pregnancy, when a spontaneous abortion may result. The infection appears in less than 1 per 1,000 live births.

If rubella does occur, estimates of the relationship between damage and timing are as follows (Sadler, 1985):

- 50 percent chance if the infection occurred during the first four weeks of pregnancy

- 20 to 25 percent following infection in the 5th to 8th week

- 10 to 15 percent in the 9th to 12th week

- 5 percent in the 13th to 16th week

- Damage to the fetus is rare during the 17th week and later

Any woman who has had German measles as a child cannot catch it a second time; she is immune. But it is wise to have a blood test taken to be on the safe side. The American Medical Association recommends that any woman of childbearing age who has not been vaccinated for German measles be immunized. These women should then avoid becoming pregnant for at least three months.

Cytomegalovirus (CMV)
A virus that can cause damage ranging from mental retardation, blindness, deafness, and even death.

Cytomegalovirus (CMV). **Cytomegalovirus (CMV)** is the most common STORCH infection, with an incidence of 10 to 20 per 1,000 live births. CMV is a disease that can cause damage ranging from mental retardation to blindness, deafness, and even death. One of the major difficulties in combating this disease is that it remains unrecognized in pregnant women. Consequently, we do not know the difference in outcome between early and late infection.

Herpes simplex
An infection that usually occurs during birth; a child can develop the symptoms during the first week following the birth. The eyes and nervous system are most susceptible to this disease.

Herpes Simplex. In the adult, type I **herpes simplex** virus usually appears in the mouth, whereas type II herpes appears in the genital area. If the disease is passed on to the fetus (usually during the passage through the birth canal), a child develops symptoms during the first week following birth. The central nervous system seems to be particularly susceptible to this disease, with serious long-term consequences. The incidence is less than 1 per 1,000 live births (Blackman, 1984).

AIDS (Acquired Immune Deficiency Syndrome)
A condition caused by a virus that invades the immune system, thus making it vulnerable to infections and life-threatening illnesses.

Thalidomide
A popular drug prescribed during the early 1960s that was later found to cause a variety of birth defects when taken by women early in their pregnancy.

The Special Case of AIDS

The final infection we wish to discuss is **AIDS** (Acquired Immune Deficiency Syndrome). There probably isn't a reader of this text who hasn't heard of AIDS. To give you some idea of the seriousness of the problem, consider these facts.

DES (diethylstilbesterol)
A synthetic hormone administered in the late 1940s and 1950s to pregnant women, supposedly to prevent miscarriage, that led to increased susceptibility to vaginal and cervical cancer in their daughters.

- About 5.5 million women of childbearing age are infected with HIV (Human Immunodeficiency Virus).

- 200,000 babies will be born this year with HIV.

The effects of teratogens: Mothers may pass the AIDS virus to their babies during pregnancy, delivery, and through breast milk. While babies of AIDS-infected mothers may not necessarily receive the virus, those who do are likely to succumb by 5 or 6 years of age.

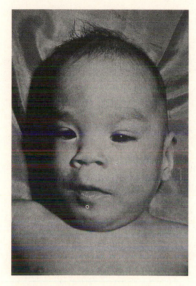

Babies born to women who drank heavily during their pregnancies may manifest distinctive characteristics such as those shown in this photo.

This cocaine-addicted baby was born prematurely and suffers from such behavior disturbances as tremulousness, irritability, and muscular rigidity.

- In the United States, 7,000 to 8,000 women infected with HIV will give birth this year.

- Of these births, 2,000 will have HIV.

- One in four babies born to HIV-infected mothers will develop AIDS.

Statistics showing that only one in four babies born of mothers infected with HIV develops AIDS have long puzzled investigators. Recent findings (Altman, 1994) have shown that these figures are directly related to the amount of the virus that the mother is carrying. That is, the more extensive the infection, the greater the chance that the baby will be born with the virus. Consequently, treatment with AZT or other treatments early in the pregnancy may help to prevent the transmission of the virus.

An infected mother can pass HIV to the fetus during pregnancy, during delivery, and after birth, occasionally through breast milk (Kelley-Buchanan, 1988). Through 1991, 1 million children worldwide had been born infected with HIV. These figures help to explain the growing and intensifying movement to provide schoolchildren with AIDS education as soon as they can grasp the concepts involved.

We know today that AIDS is a disorder that cripples the body's disease-fighting mechanisms and that the virus causing it can lie dormant for years. What triggers full-blown AIDS remains unknown, but remember that AIDS is the end stage of the infection and is not in itself a disease.

With regard to the fetus, estimates are that an infected mother transmits HIV from 30 percent to 50 percent of the time. Thus, 50 to 70 percent of these fetuses remain unaffected. When the virus is transmitted, a condition called *AIDS embryopathy* may develop. This causes growth retardation, small head size (microcephaly), flat nose, and widespread, upward-slanted eyes, among other characteristics. Also associated with AIDS are higher rates of preterm disease, low birth weight, and miscarriage.

For those fetuses who become infected, AIDS has a shorter incubation period than for adults. Symptoms may appear as early as six months after birth and include weight loss, fever, diarrhea, and chronic infections. Once symptoms appear, babies rarely survive more than five to eight months (Hochhauser & Rothenberger, 1992).

Chemicals

Many women of childbearing age in the United States use one or more of the following drugs: alcohol, cocaine, marijuana, or nicotine. Fifteen percent of these women use drugs with sufficient frequency to cause damage to a fetus during pregnancy. Estimates are that 30 to 40 percent of pregnant women smoke; 60 to 90 percent use analgesics during pregnancy; 20 to 30 percent use sedatives; and an undetermined number continue to use illicit drugs (Stimmel, 1991). Also, a number of women continue to use drugs before they realize they are pregnant.

Prescription drugs such as **thalidomide** have also produced tragic consequences. During the early 1960s, this drug was popular in West Germany as a sleeping pill and an antinausea measure that produced no adverse reactions in women. In 1962 physicians noticed a sizable increase in children born with either partial or no limbs. In some cases, feet and hands were directly attached to the body. Other outcomes were deafness, blindness, and, occasionally, mental retardation. In tracing the cause of the outbreak, investigators discovered that the mothers of these children had taken thalidomide early in their pregnancies.

DES (diethylstilbestrol) is another example of a teratogenic drug. In the late 1940s and 1950s, DES (a synthetic hormone) was administered to pregnant women, supposedly to prevent miscarriage. Researchers later found that the daughters of the women who had received this treatment were more susceptible to vaginal and cervical cancer. These daughters also experienced more miscarriages when pregnant than would be expected. Recent suspicions have arisen about the sons of DES women; they seem to have more abnormalities of their reproductive systems.

Figure 4.5

Teratogens and the timing of their effects on prenatal development. The danger of structural defects caused by teratogens is greatest early in embryonic development. This is the period of organogenesis, which lasts for several months. Damage caused by teratogens during this period is represented by the dark-colored bars. Later assaults by teratogens typically occur during the fetal period and, instead of structural damage, are more likely to stunt growth or cause problems of organ function.

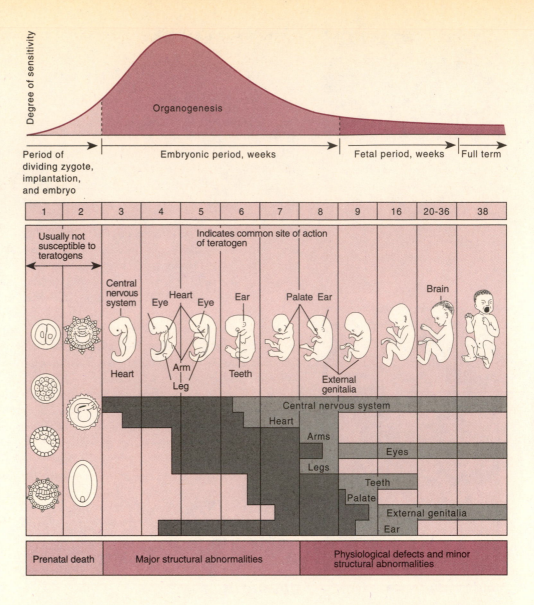

Do you think all of the warnings (smoking, drinking, etc.) that pregnant women receive have caused unnecessary alarm? Do you think undesirable emotional consequences could result?

As knowledge of the damaging effect of these agents spreads, women have grown more cautious once they realize they are pregnant. We know now that these agents pass through the placenta and affect the growing embryo and fetus. We also know that certain prenatal periods are more susceptible to damage than others; for example, the embryonic period. Figure 4.5 illustrates times of greater and lesser vulnerability.

To keep a pregnancy as safe as possible, a woman should begin by avoiding the obvious hazards. For example, as Tapley and Todd (1988) note, smoking negatively affects everything about the reproduction process: fertility, conception, possible spontaneous abortion, fetal development, labor and delivery, and a child's maturation. Smoking is probably the most common environmental hazard in pregnancy, and it results in a smaller than normal fetus. Babies of smoking mothers may have breathing difficulties and low resistance to infection, and they seem to suffer long-lasting effects after birth.

Other agents—such as alcohol, almost all drugs (including aspirin), unnecessary medication, and risky chemicals at work or at home—should be avoided (Tapley & Todd, 1988). Most pregnant women today are also cautious about the amount of caffeine and sweeteners they use (Guttmacher & Kaiser, 1987). For example, the FDA has cautioned pregnant women to moderate their consumption of caffeine-containing foods and beverages. These simple precautions will eliminate danger for most women.

Maternal Influences

Among the significant influences on prenatal development are maternal nutrition and maternal emotions.

Maternal Nutrition

IUGR

Intrauterine growth retardation; a condition that can occur when the mother's nutrient supply during pregnancy is too low.

Because the fetus depends on its mother for nourishment, most women today are keenly aware of the need to have a proper diet that will help them give birth to a healthy, happy baby. If the nutrients supplied by the mother are too low, a condition called **IUGR** (Intrauterine Growth Retardation) may occur, which can be associated with problems after birth. But a pregnant woman can't "eat for two." A rule of thumb to remember is this: For a sedentary pregnancy, add about 300 extra calories; for an active pregnancy, add about 500 extra calories. When you consider the rapidity of prenatal growth (especially from two to seven months), you can understand the importance of a mother's diet, both for her and the child she is carrying.

Women of childbearing age who wish to have children need to evaluate their weight and nutritional habits well before pregnancy. In this way they can establish good eating habits and attempt to maintain normal weight for their size. The manner in which the weight is gained is important: 1 1/2 to 3 pounds during the first three months, and then 1 pound every nine days is recommended (Cherry, 1992). Such planning will help women to accommodate the recommended 25 pounds that they will gain during their pregnancy. How much weight to gain is always an important question for pregnant women. Most doctors offer the following weight gain guide to women:

- If you are of normal weight, try to restrict weight gain to 22 to 28 pounds.

- If you are underweight, a gain of 25 to 30 pounds is acceptable.

- If you are overweight, do not gain more than 20 to 25 pounds.

A pregnant teenager may need more calories than an adult woman. A weight gain of up to 35 pounds may be necessary for her to produce a baby of normal weight. Here we see one of the problems of teenage pregnancy: A young girl is still growing and needs additional calories for herself. If she resists this need because of a concern for appearance or a desire to shield her pregnancy, the fetus may not receive enough nourishment (Jonaitis, 1988).

The woman's physician will usually recommend supplements to her regular diet, such as additional protein, iron, calcium, sodium, fiber, and vitamins. We have previously mentioned the dangers of alcohol use and cigarette smoking, and coffee, tea, and soft drinks should be taken with caution.

The effects of drugs, disease, and diet, although dramatic, are not the only influences on prenatal development. How a woman feels about her pregnancy is also highly significant.

Maternal Emotions

Most women report that delight, anxiety, worry, and irritability are common reactions during pregnancy. Mood swings are characteristic, especially during the first trimester when so much is happening to the woman (hormonal changes, increased fatigue, cravings, sickness), and produce feelings that range from delight at the pregnancy to fear of pain during delivery. These feelings usually diminish during the second trimester, when the woman is more accustomed to the changes in her body. But worry and anxiety may increase during the third trimester as sleep becomes difficult and birth draws near (Bowe, 1988).

Such reactions are normal and typically not sufficiently intense to affect the fetus. Seriously stressed mothers often have babies who are restless, irritable, and have feeding problems or bowel difficulties. Although the fetus is not perfectly insulated from the mother's stress, unless the stress that the mother experiences is unusually severe and prolonged, the effects on the fetus are usually of short duration.

No direct evidence is available that indicates a mother's emotions affect prenatal growth. Nevertheless, data continue to accumulate suggesting that a woman under stress releases hormones that may influence prenatal development. Although a definite link between maternal emotions and prenatal growth and even later neonatal behavior is still lacking, a pattern of events can be traced. Stress activates the mother's autonomic nervous system to produce hormones, which enter the mother's blood, cross the placenta, and enter the fetal bloodstream.

Women adjust to pregnancy differently. Since it is a condition that affects the total system, there is an immediate biological difference: Some women tire more easily than others and require more sleep and rest. Women differ in their more obvious physical reactions, such as nausea and vomiting: Some react better by eating several small servings rather than two or three large meals. Some women begin their pregnancies with feelings of depression, whereas others avoid depression completely. How can we explain these differences?

- The events surrounding the pregnancy—career status, money, whether the pregnancy was expected or wanted—are crucial.

- The women's personal experience with the mother-child bond probably reflects the mother's personality.

Can you think of several examples that indicate how a woman's relationship with the father of her child can affect pregnancy?

- Another major influence on the mother's personality and subsequent attitude toward the child is her relationship with the child's father.

- The mother's acceptance of pregnancy also affects her specific attitudes toward the unborn child.

- The psychological journey that women travel usually takes them from a time of intense self-preoccupation to a gradual recognition of the new person with whom they form a complex relationship.

- The mother's expectation for the child is also significant. Does she see the child as an independent human being who will forge his or her own way, or as an extension of herself?

The woman, as an individual, interprets pregnancy either as a crisis and an abnormal state of illness or as a normal occurrence and a state of health. Regardless of pregnancy, everyday life continues and most babies are born normal and healthy because their mothers coped with emotional situations without harming themselves or their child. Perhaps Nilsson and his colleagues (1987) offer the best advice when they suggest that the pregnant woman live her usual life but avoid excesses.

Nevertheless, prenatal problems arise, and today's diagnostic techniques often enable early detection of these difficulties.

Fetal Problems: Diagnosis and Counseling

Some women have a greater chance of developing difficulties during pregnancy or delivering a child with problems. To cope with these conditions, the rapidly expanding field of fetal diagnosis not only identifies problems but also offers means of treatment. Consequently, women with high-risk pregnancies have available today greater access to prenatal testing and genetic counseling, which can raise several ethical and legal issues. As Sroufe, Cooper, and DeHart (1992) note, knowledge entails responsibility.

- **Confidentiality.** Issues here include the disclosure of sensitive information to third parties and the possibility of unauthorized individuals attaining access to private information stored in data banks.

- **Autonomy.** One of the major questions about genetic and prenatal counseling is: Should such programs remain voluntary for individuals if a history of family genetic problems is known, or should they be forced to participate? Thus far, opinion is firmly tied to the principle of autonomy—people should have freedom of choice about genetic services.

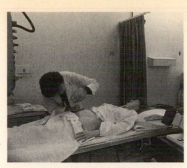

Here a pregnant woman is undergoing amniocentesis. Amniotic fluid is withdrawn and analyzed to determine sex and any chromosomal abnormalities. Amniocentesis may be done from the 15th week onward.

Amniocentesis

A process that entails inserting a needle through the mother's abdomen, piercing the amniotic sac, and withdrawing a sample of the amniotic fluid.

Fetoscopy

A procedure in which a tiny instrument called a fetoscope is inserted into the amniotic cavity, making it possible to see the fetus.

Chorionic villi sampling (CVS)

A procedure in which a catheter (small tube) is inserted through the vagina to the villi and a small section is suctioned into the tube.

As the soon-to-be mother or father, would you want to know the sex of your unborn child? Why? Why not?

Ultrasound

The use of sound waves produces an image that enables a physician to detect structural abnormalities.

- **Knowledge.** Counseling should help people become informed decision makers about their own well-being. One way of accomplishing this, of course, is to provide as much information as possible. But consider this scenario for a moment: You are the counselor involved, and in the course of obtaining data about a specific problem, you discover that the supposed father is not the biological father (Nightingale & Goodman, 1990). What do you do? There is no easy answer. If you withhold this information, you could cause future problems. If you present it objectively, you could destroy a relationship.

When a prenatal problem is suspected, both diagnostic procedures and counseling services are available. Among the diagnostic tools now available are the following.

Amniocentesis

Probably the technique you have heard most about is **amniocentesis,** which entails inserting a needle through the mother's abdomen, piercing the amniotic sac, and withdrawing a sample of the amniotic fluid. (Amniocentesis may be done from the 15th week of pregnancy on.) The fluid sample provides information about the child's sex and almost 70 chromosomal abnormalities. For example, spina bifida (see chap. 3) produces a raised level of a protein called alpha-fetoprotein (AFP), which may be detected by amniocentesis (Guttmacher & Kaiser, 1986).

Fetoscopy

In a **fetoscopy,** a tiny instrument called a fetoscope is inserted into the amniotic cavity, making it possible to see the fetus. If the view is clear, defects of hands and legs are visible. (Fetoscopy is usually performed after the 16th week.) Today, doctors avoid fetoscopy if possible because of potential injury to the fetus and use a relatively new method for obtaining fetal blood: percutaneous umbilical blood sampling. A needle is inserted through the abdomen and uterus into the blood vessels of the umbilical cord. Not only can this aid genetic diagnosis, it also permits blood transfusions to the fetus (Nightingale & Goodman, 1990).

Chorionic Villi Sampling (CVS)

The outer layer of the embryo is almost covered with *chorionic villi,* fingerlike projections that reach into the uterine lining. A catheter (small tube) is inserted through the vagina to the villi, and a small section is suctioned into the tube. **Chorionic villi sampling (CVS)** is an excellent test to determine the fetus's genetic structure and may be performed beginning at 8 weeks, usually between 8 and 12 weeks.

Ultrasound

Ultrasound is a relatively new technique that uses sound waves to produce an image that enables a physician to detect structural abnormalities. Useful pictures can be obtained as early as 7 weeks. Ultrasound is frequently used in conjunction with other techniques such as amniocentesis and fetoscopy (Sadler, 1985).

About 1 percent of infants suffer from some genetic defect, whereas another 0.5 percent suffer from defective chromosomes. As a result, prenatal testing is steadily becoming more common, especially for older women. Testing and counseling are intended to help couples who are concerned about the possibility of inherited problems.

For example, children born with cystic fibrosis or sickle-cell anemia acquire these diseases from parents who are both carriers. Tests are now available to determine whether a person is a carrier of a particular genetic disease. If both potential partners are carriers, the chances of children acquiring the disease can be calculated. The counselor would then explain how severe the problem is, what treatment is available, and what the developmental outcomes would be.

The Birth Process

The odyssey that began approximately nine months earlier reaches its climax at birth. In spite of what you may have heard, no one knows exactly what causes labor to begin or why it begins about 280 days after the first day of the last menstrual period. Before this moment arrives, the mother has to make certain decisions. Does she, for example, ask the physician to use an anesthetic, or does she want natural childbirth? Both methods have their advantages and disadvantages.

Natural childbirth provides an unforgettable experience for the mother (and father), but it is hard, painful work that some women prefer to avoid. The use of anesthesia prevents much of the birth pain, but the drug may affect the baby adversely, decreasing alertness and activity for days after birth (Maurer & Maurer, 1988).

Stages in the Birth Process

A woman usually becomes aware of the beginning of labor by one or more of these signs:

- The passage of blood from the vagina

- The passage of amniotic fluid from the ruptured amniotic sac through the vagina

- Uterine contractions and accompanying discomfort

The first two clues are certain signs that labor has begun; other pains (false labor) are occasionally mistaken for signs of true labor.

Three further stages of labor can also be distinguished:

1. Stage One: Dilation. The neck of the uterus (the cervix) dilates to about 4 inches in diameter. **Dilation** is the process responsible for labor pains and may last for 12 or 13 hours, or even longer.

    Think of the baby at this stage as enclosed in a plastic cylinder. It is upside down in the mother's abdomen, with the bottom of the cylinder under the mother's rib and the tip buried deep in her pelvis. The cervix is about one-half inch long and almost closed. Before the next stage, expulsion, occurs, the diameter of the cervix must be stretched to a diameter of 4 inches. (The comedienne Carol Burnett has said that the only way you can imagine this feeling is if you pulled your upper lip over your head!)

Dilation

Stage one of the birth process during which the cervix dilates to about 4 inches in diameter.

Answers

2. Stage Two: Expulsion. With the cervix fully dilated, the fetus no longer meets resistance and the uterine contractions drive it through the birth canal. Uterine pressure at this stage is estimated to be 60 pounds. Once the cervix is fully open, the baby passes through the birth canal. This **expulsion** phase typically lasts about 90 minutes for the first child and about 30 to 45 minutes for subsequent children (although it can last longer). This is the phase when most fathers, if they are present, become exultant. They describe the appearance of the head of the baby (called the *crowning*) as an unforgettable experience.

   Note that the times for expulsion (90 minutes and 30–45 minutes) are averages. If this second stage of labor is prolonged—with no evidence of a problem—surgical intervention remains unnecessary. Occasionally, women spend five or six hours (or more) in a normal first birth.

3. Stage Three: The afterbirth. In the **afterbirth** stage, the placenta and other membranes are discharged. This stage is measured from the birth of the baby to the delivery of the placenta and may last only a few minutes. If the spontaneous delivery of the placenta is delayed, it may be removed manually. Figure 4.6 illustrates the birth process.

When a pregnancy ends spontaneously before the 20th week, a spontaneous abortion, commonly called a **miscarriage** has occurred. After the 20th week, the spontaneous end of a pregnancy is called a **stillbirth** if the baby is born dead, or a premature birth if the baby survives. Occasionally a pregnancy occurs outside of the uterus. In an **ectopic pregnancy,** the fertilized egg attempts to develop outside the uterus, usually in one of the fallopian tubes (sometimes referred to as a *tubal pregnancy*). About 1 in every 200 pregnancies is ectopic.

Many women feel "down" a few days after giving birth. This is fairly common and is now thought to be a normal part of pregnancy and birth for some women. Called **postnatal depression,** this condition may be caused by the sudden change in hormones after birth. Also, a woman may have a sense of anticlimax after completing something she has anticipated for so many months. Women also tire easily and feel some tension about care of the baby, especially after a first birth. Postnatal depression usually leaves quickly.

For most women, the birth process, as painful as it may be, proceeds normally. Occasionally, however, problems arise.

Birth Complications

Birth can sometimes be exceptionally difficult, even dangerous. The following are a few of the more common complications.

Forceps Delivery

Occasionally, for safety, the physician will withdraw the baby with forceps during the first phase of birth. A **forceps delivery** presents some danger of rupturing blood vessels or causing brain damage but, with new guidelines, forceps delivery is considered quite safe. For example, forceps are not used unless the cervix is completely dilated and the head is within 2 inches of the mouth of the vagina (Cherry, 1992).

A decision about a forceps delivery depends on two conditions: those involving the fetus and those related to the mother. Is the fetus in distress? Is the baby in the correct position? Has the mother sufficient strength for the final push? Specifically, a forceps delivery may be called for when the woman has been in the second stage of labor for several hours or when an emergency arises for either the mother (shock, exhaustion) or the fetus (clear signs of fetal distress such as a slowing heart rate).

Expulsion

Stage two of the birth process during which the baby passes through the birth canal.

Afterbirth

Stage three of the birth process during which the placenta and other membranes are discharged.

Miscarriage

The term that describes when a pregnancy ends spontaneously before the 20th week.

Stillbirth

The term used to describe the spontaneous end of a pregnancy after the 20th week, in which the baby is born dead.

Ectopic pregnancy

A pregnancy in which the fertilized egg attempts to develop in one of the fallopian tubes; sometimes referred to as a *tubal pregnancy.*

Postnatal depression

The low, or "down" feeling many women experience a few days after giving birth.

Forceps delivery

A procedure in which the physician, for safety, will withdraw the baby with forceps during the first phase of birth.

Figure 4.6
Stages in the birth process

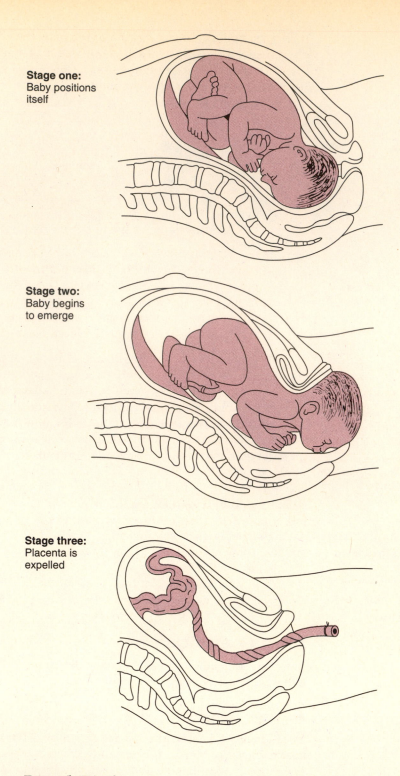

Stage one:
Baby positions itself

Stage two:
Baby begins to emerge

Stage three:
Placenta is expelled

Breech Birth

Breech birth

A birth in which the baby is born feet first, buttocks first, or in a crosswise position (transverse presentation).

During the last month of pregnancy, most babies move into a headdown (vertex) position. Most babies who don't turn during this time will be in **breech birth** presentation position. It's almost as if the baby were sitting in the uterus, head up and feet and buttocks down. Several conditions can contribute to a breech presentation: more than one fetus in the uterus, an abnormally shaped uterus, a placenta partially (or even fully) covering the uterine opening, and prematurity.

About four out of every hundred babies are born feet first, or buttocks first, while one out of a hundred are in a crosswise position (transverse presentation). These breech births can be worrisome because the baby must be carefully guided through the birth canal. Care must be taken to avoid squeezing the umbilical cord, thus restricting the flow of oxygen to the baby (Feinbloom, 1993). In spite of these concerns, most breech babies are born well and healthy. The major concern is with premature babies who, given the size of their heads in proportion to the rest of their bodies, often require a cesarean birth.

Cesarean Section

If for some reason the child cannot come through the birth canal, surgery is performed to deliver the baby through the abdomen, in a procedure called **cesarean section.** For example, a cesarean may produce a healthier baby than does prolonged labor and difficult birth. Among the conditions suggesting a cesarean are included: a pelvis too small for a safe vaginal delivery, an abnormal presentation position, and previous cesareans that increase the possibility of uterine rupture (Cherry, 1992).

Although now fairly safe, this operation is considered major surgery and is not recommended unless necessary. More than 20 percent of all live births are cesarean, a figure many consider to be excessive. Today many women attempt a vaginal delivery following a cesarean if the conditions that caused the original cesarean are no longer a concern and if only one fetus is present. The success rate for a natural delivery after having had a cesarean is from 60 percent to 80 percent.

Prematurity

About seven out of every hundred births are premature, occurring less than 37 weeks after conception. Fortunately, today it is possible to simulate womb conditions so that the correct temperature and humidity, bacteria control, and easily digestible food can be provided for the child. Still, prematurity presents real dangers, ranging from mental deficiency to death. (We'll shortly discuss this topic in more detail.)

Anoxia (Lack of Oxygen)

If something during the birth process should cut the flow of oxygen to the fetus, brain damage or death can result. A substantial need for oxygen exists during birth because pressure on the fetal head can cause some rupturing of the blood vessels in the brain. After the umbilical cord is cut, delay in lung breathing can also produce **anoxia.** Failure here can cause death or brain damage.

Controversy surrounds infants who have experienced anoxia, survived, but show evidence of mental dullness. Does anoxia cause long-term developmental impairment? A much quoted review of the literature concerning delivery and birth complications (especially the pertinent studies of anoxia) began by assuming that early cerebral oxygen deprivation would cause later intellectual difficulty (Sameroff, 1975). Youngsters were studied during infancy, at 3 years of age, and finally at 7 years.

A definite pattern emerged: A few days after birth, infants seemed impaired on visual, sensorimotor, and maturational levels. At 3 years, studied with perceptual-motor, cognitive, personality, and neurological tests, they showed lower than normal cognitive functioning and an improved performance on the other items. By 7 years, significant IQ differences had disappeared. Sameroff concludes that anoxia is a poor predictor of later intellectual functioning and that socioeconomic characteristics still remain the best single predictor of future adjustment.

The Rh Factor

Rh factor refers to a possible incompatibility between the blood types of mother and child. If the mother is Rh-negative and the child Rh-positive, miscarriage or even infant death can result. During birth some of the baby's blood inevitably enters the mother's bloodstream. The mother then develops antibodies to destroy fetal red blood cells. This usually happens after the baby is born, so the first baby may

---

Cesarean section
A surgery performed to deliver the baby through the abdomen, if for some reason the child cannot come through the birth canal.

Anoxia (lack of oxygen)
A condition that possibly can cause brain damage or death if it occurs during the birth process.

Does this study help you to take a position on the stability versus resiliency issue? In what way?

Rh factor
An incompatibility between the blood types of mother and child; if the mother is Rh-negative and the child Rh-positive, miscarriage or even infant death can result.

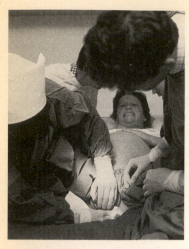

The presence of the father during birth can be a source of physical and psychological support for the mother. Fathers present during birth describe it as an "unforgettable experience."

Prepared childbirth

Combination of relaxation techniques and information about the birth process; sometimes called the Lamaze method after its founder.

escape unharmed. During later pregnancies, however, these antibodies may pass into the fetus's blood and start to destroy the red blood cells of an Rh-positive baby.

Estimates are that about 10 percent of marriages are between Rh-negative women and Rh-positive men. Today, a protective vaccine (RhoGam) has almost eliminated the possibility of Rh incompatibility when Rh-negative women are identified. In a case where the first baby's blood causes the mother to produce antibodies, exchange blood transfusions may be given to the baby while still in the uterus.

Childbirth Strategies

Most babies escape complications and experience little if any birth difficulty. To help the newly born child adjust to a new environment, Leboyer (1975) believes that we must stop "torturing the innocent." Traditionally, newborns encounter a cold, bright world that turns them upside down and slaps them. Leboyer advocates a calmer environment. He suggests extinguishing all lights in the delivery room except a small night light and making the room silent at the time of birth. Immediately after birth the child is placed not on a cold metal scale, but on the mother's abdomen, a natural resting place. After several minutes, the child is transferred to a basin of warm water. Leboyer claims that this process eases the shock of birth and that babies are almost instantly calm and happy.

Another technique, called **prepared childbirth,** or the Lamaze method after French obstetrician Fernand Lamaze, has become extremely popular with the medical profession. For several sessions women are informed about the physiology of childbirth and instructed in breathing exercises. The technique is intended to relieve fear and pain by relaxation procedures.

A range of birth options is now available to couples. Some, for example, are choosing home births under the guidance of midwives, who are trained delivery specialists. Midwives assist with about 50 percent of all nonhospital deliveries. Some hospitals are providing birthing rooms, which have a more relaxed and homelike atmosphere than the typical delivery room and may provide birthing beds or birthing chairs for greater comfort (Tapley & Todd, 1988). Still, between 95 and 99 percent of all births occur in hospitals.

The Special Case of Prematurity

The average duration of pregnancy is 280 days. Occasionally, however, some babies are born early; they are premature or preterm, often called "preemies." Formerly these babies had high mortality rates, but with today's sophisticated technology their chances of survival are much greater. Before we discuss the condition of these babies and the reasons for their early appearance, let's establish some pertinent facts.

Facts about Prematures

Prematurity

A condition that occurs less than 37 weeks after conception and is defined by low birth weight and immaturity.

In 1961 the World Health Organization (WHO) redefined **prematurity** to include those infants born before 37 weeks gestation with a birth weight of 1,500 grams (about 3 pounds) or less. Thus two criteria were suggested: immaturity and low birth weight.

Within this definition, two additional classifications are possible (Spreen & others, 1984):

- Infants born before 37 weeks whose weight is appropriate for their age; these are called preterm AGA—Appropriate for Gestational Age.

- Those born before 37 weeks whose weight is low for their age; these are called preterm SGA—Small for Gestational Age.

A third classification has recently been proposed—very low birth weight (VLBW), which is defined as below 1,500 grams (about 3 pounds).

Causes of Prematurity

About 250,000 of all infants born in the United States can be classified as premature. Although it is still impossible to predict which women will begin labor prematurely, prematurity has been linked to certain conditions (Avery & Litwack, 1983). Once a woman has given birth prematurely, the risk of prematurity in the next pregnancy is about 25 percent. If two pregnancies have ended prematurely, the risk in the third pregnancy rises to 70 percent. Is this tendency to prematurity inherited? To date, no evidence points to a genetic connection.

Multiple Births.   Multiple births—twins or triplets—usually produce babies whose birth weights are lower than that of a single baby. This condition results in prematurity and accounts for about 10 percent of premature births. Some research indicates that multiple abortions performed in the second trimester increase the risk of prematurity. Age also has been identified as a correlate of prematurity. If the mother is under 17 or over 35, the risk is substantially increased.

Low Socioeconomic Status.   Low socioeconomic status (SES) is also a frequent accompaniment of prematurity. In underdeveloped countries as many as one infant in four is born prematurely. In the United States more premature babies are born to poor than affluent women. The reasons remain a mystery, although frequent pregnancies, maternal malnutrition, and little (if any) prenatal care may be responsible.

Smoking.   Smoking is a significant factor in any discussion of prematurity. Avery and Litwack (1983) state that, regardless of social class, cigarette smoking is associated with infants of low birth weight. The relationship between prematurity and smoking is found with those who smoke one pack per day. For those women who smoke more than one pack per day, the chance of giving birth to a baby of low birth weight more than doubles.

Alcohol.   Alcohol also increases the likelihood of prematurity. About 60 percent of American women drink. For those taking 10 drinks per week while pregnant, the chance of having a low-birth-weight baby doubles. Women who consume alcohol daily during their pregnancy can produce damage in their babies, especially a condition called **fetal alcohol syndrome (FAS),** which has four clusters of clinical features (Feinbloom, 1993):

- Psychological functioning, as a result of central nervous system abnormalities, which may include mild to moderate retardation, irritability, hyperactivity, and possible learning disabilities

- Growth factors, primarily growth retardation

- Physical features such as a small head, and possible defects in limbs, joints, face, and heart

- Structural effects, which may include major malformations such as heart and genitourinary defects

Other causes of prematurity include maternal infection, cervical problems, high blood pressure, unusual stress, diabetes, and heart disease. As Avery and Litwack (1983) note, even when all of these causes are enumerated, explaining exactly what happened in any given pregnancy still is impossible. These authors emphasize that having a baby early is not usually anyone's fault.

Fetal alcohol syndrome (FAS)

A group of birth defects that can affect babies when their mothers drink alcohol during pregnancy.

With advances in the treatment of prematures (temperature control, nutrition), the outlook for these babies has greatly improved. Psychological insights into the development of prematures have led to the conclusion that parental support and stimulation are needed during the baby's hospitalization to ensure that attachment proceeds as normally as possible.

Though these children may differ from full-term babies in the early days of their development, most of these differences eventually disappear. Most prematures reach developmental levels similar to those of full-term babies. The only difference is that it takes premature babies a little longer to get there.

What can we say about the future development of these infants? Can we predict which youngsters will have later problems? If we eliminate known hazards—genetic defects and congenital malformations—prediction becomes less certain. One conclusion, however, seems inevitable: The younger and smaller the infant, the greater the risk for later difficulties.

Beckwith and her colleagues (1990) studied 55 infants born at a gestational age of 37 weeks or less and with a birth weight of 5 1/2 pounds or less. Despite birth complications and accompanying problems (respiratory difficulties, for example), the children showed intellectual development within the normal range: At the age of 12, the children had an average IQ of 108, with a range of 77 to 134. Thus they survived birth complication and developed free of any major handicaps, although 25 percent exhibited learning problems. The authors attributed the causes of learning problems versus no learning problems to differences in neurobehavioral functioning (ability to organize their behavior, visual attention) and supportive home environments.

Minde (1990), working with high-risk infants (birth weight less than 3 1/2 pounds), discovered that differences in mothers' responses to their preterms could be traced to the quality of the relationships the women had with their own mothers and their husbands. The mothers who visited their infants more when the preterms were in the hospital and spent more time with them had a strong relationship with their husbands and their mothers. Minde also found that peer group discussion helped to remove any feelings of guilt or abnormality. Of 77 families he followed until the children were 4 years old, 43 percent of the children displayed evidence of abnormal behavior. Similar to the Beckwith study just reported, the results were linked to the quality of family warmth and support.

We can best summarize our discussion by quoting Avery and Litwack:

The outlook for normal development has improved for all infants, including those born prematurely. Very small infants continue to have risks for some problems that relate to the reasons for their premature birth, or to the difficulties they may encounter during the precarious days in intensive care. Overall, 90 percent of them will be normal. The remaining 10 percent will for the most part represent the infants who are the smallest or most premature. Some will have major disabilities, such as cerebral palsy or blindness. Some will have lesser disabilities such as crossed eyes, wheezing, and perhaps some motor incoordinations. Continuing research into the causes of these problems and means of prevention remains a high priority. (1983, pp. 18–19)

Guidelines for Parents of Prematures

Although the new technology designed for prematures is marvelous, these babies need to sense parental love. This might seem next to impossible, given the technological nature of the premature nursery, but here are some guidelines parents of prematures can follow (Harrison, 1983):

- Try to understand the baby. Begin by observing carefully, learning what upsets and soothes. How does the baby respond to different types of stimulation? How long does it take to calm the baby after some upset? What kinds of clues are being given to signal discomfort (changes in skin color, muscular reaction, breathing rate)?
- Use as much body contact as possible. Since these babies came into the world early, they often seem physically insecure (when compared with the normal infant after birth). Touching the

baby with the whole hand on back or chest and stomach often relaxes the premature. Massaging both relaxes and shows affection.

- Talk to the baby. Studies have repeatedly shown that prematures, while seemingly unresponsive, show better rates of development when exposed to the mother's voice as often as possible.

When the premature infant can be taken from the incubator and given to the parent, a delicate moment has arrived. Some parents find it difficult to react positively to a premature; they feel guilty, occasionally harbor feelings of rejection, and must fight to accept the situation. They are simply overwhelmed. Usually this reaction passes quickly. On the occasion of this initial contact, parents should have been well prepared for holding a baby who is still entangled in wires and tubes.

Guided Review

14. Labor usually begins _____ days after the first day of the last menstrual period.

15. The spontaneous end of pregnancy is called a _____ if it occurs before the 20th week.

16. A fertilized egg that develops in a fallopian tube is called an _____ pregnancy.

17. _____ _____ can cause a woman to feel a little "down" for a few days following delivery.

18. Births occurring less than 37 weeks after conception are said to be _____ .

19. Lamaze's method is also referred to as _____ _____ .

20. The _____ _____ _____ has identified the criteria for prematurity.

Answers

14. 280   15. miscarriage   16. ectopic   17. Postnatal (postpartum) depression   18. premature
19. prepared childbirth   20. World Health Organization

♣ CONCLUSION

In this chapter, you have seen how a human being begins its journey through the lifespan. Nature's detailed choreography of prenatal development provides a remarkably complex yet elegantly simple means of ensuring the survival of generations. Once conception occurs, uniting the genetic contribution of both mother and father, the developmental process is under way, sheltered for the first nine months in the protective cocoon of the womb.

For some, the process is interrupted and the uterine stay is shortened. Today these prematures, thanks to technological advances, have a heightened chance of survival and of normal physical and psychological development.

♣ CHAPTER HIGHLIGHTS

The Prenatal World

- Once fertilization has occurred, implantation occurs in three stages.
- The germinal period is the time when the fertilized egg passes through the fallopian tube.
- The embryonic period is a time of rapid development and great sensitivity.
- The fetal period is a time of preparation for life outside the womb.
- The senses develop during the prenatal months and are ready to function at birth.

Influences on Prenatal Development

- Developmental risk is a term that applies to those children whose welfare is in jeopardy.
- Teratogens are those agents that cause abnormalities.
- Infectious diseases and chemical agents are the two basic classes of teratogens.
- Today AIDS is recognized as a potential danger for newborns.
- Maternal nutrition and emotions are important influences during pregnancy.

- Advancing technology has provided diagnostic tools for the detection of many fetal problems.

The Birth Process

- Birth occurs as a series of stages.
- Complications can develop during the birth process.
- Childbirth strategies are evolving that are designed to ease the transition from womb to world.
- Today the outlook for prematures is much more optimistic than in previous times.

♣ KEY TERMS

Adhesion 75
Afterbirth 89
AIDS (Acquired Immune Deficiency Syndrome) 82
Amniocentesis 87
Amniotic sac 75
Anoxia (lack of oxygen) 91
Apposition 75
Breech birth 90
Cesarean section 91
Chorionic villi sampling (CVS) 87
Cytomegalovirus (CMV) 82
DES (diethylstilbesterol) 83
Developmental risk 80
Dilation 88
Ectoderm 76

Ectopic pregnancy 89
Embryonic period 76
Endoderm 76
Expulsion 89
Fetal alcohol syndrome (FAS) 93
Fetal period 77
Fetoscopy 87
Forceps delivery 89
German measles (rubella) 82
Germinal period 75
Herpes simplex 82
Implantation 74
Invasion 75
IUGR 85
Mesoderm 76

Miscarriage 89
Organogenesis 76
Placenta 75
Postnatal depression 89
Prematurity 92
Prepared childbirth 92
Rh factor 91
Stillbirth 89
Syphilis 81
Teratogens 80
Thalidomide 83
Toxoplasmosis 81
Trophoblast 75
Ultrasound 87
Umbilical cord 75

WHAT DO YOU THINK?

1. Considerable discussion has occurred recently about the possibility of prenatal learning. Where do you stand on this issue? Be sure to support your opinion with facts from this chapter.
2. You probably have heard how careful women must be when they are pregnant. They are worried about such things as smoking and drinking. Do you think we have become too nervous and timid about these dangers? Why?

3. Turn back to table 4.2. From your own knowledge (relatives and friends, for example), indicate which of these teratogens you think are most common. Select one and explain why you think it is a common threat and what could be done to help prevent it. (Lead paint is a good example.)

4. Significant medical and ethical questions surround such techniques as fetal surgery. Assume that a physician does not inform a woman that her fetus is a good candidate for fetal surgery. The baby is stillborn. Is the doctor guilty of malpractice or any crime? Can you think of other examples?

SUGGESTED READINGS

Avery, M. C. & G. Litwack. (1983). *Born early* New York: Little, Brown. Vital data, good writing, and a positive outlook make this an excellent introduction to the topic of prematurity.

Cherry, S. (1992). *Understanding pregnancy and childbirth*. New York: Collier. This popular book, available in paperback, has been a best-seller for several years. It carefully presents detailed information about pregnancy and birth.

Kolata, G. (1990). *The baby doctors*. New York: Dell. A riveting account of the types of surgery now being performed on fetuses and newborns.

CHAPTER REVIEW TEST

1. It takes a fertilized egg about _____ _____ to travel through the fallopian tube to the uterus.
   a. 3 days
   b. 14 days
   c. 30 days
   d. 9 months

2. It then takes another _____ _____ days for the fertilized egg to implant.
   a. 3 days
   b. 7 days
   c. 14 days
   d. 30 days

3. The first two weeks following fertilization are called the _____ period.
   a. embryonic
   b. fetal
   c. germinal
   d. pregnancy

4. A _____ is a one-week-old zygote.
   a. fetus
   b. embryo
   c. blastocyst
   d. trophoblast

5. During the _____ period the nervous system develops rapidly.
   a. embryonic
   b. fetal
   c. gestational
   d. germinal

6. Which system does not develop from the mesoderm?
   a. muscular
   b. skeletal
   c. circulatory
   d. respiratory

7. The embryo is most vulnerable to outside agents during the _____ period.
   a. embryonic
   b. germinal
   c. fetal
   d. sensitive

8. The peak growth period for the fetus is during the _____ and _____ months.
   a. first, second
   b. fourth, fifth
   c. sixth, seventh
   d. eighth, ninth

9. Red blood cells transport _____ and white blood cells to combat disease.
   a. oxygen
   b. amniotic fluid
   c. teratogens
   d. villi

10. Which of the following statements is true?
   a. The earlier the damage, the greater the chance of negative long-term effects.
   b. The fetus is safe from all harm while in the womb.
   c. Babies are usually born on the day predicted.
   d. A fetus hears no sound until birth.

11. Toxoplasmosis is
   a. a sexually transmitted disease.
   b. a virus capable of causing deafness or cataracts.
   c. a disease capable of causing mental retardation or death.
   d. a problem caused by the genetic makeup of the father.

12. Which of the following will *not* result from exposure to rubella?
    a. congenital heart disorder
    b. mental retardation
    c. deafness
    d. nearsightedness

13. _____ is *not* a STORCH infection.
    a. RDS
    b. CMV
    c. herpes simplex
    d. toxoplasmosis

14. It is almost impossible for a mother to pass HIV to her baby through
    a. delivery.
    b. handling.
    c. pregnancy.
    d. breast milk.

15. It is recommended that pregnant women add _____ calories to their regular diets.
    a. 300
    b. 1,200
    c. 2,400
    d. 100

16. A woman's emotions can affect her pregnancy indirectly by a release of her
    a. villi.
    b. teratogens.
    c. hormones.
    d. Rh factor.

17. _____ is a technique in which a needle is inserted through a pregnant woman's abdomen and into the amniotic sac to obtain a fluid sample.
    a. Ultrasound
    b. Chorionic villi sampling
    c. Amniocentesis
    d. Non-stress test

18. Which statement about prematurity is *not* true?
    a. It is associated with vitamin therapy.
    b. It is associated with low SES.
    c. It is associated with multiple births.
    d. It is associated with cigarette use.

19. _____ was a pioneer in the technique of prepared childbirth.
    a. Leboyer
    b. Lamaze
    c. DeCasper
    d. Salk

20. Mental retardation, hyperactivity, and primary growth retardation can be symptoms of
    a. fetal alcohol syndrome (FAS).
    b. Rh factor.
    c. prematurity.
    d. anoxia.

21. Premature babies of very low birth weight are
    a. not normally at severe risk.
    b. not permitted visits by their parents.
    c. more likely to develop cerebral palsy.
    d. more likely to have problems later in life.

Answers

1.a 2.a 3.c 4.c 5.a 6.d 7.a 8.b 9.a 10.a 11.c 12.d 13.a 14.b 15.a 16.c 17.c 18.a 19.b 20.a 21.d

PART III

Infancy

At first, the infant, mewling and
puking in the nurse's arms.

William Shakespeare

Physical and Cognitive Development in Infancy

The bond between mother and
infant begins to form
immediately after birth.

L iz gazed at the infant girl in her arms. Although she had carried this tiny
creature within her for nine months, it was still a stranger. Would it be an
easy baby? Who would she really look like? Would she do well in school?
Of course she would be smart! As these thoughts flashed through her
mind, she remembered a course in child psychology she had taken. How had the
instructor referred to a newborn? Neonate; yes, that was it. She had read the
books on what to expect: feedings, sleep patterns, possible illnesses. But what
really was a neonate? What was an infant? Catching herself in these musings, she
began to laugh.

Liz certainly was not the first person to speculate about infancy. It is interesting
to trace several of these speculations, since they offer insights into the remarkable
changes that have occurred in our interpretation of infancy. Do you remember
Shakespeare's character Jaques in *As You Like It?* In his speech about the seven
ages of our lives, he describes an infant in the first age as "mewling and puking in
the nurse's arms."

Freud's description of infancy as richly laden with sexual experiences presents
a far different view, one that met with fierce opposition. Noting that it is a serious
error to believe that children have no sexual life and that sexuality only begins at
puberty, Freud (1966) argued that "from the very first children have a copious
sexual life." They direct their first sexual lusts and their curiosity to those who are
nearest and for other reasons dearest to them—parents, brothers, and sisters. Freud
claimed that infants give clear evidence that they expect to derive pleasure not only
from their sexual organs, but that many other parts of their body "lay claim to that
same sensitivity."

John Watson, one of America's early behaviorists, had discovered the writings of
Pavlov on classical conditioning and believed that conditioning answered all of our
questions about human behavior. Under Pavlov's influence, Watson viewed infants
as a source of potential stimulus-response connections. He believed that if you turn

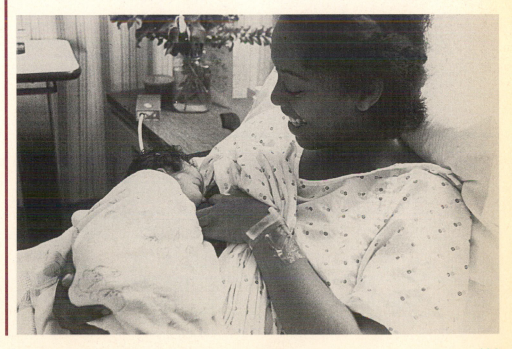

your attention to an infant early enough, you can make that infant into anything you want—it's all a matter of conditioning. His famous statement about infancy is worth repeating here.

> ■ Give me a dozen healthy infants and my own specified world to bring them up in and I'll guarantee to take any one at random and train him to become any type of specialist I might select—doctor, lawyer, artist, merchant-chief and, yes, even beggar-man and thief, regardless of his talents, penchants, tendencies, abilities, vocations, and race of his ancestors. (Watson, 1924, p. 104)

Piaget's view of infancy differed radically from Watson's. Rather than seeing children as small sponges waiting for something to be poured into them, Piaget believed that children actively construct their own views of the world during these early years. One of the first psychologists to question the apparently passive state of an infant, Piaget argued that infants are much more competent than originally thought.

Infants actually construct their view of the world, a view that changes with age. Although infants don't as yet possess language, Piaget argued that intelligence existed before language. Intelligence initially develops from infants using their bodies to explore the environment and then forming perceptions about their experiences. Piaget stated that cognitive development during infancy determines the entire course of an individual's mental growth (Piaget, 1967). During these years children build the cognitive structures that are the foundation of their intelligence.

The growing acceptance of an infant's competence has caused some to see a baby as a finely tuned computer, ready to begin such sophisticated activities as reading. That belief is far removed from an earlier concept of an infant as a passive, inert organism. Today's developmental psychologists would most likely recommend to Liz that she think of her infant daughter as an individual with her own unique personality and potential. 🌳

To help you understand an infant's world, in this chapter you'll examine the methods used to assess the well-being of infants following birth. Then you'll trace various aspects of infant development: physical, motor, perceptual, cognitive, language, and social/emotional. You'll also begin to discern the issues and themes discussed in chapter 1. For example, the issue of sensitive periods is particularly important in any discussion of infancy. Do the events that occur in infancy leave an indelible mark that lasts a lifetime?

After reading this chapter, you should be able to

- Describe those abilities that infants begin to demonstrate at birth.

- Identify critical neonatal reflexes that enhance survival and enable neonates to adapt to their environment.

- Distinguish the typical clues that signal normal physical and cognitive development.

- Appraise an infant's cognitive development by observing behavior in a variety of situations.

- Evaluate an infant's language development using the key signs of language acquisition.

Physical and Motor Development

Growing children experience changes in shape and body composition and in the distribution of tissues, and their developing motor skills influence cognitive,

Table 5.1	Neonatal Reflexes	
Name of Reflex	**How Elicited**	**Description of Response**
Plantar grasp	Pressure applied to bottom of foot	Toes tend to curl
Babinski	Gently stroke sole of foot	Toes spread in an outward and upward manner
Babkin	Press palm of hand while infant lies on back	Mouth opens; eyes close
Rooting	Gently touch cheek of infant with light finger pressure	Head turns toward finger in effort to suck
Sucking	Mouth contacts nipple of breast or bottle	Mouth and tongue used to manipulate (suck) nipple
Moro	Loud noise or sudden dropping of infant	Stretches arms and legs and then hugs self; cries
Grasping	Object or finger is placed in infant's palm	Fingers curl around object
Tonic neck reflex	Place infant flat on back	Infant assumes fencer position: turns head and extends arm and leg in same direction as head
Stepping	Support infant in upright position; soles of feet brush surface	Infant attempts regular progression of steps

psychosocial, and emotional development (Field, 1990). For example, the infant's head at birth is about a quarter of the body's total length, but in the adult it is about one-seventh of body length. Different tissues (muscles, nerves) also grow at different rates, and total growth represents a complex series of changes. At birth, of course, the infant must assume those life-sustaining functions that the mother had provided for nine months. Consequently, any analysis of an infant's physical growth must consider the important role that native reflexes play.

Neonatal Reflexes

When a stimulus repeatedly elicits the same response, that behavior is usually called a **reflex.** Popular examples include the eye blink and the knee jerk. All of the activities needed to sustain life's functions are present at birth (breathing, sucking, swallowing, elimination). These reflexes serve a definite purpose: The gag reflex enables infants to spit up mucus; the eye blink protects the eyes from excessive light; an antismothering reflex facilitates breathing.

In an attempt to rank an infant's reflexes in order of importance, Harris and Liebert (1992) note that the most crucial reflexes are those associated with breathing. Breathing patterns are not fully established at birth, and sometimes infants briefly stop breathing. These periods are called **apnea,** and although there is some concern that apnea may be associated with sudden infant death, these periods are quite common in all infants. Usually they last for about 2 to 5 seconds; episodes that extend from about 10 to 20 seconds may suggest the possibility of a problem (Berg & Berg, 1987). Sneezing and coughing are both reflexes that help to clear air passages.

Next in importance are those reflexes associated with feeding. Infants suck and swallow during the prenatal period and continue at birth. They also demonstrate the rooting reflex, in which they'll turn toward a nipple or a finger placed on the cheek and attempt to get it into the mouth. Table 5.1 describes some of the more important neonatal reflexes.

Reflex

When a stimulus repeatedly elicits the same response.

Apnea

Brief periods when breathing is suspended.

A Multicultural Perspective

As we begin our analysis of the lifespan and study the conditions under which children develop, we should keep in mind that although we are keenly aware of the influence of culture, it is almost impossible to separate culture, class, and gender. For example, African Americans, Latinos, and women are overly represented at the poverty level.

The combined forces of social and economic factors coalesce to produce social class, which holds many clues to an infant's and child's development. If different resources are available to different social classes, then we can assume the members of these classes will vary in their attitudes, values, and expectations. Working-class parents, for example, believe more in physical punishment than middle-class parents who tend to reason with their children (Sroufe & others, 1992). We should resist the temptation to make value judgments since both of these forms of discipline can carry negative consequences. Excessive reasoning can produce guilt; excessive physical punishment can lead to abuse.

Yet it is difficult to avoid the conclusion that children of poverty face obstacles that middle- and upper-class children escape. Once again, let's define our terms here. Nationally, in 1991, 11.3 percent of whites, 32.7 percent of African Americans, and 28.7 percent of Latinos had incomes below the *poverty level.* To give you an idea of what that means, in 1992 the poverty level for a family of four was $14,463. Although a number of programs are available to these families (Aid to Families with Dependent Children, Medicare, food stamps, housing subsidies, and the like), the combination of federal, state, and local aid means that a considerable discrepancy can exist between states in the level of support offered. As an example, in January of 1993, the needs standard for a family of three in the state of New Hampshire was $1,513 while it was $312 in Missouri. However we interpret these figures, they suggest a marginal level of existence at the best.

Given the undisputed differences between social classes, it is surprising that there aren't greater discrepancies in attitudes, values, and parenting practices. Differences that appear relate to feelings about power and self-direction versus helplessness and obedience to the demands of others. For example, lower-class parents place greater emphasis on respectability and obedience to authority; middle-class parents encourage curiosity, internal control, the ability to work for distant goals, and a sensitivity to relationships with others (Hetherington & Parke, 1993). What do we know about children who live in poverty?

The Children of Poverty

As far as the children of poverty are concerned, they experience more health problems, many of which can be traced to prenatal difficulties. More of these children die in the neonatal and infancy periods; they simply lack adequate health care. They suffer more accidents than do more fortunate children and are exposed to greater stress: financial, housing, dangerous neighborhoods. We know that parental stress can often translate into poor parenting practices (depression, irritability, abuse), which can lead to behavioral and emotional problems and academic difficulty. Finally, as we are aware from the daily news, these children often witness, and are the targets of, violence such as physical assault, rape, and shootings. The danger in all of this, of course, is that poverty becomes a self-perpetuating cycle. The conditions we have described put children at an immediate disadvantage: health problems in infancy, school difficulties (perhaps dropping out), low self-esteem, troublesome behavior, limited occupational opportunities, and encounters with the law. With these ideas in mind, let's turn our attention to those abilities that infants display at birth.

Newborn Abilities

If newborn infants are as competent as we now believe, do you think society should initiate formal training programs soon after birth? Explain your answer.

Neonate

Term for an infant in the first days and weeks after birth.

Imitative behavior

The tendency of infants to mimic the behavior of others.

In the days immediately following birth until about two weeks to one month, the infant is called a **neonate.** During this period, babies immediately begin to use their abilities to adapt to their environment. Among the most significant of these are the following:

- Infants display clear signs of **imitative behavior** at 7 to 10 days. (Try this: Stick out your tongue at a neonate who is about 10 days old—the baby will stick its tongue out at you!)

- Infants can see at birth and, if you capture their attention with an appropriate object (such as a small, red rubber ball held at about 10 inches from the face), they will track it as you move the ball from side to side. Infants react to color at between 2 and 4 months; depth perception appears at about 4 to 5 months.

- Infants not only can hear at birth (and prenatally), but they also can perceive the direction of the sound. In a remarkably perceptive yet simple experiment, Wertheimer (1962) sounded a clicker (similar to those children play with) from different sides of a delivery room only 10 minutes after an infant's birth. The infant not only reacted to the noise but attempted to turn in the direction of the sound.

- Infants are *active seekers of stimulation.* Although their main efforts are devoted to controlling bodily functions such as breathing and heart rate, they occasionally, for brief moments, pay close attention to the environment. These moments signal infants' search for stimulation and indicate an ability to process information.

- Compelling evidence suggests that interpersonal relationships have a powerful effect on development and research indicates that infants manifest a willingness, even a need, to interact with other human beings

Sample photographs of a model's happy, surprised, and sad expressions, and an infant's corresponding expressions.

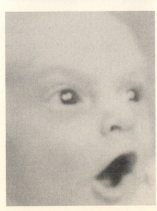

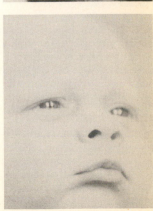

(Hinde, 1987). What has startled investigators of human relationships is the active role that infants play in controlling their parents' responses, a phenomenon called **reciprocal interactions.**

Reciprocal interactions

Similar to transactional model; recognizes the child's active role in its development (I do something to the child, the child changes; as a result of the changes in the child, I change)

- Infants, using these abilities, begin their efforts to master the developmental tasks of infancy: learning to take solid foods; learning to talk and walk.

As impressive as these accomplishments are, we must still be rather cautious to avoid overestimating an infant's abilities. Remember: Different parts of our brains mature at different rates. For example, the brain fibers for hearing develop early, but the brain parts for understanding what is heard develop much later. The brain areas controlling the upper body develop much more rapidly than those controlling other bodily areas, in a pattern having strong survival overtones.

Although all infants are born with these reflexes and abilities, not all possess them to the same degree. For example, some neonates demonstrate much weaker reflex action than others, a condition that affects their chances of surviving. Consequently, efforts to develop reliable measures of infant behavior have increased sharply.

WHAT'S YOUR VIEW?

NEONATES: COMPETENT OR HELPLESS?

Before continuing your reading, try to decide how competent you think a newborn baby is. In one view, infants are empty, unresponsive beings merely waiting for things to be done to and for them. They become active, healthy babies only because of maturation and the actions of those around them. In another view, newborns are seen as amazingly competent and capable of much more than is now expected of them. Consequently, some form of education is needed from the first months of an infant's life. In a third view, infants are seen as neither passive objects nor as superbabies, designed for instant greatness. Newborn babies are seen as bringing abilities with them into the world, a cluster of competencies that enables them to survive but also permits them to engage in a wider range of activities than was previously suspected (Brazelton, 1987).

The expectations that parents have for their babies determine how babies are treated and have important physical, cognitive, and psychosocial consequences. As we know, babies "tune into" their environments and are quite skillful in detecting the moods of those around them. Adherents of this view advise: Let them be babies, using the natural methods that have proven successful: love, attention, and warmth (Brazelton, 1987).

Which view do you think is most realistic? Which will most help infants to fulfill their potential? What's your view? Note: After you have read this chapter, return to this box and see if you would answer the question in the same way.

Neonatal Assessment Techniques

Three basic classifications of neonatal tests are used to assess infant reflexes and behavior: the Apgar scale, neurological assessment, and behavioral assessment.

Apgar

A scale to evaluate a newborn's basic life signs administered one minute after birth and repeated at three-, five- and ten-minute intervals; it uses five life signs— heart rate, respiratory effort, muscle tone, reflex irritability, skin color.

1. *The Apgar.* In 1953 Virginia Apgar proposed a scale to evaluate a newborn's basic life signs. The **Apgar** is administered one minute after birth and repeated at three-, five-, and ten-minute intervals. Using five life signs—heart rate, respiratory effort, muscle tone, reflex irritability, and skin color—an observer evaluates the infant by a three-point scale. Each of the five dimensions receives a score of 0, 1, or 2. (0 indicates severe problems, whereas 2 suggests an absence of major difficulties.)

Neurological assessment

Identifies any neurological problem, suggests means of monitoring the problem, and offers a prognosis about the problem.

2. *Neurological Assessment.* The **neurological assessment** is used for three purposes:
   - Identification of any neurological problem
   - Constant monitoring of a neurological problem
   - Prognosis about some neurological problem

Table 5.2	Physical Growth—Infancy	
Age (months)	Height (in.)	Weight (lb.)
3	24	13–14
6	26	17–18
9	28	20–22
12	29.5	22–24
18	32	25–26
24	34	27–29

Each of these purposes requires testing the infant's reflexes, which is critical for neurological evaluation and basic for all infant tests.

Brazelton Neonatal Behavioral Assessment Scale
An assessment tool that emphasizes how the infant interacts with its environment.

3. *Behavioral Assessment*. The **Brazelton Neonatal Behavioral Assessment Scale** (named after T. Berry Brazelton) has become a significant worldwide tool for infant assessment. Although the Brazelton tests the reflexes we have just discussed, its major emphasis is on how the infant interacts with its environment. In other words, it also permits us to examine the infant's behavior. Brazelton (1990) believes that the baby's state of consciousness (sleepy, drowsy, alert, fussy) is the single most important element in the examination.

Infants find these early tests quite stressful; they become irritated and start to cry. Do you think the information derived from them is worth the discomfort they cause infants?

All three of these assessment techniques provide clues about the infant's ability to function on its own. Tests such as these, plus careful observation, have given us much greater insight into infant development. These tests have also helped us to realize that infants are much more competent than we previously suspected.

To summarize, then, we can say that infant growth occurs at a rate unequaled in any other developmental period, with the possible exception of adolescence. If you recall, the average weight at birth is about 7 pounds and length is about 20 inches. Table 5.2 illustrates height and weight increases during infancy.

Brain Development

The adult human brain weighs about 3 to 4 pounds and contains about 100 billion neurons. As we have seen, nervous system development begins during the embryonic period when neurons reproduce at the rate of 25,000 per minute. During infancy, connections among the neurons begin to increase notably (as much as 100 to 1,000 connections for each of the 100 billion neurons). This amazing complexity provides the biological basis for cognitive development (Fischbach, 1992). Estimates are that the baby's brain at birth is about a quarter of its adult size. At 6 months it is about 50 percent of its adult weight, 60 percent at 1 year, 75 percent at 2 1/2 years, 90 percent at 6 years, and 95 percent at 10 years. The developmental pattern is seen in figure 5.1.

We know, however, that different parts of the brain develop at different rates. For example, the cerebellum, which controls the fine motor activities, develops more slowly than the brain areas controlling the muscles of the upper body. During the first month after birth, the cortical areas of the brain show an increasing thickness. Brain development seems to follow a definite schedule. First to show signs of development is the motor area, followed by the sensory region, the auditory area, and then the visual region. Consequently, we should expect motor development to proceed rapidly, which is just what happens.

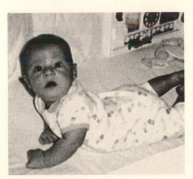

Note the steady development of body control in this picture, especially the head and upper body. Control of the lower body and legs follows by several months.

Figure 5.1
Brain development

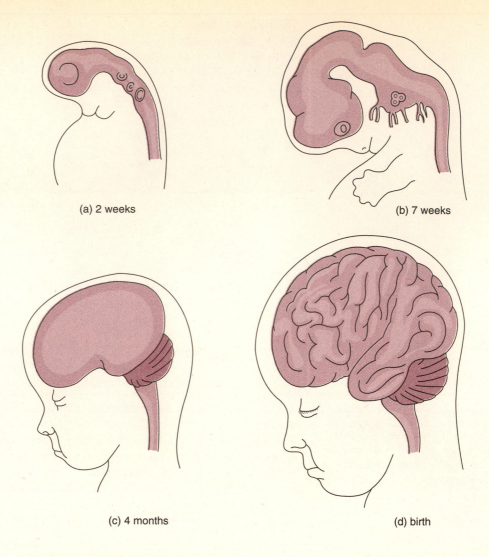

(a) 2 weeks

(b) 7 weeks

(c) 4 months

(d) birth

Motor Development

The role of motor development has assumed greater importance in understanding infant development mainly because of two crucial assumptions. First is acceptance of the concept of reciprocal interactions, which we discussed in chapter 1. Second is the belief that psychomotor development must be continuous with, and the foundation of, mental life. As a result, a new interdisciplinary field, called **developmental biodynamics,** has appeared. As Lockman and Thelen (1993) have noted, this new discipline emerged from advances in the neurosciences, biomechanics, perception, and actions. One example of the contributions that this new field has made can be seen in Bushnell and Boudreau's (1993) work. Studying the intimate relationship between perception and action, these researchers have demonstrated that the development of certain motor abilities lead to the appearance of haptic and depth perception.

Motor development proceeds at a steady pace, and the rate of motor activity seems to have a genetic component. Studying motor activity level, Saudino and Eaton (1991) used actometers—mechanical motion recorders—to assess activity level. They found that identical twins were significantly more similar in their activity levels than fraternal twins. These findings can also help parents adjust to the temperaments of their children.

Since motor development occurs in a head-to-feet direction (called *cephalocaudal*), as opposed to a *proximodistal* direction (from the center of the body to the extremities), an infant's ability to control its head signals advancing motor development. Particularly interesting in any analysis of motor development is the

Developmental biodynamics

A new method of studying motor development; stresses the relationship between perception and action.

reported motor precocity of black infants. In a study of black infants at 2 days and then at 1 month, Rosser and Randolph (1989) reported that the black infants in their study also performed well on all standard behavioral scales. This finding, which differs from those of other studies that relied on low-income samples, was attributed to the prenatal and perinatal conditions of the mothers. Of the 80 mothers, 49 were of low to lower-middle socioeconomic status (SES) and 31 were of middle SES (Rosser & Randolph, 1989).

Following are several important characteristics of motor control.

Head Control

The most obvious initial head movements are from side to side, although the 1-month-old infant occasionally lifts its head when in a prone position. Four-month-old infants can hold their heads steady while sitting and will lift their head and shoulders to a 90-degree angle when on their abdomens. By the age of 6 months, most youngsters can balance their heads quite well.

Locomotion: Crawling and Creeping

Crawling and creeping are two distinct developmental phases. In **crawling,** the infant's abdomen touches the floor and the weight of the head and shoulders rests on the elbows. Locomotion is mainly by arm action. The legs usually drag, although some youngsters push with their legs. Most youngsters can crawl after age 7 months.

Creeping is more advanced than crawling, since movement is on hands and knees and the trunk does not touch the ground. After age 9 months, most youngsters can creep.

Most descriptions of crawling and creeping are quite uniform. The progression is from propulsion on the abdomen to quick, accurate movements on hands and knees, but the sequence is endlessly varied. Youngsters adopt a bewildering diversity of positions and movements that can only loosely be grouped together.

Locomotion: Standing and Walking

After about age 7 months, infants when held will support most of their weight on their legs. Coordination of arm and leg movements enables babies to pull themselves up and grope toward control of leg movements. The first steps are a propulsive, lunging forward. Gradually a smooth, speedy, and versatile gait emerges. The world now belongs to the infant.

Once babies begin to walk, their attention darts from one thing to another, thus quickening their perceptual development (our next topic). Tremendous energy and mobility, coupled with a growing curiosity, push infants to search for the boundaries of their world. It is an exciting time for youngsters but a watchful time for parents, since they must draw the line between encouraging curiosity and initiative and protecting the child from personal injury. The task is not easy. It is, however, a problem for all aspects of development: What separates unreasonable restraint from reasonable freedom?

Table 5.3 summarizes milestones in motor development.

Crawling
Locomotion in which the infant's abdomen touches the floor and the weight of the head and shoulders rests on the elbows.

Creeping
Movement is on hands and knees and the trunk does not touch the ground.

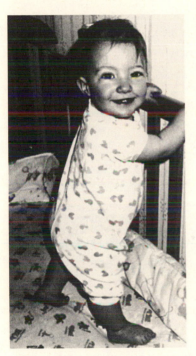

Most youngsters somewhere in the 7 to 9 month period begin to pull themselves up to a standing position. Their legs are now strong enough to support them while standing.

| Table 5.3 | Milestones in Motor Development | | | | |

Age	Head Control	Grasping	Sitting	Crawling-Creeping	Standing-Walking
1–3 months	Can lift head and chest while prone	Grasps objects; briefly holds objects; carries objects to mouth	Sits awkwardly with support		
4–8 months	Holds head steady while sitting; balances head	Develops skillful use of thumb during this period	Transition from sitting with slight support to brief periods without support		
8–12 months	Has established head control	Coordinates hand activities; handedness begins to appear	Good trunk control; sits alone steadily	Crawling movements appear (trunk touches floor); begins about 7 months	
		Handedness pronounced; holds crayon; marks lines	Can sit from standing position	Creeping (trunk raised from floor) begins at 9–10 months and continues until steady walking	Can stand holding onto something; will take steps when held; by 12 months will pull self up
14 months					Stands alone; begins to walk alone
18 months					Begins to run

An Applied View

Toilet Training—Easy or Difficult?

By the end of their child's infancy period, most parents begin to think about toilet training. One important fact to remember is that voluntary control of the sphincter muscles, which are the muscles that control elimination, does not occur until about the 18th month. (For some children, control is not possible until about 30 months.) Attempting to train children before they are ready can only cause anxiety and stress for the child and frustration for the parents.

Children really can't be trained; they learn when to use the toilet. It is not something parents do to a child; rather, parents help the child without feelings of tension and fear. Certain signs of readiness can alert parents that they can initiate the process.

- Necessary muscle control does not occur until well into the second year.
- A child must be able to communicate, either by words or gesture, the need to use the bathroom.
- At about 2 years, almost all children want to use the toilet, to become more "grown-up," and to rid themselves of the discomfort of wet or soiled diapers.

Parents should try to obtain equipment that the child feels most comfortable with—either a chair that sits on the floor or one that fits over the toilet seat. Brazelton (1981), studying the children in his clinical practice, offered the following estimates for ages of control:

- Most children start training at from 24 to 30 months.
- The average age of daytime control was 28.5 months.
- The average age of nighttime control was 33.3 months. (Girls attain nighttime control about two and a half months before boys.)

Most parents expect their children to be toilet trained by the end of infancy, usually sometime between 2 and 3 years of age (Charlesworth, 1987). Physiologically, most children are ready to learn control; socially it is desirable; psychologically it may be traumatic unless parents are careful. If youngsters are punished for a behavior that they find difficult to master, their perception of the environment is affected, which may produce feelings of insecurity. The common sense of most adults results in a combination of firmness and understanding, thus helping youngsters master a key developmental task.

Neonatal Problems

Not all infants enter the world unscathed. Occasionally the developmental sequence that we have just discussed does not run smoothly. Among the most prominent of possible problems are the following.

Failure to Thrive

Failure to Thrive (FTT)

A condition in which the weight and height of infants consistently remain far below normal (the bottom 3% of height and weight measures).

The weight and height of **failure-to-thrive (FTT)** infants consistently remain far below normal. They are estimated to be in the bottom 3 percent of height and weight measures. They account for about 3 percent of pediatric hospital admissions.

There are two types of FTT, organic and nonorganic. *Organic FTT* accounts for 30 percent of FTT cases, and the problem is usually some gastrointestinal disease. *Nonorganic FTT,* in which no physical cause for the problem can be found, is difficult to treat, and the problem may originate in family interactions (see chapter 13). The seriousness of this problem is evident from the outlook for FTT infants: Almost 50 percent of them will continue to experience physical, cognitive, and behavioral problems.

Sudden Infant Death Syndrome

Sudden Infant Death Syndrome (SIDS)

Death of an apparently healthy infant, usually between 2 and 4 months of age; thought to be a brain-related respiratory problem.

Discussion of the survival value of reflexes introduces one of the most perplexing problems facing both parents and researchers: **sudden infant death syndrome (SIDS).** An estimated 10,000 infants 2 to 4 months old die each year from SIDS. There is little warning, although almost all cases are preceded by mild cold symptoms and usually occur in late winter or early spring.

SIDS rarely occurs before age 1 month or after age 1 year; most victims are between 2 and 4 months old. Deaths peak between November and March. Boys are more vulnerable than girls, in this case by a 3-to-2 margin.

SIDS is particularly devastating for parents because of the lack of warning. These infants are apparently normal. Parents put them in a crib for a nap or for the night and return later to find them dead (hence the common name "crib death"). You can imagine the effect this has on parents, particularly the feelings of guilt: What did I do wrong? Why didn't I look in earlier? Why didn't I see that something was wrong? Today, special centers have been established to counsel grieving parents.

Since SIDS has such tragic consequences, do you think all babies should be monitored for breathing problems when they return to their homes?

Although no definite answers to the SIDS dilemma have yet been found, current research points to a respiratory problem. Control of breathing resides in the brain stem, and autopsies have indicated that the SIDS infant may not have received sufficient oxygen while in the womb. (This condition is called *fetal hypoxia.*)

Sleeping Disorders

Most sleeping disorders are less serious than FTT or SIDS. Nevertheless, infant sleeping problems negatively affect growth and trouble parents. As Ferber (1985) stated:

> ■ The most frequent calls I receive at the Center for Pediatric Sleep Disorders at Children's Hospital in Boston are from a parent or parents whose children are sleeping poorly. When the parent on the phone begins by telling me "I am at the end of my rope" or "We are at our wits' end" I can almost predict what will be said next.

Many observers believe that, in most cases of sleeping disorders, the parents are at fault. If this is true, why not tell these parents to let their children cry themselves to sleep?

Ferber goes on to explain that typically the parent has a child between the ages of 5 months and 4 years who does not sleep readily at night and wakes repeatedly. Parents become tired, frustrated, and often angry. Frequently the relationship between the parents becomes tense.

Usually a sleeping disorder has nothing to do with parenting. Also, usually nothing is wrong with the child, either physically or mentally. Occasionally problems do exist; for example, a bladder infection or, with an older child, emotional factors causing night terrors. A sleep problem is not normal and should not be waited out.

Neonates sleep more than they do anything else (usually from 14 to 15 hours per day) and have three sleep patterns: light or restless, periodic, and deep. Little if any activity occurs during deep sleep (about 25 percent of sleep). Neonates are mostly light sleepers and have the brain wave patterns associated with dreaming (although infants probably do not dream).

Some internal clock seems to regulate sleep patterns, with most deep sleep spells lasting approximately 20 minutes. At the end of the second week, a consistent and predictable pattern emerges. Neonates sleep in short stretches, about seven or eight per day. The pattern soon reverses itself, and infants assume an adult's sleep schedule.

Normal sleep patterns are as follows:

- *During the first month,* infants reduce their seven or eight sleep periods to three or four and combine two of them into one lasting about five hours. (If parents are lucky, this longer period will occur after a late evening feeding.) Infants are thus establishing a night and day routine.

- *During the third month,* sleep patterns are usually regulated. Morning and afternoon naps supplement night stretches ranging from 6 or 7 to as much as 10 or 11 hours.

- *At 5 or 6 months,* infant sleep patterns change. As part of the night sleep cycles, the infant is usually wide awake at dawn, bursting with excitement and demanding an audience.

- *By 8 months,* naps are shorter and some infants may require only one in the afternoon. A problem that most infants begin to show at this age is a reluctance to go to bed at night. They now begin to sleep most of the night.

- *At 12 months,* napping may be difficult and infants begin to set their schedules; that is, they nap only when tired. Children show continued resistance to going to bed at night, but once asleep they usually sleep through the night.

Sleep patterns in infants range from about 16 to 17 hours in the first week to 13 hours at age 2.

To determine whether a child has a sleeping problem, Ferber (1985) suggested these criteria: (1) The child's sleep patterns cause problems for parents or the infant; (2) obvious problems exist, such as an inability to sleep or, with older children, sleepwalking and sleep terrors; (3) more subtle symptoms are at work; for example excessively loud snoring may signal a breathing problem; the child is unable to go back to sleep after waking.

Respiratory Distress Syndrome

Respiratory Distress Syndrome (RDS)

A problem common with premature babies that is caused by the lack of a substance called surfactant, which keeps the air sacs in the lungs open.

The last of the disorders to be discussed is **respiratory distress syndrome (RDS)** (also called *hyaline membrane disease*). Although this problem is most common with prematures, it may strike full-term infants whose lungs are particularly immature.

RDS is caused by the lack of a substance called *surfactant,* which keeps open the air sacs in the lungs. When surfactant is inadequate, the lung can collapse. Since most babies do not produce sufficient surfactant until the 35th prenatal week, you can see why it is a serious problem for prematures. (Only 10 percent of a baby's lung tissue is developed at full-term birth.)

Full-term newborns whose mothers are diabetic seem especially vulnerable to RDS. Babies whose delivery has been particularly difficult also are more susceptible. The good news is that today 90 percent of these youngsters will survive and, given early detection and treatment, the outlook for them is excellent.

Guided Review

1. A _____ is a behavior in which a repeated stimulus elicits the same response.

2. The _____ is administered one minute after birth and measures, among other things, a newborn's muscle tone and skin color.

3. The _____ is a neonatal assessment technique that measures how an infant interacts with the environment.

4. Motor development occurs in a _____ to _____ direction.

5. The weight and height of _____ infants consistently remain below normal.

Perceptual Development

From what we've said so far, the current picture of an infant is that of an active, vibrant individual vigorously searching for stimuli. How do infants process these stimuli? Answering this question moves us into the perceptual world. For babies not only receive stimuli, they interpret them. Before attempting to chart perceptual development, let's explore the meaning of perception in a little more detail.

The Meaning of Perception

Infants acquire information about the world and constantly check the validity of that information. This process defines *perception:* getting and interpreting information from stimuli (Harre & Lamb, 1983). Infants are particularly ingenious at obtaining information from the stimuli around them. They attend to objects according to the perceptual information the objects contain.

Infants quickly begin to attend to the objects in their environments, thus constructing their views about how the world "works."

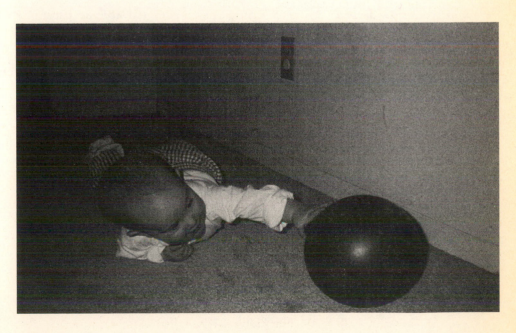

Answers

1. reflex 2. Apgar 3. Brazelton 4. head, foot 5. FTT

Seeking information leads to meaning. Objects roll, bounce, or squeak—in this way infants learn what objects are and what they do. During infancy, youngsters discover what they can do with objects, which furthers their perceptual development.

Remember: Infants are born ready to attend to changes in physical stimulation. Stimuli presented frequently cause a decrease in an infant's attention **(habituation).** If the stimuli are altered, the infant again attends, indicating awareness of the difference. For example, if you show an infant a picture (flower, birds, anything attractive), the child is first fascinated, then becomes bored; the child has habituated. If you now change the picture, you again capture the child's attention.

Infants, however, encounter a wide variety of objects, people, and events, all of which differ in many dimensions: color, size, shape. They must learn how to react to each, and how they react depends on many factors. For example, Clifton, Perris, and Bullinger (1991) found that when 6- and 7-month-old infants were in a dark setting and were presented with objects that made a sound, they reached accurately for the objects as long as they were within their reach. When the objects were out of reach, the infants were far less accurate. They thus perceive distance and direction and seem able to define their auditory space as long as an object is within reach of the body.

In a classic study, Brooks and Lewis (1976) studied how infants responded to four different types of strangers, a male and female child, a female adult, and a female midget. In this way, facial configurations and height were varied. The infants reacted to the children by continuous looking and some smiling. They reacted to the midget with considerable puzzlement but no positive response such as smiling or movement toward her. They reacted to the adult by sporadic looking, averting their eyes, frowning, and even crying. Thus the infants used size and facial configuration cues.

We may conclude, then, that perception depends on both learning and maturation. An infant's perceptual system undergoes considerable development following birth, resulting from greater familiarity with objects and events in the world as well as from growth.

Visual Perception

Humans are born able to see and quickly exhibit a preference for patterns. Recent research on vision reports the following (Aslin, 1987):

- Studies show that **variable accommodation** (focusing on objects at various distances) appears at about age 2 months.

- **Binocular coordination** appears at around 4 months. Studies indicate that a critical period may exist for the attainment of stereopsis (three-dimensional vision), since infants born with congenital esotropia (lack of ability to develop three-dimensional vision) have a greater chance of acquiring stereopsis if surgery is performed before the age of 2.

- Infants see color sometime in the 2- to 4-month age period. (A major difficulty in establishing an exact time for color recognition has been in separating color from brightness; the problem has only recently been overcome.)

- Individual differences in visual tracking ability exist at birth.

Visual Preference

Do infants prefer looking at some objects more than others? In an exciting yet simple series of experiments, Robert Fantz provided dramatic documentation of an infant's perceptual ability. Fantz (1961) stated that the best indicator of an infant's visual ability is eye activity. Infants who consistently gaze at some forms more than others show perceptual discrimination; that is, something in one form holds their attention.

Using a "looking chamber" in which an infant lies in a crib at the bottom of the chamber and looks at objects placed on the ceiling, Fantz could determine the amount of time that infants fixated on different objects.

He tested 30 infants from ages 1 week to 15 weeks on four pairs of test patterns: horizontal stripes and a bull's-eye; a checkerboard and two sizes of plain squares; a cross and a circle; and two identical triangles. The more complex patterns attracted the infants' attention significantly longer than either the checkerboard and square or the triangles.

The next step involved testing to discover whether infants preferred facial patterns. Three flat objects shaped like a head were used. One had regular features painted in black on a pink background; the second had scrambled features; the third had a solid patch of black at one end. The three forms were shown to 49 infants from 4 days old to 6 months old. Infants of all ages looked longest at the real face. The plain pattern received the least attention.

Fantz next tested pattern perception by using six objects, all flat discs 6 inches in diameter: face, bull's-eye, newsprint, red disc, yellow disc, and white disc. The face attracted the greatest attention, followed by the newsprint, the bull's-eye, and then the three plain-colored discs (none of which received much attention). Infants, then, show definite preferences based on as much complexity as they can handle (human faces are remarkably complex).

Infants' ability to detect complexity is also seen in studies by Hirshberg (1990), in which he worked with sixty-six 12-month-old infants who were responding to emotional signals given by their parents. Using toys as stimuli, the parents would give an emotional response to the infant when the child looked at them after picking up a toy. Sometimes the parent gave a happy response; at other times, with a different toy, the parent gave a fearful response; occasionally one parent gave a fearful response while the other parent gave a happy response to the infant's playing with the same toy.

The results showed that the infants did not place more emphasis on the mothers' or fathers' reactions but responded equally to the positive and negative signals of each. Infants showed the greatest decrease in toy exploration when they received conflicting signals from the parents, that is, when one gave a happy response and the other gave a fearful response. This study reinforces the belief that infants are capable of detecting considerable complexity in their surroundings.

Visual Adaptation

Studying visual development spurs speculation about how growing visual skill helps infants to adjust to their environment. Gibson and Walk (1960), in their famous "visual cliff" experiment, reasoned that infants would use visual stimuli to discriminate both depth and distance.

The visual cliff is a board dividing a large sheet of heavy glass. A checkerboard pattern is attached flush to one half of the bottom of the glass, giving the impression of solidity. The investigators then placed a similar sheet on the floor under the other half, creating a sense of depth—the visual cliff (see figure 5.2).

Thirty-six infants from ages 6 to 14 months were tested. After the infant was placed on the center board, the mother called the child from the shallow side and then the cliff side. Twenty-seven of the youngsters moved onto the shallow side toward the mother. When called from the cliff side, only three infants ventured over the depth. The experiment suggests that infants discriminate depth when they begin crawling.

Is this ability present before 6 months? Investigating the value of heart rate changes in analyzing infant behavior, Campos (1976) extended the visual cliff experiments. Noting that cardiac deceleration indicated infant attention while acceleration suggested infant fear, Campos placed infants of 1, 2, 3, and 5 months of age on the cliff. Expecting to find fear responses (cardiac acceleration) even with those

Figure 5.2
A child's depth perception is tested on the visual cliff. The apparatus consists of a board laid across a sheet of heavy glass, with a patterned material directly beneath the glass on one side and several feet below it on the other.

who were not yet crawling, Campos was surprised to discover cardiac deceleration (attention) in the 2-, 3-, and 5-month-old infants. The reactions were as follows:

- One month—no change in cardiac rate

- Two months—cardiac deceleration (attention)

- Three months—cardiac deceleration (attention)

- Five months—decreasing cardiac deceleration (decreasing attention)

- Nine months—cardiac acceleration (fear)

The pattern is fascinating and raises several questions. Prelocomotor infants perceive something at 2, 3, and 5 months, but is it depth? If they do indeed perceive depth, why don't they show fear? Thus infants demonstrate visual ability at birth and quickly show signs of increasing visual skill. Infants at 3 months also make primitive attempts to organize their visual surroundings and to integrate vision with other infant activities.

To conclude, we can state that by 2 to 4 months of age, infant perception is fairly sophisticated. Infants perceive figures as organized wholes; they react to the relationship among elements rather than single elements; they perceive color; and complex rather than simple patterns fascinate them.

🌳 Guided Review 🌳

6. The decrease in an infant's attention to stimuli presented frequently is called _____ .

7. _____ _____ , or the focusing on objects at various distances, appears at two months.

8. A child's depth perception is tested on an apparatus called a _____ _____ .

9. Neonates require about _____ hours of sleep per day.

10. Perception depends on _____ and _____ .

Cognitive Development

Can infants really think? If they can, what is their thinking like? Do they understand what is happening in the world around them? How do we explain the change in thinking from the newborn to the 2-year-old? Analyzing the way that children think led Schulman (1991) to conclude that infants, like the rest of us, are trying to answer four basic questions:

- *What's out there?* The first task infants must master is to distinguish the objects in their world: faces, voices, milk, rattles, and others (Schulman, 1991). To accomplish this task, infants discover similarities and differences and begin to recognize patterns. In a sense, this task remains with us for life; for example, you're trying to discover "what's out there" in lifespan psychology.

- *What leads to what?* Infants quickly learn that some experiences follow others: Crying leads to attention (most of the time). When infants learn about before-after sequences, they are beginning to acquire an understanding between past, present, and future.

Answers

6. habituation   7. Variable accommodation   8. visual cliff   9. 14   10. learning, maturation

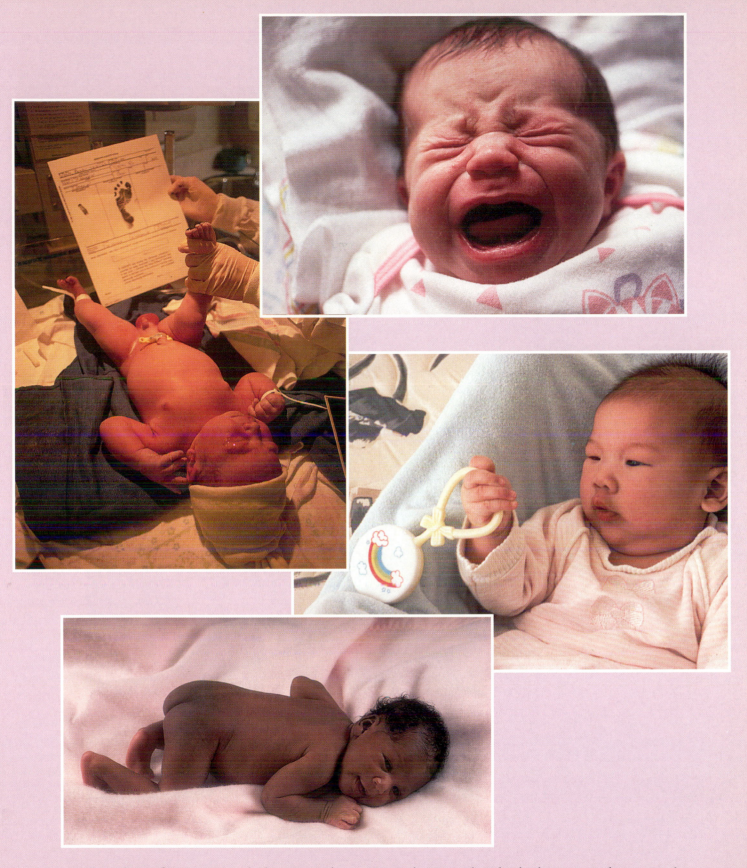

During the infancy years, babies use the native talents with which they were born until, by the end of the infancy period (about age 2), they typically are walking, talking children with an insatiable thirst for knowledge. Beginning with the reflexes that help them to survive, infants experience one of the most rapid periods of development in the human lifespan. Brain, body, and mind develop at a pace that challenges observers not only to chronicle but also to interpret the many changes that occur.

Physical growth is obvious; less so are the exciting changes that take place in the brain, thus enabling infants to acquire competencies that so dramatically appear. Crawling, standing, walking, and talking highlight motor development. These abilities, coupled with cognitive and language development, help infants to construct a picture of their world. A warm, supportive environment in which infants can attach to loved ones provides the emotional security that leads to needed self-esteem. With our current knowledge that infants are active partners in their own development has come the realization that these years have important implications for a child's future.

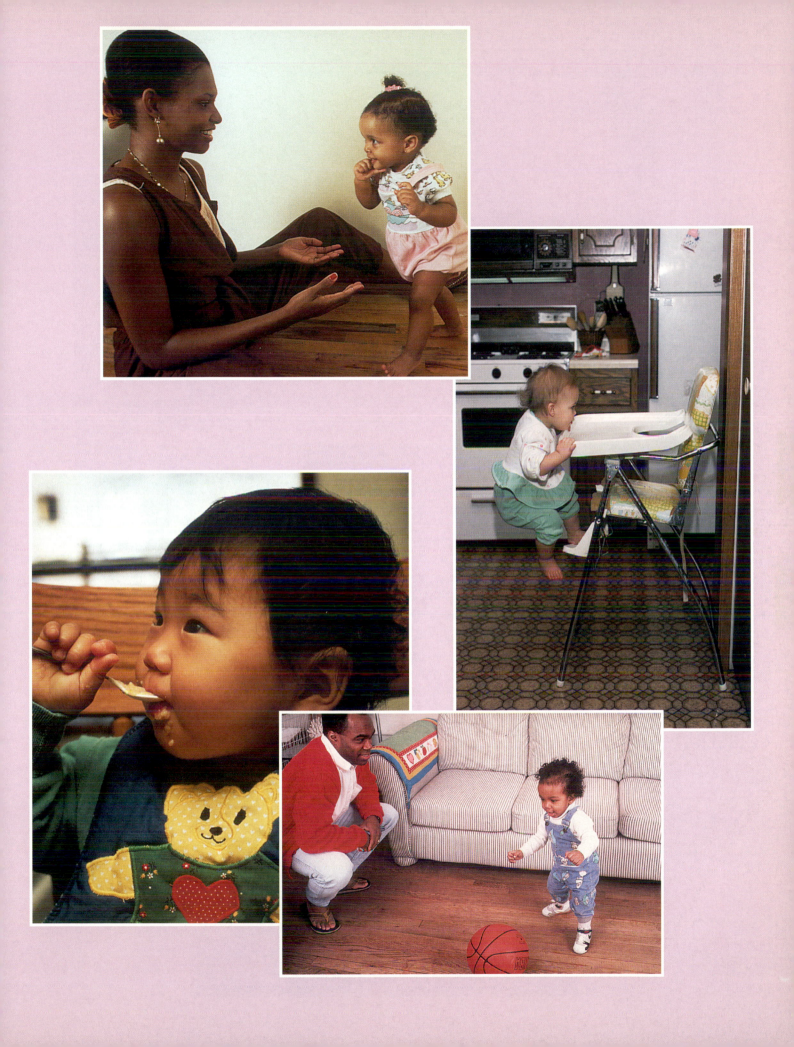

- *What makes things happen?* Infants become aware that some events cause another event; it's not just a matter of before-after. For example, pushing a toy makes it move; letting go of a doll causes it to fall. Infants also begin to realize that it is people who do things.

- *What's controllable?* Infants gradually learn that they can cause things to happen. In our discussion of reciprocal interactions, we mentioned that infants exercise control of those around them. By doing certain things such as making pleasant noises or smiling, the baby causes those around them to smile or begin to play with the baby. Thus infants begin to learn that they have the power to cause things to happen, to control their world.

How do infants develop an understanding of the objects around them? In their first year of life, they seem to proceed through several stages. In the first month, they have no idea that objects are permanent—out of sight, out of mind. From 1 to 4 months, infants will continue to stare at the spot where an object disappeared and then turn their attention to something else. From 4 to 8 months, infants begin to show signs that an object still exists even if they can't see it; they'll look for a toy after they drop it; they love playing peek-a-boo. From 8 to 12 months, infants develop the notion of **object permanence** and will continue to hunt for a hidden object (Maurer & Maurer, 1988).

Recent studies indicate that object permanence is related to later cognitive development suggesting that roots of cognition lie in infancy. For example, Rose and associates (1991) compared object permanence (among other cognitive indicators) in premature infants at 1 year with IQ measures at 5 years. They found a significant relationship between the two, suggesting developmental continuities in cognition.

To answer Schulman's four questions and to discover how infants develop such concepts as object permanence, we now turn to the work of the great Swiss scholar, Jean Piaget. You previously read about several of his important ideas in chapter 2; here we'll examine his interpretation of infancy in some detail.

Piaget's Sensorimotor Period

Piaget (1967) states that the period from birth to language acquisition is marked by extraordinary mental growth and influences the entire course of development. **Egocentrism** describes the initial world of children. Everything centers on them; they see the world only from their point of view. Very young children lack social orientation. They speak at and not to each other, and two children in conversation may be discussing utterly unrelated topics. (Likewise, egocentric adults know that other viewpoints exist, but they disregard them.) The egocentric child simply is unaware of any other viewpoint.

The remarkable changes of the **sensorimotor period** (about the first two years of life) occur within a sequence of six stages. Most of Piaget's conclusions about these stages were derived from observation of his own three children. (Jacqueline, Lucianne, and Laurent have become as famous in psychological literature as some of Freud's cases or John Watson's Albert.)

Stage 1.   During the first stage, children do little more than exercise the reflexes with which they were born. For example, Piaget (1952) stated that the sucking reflex is hereditary and functions from birth. At first infants suck anything that touches their lips; they suck when nothing touches their lips; then they actively search for the nipple. What we see here is the steady development of the coordination of arm, eye, hand, and mouth. Through these activities, the baby is building a foundation for forming cognitive structures.

Object permanence
Refers to children gradually realizing that there are permanent objects around them, even when these objects are out of sight.

Egocentrism
Child focuses on self in early phases of cognitive development; term associated with Piaget.

Are you egocentric? Isn't everyone? Is this bad?

Sensorimotor period
Piaget's term for the first of his cognitive stages of development (0 to 2 years).

Primary circular reactions
Infants repeat some act involving their bodies; term associated with Piaget's theory.

Secondary circular reactions
Infants direct their activities toward objects and events outside themselves.

Coordination of secondary schemes
Infants combine secondary schemes to obtain a goal.

Tertiary circular reactions
Repetition with variation; the infant is exploring the world's possibilities.

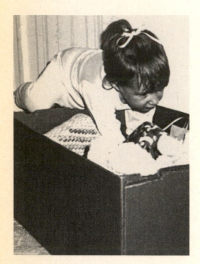

When infants begin to move things to get what they want, they are "coordinating secondary schemata." This is a clear signal of advancing cognitive development.

Stage 2. Piaget refers to stage 2 (from about 1 to 4 months) as the stage of first habits. During stage 2, **primary circular reactions** appear, in which infants repeat some act involving their bodies. For example, they continue to suck when nothing is present. They continue to open and close their hands. Infants seem to have no external goal, no intent in these actions other than the pleasure of self-exploration. But they are learning something about that primary object in their world: their own bodies.

Stage 3. **Secondary circular reactions** emerge during the third stage, which extends from about 4 to 8 months. During this stage, infants direct their activities toward objects and events outside themselves. Secondary circular reactions thus produce results in the environment, and not, as with the primary circular reactions, on the child's own body.

For example, Piaget's son, Laurent, continued to shake and kick his crib to produce movement and sound. He also discovered that pulling a chain attached to some balls produced an interesting noise, and he kept doing it. In this way, babies learn about the world "out there," and feed this information into their developing cognitive structures.

Stage 4. From about 8 to 12 months of age, infants **coordinate secondary schemes** to form new kinds of behavior. Now more complete acts of intelligence are evident (Piaget & Inhelder, 1969).

The baby first decides on a goal (finding an object that is hidden behind a cushion). The infant attempts to move objects to reach the goal. In stage 4, part of the goal object must be visible behind the obstacle. Here we see the first signs of intentional behavior.

Stage 5. **Tertiary circular reactions** appear from 12 to 18 months of age. In the tertiary circular reaction, repetition occurs again, but it is repetition with variation. The infant is exploring the world's possibilities. Piaget thought that the infant deliberately attempts to provoke new results instead of merely reproducing activities. Tertiary circular reactions indicate an interest in novelty for its own sake.

A continuing interest in novelty produces the curiosity that motivates continuous growth and change in an infant's cognitive processes. For example, how many times have you seen a baby standing in a crib and dropping everything on the floor? But listen to Piaget: Watch how the baby drops things, from different locations and different heights. Does it sound the same when it hits the floor as the rug? Is it as loud dropped from here or higher? Each repetition is actually a chance to learn. Thanks to Piaget, you will be a lot more patient when you see this behavior.

Stage 6. During stage 6, the sensorimotor period ends and children develop a basic kind of *internal representation*. A good example is the behavior of Piaget's daughter Jacqueline. At age 20 months, she approached a door that she wished to close, but she was carrying some grass in each hand. She put down the grass by the threshold, preparing to close the door. But then she stopped and looked at the grass and the door, realizing that if she closed the door the grass would blow away. She then moved the grass away from the door's movement and then closed it. She had obviously planned and thought carefully about the event before acting. Table 5.4 summarizes the accomplishments of the sensorimotor period.

Progress through the sensorimotor period leads to four major accomplishments:

- *Object permanence:* Children realize that permanent objects exist around them; something out of sight is not gone forever.

- *A sense of space:* Children realize that environmental objects have a spatial relationship.

Table 5.4	Outstanding Characteristics of the Sensorimotor Period
The Six Subdivisions of This Period	

Stage 1 During the first month the child exercises the native reflexes, for example, the sucking reflex. Here is the origin of mental development, for states of awareness accompany the reflex mechanisms.

Stage 2 Piaget referred to stage 2 (from 1 to 4 months) as the stage of *primary circular reactions*. Infants repeat some act involving the body, for example, finger sucking. (*Primary* means first, *circular reaction* means repeating the act.)

Stage 3 From 4 to 8 months, *secondary circular reactions* appear; that is, the children repeat acts involving objects outside themselves. For example, infants continue to shake or kick the crib.

Stage 4 From 8 to 12 months, the child "coordinates secondary schemata." Recall the meaning of *schema*—behavior plus mental structure. During stage 4, infants combine several related schemata to achieve some objective. For example, they will remove an obstacle that blocks some desired object.

Stage 5 From 12 to 18 months, *tertiary circular reactions* appear. Now children repeat acts, but not only for repetition's sake; now they search for novelty. For example, children of this age continually drop things. Piaget interpreted such behavior as expressing their uncertainty about what will happen to the object when they release it.

Stage 6 At about 18 months or 2 years, a primitive type of representation appears. For example, one of Piaget's daughters wished to open a door but had grass in her hands. She put the grass on the floor and then moved it back from the door's movement so that it would not blow away.

As infants acquire the ability to form representations of objects, they begin to move through their environments more skillfully.

- *Causality:* Children realize that a relationship exists between actions and their consequences.

- *Time sequences:* Children realize that one thing comes after another.

By the end of the sensorimotor period, children move from purely sensory and motor functioning (hence the name sensorimotor) to a more symbolic kind of activity.

Criticisms of Piaget

Although Piaget has left a monumental legacy, his ideas have not been unchallenged. Piaget was a believer in the stage theory of development; that is, development is seen as a sequence of distinct stages, each of which entails important changes in the way a child thinks, feels, and behaves (Scarr & others, 1986). Rest (1983), however, argued that the acquisition of cognitive structures is gradual rather than abrupt and is not a matter of all or nothing; for example, a child is not completely in the sensorimotor or preoperational stage. A child's level of cognitive development seems to depend more on the nature of the task than on a rigid classification system.

By changing the nature of the task (e.g., reducing the number of objects children must manipulate—see Gelman & Baillargeon, 1983), by allowing children to practice (e.g., teaching children conservation tasks—see Field, 1987), and by using materials familiar to children, researchers have found that children can accomplish specific tasks at earlier ages than Piaget believed (see Halford, 1989). Such criticisms have led to a more searching examination of the times during which children acquire certain cognitive abilities. For example, Piaget believed that infants will retrieve an object that is hidden from them in stage 4, from 8 to 12 months. Before this age, if a blanket is thrown over a toy that the infant is looking at, the child stops reaching for it as if it doesn't exist.

To trace the ages at which object permanence appears, Baillargeon (1987) devised an experiment in which infants between 3 1/2 and 4 1/2 months old were seated at a table where a cardboard screen could be moved back and forth, either forward (toward the baby) until it was flat on the table or backward (away from the baby) until the back of the cardboard touched the table.

Baillargeon then placed a painted wooden block behind the cardboard screen so that the infant could see the block when the screen was in a forward, flat position. But when the screen was moved backward, it came to rest on the block, removing it from the infant's sight. Occasionally Baillargeon secretly removed the block so that the screen continued backward until it rested flat on the table. The 4 1/2-month-old infants looked surprised at the change (they looked at the screen longer); even some of the 3 1/2-month-olds seemed to notice the "impossible" event. These findings suggest that infants may develop the object permanence concept earlier than Piaget originally thought.

Infants and Memory

As infants progress through these first two years, behavior appears that can only be attributed to memory. The last half of the first year appears to be a time of rapid growth in memory ability. Our discussion of Piaget's belief in the appearance of object permanence between 8 and 12 months is a good example of increasing memory ability. Analyzing the appearance of memory, Kail (1990) states that between 4 and 7 months, a marvelous change occurs in the relationship between infants and their parents. At 4 months, infants can distinguish between human and nonhuman objects in their environment (they smile and babble more to the human figures), but they are just as likely to smile at strangers as at parents. By 7 months, this has changed; infants will not smile at strangers and may appear threatened by them. (We'll discuss the psychosocial reasons for this change in chapter 6. Here we'll concentrate on cognitive explanations.)

As you can well imagine, testing infant memory is difficult because infants can't tell us whether or what they remembered. Consequently, investigators have relied on experiments that measure the time that infants look at familiar and novel objects. Kail (1990) gave the example of presenting two groups of infants with a bull's-eye pattern and a set of stripes. One group saw the bull's-eye first and then the stripes; the other group had the procedure reversed: first the stripes and then the bull's-eye. If both groups looked longer at the second presentation (the stripes for the first group and the bull's-eye for the second), it showed that they preferred the novel stimuli, thus giving evidence of infant memory. That is, they remembered the first and habituated and were then more interested in the novel stimulus.

Newborns seem to recognize events they have heard or seen before—recall the work of DeCasper and Fifer (1980) that we mentioned in chapter 4. By 2 to 3 months, infants will remember an event for several days, perhaps as long as a week. Memory continues to improve as infants "economize"; that is, rather than remembering specific events, they begin to integrate their experiences (Shields & Rovee-Collier, 1992). This helps to explain how they find hidden objects (such as in the object permanence experiments); they can now recall things and events (Kail, 1990). The growth of memory ability is a significant developmental accomplishment of the last half of the first year of life (Perris & others, 1990).

Olson and Sherman (1983) summarize infant recognition memory as follows. During the first three months, infants show growing ability to retain what they have experienced for a relatively brief time (one to several days). From ages 3 to 6 months, fairly consistent patterns of memory are present—lasting from 3 to 10 days. From ages 6 to 12 months, infants show joy when the mother returns; infants also tend to repeat first words, two practical reminders of their improving memory. From 12 to 24 months, language usage and reactions to family, friends, and strangers testify to an active, competent memory.

If memory seems to develop early in our lives, why do we have difficulty in remembering most of our experiences in infancy? You undoubtedly look with considerable skepticism at those individuals who claim to remember events from the first days of their lives. More common for all of us is a phenomenon called **infantile amnesia,** which refers to an inability to recall events from early in life. Is it that time has eroded our memory of these early experiences? Or is it that we simply did

Infantile amnesia

Our inability to recall events from early in life.

Implicit memory
Memory that affects our behavior without our being aware of it.

Explicit memory
Those events that we consciously remember.

not encode these happenings? Or have we encoded these experiences but cannot access them? Perhaps, as Newcombe & Fox (1994) speculate, as humans we have two types of memory: **implicit memory,** which affects our behavior without our being aware of it, and **explicit memory,** which are those events in our lives that we consciously remember. With our present knowledge, we're probably well advised to agree with Kail (1990) when he concludes that from early in life humans seem to be able to remember sights, sounds, and odors.

AN APPLIED VIEW

What Do Infants Think About?

Examining cognitive development in infancy may lead you to say: Well, yes, infants are much more competent than I thought, but what do they think about? What do they feel? Answering these questions takes us from the observational and experimental world we have just explored into a psychodynamic view of infancy.

A Path of Sunshine: 7:05 A.M.

■ **A space glows over there. A gentle magnet pulls to capture. The space is growing warmer and coming to life. Inside it, forces start to turn around one another in a slow dance.** (Stern, 1990, p. 55)

Stern, a sensitive interpreter of an infant's thoughts and feelings, has used these words to describe how a path of brilliant sunshine can attract an infant's attention. Infants react to attractive stimuli for all the reasons we have described in this chapter: intensity and complexity of the stimulation, visual ability, need for novelty, and so on. As we watch infants react to such stimuli, we may ask what subjective experiences accompany these behaviors.

We can't crawl inside an infant's mind, but speculating about what an infant's experiences may be like can shape our idea of what an infant is. We saw a good example of the power of these ideas in chapter 2. Freud's notion of infancy as a period seething with emotions is in stark contrast to Piaget's belief that the infant is like a little scientist busily constructing a model of its world. Both these theorists have made inferences about an infant's subjective experiences.

Is there a starting point for attempting to explain an infant's subjective experiences of its own social life? An infant's sense of self is probably the best guide for us to follow, because the qualitative changes we see in development testify to new forms of personality integration (Stern, 1985). Infants, as they undergo these changes, seem to portray a new "presence" or "social feel." For example, when an infant smiles into a parent's eyes and coos at about 3 months of age, it is more than a change of behavior. As observers, we recognize something unique and we react differently.

Stern (1985) believes that infants are predesigned to be aware of these self-organizing processes and experience four different senses of self:

• *The emergent self* appears in the time from birth to 2 months. If you observe infants of this age,

they show joy, distress, anger, and surprise—clear signs of subjective experience.
• *The core self* emerges between 2 and 4 months. Infants use memory and a growing sense of physical competence to organize their experiences. They slowly realize that their actions have consequences.
• *The subjective self* develops between 7 and 15 months. Infants begin to realize that they can share their experiences with others; for example, the mother knows the infant wants the cookies, and the child knows the mother knows. How many times have you seen a child of this age find something and smilingly show it to the mother?
• *The verbal self* follows after 15 months. From this time on, language and symbolic play are tangible clues about what is occurring in the infant's subjective world.

We should also remember, however, that the subjective world of parents also influences their children's development. Parents tend to see their children in a way that relates to their own needs, values, desires, and experiences. For example, Brazelton and Cramer (1990) have identified three parental fantasies:

• *The infant as ghost,* in which the baby reminds the parents of someone (usually dead), which in turn unleashes a flood of emotional feelings and may affect a parent's relationships with the child; Selma Fraiberg (1980) has referred to this situation as the "ghost in the nursery."
• *A parent's relationship with the infant reenacts a past mode of relationship.* Parents sometimes seek to recapture the relationships of their childhood through interactions with the infant. A mother who teased and fought with her brothers and sisters, or who might have kept a distance from them, adopts that same pattern with her children.
• *The infant as part of the parent.* Some parents attempt to project part of their selves on the infant: lazy, greedy, determined, stubborn.

The fantasy worlds of infants and parents affect children's development, and parents should be aware of such tendencies and avoid them where possible.

Language Development

In our discussion, you probably noticed that in the latter stages of the sensorimotor period, language becomes increasingly important. Indeed, one of the most amazing accomplishments of human beings is their acquisition of language. With no formal learning and often exposed to dramatically faulty language models, children learn words, meanings and how to combine them in a purposeful manner. How does this uniquely human achievement occur? Students of language, attempting to explain the richness and complexity of children's language, are convinced that this feat is possible because *children learn the rules of their language.* The process of acquiring language goes on at a furious pace until, at about the age of 5 for most children, they have acquired the fundamentals of their language. After that it's a matter of expanding and refining language skills, a task that can often define success or failure.

As an example of the world into which language development takes children, consider some of the intricacies of the English language that we, as adults, understand completely. Do you realize that you drive on a parkway and park on a driveway? Do you realize that you eat *ghoti* quite frequently? (*gh* as in tough, *o* as in women, *ti* as in nation—put them all together and you're eating *fish*.)

These examples (Pinker, 1994) illustrate what should be a stupendous task for children. But no matter how much difficulty children have with mathematics, for example, they move through their linguistic world with comparative ease. This is not to say, of course, that we all reach the heights of eloquent expression. It does, however, imply that normal children will acquire the basics of their language with comparative ease. With this brief background, let's turn our attention to what we know about language development.

All children learn their native language at about the same time and in a similar manner. During the infancy period, children at about 3 months use sounds in a similar manner to adults, and at about 1 year they begin to use recognizable words. The specific sequence of language development during infancy appears in table 5.5.

Key Signs of Language Development

In the first year, babies continue to learn the sounds of their language. During the first two months, nothing that is particularly exciting happens linguistically; babies seem to develop sounds that are associated with breathing, feeding, and crying. **Cooing** (sounds like vowels) appears during the second month. Between 5 and 7 months, babies play with the sounds they can make, and this output begins to take on the sounds of consonants and syllables, the beginning of **babbling.** At

Cooing

Early language sounds that resemble vowels.

Babbling

Infant produces sounds approximating speech between 5 and 7 months.

Table 5.5	Language Development During Infancy
Language	**Age**
Crying	From birth
Cooing	2–5 months
Babbling	5–7 months
Single words	12 months
Two words	18 months
Phrases	2 years

seven and eight months, sounds like syllables appear—*da-da-da, ba-ba-ba* (a phenomenon occurring in all languages)—a pattern that continues for the remainder of the first year. Around their first birthday, babies produce single words, about half of which are for objects (food, clothing, toys) (Pinker, 1994).

Language explosion
Rapid acquisition of words beginning at 18 months.

At 18 months children acquire words at the rate of a new word every two hours, a condition that lasts until about 3 years of age and is frequently referred to as the **language explosion.** Remember: Children know many more words than they speak. Vocabulary constantly expands, but estimating the extent of a child's vocabulary is difficult because youngsters know more words than they articulate (Woodward & others, 1994). Estimates are that a 1-year-old child may use from two to six words, and a 2-year-old has a vocabulary ranging from 50 to 250 words. Children at this stage also begin to combine two words (Pinker, 1994).

If you have the opportunity, listen to a child's speech when single words begin to appear. You will notice a subtle change before the two-word stage. *Children begin to use one word to convey multiple meanings.* For example, youngsters say "ball" meaning "give me the ball," "throw the ball," or "watch the ball roll." They have now gone far beyond merely labeling this round object as a ball.

When the two-word stage appears (at about 18 months), children initially struggle to convey tense and number. They also experience difficulty with grammatical correctness. Children usually employ word order ("me go") for meaning, only gradually mastering inflections (plurals, tenses, possessives) as they begin to form three-word sentences. A youngster's efforts to inject grammatical order into language are a good sign of normal language development.

Several things signal difficulty in language acquisition. Babbling is a good example. When children babble, they make sounds that approximate speech. For example, you may hear an "eee" sound that makes you think that the infant is saying "see." This is to be expected. Deaf children, however, continue to babble past the age when other children begin to use words. Let's now look at several language accomplishments in more detail.

Sounds to Words

At about age 4 months, children make sounds that approximate speech. These increase in frequency until the children are about a year old, when they begin to use single words. After children commence using words, babbling still appears among the simple words.

We do not yet understand the relationship between babbling and word appearance. Babbling probably appears initially because of biological maturation. (We know that deaf children babble, which would seem to suggest that babbling does not depend on external reinforcement.)

Vocables
Consistent sound patterns to refer to objects and events.

Late in the babbling period, children use consistent sound patterns to refer to objects and events. These are called **vocables** and suggest children's discovery that meaning is associated with sound. For example, a lingering *L* sound may mean that someone is at the door. The use of vocables is a possible link between babbling and the first intelligible words.

Holophrastic speech
The use of one word to communicate many meanings and ideas.

Holophrases
Children's first words that usually carry multiple meanings.

At about age 1, the first words appear. Often called **holophrastic speech** (one word to communicate many meanings and ideas), it is difficult to analyze. These first words, or **holophrases,** are usually nouns, adjectives, or self-inventive words and often contain multiple meanings. As mentioned previously, "ball" may mean not only the ball itself but "throw the ball to me."

Infants "tune into" the speech they hear and immediately begin to discriminate distinctive features. They also seem to be sensitive to the context of the language they hear; that is, they identify the emotional nature of speech. So the origins of language appear immediately after birth in infant gazes and vocal exchanges with those around them.

The precursors of language blend with babbling, which then merges into the first words, and is then continuous with the appearance of two words, phrases, and sentences. Remember: The period of single words is more than a time of merely accumulating more and more words. Although vocabularies increase, notable changes occur in both the kinds of words and the ways they are used between ages 1 and 2.

First Words

Children begin to use multiple words to refer to the things that they previously named with single words. Rather than learning rules of word combination to express new ideas, children learn to use new word forms. Later, combining words in phrases and sentences suggests that children are learning the structure of their language.

Telegraphic speech
Initial multiple-word utterances, usually two or three words.

At about 2 years of age children's vocabularies expand rapidly, and simple two-word sentences appear. Children primarily use nouns and verbs (not adverbs, conjunctions, or prepositions), and their sentences demonstrate grammatical structure. Although the nouns, adjectives, and verbs of children's sentences differ from those of adults, the same organizational principles are present. These initial multiple-word utterances (usually two or three words: "Timmy runs fast") are called **telegraphic speech.** Telegraphic speech contains considerably more meaning than superficially appears in the two or three words.

Word order and inflection (changing word form: e.g., "word"/"words") now become increasingly important. During the first stages of language acquisition, word order is paramount. At first, children combine words without concern for inflections, and it is word order that provides clues as to their level of syntactic (grammatical) development.

Once two-word sentences are used, inflection soon appears, usually with three-word sentences. The appearance of inflections seems to follow a pattern: first the plural of nouns, then tense and person of verbs, and then possessives.

Language Acquisition: The Theories

Many of the language achievements we take for granted are actually amazing accomplishments that defy easy explanation. Imitation, although a powerful linguistic force, does not seem to be the sole explanation for a youngster's intuitive grasp of grammar, because a child hears so many incorrect utterances. Nor does imitation explain how thoughts are translated into words. Although we don't have a totally satisfactory explanation of how children acquire their language, four major theories have been proposed.

Biological Theory

Nativist theory
A biological explanation of language development.

A *biological,* or **nativist theory,** explanation focuses on innate language mechanisms that automatically unfold. Linguistic achievements that cannot be explained by imitation or some other cause have led some to a biological interpretation of language. What else but an innate capacity for language can explain the innovative nature of language? Children do not merely imitate those around them. If you listen carefully to young children, you will distinguish unique combinations of words, combinations that they never heard before. For example, they may have heard the words *man, doll,* and *walk,* but never the combination "man walk doll." Such novel utterances testify to the creative aspects of language.

The work of Eric Lenneberg offers insights into the biological bases of the capacity for language (1967). Although the specific causal elements and the underlying cerebral mechanisms for the language explosion are still unknown, Lenneberg believed that imitation, conditioning, and reinforcement—all external factors—are inadequate explanations for language development, and that anatomical and physiological agents—internal factors—play a major part.

Lenneberg postulated that language development follows a biological schedule, which is activated when a state of "resonance" exists; that is, when children are "excited" in accordance with the environment, the sounds that they have been hearing suddenly assume a new, meaningful pattern. Consequently, if children of an appropriate age are placed in any language community, they will immediately and with little difficulty acquire that language.

Cognitive Theory

Piaget's *cognitive* explanation of language development views language as part of a child's emerging cognitive abilities. Piaget believed that language emerges not from a biological timetable, such as Lenneberg suggests, but from existing cognitive structures and in accordance with the child's needs. Piaget began his basic work on language, *The Language and Thought of the Child* (1926), by asking, What are the needs that children tend to satisfy when they talk? What is the function of language for a child? Piaget answered this question by linking language to his belief in cognitive structures.

Recording the speech of two 6-year-old children, Piaget identified two major speech categories of the preoperational child: egocentric speech and socialized speech. Children engage in **egocentric speech** when they do not care to whom they speak, or whether anyone is listening to them (Piaget, 1926). Children use **socialized speech** when they exchange views with others, criticize one another, ask questions, give answers, and even command or threaten. Piaget estimated that about 50 percent of the 6-year-old's speech is egocentric and that what is socialized is purely factual. He also warned that although most children begin to communicate thought at between 7 and 8 years of age, their understanding of each other is still limited.

Seven or 8 years of age is the beginning of the slow but steady disappearance of egocentrism, except in verbal thought, in which traces of egocentrism remain until about 11 or 12 years of age. Usage and complexity of language increases dramatically as children pass through the four stages of cognitive development. Piaget insisted that the striking growth of verbal ability does not occur as a separate developmental phenomenon but reflects the development of cognitive structures.

A different cognitive interpretation has been proposed by Vygotsky (1962), who argued that the roots of language and thought are separate and only become linked as development proceeds through interactions with the environment. Thought isn't just expressed in words; it comes into existence *through* words. Vygotsky also sharply disagreed with Piaget's explanation of egocentric speech. Rather than seeing it as contributing little to cognitive development, Vygotsky believed that children use egocentric speech to "grasp and remedy the situation", that is, to solve problems.

■ Where's the pencil? I need a blue pencil. Never mind, I'll draw with the red one and wet it with water; it will become dark and look like blue. (1962, p. 16)

Egocentric speech
Piaget's term to describe children's speech when they do not care to whom they speak.

Socialized speech
Piaget's term for the time when children begin to exchange ideas with each other.

Egocentric speech (now more commonly called *private speech*), which Vygotsky believed is a form of social communication, gradually becomes internalized. Thus the true direction of thought and language is not from the individual to the socialized, but from the social to the individual (Vygotsky, 1962).

This social interaction viewpoint has also been advocated by Jerome Bruner (1990) who has called the language support offered to a child a **language acquisition support system (LASS).** For example, parents and other adults play nonverbal games with babies (peek-a-boo), which teaches them about turn taking. With this help, infants thus become capable of behavior that they couldn't otherwise manage, a process called **scaffolding.** Parents also modify their speech when talking to their children, a phenomenon referred to as **motherese** (very simple words and sentences, higher pitch).

Psycholinguistic Theory

A **psycholinguistic** interpretation attempts to explain how native speakers can understand and produce sentences that were never spoken or written. Noam Chomsky, a professor of linguistics at the Massachusetts Institute of Technology, believed that all humans have an innate capacity to acquire language as a result of their biological inheritance. Trained in linguistics, mathematics, and philosophy, Chomsky went further than Lenneberg in his biological views: Not only do we have a biological predisposition for language, we also have an innate knowledge of language. He called it our **language acquisition device (LAD).** Chomsky (1965) also stated that no one acquires a language by learning billions of sentences of that language. Rather, children acquire a grammar that can generate an infinite number of sentences in their native language.

Chomsky's work is usually referred to as psycholinguistics, a combination of psychology and linguistics. Linguistics is the study of the rules of any language, whereas psychology focuses on behavior. Linguists assume that the rules of language are part of our knowledge; psychologists have attempted to discover how these rules are represented in our minds (especially the capacities that children must have to master the rules of their language). The combination of the two approaches has produced the field of psycholinguistics (Gardner, 1982b).

Children possess an innate competence for language acquisition, just as they possess an innate capacity for walking. No one has to tell children how to walk—they walk and talk without consciously knowing how they did either. Although all normal children possess approximately the same language competence, their performance, or use of language, varies increasingly as they grow older. This variation is largely due to differences in opportunities to learn how to use language, which includes not only speaking but also listening, writing, and reading.

Behaviorist Theory

A *behavioristic* explanation concentrates on language as a learned skill. Children utter sounds that are reinforced and shaped by the environment, especially parents and teachers, and gradually learn to make distinguishable sounds and to form correct sentences. B. F. Skinner (1957), a leading behaviorist, proposed a detailed behavioristic theory of language acquisition in one of his early books.

Note how frequently we have said that cognitive development and language development occur in relation to other people. Huttenlocher and associates (1991) have found that parental speech input at 16 months accounts for considerable variation among children in vocabulary growth. This finding points to the critical role that social development plays in an infant's growth.

Table 5.6 summarizes several of the developmental highlights we have discussed in this chapter.

Language acquisition support system (LASS)

Bruner's term for the support children get in acquiring their language.

Scaffolding

Developing a support system to help children acquire their language.

Motherese

Using simple words when talking to children.

Psycholinguistic theory

A combination of psychology and linguistics, which attempts to explain how native speakers acquire language.

Language acquisition device (LAD)

Chomsky's term for the biological predisposition to acquire language.

Table 5.6			Developmental Characteristics of Infancy		
Age (months)	Height (in.)	Weight (lb.)	Language Development	Motor Development	Cognitive (Piaget)
3	24	13–14	Cooing	Supports head in prone position	Primary circular reactions
6	26	17–18	Babbling—single-syllable sounds	Sits erect when supported	Secondary circular reactions
9	28	20–22	Repetition of sounds signals emotions	Stands with support	Coordinates secondary schemata
12	29.5	22–24	Single words—"mama," "dada"	Walks when held by hand	Same
18	32	25–26	3–50 words	Grasps objects accurately, walks steadily	Tertiary circular reactions
24	34	27–29	50–250 words, 2–3 word sentences	Runs and walks up and down stairs	Representation

As we complete this initial phase of examining infant development, remember that all phases of development come together in an integrated manner. Motor development is involved when a child moves excitedly toward its mother on her return. Language development is involved when infants intensify their relationships with their mothers by words that are now directed toward her. Cognitive development is probably less obvious but just as significant: Children are excited by their mothers' return because they remember their mothers. Consequently, a sound principle of development remains—all development is integrated.

Guided Review

16. _____ is sounds that approximate speech.

17. One word used to communicate many meanings is called _____ speech.

18. Lenneberg uses a _____ explanation to account for language development in children.

19. Piaget identified two major speech categories: _____ and _____ .

20. The combination of psychology and linguistics is called _____ .

Answers

16. Babbling   17. holophrastic   18. biological (nativist)   19. egocentric, socialized
20. psycholinguistics

CONCLUSION

You should now view an infant as an individual of enormous potential, one whose activity and competence is much greater than originally suspected. It is as if a newborn enters the world with all its systems ready to function and eager for growth. What happens during these first two years has important implications for future development. Setbacks—both physical and psychological—will occur, but they need not cause permanent damage. From your reading in chapter 1,

you realize that human infants show remarkable resiliency.

How do infants first learn that they can trust those around them? The answer lies in the way their initial needs are satisfied. They have the ability to detect and react to parental signals. In chapter 2 you read about Erikson's stages of development. In light of what you now know about infant potential, it is easier to accept Erikson's great contribution

to our understanding of infants' development of trust.

You are also now aware that proper need satisfaction entails psychological as well as physical comfort. These first parent-infant interactions furnish the basis for attachment, the knowledge that others can be trusted. In chapter 6, we turn to an infant's social development and analyze how interactions with others affect development.

CHAPTER HIGHLIGHTS

Physical and Motor Development

- Newborns display clear signs of their competence: movement, seeing, hearing, interacting.
- Infants' physical and motor abilities influence all aspects of development.
- Techniques to assess infant competence and well-being are widely used today.
- Motor development follows a well-documented schedule.
- Infants can develop problems such as SIDS and FTT for a variety of reasons.

Perceptual Development

- Infants are born with the ability to detect changes in their environment.
- Infants are capable of acquiring and interpreting information from their immediate surroundings.
- Infants from birth show preferences for certain types of stimuli.

Cognitive Development

- Infants, even at this early age, are attempting to answer questions about their world, questions that will continue to occupy them in more complex and sophisticated forms throughout their lives.

- One of the first tasks that infants must master is an understanding of the objects around them.
- Piaget's theory of cognitive development has shed considerable light on the ways that children grow mentally.
- A key element in understanding an infant's cognitive development is the role of memory.

Language Development

- Infants show rapid growth in their language development.
- Language acquisition follows a definite sequence.
- Language behaviors in infancy range from crying to the use of words and phrases.

KEY TERMS

Apgar   106
Apnea   103
Babbling   122
Binocular coordination   114
Brazelton Neonatal Behavioral Scale   107
Cooing   122
Coordination of secondary schemes   118
Crawling   109
Creeping   109
Developmental biodynamics   108
Egocentric speech   125
Egocentrism   117
Explicit memory   121
Failure to thrive (FTT)   111

Habituation   114
Holophrases   124
Holophrastic speech   124
Imitative behavior   105
Implicit memory   121
Infantile amnesia   120
Language acquisition device (LAD)   126
Language acquisition support system (LASS)   126
Language explosion   123
Motherese   126
Nativist theory   124
Neonate   105
Neurological assessment   106
Object permanence   117

Primary circular reactions   118
Psycholinguistic theory   126
Reciprocal interactions   106
Reflex   103
Respiratory distress syndrome (RDS)   112
Scaffolding   126
Secondary circular reactions   118
Sensorimotor period   117
Socialized speech   125
Sudden infant death syndrome (SIDS)   111
Telegraphic speech   124
Tertiary circular reactions   118
Variable accommodation   114
Vocables   123

🌳 WHAT DO YOU THINK?

1. The shift from considering an infant as nothing more than a passive sponge to seeing infants as amazingly competent carries with it certain responsibilities. We can't be overly optimistic about a baby's abilities. Why? What are some of the more common dangers of this viewpoint?
2. Testing infants has grown in popularity these past years. You should consider some cautions, however. Remembering what you have read about infants in this chapter, mention several facts you would be careful about.
3. You have been asked to babysit your sister's 14-month-old baby. When you arrive, the mother is upset because she has been repeatedly picking up things that the baby has thrown out of the crib. With your new knowledge, you calm her down by explaining the baby's behavior. What do you tell her?
4. After reviewing the infancy work, what do you think about this period as "preparation for the future"? Select one phase of development (e.g., cognitive development) and show how a stimulating environment can help to lay the foundation for future cognitive growth.

🌳 SUGGESTED READINGS

Field, T. (1990). *Infancy*. Cambridge, MA: Harvard University Press. A clear, simple, and carefully written account of infancy by a well-known commentator on these years.

Harris, J. R. & Liebert, R. (1992). *Infant & child*. Englewood Cliffs, NJ: Prentice-Hall. A thorough, well-documented account of the early years; particularly strong in its use of the transactional model.

Maurer, D. & Mowrer, C. (1988). *The world of the newborn*. New York: Basic Books. A fascinating explanation of the newborn's experiences—scientifically sound and enjoyable to read.

Osofsky, J. (Ed.). (1987). *Handbook of infant development*. New York: Wiley. This book is really the "bible" of infancy. If you have any questions about infant behavior, this is the text to use.

Pinker, S. (1994). *The language instinct*. New York: Morrow. A fascinating, well-written account of the nature of language and how humans acquire their language.

🌳 CHAPTER REVIEW TEST

1. Which of the following is not a reflex?
   a. breathing
   b. sucking
   c. swallowing
   d. laughing

2. A _____ reflex is elicited by gently touching the infant's cheek.
   a. Moro
   b. rooting
   c. Babkin
   d. Babinski

3. _____ are brief periods when an infant stops breathing.
   a. Apnea
   b. Rooting
   c. Babbling
   d. Primary circular reactions

4. Depth perception in infants appears at
   a. birth.
   b. 7 to 10 days.
   c. 2 to 4 months.
   d. 4 to 5 months.

5. The Brazelton test assesses an infant's
   a. interaction with the environment.
   b. respiratory effort.
   c. reflex irritability.
   d. hearing.

6. Neurological assessment is *not* used for which of the following purposes?
   a. identification of a neurological problem
   b. treatment of a neurological problem
   c. monitoring a neurological problem
   d. prognosis about a neurological problem

7. The final area of the brain to develop is the
   a. sensory region.
   b. motor area.
   c. visual area.
   d. auditory area.

8. _____ is a disorder caused by the lack of a substance called surfactant.
   a. SIDS
   b. RDS
   c. AIDS
   d. FTT

9. Infants see color at
   a. the neonatal period.
   b. 2 to 4 months.
   c. 6 to 7 months.
   d. 9 to 12 months.

10. A child's exploration of a new toy was most influenced by which of the following parental responses?
    a. happy response from the mother
    b. fearful response from the father
    c. mixed response from mother and father
    d. happy response from mother and father

11. Infants show preferences for certain types of stimuli from
    a. birth.
    b. 10 days.
    c. 2 months.
    d. 6 months.

12. An infant's search for novelty during the sensorimotor period is seen in
    a. object permanence.
    b. secondary circular reactions.
    c. coordination of secondary scemata.
    d. tertiary circular reactions.

13. Infants initially show memory ability during
    a. the first and second weeks.
    b. the first three months.
    c. third to sixth month.
    d. sixth to twelfth month.

14. In the development of language, children about 1 year of age begin to use recognizable
    a. vocables.
    b. holophrases.
    c. words.
    d. sentences.

15. According to Piaget, the acquisition of language in children depends on
    a. cognitive structures.
    b. biology.
    c. reinforcement.
    d. language acquisition devices.

16. By _____ months a child begins to run.
    a. 9
    b. 12
    c. 24
    d. 18

17. Which of the following is *not* a major accomplishment of the sensorimotor period?
    a. reversibility
    b. sense of space
    c. causality
    d. time sequence

18. _____ believes infants experience four different sense of self: emergent, core, subjective, and verbal.
    a. Erikson
    b. Skinner
    c. Piaget
    d. Stern

19. A 2-year-old child may have a vocabulary of as many as _____ words.
    a. 250
    b. 500
    c. 1,000
    d. 2,000

20. _____ believed the roots of language and thought were separate and only become linked through development.
    a. Chomsky
    b. Lenneberg
    c. Vygotsky
    d. Piaget

Answers

1.d 2.b 3.a 4.d 5.a 6.b 7.c 8.b 9.b 10.d 11.a 12.d 13.d 14.c 15.a 16.d 17.a 18.d 19.a 20.c

CHAPTER 6

Psychosocial Development in Infancy

Chapter Outline

Beginning at about six months of age, infants show signs of distress when approached by a stranger.

Janice watched with exasperation as her 1-year-old son, Joseph, sat crying. Her friend Laura had dropped in for a cup of coffee and had started to play with Joseph when he began to cry and pull away from her. Janice had noticed this happening often lately and was concerned that something was bothering him. She could tell that her friend, who had no children, was hurt; Janice wondered whether the problem was serious enough to call her doctor for advice. Joseph looked fine and seemed to show no symptoms of any illness, which made her hesitate.

Later that day, after her friend had left and Joseph was taking his nap, Janice thought about his behavior. If he wasn't sick, what was the problem? She was concerned that he might be so shy that he could have difficulty with relationships and in making friends. She was also bothered that she could be doing something wrong. Joseph was a first child; could she be keeping him too close to her and perhaps subconsciously resisting any contacts he might have with others?

Janice decided to take Joseph shopping the following day and visit the local bookstore. The next morning, Joseph was bright and cheerful and kept himself busy with a toy while Janice browsed through the books in the child-care section of the bookstore. At first she turned to those books that dealt with specific problems, but she didn't know what to look for, so she turned to more general discussions of child rearing. Still not satisfied, she was about ready to give up when she came across a book that described the milestones that occur during infancy.

Sure enough, there it was. "Beginning in the second half of the first year, infants start to show anxiety in the presence of strangers. This behavior is probably the first clue you will notice that tells you attachment is developing." Janice read the words again, relieved and delighted; Joseph was perfectly normal. Now, however, she was determined to learn more about attachment. 🌳

In chapters 1 and 5, we noted that infants are much more actively involved in their own development than we had previously realized. This knowledge has enabled us to examine an infant's psychosocial development from a totally new and exciting perspective. Not only do infants attempt to make sense of their world as they develop cognitively, they also "tune into" the social and emotional atmosphere surrounding them and immediately begin to shape their relationships with others.

A growing recognition exists today that relationships with others are the basis of our social development, commencing in those first days after birth. Joseph's relationship with his mother (the bond with her that's usually called *attachment*) will become the basis for his relations with others. The attachment that forms, typically between mother and child, tells the child what to expect from others. (Usually the bond is between the mother and child, although occasionally it may be between the child and someone else—father, grandparent.)

Think for a moment of what you have read about infants, especially their rapid brain and cognitive development. Infants take in information, and some of this information concerns how others, especially their mothers, treat them. Although they may not grasp the significance of what's going on around them, infants can understand the quality of their treatment. It is what Erikson has called the time of trust, which means that children acquire confidence in themselves as well as others. The degree of trust acquired does not depend as much on nutrition and displays of love as it does on the quality of the parent-child relationship. Parents can encourage a sense of trust by responding sensitively to their infant's needs. Physical contact and comfort are crucial for trust to develop.

Gradually, as children master motor control, they learn to trust their bodies, thus increasing their psychological sense of security. With the aid of their parents, and their own growing competence, children begin to think of the world as a safe and orderly place. An infant's relationships usually begin with its mother and then extend to father, siblings, friends, and so on. We know now that the entire range of a child's relationships contributes to social development.

Growing knowledge about the emergence of relationships, how they change, and how they affect development has become a key component of developmental research. For example, everyone in your family is a unique individual, a quite different personality. While growing up one child might have been exceptionally active, whereas another was shy and quiet. These temperamental differences caused your parents to treat each of you differently.

To help us untangle this important network, in this chapter we'll first present several basic ideas about relationships (such as the active role that infants play in their own development). We'll then analyze the meaning of relationships: What are they and what do they consist of? Next, we'll examine the source of those first relationships and how they develop and influence later relationships. Finally, we'll explore the research on attachment that has attracted so much attention these past few years. Let's begin by looking at several basic ideas about relationships.

After reading this chapter, you should be able to

- Describe how theory and research have contributed to our understanding of relationships.

- Assess the role of reciprocal interactions in any relationship.

- Distinguish the characteristics of a relationship.

- Identify the givens in a relationship.

- Trace the origins of relationships.

- Evaluate the significance of the parent-infant relationship.

- Analyze the impact of attachment on psychosocial development.

Have the relationships you developed over the years helped or hindered you? That is, did your friends cause you to get into trouble? Did any of your friends help you in school? Did any friends help you in important choices you have made?

Infants immediately begin to take in information from their environment, and mothers are an important source of this information. From mothers, infants begin to develop a sense of how the world will treat them.

Relationships and Development

Consider for a moment all that a single relationship incorporates: *Physical aspects* of development such as walking, running, and playing with a peer; *language aspects*, which enable youngsters to share one anothers' lives; *cognitive aspects*, which allow them to understand one another; *emotional aspects*, which permit them to make a commitment to another; and *social aspects*, which reflect both socialization and individuation.

All of these features combine as youngsters interact with a remarkable variety of individuals, from those first crucial days with parents to later interactions with siblings, other family members, peers, teachers, and many others. Children continue to widen their circle of relationships as they grow. Our concern here, however, is with the origin of relationships in infancy, a concern that has grown out of the changing view of infancy we discussed. For example, how has the changing view of infancy we discussed in chapter 5 led to the current interest in the role of relationships? Let's briefly review several of the developmental concepts we discussed previously that have contributed to a greater understanding of how relationships develop.

Background of the Relationship Research

One of the major reasons for the interest in relationships is that developmental psychologists became dissatisfied with studying "the relationship" between mother and child. Greater precision was demanded: What do we know about the content of the interactions between mother and child? Can we study the quality of these interactions? Is it possible to determine the mother's commitment to the relationship? What does relationship mean?

Another important influence on relationship research has been the acceptance of a reciprocal interaction (or a *transactional* model) of development, which recognizes the child's active role in its development (Brazelton, 1984, 1987; Brazelton & Cramer, 1990). As defined previously, *reciprocal interactions* means that I do something to the baby and the baby changes; as a result of the infant's change, I change; the process continues indefinitely. The unique temperamental distinctions that infants display at birth cause unique parental reactions. For example, the easy or difficult infant has a decided impact on parents. Visualizing how parents respond differently to a crying or cooing infant doesn't take much effort. (See chapter 1.)

When parents change their behavior according to their child's behavior, they signal pleasure, rejection, or uncertainty about what their child is doing. Children act on their parents and change the parents; these changes are then reflected in how parents treat their children. The tone of the interactions between children and parents assumes a definite structure that will characterize the relationship for the coming years. Figure 6.1 illustrates the back-and-forth reaction of parents and their children.

Figure 6.1
Transactional analysis, or reciprocal interactions

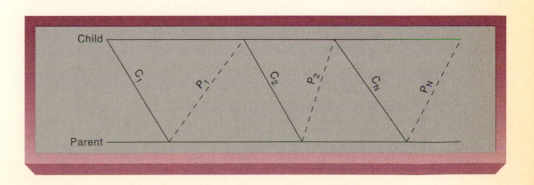

Remember: In any adult-child interactions, infants also exercise some control over the interactions. We, as adults, respond to infants partly because of the way that they have responded to us. An infant's staring, cooing, smiling, and kicking can all be employed to maintain the interactions. Thus these early interactions establish the nature of the relationship between parent and child, giving it a particular tone or style.

A MULTICULTURAL VIEW

Different Cultures, Different Interactions

In a thoughtful review of the literature analyzing minority infants (African American, Hispanic American, Asian American, Native American, Alaskan native, and Pacific Islander), Garcia-Coll (1990) notes that during the first three years of life, infants develop those psychomotor, cognitive, and psychosocial skills that enable them to become accepted members of their cultural and social systems. Because of their families' backgrounds, minority infants are exposed to unique experiences that can influence their developmental outcomes in ways not yet understood.

Parents from a particular culture share a common system of beliefs, values, practices, and behaviors that differ from those of parents in other cultures. Parents from different cultural backgrounds differ in their views of infant competence, how to respond to crying, and what developmental skills are most significant (Garcia-Coll, 1990). Consequently, infants are subject to different parental behaviors that are shaped by a particular culture.

Many interactions between parents and their infants are universal, such as baby talk, facial expressions, and play. Behaviors such as baby talk are so common that a

mother's behavior may seem infantile. Many other maternal behaviors, however, are not that common. Eye contact and face-to-face talk are avoided in some cultures (Field, 1990). Specific examples include Chisholm's study (1983) of the use of cradle boards with Navajo infants. The arousal level and activity level of these infants seems to be lower than infants from other cultures, which affects mother-infant interactions. Mother-infant interactions are fewer and less intense. Chisholm (1983) also found that Navajo infants have fewer contacts with strangers and are less fearful of them in the first year than Caucasian infants, but the pattern reverses in the second year.

Studying mother-infant interactions of 51 low-socioeconomic-status Mexican American mothers in the Los Angeles area, Zepeda (1986) discovered that tactile stimulation was used more frequently than vocalizations. This study is consistent with other findings that the early interactions of Mexican American mothers with their infants are mainly nonverbal. These differences in parental behaviors may have important developmental outcomes, but as yet research has not provided specific answers.

Can you think of times when you exhibited sensitive responsiveness (even before you knew the meaning of the term)? Did you react in a particular way to a child because you recognized something different in that child's behavior?

Sensitive responsiveness
Refers to the ability to recognize the meaning of a child's behavior.

A third influence evident in studying relationships, the recognition that mothers react differently to different children, has introduced the concept of sensitive responsiveness. For example, we now know that babies are temperamentally different at birth. An example of **sensitive responsiveness** would be that although most infants like to be held, some dislike physical contact. How will a mother react to an infant who stiffens and pulls away, especially if previous children liked being held? This research has contributed to a greater understanding of the role of relationships in development.

We know now that children are temperamentally different at birth and instantly tune in to their environment. They give clues to their personalities so that a mother's and father's responses to their child's signals must be appropriate for *that* child. As Isabella (1993) has noted, maternal sensitivity is an all-important characteristic of reciprocal interactions that is consistently linked to attachment security.

The final influence came when investigators realized that, from birth, children are active processors of information. *Active processors of information* means that children don't only react to stimuli; they see and hear at birth and immediately begin the task of regulating their environment. They fight to control their breathing, and they struggle to balance digestion and elimination. But brief, calm periods appear after birth when infants take in information from the surrounding world. These fleeting but significant periods are the foundation for the appearance of key developmental milestones during the infancy period.

Infants are ready to respond to social stimulation. It is not only a matter of responding passively; infants in their own way can initiate social contacts. Many of their actions (such as turning toward their mothers or gesturing in their direction) are forms of communication. Hinde (1987), too, notes that the interchange between infants and their environments is an active one. Those around infants try to attract their attention, but the babies actively select from these adult actions. In other words, infants begin to structure their own relationships according to their individual temperaments.

We can usually label relationships, using adjectives such as warm, cold, rejecting, and hostile. But we must be cautious. Any relationship may be marked by apparently contradictory interactions. A mother may have a warm relationship with her child as evidenced by hugging and kissing, but she may also scold when scolding is needed for the child's protection. *To understand the relationship, we must understand the interactions.*

WHAT'S YOUR VIEW?

INITIAL ENCOUNTERS: SIGNIFICANT OR FLEETING?

We cannot exaggerate the importance of the initial encounters that infants have with the adults around them. In a particularly significant study that was one of the first to focus on the lingering effects of these early interactions, Osofsky (1976, 1987) examined the link between neonatal characteristics and early mother-infant relations in 134 mothers and their 2- to 4-day-old infants.

Osofsky observed the infants at a scheduled feeding and in a 15-minute stimulation situation, during which the mothers presented tasks from the Brazelton Neonatal Assessment Scale to their children. The infants were next evaluated (between 2 and 4 days of age) using the full Brazelton scale.

A particularly significant finding showed that the overall pattern of interactions indicates consistent maternal and infant styles that appear soon after birth. Infants who were highly responsive during the Brazelton assessment were also highly responsive during the stimulation periods. Osofsky also found strong correlations between the mother's stimulation and the child's responsiveness: More sensitive mothers have more responsive infants.

Again, note the evidence supporting the importance of the mother-infant interactions. Osofsky concluded that both infant and mother contribute to the style of the relationship. With the pattern of interactions formed almost from birth, a clearly defined relationship is set that will undoubtedly shape the course of social development. Do you agree with Osofsky's conclusion that the early mother-infant relationship shapes future relationships? What's your view?

Once developmental psychologists accepted these four views, investigations into bonding, attachment, first relationships, and peer relationships could be subjected to more precise and meaningful analysis. With this background, we can now turn to an analysis of the role of relationships in development. First, however, just what do we mean by relationships?

🌳 Guided Review 🌳

1. Beginning at _____ children begin the task of regulating their environment.

2. Infants begin to structure their relationships according to their individual temperaments. This is also known as _____ processing of information.

3. A child's first relationship is usually with his or her _____ .

4. An adult's appropriate response to an infant is called _____ _____ .

5. The new model of looking at all aspects of development is known as the _____ model.

Answers

1. birth   2. active   3. mother   4. sensitive responsiveness   5. biopsychosocial

The Meaning of Relationships

Think for a moment about your friends. What type of relationship do you have with them? with your parents? with a husband or wife? with a child? Now consider this classic definition of a relationship.

> ■ A relationship implies a pattern of intermittent interactions between two people involving interchanges over an extended period of time. (Hinde, 1979, p. 14)

Interactions

Behaviors involving two or more people.

If you have a true relationship with someone, that relationship has continuity. That is, you can continue to maintain a relationship with a friend you have not seen for years. An extended series of **interactions,** however, does not necessarily constitute a relationship. The cashier you frequently see at the supermarket, the attendant at the gas station, the receptionist at your dentist's office with whom you exchange pleasantries—none of these become partners in a relationship. If the interactions are nothing more than an exchange of money and a thank you, they cannot be classified as relationships.

Although the history of the interactions defines a relationship, it is still more than the sum of these interactions. In a relationship, the interactions are integrated differently from the separate interactions. It isn't just a matter of saying "Good morning. Isn't it a nice day?" to the cashier. A relationship also involves your perceptions, your mental picture, and your feelings for the other person. What one says or does is significant, but how the partner perceives and judges that behavior is even more important.

These ideas help us to understand the developing relationship between parents and infants. We think today that infants "tune into" their environment from birth. Thus they react to far more than their parents' behavior; the quality of the interactions instantly begins to establish the nature of the relationship.

The Characteristics of a Relationship

Hinde (1979, 1987), a noted investigator of the role of relationships in development, has identified eight categories that are useful for analyzing relationships: the content of interactions, the diversity of interactions, the qualities of interactions, the relative frequency and patterning of interactions, reciprocity versus complementarity, intimacy, interpersonal perception, and commitment. Table 6.1 describes the meanings of these categories.

The value of Hinde's classification is that we no longer need to be satisfied with just observing the mother-infant relationship. We can now examine specific features of the relationship (content, quality, etc.), study them, conduct research, and determine how, or if, these eight categories are integrated. Hinde's categories are also valuable for discovering just what might be wrong in a relationship. This work promises to help us achieve much deeper insights into the dynamics of relationships.

Understanding relationships is a critical issue for developmental psychology because relationships affect individual characteristics (e.g., maternal practices and a child's behavior) differently at different stages of development. Fear, for example, may develop because of a parent's reaction to thunder and lightning, which a child may outgrow with increasing experience (Hinde, 1992).

The Givens in a Relationship

In the mother-infant (or father-infant) relationship, both individuals bring to the relationship physical and biological characteristics ranging from appearance to hereditary endowment—the givens in any relationship. Since we have previously discussed genetic contribution, here we can focus on personal characteristics, such as personal appearance and temperament.

Table 6.1	Categories of Interactions
Category	**Meaning**
1. Content	a. What the partners do together. b. May distinguish different relationships—mother-child, father-child. c. Enables us to label the relationship.
2. Diversity	a. Indicates the types of interactions making up the relationship. b. The number of things mother and child do together contributes to infant's understanding of others.
3. Quality	a. Not only what partners are doing but also how they are doing it. b. A mother may handle an infant gently or roughly.
4. Relative frequency and patterning of interactions	a. Frequency of interactions but in relation to other types of interactions. b. A pattern of warm interactions may demand hugging and scolding.
5. Reciprocity versus complementarity	a. Doing the same things simultaneously or taking turns. Children's play is an example of reciprocity. b. Interactions are complementary when they are different yet blend together, such as a mother changing or feeding an infant.
6. Intimacy	a. Extent to which partners are prepared to reveal themselves to each other—probably never totally. b. Meaningless for infants, but changes quickly with development.
7. Interpersonal perception	a. How the partners see each other. b. Since our sense of self is shaped by reactions of others, the importance of first relationships is clearly evident.
8. Commitment	a. Acceptance of relationship—infant and child have little choice. or b. Decision to work toward continuing a particular relationship.

Personal Appearance

Have you ever reacted to a child because of the way that child appeared? How would you evaluate that type of behavior now?

Physical appearance has a powerful effect on a relationship. For good or ill, physical appearance affects how others react to us. Attractiveness is as important for infants as it is for adults (Ritter & Langlois, 1988).

You know how appealing the mere sight of a happy baby can be. Their facial expressions and the shape of their features are attractive to most people and help to ensure an infant's survival, given their immaturity and helplessness. The appearance of a sick baby generates concern. We almost instinctively react to their distress. We respond in yet a different manner to an unhappy, crying baby. Tired, frustrated parents may find it difficult to react positively, tending instead to be abrupt and stiff with the baby. Again, an infant's appearance structures our interactions. From what we know of a baby tuning into its environment, we can understand how easily appearance can affect those first relationships.

The first mother-infant interactions quickly establish the style and tone of the relationship. If the infant's physical attractiveness alters the interactions, sensitive responsiveness becomes a matter of prime concern. Given the importance of reciprocal interactions, mothers can initiate a relationship in which an infant quickly realizes that something is wrong with the quality of the interactions.

As babies begin to interact with their mothers, a pattern for future relationships is established. The more diverse the interactions that a baby engages in with its mother, the richer the relationship becomes.

Temperament
A child's basic personality, which is now thought to be discernible soon after birth.

New York Longitudinal Study
Long-term study by Chess and Thomas of the personality characteristics of children.

Easy children
Term used to describe calm, relaxed children; associated with Chess and Thomas.

Difficult children
Term to describe restless, irritable children; associated with Chess and Thomas.

Slow-to-warm-up children
Term used to describe children with low intensity of reactions; may be rather negative when encountering anything new.

Temperament

Temperament is an individual's unique behavioral style in interacting with the environment, which immediately begins to structure infants' relationships with those around them. Goldsmith and Campos (1990) viewed temperament as individual differences in tendencies to express the primary emotions, which helps to explain an infant's behavioral patterns. Thus temperament is a critical personality trait, especially in the first days and weeks after birth.

Today's acceptance of the importance of temperament reflects the basic work of Chess and Thomas (1987), who believed that in the first half of the twentieth century psychologists overemphasized the role of the environment in development. These authors were struck by the individuality of their own children in the days immediately following birth, differences that could not be attributed to the environment.

To test their hypothesis, Chess and Thomas designed a longitudinal study called the **New York Longitudinal Study.** In 1956 they began collecting data on 141 middle-class children. They observed the behavioral reactions of infants, determined their persistence, and attempted to discover how these behavioral traits interacted with specific elements in the infants' environments. From the resulting data they found nine characteristics that could be reliably scored as high, medium, or low:

- The level and extent of motor activity

- The rhythmicity, or degree of regularity, of functions such as eating, sleeping, and elimination

- The response to a new object or person (approach versus withdrawal)

- Adaptability of behavior to environmental changes

- Sensitivity to stimuli

- Intensity of responses

- General mood or disposition (friendly or unfriendly)

- Degree of distractibility

- Attention span and persistence in an activity

These ratings provided a behavioral profile that was apparent in the children by 2 or 3 months of age. Certain characteristics clustered with sufficient frequency for the authors to identify three general types of temperament:

- **Easy children,** characterized by regularity of bodily functions, low or moderate intensity of reactions, and acceptance of, rather than withdrawal from, new situations (40% of the children)

- **Difficult children,** characterized by irregularity in bodily functions, intense reaction, and withdrawal from new stimuli (10% of the children)

- **Slow-to-warm-up children,** characterized by a low intensity of reactions and a somewhat negative mood (15% of the children)

The authors were able to classify 65 percent of the infants, leaving the others with a mixture of traits that defied categorization. Knowing what kind of temperament their child has can help parents to adjust their style (way of doing things) to their child's. This can be a distinct advantage in forming positive parent-child relationships. The Thomas and Chess work suggests that infants immediately bring definite temperamental characteristics to the mother-infant relationship, characteristics that do much to shape those critical initial interactions.

The Origins of Temperament. Temperament appears to have a constitutional component that is observable, at least partially, during the first few days of life. Results of the *Colorado Adoption Project*, which compared adopted and nonadopted children, showed a genetic influence on temperament (Plomin & others, 1988). Twin studies also illustrate the immediate appearance of temperament. For example, Matheny (1980), in the *Louisville Twin Study*, studied twin temperament and discovered differences at each age among the nonidentical twins. But Matheny found in his work with identical twins that they were remarkably alike in temperamental characteristics at all ages.

In another significant twin study, Torgersen (1982) studied the nine categories of temperament identified by Thomas and Chess in a sample of 53 same-sex twins at 2 and 9 months. The mothers were also asked about similarities and differences between their twins. All temperamental variables for the identical twins at both ages were more similar than those for the nonidentical twins, with more marked similarities at 9 months.

Torgersen (1982) next reported a follow-up study of the same twins at 6 years of age. Again using eight of the categories proposed by Thomas and Chess, Torgersen found the identical twins to be more alike than the nonidentical. Summarizing the data, Torgersen stated that temperament showed a strong genetic thrust in infancy, and at 6 years of age, a genetic influence was still evident in many of the categories.

The ongoing *MacArthur Longitudinal Twin Study*, designed to study more than 330 same-sex twin pairs, has initially reported genetic influences on individual differences at 14 months of age; for example, behavioral inhibition and observed shyness showed a significant genetic influence (Emde & others, 1992).

As Kagan (1992) noted, given the individual differences in the biochemistry of the brain, it is little wonder that a child could be vulnerable to either sadness or anxiety. Thus, evidence continues to suggest a genetic role in temperament, with all that implies for the mother-infant relationship (Saudino & Eaton, 1991). What are some implications of these temperamental differences, and how do they influence parent-child relationships?

Goodness of fit

Compatibility between parental and child behavior; how well parents and their children get along.

Goodness of Fit. Compatibility between parental and child behavior introduces the concept of **goodness of fit.** As Chess and Thomas (1987) searched for some unifying theme to explain why a child's development was proceeding smoothly or not, they found that a goodness of fit existed when the demands and expectations of parents were compatible with their child's temperament. Goodness of fit signifies the match between the properties of the environment with its expectations and demands, and the child's capacities, characteristics, and style of behaving. Poorness of fit exists when parental demands and expectations are excessive and not compatible with a child's temperament, abilities, and other characteristics. Poorness of fit produces stress and is often marked by developmental problems (Chess & Thomas, 1987). A simple way of phrasing this concept is to ask parents and their children how they get along together.

To help parents avoid the stress and developmental problems associated with poorness of fit, Thomas and Chess designed intervention programs to alter the nature of the parent-child relationship to one more closely approximating goodness of fit. For intervention to be successful, parents need to be reassured that nothing is wrong with their behavior (if this is the case). With a child of a different temperament, they might have done quite well.

Parents need to be aware of the link between temperament and an infant's early behavior. For example, Vaughn and associates (1992) attempted to discover any association between security of attachment and an infant's temperament. They studied 555 children ranging in age from 5 months to 42 months and found a significant relationship between temperament and attachment at all ages. These researchers conclude that attachment and temperament are not isolated entities but influence each other.

Although goodness of fit established in infancy produces a good beginning for a child, no guarantee exists that this fit between parental demands and expectations and a child's temperament and capacities will last (Chess & Thomas, 1987). Children change and so do their parents' expectations, and as relationships become more complex (e.g., during adolescence) the goodness of fit may also change. For example, the parents of an infant with a low threshold for stimulation—a door closing or a light coming on may disturb her—may have adapted to her temperament. Later in school, however, the child may need extra time for homework or lose attention during a long lesson. Unless such environmental demands are made in light of the child's temperament, the goodness of fit could rapidly deteriorate.

YOUR VIEW?

WHAT'S

ATTRACTIVE OR UNATTRACTIVE— DOES IT MATTER?

In an interesting experiment, Langlois and associates (1991) demonstrated that infants discriminate among adult female faces on the basis of attractiveness. These findings were surprising to many, because infants were not expected to make such subtle discriminations (Langlois & others, 1991). In addition, most researchers believed that children only gradually learn what their culture has identified as "attractive."

Working with 60 infants who were 6 months old, the researchers presented them with color slides of 16 adult males and 16 adult females. Half of the slides of each sex were attractive; half were unattractive. (Attractiveness and unattractiveness were rated by 40 undergraduate men and women.) The infants consistently looked longer at the faces judged to be attractive.

In a second phase of their study, Langlois and her colleagues used the faces of black adult women as stimuli. They tested 43 infants who were 6 months old. Both black and white adults rated 16 slides for attractiveness and unattractiveness. The infants looked longer at the faces of attractive black women. In the final phase of their study, the researchers used slides of attractive and unattractive babies as stimuli for 52 six-month-old infants. Once again, the infants preferred the more attractive faces.

The results from these studies showed that infants discriminate attractive from unattractive and that they prefer the attractive faces of diverse types (Langlois & others, 1991). What is particularly interesting about these studies is that the infants treated attractive faces as distinctive regardless of sex, color, or age. They reacted this way although most of the infants had little experience with some of the types of faces they viewed and little idea of what their culture considered attractive or unattractive. These infants were clearly demonstrating visual preference.

Using the concept of reciprocal interactions to explain how both partners influence a relationship raises the question: What do adults think about the attractiveness of infants? Less attractive and older-appearing infants are trapped in a vicious cycle of unrealistic expectations and apparently immature behavior. Their failure to behave as expected only increases negative evaluations by adults. Studying adult responses to infant attractiveness, Ritter, Casey, and Langlois (1991) found that adults thought that attractive infants were younger than they actually were. They also assumed unattractive infants were older than they actually were, which led them to expect more advanced behaviors from these infants. Do you agree that attractiveness can affect the relationships between children and adults? What's your view?

Having considered the nature and givens of relationships, we can now ask, what is the source of the interactions that lead to social relationship? How do an infant's first relationships develop?

Guided Review

6. Hinde argues for _____ categories of interactions in a relationship.

7. _____ and her colleagues demonstrated that infants discriminate among adult female faces on the basis of attractiveness.

8. _____ is an individual's behavioral style in interacting with the environment.

9. Compatibility between parental and child behavior is known as _____ _____ _____ .

10. The _____ of interactions is characterized not only by what the partners are doing but also how they are doing it.

Answers

6. eight   7. Langlois   8. Temperament   9. goodness of fit   10. quality

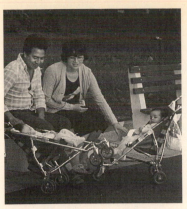

As the number of relationships within the family increases, the interactions among family members grow dramatically. Parents, employing the concept of "sensitive responsiveness," engage in reciprocal interactions with their children, thus influencing the path of psychosocial development.

First Relationships

In an intriguing statement about how early relationships develop, Brazelton and Cramer (1990) stated:

> For all parents-to-be, three babies come together at the moment of birth. The imaginary child of their dreams and fantasies and the invisible but real fetus, whose particular rhythms and personality have been making themselves increasingly evident for several months now, merge with the actual newborn baby who can be seen, heard, and finally held close. The attachment to a newborn is built on prior relationships with an imaginary child, and with the developing fetus which has been part of the parents' world for nine months. (p. 3)

These interactions help infants to form their first relationships and influence how they relate to others. But how do these first relationships actually begin?

How Do Children Develop Relationships?

Infants typically react by general states of excitement and distress, which swiftly focus on the mother as infants recognize their mothers as sources of relief and satisfaction. Mothers rapidly discriminate their infants' cries: for hunger, attention, or fright. Thus infants learn to direct their attention to their mothers. Once the pattern is established, infants begin to evaluate the emerging interactions.

Three motives seem to be at work:

- *Bodily needs*—food, for example—lead to a series of interactions that soon become a need for social interaction. But these basic bodily needs are not the only source of the need for interactions. If you have ever witnessed mother-infant interactions during feeding, you may have been amazed by the infant's intensity in satisfying a basic need. Yet if you move to a position where the infant can see you, the baby may momentarily stop sucking to attend to the novel sight.

- *Psychological needs* can cause infants to interrupt one of their most important functions, such as feeding. Consequently, in regard to the origin of relationships, the satisfaction of bodily needs is only the beginning. Children, from birth, seem to seek novelty; they require increasingly challenging stimulation. For infants, adults become the source of information as much as the source of bodily need satisfaction.

- *Adult response needs*. The preceding two needs alone are inadequate to explain why, for most of us, relationships with other people are the most important part of our lives. Adults, usually mothers, satisfy needs, provide stimulation, and initiate communication, thus establishing the basis for future social interactions.

The Developmental Sequence

These three influences at work during the infant's early days—bodily need satisfaction, a search for novelty, and adult responses to their overtures—form a basis for the appearance of social interactions similar to the following sequence.

- During the first three weeks of life, infants are not affected much by an adult's appearance. The only exception, as noted, is during feeding periods.

Figure 6.2

The origin and development of relationships

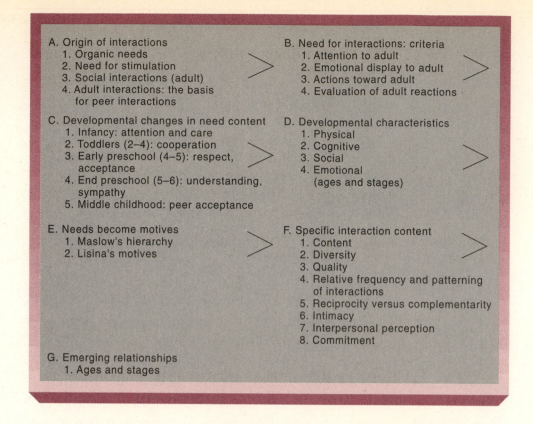

A. Origin of interactions
  1. Organic needs
  2. Need for stimulation
  3. Social interactions (adult)
  4. Adult interactions: the basis for peer interactions

B. Need for interactions: criteria
  1. Attention to adult
  2. Emotional display to adult
  3. Actions toward adult
  4. Evaluation of adult reactions

C. Developmental changes in need content
  1. Infancy: attention and care
  2. Toddlers (2–4): cooperation
  3. Early preschool (4–5): respect, acceptance
  4. End preschool (5–6): understanding, sympathy
  5. Middle childhood: peer acceptance

D. Developmental characteristics
  1. Physical
  2. Cognitive
  3. Social
  4. Emotional
     (ages and stages)

E. Needs become motives
  1. Maslow's hierarchy
  2. Lisina's motives

F. Specific interaction content
  1. Content
  2. Diversity
  3. Quality
  4. Relative frequency and patterning of interactions
  5. Reciprocity versus complementarity
  6. Intimacy
  7. Interpersonal perception
  8. Commitment

G. Emerging relationships
  1. Ages and stages

- From about the beginning of the fourth week, infants begin to direct actions at the adults. Emotional reactions also appear at this time, with obvious signs of pleasure at the sight and sound of adults, especially females.

- During the second month, more complex and sensitive reactions emerge, such as smiling and vocalizations directed at the mother, plus animated behavior during interactions.

- By 3 months of age, the infant has formed a need for social interactions. That need continues to grow and be nourished by adults until the end of the second or beginning of the third year, when a need for peer interactions develops (Lisina, 1983).

Figure 6.2 illustrates the sequence by which the first interactions, combined with developmental changes, gradually lead to specific relationships.

AN APPLIED VIEW
The Significance of the Mother-Infant Interaction

In a series of sensitive statements describing mother-infant interactions, Stern (1977, 1985) identified certain characteristics that both mothers and infants bring to the relationship.

The Caregiver's Repertoire

- *Facial expressions.* Facial expressions such as smiling, frowning, showing sympathy, and demonstrating surprise all have social consequences: They are intended to encourage the relationship or, with some mothers and their infants, to avoid interacting.
- *Vocalizations.* Mothers typically exaggerate their speech to their infants and vary its speed. These early speech behaviors seem to have as much a bonding function as they are an effort to convey information.
- *Gaze.* Mothers and infants gaze at each other for relatively long periods, sometimes introducing vocalizations. These behaviors also further the relationship.
- *Face presentations and head movements.* Peek-a-boo and all its variations seem to have both emotional and cognitive consequences: Infants enjoy them and learn from them.

The Infant's Repertoire

- *Facial expressions.* From the time of Darwin, the variety and revealing nature of facial expressions have impressed investigators. Conveying a range of emotions from pleasure to displeasure, infants communicate with those around them, firmly establishing a pattern of human relatedness.
- *Gaze.* With steadily improving sight, infants include both people and objects as stimulation. When this occurs, the nature of interactions also

changes, since infants can now exercise more control over their partner.

As these early interactions commence, several characteristics begin to identify the emergence of a successful relationship (Brazelton & Cramer, 1990). The first of these is **synchrony,** which refers to the ability of parents to adjust their behavior to that of an infant. Immediately after birth, infants are mostly occupied by their efforts to regulate such systems as breathing and heart rate, which demands most of their energy and attention. Once parents recognize these efforts—the baby's "language" (Brazelton & Cramer, 1990)—they can use their own behavior to help their infants adapt to environmental stimuli. This mutual regulation of behavior defines synchrony.

Another characteristic is **symmetry,** which means that an infant's capacity for attention and style of responding influence any interactions. As Brazelton and Cramer (1990) note, in a symmetric dialogue parents recognize an infant's thresholds, that is, what and how much stimuli an infant can tolerate.

Other characteristics include **contingency,** which refers to the effects of a parent's behavior on the infant's state. **Entrainment** is a characteristic that identifies the rhythm that is established between a parent's and infant's behavior. For example, when the infant reaches toward the mother, the mother says something like, "Oh, yes, Timmy." The sequence involved in entrainment leads to playing games such as the mother making a face at the baby and the infant trying to respond similarly. Once infants realize that they have a share in controlling the interactions (about 6 months of age), they begin to develop a sense of **autonomy.** With these interactions, infants are beginning to form relationships and learn about themselves.

Synchrony
The ability of parents to adjust their behavior to that of an infant.

Symmetry
An infant's capacity for attention and style of responding influence any interactions.

Contingency
The effects of a parent's behavior on the infant's state.

Entrainment
Term used to describe the rhythm that is established between a parent and an infant's behavior.

Autonomy
Infants realize that they have a share in controlling their interactions with others.

As the interactions between mother and child increase and become more complex, an attachment develops between the two. With the preceding ideas in mind, we can turn now to the special topic of attachment.

Guided Review

11. Infants' interactions with their mothers are motivated by three categories of needs: _____ , _____ , _____ .

12. _____ is the ability of parents to adjust their behavior to that of an infant.

13. The need for peer interactions develops at the end of the _____ year.

14. Infants' capacity for attention and style of responding that influences their interactions is called _____ .

15. The effects of a parent's behavior on an infant's state is _____ .

Answers
11. bodily, psychological, adult response   12. Synchrony   13. second   14. symmetry   15. contingency

Attachment

Because the roots of future relationships are formed during the first days of life, we may well ask, How significant is the mother-infant relationship in the minutes and hours after birth? We know that infants who develop a secure **attachment** to their mothers have the willingness and confidence to seek out future relationships. One of the first researchers to recognize the significance of relationships in an infant's life was John Bowlby.

Attachment

Behavior intended to keep a child (or adult) in close proximity to a significant other.

Both mother and child bring their own characteristics to the relationship (facial expressions, movements, vocalizations), and as they do, the interactions between the two become more complex and an attachment slowly develops between the two.

Bowlby's Work

The traditional notion of attachment was developed with great insight by John Bowlby (1969). Early in his professional career, Bowlby had been affected by the plight of children who had suffered negative family experiences (such as separation) early in life (Bretherton, 1992). This led to his basic premise: A warm, intimate relationship between mother and infant is essential to mental health because a child's need for its mother's presence is as great as its need for food. A mother's continued absence can generate a sense of loss and feelings of anger. (In his 1969 classic, *Attachment*, Bowlby stated quite clearly that an infant's principal attachment figure can be someone other than the natural mother.)

Background of Attachment Theory

Bowlby and his colleagues, especially James Robertson, initiated a series of studies in which children aged 15 to 30 months who had good relationships with their mothers experienced separation from them. A predictable sequence of behaviors followed.

- *Protest*, the first phase, may begin immediately and persist for about one week. Loud crying, extreme restlessness, and rejection of all adult figures mark an infant's distress.

- *Despair*, the second phase, follows immediately. The infant's behavior suggests a growing hopelessness: monotonous crying, inactivity, and steady withdrawal.

- *Detachment*, the final phase, appears when an infant displays renewed interest in its surroundings, a remote, distant kind of interest. Bowlby describes the behavior of this final phase as apathetic, even if the mother reappears.

From observation of many similar cases, Bowlby defined attachment as follows:

■ Attachment behavior is any form of behavior that results in a person attaining or maintaining proximity to some other clearly identified individual who is conceived as better able to cope with the world. It is most obvious when the person is frightened, fatigued, or sick, and is assuaged by comforting and care-giving. At other times the behavior is less in evidence. (1982, p. 668)

Bowlby also believed that while attachment is most obvious in infancy and early childhood, it can be observed throughout the life cycle. Table 6.2 presents a chronology of attachment behavior.

Table 6.2	Chronology of Attachment Development	
Age	**Characteristics**	**Behavior**
4 months	Perceptual discrimination; visual tracking of mother	Smiles and vocalizes more with mother than anyone else; begins to manifest distress at separation
9 months	Separation anxiety, stranger anxiety	Cries when mother leaves; clings at appearance of strangers (mother is primary object)
2–3 years	Intensity and frequency of attachment behavior remains constant; increase in perceptual range changes circumstances that elicit attachment	Notices impending departure, signaling a better understanding of surrounding world
3–4 years	Growing confidence; tendency to feel secure in a strange place with subordinate attachment figures (relatives)	Begins to accept mother's temporary absence; plays *with* other children
4–10 years	Less intense attachment behavior but still strong	May hold parent's hand while walking; anything unexpected causes child to turn to parent
Adolescence	Weakening attachment to parents; peers and other adults become important	Becomes attached to groups and group members
Adult	Attachment bond still discernible	In difficulty, adults turn to trusted friends; elderly direct attachment toward younger generation

Source: From John Bowlby, "Attachment and Loss: Retrospect and Prospect" in *American Journal of Orthopsychiatry,* 52:664–678. Reprinted, with permission, from the American Journal of Orthopsychiatry. Copyright © 1982 by the American Orthopsychiatric Association, Inc.

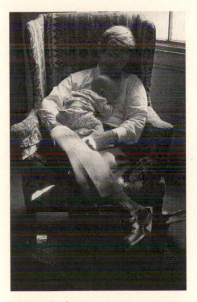

Although the interactions between a mother and her child and a father and his child may appear quite different, a child will attach to both mother and father.

Think of instances in which you saw a child stay close to one parent even when the other parent was present. Do you think this is an example of a hierarchy of attachment behaviors?

Other Explanations of Attachment

Bowlby's is not the only explanation of attachment. As you might expect from your reading of the developmental theories in chapter 2, other theorists have commented on the appearance of attachment.

- *Psychoanalytic theorists,* following Freud, hold that infants become attached to those who provide them oral satisfaction. Thus infants attach to their mothers because mothers usually feed them. Erikson, while accepting the traditional psychoanalytic interpretation of the importance of feeding, also believed that a developing sense of trust between mother and infant contributed to attachment between the two.

- *Behaviorists,* following Skinner, emphasize the importance of reinforcement. For behaviorists, feeding is only one form of reinforcement and not terribly important. Physical contact, comforting, and appropriate types of stimulation (visual, vocal) are equally important. The total range of reinforcement parents or caregivers provide explains attachment.

- *Cognitive theorists,* following Piaget and Kohlberg, believe that attachment is more of an intellectual achievement involving cognitive concepts such as object permanence and a developing sense of competence.

Attachment Research

Ainsworth (1973, 1979; Ainsworth & Bowlby, 1991), who accepts Bowlby's theoretical interpretation of attachment, devised the strange situation technique to study attachment experimentally. Ainsworth defines attachment as follows:

■ The hallmark of attachment is behavior that promotes proximity to or contact with the specific figure or figures to whom the person is attached. Such proximity-and-contact-promoting behaviors are termed attachment behaviors. Included are signaling behavior (crying, smiling, vocalizing), orienting behavior such as looking, locomotions relative to another person (following, approaching), and active physical contact behavior (climbing up, embracing, clinging). (1973, p. 2)

These behaviors indicate attachment only when they are differentially directed to one or a few persons rather than to others. This is especially noticeable when infants first direct their attention to their mothers, which is the infant's way of initiating and maintaining interaction with its mother. Children also attempt to avoid separation from an attachment figure, particularly if faced with a frightening situation.

The Strange Situation Technique

To assess the quality of attachment by the strange situation technique, Ainsworth had a mother and infant taken to an observation room. The child was placed on the floor and allowed to play with toys. A stranger (female) then entered the room and began to talk to the mother. Observers watched to see how the infant reacted to the stranger and to what extent the child used the mother as a secure base. The mother then left the child alone in the room with the stranger; observers then noted how distressed the child became. The mother returned and the quality of the child's reaction to the mother's return was assessed. Next the infant was left completely alone, followed by the stranger's entrance, and then that of the mother. These behaviors were used to classify children as follows:

- *Group A infants (avoidantly attached)*, who rarely cried during separation and avoided their mothers at reunion. The mothers of these babies seemed to dislike or were indifferent to physical contact.

- *Group B infants (securely attached)*, who were secure and used the mother as a base from which to explore. Separation intensified their attachment behavior; they exhibited considerable distress, ceased their explorations, and at reunion sought contact with their mothers.

- *Group C infants (ambivalently attached)*, who manifested anxiety before separation and who were intensely distressed by the separation. Yet on reunion they displayed ambivalent behavior toward their mothers; they sought contact but simultaneously seemed to resist it.

Examining the nature of these mother-infant interactions, Ainsworth (1979) stated that feelings, close bodily contact, and face-to-face interactions seem to be equally important in the child's expectations of the mother's behavior.

Ainsworth also believed that attachment knows no geographic boundaries. Reporting on her studies of infant-mother attachment in Uganda, Ainsworth (1973) reported that of 28 infants she observed, 23 showed signs of attachment. She was impressed by the babies' initiative in attempting to establish attachment with their mothers and noted that the babies demonstrated this initiative even when no threat of separation or any condition that could cause anxiety existed. In tracing the developing pattern of attachment behavior, Ainsworth (1973) stated:

> ■ The baby did not first become attached and then show it by proximity-promoting behavior, but rather that these are the patterns of behavior through which attachment grows. (p. 35)

Ainsworth reported other studies conducted in Baltimore, Washington, and Scotland indicating that cultural influences may affect the ways in which different attachment behaviors develop. Nevertheless, although these studies used quite different subjects for their studies, all reported attachment behavior developing in a similar manner.

The Klaus and Kennell Studies

A different interpretation of attachment led some investigators to believe that the initial, intense contacts with the mother have a critical and long-lasting influence on a child's development. Two physicians, Marshall Klaus and John Kennell, both professors of pediatrics at Case Western Reserve University School of Medicine, conducted a series of studies (1976, 1983) concerning the impact of immediate post-birth experiences.

In Klaus and Kennell's initial work (1976), 14 mothers of newborns were given extended contact with their infants. Heat shields (a panel to provide heat) were placed over the mothers' beds, and the mothers were given their naked infants for 1 hour of the first two hours after birth and then for 5 hours on each of the next three days, for a total of 16 hours. Fourteen other mothers, matched for age, marital status, and socioeconomic status, received the more standard hospital treatment: They were shown the baby immediately after birth, six or seven hours later they briefly held the baby, and they fed their infants about every four hours.

Kennell controlled the conditions as tightly as possible. The women were randomly assigned to each group, given identical explanations for the study, provided with heat shields (both groups), and had no idea that the mother-infant contacts differed during the three days. The question that Klaus and Kennell pursued was: Did the differences in mother-infant contact cause differences in the later mother-child relationship?

One month after giving birth, all of the mothers returned to the hospital for an interview, a physical examination of the child, and a film of the mother feeding her infant. Klaus and Kennell reported that the extended-contact mothers touched their children more frequently, stood and watched the physical examination more closely, and seemed reluctant to leave their infants with anyone else. Returning at one year after birth for the infant's examination, the extended-contact mothers soothed their youngsters more when they cried. They also seemed to want to remain closer to their infants than the control mothers.

Two years after their child's birth, five mothers from each group were randomly selected and interviewed. The extended-contact mothers employed richer language with their children, using more words and asking more questions than the other mothers. When the children were 5 years old, Klaus and Kennell compared nine of the extended-contact children with ten of the control group children. Children of the extended-contact mothers had significantly higher IQs and higher scores on language tests. In other words, the extra 16 hours of contact during the first three days of life affected maternal behavior for at least one year after birth (possibly longer) and seemed to have important developmental consequences for the infant.

We should accept the conclusions of Klaus and Kennell with some reservations. Although the authors used careful techniques, one may want to question how different the mothers of the two groups were before the infants' births. Were some mothers more sensitive to their infant's reactions than others? Were the infants temperamentally different at birth, enough to cause different behavioral responses?

Fathers and Attachment

Although we have concentrated on the mother in our discussion of attachment, the father's role in the process has attracted growing interest. As fathers become more involved in child care (in the 1990s, about 90% of mothers will work full- or part-time), questions have arisen about an infant's attachment to both mother and father. Do infants react differently to each parent?

Commenting on the attachment between father and child, Bowlby (1988) noted that the patterns closely resembled those between mothers and their children. A finding that intrigued Bowlby was that no correlation existed between the attachment patterns for each parent; that is, an infant may have a secure attachment with the mother but not the father or with the father but not the mother.

Other comparisons between the attachment of infants to mothers and fathers support Bowlby's conclusions. For example, a study of 15-month-old Dutch infants showed that the attachment behaviors directed toward mothers and fathers were linked (Goossens & Van Ijzendoorn, 1990). This, and other studies, suggests that although the mother usually remains the primary attachment figure, both mother and father have the potential to induce attachment (Fox & others, 1991).

The interactions between a father and his child tend to be more physical than those between a mother and her child. The qualitatively different types of stimulation a child receives from each parent would seem to suggest implications for the staffing of day-care centers and preschool facilities.

We can summarize these findings by stating that at 7 or 8 months of age, when attachment behavior (as defined by Bowlby and Ainsworth) normally appears, infants are attached to both mothers and fathers and prefer either parent to a stranger. The evidence indicates, then, that fathers can establish a close and meaningful relationship with their infants immediately from birth (Cox & others, 1992; Phares, 1992).

Research has also focused on demonstrating the differences between mothers' and fathers' behavior (nurturant versus playful), the similarity between parental behaviors (both exhibit considerable sensitivity), and the amount of involvement in the infant's care. For example, fathers tend to engage in more exciting activities such as bouncing, lifting, and tossing their infants into the air. Mothers are more verbal, tend to provide toys, and play more conventional games (Sroufe & others, 1992).

In spite of fathers' increased involvement, most fathers still spend a limited amount of time with their infants and only occasionally are they involved with physical care. As you can tell from this brief summary, more research is needed to help us understand the dynamics of the interaction between fathers and their infants.

New Directions in Attachment Research

Several attachment topics are currently attracting considerable interest. The cognitive aspects of attachment have led to a closer scrutiny of how representations of a person's attachment history influence development. Studying 85 Icelandic children, Jacobsen, Edelstein, and Hofmann (1994) measured attachment representation at 7 years of age and then assessed cognitive functioning at 7, 9, 12, 15, and 17 years of age. They found that children with a secure attachment representation at age 7 did well on tests of concrete and formal operational thinking in childhood and adolescence. Those identified with an insecure-disorganized attachment representation at age 7 did poorly on cognitive tasks, especially deductive reasoning, in childhood and adolescence.

The intergenerational transmission of attachment patterns has also become a source of research interest. In other words, what are the internal models of attachment that influence how we treat our own children? Does deprivation in one generation lead to problems in the next? Evidence points to the reality of **intergenerational continuity,** that is, the connection between childhood experiences and adult parenting behavior. For example, studies have shown that children raised in unhappy or disrupted homes are more prone to unhappy marriages and divorce. A similar pattern has been found among parents who batter their children: These parents suffered seriously disturbed childhoods marked by neglect, rejection, or violence (Rutter, 1981).

In an attempt to discover if parental behaviors reach across generations, Ricks (1985) has examined the evidence from two perspectives: the impact of separation or disruption, and parental reports of their childhood attachments. Ricks was concerned with the time involved in these studies. Memory, for example, poses an obstacle because our current thinking, our present mood, and our present status may well affect our recall of the past. As Ricks (1985) asked: Do childhood memories accurately reflect childhood experiences?

With these cautions, Ricks then examined the separation and disruption studies. Two findings emerged:

- Separation from parents in the family of origin (i.e., the parents' original family) was related to problems in parenting.

- Separation in the family of origin seemed to be associated with marriage problems and with depression in the mother.

A key factor in intergenerational effects was disruption (parents remain together but fight and are basically unhappy). Mothers from disrupted families of origin did not manifest the warm relationships with their children that mothers from nondisrupted families manifested. Preschool children of mothers from disrupted families

Intergenerational continuity

Term used to describe the connection between childhood experiences and adult behavior.

had poorer language skills than youngsters whose mothers had not come from disrupted families. Disruption, divorce, or long-term separation in the mother's family of origin adversely affected the early attachment relationship.

In the second phase of her study, Ricks turned to the recollections that mothers had of their own relations with their parents. She consistently found significant relations between a mother's recollection of her childhood attachments and her present ability to serve as a secure base for her child. In the development of social relationships, those first bonds, the initial relationships, have a critical function that may carry across generations.

A link has also been discovered between the way a mother recalls her childhood experiences and the present quality of the relationship with her child. Studying 100 pregnant women, Fonagy, Steele, and Steele (1991) wanted to assess how the attachment experiences of these women affected attachment with their children at 1 year of age. They found that 75 percent of the women who had been securely attached now had securely attached children. Of the remaining mothers, 23 percent had insecurely attached children. The researchers conclude that the internal representations of childhood attachment seem to carry to the next generation.

This, in turn, has caused researchers to examine patterns of adult attachment. For example, parents were asked about their attachment relationships in childhood and how these early relations affected their own development (Main & Goldwyn, 1990). The attachment found in the adults corresponded to Ainsworth's categories we previously mentioned.

The attachment relationship among adults promises to provide insights into attachment across the lifespan. For example, those adults who described themselves as secure, avoidant, or ambivalent in their marital or romantic relationships also report different attachment patterns in the families of origin. Studies of adult attachment have also turned to the relationships between middle-aged children and their elderly parents, and to the relationships between siblings, to members of families with depression, families with maltreatment, those with children exhibiting behavior problems, and between fathers and children (Bretherton, 1992).

Guided Review

16. An early researcher into the significant relationships in an infant's life was
_____ .

17. Following separation from their mothers, Bowlby found a predictable sequence of behaviors: _____ , _____ , _____ .

18. Attachment characterized by separation or stranger anxiety usually begins at the age of _____ months.

19. Studies have shown that by _____ months of age, infants are attached to both parents.

20. _____ is known for her work in attachment across generations.

Early Emotional Development

As you read about the impact of attachment and early relationships on psychosocial development, you can understand how a child's emotional life is also affected. The study of emotions has had a checkered career in psychology. From the peaks of popularity, interest in emotions and their development plunged to the depths of neglect. Today we see once again a resurgence of enthusiasm for the study of emotional development.

Answers

16. Bowlby 17. protest, despair, detachment 18. 9 months 19. 8 20. Ricks

Signs of Emotional Development

Emotional development seems to move from the general (positive versus negative emotions) to the specific: General positive states differentiate into such emotions as joy and interest; general negative states differentiate into fear, disgust, or anger. These primary emotions emerge during the first six months. Sometime after 18 months of age (recall Piaget's explanation of cognitive development), secondary emotions appear, which are associated with a child's growing cognitive capacity for self-awareness. For emotions such as embarrassment to appear, a self system, which a child can use as a reference point, is necessary (Lewis, 1989).

One of the first signs of emotion is a baby's smile, which most parents immediately interpret as a sign of happiness. Two-month-old infants are often described as "smilers." Although smiles appear earlier, they lack the social significance of the smile that emerges at 6 weeks. Babies smile instinctively at faces—real or drawn—and this probably reflects the human tendency to attend to patterns. Infants gradually learn that familiar faces usually mean pleasure, and smiling at known faces commences as early as the fifth month. Smiling seems to be a key element in securing positive reinforcement from those around the infant.

Smiling has a developmental history and "for no reason" appears soon after birth (Kagan, 1984). These smiles are usually designated as "false" smiles because they lack the emotional warmth of the true smile. By the baby's third week, the human female voice elicits a brief, real smile. By the sixth week, the true social smile appears, especially in response to the human face. Babies smile at a conceptual age of 6 weeks, regardless of chronological age.

Why do infants smile? Several possible explanations are:

- Infants smile at human beings around them.

- Infants smile at any high-contrast stimuli, thus eliciting attention from those around them. The infant then links the human face with pleasure.

- Infants smile at discovering a relationship between their behavior and events in the external world.

These behaviors suggest that infants' emotions are much more organized than previously suggested. Tronick (1989) questioned how some infants become sad and withdrawn, whereas others become happy, curious, and affectionate. To answer this question and to understand emotional development, Tronick turned to the nature of infant-caretaker emotional communication, in which both are active participants. (Again, note the importance of understanding that development is an integrated process—physical, cognitive, social, and emotional—and how important reciprocal interactions are to healthy growth.)

To begin his analysis, Tronick noted that infants, like all of us, have multiple goals: interacting with others, maintaining proximity to attachment figures, establishing homeostatic control, among others. To attain these goals, infants process information about themselves; in other words, there is an almost immediate cognitive input. Infants who attain their goals acquire a positive emotional state that encourages them to engage in additional interactions. Infants who determine that their goals are not being met experience negative emotions and begin to withdraw from any additional interactions. Obviously, infants can't reach these objectives on their own; they are too immature and limited in their abilities. They can, however, engage in reciprocal interactions that motivate others to help them.

Interactions between an infant and, usually, its mother display both coordination and miscoordination. When miscoordination occurs—a mother misinterprets her child's behavior—the infant may turn away, frown, or whimper. Tronick labels these interactions as **interactive errors,** which can be corrected by **interactive repair,** thus returning the interactions to a positive state. Infants who consistently experience miscoordinated interactions gradually tend to distort their interactions with other people; they increasingly become more negative in their lifestyles. The nature of these interactions ultimately determines whether a child will be happy and cheerful, or sad and depressed.

This 3-month-old infant is responding to its mother's face by smiling. In these interactions we see the roots of a child's psychosocial development.

Interactive errors
Interactions between a mother and child that result in a miscoordination.

Interactive repair
Correcting negative interactions and returning them to a positive state.

First Feelings

As you can tell from this brief excursion into emotional development, recent interest has yet to be matched by hard evidence. But given the changes in developmental research that we've described in these first chapters, it can be only a matter of time before the path of emotional development becomes less obscure.

We have previously noted the current view of an infant as an active partner in development and have also described an infant's state with all of its meaning (Tronick, 1989). Today we are aware of the number of abilities an infant brings into the world. Using these insights, Greenspan and Greenspan (1985) have begun to probe into the origins of emotions. They believe that the six emotional milestones they have identified can lead to parental practices that will help infants to establish more satisfying relationships with others.

- *Birth to 3 months*. The Greenspans believe that the major features of this period are self-regulation and interest in the world. For normal infants, each of these tasks supports the other.

- *2 to 7 months*. This is the infant's time of falling in love. The baby begins to focus on its mother and is delighted by her appearance, voice, and actions.

- *3 to 10 months*. During these months, an infant attempts to develop intentional communication. It is a time of reciprocal interactions. The mother and infant are responding to each other's signals. When adults (usually the mother) respond to the baby's signals, the infant learns that its actions can cause a response.

- *9 to 18 months*. This is a time of dramatic observable achievements: standing, walking, talking. An organized sense of self begins to emerge. For example, when the mother returns to her infant, at this stage the baby may no longer look at her. An infant of this age may walk to the mother, touch her, and perhaps say a word or two. The baby has put together several behaviors in an organized manner.

- *18 to 36 months*. Called the time of creating emotional ideas, this is a period of rapid mental growth. Children can form images of the mother in her absence. They now link these cognitive capacities to the emotional world. They remember their mother's reading to them last night—why not tonight? They remember their father wrestling with them last night—why not tonight?

- *30 to 48 months*. The Greenspans believe that the emotional thinking of these months forms the basis for fantasy, reality, and self-esteem. In other words, children can use their ideas to form a cause-and-effect understanding of their own emotions.

Several theories have been proposed to explain emotional development.

Theories of Emotional Development: A Summary

An early theory of emotional development was proposed by Bridges (1930). She believed that neonates demonstrated only one type of emotion: general excitement. Bridges believed that as infants grow, specific positive and negative emotions appear: Distress is shown at 3 weeks, anger grows out of distress at 4 months, disgust follows anger at 5 months, and fear follows disgust at about 6 months. More recently, as researchers have observed specific emotions in the neonate, interest in Bridges' work has faded.

Other theorists (Izard & others, 1991), believed that infants demonstrate specific emotions. Using an infant's facial expressions as the basis for his work, Izard stated that emotions emerge as an infant needs them to adapt, and that emotional development follows a definite pattern:

- The newborn shows startle, interest, disgust, and distress.

- During the next four months anger, surprise, and joy appear.

- Fear and shyness emerge during the 6- to 12-month period.

Izard and his colleagues (1991) believed that emotions are the keystone of adaptation and the motivational component of personality and social relationships. Studying 114 mothers and their infants, these researchers found that the mothers' emotional experiences and emotional behavior predicted the quality of attachment: Those mothers who expressed positive emotions around their children had securely attached infants.

In a thoughtful statement about emotional development, Kagan (1984) stated that during the first three or four months infants display reactions that suggest emotions, but most likely these behaviors reflect some kind of internal change we as yet don't understand. For example, widening of the eyes and an increase in heart rate is often referred to as "surprise to novelty." Between 4 and 12 months of age, cognitive development (especially memory) helps infants to produce new emotional reactions. For example, unexpected events cause 8-month-old infants to show facial expressions of wariness, a cessation of playing, and perhaps crying (Kagan, 1984). As Kagan noted, during these first years, emotions are mainly caused by external events. If infants are securely attached and have begun to establish positive, emotionally rewarding relationships with those around them, their psychosocial development has had a promising start.

Guided Review

21. According to Izard, _____ are the keystones to and the motivational component of personality and social relationships.

22. One of the first signs of emotions is a baby's _____ .

23. An infant's smile appears soon after _____ .

24. The Greenspans have identified _____ emotional milestones in an infant's emotional development.

25. The Greenspans would describe the period of _____ to _____ months as a period of self-regulation and interest in the world.

Answers

21. emotions 22. smile 23. birth 24. six 25. birth, 3

🌳 CONCLUSION

The role of relationships in development has finally achieved a prominent place in our attempts to understand a child's growth. From the initial contacts with the mother to the ever-expanding network of siblings and peers at all ages, relationships exert a powerful and continuing influence on the direction of development.

We are slowly acquiring data about the function of relationships. For example,

we have seen how important and persistent are the first interactions with parents. They set a tone for future relationships and set the direction for social and emotional development. Recent research has led to significant findings about the quality of relationships.

In this chapter, you were asked to become familiar with the beginnings of relationships. As you continue your

reading and we move into the early childhood period, you'll consider the function of relationships in children's play and their first experiences with school. In middle childhood and adolescence, the effect of peer relationships becomes even more significant. For now, however, we turn our attention to early childhood.

🌳 CHAPTER HIGHLIGHTS

Relationships and Development

- Acceptance of the transactional model of development and the idea of sensitive responsiveness has helped us to understand how children form relationships.
- Infants, as active partners in their development, help to shape their relationships.

The Meaning of Relationships

- Analyzing relationships by a system of categories such as Hinde's helps to make both theory and research more precise.
- Certain characteristics such as appearance and temperament are intrinsic parts of any relationship.
- Appearance affects our initial impression of an individual.
- An infant's temperament immediately affects interactions with adults.

- The work of Chess and Thomas has helped us to understand the concept of goodness of fit—the match between an infant's and parents' temperaments.

First Relationships

- Developing relationships follow a sequence that incorporates all aspects of development: physical, cognitive, and psychosocial.

Attachment

- Bowlby and his colleagues, studying the separation of children from their parents, identified attachment as an important part of psychosocial development.
- Other explanations of attachment include the psychoanalytic, behavioral, and cognitive.

- Ainsworth's strange situation technique was designed to assess the security of an infant's attachment.
- Attachment is a cross-cultural phenomenon that knows no geographic boundary.
- Attachment develops early in life and offers clues as to psychosocial development.
- The sensitivity of the infant-mother relationship in the moments following birth has led to considerable controversy.
- A mother's attachment to her infant seems to be influenced by the security of her attachment to her own mother.

Early Emotional Development

- Smiling is one of the first clues to emotional development.
- The Greenspans have identified several milestones of early emotional development.

🌳 KEY TERMS

Attachment   144
Autonomy   143
Contingency   143
Difficult children   138
Easy children   138
Entrainment   143

Goodness of fit   139
Interactions   136
Interactive errors   150
Interactive repair   150
Intergenerational continuity   148
New York Longitudinal Study   138

Sensitive responsiveness   134
Slow-to-warm-up children   138
Symmetry   143
Synchrony   143
Temperament   138

🌳 WHAT DO YOU THINK?

1. Probably the basic issue for you to grasp is the extent of an infant's abilities: physical, social, and psychological. Do you think that infants are as we have described them in chapters 5 and 6, or do you think that we have over- or underestimated their competencies?

2. Depending on your answer to question 1, explain how you interpret an infant's participation in developing relationships. That is, given an infant's ability to smile, coo, and make physical responses, how much control do you believe infants exercise in their interactions with adults?

3. Think about the role of appearance and temperament in developing relationships. A well-known psychologist once said that some children are so difficult to love that parents may have to fake it. How do you react to this statement? Do you think an infant could detect such parental behavior?

4. Once the Klaus and Kennell studies received wide coverage (which they did in the press and television), many mothers experienced feelings of guilt because their children had not received such treatment immediately after birth. They were afraid that their children would be at a disadvantage. What would you tell them? How would you attempt to relieve their feelings of guilt?

🌳 SUGGESTED READINGS

Bowlby, J. (1969). *Attachment*. New York: Basic Books. Here is Bowlby's classic statement about attachment. This book is very readable and is a reference with which you should be familiar.

Brazelton, T. B. & B. Cramer (1990). *The earliest relationship*. Reading, MA: Addison-Wesley. An excellent, readable account of how relationships develop, presented from both a pediatric and psychoanalytic perspective.

Manchester, W. (1983). *The last lion: Winston Spencer Churchill*, 1874–1932. A particularly revealing look at Churchill's difficult boyhood and his desperate attempt to please indifferent parents.

Maurer, D. & C. Maurer. (1989). *The world of the newborn*. New York: Basic Books. This book contains readable summaries of many of the crucial developmental milestones of infancy that we have discussed.

🌳 CHAPTER REVIEW TEST

1. A reciprocal interactions model is also known as a (an) _____ model.
   a. transactional
   b. interaction
   c. main effects
   d. developmental

2. Which of the following statements is not in agreement with an understanding of sensitive responsiveness?
   a. All children are temperamentally similar at birth.
   b. Children instantly tune into their environment.
   c. Children give clues to their personalities.
   d. Children, from birth, engage in reciprocal interactions.

3. A true relationship has
   a. reciprocity.
   b. continuity.
   c. spontaneity.
   d. longevity.

4. More sensitive mothers have infants who are more
   a. restless.
   b. nervous.
   c. detached.
   d. responsive.

5. The content of interactions as described by Hinde would *not* include
   a. what the partners do together.
   b. how the partners see each other.
   c. distinguishing different relationships.
   d. labeling the relationship.

6. Langlois demonstrated that infants discriminate among adults female faces based on
   a. a smile.
   b. skin color.
   c. gender.
   d. attractiveness.

7. Children's _____ contribute significantly to their interactions with their environments.
   a. ages
   b. gender
   c. temperaments
   d. culture

8. Chess and Thomas described a child with a low intensity of reactions and a somewhat negative attitude as
   a. slow to warm up.
   b. difficult.
   c. easy.
   d. depressed.

9. Which of the following influences is *not* at work during the first days of an infant's life?
   a. bodily needs
   b. psychological needs
   c. cognitive needs
   d. adult response needs

10. By the age of _____ the infant has formed a need for social interactions.
    a. 3 months
    b. 1 week
    c. 6 months
    d. 1 year

11. _____ is a characteristic that identifies the rhythm that is established between a parent's and infant's behavior.
    a. Synchrony
    b. Autonomy
    c. Entrainment
    d. Symmetry

12. According to Bowlby, _____ behavior is any form of behavior that results in a person attaining or maintaining proximity to some other clearly identified individual who is conceived as better able to cope with the world.
    a. detachment
    b. attachment
    c. protest
    d. emotional

13. Which statement is true?
    a. Only mothers have the potential to induce attachment.
    b. Fathers and mothers act quite differently with their infants.
    c. There is a sensitive period for parent-infant bonding.
    d. No sensitive period exists for parent-infant bonding.

14. The connection between childhood experiences and adult parenting behavior is described in
    a. intergenerational continuity.
    b. the New York Longitudinal Study.
    c. the origins of temperament.
    d. goodness of fit.

15. A smile is an early sign of a baby's
    a. cognitive development.
    b. emotions.
    c. physical needs.
    d. attachment.

16. The true social smile appears by the
    a. third day.
    b. third week.
    c. sixth week.
    d. third month.

17. Which is *not* a possible explanation of an infant's smile?
    a. Infants smile at human beings around them.
    b. Infants smile at high-contrast stimuli.
    c. Infants smile at discovering a relationship between their behavior and external events.
    d. Infants smile at the sound of rhythmic music.

18. According to Kagan, during the first years of a child's life, emotions are mainly caused by
    a. fear.
    b. cognitive development.
    c. external events.
    d. sensitive responsiveness.

19. According to the Greenspans, the age 3 to 10 months is characterized by
    a. standing, walking, and talking.
    b. an attempt to develop intentional communication.
    c. the infant falling in love.
    d. creating emotional ideas.

20. Early relationships
    a. can influence later relationships.
    b. are based on physical needs.
    c. are preprogrammed.
    d. are characterized by shyness.

Answers

1. a 2. a 3. b 4. d 5. b 6. d 7. c 8. a 9. c 10. a 11. c 12. b 13. d 14. a 15. b 16. c 17. d 18. c 19. b 20. a

PART IV

Early Childhood

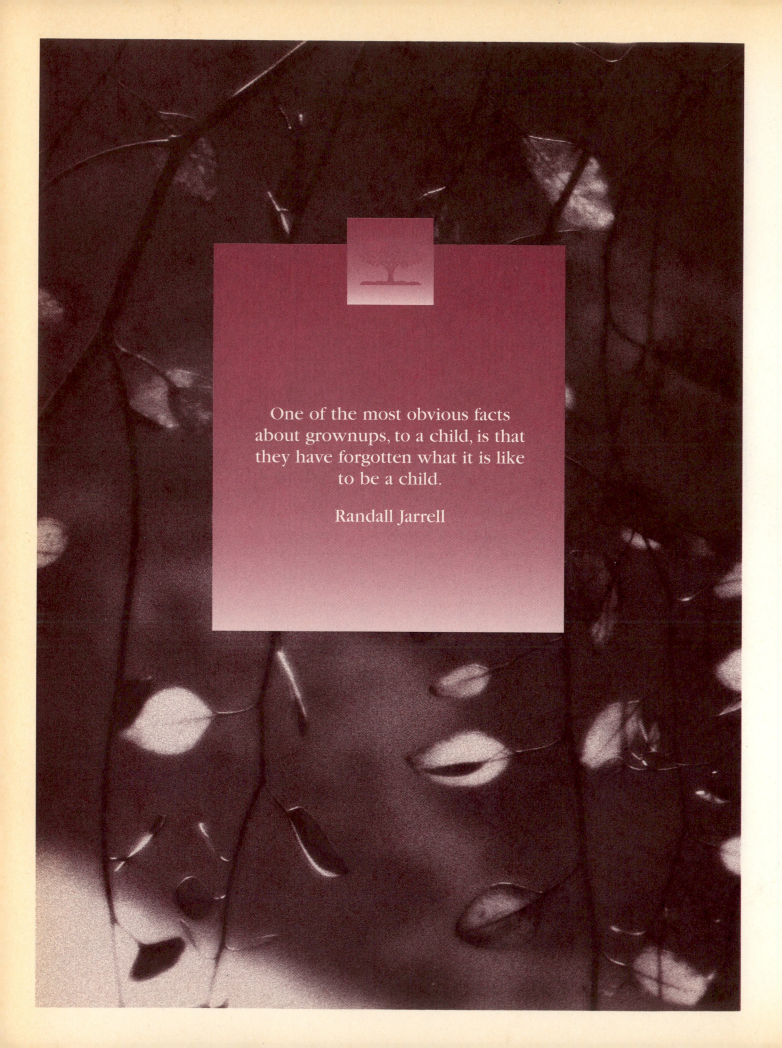

One of the most obvious facts
about grownups, to a child, is that
they have forgotten what it is like
to be a child.

Randall Jarrell

Physical and Cognitive Development in Early Childhood

Chapter Outline

Children pass through periods when they want to test their developing abilities against any restrictions they perceive. The "terrible twos" are a good example.

iz, whom we met in chapter 5, felt she now had a good idea of what perpetual motion meant. Her two children, 3-year-old Maddi and 5-year-old Jackie, engaged in nonstop activities from the time they woke up in the morning until they went to bed—with great reluctance. (Be thankful for small favors, she thought; Maddi still took a long afternoon nap.) At least you could talk to Jackie, who was excited about entering kindergarten in September.

But Maddi—oh, that Maddi! She had discovered the thrill of saying "no" loudly and emphatically, was into everything, and sometimes pretended not to hear Liz's warnings. Liz was worried about what seemed to be a steady stream of threats directed at Maddi. She was concerned that so many negative incidents could affect her relationship with Maddi.

These thoughts came to Liz as she opened a letter from the preschool where Maddi was registered for the fall. Also included was a form for her to fill out, and as she read the items, she became even more concerned.

The first item asked for a description of Maddi. Liz answered honestly that she was healthy, vigorous, active, and seemed to be progressing well. She was toilet trained, helped in dressing herself, and seemed quite independent. Liz thought Maddi was unusually curious, always poking into things, opening drawers, and looking into closets. Liz was often embarrassed by this behavior when she and Maddi visited other homes. On the other hand, Maddi was putting her words together nicely and played fairly well with other children.

In the next part of the form, Liz was asked several specific questions: How independent was Maddi? Was she left-handed or right-handed? Were there particular activities that Maddi really enjoyed, such as drawing? Did she like pretend play?

Liz answered the questions carefully: Maddi seemed quite independent; she didn't cling and could play by herself. She used her right hand for drawing and throwing. She loved to draw and Liz was able to understand what Maddi was trying to tell in her pictures. In her games and play, she often used objects for different purposes, such as a stick for a broom.

As Liz responded to the questions, she realized that Maddi seemed to be a fairly normal 3-year-old (whatever that might mean, Liz thought a little gloomily). Still, she was bothered by Maddi's incessant questioning and outbursts of negativism. Since she and Maddi were scheduled for an interview at the preschool the next week, Liz decided to mention her worries to the instructor who would be interviewing them. After all, preschool teachers worked constantly with children of this age.

The following week, while Liz talked with one of the instructors, Maddi played happily with a variety of toys. When the instructor commented that Maddi seemed quite well adjusted, Liz had the opportunity to mention how worried she was. The instructor listened and then began to laugh, saying that Maddi seemed to be perfectly normal for her age. She mentioned that Maddi was at that age when she wanted as much information as possible to feed her inquiring mind, which was steadily becoming involved in more symbolic activities, such as telling a story with her drawings and using one thing to represent another.

As Liz listened, she was delighted because these were just the things that Maddi was doing. She was acting as most youngsters of her age do. The instructor then went on to describe what Liz could expect for the next year or so. 🌳

Liz's concerns and what she was learning about these years is our task for the next two chapters. Bursting with energy, constantly curious, and searching for novelty are all characteristics of children from 2 to 6 years of age. The rounded bodies of infancy give way to the slimmer torsos of early childhood, muscles begin to firm, bones begin to harden, and continued brain development provides a foundation for a world of symbolic promise. When these changes combine with strong feelings of competence and mastery, parents and other adults working with children of this age face challenges that can try their patience.

By age 2 typical children walk, talk, and eagerly explore their environment. Early childhood youngsters gradually acquire greater mastery over their bodies. More coordinated, skillful movements replace the clumsy actions of infancy. With walking and talking, new directions in development become more obvious. Children's personalities take on definite shadings.

Children's interactions with those around them begin to take shape, setting the stage for the kind of relationships they will form in the future. They now begin the process of widening their circle of relationships. Children from 2 to 6 will make new friends and, in our society today, almost inevitably have experience with preschool teachers. Some youngsters of this age are also faced with adjusting to a new sibling (or siblings), which can be a time of great frustration if not handled carefully.

To help you understand the rapid changes that occur during these years, we'll first trace the important physical changes of the period. We'll then analyze cognitive development and trace the growing symbolic ability of the early childhood youngster. Finally, during these years children experience the "language explosion" with all that it implies for development, so we'll conclude by discussing this critical phase.

After reading this chapter, you should be able to

- Describe the outstanding physical and cognitive characteristics of the period.

- Analyze the importance of brain lateralization in a child's development.

- Identify the key phases in cognitive development during the preoperational period.

- Contrast Piaget's view of cognitive development with information-processing explanations.

- Designate the language milestones of the early childhood years.

- Indicate the speech irregularities that can occur in the early childhood period.

Early childhood youngsters find the world a fascinating place. Giving these children the freedom to explore and learn, coupled with sensible restrictions, encourages the development of mastery.

Features of the Early Childhood Years

Early childhood, extending from age 2 to age 6, is a time of rapid change: Height increases about 10 to 12 inches, weight by about 15 pounds; language grows at a phenomenal rate; cognitive changes appear in both thought and language; personality and social development enter a new, distinct phase; feelings of mastery and independence may conflict with the directions of parents and teachers. Early childhood is Erikson's time of *autonomy* and *initiative* and Piaget's **preoperational period.** Children continue their mastery of toilet training, get ready to read, demonstrate symbolic thinking, improve their use of language, and begin to distinguish right from wrong.

Preoperational

Piaget's second stage of cognitive development, extending from about 2 to 7 years of age.

A Multicultural Perspective

Any discussions of social-cultural influences on development stress that cultures differ in their views of acceptable childrearing practices. We also know that the effects of culture, health, socioeconomic status, and biological factors interact with each other and produce varying, but normal, developmental outcomes. As Bruner (1990) has noted, culture is a major factor in giving form to the minds of those under its sway. Russian psychologist Vygotsky has argued in a similar manner: Mental functioning can only be understood by examining the surrounding social and cultural processes (Wertsch & Tulviste, 1992).

Vygotsky's ideas concerning how culture affects development (which we discussed in chapter 2) help us to realize that we cannot understand development without considering the social processes acting on children. Vygotsky traces mental development to the interactions between changing social conditions and a biological organism. His fundamental claim is that human mental processes can only be understood by considering how and where they occur (Wertsch, 1985). Thus, understanding human development requires knowledge of that culture where development occurs.

As we have seen, Vygotsky (1978) believed that cognitive development occurs in those circumstances where an adult or more experienced peer guides a pupil's thinking (Rogoff, 1990). These skilled adults (parents, teachers) aid cognitive development by using cultural tools (e.g., language and mathematics). Institutions such as the school and inventions such as the computer provide critical help in a pupil's cognitive development. For Vygotsky, children depend on social interactions to develop cognitively (Rogoff, 1990). Vygotsky's ideas are similar to Bruner's explanation of the role of symbols in cognitive development.

Language as an Example

Bruner (1990) has argued that culture shapes cognitive development by imposing its symbolic systems—language, for example, which we'll again discuss in this chapter—on the child's developing mind. Turning to language, Bruner urged that we not be swept away by biological interpretations of language development because children need considerable interactions with others in acquiring their language. As he has stated, language is a major part of the "cultural tool kit" that organizes the child's thinking; that is, learning language is learning how to do things with words.

Children come into the world prepared to acquire their language, but different cultures shape the way language is constructed. For example, studying children's (15 to 39 months old) responses to yes-no questions, Choi (1991) found that many similarities as well as differences occurred in the way that English, French, and Korean children used their native answering systems. In all three languages, the same answering system applies to affirmative questions, but the answering systems to negative questions differ in the three languages.

Choi used the examples of an affirmative question—"Is this a cat?"—and a negative question—"Isn't this a cat?" All the children from the three countries learned the interpretative-functional meaning of yes-no questions before the truth-functional meaning. The children differed in the way they responded to negative questions because of their interpretation of the question, which seemed to be a cultural phenomenon. In English, negative questions are used when the questioner believes the positive; that is, negative questions have a rhetorical function. For example, "Wasn't John at the party?" implies that the questioner believes John *was* at the party. Neither Korean nor French children reacted this way; that is, negative questions are rarely used rhetorically. The Korean and French children interpret the question to indicate doubt about its truthfulness—John was *not* at the party.

Tobin, Wu, and Davidson (1989) offered another example of cultural influence on cognitive and language development. Studying 4-year-old children in China, Japan, and the United States, these investigators noted that in China and the United

Table 7.1 — Some Developmental Characteristics of Early Childhood

Age (years)	Height (in.)	Weight (lb.)	Language Development	Motor Development
2 1/2	36	30	Identifies object by use; vocabulary of 450 words	Can walk on tiptoes; can jump with both feet off floor
3	38	32	Answers questions, brief sentences; may recite television commercials; vocabulary of 900 words	Can stand on one foot; jumps from bottom of stairs; rides tricycle
3 1/2	39	34	Begins to build sentences; confined to concrete objects; vocabulary of 1,220 words	Continues to improve 3-year-old skills; begins to play with others
4	41	36	Names and counts several objects; uses conjunctions; understands prepositions; vocabulary of 1,540 words	Walks downstairs, one foot to step; skips on one foot; throws ball overhand
4 1/2	42	38	Mean length of utterance (morphemes) 4.5 words; vocabulary of 1,870 words	Hops on one foot; dramatic play; copies squares
5	43	41	Begins to show language mastery; uses words apart from specific situation; vocabulary of 2,100 words	Skips, alternating feet; walks straight line; stands for longer periods on one foot
5 1/2	45	45	Asks meanings of words; begins to use more complex sentences of 5 or 6 words; vocabulary of 2,300 words	Draws recognizable person; continues to develop throwing skill
6	46	48	Good grasp of sense of sentences; uses more complex sentences; vocabulary of 2,600 words	Jumps easily; throws ball overhand very well; stands on each foot alternately

States, adults believe that preschool experiences should help children develop their language skills and learn appropriate ways to express themselves. In Japan, however, the preschool language experience is seen less as a vehicle for self-expression than as a way of developing and expressing group solidarity and shared social goals. Although these views about the powerful influence of culture on learning and development probably come as no surprise to you, keep them in mind as you analyze the various topics in this chapter.

We may casually observe early childhood youngsters and comment on their energy. But by examining them psychologically, we can see the interplay of movement, activity, and cognitive curiosity that produces constant improvement in competence. Table 7.1 summarizes many characteristics of these youngsters.

🌳 Guided Review 🌳

1. The early childhood years coincide with Piaget's _____ period.
2. The period of early childhood extends from the age of _____ to the age of _____ .
3. During this period a child can grow as much as _____ inches and gain _____ pounds.
4. We now recognize that the _____ as well as the biological helps to produce normal development.

Answers

1. preoperational   2. 2, 6   3. 10–12, 15   4. cultural

Figure 7.1
The human growth curve

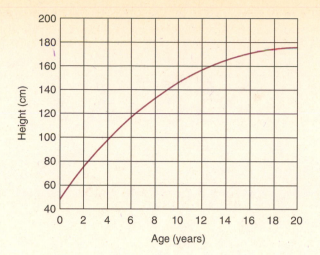

Physical and Motor Development

As you can see from table 7.1, growth in childhood proceeds at a less frantic pace than in infancy. Children during this period grow about another 12 inches and continue to gain weight at the rate of about 5 pounds a year. Body proportions are also changing, with the legs growing faster than the rest of the body. By about age 6, the legs make up almost 45 percent of body length. At the beginning of this period, children usually have all their baby teeth; and at the end of the period, children begin to lose them. Boys and girls show about the same rate of growth during these years.

Characteristics of Physical Development

Children's rapidly developing motor skills are clearly seen in their drawings from uncontrolled scribbling to controlled "within the lines" attempts to their own creative expressions.

Look at figure 7.1, the human growth curve. (Note that 10 centimeters equal 4 inches.) This curve strikingly illustrates the regularity of physical growth. Most parts of the body (except the brain and the reproductive organs) follow this pattern (Tanner, 1989). With the exception of the two spurts at infancy and adolescence, growth is highly predictable for almost all boys and girls, given satisfactory conditions.

The Sequence of Early Childhood Growth

Thinking of children you know, do you believe that growth is regular and orderly? How would you support your opinion?

We are concerned here with physical growth and development. Optimum growth requires proper nutrition, temperature, and rest to stimulate the genetic elements and growth hormones. Tanner (1989) noted that the growth process is self-stabilizing. It is governed by the control system of the genes and fueled by energy absorbed from the environment. If malnutrition or illness deflects children from the normal growth path—physical, social, cognitive—but a corrective force (adequate diet or termination of illness) intervenes, the normal course of development will accelerate until the children "catch up"; thereupon, growth slows. Children who experience an interruption in their normal growth plan are often called **developmentally delayed.**

Developmentally delayed

A term that describes children who experience a developmental lag because of either physical or psychological causes; these children usually "catch up."

Different cells, tissues, and organs grow at different rates. (Some tissues never lose the ability to grow, such as hair, skin, and nails.) In humans, for example, body length at birth is about four times the length of the face at birth, so the head is relatively large. But the head grows more slowly than the trunk or limbs, so that at age 25 body length is about eight times that of face length.

Parents and children alike are quite conscious of the appearance and loss of "baby" teeth and the arrival of the first permanent teeth. At about 2 1/2 years all of the primary teeth have come through, which most children begin to lose between 5 and 6 years. At about this time, the first permanent teeth, the molars, appear. Children continue to lose their primary teeth and gain new permanent teeth at

Figure 7.2
Lateralization of handedness

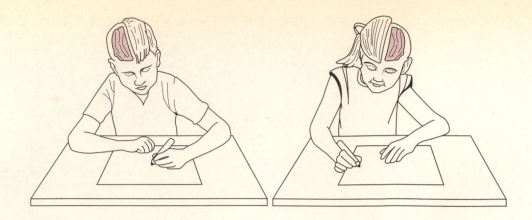

about the same time. The timing can be different for some children, however, so that gaps between teeth may appear or new teeth arrive before the baby teeth have fallen out, causing a space problem that may require professional attention.

Continuing Brain Development

During the early childhood years, as the brain continues to grow, exercising its powerful control of behavior, children show a decided preference for using one hand or foot over the other. This preference, called **handedness,** starts to appear toward the end of infancy and becomes well established by the age of 5 or 6.

Lateralization

Which hand do you use for writing? If you were to kick a football, would you use the leg on the same side of your body as the hand you use for writing? Pick up a pencil or ruler and pretend it is a telescope. Which eye do you use? Are you using the same side of the body that you used for writing and kicking? Your answers to these questions should give you some idea of the meaning of cerebral **lateralization.**

We tend to think of the brain as a single unit, but actually it consists of two halves: the cerebral hemispheres (Fischbach, 1992). The two halves are connected by a bundle of nerve fibers (the corpus callosum). The left hemisphere controls the right side of the body; the right hemisphere controls the left side of the body. The right hemisphere functions more globally than the left, which tends to break things into their component parts.

Language is a good example. If you recall our earlier discussion in chapter 5, language entails the combining of discrete elements—letters, syllables, words. Since this fits the functioning of the left hemisphere, about 95 to 99 percent of right-handed people and about 70 percent of left-handed people are left lateralized for language.

Consequently, although the hemispheres seem to be almost identical, our discussion reveals important differences between the two. These differences are clues to your brain's organization. If you are right-handed, for example, your left cerebral hemisphere is lateralized for handedness and also for control of your speech—you are "left lateralized." Figure 7.2 illustrates lateralization.

Much of our knowledge of cerebral lateralization has resulted from studies of brain-damaged patients. Patients with left hemisphere damage, for example, typically have speech difficulties; damage to the right hemisphere frequently causes perceptual and attentional disorders (Gershon & Rieder, 1992). Because as humans we rely so heavily on language, the left hemisphere came to be thought of as the dominant or "major" hemisphere. Today, however, we recognize the right hemisphere's control of visual and spatial activities.

Handedness
Children's preference for using one hand over the other.

Are you left-handed, right-handed, or ambidextrous? In everything? How do you explain people who use their right hand to write but throw a ball left-handed?

Lateralization
Refers to a preferred side of the brain for a particular activity.

Physical Development in Early Childhood

In an excellent overview of physical development, Tanner (1989) discussed how the interaction of heredity and environment produces the rate and kinds of physical growth. Among the chief contributing forces are the following:

- *Genetic elements*. Hereditary elements are of immense importance to the regulation of growth. The genetic growth plan is given at conception and functions throughout the entire growth period.

- *Nutrition*. Malnutrition delays growth and, if persistent, can cause lasting damage. Children in Stuttgart, Germany, were studied each year from 1911 to 1953. From 1920 to 1940 there was a uniform increase in average height and weight, but in the later years of each war (World Wars I and II) average height declined as food was curtailed. These children recovered, but questions remain about the effects of chronic malnutrition. For example, does chronic malnutrition produce permanent brain damage in the fetus and the 1- or 2-year-old child?

- *Disease*. Short-term illnesses cause no permanent retardation of the growth rate, although they may cause some disturbance if the child's diet is consistently inadequate. Major disease usually causes a slowing of growth, followed by a catch-up period if circumstances become more favorable.

- *Psychological disturbance*. Stress can slow development and occasionally lead to deprivation dwarfism. Small children under uncompromising strain such as divorce seem to "turn off" their growth hormone and become almost dwarfed.

- *Socioeconomic status*. Children from different social classes differ in average body size at all ages. Tanner gives the example of differences in height between British children of the professional class and those of laborers. Children of the professional class are from 1 inch taller at age 3 to 2 inches taller at adolescence. A consistent pattern appears in all such studies, indicating that children in more favorable circumstances are larger than those growing up under less favorable economic conditions. The difference seems to stem from nutrition, sleep, exercise, and recreation.

- *Secular trends*. During the past hundred years the tendency has been for children to become progressively larger at all ages. This is especially true in Europe and America.

This brief overview of physical development again illustrates the importance of the biopsychosocial model. For example, you may be tempted to think that physical growth is essentially biological, mainly determined by heredity. Note, however, the role played by nutrition and socioeconomic status. The interaction among biological, psychological, and social influences testifies to the power of the biopsychosocial model in explaining development.

Growing Motor Skills

When early childhood children reach the age of 6, no one—neither parents nor teachers—is surprised by what they can do physically. Think back to the infancy period and recall how often we referred to what children couldn't do. Stand, walk, run. We tend to take the accomplishments of the 6-year-old for granted, but a great deal of neuromuscular development had to occur before these motor skills became so effortless.

We are concerned here with two types of motor skills: *gross* (using the large muscles) and *fine* (using the small muscles of the hands and fingers). The well-known chronicler of children's development, Arnold Gesell (1940), stated that

The energy of the early childhood years is seen in the physical activities of the period: constant motion followed by periods of rest and nutrition.

Table 7.2	The Emergence of Motor Skills	
Age	**Gross Skills**	**Fine Skills**
2	Runs, climbs stairs, jumps from object (both feet)	Throws ball, kicks ball, turns page, begins to scribble
3	Hops, climbs stairs with alternating feet, jumps from bottom step	Copies circle, opposes thumb to finger, scribbling continues to improve
4	Runs well, skillful jumping, begins to skip, pedals tricycle	Holds pencil, copies square, walks balance beam
5	Hops about 50 feet, balances on one foot, can catch large ball, good skipping	Colors within lines, forms letters, dresses and undresses self with help, eats more neatly
6	Carries bundles, begins to ride bicycle, jumps rope, chins self, can catch a tennis ball	Ties shoes, uses scissors, uses knife and fork, washes self with help

This child is using his right hand to dig, signaling that his left cerebral hemisphere is lateralized for handedness and control of speech.

thanks to perceptual and motor development, 3- and 4-year-old children can hold crayons, copy triangles, button their clothes, and unlace their shoes. Table 7.2 summarizes the development of motor skills.

Cratty (1986) discussed several motor skills as follows:

- *Running.* The 18-month-old child has a hurried walk. The true run appears between ages 2 and 3. By the age of 5 or 6, youngsters run rapidly (about 11.5 feet per second), employing considerable arm action.

- *Jumping.* At about age 18 months, youngsters step off a low object with one foot, hesitating slightly before placing it on the ground. At age 2 youngsters use what Cratty calls "the two-feet takeoff." Soon they begin to jump over low barriers, and by age 5 they are skillful jumpers (they can broad jump three feet and hurdle 1-foot objects).

- *Hopping, skipping, galloping.* Hopping may be on one foot in place, using alternate feet, or hopping for distance. Some time after age 3 or 4, youngsters can hop from one to three steps on their preferred foot, and by age 5 they can extend hopping to about ten steps. Girls acquire this skill slightly earlier and more successfully than boys. Skillful skipping and galloping appear between the ages of 6 and 7.

- *Balancing.* Balancing, a measure of nervous system integrity, appears quite early. Three-year-olds can walk a reasonably straight line. Five-year-olds can maintain control while standing on one foot with their arms folded. Girls are slightly superior on this task.

The early childhood years are a time when children show a great love for drawing. Not only are their drawings a sign of motor development, but they also indicate levels of cognitive development and can be emotionally revealing.

Random scribbling

Drawing in which children use dots and lines with simple arm movements.

Controlled scribbling

Drawing in which children carefully watch what they are doing, when before they looked away.

Do you still like to draw? If not, what do you think happened? Do you agree with Gardner's explanation?

The physical picture of the early childhood youngster is one of energy and growing motor skill. Parents often worry that their child is not eating enough, but given the slower growth rate of the early childhood years, less food is needed; rather, it is the quality of children's intake that is important (junk food and excessive fats and sugars are to be avoided). Some parents in developed countries have children who are on vegetarian diets. In certain cases, the children themselves dislike meat or avoid it because of their love of animals. Although vegetarian diets are in many ways desirable, care must be taken that nutrients such as iron and zinc are obtained. Also, some fat is necessary because when the fat content of a diet falls below 20 percent, growth can be stunted.

Adequate rest is critical and parents should establish a routine to avoid problems. For example, to reconcile a rambunctious child with the necessity of sleep, parents should minimize stimulation through a consistent, easily recognized program: washing, tooth brushing, storytelling, and gentle but firm pressure to sleep. Careful and thoughtful adult care should prevent undue difficulties.

The Special Case of Drawing

Children love to draw. No one has to teach them. In a finely tuned sequence, children move from random scribbles to skillful creations. When something is as natural and fascinating for children as drawing, we can only wonder why the vast majority of youngsters lose this desire and skill.

Children's drawings go through a sequence of stages: Two-year-olds grab markers and scribble enthusiastically (using dots and lines) and seem fascinated by their ability to produce lines as a result of their movements. This **random scribbling** continues until about age 3. Three-year-olds begin to use their wrists, typically using the whole hand to hold a crayon, which permits them to draw curves and loops. They become engrossed with geometric figures and are beginning to realize their lines can represent objects. This phase, called **controlled scribbling**, lasts until about age 4.

Four- and 5-year-olds show greater control and attention to what they are doing, deliberately attempting to create representations of objects. Young children produce exciting creations, until the peak of artistic expression is reached by the end of the early childhood period. During these years, children begin to paint and hold the brush with thumb and fingers. They hold the paper in place with the free hand. They give names to their drawings and begin to show representation (using one thing for another—see the cognitive section of the chapter).

Well-known psychologist Howard Gardner (1980, 1982) has written sensitively about children's drawing and raised several important questions. Noting how drawings develop—from the scribbles of the 2-year-old to the 3-year-old's interest in design to the 4- and 5-year-old's drawing representations—Gardner commented on the liveliness and enthusiasm of their work. And then suddenly it stops! The end of the early childhood period sees the end of creative expression, except for a select few. Why?

Gardner (1982a) has argued that children limit their artistic efforts to copying forms or cease drawing altogether after the peak of creativity has been reached. This "reach for realism" may be a critical stage of development during which children reflect their cognitive level by following rules and obeying the dictates of convention. With growing cognitive ability, and a decrease in egocentrism, children may well compare their efforts with those of others and become discouraged—their work just isn't as good—and they lose interest. It is not until adolescence that a small number of children again manifest that creative spark. At this time inborn talent and a supportive environment can help a child develop those skills needed to withstand immersion in rules and correct thinking.

Children's drawings not only are good clues to their motor coordination but, as we'll see, also provide insights into their cognitive and emotional lives, another example of how a biopsychosocial perspective helps us to understand development.

🌳 Guided Review 🌳

5. Optimum growth requires proper _____ , _____ and _____ to stimulate growth hormones.

6. Children whose growth has been temporarily interrupted by insufficient diet or illness are called _____ _____ .

7. _____ scribbling continues until about 3 years of age.

8. A child using his/her left hand to draw signals that his or her _____ cerebral hemisphere is lateralized for handedness.

9. Motor skills fall into two types _____ and _____ .

10. Gardner has attributed the loss of a child's artistic creativity to the "_____ _____ _____ ."

Cognitive Development

Physical development during early childhood, while observable and exciting, is not the only significant change occurring. Early childhood youngsters expand their mental horizons by their increasing use of ideas and by rapid growth in language. This growing cognitive ability is a fact; explaining it is much more difficult. To help us understand what is happening and how it happens, we turn once more to Piaget.

Piaget's Preoperational Period

For Piaget, *preoperational* refers to a child who has begun to use symbols but is not yet capable of mentally manipulating them. Children who cannot take two things into consideration at the same time—take something apart and put it together again; who cannot return to the beginning of a thought sequence, that is, who cannot comprehend how to reverse the action of 2 + 2; who cannot believe that water

These children, playing doctor and patients, are furthering all aspects of their development. They are discovering what objects in their environment are supposed to do, they are learning about the give and take of human relationships, and they are channeling their emotional energies into acceptable outlets.

Answers

poured from a short, fat glass into a taller, thinner one retains the same volume—these children are at a level of thinking that precedes operational thought. Several examples of preoperational thinking are as follows:

Realism

Refers to when children learn to distinguish and accept the real world.

Animism

Refers to when children consider a large number of objects as alive and conscious that adults consider inert.

Realism, which means that children slowly distinguish and accept a real world. They now have identified both an external and internal world.

Animism, which means that children consider a large number of objects as alive and conscious that adults consider inert. For example, a child who sees a necklace wound up and then released explains that it is moving because it "wants to unwind." Children overcome this cognitive limitation when they refuse to accept personality in things. Piaget believed that comparison with the thoughts of others slowly conquers animism as it does egocentrism. He identified four stages of animism:

- Almost everything is alive and conscious.
- Only those things that move are alive.
- Only those things that manifest spontaneous movements are alive.
- Consciousness is limited to the animal world.

Artificialism

Refers to when children attribute human life to everything.

Artificialism, which consists of attributing human creation to everything. For example, when asked how the moon began, some of Piaget's subjects replied, "because we began to be alive." As egocentrism decreases, youngsters become more objective and they steadily assimilate objective reality to their cognitive structures. They proceed from a purely human or divine explanation to an explanation that is half natural, half artificial: The moon comes from the clouds but the clouds come from people's houses. (The decline of artificialism parallels the growth of realism.)

Features of Preoperational Thought

For Piaget, the great accomplishment of the preoperational period is a growing ability to represent, which is how we record or express information. For example, the word *car* is a **representation** because it represents a certain idea. Pointing an index finger at a playmate and saying "Stick 'em up" is also an example of representation.

Representation

Child's growing ability to engage in abstract thinking.

Other activities typical of preoperational children reflect their use of internal representation (Piaget & Inhelder, 1969) and include the following.

Deferred imitation

Imitative behavior that continues after the disappearance of the model to be imitated.

Deferred imitation. Preoperational children can imitate some object or activity that they have previously witnessed; for example, they walk like an animal that they saw at the zoo earlier in the day. Piaget gives the example of a child who visited his home one day and while there had a temper tantrum. His daughter Jacqueline, about 18 months old, watched, absolutely fascinated. Later, after the child had gone, Jacqueline had her own tantrum. Piaget interprets this to mean that Jacqueline had a mental image of the event.

Symbolic play

The game of pretending; one of five preoperational behavior patterns.

Symbolic play. Children enjoy pretending that they are asleep, or that they are someone or something else. Piaget argued eloquently for recognizing the importance of play in a youngster's life. Obliged to adapt themselves to social and physical worlds that they only slightly understand and appreciate, children must make intellectual adaptations that leave personality needs unmet. For their mental health, they must have some outlet, some technique that permits them to assimilate reality to self, and not vice versa. Children find this mechanism in play, using the tools characteristic of symbolic play. (We'll discuss the role of play in greater detail in chapter 8.)

Drawing

Piaget's use of the term to indicate a growing symbolic ability.

Drawing. We have previously discussed drawing in a broad context but here Piaget concentrated solely on its cognitive elements. Children of this age project their mental representations into their drawings. Highly symbolic, their artwork reflects the level of their thinking and what they are thinking. Encourage children to talk about their art.

Mental images. Mental images appear late in this period because of their dependence on internalized imitation. Piaget's studies of the development of mental images between the ages of 4 and 5 showed that mental images fall into two categories. **Reproductive images** are images restricted to those sights previously perceived. **Anticipatory images** are images that include movements and transformations. At the preoperational level, children are limited to reproductive images.

A good illustration of the difference between the two is Piaget's famous example of matching tokens. Piaget showed 5- and 6-year-old children a row of red tokens and asked them to put down the same number of blue tokens. At this age, children put one blue token opposite each red one. When Piaget changed the arrangement, however, and spread out the row of red tokens, the children were baffled because they thought there were more red tokens than blue. Thus, children of this age can reproduce but not anticipate, which reflects the nature of their cognitive structures and level of cognitive functioning.

Language. For preoperational children, language becomes a vehicle for thought. Children of this age need ample opportunities to talk with adults and with each other.

Limitations of Preoperational Thought

Although we see the steady development of thought during this period, preoperational thought still has limitations. As the word *preoperational* implies, this period comes before advanced symbolic operations develop. Piaget has stated consistently that knowledge is not just a mental image of an object or event.

To know an object is to act on it, to modify it, to transform it, and to join objects in a class. The action is also reversible. If two is added to two, the result is four; but if two is taken away from four, the original two returns. The preoperational child lacks the ability to perform such operations on concepts and objects.

Several reasons can account for the restricted nature of preoperational thought. In the period of preoperational thought, children cannot assume the role of another person or recognize that other viewpoints exist, a state called **egocentrism.** This differs from sensorimotor egocentrism, which is primarily the inability to distinguish oneself from the world. For example, children may believe that the moon follows *them* around; everything focuses on them.

A striking feature of preoperational thought is the centering of attention on one aspect of an object and the neglecting of any other features—called **centration.** Consequently, reasoning is often distorted. Preoperational youngsters are unable to decenter, to notice features that would give balance to their reasoning. A good example of this is the process of **classification.** When youngsters from age 3 to age 12 are asked, "What things are alike?", their answers proceed through three stages. First, the youngest children group *figurally,* that is, by similarities, differences, and by forming a figure in space with the parts. Second, children of about age 5 or 6 group objects *nonfigurally.* They form the elements into groups with no particular spatial form. At this stage, the classification seems rational, but Piaget and Inhelder (1969) provide a fascinating example of the limitations of classification at this age. If in a group of 12 flowers, there are 6 roses, preoperational youngsters can differentiate between the other flowers and the roses. But when asked if there are more flowers or more roses, they are unable to reply because they cannot distinguish the whole from the part (see figure 7.3). This understanding does not appear until the third phase of classification, at about the age of 8.

Reproductive images
Mental images that are faithful to the original object or event being represented; Piaget's term for images that are restricted to those sights previously perceived.

Anticipatory images
Piaget's term for images (which include movements and transformation) that enable the child to anticipate change.

Egocentrism
Piaget's term that refers to a child's focus on self in early phases of cognitive development.

Centration
A feature of preoperational thought—the centering of attention on one aspect of an object and the neglecting of any other features.

Classification
The ability to group objects with some similarities within a larger category.

Figure 7.3

Lack of genuine classification

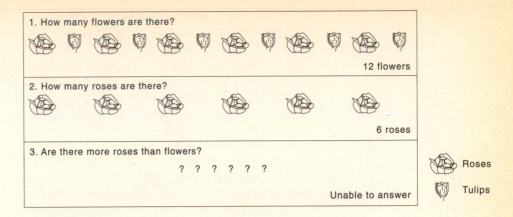

1. How many flowers are there?

12 flowers

2. How many roses are there?

6 roses

3. Are there more roses than flowers?

? ? ? ? ? ?

Unable to answer

Roses

Tulips

Figure 7.4

Piaget used the beaker task to determine whether children had conservation of liquid. In I, two identical beakers (A and B) are presented to the child; then the experimenter pours the liquid from B into beaker C, which is taller and thinner than A and B. The child is asked if beakers B and C have the same amount of liquid. The preoperational child says no, responding that the taller, thinner beaker (C) has more.

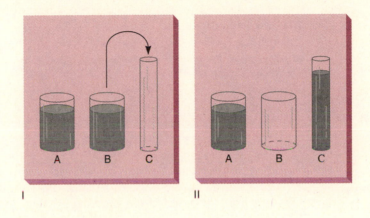

A   B   C

A   B   C

I

II

Conservation

The ability to understand that something may remain the same even though surface features may change.

Reversibility

The inability to reverse thinking, that is, to solve a problem and then proceed in reverse, tracing the steps back to the original question or premise.

Another limitation of the period is the lack of **conservation.** Conservation means understanding that an object retains certain properties, no matter how its form changes. The most popular illustration is to show a 5-year-old two glasses, each half filled with water. The child agrees that each glass contains an equal amount. But if you then pour the water from one of the glasses into a taller, thinner glass, the youngster now says that the new glass contains more liquid (see figure 7.4). Youngsters consider only the appearance of the liquid and ignore what happened. They also do not perceive the reversibility of the transformation. In their minds they do not pour the water back into the first glass.

Finally, preoperational thought lacks **reversibility.** A truly cognitive act is reversible if it can use stages of reasoning to solve a problem and then proceed in reverse, tracing its steps back to the original question or premise. The preoperational child's thought is irreversible and entangles the child in a series of contradictions in logic.

In the water-level problem, for example, the child believes that the taller, thinner glass contains more water. Youngsters cannot mentally reverse the task (imagine pouring the contents back into the original glass). At the conclusion of the preoperational period, children slowly decenter and learn reversibility as a way of mental life.

Challenges to Piaget

As we mentioned in our previous discussion of Piaget's sensorimotor period (see chapter 5), recent research has raised questions about Piaget's assumptions concerning the cognitive abilities of young children. For example, as we explained in the matching tokens problem, children of this age are likely to say that the spread-out row now has more tokens. Piaget believed that the children concentrated on the length of the row because they lacked a concept of number.

When Gelman and Baillargeon (1983) used similar problems with a smaller number of objects (up to four), however, children of this age successfully answered questions about the number of objects involved. Evidence continues to mount supporting the conclusion that Piaget underestimated the cognitive abilities of young children: They conserve, classify, and overcome egocentrism earlier than Piaget realized (Gardner, 1983). How can we explain these differences? One explanation points to the complexity of Piaget's tasks—they were more difficult than those used by modern psychologists. Also, his reliance on verbal cues may have confused some of the children he tested.

As Flavell (1992, p. 999) has noted, young children are quite competent—they are not as "pre this or pre that" as we used to think. He gives the example of 2-year-olds who know that a blindfolded person will not see what they themselves are looking at. Their understanding of numbers and their mental states are more advanced than previously realized. For example, we now think that children construct their own ideas of how their minds work, a theory of mind frequently referred to as **metacognition.**

Although interest in metacognition is relatively recent, its content has always been with us; for example, our thoughts about a decision we made or "how we are doing on a project" all entail metacognitive processes. Metacognitive skills seem to be involved in many mental activities: comprehension, evaluation, reading, writing, and problem solving among others. Flavell (1985) has analyzed metacognition by two domains: **metacognitive knowledge** and **metacognitive experiences.**

Metacognitive knowledge refers to a child's knowledge and beliefs about cognitive matters gained from experiences that are then stored in long-term memory (Flavell, 1985). Children acquire metacognitive knowledge about *people, tasks,* and *strategies*. For example, they may have come to believe that a particular person just does not like them; pupils may decide that a teacher has little confidence in their ability.

With regard to tasks, children gradually learn that the nature of a task forces them to think about how they will attack it. If it's difficult, perhaps they will need more time, or perhaps they will take a different approach or seek adult help. As for strategies, children learn to make a distinction between cognitive strategies (achieving a goal) and metacognitive strategies (monitoring progress toward that goal). Over time, they will continue to learn about what strategies are best suited for success on a particular task.

Metacognitive experiences are either cognitive or affective experiences that relate to cognitive activities. For example, children, after studying, may feel a little uncertain or doubtful about one of the topics or may be concerned that they didn't understand it. As Flavell (1985) noted, metacognitive experiences are most likely to occur when careful, conscious monitoring of cognitive efforts is required.

You can see, then, how valuable these metacognitive experiences can be for children. If something puzzles them, then their sense of uncertainty will cause them to read the section again, perhaps discuss it, or bring up questions to adults. Children who lack skill in this ability (perhaps because they are impulsive or have missed valuable experiences) are at a serious disadvantage. By urging children to become aware that they can "think about their thinking," you will also help them to improve those cognitive behaviors that result in better adjustment in all aspects of their lives.

Despite challenges to Piaget's assumptions, his ideas have been one of the resources for early childhood education programs.

Metacognition

The theory of mind that refers to children's ability to construct their own ideas of how their minds work.

Metacognitive knowledge

A child's knowledge and beliefs, gained from experience, about cognitive matters.

Metacognitive experiences

Responses to cognitive stimuli.

AN APPLIED VIEW

Children and Their Humor

■ "Why did daddy tiptoe past the medicine cabinet?"
"Because he didn't want to wake the sleeping pills."

Jokes such as these have spurred Paul McGhee (1979, 1988) to analyze children's humor and trace its developmental path. Noting that little is known about how children develop humor, McGhee turned to cognitive development as a possible explanation. Although humor also has psychodynamic and social features, McGhee believed that its cognitive properties offer the best basis for unraveling its secrets.

McGhee began by noting that the basis of most children's humor is incongruity, which is the realization that the relationship between different things just isn't "right." Using this as a basis, he traces four stages of incongruous humor. He treated stages as did Piaget: The sequence of stages remains the same, but the ages at which children pass through them varies.

Stage 1: Incongruous Actions toward Objects. Stage 1 usually occurs sometime during the second year, when children play with objects. They are able to form internal images of the object and thus start to "make believe." For example, one of Piaget's children picked up a leaf, put it to her ear, and talked to it as if it were a telephone, laughing all the time. One of the main characteristics of stage 1 humor is the child's physical activity directed at the object.

Stage 2: Incongruous Labeling of Objects and Events. Stage 2 humor is more verbal, which seems to be its most important difference from stage 1. McGhee (1979) noted

that the absence of action toward objects is quite noticeable. Piaget's 22-month-old daughter put a shell on the table and said, "sitting." She then put another shell on top of the first, looked at them and said, "sitting on pot." She then began to laugh. Children in this stage delight in calling a dog a cat, a foot a hand, and then start laughing.

Stage 3: Conceptual Incongruity. Around age 3 most children begin to play with ideas, which reflects their growing cognitive ability. For example, stage 3 children laugh when they see a drawing of a cat with two heads.

Stage 4: Multiple Meanings. Once children begin to play with the ambiguity of words, their humor approaches the adult level.

■ "Hey, did you take a bath?"
"No. Why, is one missing?"

Children at stage 4 (usually around age 7) understand the different meaning of *take* in both instances. Stage 3 children could not understand the following joke:

■ "Order! Order! Order in the court."
"Ham and cheese on rye, your honor."

Stage 4 youngsters appreciate its ambiguity.

You can see how cognitive development is linked to humor. McGhee (1988) stated that the effective use of humor with children can help stimulate new learning and creative thinking, instill an interest in literature, facilitate social development, and enhance emotional development and adjustment.

Guided Review

11. According to Piaget, _____ is the means that permits children to assimilate reality to self.

12. Attributing human activity or creation to things is known as _____ .

13. To understand that an object retains properties no matter how its form changes is called _____ .

14. Children's tendency to construct their own theories of mind is also called _____ .

Early Childhood Education

Early education programs, often referred to as preschool and kindergarten programs, usually take one of two directions. They are either physically, socially, and emotionally oriented or more cognitively centered, which is not to say that programs are exclusively social or cognitive; typically elements of both occur in all programs. But it is usually possible to detect greater emphasis on the social or the

Answers

11. play   12. artificialism   13. conservation   14. metacognition

cognitive, which reflects an underlying educational philosophy. Given today's concern with educational achievement, more preschool programs rely on the ideas of individuals such as Piaget or Montessori.

Piaget and Montessori

In these programs, which are based on a developmental theory of behavior, children are encouraged to learn through interacting with their environments and to be active participants in constructing knowledge. Early childhood programs stress integrated subject matter; for example, mathematics is taught by having the children weigh different objects and measure amounts to cook. Peer relationships are stressed and the line between work and play fades. Teachers encourage, mediate, and try to extend children's thinking (Hauser-Cram & others, 1991).

Although Piaget himself never advocated using his developmental theory in this manner, you can see how his ideas could form the basis for early childhood programs. His emphasis on a child's progression through intellectual stages of development has clearly defined program implications (use of concrete materials, etc.). Since Piaget's is an *interactive* theory, children's energy and activities can be directed at interesting cognitive outcomes rather than having children passively accept facts.

In contrast, Montessori (1967) was a strong proponent of early childhood programs. She believed that developing children pass through different physical and mental growth phases that alternate with periods of transition, suggesting that children possess different types of minds at different periods. These periods differ so sharply that Montessori referred to them as a series of new births. She described three major periods of development. The first stage, which is called the **absorbent mind** phase to indicate a child's tremendous ability to absorb experiences from its environment, extends from birth to age 6.

The second stage, which is referred to as the **uniform growth** phase to identify these years as a time of considerable stability, extends from age 6 to age 12. Finally, the third stage extends from 12 to 18 years. A youngster reaches this level by what Montessori calls the **prepared environment.** For children under age 6, the prepared environment includes sensorial materials, such as rods to teach lengths, cubes to teach size, and bells to teach musical pitch; materials for the acquisition of cultural geography, history, art, and arithmetic; and materials and techniques necessary for the development of a child's religious life. Montessori also devised concrete materials to encourage learning in 6- to 12-year-old children.

Montessori maintained that a prepared environment allowed children to learn independently and at an optimal pace for each individual. Montessori believed that children develop inner discipline and a love of learning in a properly prepared environment. She thought that children could develop, through sensory training, those skills necessary for later learning. Children also receive tremendous satisfaction from perceiving order in their environment, which increases their understanding of the world around them.

The stages we have just described lead to what is perhaps the best known of Montessori's ideas, that of sensitive periods. Montessori believed that there were times when a child was especially *sensitive* or ready for certain types of learning. One of the earliest and most vital of these periods is concerned with the attainment of language. To understand more graphically what language implies, picture yourself trying to learn German, Russian, or Swahili. No matter how young you are, you will still have difficulty, typically never mastering all the subtleties that a native-born speaker comes by so naturally. But, as we have seen, children acquire their language effortlessly, a good example of Montessori's sensitive periods. Preschool programs, such as Head Start, have also helped disadvantaged children.

Absorbent mind
Montessori's term for a child's ability to absorb experiences from the environment (0 to 6 years).

Uniform growth
Montessori's term to describe the developmental period in which children show considerable stability.

Prepared environment
Use of age-appropriate materials to further cognitive development.

Would you want your child in a preschool program based on Montessori or Piaget? Why?

Project Head Start

Head Start
Early intervention program intended to provide educational and developmental services to disadvantaged children.

Originally conceived as part of President Lyndon Johnson's War on Poverty in the 1960s, **Head Start** was headed by Sargent Shriver, who had been astounded on examining the distribution of poverty in the United States. Data indicated that about one-half of the nation's 30 million poor were children and most of these were under age 12. Shriver's main objective thus became the preparation of poor children for entrance into kindergarten and the first grade. As Hauser-Cram and others (1991) noted, Head Start was intended to provide educational and developmental services to preschool children from low-income families.

Improving children's health became a primary goal; children received pediatric and neurological assessments plus two nutritious meals a day (Zigler & Muenchow, 1992). Head Start programs had six components: preschool education, health screening and referral, mental health services, nutrition education and hot meals, social services for the child and family, and parental involvement (Zigler & Styfco, 1994). Since its beginning, Head Start has served more than 13 million children.

Unfortunately, several of the early claims about the gains to be realized from Head Start programs revolved around changes in IQ; some proponents stated that as a result of participation in Head Start, a child's IQ would increase one IQ point a month. In the mid-1960s, critical evaluations of intelligence tests had not reached today's level of sophistication, but even then certain individuals such as Edward Zigler, a member of the Head Start Planning Committee, deplored reliance on increases in IQ scores as the means of evaluating Head Start.

His fears were quickly justified as follow-up studies of Head Start children showed a "fadeout effect." That is, although graduates of these preschool programs showed immediate gains in intelligence and achievement test scores, after several months in the public schools, the Head Start children seemed to lose these cognitive benefits (Zigler & Styfco, 1994). Nevertheless, even if Head Start graduates do not maintain *academic* gains, they have improved their readiness for school and the advantages of Head Start extend to other parts of their lives.

For example, Lazar and Darlington (1982) studied the long-term results of 12 Head Start programs and reported significant effects on school competence, families, and attitudes about self and school. Among the techniques employed by the

Head Start was designed to offer developmental and educational services to preschool children from low-income families. With the increasing number of children living in poverty, such programs can provide much needed services.

various programs were constant communication with parents, training of mothers in the use of educational activities in the home, and periodic home visits. Pooling the data from these studies, Lazar and Darlington (1982) discovered that children who attended these programs were less likely to be retained in grade and more likely to meet their schools' requirements. They also attained higher IQ scores than their controls, demonstrated higher self-concepts, and were proud of their school accomplishment. The mothers of program graduates were more satisfied with their child's school performance than control mothers; they also had higher occupational aspirations for their children than control mothers. These results were obtained several years after the children had left the program and suggest the benefits of positive parental involvement in school affairs.

Do you believe that programs such as Head Start should be a vital part of national social policy? Include in your answer relevent facts such as outcomes, duration, and behaviors.

Today, with the rapid increase in the number of working women and the stunning rise of children living in poverty, the need for early intervention programs to aid these children seems more compelling than ever. In her summary of the need for greater support of preschool programs, Kassebaum (1994) pointed out that 21 percent of all American children live in poverty; 25 percent of all children live with a single parent; 25 percent of all babies are born to unmarried mothers; every night at least 100,000 children are homeless; the United States ranks 20th in the world with regard to infant mortality.

These statistics cry out for attention because the children they represent not only suffer educational disadvantages but they also face other developmental difficulties. For example, as we have seen, they are more frequently the premature babies; their families suffer devastating and widespread deprivation; the children themselves are more subject to physical illness and lowered cognitive performance. As more of these children enter the public schools, is it any wonder they are unable to meet the ordinary demands of the classroom (Hauser-Cram & others, 1991)? It is in meeting their needs that we see the value of programs such as Head Start and the hope of bringing these children successfully into the mainstream of school life and the wider community. If we are to succeed, we must identify the skills, both academic and social, that our students need.

Finally, a frequently mentioned concern has been that preschool programs may expose young children to too much pressure (Piccigallo, 1988). Elkind (1987), for example, has stated that, too often, educating preschoolers reflects the parents' needs and that preschool programs can offer inappropriate experiences leading to excessive pressure on children. Yet carefully designed and executed programs, regardless of their nature (Piagetian, Montessori), share common characteristics.

For example, several features distinguish good preschools: low teacher-child ratio, specially trained teachers, availability of resources, and recognition of children's individual differences. These programs are all child centered; that is, they are designed to emphasize individual children and to provide children with enriching, enjoyable experiences suitable for their years, which is especially desirable given the social needs of early childhood youngsters. Most studies of peer relationships during the early childhood period (2–6 years) have been conducted in day-care centers and nursery schools. Note the age progression in developing relationships: Social contacts occur more frequently among 5-year-olds than 3-year-olds. Aggressive interactions are quite common in the period, although aggression decreases in proportion to friendly interactions (especially true among middle-class boys).

Particularly interesting are the changes in quarreling during these years. As in their other social exchanges, older youngsters (4, 5, and 6 years) engage in fewer but longer quarrels with members of their own sex (Hartup, 1983). Boys quarrel more frequently among themselves than girls, usually over objects, gradually changing from physical to verbal aggression toward the end of the period. Although solitary activity persists, older children of this period are more obviously bidding for the attention of their peers.

As you can tell from our discussion thus far, children of these years have marched firmly into a symbolic world, a major part of which is language.

Language Development

Youngsters soon acquire their native language, a task of such scope and intricacy that its secrets have eluded investigators for centuries. During the early childhood period, language figuratively "explodes." Remember: Children don't learn to speak by imitating adults, nor do most parents reward their children for good grammar (deCuevas, 1990). All children, however, learn their native language. At about the same age they manifest similar patterns of speech development, whether they live in a ghetto or in a wealthy suburb. Moskowitz (1979) states that within a short span of time and with almost no direct instruction, children completely analyze their language. Although refinements are made between ages 5 and 10, most children have completed the greater part of the process of language acquisition by the age of 4 or 5. Recent findings have also shown that when children acquire the various parts of their language, they do so in the same order. For example, in English, children learn *in* and *on* before other prepositions, and they learn to use *ing* as a verb ending before other endings such as *ed* (Gleason, 1985).

Language acquisition is a tremendous accomplishment; if you remember how you may have tried to learn a foreign language as an adult, you'll recall how difficult it was to acquire vocabulary and to master rules of grammar and the subtleties of usage. Yet preschool children do just this with no formal training. By the time they are ready to enter kindergarten, most children have a vocabulary of about 8,000 words; use questions, negative statements, and dependent clauses; and have learned to use language in a variety of social situations (Gleason, 1985).

Language as Rule Learning

As children acquire the basics of their language, they are also learning the guidelines that make language such a powerful tool. For example, by the age of 4 or 5, children will have discovered that rules exist for combining sounds into words, that individual words have specific meanings, and that there are rules for combining words into meaningful sentences and for participating in a dialogue. These rules help children to detect the meaning of a word with which they are unfamiliar. Called **fast mapping,** this technique enables children to use context for a word's meaning, thus helping them to continue rapid vocabulary development.

We can summarize these accomplishments as follows:

- The rules of **phonology** describe how to put sounds together to form words.

- The rules of **syntax** describe how to put words together to form sentences.

- The rules of **semantics** describe how to interpret the meaning of words.

- The rules of **pragmatics** describe how to take part in a conversation.

The attention that adults (especially parents) give children encourages positive interactions and leads to satisfactory and fulfilling relationships. Adult attention will also further language development and enhance a child's self-concept.

Fast mapping
Techniques to help children detect word meanings.

Phonology
Describes how to put sounds together to form words.

Syntax
Describes how we learn to put words together to form sentences.

Semantics
Describes how to interpret the meaning of words.

Pragmatics
Describes how we learn to take part in a conversation.

Answers

15. cognitive; physical, social, emotional   16. Piaget, Montessori   17. health

WHAT'S YOUR VIEW?

WHOLE LANGUAGE: LASTING IMPROVEMENT OR PASSING FAD?

Building on a growing knowledge of language development, many educators, long dissatisfied with the teaching of reading and writing, have adopted a new strategy. Called **whole language,** this strategy refers to a technique by which all language processes (speaking, listening, reading and writing—including spelling and handwriting) are studied in a more natural context, as a whole and not as a series of isolated facts. For example, oral and written language are best acquired through actual use in meaningful situations. Instruction should be guided by the needs and interests of the learners and real literature should be used as much as possible (Giddings, 1992).

The proponents of whole language believe that it is consistent with Piaget's theory of human development because a child's use of language materials matches that child's level of cognitive development. Proponents also claim that it is consistent with Vygotsky's work because of the important role that context plays in a child's attempts to master reading and writing (McCaslin, 1989).

How the Whole Language Concept "Works"

Shifting from dependence on a basal language series to whole language requires teachers to rethink their assumptions about literature and language learning. For example, in the whole language strategy, many teachers will work with themes: friendship, loyalty, and honesty. First children will read a story that illustrates the theme. This is known as *experiencing the literature.* Next the teacher may read a related story or poem; pupils are *listening to the literature.*

Now the teacher may attempt to *expand* the concepts that the children experienced in their literature and simultaneously work on vocabulary using various techniques. Next children may read the selection cooperatively (taking turns with their partners or reading aloud about a particular character in the story). They can then discuss the characters in the story.

At this point, the children may *respond* to the literature by completing a story form (sentences with missing words, explaining the beginning and ending, telling how the story's problem was solved). The teacher may ask them to evaluate the characters' actions in the story or give their own opinions about the story. Some children may explore language; that is, if they need help with vocabulary or phonics, or with general reading strategies, they are now guided to appropriate activities.

The children now shift from reading to writing. For example, they may write a paragraph explaining a particular part of the story. They use the words they have learned in their reading and apply them to their writing. They can be taught how to proofread and to revise in this phase.

With their reading and writing experiences completed, and if time permits, children may *extend their reading experiences.* That is, if the theme of their work was friendship, they may do independent research that could include examples of friendship in stories, friendship between leaders of nations, or friendship between people of different cultures.

The ideal time for the introduction of whole language is during the early childhood period. Children of this age are experiencing a rapid natural growth of language and enjoying the newfound power that language confers, which is the rationale for harnessing this exuberance and using it to further their learning.

Critics of the whole language approach believe that children can miss many necessary fundamentals because of the lack of a structured curriculum. What's your view?

Whole language

A method in which students learn to read by obtaining the meaning of words, with phonics being introduced when needed from context.

Receptive language

Language that children use to show an understanding of words without necessarily producing them.

Expressive language

Language that children use to express their own ideas and needs.

As we trace the path of language development in the early childhood years, you should remember a basic distinction that children quite clearly demonstrate. At about 1 year (the infancy period), children show an ability for **receptive language** ("show me your nose"—they receive and understand these words). Now, in early childhood, they produce language themselves, **expressive language.** How do children acquire these language milestones?

The Pattern of Language Development

As mentioned earlier, all children learn their native tongue, and at similar ages they manifest similar patterns of language development. The basic sequence of language development during early childhood is that at about 2 1/2 years, most children produce complete sentences, begin to ask questions, and use negative statements. At about 4 years they have acquired the complicated structure of their native tongue, and in about two or three more years they speak and understand sentences that they have never previously used or heard.

As children grow, specifying the extent of their vocabularies is difficult. Do we mean spoken words only? Or do we include words that children may not use but clearly understand? Building a vocabulary is an amazing accomplishment. For example, the vocabulary of every language is categorized; that is, some words are nouns, some are verbs, still others are adjectives, prepositions, or conjunctions. If English had only 1,000 nouns and 1,000 verbs, we could form 1 million sentences (1,000 × 1,000). But nouns can be used as objects as well as subjects. Therefore the number of possible three-word sentences increases to one billion (1,000 × 1,000 × 1,000).

One billion sentences is the result of a starkly impoverished vocabulary. The number of sentences that could be generated from English, with its thousands of nouns and verbs, plus adjectives, adverbs, prepositions, and conjunctions, staggers the imagination. Estimates are that it would take trillions of years to say all possible English sentences of 20 words. In this context, the ability of children to acquire their language is an astounding achievement. Although most youngsters experience problems with some tasks during this period—difficulty with reading or mathematics—they acquire their language easily and in just a few years. Remember, don't confuse youngsters who demonstrate a serious language problem (such as lack of comprehension) with those who experience temporary setbacks.

Overextensions

Children's tendency to apply a word too widely.

When speech emerges, certain irregularities appear that are quite normal and to be expected. For example, **overextensions** mark children's beginning words. Assume that a child has learned the name of the house pet, *doggy*. Think what that label means: an animal with a head, tail, body, and four legs. Now consider what other animals "fit" this label: cats, horses, donkeys, and cows. Consequently, children may briefly apply *doggy* to all four-legged creatures; they quickly eliminate overextensions, however, as they learn about their world.

Overregularities

Children's inappropriate use of language rules they have learned.

Overregularities are a similar fleeting phenomenon. As youngsters begin to use two- and three-word sentences, they struggle to convey more precise meanings by mastering the grammatical rules of their language. For example, many English verbs add *ed* to indicate past tense.

> I want to play ball.
> I wanted to play ball.

Other verbs change their form much more radically.

> Did Daddy come home?
> Daddy came home.

Most children, even after they have mastered the correct form of such verbs as *come, see,* and *run,* still add *ed* to the original form. That is, youngsters who know that the past tense of *come* is *came* will still say:

> Daddy comed home.

Again, this phenomenon persists only briefly and is another example of the close link between language and thought. We know that from birth, children respond to patterns. They look longer at the human face than they will at diagrams because the human face is more complex. (Remember the Fantz study?) Once they have learned a pattern such as adding *ed* to signify past tense, they have considerable difficulty in changing the pattern.

The path of language development is similar for all children. A particular culture has little to do with language emergence, but it has everything to do with the shape that any language assumes. Children will not speak before a certain time—this is a biological given and nothing will change it. But once language appears, it is difficult to retard its progress. Usually only some traumatic event such as brain damage (which we have discussed) or dramatically deprived environmental conditions can hinder development.

Summarizing, then, as children come to the end of the early childhood period, several language milestones have been achieved:

- Children become skillful in building words; adding suffixes such as *er, man,* and *ist* to form nouns (the person who performs experiments is an *experimenter*).

- They begin to be comfortable with passive sentences (the glass *was broken* by the wind).

- By the end of the early childhood period, children can pronounce almost all English speech sounds accurately.

- As we have noted, this is the time of the "language explosion" and vocabulary has grown rapidly.

- Children of this age are aware of grammatical correctness.

Metalinguistic Awareness

Metacognition, as mentioned earlier, refers to children's ability to step back and look at the various cognitive skills that they have developed. One of these cognitive skills is language, and probably nothing reveals the close link between cognitive and language development more than a youngster's acquisition of metalinguistic awareness (Dash & Mohanty, 1992). At about the age of 6, youngsters acquire this ability to "look at language and not through it," which is the meaning of **metalinguistic awareness.**

Metalinguistic awareness
A capacity to think about and talk about language.

The stages in the acquisition of metalinguistic awareness have been summarized as follows by Bullinger and Chatillon (1983).

- *For 4-year-olds,* words exist on the same plane as the things to which they refer. "Train is a long word because a train has a lot of cars."

- *From 5 to 6 years,* children identify words with the activity of speaking. "A word is when you talk."

- *From 6 to 7 years,* words are differentiated from what they represent. Youngsters now begin to show an understanding of language.

A good example of metalinguistic awareness is seen in the developmental progression of listening skills (McDevitt & others, 1990). In a study of first, third, and fifth graders, researchers found that the older children relied less on behavioral cues and more on comprehension. Children of all ages responded to speakers by combining their judgments of the speaker's competence with the norms of the situation (home, school).

Another example of how children's understanding their language affects their accomplishments is the work of Dresher and Zenge (1990) on the relationship between metalinguistic awareness and reading success. Studying 65 first graders, these investigators found that the students with greater metalinguistic ability were superior readers in the third and fifth grades. These researchers conclude that metalinguistic awareness is a good predictor of later reading success.

Bilingualism

Finally, we must recognize that many children in the United States do not speak or write English as their native language, and the number is growing. All evidence points to the conclusion that our country today is more diverse ethnically and linguistically than ever before. For example, while the country's population increased by 11.6 percent between the years 1970 and 1980, the Asian American community increased by 233 percent, Native Americans by 71 percent, Hispanics by 61 percent, and African Americans by 17.8 percent. Moreover, estimates are that at least 3.4 million pupils are limited in English language skills in a school system primarily designed for those who speak English (Lindholm, 1990).

To help make these figures more meaningful, consider this: The New York City school system, in the last four years, has enrolled 138,000 immigrant children and in the year in which this is written, 1994–95, will enroll 18,000 more. But suburban school systems are also experiencing the same increase. In one system of 5,300 students, the children speak 25 languages; in a larger Northeast system, the children speak 46 languages. How have the schools responded to these challenges?

AN APPLIED VIEW

The Case of Genie

The startling case of Genie illustrates the durability of language but also demonstrates its vulnerability. Discovered in the upstairs room of a suburban Los Angeles home, Genie was 13 years old and weighed only 60 pounds when found. She could not stand or chew solid food, nor was she toilet trained (Curtiss, 1977).

From the age of 20 months she had been confined to a small, shaded room where she had been kept in a crib or tied to a chair. Any noises that she made were greeted with a beating. Few, if any, words were exchanged with her parents; the home had no radio or television set. She was usually fed baby food. Genie also had a congenital hip problem that caused her father to think that she was severely retarded. She had emotional difficulties but had normal hearing and vision. Her language comprehension and usage were almost nonexistent.

After treatment in the Children's Hospital of Los Angeles, Genie was placed in a foster home where she acquired language, more from exposure than any formal training. Estimates are that she has acquired as much language in eight years as the normal child acquires in three. She continues to have articulation problems and difficulty with word order.

Although Genie has made remarkable language progress, difficulties persist. For example, she does not appear to have mastered the rules of language (her grammar is unpredictable), she continues to use the stereotypic speech of the language-disabled child, and she seems to understand more language than she can produce. Thus the case of Genie suggests that while language is difficult to retard, sufficiently severe conditions can affect progress in language. Here we see the meaning of a sensitive period when applied to language development.

Bilingual Education Programs

In a landmark decision in 1974 (*Lau v. Nichols*), the U.S. Supreme Court ruled that LEP (Limited English Proficiency) students in San Francisco were being discriminated against because they were not receiving the same education as their English-speaking classmates. The school district was ordered to provide means for LEP students to participate in all instructional programs. The manner of implementing the decision was left to the school district under the guidance of the lower courts. This decision provided the impetus for the implementation of bilingual education programs in the United States.

Two different techniques for aiding LEP pupils emerged from this decision. The *English as a Second Language* (ESL) program usually has students removed from class and given special English instruction. The intent is to have these pupils acquire enough English to allow them to learn in their regular classes that are taught in English. With the *bilingual* technique, students are taught partly in English and partly in their native language. The objective here is to help pupils to learn English by subject matter instruction in their own language and in English. Thus they acquire subject matter knowledge simultaneously with English. In today's schools, bilingual education has become the program of choice.

Bilingual education programs can also be divided into two categories. First are those programs (sometimes called *transitional* programs) in which the rapid development of English is to occur so that students may switch as soon as possible to an all-English program. Second are those programs (sometimes referred to as *maintenance* programs) that permit LEP students to remain in them even after they have become proficient in English. The rationale for such programs is that students can use both languages to develop mature skills and to become fully bilingual.

The difference between these two programs lies in their objectives. Transitional programs are basically compensatory; that is, they use the students' native language only to compensate for their lack of English. Maintenance programs, however, are intended to bring students to the fullest use of both languages. As you can well imagine, transitional programs are the most widely used in the schools.

Since the use of two languages in classroom instruction actually defines bilingual education, several important questions must be answered.

- What is an acceptable level of English that signals the end of a student's participation?

- What subjects should be taught in each language?

- How can each language be used most effectively? (That is, how much of each language is to be used to help a student's progress with school subjects?)

- Should English be gradually phased in or should students be totally immersed in the second language (which, for most of the students we are discussing, would be English)?

One reason for the controversy surrounding these programs is that research has yet to grapple with many of the important variables. For example, what should be evaluated, English proficiency or subject matter success? How can the quality of the program be assessed? How alike are the children in any program (ability, SES, proficiency in their native languages, the level of English on entering the program)?

While the answers to these and other questions continue to spark controversy, bilingual programs allow students to retain their cultural identities while simultaneously progressing in their school subjects. These programs also offer the opportunity for pupils to become truly bilingual, especially if programs begin early. Given the early childhood youngster's ability to acquire language, early childhood is an ideal time to introduce a new language, both to help a child's adjustment and to prepare for school instruction.

Many misconceptions have surrounded the educational progress of students with an ability to speak two or more languages. For example, introducing a second language does *not* hurt the development of a student's primary language. Bilingual children will *not* become confused by the use of two languages. In the past, a common practice has been to emphasize English and minimize the student's primary language, which has caused McLaughlin (1990) to note the following:

■ Educational programs that do not attempt to maintain the child's first language deprive many children of economic opportunities they would otherwise have as bilinguals. This is especially true of children who speak world languages used for international communication such as Spanish, Japanese, Chinese, and the like. If these children's first languages are not maintained, one of this country's most valuable resources will be wasted. (p. 74)

🌳 Guided Review 🌳

18. Most children have completed the greater part of language acquisition by the age of _____ .

19. _____ describes how to put sounds together to form words.

20. Calling all four-legged, furry animals *doggy* would be an example of _____ .

21. The ability for receptive language demonstrated in the infancy period is advanced to include _____ language in early childhood.

22. The development of language can be hindered by _____ _____ or _____ _____ _____ .

23. The two chief methods for instructing non-English-speaking students are _____ _____ and _____ .

Answers

18. 5   19. Phonology   20. overextension   21. expressive   22. brain damage, deprived environmental conditions   23. bilingual education, ESL.

TEACHING NON-ENGLISH-SPEAKING STUDENTS: BILINGUAL EDUCATION OR ESL?

By the turn of the century, about 40 percent of public school students will be from ethnically diverse backgrounds, and these students may be at risk because of an English language deficit. Bilingual education, which offers these students course instruction in their native language while they study English separately, is a major commitment because academic fluency takes about seven years. Many issues concerning bilingual education generate conflicting, often heated, opinions such as the following:

■ Issue: Bilingual education is the way American public schools should educate non-English-speaking students.

Answer—Pro Students in bilingual education are not penalized because of a language deficit. They are able to stay current with their studies because they are taught in their native language, which helps to maintain students' self-esteem while they gain proficiency in English.

Answer—Con Bilingual education is not that helpful to these students. Students who eventually succeed in the marketplace are proficient in English. Bilingual education wastes valuable time reinforcing students' native languages instead of teaching them English.

■ Issue: English as a Second Language (ESL) is a good alternative program to bilingual education.

Answer—Pro ESL is a desirable program because most of a student's course work is in English, with separate time allotted for specific English language instruction. Students are grouped according to grade level and the ESL teacher uses the student's classroom curriculum.

Answer—Con ESL does not give students support in their native language. In spite of English language training these students fall behind. Older students in particular may have difficulty with this technique.

■ Issue: Since English is the official language of government and commerce in the United States, classroom instruction in public school classrooms should be in English.

Answer—Pro One of the goals of public school education is fluency in spoken and written English. If students are in an environment where only English is spoken, they will learn the language more quickly. These students may have initial difficulty but once they have acquired English proficiency, they typically catch up.

Answer—Con Non-English-speaking students are often put in with students younger than themselves while gaining English proficiency. Or if they are put in with their peers, they suffer because they cannot keep up with the course work. Both of these conditions result in a loss of self-esteem for the students, which can then affect total academic performance and may cause the student(s) to drop out of school altogether.

What's your view?

CONCLUSION

Thus far in our discussion of the early childhood years, we have seen that although the rate of growth slows somewhat, it still continues at a steady pace. Physical and motor skills become more refined. Cognitive development during these years leads to a world of representation in which children are expected to acquire and manipulate symbols. Language gradually becomes a powerful tool in adapting to the environment.

Other aspects of development, however, affect the direction a child's development takes. Youngsters in early childhood seem to "come into their own." Their emerging personalities take on definite dimensions in these years. They must learn to adjust to family members—perhaps a new brother or sister. Many children of this age experience the shock of parental separation and divorce, with its developmental overtones. For many, the idea of family takes on new meaning. These are among the important topics to which we now turn.

CHAPTER HIGHLIGHTS

Features of the Early Childhood Years

- Children of these years, aware of their growing competence, often clash with the wishes of their parents and teachers.
- Understanding early childhood development requires knowledge of the physical, cognitive, and social processes affecting children.

Physical and Motor Development

- Growth continues at a steady, less rapid rate during these years.

- Brain lateralization seems to be well established by the age of 5 or 6.
- Height is a good indicator of normal development when heredity and environment are considered in evaluating health.

- Increasing competence and mastery are seen in a child's acquisition of motor skills.

Cognitive Development

- These years are the time of Piaget's preoperational period and the continued appearance of symbolic abilities.
- Children's growing cognitive proficiency is seen in their use of humor.
- Many current early childhood programs have a cognitive orientation.

Early Childhood Education

- Many preschool programs are based on the ideas of Piaget and Montessori.
- Project Head Start was originally designed to offer educational and developmental services to disadvantaged children.
- Several positive social and emotional outcomes seem to be associated with Head Start programs.

Language Development

- Children acquire the basics of their language during these years with little, if any, instruction.
- All children seem to follow the same pattern in acquiring their language.
- Children whose native language is not English need a carefully designed program to support their native language and to help them acquire English as efficiently as possible.

🌳 KEY TERMS

🌳 WHAT DO YOU THINK?

1. As you can tell from the data presented in this chapter, early childhood youngsters continue their rapid growth, although at a less frantic rate than during infancy. Consider yourself a parent of a child of this age (boy or girl) for a moment. How much would you encourage them to participate in organized, directed physical activities (swimming, dancing, soccer, etc.)? Be sure to give specific reasons for your answer.

2. As you read Paul McGhee's account of the development of children's humor, could you explain his stages by comparing them with Piaget's work? Do you think this is a logical way to proceed? Why?

3. When you consider the tragic case of Genie compared to the enormous language growth of most children, what comes to your mind? Does it change your opinion about how language develops? In what way? What do you think this case implies for the existence of a sensitive period for language development?

🌳 SUGGESTED READINGS

Hauser-Cram, P., Pierson, D., Klein Walker, D., & Tivnan, T. (1991). *Early education in the public schools.* San Francisco: Jossey-Bass. An excellent review of early childhood programs designed according to developmentally appropriate principles.

Moskowitz, B. (1979). The acquisition of language. *Scientific American, 239,* 92–108. If you are like most readers encountering the basics of language development for the first time, you could use a good summary of the process. This article, still one of the best, is clear, thorough, and well written. You will find it helpful.

Zigler, E. & Muenchow, S. (1992). *Head Start.* New York: Basic Books. A fascinating, well-written history of the early intervention movement and its role in attempting to prepare disadvantaged children for a successful school experience.

🌳 CHAPTER REVIEW TEST

1. By the age of 4 a child should be able to
   a. walk on tiptoes.
   b. draw a recognizable person.
   c. skip.
   d. throw ball overhand.

2. The early childhood period coincides with Erikson's time of autonomy and
   a. sensitive responsiveness.
   b. attachment.
   c. initiative.
   d. goodness of fit.

3. A 5-year-old may have as many as _____ words in his/her vocabulary.
   a. 5,000
   b. 2,100
   c. 500
   d. 900

4. During the early childhood period
   a. girls grow at a faster rate than boys.
   b. girls and boys grow at about the same rate.
   c. boys grow at a faster rate than girls.
   d. boys grow at a faster rate until age 4.

5. Children whose normal growth is interrupted are called
   a. disturbed.
   b. motorically lazy.
   c. developmentally delayed.
   d. slow learners.

6. Which of the following factors is *not* known to influence physical development?
   a. genetic elements
   b. SES
   c. disease
   d. ethnicity

7. Which of the following would *not* be considered a motor skill?
   a. running
   b. skipping
   c. tying shoes
   d. singing

8. Children's drawings provide clues to all but one of the following. Which one?
   a. cognitive life
   b. social life
   c. emotional life
   d. motor coordination

9. Which of the following behaviors is *not* associated with the preoperational period?
   a. symbolic play
   b. drawing
   c. language
   d. walks steadily

10. A child's belief that inanimate objects are real and conscious is known as
    a. artificialisim.
    b. delusion.
    c. animism.
    d. centration.

11. By the time children are ready to enter kindergarten they are at the
    a. absorbent mind phase
    b. conservation phase
    c. reversibility phase
    d. uniform growth phase

12. McGhee notes that the basis of most children's humor is
    a. irony.
    b. play on words.
    c. incongruity.
    d. sarcasm.

13. Effective use of humor is not credited with stimulating
    a. motor development.
    b. creative thinking.
    c. social development.
    d. emotional development.

14. Montessori's ideas concerning _____ periods are important in planning preschool programs.
    a. lengthy
    b. class
    c. sensitive
    d. time

15. Project Head Start was initiated in the
    a. 1960s.
    b. 1970s.
    c. 1980s.
    d. 1990s.

16. "Looking at language and not through it" refers to
    a. whole language.
    b. language acquisition.
    c. language rules.
    d. metalinguistic awareness.

17. The rules of _____ describe how to put words together to form sentences.
    a. phonology
    b. semantics
    c. syntax
    d. pragmatics

18. A child can use short sentences and questions by the age of _____ years.
    a. 2
    b. 3
    c. 4
    d. 5

19. A 3-year-old stating, "Daddy camed home" is an example of
    a. overextension.
    b. mispronunciation.
    c. overregulation.
    d. delayed development.

20. By the end of the early childhood period children still cannot
    a. appreciate jokes and riddles based on ambiguities in syntax.
    b. pronounce almost all English speech sounds.
    c. increase their vocabulary greatly.
    d. gain awareness of grammatical correctness.

Answers

1. a 2. c 3. b 4. b 5. c 6. d 7. d 8. b 9. d 10. c 11. a 12. c 13. a 14. d 15. a 16. d 17. c 18. b 19. c 20. a

 **8**

Psychosocial Development in Early Childhood

Chapter Outline

The physical activities of the early childhood years are a time not only for play and games but also for learning and adjustment.

Barbara is a former nurse who now takes care of four neighborhood children, ranging in age from 9 months to 4 years. A neat, careful person who loves children (she has two of her own away at school), she is sensitive to their needs and aware of the developmental changes constantly occurring in her four children. Barbara is in great demand by neighborhood families because of these traits, but she refuses to take more than four children at a time.

It's eight o'clock in the morning and Gina, a 4-year-old dynamo, is at the door with her mother, Janice. Janice takes courses at the local college and leaves Gina with Barbara three days each week. Barbara smiles at the thought of Gina. Pretty, bright, and active, with springs in her legs, Gina usually leads the other children (and Barbara) on a merry chase. When you talk to her, Gina constantly bounces up and down.

Janice and Gina walk into the front room, which is spotless and filled with toys arranged attractively along the walls. It's apparent that this home is designed for children: bright, cheerful, and safe. Janice and Barbara talk about Gina for a few minutes; she had a cold the previous day and had a restless night, but Janice says she seems fine now. Upon seeing her 3-year-old friend, Amy, Gina darts over and begins to hug her.

Barbara and Janice watch as Gina asks Amy if she wants to see her new dance. (Gina takes a dance class and will be in a recital soon.) Without waiting for an answer, she goes through her dance and takes a deep bow. Amy laughs happily as Janice and Barbara applaud. Gina then takes Amy's hand and pulls her toward the backyard with its swings and sandbox.

It's so easy to tell how Gina feels by observing her play, Barbara thinks. Today she seems to be feeling better, has her energy back, and wants to play physically. At other times, Barbara has seen Gina working out a conflict with Janice by playing with dolls and assigning them mother-daughter roles. In her pretend play world, there were "mommy" dolls, "good" dolls, "bad" dolls, and "napping" dolls. As Barbara watches, she thinks to herself, as she does so often, what a wonderful time these years are. 🌳

During the early childhood years, youngsters blossom into distinct personalities. Although temperamental differences are apparent at birth, they now flourish until even the casual observer notices a child's "personality." Early childhood youngsters begin a period in which they must reconcile their individuality with the restrictions of the world around them.

This period is often described as one of socialization versus individuation. **Socialization** means the need to establish and maintain relations with others and to regulate behavior according to society's demands. **Individuation** refers to the fullest development of one's self. These two functions seem to pull in opposite directions. Society has certain regulations that its members must follow if chaos is to be avoided. Yet these rules must not be so rigid that the individual members who constitute the society cannot develop their potential to the fullest.

Any society, ours included, demands resolution of the tension between the two. Each needs the other. In chapter 7, individuation was stressed, the emergence of individual physical and cognitive abilities. In this chapter, we'll explore the expression of those talents within a societal context and trace the possible sources of tension.

In a thoughtful essay on children in our society today, Neil Postman (1982) argued that childhood has actually disappeared. Citing highly paid 12-year-old models, toddlers in designer jeans, and the growing absence of children's games, Postman lamented the disappearance of childhood. In a highly technological society with instant and open communication, nothing is withheld from youngsters. Calling television the "total disclosure medium," Postman believed that the lines separating adulthood from childhood are being erased. This loss of a distinct childhood results in a loss of shame. Everything is revealed to children; there are no secrets.

To come to grips with these issues, in this chapter we'll examine the modern family, tracing the stages through which it proceeds, the impact of parenting on children, the effect of divorce on development, and the growing importance of day care in our society. Throughout these years, a child's sense of personal identity is gradually emerging. Its inherent temperamental characteristics are tempered by the reactions of family members, teachers, and peers. Finally, we'll comment on the significance of play to children of this age.

Socialization

Refers to the need to establish and maintain relations with others and to regulate behavior according to society's demands.

Individuation

Refers to the fullest development of one's self.

Do you think today's parents (those you know) are doing a good job in helping their children recognize the distinction between socialization and individuation? Give specific examples.

Television, one of the major socializing agents in a child's life, can have both prosocial and antisocial consequences. Consequently, parents should carefully monitor what their children watch.

After reading this chapter, you should be able to

- Assess the impact of the family on a child's development.
- Evaluate the influence of parenting behavior on a child's development.
- Compare the various types of day-care centers.
- Describe the role of preschool education during the early childhood years.
- Determine the importance of self-esteem in a child's life.
- Appraise the function of play in a child's development.

Our initial task, though, is to examine that great socializing agent—the family.

The Family in Development

This section could have been written for any chapter in a lifespan book, but it is particularly pertinent here because the family is still recognized as the great socializing agent. Before we begin our analysis, it would be well to remember that any family is dynamic, not static. Families change, and as they do, they exercise different effects on a child's development—some significant, others not so (Scarr, 1992).

For example, children who remain in an intact family, or who experience the death of a parent, or who go through a parental divorce all undergo unique experiences that must affect development. We need not be so dramatic, however. All families sustain normal change in the course of the lives of their members.

The Changing Family

As social conditions change—working mothers, single-parent families—fathers have become more involved in child care. Children thus see their parents in roles different from the more stereotypical views of the past.

Defining "family" in our changing society is becoming increasingly difficult. As Garbarino (1992) noted, family takes many different forms, both across cultures and within societies. Traditionally, a man and woman marry and raise children. Today, however, we see many variations of this basic theme. Most of us are born into a family—the family of origin—and later in life usually start a family of our own—the family of procreation. You can see, then, that most people spend much of their lives in family units of one type or another.

The nature of that unit has changed dramatically. For example, in 1970, 70 percent of all households in the United States had married couples; in 1990, that figure had dropped to 56 percent. In 1970, 40 percent of married couples had children; in 1990, that figure had dropped to 26 percent. In 1970, 18 percent of families had three or more children; in 1990, that figure had dropped to 7 percent (U.S. Bureau of Census, 1991). About half of all children will spend some time in a single-parent household before they are 18.

Noting that these changes make defining a family a difficult task, Garbarino and Abramowitz (1992) used the following criteria: A family is any two people related by blood, marriage, or adoption. Whatever the particular type of family, The National Commission on Children (1991) has identified several characteristics of a strong family:

- Open and frequent communication among family members
- A feeling of belonging to a warm, supportive social unit
- Respect for individual members
- An ability to cope with stressful events
- Well-defined roles and responsibilities

Remember: Any analysis of family life contains two major themes. First is the nature of the family itself. In the late twentieth century, the identification of various forms of family living has sharply altered our view of the traditional family. Different family styles have always existed. Population projections and estimates of family styles present a fairly consistent pattern: Change will continue, but it will represent a modification of current styles. For example, the number of single mothers will increase, but as governmental support also increases, there will undoubtedly be more and better day-care services, increased after-school programs for the older children, and perhaps greater flexibility in the work schedules of working parents. The second major theme is the developmental consequences of these changes. Here we find much less certainty, since it is simply too soon to make definite statements.

As society changes, how families respond also changes. Children cannot escape the results, positive or negative, of these twists and turns of family living. We also know that one of the most important characteristics of any family is the way that parents treat their children. For example, Dekovic and Janssens (1992) found that popular and rejected children had different experiences. Parents of popular children used an authoritative/democratic style when interacting with their children, relying on verbal persuasion, positive reinforcement, and indirect methods of control. Parents of rejected children tended to be authoritarian/restrictive; that is, they were more critical and controlling.

Parenting Behavior

In a careful analysis of the relationship between parental behavior and children's competence, Baumrind (1967, 1971, 1986, 1991) discovered three kinds of parental behavior: authoritarian, authoritative, and permissive. Here is what she means by each of the types.

Authoritarian Parents

Authoritarian parents are demanding, and for them instant obedience is the most desirable child trait. When there is any conflict between these parents and their children (Why can't I go to the party?), no consideration is given to the child's view, no attempt is made to explain why the youngster can't go to the party, and often the child is punished for even asking.

Authoritative Parents

Authoritative parents respond to their children's needs and wishes. Believing in parental control, they attempt to explain the reasons for it to their children. Authoritative parents expect mature behavior and will enforce rules, but they encourage their children's independence and search for potential. They try to have their youngsters understand that both parents and children have rights. In the resolution of socialization versus individuation, authoritative parents try to maintain a happy balance between the two.

Permissive Parents

Baumrind believed that **permissive parents** take a tolerant, accepting view of their children's behavior, including both aggressive and sexual urges. They rarely use punishment or make demands of their children. Children make almost all of their own decisions. Distinguishing indulgence from indifference in these parents can be difficult. Table 8.1 summarizes the relationship between Baumrind's categories of parenting behavior and levels of control, clarity of communication, maturity demands, and nurturance.

As you can see, authoritative parents are high on control (they have definite standards for their children), high on clarity of communication (the children clearly understand what is expected of them), high in maturity demands (they want their children to behave in a way appropriate for their age), and high in nurturance (a warm, loving relationship exists between parents and children). Thus, according to Baumrind's work, authoritative parents are most desirable. Table 8.2 presents the relationship between Baumrind's classes of parenting behavior and children's characteristics.

Authoritarian parents
Baumrind's term for parents who are demanding and want instant obedience as the most desirable child trait.

Authoritative parents
Baumrind's term for parents who respond to their children's needs and wishes; believing in parental control, they attempt to explain the reasons for it to their children.

Permissive parents
Those parents who take a tolerant, accepting view of their children's behavior.

How would you categorize the behavior of your parents? Do you think your parents' behavior affected you, either positively or negatively?

Table 8.1	Patterns of Child-Rearing Behavior					
	Authoritarian		Authoritative		Permissive	
	High	*Low*	*High*	*Low*	*High*	*Low*
Control	•		•			•
Clarity of communication		•	•		•	
Maturity demands	•		•			•
Nurturance		•	•		•	

Table 8.2	Parental Behaviors and Children's Characteristics		
	Parental Behaviors		
	Authoritarian	*Authoritative*	*Permissive*
Children's characteristics	Withdrawn Lack of enthusiasm Shy (girls) Hostile (boys) Low need achievement Low competence	Self-assertive Independent Friendly Cooperative High need achievement High competence	Impulsive Low self-reliance Low self-control Low maturity Aggressive Lack of responsibility

Secure parents

Those parents who are confident of their techniques; they assume they will cope successfully and look on parenting as an exciting challenge.

Insecure parents

Those parents who believe everything they do inevitably influences their child's destiny; they feel overwhelmed by the difficulties of parenting.

Intimidated parents

Those parents who lack the ability to be firm with their child.

Overinterpretive parents

Those parents who feel they must explore in depth the complex psychological meanings behind their child's behavior.

Victimized parents

Those parents who believe it just isn't fair if their child shows any sign of a problem after all *they* have done for the child.

Today, most developmental psychologists believe that there are two kinds of permissive parents: permissive-indulgent and permissive-indifferent (Maccoby & Martin, 1983). *Permissive-indifferent* refers to those parents who are not interested in their children's lives. *Permissive-indulgent* applies to those parents who are quite involved with their children but who are tolerant and accepting and who avoid using their authority and rarely punish their children.

Baumrind's findings have held firm over the years. As Dornbusch and others (1987) stated, authoritative parents have adolescents who achieve better and demonstrate more positive social adjustment than children whose parents adopted either authoritarian or permissive parenting styles. Yet these findings apply to white, middle-class families with both parents present. Children reared in single-parent families may experience quite different parenting behaviors. (See the section "Children of Divorce" that follows later.)

For example, examining the various types of families in a modern society, Chess and Thomas (1987) have identified the following six parenting styles. In so doing they have attempted to differentiate the behaviors a parent brings to child rearing from those that are a reaction to a child's behavior. **Secure parents** are confident of their techniques; if they make mistakes, they can change with no harm done. They assume they will cope successfully and look on parenting as an exciting challenge. This is not to state that all secure parents have the same parenting style, but the one defining theme is their security.

Insecure parents believe everything they do inevitably influences their child's destiny. The difficulties of parenting overwhelm them; when things turn out positively, they attribute it to luck. *Anything* to do with their child becomes a major issue. **Intimidated parents** lack the ability to be firm with their child. Whether from fear, guilt, or stress, their parenting style can only be described as one of appeasement. **Overinterpretive parents** feel they must explore in depth the complex psychological meanings behind their child's behavior. **Victimized parents** believe it just isn't fair if their child shows any sign of a problem after all *they* have

Pathological parents
Those parents who actually suffer from a form of mental illness, which does not necessarily mean that their child will be subject to psychological disturbances.

done for the child; that is, it must be their child's fault. **Pathological parents** are those who actually suffer from a form of mental illness, which does not necessarily mean that their child will be subject to psychological disturbances.

These different styles will *not* determine a child's psychological development. Rather it is the match between parenting behaviors and a child's temperament that is decisive, the *goodness of fit* that we discussed in chapter 6. For example, the parents of minority children may have different goals and expectations for their children than did the parents in Baumrind's study, which implies that the goodness of fit will be different.

A good example can be seen in the work of Lin and Fu (1990) who studied childrearing practices among Chinese, immigrant Chinese, and Caucasian American parents of early childhood youngsters. They found a shifting pattern of parenting behaviors among the parents of Chinese origin, especially with regard to fostering independence in their children. Contrary to earlier research findings, they discovered both groups of Chinese parents had higher ratings on encouraging independence in their children than did the Caucasian American parents. Yet these same parents also reflected traditional values such as exerting greater control over their children and having higher academic expectations for their children than did the American sample.

Finally, we must assess the question of how much children's temperaments affect the way they are treated; in other words, what the interaction is between a child's temperament and parenting behavior. In his elegant treatise on temperament, Kagan (1994), although arguing that temperament cannot be reduced to biology, noted that neither can physiology be removed from any analysis of temperament. That is, we cannot say that because a child is aggressive and uninhibited that parenting behaviors are solely at fault. The biological input into temperament must also be considered. The critical question is: *How* do temperament and parenting behavior interact and *what* will be the resulting behavior? Baumrind has acknowledged the influence of temperament but has also argued that parenting behavior must have a decided impact on a child's behavior.

Next in our discussion of the role of family in development is a growing phenomenon in our society, one that affects an increasing number of children—homelessness.

Homeless Children

Traditional definitions of homelessness focused on the lack of a permanent place to live. Researchers now, however, tend to be more specific and concentrate on those who rely on shelters for their residence, or who live on the streets or in parks. The homeless today represent a different population from the days when they were seen as alcoholic men clustered together on skid rows. The so-called new homeless population is younger and much more mixed: more single women, more families, and more minorities. Families with young children may be the fastest-growing segment of today's homeless. On any given night, 100,000 children in this country will be homeless (Walsh, 1992). The homeless are also characterized by few social contacts, poor health, and a high level of contact with the criminal justice system. Although the paths to homelessness are many, we cannot avoid discussing the role that poverty plays in this growing phenomenon.

The Children of Poverty

Children of poverty experience more health problems, many of which can be traced to prenatal difficulties, than children who do not live in poverty. More of these children die in the neonatal and infancy periods; they simply lack adequate health care. They suffer more accidents than more fortunate children and are exposed to greater stress: occupational, financial, housing, dangerous neighborhoods. We know that parental stress can often translate into poor parenting practices (depression, irritability, abuse), which can lead to behavioral and emotional problems and academic difficulty. Finally, as we are aware from the daily news, these children often witness, and are the targets of, violence such as physical assault, rape, and shootings. The danger in all of this, of course, is that poverty becomes a self-perpetuating cycle (Huston & others, 1994). The conditions we have described put children at an immediate disadvantage: school difficulties (perhaps dropping out in the upper grades), low self-esteem, troublesome behavior, limited occupational opportunities, and encounters with the law. Erratic employment contributes to poverty and the cycle commences again.

Analyses of the children of poverty typically focus on income, education, occupation, and social status, yet other, potentially more powerful, psychological forces are also at work. For example, can children living in poverty avoid feelings of powerlessness? It doesn't take them long to perceive that they have little influence in their society, have access to fewer societal opportunities, and are more likely to have their lives directed by others.

How do these facts translate into meaningful differences in the lives of these children? Classroom performance is a good example. Although our interpretation and use of intelligence tests has changed dramatically, these tests remain an indicator of achievement. Today children at a lower socioeconomic level score 10 to 15 IQ points below middle-class children; these differences are not only *present by the first grade,* they persist throughout the school years. Since the differences in these scores undoubtedly reflect social class distinctions, efforts have been made to discover any patterns that may exist. Profiles drawn from the data suggest that social class may cause an increase in scores, but the general pattern of intellectual ability was similar. That is, when profiles of lower-class children were drawn, they showed the children were like the middle-class children but they were lower on all abilities (Hetherington & Parke, 1993).

Consequently, socioeconomic status remains a reliable predictor of school achievement and suggests that students from the same social class will perform in a remarkably similar manner. For example, in a study of eighth graders, low SES white children are as likely as African American and Latino students to have poor grades. In this same study, low SES Asian American students did not achieve much better than other low SES students (Weiss & others, 1989). These and similar results testify to the conclusion that socioeconomic status, more than any other variable, predicts educational outcome.

Paths to Homelessness

Families seem to move into homelessness in one of three ways. First is the family that quickly shifts from stable housing to homelessness. These families usually have been evicted or have experienced rent difficulties; their rent exceeded a public allowance they were receiving. Second is the family caught in a "slow shift" from stable housing to homelessness. These families usually had lost permanent housing about a year earlier and had doubled up with another family but could contribute nothing to the rent and had to move to a shelter. Finally, there are those families, usually headed by young mothers, that had never maintained permanent housing (Weitzman & others, 1990).

The rates of alcohol, drug, and mental disorders are much higher among the homeless than in the general population: Alcohol disorders are found in about two-thirds of the homeless, drug and mental disorders in about half of homeless adults (Fischer & Breakey, 1991). These problems are often found together; alcoholics are frequently drug abusers. When you consider these figures and then realize that 30 percent of the homeless population in the cities are families, you begin to realize the impact that homelessness can have on a child's development.

The Impact of Homelessness on Development

Saying that the well-being of homeless children is seriously threatened is no exaggeration. Defining the homeless as those in emergency shelter facilities with their families, Rafferty and Shinn (1991) stated that these children are particularly vulnerable to health problems, hunger and poor nutrition, developmental delays, psychological problems, and educational underachievement. As we analyze these potential problems, it is well to remember that homelessness is a composite of several conditions and events: poverty; changes in residence, schools, and services; loss of possessions; disrupted social lives; and exposure to extreme hardship (Molnar & Rubin, 1991). Any one of these conditions, or any combination, may produce different effects on children.

- *Health problems.* Homeless children have much higher rates of acute and chronic health problems, which may have their roots in the prenatal period. For example, homeless women have significantly more low-birth-weight babies and experience greater levels of infant mortality. Their children are more susceptible to asthma, ear infections, diarrhea, and anemia. As you might expect, these children are also subject to immunization delays.

- *Hunger and poor nutrition.* Rafferty and Shinn (1991) summarized recent research on this topic when they described a homeless family's struggle to maintain an adequate and nutritionally balanced diet while living in a hotel: no refrigerator, no stove, poor food, and lack of food. Homeless children and their families often depend on emergency food assistance. But many times those facilities are themselves suffering from a lack of resources, with the result that the children, and their families, go hungry.

- *Developmental delays.* Homeless children experience, to a significantly higher degree than typical children, coordination difficulties, language delays, cognitive delays, social inadequacies, and a lack of personal skills (e.g., do not know how to eat at a table). The instability of their lives, the disruptions in child care, an erratic pattern of schooling, and how parents adapt to these conditions also impede development (Molnar & Rubin, 1991).

- *Psychological problems.* Homeless children seem to suffer more than typical children from depression, anxiety, and behavioral problems. Again, remember the composites of homelessness discussed earlier that may contribute to these psychological problems. Data are simply lacking that enable us to identify the particular aspect of homelessness that causes a child's anxiety or depression. We must also consider that parental depression affects children, and that children's problems may reflect the parents' feeling of helplessness.

- *Educational underachievement.* Little research has been done on this issue other than to show that homeless children do poorly on reading and mathematics tests. This finding should come as no surprise, given that these children have difficulty in finding and maintaining free public education for substantial periods. Missing educational opportunities is bad enough, but with the frequent moves their families make, these children also miss the remedial work they so urgently need. As Rafferty and Shinn (1991) noted, school is especially critical for homeless children because it can produce a sense of stability that is otherwise lacking.

In her interviews with homeless children, Walsh (1992) noted that children, because of their status and lack of power, cannot directly solve the problem of homelessness. Instead they concentrate on coping with the emotions that arise from becoming homeless, perhaps by restructuring the circumstances surrounding their homelessness. Younger children, for example, may unrealistically attribute their problems to some external event that is unrelated to them or their parents. Older children may try to explain away the cause, especially if it pertains to a parent. For example, rather than blame a parent's alcoholism or drug use, a youngster may say that the parent is sick or has problems.

Do you think the schools should play a greater role in the development of low SES children? How? Give specific examples and defend your reasons.

■ Homelessness and poverty have robbed these children of a good part of their childhood. They have been forced to worry about the things that most children take for granted—food, safety, and a roof over their heads. Some become "little adults" in their efforts to help themselves and their families to survive. And yet, as their stories remind us, they are children. They cherish their toys, they play at the hint of any opportunity, they rush to get lost in the world of fantasy. They think in the magical and concrete ways of children, constructing their world with the logic of childhood. And they make clear in their stories that they would like to be treated as children—to be less burdened by worry and more able to depend on adults for the basics of survival. (Walsh, 1992, p. 178)

Guided Review

1. The early childhood years are frequently described as a period of socialization versus _____ .

2. A family, as defined by Garbarino and Abramowitz, is any two people related by _____ , _____ , or _____ .

3. Parents who rely on verbal persuasion, positive reinforcement, and indirect methods of control are demonstrating _____ parenting behavior.

4. Today's new homeless are characterized by few_____ contacts, poor _____ , and a high level of contact with the _____ _____ _____ .

5. Although homelessness has many causes, _____ remains a major contributing factor.

Children of Divorce

Divorce, as an increasingly important aspect of family life, affects children in many ways. Not only is their physical way of life changed (perhaps a new home or reduced standard of living) but their psychological lives are touched also (Hetherington & others, 1985). Adults have a tendency to underestimate the circumstances that a child experiences, especially if the divorce is followed by a remarriage, which is true for 75 percent of divorced mothers and 80 percent of divorced fathers.

Another distressing fact children must face is that the divorce rate following a remarriage is higher than that in first marriages. So children can experience the effects of divorce, usually several years in a single-parent home, and then the changed circumstances of a remarriage (Hetherington & others, 1989). Before examining these effects, let's look first at the divorce phenomenon.

Facts about Divorce

Nearly half of today's marriages will end in divorce and an estimated 50 percent of our children will live with a single parent before the age of 18. As mentioned earlier, any discussion of the effects of divorce (or any traumatic event) must begin with the child's level of cognitive development. Remember that early childhood youngsters are at Piaget's preoperational level. Their ability to engage in abstract thinking is still limited, and they lack that vital aspect of cognition—the ability to reverse their thinking. This colors their reaction to their parents' divorce.

In about two or three years following the divorce, most children adjust to living in a single-parent home. This adjustment, however, can once again be shaken

Answers

1. individuation 2. blood, marriage, adoption 3. authoritative 4. social, health, criminal justice system 5. poverty

by what a parent's remarriage means: losing one parent in the divorce, adapting to life with the remaining parent, the addition of at least one family member in a remarriage (Hetherington & others, 1989).

Studying the long-term effects of divorce on children, Hetherington and her colleagues (1985, 1989) concluded that divorce has more adverse, long-term effects on boys. Remarriage of a mother who has custody of the children, however, is associated with an increase in girls' behavior problems and a slight decrease in boys' problems (Hetherington, 1991).

The transition period in the first year following the divorce is stressful economically, socially, and emotionally. Conditions then seem to improve, and children in a stable, smoothly functioning home are better adjusted than children in a nuclear family riddled with conflict. Nevertheless, school achievement may suffer and impulsivity increases. In an interesting comment about the relationship between divorced mothers and their children, Hetherington and Parke (1986) stated:

> ■ Divorced mothers may have given their children a hard time, but divorced mothers got rough treatment from their children, particularly their sons. In comparison with divorced fathers and parents in nuclear families, the divorced mother found that in the first year following divorce her children didn't obey, affiliate, or attend to her. They nagged and whined, made more dependency demands, and were more likely to ignore her. The aggression of boys with divorced mothers peaked at one year following divorce, then dropped significantly, but at six years after divorce was still higher than that of boys in nuclear families. (p. 524)

Other conditions also affect children's reactions to their parents' divorce (Wallerstein & Blakeslee, 1989):

- The bitterness of conflict before the divorce

- The child's reaction to the loss of the parent who leaves

- Any change in the relationship between the child and the departed parent

- The effect the divorce has on the parent who retains custody of the children

- Any change in behavior toward the children on the part of the parent who retains custody

Commonly reported reactions of early childhood youngsters to divorce are shock, depression, and loyalty conflict (Buchanan & others, 1991). They fear that their parents no longer love them and are actually abandoning them. These reactions fit the pattern of preoperational thinking. Early childhood youngsters' cognitive egocentrism prevents them from seeing the problem from their parents' perspective. They cannot realize that their mother or father loves them just as much even though they are leaving. Thus divorce centers on the children.

Second Chances

Wallerstein and Blakeslee (1989) reported findings similar to those of Hetherington and others. Beginning in 1971, Wallerstein studied 60 families that had experienced divorce. She worked with 131 children who were between the ages of 2 1/2 and 18 at the time their parents separated. Her analysis of the 34 youngsters who were in preschool at the time of parental breakup reveals important information about early childhood youngsters.

When the parents separated, their children were seriously upset. Acute separation anxiety appeared. Eighteen months later, about half of the group was still quite troubled, with boys showing the most severe problems. Five years later, the children's adjustment seemed to be tied to the quality of life in the postdivorce or remarried family. About one-third of the group showed signs of depression. Ten

Reconciliation fantasies
Children wish their parents could get together again following divorce.

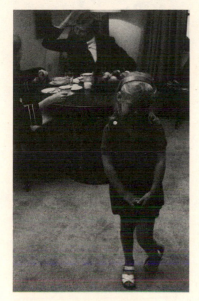

Children develop within a complex network of family relationships. What they are exposed to during these years can have long-lasting consequences.

Do you know any children of divorced parents? How would you assess their development? Can you relate your answer to the relationship between the parents and/or the children's living arrangements?

Day Care
Locations providing services and care for children.

years later, the children claimed little memory of the circumstances surrounding the divorce. Wallerstein, however, in analyzing their replies to questions, found a high degree of repression in their conversations. Wallerstein also discovered a phenomenon she called **reconciliation fantasies.** Although the divorce had occurred 10 years earlier, many of the children stated poignantly that they wished their parents could get together again. Wallerstein concluded that early childhood youngsters who live through the divorce of their parents are less burdened in the future than those who are older at the time of the divorce.

Does Divorce Cause Childhood Problems?

We have one final comment about the difficulties children have after divorce. In a carefully designed study, Block, Block, and Gjerde (1986) have raised questions about problems that children have after parental divorce. Beginning with data indicating that some youngsters do and others do not have problems, the authors state that one fault of the divorce studies is that they are almost all retrospective; that is, they "look back." Consequently, they are at the mercy of faulty memories and perhaps an adolescent's or adult's unwillingness to speak of painful experiences.

The authors were able to design a prospective study (looking ahead) of children's personalities before the divorce. They found that 3-year-old boys whose parents eventually divorced already were showing problems, especially in self-control. When they were 7 years old, they were still showing the same behavior. Three-year-old girls whose parents would divorce seemed competent, skillful, and competitive. But by age 4 their behavior had changed: They didn't get along with others, were overly emotional, and tended to withdraw. By age 7 these behaviors were still evident, but the girls also showed continuing cognitive competence.

The authors' findings point to several important conclusions:

- Researchers cannot focus on the divorce itself as the cause of children's later problems.

- Some youngsters show these same problems years before the divorce.

- Events preceding the divorce, especially the stress and conflict involved, may be responsible for problems that appear after the divorce.

- Girls may not be as immune to marital turmoil as we thought. They may simply display their feelings in a manner "appropriate" for girls: being anxious, withdrawn, extremely well-behaved.

Hetherington's excellent earlier study (1972) of father absence supports this last conclusion. Girls whose fathers died or who left because of divorce showed little disruption of appropriate sex-role behavior but had later problems in adolescence in relating to males. Daughters of divorced women sought more attention from boys, actively seeking contact with them. Daughters of widows avoided boys and preferred female friends and activities.

Day Care

Almost two-thirds of women with children under age 14, and more than one-half of mothers with children under age 1, are in the labor force. In fact, the single largest category of working mothers is those with children under age 3 (Zigler & Lang, 1991). What happens to children while their mothers are at work? Obviously someone must be taking care of these youngsters, and it is precisely here that questions are raised about **day care.** How competent are the individuals who offer these services? Is the day-care center healthy and stimulating? Is it safe? What are the long-term developmental consequences of day-care placement? In light of recent exposures of the sexual abuse of children in some centers, America's parents are demanding answers to these questions.

(a) Day care has become an important phenomenon in our society as more and more mothers join the workforce. Research indicates that developmental outcomes are closely linked to the quality of day care. (b) Among the variety of day-care settings, home day-care centers are quite numerous. Often run by a family member or neighbor, they are smaller and more informal than large centers.

(a)

(b)

Facts about Day Care

Reliable facts about day care are hard to come by, chiefly because of the lack of any national policy that would provide hard data. About 35,000 to 40,000 "places" provide day-care services (i.e., principal income is from offering child care). "Places" is perhaps the best way to describe these facilities because of the wide variety of circumstances that exist: Zigler and Lang (1991) referred to them as a "patchwork of arrangements." For example, one mother may charge another mother several dollars to take care of her child. A relative may care for several family children. Churches, businesses, and charities may run large operations. Some may be sponsored by local or state government as an aid to the less affluent. Others are run on a pay-as-you-go basis. Almost everyone agrees that the best centers are staffed by teachers who specialize in day-care services (about 25% of day-care personnel).

The following figures, based on data from the U.S. Bureau of Labor Statistics (1991), will give you an idea of the types of child-care arrangements and the number of children under 5 years of age in day care with employed mothers.

Care Outside of Home	
Mother cares for child at work	6.7%
Kindergarten	1.2%
Nursery/preschool	6.4%
Group care centers	14.7%
Care in Another Home	
By grandparent	11.5%
By other relative	6.0%
By nonrelative	23.8%
Care in Child's Home	
By father	14.2%
By grandparent	6.7%
By other relative	2.7%
By nonrelative	6.0%

Note that the majority of these children are cared for in private homes. This may help to explain why we are uncertain about the influence of day care on development, since most research is done with children from day-care centers.

If we now sort out what is known about types of day-care centers, we can group them as follows (Clarke-Stewart, 1993). (Remember: Most states now have minimum standards for day-care operation.)

Care in the Child's Home. In this type of care, a relative is usually the caregiver, which is fairly common, but as Clarke-Stewart noted, we probably know less about this care than any other. Although such an arrangement has several advantages (e.g., the child is familiar with the setting and the caregiver, the schedule can be flexible), several disadvantages also occur (e.g., the caregiver is usually untrained, the child misses peer activities).

Family Day Care.   Here caregivers provide service in their homes, which may or may not be licensed, and the number of children may range from 1 (family day-care home) to 12 (group day-care home). As Clarke-Stewart stated, family day-care homes are the most numerous and the least expensive. They are typically located near the child's home so transportation is no problem. A family atmosphere exists while simultaneously enabling a child to interact with a limited number of children of various ages. A major disadvantage is that the provider is the least accountable of providers. These settings typically are informal, unprofessional, and short-lived (Clarke-Stewart, 1993).

Day-Care Centers.   These centers are what people mean when they refer to "day care." They may be for profit (the number of these is increasing), or they may be nonprofit. They may provide for fewer than 15 or more than 300 children, whom they group by age. Here is a summary of many of the day-care centers.

- *Private day-care centers* run for profit have no eligibility requirements and will accept almost anyone who can pay the fee. Typically staffed by two or three people (usually not professionally trained), these centers may operate in a converted store or shop. They probably are minimally equipped with toys and educational activities and usually offer no social or health services.

- *Commercial centers* are also private and run for profit. They may be part of a national or regional chain with uniform offerings and facilities. They usually are well equipped with good food and activities. The centers are a business, much like a McDonald's or Burger King. KinderCare, for example, runs about 900 centers.

- *Community church centers* are often, but not always, run for children of the poor. The quality of personal care (attention, affection) is usually good, but church centers often have minimal facilities and activities.

- *Company centers* are often offered as fringe benefits for employees. They are usually run in good facilities with a well-trained staff and a wide range of services.

- *Public service centers* are government sponsored, well run, and have high quality throughout. Unfortunately, few of these are available and they are designed to serve children of low-income families.

- *Research centers* are usually affiliated with some university and represent what the latest research says a day-care center should be. Most studies of day care have been conducted in these centers. But since the centers are of the highest quality, the results of such studies do not give a true picture of day care throughout the country.

- *Other centers* include the family-run centers mentioned earlier and cooperative centers where parents rotate responsibility for child care under professional guidance. In another fairly popular form of care, a neighborhood mother, usually a former nurse or teacher, takes care of two or three children, thus avoiding state requirements concerning number of children, facilities, or insurance.

AN APPLIED VIEW

Desirable Qualities of Day-Care Centers

For those who want guidelines to identify important features in a day-care setting, here are several specific suggestions by the National Association for the Education of Young Children (1986).

1. Adult Caregivers
   - Adults should understand how infants and young children grow.
   - The number of adults available to meet the individual needs of the children should be adequate (see table 8.3).
   - Good records should be kept for each child.
2. The Program Itself
   - The setting should facilitate the growth and development of young children working and playing together.
   - Equipment and play materials should be adequate and readily available.
   - Instructors should be sufficiently skilled to aid youngsters in their language and social development.
3. Relations with Clients and Community
   - Parents should be actively involved with the center.
   - The community should be aware of activities at the center, and the center should be aware of community resources (recreational, learning centers).
4. The Ability to Meet the Demands of All Involved
   - The health of all members—children, staff, and parents—should be both protected and promoted.
   - Safety should be a primary concern.
   - Adequate space should be available to serve all activities (35 square feet of usable playroom floor space indoors per child and 75 square feet of play space outdoors per child).

Table 8.3	Suggested Ratio of Staff to Children		
	Age	Maximum Size	Staff-Child Ratio
For Centers	0–2	6	1:3
	2–3	12	1:4
	3–6	16	1:8
For Homes	0–2	10	1:5
	2–6	12	1:6

A National Concern

As you can see, the country is moving into a different era with regard to day care. Working mothers are now in the majority, and their numbers promise to increase. Given these events, regulation of day care has taken on new urgency. Legislative battles over standards for day-care centers have been constant, but the best the federal government has been able to do is to propose general standards, such as the suggested ratio of staff to children, which is illustrated in table 8.3.

Despite the minimal salaries of day-care workers, costs are high because day care is labor intensive. Staff-child ratios usually average from 1:8 to 1:10, much too high considering children's needs and safety. But a new attitude is developing, one with political consequences. National surveys have consistently shown that more than one-half of the voters think a national policy regarding day care should be formulated.

Developmental Outcomes

Regardless of what you may have heard or read, no definite conclusions have been reached concerning the long-term developmental consequences of day care. One reason is that careful follow-up of children from day care is not yet available (Clarke-Stewart, 1993).

Such studies are only beginning to appear. For example, Belsky and Rovine (1988) reported on the results of two longitudinal studies of infants and their families. They found that when infants were 12 to 13 months old and had 20 or more hours of nonmaternal care per week, some of the infants were insecurely attached. These same infants were more likely to be aggressive and tended to withdraw. Yet this report also contains puzzling data. More than one-half of the infants who had the 20 hours of nonmaternal care were securely attached. These data reveal the uncertainty of our present knowledge and reinforce our conclusion that we must be careful about either positive or negative statements about day care (Lamb & Sternberg, 1990).

Another obstacle to definite conclusions has been the use of university-sponsored research centers to study children. These centers are usually lavishly equipped and overstaffed; they simply do not reflect the national norm. Despite this, some conclusions have been drawn.

- The type of care is significant.

- Effects depend on the child's total environment.

- A child's personal characteristics affect the day-care experience (Zigler & Hall, 1989).

Given a good day-care center, do you believe all children will do well there? What do you think about the age of placement?

Clarke-Stewart (1993) has summarized these findings as follows: With regard to *physical development,* disadvantaged children gain height and weight more rapidly and advance their motor skills in a day-care setting; time spent in a day-care setting has no negative *intellectual outcomes* and benefits children from 2 to 4 years from disadvantaged homes; skills in social competence may increase, although children may display more aggression than others. These are shaky findings and may very well be reversed by additional research.

Guided Review

6. Nearly _____ of today's marriages will probably end in divorce.

7. According to Hetherington and her colleagues divorce has more adverse, long-term effects on _____, whereas remarriage is associated with an increase in _____ behavior problems.

8. Reliable facts about day care are hard to come by because of the lack of _____ _____ .

9. The developmental outcomes of day care are difficult to assess because most children are in _____ settings.

10. _____ day-care settings are the most numerous probably because they are the least _____ .

The Self Emerges

"You are who you are." This oft-repeated statement summarizes what personality means. Psychologists define personality as the "dynamic organization of those psychophysical systems that define a person's behavior and thought." Our concern is how children acquire this sense of self.

In chapter 6 we mentioned the growing belief that humans come into this world with inborn temperamental differences. These differences, then, are the foundation on which children build their unique personalities. Children form their personalities by using their genetic endowment that defines their potential, both

Answers

6. one-half   7. boys, girls   8. follow-up studies   9. private   10. Family, expensive

physical and intellectual. Children also learn about themselves from those around them. The reactions of others contribute greatly to what children think of themselves (Damon, 1983).

The Development of Self

To understand development, you must always remember it is an integrated process (Harter, 1983). All aspects—physical, cognitive, social, and emotional—contribute to smooth growth. Nowhere is this more evident than in the analysis of self-development.

- If a youngster has normal physical growth, a sense of mastery develops, increasing self-confidence.

- If cognitive development progresses satisfactorily, children acquire vital knowledge that helps them to adjust to their world, increasing self-confidence.

- If relations with others are mostly pleasant, children learn about others and themselves, increasing self-confidence.

The infant shown here touching his nose and mouth against the mirror reveals the development of a sense of self, which most infants accomplish by about 18 months of age.

Children distinguish themselves from others at about age 18 months, perhaps even a little earlier. In their famous experiment, Lewis and Brooks-Gunn (1979) put rouge on the noses of children aged 15 to 18 months. When placed before a mirror, the children touched the rouge on their noses, indicating that they knew who they were. They recognized themselves.

Think of what you have learned about cognitive development: Children are becoming less egocentric; they are distinguishing themselves from the world. Emotionally, they have begun the process of separating from their mothers, recognizing that mothers are also individuals. Language is flourishing and others are speaking to them. The convergence of developmental paths helps to further the sense of self. Their growing cognitive ability helps children to represent things, to separate from mothers and the world in general. This leads to acceptance—through cognition, language, and developing relations—of an independent world "out there."

Kagan (1984) has attributed the development of a child's self-concept during the early childhood years to two sources. First is a child's slowly emerging awareness of feelings, intentions, and sense of having certain specific characteristics. For example, children know when they are happy, that they are either a boy or a girl, that their hair is red or brown, that their eyes are brown or blue. Intention is particularly interesting. When children want their parents to do something (make a funny noise, look at them), they are as much concerned with influencing their parents' behavior as producing a funny sound (Kagan, 1984). As they come to the end of the early childhood period, children use the second source of their self-development: comparative evaluations of self with others. "I'm smarter than my brother, Timmy." Again note the cognitive input—the switch from bodily actions to the use of ideas as a means of differentiating the self.

The Special Case of Self-Esteem

Developmental psychologists, educators, parents, and almost everyone who works with children have come to accept the vital role that a child's self-esteem plays in development. What do we mean by self-esteem? A technical definition would be that self-esteem is the evaluative and affective dimension of self-concept (Santrock & Yussen, 1992). A simpler way of defining it would be to say that self-esteem is how children feel about themselves, how they value themselves. These authors give a good example of self-esteem when they describe the girl who realizes that she is not just a student but a good student, the boy who realizes that he is not just a basketball player but a good basketball player.

A close relationship seems to exist between the way parents treat a child and that child's self-esteem. Coopersmith (1967), in an enduring study, found that high self-esteem in boys was associated with expressions of affection, concern with a child's problems, a happy home life, clearly established rules, reasonable amounts of freedom, and a structured environment that provided help when needed. Remember: These characteristics don't *cause* high self-esteem; they are related to it.

During the preschool years, children seem to distinguish between two types of self-esteem—social acceptance and competence—but as yet don't identify competence in particular activities. This ability appears at about 7 or 8 years of age and suggests that developmental changes occur in self-esteem. A child coming from a supportive home typically has an inflated sense of self-esteem before beginning school. It isn't until the second grade that pupils' estimation of their self-esteem matches the opinions of those around them; that is, children's estimations correlate with teacher ratings, test scores, and direct observations (Berk, 1994).

Self-esteem seems to be composed of several elements that contribute to a child's sense of worth.

- A sense of physical safety. Children who feel physically secure aren't afraid of being harmed, which helps to develop feelings of confidence.

- A sense of emotional security. Children who aren't humiliated or subjected to sarcasm feel safe emotionally, which translates into a willingness to trust others.

- A sense of identity. Children who know "who they are" have achieved a degree of self-knowledge that enables them to take responsibility for their actions and relate well with others.

- A sense of belonging. Children who are accepted by others are comfortable in seeking out new relationships and begin to develop feelings of independence and interdependence.

- A sense of competence. Children who are confident in their ability to do certain things are willing to try to learn to do new things and persevere until they achieve mastery (Youngs, 1991).

Another powerful input into a child's sense of self is that of maleness and femaleness.

The Role of Gender in Development

We realize today that gender identity results from a complicated mix of culture and biology. For example, children, at an early age, construct social categories from the world around them, attach certain characteristics to these categories, and then label the category. This process may be positive, since it helps children to organize their world; it may also be negative if the characteristics associated with the category are limiting—"girls just can't do math" (Serbin & others, 1993).

One of the first categories children form is sex related; there is a neat division between male and female. Children then move from the observable physical differences between the sexes and begin to acquire gender knowledge about the behavior expected of male and female. Depending on the source of this knowledge, gender role stereotyping has commenced and attitudes toward gender are being shaped. As Serbin and her colleagues (1993) noted, despite the societal changes we have seen in acceptable gender roles, gender role stereotypes have remained relatively stable. What do we know about this process?

ACQUIRING GENDER IDENTITY: HEREDITY OR ENVIRONMENT?

Before beginning our discussion of the role that gender plays in development, you may find clues to the current status of women by examining the processes by which boys and girls acquire their sense of gender identity. The contributions of biology and the environment, however, interact in a complex, interactive manner, one that continues to cause controversy. Most psychologists today believe in a reciprocal interaction model of development to explain our behavior. That is, we respond to those around us and they change; their responses to us then change and we in turn change. The process is constant and you can see how the reactions to ideas of gender, particularly if they are stereotypical, can influence gender identity and also *behavior.* If girls are told that "girls don't make good scientists," then possibly their achievement in science classes will suffer. The first component of the heredity–environment interaction is biology.

Does Biology Count?

Whatever your ideas on gender identity, we start with an unavoidable premise: Parts of the sexual agenda are biologically programmed. John Money (1980), working in a Johns Hopkins clinic devoted to the study of congenital abnormalities of the sex organs, believed that sexual differentiation occurs through a series of four stages. First is *chromosomal sex.* The biological sexual program is initially carried by either the X or Y sex chromosome. Second is *gonadal sex,* in which the XX or XY combination pass on the sexual program to the undifferentiated gonads. Third is *hormonal sex.* Once the testes or ovaries are differentiated, they begin to produce chemical agents called sex hormones. Males produce more of the sex hormones called androgens than females, whereas females produce more estrogens (the female sex hormone). Fourth is *genital sex.* A

baby's sex is determined not only by chromosomes and hormones but also by its external sex organs. As you can well imagine, genital or morphological sex determines how society will treat the newly born baby. With these as the biological givens, we turn now to the role of socialization.

Does the Environment Count?

It doesn't take children long to discover what behavior "fits" boys and which "fits" girls (Fagot & others, 1992). If you think about children's cognitive competencies and realize that they acquire their sex identity by 2 to 3 years of age, you can understand their rapid assignment of appropriate behavior to either male or female. Lott (1989) reports that by preschool age, most children are well aware of their own gender, which parent they are most like, and the gender of family members and peers.

For an idea of how soon children begin to make decisions based on sex, Lott (1989) reported the result of a study that required children 2 to 7 years of age to assign various occupations to either a male or female doll. As early as 2 years of age, they assigned male occupations to male dolls. For example, 67 percent of 2- and 3-year-olds chose the male doll for doctors.

In an attempt to explain these and similar findings, Martin, Wood, and Little (1990) found a developmental sequence to the appearance of gender stereotypes. In the first stage, children learn what kinds of things are associated with each sex (boys play with cars; girls play with dolls). From the ages 4 to 6 years, children move to the second stage where they begin to learn the more complex associations for their own sex (different kinds of activities associated with a toy). By the time of the third stage (roughly 6 to 8 years), children make the same types of associations for the opposite sex.

Do these views result from biology? Or from the environment? Or from both? What's your view?

Family

Evidence clearly suggests that parents treat boy and girl babies differently from birth. Adults tend to engage in rougher play with boys, give them stereotypical toys (cars and trucks), and speak differently to them. By the end of the second year, parents respond favorably to what they consider appropriate sexual behavior (i.e., stereotypical) and negatively to cross-sex play (boys engaging in typical girl's play and vice versa). For example, Fagot (1985a; Fagot & Hagan, 1991) observed toddlers and their parents at home and discovered that both mothers and fathers differentially reinforced their children's behavior. That is, parents reinforced girls for playing with dolls and boys for playing with blocks, girls for helping their mothers around the house and boys for running and jumping.

Lips (1993) believed that parents were unaware of the extent to which they engaged in this type of reinforcement. In a famous study (Will & others, 1976) 11 mothers were observed interacting with a 6-month-old infant. Five of the mothers played with the infant when it was dressed in blue pants and called "Adam." Six mothers later played with the same infant when it wore a pink dress and was called

Siblings play a major role in development. For those children with brothers and sisters, older siblings can act as models, help younger brothers and sisters in times of difficulty, and help smooth relations with adults.

Sex cleavage
Youngsters of the same sex tend to play and do things together.

Children quickly learn what objects, activities, and friends are gender appropriate.

"Beth." The mothers offered a doll to "Beth" and a toy train to "Adam." They also smiled more at Beth and held her more closely. The baby was actually a boy. Interviewed later, all the mothers said that boys and girls were alike at this age and *should be treated identically*.

Siblings also influence gender development. Brothers and sisters differ markedly in personality, intelligence, and psychopathology in spite of shared genetic roots. Since about 80 percent of children have siblings and spend considerable time with each other, these relationships exercise a considerable influence (Dunn, 1983). An older brother showing a younger brother how to hold a bat; a younger sister watching her older sister play with dolls; quarrelling among siblings—each of these examples illustrates the impact that sibling relationships have on gender development.

Perhaps no one has summarized the importance of this differential treatment of sons and daughters better than Block (1983). Noting the reality of this parental behavior, Block stated that males and females grow up in quite different learning environments with important psychological implications for development. Peers are an important part of these different learning environments.

Peers

When children start to make friends and play, these activities foster and maintain sex-typed play. Studies show that by the age of 3, children reinforce each other for sex-typed play (Langlois & Downs, 1979). When they engage in "sex-inappropriate" play (boys with dolls, girls with a football), their peers immediately criticize them and tend to isolate them. This tendency increases with age until most adolescents react to intense demands for conformity to stereotypical gender roles.

Here, again, we see the influence of imitation and reinforcement. During development, youngsters of the same sex tend to play together, a custom called **sex cleavage** and one that is encouraged by parents and teachers. If you think back on your own experiences, you can remember your friends at this age—either all male or female. In adolescence, despite dating and opposite sex attraction, both males and females want to live up to the most rigid interpretations of what their group thinks is ideally male or female. You can understand, then, how imitation, reinforcement, and cognitive development come together to intensify what a boy thinks is masculine and a girl thinks is feminine (Dunn, 1983).

Media

Another influence on gender development, one that carries important messages about what is desirable for males and females and one that reaches into the home, is the media, especially television. Television has assumed such a powerful place in the socialization of children that it is safe to say that television is almost as significant as family and peers. What is particularly bothersome is the stereotypical behavior that it presents as both positive and desirable. As Lips (1993) has stated flatly, television teaches gender stereotypes. The more television children watch, the more stereotypical is their behavior.

In spite of such shows as *Murphy Brown* and *Murder, She Wrote,* the central characters of shows are much more likely to be male than female, the theme will be action-oriented for males, and the characters typically engage in stereotypical behavior (men are the executives and leaders, women are the housewives and secretaries). Much the same holds true for television commercials. There is little doubt that children notice the different ways television portrays males and females. When asked to rate the behavior of males and females, children aged 8 to 13 responded in a rigidly stereotypical manner: Males were brave, adventurous, intelligent, and made good decisions. Females, on the other hand, cried easily and needed to be protected (Lips, 1993).

These distinctions apply to other, much more subtle, features of television programming. For example, to understand a television program, children must know something about story form—how stories are constructed and presented. They use their knowledge of the world and general knowledge about situations and events in order to grasp television's content, which often reinforces what they are watching. They must also have knowledge of television's forms and conventions to help them understand what is happening on the screen. Music and visual techniques, plus camera angles, all convey information (Liebert & Sprafkin, 1988).

In other words, children learn more than the contents of a program from television. They learn the many cues that signal male or female. Loud music, rapid scene changes, multiple sound effects, and frequent cuts mean just one thing—a male-oriented show. Shows designed for females have soft background music, gentle cuts, and soothing sound effects. Children as young as 6 years can use these cues to identify shows that are intended for either males or females (Lips, 1993). Children understand television programs according to their level of development, and their level of development is affected by their television viewing, with all that implies for gender development. Let's now turn our attention to several theories that attempt to explain gender development.

Theories of Gender Development

Several theories of gender development have generated most of the research during the past 10 years: social learning theory, cognitive development, and gender schema theory. *Social learning theorists* believe that parents, as the distributors of reinforcement, reinforce appropriate gender-role behaviors. By their choice of toys, by urging "boy" or "girl" behavior, and by reinforcing this behavior, parents encourage their children to engage in gender-appropriate behavior. If the parents have a good relationship with their children, they become models for their children to imitate, encouraging them to acquire additional gender-related behavior. Thus children are reinforced or punished for different kinds of behavior. They also learn appropriate gender behavior from other male and female models (such as those in television shows) who display different kinds of behavior.

A second explanation, quite popular today, is *cognitive-developmental,* which derives from Kohlberg's speculations about gender development (1966). We know from Piaget's work that children engage in symbolic thinking by about 2 years of age. Using this ability, children acquire their gender identity and then, Kohlberg believed, they begin the process of acquiring sex-appropriate behavior. In other words, as a result of cognitive development—in a sense, constructing their own world—children begin to build the concepts of maleness and femaleness.

A newer, and different, cognitive explanation is called *gender schema* theory. A schema is a mental blueprint for organizing information, and children develop a schema for gender. This schema helps them to develop their gender identity and formulate an appropriate gender role. Consequently children develop an integrated schema or picture of what gender is and should be. With this brief examination of the biological and environmental forces that contribute to gender and the theories that attempt to explain the process, let's next look at what happens when gender stereotypes are formed.

Gender Stereotyping

We previously defined gender stereotyping as the beliefs that we have about the characteristics and behavior associated with male and female. In other words, from an early age we form an idea of what a male and female should be, begin to accumulate characteristics about male and female, and assign a label to that category. This process certainly simplifies our ability to deal with our world: That rough, noisy person is a boy; that gentle, soft-spoken, obedient person is a girl. (As a result of such stereotyping, the "feminine" boy or "masculine" girl often has difficulties with peers.)

Problems can arise, however, when the characteristics associated with a label create a negative image. "Oh, girls can't do math; girls can't do science; girls are

Children often find opposite-sex toys extremely attractive. Many parents encourage the use of such toys to help their children avoid the development of stereotypical gender-role attitudes.

always crying, girls can't be leaders." At this point we start to treat the individual according to the characteristics we associate with male or female. If you think about this for a moment, you can see some potential pitfalls, especially in the classroom. (For an excellent summary of the place of women in education, see Sadker & Sadker, 1994, pp. 15–41).

Although sexual equality is widely accepted today—legally, professionally, and personally—gender stereotyping is still alive and well. But are males and females actually that different?

Gender Similarities and Differences

As knowledge about gender behavior increases, a growing consensus has emerged that the differences between the sexes are not as great as once thought. In a benchmark study of gender differences published in 1974, Maccoby and Jacklin concluded that males were superior in mathematical and visual-spatial skills, and females had better verbal skills. (Recent studies have continued to identify gender similarities and differences; for a summary of this research, see Berk, 1994.) We can capsulize this research by stating that many more similarities exist than you probably expected, and that differences aren't necessarily caused by biological forces.

As an illustration of similarities, consider the recent work of Pinker (1994) who noted that anthropologists frequently stress differences between peoples (the "strange behaviors" of others) and often understate the many similarities among all humans. For example, Pinker specified such universal human characteristics as humor, insults, fear, anger, storytelling, laws, dreams, words for common objects, binary distinctions, measures, common facial expressions (happy, sad, angry, fearful), crying, displays of affection, and on and on. What we have here is a list of complex interactions between a universal human nature and the conditions of living in a human body on this planet (Pinker, 1994). Obviously, the point of this discussion is that humans are quite similar, regardless of any male-female distinctions.

Nevertheless, differences do exist, as seen in table 8.4. By the way, we should point out that these differences are not fixed; that is, changes occur as more sophisticated research techniques produce new data. One example of this is the realization that differences in mathematical abilities are not as great as once thought.

Table 8.4	Observed Gender Differences
Characteristic	**Gender Difference**
Physical differences	Although almost all girls mature more rapidly than boys, by adolescence boys have surpassed girls in size and strength.
Verbal ability	Girls do better on verbal tasks beginning in the early years, a superiority that is retained. Boys also exhibit more language problems than girls.
Spatial skill	Boys display superiority on spatial tasks, a superiority that continues throughout schooling.
Mathematical ability	Little, if any, difference exists in the early years; boys begin to demonstrate superiority during the high school years.
Science	Gender differences seem to be increasing; females are falling more behind, whereas the performance of males is increasing.
Achievement motivation	Differences here seem to be linked to task and situation. Boys do better in stereotypical "masculine" tasks (math, science), girls on "feminine" tasks (art, music). In direct competition between males and females beginning around adolescence, girls' need achievement seems to drop.
Aggression	Boys appear to be innately more aggressive than girls, a difference that appears early and is remarkably consistent.

An important part of the early childhood youngster's life is the role of play in physical, cognitive, social, and self development.

Guided Review

11. Development is the integration of all aspects of growth: _____ , _____ , _____ , and _____ .

12. The evaluative and affective dimension of self-concept is known as _____ .

13. During preschool years, children seem to distinguish between two types of self-esteem: _____ _____ and _____ .

14. When children develop a mental blueprint concerning gender, this is called _____ _____ _____ .

15. Psychologists today are more alert to the proper use of the terms _____ and _____ to indicate the interaction of _____ and _____ to explain gender.

The Importance of Play

Children yelling; children running; children chasing each other; children busy at games. All of these activities seem to fit what we mean by **play.** This seemingly simple, happy behavior is, nevertheless, difficult to define with any degree of precision. As Garvey (1990) stated, several descriptive characteristics of play are critical to its definition:

- Play must be enjoyable and valued by the player.

- Play has no extrinsic goals; that is, play is intrinsically motivated.

Play

Play is an activity that children engage in because they enjoy it for its own sake.

Answers

11. physical, cognitive, social, emotional   12. self-esteem   13. social acceptance, competence
14. gender schema theory   15. sex, gender; biology, environment

- Play is spontaneous and voluntary; no one is forcing a child to play; it is freely chosen by the child.

- Play demands that a child be actively engaged.

- Play has systematic relations to other behavior that is not play.

We'll see later that play is linked to other developmental considerations such as cognition, emotion, and the like. Probably a definition that is as good as any is that *play is an activity that children engage in because they enjoy it for its own sake.* As we begin our analysis of play, remember that play affects all aspects of development—physical, cognitive, social, and emotional.

But how can we be sure that what we see is actually play? In their exhaustive survey, Rubin, Fein, and Vandenberg (1983) have identified several dispositional features of play:

- Play is not forced on children; they do it because they like it.

- They are not concerned with outcome; they enjoy the act of playing.

- Play has an "as if" quality; reality is suspended and children get great enjoyment from pretending.

- When children play, they are active; they are not daydreaming.

The Meaning of Play

Beginning with the notion that play has widespread consequences, we can say that play allows children to explore their environment on their own terms and to take in any meaningful experiences at their own rate and on their own level (e.g., running through a field and stopping to look at rocks or insects). Play also permits children to relieve tension and helps them to master anxiety. You probably remember the story of the child playing dentist after a visit to a dentist's office.

Children also play for the sheer exuberance of it, which enables them to exercise their bodies and improve motor skills. In our discussion, remember to note the interactive nature of play: For example, children can't play certain kinds of games until they reach a certain cognitive level, but they can't reach that level without environmental encouragement, some of which comes through their play.

With this interactive model in mind, we can see that children play for various reasons, such as the following.

Cognitive Development

Play aids cognitive development; cognitive development aids play. Through play, children learn about the objects in their world, what these objects do (balls roll and bounce), what they are made of (toy cars have wheels), and how they work. To use Piaget's terms, children "operate" on these objects through play and also learn behavioral skills that will help them in the future.

Social Development

Play helps social development during this period because the involvement of others demands a give-and-take that teaches early childhood youngsters the basics of forming relationships. Social skills demand the same building processes as cognitive skills. Why are some 5- and 6-year-olds more popular with their classmates than others? Watching closely, you can discover the reasons: decreasing egocentrism, recognition of the rights of others, and a willingness to share. These social skills do not simply appear; they are learned, and much of the learning comes through play.

Emotional Development

Play provides an emotional release for youngsters (Fischer & others, 1990). There are not the right or wrong, life-and-death feelings that accompany interactions with adults. Children can be creative without worrying about failure. They can also work out emotional tensions through play.

Caplan and Caplan (1984) stated that play is a powerful developmental instrument for several reasons:

- Play aids learning because children have the freedom to explore and enjoy.

- Play is investigative because children, lacking knowledge, must search for and discover what works and what doesn't.

- Play is voluntary, with no fixed directions.

- Play can provide an imaginary, escape world, which children sometimes need.

- Play helps to build interpersonal relationships.

Aside from these more formal characteristics, Elkind's ideas seem particularly pertinent.

■ But children need to be given an opportunity for pure play as well as work. At all levels of development, whether at home or at school, children need the opportunity to play for play's sake. Whether play is the symbolic play of young children, the games with rules and collections of the school-age child, or the more complicated intellectual games of adolescence, children should be given the time and encouragement to engage in them. (1981, p. 97)

The Development of Play

Does play change over time? Are there age-related features of play that we can identify? Linking a specific kind of play to a specific age is difficult, if not impossible. But the kinds of play can be linked with the characteristics of a particular level (e.g., early childhood, middle childhood).

Until the age of 18 months to 2 years, children's play is essentially sensorimotor; that is, a great deal of repetition involving the body occurs (e.g., doing the same things with a toy). Gardner (1983) stated that at age 2 a great divide is passed because children can engage their world symbolically: letting one thing represent another, adopting different types of roles, and indulging in fantasy and pretend activities. Children may pretend to drink from play cups, or feed a doll with a spoon, or use a clothespin as a doll (Sutton-Smith, 1988).

Play also becomes more social; interactions with other children become more important in play. With the beginning of the school years, play becomes even more social and rule dominated. Games with rules become important, which reflects children's ability to use abstract thinking in playing games. A strike in baseball, for example, is a ball thrown over the plate, one that a batter swings at and misses, or a "foul ball." School-age children, with their increased symbolic ability, understand these rules and apply them in their games.

Pretend play, however, seems most characteristic of the early childhood years. Children of Piaget's preoperational period show an increasing ability to represent. They are better able to engage in abstract thinking, to let one thing represent another. The extent of pretend play is illustrated in table 8.5.

Pretend play peaks during the early childhood years. It is a way for children to explore the varieties of familiar events and to speculate about the less familiar.

Table 8.5	Pretend Play in the Early Childhood Years
Age	**Group Pretend Play**
3	70%
4	74–80%
5	68–71%
6	65%

Source: Data from K. Rubin, G. Fein, and B. Vandenberg, "Play" in *Handbook of Child Psychology,* edited by P. Mussen, Wiley & Sons, New York, 1983.

Children of these years obviously can pretend and Rubin, Fein, and Vandenberg (1983) stated that pretend play becomes more social with age, entailing a three-stage sequence:

1. Pretend play becomes increasingly dramatic until the early elementary school years.

2. Pretend play becomes more social with age.

3. Pretend play gradually declines and is replaced by games with rules during middle childhood.

Pretend play begins with simple actions such as pretending to be eating or asleep. But as symbolic ability increases during the early childhood years, the nature of pretending changes. Youngsters will use toy telephones to talk. Later, they will pick up a banana and pretend to talk on the telephone. Pretend play steadily becomes more elaborate. Youngsters will serve tea to a group of dolls or feed soldiers; they also begin to enact the role of others. You can see, then, how play affects all aspects of development.

Guided Review

16. Any analysis of play must take into consideration that children play because they _____ it for its own sake.

17. Play is associated with three aspects of development: _____, _____, and _____.

18. Early childhood youngsters seem to be especially involved in _____ play.

19. The _____ nature of play suggests play aids development, but also that development permits different aspects of play.

20. During infancy, play is essentially _____; during early childhood, _____ play dominates, which gradually leads to _____-_____ play.

Answers

16. enjoy   17. cognitive, social, emotional   18. pretend   19. interactive   20. physical, pretend, rule governed

♣ CONCLUSION

At the beginning of the early childhood years, most children meet other youngsters. By the end of the period, almost all children enter formal schooling. Their symbolic ability enriches all of their activities, although limitations still exist. Given their boundless energy and enthusiasm, early childhood youngsters require consistent and reasonable discipline. Yet they should be permitted to do as many things for themselves as possible to help them gain mastery over themselves and their surroundings.

By the end of the early childhood period, children have learned much about their world and are prepared to enter the more complex, competitive, yet exciting world of middle childhood.

♣ CHAPTER HIGHLIGHTS

The Family in Development
- The meaning of "family" in our society has changed radically.
- How parents treat their children has a decisive influence on developmental outcomes.
- Baumrind's types of parenting behavior help to clarify the role of parents in children's development.
- Research has demonstrated how divorce can affect children of different ages.

- Divorce plus remarriage produces a series of transitions to which children must adjust.
- Many children attend some form of day care, and the developmental outcomes of these experiences are still in question.

The Self Emerges
- The emergence of the self follows a clearly defined path.
- Self-esteem plays a crucial role in a child's development.

- Youngsters acquire their gender identity during the early childhood years.
- Children initially seem to acquire an understanding of gender before they manifest sex-typed behavior.

The Importance of Play
- Play affects all aspects of development: physical, cognitive, social, and emotional.
- The nature of a child's play changes over the years, gradually becoming more symbolic.

♣ KEY TERMS

Authoritarian parents 190
Authoritative parents 190
Day care 197
Individuation 188
Insecure parents 191

Intimidated parents 191
Overinterpretive parents 191
Pathological parents 192
Permissive parents 190
Play 208

Reconciliation fantasies 197
Secure parents 191
Sex cleavage 205
Socialization 188
Victimized parents 191

♣ WHAT DO YOU THINK?

1. With today's accepted changes in the gender roles of males and females, do you think that a boy or girl growing up in these times could become confused about gender identity? Does your answer also apply to gender roles? Why?
2. Think back on your days as a child. Can you put your parents' behavior in any of Baumrind's categories? Do you think it affected your behavior? Explain your answer by linking your parents' behavior to some of your personal characteristics.
3. In this chapter you read about the "sleeper" effect of divorce (effects show up quite a bit later). Do you agree with these findings? Can you explain them by the child's age at the time of the divorce? (Consider all aspects of a child's development at that age.)
4. You probably have read about child abuse in some day-care centers. Do you think there should be stricter supervision? Why? By whom?

SUGGESTED READINGS

Ambrose, S. (1983). *Eisenhower.* (Vol. I). New York: Simon & Schuster. Includes the boyhood days of the man who would become soldier, general, and president. A revealing account of the family and community forces that helped to shape his destiny.

Brazelton, T. B. (1981). *On becoming a family: The growth of attachment.* New York: Delacorte. An engrossing account of the development of family relationships by one of America's most renowned pediatricians.

Garvey, C. (1990). *Play.* Cambridge, MA: Harvard Univ. Press. A brief, thorough examination of what we mean by play and how children play with objects, language, and rules, among others.

Wallerstein, J. & Blakeslee, S. (1989). *Second chances.* New York: Simon & Schuster. This book is must reading for anyone interested in the effect of divorce on children. It summarizes Wallerstein's 10-year follow-up of the children of divorced parents and furnishes insights into the entire spectrum of divorce in our society today.

CHAPTER REVIEW TEST

1. The National Commission on Children has identified several characteristics of a strong family. Which of the following is *not* included?
   a. open and frequent communication among members
   b. respect for individual members
   c. an ability to cope with stressful events
   d. extended generational membership

2. A child who is aggressive and demonstrates a lack of responsibility is associated with _____ parenting behavior.
   a. authoritative
   b. permissive
   c. indifferent
   d. doting

3. Conditions associated with homelessness can produce hardships on children. Which of the following conditions is *not* necessarily associated with homelessness?
   a. health problems
   b. hunger and poor nutrition
   c. lower intelligence
   d. developmental delays

4. _____ percent of divorced mothers remarry.
   a. Seventy-five
   b. Eighty
   c. Fifty
   d. Twenty-five

5. Almost _____ percent of today's marriages will end in divorce.
   a. 25
   b. 50
   c. 10
   d. 75

6. Which one of the following is *not* a commonly reported reaction of early childhood youngsters to divorce?
   a. lowered cognitive competence
   b. shock
   c. depression
   d. loyalty conflict

7. Wallerstein discovered that even after 10 years following a divorce, children wished their parents would get together again. This phenomenon is called
   a. reconciliation fantasy.
   b. divorce related depression.
   c. cognitive incompetence.
   d. separation anxiety.

8. Almost _____ of women with children under age 14 are in the labor force.
   a. 1/2
   b. 3/4
   c. 2/3
   d. 1/3

9. Most children in day care are being cared for
   a. by a father at home.
   b. by a grandparent in another home.
   c. by a nonrelative in another home.
   d. in a nursery/preschool.

10. A long-term developmental consequence of day care is
    a. insecurity.
    b. adaptability.
    c. self-sufficiency.
    d. No definite conclusion is possible.

11. There are about _____ places providing day-care services.
    a. 20,000–25,000
    b. 25,000–30,000
    c. 30,000–35,000
    d. 35,000–40,000

12. Probably the best type of day care is found in the _____ center, which may not provide an accurate picture of all centers.
    a. research
    b. company
    c. commercial
    d. family run

13. _____ is how children feel about themselves and how they value themselves.
    a. Self-identity
    b. Self-esteem
    c. Sense of belonging
    d. Sense of competence

14. Social learning theory states that parents _____ appropriate gender-role behavior.
    a. discuss
    b. analyze
    c. reinforce
    d. ignore

15. In cognitive development theory, children first acquire their
    a. gender identity.
    b. appropriate gender behavior.
    c. psychic stability.
    d. conditioned behavior.

16. Social learning theory depends on the concept of _____ to explain the acquisition of appropriate gender behavior.
    a. schema
    b. assimilation
    c. reinforcement
    d. adaptation

17. When children of the same sex tend to play together, it is referred to as
    a. sex differentiation.
    b. sex cleavage.
    c. sex bias.
    d. sex dichotomy.

18. Pretend play becomes more _____ with age.
    a. physical
    b. cognitive
    c. emotional
    d. social

19. As much as _____ percent of a 6-year-old's play is pretend play.
    a. 65
    b. 50
    c. 25
    d. 10

20. The most typical type of play during the early childhood years is
    a. social.
    b. physical.
    c. adult sponsored.
    d. pretend.

Answers

1.d 2.b 3.c 4.a 5.b 6.a 7.a 8.c 9.c 10.d 11.d 12.a 13.b 14.c 15.a 16.c 17.b 18.d 19.a 20.d

PART V

Middle Childhood

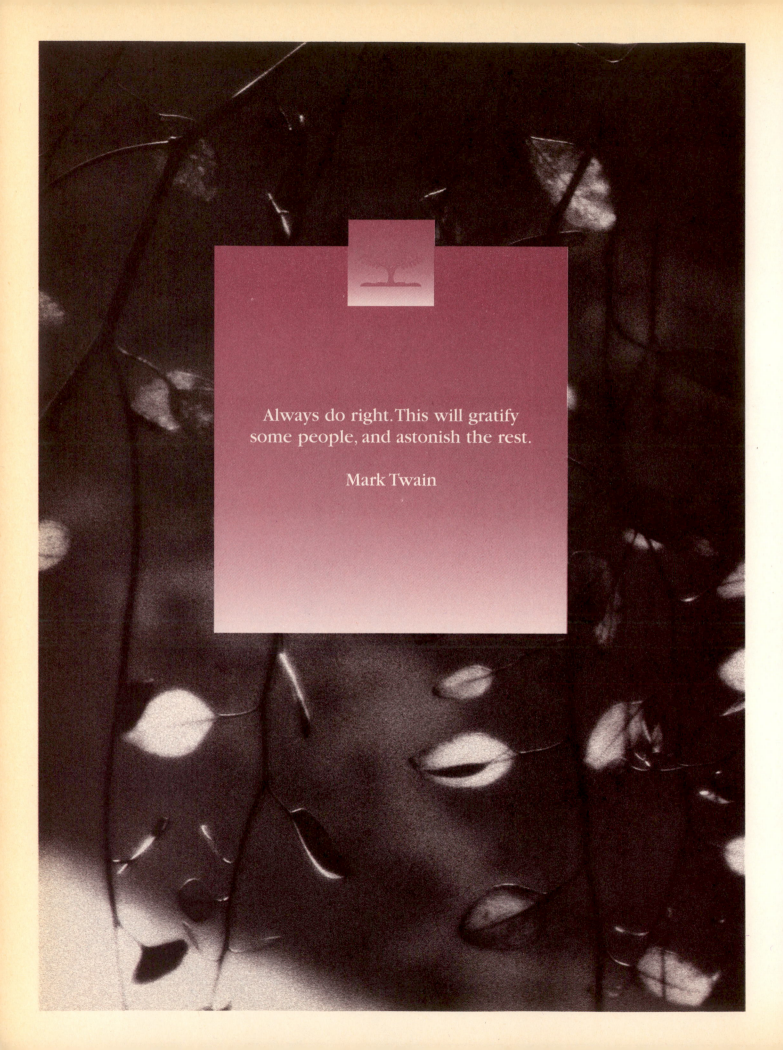

Always do right. This will gratify
some people, and astonish the rest.

Mark Twain

CHAPTER 9

Physical and Cognitive Development in Middle Childhood

Chapter Outline

Cognitive theory has made us aware that children's language reveals much about their level of mental functioning.

It was the week after school opened and 5-year-old Kenny Wilson and his 11-year-old sister Alice had just transferred to the Brackett School District. Mrs. Allan, the principal, took both pupils to their new classrooms and introduced them to their teachers.

"Good morning, Kenny. I'm delighted that you're going to be in this classroom," said Mrs. Groves, the first-grade teacher. "Some of the boys and girls in this room live near you. By the way, do you like your new house?"

Kenny, at first nervous, began to respond to Mrs. Groves' warm manner. "Oh, yes. I have my own bedroom. It has big windows."

Mrs. Groves laughed. "Can you see the moon from your window?" she asked.

"You bet. It follows me around the room," said Kenny.

At the same time, Alice was talking with Mr. Gallo, the sixth-grade teacher. "Welcome to the Brackett sixth grade, Alice. I think you'll enjoy being here," said Mr. Gallo. "Can you give me an idea of the kind of work you were doing?"

"Well, the social studies teacher was helping us with research skills," said Alice. "We were doing a project on Egypt and we had to pick one specific topic like housing. Then we outlined it and made a report to the class."

"That sounds as if you were doing good work, Alice. You'll like it here; we're doing a lot of the same things."

Both teachers were listening to and observing their pupils as they spoke, searching for clues that would help them work with these new pupils in their classrooms. And the clues were there, as you can tell from both conversations. Although each pupil spoke well, there are significant differences in both the thinking and speech of the two students. For example, Kenny's statement that the moon follows him around furnishes clues to his level of cognitive development, which we described in chapter 7 when we discussed cognitive development during the early childhood years.

Alice's skillful explanation of her use of research methods also revealed a level of cognitive development that one would expect of a typical sixth grader. Understanding the cognitive achievements of children Alice's age—in middle childhood—will be our task in the next two chapters. 🌳

This chapter, which analyzes the physical, cognitive, and moral milestones of middle childhood, will often take on the appearance of a mystery. Much is happening to 6- to 12-year-old youngsters that eludes initial detection. Cognitive complexities and subtle moral reasoning characterize these years between childhood and adolescence.

To help you discover clues to important developmental achievements, in this chapter we begin by tracing physical and motor development during the middle childhood years. We'll then turn again to Piaget and analyze his concrete operational period, that time of cognitive development when youngsters begin to engage in truly abstract thinking. Here we'll pause and examine the world of intelligence testing, which has caused so much controversy. But today's children are expected to do much more with their intelligence than just sit and listen and memorize: They're expected to develop thinking skills and to solve problems. We'll explore both of these worlds (cognitive and problem solving) and then trace the moral and language development of middle childhood youngsters.

As observers of this phase of lifespan development, we cannot allow ourselves to be deceived by an apparent lull in development. Too much is going on. Deep-seated developmental currents are changing the very process by which children reason and make their moral decisions.

In following the developmental path of children during these years, we can find significant signposts in fiction. Can anyone describe the cognitive ability of a middle childhood youngster better than Mark Twain? Do you recall the memorable scene where Tom Sawyer was desperately trying to avoid whitewashing Aunt Polly's fence? One of his friends, Ben Rogers, passed by, imitating the "Big Missouri" riverboat. When Ben sympathized with him, Tom looked at him and said, "What do you call work?"

His friend asked, "Why ain't that work?" Tom neatly dodged the question and asked, "Does a boy get a chance to whitewash a fence every day?" By that time Ben was jumping up and down in his eagerness to paint. When that happened,

> ■ Tom gave up the brush with reluctance in face but alacrity in his heart. And while that late steamer Big Missouri worked and sweated in the sun, the retired artist sat on a barrel in the shade close by, dangled his legs, munched his apple, and planned the slaughter of more innocents. (Twain, 1980)

What else can we do but acknowledge a sophisticated and subtle mind at work?

Do you remember Huck Finn meeting the Duke and the Dauphin? Not believing their stories about lost titles, Huck makes a decision:

> ■ It didn't take me long to make up my mind that these liars warn't no kings nor dukes at all, but just lowdown humbugs and frauds. But I never said nothing, never let on; kept it to myself; it's the best way; then you don't have no quarrels and don't get into no trouble. (Twain, 1979)

As we'll see a little later, such thinking reflects a certain level of moral reasoning. Children of these years use their previous experiences with rewards and punishments and their growing cognitive ability to reach moral decisions.

Think about what you read in this chapter; probe into what lies behind a child's behavior. It will help you to understand the developmental achievements that prepare a youngster to move from these last years of childhood to the different demands of adolescence.

After reading this chapter, you should be able to

- Describe the physical development and growing motor skills of middle childhood youngsters.

- Indicate the cognitive accomplishments of the concrete operational period.

- Evaluate the importance of thinking skills in a child's life.

- Discriminate the skills involved in problem solving.

- Contrast theories of moral development.

- Assess language achievement in the middle childhood years.

- Identify the strategies children use as they begin to read.

Physical Development

In contrast to the rapid increase in height and weight during the first years of life, physical development proceeds at a slowed pace during middle childhood. As you can see from table 9.1 on pg. 221, most children gain about 2 inches in height per year. The same pattern applies to weight gains. By 6 years of age, most children are about seven times their birth weight.

Middle childhood youngsters show steady growth, usually good health, and an increasing sense of competence. Physical growth is relatively slow until the end of the period, when girls' development may spurt. Variables such as genetic influence, health, and nutrition can also cause wide fluctuations in the growth of these children. Two youngsters may show considerable physical variation and yet both be perfectly normal. As Garcia Coll (1990) has reminded us, although most children achieve the major developmental milestones, the rate and content of development may well differ between cultures, subcultures, and ethnic groups.

A Multicultural Perspective

As we begin to examine development during the middle childhood years, our attention will be drawn to the obvious competencies (physical, cognitive, and psychosocial) that children acquire. Yet we are also aware that successful adjustment to school, friends, and family requires multiple skills. For some children, the path to understanding and esteem can be difficult. As Billingsley (1992) has noted, African American families are caught between conflicting tensions: the economic, physical, social, psychological and spiritual demands of its members on the one hand and the demands of a dominant society on the other. That is, the struggle for better housing and schools, higher incomes, and more satisfying occupations requires adjustment to a different lifestyle (Jaynes & Williams, 1989).

Some psychologists insist that too much importance has been made of the role of self-esteem in development. Do you agree or disagree? Why? Be specific.

If we agree with Garbarino and Benn (1992) that a child's single most important psychological necessity is self-esteem, then it becomes apparent that rejection can only frustrate the development of a positive self-regard. The notion of rejection as an obstacle to the development of healthy self-esteem is not confined to individuals (e.g., as when a mother or a father rejects a child). Rejection because you are a member of a particular group can work in exactly the same way.

When children interact with individuals from other cultures, their self-identity broadens to accept those with different customs, languages, and ideas. Although this may sound idealistic, helping youngsters to achieve this objective is the social goal of multicultural education. In this way, children are encouraged to form positive cultural, racial, and class identities, which in turn leads to high self-esteem and the ability and willingness to interact with diverse others. Ultimately, then, children develop a sense of social responsibility and an active concern for the welfare of others, both an idealistic and practical outcome.

In commenting on the need to acquire a growing understanding of others, Ramsey (1987) stated:

> While knowledge of unfamiliar people and lifestyles may reduce children's fears and avoidance of differences, their motivation for reaching beyond cultural, racial, and class barriers largely rests on their self-confidence, their ability to empathize with others' experiences and feelings, and their anticipation of pleasure and satisfaction to be derived from expanding their social relationship. (p. 112)

Those working with children of various cultures have a unique opportunity to further a positive multicultural perspective during these years of enthusiasm and rapid learning. As an example of steps that could be taken, Yao (1988) offered several suggestions for working with Asian immigrants. She began by urging adults to take the time to familiarize themselves with the physical, social, cultural, and personality traits that make these children and their parents unique. Ask yourself questions such as:

- Do I have any prejudices toward this group?

- What stereotypes do I associate with Asian Americans (for example, they're all superior in math and science)?

- What do I know about their culture?

- Will there be any conflict between my values and theirs?

These and similar questions can act as guidelines to help us adapt to those of different cultures and also help these children adapt to rules and procedures that may seem strange to them. The middle childhood years are an ideal time to foster positive interactions with multicultural children so that their energy and enthusiasm can be directed to optimum development, learning, and adjustment.

Physical Changes in Middle Childhood

Changes in height and weight are not the only noticeable physical differences. Body proportion changes also. Head size comes more in line with body size. An adult's head size is estimated to be about one-seventh of total body size; the preschooler's is about one-fourth. This difference gradually decreases during the middle childhood years. Also, the loss of baby teeth and the emergence of permanent teeth change the shape of the lower jaw. By the end of the period, the middle childhood youngster's body is more in proportion and more like an adult's (Tanner, 1989).

Changes in arms, legs, and trunk size also occur. The trunk becomes thinner and longer, and the chest becomes broader and flatter. Arms and legs begin to stretch but as yet show little sign of muscle development. Hands and feet grow more slowly than arms and legs, which helps to explain some of the awkwardness that we see during these years. These children are tremendously active physically and gradually display a steady improvement in motor coordination (Tanner, 1989).

Healthy, active children of this age—both boys and girls—also demonstrate considerable motor skill. Lansdown and Walker (1991) summarized motor development during these years:

- Skill increases with maturity until, by the end of the period, some youngsters are highly skilled and much in demand for various sports.

- Boys are stronger than girls.

- Girls may be more graceful and accurate.

- Sex differences—especially strength—become more obvious toward the end of the period.

- Balance matures by the end of the period.
- Fine motor skills (writing and drawing) improve noticeably.

Table 9.1 summarizes the major physical/motor changes in middle childhood.

Table 9.1	Physical Motor Development in Middle Childhood			
Age (years)	**Height (in.)**		**Weight (lb.)**		**Motor Development**
	Girl	*Boy*	*Girl*	*Boy*	
7	48	49	52	53	Child has good balance; can hop and jump accurately
8	51	51	60	62	Boys and girls show equal grip strength; great interest in physical games
9	52	53	70	70	Psychomotor skills such as throwing, jumping, running show marked improvement
10	54	55	74	79	Boys become accurate in throwing and catching a small ball; running continues to improve
11	57	57	85	85	Boys can throw a ball about 95 feet; girls can run about 17.5 feet per second
12	60	59	95	95	Boys can run about 18.5 feet per second; dodge ball popular with girls

The middle childhood years are a time when children demonstrate considerable competence; their continuing mastery of their bodies and their environment lead to emerging skills that are readily observable.

Guided Review

1. A child's single most important psychological necessity is _____ .
2. One of the greatest obstacles to the development of positive self-esteem is _____ .
3. Changes in height, weight, and _____ _____ are major physical changes in middle childhood.

Answers

1. self-esteem   2. rejection   3. body proportion

Cognitive Development

During the middle childhood years, children's cognitive abilities become remarkably complicated and sophisticated, reflecting in more observable form the complex mixture of heredity and environment (Cardon & others, 1992). For example, in a series of studies, Rose and associates (1991) found that measures of object permanence made at 1 year of age were significantly related to cognitive performance at 5 years of age, suggesting that some of the roots of later cognition can be found in infancy.

Middle childhood youngsters now enter formal education, and their cognitive abilities should enable them to meet the more demanding tasks set by the school. We shall continue our practice of examining the cognitive abilities of children by beginning with Piaget and his explanation of these years—the **concrete operational period.**

Piaget and Concrete Operations

During the period of concrete operations, children gradually employ logical thought processes with concrete materials, that is, with objects, people, or events that they can see and touch. They also concentrate on more than one aspect of a situation, which is called **decentering.** Children likewise acquire conservation and can now reverse their thinking. Think of the water jar problem (see chapter 2). Now they can mentally pour the water back.

Several notable accomplishments mark the period of concrete operations:

- **Conservation** appears. In Piaget's famous water jar problem, children observe two identical jars filled to the same height. While they watch, the contents of one container are poured into another, taller and thinner jar so that the liquid reaches a higher level. Seven-year-old children typically state that the contents are still equal. They conserve the idea of equal amounts of water by decentering, focusing on not only one part of the problem but both. They can now reverse their thinking and mentally pour the water back into the original container.

- **Seriation** means that concrete operational children can arrange objects by increasing or decreasing size.

- **Classification** enables children to group objects with some similarities within a larger category. Brown wooden beads and white wooden beads are all beads.

Concrete operational period

Piaget's third stage of cognitive development during which children begin to employ logical thought processes with concrete material.

Decentering

The process in which concrete operational children concentrate on more than one aspect of a situation.

Conservation

The understanding that an object retains certain properties, no matter how its form changes.

Seriation

The process in which concrete operational children can arrange objects by increasing or decreasing size.

Classification

The process in which concrete operational children can group objects with some similarities within a larger category.

Middle childhood youngsters are at Piaget's stage of concrete operations. Now they demonstrate increasing mental competence, such as classifying.

Features of Concrete Operational Thinking

Children at the level of concrete operations can solve the water-level problem, but the problem or the situation must involve concrete objects, hence the name of the period. In the water-level problem, for example, children no longer concentrate solely on the height of the water in the glass; they also consider the width of the glass. But as Piaget noted, concrete operational children nevertheless demonstrate a true logic, since they now can reverse operations. Concrete operational children gradually master conservation—that is, they understand that something may remain the same even if surface features change.

Figure 9.1 illustrates the different types of conservation that appear at different ages. For

Figure 9.1

Different kinds of conservation appear at different ages.

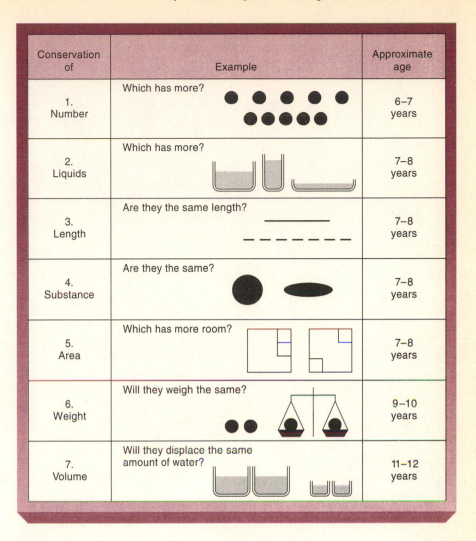

Conservation of	Example	Approximate age
1. Number	Which has more?	6–7 years
2. Liquids	Which has more?	7–8 years
3. Length	Are they the same length?	7–8 years
4. Substance	Are they the same?	7–8 years
5. Area	Which has more room?	7–8 years
6. Weight	Will they weigh the same?	9–10 years
7. Volume	Will they displace the same amount of water?	11–12 years

example, if preoperational children are given sticks of different lengths, they cannot arrange them from smallest to largest. Or if presented with three sticks, A, B, and C, they can tell you that A is longer than B and C, and that B is longer than C. But if we now remove A, they can tell you that B is longer than C, but not that A is longer than C. They must see A and C together. The child at the level of concrete operations has no difficulty with this problem.

But limitations remain. Piaget (1973) gave the example of three young girls with different colored hair. The question was: Who has the darkest hair of the three? Edith's hair is lighter than Suzanne's but darker than Lili's. Who has the darkest hair? Piaget believed that propositional reasoning is required to realize that it is Suzanne and not Lili. Youngsters do not achieve such reasoning until about 12 years of age.

Concrete operational children can also classify; that is, they can group different things that have something in common. For example, wooden objects may include both a table and a chair. In a classic experiment illustrating mastery of classification, Piaget showed a girl about 20 brown wooden beads and two or three white wooden beads. He then asked her to separate the brown from the white beads. Children at both the preoperational and concrete levels can do this. But then he asked her, "Are there more brown beads or wooden beads?" The preoperational child answered brown, whereas an older child answered correctly.

Numeration

The process in which concrete operational children grasp the meaning of number, the oneness of one.

Another interesting feature of this period is the child's acquisition of the number concept, or **numeration.** This is not the same as the ability to count. If five red tokens are more spread out than five blue ones, preoperational children, although able to count, still think there are more red than blue tokens. Piaget then constructed an ingenious device that enabled a child to trace the blue to the red. The

Figure 9.2
Encouraging acquisition of
number concept.

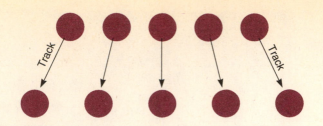

preoperational child can actually move the blue token to the corresponding red, but still thinks there are more red tokens! During the concrete operational period children understand oneness—that one boy, one girl, one apple, and one orange are all one of something (see figure 9.2).

Piaget's Legacy

As we end our work on Piaget's analysis of cognitive development, what can we conclude? Two major contributions of Piaget come immediately to mind: Thanks to Piaget we have a deeper understanding of children's cognitive development. He also has made us more alert to the need for greater comprehension of how children think (the processes that they use) and not just what they think (the products of their thinking).

As we have seen, serious questions have emerged about Piaget's beliefs. By changing the nature of the task (e.g., reducing the number of objects children must manipulate—see Gelman & Baillargeon, 1983), by allowing children to practice (e.g., teaching children conservation tasks—see Field, 1987), and by using materials familiar to children, researchers have found that children can accomplish specific tasks at earlier ages than Piaget believed (Halford, 1989).

Although Piaget has left an enduring legacy, his ideas are not the only way of analyzing cognitive development. Other psychologists, not entirely happy with Piaget's views, have devised new ways of explaining children's cognitive abilities.

New Ways of Looking at Intelligence

In our discussion of cognitive development from infancy through the middle childhood years, we have identified limitations in Piaget's theory. Addressing these shortcomings, several recent theories have been proposed to explain intelligence and cognitive development. Two of these seem particularly significant.

Sternberg's Triarchic Model of Intelligence

Robert Sternberg (1988) has designed a **triarchic model of intelligence** to answer three questions:

- What is the relationship of intelligence to our internal world? What are the inner processes and strategies that we use?

- What is the relationship of intelligence to our external lives? How does the environment affect intelligence?

- What is the relationship of intelligence to our experiences? How does what we do help to shape our intelligence?

To answer these questions, Sternberg (1986) devised the following threefold model of intelligence:

1. *The components of intelligence.* Sternberg has identified three types of information-processing components: **metacomponents,** which help us to plan, monitor, and evaluate our problem-solving strategies; **performance components,** which help us to execute the instructions of the metacomponents; and **knowledge-acquisition components,**

Has your knowledge of Piaget changed the way you think about children? How? Give examples.

Triarchic model of intelligence
A three-tier explanation of intelligence proposed by Robert Sternberg.

Metacomponents
Sternberg's term for those components that help us to plan, monitor, and evaluate our problem-solving strategies.

Performance components
Sternberg's term for those components that help us to execute the instructions of the metacomponents.

Knowledge-acquisition components
Sternberg's term for those components that help us to learn how to solve problems in the first place.

Figure 9.3

The relationship among the components of intelligence.

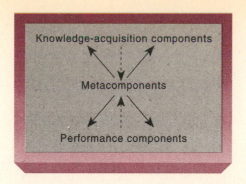

which help us to learn how to solve problems in the first place (Sternberg, 1988). These three components are highly interactive and generally act together.

For example, consider writing a term paper. The metacomponents help you to decide on the topic, plan the paper, monitor the actual writing, and evaluate the final product. The performance components help you in the actual writing of the paper. You use the knowledge-acquisition components to do your research. Figure 9.3 illustrates how the components work together.

2. *Experience and intelligence.* Sternberg's second aspect of intelligence includes our experiences, which improve our ability to deal with novel tasks and to use pertinent information to solve problems.

3. *The context of intelligence.* The third aspect of intelligence in Sternberg's model refers to our ability to adapt to our culture. The major thrust of contextual intelligence is *adaptation*. Adaptation, for Sternberg, has three meanings:

   - *Adapting to existing environments,* so that you adjust to current circumstances

   - *Shaping existing environments,* which implies changing the present environment to meet your needs

   - *Selecting new environments*

If you apply these descriptions to yourself and others you know, you probably can identify which aspect of intelligence predominates in each person. For example, if you excel in analytical thinking, you probably do quite well on traditional IQ tests.

Although Sternberg did not apply his theory directly to children, you can see how his work relates to the developing cognitive competence of the middle childhood youngster. To take one example, with their growing symbolic activity, children can think about their thinking; that is, they are employing metacomponents. Sternberg (1988) has also compiled a list of reasons why we too often fail, which has important implications for children of this age.

Noting that all of us, children and adults, let self-imposed obstacles frustrate us, Sternberg stated that what is important is not the level of our intelligence but what we achieve with it. Sternberg has identified the most common obstacles:

- *Lack of motivation.* If children aren't motivated, it really doesn't matter how much talent they have. In a typical classroom situation, for example, the range of intelligence may be fairly narrow and differences in motivation spell success or failure.

- *Using the wrong abilities.* Although children acquire greater cognitive ability, they frequently don't use it or else fail to recognize exactly what is needed. For example, faced with a math test, they may fail to review solutions to word problems (knowledge-acquisition components) and instead depend on their previous experiences.

- *Inability to complete tasks.* Regardless of how skilled children may be in their use of Sternberg's components, if they are unable to sustain their efforts—for whatever reason—they are in danger of failure. The worry here is that this tendency may become a way of life, ensuring difficulty, frustration, and failure.

- *Fear of failure*. Some youngsters may develop a fear of failure early in life. This can prevent them from ever fulfilling their intellectual potential.

These are among the obstacles that adults should be aware of, so they can help middle childhood youngsters develop to the fullest.

Gardner and Multiple Intelligences

Multiple intelligences
Gardner's theory that attributes seven types of intelligence to humans.

Howard Gardner (1983, 1985, 1991, 1993) has forged a tight link between thinking and intelligence with his theory of **multiple intelligences.** An especially intriguing aspect of his theory concerns understanding an individual who is capable of penetrating mathematical insights but who is baffled by the most obvious musical symbols. Gardner attempted to explain this apparent inconsistency by identifying seven equal intelligences.

1. *Linguistic intelligence*. The first of Gardner's intelligences is language—linguistic intelligence. For example, we can trace the effects of damage to the language area of the brain; we can identify the core operations of any language (phonology, syntax, semantics, and pragmatics); and language development in humans has been well documented and supported by empirical investigations. Gardner considered language a preeminent example of human intelligence.

   As we will soon see, during these years children change their use of language to a more flexible, figurative form. Gardner commented on this by noting that middle childhood youngsters love to expand on their accomplishments. They use appealing figures of speech: "I think I'll get lost," meaning that they're about ready to leave.

2. *Musical intelligence*. One has only to consider the talent and career of Yehudi Menuhin to realize that musical ability is special. At 3 years of age, Menuhin became fascinated by music, and by 10 he was performing on the international stage. The early appearance of musical ability suggests some kind of biological preparedness—a musical intelligence. The right hemisphere of the brain seems particularly important for music, and musical notation clearly indicates a basic symbol system. Although not considered intelligence in most theories, musical skill satisfies Gardner's criteria and so demands inclusion.

Relationships with peers, abstract activities, and developing physical skills all occupy middle childhood youngsters. The success that children achieve in these activities contributes significantly to an emerging sense of competence.

In regard to the middle childhood years, Gardner noted that most children (except for those who are musically talented) cease musical development after school begins. For the talented, up to the age of 8 or 9, talent alone suffices for continued progress. Around 9 years of age, serious skill building commences, with sustained practice until adolescence, when these children must decide how much of their lives they want to commit to music. In general, society accepts musical illiteracy.

3. *Logical-mathematical intelligence.* Unlike linguistic and musical intelligences, logical-mathematical intelligence, Gardner believed, evolves from our contact with the world of objects. In using objects, taking them apart, and putting them together again, children gain their fundamental knowledge about "how the world works." By this process, logical-mathematical intelligence quickly divorces itself from the world of concrete objects. Children begin to think abstractly.

    Gardner then used Piaget's ideas to trace the evolution of thinking. The development of logical-mathematical thinking, as explored by Piaget, is used as an example of the scientific thinking so characteristic of logical-mathematical intelligence. You may want to review Piaget's ideas concerning the unfolding of intelligence to better understand Gardner's views.

4. *Spatial intelligence.* Brain research has clearly linked spatial ability to the right side of the brain. Here Gardner relied heavily on Piaget, noting that an important change in children's thinking occurs during these years, especially with the appearance of conservation and reversibility. Middle childhood youngsters can now visualize how objects seem to someone else. During these years, children can manipulate objects using their spatial intelligence, but this ability is still restricted to concrete situations and events.

5. *Bodily-kinesthetic intelligence.* As Gardner noted, describing the body as a form of intelligence may at first puzzle you, given that we normally divide the mind and reasoning from our physical nature. This divorce between mind and body is often accompanied by the belief that our bodily activities are somehow less special.

    Gardner urged us to think of mental ability as a means of carrying out bodily actions. Thus thinking becomes a way of refining motor behavior. Our brain's control of our bodily functions has been well documented. Also, the developmental unfolding of bodily movements has been thoroughly recorded. Gardner stated that our control of bodily motions and the ability to handle objects skillfully are defining features of an "intelligence"—bodily-kinesthetic intelligence.

    We have commented that middle childhood is the beginning of the emergence of bodily skills, to the point where they can dominate some children's lives. Gardner posed an age-old question to which we still have no definite answer: Does increasing mental ability affect the performance of a bodily skill?

6 & 7. *Interpersonal and intrapersonal intelligence.* Gardner referred to interpersonal and intrapersonal intelligences as the personal intelligences. Interpersonal intelligence builds on an ability to recognize what is distinctive in others, while intrapersonal intelligence enables us to understand our own feelings. Autistic children are good examples of a deficit in this intelligence. Often competent in a certain skill, they may be utterly incapable of ever referring to themselves.

    The middle childhood years are a time of greater social sensitivity, a keener awareness of others' motivations, and a sense of one's own

Table 9.2	Gardner's Multiple Intelligences
Type of Intelligence	**Meaning**
Linguistic	Communication, a preeminent example of human intelligence
Musical	Linked to brain location and a basic symbol system
Logical-mathematical	What we usually mean by "intelligence"
Spatial	Linked to brain location and symbol systems
Bodily-kinesthetic	Smooth development of bodily movements and adaptation
Interpersonal and intrapersonal	Linked to frontal lobe of brain; recognize what is distinctive in others

Gardner's theory of intelligence has become quite popular. Do you find his idea of multiple intelligences appealing and useful? Why?

competencies. Children begin to develop friendships and devote considerable time and energy to securing a definite place in a circle of friends. This effort can only increase their sensitivity to interpersonal relations. At the same time, they become more aware of themselves, furthering the development of their intrapersonal intelligences. If children of this age do not succeed in establishing harmonious relationships, they may develop feelings of inadequacy and isolation. This fuels a fear of failure that can produce diminished expectations. (Table 9.2 illustrates Gardner's multiple intelligences.)

A MULTICULTURAL VIEW

Immigrant Children and Tests

Children's ability to take tests often powerfully influences the results of the test, especially intelligence tests. Tests can scare students or cause them anxiety. Whatever the reason for test anxiety—parental pressure, their own concerns, or the testing atmosphere—merely taking a test can affect performance. This is especially true for pupils with different cultural experiences. Language, reading, expectations, and behavior all may be different and influence test performance (Stigler & others, 1990). One publication, *New Voices: Immigrant Students in U.S. Public Schools* (1988), describes many of these pupils as having experienced wars, political oppression, economic deprivation.

These children want to succeed, as reflected in interviews with many of them: Almost 50 percent were doing one to two hours of homework every night. (Twenty-five percent of the Southeastern Asian students reported more than three hours each night.) We have spoken throughout our work of the need for sensitive responsiveness. Here is an instance in which being sensitive to the needs of multicultural children can only aid their adjustment and achievement in school.

In an effort to ensure equity in testing, a new national system of authentic assessment has been proposed (Madaus, 1994). These tests supposedly engage students in real world tasks rather than multiple-choice tests (Darling-Hammond, 1994). For example, President Clinton's Goals 2000 rests on the assumption that the federal government can help state and local communities in their striving for educational reform by specifying goals, providing financial support to attain these goals, and establishing a voluntary assessment mechanism for

accountability (Pullin, 1994). The intent is to ensure that *all* students will be competent in the core academic subjects, which can only occur if each disadvantaged group has an effective and complete opportunity to learn.

The goals are clear; the task itself is difficult. As Madaus (1994) noted, since social and cultural groups differ in the extent to which they share the values that underlie testing and the values that testing promotes, any national testing system raises questions of equity. The values of the test makers and the test takers aren't necessarily identical. For example, different cultural groups may have different intellectual traditions that tests, of whatever design, may not measure. As Madaus (1994) pointed out, who gains and who loses once again raises the issue of equity.

When children feel comfortable, they do better; this is particularly true for test taking. Multicultural children need information about why the test is being given, when it is being given, what material will be tested, and what kinds of items will be used. These are just a few topics to consider. In addition, language should not be a barrier to performance. For example, children need to understand the terms in the directions of the test—what *analyze* means; what *compare* means; what *discuss* means.

Helping multicultural students in this way means extra time and effort for teachers. But it is teaching, just as teaching English or history is teaching. As more and more multicultural students become users of classroom tests, they shouldn't do poorly because they don't understand the mechanics of the test.

Thinking and Problem Solving

Advanced societies demand citizens who can do more with their intelligence than just survive. Rapid change requires the ability to cope. Yet 25 percent of the 14- to 18-year-old group are no longer in school. We can only question how many young people are adapting. Concern about these and similar statistics has prompted renewed interest in two topics that have been with us for years: critical thinking and problem solving.

An Applied View

How Would You Answer These Questions?

1. Imagine that you were lucky enough to obtain two tickets to the great Broadway musical *Phantom of the Opera* for $100. As you walk down the street to the theater, you discover that you have lost the tickets. You can't remember the seat numbers. Would you go to the ticket window and buy another pair of tickets for $100?
2. Imagine that you are on the way to the theater to buy tickets for the Broadway play *Phantom of the Opera*. They will cost you $100. As you approach the ticket window, you discover that you have lost $100. Would you still pay $100 for the tickets?

These questions, originally posed by Tversky and Kahneman (1981) elicit some interesting answers. How did you answer them? Among their subjects, 46 percent answered yes to question 1, while 88 percent answered yes to question 2. Note that many more people said they would buy new tickets if they had lost the money rather than the tickets. Yet the two situations are almost identical—in each instance you would have lost $100.

How can we explain the difference in the responses? Tversky and Kahneman believed that the way a problem is framed helps to explain our response. As they stated:

> The frame that a decision-maker adopts is controlled partly by the formulation of the problem and partly by the norms, habits, and personal characteristics of the decision-maker. (1981, p. 453)

The point here is that our personal characteristics (such as motivation, persistence, and the like) and how questions and problems are structured influence our decisions. We can help children reach better decisions by teaching them the skills and strategies discussed in this chapter.

Thinking Skills

As our society moves from an industrial base to one committed to an information technology, the skills that children need to adapt to these new directions likewise change. Unless parents and teachers equip themselves with the ability to teach innovative skills, children will be woefully unprepared to meet new demands. Since a swift proliferation of knowledge characterizes an information technology, mastery

Answers

4. concrete operations   5. conservation, seriation, classification   6. metacomponents, performance, knowledge acquisition   7. Gardner   8. interpersonal

of available content will not suffice once children leave home and school and attempt to become productive citizens. Rather, they need skills and strategies that will enable them to adapt to constant change. That is, critical thinkers are self-correcting; they discover their own weaknesses and act to remove obstacles and faults.

What do we mean by **critical thinking?** Robert Sternberg has proposed a working definition that reflects his psychological concerns about thinking and intelligence (as we have just seen).

Critical thinking
Those mental processes that help us to solve problems and make decisions.

> ■ Critical thinking comprises the mental processes, strategies, and representations people use to solve problems, make decisions, and learn new concepts. (Sternberg, 1985, p. 46)

As Sternberg noted, his definition emerged from a psychological analysis of critical thinking, especially as it is related to intelligence. Using this definition as a basis, parents and teachers can take several steps to help children sharpen their thinking skills by using games and exercises such as those found in the accompanying box.

AN APPLIED VIEW

Sharpening Thinking Skills

Given the importance of developing and using thinking skills in our society today, parents and teachers can help children to develop the habit of analyzing, that is, to identify the parts in a problem or situation and to see how they relate to the whole. This is common in math and science classes, but children should apply these techniques in all aspects of their lives.

- Teach children not to be satisfied with the first thing they do. For example, in doing a homework assignment, students should learn to evaluate the work according to certain criteria: Did I get all the information I could? Does it "fit" the topic? Is it what I was supposed to do?
- Ask children to invent something they can use in their homes. Give them simple examples, such as the need for a back-scratching instrument or a device that will pick up pins and needles from the floor. You can structure it in the form of a "back-to-the-future" game. *But make them justify their invention:* Is it necessary? What is the problem it will solve? Are materials available to build it? How much will it cost? You are forcing them to examine the basis of their judgments.

- Teachers could have groups of students research the countries of origin of several of their classmates and create a "cultural corner" where one group at a time places their reports, magazines, pictures, literature about the country, and any other materials they may have collected. They could design holiday cards for the special holidays of that country and then specify class time for oral reports.
- Children should be aware of current environmental concerns by discussing news accounts of dangerous incidents, such as oil spills, toxic waste, and so on. Have them write letters to the local papers expressing their concerns. In this way, you are encouraging them to work together to solve problems.

Parents and teachers can encourage a middle childhood youngster's cognitive potential to think critically. By appealing to a child's enthusiasms and abilities, adults can encourage these youngsters to begin using "a thinking disposition."

Problem-Solving Skills

Do you think the schools should devote blocks of time to teaching thinking skills as a separate subject? Give specific reasons for your answer.

Middle childhood youngsters can use their newly developed cognitive accomplishments, such as ability in critical thinking, to solve the problems they face in their daily lives. To give you an idea of what we're talking about, see how good you are at solving the problem in the accompanying box.

AN APPLIED VIEW

Try This Problem

Do you think you're a good problem solver? Before you answer, try to solve the following problem.

    ■ Two motorcyclists are 100 miles apart. At exactly the same moment, they begin to drive toward each other for a meeting. Just as they leave, a bird flies past the first cyclist in the direction of the second cyclist. When it reaches the second cyclist, it turns around and flies back to the first. The bird continues flying in this manner until the cyclists meet. The cyclists both traveled at the rate of 50 miles per hour while the bird maintained a constant speed of 75 miles per hour. How many miles will the bird have flown when the cyclists meet?

    Many readers, after examining this problem, immediately begin to calculate distance, miles per hour, and constancy of speed. Actually this is not a mathematical problem; it is a word problem. Carefully look at it again. Both riders will travel for one hour before they meet; the bird flies at 75 miles per hour; therefore the bird will have flown 75 miles. No formulas, no calculations, just a close examination of what is given.

As children's decision-making abilities improve with age, they can be further aided by helping them to improve their thinking and problem-solving skills.

Teaching children the basics of problem solving will improve their abilities to recognize and solve problems, both in and out of the classroom.

Obviously some people are better at problem solving than others due to intelligence, experience, or education. But anyone's ability to solve problems can be improved, even children's. Some children and adults don't do well with problems because they're afraid of them. "I'm just not smart enough"; "I never could do these." Here is a good example. Group the following numbers in such a way that when you add them, the total is 1,000.

8 8 8 8 8 8 8 8

Unintimidated elementary school children get the answer almost immediately. Some of you won't even bother trying; others will make a halfhearted effort; still others will attack it enthusiastically. What is important is how you think about a problem. Step back and decide what you have to do; then decide on the simplest way to get the answer.

In the eights problem, think of the only number of groups that would give you 0 in the units column when you add them—five. Try working with five groups and you will eventually discover that $888 + 88 + 8 + 8 + 8$ gives you 1,000.

Many of the daily problems children face are vague and ill defined. If children lack problem-solving strategies, their task is next to impossible. This is one of the major reasons schools are under increasing pressure to teach problem-solving skills, either as a separate course or as a part of another course's content. Adults can help children to become better problem solvers by teaching them a problem solving method such as the DUPE technique.

The DUPE Model

Many models have been proposed to help people solve a wide variety of problems. Often these models employ acronyms to assist people in problem solving (e.g., SAC—Strategic Air Command; NATO—North Atlantic Treaty Organization; HOMES—The names of the Great Lakes: Huron, Ontario, Michigan, Erie, Superior). For our purposes we'll use an acronym that you can remember easily and that you can transfer to any problems (or teach to a child). The acronym is **DUPE** and its intent is to convey the message: **Don't let yourself be deceived.** The meaning of each letter is as follows:

D—*Determine* just exactly what is the nature of the problem. Too often meaningless elements in the problem deceive us; it is here that attention to detail is so important. How would you go about solving this problem?

■ There is a super psychic who can predict the score of any game before it is played. Explain how this is possible.

This problem, taken from Bransford and Stein (1984), poses a challenge to most of us because, as the authors noted, a reasonable explanation is difficult to generate. If you are having difficulty, it is probably because you have made a faulty assumption about the nature of the problem. You were not asked about the final score; the score of any game before it is played is 0 to 0. We deliberately presented a tricky problem to stress that you must attend to details.

U—*Understand* the nature of the problem. Realizing that a particular problem exists is not enough; you must also comprehend the essence of the problem if your plan for solution is to be accurate. For example, we frequently hear that a pupil's classroom difficulties are due to hyperactivity. Thus the problem is determined; but understanding the cause of the hyperactivity—physical, social, psychological—requires additional information. Here is an example of the need to understand the nature of a problem.

■ Tom either walks to work and rides his bicycle home or rides his bicycle to work and walks home. The round trip takes one hour. If he were to ride both ways, it would take 30 minutes. If Tom walked both ways, how long would a round trip take?

This problem illustrates a basic problem-solving strategy of dividing a problem's information into subgoals to help understand what's required. Think for a moment: What are the givens? How long would it take to ride one way? (15 minutes) How long is a round trip? (1 hour) How long does it take to walk one way? (45 minutes) How long is the round trip if Tom walked both ways? (45 + 45 = 90 minutes)

P—*Plan* your solution. Now that you know that a problem exists and you understand its nature, you must select strategies that are appropriate for the problem. It is here that memory plays such an important role. The accompanying box illustrates various memory strategies that aid memory.

E—*Evaluate* your plan, which usually entails two phases. First you should examine the plan itself in an attempt to determine its suitability. Then you must decide how successful your solution was.

All of these techniques, however, are useless unless children are motivated to use them.

DUPE

Problem-solving model (Determine a problem exists, Understand its nature, Plan for its solution, and Evaluate the solution).

The Role of Memory

One of the most powerful strategies in solving problems is the efficient use of memory. All memory strategies, however, are not equally effective. The appropriateness of the strategy depends on what you are asked to do. Try this memory problem.

■ The following list contains 25 words. Take 90 seconds to study these words. When time runs out, write as many of the words as you can without looking at the list.

paper	fruit	street	wheel
white	step	juice	time
spoke	shoe	car	note
ball	word	judge	run
banana	touch	hammer	table
dark	page	bush	official
walk			

How did you do? Or more importantly from our perspective, how did you do it? Were these among the strategies you used?

1. Rehearse each word until you have memorized it: car, car, car.

2. Rehearse several words: paper, white, spoke; paper, white, spoke.

3. Organize the words by category. Note that several words are related to cars; others could be grouped as fruit; still others could be categorized as relating to books.

4. Construct a story to relate as many of the words as possible.

5. Form images of words or groups of words.

You may have tried one or a combination of these strategies, but note that you were not told to memorize them in any particular manner. If you had received specific instructions, each of these strategies would not have been equally effective. For example, when we are asked to remember a particular telephone number, the tendency is to rehearse it for as long as we need to recall it. If you had been directed to memorize the words in the list in a certain order (e.g., the way that they were presented), grouping them by categories would not have been efficient. Thinking of a story to link them in the correct order would have been much more efficient.

Children and Motivation

These new ways of examining intelligence and the renewed interest in critical thinking, problem solving, and motivation seem particularly pertinent to middle childhood youngsters. With their developing cognitive sophistication, they are equal to the challenge posed by new ideas and welcome the opportunity to sharpen their mental skills, *provided they are motivated to do so.*

What Is Motivation?

When people ask about motivation, they want to know what causes a child to act in a particular way. To answer this question, we must first attempt to understand what motivation, a central construct in psychological research for the past 60 years, means (Weiner, 1990). No single best definition of motivation is recognized; thus to help us in our work, we'll think of motivation as consisting of three interrelated components: *personal goals, personal agency beliefs,* and *emotions* (Ford, 1992).

Personal agency beliefs refer to children's beliefs that they have the ability to attain personal goals. The beliefs must be realistic; that is, children must believe they are sufficiently competent to attain a goal. For example, let's say a student decides to enter an essay contest on "The Changing Face of America." Motivated by her belief that this is something that she can do, plus her willingness to work at it, she feels more confident because of the support she receives, for example, a teacher's guidance in a computer search for appropriate immigration data and help with editing the final version of the paper. Consequently, the student's assessment of her ability and her realization that she will receive important assistance from her teacher should help this student to feel confident about submitting an essay worthy of careful consideration.

You are probably aware of the role of emotions in arousing behavior but are probably less familiar with the close association between goals and emotions (Ford, 1992). How does this relate to motivation? Think for a moment: How do you feel when you attain something that you worked hard for? You *feel* good; the subjective nature of your emotional reaction reveals the degree of success or failure that you have achieved. Children react in the same way: They *feel* pleased and competent when they have achieved a worthwhile goal.

We can now use these ideas to define motivation. *Motivation arouses, sustains, directs, and integrates behavior.* When you are motivated, or when children are motivated, you usually can discover what conditions caused the behavior. Something acted on you to produce a certain kind of behavior, which was maintained at a certain level of intensity, and which was directed at a definite goal. For example, a teenager may have been promised a ticket to a rock concert for passing an algebra course. Here a certain type of behavior was aroused and maintained long enough to achieve a specific goal, which raises the topic of intrinsic and extrinsic motivation.

Intrinsic and Extrinsic Motivation

Psychologists have long argued about the relative merits of intrinsic versus extrinsic motivation: Should children always be intrinsically motivated? Should adults avoid extrinsic motivation when working with children, since it may frustrate the development of intrinsic motivation? Or should we stress the role of the environment and learn as much as possible about the use of rewards to further learning?

Intrinsic motivation means that children themselves want to do something to achieve a specific objective. Obviously this is an ideal state that results in considerable learning. You can help children acquire intrinsic motivation by relating your knowledge of their abilities, needs, and interests to meaningful goals. For example, when a parent, teacher, or counselor recognizes that a child is interested in the medical field, knowing that child's ability enables them to channel that interest in an appropriate direction.

Although this is ideal, intrinsic motivation can be elusive. Consequently, marks, prizes, and other tangible rewards are used. Since rewards and inducements are external to a child, they are characterized as *extrinsic* motivation. Even when adults use these methods, they should always attempt to have children transfer these temporary external devices to intrinsic motives. How? By making sure that children succeed at some level and being there to reinforce their efforts.

Any society can ill afford to ignore the significance of motivated children if it desires harmony in the home, school, and community. Remember: Children are always motivated to do something, and if this energy is not focused on worthwhile goals, delinquency, violence, and maladjustment often, if not always, result.

As middle childhood youngsters think better, reason more maturely, and evaluate their actions, moral development becomes a matter of increasing importance.

🌳 Guided Review 🌳

9. A workable definition of critical thinking was formulated by _____ .

10. A memory strategy in which you go over material repeatedly is called _____ .

11. The goal of the DUPE model is _____ _____ _____ _____ _____ .

12. Good problem solvers share distinct characteristics such as a positive _____ and a concern for _____ .

13. The letters in DUPE mean _____ , _____ , _____ , and _____ .

Answers

9. Sternberg 10. rehearsal 11. don't let yourself be deceived 12. attitude, accuracy 13. determine, understand, plan, evaluate

Moral Development

The beginnings of moral development emerge as a consequence of learning: Children are rewarded for what their parents believe is right and are punished for wrongdoing. Recent research indicates that parents may be more influential than originally thought in a child's moral development. Parents who encourage children to express their opinions about a real dilemma and who themselves present a higher level of moral reasoning help to advance their children's moral development (Walker & Taylor, 1991). With cognitive growth, reasoning appears and control of behavior gradually begins its shift from external sources to more internal self-control.

Piaget's Explanation

Youngsters realize that the opinions and feelings of others matter: What they do might hurt someone else. By the end of the period, children clearly include intention in their thinking. For 6-year-olds, stealing is bad because they might get punished; for the 11- or 12-year-old, stealing may be bad because it takes away from someone else. During these years, children move from judging acts solely by the amount of punishment to judging acts based on intention and motivation.

As might be expected, Piaget examined the moral development of children and attempted to explain it from his cognitive perspective. Piaget formulated his ideas on moral development from observing children playing a game of marbles. Watching the children, talking to them, and applying his cognitive theory to their actions, he identified how children actually conform to rules.

- In the first stage, children simply played with the marbles, making no attempt to conform to rules. Piaget (1932) referred to this as the *stage of motor rules*.

- In the second stage, at about ages 3 to 6, children seemed to imitate the rule behavior of adults, but they still play by themselves and for themselves. Piaget called this the *egocentric stage*.

- Between ages 7 and 8, children attempted to play by the rules, even though rules are only vaguely understood. This is Piaget's *stage of incipient cooperation*.

- Finally, between the ages of 11 and 12, which Piaget called the *stage of codification of rules*, children played strictly by the rules.

According to Piaget, after youngsters reach the fourth stage, they realize that rules emerge from the shared agreement of those who play the game and that rules can be changed by mutual agreement. Children gradually understand that intent becomes an important part of right and wrong, and their decreasing egocentrism permits them to see how others view their behavior. Peers help here because in the mutual give-and-take of peer relations, children are not forced to accept an adult view.

While observing the children playing marbles Piaget also asked them their ideas about fairness and justice, what is a serious breach of rules, and how punishment should be administered. From this information, he devised a theory of moral development:

- Up to about 4 years, children are not concerned with morality. Rules are meaningless, so they are unaware of any rule violations.

- At about 4 years, they begin to believe that rules are fixed and unchangeable. Rules come from authority (e.g., parents, God) and are to be obeyed without question. This phase of moral development is often called *heteronomous morality* (or moral realism). Children of this age make judgments about right or wrong based on the consequences of behavior; for example, it is more serious to break five dishes than one. They also believe in immanent justice; that is, anyone who breaks a rule will be punished immediately—by someone, somewhere, somehow!

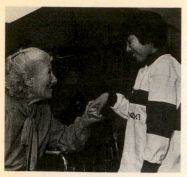

A major objective for those working with children should be to make them sensitive to their relationships with others, to recognize those times when a "helping hand" is needed.

Moral dilemma

A modified clinical technique used by Kohlberg in which a conflict is posed for which subjects justify the morality of their choices.

• From 7 to about 11 years of age, children begin to realize that individuals formulate social rules, which can be changed. This phase is referred to as *autonomous morality* (or the morality of reciprocity). At this age, children think punishment for any violation of rules should be linked to the intent of the violator. The person who broke five cups didn't mean to, so should not be punished any more than the person who broke one.

Piaget's ideas about moral development led to the advancement of a more complex theory that Lawrence Kohlberg devised.

Kohlberg's Theory

Among the more notable efforts to explain a child's moral development has been that of Lawrence Kohlberg (1975, 1981). Using Piaget's ideas about cognitive development as a basis, Kohlberg's moral stages emerge from a child's active thinking about moral issues and decisions. Kohlberg formulated a sophisticated scheme of moral development extending from about 4 years of age through adulthood.

To discover the structures of moral reasoning and the stages of moral development, Kohlberg (1975) employed a modified clinical technique called the **moral dilemma,** in which a conflict leads subjects to justify the morality of their choices. In one of the best known, a husband needs a miracle drug to save his dying wife. The druggist is selling the remedy at an outrageous price, which the woman's husband cannot afford. He collects about half the money and asks the druggist to sell the drug to him more cheaply or allow him to pay the rest later. The druggist refuses. What should the man do: steal the drug or permit his wife to die rather than break the law? By posing these conflicts, Kohlberg forces us to project our own views.

Kohlberg's theory traces moral development through six stages by successive transformations of cognitive structures (see table 9.3). Middle childhood youngsters are typically at Kohlberg's *preconventional level of morality*. Only as they approach

Table 9.3	**Kohlberg's Stages of Moral Development**
Level I. Preconventional (about 4 to 10 years) During these years children respond mainly to cultural control to avoid punishment and attain satisfaction. There are two stages: *Stage 1.* Punishment and obedience. Children obey rules and orders to avoid punishment; there is no concern about moral rectitude. *Stage 2.* Naive instrumental behaviorism. Children obey rules but only for pure self-interest; they are vaguely aware of fairness to others but only for their own satisfaction. Kohlberg introduces the notion of reciprocity here: "You scratch my back, I'll scratch yours." **Level II. Conventional** (about 10 to 13 years) During these years children desire approval, both from individuals and society. They not only conform, but actively support society's standards. There are two stages: *Stage 3.* Children seek the approval of others, the "good boy-good girl" mentality. They begin to judge behavior by intention: "She meant to do well."	*Stage 4.* Law-and-order mentality. Children are concerned with authority and maintaining the social order. Correct behavior is "doing one's duty." **Level III. Postconventional** (13 years and over) If true morality (an internal moral code) is to develop, it appears during these years. The individual does not appeal to other people for moral decisions; they are made by an "enlightened conscience." There are two stages: *Stage 5.* An individual makes moral decisions legalistically or contractually; that is, the best values are those supported by law because they have been accepted by the whole society. If there is conflict between human need and the law, individuals should work to change the law. *Stage 6.* An informed conscience defines what is right. People act, not from fear, approval, or law, but from their own internalized standards of right or wrong.

Source: Based on L. Kohlberg, "A Cognitive-Developmental Analysis of Children's Sex-Role Concepts and Attitudes" in *The Development of Sex Differences,* edited by E. Maccoby, Stanford University Press, Stanford, Calif., 1966.

ages 10 to 12 do they begin to edge into the *conventional level of morality,* where acts are right because that's the way it's supposed to be (determined by adult authority). The *postconventional level of morality* comes at age 13 and over.

According to Kohlberg, moral judgment requires us to weigh the claims of others against self-interest. Thus youngsters must overcome their egocentrism before they can legitimately make moral judgments. Also, anyone's level of moral development may not be the same as their moral behavior. To put it simply, people may know what is right but do things they know are wrong. Not all students of moral development agree with Kohlberg. Strenuous objections have been made to Kohlberg's male interpretation of moral development, especially by Carol Gilligan.

AN APPLIED VIEW — Schools and Character Development

Addressing the issue of a troubled society and our schools' role in that society, Lickona (1991, 1993) argued that the schools cannot be ethical bystanders. With the realization that our young people are experiencing difficult times, schools are beginning to become concerned once more with the issue of character development. As educators cautiously commence work on this topic, they are attempting to avoid the controversies that surrounded the values clarification movement of the 1960s, whose programs were intended to help children clarify their own values. Today's efforts are directed at identifying and building into programs such universal values as honesty, kindness, responsibility, and respect, concepts that teachers have traditionally introduced into their work.

As Lickona (1993) noted, character development in the classroom ranges from a teacher treating students with love and respect, with students treating each other with care and concern, and involving students in a democratic classroom (accepting responsibility) to encouraging students to extend these ideas beyond the classroom. In a similar manner, Brooks and Kann (1993) urged teachers to be sure their students understand the meaning of the concepts they are trying to instill in their students. For

example, do students really know what *courage, responsibility,* and *respect* mean?

Because there's no way to really know what another person is thinking, we can identify good character only by watching and listening to our students (Wynne, 1988). Therefore it makes sense for schools to encourage and reward the good conduct of their students. For example, the *For Character* program developed in the Chicago area publicly acknowledges the good conduct and academic efforts of its students, including such character-building activities as tutoring peers or students in other grades, serving as a crossing guard, acting as a student aide, acting as a class monitor, and joining school or community projects.

The program also provides opportunities for motivating students: public recognition through awards and ribbons presented at school assemblies and through mention over the school's public address system, and in school bulletins. Such recognition is given to individual pupils, groups of students, and entire classes. The relationship between academic learning and character development is mutually supportive because educators get back what they put into their work (Wynne, 1988).

Gilligan's "In a Different Voice"

Carol Gilligan (1982) has questioned how accurate Kohlberg's theory is in relation to women. Gilligan believed the qualities associated with the mature adult (autonomous thinking, clear decision making, and responsible action) are qualities that have traditionally been associated with masculinity rather than femininity. (Kohlberg, for example, placed most women at the third stage of his hierarchy because of their desire for approval, their need to be thought nice.) The characteristics that traditionally define the good woman (gentleness, tact, concern for the feelings of others, display of feelings) all contribute to women's lower scores for moral development.

Noting that most women's moral decisions are based on an ethic of caring rather than a morality of justice, Gilligan argued for a different sequence for the moral development of women. For boys and men, separation from mothers is essential for the development of masculinity; for girls, femininity is defined by attachment to mothers. Consequently, women define themselves through a context of human relationships and judge themselves by their ability to care (Gilligan, 1982).

Gilligan noted that a special interpretation of human relationships masks a woman's development. A shift in imagery occurs. For example, whereas cognitive and moral theory clearly traces an 11-year-old boy's thinking, that same theory "casts scant light on that of the girl" (Gilligan, 1982, p. 25). When the 11-year-old boy, Jake, is confronted with the dilemma of the overpriced drug in Kohlberg's scenario, he has no hesitation—"steal it." The response of the girl, Amy, is quite different. The husband should not steal the drug; rather, he should seek other, legal ways of obtaining it. Consequently, Gilligan believed that a new interpretation of a woman's moral development is needed, one that is based on the imagery of a female's thinking.

As a result of her studies, Gilligan formulated a developmental sequence based on the ethic of care. According to Gilligan, when the outline of women's morality is sketched, the results differ from Kohlberg's speculations about men. Gilligan described a morality of responsibility based on a concept of harmony and nonviolence and a recognition of the need for compassion and care for self and others (Brabeck, 1983). Gilligan did not argue for the superiority of either the male or female sequence but urged that we recognize the difference between the two. By recognizing two different modes, we can accept a more complex account of human experience.

Continuing to refine her ideas about the sequence of moral development for women, Gilligan, Lyons, and Hanmer (1990) noted that adolescent girls face problems of connections: What is the relationship among self, relationships, and morality? Must women exclude themselves and be thought of as a "good woman," or exclude others and be considered selfish? The answer seems to reside in the nature of the connections that women make with others.

🌐 YOUR VIEW?

WHAT'S

Teaching Moral Values: In the School or in the Home?

Increasing crime and violence in this country is an issue of national attention. In particular, incidences of violence in American schools have never been higher. Many feel the time has come to formally teach moral values in our classrooms, but others disagree.

■ **Issue:** A formal in-school program of moral education should be mandatory in all schools.

Answer—Pro A growing consensus has emerged that violence, particularly among the young, is a national problem. As such, the schools, which contact all of our children, would be a logical place to introduce formal programs devoted to moral education. Such programs would guarantee all students access to these ideas and behaviors and would maintain uniformity of the content.

Answer—Con The school day is already too short. Something we are now teaching would have to be eliminated to include another subject. An informal treatment of these issues, designed to suit the problems of individual communities and integrated across the curriculum of the community's schools makes better sense.

■ **Issue:** Educators are best suited to develop and implement a program that instills values for children.

Answer—Pro Educators understand best how to develop and teach ideas. Since children spend the greatest part of the day in school, they should receive moral education within the educational system.

Answer—Con More and more schools are being asked to take up the responsibilities that have traditionally rested with the family, which is one reason that achievement scores have fallen. The schools can only do so much. Families and religious settings are the best contexts within which to impart moral values, not the public school.

■ **Issue:** Educators are well suited to develop the content of a moral education curriculum.

Answer—Pro Since teachers are assuming more and more responsibility for all aspects of their students' lives, they are the ideal choice to determine what their students need in a program of moral education. Schools can present a developmentally sensitive curriculum using aspects of ideas like respect, service, and integrity appropriately.

Answer—Con Whose values or morality will the school teach? We are an ever-increasing multicultural nation. Our many backgrounds mean we have many ways of looking at these issues. How do we decide whose view to choose?

What's your view?

Whether the label is values, morals, or character, do you think the schools should become involved? This is a controversial issue, so think carefully about the reasons for your answer.

Whether boy or girl, middle childhood youngsters, through their rapid cognitive development, are aware of right and wrong. How do we know this? They write answers to questions; they talk to us. Thus, language development is another clue to their growing maturity.

Guided Review

14. According to Piaget, the attempt by 7- and 8-year-olds to play by even vague rules is the stage of _____ _____ .
15. The phase of moral development when children realize that individuals formulate social rules is known as _____ _____ .
16. A _____ _____ was Kohlberg's clinical technique whereby a conflict leads subjects to justify the morality of their choices.
17. Middle childhood youngsters are, for the most part, at Kohlberg's _____ level of morality.
18. _____ has challenged Kohlberg's theory with regard to women.

Language Development

In middle childhood we find children immersed in a verbal world. By the age of 7, almost all children have learned a great deal about their language. They appear to be quite sophisticated in their knowledge; as Menyuk (1982) noted, however, considerable development is still to come. During the middle childhood years, children improve their use of language and expand their structural knowledge. By the end of the period, they are similar to adults in their language usage.

Changes in Usage

Three types of change in language usage occur during these years (Menyuk, 1982):

- *Children begin to use language for their own purposes,* to help them remember and plan their actions. They move from talking aloud when doing something, to inner speech. From about age 7 on, children use language to help them recall things. This applies not only to individual items (such as lists) but also to the relations between objects or actions (psychologists call this **encoding**).

- *Language during these years becomes less literal.* We saw the beginnings of this change in chapter 7, when we discussed children's humor. Now they use language figuratively. On going to bed, an 11-year-old may say, "Time to hit the sack." Children display this type of language by a process called **metalinguistic awareness,** which means a capacity to think about and talk about language. You can see how this is impossible until children acquire the cognitive abilities that we just discussed.

- *Children are able to communicate with others more effectively.* They understand relationships; they can also express these relationships accurately, using appropriate language. In a sense, more effective communication is the product of the interaction of many developmental forces: physical growth as seen in the brain's development; cognitive development as seen in the ability to use symbols and to store them; and

Encoding
Translating speech sounds into meaningful language.

Metalinguistic awareness
A capacity to think about and talk about language.

Answers

14. incipient cooperation   15. autonomous morality   16. moral dilemma   17. preconventional   18. Gilligan

language development as seen in vocabulary development and usage. Language has now become an effective tool in adapting to the environment.

In regard to changes in structural knowledge, most middle childhood youngsters, especially by the end of the period, begin to use more complexly derived words. Remember when we spoke of the acquisition of morphological rules? Adding *er* to *old* changes its meaning. Children begin to change word stems, which can produce syntactic changes as well.

I really like history.
I really like historical books.

They now understand the rules that allow them to form and use such changes.

The same process applies to compound words. What does your instructor write on? Usually it's a blackboard. Middle childhood youngsters realize that a blackboard in this meaning is not a black piece of wood. The awareness of relations helps them to learn that the same relationship can be expressed in different ways.

Liz slapped Janie.
Janie was slapped by Liz.

As Menyuk (1982) states, much of children's language development during these years results from their awareness of language categories and the relationships among them.

During middle childhood the relationship of language development (in the sense of mastering a native tongue) to reading becomes crucial. Between the ages of 6 and 10, children must interpret written words wherever they turn: from signs on buses and streets as they go to school, to schooling that is massively verbal. When you consider a middle childhood youngster's competence, especially cognitive and linguistic, you conclude that they should be able to read effectively. The topics that engage reading researchers reflect the cognitive abilities of these children.

The Importance of Reading

In summarizing the reading research of the last decade, we can make several generalizations:

- *Reading is a constructive process,* which clearly implies that readers construct meaning from what they read (Mason & Au, 1990). The meaning that children glean from their reading also depends on their previous experiences, which may be rich or deficient. A related problem here is that even if children possess relevant knowledge about what they are reading, they may not use it.

- *Reading must be fluent,* which means that children must be able to decode quickly and accurately. We'll discuss this shortly.

- *Reading must be strategic,* which means that good readers, for example, adapt their reading techniques to the difficulty of the text and the purpose of their reading (Mason & Au, 1990).

- *Reading requires motivation,* which demands that reading materials be interesting and teaching be innovative and challenging.

- *Reading is a continuously developing skill,* which suggests that instruction and materials must match the changing abilities and skills of children.

Every effort should be made to instill a love of reading in children, both for academic success and the lifelong pleasure reading affords.

With these guidelines, researchers are investigating topics such as the following.

Decoding, a controversial and elusive topic, refers to the technique by which we recognize words. Some reading theorists argue that children should focus on the whole word; others believe that individual letters must be taught—the phonics method. Research today indicates that early phonics instruction produces the most satisfactory results. Do middle childhood youngsters possess this ability? Absolutely.

Vocabulary, or word meaning, refers to teaching the meaning of a word, not how to pronounce it. Pause for a moment and consider the ramifications of this statement. Knowledge of vocabulary is highly correlated with intelligence, which is highly correlated with reading performance and school success. Is it any wonder, then, that the acquisition of vocabulary is high on any list of reading priorities?

Reading comprehension, which is the ultimate objective in any type of reading instruction, means that a reader not only recognizes words but also understands the concepts that words represent. Children of this age should have the capacity to understand the meaning of appropriate words. Wolf and Dickinson (1985) furnished a good example.

■ Imagine if you will, a small group of children ranging in age from 3 to 10, huddled around a piece of paper with *die Katze* written in bold letters upon it. The youngest child squeals, "A picture!" A slightly older 4-year-old child shouts, "Book!" A first grader quickly tries to pronounce it, then says slowly with a puzzled expression, "It isn't a picture or a book. It's funny letters. I think it's funny words." The oldest child smiles knowingly and with the slightest disdain says, "It's a word all right, but it isn't in English. I'm pretty sure it means cat, but in Italian, maybe French, too." (p. 227)

The 10-year-old knows this word is different. To reach the understanding, illustrated in the preceding example, Chall (1992) believed, children pass through a series of stages:

- In the prereading stage, children up to 6 years of age learn letter and number discrimination and basics of reading.

- In stage 1 (grades 1.5–2.5), the major emphasis is on decoding as it applies to single words and simple stories.

- In stage 2 (grades 2.5–4), reading becomes much more fluent and understanding what is read becomes increasingly important.

- In stage 3 (grades 4–8), reading should be automatic and effort should be put into the comprehension of more complex material.

- Chall's stages 4 and 5 apply to adolescents and adults.

The goal of reading instruction during these years should be to enable children to control their own reading by directing attention where it is needed.

Strategies of Maturing Readers

In discussing the strategies that children of all ages use to obtain meaning from words, Booth (1994) stated that readers sample the text, confirming or rejecting possible meanings. They read along, pause to reflect on what they've read, perhaps skip words that they'll come back to, and reread to clarify meaning. As they do, they search for several types of cues in the text. The first type of cue that Booth (1994) identified are *pragmatic cues,* that is, those practical signals that help discover meaning. For example, a novel differs from a textbook, a shopping list differs from a statistical table.

Readers then relate the words themselves to what they signify, that is, to known facts and ideas. Using these *semantic cues,* readers integrate this new information with what they already understand, which is remarkably similar to Piaget's discussion of assimilation and accommodation. *Syntactic cues* enable readers to apply the rules of oral language that they have acquired to predict the meaning of words. Finally, readers use *phonographemic cues* to assess the relationship between the sounds of words and their written symbols.

Using these cues to assess reading capacity, Booth (1994) has identified several levels of reading ability. First are the *emergent readers,* who can identify letters and recognize some common words. They know what books "do" and they attempt to read by using segmental and syntactic cues. Next are *developing readers,* who are beginning to understand the relationship between sound and symbol. They pay close attention to the print in their efforts at decoding. Readers at this level use all four of the cueing systems previously mentioned. Finally, there are *independent readers,* who can read ably and without assistance using all of the cueing systems.

As children come to the end of the middle childhood years, they are in the independent reader category. They use their language more symbolically and understand abstract concepts such as time. (Again, note the agreement with Piaget's description of the concrete operational years.) Through these years, which are the elementary school years, children continue to expand the length of their oral sentences and continue to refine their understanding of the structure and function of language (Barchers, 1994).

You can understand why reading is so important to children of this age. As they move through the school curriculum, their work becomes increasingly verbal: They read about the history of their country, the story of science, the symbols of mathematics, or any subject you can mention. A youngster who has a reading problem is a youngster in trouble. To help such children, a new technique called *Reading Recovery* is achieving widespread use. Teachers are specially trained to work with children who need extra help, particularly during their early years in elementary school, by helping them develop the strategies of good readers.

A *Reading Recovery* lesson involves independent reading, writing stories, and fixing cut-up stories. The program runs for 20 weeks and thus far has shown considerable success: Students in the program have attained the level of typical readers of their age. Estimates are that as many as 60,000 children in North America were in *Reading Recovery* programs in 1993–1994. (If you are interested in reading more about this program, see Clay, 1993.)

🌳 Guided Review 🌳

19. Middle childhood youngsters begin to use language for their own _____ .

20. Readers construct meaning from what they read, which means that reading is a _____ _____ .

21. When readers adapt their techniques to the difficulty of the text, this shows that reading is also a _____ _____ .

22. The process by which we recognize words is called _____ .

23. According to Booth, _____ cues help readers to discover meaning.

Answers

19. purposes   20. constructive process   21. strategic process   22. decoding   23. pragmatic

🌳 CONCLUSION

From our discussion so far, we know several things about middle childhood youngsters. But are they capable of meeting the problems they face? Yes and no. They can assimilate and accommodate the material they encounter but only at their level. For example, elementary school youngsters up to the age of 10 or 11 are still limited by the quality of their thinking. They are capable of representational thought but only with the concrete, the tangible. They find it diffi-cult to comprehend fully any abstract subtleties in reading, social studies, or any subject.

According to Erikson, the middle childhood period should provide a sense of industry; otherwise, youngsters develop feelings of inferiority. With all of the developmental accomplishments of the previous six or seven years, youngsters want to use their abilities, which means that they inevitably experience failure as well as success, especially in their school work. The balance between these two outcomes decisively affects a child's self-esteem.

Physically active, cognitively capable, and socially receptive, much is expected of these children, especially in school. Their widening social horizons, with increasingly influential peer input, introduce joy and excitement but also stress and anxiety. We turn to these concerns in the next chapter.

🌳 CHAPTER HIGHLIGHTS

Physical Development

- These are good years physically as middle childhood youngsters consolidate their height and weight gains.
- Middle childhood youngsters develop considerable coordination in their motor skills.

Cognitive Development

- Among the major cognitive achievements of this period are conservation, seriation, classification, and numeration.
- Children of this age show clear signs of increasing symbolic ability.

- Sternberg and Gardner have proposed new ways of explaining intelligence.

Thinking and Problem Solving

- Children today need critical thinking skills to adapt to sophisticated, technological societies.
- Good problem solvers have several observable characteristics.
- The DUPE model offers suggestions for improving problem-solving skills.

Moral Development

- Piaget formulated a four-stage theory of moral development that is tightly linked to his explanation of cognitive development.
- Kohlberg proposed six levels of moral development that follow a child's progress from about 4 years of age to adulthood.
- Gilligan has challenged the male-oriented basis of Kohlberg's work.

Language Development

- Children's language growth during these years shows increasing representation and facility in conversing with others.
- During these years children develop several strategies to help them with their reading.

🌳 KEY TERMS

Classification 222
Concrete operational period 222
Conservation 222
Critical thinking 230
Decentering 222
DUPE 232

Encoding 239
Knowledge-acquisition components 224
Metacomponents 224
Metalinguistic awareness 239
Moral dilemma 236

Multiple intelligences 226
Numeration 223
Performance components 224
Seriation 222
Triarchic model of intelligence 224

🌳 WHAT DO YOU THINK?

1. Imagine an 11-year-old boy—let's call him Tom—who lives in the suburbs of a large northeastern city. He shows signs of becoming a great baseball player (a pitcher). His father realizes that his son could eventually win a college scholarship and go on to become a professional if he continues to develop. He decides that Tom should not play pickup games with his friends, because he might hurt himself. He also decides that the family should move to the South so Tom can play ball all year. Neither his wife nor Tom's sister wants to move. As a family friend, you have been asked for advice. What would you suggest?

2. You are a fourth-grade teacher and you turn to Janice and say, "Janice, Barbara is taller than Janie, who is taller than Liz. Who's the tallest of all?" Janice just looks at you. You sigh and think, "Where's Piaget when I need him?" How would you explain Janice's behavior?

3. Billy (9 years old) cuts through the parking lot of a supermarket on the way home from school. In the bike rack by the wall he sees a beautiful racing bike that he really wants. It seems to be unlocked and no one is around. With Kohlberg's work as a guide, what do you think is going through Billy's mind?

🌳 SUGGESTED READINGS

Bransford, B. & Stein, B. (1993). *The IDEAL problem solver*. New York: Freeman. An excellent little book that explores the mysteries of problem solving in an engaging and practical way.

Gardner, H. (1983). *Frames of mind*. New York: Basic Books. Gardner's book, which is available in paperback, is an excellent example of the new perspective on studying intelligence. Recognizing that we all seem to demonstrate different abilities, Gardner makes an appealing case for the existence of several intelligences.

Young, J. (1988). *Steve Jobs: The journey is the reward*. New York: Lynx. A penetrating account of the restless, inquiring mind of the middle childhood years that eventually led to the founding of Apple Computer.

🌳 CHAPTER REVIEW TEST

1. Psychological characteristics of middle childhood include all but
   a. seriation.
   b. numeration.
   c. moral reasoning.
   d. random scribbling.

2. An average 11-year-old who stands 57 inches weighs about _____ pounds.
   a. 50
   b. 85
   c. 100
   d. 115

3. Which statement is *not* true?
   a. Girls and boys in the middle childhood years show equal strength.
   b. Boys are stronger than girls during middle childhood.
   c. Middle childhood boys and girls show equal interest in physical games.
   d. Balance matures by the end of middle childhood.

4. Which of the following is out of order? Conservation of
   a. number
   b. volume
   c. liquids
   d. length

5. The acquisition of the number concept is known as
   a. classification.
   b. seriation.
   c. numeration.
   d. conservation.

6. Sternberg's theory is based on components, experience, and
   a. context.
   b. gender.
   c. age.
   d. chromosomes.

7. According to Sternberg, obstacles to realizing the potential of our intelligence include all but
   a. lack of motivation.
   b. using wrong abilities.
   c. fear of failure.
   d. physical disability.

8. Howard Gardner's theory of multiple intelligences includes _____ equal intelligences.
   a. 4
   b. 5
   c. 7
   d. 10

9. In Sternberg's theory, learning how to solve problems is a function of
   a. metacomponents.
   b. genetic endowment.
   c. environment.
   d. knowledge-acquisition components.

10. When we plan, monitor, and evaluate our problem-solving strategies, we are using
    a. knowledge-acquisition components.
    b. performance components.
    c. metacomponents.
    d. general intelligence.

11. According to Sternberg, adapting to our culture is called the context of
    a. intelligence.
    b. organization.
    c. assimilation.
    d. accommodation.

12. Recognizing what is distinctive in others is an example of which of Gardner's intelligences?
    a. linguistic
    b. interpersonal, intrapersonal
    c. logical-mathematical
    d. bodily-kinesthetic

13. Which of Gardner's intelligences results from contact with the objects of the world?
    a. musical
    b. interpersonal, intrapersonal
    c. linguistic
    d. logical-mathematical

14. Which of Gardner's intelligences is linked to the right side of the brain?
    a. spatial
    b. interpersonal
    c. linguistic
    d. logical-mathematical

15. One problem with tests is that test takers and test makers may differ in their
    a. relationships.
    b. circumstances.
    c. conditions.
    d. values.

16. Our response to problems may be determined by how the problem is
    a. framed.
    b. referenced.
    c. refined.
    d. filtered.

17. Gilligan's developmental sequence is based on
    a. social justice.
    b. female superiority.
    c. an ethic of care.
    d. moral reasoning.

18. Piaget's ideas on moral development came from
    a. structured interviews with children.
    b. moral dilemmas.
    c. an ethic of care.
    d. observations of children playing marbles.

19. During the years 7 to 11, Piaget believed that children develop a form of morality he called
    a. autonomous.
    b. heteronomous.
    c. individualized.
    d. group-oriented.

20. Which statement is *not* accurate?
    a. Knowledge of vocabulary is highly correlated with intelligence.
    b. Intelligence is correlated with reading performance.
    c. Reading performance is highly correlated with gender.
    d. Intelligence is highly correlated with school success.

Answers

1. d 2. b 3. a 4. b 5. c 6. a 7. d 8. c 9. d 10. c 11. a 12. b 13. d 14. a 15. d 16. a 17. c 18. d 19. a 20. c

10 Psychosocial Development in Middle Childhood

Chapter Outline

Loyalty to friends rapidly becomes a powerful influence during the middle childhood years, often causing emotional conflicts and moral dilemmas for children.

Tim Owens, who was in the sixth grade at the Brackett School, kept staring at the ground in the school's parking lot. Although all the students in the school were milling around, talking and trying to discover the exact location and cause of the fire, Tim stayed by himself. With a troubled expression, he watched the firefighters quickly extinguish the small blaze. He knew who had set the fire.

Earlier in the day, Tony Larson, another sixth grader, had said to Tim, "Let's get something started around here. It's been pretty dull lately. B-o-r-i-n-g. Watch what happens in science today."

"What's up, Tony? You're not going to try anything in Evans's class, are you? (Mildred Evans was the sixth-grade science teacher.) She's a pretty good person."

"What difference does that make? Let's liven things up. This place is really dullsville."

When the officials from the fire department gave the all clear and the students returned to the building, Tim walked by the science lab and saw the damage caused by the small fire. He looked around, worried; he was pretty sure he knew what had happened. He liked Mrs. Evans; she had always been fair to him.

Mildred Evans saw him standing at the doorway and said, "This is a tough one, Tim. The fire inspector said it was set. I can't believe anyone would do this. Think of the damage and what could have happened to some of the students. Who could possibly do something like this?"

Tim looked at the teacher. He knew that Tony Larson wasn't really bad; Tony just didn't think that others really liked him, so he was always looking for attention. "Why, he even told me something would happen, just to make sure somebody would know," thought Tim. "If I tell Mrs. Evans what I know, maybe she could straighten him out. But he could be in a lot of trouble, maybe even expelled." Tim stood there, not sure what to do next.

Torn between loyalty to a friend and yet knowing that his friend's actions are wrong, Tim is faced with a dilemma that has strong implications for psychosocial development. If he decides to confide in the teacher, whom he likes, what will the rest of his friends think? Peer influence at this age is becoming a powerful motivator of behavior. Yet, as you realize from reading about Piaget's work, a pupil of this age knows when something is wrong. Can Tim reconcile his behavior with what he thinks, and at the same time be trusted by his friends? Or will he compromise what he believes to be right to stay "in" with his friends? Moral implications also exist, as we have just seen in chapter 9. 🌳

Consider the developmental accomplishments that we described in chapter 9. Children's skills—physical, motor, cognitive, linguistic—are beginning to flourish. Now children want an opportunity to demonstrate their prowess and to win recognition from others. But if their efforts meet only failure, the result can be feelings of inferiority. Their experiences with their families, friends, and in school should provide the opportunities for the further development of competence.

With these personal changes children's social contacts expand—perhaps the addition of brothers and sisters, new friends, new adult figures, and school with its challenges and achievements. All of these new contacts—siblings, friends, and teachers—become important influences on a child's development since we know that the great socializing agents of childhood are family, peers, school, and the media.

One type of positive social contact that a youngster of this age can make is in forming relationships with the elderly. Children 10 or 11 years old visit nursing homes where they find "writing partners," elderly citizens with varied cultural backgrounds and rich personal experiences. The partners write stories and poems that the children use in their language classes. These interpersonal relationships give the children insights into a group they rarely encounter (with the possible exception of grandparents). Such experiences help children to develop those prosocial behaviors so needed in our society: caring, sharing, a sense of responsibility, and a sensitivity to the needs of others. The children also help the elderly. With the enthusiasm and energy of these years, they bring interest and excitement to many whose lives are limited. Here we have an excellent example of what middle childhood youngsters can accomplish and give to others as they begin to move into a wider social context.

In tracing the impact that different individuals have on development, it is perhaps wise to begin with those closest to home—siblings. We'll then turn our attention to peer influence. Following that, we'll examine those two great socializing agents: school and television. But we know that children are growing up in difficult times, so we should also consider how stress affects development.

After reading this chapter, you should be able to

- Assess the influence of siblings on development.

- Analyze the role of peers in middle childhood development.

- Compare the different kinds of influence that schools exercise during the middle childhood years.

- Describe television's effect on the different aspects of development in middle childhood.

- Define the different kinds of stress that can affect children during this period.

- Distinguish the causes of violence in middle childhood youngsters.

Siblings and Development

■ Children grow up within a network of relationships—with parents, grandparents, friends, and for 80% of children in the United States and Britain, siblings. How does this experience of being a sibling affect their development? (Dunn, 1985, p. 787)

Siblings
Brothers and sisters.

Older siblings can help their younger brothers and sisters and ease many of the normal upsets in development. By being models, offering advice, and interceding with adults, siblings form bonds that survive distance and time.

With these words, one of the leading students of **sibling** relationships, Judy Dunn, emphasizes the importance of brothers and sisters in a child's development. Of one thing we can be very sure: Growing up with brothers and sisters is quite different from growing up without them. Brothers and sisters, because of their behavior toward one another, create a different family environment. As Dunn stated (1988), the sibling relationship provides a context in which children demonstrate their varied abilities with frequency and intensity. During their early years, for example, siblings probably spend more time with each other than they do with their parents. An older sibling may spend considerable time taking care of younger brothers and sisters. These relationships last a lifetime, longer in most cases than those between husband and wife or parent and child (Dunn, 1988).

When you examine sibling relationships from this perspective, you can see how they affect development. In the early years, young brothers and sisters can provide security for babies who may feel frightened by strangers or anything different. (The attachment literature we discussed in chapter 5 shows that siblings definitely can attach to each other.) Older siblings are also models for younger children to imitate. They can become sounding boards for their younger brothers and sisters; that is, the younger siblings can try out something before approaching a parent. Older siblings often ease the way for the younger by trying to explain to parents that what happened wasn't all that bad. In this way, bonds are formed that usually last a lifetime (Hinde, 1987).

The Developing Sibling Bond

Attempts to analyze the influence of sibling relationships on development must reckon with age differences, friendships outside of the family, school experiences, sickness, accidents, gender differences, and socioeconomic status. Basic to all of these factors is the inborn temperamental disposition that each child brings to any relationship, which helps to explain the contradictions that seem to exist in the way that siblings relate to each other, sometimes affectionately and warmly, at other times hostilely.

Several cultural factors have contributed to the formation of a lifelong bond between siblings. For example, *longer lifespans* mean that brothers and sisters spend a longer period of their lives together than ever before, as long as 70 or 80 years! When parents have died, the siblings' own children have left, and spouses have died, siblings tend to tighten the bond and offer each other needed support. *Geographic mobility* means unavoidable separation. Friendships are broken; schools and teachers change; adjustments to new situations must be made. For many children, the one anchor to be found is a brother or sister. *Divorce and remarriage* typically bring unhappiness and hurt. Relationships change, which causes most children to experience emotions ranging from relief to fear.

How Siblings Help Each Other

As you might conclude from what we've said about siblings, conditions may exist that link siblings in a lifelong relationship. After all, why not? Think of the functions that siblings perform for one another, functions that contribute to the cementing of the bond. Among them are the following (Banks & Kahn, 1982):

1. *Identification and differentiation.* If identification is the glue of the sibling relationship, then the process by which one youngster learns from a sibling's experiences is a powerful phenomenon. Observing, imitating, and tentative trials, on the younger sibling's own terms (i.e., without parental pressure), can become an effective means of acquiring competence. Accepting some of an older sibling's behaviors and rejecting others leads to differentiation, an important and necessary step in developing a healthy self-concept.

2. *Mutual regulation.* Siblings can act as nonthreatening sounding boards for each other. New behaviors, new roles, and new ideas can be tested on siblings, and the reactions, whether positive or negative, lack the doomsday quality of many parental judgments. The emotional atmosphere is less charged. These simple experiments can give children confidence or prevent them from embarrassing incidents (Sroufe & others, 1992).

3. *Direct services.* Cooperative siblings can ease many burdens. From the exchange of clothes as teenagers, to the borrowing of money before a paycheck, to support in life's crises, siblings provide valuable services for each other.

4. *Dealing with parents.* Sibling subsystems are the basis for the formation of powerful coalitions, often called the *sibling underworld.* Older siblings can warn their younger brothers and sisters about parental moods and prohibitions, thus averting problems. Older siblings frequently provide an educational service to parents by informing them of events outside the home (Eisenberg, 1992).

Siblings perform many functions for each other. Not only do they directly help each other, but by observing older sibling's behaviors, younger siblings decide what to accept and what to reject, thus contributing to their own sense of identity.

We also know, however, that sibling relationships can be negative. *Rivalry*, whatever the cause, may characterize any bond. An older sibling can contribute to those feelings of inferiority that Erikson so elegantly describes as contributing to the crises of this period. Imagine the difficulty of a firstborn sibling forced to share parental attention, especially if the spacing between the children is close (less than two years). If the firstborns must also care for younger children, they can become increasingly frustrated.

The causes for rivalry are not one-sided. Younger children may only see the apparent privileges that are extended to the oldest: a sharing in parental power, authority, and more trivial matters such as a later bedtime or greater use of the television set. As Eisenberg noted (1992), although the bond remains, siblings who help each other, share things, and frequently cooperate still have conflicts.

In fact, sibling discord is one of the problems that parents most frequently report. Researchers now realize that sibling conflict has multiple causes (Brody & others, 1992). For example, marital quality and conflict and the family's emotional quality seem to be related to sibling conflict. Studying 152 white children, Brody and his colleagues (1992) attempted to determine whether the way parents treated trouble between their children had any long-term consequences on sibling conflict. The researchers found that family harmony during discussions about sibling problems, and the father's impartiality, reduced sibling conflicts.

How Siblings Affect Development

In an early and careful investigation, Koch (1960) found that school-age children have unique attitudes toward their siblings. For example:

- Some children said they played frequently with their brothers and sisters; others rarely did.

- About one-third of the children said they fought constantly; another one-third said they seldom quarreled.

- Some said they liked playing with a sibling; others much preferred a friend.

When Koch specifically asked the youngsters if they would be happier without their siblings, she received definite answers. One-third replied they would be happier without the sibling. (Could you make her disappear? She's too bossy.) The majority, however, said they preferred keeping the sibling (although they phrased their answers in less than glowing terms: "I'll keep him. He's bad but not that bad").

The children's replies reflected many of the functions that siblings provided—help, money, support. Those who preferred life without a sibling commented on conflicts, bossiness, and abuse. ("He makes me cry." "She's so mean.") The emotional quality of the relationship was apparent in both the positive and negative responses, much more so than when referring to anyone else. Commenting on Koch's findings, Dunn (1985) states:

> ▬ The children talked about affection, comforting, and helping, but also about antagonism and quarreling. And it is striking that these different qualities of the relationship were not closely linked. Children who described their relationship with a brother or sister as very warm, close and affectionate, for instance, were not necessarily those children who experienced little conflict with the sibling or who expressed little rivalry with each other. And the children who fought a great deal with their siblings were not necessarily the children who reported much jealousy about the parents. (p. 51)

Analyzing how children perceive their relations with their brothers and sisters, Furman and Buhrmester (1985) conducted two studies that attempted to discriminate the quality of these relationships. In the first study of 49 fifth- and sixth-grade children (using individual interviews), the investigators developed a list of the primary qualities of sibling relationships. They discovered that the most common positive qualities mentioned were *companionship* (93% of the children identified this quality), *admiration* (81%), *prosocial behavior* (77%), and *affection* (65%). The most negative qualities mentioned were *antagonism* (91%) and *quarreling* (79%).

In their second study, Furman and Buhrmester developed a self-report questionnaire to assess children's perceptions of their sibling relationships. Their subjects were 198 fifth- and sixth-grade children. The researchers found that the questionnaire assessed the nature of the children's interactions in many different social contexts. Four dimensions were particularly significant:

- *Warmth/closeness*. Children felt closer to same-sex siblings, although this finding became less significant as the ages between siblings increased.

- *Relative status/power*. Age had a strong effect on perceptions of status and power. The older siblings reported greater nurturance of and dominance over younger members.

- *Conflict*. Age was a significant factor here. More conflict occurred between narrow-spaced siblings than wide-spaced pairings. Children also perceived older siblings of the same sex to be more dominant than older siblings of the opposite sex.

- *Rivalry*. Children reported greater rivalry and parental partiality when siblings were younger. The authors believe that the attention and treatment by others outside of the sibling pair may be more important than in other types of relationships.

What specific developmental implications can we draw from our discussion? First, the early affective quality of the relationship persists through the years. The content of the interactions between siblings will obviously change throughout the years, but its affective quality remains consistent. Second, younger siblings tend to imitate older brothers or sisters. For example, second-borns imitate most frequently, especially if the firstborn had been affectionate. Same-sex pairs imitate each other more frequently than mixed-sex pairs (Dunn, 1985).

Do you have either brothers or sisters? Being as objective as you can, do you think they had a positive or negative effect on your development?

Here we may ask: Does the nature of the sibling relationship persist? In a study of sibling relationships from preschool through middle childhood to the beginning of adolescence, Dunn, Slomkowski, and Beardsall (1994) commented on the individual differences in children's relationships in middle childhood: Some are characterized by affection, others by hostility. Are these characteristics part of a pattern that began in early childhood? Considering our discussion thus far, you can see how it is possible to argue for continuity (yes, the nature of the sibling relationship is basically the same), since a child's personality and family dynamics usually remain stable. It is also possible to argue for discontinuity (no, the relationship changes over the years), since children's social relationships change over the years (e.g., they make new friends in and out of school) as do their perceptions of self.

Dunn and her associates (1994) found considerable continuity from early childhood to the beginning of adolescence in the positive and negative feelings of siblings toward each other. Many reasons contribute to the stability of these behaviors, especially the ongoing family dynamics. The siblings seemed to grow closer with adversity; that is, when one sibling had troubles with someone at school or became ill, other siblings offered support and sympathy. Gender differences also appeared: Adolescent sisters were closer to their younger sisters than were adolescent boys, who became more intensely involved with their male peer group.

Middle childhood youngsters will bring to their interactions with those outside of the family the characteristics that they formed within the family circle. With this in mind, let's turn now to the impact of peers on development.

🌳 Guided Review 🌳

1. Among the cultural changes contributing to a strengthening of sibling relationships are the following: _____ _____ , _____ _____ , and _____ .

2. Siblings act as nonthreatening sounding boards for each other, which is called _____ _____ .

3. One way siblings help each other is by learning from each other's experiences. Banks and Kahn called this _____ and _____ .

4. Sibling conflict seems to be related to _____ .

5. The most common quality found in siblings' relationships was _____ .

The Influence of Peers

Peers
Refers to youngsters who are similar in age to other children, usually within 12 months of one another.

We typically use the word **peers** to refer to youngsters who are similar in age, usually within 12 months of each other. But equal in age does not mean equal in everything, for example, intelligence, physical ability, or social skills. Also, research shows that many of a child's interactions are with those who are more than 12 months older, although we know little about the nature of these relationships (Hartup, 1989).

With these cautions, we turn now to the influence of peers during middle childhood. (Here you may want to return briefly to chapter 5 and the analysis of relationships. We'll assume that you understand the basics of a relationship at this point.) When we turn to same-sex and mixed-sex interactions, we can summarize the obvious findings quickly. Children of all ages associate more frequently with members of their own sex. Why? Adults encourage such relationships. Children of the same sex also share more mutual interests, and gender-role stereotypes operate powerfully to reinforce same-sex relationships.

Children's Friendships

Friend
A nonfamilial relationship that offers feelings of warmth and support.

In his engaging book *Children's Friendships,* Rubin (1980) stated that the word **friend** reflects the common functions of peer relationships for people of all ages. It refers to nonfamilial relationships that are likely to foster a feeling of belonging and a sense of security. How youngsters think about friends, of course, changes with age.

Middle childhood youngsters, with the abilities that we have traced, can reach logical conclusions about their friends. Children of this age search for friends who are psychologically compatible with them. For example, does Jimmy share my interests? Does he want to do the same things I do? Children begin to realize, especially toward the end of the middle childhood period, that friends must adapt to each other's needs.

Children who feel rejected by their peers frequently are plagued by problems. For example, in studying 452 five- to seven-year-old children, Cassidy and Asher (1992) found that children who believed that they had few friends were troubled by feelings of loneliness. Even the younger children in the study recognized that they had peer relationship problems and experienced unhappiness with their rejection. This study, with its focus on loneliness, testifies to the significance of peer relations to normal social development.

In a similar study, Parker and Asher (1993) analyzed the relationship between group acceptance and friendship and concluded that problems with group acceptance doesn't necessarily doom the possibility of satisfactory friendships. The

Answers

1. longer lifespan, geographic mobility, divorce   2. mutual regulation   3. identification, differentiation   4. age   5. companionship

During middle childhood, peer relationships become increasingly important for social development. Children are attracted to those who share their interests, who play well with them, and who help them to learn about themselves.

authors discovered that not all highly accepted children had close friends and that friendships had a more powerful impact on children's feelings of loneliness than did peer group acceptance. For example, children without best friends were more lonely than children with best friends regardless of how well accepted they were. Parker and Asher (1993) concluded that feelings of loneliness arise from several sources—poor acceptance by peers, lacking a friend, or having a friendship that fails to meet relationship needs—that either singly or in combination can seriously undermine children's feelings of well-being.

These findings were confirmed by Morison and Masten's (1991) longitudinal study of peer reputation as a predictor of later adaptation. Believing that the ability to get along with peers is a critical developmental task of middle childhood, these authors studied 207 third to sixth graders, and seven years later restudied 88 percent of the group. They found that peer reputation assessed in middle childhood was a significant predictor of adolescent adjustment. Disruptive, aggressive, sensitive, and isolated behavior during the early childhood years were associated with antisocial, incompetent behavior in adolescence.

Rubin (1980) believed that friends provide children certain resources that adults can't provide, such as the following:

- *Friends offer opportunities for learning skills.* They teach children how to communicate with one another, which gradually leads to the ability to recognize the other person's needs and interests. (We'll discuss this shortly with Selman's work.) Friendship also means that a child has to learn how to cooperate and how to deal with conflict.

- *Friends give children the chance to compare themselves with others.* "I can run faster than you" is not just a competitive statement. It's also a means of evaluating oneself by comparison with others.

- *Friends give youngsters the chance to feel that they belong to a group.* By age 10 or 11, groups have become important, and, as we saw earlier in our discussion of gender, sex cleavage is the rule. Here children find a social organization that includes not just individual friendships but roles, collective participation, and group support for activities. You can see, then, how being included in a group can further development, and how feelings of isolation and self-doubt can come from being excluded. Friendships are one means of traveling the normal path of social development.

Peers in Middle Childhood

Think of the world these children are now encountering. Physical and cognitive abilities enable them to move steadily, although slowly, toward others such as neighborhood friends. Upon entering school, they increase their contacts and begin to realize that other children have ideas that may differ from their own. How children react to these different opinions may reflect their own home conditions. Cassidy and her colleagues (1992) discovered that children whose parents are warm, responsive, and consistent disciplinarians have children who are more competent with peers than children whose parents are harsh and rejecting or overly permissive. Cognitive development also helps middle childhood youngsters to accept differences. For Piaget, one of the major obstacles to more mature thinking is egocentrism, that tendency to relate everything to "me." With its decline during middle childhood, children gradually see that other points of view exist. This in itself is an important developmental phenomenon, one that Robert Selman (1980) has carefully explored.

In his efforts to clarify emerging interpersonal relationships, Selman has developed a theory of **social perspective taking** that springs from a social cognitive developmental framework. Selman (1980) stated that you can't separate children's views on how to relate to others from their personal theories about the traits of others. Thus, children construct their own version of what it means to be a self or other.

As a result of careful investigations of children's interactions with others, and guided by such theorists as Piaget, Flavell, Mead, and Kohlberg, Selman has identified several levels of social perspective taking and noted that in the middle childhood years a youngster gradually realizes that other people are different and have ideas of their own. By the end of middle childhood, a youngster's views of a relationship include self, someone else, and the kind of relationship between them.

We have mentioned cognitive development, diminished egocentrism, and a striving for competence as factors in getting along with others. Youngsters of this age are also better able to communicate with one another and to use reinforcements from their peers to shape their own behavior (Boivin & Begin, 1989). Because of their cognitive, language, and perspective-taking skills, middle childhood youngsters cooperate better with one another than younger children can, and aggression decreases somewhat. The desire to conform becomes important, especially at the end of the period.

Given the increase in friends during the school years, we can question the role of schooling itself. How does it influence the development of middle childhood youngsters?

Social perspective taking
The idea that children's views on how to relate to others emerge from their personal theories about the traits of others.

How influential were peers at different times in your life? Give examples.

Guided Review

6. Children who are within 12 months of age of each other are called
   _____ .

7. Friends give children the chance to feel that they belong to a _____ .

8. Children who believed they had few friends were troubled by feelings of
   _____ .

9. Selman's theory is referred to as _____ _____
   _____ .

10. Children in middle childhood gradually come to see that other points of view exist due to diminishing _____ .

Answers

6. peers 7. group 8. loneliness 9. social perspective taking 10. egocentrism

School is an important milestone for all aspects of development. Children must learn to respond appropriately to authority outside of the family and to get along with peers. It is an important part of psychosocial as well as cognitive development.

Schools and Middle Childhood

Do schools affect development during these years? Given the physical, cognitive, and social changes that occur in children of these years, it is only reasonable to expect schools to play a decisive role. Let's first examine several of the academic issues that affect children in our schools.

Middle Childhood and Educational Change

As children pass through the elementary grades, they will encounter constant change as educators strive to devise methods that will meet the demands of twentieth-century America.

Reading and Writing

For example, a major change in the teaching of reading and writing can be seen in the *whole language* technique (see chapter 7). Rather than learning phonics isolated from meaning, students learn to read by obtaining the meaning of words from context, with phonics introduced as needed. If while reading a story a pupil has difficulty with the word *dish,* the teacher stops and sounds it out. Students don't use basal readers; they read appropriate-level literature about themes that interest them and then write about these ideas. Teachers who have begun to use this new technique believe that it motivates their pupils better than the older methods. Not everyone agrees with this approach, however.

Mathematics

International comparisons of students on *mathematics* achievement tests have repeatedly found Americans at or near the bottom. As a result, the country will soon experience another wave of publicity about a revision of the mathematics curriculum. You may have heard about the "new math" of the 1960s, followed a few years

Psychosocial Development in Middle Childhood **257**

later by the "back-to-basics" movement. One of the reasons that the new math was not an unqualified success was that public school teachers had little to say about it. It was simply imposed on them.

Today's emphasis is less on skills for their own sake and more on thinking about and understanding the meaning of numbers. For example, mathematician J. Paulos (1988) quoted a couple as saying they're not going to Europe because of all the terrorists. In 1985, 17 of the 28 million Americans who traveled abroad that year were killed by terrorists. That same year, 45,000 people were killed on American highways (thus, the couple had 1 chance in 5,300 of being killed in a car crash). Understanding the numbers involved helps you to evaluate which situation contains the greatest potential danger. The National Council of Teachers of Mathematics recommends that students use calculators at all times and urges teachers to emphasize problem-solving skills and the practical side of mathematics. The goal is to make mathematics seem less threatening and more useful.

Science

When we turn to *science,* estimates are that although most of us shake our heads at the "scientific illiteracy" of our youth, less than 10 percent of high school graduates still have the skills necessary to perform satisfactorily in college-level courses. Attempting to combat this trend, many science educators are today turning to a more "hands-on" approach to their teaching. Instead of having their students memorize lengthy formulas, they have them do experiments, starting in the early grades. For example, instead of reading about the principle of buoyancy, students make lumps of clay into various shapes, put them in plastic bags, and discover which shapes float and which sink.

You may argue that there's nothing new in this technique; good teachers have been doing it for years. There are differences, however. Where this approach has been successful, teachers have acted as facilitators, not directors. Teachers are not forced to teach a specific amount of material; in a sense, teaching less can result in teaching more. That is, by teaching generalizable problem-solving strategies along with the concepts of basic subject matter, and by emphasizing that learners should know themselves, teachers can prepare students for a lifetime of learning. Also, these school systems have been totally committed to scientific discovery from the elementary grades through high school.

Grade Retention

Do you think children should ever be retained in a grade? In your answer, consider both positive and negative aspects of retention.

Consider this possible future scenario. You are meeting with the teacher of one of your children, and you are told that your child should be retained in third grade. How would you react? Making pupils repeat a year's work has come under heavy attack recently, with opponents claiming that it usually doesn't work. After reviewing studies comparing the education of students who were retained with students of comparable achievement and maturity who were promoted, Holmes (1990) concluded that retained students were no better off than those who went on to the next grade. *Grade retention,* either because of immaturity or lack of achievement, is a common practice in our schools that raises many questions (Medway & Rose, 1986):

- Does grade retention produce academic achievement superior to that found in comparable students who are promoted?
- Do students who have been retained drop out of school more frequently than comparable students who were promoted?
- Does a policy of retention discriminate against particular groups of students?
- What evidence does a school use in its decision to retain?
- Does eliminating grade retention mean a return to a policy of social promotion?
- What are the legal ramifications of grade retention?

Although evidence is accumulating that retention has not been a uniformly successful policy, the issue today is widely debated.

Homework

Another change to discuss is *homework,* which is once again enjoying renewed acceptance. (Homework usually refers to school-assigned academic work that is to be completed outside of school, usually in the home.) At the turn of the twentieth century, homework was considered vital; its popularity declined in the 1940s. Homework reemerged in the 1950s (after Sputnik), fell into disfavor in the 1960s because it was seen as a form of useless pressure, and now, with reports of the poor achievement of American students, is once more viewed as essential. Research shows that for high school students two or more hours of homework increases achievement, junior high school students benefit from one to two hours of homework, and a slight relationship seems to exist between homework for elementary school pupils and improved achievement (Cooper, 1989). Homework at the elementary school level, however, brings home and school closer together and encourages pupils to realize that they can learn on their own. Homework should not be a burden for students and their parents but should be assigned to meet demonstrated needs.

Quality of Schools

Total Quality Management (TQM)

A concept to improve the quality of learning in our schools.

Finally, the issue of the quality of our schools cannot be ignored. In the light of mounting criticism, many educators have endorsed the idea of **Total Quality Management.** Sometimes referred to as **TQM,** this concept is usually linked to the work of W. Edwards Deming in Japan following World War ll. Deming helped Japanese business leaders move from turning out careless, shoddy products to a level of quality production that inspired worldwide envy. With the present concerted effort to improve our schools, more and more educators are turning to TQM.

Thus, with growing maturity, middle childhood youngsters face greater demands and higher expectations. From our brief discussion, you can see how the schools should contribute to the youngster's sense of competence, which Erikson identified as the psychosocial strength of these years. Competence is not confined to academics but extends into the physical and social worlds, helping middle childhood youngsters develop a needed self-confidence.

Schools and Social Development

Schools are different social contexts at preschool, elementary, and secondary levels. They are organized differently, children perceive them differently, and different aspects of social behavior appear to meet pupils' changing needs (Minuchin & Shapiro, 1983). Preschool experiences are more protective and caring than educational. The children interact with one or two teachers, perhaps an equal number of aides, and several peers. During the middle childhood years, the elementary school classroom becomes more of a true social unit, with more intense interactions between teacher and pupil and among peers (Travers, 1982). Teachers, as authority figures, establish the climate of the classroom and the kinds of relationships permitted. Peer group relationships stress friendship, belongingness, and status (Adalbjarnardottir & Selman, 1989).

Two different types of interactions can be identified, both of which shape the direction of a middle childhood youngster's growth. First is the relationship with the teacher: usually intense, goal-directed, and subject to evaluation. Second is the relationship with peers, which opens up a new world. When you examine these relationships objectively, the school's role in development for children of these years seems critical.

Think now of the many aspects of development that we have mentioned: the inborn temperamental disposition of children, the pattern of childrearing behavior

The first day of school is stressful for youngsters. For most children, however, this upset to their psychological equilibrium passes and they adapt quickly.

TQM: PANACEA OR ILLUSION?

Is Total Quality Management the solution for effective schools? As the search for answers to questions about the effectiveness of our schools continues, more and more educators are turning to new ideas: cooperative learning, authentic assessment, portfolio assessment, thinking skills and, more recently, Total Quality Management. Some educators are attracted to the concept because they see a conceptual framework that helps them to understand a complex system (Brandt, 1992). Psychologists are examining it carefully because of its implications for programs that address individual differences, intrinsic and extrinsic motivation, and methods of assessment.

■ **Issue:** TQM is another of the "fads" that intrigue educators.

Answer—Pro Following the principles of TQM means that teachers must change many traditional practices. For example, many teachers will find it difficult, if not impossible, to abandon their dependence on grades. Will administrators be willing to take the time and devote precious resources to the commitment that must be made? Although the plan may have potential, the many obstacles it faces make it unlikely that TQM will succeed.

Answer—Con Our schools cannot continue as they are now. TQM can provide many of the answers that we are presently searching for. TQM has succeeded in business and, with modifications, can improve the quality of learning in our schools, even though problems will occur and delays will happen. For example, a key element obviously is the teaching force. If our teachers can be persuaded of TQM's value through workshops, seminars, and modeling, then it has an excellent chance of bringing change to our schools.

■ **Issue:** TQM lends itself to a greater understanding of how motivation functions in a classroom.

Answer—Pro Total quality management would lead to a lessening of teachers' reliance on extrinsic motivation (stars, grades, etc.) and place much more emphasis on intrinsic motivation. Extrinsic motivation can be destructive because it fosters competition and hurts those who are excluded.

Answer—Con Reliance on intrinsic motivation quickly leads to a lack of attention, faulty classroom control, and poor learning. To assume that students will come to every class enthusiastic and eager to learn is simply not realistic. A carefully planned sequence of rewards that addresses specific behaviors can lead eventually to intrinsic motivation.

What's your view?

---

parents adopt, the relationships within the family. All of these determine how a child reacts to what happens in a classroom. For example, during the kindergarten and elementary school years, pupils are being socialized. They are learning to respond to teachers and get along with their peers while being taught the basic skills. Discipline is typically not a major concern, since youngsters of this age usually react well to authority and seek teacher praise and rewards. Adjustment to the school as a major socializing agent and mastery of the fundamentals are the two chief tasks of these years.

Pupils in the middle elementary school grades know a school's routine and have worked out their relationships with their peers. They must concentrate on curricular tasks in a clearly defined classroom atmosphere (Minuchin & Shapiro, 1983). During the upper elementary years, however, peer pressure mounts and most youngsters are concerned with pleasing friends. Teachers are authority figures and more challenging to students; thus classroom control becomes more of an issue. Another issue that schools face is the increasing role that television plays in children's lives.

A MULTICULTURAL VIEW

Poverty, Culture, and Education

In his biting commentary on current conditions in America's schools, Kozol (1991) drew some vivid comparisons. In schools populated with children of the poor, students are crowded into small, squalid spaces, and in some cities overcrowding is so bad that some schools function in abandoned factories. Students eat their lunches in what was previously the building's boiler room. Reading classes are taught in what used to be a bathroom; science classes have no microscopes; one counselor serves 3,600 students in the elementary grades. In the high school of this district, a single physics section exists for 2,200 students; two classes are being taught simultaneously in one classroom.

As an example of these kinds of schools, listen to Kozol's words.

> The city was so poor there had been no garbage pickup for four years. . . . On the edge of the city is a large chemical plant. There is also a very large toxic waste incinerator, as well as a huge sewage treatment plant. . . . The city has one of the highest rates of infant mortality in Illinois, the highest rate of fetal death, and also a very high rate of childhood asthma.
>
> The schools, not surprisingly, are impoverished. . . . The entire school system had been shut down after being flooded with sewage from the city's antique sewage system. "I did meet several wonderful teachers in the school, and I thought the principal of the school was excellent. The superintendent is also a very impressive person" (Kozol, 1991, p. 5).

A more affluent district in the same state presents a different picture. A greenhouse is available for students interested in horticulture; the physical sciences department offers 14 courses; there are 18 biology electives. The school's orchestra has traveled to the former Soviet Union. Beautifully carpeted hallways encourage students to sit and study; computers are everywhere. The ratio of counselors to students is 1 to 150. Parents of these students recently raised money to send the school choral group to Vienna. Given these different conditions, is it any wonder that different educational outcomes are inevitable?

If, as frequently described, the school is a middle-class institution staffed mainly by white middle-class teachers, then students from different social classes immediately begin their schooling at a disadvantage (Hetherington & Parke, 1993). From everything we have said, you can understand that middle-class teachers can be expected to have different values and expectations than their economically deprived students.

These conditions can either be improved or made worse by the family's belief in education. As Garbarino and Benn noted (1992), parents may not be present in the classroom but they have a profound influence on the ways their children view school and learning. The extent to which the family supports the school's objectives directly affects their child's academic performance. Too often low parental expectations for their children reflect the parents' own educational experiences. If parents had encountered difficulties in school, they may exercise a negative impact on their children's attitudes, expectations, and performance. The reverse also holds true.

These conclusions are particularly significant for immigrant students. Their backgrounds, frequently composed of crushing poverty, can be almost impossible for American teachers to understand. The economic hardships these immigrants previously lived with may continue here and they undoubtedly face a bleak economic future in the United States, especially when we realize minorities reach the poverty level at an ever-increasing rate. These facts point to an inescapable conclusion: Our schools must be as good as possible because they frequently are the only escape routes from poverty, crime, and violence.

Guided Review

11. Some of the major changes occurring in our schools include: teaching reading by the _____ _____ method and an emphasis on _____ .

12. A controversial policy of our schools is _____ _____ .

13. Parents often, and sharply, disagree about the role of _____ in their children's education.

14. _____ _____ _____ is a concept, formulated for the business world, intended to improve the quality of our schools.

15. Although schools are best known for their efforts to improve the cognitive development of their students, they also contribute significantly to the _____ _____ of children.

Answers

11. whole language, mathematics   12. grade retention   13. homework   14. Total Quality Management   15. social development

Television has become one of the great means of socialization in a child's life. As such, and recognizing the relationship between program content and a child's age, adults should be particularly careful in what children watch.

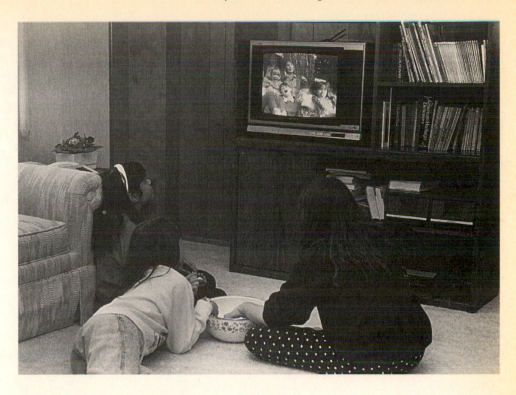

Television and Development

Do you have a television set in your home? Did you laugh at what appears to be a ridiculous question? You probably have at least one, more likely two or three. When you consider that American homes have at least one set and realize the colorful appeal of TV, you can better understand why television has become the school's great competition (Pinon & others, 1989).

 **AN APPLIED VIEW**   *The Extent of Television Watching*

For an idea of the role that television plays in our society, try to answer these questions, which have been drawn from several national surveys:

1. What percentage of American homes have a TV set?
2. How long (on the average) is the set on per day?
3. By age 85 how many years of television has the average viewer seen?
4. How many hours of TV does the average viewer watch per week?
5. By age 18 a student has watched how many hours of TV?
6. By age 15 how many killings has a child seen on television?
7. Can television influence a child's behavior?

If you had any doubts about the extent of television viewing, these figures should dispel them.

1. 99%   2. 6 hours   3. 9 years   4. 28 hours   5. 15,000 hours   6. 13,000 killings   7. yes

In the Surgeon General's report on television viewing, *Television and Behavior: Ten Years of Scientific Progress and Implications for the Eighties* (U.S. Department of Health and Human Services, 1982), one of the questions asked was, Who watches television? The answer was simple: almost everyone. Elementary school children watch at least four hours each day. Today television viewing may be the most frequently shared activity among family members (St. Peters & others, 1991).

The beginning of school attendance slows the time spent watching, but at about age 8 the rate increases dramatically. What is particularly interesting is the match between children's ages and program content. For example, Comstock and Paik (1991) reported that the popularity of *Sesame Street* declined between the ages of 3 to 5 from 30 percent to 13 percent. *The Flintstones* rose in popularity in these same years, from 11 percent to 36 percent. Are there developmental effects from all this viewing?

The 1982 Surgeon General's report reflects the pattern of development discussed thus far. Babies are briefly attracted by the color and sound; 2- and 3-year-olds watch longer and with some understanding; elementary school children watch for long periods; and teenagers spend less time watching television. These viewing habits are fairly well established. Specifically, the report presented several findings related to development.

Television and Cognitive Development

The moment we concede that children learn from watching television, certain questions arise:

- How active are children in the process?

- To what do they attend?

- How much do they understand?

- How much do they remember?

Answering these questions gives us insight into how TV watching and cognitive development are associated. For example, when you studied Piaget's work, especially his views on operations, you saw how Piaget insisted that children were active participants in their cognitive development. They actively construct their cognitive world.

The same is true of their TV watching. They bring a unique set of cognitive structures to the TV set, structures that reflect their level of cognitive development. Remember what we said about middle childhood youngsters: Attention span lengthens, memory improves, and comprehension increases. Children don't drop these abilities when they watch TV; they apply them to what they are seeing (Liebert & others, 1988). Specifically, we know that

- *Children remember what is said,* even when they are not looking at the screen. Auditory attention is also at work (voices, sound changes, laughing, and applause).

- *The amount of time spent looking at the set is directly related to age.* By age 4 children attend to TV about 55 percent of the time, even when there are many other distractions in the room.

- *Specific features of programs attract children:* women, movement, and camera angles; they look away during stills and animal shots.

- *Children quickly learn to relate sound to sight:* Chase music means a chase scene. (Note the ideal combination of auditory and visual effects that produces powerful attractions.)

- *Comprehension depends on age and experience* (Comstock & Paik, 1991). To understand television, children need three accomplishments. First, they must know something about story form—how stories are constructed and understood. Second, they must have world knowledge or general knowledge about situations and events in order to grasp television's content. Finally, they must have knowledge of television's forms and conventions to help them understand what is happening on the screen. Music, visual techniques, and camera angles all convey information (Liebert & others, 1988).

Consideration of these three requirements helps to put children's viewing in perspective: They simply lack the maturity and experience to grasp fully much of what they are watching. For example, children have the perceptual skills to see and recognize a car moving away. But then the camera may cut to another scene (the sky, a police officer, or the corner of a house). The significance of the cut introduces another theme, embedded in the story, that completely eludes youngsters.

When you were in elementary and high school, how much television did you watch? How much do you watch now? Do you think that television viewing has hindered your achievement in school?

We can conclude, then, that much of what children see on television is not just content. They also learn TV's codes: sound effects, camera techniques, and program organization. Some researchers believe that changes in children's behavior following the viewing of televised violence come from their responding to fast action, loud music, and camera tricks. Children understand television programs according to their level of development, and their level of development is affected by their television viewing.

Television and Violence

If we were to summarize the Surgeon General's report (U.S. DHHS, 1982), we would say:

■ BE CAREFUL OF WHAT CHILDREN WATCH; TELEVISION MAY BE HARMFUL TO THEIR HEALTH.

The key word here is *may*. Although research and theory point to television's role in aggressive behavior, almost total agreement exists that television is *a* cause, not *the* cause of aggressive behavior (Comstock & Paik, 1991). Nevertheless, after decades of research, we can safely conclude that televised violence causes aggressive behavior in the children who observe it (Parke & Slaby, 1983). Are children exposed to much television violence?

Remember that almost every American home has at least one television set, which children watch for many hours each day. Recall also that much of television's programming contains violence as a common feature. Consequently, we cannot ignore the possible negative effects, particularly when you realize the power of observational learning. Most children watch television with few, if any, parental restrictions. (Our concern here is with middle childhood youngsters who tend to watch adult shows.) Thus, it's difficult to disagree with Parke and Slaby (1983) when they concluded that televised violence increases children's level of aggression and televised violence increases children's passive acceptance of the use of aggression by others.

Can the American public force television producers to decrease the level of violence in their programming, a level that slowly but steadily seems to be increasing? For many reasons, ranging from the appeal of violence to issues of free speech, this is a difficult question to answer. But all responsible adults can take one step with far-reaching consequences: Be alert to what children are watching, because television affects development.

WHAT'S

YOUR VIEW?

TELEVISION'S IMPACT: BY UNDERSTANDING OR MODELING?

We have repeatedly noted how different theorists (especially the major theorists discussed in chapter 2) can interpret the same data differently. Television violence is a good example. Two theories have been widely used in attempts to understand television's impact on children: cognitive and behaviorist.

Cognitive theorists, reflecting Piaget's views, believe that children understand what they see according to their level of cognitive development. The cognitive structures that children form can be altered by what they see on television. Children attend to what they see; they learn from what they see; and they remember what they see. They can also apply these new ideas in new settings. Since we have discussed cognitive theory in detail, let's turn to the behaviorists.

Behaviorists, especially in the social learning theory of Bandura (1986), offer a different interpretation. Bandura believed that considerable evidence exists to show that learning can occur by observing others, even when the observer doesn't reproduce the model's responses. Referring to this as **observational learning,** Bandura stated that the information we obtain from observing other things, events, and people influences the way we act.

On what does Bandura base his conclusions? With his colleagues (Bandura & others, 1963), Bandura conducted a now-famous experiment (discussed earlier in chapter 2). Preschool children observed a model displaying aggression toward an inflated doll under three conditions: In one situation the children saw a film of a human model being aggressive toward the doll. In the next, children witnessed filmed cartoon aggression. Finally, live models exhibited the identical aggressive behavior. The results: Later, all children exhibited more aggression than youngsters in a control group!

Which theory do you think offers the best explanation? What's your view?

Observational learning
A term associated with Bandura, meaning that we learn from watching others.

Prosocial behavior
Refers to such behaviors as friendliness, self-control, and being helpful.

Television and Prosocial Behavior

The Surgeon General's report also refers to television's potential for encouraging **prosocial behavior** in children. Prosocial behavior includes such things as helping, sharing, and comforting behaviors (Eisenberg, 1992).

Testing this potential, Sprafkin, Liebert, and Poulos (1975) selected two episodes from the *Lassie* series. One of these episodes had the lead child character risk his life to save a puppy. The other episode had no such dramatic incident. An episode from the *Brady Bunch* show was also used. The researchers created a situation in which children would have to make a choice between alerting adults that an animal needed help or continuing to work on a task that could win them a prize. If they pushed a help button, they lost time on their task (a game). They had to make a choice, then, between sacrifice or self-interest.

The children who had seen the prosocial *Lassie* episode were more willing to help than those who watched either of the other two programs. They pressed the help button for 93 seconds compared with 52 and 38 seconds for those who had watched the other programs.

> ▄ Clearly, television can be a negative influence on children; but can it also be a positive influence? If children model and learn from violent television shows and movies, they would be expected to learn positive behaviors and values from shows depicting helpfulness, generosity, cooperation, self-sacrifice, and the like. Recent studies suggest that the media can be used to foster development, although the effects of viewing prosocial television programming appear to be somewhat weaker than the effects of viewing violent programming. (Eisenberg, 1992)

A new brother or sister, budding friendships, school challenges, televised violence, inevitable upset at home—put them all together and they spell stress.

WHAT'S YOUR VIEW?

PROSOCIAL TELEVISION: FOR BETTER OR WORSE?

Should television be used as a prosocial agent? Your initial response to this question is probably a firm yes. Would everyone agree with you? We're not so sure.

In 1975 the United Methodist Church provided money for producing 30-second television spots intended to help children become more cooperative. Psychologists and experienced television personnel combined to make as professional a presentation as possible. The format was identical to that of regular commercials.

Children, ages 4 to 10, watched television while sitting on a comfortable sofa in a relaxed, denlike setting with natural distractions such as toys and books. They were later tested for comprehension of the program and were observed playing.

In the best-known spot, "The Swing," a boy and a girl about 10 years old both run to a swing. They argue and struggle over it, each claiming the first ride. They scowl and look menacingly at each other. Suddenly one of them steps back and suggests that the other go first. They are then shown taking turns, happily swinging through the air. The announcer's voice concludes that "this is how you (children) should behave" (Liebert & others, 1988).

Tens of millions of children all over the world saw "The Swing." After seeing the film, children's cooperation increased and all seemed well. Then a reaction set in amid charges of psychological behavior control. Who has a right to impose values on children? Should all children be taught cooperation? Don't some youngsters need to be aggressive to survive? Isn't this brainwashing children? Are we infringing on that fundamental right we all cherish in our society—the right to freedom?

Would you still answer the first question in the same way? What's your view?

Guided Review

16. Television can alter a child's cognitive _____ .
17. Bandura's belief that learning can occur by watching others is called _____ _____ .
18. Watching television requires certain cognitive abilities, such as understanding a _____ _____ .
19. Television can also increase a child's _____ behavior.

Stress in Childhood

As youngsters of this age spend more of their time away from home, new contacts and new tasks can upset them. There is no escape; we all have faced similar circumstances. Were we scarred for life by these encounters? Probably not. Yet for some children, an inability to cope with stress has serious consequences, and today we are more alert to the signs of childhood stress. In her excellent and practical analysis of childhood stress, Brenner (1984) described a spectrum of stressors:

Ordinary	Moderate	Severe
Jealousy of sibling	One-parent home	Separation from parent
Typical school anxiety	Multiple parents (biological mother, stepmother, biological father, stepfather)	(divorce, death, illness)
		Abuse
		Parental alcoholism

But first, let's link what is known about childhood stress to development. We begin by admitting that no definition of stress exists that everyone agrees with. Let's use this definition: **Stress** is anything that upsets our equilibrium—both psychological and physiological.

Stress
Anything that upsets our equilibrium—both psychological and physiological.

Abused Children

Most people consider the United States to be a nation of child lovers. Therefore, discussing child abuse always comes as a shock. Before we begin to discuss this topic, we should agree on what is meant by the term. Six major types of abuse are commonly identified: physical abuse, sexual abuse, emotional abuse, physical neglect, emotional neglect, and educational neglect.

Child abuse has always been with us, but it has only been a matter of public awareness for the past quarter-century. Abuse still remains an elusive subject that defies precise definition because of its many forms. Physical and sexual abuses that leave evidence are easy to detect and describe (if they are reported), but other forms of abuse that emotionally wound youngsters are perhaps never detected. Professionals believe that abusive behavior involves direct harm (physical, sexual, deliberate malnutrition), intent to harm (which is difficult if not impossible to detect), and intent to harm even if injury does not result.

Another troublesome issue is that of incidence. Figures show tremendous variability. The actual data are only for reported cases and undoubtedly represent only the tip of the iceberg. The true extent of the problem may be staggering. For example:

- In 1990 more than 2.5 million cases of child abuse were reported, an increase of 100 percent since 1980.

- Estimates of national child abuse and neglect range from 35 percent to 53 percent of the child population.

- A 1990 state survey of child abuse indicated that 27 percent of reported abuse cases were due to physical abuse, 45 percent to neglect, 15 percent to sexual abuse, and 13 percent to emotional abuse.

- In 1990 an estimated 1,211 children from 39 states died from abuse or neglect. Ninety percent of these children were under age 5, and 50 percent were infants under age 1 (Hearings on the Child Abuse Prevention, Adoption, and Family Services Act, 1992).

The Nature of the Problem

Although child abuse is an age-old problem, not until recently did it become widely publicized. In the 1920s Dr. John Caffey, studying bone fractures and other physical injuries, suggested that parents might have caused the injuries. The skepticism that greeted his conclusions prevented him from officially reporting his findings until the late 1940s. In 1961 C. Henry Kempe and his associates startled the annual meeting of the American Academy of Pediatrics by their dramatic description of the battered child syndrome.

You may well ask, What kind of person could ever hurt a child? Although the parental characteristics leading to child abuse are not rigidly defined, several appear with surprising frequency. Here are some of the most frequently found characteristics:

- The parents themselves were abused as children.

- They are often loners.

- They refuse to recognize the seriousness of the child's condition.

- They resist diagnostic studies.

- They believe in harsh punishment.

- They have unreasonable expectations for the child. (Children should never cry or drop things.)

- They lack control and are often immature and dependent.

- They feel personally incompetent.

A cycle of abuse becomes clear. The most consistent feature of the histories of abusive families is the repetition, from one generation to the next, of a pattern of abuse, neglect, and parental loss or deprivation. In each generation we find, in one form or another, a distortion of the relationship between parents and children that deprives children of the consistent love and care that would enable them to develop fully. Parents perceive the child as disappointing or unlovable, especially in times of stress and crisis. Finally, for most children, no lifeline exists; that is, no helpful sources can be accessed in times of crisis.

But what of the children themselves? Some observers believe that certain types of children are more prone to be abused than others. Remember: Children shape their parents as much as parents shape their children. If a child's actions or appearance irritate a parent predisposed to violence, then the results of the parent-child interaction may be preordained (which does not mean that the child is at fault).

Children growing up in a hostile environment feel that to survive they must totally submit to their parents' wishes. They often exhibit continual staring and a passive acceptance of whatever happens. Only later, in a permissive setting, does the pent-up fury explode. Abused children slowly develop complete distrust of others, which often translates into school problems.

When you consider the factors that may trigger abuse—parents, children themselves, poor family relations, socioeconomic conditions, lack of support—understanding the problem clearly requires considerable and careful research.

The Special Case of Sexual Abuse

Sexual abuse

Any sexual activity between a child and adult, whether by force or consent.

Sexual abuse refers to any sexual activity between a child and an adult whether by consent or force. It includes fondling, penetration, oral-genital contact, intercourse, and the use of children in pornography (Kelley, 1986). Estimates are that between 50,000 and 500,000 children are sexually abused each year. Most of the victims are female, but the number of male victims is on the rise.

Abused children feel that they have lost control and are helpless when an adult sexually abuses them. All of their lives children have been taught to obey adults, so they feel forced to comply. This is particularly sensitive because most abusers are known to the family: a relative, friend, or some authority known to the children.

What are the developmental effects of an adult's violation and betrayal of a child? Browne and Finkelhor (1986), summarizing several major studies, report the results of both short-term and long-term effects of sexual abuse. Different ages seem to suffer different types of effects. For example, the highest rate of problems was found in the 7- to 13-year-old group. Forty percent of the abused children of this age group showed serious disturbances; 17 percent of the 4- to 6-year-old group manifested some disturbance. About 50 percent of the 7- to 13-year-old group showed greatly elevated levels of anger and hostility compared with 15 percent of the 4- to 6-year-olds. Increase of anxiety, fear, and distress were common to all age groups.

Do adults who were sexually abused as children suffer long-term consequences? Among the possible effects are the following: depression (probably the most common finding), above-normal levels of tension, a negative self-concept, and sexual problems.

Sexual abuse is a problem that every reader will find repugnant. Yet we can offer some positive conclusions. We are now better able to identify these children and provide help. Treatment techniques offer hope for the future. As the problem becomes more widely publicized, parents, teachers, and concerned adults are becoming more sensitive to the possibility of the occurrence of sexual abuse.

Types of Stress

Do you think there are times that the courts should remove chidren from their parents? Given the seriousness of this issue, give detailed and specific reasons for your answer.

Different kinds of stress can cause similar reactions. Think of a time when your parents were really angry with you, or when you were faced with a severe challenge (perhaps speaking before a large group for the first time; or just after you had been

Table 10.1	Specific Childhood Stressors
Type	**Example**
Two-parent families	Changes associated with normal growth: new siblings, sibling disputes, moving, school, working parents
One-parent families	Multiple adults, lack of sex-role model, mother vs. father, financial difficulties
Multiparent families	New relationships, living in two households
Death, adoption	Parental death, sibling death, possible institutional placement, relationships with different adults
Temporary separation	Hospitalization, health care, military service
Divorce	Troubled days before the divorce, separation, the divorce itself
Abuse	Parental, sibling, institutional; sexual, physical, emotional
Neglect	Physical (food, clothes), emotional (no response to children's needs for attention and affection)
Alcoholism	Secrecy, responsibility for alcoholic parent, suppress own feelings

given some bad news). Some children react in the same way to all of these events, either with high anxiety, fear, avoidance, weakness, or vomiting. The types of stress that cause these reactions include: internal sources (usually illness); external sources, such as family, school, or peers; or chronic sources, such as the child who is trapped for years with an alcoholic or abusive parent or with an insensitive teacher. Table 10.1, based on Brenner (1984), summarizes specific childhood stressors.

When each of us is faced with stress, we react differently. To begin with, not all of us would agree on what stress is. For example, some people are probably terrified of flying, whereas others see it as a pleasant, relaxing adventure. Although many reasons account for these different responses, we can isolate several important individual differences.

Sex

As we have repeatedly seen, boys are more vulnerable than girls. This includes their reaction to stress. Select any event that is likely to induce stress, and boys are more susceptible: death, divorce, new sibling, or hospital admission.

Age

Children of different ages respond differently to stress. Good evidence suggests that infants are relatively immune to the stress of hospital admission; the age of greatest risk is from age 6 months to 4 years. Children above the age of 4 can rationalize that hospitalization, for example, does not mean parental abandonment. Middle childhood youngsters are less vulnerable to the stress a new sibling causes, whereas younger children show a great deal of clinging.

The grief reactions of young children are shorter and milder than those of older youngsters. Cognitive level probably explains the difference; younger children can't understand the concept of death itself (Rutter, 1988). Long-term effects may be greater if family breakup causes change in socioeconomic status, and if moving is involved.

Temperament

Recall that we are all born with unique temperaments, differences that affect the way we interact with the environment. Consequently, children's temperament influences the intensity of their reactions after a stressful event, for example, parental separation.

These are but a few of the many factors that help to explain different reactions to stress. But what can we say about their developmental effects?

Developmental Effects of Stress

If we attempt to link development and vulnerability to stress, we reach certain conclusions. For example, Maccoby (1988) notes that we cannot be upset by events whose power to harm us we do not understand. We cannot be humiliated by failure to handle problems whose solutions are someone else's responsibility. Maccoby compares why some events are stressful and others are not and formulates several hypotheses. First, *age changes alone don't explain vulnerability.* Although the events that cause stress change with age, we all experience periods of stabilization and destabilization. In other words, we may be more vulnerable to change at certain times (e.g., we may react emotionally to bad news if we have been quite sick).

Second, *the environment can lessen vulnerability.* Youngsters can handle stress better if all other parts of their lives are stable. For example, entering school is stressful for almost all children. Home conditions that are warm and supportive help to ease what can be a difficult transition. But if parents have separated during these days, children can find school entrance quite painful.

Next, *although middle childhood youngsters face more stressful situations than younger children, they have learned better ways to cope.* In addition, as they move away from sole dependence on parents as attachment figures, peers begin to form a strong supportive network, especially toward the end of middle childhood. Also, *recognizing adults as authority figures* gives children a sense of security, which acts as a buffer against stress.

Finally, *with their growing cognitive ability,* children of this age begin to develop coping skills that help them to combat stress. Think of our discussion of this growing cognitive capacity: the ability to think abstractly, solve problems, reach decisions, and to plan ahead. All of these abilities help to combat stress.

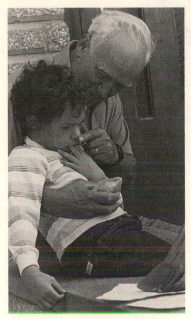

Children need emotional support from those in their environment. Even under the most difficult circumstances (divorce, death of a parent, hospitalization), the presence of a "significant other" can help a child to cope, to deal with stress in an appropriate manner for the child's developmental level.

Children and Violence

On June 3, 1986, the state of Florida charged 9-year-old Jeffrey Bailey with murder. Making sure that no one else was around, he had pushed a 3-year-old boy who couldn't swim into a pool. He pulled up a chair to watch the boy drown. Later, when the police had pieced together the circumstances of the murder, they arrested Jeffrey, who was described as calm, nonchalant, and enjoying the attention (Magid & McKelvey, 1987).

This startling story is true, and others like it are appearing with increasing frequency in our nation's newspapers. Murder is the most dramatic example of a life gone wrong, but the increasing rate of assaults, robberies, and arson raises a basic question: What has happened to these children to turn them into killers, thieves, and arsonists?

Theories of Early Criminal Behavior

In their massive study of crime and human nature, Wilson and Herrnstein (1985) note that the majority of all young males have broken the law at an early age. Unfortunately, there is clear evidence of the positive association between past and future criminal behavior, which gives rise to this maxim: The best predictor of crime is past criminal behavior. Today's criminologists believe that a tendency to commit crime is established early in life, perhaps as soon as the preschool years (Nagin & Farrington, 1992).

The Causes of Crime

Although ample evidence exists concerning the early appearance of crime, the evidence is merely descriptive, telling us little about the roots of violence. Most theorists have identified a cluster of possible causes that should come as no surprise: constitutional (more males than females commit crimes and more younger males than older males), developmental (broken families), and community (gangs, drugs). No one element can be considered the cause, so it is best to think of the causes of

The majority of young males who have broken the law have done so at an early age.

crime as complex, multiple, and interactive. One conclusion, however, is possible: No matter the circumstances, an individual, when faced with a choice, will choose the preferred course of action (Wilson & Herrnstein, 1985).

Attempts to identify the causes of crime always begin with the individual child. If two boys are from the same family, with the same opportunities, why does one turn to a life of crime while the other leads a law-abiding life? Was there some subtle genetic transmission? Were the family relations similar for both boys? Were their friends radically different? Examining each case helps us to identify the causes of crime for *that* child. Family conditions may be the cause for one child but not another; that is, one child may experience the environment quite differently than another.

With these ideas in mind, we may well ask whether youthful criminals are different from nondelinquents. What are some characteristics of children who become delinquent? Among the major characteristics found by Wilson and Herrnstein (1985) are the following:

- Constitutional factors seem to be at work; for example, both members of identical twin pairs are more likely to be involved in delinquency than nonidentical twins.

- Males are more prone to criminal behavior than females, and younger males are more likely to commit crimes at a higher rate than older males; age is a major factor in understanding criminal behavior (Regoli & Hewitt, 1991).

- Attitudinally, delinquents are hostile, defiant, resentful, suspicious, and resistant to authority.

- Psychologically, delinquents are more interested in the concrete than the abstract and are generally poor problem solvers.

- Socioculturally, delinquents are frequently reared in homes that offer little understanding, affection, stability, or moral clarity. For example, some parents frequently reinforce aggressive behavior in an effort to defuse an explosive situation. The mother may tell a child to do something; the child refuses and becomes aggressive toward the mother. The mother may then "back off" and the child's aggressive behavior has been positively reinforced (Morton, 1987).

We can interpret these conclusions to mean that although any one of these elements can cause an individual's delinquency, usually a high probability of delinquency depends on the interplay of all of them. For example, in the stimulating but culturally inconsistent milieu of underprivileged areas, those with delinquent tendencies express their impulses and desires with little thought of self-control, which can become a type of psychopathology (Crowell, 1987).

Some theorists today are probing into the infancy years, searching for the roots of violence. For example, Magid and McKelvey (1987) stated that those who do not form bonds with anyone (see the attachment sections in chapter 6) constitute one of the largest deviant populations in the country. These are the children who cannot form relationships; they describe their reactions to others as making "no connections." The words of convicted serial killer Ted Bundy are revealing:

> ■ **I didn't know what makes things tick. I didn't know what made people want to be friends. I didn't know what made people attractive to one another. I didn't know what underlay social interactions. (Magid & McKelvey, 1987)**

As children become more and more involved in crime and violence, identifying the causes of such behavior and formulating the means to prevent it become more urgent. The task is difficult, expensive, and lengthy but well worth it to prevent violence from becoming an accepted part of children's lives.

A warning is necessary here, however. Note that Magid and McKelvey referred to children *who did not form a bond with anyone,* which is not the same as saying that a child has an insecure relationship with parents. In an excellent and timely caution, Fagot and Kavanagh (1990) urge us not to predict adolescent and adult problems with children who have an insecure relationship with parents. Studying 89 children who were clearly classified as insecure/avoidant or securely attached, the authors found that the parents of both groups reported the same number of problems (defiant, aggressive). Nor do the children in both groups show any differences in problem behaviors at home or in play. The authors conclude that although continuities may exist between attachment and later interactional styles, the data do not warrant predictions or any type of intervention.

There are no guarantees of successful coping, for obvious reasons: the intensity of the stress, the immaturity of the children, and the amount of support they receive. Yet we also know that a small number of children seem oblivious to stress, at least for a time.

AN APPLIED VIEW

A Life of Crime

How does a child become entrapped in a life of crime? In an insider's account of organized crime in the United States, Peter Maas has written a book called *The Valachi Papers.* In a fascinating tale of violence and crime, Valachi (a member of organized crime) portrays how he was drawn into the criminal network.

He recalls that his "was the poorest family on earth—three rooms, no hot water, only a toilet out in the hall." This was for a family of eight. Valachi was constantly truant from school, and when he was 11, he hit the teacher in the eye with a rock. He was then sent to a disciplinary school, returned to the public schools, and then left school for work after completing only the sixth grade.

Then he started to steal, because his father took his money. By the time he was 18, Valachi's petty thefts had earned him membership in a burglary gang. At 19 he was arrested and sent to the notorious Sing Sing prison. Released, rearrested, and returned to Sing Sing, Valachi made his first contact with members of the crime syndicate.

The road Valachi traveled is clear—poor, needing money, truant, petty theft, making the contacts that lead to organized crime, acceptance into the syndicate, and, finally, murder. Most cases are not so clear and dramatic, but the pattern is similar for those for whom the environment is the chief cause.

Resilient Children

The mother of three children was beset by mental problems. She refused to eat at home because she was sure someone was poisoning her. Her 12-year-old daughter developed the same fear. Her 10-year-old daughter would eat at home only if the father ate with her. Her 7-year-old son thought they were all crazy and always ate at home. The son went on to perform brilliantly in school and later in college and has now taken the first steps in what looks like a successful career. The older daughter is now diagnosed schizophrenic, whereas the younger girl seems to have adjusted after a troubled youth. Why? How?

Answering these questions takes us into uncharted territory. We simply don't know why some children seem so resilient. But what is known points to the ability to recover from either physiological or psychological trauma and return to a normal developmental path.

Identifying Resilient Children

Resilient children

Children who sustain some type of physiological or psychological trauma yet remain on a normal developmental path.

Who are these **resilient children** who grow up in the most chaotic and adverse conditions, yet manage to thrive? They seem to possess some inner quality that protects them from their environment and enables them to reach out to an adult who can offer critical support (Garmezy, 1987). The ratio seems to be about 1 in 10; that is, for every 10 children who succumb to adverse conditions, one, who has the necessary emotional support, develops normally (Garmezy, 1987).

These children seem to possess winning personalities. (Remember the discussion of inborn temperamental differences in chapter 6.) They also seem to have a special interest or talent. For example, some of these youngsters were excellent swimmers, dancers, and artists; others had a special knack for working with animals; some showed talent with numbers quite early. Whatever their interest, it served to absorb them and helped to shelter them from their environment. Such characteristics—a genuinely warm, fairly easygoing personality, an absorbing interest, and the ability to seek out a sympathetic adult—helped these children to distance themselves emotionally from a drugged, alcoholic, or abusive parent (sometimes a parent with all of these problems). Recent studies have shown that children who are emotionally close to a disturbed parent frequently develop problems.

Michael Rutter (1987b), a leading researcher in the study of invulnerable children, has attempted to sort out some of the characteristics that help to explain either invulnerability or vulnerability:

- *Sex.* As with any other problem we discuss, boys are more vulnerable than girls. Whether or not psychological vulnerability is innate is difficult to determine. Boys tend to be exposed to psychological stress more than girls and typically display disruptive behavior.

- *Temperament.* Children with negative personality features are more frequently the target of a disturbed parent. Parents with a problem do not take it out equally on all children.

- *Parent-child relationship.* Although not much is known about this characteristic, a good relationship with one parent acts as a buffer for the child.

- *Positive school experience.* The experience could be either academic or nonacademic. The pleasure associated with success seems to help raise a youngster's sense of self-esteem.

- *Early parental loss.* The results of losing a parent, especially a mother, do not become evident until later in life. Even then its effects are not apparent unless combined with another threatening event.

Table 10.2	Children's Patterns of Coping	
Avoiding Stress		**Facing Stress**
Denial: Children act as though the stress does not exist; may use fantasy (imaginary friends to talk to).		*Altruism:* By helping others, children ease their own pain.
Regression: Children act younger than their years, show greater dependency.		*Humor:* Children joke about their problems.
Withdrawal: Children remove themselves, either physically or mentally; they may run away, or attempt to fade into the background.		*Suppression:* Children push their troubles from their minds; they may play unconcernedly for a while.
Impulsive acting out: Children speak and act impulsively to avoid thinking about reality; by making others angry they attract attention, thus temporarily easing pain.		*Anticipation:* These children plan how to meet stress; they tend to protect themselves and accept what can't be avoided.

Table 10.3	Characteristics of Resilient Children
Age	**Characteristics**
At birth	Alert, attentive
1 year	Securely attached infant
2 years	Independent, slow to anger, tolerates frustration well
3–4 years	Cheerful, enthusiastic, works well with others
Childhood	Seems to be able to remove self from trouble, recovers rapidly from disturbance, confident, seems to have a good relationship with at least one adult
Adolescence	Assumes responsibilities, does well in school, may have part-time job, socially popular, is not impulsive

Vulnerable children need to be taught the methods of stress reduction and opportunities to gain success and pleasure in other activities. They need emotional support and help to acquire a greater sense of self-esteem by offering a secure relationship and an opportunity for successful achievements.

How Children Cope

Before we begin to discuss coping in childhood, we should remember that for most children psychosocial stress is the villain. That is, a child's hospital admission or a mother's temporary absence is really not the issue here. In most cases of psychosocial stress, the tension is persistent and unrelenting. The child with an alcoholic father or abusive mother has little chance of escaping. Table 10.2 illustrates children's ways of coping with stress.

Yet some children seem remarkably resistant to stress, which is not to imply that these are superchildren who can resist all stress.

> ■ There is no single set of qualities or circumstances that characterizes all such resilient children. But psychologists are finding that they stand apart from their more vulnerable siblings almost from birth. They seem to be endowed with innate characteristics that insulate them from the turmoil and pain of their families and allow them to reach out to some adult—a grandparent, teacher, or family friend—who can lend crucial emotional support. (Goleman, 1987, p. 82)

Continuing deprivation or problems will eventually scar resilient children, but these children are better able to function in settings that disable other children. The characteristics of these children are summarized in table 10.3 (based on work by Farber & Egeland, 1987).

We can best summarize all that we know about coping skills and child development in this list of guidelines for adults:

- To encourage coping skills in children, demonstrate these skills yourself, especially self-control.

- Encourage children to develop self-esteem.

- Be sympathetic to children's feelings and learn to recognize when a child is under stress.

- Urge children to adopt a positive attitude, which then helps them to search for solutions.

- Talk to children; get them to examine their problems openly so that they can obtain any available support.

🌳 Guided Review 🌳

20. Anything that upsets our equilibrium, both psychological and physiological is known as _____ .

21. The highest rate of problems resulting from sexual abuse was found in children aged _____ to _____ .

22. _____ , _____ , and _____ are examples of external sources of stress.

23. Gender must be considered in responding to stress. _____ are more vulnerable to stress than _____ .

24. Children who succeed under adverse conditions are called _____ children.

Answers

20. stress   21. 7, 13   22. Family, school, peers   23. Males, females   24. resilient

---

🌳 CONCLUSION

In this chapter, we followed middle childhood youngsters as they moved away from a sheltered home environment and into a world of new friends, new challenges, and new problems. Whether the task is adjusting to a new sibling, relating to peers and teachers, or coping with difficulties, youngsters of this age enter a different world.

But the timing of their entrance into this novel environment is intended to match their ability to adapt successfully, to master those skills that will prepare them for the next great developmental epoch, adolescence. From Tom Sawyer's subtlety to children learning to cope with stress, middle childhood youngsters require those skills that will enable them to deal with their widening social world.

Inevitably, though, they face times of turmoil, which, as we have seen, can come from internal or external sources. For some youngsters, these periods of stress are brief interludes; for others, there is no relief for years. Children cope uniquely using temperamental qualities and coping skills as best they can.

🌳 CHAPTER HIGHLIGHTS

Siblings and Development

- Sibling relationships have an enduring and significant impact on development.
- Most children respond positively when questioned about the quality of their sibling relationships.

The Influence of Peers

- During the middle childhood years, children begin to form close friendships.
- Children who have difficulty with their peers are often bothered by personal problems.

- Middle childhood youngsters learn to recognize the views of others.

Schools and Middle Childhood

- Children form and test social relations during these years.

- Children must learn to adjust to a wide variety of classmates, many of whom may be children of different cultures.
- School-age children are encountering considerable change in both curriculum and instructional methods.

Television and Development

- Television is the school's great competitor for children's time and attention.

- Some children spend more time watching television than they do in school-related activities.
- Controversy surrounds the issue of the effects of television violence.
- Television is also credited with the potential for encouraging prosocial behavior.

Stress in Childhood

- Children react differently to stress according to age, gender, and temperament.

- Some children, called resilient children, overcome the adverse effects of early stressors.
- Several theories have been proposed to explain how children become violent.
- Researchers are currently examining infant experiences, especially the quality of attachment, for an explanation of early violence.
- Children acquire coping skills that enable them to adjust to stress in their lives.

KEY TERMS

Friend   253
Observational learning   264
Peers   253
Prosocial behavior   264

Resilient children   272
Sexual abuse   267
Sibling   249

Social perspective taking   255
Stress   265
TQM (Total Quality Management)   258

WHAT DO YOU THINK?

1. Recall your relationship with your brothers and sisters. How would you evaluate the experience, positively or negatively? Why? Does your answer reflect some of the topics mentioned in this chapter? If you are an only child, do you think you missed out on something? Why?
2. It is generally accepted that friendships and groups become more important during the middle childhood years. With your knowledge of the developmental features of these years, do you think children of this age are ready for group membership?
3. For individuals to experience stress, they must understand the forces that are pressing on them. Do you think middle childhood youngsters are capable of such an interpretation of the events surrounding them?
4. Great concern exists today about the increasing rate of violence among children. Do you think the problem is as serious as the media indicate? From your knowledge of this topic, do you think the predictors of early criminal behavior are useful?

SUGGESTED READINGS

Liebert, R. & Sprafkin, J. (1988). *The early window*. 3d ed. New York: Pergamon. This paperback is one of the best single sources on the impact of television on our society today. Once you read this, you'll understand why TV is considered a major socializing force in a child's life.

Magid, K. & C. McKelvey (1987). *High risk: Children without a conscience*. New York: Bantam. An excellent, readable account of the development of violent children. Valuable case studies.

Parmet, H. (1980). *Jack: The struggles of John F. Kennedy*. New York: Dial. An insightful glimpse of those childhood years when the give-and-take of family interactions was colored by a constant sense of "great expectations."

Ward, G. (1989). *A first-class temperament: The emergence of Franklin Roosevelt*. New York: Harper & Row. To the end of her days, Eleanor Roosevelt felt that no one loved her for herself. In this intriguing account of the young Roosevelts, Ward traces the effect of an alcoholic father and an indifferent mother on the emotional life of a young girl.

CHAPTER REVIEW TEST

1. Older siblings can help their brothers and sisters by all but one of the following. Which will *not* help?
   a. being a role model
   b. offering advice
   c. interceding with adults
   d. borrowing their clothes
2. A peer is defined as one who is
   a. equal in intelligence.
   b. in the same grade.
   c. within 12 months of age.
   d. in a nearby house.
3. Attempts to improve the level of quality production in the schools is referred to as
   a. management directives.
   b. parents, teachers, students coalition.
   c. school-based control.
   d. Total Quality Management.

4. _____ _____ is a term used by Eisenberg to describe warnings of parental moods and prohibitions from older siblings to their younger brothers and sisters.
   a. Sibling rivalry
   b. Sibling underworld
   c. Sibling bond
   d. Sibling network

5. Friends provide certain resources for children that adults lack. Which of the following is *not* a resource provided by friends?
   a. role model
   b. opportunity for learning skills
   c. chance to compare self with others
   d. chance to belong to a group

6. Selman's theory of interpersonal relationships is known as
   a. observational learning.
   b. social perspective taking.
   c. linguistic interpretation.
   d. accommodation.

7. The National Council of Teachers of Mathematics recommends that students use _____ at all times.
   a. computers
   b. tables
   c. slide rules
   d. calculators

8. Schools are different _____ contexts at different levels.
   a. social
   b. individual
   c. constructive
   d. physical

9. The author of a scathing criticism of schools in low SES environments is
   a. Bruner.
   b. Skinner.
   c. Kozol.
   d. Deming.

10. A controversial television spot that emphasized prosocial behavior was
    a. "No Violence Today."
    b. "Look to the Future."
    c. "The Swing."
    d. "Children in Danger."

11. Which of the following is *not* a requirement for a child to be able to understand what they see on television?
    a. must know something about story form
    b. must have general knowledge about situations and events
    c. must have knowledge about television forms and conventions
    d. must be able to predict outcomes

12. Which of the following is *not* considered a severe stressor of childhood?
    a. parental alcoholism
    b. one-parent home
    c. abuse
    d. separation from parent

13. Child abusers often share parental characteristics. Which of the following is *not* such a characteristic?
    a. perpetrator abused as a child
    b. have unreasonable expectations for the child
    c. often immature and dependent
    d. low SES

14. There are as many as _____ sexually abused children per year in the United States.
    a. 75,000
    b. 250,000
    c. 500,000
    d. 1,000,000

15. Which is *not* a long-term effect of sexual abuse?
    a. permissive parenting
    b. depression
    c. negative self-concept
    d. sexual problems

16. _____ notes that we cannot be upset by events whose power to harm us we do not understand.
    a. Maccoby
    b. Brenner
    c. Eisenberger
    d. Bruner

17. _____ is a way a child avoids coping with stress by acting younger than their years.
    a. Denial
    b. Regression
    c. Withdrawal
    d. Impulsivity

18. Children can successfully cope with stress by protecting themselves and accepting what can't be avoided. This is called
    a. altruism.
    b. humor.
    c. suppression.
    d. anticipation.

19. Children react differently to stress according to all but
    a. age.
    b. gender.
    c. temperament.
    d. race.

20. One explanation of violence being researched currently is
    a. quality of attachment.
    b. emotional control.
    c. confidence.
    d. peer influence.

Answers

1. d 2. c 3. d 4. b 5. a 6. b 7. d 8. a 9. c 10. c 11. d 12. b 13. d 14. c 15. a 16. a 17. b 18. d 19. d 20. a

PART VI

Adolescence

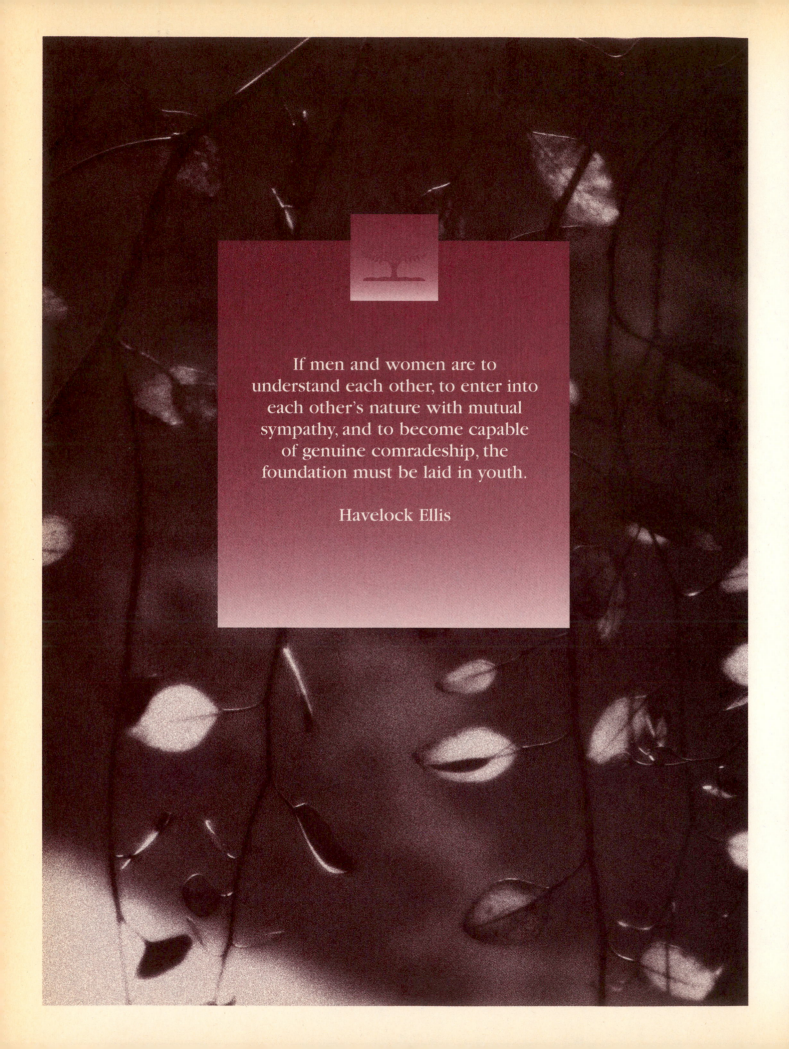

If men and women are to
understand each other, to enter into
each other's nature with mutual
sympathy, and to become capable
of genuine comradeship, the
foundation must be laid in youth.

Havelock Ellis

W ho are you?" said the caterpillar. Alice replied, rather shyly, "I—I hardly know, Sir, just at present—at least I know who I was when I got up this morning, but I must have changed several times since then."

Lewis Carroll, *Alice in Wonderland,* 1865

Most American adolescents come through the critical years from ages ten to twenty relatively unscathed. With good schools, supportive families, and caring community institutions, they grow to adulthood meeting the requirements of the workplace, the commitments to family and friends, and the responsibilities of citizenship. Even under less-than-optimal conditions for healthy growth, many youngsters manage to become contributing members of society.

Carnegie Corporation, *Adolescence,* 1990, p. 1 🌳

Some writers have suggested that like Alice, adolescents experience life as a constant swirl of adjustments. Is adolescence a time of topsy-turvy change, marked by abrupt emotional crises, or is this only a stereotype, as the preceding quote from the Carnegie report indicates? This question has caused a great deal of debate among scientists who study this fascinating period of life.

Another major concern focuses on when (at what age or with what event) this stage of life begins, and when it ends. A third debate addresses the question, "What are the best ways of answering questions about adolescence?" Resolving each of these controversies would help us to agree on a definition of adolescence and would go a long way toward helping us to understand it. In this chapter we consider each of these questions, starting with the first one. In the last two sections of the chapter, we examine the changing roles of adolescents' families, as well as the disturbing problem of the increase in the suicide rate among teens.

As a result of having read this chapter, you should be able to

- Identify ways in which your own adolescence was different from or similar to that of today's teens.

- Describe how adolescence was viewed in ancient times, during the Middle Ages, during the "Age of Enlightenment," and in the present century.

- Explain the value of studying adolescence in two stages, early and late, rather than as one stage.

- State what you believe to be the best definitions of the beginning and end of adolescence.

- List G. S. Hall's four stages of development.

- Discuss Hall's notion of "storm and stress."

- State the contributions of Anna Freud and Robert Havighurst to adolescent theory.

- Detail the special importance Erik Erikson's psychosocial theory has for adolescence.

- Name the five main functions that have been lost by the family, as well as the role that remains.

- Explain the increase in age-related activities.

- Describe the effects of divorce on adolescents.

- Establish the prevalence of suicide among teens and identify the meanings suicide attempts have for some of them.

- Discuss these issues from an applied, a multicultural, and your own point of view.

AN APPLIED VIEW

An Average Day in the Life of Some North American Teens

Today (and every other day this year):

- 7,742 teenagers have become sexually active.
- 623 teenagers have gotten syphilis or gonorrhea.
- 2,740 teenagers have gotten pregnant.
- 1,293 teenagers have given birth to a child.
- 1,105 teenagers have had an abortion.
- 369 teenagers have miscarried.
- 1,375 teenagers have dropped out of school before graduation.
- 3,288 have run away from home.
- 1,629 teenagers are locked up in adult jails.
- 6 teenagers have died of suicide.
- ? teenagers are being beaten or psychologically or sexually abused.
- ? teenagers have parents who are or soon will be divorced. (Children's Defense Fund, 1989)

On the other hand, today (and every other day this year), teenagers have engaged in many kinds of activities that enrich their own lives and those of the people around them. It is impossible to know exactly how many are involved in each of these activities. (It is interesting that we know much more about teenagers' negative actions, isn't it?) Here are some examples:

- Have joined a service-oriented club (e.g., Scouts, 4-H, Future Farmers of America)
- Became members of Junior Achievement
- Competed in an athletic event
- Became a candy-striper (volunteer nurse's aide)
- Joined Students Against Drunk Driving
- Taught another teen in a peer tutor program
- Served food in a shelter for the homeless
- Volunteered at a day-care center or a nursing home for the elderly
- Answered phones on a drug abuse or suicide hotline
- Delivered newspapers, stocked supermarket shelves, or in some other way earned money at a part-time job

Obviously, we would wish that all adolescents were more interested in the ideals represented by these activities. Can you think of ways that you could help make this happen?

How Should We Define Adolescence?

In this section we consider the definition of adolescence by reviewing ideas about when it starts and by examining its history.

Is interest in the opposite sex the best sign that a young person has reached puberty? What other indicators could you name?

When Does It Start?

At what point did your adolescence begin? Many answers have been offered:

- When you began to menstruate, or when you had your first ejaculation

- When the level of adult hormones rose sharply in your bloodstream

- When you first thought about dating

- When your pubic hair began to grow

- When you became 11 years old (if a girl); when you became 12 years old (if a boy)

- When you developed an interest in the opposite sex

- When you (if a girl) developed breasts

- When you passed the initiation rites set up by society: for example, confirmation in the Catholic Church; bar mitzvah and bas mitzvah in the Jewish faith
- When you became unexpectedly moody
- When you became 13
- When you formed exclusive social cliques
- When you thought about being independent of your parents
- When you worried about the way your body looked
- When you entered seventh grade
- When you could determine the rightness of an action, independent of your own selfish needs
- When your friends' opinions influenced you more than your parents' opinions
- When you began to wonder who you really are

Although at least a grain of truth exists in each of these statements, they don't help us much in defining adolescence. For example, although most would agree that menstruation is an important event in the lives of women, it really isn't a good criterion for determining the start of adolescence. The first menstruation (called *menarche*) can occur at any time from 8 to 16 years of age. We would not say that the menstruating 8-year-old is an adolescent, but we would certainly say the non-menstruating 16-year-old is one.

Probably the most reliable indication of the onset of adolescence is a sharp increase in the production of the four hormones that most affect sexuality: progesterone and estrogen in females, testosterone and androgen in males. But determining this change would require taking blood samples on a regular basis, starting when youths are 9 years old. Not a very practical approach, is it?

Clearly, identifying the age or event at which adolescence begins is not a simple matter. We will need to look at it much more closely, from the standpoints of biology, psychology, sociology (the biopsychosocial model), and several other sciences, and we will do so in other chapters in this book.

■ **These are the best years of your life! You'd better enjoy them now, because before you know it, you'll be weighed down with adult responsibilities!**

Can you remember your parents saying this, or something like it? At some time during their teen years, most people are advised not to waste their youth. In the past, a common belief was that adolescence is a carefree period, a stage of life when people "sow their wild oats" before settling down to the more rigorous demands of adult maturity.

This view is not so common any more. In fact, some observers believe that adolescence has become the worst time of life. Is it an unusually difficult period of life? Are the changes that accompany it more abrupt and disruptive than those of earlier and later stages?

Obviously, adolescence is a very bad time for some people. But does that mean that adolescents in general are becoming more of an affliction to themselves and to society? Do average adolescents have a harder time of it than their predecessors? For an answer, let's use the perspective of history. What follows is a brief summary of the ways that Western civilizations in earlier times viewed adolescence.

Ancient Times

It appears that teenagers were no more popular with early writers than they are with many people today. Take, for example, this rather cranky statement written in the eighth century B.C. by the Greek poet Hesiod:

> ■ I see no hope for the future of our people if they are dependent on the frivolous youth of today, for certainly all youth are reckless beyond words. When I was a boy, we were taught to be discreet and respectful of elders, but the present youth are exceedingly wise and impatient of restraint.

The famous Greek philosopher and renowned teacher of the young, Socrates, was no great fan either. He wrote this in the fifth century B.C.:

> ■ Our youth now love luxury. They have bad manners, contempt for authority; they show disrespect for their elders and love chatter in place of exercise. They no longer rise when others enter the room. They contradict their parents, chatter before company, gobble up their food and tyrannize their teachers.

Socrates' notable student, Plato, had a more positive outlook. In his view of the lifespan, childhood is the time of life when the spirit (meaning life values) develops, and so children should study sports and music. In the teen years, the reason starts to mature, and so youth should switch to the study of science and mathematics. For Plato's student, Aristotle, the teens are the years in which we develop our ability to choose, to become self-determining. This passage is not an easy one, however, and he felt it caused youth to be impatient and unstable.

The Middle Ages

During the Middle Ages, the concept of human development became unrelentingly negative. Children came to be seen as "miniature adults." Children rarely appear in paintings from those times, but when they do, they are always dressed in cut-down versions of their parents' clothes. It was generally agreed that the way to help them become mature adults was through strict, harsh discipline, so that they could overcome the natural evils of the childish personality.

The word *teen,* meaning a person from 11 to 19 years old, is an inflected form of *ten,* used as a suffix (e.g., four-teen). In Middle English, however, there was a word teen that meant "injury; misery, affliction; grief." The obsolete *teen* and the suffix *-teen* are not related. But coincidentally, teen is an accurate description of how youth was looked at in the period from the Romans to the Renaissance in Western culture.

The "Age of Enlightenment"

The beginning of the Age of Enlightenment (from the 1600s to the early 1900s) brought no major change from the previous period in the view of adolescence. For example, Hesiod's and Socrates' observations were echoed by an old shepherd in Shakespeare's *The Winter's Tale* (1609):

> ■ I would there were no age between ten and three-and-twenty, or that youth would sleep out the rest; for there is nothing in the between but getting wenches with child, wronging the ancientry [elderly], stealing, fighting.

This position held sway until the 1700s, when Jean-Jacques Rousseau argued forcibly through his book *Emile* (1762) that children and youth need to be free of

Prior to the twentieth century, it appears that children moved directly from childhood into adulthood with no period of adolescence in between.

Historically adolescents have been viewed rather negatively. Do you think this treatment is warranted, or does the problem lie with the adult misperceptions?

adult rules so they can experience the world naturally. Rousseau compared childhood to the lives of the American Indians, whom he referred to as "noble savages." He believed that both groups are basically good and that Indians grow into kind and insightful adults because they are not corrupted by civilization.

In early America, this view did not gain much support. Life for the colonists was not easy, and everyone was expected to work hard, including children. Most youths worked on farms, but as the population grew, more and more went into apprenticeships in the cities.

By the nineteenth century, however, a dual pattern began to emerge. The country was clearly splitting into a large lower and middle class by the 1840s. The children of the poor continued in the old apprenticeship mold, but middle-class youth began to stay in school longer and longer. The technical demands of the Industrial Revolution called for more extensive education. The reform movement of the "muckrakers" at the turn of the twentieth century, which brought about stricter labor and compulsory education laws, created a more equitable situation between the two social classes. Only in the early 1900s did adolescence, as we know it today, begin.

A MULTICULTURAL VIEW

Is Adolescence a Cultural Phenomenon?

In Western cultures, extended schooling keeps children out of full-time productive work so they do not start observing and participating in the adult economic world as they do in, for example, Guatemala. Schooling has become a substitute for adult roles. For instance, a college student spends years studying nursing (chemistry, psychology), but he is not a nurse (chemist, psychologist). Extended schooling, then, artificially stretches the period from childhood to adulthood. This delay or waiting period is unique in human history. Combined with the decreasing age of reaching menarche

in middle-class Western girls, adolescence can be prolonged more than 10 years! Compare this to the Efe, hunters and gatherers in Zaire, who marry and assume adult roles soon after puberty. Is adolescence just a theoretical construct (see chapter 2)? Is it peculiar to cultures with extended schooling? Has an extended adolescence altered our definition of maturity? What if our increasing need for high-level education were to extend adolescence into the middle or even late twenties? Would this change the meaning of adolescence? What do you think?

The Twentieth Century

Empiricism

The process of making careful observations.

Now began the age of **empiricism.** Early in our century, those who were interested in understanding youth ceased speculating about the nature of adolescence and began to make careful observations of them. This is what empiricism means.

Psychology itself began only in the late nineteenth century. It took as its first task learning how the brain perceives the environment around us but soon turned

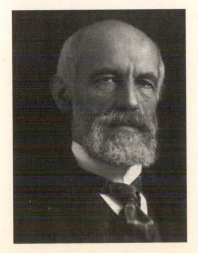

G. S. Hall was the first American to publish research on the teen years, with his book *Adolescence* (1904).

to studying human development. The new science quickly accepted the challenge of explaining the transition from childhood to adulthood. In this task, psychology was greatly influenced by the writings of G. Stanley Hall and a number of other social scientists who followed him.

G. S. Hall and the Theory of Recapitulation

G. Stanley Hall (1844–1924) is known as the father of adolescent psychology. Building on Charles Darwin's theory of evolution, Hall constructed a psychological theory of teenage development, published in two volumes and entitled *Adolescence* (1904).

Hall posited four periods of development of equal duration, which he felt correspond to the four lengthy stages of development of our species: infancy/animal, childhood/anthropoid (humanlike apes), youth/half-barbarian, and adolescence/civilized.

- Infancy: birth to 4 years. In this stage children recapitulate the animal stage, in which mental development is quite primitive. Sensory development is the most important aspect of this period, together with the development of sensorimotor skills.

- Childhood: 4 to 8 years. Hunting and fishing, using toy weapons, and playing with dolls are common activities of childhood. Language and social interaction begin to develop rapidly, as they did during the nomadic period of the human race.

- Youth: 8 to 12 years. This period corresponds to the more settled life of the agricultural world of several thousand years ago. This is the time when children are willing to practice and to discipline themselves; this is when routine training and drills are the most appropriate—especially for language and mathematics.

Storm and stress
G. Stanley Hall's term used to describe the state of adolescence.

- Adolescence: 12 to 25 years. **Storm and stress** typify human history for the past 2,000 years, as well as this developmental period. Adolescence is a new birth, for now the higher and more completely human traits are born.

Hall believed that each person's development passes through the same four stages as the human species. He thought that all development is determined by physiological (i.e., genetic) factors. Development occurs in an unchangeable, universal pattern, and the effects of the environment are minimal. For example, Hall argued that some socially unacceptable behavior in children, such as fighting and stealing, is inevitable. He urged parents to be lenient and permissive, assuring them that children must have this catharsis, and that when they reached the later developmental stages, these behaviors would simply drop out of existence.

Hall felt that the development of most human beings stopped short of the fourth stage, in which appreciation of music and art is achieved. Most people seemed fixated at the third stage, in the dull routine of work. A social reformer, Hall believed that adolescence is the only period in which we have any hope of improving our species. He felt that placing teenagers in enriched environments would improve their genes, which their children would then inherit. Hence we could become a race of superanthropoids.

Recapitulation theory
G. Stanley Hall's psychological theory of teenage development.

Psychologists today argue that **recapitulation theory** is an interesting but quite inaccurate picture of human social development. They believe Hall tried to force reality to fit an outmoded conception of evolutionary development. His theory is considered wrong for several reasons. It most particularly does not present a true picture of adolescence. Although the majority of youth in his time may not have had much appreciation for civilized culture, this was clearly due not to genetic imperfections, but to such factors as having been forced to leave school to work on the farm. In addition, Hall's belief in the genetic transmission of acquired (improved) characteristics is scientifically false. Since Hall looked only at American culture, and since most individuals in the culture did develop similarly, he mistakenly thought that genes were responsible for this similarity. Later studies of other cultures have shown wide differences in developmental patterns. We can conclude that from the standpoint of the biopsychosocial model, Hall overemphasized the biological aspect.

Although Hall is to be admired for his efforts to bring objectivity to adolescent psychology through the use of empiricism, it has been suggested that he had several personal agendas. He was a strong preacher against what he viewed to be teenage immorality and was especially concerned that educators try to stamp out the "plague of masturbation," which he considered to be running rampant among male youth. Here is a little speech that he recommended high school teachers and clergy give to their youthful charges:

> ■ If a boy in an unguarded moment tries to entice you to masturbatic experiments, he insults you. Strike him at once and beat him as long as you can stand, etc. Forgive him in your mind, but never speak to him again. If he is the best fighter and beats you, take it as in a good cause. If a man scoundrel suggests indecent things, slug him with a stick or a stone or anything else at hand. Give him a scar that all may see; and if you are arrested, tell the judge all, and he will approve your act, even if it is not lawful. If a villain shows you a filthy book or picture, snatch it; and give it to the first policeman you meet, and help him to find the wretch. If a vile woman invites you, and perhaps tells a plausible story of her downfall, you cannot strike her; but think of a glittering, poisonous snake. She is a degenerate and probably diseased, and even a touch may poison you and your children. (1904, p. 136)

Is a Bias Built into Adolescent Research?

Hall is hardly the only adolescent psychologist who can be accused of bias in his thinking. In a fascinating study, Enright and colleagues (1987) looked at 89 articles published during two economic depressions and two world wars to see if these events had an influence on research. The results were striking:

> ■ In times of economic depression theories of adolescence emerge that portray teenagers as immature, psychologically unstable, and in need of prolonged participation in the educational system. During wartime, the psychological competence of youth is emphasized and the duration of education is recommended to be more retracted than in depression. (p. 541)

Is it likely that youth were viewed as immature during depressions to keep them from competing with adults for scarce jobs, and that their maturity is seen as greater during wartime because they are needed to perform such adult tasks as soldiering and factory work? If so, is this bias conscious or unconscious? What do you think?

As you read the other theories in this chapter, see if you can spot what you believe to be biases in them.

To conclude this brief excursion into the historical point of view, let us say that distrust of adolescence has not died in the second half of this century. As noted adolescent sociologist Edgar Friedenberg remarked in 1959:

> ■ A great many young people are in very serious trouble throughout the technically developed world, and especially the Western world. Their trouble, moreover, follows certain familiar common patterns; they get into much the same kind of difficulty in very different societies. (p. 6)

We cannot accept these historical views with confidence, however, because each of them suffers from the same critical flaw: They are primarily reflections of subjective opinion, not of scientifically objective measurement. Many more factors must be considered before we can honestly say we have an acceptable definition of adolescence. For an understanding of the most important of these factors, we turn to several experts on adolescence.

Guided Review

1. G. S. Hall, the father of adolescent psychology, saw child development paralleling the development of the human race, with adolescence being a time both of civilization and of storm and _____ .

2. During the Middle Ages children were regarded as _____ _____ .

3. During this time period it was agreed that helping children become mature adults required strict _____ .

4. The four periods of development outlined by G. S. Hall are infancy, childhood, _____ , and adolescence.

Theories of Adolescence

In this section, the theories of three famous adolescent theorists are reviewed.

Anna Freud

A trained psychoanalyst like her father, Anna Freud (1895–1983) believed that his definition of adolescence was too sketchy. She suggested (1968) that her father had been too involved with his discovery that sexuality begins not at puberty but in early infancy. As a result, he overemphasized the importance of that earlier stage in the total developmental picture. Anna Freud spent the major part of her professional life trying to extend and modify psychoanalytic theory as applied to adolescence.

Anna Freud saw the major problem of adolescence as being the restoration of the delicate balance between the ego and the id, which is established during latency and disrupted by puberty. Latency, she felt, is the time when children adopt the moral values and principles of the people with whom they identify. Childhood fears are replaced with internalized feelings of guilt that are learned during this period. The id is controlled during latency by the strength of the superego. At puberty, however, the force of the id becomes much greater and the delicate balance is destroyed.

The problems brought about by this internal conflict cause the adolescent to regress to earlier stages of development. A renewed Oedipal conflict (see chapter 2) brings about fears that are entirely unconscious and often produce intense anxiety. Therefore, the unconscious defenses of the ego tend to multiply rapidly, especially the typical ones of repression, denial, and compensation. The problem, of course, is that the use of these defense mechanisms causes new stresses within the individual and tends to further increase the level of anxiety.

Anna Freud described two additional adolescent defense mechanisms:

- *Asceticism,* in which, as a defense against the sexual, "sinful" drives of youth, the teenager frequently becomes extremely religious and devoted to God

- *Intellectualization,* in which the adolescent defends against emotionality of all kinds by becoming extremely intellectual and logical about life

Anna Freud may be seen as emphasizing the psychological aspect of the biopsychosocial model.

Robert Havighurst

By the 1950s and 1960s, several new theories developed as a reaction to the earlier viewpoints. Robert Havighurst (b. 1900), a sociologist at the University of Chicago,

Sociologist Robert Havighurst suggested a series of developmental tasks for each stage of life.

Answers

1. stress 2. miniature adults 3. discipline 4. youth

Developmental tasks

Havighurst suggests these specific tasks at each stage of life, which lie midway between the needs of the individual and the ends of society. These tasks, such as skills, knowledge, functions, and attitudes, are needed by an individual in order to succeed in life.

In what ways is adolescent development caused by the adolescent's environment? By heredity?

became a major spokesperson of the new view. He suggested that specific **developmental tasks,** which lie midway between the needs of the individual and the ends of society, occur at each stage of life. He defined these tasks as skills, knowledge, functions, and attitudes that an individual needs to succeed in life. As with Freudian theory, the inability to negotiate successfully any particular stage interferes with success at all succeeding stages.

For the adolescent period, Havighurst (1951) described nine developmental tasks:

- Accepting one's physique and accepting a masculine or feminine role
- Forming new relations with age-mates of both sexes
- Achieving emotional independence of parents and other adults
- Achieving assurance of economic independence
- Selecting and preparing for an occupation
- Developing intellectual skills and concepts necessary for civic competence
- Desiring and achieving socially responsible behavior
- Preparing for marriage and family life
- Building conscious values in harmony with an adequate scientific world picture

Although written 40 years ago, Havighurst's list holds up rather well today. Research has lent considerable support to Havighurst's theory, and educators and therapists have found his ideas useful. He clearly emphasized the social component of the biopsychosocial model.

Erik Erikson

According to Erik Erikson (1902–1994), the main task of the adolescent is to achieve a **state of identity.** Erikson (1958, 1959, 1963, 1968, 1969), who originated the term **identity crisis,** used it in a special way. In addition to thinking of identity as the general picture one has of oneself, Erikson referred to it as a state toward which one strives. If you were in a state of identity, the various aspects of your self-images would be in agreement with each other; they would be identical.

Repudiation of choices is another essential aspect of a person's identity. Striving for identity means that we have to repudiate (give up) all the other possibilities, at least for the present. All of us know people who seem unable to do this. They cannot keep a job, they have no loyalty to their friends, they are unable to be faithful to a spouse. For them, "the grass is always greener on the other side of the fence." Thus they must keep all their options open and must not repudiate any choices, lest one of them should turn out to have been "the right one."

Erikson suggested that identity confusion is far more likely in a democratic society because so many choices are available. In a totalitarian society, youths are usually given an identity, which they are forced to accept. The Hitler Youth Corps of Nazi Germany in the 1930s is an example of a national effort backed by intense propaganda to get all the adolescents in the country to identify with the same set of values and attitudes. In democratic societies, where more emphasis is placed on individual decision making, choices abound; some children may feel threatened by this overabundance of options. Nevertheless, a variety of choices is essential to the formation of a well-integrated identity.

Further, it is normal for identity confusion to cause an increase in self-doubt during early adolescence (Seginer & Flum, 1987; Shirk, 1987). Shirk states that such doubts should decrease during the middle teen years, "as social norms for self-evaluation are acquired through role-taking development" (p. 59). He studied self-doubt in 10-, 13-, and 16-year-olds and found significant decreases with advancing age.

State of identity

According to Erikson, the main goal of adolescence.

Identity crisis

Erikson's term for the situation, usually in adolescence, that causes us to make major decisions about our identity.

Repudiation

Choosing an identity involves rejecting other alternatives.

You may recall that in chapter 2 we described Erikson's complete theory as "an amazingly perceptive and at times poetically beautiful description of human life." He probably has done more research and writing on this fifth stage of identity formation than on all the others combined. We believe that most psychologists would call him the foremost theorist on adolescence today. This does not mean, however, that all agree with his view that adolescence is a time of identity crisis.

The Search for Identity

Goethals and Klos (1976) argued that if an identity crisis exists at all, it comes only at the end of adolescence:

> ■ It is our opinion that college students do not typically have a firm sense of identity and typically have not undergone an identity crisis. College students seem to be in the process of identity seeking, and experience identity crisis toward the end of senior year and in their early post-college experience. A male or female's disillusionment with their job experience or graduate study, a female's disappointment at being at home with small children, is often the jolt that makes them ask what their education was for, and why they are not as delighted with their lives as they had been led to believe they would be. (p. 129)

Erikson, who himself had an extensive and rather difficult identity crisis in his youth, supposed that "My friends will insist that I needed to name this crisis in everybody else in order to really come to terms with it" (1975, p. 26). Born Erik Homberger, he seems to have rejected his past, which was a difficult one. His Danish mother remarried a German Jew, and he found himself rejected both by Jewish and Christian children. His identity crisis was resolved by the creation of a brand-new person with a new name, religion, and occupation. Some biographers (e.g., Berman, 1975; Roazen, 1976) have suggested that the surname he chose, Erikson, means he is the "son of himself." His experiences no doubt colored his theory. At the same time, the intensity and degree of his identity crisis made him extremely sensitive to the problems that all adolescents go through.

Perhaps the best conclusion we can reach, based on the available evidence, is that though the teen years are definitely a time of concern over one's identity, many may postpone major decisions about it until they reach early adulthood. This is probably truer today than ever, because of the phenomenon that Erikson called the **moratorium of youth,** which seems to be lasting longer and longer.

The Moratorium of Youth

Erikson saw adolescence as a period of moratorium—a "time out" period during which the adolescent experiments with a variety of identities, without having to assume the responsibility for the consequences of any particular one. We allow adolescents this moratorium so that they can try out a number of ways of being, the better to come to their own particular identity. The moratorium period does not exist in preindustrial societies. Some have suggested that only Western industrial societies can afford the luxury of a moratorium. Others say that only because the values in Western industrial societies are so conflicted do adolescents need a moratorium.

Erikson stated that indecision is an essential part of the moratorium. Tolerance of it leads to a positive identity. Some youth, however, cannot stand the ambiguity of indecision. This leads to **premature foreclosure.** The adolescent who makes choices too early usually comes to regret them. He or she is especially vulnerable to identity confusion in later life.

Erikson suggested that religious initiation ceremonies such as Catholic confirmation and Jewish bar and bas mitzvah can limit the young, forcing them into a narrow, negative identity. This can happen if the ceremony dogmatically spells out the specific behaviors that adults expect. On the other hand, such ceremonies can

---

Moratorium of youth

A "time-out" period during which the adolescent experiments with a variety of identities, without having to assume the responsibility for the consequences of any particular one.

Premature foreclosure

A situation in which a teenager chooses an identity too early, usually because of external pressure.

Members of the Hitler Youth Corps were victims of "premature foreclosure," in which their identity was designed for them without their having any choice. They were taught exactly what to wear, how to act, what to think. Some actually turned their parents in to the secret police for what they believed to be violations of Hitler's creed.

Negative identity

Persons with a negative identity adopt one pattern of behavior because they are rebelling against demands that they do the opposite.

Erikson suggests that the young Martin Luther was an excellent example of his concept of negative identity. Because of what happened in his youth, he spent his adulthood rebelling against what he had been taught. Here Frau Cotta, the woman who cared for him when he was 11 (in 1494) introduces the shy boy to her family.

suggest to youths that the adult community now has more confidence in their ability to make decisions. The effect depends on the explanation of the goals of the ceremony.

Although some youths tend to be overly idealistic, Erikson believed that idealism is essential for a strong identity. In young people's search for a person or an idea to be true to, they are building a commitment to an ideology that will help them unify their personal values. They need ideals to avoid the disintegration of personality that is the basis of most forms of mental illness.

Negative Identity

Although most adolescents do not go through changes as great as Erikson did in his youth, many do take on what he calls a **negative identity.** People with negative identities adopt one pattern of behavior because they are rebelling against demands that they do the opposite. An example is the boy who joins a gang of shoplifters, not because he wants to steal, but because he doubts his masculinity and seeks to prove, through the dangerous act of theft, that he is not a coward. Another example is the sexually permissive girl who is punishing her mother for trying to keep unreasonably strict control over her. Sex is not her goal; proving that she is no longer her mother's baby is.

In his psychohistorical biography of German religious leader Martin Luther (1483–1546), called *Young Man Luther* (1958), Erikson painted a somber picture of negative identity. Luther's greatness as a leader, says Erikson, was partly built on the enormous anger and unresolved conflict he experienced in his late teens. Luther's decision to become a monk and enter the monastery was the assumption of a negative identity. The choice expressed his rejection of fifteenth-century society rather than his devotion to Catholicism. Luther indulged in further contrariness by trying to be a better monk than anyone else. Luther's strong internal conflict is illustrated by the story of his falling into a faint while performing in the choir. As he fell to the ground, he is said to have cried out, "It isn't me!" Many other incidents also indicate that he couldn't accept being who he was.

 A MULTICULTURAL VIEW

Ethnic Self-Concept

One African American male recalls, "Much of my junior and high school years were difficult because, on top of the typical problems of this time period, I had to combine the struggle of being Black and having my race always looked down upon, expected to fail, expected to cause trouble, and expected to be unproductive. During this time, I had to fight to maintain my confidence. I did not know who I was . . . I was confused." He went on to describe how he was kicked off the football team for a failing grade, but when his parents spoke to the teacher, it was discovered that he actually had a C+. "He had given me an F not because I earned it, but because he expected me to deserve it" (John B. Diamond in Schoem, 1991).

A Mexican American male stated, "As I moved to junior high, the issue of my ethnicity became a problem. I remember thinking that I would be a great deal more

popular if only I had Bobby's face and body and brains. I would look in the mirror and imagine what I would look like. The mythical Bobby was, of course, always white and popular with girls. This fantasy ate away at my self-esteem, and I found myself bitterly questioning why I had been born a brown-faced Mexican. . . . From this point on, all my energies were spent on the elusive quest for acceptance by my peers—and unconsciously, by myself" (Carlos Manjarrez in Schoem, 1991).

Do you think ethnic prejudice can make the development of self-concept and positive self-esteem difficult? Do you think the African American teen felt that he mattered to his teacher? What are the social expectations for him and how might they influence self-concept? What values of American society make the development of self-concept and positive self-esteem challenging for adolescents of color?

Given Erikson's concept of negative identity, do you think an adolescent who is consistently disruptive and rebellious in school should be removed from the school? What should be done with him/her?

Identity status

Refers to Marcia's four types of identity formation.

Identity confusion

Marcia's initial status, in which no crisis has been experienced and no commitments have been made.

Identity foreclosure

One of Marcia's statuses, in which no crisis has been experienced, but commitments have been made, usually forced on the person by the parent.

Identity moratorium

One of Marcia's statuses of adolescence, in which considerable crisis is being experienced but no commitments are yet made.

Identity achievement

Marcia's final status, in which numerous crises have been experienced and resolved, and relatively permanent commitments have been made.

Erikson believed that Luther had an extended identity crisis. His monkhood was used as the time and place for working out a positive identity. As his identity evolved, Luther devoted himself without reluctance to God and turned all his fury against the pope, fomenting the Protestant religious upheaval. Like Erikson, Luther's identity crisis was not resolved until he reached 30.

Erikson recognized the role of biology in his theory, through his description of eight stages that invariably follow the same sequence for everyone. However, he put more emphasis on the psychological and social aspects of the biopsychosocial model. Would you agree that his theory is, therefore, better balanced than the others?

Identity Status

Erikson's ideas on adolescence have generated considerable research on identity formation. The leader in this field is James Marcia, who has made a major contribution to our understanding through his research on **identity status.** He and his colleagues have published numerous studies on this topic (Marcia, 1966, 1967, 1968, 1980, 1983; Cote & Levine, 1988; Craig-Bray & others, 1988; Dellas & Jernigan, 1987; Kroger & Haslett, 1988; Raphael & others, 1987; Rogow & others, 1983; Rowe & Marcia, 1980; Schiedel & Marcia, 1985; Slugoski & others, 1984).

Marcia believes that two factors are essential in the attainment of a mature identity. First, the person must undergo several crises in choosing among life's alternatives, such as the crisis of deciding whether to hold or to give up one's religious beliefs. Second, the person must come to a commitment, an investment of self, in his or her choices. Since a person may or may not have gone through the crisis of choice and may or may not have made a commitment to choices, four combinations, or statuses, are possible for that person to be in:

Status 1. **Identity confusion:** No crisis has been experienced and no commitments have been made.

Status 2. **Identity foreclosure:** No crisis has been experienced, but commitments have been made, usually forced on the person by the parent.

Status 3. **Identity moratorium:** A number of crises have been experienced, but no commitments are yet made.

Status 4. **Identity achievement:** Numerous crises have been experienced and resolved, and relatively permanent commitments have been made.

 **AN APPLIED VIEW** — *Identity Rating*

Try placing people you know into one of Marcia's four statuses. Choose 10 friends and write their names in the spaces below. Put the number of the identity status you choose for each person after his or her name. Do the rating quickly, without thinking about it too much—this tends to make the rating more accurate.

Name	Status
1.	
2.	
3.	
4.	
5.	

Name	Status
6.	
7.	
8.	
9.	
10.	

Notice how many of your ratings fall into each category. Were most of them in the fourth category, identity achievement? If so, was this because most of the friends you chose for this activity have an achieved identity, or perhaps because you unconsciously chose them on that basis? Have most adults achieved identity? Have you? Once achieved, is identity a permanent state?

Table 11.1	Summary of Marcia's Four Identity Statuses			
	Identity Status			
	Confusion	*Foreclosure*	*Moratorium*	*Achievement*
Crisis	Absent	Absent	Present	Present
Commitment	Absent	Present	Absent	Present
Period of adolescence in which status often occurs	Early	Middle	Middle	Late

Table 11.1 summarizes these definitions.

Erikson's eight stages (in addition to the six mentioned earlier, there are the stages of generativity and integrity) follow each other in a more or less unchangeable sequence. Research indicates that Marcia's identity statuses have a tendency toward an orderly progression, but not so clearly as Erikson's stages. For example, Meilman (1979) studied males at the ages of 12, 15, 18, 21, and 24. They were rated on attitudes toward occupation, religion, politics, and, for the older subjects, sexual matters. For each of these areas, the older the group, the fewer the individuals in the confusion status and the more in the achieved status.

In fact, most of Meilman's results fit Marcia's theory well. For instance, the number of teens in the achievement category increased progressively through age 24. The largest percentages of those in the identity confusion category were age 12, 68 percent, and age 15, 64 percent; at age 18, 48 percent were still seen to be in this category. The foreclosure category was also greater in the younger age brackets: age 12, 32 percent; age 15, 32 percent; and age 18, 24 percent. None of the 12-year-olds were found to be in the achievement category, and only 4 percent of the 15-year-olds were. The moratorium category also increased in each of the age brackets.

Grotevant, Thorbeck, and Meyer (1982) have expanded Marcia's research into the interpersonal realm, including friendships, dating, and sex roles. They suggested that before forming intimate relationships, adolescents explore and commit themselves to interpersonal relationships as part of their identity formation.

Carol Gilligan (1982) and others have focused on possible gender differences in identity formation. They have concluded that women are less concerned than men with achieving an independent identity status. Women are more likely to define themselves by their relationships and responsibilities to others. Society gives women the predominant role in transmitting social values from one generation to the next. This role requires a stable identity, and therefore a stable identity appears to be more important to women than it is to men.

In summary, it may be said that the adolescent's personality is undergoing many changes, but these changes are probably no more traumatic than at any other stage of life. The major concern is to begin to form an adult identity, which means choosing certain values and repudiating others. A danger does exist of staying in the moratorium period too long, and of forming a negative identity. It is considered necessary to work one's way from identity confusion through the moratorium to an achieved identity, while avoiding foreclosure. In the next half of this chapter, we will be dealing with the two foundations of the identity process: relationships with family and peers.

5. Anna Freud sees adolescence as a time to restore the delicate balance between the ego and the id, and sees _____ and intellectualization as two defense mechanisms unique to the period.

6. Robert Havighurst continues his articulation of developmental tasks into adolescence, including achieving _____ independence from parents and desiring and achieving socially responsible behavior.

7. The phrase "identity crisis" is associated with _____ _____ and is his fifth stage of development.

8. Identity status is achieved through crises and commitment in four stages: identity confusion, identity foreclosure, identity _____ , and identity achievement.

9. Marcia believes that to attain a mature identity, a person must undergo several crises in choosing from life alternatives and come to a _____ in his/her choices.

Changing American Families and Their Roles in Adolescent Life

◼ It is, after all the simplest things we remember: A neighborhood softball game, walking in the woods at twilight with Dad, rocking on the porch swing with Grandma.

Now, no one has time to organize a ballgame. Our woods have turned to malls. Grandma lives three states away. How will our children have the same kind of warm memories we do? (B. F. Meltz, "Saving the Magic Moments," 1988)

Of all the changes in American society in recent years, those affecting families have probably been the most extensive (also see chapter 8). Curiously, researchers have spent little of their time studying adolescent-parent relations—until recently. Steinberg (1987) offered an explanation for the change:

◼ The reasons for the rekindled interest in adolescents' relations with mothers and fathers are many, but among them surely is the increased public attention that family issues in general (e.g., divorce, stepfamilies, maternal employment, family violence) have received during the past five years. (p. 192)

Let's begin with a look at the changing roles of families in modern society.

The Loss of Functions

In 1840 the American family fulfilled six major functions (Sebald, 1977). Table 11.2 lists those functions and suggests which elements of society now perform them. Today professionals have taken over the first five functions—economic-productive, educational, religious, recreational, medical. It appears that the family has been left to provide but one single function—affection for its members. In the nineteenth century, parents and children needed each other more than now, for the following three major reasons (Coleman, 1961):

- *Vocational instruction*. For both males and females, the parent of the same sex taught them their adult jobs. Most men were farmers and most women, housewives. Parents knew all the secrets of work, secrets passed on from

Answers

5. asceticism   6. emotional   7. Erik Erikson   8. moratorium   9. commitment

Table 11.2	The Changing Roles of Families
Former Family Roles	**Societal Elements That Perform Them Now**
Economic-productive	Factory, office, and store
Educational	Schools
Religious	Church or synagogue
Recreational	Commercial institutions
Medical	Doctor's office and hospital
Affectional	Family

generation to generation. Today nearly 100 percent of men work at jobs different from their fathers, and an increasing percentage of women are not primarily housewives, as their mothers were.

- *Economic value*. Adolescents were a vital economic asset on the farm; without children, the farm couple had to hire others to help them. Work was a source of pride to the children. It was immediately and abundantly clear that they were important to the family. Today, instead of being an economic asset, most children are an economic burden on the family's resources.

- *Social stability*. When families almost never moved from their hometowns, parents were a crucial source of information about how to live in the town, knowing all the intricacies of small-town social relationships. One depended on one's parents to know what to do. Today, when the average American moves every five years, the adults are as much strangers in a new place as the children. In fact, with Dad, and now frequently Mom, driving out of the neighborhood to work, the children may well know the neighborhood better than their parents do.

The Increase in Age-Related Activities among Older Adolescents

The change from family to peer group influence during middle adolescence is accelerating these days. This is mainly caused by the specialization of the entertainment industry and the media. Both participatory entertainment, such as sports, and spectator entertainment, such as television, are more and more aimed at specific age groups. Therefore, everyone, teenagers included, tends to watch or participate in recreational activities only with members of their own age group.

Television has been especially powerful in this changeover. When teenagers reach the age of 18, they typically will have watched twice as many hours of television as they will have spent in the classroom. These activities isolate teenagers more and more from adults (who spend less time watching television) and force them to rely on friends for security and values orientation.

Bronfenbrenner (1977) found that as teenagers depend more on their friends, they are more likely to view their parents as lacking in affection and not very firm in discipline. Teens also show greater pessimism about the future, rank lower in responsibility and leadership, and are more likely to engage in antisocial behavior. Even when such detrimental tendencies are not present, life changes that the child and parents usually are undergoing can make life difficult, particularly when divorce is involved.

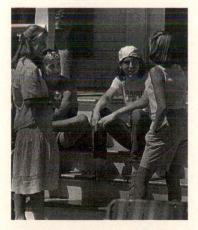

Bronfenbrenner suggests that teenagers today depend more on their friends and less on their families for their values than in earlier times. Possibly because of this, they seem to have less positive feelings toward their parents.

The Effects of Divorce

A smoothly functioning family can provide support and nurturance to an adolescent during times of stress. But when the family is itself in a state of disarray, such as during a divorce, not only is the support weakened, but the family often becomes a source of stress.

Divorce has become commonplace in American society. Even with slight decreases in the divorce rate in recent years, more than one million divorces still occur every year, which is roughly half the number of marriages performed during the same time (U.S. Bureau of Census, 1986). Divorce tends to occur most in families with a newborn, and second most in families with an adolescent present. Estimates suggest that divorce affects as much as one-third to one-half of the adolescent population (Jurich & others, 1987).

What, then, are the effects of divorce on the development of the adolescent? Unfortunately, conclusions are often based as much on speculation as on research findings, due to problems in the research. Divorcing parents often refuse to let themselves or their children participate in such studies, which makes random samples difficult to obtain (Santrock, 1987).

Nevertheless, the divorcing family clearly contributes additional stress to a developing adolescent. One obvious effect is economic. The increased living expenses that result from the need to pay for two domiciles most often leads to a significant decrease in the standard of living for the children. Most adolescents, particularly young adolescents, are extremely status conscious, and status is often obtained with the things money can buy (clothes, stereos, cars, etc.). Young adolescents may well resent being unable to keep up with their peers in this regard. Older adolescents are better equipped to cope with this type of additional stress, both psychologically and financially, since they can enter the workforce themselves.

Another obvious effect of a divorce is the absence of one parent. Often custodial rights are given to one parent (usually the mother), and so the children are likely to lose an important source of support (usually that of the father). What support the noncustodial parent provides is sometimes jeopardized by the degree of acrimony between the divorced parents. One or both of the parents may attempt to "turn" the adolescent against the other parent. This sometimes results in disturbing, negative tales about a mother or father, forcing adolescents to cope with adult realities while they are still young.

Such distractions also can disrupt the disciplinary process during adolescence. Under any circumstances, administering consistent and effective discipline during this time often requires the wisdom of King Solomon. A difficult job for two parents becomes the primary responsibility of one. Preoccupied parents, perhaps feeling guilty over subjecting the child to a divorce, find it difficult to provide the consistent discipline that the child was used to previously.

Because the father typically leaves a family during divorce, there are often more negative effects for males than for females (Hetherington & others, 1989). During the teenage years, the father often assumes primary responsibility for disciplining the male adolescents in the family. An abrupt change in disciplinary patterns can lead some adolescents to exhibit more antisocial and delinquent behavior. For example, divorce may force adolescents into growing up faster and disengaging from their families. Early disengagement from a family can actually be a good solution for teens, if they can devote themselves to school activities and rewarding relationships with friends or teachers (Hetherington & others, 1989).

Young adolescents often have difficulty accepting remarriage. Older adolescents, because of their greater maturity and self-confidence, seem to have an easier time accepting remarriage but are likely to confront or question aspects of the new family arrangements. In addition, their acute awareness of sexuality may foster resentment of the new marital closeness of their parents (Hetherington & others, 1989).

Despite the negative aspects we've outlined, you should keep in mind that not all aspects of a divorce have a negative impact on adolescents. Divorce is often a

In what ways does having two working parents affect adolescents?

Some single parents find life without their spouse quite difficult; others find they like it. Regardless of the effect on the parents, the children in a divorce virtually always suffer.

better alternative than keeping a stressful, unhappy family intact. In fact, the few studies that have compared adolescents from the two groups have shown that teenagers from divorced families do better in general than adolescents from intact but feuding families (Hetherington & others, 1989). Obviously the ability of the two parents to resolve their divorce as amicably as possible is an important factor in lessening the burden on the children. And although too many new or inappropriate responsibilities may inhibit ego formation, some added responsibilities may increase self-esteem and independence in the long run. It is also the case that many of the negative consequences of the single-parent family are relieved by a remarriage, though this is by no means always the case (Hetherington & Camara, 1984).

The Effects of Gender

A spate of new studies have investigated the part that gender plays in family life, which lead to three generalizations (Steinberg, 1987):

- Boys and girls do not differ markedly in the way they relate to their families in general (Hauser & others, 1987; Hill & Holmbeck, 1987; Montemayor & Brownlee, 1987). An important exception is that for healthy development, many females need to become more emotionally independent from the family, whereas males do better when they maintain close ties (Cooper & Grotevant, 1987; Hakim-Larson & Hobart, 1987; Hill & Holmbeck, 1987; Silverberg & Steinberg, 1987).

- Mothers and fathers relate to their families quite differently. Fathers are more likely to be helpful in family discussion than mothers (Hauser & others, 1987); fathers spend most of their time with their adolescent children playing, while mothers spend about half of their time with them in household matters (Montemayor & Brownlee, 1987); and mothers are more likely to be involved in conflicts (Silverberg & Steinberg, 1987).

- Mother-daughter relationships are the most intense, positively and negatively, and father-daughter relationships are the most bland (Silverberg & Steinberg, 1987; Youniss & Smollar, 1985).

The Nurturing Parent

As we discussed in chapter 8, most family researchers have agreed that three styles of parenting exist (Baumrind, 1986): the **authoritarian, permissive,** and **authoritative parenting styles.** In an extensive study of 56 families in which at least one of the adolescents was highly creative (Dacey & Packer, 1992), a picture of a fourth style clearly emerged. The parents in these families were found to be devotedly interested in their children's behavior, but they seldom make rules to govern it. Instead, by modeling and family discussions, they espouse a well-defined set of values and expect their children to make personal decisions based on these values.

After the children make decisions and take actions, the parents let the children know how they feel about what was done. Even when they disapprove, they rarely punish. Most of the teens in the study said that their parents' disappointment in them was motivation enough to change their behavior. All of the parents agreed that if their child were about to do something really wrong, they would stop her or him, but that this virtually never happens. We call this the **nurturing parenting style** (Dacey & Packer, 1992). Only some of the parents in the study are themselves creative, but all appear committed to this approach.

In addition to fostering values formation, nurturing parents also cultivate certain personality and intellectual traits that help children to make sound, insightful decisions. Among the traits are tolerance of ambiguity, risk-taking, delay of gratification, androgyny, problem-solving skills, and balanced use of brain hemispheres.

The success of nurturing parents is based on a well-established principle: People get better at what they practice. These parents provide their children with

---

Some adolescents are raised by two same-gender parents. In general, society has expressed concern over this issue. What would be the reasons for this concern, and are they warranted?

Authoritarian parenting style

Parents strive for complete control over their children's behavior by establishing complex sets of rules.

Permissive parenting style

Parents have little or no control over their children and refrain from disciplinary measures.

Authoritative parenting style

The most common parenting style, in which parents are sometimes authoritarian and sometimes permissive, depending to some extent on the parents' mood. Parents believe that both parents and children have rights but that parental authority must predominate.

Nurturing parenting style

The style of parenting in which parents use indirect methods such as discussion and modelling rather than punishment to influence their child's behavior. Rules are kept to a minimum.

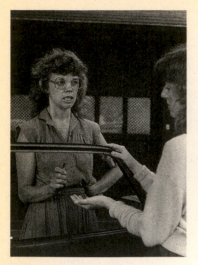

Authoritarian parents insist on strict adherence to the rules they set. The authoritarian parent is unlikely to cultivate her child's creativity.

ample opportunities to practice decision-making skills, self-control, and, most vital of all, creative thinking. They serve as caring coaches as their children learn how to live. This research demonstrates the profoundly positive effects a healthy family can have on a person.

🌳 Guided Review 🌳

10. Coleman lists three functions that were provided by the family but are now provided elsewhere: vocational instruction, economic value, and _____ stability.

11. Within families that experience divorce, there are some interesting gender differences. Divorce generally has more adverse effects on _____ than on _____ .

12. In a study on parenting styles in which at least one of the adolescents in a family was highly creative, parents were found to employ a style of parenting called _____ .

13. Divorce tends to occur most often in families with a newborn and second most in families with an _____ .

14. The three styles of parenting most often identified by researchers are authoritarian, permissive, and _____ .

The feeling that they appear foolish to everyone is a reason given by some adolescents to explain why they have attempted to kill themselves. Unfortunately, this is also a topic we must consider when trying to understand the world of teens.

Suicide—The Leading Cause of Death in the Teen Years?

Suicide and attempted suicide among contemporary adolescents is cause for growing concern (see table 11.3). Suicide is known to be at least the second leading cause of death in this age group. Some experts believe that because it is sometimes hard to determine (was a car crash intentional or not?) and sometimes covered up by friendly police and coroners, it may well be the most prevalent cause. Whites are more likely to attempt suicide than African Americans and Native Americans are more likely than whites (Berman & Jobes, 1991). Athletes were more likely than nonathletes to possess certain behavioral and psychological correlates of eating disorders and the use of pathogenic weight control techniques (Taub & Blinde, 1992). Poor teens are more likely than other teens to try to kill themselves (McCall, 1991). Although females are three times as likely as males to attempt suicide, males are almost four times as likely to die of it, because of the methods they use (such as guns and car crashes) (Sanders & Mullis, 1988). These unhappy facts make it necessary that we discuss this topic as part of the context in which today's teens are living.

The Meaning of Suicide Attempts among Teenagers

Only a small percentage of teenagers who make suicide attempts actually die. Several studies have explored the lethal intent in adolescent suicide attempts. For example, Curran (1984) asked teenagers who attempted suicide if they thought that adolescents who attempt suicide intend to die. Only 16 percent named "wish to die" as the primary motive.

Answers

10. social   11. boys, girls   12. nurturing   13. adolescent   14. authoritative

| Table 11.3 | Suicide Deaths per 100,000 among U.S. Adolescents Ages 10 to 14 and 15 to 19, 1979–87 |

Suicide Deaths/100,000 Population

| | Ages 10 to 14 | | | | | | Ages 15 to 19 | | | | | |
	Total	Male	Female	White	Black	Other	Total	Male	Female	White	Black	Other
1979	0.81	1.09	0.59	0.91	0.26	1.21	8.35	13.32	3.2	8.92	4.38	12.13
1980	0.76	1.21	0.29	0.86	0.33	0	8.51	13.82	3.02	9.29	3.59	11.02
1981	0.89	1.23	0.54	1.01	0.22	0.79	8.63	13.56	3.54	9.45	3.53	11.28
1982	1.09	1.71	0.44	1.13	0.81	1.29	8.7	14.07	3.15	9.58	3.86	8.26
1983	1.09	1.58	0.57	1.1	1.0	1.23	8.7	13.98	3.24	9.4	4.15	12.32
1984	1.28	1.91	0.63	1.38	0.71	1.51	9.01	14.26	3.54	9.92	3.8	10.12
1985	1.61	2.31	0.87	1.76	0.83	1.62	9.97	15.98	3.73	10.81	4.86	12.07
1986	1.5	2.3	0.66	1.58	0.96	2.05	10.18	16.36	3.76	11.28	4.59	8.36
1987	1.5	2.3	0.6	1.6	1.0	0	10.3	16.2	4.2	11.2	5.8	0.7

Source: *Adolescent Health* (vol. 1–3), Office of Technology Assessment, Washington, D.C., 1991.

What is the best response to a teen who speaks of committing suicide?

Self-poisoning (usually through drug overdose) is by far the most common mode of attempting suicide among female and younger adolescents in general. Self-poisoning, however, is rarely of high lethality. McIntire (1980) reported that only 12 percent of cases intended to cause death.

It is safe to say that most teenage injuries to self are not attempts to end life. What then is the actual meaning of and reasons for such dramatic acts? What are the hoped-for effects of the suicidal act of low lethality?

The finding that teenage suicide attempts are usually of low lethality in no way diminishes the seriousness of the action. The adolescent who attempts suicide is a needy person whose act should be treated with the utmost seriousness. This is also true for those who "only talk about committing suicide." Their remarks should always be referred to qualified personnel.

Adolescent suicide and attempted suicide can derive from a variety of conditions. However, certain common factors have been found. In every case, suicidal behavior occurs as the culmination of multiple, long-standing, significant problems, both within the person and between that person and the environment. The problems involve three major areas: personality problems, family problems, and societal problems.

Guided Review

15. The ethnic group most likely to commit suicide is _____ .

16. One study showed that about _____ percent of adolescents admitted to hospitals for self-poisoning reported later that they had wished to die as a result.

17. Of poor, middle-class and wealthy teens, those who are _____ are most likely to attempt suicide.

Answers

15. whites 16. 12 17. poor

🌳 CONCLUSION

Being an adolescent is no easy task these days. It probably never was, but now, with so many choices, the temptation is great to try and take them all! Whether adolescent peer group relationships are all that different from earlier times is unclear, but the family in the United States appears to be undergoing major alterations. What is clear is that with every passing year, the peer group plays a greater and greater role in the adolescent's life, while the roles of families and other societal systems (the media, the workplace, etc.) continue to change.

As Nightingale and Wolverton put it in their report to the Carnegie Council on Adolescent Development (1988),

🟥 Adolescents have no prepared place in society that is appreciated or approved; nonetheless they must tackle two major tasks, usually on their own: identity formation, and development of self-worth and self-efficacy. The social environment of adolescents today makes both tasks very hard. . . . We must change the view that many people hold of all youth as troubled and harmful to the rest of society. (pp. 1, 16)

In this chapter, we have given an overview of the personality and social development of adolescents. This is only half of the picture, though. Of at least equal importance are the critical factors of physical and mental development, which we report on in the next chapter.

🌳 CHAPTER HIGHLIGHTS

How Should We Define Adolescence?

- There are fewer adolescents in the 1990s than there used to be, and they make up a smaller proportion of the total population.
- Thinking back on your own adolescence can help you to have a deeper understanding of today's teenagers.
- In ancient times, some philosophers believed that youths were frivolous and irresponsible, whereas others emphasized their growing intellectual skills and self-sufficiency.
- From the Middle Ages until the start of the twentieth century, strict discipline was believed necessary to force young people to take on adult responsibilities as early as possible.
- Two early twentieth-century concepts changed our view of adolescence: compulsory education and labor laws.
- Most experts state that the majority of adolescents are happy and productive members of their families and communities (see the Carnegie Report, 1990).

- According to G. Stanley Hall, all human beings pass through four periods of development: birth to 4 years, 4 to 8 years, 8 to 12 years, and 12 to 25 years.
- Hall's interpretation of adolescent development was greatly influenced by his observation that it is a period of storm and stress.

Theories of Adolescence

- Anna Freud believed that the delicate balance between the superego and the id, being disrupted by puberty, causes the adolescent to regress to earlier stages of development.
- According to Robert Havighurst, each stage in development had specific developmental tasks—skills, knowledge, functions, and attitudes—that are needed by a person to succeed in life.
- Human life progresses through eight "psychosocial" stages, each of which is marked by a crisis and its resolution. The fifth stage applies mainly to adolescence.
- Although the ages at which one goes through each stage vary, the sequence of stages is fixed. Stages may overlap, however.

- A human being must experience each crisis before proceeding to the next stage. Inadequate resolution of the crisis at any stage hinders development.

Changing American Families and Their Roles in Adolescent Life

- American families have lost five of their six main functions; the only remaining one is providing affection for family members.
- A significant rise in age-related activities has tended to reduce effective communication within families.
- A number of effects of divorce pertain only to adolescents.

Suicide

- Suicide is most common among middle-class whites, but the suicide rate for African American males has increased in recent years.
- Females are more likely to attempt suicide, but males are more likely to die from it.
- The causes of suicide include personality, family, and societal problems.

🌳 KEY TERMS

Authoritarian parenting style   295
Authoritative parenting style   295
Developmental tasks   287
Empiricism   283
Identity achievement   290
Identity confusion   290
Identity crisis   287

Identity foreclosure   290
Identity moratorium   290
Identity status   290
Moratorium of youth   288
Negative identity   289
Nurturing parenting style   295

Permissive parenting style   295
Premature foreclosure   288
Recapitulation theory   284
Repudiation   287
State of identity   287
Storm and stress   284

🌳 WHAT DO YOU THINK?

1. Do you believe you have had an "identity crisis"? If so, what makes you think so?

2. Research indicates that adolescence is no more stormy or stressful than any other period of life—each period has its ups and downs. Why, then, are the teen years so often characterized in the popular literature and media as being filled with disruptive conflicts?

3. What would you say are the characteristics of an adolescent? Try to include examples of actual behavior in your response.

4. In what ways do you think adolescence may have changed over the centuries?

5. Do you know anyone whom you feel has a negative identity? What is this person like?

6. In what ways is your nuclear family different from your mother's or your father's?

7. Think back to the last time you were "down in the mouth" about something. Now suppose it were five times worse than it actually was. How would you feel? How would you act? How would others treat you?

🌳 SUGGESTED READINGS

Auel, J. (1981). *Clan of the cave bear.* New York: Bantam. Auel's wonderful imagination and excellent knowledge of anthropology make this book on the beginnings of the human family a winner. In fast-paced fiction, she describes the relationships between two types of primitive peoples—those who communicate by voice and those who do so with their hands!

Erikson, E. (1958). *Young man Luther.* New York: Norton. Erikson picked Martin Luther as a subject because, in Erikson's view, he was a famous case of negative identity. This book also closely examines the Protestant Reformation and so may appeal to you if you are interested in the beginnings of the Protestant religions.

Goldman, W. (1962). *Lord of the flies.* New York: Coward-McGann. This tale of a group of teenage boys whose plane crashes on a Pacific island, killing the adults, is must reading. You watch the subgroups develop and proceed to the shocking ending.

McCullers, C. [1946] (1985). *Member of the wedding.* New York: Bantam. Twelve-year-old Frankie yearns desperately to join her brother and his bride on their honeymoon. She learns a great deal about the transition from childhood to maturity from the devoted housekeeper.

Moravia, A. (1958). *Two women.* New York: Farrar, Straus & Giroux. This moving, compassionate tale describes the relationship between a peasant mother and her daughter in war-torn Italy. It involves the struggles of the mother to deal with her adolescent daughter's needs under these extremely trying circumstances.

Plath, S. (1971). *The bell jar.* New York: Bantam. This famed book tells the story of Esther Greenwood's painful month in New York City, which leads eventually to her insanity and attempted suicide.

Rebeta-Burditt, J. (1986). *The cracker factory.* New York: Bantam. This novel humorously describes the difficulties of a young woman who takes to drinking because of the pressures in her life and is eventually institutionalized because of an attempted suicide.

Wright, R. (1945). *Black boy.* New York: Harper & Row. This is a moving autobiography of the novelist's adolescence in the deep South. Its insights are entirely relevant to today's world.

CHAPTER REVIEW TEST

1. During the Middle Ages the attitude toward children was
   a. that they are in a time of life when their spirit develops.
   b. that children are "miniature adults" and only through harsh discipline can they overcome the natural evils of childhood.
   c. that children were "noble savages."
   d. they should work hard and follow in the footsteps of their parents through vocational training.

2. G. Stanley Hall held that his four periods of development corresponded to the
   a. developmental tasks proposed by Havighurst.
   b. cognitive stages of development.
   c. four stages of development of our species.
   d. four types of identity status.

3. Anna Freud described adolescent defense mechanisms of
   a. asceticism and intellectualization.
   b. intellectualization and denial.
   c. asceticism and denial.
   d. repression and compensation.

4. According to Robert Havighurst, what lies midway between the needs of the individual and the ends of society?
   a. identity confusion
   b. a developmental task
   c. identity crisis
   d. crises and commitment

5. The final developmental task, according to Havighurst is
   a. desiring and achieving socially responsible behavior.
   b. developing intellectual skills necessary for civic competence.
   c. preparing for marriage and family life.
   d. building conscious values in harmony with an adequate scientific world picture.

6. Erik Erikson believed that the main task of the adolescent is to achieve a state of
   a. generativity.
   b. intimacy.
   c. competence.
   d. identity.

7. Repudiation is an essential aspect of achieving
   a. foreclosure.
   b. moratorium.
   c. identity.
   d. a developmental task.

8. According to Erikson, religious initiation ceremonies can
   a. assist adolescents in achieving identity.
   b. force adolescents into a negative identity.
   c. promote identity crises.
   d. lead to a positive identity.

9. The boy who joins a gang because he doubts his masculinity, and wants to prove to his father that he is not a coward, has taken on a
   a. repudiation.
   b. developmental task.
   c. defense mechanism.
   d. negative identity.

10. In Marcia's _____ , a crisis is present and a commitment is absent.
    a. theory of identity formation
    b. explanation of identity confusion
    c. development of negative identity
    d. identity status of moratorium

11. Affection for its members is the only role that still exists for
    a. the peer group.
    b. the social network.
    c. the family.
    d. None of the answers are correct.

12. During the nineteenth century the major functions of the family were
    a. vocational instruction and social stability.
    b. vocational instruction, economic value, and social stability.
    c. economic value and social stability.
    d. vocational instruction and affectional needs.

13. Fathers are more likely to be helpful in _____ , whereas mothers are more likely to be involved in _____ .
    a. skills training; moral development
    b. moral development; skills training
    c. family discussions; conflicts
    d. conflicts, family discussions

14. Most family researchers have agreed that the three styles of parenting are
    a. authoritarian, permissive, and devoted.
    b. permissive, aggressive, and impassive.
    c. authoritarian, authoritative, and permissive.
    d. aggressive, impassive, and devoted.

15. Research indicates that for healthy development many females need to _____ , and males need to _____ .
    a. become emotionally independent from their families; maintain close ties
    b. maintain close ties to their families; become emotionally independent
    c. maintain close ties; become financially independent
    d. None of the answers are correct.

16. Parents who practice a nurturing parenting style are
    a. interested in their child's behavior but seldom prescribe rules, relying instead on modeling and family discussions to instill a well-defined set of values.
    b. controlling but loving in guiding their children through development.
    c. nurturing but providing little structure in the family.
    d. nurturing yet controlling of the way in which the family functions.

Answers

1.b 2.c 3.a 4.b 5.d 6.d 7.c 8.b 9.d 10.d 11.c 12.b 13.c 14.c 15.a 16.a

CHAPTER 12

Physical and Cognitive Development in Adolescence

Gretchen, my friend, got her period. I'm so jealous, God. I hate myself for being so jealous, but I am. I wish you'd help me just a little. Nancy's sure she's going to get it soon, too. And if I'm last, I don't know what I'll do. Oh, please, God. I just want to be normal.

Judy Blume, *Are You There, God? It's Me, Margaret,* 1970

If you want to understand adolescence, you'll surely need to know quite a bit about puberty. In this chapter, we'll explain its biological basis, the sequence of events that make it up, the contrast of changes for males and females, and the effects of timing. We'll also be examining stages of cognitive development, as well as research on egocentrism and critical and creative thinking.

When you have finished studying this chapter, you will be able to

- Identify the important parts of the male and female reproductive systems and explain their functions.

- List the normal sequence of events in puberty for males and females.

- Contrast male and female development in puberty.

- Describe the influence of timing on individual adolescents' emotional reactions to the physical changes of puberty.

- Identify the symptoms associated with anorexia nervosa and bulimia.

- Describe four factors that contribute to the development of eating disorders.

- List and identify Piaget's four main stages of cognitive development.

- Explain the cognitive development that takes place in early and late phases of the formal operations stage.

- Describe the major elements of egocentric thinking: the imaginary audience and the personal fable.

- Identify the differences between critical thinking and creative thinking and discuss the importance of each.

- Show why the use of metaphor is important, especially for creative thinking.

- State your position on whether psychopathology is normal during adolescence and list the types of mental disorders that adolescents suffer.

Puberty
A relatively abrupt and qualitatively different set of physical changes that normally occur at the beginning of the teen years.

Physical Development

To better understand **puberty,** we'll answer the following questions in this section: What parts of our body are involved? When does puberty start? What are the effects of timing?

Early Studies

> ■ The girls are clearly beginning to look like young ladies, while the boys with whom they have thus far played on scarcely equal terms now seem hopelessly stranded in childhood. This year or more of manifest physical superiority of the girl, with its attendant development of womanly attitudes and interests, accounts in part for the tendency of many boys in the early teens to be averse to the society of girls. They accuse them of being soft and foolish, and they suspect the girls' whispering and titterings of being laden with unfavorable comments regarding themselves. (King, 1914, p. 13)

This quaint description of the differences between males and females is typical of many of the adolescent theorists of the early twentieth century (e.g., Boas, 1911; Bourne, 1913; Burnham, 1911; King, 1914). Understandably, these writers had far less data available than we do today, and their opinions were largely subjective. For example, King (1914) suggested that the major cause of **delayed puberty** was "excessive social interests, parties, clubs, etc., with their attendant interference with regular habits of rest and sleep" (p. 25).

Delayed puberty
The stages of pubertal change do not begin until a significant time after the normal onset.

Your Reproductive System

Today more is known about many aspects of puberty, such as how the organs of our reproductive system function together. Just as important, we are learning how to present this knowledge to adolescents effectively.

The Female Sexual System

The parts of the female sexual system are defined here and are illustrated in figure 12.1.

- *Bartholin's glands.* A pair of glands located on either side of the vagina. These glands provide some of the fluid that acts as a lubricant during intercourse.

- *Cervix.* The opening to the uterus located at the inner end of the vagina.

- *Clitoris.* Comparable to the male penis. Both organs are similar in the first few months after conception, becoming differentiated only as sexual

Figure 12.1
The female reproductive system

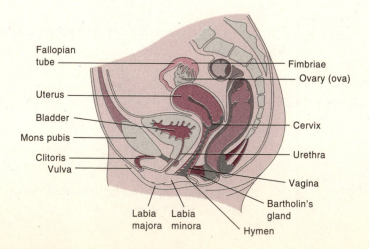

determination takes place. The clitoris is the source of maximum sexual stimulation and becomes erect through sexual excitement. It is above the vaginal opening, between the labia minora.

- *Fallopian tubes.* Conduct the ova (egg) from the ovary to the uterus. A fertilized egg that becomes lodged in the fallopian tubes, called a fallopian or ectopic pregnancy, cannot develop normally and if not surgically removed will cause the tube to rupture.

- *Fimbriae.* Hairlike structures located at the opening of the oviduct that help move the ovum down the fallopian tube to the uterus.

- *Hymen.* A flap of tissue that usually covers most of the vaginal canal in virgins.

- *Labia majora.* The two larger outer lips of the vaginal opening.

- *Labia minora.* The two smaller inner lips of the vaginal opening.

- *Mons pubis* or *mons veneris.* The outer area just above the vagina, which becomes larger during adolescence and on which the first pubic hair appears.

- *Ova.* The female reproductive cells stored in the ovaries. These eggs are fertilized by the male sperm. Girls are born with more than a million follicles, each of which holds an ovum. At puberty, only 10,000 remain, but they are more than sufficient for a woman's reproductive life. Since usually only one egg ripens each month from the midteens to the late forties, a woman releases fewer than 500 ova during her lifetime.

- *Ovaries.* Glands that release one ovum each month. They also produce the hormones estrogen and progesterone, which play an important part in the menstrual cycle and pregnancy.

- *Pituitary gland.* The "master" gland located in the lower part of the brain. It controls sexual maturation and excitement and monthly menstruation.

- *Ureter.* A canal connecting the kidneys with the bladder.

- *Urethra.* A canal leading from the bladder to the external opening through which urine is excreted.

- *Uterus.* The hollow organ (also called the *womb*) in which the fertilized egg must implant itself for a viable pregnancy to occur. The egg attaches itself to the lining of the uterus from which the unborn baby draws nourishment as it matures during the nine months before birth.

- *Vulva.* The external genital organs of the female.

The Male Sexual System

The parts of the male sexual system are defined here and are illustrated in figure 12.2.

- *Cowper's glands.* Located next to the prostate glands. Their job is to secrete a fluid that changes the chemical balance in the urethra from an acidic to an alkaline base. This fluid proceeds up through the urethra in the penis, where it is ejaculated during sexual excitement just before the sperm-laden semen. About a quarter of the time, sperm also may be found in this solution, sometimes called *preseminal fluid.* Therefore, even if the male withdraws his penis before he ejaculates, it is possible for him to deposit some sperm in the vagina, which may cause pregnancy.

- *Epididymis.* A small organ attached to each testis. It is a storage place for newly produced sperm.

Figure 12.2
The male reproductive system

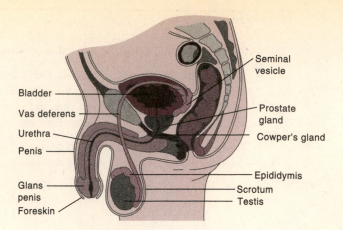

- *Foreskin*. A flap of loose skin that surrounds the glans penis at birth, often removed by a surgery called circumcision.

- *Glans penis*. The tip or head of the penis.

- *Pituitary gland*. The "master" gland controlling sexual characteristics. In the male it controls the production of sperm, the release of testosterone (and thus the appearance of secondary sexual characteristics such as the growth of hair and voice change), and sexual excitement and maturation.

- *Prostate glands*. Produce a milky alkaline substance known as semen. In the prostate the sperm are mixed with the semen to give them greater mobility.

- *Scrotum*. The sac of skin located just below the penis, in which the testes and epididymis are located.

- *Testes*. The two oval sex glands, suspended in the scrotum, that produce sperm. Sperm are the gene cells that fertilize the ova. They are equipped with a tail-like structure that enables them to move about by a swimming motion. After being ejaculated from the penis into the vagina, sperm attempt to swim through the cervix into the uterus and into the fallopian tubes, where fertilization takes place. If one penetrates an egg, conception occurs. Although the testes regularly produce millions of sperm, the odds against any particular sperm penetrating an egg are enormous. The testes also produce testosterone, the male hormone that affects other aspects of sexual development.

- *Ureter*. A canal connecting each of the kidneys with the bladder.

- *Urethra*. A canal that connects the bladder with the opening of the penis. It is also the path taken by the preseminal fluid and sperm during ejaculation.

- *Vas deferens*. A pair of tubes that lead from the epididymis up to the prostate. They carry the sperm when the male is sexually aroused and about to ejaculate.

When Does Puberty Start?

Is the beginning of adolescence marked by any one physiological event? The sequence of bodily changes in puberty is surprisingly constant. This holds true whether puberty starts early or late and regardless of the culture in which the child is reared. Table 12.1 lists the sequences of physiological change.

Table 12.1	**The Sequence of Physiological Change in Males and Females**

Females

- Change in *hormonal balance*
- The beginning of rapid *skeletal growth*
- The beginning of breast development
- The appearance of straight, pigmented pubic hair
- The appearance of kinky, pigmented pubic hair
- *Menarche* (first menstruation)
- *Maximum growth spurt* (when growth is at its fastest rate)
- The appearance of hair on the forearms and underarms

Males

- Change in hormonal balance
- The beginning of skeletal growth
- The enlargement of the genitals
- The appearance of straight pigmented pubic hair
- Early voice changes (voice "cracks")
- First ejaculations (wet dreams, nocturnal emissions)
- The appearance of kinky, pigmented pubic hair
- Maximum growth spurt
- The appearance of downy facial hair
- The appearance of hair on the chest and underarms
- Late voice change (the voice deepens)
- Coarse, pigmented facial hair

Note: For more on these physiological changes, see Muuss (1982).

Hormonal balance

One of the triggering mechanisms of puberty that may be used to indicate the onset of adolescence.

Skeletal growth

The development of the bone structure in the body.

Menarche

Onset of menstruation.

Which of these physical events in the life of the adolescent might we choose as the actual beginning of puberty? Change in **hormonal balance** is first, but its beginning is difficult to pinpoint. **Skeletal growth,** genital growth, pubic hair, breast development, voice change, growth spurt—all are inconvenient to measure. **Menarche** has been suggested as the major turning point for girls, but many women do not recall menarche as a particularly significant event. Sometimes the first ejaculation is suggested as the beginning of adolescent puberty for males, but this too is often a little-remembered (and possibly repressed) event.

Despite the fact that puberty is primarily thought of as a physical change in an adolescent, the psychological impact can be significant. This is especially true with menstruation. Even in these "enlightened" times, too many girls experience menarche without being properly prepared. As a result, an event in a young girl's life that should be remembered as the exciting, positive beginning of the transition to adulthood is instead viewed as a negative, sometimes frightening, experience. Research suggests that better preparation for first menstruation results in more positive attitudes about it (Koff & others, 1980). The same is probably also the case for a male's first ejaculation.

Given our understanding of the physiology of adolescents and differences in individual psychology and culture, we would have to conclude that no single event but, rather, a complex set of events marks the onset of puberty, a process whose effects may be sudden or gradual.

Figure 12.3
Comparison of male and female growth (King, 1914)

Normal range of development
The stages of pubertal change occur at times that are within the normal range of occurrence.

Maximum growth spurt
The period of adolescence when physical growth is at its fastest.

Maturation
The process of physical and mental development due to physiology.

Throughout the years, puberty has been regarded as one of the more difficult times in a person's life. Do you agree or disagree that this is such a serious problem?

The Effects of Timing on Puberty

In a general sense, the onset of puberty affects all adolescents in the same way. However, the age at which these changes begin has some very specific effects on the adolescent's life. (The photograph in figure 12.3, taken in 1912, illustrates how 14-year-old adolescents can differ greatly in their stage of physiological development—and did so even many years ago!)

In this section, eight adolescents (four females and four males) are compared to illustrate the differences that often occur among children even though they are all in the **normal range of development.** Each adolescent is 14 years old. The first female and male are early maturers, the second are average maturers, and the third are late maturers. They all fall within the typical range of all adolescents. The fourth female and male represent average adolescents of one hundred years ago.

The Early-Maturing Female: Ann

At 5 feet, 5 inches and 130 pounds, Ann is considerably bigger than her age-mates. Her growth accelerated when she was 8 years old, and by the time she was 10 1/2, her **maximum growth spurt** crested. She is still growing taller but at a slower rate. Her motor development (coordination and strength) had its greatest rate of increase two years ago. She is stronger than her age-mates, but her strength and coordination have reached their maximum.

She started menstruating three years ago, at age 11, and her breasts are already in the secondary (adult) stage. Her pubic and underarm hair are also at an adult stage.

Ann is confused about the way her body looks. She feels conspicuous and vulnerable because she stands out in a crowd of her friends. Her greater interest in boys, and their response, often causes conflicts with other girls. They envy the interest the boys show in Ann's more mature figure. She often has negative feelings about herself because she is "different."

Other girls tend to avoid her now because her early **maturation** makes her seem older than they are. In later adolescence, she may experience some difficulties; she may find herself in situations (such as with drugs, sex, or drinking) she is not yet ready for. We can say that Ann is experiencing difficulties with her early maturity, but she will begin to feel better about herself as her contemporaries catch up with her developmentally.

The Average-Maturing Female: Beth

Although Beth is also 14, she is different in almost every way from Ann. She represents the typical adolescent today in the sense of being average in her measurements and physical change. It is clear that from the standpoint of personality and behavior, no "average" adolescent exists.

Beth is 5 feet, 3 inches tall and weighs 120 pounds. She reached her maximum growth spurt two years ago and is also starting to slow down. She is presently at the peak of her motor development.

Her breasts are at the primary breast stage; she is beginning to need a bra, or thinks she does. She started menstruating two years ago. She has adult pubic hair, and her underarm hair is beginning to appear.

She feels reasonably happy about her body, and most, but not all, of her relationships with her peers are reasonably satisfying. Although she does have some occasional emotional problems, they are not related to her physical development as much as are Ann's.

Girls who reach puberty late are usually unhappy about it, but not as unhappy as boys who are late. Boys who reach physical maturity early are usually quite happy about it—more happy than girls who are early.

The Late-Maturing Female: Cathy

Cathy is at the lower end of the normal range of physical development for a 14-year-old girl. She is only 4 feet, 8 inches tall, weighs 100 pounds, and is just beginning her growth spurt. She is not too happy about this; she feels that the other girls have advantages in relationships with boys.

Cathy's breasts are at the bud stage; her nipples and encircling areolae are beginning to protrude, but she is otherwise flat-chested. She has just begun menstruation. Pubic hair growth has started, but as yet no hair has appeared under her arms.

Other girls tend to feel sorry for her, but they also look down on her. She is more dependent and childlike than the others. She feels a growing dislike for her body, and she is becoming more and more introverted and self-rejecting because of it. At this stage her immaturity is not a great disability; at least she is more mature than some of the boys her age. As she reaches later adolescence, her underdeveloped figure may be a more serious source of unhappiness for her if she accepts conventional standards of sexual desirability.

 ## A MULTICULTURAL VIEW

Culture and the Imaginary Audience

" 'Chin, chong, chin, chong, ah so! Yellow-face, can you see out of those eyes?!' Every day for nearly one year, I heard those words as I rode the bus to middle school. I was 11 years old in the seventh grade." This story was related by a young Korean girl. At that time she believed that she must have done something to deserve such anger. She experienced immense humiliation and pain. She wanted to be like the other children. "With the onset of puberty, my body began to change, and I did not want to change into something even more different from the other girls." Since she could not change her slanty eyes or her skin color, she decided she must learn to speak perfect English.

When she was 14, however, she rejected the ways of her white classmates, staying home on the weekends with her mother, who only spoke Korean. She made an effort to improve her Korean, rather than to hide and resent her accent.

When she was 11, this young woman worked hard on her English to please an imaginary audience—all those peers whom she imagined were watching her every move. By the time she was 14, their opinion became much less important to her, and she began to feel pride in her ethnic identity.

Phinney (1993) has found that ethnic identity development has stages that parallel those of Marcia's ego statuses in adolescents: a combined foreclosure-diffusion stage in which teenagers had not explored their ethnic identity yet; ethnic identity search/moratorium; and ethnic identity achievement (see chapter 11). This study found that the greater a teen's ethnic identity achievement, the higher was her or his self-esteem. In an interesting series of studies, Rotheram-Borus (1993) found that in an integrated school, *biculturalism* (identification with American culture and with the ethnic background of their parents) was common (44–45%). In a school with high cross-ethnic tension, however, most students (over 70%) were most strongly committed to the ethnic identity of their parents. Ethnicity, then, seems to become a more powerful conditioner of one's identity if one experiences strong ethnic tension in one's surroundings.

The Average Adolescent Female of 100 Years Ago: Dorothy

Although records of adolescent physical development of 100 years ago are less than adequate, we can be fairly certain about some of the data. Dorothy, who was typical for her time, was physically much like Cathy is now. At 4 feet, 7 inches, she was one inch shorter, and at 85 pounds, she weighed 15 pounds less than Cathy.

At age 14, Dorothy would still have had four years to go before her peak of motor development, and she would not have started to menstruate for another year. In all the other physical ways, she looked a great deal like Cathy. The major difference between the two girls is that while Cathy is unhappy about her body's appearance, Dorothy, who was typical, felt reasonably good about hers.

The Early-Maturing Male: Al

Al finds that at 5 feet, 8 inches tall, he towers over his 14-year-old friends. He reached his maximum growth spurt approximately two years ago and weighs 150 pounds. He is now about two years before the peak of his motor development. His coordination and strength are rapidly increasing, but contrary to the popular myth he is not growing clumsier.

As adolescents reach their peak of motor development, they usually handle their bodies better, although adults expect them to have numerous accidents. It is true that when one's arms grow an inch longer in less than a year, one's hand-eye coordination suffers somewhat. However, the idea of the gangling, inept adolescent is more myth than fact.

Al's sexual development is also well ahead of that of his age-mates. He already has adult pubic hair, and hair has started to grow on his chest and underarms. He began having nocturnal emissions almost two years ago, and since then the size of his genitals has increased almost 100 percent.

Because our society tends to judge male maturity on the basis of physique and stature, Al's larger size has advantages for him. He is pleased with his looks, although once in a while he is bothered when someone treats him as though he were 17 or 18 years old. Nevertheless, he uses the advantages of his early maturity whenever possible.

His friends tend to look up to him and to consider him a leader. Because size and coordination often lead to athletic superiority, and because success in school sports has long meant popularity, he has the most positive self-concept of all the adolescents described here, including the females. He has a good psychological adjustment, although he is sometimes vain, and is the most confident and responsible of this group. He engages in more social activities than the others, which also occasionally gets him into trouble, because he is not psychologically ready for some of the social activities in which he is permitted to participate.

The Average-Maturing Male: Bob

Interestingly, Bob is exactly the same height as his "average" female counterpart, Beth, at 5 feet, 3 inches tall. At 130 pounds, he outweighs her by 10 pounds. He is currently in the midst of his maximum growth spurt and is four years away from reaching the peak of his coordination and strength.

His sexual development began about a year ago with the start of nocturnal emissions, and he is just now starting to grow pubic hair. As yet he has no hair on his chest or under his arms. However, his genitals have reached 80 percent of their adult size.

Bob gets along well with his age-mates. He is reasonably happy with the way his body has developed so far, although there are some activities that he wishes he could excel in. Most of the attributes that he aspires to are already possessed by Al, whom he envies. This causes few problems, since Bob still has every reason to hope his body will develop into his ideal physical image.

The Late-Maturing Male: Chuck

Chuck is also similar in stature to his counterpart, Cathy. They are both 4 feet, 8 inches tall, although at 90 pounds, Chuck is 10 pounds lighter than Cathy. He is a year and a half away from his maximum growth spurt and must wait six years before his motor development will peak.

Chuck's sexual development is also lagging behind those of the other two boys. His genitals are 50 percent larger than they were two years ago, but as yet he has no pubic, chest, or underarm hair. He has not yet experienced nocturnal emissions, although these are about to begin.

Of the adolescents described here, Chuck is the least happy with his body. His voice has not yet changed, he is not as strong and coordinated as the other boys, and he is much smaller than they are. They tend to treat him as a scapegoat and often ridicule him. He chooses to interact with boys who are younger than himself and is attracted to activities in which mental rather than physical prowess is important, such as chess and band. He avoids girls, almost all of whom are more physically mature than he. This lack of heterosexual experience may later affect his self-concept.

Chuck lacks confidence in himself and tends to depend on others. He was of almost average size in grammar school and now feels he has lost prestige. He frequently does things to gain the attention of others, but these actions seldom bring him the acclaim he craves. Probably as a result, he is more irritable and restless than the others and engages in more types of compensating behaviors.

AN APPLIED VIEW

Dealing with Early or Late Development

Petersen & others (1988) found an increased risk of sexual abuse for the early-maturing female. Significantly early or late development has been linked to depression and eating disorders in both boys and girls (Rierdan & others, 1988), so it is important for practitioners working with adolescents to be aware of negative reactions to their physical change (or lack of it). If you know a teen who is significantly early or late in body development, be on the lookout for psychological problems. If you find evidence of such problems, make arrangements for the youth to have access to appropriate professional attention.

On the other hand, you should understand that "normal" covers a wide band of developmental time. We should help teens who "hate" their bodies because they are not perfectly average to be more accepting. Finally, if you do feel there is a problem, say nothing to the teen until you have an experienced person's advice on the best course of action.

The Average Adolescent Male of 100 Years Ago: Dan

At 4 feet, 7 inches, Dan was shorter than Chuck by 1 inch and weighed the same, 90 pounds. He trailed Chuck in sexual development by two years, and, at age 14, his genitals had increased only 20 percent in size.

However, the major difference between Chuck and Dan lies in self-satisfaction. Whereas Chuck is extremely unhappy about the way he is developing, Dan was as happy as Bob is now, because he was quite average for that time. Although we cannot know what his relationship with peers was like or how he viewed himself, we can guess that these were quite similar to Bob's.

The preceding descriptions illustrate the great variability in adolescent growth and in adolescent responses to growth. Keep in mind, however, that self-image and peer relationships are not entirely determined by physique. "Average-sized" adolescents do not always lead a charmed life, and many late and early maturers are quite comfortable with themselves. Adolescents who have clarified their values and set their own standards are not likely to be overly affected by pubertal changes or the peer approval or disapproval brought about by them.

Figure 12.4

Normal age ranges of puberty

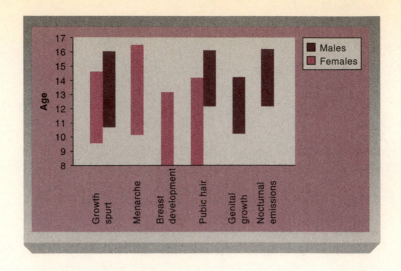

The Secular Trend

The small size of Dorothy and Dan, who were average teenagers 100 years ago, is
part of the phenomenon called the **secular trend.** The secular trend refers to the
decreasing age of the onset of puberty, including a significant drop in the average
age at which females in a particular country reach menarche. In Western countries,
the average age of menarche has declined about three months per decade over the
past hundred years. In the United States, 17 was the average age in the late eighteenth and early nineteenth centuries (Vaughan & Litt, 1990).

Today the average age of onset is 12.5 years. Most researchers feel that
improved nutrition, sanitation, and health care are responsible for the trend, and
that we are now at a period of leveling off (Brooks-Gunn & others, 1985). We think
nutrition is involved because girls must typically achieve a certain proportion of
body fat before they can menstruate (Frisch, 1988). Studies of female athletes and
dancers have shown that a lack of fat can delay menarche or can stop menstruation after it has begun (Brooks-Gunn, 1987).

Will the secular trend continue in future years? No, the trend likely is a special
case that pertains only to the period from the 1700s to today and is the result of
improvements in nutrition, medicine, and health care in general.

Figure 12.4 details the age ranges considered normal for development.
Adolescents who experience these changes earlier or later may have no medical
problem, but consulting a doctor is probably a good idea. If a glandular imbalance
exists, the doctor can usually remedy the problem with little difficulty.

In summary, we may say that the vast majority of human bodies proceed
toward maturity in the same way, but that in the last few centuries the timing of
the process in females has changed radically. Although timing is affected mainly
by biology, psychological and social forces clearly influence it, too. Another
aspect of physical development that psychological and social forces affect is the
eating disorder.

Eating Disorders

Although still rather rare, eating disorders are so serious (about one-third of those
who develop an eating disorder die) it is necessary to review what we know about
them here. There are two main types, known as anorexia and bulimia nervosa.

Anorexia Nervosa

Anorexia nervosa is a syndrome of self-starvation that mainly affects adolescent
and young adult females, who account for 95 percent of the known cases.
Professionals suspect that many males may also be victims (e.g., those who must

Anorexia nervosa has become an increasingly frequent problem among adolescent females.

maintain a low weight for sports), but their illness is covered up (Larson & Johnson, 1981; Mintz & Betz, 1988). Anorexia is characterized by an "intense fear of becoming obese, disturbance of body image, significant weight loss, refusal to maintain a minimal normal body weight, and amenorrhea [suppressed menstruation]. The disturbance cannot be accounted for by a known physical disorder" (American Psychiatric Association, 1985).

Health professionals have seen an alarming rise in the incidence of this disorder among young women in the last 15 to 20 years (Anderson & others, 1992; Malowald, 1992; Rosen & others, 1987). Whether anorexia nervosa has actually increased or whether it is now being more readily recognized has yet to be determined.

The specific criteria for anorexia nervosa are the following:

- Onset prior to age 25

- Weight loss of at least 25 percent of original body weight

- Distorted, implacable attitudes toward eating, food, or weight that override hunger, admonitions, reassurance, and threats, including
  - Denial of illness, with a failure to recognize nutritional needs
  - Apparent enjoyment in losing weight, with overt manifestations that food refusal is a pleasurable indulgence
  - A desired body image of extreme thinness, with evidence that it is rewarding to the person to achieve and maintain this state
  - Unusual hoarding and handling of food

- No known medical illness that could account for the anorexia and weight loss

- No other known psychiatric disorder, particularly primary affective disorders, schizophrenia, or obsessive, compulsive, or phobic (fearful) neuroses. (Even though it may appear phobic and obsessional, food refusal alone is not sufficient to qualify as an obsessive, compulsive, or phobic disorder.)

- At least two of the following manifestations: amenorrhea (loss of menses); lanugo (soft downy hair covering body); bradycardia (heart rate of less than 60); periods of overactivity; vomiting (may be self-induced).

Bulimia Nervosa

Bulimia nervosa is a disorder related to anorexia nervosa and sometimes combined with it. It is characterized by

> ... episodic binge-eating accompanied by an awareness that the eating pattern is abnormal, fear of not being able to stop eating voluntarily, and depressed mood and self-deprecating thoughts following the eating binges. The bulimic episodes are not due to anorexia nervosa or any known physical disorder. (American Psychiatric Association, 1985)

Bulimia has been observed in women above or below weight, as well as in those who are normal (Lowenkopf, 1982). The specific criteria of bulimia are the following:

- Repeated episodes of binge-eating

- Awareness that one's eating pattern is abnormal

- Fear of not being able to stop eating

- Depressed mood and self-deprecation after binges

Bulimia nervosa

This disorder is characterized by "episodic binge-eating accompanied by an awareness that the eating pattern is abnormal, fear of not being able to stop eating voluntarily, and depressed mood and self-deprecating thoughts following the eating binges."

In what ways, if any, do you think the media has contributed to the spread of anorexia nervosa and bulimia in recent years?

Anorectics and bulimics share emotional and behavioral traits, despite their clinical differences. The most characteristic symptoms specific to these disorders are the preoccupation with food and the persistent determination to be slim, rather than the behaviors that result from that choice (Bruch, 1981).

A number of new approaches to treatment and therapy are currently being researched (Scott, 1988). Although success rates are not high, the situation in either disorder is usually so complex and potentially hazardous that only qualified personnel should attempt to treat victims.

🌳 Guided Review 🌳

1. Puberty is a relatively abrupt and qualitatively different set of physical changes in boys and girls that usually occurs at the beginning of the _____ years.

2. Although there is a rather wide normal range of development as relates to the onset of puberty, early- or late-maturing children can be affected socially and
_____ .

3. _____-maturing boys are often peer group leaders.

4. One hundred years ago the average-maturing girl was physically much like the late-maturing girl today. This phenomenon is called the _____
_____ .

5. _____ _____ is a syndrome of self-starvation characterized, in part, by an intense fear of becoming obese, disturbance of body image, and significant weight loss.

Cognitive Development

■ I was about twelve when I discovered that you could create a whole new world just in your head! I don't know why I hadn't thought about it before, but the idea excited me terrifically. I started lying in bed on Saturday mornings till 11 or 12 o'clock, making up "my secret world." I went to fabulous places. I met friends who really liked me and treated me great. And of course I fell in love with this guy like you wouldn't believe! (Susan Klein, an eighth-grade student)

Adolescence is a complex process of growth and change. Because biological and social changes are the focus of attention, changes in the young adolescent's ability to think often go unnoticed. Yet it is during early and middle adolescence that thinking ability reaches Piaget's fourth and last level—the level of abstract thought (see chapter 2). To understand how abstract thought develops, we have to know more about cognition itself.

Variables in Cognitive Development: Piaget

Let us pause to review Jean Piaget's theory (described in chapter 2). He argued that the ability to think develops in four stages:

- The *sensorimotor stage (birth to 2 years),* in which the child learns from its interactions with the world.

- The *preoperational stage (2 to 7 years),* in which behaviors such as picking up a can are gradually internalized so that they can be manipulated in the mind.

Answers

1. teen 2. psychologically 3. Early 4. secular trend 5. Anorexia nervosa

The ability to understand that the rules of games can be fairly changed is an aspect of the formal operation stage. Even though these young men are unlikely to change the rules of their chess game, they are now at the intellectual level at which they recognize this is a possibility.

- The *concrete operational stage (7 to 11 years),* in which actions can be manipulated mentally, but only with things. For example, a child of 8 is able to anticipate what is going to happen if a can is thrown across the room without actually having to do so.

- The *formal operational stage (11 years +),* in which groups of concrete operations are combined to become formal operations. For example, the adolescent comes to understand democracy by combining concepts such as putting a ballot in a box and hearing that the Senate voted to give money for the homeless. This is the stage of abstract thought development.

We are like other animals, especially the primates, in many ways. They, too, can make plans, can cooperate in groups, and may well have simple language systems. But the ability to perform formal operations is what truly separates us (although we cannot say that all humans reach this stage, either). Piaget's conception of the formal operation is a remarkable contribution to psychology.

It was also Piaget who first noted the strong tendency of early adolescents toward democratic values because of this new thinking capacity. This is the age at which youths first become committed to the idea that participants in a group may change the rules of a game, but once agreed on, all must follow the new rules. This tendency, he believes, is universal; all teenagers throughout the world develop this value.

Having considered Piaget's ideas about adolescent cognition in some detail earlier in this book, let us turn now to a review of the findings of those researchers who have been diligently following him.

Culture and gender can also influence cognitive development. Piaget's theory seems to assume that the ideal person at the end point of cognitive development resembles a Swiss scientist. Most theorists focus on an ideal end point for development that, not too surprisingly, ascribes their own valued qualities to maturity.

Piaget (1973) acknowledged that his description of the end point might not apply to all cultures, since evidence had showed cultural variation. If one stresses the influence of context (sociocultural and individual) on development as Vygotsky (1978) and Barbara Rogoff (1990) do, then one sees multiple directions for development rather than only one ideal end point. For example, it may well be that for some agricultural societies, sophisticated development of the concrete operational stage would be far more useful than minimal formal operational thinking. That is, an understanding of the complicated workings of a machine may be concrete, but that does not make that type of thinking inferior to another person's ability to do formal operations. Thus believing that the formal operations stage is always superior would be intellectual snobbism.

Gender also plays a role in the definition of formal operations. Gilligan (1982) said that most theories of development define the end point of development as being male only, and that they overlook alternatives that more closely fit the mature female. She believed that if the definition of maturity changes, so does the entire account of development. Using men as the model of development, independence and separation are seen as the goals of development. But if women are used as the models, relationship with others or interdependence are the goals of development.

A MULTICULTURAL VIEW

Personality Factors, Achievement, and Ethnicity

It is often assumed that economic disadvantages and poor academic achievement have led people of color in the United States to have low expectations for the future and negative self-concepts. A number of recent studies have examined the relationships among several personality factors and achievement as they are related within several ethnic groups. For example, Graham (1994) learned that although motivational factors are believed to be as important as intellectual competencies in understanding achievement in all people, this is especially so among African Americans. Graham's research reviewed 140 studies on motivation in African Americans covering strength of achievement motive, locus of control, causal attributions, levels of expectancy, and self-concept.

Graham concludes from this research that African Americans do not lack the motive to strive for success. Even in studies where African Americans appeared to be lower in achievement motive (and no studies after 1970 showed differences favoring whites over African Americans), African Americans reported educational and vocational aspirations equal to or higher than their white counterparts. They were just as likely as whites to aspire to go to college and/or enter high status professions. For all subjects, motive scores increased with higher social status. When socioeconomic class (SES) was controlled, differences between African Americans and whites diminished or reversed. In other words, high SES African American boys had higher achievement motive scores than did boys in a number of low SES white groups.

Other studies found equally low motive scores for African Americans and whites in the lowest SES groups.

People with internal locus of control (those who see themselves as the main cause of what happens to them) are considered less susceptible to social influence, better information seekers, more achievement-oriented, and better psychologically adjusted. Graham's review found less internality among African Americans. However, studies examining the relationship between locus of control and other achievement-related variables did not support the argument that this lack of internality is a problem for African Americans. In fact, there appear to be positive consequences of this perception, such as increased social activism and militance.

African Americans and whites were equal in displaying an adaptive pattern by attributing success to one's ability and effort, and failure to one's lack of effort. Data also show African American subjects remained optimistic about the future even after achievement failure. Research on general self-concept in African Americans does not support the view that they have negative self views; they have consistently been shown to be equal to or higher than whites on a variety of self-concept measures.

Graham's overview of past research is generally supported by Taylor and associates (1994), who studied a sample of African Americans, by Lease and Robbins (1994), whose research was on Southeast Asian adolescent refugees, and by Yan and Gaier (1994), who studied Chinese, Japanese, Korean, and Southeast Asian college students.

How do sociocultural influences impact adolescent cognitive development? How do these influences differ for girls and boys?

Adolescent egocentrism
The reversion to the self-centered thinking patterns of childhood that sometimes occurs in the teen years.

Imaginary audience
Adolescents' perception that the world is constantly scrutinizing their behavior and physical appearance.

Adolescent Egocentrism

Parents often feel frustrated at the seemingly irrational attitudes and behaviors of their adolescent children. One explanation is the reemergence of a pattern of thought that marked early childhood, egocentrism. **Adolescent egocentrism,** a term coined by Elkind (1978), refers to adolescents' tendency to exaggerate the importance, uniqueness, and severity of social and emotional experiences. Their love is greater than anything their parents have experienced. Their suffering is more painful and unjust than anyone else's. Their friendships are most sacred. Their clothes are the worst or the best. Developmentally speaking, adolescent egocentrism seems to peak around the age of 13 (Elkind & Bowen, 1979), followed by a gradual and sometimes painful decline.

Elkind sees two components to this egocentrism. First, teenagers tend to create an **imaginary audience.** They feel they are on center stage, and the rest of the world is constantly scrutinizing their behavior and physical appearance. This

Divergent thinking is an important aspect of critical thinking as well as creative problem solving.

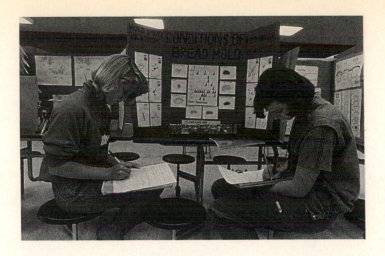

accounts for some of the apparently irrational mood swings in adolescence. The mirror may produce an elated, confident teenager ready to make an appearance. Then one pimple on the nose can be cause for staying inside the house for days. In fact, school phobia can become acute during early adolescence because of concerns over appearance.

Personal fable

Adolescents' tendency to think of themselves in heroic or mythical terms.

The second component of egocentrism is the **personal fable.** This refers to adolescents' tendency to think of themselves in heroic or mythical terms. The result is that they exaggerate their own abilities and their invincibility. This type of mythic creation on the part of an adolescent can sometimes lead to increased risk-taking, such as drug use, dangerous driving, and disregard for the possible consequences of sexual behavior. Many teenagers simply can't imagine an unhappy ending to their own special story.

Critical Thinking

Although we discussed critical thinking at some length in chapter 9, we should make a number of points about its role in adolescence. Guilford's (1975) distinction between convergent and divergent thinking is helpful here, because critical thinking is made up of these two abilities.

Convergent thinking

Thinking used to find one correct answer.

Convergent thinking is used when we solve a problem by following a series of steps that close in on the correct answer. For example, if we were to ask you to answer the question, "How much is 286 times 469?" you probably could not produce it immediately. However, if you used a pencil and paper or a calculator, you would almost certainly converge on the same answer as most others trying to solve the problem. Only one answer is correct. Critical thinking uses convergent thinking. As Moore and Parker (1986) state, it is "the correct evaluation of claims and arguments."

Divergent thinking

Thinking used when a problem to be solved has many possible answers.

Divergent thinking, on the other hand, is just the opposite. This is the type of thinking used when the problem to be solved has many possible answers. For example, what are all the things that would be different if it were to rain up instead of down?

Other divergent questions are "What would happen if we had no thumbs?" and "What should we do to prevent ice buildup from snapping telephone lines?" Divergent thinking can be right or wrong, too, but considerably greater leeway exists for personal opinion than with convergent thinking. Not all divergent thinking is creative, but it is more likely to produce a creative concept. To be a good critical thinker, analyzing statements accurately is not enough. Often you will need to think divergently to understand the possibilities and the implications of those statements, too.

Because adolescents are entering the formal operations stage of intellectual development, they become vastly more capable of critical thinking than younger children. As they move through the teen years, they grow in their ability to make effective decisions. This involves five types of newly acquired abilities (Moore & others, 1985):

Phase 1. Recognizing and defining the problem (e.g., a 13-year-old boy notices that girls seem to avoid him, and when he stands near them, they move away)

Phase 2. Gathering information (he asks other boys if they get the same reaction, and several mention that he gets that reaction because he has body odor)

Phase 3. Forming tentative conclusions (he wonders if he should shower more than twice a week and change his clothes more often)

Phase 4. Testing tentative conclusions (he showers and changes clothes daily, and then strikes up conversations with several girls)

Phase 5. Evaluation and decision making (since he no longer experiences avoidance, he decides to continue his cleanliness program)

In the next section, we make a distinction between critical and creative thinking, but it is important that we not make too great a distinction. Paul (1987) describes this concern well:

> ■ Just as it is misleading to talk of developing a student's capacity to think critically without facing the problem of cultivating the student's rational passions—the necessary driving force behind the rational use of all critical thinking skills—so too it is misleading to talk of developing a student's ability to think critically as something separate from the student's ability to think creatively. . . . The imagination and its creative powers are continually called forth. (p. 143)

Creative Thinking

> ■ This is the story about a very curious cat named Kat. One day Kat was wandering in the woods where he came upon a big house made of fish. Without thinking, he ate much of that house. The next morning when he woke up he had grown considerably larger. Even as he walked down the street he was getting bigger. Finally he got bigger than any building ever made. He walked up to the Empire State Building in New York City and accidentally crushed it. The people had to think of a way to stop him, so they made this great iron box which made the cat curious. He finally got inside it, but it was too heavy to get him out of again. There he lived for the rest of his life. But he was still curious until his death, which was 6,820,000 years later. They buried him in the state of Rhode Island, and I mean the whole state. (Ralph Titus, a seventh-grade student)

The restless imagination, the daring exaggeration, the disdain for triteness that this story demonstrates—all are signs that its young author has great creative potential. With the right kind of encouragement, with the considerable knowledge we now have about how to foster creativity, this boy could develop his talents to his own and society's great benefit.

Creative thinking appears to have many elements—divergent thinking, fluency, flexibility, originality, remote associations. We will look more closely at these elements when we get to adult creativity later in this book, but one element that seems to be of special importance in adolescence is the use of metaphor.

The Use of Metaphor

A *metaphor* is a word or phrase that by comparison or analogy stands for another word or phrase. Common sense suggests a relationship between efficient metaphor use and creativity. Using a metaphor in speech involves calling attention to a

What are some ways that a school curriculum can enhance creative thinking at the junior and senior high school levels?

similarity between two seemingly dissimilar things. This suggests a process similar to divergent thinking, and a growing body of research shows support for this relationship (Jaquish & others, 1984; Kogan, 1973, 1983; Wallach & Kogan, 1965).

Kogan (1983) believes that the **use of metaphor** can explain the difference between ordinary divergent thinking and high-quality divergent thinking. A creative person must be able not only to think of many different things from many different categories but also to compare them in unique, qualitatively different ways. Although metaphors are typically first used by older children and adolescents, research has looked at the symbolic play of very young children and how it relates to creativity (see Kogan, 1983, for a good review). The early imaginative play of children is now being viewed as a precursor of later metaphor use and creativity.

Howard Gardner and his associates at Harvard University have studied the role of metaphor. Gardner's seminal *Art, Mind, and Brain: A Cognitive Approach to Creativity* (1982) offers many insights into the process (see also Gardner, 1993a, 1993b). Gardner has based his research on the theories of three eminent theorists: Jean Piaget, Noam Chomsky, and Claude Levi-Strauss. He states that "These thinkers share a belief that the mind operates according to specifiable rules—often unconscious ones—and that these can be ferreted out and made explicit by the systematic examination of human language, action, and problem solving" (p. 4).

Gardner's main efforts have focused on the relationship between children's art and children's understanding of metaphor, both in normal and brain-damaged children. He describes talking to a group of youngsters at a seder (the meal many Jews eat to commemorate the flight of the Hebrews from Egypt). He told the children how, after a plague, Pharaoh's "heart was turned to stone." The children interpreted the metaphor variously, but only the older ones could understand the link between the physical universe (hard rocks) and psychological traits (stubborn lack of feeling). Younger children are more apt to apply magical interpretations (God or a witch did it). Gardner believes that the development of the understanding of metaphoric language is as sequential as the stages that Piaget and Erikson proposed and is closely related to the types of development treated in those theories.

Examining children's metaphors such as a bald man having a "barefoot head" and an elephant being seen as a "gas mask," Gardner and Winner (1982) found clear changes with age in the level of sophistication. Interestingly, two opposing features appear:

- When you ask children to explain figures of speech, they steadily get better at it as they get older. This ability definitely increases as the child attains the formal operations stage.

- However, very young children seem to be the best at making up their own metaphors. Furthermore, their own metaphors tend to be of two types (Gardner & Winner, 1982):

■ **The different patterns of making metaphors may reflect fundamentally different ways of processing information. Children who base their metaphors on visual resemblances may approach experience largely in terms of the physical qualities of objects. On the other hand, children who base their metaphors on action sequences may view the world in terms of the way events unfold over time. We believe that the difference may continue into adulthood, underlying diverse styles in the creation and appreciation of artistic form. (p. 164)**

It is exciting to think that this discovery by Gardner and Winner may explain why some people become scientists and others writers. If this is so, it certainly is an important key to fostering such talent. Of course, this is not to say that they have the answers to such questions as why children develop one of the two forms of "metaphorizing" (or neither), but their work appears to be a giant step in the right direction.

Use of metaphor
The ability to think of a word or phrase that by comparison or analogy can be used to stand for another word or phrase.

Studying the stories of the Bible is an excellent way to learn about metaphors.

These researchers believe that the spontaneous production of metaphors declines somewhat during the school years. This is probably because the child, having mastered a basic vocabulary, has less need to "stretch the resources of language to express new meanings" (Gardner & Winner, 1982, p. 165). In addition, teachers and parents exert greater pressure on children to get the right answers, so they take fewer risks in their language. Gardner and Winner point to the *Shakespeare Parallel Text Series,* which offers a translation of the bard's plays into everyday English ("Stand and unfold yourself" becomes "Stand still and tell me who you are"), as a step in the wrong direction. "If, as we have shown, students of this age have the potential to deal with complex metaphors, there is no necessity to rewrite Shakespeare" (p. 167).

Creativity, Giftedness, and the IQ

As Feldman (1979) has pointed out, many studies of "giftedness" have been conducted, but only a few of exceptionally creative, highly productive youth have been undertaken. This is a serious omission because, as you will see later in this book, adolescence is a sensitive period in the growth of creative ability. Feldman believes that this unfortunate situation is mainly the fault of "the foremost figure in the study of the gifted," Lewis M. Terman. Terman (1925) was well known for his research on 1,000 California children whose IQs in the early 1920s were 135 or higher. Terman believed these children to be the "geniuses" of the future, a label he kept for them as he studied their development over the decades. His was a powerful investigation and has been followed by scholars and popular writers alike.

Precisely because of the notoriety of this research, Feldman argues, we have come to accept a numerical definition of genius (an IQ above 135), and a somewhat low one at that. Feldman notes that the *Encyclopedia Britannica* now differentiates two basic definitions of genius: the numerical one fostered by Terman; and the concept first described by Sir Francis Galton (1870, 1879): "creative ability of an exceptionally high order as demonstrated by actual achievement."

Precociousness

The ability to do what others are able to do, but at a younger age.

Prodigiousness

The ability to do *qualitatively* better than the rest of us are able to do; such a person is referred to as a prodigy.

Feldman (1979) says that *genius,* as defined by IQ, really only refers to **precociousness**—doing what others are able to do, but at a younger age. **Prodigiousness** (as in child prodigy), on the other hand, refers to someone who is qualitatively higher in ability from the rest of us. This is different from simply being able to do things sooner. Further, prodigiousness calls for a rare matching of high talent and an environment that is ready and open to creativity. If such youthful prodigies as Mozart in music or Bobby Fischer in chess had been born 2,000 years earlier, they may well have grown up to be much more ordinary. In fact, if Einstein had been born 50 years earlier, he might have done nothing special—particularly since he did not even speak well until he was five!

Child prodigies are distinguished by the passion with which they pursue their interests. Here we see the young Wolfgang Amadeus Mozart performing for a group of admiring adults. He was not merely precocious—able to perform at levels typical of older children; he was prodigious—able, at a young age, to write music that professional musicians still perform.

So if prodigies are more than just quicker at learning, what is it that truly distinguishes them? On the basis of his intensive study of three prodigies, Feldman states that

■ Perhaps the most striking quality in the children in our study as well as other cases is the passion with which excellence is pursued. Commitment and tenacity and joy in achievement are perhaps the best signs that a coincidence has occurred among child, field, and moment in evolutionary time. No event is more likely to predict that a truly remarkable, creative contribution will eventually occur. (1979, p. 351)

What types of special programs should schools provide for gifted and creative students? Should these students be mainstreamed with other students?

In summary, critical and creative thinking are similar in that they both employ convergent and divergent production. The main difference between them is that critical thinking aims at the correct assessment of existing ideas, whereas creativity is more aimed at the invention and discovery of new ideas. Although each requires a certain amount of intelligence, creativity also depends on such traits as metaphorical thinking and an independent personality.

AN APPLIED VIEW

Guidelines for Improving Your Own Creativity

Here are some suggestions (Dacey, 1989a) that should help you become a more creative problem solver yourself and that you could teach to adolescents you work with:

- Avoid the "filtering out" process that blocks problems from awareness. Become more sensitive to problems by looking for them.
- Never accept the first solution you think of. Generate a number of possible solutions; then select the best from among them.
- Beware of your own defensiveness concerning the problem. When you feel threatened by a problem, you are less likely to think of creative solutions to it.
- Get feedback on your solutions from others who are less personally involved.
- Try to think of what solutions someone else might think of for your problem.
- Mentally test out opposites to your solutions. When a group of engineers tried to think of ways to dispose of smashed auto glass, someone suggested trying to find uses for it instead. Fiberglass was the result!
- Give your ideas a chance to incubate. Successful problem solvers report that they frequently put a

problem away for a while, and later on the solution comes to them full blown. It is clear that they have been thinking about the problem on a subconscious level, which is often superior to a conscious, logical approach.
- Diagram your thinking. Sometimes ideas seem to fork, like the branches on a tree, with one idea producing two more, each of which produces two more, and so on. Diagramming will let you follow each possible branch to its completion.
- Be self-confident. Many ideas die because the person who conceived them thought they might be silly. Studies show that females have been especially vulnerable here.
- Think about the general aspects of a problem before getting to its specifics.
- Restate the problem several different ways.
- Become an "idea jotter." A notebook of ideas can prove surprisingly useful.
- Divide a problem, then solve its various parts.
- Really good ideas frequently require some personal risk on the part of the problem solver. In this we are like the turtle, which can never move forward until it sticks its neck out.

Robert Sternberg (1990) said the intelligent person can recall, analyze, and use knowledge, whereas the creative person goes beyond existing knowledge and the wise person probes inside knowledge and understands the meaning of what is known (see chapter 18). It should be noted that these conclusions appear to hold true not only for adolescence, but for all periods of the lifespan.

Mental Health Issues

A number of psychologists and psychoanalysts (most notably Freud) have suggested that having distressing, turbulent, unpredictable thoughts that in an adult would be considered pathological is normal in adolescence. Here is an example of this view:

> ■ The fluidity of the adolescent's self-image, his changing aims and aspirations, sex drives, unstable powers of repression, and his struggle to adapt his childhood standards of right and wrong to the needs of maturity, bring into focus every conflict, past and present, that he has failed to solve. Protective covering of the personality is stripped off, and the deeper emotional currents are laid bare. (Ackerman, 1958, pp. 227–28)

This disruptive state is partly characteristic of the identity stages of confusion and moratorium. Identity confusion is sometimes typified by withdrawal from reality (Erikson, 1958, 1968). Occasional distortions in time perspective can occur. Mental disturbance also often makes intimacy with another person impossible. These characteristics are also seen in the moratorium stage, but they tend to be of much shorter duration.

How common and how serious are these problems? The picture is not clear. Summarizing decades of research, Kimmel and Weiner (1985) concluded that true psychopathology (mental illness) is relatively rare during adolescence. It is impossible to determine the frequency of mental illness, however, because of current disagreements over its definition. Weiner (1970) summarized numerous studies, which give us considerable reason to believe that "adolescent turmoil," though common, does not really constitute psychopathology.

Studies do indicate that when adolescents become seriously disturbed and do not receive appropriate treatment quickly, the chances of their "growing out" of their problems are dim (Walker & Greene, 1987; Wilson, 1987). Weiner (1970) warned that

> ■ An indiscriminate application of "adolescent turmoil" and "he'll-grow-out-of-it" notions to symptomatic adolescents runs the grave risk of discouraging the attention that may be necessary to avert serious psychological disturbance. (p. 66)

Types of Mental Disorders

The question of what kinds of mental illness afflict adolescents has not received much attention recently. A study by Rosen and colleagues (1965), though dated, examined a very large number of cases. It gives us an idea of the types of mental disorders that adolescents suffer, and there is no reason to assume that these data have changed greatly. Approximately 4 percent of the illnesses of both males and females were accounted for by acute and chronic brain disorders (a malfunction of some part of the brain), 10 percent by mental retardation, and 6.5 percent by schizophrenia (a serious distortion of reality).

In Britain, Rutter (1980) reviewed surveys and found that psychiatric disorders afflicted about 15 percent of 15-year-olds, although as many as 6 percent more went undetected. In a more recent study, Horwitz and White (1987) studied differences between male and female adolescents. They found that 11 percent of the males suffered from neurotic disorders, such as anxiety, depression, and obsessive-compulsive reaction, compared with 18 percent of the females.

Guided Review

6. In exploring cognitive development, we examine Piaget's four stages of cognitive development: sensorimotor, preoperational, _____ operational, and formal operational.

7. Formal operational means that a person can form _____ mental operations.

8. Elkind presents the concept of adolescent egocentrism, which includes an _____ _____ and the personal fable.

9. Thinking skills can be separated into convergent (coming together with a single correct answer) and _____ (exploring the many possible answers to a question).

10. David Feldman claims that some children are precocious (doing what others do, but at a younger age), while other children are _____ (having a qualitatively greater ability than the rest of us).

11. _____ _____ is sometimes typified by withdrawal from reality.

Answers

6. concrete   7. abstract   8. imaginary audience   9. divergent   10. prodigious   11. Identity confusion

CONCLUSION

We wish that all children could complete puberty with a normal, healthy body and body image. We wish they could negotiate adolescence so successfully that they become energetic, self-confident adults.

Unfortunately, we know that this is not always the case. Some youths suffer from a negative self-concept because, although they differ from the norm only slightly in their body development, they perceive this as "catastrophic." Others deviate significantly from the norm because of some physiological problem. Of particular concern for females is our society's obsession with thinness. Taken together, the various aspects of puberty can cause the adolescent quite a bit of chagrin.

The only solution is to get some perspective on these problems. The good news is that just when they need it, most adolescents develop improved mental abilities that enable them to get a more realistic view of themselves.

Cognitive development is a complex matter, one about which we understood very little prior to this century. Our best evidence is that the intellect develops in stages. Contrary to earlier beliefs, thinking in childhood, adolescence, and adulthood are qualitatively different from each other. Furthermore, cognitive development has a number of other aspects: social cognition, information processing, egocentric thinking, critical thinking, and creative thinking.

Although most adolescents are healthy and have relatively untroubled lives, the advent of changes in peer relations, sexuality, pregnancy, substance abuse, sexually transmitted diseases and criminal associations pose serious psychosocial challenges for most. In the next chapter, we examine these important relationships.

CHAPTER HIGHLIGHTS

Physical Development

- Theories of adolescence in the early twentieth century were largely based on personal bias, because little empirical data existed.
- Those who work with adolescents need complete knowledge of the reproductive systems of both sexes.
- The order of physical changes in puberty is largely predictable, but the timing and duration of these changes are not.

- The normal range in pubertal development is very broad, and includes early, on-time, and late maturers.
- The adolescent's own perception of being normal has more influence on self-esteem than objective normality.
- Maturity of appearance affects whether adolescents are treated appropriately for their age.
- Early maturing is a positive experience for boys but may be negative for girls.
- Late maturing is often difficult for both boys and girls.

- Two of the most disruptive problems for adolescents are the eating disorders known as anorexia and bulimia nervosa.
- Adolescent girls develop eating disorders more than any other group.
- Developmental, cultural, individual, and familial factors are associated with the development of eating disorders.

Cognitive Development

- Piaget focused on the development of the cognitive structures of the intellect during childhood and adolescence.

- The infant and child pass through Piaget's first three stages: sensorimotor, preoperational, and concrete operational.
- Piaget's highest stage of cognitive development, that of formal operations, begins to develop in early adolescence.
- Adolescents focus much attention on themselves and tend to believe that everybody is looking at them. This phenomenon is called the imaginary audience.
- Many adolescents also hold beliefs about their own uniqueness and invulnerability. This is known as the personal fable.

- Critical thinking combines both convergent thinking, in which there is only one correct answer, and divergent thinking, in which there are many possible answers to a problem.
- Effective decision making, a formal operational process, is a part of critical thinking.
- Creative thinking includes divergent thinking, fluency, flexibility, originality, and remote associations.
- In adolescence, the understanding and use of metaphor appears to be an important aspect of creative thinking.

- Conventional schooling often has a dampening effect on students' willingness to risk doing creative, metaphorical thinking.
- Criticism of genius, as defined by IQ, holds that IQ indicates only precociousness but cannot account for prodigiousness.
- The idea that those who develop mental illness during adolescence will "grow out of it" is not supported by research.
- It appears that between 15 and 20 percent of teens suffer from some types of mental illness at some point during their adolescence.

🌳 KEY TERMS

🌳 WHAT DO YOU THINK?

1. Should children be taught about their body functions in school? Should this teaching include sexuality? If so, at what grade should it start?
2. What was the beginning of puberty for you? Why do you think so?

3. Why do you suppose people develop eating disorders?
4. Why should adolescents be more prone than other age groups to having "imaginary audiences" and "personal fables"?

5. Do you believe you can "disinhibit" (free up) your creative abilities? How should you start? Why don't you?
6. What are some of the ways we can help adolescents to have better mental health?

🌳 SUGGESTED READINGS

Blume, J. (1970). *Are you there, God? It's me, Margaret*. New York: Bradbury. Although written for teens, this book has a wealth of insights into pubertal change, at least for females. Our women friends tell us that Blume really understands.

Clavell, J. (1981). *The children's story*. New York: Delacorte. Illustrates the way children and youths tend to accept things without question, whereas adults are more likely to fear change and be suspicious of any deviation from the norm.

Curtis, R. H. (1986). *Mind and mood: Understanding and controlling your emotions*. New York: Scribner's. According to Curtis, knowing more about emotions and how they affect the body can help in understanding and controlling them. This book has chapters that describe the nervous system and endocrine system, addressing the physiological impact on emotions; a chapter on behavior modification; and a section with personality tests that you can take.

Erikson, E. (1969). *Gandhi's truth*. New York: Norton. This is one of the best examples of "psychohistory," which is the biography of a person as seen from the two disciplines of psychology and history. Mahatma Gandhi's quest to free India from British domination makes for good reading. The stories about the forces that influenced his youthful thinking are particularly instructive.

Gibson, M. (1980). *The butterfly ward*. New Orleans: Louisiana State University Press. This set of short stories tells what it is like to be between sanity and insanity. It is a sensitive look at the world of the mentally ill, both in and out of institutions.

McCoy, K. & Wibbelsman, C. (1987). *The teenage body book.* Los Angeles, CA: The Body Press. An excellent reference book for teenagers and those who work with them.

Potok, C. (1967). *The chosen.* New York: Fawcett. This is the story of a boy whose father is a rabbi in the strict Hassidic (Jewish) religion. It chronicles the struggle he has over his desire to be a good student and still be "normal." Also *The gift of Asher Lev,* 1990.

🌳 CHAPTER REVIEW TEST

1. Which of the following is part of the male reproductive system?
   a. fimbriae
   b. vas deferens
   c. cervix
   d. ova

2. What controls sexual characteristics in both males and females?
   a. pituitary gland
   b. Bartholin's glands
   c. Cowper's glands
   d. epididymis

3. What marks the onset of puberty?
   a. menarche for females; the first ejaculation for males
   b. the growth spurt for females and males
   c. the beginning of breast development for females; the enlargement of the genitals for males
   d. No single event marks the onset of puberty.

4. Adolescents who are dependent and childlike, feel a growing dislike for their bodies, and become more introverted and self-rejecting because of it are most likely to be
   a. early-maturing males.
   b. early-maturing females.
   c. average-maturing males.
   d. late-maturing females.

5. How does the average adolescent female of 100 years ago differ from the late-maturing female of today?
   a. The female 100 years ago weighed more than the female of today.
   b. The female 100 years ago was taller than the female of today.
   c. The female 100 years ago did not feel good about her body's appearance, whereas the female of today does.
   d. The female 100 years ago felt good about her body's appearance, whereas the female of today does not.

6. The decreasing age of the onset of puberty is referred to as
   a. early physical maturation.
   b. early psychological maturity.
   c. the evolutionary trend.
   d. the secular trend.

7. Specific criteria for anorexia nervosa include
   a. weight loss of at least 25 percent of original body weight.
   b. onset prior to age 25.
   c. distorted attitudes toward eating and weight.
   d. All of the answers are correct.

8. Fear of not being able to stop eating, depressed moods, and eating binges are characteristic of
   a. bulimia nervosa.
   b. eating disorders.
   c. anorexia nervosa.
   d. negative body image.

9. The formal operational stage is the _____ of Piaget's cognitive stages of development.
   a. first
   b. second
   c. third
   d. fourth

10. What occurs during Piaget's formal operational stage?
    a. Concrete operations combine to become formal operations.
    b. Preoperations combine to become formal operations.
    c. Parts of the sensorimotor stage combine to become formal operations.
    d. The preoperational stage and the concrete operational stage combine to become formal operations.

11. One of the criticisms of Piaget's theory of cognitive development is that
    a. it is too broad.
    b. it does not address abstract thought.
    c. it is too complex.
    d. it does not account for culture and gender influences.

12. To think of oneself in heroic or mythical terms is known as
    a. egocentrism.
    b. imaginary audience.
    c. the personal fable.
    d. invincibility.

13. When teenagers believe they are being scrutinized for their behavior and physical appearance they are
    a. egocentric.
    b. creating a personal fable.
    c. creating an imaginary audience.
    d. exaggerating their abilities and skills.

14. Divergent thinking is used when
    a. we solve a problem by following a series of steps.
    b. there is only one correct answer.
    c. we are doing critical thinking.
    d. the problem to be solved has many possible answers.

15. To solve problems that have only one correct answer, we are using
    a. divergent thinking.
    b. convergent thinking.
    c. creative thinking.
    d. critical thinking.

16. New ideas are to creative thinking as existing ideas are to
    a. convergent thinking.
    b. critical thinking.
    c. divergent thinking.
    d. concrete operational thinking.

Answers

1.b 2.a 3.d 4.b 5.d 6.d 7.d 8.a 9.d 10.a 11.d 12.c 13.c 14.d 15.b 16.b

Chapter Outline

Egocentric interests

The self-interested attitudes that Piaget believed characterize children but that Vygotsky saw as typical of adolescents.

Social interests

The interest in others that Piaget believed characterizes children but that Vygotsky saw as typical of adolescents.

Introspection

The ability to observe one's own thoughts, feelings, and behavior and to make judgments of them.

As a result of his studies of social thinking patterns of Swiss children, Jean Piaget came to believe that humans progress from **egocentric interests** in childhood (self-interest) to **social interests** (interest in others) in adolescence. Lev Vygotsky's studies of the development of social behavior among Russian children led him to precisely the opposite conclusion (see chapter 2 for an overview of the theories of Piaget and Vygotsky). Who is right? Could it be that they both are?

Piaget reached his conclusion because, in watching children play, he saw that when they "converse" with each other, they seldom pay much attention to what the other is saying. They just babble on without regard for the words spoken by their playmates. Adolescents, on the other hand, are intensely concerned with what others are thinking. Hence they are "socially minded." Vygotsky interpreted the same behavior in the opposite way. Children, he believed, seldom think about themselves. Instead, they are most involved in what other children are doing. They may not *talk* about it in a mutual way, but they are most oriented in their thinking toward the actions of others. It is only in adolescence that we see the beginnings of **introspection** (observation of one's own thoughts, feelings and actions). At this stage, human thought turns inward, and self-examination gains priority over social examination. Hence for Vygotsky, development goes from social to egocentric interests.

Today most social scientists believe that Piaget and Vygotsky are both right; the answer depends on what aspects of thought and behavior we are looking at. The topics in this chapter, beginning with peer relations, offer ample expansion on this point.

Following a discussion of peer relations, we turn to three other aspects of adolescence that have undergone many important changes. We look closely at what have been called the three stages of sexuality: autosexuality, homosexuality, and heterosexuality. We also cover four topics of psychosocial development that no one is happy about: sexually transmitted diseases, teenage pregnancy, substance abuse and criminal behavior.

After reading this chapter, you will be able to

- List positive influences that the peer group can have on an adolescent's growth.

- Describe the developmental patterns of peer groups.

- List the functions of peer groups.

- Specify the various concerns that adults have about adolescents engaging in sexual intercourse.

- Define the "sexual revolution."

- Discuss three theories of the origin of homosexuality and their implications for those who work with gay teens.

- Discuss reasons that teenagers engage in premarital sexual activity.

- Explain why some adolescents become runaways, prostitutes, or both.

- List the prevalence, symptoms, consequences, transmission, and treatment of sexually transmitted diseases found in adolescents.

- Discuss factors associated with causes and consequences of teenage parenthood.

- Explain the role of the family in teen pregnancies.

- Describe the prevalence of drug use among different groups of adolescents and between different types of drugs, and state any major differences between groups.

- Describe the connection between school performance (including learning disabilities) and delinquent behavior.

- List and describe at least three reasons that youth join gangs.

Peer Relations

Important debates have existed in the field of adolescent psychology concerning the value and influence of peer and parental relationships during adolescence. Recent research has helped to resolve some of these debates. The importance of parent and peer relationships and the ways in which peer relationships change during the adolescent years will be the focus of this section.

Developmental Patterns of Peer Groups

Peer groups are important in adolescent development. Although it is clear that friendships are vital throughout life, there seems to be something special about the role of the peer group during adolescence.

The role of peers as a source of activities, support, and influence increases greatly (Savin-Williams & Berndt, 1990). Perhaps it is for these reasons that adults and the media have been interested in and anxious about the role of the peer group. Brown (1990) described four specific ways in which the peer group changes from childhood to adolescence.

1. As previously mentioned, adolescents spend much more time with peers than do younger children. As early as sixth grade, the early adolescent begins withdrawing from adults and increases time spent with peers. During high school, middle adolescents spend twice as much time with their peers as they spend with parents and other adults.

2. Adolescent peer groups receive less adult supervision and control. Teenagers try to avoid close supervision by parents and teachers and are more independent and find places to meet where they are less closely watched. Even at home, teenagers seek privacy and places where they can talk to friends without being overheard by parents and siblings.

3. Adolescents begin interacting more with peers of the opposite sex. Although boys and girls participate in different activities and friendship groups during middle childhood, the sexes mix increasingly during the adolescent years. Interaction with members of the opposite sex seems to increase at the same time as adolescents distance themselves from their parents.

4. During adolescence, peer groups become more aware of the values and behaviors of the larger adolescent **subculture.** They also identify with certain **crowds,** which are groups with a reputation for certain values, attitudes, or activities. Common crowd labels among high school students include "jocks," "brains," "druggies," "populars," "nerds," "burnouts," and "delinquents." Interestingly, while the adolescent subculture changes over time, these crowds seem to exist in some form across all periods in which the adolescent subculture has been studied.

Subculture

A subgroup within a culture, in this case a social culture.

Crowds

Groups known for certain values, attitudes, or activities.

Although rigidly segregated into gender groups during middle childhood, boys and girls become much more willing to interact with each other as adolescence proceeds.

Why do adolescent peer groups receive less supervision than they used to?

Brown (1990) also thought about why peer groups change in the preceding ways during adolescence and suggested several explanations. He maintained that the biological, psychological, cognitive, and social changes of adolescence affect the development of a teenager's peer relationships. First, puberty seems to increase adolescents' interest in the opposite sex and contributes to withdrawal from adult activities and increased time with peers. While adolescents are in the process of becoming less dependent on their parents they tend to increase their dependence on peers.

An adolescent's definition of a friend is quite different from a child's. Although both a 5-year-old and a 15-year-old might say a friend is "someone who is close to you," the same words would mean very different things to each. If questioned more carefully about what they mean by "close," the younger child might say it means "someone who lives near you, that you play with." The adolescent would have a much fuller set of requirements, which would not necessarily include living close by. By the teen years, the young person includes many psychological dimensions in her definition of a friend. These would include such things as values and interests in common, as well as the idea that a friend is someone to be trusted with very personal information (Selman & Schultz, 1990).

Recently Tedesco and Gaier (1988) studied what 204 adolescents in grades 7, 9, and 12 appreciate most in their friends. The 100 female and 104 male students gave written replies to 10 open-ended questions about friendship values. For example, two of the questions were: "What is it about your best friend that you like most?" and "What are the most important things to consider in judging people?" Three categories emerged from the students' answers: interpersonal qualities, achievement, and physical qualities. A comparison of the responses for the different grade levels revealed what the researchers call "an interesting developmental phenomenon." Although all ages of students gave some answers that showed high regard for interpersonal qualities, the older a student was, the more he or she valued these qualities, and the less weight he or she gave to attributes of achievement or physical appearance and dress.

Functions of Peer Groups

In contrast with the popular view that peers are a negative influence during adolescence, Hartup (1985) noted that peer influence serves important social and psychological functions. When adolescents do not have the chance to be part of a peer group, they miss out on important learning experiences. Kelly and Hansen (1990) described six important positive functions of the peer group. The group can help teens to:

- *Control aggressive impulses.* Through interaction with peers, children and adolescents learn how to resolve differences in ways other than direct aggression. Observing how peers deal with conflict can be helpful in learning assertive, rather than aggressive or "bullying," behavior.

- *Obtain emotional and social support and become more independent.* Friends and peer groups provide support for adolescents as they take on new responsibilities. The support adolescents get from their peers helps them to become less dependent on their family for support.

- *Improve social skills, develop reasoning abilities, and learn to express feelings in more mature ways.* Through conversation and debate with peers, adolescents learn to express ideas and feelings and expand their problem solving abilities. Social interactions with peers give adolescents practice in expressing feelings of caring and love, as well as anger and negative feelings.

- *Develop attitudes toward sexuality and gender-role behavior.* Sexual attitudes and gender-role behaviors are shaped primarily through peer interactions (Hartup, 1983). Adolescents learn behaviors and attitudes that they associate with being young men and women.

- *Strengthen moral judgment and values.* Adults generally tell their children what is right and what is wrong. Within the peer group, adolescents are left to make decisions on their own. The adolescent has to evaluate the values of peers and decide what is right for him or her. This process of evaluation can help the adolescent to develop moral reasoning abilities.

- *Improve self-esteem.* Being liked by a large number of peers helps adolescents feel good about themselves. Being called up on the telephone or being asked out on a date tells adolescents that they are liked by their peers, thereby enhancing feelings of positive self-esteem.

 A MULTICULTURAL VIEW

Racial Influences on Peer Groups

In a recent study, Steinberg (1990) examined whether parental or peer influence on academic values is stronger for adolescents of different races. Steinberg and his colleagues studied 15,000 high school students from nine different high schools in Wisconsin and California. They found that parental influence on academics was stronger only for the white students. For African American, Latino, and Asian American students, the peer group had a greater influence on school attitudes and behavior, including how much time students spent on their homework, whether they enjoyed school, and how they behaved in class. Fortunately for the Asian students, their peers generally valued academic achievement and positively influenced academic achievement. For African American and Latino adolescents, it was more difficult to find and join a peer group that rewarded academic success. Consequently, these youths often experienced conflict between the positive values of their parents for academic achievement and the negative values held by their peers and did less well in school.

Similarly, Fordham and Ogbu (1986) found that African American students felt that to be popular, they could not do well in school. When African American students of high ability attended school with only high-achieving students, they were no longer anxious about losing peer support and were more successful.

Further, the African American teen subculture does appear to promote a greater sense of loyalty and support among its members than does the white teen subculture. This provides a climate that helps nurture a positive identity and self-confidence.

Although the peer group gains influence during adolescence, adults continue to play an important role in adolescents' lives. Adult and peer relationships seem to fulfill different needs in adolescent development (Savin-Williams & Berndt, 1990). Adolescents, for example, often talk with adults about their school progress and career plans. Adults provide an important source of guidance and approval in forming values and setting future goals. With peers, adolescents learn about social relationships outside of the family. They talk about more personal experiences and concerns, such as dating and views on sexuality. Adolescents generally feel more comfortable talking with peers about these concerns. They believe that peers will understand their feelings better than adults. Also, teens are afraid they may appear foolish to the adults whose approval they seek.

It is clear that the formation of intimate friendships is an important adolescent goal. One of the most important aspects of these friendships during adolescence is the growing trend for them to become sexual.

Guided Review

1. Brown describes four ways in which the peer group changes from childhood to adolescence. These are (a) adolescents spend more time with peers; (b) adolescent peer groups receive less adult supervision; (c) adolescents begin interacting more with peers of the _____ _____ ; and (d) peer groups become aware of values of the larger adolescent subculture.

2. When describing what they like best about their "best friend," adolescents state that they like interpersonal qualities, _____ , and physical qualities.

3. The influences of the peer group serve important social and _____ functions.

4. Whereas peers teach adolescents about social relationships outside the family, adults provide a source of guidance in forming _____ and setting goals.

Sexual Behavior

Few aspects of human behavior have changed more in this century than sexual behavior. Until the 1970s the popular belief about sex was, "They're talking more about it now, but they're not doing anything more about it!" This may have been true earlier in this century, but no longer. The situation has changed so much that it is reasonable to call it a **sexual revolution.**

The Sexual Revolution

Seeing their elders flounder in a sea of confused values, adolescents have begun to consult one another more often on important matters like sex. Edgar Friedenberg, a visionary sociologist, saw the beginning of this change as early as the late 1950s. He described these new attitudes in *The Vanishing Adolescent* (1959). The yearning for love and world peace, perennially scorned by some cynical older adults, began to flourish among late teens and young adults in the 1960s. Many middle-age adults came to the disconcerting realization that they were beginning to admire and even emulate the values of their adolescent children. As the spirit of "love among brothers and sisters" grew, so did its consequence, more open sexuality. And a great many adults were no longer sure this was wrong.

Sexual revolution
The extraordinary change in human sexual behavior that occurred in the 1960s and 1970s.

Answers

1. opposite sex 2. achievement 3. psychological 4. values

After all, that teens should have sexual feelings is entirely normal. As one expert puts it, "sexuality is clearly tied to the developmental tasks of this age period—formation of identity, a growing need for intimacy, and development of social skills" (Mendes, 1992, p. 7). As most adolescents move toward adulthood, interest in sex is biologically, psychologically, and socially inevitable.

Although most teenagers are not ready for mature love, sexual feelings are unavoidable, and for many they are extremely frightening. Now comes one of the most difficult decisions of life: Shall I say yes or no to premarital sex? Parents, clergy, teachers, police, and other adults used to be united in their resistance to it. But now, possibly for the first time in history, adult domination of the values of youth has faltered. As Williams (1989) expressed the change:

> ■ Even as adults in America moderate their sexual activity in response to the threat of AIDS and shifting standards of behavior, teen-agers in the last decade have developed a widely held sense that they are entitled to have sex. (p. 13)

Evidence shows that the forces that traditionally kept the majority of adolescents from engaging in sex are no longer powerful. Available data show that U.S. adolescents are becoming sexually active at increasingly earlier ages. According to a recent analysis (Office of Technology Assessment, 1991), the proportion of 15- to 19-year-old females who report having premarital sexual intercourse has increased steadily since 1970, from 28.6 percent to 36.4 percent in 1975, 42 percent in 1980, 44.1 percent in 1985, and 51.5 percent in 1988. The largest increase was among 15-year-old females (4.6% in 1970 to 25.6% in 1988). For males, data from 1988 (Sonnenstein & others, 1990) found that 64 percent of 15- to 18-year-olds had experienced sexual intercourse, 33 percent by age 15. A more recent study (Kann & others, 1993) found that for both sexes, 67 percent had experienced intercourse by the twelfth grade. Early sexual activity may have declined recently, however, due to a growing concern about AIDS and other sexually transmitted diseases (Koyle & others, 1989). Results of studies vary, but the most likely percentage of college sophomores who are no longer virgins is about 75 percent for both males and females.

Stages of Sexuality

Many psychologists believe that human sexuality develops in three steps:

1. Love of one's self (**autosexuality**)

2. Love of members of one's own sex (**homosexuality**)

3. Love of members of the opposite sex (**heterosexuality**)

These stages appear to be natural, although some argue that it is as natural to stay in the second stage as to go on to the third.

In the autosexual stage, the child becomes aware of himself or herself as a source of sexual pleasure and consciously experiments with masturbation. The autosexual stage begins as early as 3 years of age and continues until the child is about 6 or 7, although in some children it lasts for a considerably longer period of time.

When the child enters kindergarten, the homosexual phase comes to the fore (please note that this does not necessarily refer to sexual touching, but rather to the direction of feelings of love). For most children from the age of 7 to about 13, best friends, the ones with whom he or she dares to be intimate, are people of the same sex. Feelings become especially intense between ages 10 and 12, when young people enter puberty and feel a growing need to confide in others. They naturally are more trusting with members of their own sex, who share their experiences. Occasionally these close feelings result in overt sexual behavior (one study found this to be true more than one-third of the time). In most cases, however, it appears that such behavior results from curiosity rather than latent homosexuality of the adult variety.

Autosexuality

The love of oneself; the stage at which the child becomes aware of himself or herself as a source of sexual pleasure, and consciously experiments with masturbation.

Homosexuality

Love of members of one's own sex.

Heterosexuality

Love of members of the opposite sex.

The great majority of teenagers move into the third stage, heterosexuality, at about 13 or 14 years, with girls preceding boys by about a year. We discuss these three phases in the following sections.

Autosexual Behavior

Psychologists have been debating autosexual behavior since the dire warnings of G. S. Hall (see chapter 11). Today many people, especially females, would disagree with Hall about masturbation:

> ▪ From the moment we were born we all began making ourselves feel good by touching and playing with our bodies. Some of these experiences were explicitly sexual. From our parents and later, our schools and churches, many of us learned that we were not to continue this pleasurable touching. Some of us heeded their messages and some of us did not. But by the time we were teenagers, whether we masturbated or not, most of us thought it was bad. (Boston Women's Health Book Collective, 1984, p. 47)

Masturbation is probably universal to human sexual experience. Although most people still consider it an embarrassing topic, it has always been a recognized aspect of sexuality, legitimate or not. Kinsey, in his 1948 study of male sexuality, found that 97 percent of all males masturbated. As for women, approximately two-thirds have masturbated to orgasm by the time they reach 16 (Gagnon & Simon, 1969). Most 4- to 5-year-olds masturbate, are chastised for it, and stop, then start again at an average age of 14 (Masters & Johnson, 1966). If masturbation is so popular, why has it been considered such a problem?

For one reason, many believe that the Bible forbids masturbation. Dranoff (1974) pointed out that the Latin word *masturbari* means "to pollute oneself." For generations, people have taken as a prohibition the passage in Genesis 38:8 in which Onan is slain by the Lord because "he spilled his seed upon the ground." Dranoff argues that Onan was not slain by the Lord for masturbating, but because he refused to follow God's directive to mate with his brother's wife. Instead, he practiced coitus interruptus (withdrawal from the vagina before ejaculation).

In addition to the biblical restrictions, for centuries the medical profession believed that masturbation caused disease. In 1760 Tissot asserted that a common consequence of masturbation is "locomotor ataxia and early insanity." Many myths surround masturbation: It causes one to go mad; it causes hair to grow on one's palms; it causes one to reject sex with anyone else. No research evidence shows that masturbation has any intrinsic bad effects. In fact, the American Psychiatric Association has stated that it should not be considered the sole cause of any particular psychiatric problem (American Psychiatric Association, 1985).

Although most psychiatrists feel that no intrinsic harm exists in masturbation and believe it to be a normal, healthy way for adolescents to discharge their sexual drive, some teens (mainly boys) feel such a sense of shame, guilt, and fear that they develop the "excessive masturbation" syndrome. In this case, masturbation is practiced even though the child feels very bad about it. These feelings are reinforced by solitude and fantasy, which leads to depression and a debilitating sense of self-condemnation. Some teens are now being treated for an addiction to making 900 phone line sex calls.

In summary, most psychiatrists argue that masturbation in childhood is not only normal but helpful in forming a positive sexual attitude. It cannot be obsessive at 4, so it should be ignored at that age. However, it can be obsessive at 14, and if the parents suspect this to be the case, they should consult a psychologist.

Clearly, some of the stereotypes about homosexuals are untrue and unfair. What generalizations, if any, do you believe can fairly be made about all homosexuals?

Causes of Homosexuality

A number of suggestions have been put forth about why people become homosexuals. The three most often cited explanations are the psychoanalytic theory of homosexuality, the learning theory of homosexuality, and the genetic theory of homosexuality.

The Psychoanalytic Theory of Homosexuality

Psychoanalytic theory of homosexuality

Freud's theory suggests that if the child's first sexual feelings about the parent of the opposite sex are strongly punished, the child may identify with the same-sex parent and develop a permanent homosexual orientation.

Freud's **psychoanalytic theory of homosexuality** suggested that if the child's first sexual feelings about the parent of the opposite sex are strongly punished, the child may identify with the same-sex parent and develop a permanent homosexual orientation. Because researchers have noted many cases in which the father's suppression of the homosexual's Oedipal feelings was not particularly strong, this theory is not held in much regard today.

The Learning Theory of Homosexuality

Learning theory of homosexuality

The belief that homosexuality is the result of learned experiences from significant others.

The **learning theory of homosexuality** offers another explanation: Animals that are low on the mammalian scale follow innate sexual practices. Among the higher animals, humans included, learning is more important than inherited factors. According to this theory, most people learn to be heterosexual, but for a variety of little-understood reasons, some people learn to be homosexual.

The Genetic Theory of Homosexuality

Genetic theory of homosexuality

The theory that homosexuality is caused by some factor in a person's DNA.

No direct proof exists that people become homosexual because of genetic reasons. However, in a review of the literature about homosexuality, Buunk and van Driel (1989) noted that researchers are looking at what is known about homosexuality in other species for clues. Recently interest in the influence of hormones during fetal development has emerged (Money, 1987). These theories argue that how the fetus's brain reacts to sex hormones during the second through sixth month of gestation may create a genetic tendency toward homosexuality. They argue that persons born with this tendency (called a *predisposition*) can be influenced by the environment to either select or avoid homosexuality. In other words, those who favor a **genetic theory of homosexuality** suggest that if the biological predisposition is present (a genetic tendency) and certain psychological and social factors (as yet unknown) are in place, then the contention of many homosexuals that their sexual orientation was not a matter of choice would be confirmed.

The Onset of Homosexuality

For a long time, psychologists believed that homosexuality does not manifest itself until adulthood. Recent studies of male homosexuals reviewed in the *Journal of the American Medical Association* (Remafedi, 1988), however, indicate that this belief was the result of interviews with teens, most of whom were ashamed or otherwise unwilling to tell about their feelings on the subject. The current studies, using better methods, are in remarkable agreement that at least one-third of all males have had "a homosexual experience that resulted in an orgasm" at least once during their adolescent years. About 10 percent "are exclusively homosexual for at least three years between the ages of 16 and 55" (p. 222).

WHAT'S YOUR VIEW?

IS HOMOSEXUALITY A MATTER OF CHOICE?

We have the behaviorists and the psychoanalysts giving their explanations of homosexuality. We have many homosexuals who believe that their sexual orientation became clear so early in life that it could only have been caused genetically. Proponents of each of these positions agree that being homosexual is not a matter of choice for the homosexual. Thus it is argued that they should be accepted the same as heterosexuals, or at the very least be given sympathy, because their role in today's society is not an easy one.

Others believe that homosexuality is a matter of free choice and that those who choose it are behaving in an immoral way. Homosexuals don't have to be that way; they want to. Because they are immoral and because they disrupt the "natural order of things," they deserve society's condemnation. What's your view?

Most adult homosexuals remember feeling that they were "different" at about 13 years old, the age when most boys are beginning to notice girls. One study followed boys who were seen by medical personnel because of gender-atypical behavior (dressing in girls' clothes, playing with dolls, etc.) between the ages of 3 and 6. The majority developed a homosexual identity during adolescence or adulthood.

Remafedi (1988) summed up the situation:

> Professionals may deny the existence of gay or lesbian teenagers for a number of reasons, some benign and others more malignant. It is both reasonable and judicious to avoid applying potentially stigmatizing labels to children and adolescents. It is also understandable . . . to adopt a 'wait and see' approach to a teenager's homosexuality, while providing appropriate preventative and acute health care. However, the reluctance of some professionals to acknowledge the existence and the needs of homosexual adolescents is primarily related to the emotionalism surrounding the issue. (p. 224)

Two other studies reinforce Remafedi's position: those by Harry (1986) and Sullivan and Schneider (1987).

Whatever one believes about homosexuality being a natural stage of sexual development, the great majority of people in the United States today do engage in heterosexual behavior sooner or later—and the evidence indicates that they begin much sooner than they used to.

Heterosexual Behavior

At the beginning of this section, we presented some statistics on teen sexuality that may have surprised you. To get a clearer picture of this situation, you will need to look at the data that a number of other studies have provided on heterosexual teen behavior.

One societal change that seems to have strongly affected adolescent sexuality is maternal employment. Hansson and colleagues (1981) conducted a study to determine whether maternal employment is associated with teenage sexual attitudes and behaviors and whether it increases the likelihood of pregnancy. They found that those girls whose mothers are employed outside the home have a greater tendency to begin sexual relations before the age of 19.

Research suggests that girls whose mothers are employed outside the home tend to begin sexual relations at an earlier age. Are there reasons other than mother's absence for this?

Wagner (1980) found that sexuality becomes a part of the adolescent's concept of self, regardless of their personal experience or knowledge. She summarizes what we currently know about certain aspects of adolescent sexuality:

- *Knowledge about sexuality*. Some evidence indicates that teenagers who receive sex information from their parents or someone important to them behave more conservatively and responsibly. Males and females are about equally informed, but neither group knows as much as they need to. Peers and books are the most common sources of information.

- *Attitudes, values, and standards*. Current research reveals a trend toward change in sexual mores among the young. In general, having sex with one person, for whom "love" is felt, is emerging, at least among older teens, as the most popular standard. Adolescent sexuality appears to be affected as much by social change and historical events as by separation and identity formation.

- *Male-female differences*. Differences in heterosexual specific practices are more evident in younger than in older adolescents. Tremendous variability exists among adolescents in specific sexual practices. More advanced types of sexual behavior (such as petting and intercourse) are occurring at earlier and earlier ages. Although male promiscuity has declined, female permissiveness has increased.

Wagner concludes that each new sexual experience provides the adolescent with opportunities to test autonomous behavior in a conflict situation. She states that societal changes in attitudes, standards, and behavior have all been reflected in sexuality among adolescents.

First Coitus

Although sexuality develops throughout life, most people view first intercourse as the key moment in sexual development. When do most Americans first experience intercourse? The statistics vary, but all research confirms that this experience occurs at a younger age than it did for previous generations. Table 13.1 makes this evident.

Why are adolescents engaging in sex at earlier ages? Some theorists point to changes in social context (Walsh, 1989). They argue that today's youths learn about sexuality much earlier and from more sources than in the past. Sexually explicit magazines, rock music videos, advertisements displaying sexual situations, and movies depicting sexually graphic material are all part of the everyday culture of teenagers today. In the 1950s such materials weren't commonly available. The women's movement and its focus on double standards about sexuality also contributed to the social context of teens today. Early feminists questioned the **double standard** that engaging in sexual relations was acceptable for males but not for females. Together these factors create a social context that provides developing adolescents with information about sex beyond what they learn from their peers and family. It is in this new social context that adolescents make decisions about when first to engage in sexual relations.

Factors that increase the likelihood that a teen will engage in premarital sex include coming from a one-parent home, living in poverty, being without religious affiliation, and living in a family where educational discussions about sex never occur. Researchers studying race and premarital sex have found that by itself, race or ethnic affiliation is not related to premarital sex (Wyatt, 1989). In many urban areas, it is people of color who live in poverty. Teens from those families are most likely to experience first coitus at an early age (Forste & Heaton, 1988; Wyatt, 1989).

Double standard
The belief that the standards for female sexual behavior should be higher than those for males.

Reflective listening
A method of talking to others; you rephrase the person's comments to show you understand.

Table 13.1	Percentage of High School Students Who Have Had Sexual Intercourse		
	Ever had sexual intercourse	**Have had 4 or more sex partners**	**Currently sexually active**[1]
Sex			
Female	50.8	13.8	75.3
Male	57.4	23.4	64.1
Grade			
9	39.0	12.5	57.5
10	48.2	15.1	68.9
11	62.4	22.1	69.4
12	66.7	25.1	75.9
Race or ethnicity			
White	50.0	14.7	67.9
Black	81.5	43.1	72.9
Hispanic	53.1	16.8	69.6

[1]Of those who had ever had sexual intercourse, the percentage who had had intercourse during the 3 months preceding the survey.

Source: L. Kann, W. Warren, J. L. Collins, J. Ross, B. Collins, and L. J. Kolbe, "Results from the National School-Based 1991 Youth Risk Behavior Survey and Progress Toward Achieving Related Health Objectives for the Nation" in *Public Health Reports, vol. 108,* supp. 1, 1993, pages 47–55.

AN APPLIED VIEW

How to Talk to Teens about Sex (or Anything Else, for That Matter)

Adolescents are more likely to talk to adults who know how to listen—about sex, alcohol, and other important issues. But certain kinds of responses, such as giving too much advice or pretending to have all the answers, have been shown to block the lines of communication.

Effective listening is more than just "not talking." It takes concentration and practice. Below are six communication skills that are useful to anyone who wants to reach adolescents. By the way, these skills can also enhance communication with other adults.

Rephrase the person's comments to show you understand. This is sometimes called **reflective listening.** Reflective listening serves four purposes:

- It assures the person you hear what she or he is saying.
- It persuades the person that you correctly understand what is being said (it is sometimes a good idea to ask if your rephrasing is correct).
- It allows you a chance to reword the person's statements in ways that are less self-destructive. For example, if a person says "My mother is a stinking drunk!" you can say "You feel your mother drinks too much." This is better, because the daughter of someone who drinks too much usually can have a better self-image than the daughter of a "stinking drunk."
- It allows the person to "rehear" and reconsider what was said.

Watch the person's face and body language. Often a person will assure you that he or she does not feel sad, but a quivering chin or too-bright eyes will tell you otherwise. A person may deny feeling frightened, but if you put your fingers on her or his wrist, as a caring gesture, you may find that the person has a pounding heart. When words and body language say two different things, always believe the body language.

Give nonverbal support. This may include a smile, a hug, a wink, a pat on the shoulder, nodding your head, making eye contact, or holding the person's hand (or wrist).

Use the right tone of voice for what you are saying. Remember that your voice tone communicates as clearly as your words. Make sure your tone does not come across as sarcastic or all-knowing.

Use encouraging phrases to show your interest and to keep the conversation going. Helpful little phrases, spoken appropriately during pauses in the conversation, can communicate how much you care:

"Oh, really?"

"Tell me more about that."

"Then what happened?"

"That must have made you feel bad."

Remember, if you are judgmental or critical, the person may decide that you just don't understand. You cannot be a good influence on someone who won't talk to you.

The Many Nonsexual Motives for Teenage Sex

In recent years researchers have begun to pay more attention to the notion that teens engage in sex for many reasons other than the satisfaction of their prodigious sexual drives. In one of the most enlightening articles on this subject, two therapists who work with adolescents (Hajcak & Garwood, 1989) concluded that for many adolescents, orgasm becomes a "quick fix" for a wide variety of other problems. Among these alternative motives for sex are the desire to do the following:

- *Confirm masculinity/femininity.* For some teens, having sex with one or more partners (sometimes called "scoring") is taken as evidence that their sexual identity is intact. This is particularly relevant to those (especially males) who consciously or unconsciously have their doubts about it.

- *Get affection.* Usually some aspects of sexual behavior include physical indications of affection, such as hugging, cuddling, and kissing. To the youth who gets too little of these, sex is not too high a price to pay to get them.

- *Rebel against parents or other societal authority figures.* There are few more effective ways to "get even" with parents than to have them find out that you are having sex at a young age, especially if it leads to pregnancy.

- *Obtain greater self-esteem.* Many adolescents feel that if someone is willing to have sex with them, then they are held in high regard. Needless to say, this is often an erroneous conclusion.

- *Get revenge on or to degrade someone.* Sex can be used to hurt the feelings of someone else, such as a former boyfriend. In more extreme cases, such as "date rape," sex can be used to show the person's disdain for the partner.

- *Vent anger.* Because sex provides a release of emotions, it is sometimes used to deal with feelings of anger. Some teens regularly use masturbation for this purpose.

- *Alleviate boredom.* Another frequent motive for masturbation is boredom.

- *Ensure fidelity of girlfriend or boyfriend.* Some teens engage in sex not because they feel like it, but because they fear their partner will leave them if they don't comply.

Using sex for these reasons often has an insidious result. As Hajcak and Garwood (1989) described it:

> Adolescents have unlimited opportunities to learn to misuse sex, alone or as a couple. This happens because of the powerful physical and emotional arousal that occurs during sexual activity. Adolescents are very likely to ignore or forget anything that transpired just prior to the sex act. Negative emotions or thoughts subside as attention becomes absorbed in sex. . . . The end result is that adolescents condition themselves to become aroused any time they experience emotional discomfort or ambiguity . . . sexual needs are only partially satisfied [and] the nonsexual need (for example, affection or to vent anger) is also only partially satisfied, and will remain high. . . . The two needs become paired or fused through conditioning. . . . Indulging in sex inhibits their emotional and sexual development by confusing emotional and sexual needs and, unfortunately, many of these teens will never learn to separate the two. (pp. 756–58)

This is not to say that adolescents don't experience genuine sexual arousal. They definitely do, but this does not by itself justify sexual activity. These therapists

Table 13.2	Age of First Full Sexual Experience by Section of the United States			
	Northeast	**South**	**Midwest**	**West**
N =	*558*	*928*	*661*	*573*
By age 10	2%	1%	0%	3%
11–14	12	16	7	11
15–18	44	65	51	51
19–25	39	17	37	34
26+	3	1	5	1
By age 14	14	17	7	14
Over age 18	42	18	42	35

From S. Janus and C. Janus, *The Janus Report on Sexual Behavior.* Copyright © 1993 Wiley & Sons, New York. Reprinted by permission of John Wiley & Sons, Inc.

argue that teens need to be taught to understand their motives and to find appropriate outlets for them. In fact, this has led some experts to recommend sex education that teaches alternatives to premarital sex.

The Janus Report

The largest, most scientifically designed study of sexuality since the Kinsey Report in the late 1940s was recently published. The *Janus Report of Sexual Behavior* (1993) was compiled by Cynthia Janus, MD, and her husband, Samuel Janus, Ph.D. The study covered a wide range of sexual topics, using questionnaire and interview methods. Its sample of nearly 3,000 adults closely resembles the adult population described in the 1990 U.S. Census. Unfortunately, because of the legal problems involved in questioning children and adolescents, the researchers sought answers only from persons 18 or older. A number of questions did involve the subjects' teen years, however. Here are some of the Janus Report's most important findings:

- Nearly 20 percent of men, but only 7.5 percent of women, reported they had had full sexual relations by age 14.

- Younger women responding to the questionnaire reported much younger ages at which they had their first full sexual experience than older women, thus indicating a continuing downward trend.

- Compared with phase 1 of the study (1983 to 1985), in phase 2 (1988 to 1992) 12 percent fewer men and women remained virgins until age 18.

- The South has the earliest ages of sexual initiation and the most reported premarital sex (see table 13.2).

- Asked whether they had had at least one homosexual experience, 22 percent of men (15% lower than Kinsey reported in the late 1940s), 17 percent of women, and twice as many career women as women who were homemakers answered yes.

- An amazing 11 percent of men and 23 percent of women reported having been sexually molested as children.

- Of the women who had had abortions, almost 20 percent had their first before they reached 18 years of age.

The results of this most recent study appear to indicate that several types of sexual experience are occurring even earlier than previous studies show. We will summarize the rest of the-major findings of this report in chapters 16 and 20 in the relevant sections.

Sexual Abuse

When adolescents are abused, typically it is by someone they know and trust. It is often just a continuation of abuse that started during childhood. The most common type of serious sexual abuse is incest between father and daughter (Alexander & Kempe, 1982). This type of relationship may last for several years. The daughter is often manipulated into believing it is all her fault and that if she says anything to anyone, she will be seen as a bad person, one who may even be arrested and jailed. The outcome is usually another adolescent statistic: a runaway or even a prostitute.

Most sexual offenses were discussed with a friend or with no one (Alexander & Kempe, 1982). Very few were reported to parents, police, social workers, or other authorities. It has also been found that the effects of abuse may influence a youth's future relationships. Directly following the experience, children may engage in such "acting out" behaviors as truancy, running away, sexual promiscuity, and damage to school performance and family relationships.

Gruber, Jones, and Freeman (1982) interviewed a group of female teenagers ranging in age from 13 to 17 who had been sexually abused. These young women were involved in a residential intervention program. Gruber and colleagues found that the victims sustained a diminished self-worth and poorer interpersonal relationships with males. In addition, VanderMay and Neff (1982), in reviewing research and treatment of adult-child incest, concluded that the long-term effects may result in promiscuity, alcoholism, sexual dysfunction, drug abuse, prostitution, depression, and even suicide.

VanderMay and Neff call for improved education to sensitize people to prevent incest, as well as improved reporting systems, legal definitions, and treatment of victims. These may help us better understand and intervene, so that victims can receive professional attention earlier that may reduce the long-term effects of abuse.

Sexuality in the lives of late adolescents and young adults in the last decade of this century is very different from in earlier decades (although perhaps not so different from several centuries ago). What is the relationship between this fact and the problem covered in the next section, sexually transmitted disease? That is a complex question.

Sexually abused children and adolescents are typically abused by someone they know. How do we best teach children and adolescents about sexual abuse without instilling fear and mistrust in others?

Very few cases of sexual molestation are actually reported to the authorities.

Sexually Transmitted Diseases

In this section, we cover research on AIDS and other diseases that are passed on sexually.

AIDS

Sexually transmitted diseases

A class of diseases that are transmitted through sexual behavior.

AIDS (Acquired Immune Deficiency Syndrome)

A condition caused by a virus that invades the body's immune system, making it vulnerable to infections and life-threatening illnesses.

Not long ago, when people thought about **sexually transmitted diseases** (STDs), gonorrhea came to mind. In the 70s, it was herpes. Today, **AIDS** (Acquired Immune Deficiency Syndrome) causes the most concern (Forestein, 1989).

AIDS was first diagnosed at Bellevue-New York University Medical Center in 1979 and has quickly approached epidemic proportions. What is known about AIDS is that a virus attacks certain cells of the body's immune system, leaving the person vulnerable to any number of fatal afflictions such as cancer and pneumonia. In addition, the disease can directly infect the brain and spinal cord, causing acute meningitis.

As of July 1989, 100,000 cases of AIDS had been reported since the first diagnosis. Of these 100,000 reported cases, about 60,000 of the patients have since died. AIDS now ranks 15th among the leading causes of morbidity and mortality in children and young adults. The first 50,000 cases of AIDS were reported from 1981 to 1987. The second 50,000 were reported in just the following two years (CDC, 1989b). Table 13.3 presents current statistics. Keep in mind that these are only *reported* cases of the full-blown AIDS disease. A combination of underdiagnosis and

First diagnosed in 1979, AIDS has quickly approached epidemic proportions.

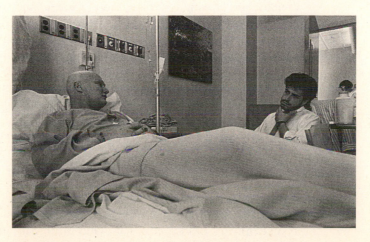

Answers

5. homosexuality 6. learning 7. 70 8. masculinity, femininity 9. sexual intercourse

Table 13.3	Current AIDS Statistics	
HIV-positive Patients (in thousands)		
	In 1981	*In 1992*
Age 13–29	23	194
% Male	93	86
% Female	7	14
% White	60	49
% Black	26	35
% Latino	14	15
Other	1	1
AIDS Deaths by Age		
Age	*1981*	*1992*
0–4	96	192
5–12	10	36
13–29	1329	3809
30–39	3013	10265
40–49	1396	5855
50–59	590	1760
60+	248	758

Source: *Statistical Abstract of the United States,* U.S. Department of Commerce, Washington, D.C., 1994.

underreporting makes these estimates conservative at best. The CDC estimates that 1 to 1.5 million people in the United States are currently infected with the initial virus. Studies suggest that about 50 percent of these people will develop the full-blown AIDS disease within 10 years of infection, and that 99 percent will eventually develop the disease (Lifson & others, 1989).

Trends include increased reporting of AIDS in intravenous drug users, women, children, the elderly, African Americans, Latino Americans, heterosexuals, small cities, and rural areas (Catania & others, 1989; CDC, 1989a; Kirkland & Ginther, 1988). The only segment of society in which the incidence of AIDS is decreasing are homosexuals with no history of intravenous drug use.

Human immunodeficiency virus (HIV)
The virus that leads to AIDS.

The virus that leads to AIDS—**human immunodeficiency virus (HIV)**—is transmitted through the transfer of substantial amounts of intimate bodily fluids such as blood and semen. The virus is most likely to be transferred through sexual contact, the sharing of hypodermic needles, and, much less likely, through blood transfusions (a test for AIDS is now available at blood banks and hospitals). In addition, the virus can be transmitted from an infected mother to an infant during pregnancy or birth. Figure 13.1 shows the concentrations of AIDS in each of these groups, as well as the percentages of cases by race/ethnicity.

In the initial stages of the spread of the disease in this country, HIV has most often been found in certain segments of the population such as male homosexuals and intravenous drug users and, to a much lesser degree, among hemophiliacs. But that could easily change over time. In some Central African countries, where AIDS is thought to have originated, HIV is found equally among men and women throughout the population.

Although there is no cure for AIDS, the disease can be effectively controlled through preventive measures. Use of condoms during sexual intercourse and clean, unused needles during intravenous drug use can drastically reduce the risk of contracting the virus. Figure 13.2 reflects the improvement in protection through use of contraceptives. After a slow start, large-scale education efforts by grassroots organizations, as well as by state and federal government agencies, have begun to get these messages out, but the problems remain extremely serious.

Figure 13.1

Percentage of 13- to 19-year-old AIDS victims in the United States, by race/ethnicity

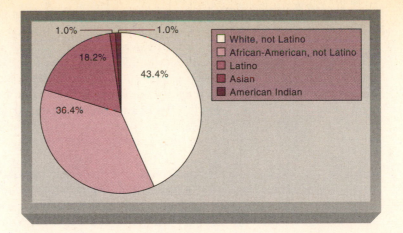

Figure 13.2

Contraceptive use among United States teenage males. The chart shows the percentage of 17- to 19-year-olds who say they used (or didn't use) contraceptives during their last sexual intercourse.

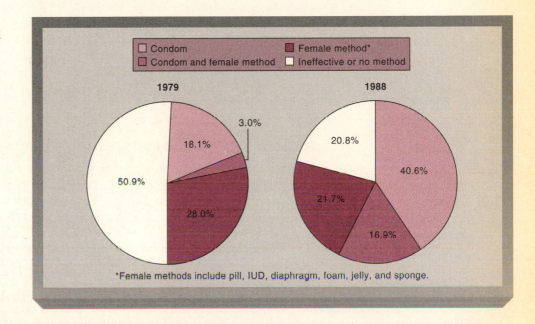

*Female methods include pill, IUD, diaphragm, foam, jelly, and sponge.

AN APPLIED VIEW — How Adolescent Hypocrisy Can Affect Condom Use

Between 1989 and 1991, the incidence of HIV infection among adolescents rose 77 percent while at the same time condoms, the only effective preventative against HIV for those engaged in sex, are used every time they have sex by only 17 percent of teens (Azar, 1994a). Why the discrepancy?

University of California researcher Eliot Aronson believes this occurs because of two widespread hypocrisies:

- Obsession with sex versus the puritanical view of sex
- Condom use promotes early sexual practices versus condoms provide safety

Denial, Aronson believes, is the mechanism that makes otherwise savvy students accept these obviously hypocritical positions. Neither threatening adolescents with dire results nor trying to "eroticize" condoms was found to have any lasting effects (Azar, 1994b). Therefore Aronson tried a different approach: He got groups of college students to make videotapes promoting safe sex and then use these tapes to teach high school students. Compared with a control group of college students who simply made videotapes, the "teachers" reduced unsafe sex practices significantly. Apparently actually talking to others made it harder for them to use denial, and thus they were more likely to change their own behavior.

First, as mentioned, the virus has been identified with a few select groups. If you're not gay or a drug user, you might think you don't have to consider preventive measures. However, a person exposed to HIV may not show any symptoms for as much as 15 years. Further, this same person can expose other people to the virus during this incubation phase. Some people have reacted to this by becoming more particular about their sexual partners. Monogamous relationships have been on the rise again during the 1980s, after the "liberated" days of the sexual revolution of the 1960s and 1970s. And the educational message seems to be getting through as condom use increases. But many still ignore the dangers, and the consequences may be years away.

This may be particularly true among adolescents. Adolescents currently constitute only about 1 percent of all diagnosed cases of AIDS in the United States. But given the long incubation period and the research findings that suggest that adolescents are not very well informed about AIDS, many researchers think this may be an underestimation. Adolescents are also more prone than the general public to misconceptions and prejudices generated by the frightening new disease.

For example, some adolescents have the misconception that AIDS can be transmitted through casual contact such as kissing or hugging someone with AIDS, or sharing their utensils or bathroom facilities. Such misconceptions unnecessarily increase fear and anxiety in everyone. AIDS prevention efforts aimed at adolescents often have as their main goal the dispelling of such myths (DiClemente & others, 1987).

Other Sexually Transmitted Diseases

Often lost in the public focus on the burgeoning AIDS problem is a truly epidemic increase in the prevalence of other STDs. Because of its fatal nature, AIDS gets most of the press and the major funding. But STDs such as gonorrhea, syphilis, chlamydia, and herpes are running rampant compared with AIDS, particularly among adolescents. The effects of such venereal diseases range from the mildly annoying to the life-threatening. More than 50 diseases and syndromes other than AIDS account for over 13 million cases and 7,000 deaths annually (National Institute of Allergy and Infectious Diseases, 1987).

Some of the more common STDs (other than AIDS) include the following:

Chlamydia
Now the most common **STD**, with about 5 to 7 million new cases each year. There often are no symptoms; it is diagnosed only when complications develop.

- *Chlamydial infection.* **Chlamydia** is now the most common STD, with about 5 to 7 million new cases each year (Subcommittee on Health and the Environment, 1987). In one state, black and Hispanic female teens have rates of chlamydia infection more than 10 times higher than rates reported in white female teens (Massachusetts Department of Public Health, 1991). Often chlamydia has no symptoms. It is diagnosed only when complications develop. It is particularly harmful for women and is a major cause of female infertility, accounting for 20 to 40 percent of all cases (Hersch, 1991b). Untreated, chlamydia can lead to pelvic inflammatory disease (see the information to follow). As with all of these diseases, it can be transmitted to another person whether symptoms are present or not. The news about this infection, however, is excellent. A single-dose antibiotic treatment has been found to be very effective (Martin & others, 1992).

Gonorrhea
Well-known venereal disease accounting for between 1.5 and 2 million cases per year.

- *Gonorrhea.* The well-known venereal disease **gonorrhea** infects between 1.5 and 2 million persons per year. One quarter of the cases reported are adolescents (Klassen & others, 1989). Gonorrhea is caused by bacteria and can be treated with antibiotics. When penicillin was introduced in the 1940s, the incidence of gonorrhea declined dramatically. Today, however, the number is rising and has reached the highest level in 40 years (Hersch, 1991a). The most common symptoms are painful urination and a discharge from the penis or the vagina.

Pelvic inflammatory disease (PID)
Disease that often results from chlamydia or gonorrhea, and frequently causes prolonged problems, including infertility.

Genital herpes
An incurable sexually transmitted disease, with about 500,000 new cases every year.

Syphilis
A sexually transmitted disease that presents a great danger in that in its early stage there are no symptoms. If untreated, it can be fatal.

Hepatitis B
A viral disease transmitted through sex or shared needles.

- *Pelvic inflammatory disease (PID).* **Pelvic inflammatory disease** frequently causes prolonged problems, including infertility. It is usually caused by untreated chlamydia or gonorrhea. These infections spread to the fallopian tubes, resulting in PID. The scarring the infection causes often prevents successful impregnation. More than 1 million new cases per year occur in the United States (Washington & others, 1986). Women who are most likely to get it are those who use an intrauterine device for birth control, have multiple sex partners, are teenagers, or have had PID before. PID is so widespread that it causes $2.6 billion in medical costs per year!

- *Genital herpes.* **Genital herpes** is an incurable disease, with about 500,000 new cases every year. Spread by a virus during skin-to-skin contact, the major symptom of genital herpes is an outbreak of genital sores, which can occur as often as once a month. Estimates suggest about 30 million people in this country suffer from this infection. Unlike chlamydia, problems associated with herpes are mainly emotional and social rather than medical (Hersch, 1991b). People with herpes often experience embarrassment and low self-esteem about their bodies.

- *Syphilis.* Like gonorrhea, **syphilis** is no longer the killer it was before penicillin. However, this sexually transmitted disease still accounts for 70,000 new cases per year. In the state of Massachusetts, 76 percent of these cases were teens of color (Massachusetts Department of Public Health, 1991). Caused by bacteria, the first sign of syphilis is a *chancre* ("shan-ker"), a painless open sore that usually shows up on the tip of the penis and around or in the vagina. This disease must be treated with antibiotics or it can be fatal.

- *Hepatitis B.* About 200,000 new cases of **hepatitis B** occurred in the United States in 1990, and 300,000 were predicted to occur in 1991 (Hersch, 1991a). This viral disease is transmitted through sexual contact and also through the sharing of infected needles. Although a preventive vaccine is available, those who are most at risk for hepatitis B (intravenous drug users, homosexual men, and inner-city heterosexuals) usually do not have the vaccine readily available to them.

Figure 13.3 depicts the relative percentage of new cases of each type of STD in the United States each year.

Figure 13.3
The relative percentage of new cases of each type of STD in the United States each year

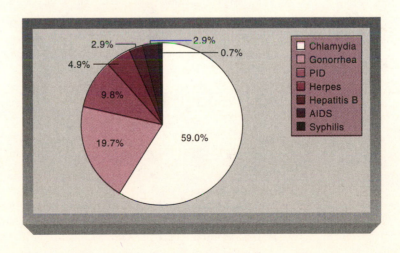

Studies have shown that the age group at greatest risk for STDs are individuals between 10 and 19 years old (National Institute of Allergy and Infectious Disease, 1987). This age group is particularly difficult to educate in any area concerning sexuality. The obstacles to education include individuals who refuse to take the information seriously, and parents who won't let the information be taught.

The AIDS crisis and the STD epidemic have several features in common. On the negative side, misconceptions contribute to both problems. Many young people believe that only promiscuous people get STDs, and that only homosexuals get AIDS. Having multiple sexual partners does increase the risk of contracting STDs, but most people do not view their sexual behavior, no matter how active, as being promiscuous. Recent research also suggests machismo gets in the way of proper condom use, an effective prevention technique for all STDs. A "real man" doesn't use condoms. And, finally, when people do contract a disease, strong social stigmas make accurate reporting difficult.

On the positive side, the preventive and educational measures are basically the same for AIDS and other STDs: Dispel the myths, increase general awareness and acknowledgment of the problem, and encourage more discriminating sexual practices. Perhaps some of the educational efforts made on behalf of AIDS prevention and treatment will have a helpful effect on the current STD epidemic. Historically the health focus on STDs has been on treatment, typically with antibiotics, but recently the Public Health Service has shifted its focus for all STDs to prevention. So perhaps comprehensive efforts of this kind that emphasize all STDs will prove fruitful.

In summary, it seems safe to say that major changes in adolescent sexual practices have occurred in recent decades. Many of them must be viewed with considerable alarm, especially when you consider the tragic increases in STDs and pregnancy.

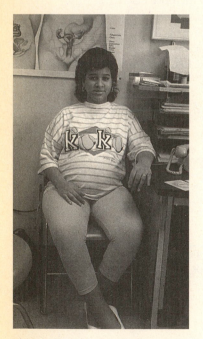

Except for the youngest adolescents, birthrates for adolescents have been dropping in recent years. However, the extent to which young adolescents have been becoming pregnant is certainly a cause for great concern because physically, emotionally, and economically, they are at the greatest risk.

Guided Review

10. The nature of our concern about sexually transmitted diseases has changed since the spread of AIDS, or _____ _____ _____ syndrome.

11. HIV attacks the body's _____ _____ , thus leaving the person vulnerable to a number of fatal afflictions.

12. Other sexually transmitted diseases include chlamydia, _____ , pelvic inflammatory disease, syphilis, genital herpes, and hepatitis B.

13. Studies show that the age stage at greatest risk for sexually transmitted diseases is _____ .

The Teenage Parent

■ "You're pregnant," the doctor said, "and you have some decisions to make. I suggest you don't wait too long to decide what you'll do. It's already been seven weeks, and time is running out!"

"Look, it just can't be true!" I replied. I was trying to convince myself that the clinic doctor was lying. It wasn't supposed to be like this! I was tired of the bitter quarrel I had been having with the doctor. I resented him with every passion. How could I let myself be seen like this?

I had been fearing this answer. I suppose I knew the truth all along, but I really didn't want to face it. I didn't want an abortion, that much I was sure of. Besides, where would I get the money?

Answers

10. acquired immune deficiency 11. immune system 12. gonorrhea 13. adolescence

For ages now, I had been thinking my period would come any day. Now the truth was in the open! I walked out of the office and headed aimlessly down the street. I looked around and saw only ugliness. I thought about God and how even He had deserted me. It all hurt so much.

"How could this have happened to me?" I thought. "Good girls don't get pregnant!" All of the things my mother had told me were lies. According to her, only the "fast girls got pregnant." The ones who stayed out late and hung around with boys. I wasn't part of that category!

I looked down at my stuffed belly and thought about my family. Would they be understanding? After all, they had plans for my future. They would be destroyed by the news.

"I'm not a tramp," I said to myself. "Then again, I'm only 16 and who would believe that Arthur and I really are in love?"

The feelings of this unmarried girl are all too typical. Children born of these pregnancies have it even harder (Garn & Petzold, 1983). Harvard biological anthropologist Melvin Kohner (1977) sums it up:

■ As maternal age drops from age 20, mortality risk for mother and child rise sharply as does the probability of birth defects. Offspring of adolescent mothers, if they survive, are more likely to have impaired intellectual functioning. Poverty, divorce, inept parenting, child neglect, and child abuse are all more frequent in teenage parents. (p. 38)

Trends in Behavior

As figure 13.4 makes clear, out-of-wedlock child bearing is on the increase in all age groups for both white and African American teenage females. As would be expected, the rate is highest for those under 15. In most states, 10 to 20 percent of all females have been pregnant at least once by the time they reach their 19th birthday. Clearly this is unfortunate, but the rate for 15- to 17-year-olds, which is about one-third as high, might even be described as catastrophic. The largest increases in

A number of large, urban high schools are creating day-care facilities for the babies and children of high school students. Do you think public schools should be providing these services? What services, if any, should junior and senior high schools provide to teenage parents?

Figure 13.4

Trends in out-of-wedlock child bearing among U.S. females under age 20 by race, 1969–87

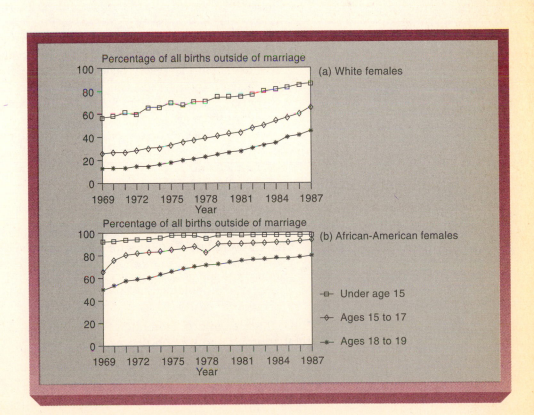

Table 13.4	Adolescent Fathers Who Reported Having Fathered a Child Before the Age of 20, by Father's Age at Child's Birth and Marital Status at Conception					
Father's age at child's birth	**Males who reported having fathered a child before age 20** N = 555		**Single at conception** N = 446		**Married at conception** N = 109	
Age 11 to 16	66	(10.1%)	66	(12.7%)	0	(0.0%)
Age 17	85	(15.8)	76	(18.3)	9	(5.8)
Age 18	181	(30.6)	158	(32.8)	23	(22.1)
Age 19	223	(43.5)	146	(36.2)	77	(72.0)
Age 11 to 19	555	(100.0)	446	(100.0)	109	(100.0)

Source: *Adolescent Health* (vol. 1–3), Office of Technology Assessment, Washington, D.C., 1991.

teen pregnancy rates have occurred in those under the age of 15 (Westoff & others, 1983) and overall, more unmarried teens become parents than ever (Furstenberg, 1990).

Currently more than 1 million teenagers become pregnant in this country every year. One in 10 girls becomes pregnant before the age of 20 (Foster, 1988). The ramifications of this social problem extend into other social problems. Pregnancy is considered the number-one reason for adolescent females dropping out of school (Strobino, 1987). The most likely profile of a pregnant teenager is a girl of color, raised in a poor, single-parent home, who has low academic and occupational aspirations (Polit, 1985). To further complicate things, the younger the father at the time of the child's birth, the less likely he is to be married (see table 13.4 for data on this).

Many stereotypes have been suggested for the causes of this epidemic. Some point to earlier menstruation; others talk of the crumbling morals of today's youth. We can say that the images of the fast and easy girl and the sex-obsessed boy are surely false (Herz & Reis, 1987; Kinard & Reinherz, 1987; Klein & Cordell, 1987; Stiffman & others, 1987). Most of these couples have had a substantial relationship prior to the pregnancy, usually for at least six months.

Adolescents in the United States have rates of pregnancy that are among the world's highest; this is especially true of inner-city adolescents (Colletta, 1982; Garcia-Coll & others, 1987; Herz & Reis, 1987; Silber, 1980; Stiffman & others, 1987). Six percent of them give birth each year. Of these, one-third give birth out of wedlock, one-third conceive before marriage, and one-third conceive after marriage. In one study, researchers interviewed a thousand 30-year-olds and found that 10 percent of the men and 31 percent of the women had had a child during adolescence (Russ-Eft & others, 1979).

As Lancaster and Hamburg (1986) point out:

Except for the very youngest adolescents, contraception and abortion have lowered the birthrates for adolescents since 1970 to levels that are somewhat lower than those in the 1920s and 1950s. However, the rate of adolescent childbearing outside of marriage has shown steep increases. (p. 5)

What this means is that more and more children are being born without the cultural approval and support that marriage brings.

The Role of Family in Teen Pregnancies

Rosen (1980) examined the extent to which teenagers involve their parents in decision making in resolving unwanted conceptions. Data were obtained from a questionnaire given to 432 unmarried 12- to 17-year-olds with unwanted conceptions. Although few subjects consulted their parents when they first thought they might be pregnant, more than half did involve their mothers in deciding what to do about the pregnancy. The findings indicate that less of a generation gap may exist between parents and teenagers than is often supposed.

However, there is some doubt that communication about any sexual topics makes much difference. On the basis of their study of 287 African American and white teens, Furstenberg (1990) concluded that

> ■ most parents do not want to get directly involved and, certainly, most teenagers are reluctant to encourage involvement. . . . [Most parents] are relieved to discover that their teenagers are obtaining contraception. Beyond that, it seems that most are either willing or prefer to respect the adolescent's privacy. (p. 241)

Held (1981) conducted a study of 62 girls, none more than 17 years old, who were in the third trimester of pregnancy. Twenty-two percent were white; 56 percent African American; and 16 percent Mexican American. Each adolescent completed the self-esteem inventory and rated her perception of the reactions of significant people in her life to the pregnancy.

A MULTICULTURAL VIEW

The Role of Ethnicity in Teen Pregnancy

Many studies have reported that teens of color are at great risk of having unwanted pregnancies. To understand this finding, however, it is important to sort out ethnic values from socioeconomic factors. Poor teens, whether African American, Asian American, Native American, white, or Latino, are three to four times as likely to become unwed teens than economically advantaged teens (Children's Defense Fund, 1989).

The higher rates of teenage parenthood among economically disadvantaged youth are understandable. Teens who are behind in school, who lack basic skills, and who see few opportunities for their future are more likely to become parents as teenagers. For adolescents lacking educational and job opportunities, parenting may be one of the few available ways of achieving adult status. Unfortunately, becoming pregnant as teenagers often makes their lives and the lives of their young children more difficult.

To solve the problem of teenage parenthood, we have to solve problems of education and job opportunities for all teenagers, regardless of ethnicity. We must also consider ways to help teenage mothers provide their babies with the needed emotional, intellectual, and physical care, while also enabling the mothers to continue their education. These factors, as you will recall from our discussion of the consequences of teenage pregnancy, often make a difference in the futures of the mothers and their children. Support from family members can be important.

The person on whom these subjects depended most was the mother; the prospective grandmother was the most disapproving. Social support among the three ethnic groups differed: The African American woman who was keeping her baby had the highest self-esteem, but she and her mother were least likely to rate the pregnancy as "good" or "OK." White women more often rated the pregnancy highly but had lower self-esteem. The 10 Mexican Americans reported the least disapproval.

Gabriel and McAnarney (1983) compared the decision about parenthood in two study groups in Rochester, New York: 17 African American, low-income adolescents (age 15 to 18 years) and 53 white, middle-class adult couples. The researchers' observations showed that the decision to become parents was related to different subcultural values. In contrast to the white adults, the African American subjects did not see marriage as a prerequisite for motherhood, nor did they view completion of schooling and economic independence as phases of maturation that should precede parenthood.

Instead, these subjects expected that becoming mothers would help them to achieve maturation and acceptance as adults. This may have been because the African American subjects did not see other adult roles as available, whereas middle-class white couples did. At the same time, adolescent pregnancy and out-of-wedlock motherhood were not viewed negatively among the low-income African American subjects. Health care programs that encourage birth control to avoid "unwanted pregnancies" may be ineffective because they do not address the needs of African American clients in terms of the values of their own subculture.

AN APPLIED VIEW

Talking to Teens about Pregnancy

Nurses, teachers and counselors frequently have opportunities to help teens to clarify their attitudes toward pregnancy, whether they are currently involved with a pregnancy or not. For a number of reasons, these conversations seldom take place, however.

Sometimes those who work with teens feel that discussing pregnancy with them means pushing their own values on them. Others feel that this subject is very delicate and should not be discussed outside the church or home. Others refrain from discussing it because they

feel like they just don't know enough (readers of this book, of course, will not have to be concerned about this problem!). It does seem reasonable to make sure that teens have the objective facts about pregnancy and its repercussions for baby, mother, and father. Does this make sense to you?

It should be noted that some of the suggestions for talking to teens about sex in the box on page 335 are useful here, too.

In summary, one note of caution: In an extensive review of the literature on adolescent pregnancy, McKenry, Walters, and Johnson (1979) made an important point about racial difference. They found that whereas studies of low-income non-white girls tended to focus on social factors, studies of white, middle-class girls tended to search for psychological explanations for the pregnancies and their outcomes. It is important to remember that although racial and social class differences have been reported in the research, some of these differences may have more to do with the researchers than with the teenagers themselves.

Guided Review

14. A large increase in the pregnancy rate is occurring in those under the age of _____ .

15. The ramifications of teen pregnancies extend into numerous other _____ problems.

16. Most teenagers who become pregnant had been in a relationship for at least _____ _____ , contrary to the stereotype.

17. McHenry and colleagues found that whereas adolescent pregnancy studies of low-income nonwhite girls tended to focus on _____ factors, studies of white, middle-class girls tended to search for _____ explanations for the pregnancies and their outcomes.

Answers

14, 15. social   16. six months   17. social, psychological

Figure 13.5
High school seniors reporting having ever used selected drugs

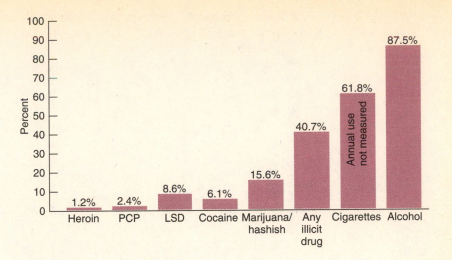

Illegal Behavior

Although they are not necessarily developmental in nature, we include brief sections on substance abuse and criminal behavior in this chapter because they often play a role in other aspects of development during adolescence. For the most part, clearly, that role is negative.

Substance Abuse

It is difficult to say precisely how widespread substance abuse is. Studies differ from year to year, from region to region, and disappointingly, from one another (even when year and region are the same). One of the best studies of high school seniors (Office of Technology Assessment, 1991) found a slight decrease in marijuana, stimulants, hallucinogens, sedatives, tranquilizers, cocaine, and crack cocaine, and a leveling off in alcohol (which at 90.7 percent could not get a lot higher than it is). Figure 13.5 presents the most recent data on substance use.

Criminal Behavior

Although much could be said about juvenile delinquency, it is so changeable and varying by region, gender, and social class that we will not be able to go into it here. Instead, we will limit this discussion to one aspect of adolescent criminal behavior, gang behavior, which has been moving in a most disturbing direction lately.

Gangs often offer youths the fulfillment of basic needs. Some of their functions clearly coincide with those of the larger society. Gangs typically provide protection, recognition of the desire to feel wanted, and rites of passage that mark achievement, status, and acceptance, such as the initiation rite of a potential gang member. Thus we may say that the gang is a kind of subculture, a "subculture of violence" (Hammond & Yung, 1993, p. 145).

According to a study the New York City Youth Board (1989) commissioned, urban gangs possess the following characteristics:

- Their behavior is normal for urban youths; they have a high degree of cohesion and organization; roles are clearly defined.

- They possess a consistent set of norms and expectations, understood by all members.

- They have clearly defined leaders.

- They have a coherent organization for gang warfare.

In what cases should juvenile offenders be tried as adults? Should they always be treated as adults? Should they be treated differently because of their age? What things need to be considered?

After a period of decline, urban gangs are again on the rise.

The gang provides many adolescents with a structured life they never had at home. What makes the gang particularly cohesive is its function as a family substitute for adolescents whose strong dependency needs are displaced onto the peer group. The gang becomes a family to its members (Burton, 1978).

The formation of juvenile gangs typically follows a sudden increase in this country of new ethnic groups due to immigration. The children of new immigrants have a difficult time breaking through cultural barriers such as a new language and racism. Perceiving their prospects of succeeding in the new society as bleak, some of these children form gangs, which provide the structure and security discussed, but also serve as an outlet to attack the society that seemingly will not accept them. In times past, these gangs were composed of Jewish, Irish, and Italian Americans. Today's gangs are frequently formed by Latinos, Asian Americans, and African Americans (Burke, 1990; Vigil, 1988). The gang becomes a vehicle for tearing its members away from the main social structures and authorities, in particular the family and school.

But today's gangs have some disturbing differences from those of years past. They are much more heavily armed and seemingly much more willing to use their weapons. Movies like *West Side Story* (1961) depict gang members carrying knives, chains, and pipes. Today's urban gangs are often armed with AK-47 assault rifles and UZI submachine guns, grenades, and even cluster bombs.

Gang violence has increased dramatically in this decade. Urban gangs commit 25 percent of all juvenile crimes. Los Angeles, with more than 200 gangs with 12,000 members, has perhaps suffered most from this upsurge in violence. That city saw gang-related homicides increase from an already staggering 150 in 1985 to an unfathomable 387 in 1987. Of course, the days of rioting in 1992 eclipse even these statistics.

Law enforcement officials have noted that attacks by gangs on police officers are now quite common and continue to increase (Gates & Jackson, 1990; Sessions, 1990). Many innocent bystanders are also injured or killed by violent gangs, often in **drive-by shootings.** Statistics from the Los Angeles Police Department indicate that 50 percent of the victims of gang violence have no connection at all with any gang activity (Gates & Jackson, 1990). In addition to killing members of rival gangs, gang members also frequently kill one another, even within their own "set"

Drive-by shootings

Shootings committed by someone riding in a car past the victim.

or subdivision. This is especially true of large gangs like the Crips and the Bloods of Los Angeles (Bing, 1991; Ewing, 1990) (although these two gangs have recently sought to establish a peaceful truce between them—Barnicle, 1992).

Gangs are also no longer limited to the large urban areas. Smaller cities and towns in the United States have recently seen an increase in the formation of juvenile gangs (Takata & others, 1987). These gangs are often related to other, well-established gangs from the larger cities. So in effect, a gang such as L.A.'s Crips can set up "franchises" in cities such as Seattle and Shreveport. Suburban gangs have also been on the upswing (Muehlbauer & Dodder, 1983). These suburban gangs usually don't exhibit the same degree of organization or formality. They typically get their "kicks" from the malicious destruction of property.

🌳 Guided Review 🌳

18. Some of the functions of a gang include protection, recognition of desire to feel wanted, rites of passage that mark _____ , status, and acceptance.

19. Gangs can be cohesive because of their function as a _____ _____ for adolescents with strong dependency needs.

20. Gangs can become a vehicle for tearing their members away from the main _____ _____ of society.

Answers

18. achievement   19. family substitute   20. social structures

---

🌳 CONCLUSION

For each of the aspects of social interaction reviewed in this chapter—peer relations, sexual behavior, sexually transmitted diseases, teenage parenthood, criminal behavior—all adolescents must deal with one consistent trend: fast-paced change. Some of this change derives from ground swells in today's society, and some results from the nature of adolescence itself. Thus again we see the biopsychosocial model demonstrated.

Interactions among teenaged peers alter with each generation. Gang behavior is a growing threat to healthy development. Yet perhaps nothing has had a more resounding impact on adolescent life than the recent changes in our attitudes toward sexuality. The four areas of greatest change have been in homosexuality, sexually transmitted diseases (including AIDS), the earlier and more widespread participation in sex by teenage females, and the increase in pregnancy and child bearing among younger teenagers.

Some observers have suggested that the biggest problem facing adolescents today, and one intertwined with those just listed, is the difficulty in knowing when childhood and youth have ended and adulthood has begun. When the societal lines between these stages of development are blurred, youth cannot be blamed for not knowing how to behave. A clearer induction into adult life has been advocated. This will be the main topic of the next chapter.

🌳 CHAPTER HIGHLIGHTS

Peer Relations

- Peer groups provide adolescents with a source of social activities and support, and an easy entry into opposite-sex friendships.
- The biological, psychological, cognitive, and social changes of adolescence affect the development of a teenager's peer relationships.
- Peer groups serve to control aggressive impulses, encourage independence, improve social skills, develop reasoning abilities, and form attitudes toward sexuality and sexual behavior. They may also strengthen moral judgment and values and improve self-esteem.
- Peer groups also aid in the development of self-concept and allow an adolescent to try out a new identity.

Sexual Behavior

- The "sexual revolution" has led to many teenagers becoming sexually active at increasingly younger ages.
- Sexuality develops in three stages, from love of self to love of members of the same gender to love of members of the opposite gender.

- Masturbation is believed to be a harmless and universal form of human sexual expression.
- Homosexual behavior has been surrounded by many myths throughout history.
- Several theories suggest different origins of homosexual orientation: psychoanalytic, learning, and genetic.
- Many researchers now believe that homosexual orientation may already be set by adolescence.
- Many teens still obtain a great deal of information and misinformation about sex from their peers.
- First intercourse is now occurring earlier than it did in past generations.
- Youths from stable family environments are less likely to engage in premarital sexual relations.
- Effective listening skills are essential for parents who wish to maintain good communication with their adolescents.
- Teenagers misuse sex for many nonsexual reasons, including a search for affection, rebellion against parents, venting anger, and alleviating boredom.
- Many adolescent runaways and prostitutes are the products of

sexual abuse, often by someone they know, a family member or parent.

Sexually Transmitted Diseases

- Today a high prevalence of sexually transmitted diseases (STDs) is found in sexually active adolescents.
- AIDS (acquired immune deficiency syndrome) causes the most concern, because it is currently incurable and often fatal. As yet it is not very common in adolescents, but because it usually lies dormant for 10 to 15 years, it is a cause for great concern.
- Other STDs that affect adolescents are increasing in epidemic proportions, including chlamydia, gonorrhea, genital herpes, syphilis, and hepatitis B.
- In spite of increased availability and information about contraceptive methods, many teenagers continue to engage in unprotected sex.

The Teenage Parent

- Teenage pregnancy and parenthood are on the rise among younger teens. With rare exceptions, this situation causes a lot of heartache for the teenage parents, their parents, and their child.

- Teenage mothers who receive emotional support from their families, who continue in school, and who have no additional children while they are still teenagers are likely to have better-adjusted children and avoid the cycle of poverty.
- When teens possess strong self-esteem, feelings of hope concerning the future, and job and academic skills for entry into the job market, they are less likely to become teenage parents.

Illegal Behavior

- Drug and alcohol abuse is still prevalent, although some important changes have been noted. For example, tobacco use is on the rise among teenagers, whereas marijuana use is on the decline.
- Gangs typically have a high degree of cohesion and organization, a consistent set of norms, clearly defined leaders, and coherent organization for warfare.
- Gangs have become much more violent in the past decade, probably in part as a response to increased drug trafficking.

🌳 KEY TERMS

AIDS (acquired immune deficiency syndrome)   339
Autosexuality   330
Chlamydia   342
Crowds   326
Double standard   334
Drive-by shootings   350
Egocentric interests   325
Genetic theory of homosexuality   332

Genital herpes   343
Gonorrhea   342
Hepatitis B   343
Heterosexuality   330
Homosexuality   330
Human immunodeficiency virus (HIV)   340
Introspection   325
Learning theory of homosexuality   332

Pelvic inflammatory disease (PID)   343
Psychoanalytic theory of homosexuality   332
Reflective listening   335
Sexual revolution   329
Sexually transmitted diseases   339
Social interests   325
Subculture   326
Syphilis   343

🌳 WHAT DO YOU THINK?

1. Do you think that your adolescent peer group followed the developmental patterns described in this chapter?
2. What are some of the most important effects that your teenaged peer group had on your life?
3. Do you agree with the theorists who claim that there are three stages in the development of love and

sexuality and that this development is natural?
4. Why do you think we are seeing such widespread changes in the sexual aspects of our lives?
5. If you were the mayor of a medium-size city, what actions would you take to try to reduce the incidence of sexually transmitted diseases?

6. If you were the mayor of a medium-size city, what actions would you take to try to reduce the incidence of teenage parenthood?
7. If you were the mayor of a large-size city, what actions would you take to try to reduce the incidence of gang violence?

SUGGESTED READINGS

Angelou, M. (1970). *I know why the caged bird sings*. New York: Random House. Ms. Angelou recounts her childhood in rural Arkansas. Her strength and resilience model the building of a strong personal and cultural identity.

Auel, J. (1981). *Clan of the cave bear*. New York: Bantam. Auel's wonderful imagination and excellent knowledge of anthropology make this book on the beginnings of the human family a winner. In fast-paced fiction, she describes the relationships, sexual and otherwise, of early humans who, she speculates, were unaware that sex causes pregnancy!

Calderone, M. S. & Ramsey, J. (1981). *Talking to your child about sex*. New York: Ballantine. This book offers a creative interpretation of human sexuality in a family setting.

Capote, T. [1948] (1988). *Other voices, other rooms*. New York: Signet. Written when Capote was 23 years old, this book is considered by many to be his best work. It is the story of a 13-year-old boy who goes to live with his father in Louisiana and meets many eccentric characters. Through this experience he becomes aware of the adult world and his own homosexuality.

Cohen, S. & Cohen, D. (1986). *A six-pack and a fake I.D.: Teens look at the drinking question*. New York: M. Evans. According to the authors of this book, the decision to drink or not to drink is personal rather than moral. They recognize the tragedy that alcohol can bring into people's lives, but they still "do not see moderate drinking as a problem; indeed, it is often a positive pleasure." They do, however, feel that before coming to conclusions about the use of alcohol, you should have reliable and believable information to help you make the best and most informed decision.

Fromm, E. (1968). *The art of loving*. New York: Harper & Row. Although most of us think of love as a very personal topic, it would be hard to think of anything that has been the subject of more novels, articles, poems, plays, and psychological treatises. Most of these are not particularly helpful, and many are downright corny. Fromm's book is a distinct exception. You will understand what love is and how to give and receive it much better when you have finished reading it.

Harris, J. (1987). *Drugged athletes: The crisis in American sports*. New York: Four Winds Press. Athletes take drugs to increase speed, strength, and accuracy; to mask pain; to relax muscles; to relieve stress; to improve performance; and to gain pleasure. Harris provides an overview and discusses specific problems of drugs in sports at all levels.

Jacoby, A. (1987). *My mother's boyfriend and me*. New York: Dial Books. Sixteen-year-old Laurie doesn't know how to handle it when her mother's 27-year-old, handsome, blue-eyed boyfriend starts making advances.

Janus, S. & Janus, C. (1993). *The Janus report on sexual behavior*. New York: Wiley. A wide-ranging survey of attitudes and behavior.

Tannahill, R. (1980). *Sex in history*. New York: Ballantine. This lively book describes the role of sex down through the ages.

Walker, A. (1982). *The color purple*. New York: Harcourt Brace Jovanovich. This disturbing story of African American teenage pregnancy in the South was hailed by all the reviewers for its insight.

CHAPTER REVIEW TEST

1. Brown (1991) states that the peer group can change in four ways during adolescence: adolescents spend more time with peers; they receive less adult supervision; they interact more with peers of the opposite sex; and
   a. they interact with peers in a work setting.
   b. they become sexually active.
   c. they begin to identify with certain crowds.
   d. they interact more with peers in school and service activities.

2. An adolescent's definition of a friend is likely to include
   a. someone who lives in the neighborhood.
   b. someone who shares similar values and interests.
   c. someone in class.
   d. someone whom they work with.

3. What reason is cited in the text for why there may be a decline in early sexual activity?
   a. concern about AIDS and other STDs
   b. prevailing conservative attitudes
   c. more people devoting time to making money
   d. the increasing influence of religion

4. The first stage of sexuality
   a. is heterosexuality.
   b. is homosexuality.
   c. is autosexuality.
   d. depends on the individual.

5. Adolescents are engaging in sex at earlier ages
   a. because they want to experiment with sex.
   b. because there is an increased level of alcohol and drug use among this population.
   c. due to changes in our social context.
   d. to be rebellious.

6. The genetic theory on homosexuality claims that
   a. people learn to be homosexual.
   b. as children homosexuals identified with the same-sex parent.
   c. persons born with a predisposition toward homosexuality can be influenced by the environment to either select or avoid homosexuality.
   d. many homosexuals are in denial about their genetically predisposed orientation.

7. Although he has a girlfriend, Steve wants to prove to his friends that he can "score" with a number of different girls in school. Steve's nonsexual motive for sex is to
   a. get affection.
   b. confirm his masculinity.
   c. ensure fidelity of his girlfriend.
   d. obtain greater self-esteem.

8. A female adolescent who "acts out" by running away, engaging in sexual promiscuity, or damaging her school performance may be a victim of
   a. drug abuse.
   b. peer pressure.
   c. extreme loneliness.
   d. sexual abuse.

9. The CDC estimates how many people in the United States are currently infected with the initial virus of AIDS?
   a. 50,000
   b. 100,000
   c. 500,000 to 600,000
   d. 1 to 1.5 million

10. Intravenous drug users, homosexual men, and inner-city heterosexuals are groups most at risk for contracting
    a. syphilis.
    b. genital herpes.
    c. hepatitis B.
    d. gonorrhea.

11. The highest rates of teen pregnancy occur for those
    a. under age 15.
    b. 15 to 16 years of age.
    c. 16 to 18 years of age.
    d. 18 to 19 years of age.

12. Sara is an African American teenager who grew up in a poor, single-parent home, and has low occupational aspirations. Sara fits the profile of a
    a. drug abuser.
    b. gang member.
    c. pregnant teenager.
    d. domestic abuse victim.

13. Held (1981) conducted a study of teenage girls in the third trimester of pregnancy. It was found that social support among the ethnic groups differed in that _____ keeping their baby had the highest self-esteem.
    a. Mexican Americans
    b. whites
    c. African Americans
    d. None of the answers are correct.

14. Important racial differences can be found in recent research on teenage pregnancy. It seems that studies of low-income nonwhite girls focus on societal factors, whereas studies of white, middle-class girls tend to focus on
    a. social causes.
    b. cognitive ability causes.
    c. psychological causes.
    d. moral reasoning ability causes.

15. John joins a gang because it serves as a pseudo-family for him. Most likely John has strong _____ needs that are being displaced onto the peer group.
    a. dependency
    b. friendship
    c. financial
    d. All of the answers are correct.

16. Recent research indicates that gangs have which of the following characteristics?
    a. They possess a consistent set of norms and expectations that are understood by all gang members.
    b. Members have lower expectations of success than do nonmembers.
    c. Members are as likely to have divorced parents as are nonmembers.
    d. Members are more likely to score high on IQ tests than are nonmembers.

Answers

1. c 2. b 3. a 4. c 5. c 6. c 7. b 8. d 9. d 10. c 11. a 12. c 13. c 14. c 15. a 16. a

PART VII

Early Adulthood

You grow up the day you have the
first real laugh—at yourself.

Ethel Barrymore

All the young men standing in the living room of the old fraternity house had solemn faces. As the fraternity president began intoning the sacred words that would lead to their induction, Dave and Bill looked at each other out of the corners of their eyes. The two "pledges" were in the front row, waiting along with nine other sheepish-looking freshmen. Each knew the other was remembering the same thing—the long ordeal of their pledge period, which had begun at the start of the semester.

For weeks they had to wear ridiculous beanies on their heads and act as virtual slaves to the fraternity brothers. Despite their best efforts to obey the complex rules, each had incurred numerous violations, which the brothers had noted in their pledge books.

Last night, for the initiation opener, they had endured one blow from a thick magazine, rolled up and taped for the purpose, for each of their rule violations. Bent over and holding their ankles, they had managed to get through the bottom-beatings without crying out, but not without becoming very black and blue. Then they were taken as a pair and dropped off in the middle of a dark woods with instructions to get back to the frat house by 10 A.M. if they wanted to be initiated.

After numerous scares and mishaps, they made it to the main road and hitched into town. On their return to the house, they thought their initiation was finished, but the ordeal was far from over. Now came a series of lesser trials, including

- Being made to lie on their backs while tablespoons of baking soda and then vinegar were poured into their open mouths. They were ordered to close their mouths and keep them that way no matter what. The brothers laughed uproariously when, inevitably, the mixture exploded, shooting a geyser from their tightly pressed lips high into the air.

- Being blindfolded and made to eat warm "dog manure." Actually they had eaten doughnuts soaked in warm water, but the bag of manure held under their noses made them believe it was the real thing.

- Having a mixture of Liederkranz cheese and rotten eggs smeared on their upper lips, then being made to run around while inhaling the dreadful odor.

Now, as the torture was over, and the final ceremony was under way, both Dave and Bill had the same thought in their minds: I've done it! I've survived! I'm in! 🌳

This chapter investigates three important factors in adult life: the Western passage to maturity, criticisms of it, and alternatives to it; sexual identity and gender roles; and stress, which is placed in this chapter not because young adults are under more stress than other age groups, but because this is the age when people must begin learning how to manage the many sources of stress in life, relying mainly on their own resources.

When you finish this chapter, you will be able to

- Discuss the purpose of initiation rites and the effects on adolescents of there being no formal rite of passage into adulthood in our culture.

- Describe the components of some initiation rites in preindustrial societies.

- List activities in our own society that may be parallel to these rites.

- Discuss the concept of the adolescent moratorium, its strengths and weaknesses.

- Specify some activities that could serve some of the purposes of an initiation rite.

- Distinguish between sexual identity and gender role.

- Define three aspects of gender role, as well as the concept of androgyny.

- Demonstrate awareness of gender-role stereotypes and how they influence adolescent behavior.

- Define stress and identify common sources of stress during the teenage years.

- Describe the relationship between stress, physical illness, and mental health.

- List the three stages of Selye's general adaptation syndrome.

- Explain the relationship between risk and resiliency.

Initiation Rites

The horrors of the fraternity initiation have been softened by legal restrictions and by more humane attitudes. For example, Baier and Williams (1983) surveyed 440 active members and 420 alumni members of the fraternity system of a large state university. They compared attitudes of these men toward 22 **hazing practices** (such as those just described) known to be used by the frats. They found the active members were considerably opposed to more of the practices than the alumni.

Hazing practices
The often dangerous practices used by some fraternities to initiate new members.

Nevertheless, most of us have heard of recent cases of maimings and even deaths of young men who have been put through hazing. People at all socioeconomic levels and racial and ethnic backgrounds hold such trials. They are organized by sports teams and criminal gangs and are not limited to males, either.

Nor is the problem limited to the United States. For example, in his study of French juvenile delinquents, Garapon (1983) saw a "symbolic, sacrificial dimension" to their crimes. He noted that often cars and other stolen goods are either dumped in the canals or burned, which he feels parallels the sacrifices of prized goods that preindustrial tribes carried out with fire and water. He pointed out other links to tribal initiations: Most crimes are committed at night and wind up in courtrooms, where there are symbolic costumes such as the judge's robes. In Germany, Zoja (1984) has suggested similar parallels in the path to drug addiction. He states that "Drug addiction can be an active choice, allowing the user to acquire a solid identity and social role, that of the negative hero, as well as access to an esoteric glimpse of an 'other world'" (p. 125).

Why do some people, and the groups they wish to be associated with, seem to enjoy holding initiation rites so much? And why are so many adolescents, many of them otherwise highly intelligent and reasonable, willing and eager to endure such pain? Is it simply because they want to join the group, to feel that they belong? There seems to be more to it than that. Throughout the world, adolescents readily engage in such activities because they seem to want to be tested, to prove to themselves that they have achieved the adult virtues of courage, independence, and self-control. And the adults seem to agree that adolescents should prove they have attained these traits before being admitted to the "club of maturity." Compare the activities that Dave and Bill were put through with those of Yudia and Mateya, two members of the Kaguru African tribe (see page 360).

Analysis of an Initiation Rite

Before discussing the implications of American initiation rites (or the lack of them), we'll provide a more detailed description of the purposes and components of such rites.

The first analysis of initiation ceremonies in preindustrial societies such as the Kaguru was completed by anthropologist Arnold Van Gennep in 1909 (Van Gennep, 1960). His explanation is still highly regarded, as can be seen in more recent studies (e.g., Anderson & Noesjirwan, 1980; Hill, 1987; Kitahara, 1983; Lidz & Lidz, 1984; Morinis, 1985; Ramsey, 1982). Van Gennep argued that the purpose of the **initiation rites,** as with all rites of passage (marriage, promotion, retirement, etc.), is to cushion the emotional disruption caused by a change from one status to another. For males, this transition also involves the end of dependence on their mothers and other older women and the beginning of their inclusion in the world of men.

This ceremony is often scheduled to coincide with the peak in adolescent physiological maturation and therefore has often been called a **puberty rite.** Van Gennep argued that this is inappropriate, since initiation may be held by one tribe when the children are 8 years old and in another at 16. Children of 8 have not yet started puberty; those of 16 are halfway through it. Also, the age at which puberty starts differs from individual to individual and now occurs approximately three years earlier than it did 100 years ago (see chapter 12). Nevertheless, the initiation rite is usually held at one age within each tribe, regardless of the physical maturity of the individual initiates.

Serving as an introduction to sexuality and separation from mother is one purpose of the initiation rite. Several other purposes have been suggested. In his classic text *Totem and Taboo* (1914/1955), Sigmund Freud offered the psychoanalytic explanation. In his view, such ceremonies are necessitated by the conflict between fathers and sons over who will dominate the women of the tribe. Adolescent males are seen as challenging the father's authority and right to control the women.

To make clear their supremacy in the tribe and to ensure the allegiance of the young males, the adults set a series of trials for the youth at which the adults are clearly superior. The ultimate threat held over the young is castration, the loss of sexual power. Most rites include trials of strength, endurance, prowess, and courage. These usually involve forced ingestion of tobacco and other drugs, fumigations, flagellations, beatings with heavy sticks (running the gauntlet), tattooing, cutting of the ears, lips, and gums, and that most Freudian of inflictions, the circumcision of the foreskin of the penis.

The message is clear: "We, the adult males, are in charge. Join us and be loyal, or else!" Psychologist Bruno Bettleheim (1969) agrees with Freud that a fear of castration exists among the males but argues that the main role of the initiation rite is to ease, not to exaggerate, the stress of becoming an adult.

In these explanations of initiation rites, biological, psychological, and social factors are emphasized to varying degrees. Can you say what these factors are?

After months of grueling training, teenage members of most preindustrial tribes, such as these San Carlos Apaches, are inducted into adulthood.

Initiation rites

A cultural and sometimes ceremonial task that signals the entrance to some new developmental stage. Such rites can indicate the passage from adolescence to adulthood.

Puberty rite

An initiation ceremony often scheduled to coincide with the peak in adolescent physiological maturation.

Answers

1. rituals   2. independence

A MULTICULTURAL VIEW

Yudia and Mateya Come of Age

Yudia cannot believe how rapidly her feelings keep changing. One moment she is curious and excited, the next, nervous and afraid. Tonight begins her *igubi,* the rite that celebrates her induction into adulthood. Yudia has longed for this day most of her 11 years, but now she wonders if she really wants the responsibilities of a grown-up.

Though it seems much longer, only a week has passed since the excruciating beginning of her initiation. The memory of it is already dimming: the bright fire, her women relatives pinning her down on the table, her grandmother placing a thin sharp stone against her vulva, the searing pain.

The women had held and consoled her, empathizing fully with her feelings. Each had been through the same agony. For them, too, it occurred shortly after their first menstruation. They had explained to her that this was just the beginning of the suffering she must learn to endure as an adult woman. All during the past week, they had been teaching her—about the pain her husband would sometimes cause her, about the difficulties of pregnancy and childbirth, about the many hardships she must bear stoically. For she is Kaguru, and all Kaguru women accept their lot in life without complaint.

It has been a hard week, but tonight the pleasure of the igubi will help her forget her wound. There will be singing, dancing, and strong beer to drink. The ceremony, with its movingly symbolic songs, will go on for two days and nights. Only the women of this Tanzanian village will participate, intoning the time-honored phrases that will remind Yudia all her life of her adult duties.

In a large hut less than a mile from the village, Yudia's male cousin Mateya and seven other 13-year-old Kaguru boys huddle close, even though the temperature in the closely thatched enclosure is a stifling 110 degrees. Rivulets of sweat flow from their bodies and flies dot their arms, backs, and legs. They no longer pay attention to the flies, nor the vivid slashes of white, brown, and black clay adorning all their faces. Their thoughts are dominated by a single fear: Will they cry out when the elder's sharpened stone begins to separate the tender foreskin from their penises? Each dreams of impressing his father, who will be watching, by smiling throughout the horrible ordeal.

Three months of instruction and testing have brought the young men to this point. They have learned many things together: how to spear their own food, how to tend their tiny gardens, how to inseminate their future wives, and most important, how to rely on themselves when in danger.

The last three months have been exhausting. The boys have been through many trials. In some, they had to prove they could work together; in others, their skill in self-preservation was tested. For most of them, being out of contact with their mothers was the hardest part. They have not seen any of the female members of their families since they started their training. Unlike Yudia's initiation, which is designed to draw her closer to the adult women of the tribe, Mateya's initiation is designed to remove him forever from the influence of the females and to align him with the adult men.

Now it is evening. Mateya is the third to be led out to the circle of firelight. Wide-eyed, he witnesses an eerie scene. His male relatives are dancing in a circle around him, chanting the unchanging songs. The grim-faced elder holds the carved ceremonial knife. Asked if he wishes to go on, the boy nods yes. Abruptly the ritual begins: The hands of the men hold him tight; the cold knife tip touches his penis; a shockingly sharp pain sears his loins; he is surprised to hear a piercing scream; then, filled with shame, he realizes it comes from him.

Thus far, Yudia's and Mateya's initiations have been different. Mateya's has been longer and harder than Yudia's. She is being brought even closer to the women who have raised them both, but Mateya must now align himself with the men (for more on this, see Lidz & Lidz, 1984).

The initiations are similar, though, in that both youths have experienced severe physical pain (for more on this, see Morinis, 1985). In both cases, the operations were meant to sensitize them to the vastly greater role sex will now play in their lives. Furthermore, their mutilations made them recognizable to all as adults of the Kaguru tribe.

At this "coming out" ceremony, males and females also receive new names, usually those of close ancestors. This illustrates the continuity of the society. The beliefs of the tribe are preserved in the continuous flow from infant to child to adult to elder to deceased and to newborn baby again. When all is done, Yudia and Mateya can have no doubt that they have passed from childhood to adulthood.

Guided Review

3. According to Van Gennep, the purpose of initiation rites is to cushion the _____ _____ caused by a change from one status to another.

4. An additional purpose of the initiation rite is to serve as an introduction to _____ and separation from mother.

Answers

3. emotional disruption   4. sexuality

The Passage to Adulthood in Western Countries

How are Western youths inducted into adulthood? Are Western initiation rites adequate? These are questions we will now address.

The Transition to Adulthood in the United States

In the industrial past of the United States, it used to be fairly clear when one became an adult. In their late teens, boys and girls usually got married and assumed an adult role. Males were accepted as partners in the family farm or business; females became housewives. This has changed in many ways. What Black (1974) has suggested is still true:

> Today, in modern society, initiation of the boy and girl into adult life is far more complicated. Society is fast, heterogeneous, a network of interdependent groups with many different backgrounds, traditions, and outlooks, the products of religious, racial, national, and class differences. In our age of technology, the young have to learn to deal with cars and trains and planes, machines and other electronic equipment, typewriters, television sets, computers, and mass production assembly lines. They face high concentrations of population, high mobility, and relationships on regional, national, and global levels. All this they have to know and understand at a time when customs, laws and institutions are undergoing drastic and rapid change in the midst of a high degree of human differences and human conflict. (p. 25)

No specific rituals are comparable to those in preindustrial societies to help Western youth through this difficult period. For example, religious ceremonies like confirmation and bar mitzvah no longer seem to play the role they had in earlier times. Kilpatrick (1975) argued that

> at some point we grew too sophisticated, at some point the rituals lost their vitality and became mere ornaments. We may still keep their observance, but they are like old family retainers, kept on in vague remembrance of their past service. (p. 145)

In his anthology of adolescent literature, Thomas Gregory (1978) pointed out that many modern writers find the decline of the initiation rite in the United States a noteworthy theme. He describes their thinking as follows:

> Today's adolescents are faced with not knowing when they have reached maturity . . . the absence of a formal rite of passage ceremony necessitates a larger and more uncertain transition, with much groping, as adolescents not only try to establish their new adulthood, but also their identity. (p. 336)

Types of Initiation Activities in the United States

This is not to say that Americans have no activities that signal the passage to maturity. We have a number of types of activities, which usually happen at various stages and ages of adolescence. Here is a list of the types and some examples of each:

Religious
Bar mitzvah or bas mitzvah
Confirmation
Participating in a ceremony, such
   as reading from the Bible

Sexual
Menarche (first menstruation)
Nocturnal emissions (male "wet
   dreams")
Losing one's virginity

Societal changes have led to a change in the nature of initiation rites for adolescents. As a result, are adolescents better off today or should we try to return to the family and societal structures of the past?

The tuxedo and party dress might be considered costumes in one of America's initiation rites.

Social
"Sweet Sixteen" or debutante
    parties
Going to the senior prom
Joining a gang, fraternity, or
    sorority
Beginning to shave
Being chosen as a member of a
    sports team
Moving away from one's family
    and relatives
Joining the armed forces
Receiving a bridal shower
Getting married

Becoming a parent
Voting for the first time

Educational
Getting a driver's license
Graduating from high school
Going away to college

Economic
Getting a checking or credit card
    account
Buying a first car
Getting a first job

Adolescent moratorium

A "time-out" period during which the adolescent experiments with a variety of identities, without having to assume the responsibility for the consequences of any particular one.

The Adolescent Moratorium

In the late twentieth century, the attitude that youths need a "time out" period to explore possibilities and to continue education has become widespread. This phase of life is known as the **adolescent moratorium** (see chapter 11).

Perhaps it is natural that we have discarded rites of passage into adulthood for the more leisurely moratorium. In preindustrial societies, children must take over the responsibilities of adulthood as quickly as possible. The survival of the tribe depends on getting as much help from all individuals as possible. In industrial societies, and even more so in our information-processing society, the abundance of goods makes it less necessary that everyone contribute to the society. More extensive schooling is also needed in preparation for technical types of work. The moratorium, then, comes about because of our advanced economic system. Furthermore, our society values choice. Our children are not expected to follow in their parents' footsteps. It should be noted that poor adolescents, who have fewer choices, also have a shorter moratorium. For these reasons, the initiation ritual has declined considerably since the nineteenth century. Is our society the better or worse for this change?

Implications of the Lack of an Initiation Ceremony

Today we have doubts that this moratorium is turning out to be effective. In fact, it appears that crime is one of the ways that some youth are initiating themselves into adulthood. Males especially seem to need to do something dangerous and difficult. Males raised without fathers or father substitutes are especially vulnerable to the attractions of criminality (Dacey, 1986). When they are leaving adolescence, many of them seem to feel they must prove their adulthood by first proving their manhood in risk-taking behavior.

In the 1960s and early 1970s, American youths sought to establish their identities by imitating the very rituals of the preindustrial tribes described earlier in this chapter. Known as "hippies" and "flower children," they attempted to return to a simpler life. Many of them returned to the wilderness, living on farms and communes away from the large cities in which they were brought up. Many totally rejected the cultural values of their parents. The most famous symbol of their counterculture was the Woodstock musical marathon in 1969. With its loud, throbbing music, nudity, and widespread use of drugs, the event was similar to many primitive tribal rites. Yet these self-designed initiation rites also seem to be unsuccessful as passages to maturity. Most of the communes and other organizations of the youth movement of the 1960s have since failed. Most American youths have decided "you can't go back again."

It has been suggested that sports play the same role in life as the arduous tasks performed by youths in centuries past: learning coordination, cooperation, and the other skills necessary in adult work. Can you think of ways that sports might serve as initiation rites?

Organized sport is another attempt to include initiation rites in American life. The emphasis on athletic ability has much in common with the arduous tasks given to preindustrial youth. In particular, we can see a parallel in the efforts by fathers to get their sons to excel in Little League Baseball and Pop Warner Football. Fathers (and often mothers) are seen exhorting the players to try harder, to fight bravely, and when hurt, to "act like a man" and not cry.

Thus, in delinquency, the counterculture, and sports, we see evidence that members of several age groups today yearn for the establishment of some sort of initiation rite. Adolescents and adults alike seem to realize that something more is needed to provide assistance in this difficult transitional period. But what?

Traditional initiation rites are inappropriate for American youth. In preindustrial societies, individual status was ascribed by the tribe to which the person belonged. Social scientists call this an *ascribed identity*. The successes or failures of each tribe determined the prestige of its members. Family background and individual effort usually made little difference. In earlier times in the United States, the family was the prime source of status. Few children of the poor became merchants, doctors, or lawyers. Today, personal effort and early commitment to a career path play a far greater role in the individual's economic and social success. This is called an *achieved identity*. For this reason (and others), preindustrial customs are not compatible with Western youth today.

A MULTICULTURAL VIEW

The Cultural Role of the Bridal Shower

Although numerous differences occur in the ways our different religious and ethnic cultures unite men and women in marriage, one aspect of the wedding festivities that is common among most American ethnic groups is the bridal shower. Cheal (1989) has suggested that this is because all these groups use the shower, in which brides-to-be receive tokens of their new status such as kitchen utensils and household furnishings, to reenact the dependence of women on men. They also emphasize the interdependence of women on each other. In this view, bridal showers are a rite of passage designed to subjugate women to male dominance. What do you think?

Roy (1990) suggested that the regular inclusion of family rituals, of which rites of passage are one type, promote communication and healing within the family system. (Examples might be allowing a child to stay home alone, and a parent teaching a child to drive.) Through the marking of change in an individual, the family also realizes that it itself is changing. By traveling the developmental road together, it seems that adolescents and their families are able to adjust to the inherent difficulties of transition more readily.

The use of initiation rites has valuable implications for therapists and others. Roy claimed that

> ■ clergy and therapists can increase their effectiveness by promoting change through rituals. Rites of passage are the most obvious arena for change, individual as well as family. . . . Family members [can decode] family disputes around a rite of passage and facilitate the entry or exit of family members from nuclear family units. (p. 63)

With the apparent conflict that surrounds families with adolescents, it seems a natural option for them to create and employ meaningful rites of passage for the sake of healthy growth and family harmony.

A number of prominent thinkers have suggested that human development could be enhanced if the transition from adolescent to adult were clearer. But how to do it? Here are two suggestions that have been studied.

Two Proposals

The following two ideas on initiation procedure have lately been gaining in popularity. As you read about them, question whether either or both would fulfill the need for some kind of initiation into adulthood.

Outward Bound

Outward Bound

A program in which people learn to deal with their fears by participating in a series of increasingly threatening experiences.

Although they hardly know each other, these boys will find that working together to achieve the goals of this Outward Bound program quickly serves to break down the boundaries society establishes between strangers.

The **Outward Bound** program (Outward Bound, 1988) was founded during World War II to help merchant seamen in England survive when their ships were torpedoed. Early in the war, it was learned that many sailors died because they became paralyzed with fear when their ship was hit. Outward Bound was designed to prepare these men to handle their fears in dangerous situations. The program was so successful that after the war it was redesigned for much broader use.

Outward Bound's basic premise is that when people learn to deal with their fears by participating in a series of increasingly threatening experiences, their sense of self-worth increases and they feel more able to rely on themselves. The program uses such potentially threatening experiences as mountain climbing and rappeling, moving about in high, shaky rope riggings, and living alone on an island for several days. Some of the experiences in the program also involve cooperation of small groups to meet a challenge, such as living in an open rowboat on the ocean for days at a time.

Outward Bound has grown rapidly in recent years and has installations throughout the country. Each program emphasizes the use of its particular surroundings. For example, the Colorado school emphasizes rock climbing, rappeling, and mountaineering. The Hurricane Island school in Maine uses sailing in open boats on the ocean as its major challenge. The school in Minnesota emphasizes reflection and development of appropriate spiritual needs.

Outward Bound has proven its special worth for teenagers. It originally started with males, but most of its sessions now include equal numbers of males and females. The program operates as a basic rite of passage by offering a chance to

Recidivism rates
The percentage of convicted persons who commit another crime once they are released from prison.

Although initially successful, programs like Outward Bound seem to lose their effectiveness once the participant returns to his or her home environment. What are some ways that the lessons learned can be reinforced once someone completes such programs?

prove one's self-worth and to have this feeling validated by others. The philosophy of the program is that participants cannot be told what they are capable of but must discover it for themselves.

If the Outward Bound experience can effectively reduce **recidivism rates** (the percentage of convicted persons who commit another crime once they are released from prison), it would have widespread implications in treating juvenile delinquents. This program is not punitive as reform schools are and is considerably less expensive than prison. However, the effectiveness of the program decreases significantly after the enrollees have spent some time back in their neighborhoods (Outward Bound, 1988). Perhaps this just means that they must be brought back for "booster" sessions from time to time.

Although there is a lack of extensive experimental evidence on the effects of Outward Bound, there is no scarcity of testimony from the participants themselves. As one short teenager put it, "Size really doesn't matter up there. What really counts is determination and self-confidence that you can do it!"

AN APPLIED VIEW — *The Components of Maturity*

Think of the woman and the man who are the most mature persons you know—people with whom you are personally familiar, or people who are famous. Then ask yourself, "Why do I think these people are so much more mature than others?" In the spaces to the right, for both the male and the female, create a list of the characteristics that seem to distinguish them in their maturity.

How much do the lists differ? Is male maturity significantly different from female maturity? Which of the two people is older? Which of the two do you admire more? Which of the two are you more likely to want to imitate? Were you able to think of many candidates for this title of "most mature adult," or was it difficult to think of anyone? Are either or both of the people you picked professionals? Are either or both of these persons popular with their own peer group? What is the significance of your answers to you?

Female	Male
1.	1.
2.	2.
3.	3.
4.	4.
5.	5.
6.	6.
7.	7.
8.	8.
9.	9.
10.	10.

Many graduates say that they find life less stressful and feel more confident about their everyday activities as a result of participating in Outward Bound. One of the most positive aspects of the program is its effect on women. Many say that they are surprised to discover how much more self-reliant they have become. Probably the most important result is that most graduates say they feel more responsible and grown-up after having been through the experience.

Walkabout
Originally an aborigine initiation rite; the American version attempts to focus the activities of secondary school by demonstrating to the student the relationship between education and action.

The Walkabout Approach

In the remote regions of Australia, the aborigines have a rite of passage for all 16-year-old males. It is known as the **walkabout.** In the walkabout, the youth, having received training in survival skills throughout most of his life, must leave the village and live for six months on his own. He is expected not only to stay alive, but to sustain himself with patience, confidence, and courage. During this six-month

The Australian aborigines train their teenaged youth, such as this boy learning to spear a ray, to subsist while on a solo "walkabout," an extended initiation rite. The walkabout has been used as a model to induct American youths into adulthood.

estrangement from home and family, he learns to strengthen his faith in himself. He returns to the tribe with the pride and certainty that he is now accepted as an adult member.

According to educator Maurice Gibbons (1974),

■ the young native faces an extreme but appropriate trial, one in which he must demonstrate the knowledge and skills necessary to be a contributor to the tribe rather than a drain on its meager resources. By contrast, the young North-American is faced with written examinations that test skills very far removed from actual experience he will have in real life. (p. 597)

As a result of Gibbons's article, Phi Delta Kappa (PDK), the national education fraternity, set up a group to see what could be done about promoting walkabouts for boys and girls in this country. Although this approach is now somewhat dated, organizations in this country still share the various types of walkabouts that students in participating schools have devised. A booklet has been produced that makes specific suggestions. In it, the PDK Task Force suggests that

■ the American walkabout has to focus the activities of secondary school. It does so by demonstrating the relationship between education and action. It infuses the learning process with an intensity that is lacking in contemporary secondary schools. The walkabout provides youth with the opportunity to learn what they can do. It constitutes a profound maturing experience through interaction with both older adults and children. The walkabout enriches the relationship between youth and community. (Task Force, 1976, p. 3)

The walkabout process has three phases: pre-walkabout, walkabout, and post-walkabout. Each of these phases calls for learning specific skills. In the pre-walkabout, adolescents study personal, consumer, citizenship, career, and lifelong learning skills. In the walkabout itself, the skills to be mastered are logical inquiry, creativity, volunteer service, adventure, practical skills, world of work, and cognitive development. The task force suggests a great number of activities that foster learning in each of these skills. Most involve at least six months of supervised study and activity outside the school, such as working in a halfway house for mental patients.

The post-walkabout is a recognition that the student has engaged in a major rite of passage on his or her way to adulthood. It is not enough to recognize this experience in a ceremony where members are confirmed en masse, such as the typical graduation. Instead, an individual ceremony involving the graduate's family and friends is held for each walkabout the student undergoes.

■ The celebration of transition could take a variety of forms. The ceremonies are varied according to family tastes and imagination, but in each celebration the graduate is the center of the occasion. Parents and guests respond to the graduate's presentation. Teachers drop by to add their comments and congratulations. The graduate talks about his or her achievements, sharing some of the joys and admitting the frustrations. (Task Force, 1976, p. 34)

The Outward Bound and walkabout procedures are becoming popular, and they will almost certainly help to alleviate the need for transitional activities, but they are clearly not sufficient in themselves. The complexity of American adulthood requires a variety of such approaches, if we are to develop in our youth the kind of mature women and men we want. For example, a growing call to require universal public service of all youth for one year has emerged. What do you think about this idea?

WHAT'S

YOUR VIEW?

SHOULD SCHOOL CURRICULA BE RESTRICTED TO INTELLECTUAL MATTERS?

A number of prominent educators believe that schools should concern themselves only with intellectual matters, not with personal and social development. Do you

agree? These educators are opposed to ideas like Outward Bound and walkabout. How do you feel about these two ideas? If you like these ideas, can you use them as a springboard to other methods by which we adults might help youth in their "passage to maturity"?

As this section attempts to make clear, some kind of formal initiation into adulthood appears to be useful to the goal of a smooth and effective transition from adolescence. In the following sections we deal with several aspects of what it means to be a mature adult: a clear sense of one's sexual identity and gender role, and the ability to deal with stress without the constant guidance of parents, teachers, and other helpers.

🌳 Guided Review 🌳

5. In the United States today, initiation activities occur in religious, _____ , social, educational, and _____ settings.

6. The "time out" period, when adolescents explore possibilities and continue their education, is called the adolescent _____ .

7. This moratorium period comes about in our society because of our advanced _____ system which, in part, requires adolescents to acquire more extensive schooling to prepare for technical types of work.

8. Organized sports, countercultural involvement, and _____ _____ are evidence that adolescents yearn for the establishment of some form of initiation rite.

9. In U.S. society today, personal effort and commitment to a _____ _____ play an important role in the development of one's achieved identity.

10. Outward Bound and the _____ approach are two different contemporary ways to reintroduce rites of passage.

Sexual Identity and Gender Roles

■ The problem lay buried, unspoken, for many years in the minds of American women. It was a strange stirring, a sense of dissatisfaction, a yearning that women suffered in the middle of the twentieth century in the United States. Each suburban wife struggled with it alone, as she made the beds, shopped for groceries, matched slipcover material, ate peanut butter sandwiches with her children, chauffeured Cub Scouts and Brownies, lay beside her husband at night—she was afraid to ask even of herself the silent question—"Is this all?" (Betty Friedan, 1963, p. 1)

This paragraph, which opened Betty Friedan's famous book, *The Feminine Mystique* (1963), marked the beginning of a major reexamination of the female gender role. Today we are still undergoing a searching societal inquiry into the appropriate gender roles of both sexes. But are we any nearer to the answers we seek?

Answers

10. walkabout
5. sexual, economic   6. moratorium   7. economic   8. delinquent activities   9. career path

The beginning of the "feminist revolution" in the 1960s opened an era of changing views toward gender roles. Do you believe that society's views of gender roles are significantly different today from what they were ten years ago?

Consider this statement that the famed Greek philosopher Aristotle made more than 2,000 years ago: "Woman may be said to be an inferior man." Most of us would disagree with his viewpoint publicly. On the other hand, its underlying attitude is still widespread. People today are far less willing to admit to a belief in female inferiority, but many still act as though it were so. However, the influence of the women's movement, as well as of science and other forms of social change, is profoundly affecting the way we view sexual identity and gender role.

First, we should make a distinction between the two. **Sexual identity** results from those physical characteristics that are part of our biological inheritance. They are the genetic traits that make us males or females. Genitals and facial hair are examples of sex-linked physical characteristics. **Gender role,** on the other hand, results largely from the specific traits in fashion at any one time and in any one culture. For example, women appear to be able to express their emotions through crying more easily than men, although no known physical cause accounts for this difference.

People may accept or reject their sexual identity, their gender role, or both. For example, Jan Morris (1974), a British author, spent most of her life as the successful author James Morris. Although born a male, she deeply resented the fact that she had a male sexual identity and hated having to perform the male gender role. She always felt that inside she was really a woman. The cause of these feelings may have been psychological—something that happened in her childhood, perhaps. Or the cause may have been genetic—possibly something to do with hormone balance. Such rejection is rare, and no one knows for sure why it happens. Morris decided to have a **transsexual operation** that changed her from male to female. The change caused many problems in her life, but she says she is infinitely happier to have her body match her feelings about her gender role.

Aspects of Gender Role

Some people are perfectly happy with their sexual identity but don't like their gender role. Gender role itself has three aspects:

- **Gender-role orientation.** Individuals differ in how confident they feel about their sex identity. Males often have a weaker gender-role orientation than females. (This will be discussed later in the chapter.)

- **Gender-role preference.** Some individuals feel unhappy about their gender role, as did Jan Morris, and wish either society or their sex could be changed, so that their gender role would be different. The feminist movement of the last few decades has had a major impact on many of the world's societies in this regard.

Sexual identity

Sexual identity results from those *physical characteristics* and *behaviors* that are part of our biological inheritance. They are the traits that make us males or females.

Gender role

A pattern of behavior that results partly from genetic makeup and partly from the specific traits that are in fashion at any one time and in any one culture.

Transsexual operation

An operation that changes the physical characteristics of an individual to those of the opposite sex.

Gender-role orientation

Individuals differ in how *confident* they feel about their sexual identity. Those with low confidence have a weak orientation toward their gender role.

Gender-role preference

Some individuals feel unhappy about their gender role, and wish either society or their gender could be changed, so that their gender role would be different.

Some people are so unhappy with their sexual identity that they have it changed surgically. Renee Richards (a) before the surgery, and (b) the female tennis star, used to be a man by the name of Richard Raskind.

(a)

(b)

Gender-role adaptation

Defined by whether the individual's behavior may be seen as in accordance with her or his gender.

If you were in charge of the human race, which aspects of gender roles would you get rid of, and which would you keep?

Chromosome failure

A genetic abnormality such as gynecomastia (breast growth in the male) or hirsutism (abnormal female body hair).

- **Gender-role adaptation.** Adaptation is defined by whether other people judge individual behavior as masculine or feminine. If a person is seen as acting "appropriately" according to her or his gender, then adaptation has occurred. People who dislike their gender role, or doubt that they fit it well (e.g., the teenage boy who fights a lot because he secretly doubts he is masculine enough), may be said to be poorly adapted.

The more traditional view (e.g., Diamond, 1982) holds that sexual identity is the result of interaction between sex chromosome differences at conception and early treatment by the people in the child's environment. However, Baker (1980), in her review of the main body of research on this topic, is unequivocal: She stated that sexual identity depends on the way the child is reared, "regardless of the chromosomal, gonadal, or prenatal hormonal situation" (p. 95).

Once culture has had the opportunity to influence the child's sexual identity, it is unlikely to change, even when biological changes occur. Even in such extreme cases of **chromosome failure** as gynecomastia (breast growth in the male) and hirsutism (abnormal female body hair), sexual identity is not affected. In almost all cases, adolescents desperately want medical treatment so they can keep their sexual identities.

Although sexual identity becomes fixed rather early in life, gender roles usually undergo changes as the individual matures. The relationships between the roles of the two sexes also change and have altered considerably in the past few decades.

Erik Erikson's Studies

Erik Erikson's ideas (see chapters 2 and 11) about the biological determinants of male and female gender roles came from his studies of early adolescents (1963). He tossed wooden blocks of various shapes and sizes on a table and asked each child to make something with them. Girls, he found, tend to make low structures like the rooms of a house. Having finished these structures, the girls then use other blocks as furniture, which they move around in the spaces of the rooms. Boys, on the other hand, tend to build towers, which, after completion, they usually destroy.

Erikson likens the roomlike structures of the girls to their possession of a womb, and the towerlike structures of the boys to their possession of a penis. He feels that these differences account for greater aggressive behavior in males. Penis and tower alike are seen as thrusting symbols of power. He attributed these behaviors to inherited tendencies of the two sexes. As you would expect, many researchers and most feminists disagree with his interpretation, arguing that his findings are more likely the result of learning that occurred in the childhoods of his subjects.

AN APPLIED VIEW

The Young Adolescent's Rigid View of Gender

The term *gender* is used all the time. But what does it mean? Gender refers to our conceptions of what it means to be male or to be female. In a recent article, Ronald Slaby (1990) explored gender as a social category system. By that he means a mental filing system; that is, we use the categories of male and female to organize the information we receive. Slaby argued that gender categories are loaded with meaning. For example, when we hear of a person named Mary, before even meeting her, we hold certain preconceptions of what she will be like. She will (probably) always be female (and there are few traits that remain so stable). If you're female, then a person named Mary shares with you the things you think that all females experience. If you're male, then there are things that you think only males experience that you feel certain a person named Mary does not experience. In this manner, gender acts as a powerful organizing system. As Sandra Bem (1975) described it, once we have our sexual identity, we begin to view the world through gender

"filters." All new stimuli are processed through these filters according to gender roles.

Most adolescents wrestle with what it means for them personally to be male or female. In doing so, they develop their gender categories. Studies of the adolescents' ideal men and women reflect very stereotyped notions of the sexes. According to Slaby, this is due to the inflexibility of their developing gender categories. When children and adolescents are just forming their concepts of gender, they are more likely to use **gender-role stereotypes** of male and female in a rigid manner. That clarity helps adolescents solidify their understanding of gender. When they become confident and comfortable in their ability to figure out maleness or femaleness, then they become able to use the gender categories more accurately. Then they are able to understand that even though Mary might fit their category of female in most ways, in some ways she may not.

Our gender-role stereotypes define what actions are and are not appropriate for each sex. What would most people say if they saw this young woman chopping wood? What would people have said a hundred years ago?

Androgyny

One gender-role researcher, Sandra Bem (1975), has argued that typical American roles are actually unhealthy. She says that highly masculine males tend to have better psychological adjustment than other males during adolescence, but as adults they tend to become highly anxious and neurotic and often experience low self-acceptance. Highly feminine females suffer in similar ways.

Bem believes we would all be much better off if we were to become more *androgynous.* The word is made up of the Greek words for male, *andro,* and for female, *gyne.* It refers to those persons who are more likely to behave in a way appropriate to a situation, regardless of their sex.

For example, when someone forces his way into a line at the movies, the traditional female role calls for a woman to look disapproving but to say nothing. The androgynous female would tell the offender in no uncertain terms to go to the end of the line. When a baby left unattended starts to cry, the traditional male response is to try to find some woman to take care of its needs. The androgynous male would pick up the infant and attempt to comfort it.

Androgyny is not merely the midpoint between two poles of masculinity and femininity. Rather, it is a more functional level of gender-role identification than either of the more traditional roles. Figure 14.1 illustrates this relationship. In discussing the concept of androgyny, we assume that we know what the essential qualities of a male and female are. Critics of Bem have suggested that her concept of androgyny portrays women more like men.

Gender-role stereotypes

Behavior common in our culture that can be identified as typically either male or female.

Androgyny

Refers to those persons who have higher than average male *and* female elements in their personalities.

Figure 14.1
Relationships among the three gender roles

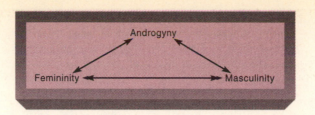

The androgynous man is not afraid to be seen being kind to an infant.

Before we can speculate on what gender roles are most appropriate in adulthood, perhaps we need a clearer idea of the successful adult. To put this another way: "What is a mature person?" This question has intrigued thinkers throughout recorded history. Maturity has been variously described as a search for peace, for the knowledge of God, for satori, for nirvana, for self-actualization, or for wisdom. We will be exploring the many aspects of maturity in the chapters that follow, but first we want to consider one other aspect of "growing up," the ability to deal with the stresses of adult life in a mature way.

Guided Review

11. With regard to gender roles, many people are not willing to admit a belief in female _____ but act as if it were so.

12. Sexual identity refers to our physical characteristics, whereas gender roles refer largely to the specific social _____ in fashion at a given time in a culture.

13. The three parts of gender identity are: gender-role_____ , gender-role preference, and gender-role adaptation.

14. Erik Erikson believes that gender differences are _____ determined, based on his experiments with girls and boys as they played with building blocks.

15. According to Bem, _____ is characterized by more functional levels of role identification than by either male or female roles.

Dealing with the Stresses of Adulthood

In chapter 11, we cited the oft-repeated warning of parents that adolescence is the last chance to have fun, because becoming an adult means taking on the heavy responsibilities of maintaining a job and a family. Well, this is not to say that infancy, childhood, and the teen years are free of stress—far from it! Adolescent psychologist David Elkind (1989) summarized the current situation:

■ Young teen-agers today are being forced to make decisions that earlier generations didn't have to make until they were older and more mature— and today's teen-agers are not getting much support and guidance. This pressure for early decision-making is coming from peer groups, parents, advertisers, merchandisers and even the legal system. (p. 24)

The section that follows applies to these years, too. But we have included this section in the adult part of our book because the stresses of adulthood are different in one important way: More and more, adults are expected to deal with stress entirely on their own. True, we adults can and should expect help from others, but an increasing number of crises call for independent decisions and actions. For example, many more families today exist in a state of ongoing, unending crisis. These families often have only one parent, who is unable to work and therefore is below the poverty level, and who has one or more handicapped or highly disruptive children (Smith, 1990).

Answers

11. inferiority 12. characteristics 13. orientation 14. biologically 15. androgyny

Sometimes stress may be due to childhood traumas that begin to manifest themselves only during adulthood. This may be due to psychological defense mechanisms such as denial (see chapter 18). Brown, Bhrolchain, and Harris (1975) studied depression in working-class English women. A high incidence of separation from or loss of their mothers by death in early childhood existed among those women who suffered with depression. Many of these women had been born before or during World War II and, as a result of the Battle of Britain, were sent as children to the countryside or to other countries to protect them from the German bombing of the major British cities. Even today, many children in the world must face such trauma. In North America, abuse is a more likely stressor. Knowing how stress works, and how to handle it effectively, is a necessary building block in the process of maturation.

As should be clear by now, stress has many sources, regardless of your age. Mainly, stress is due to change. It is the nature of human development to produce inexorable change in every aspect of our existence. This situation is difficult enough when we are young, but at least then we have the support of parents, teachers, and other adults, as well as a more resilient body. More stress does seem to occur as we get older. As we move from early to late adulthood, we must rely more and more on knowledge and insight to avoid having a stressful life. What follows is a detailed description of just what stress is, and how humans try to deal with it. Table 14.1 contains a list of common life events and the ratings they have been given. To evaluate the amount of stress you are under, check the events that you have experienced in the past year. Total your score; it will be explained later in the chapter.

Change as a Source of Stress

> ■ If the last 50,000 years of man's existence were divided into lifetimes of approximately 62 years each, there have been about 800 such lifetimes. Of these 800, fully 650 were spent in caves. Only during the last 70 lifetimes has it been possible to communicate effectively from one lifetime to another—as writing made it possible to do. Only during the last six lifetimes did masses of men ever see a printed word. Only during the last four has it been possible to measure time with any precision. Only in the last two has anyone anywhere used an electric motor. And the overwhelming majority of all the material goods we use in daily life have been developed within the present, the 800th, lifetime. (Toffler, 1970, p. 148)

With the incredible amount of change in this current "lifetime," it is not surprising that the twentieth century has been called the most stressful in which humans have ever lived. So great have been the results of change in terms of stress that sociologist Alvin Toffler (1970, 1984) has labeled it a new disease: **future shock.** Future shock is the illness that results from having to deal with too much change in too short a time. Toffler compares it to culture shock, the feeling we get when arriving in a foreign country for the first time. We become disoriented and anxious, but in the back of our minds, we know that if this discomfort becomes too great, we have only to get on the plane and go back to our own culture where we can feel safe again. Future shock causes the same kind of stressful feeling, except there is no going home to escape from it.

Why is change so stressful? Toffler suggested that the stress results not so much from the direction or even the kind of changes we are faced with in this century, but rather from the incredible rate of change in our daily lives. He suggested that the rate of change has three major aspects, each of which is rapidly increasing:

Future shock

The illness that results from having to deal with too much change in too short a time.

Transience

Toffler's term for the lack of permanence of things in our lives that leads to increased stress.

- **Transience.** There is a lack of permanence of things in our lives. Toffler documents in great detail how much more transient (fast-moving) our lives have become in this century.

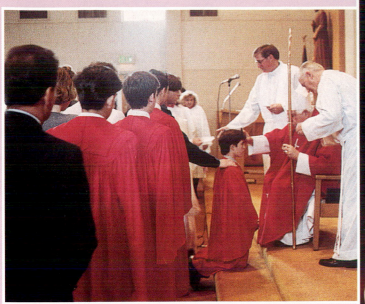

THE PASSAGE TO ADULTHOOD

In this book we have noted from time to time the variations in human behavior
that occur in different cultures. Underlying these behaviors, however, we often find clear
similarities in the goals of those cultures, both throughout the world and throughout human
history. The need to help our young people move from the status of a child to the status of
an adult appears to be a universal aspect of human development.

    No societies have ceremonies designed to pass infants into the tod-
dler's world. Movement from early to middle to late adulthood throughout
the world is relatively gradual. Why, then, should we feel the need to induct
young people, usually at some point in their adolescent years, into adult life?

    A number of suggestions have been offered to explain the "initiation
rite." Some believe its goal is to help us move from the world of play

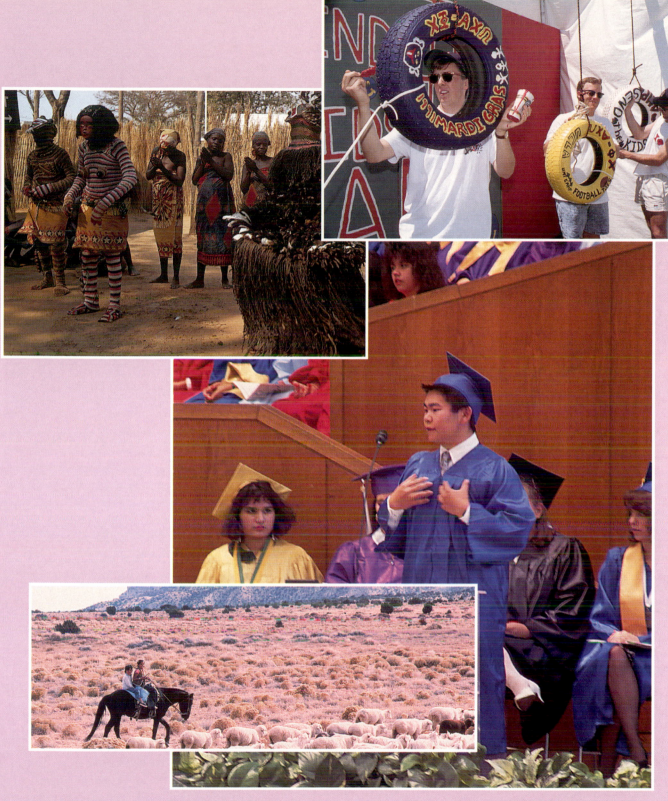

into the world of work. Others argue that the transformation from being cared for as a child to giving care as a parent is so important that it must be formally marked. Reflecting the Freudian position, Brain and associates (1977) stated that:

The particular problem being dealt with is the change from childhood, seen as asexual, to adulthood, seen as sexual. Further, sex is threatening, since it is connected with death and with the unique human knowledge of mortality.

Whatever the reason, a great deal of variety exists among cultures, as they try to assist their young with the passage to maturity (see Chapter 14). A number of these variations are depicted on these pages. As you look at these pictures, try to make up your mind as to why we humans provide these initiation rites. Ask yourself which of them is most effective and which is least effective. Finally, imagine that you are the chief of initiation rites for all the young in our society. You can design any procedure you wish. What would you do?

Table 14.1	Social Readjustment Rating Scale	
Life Events		**Life Change Units**
1. Death of spouse	100	
2. Divorce	73	
3. Marital separation	65	
4. Jail term	63	
5. Death of close family member	63	
6. Personal injury or illness	53	
7. Marriage	50	
8. Fired at work	47	
9. Marital reconciliation	45	
10. Retirement	45	
11. Change in health of family member	44	
12. Pregnancy	40	
13. Sex difficulties	39	
14. Gain of new family member	39	
15. Business readjustment	39	
16. Change in financial state	38	
17. Death of close friend	37	
18. Change to different line of work	36	
19. Change in number of arguments with spouse	35	
20. Mortgage over $10,000	31	
21. Foreclosure of mortgage or loan	30	
22. Change in responsibilities at work	29	
23. Son or daughter leaving home	29	
24. Trouble with in-laws	29	
25. Outstanding personal achievement	28	
26. Wife begins or stops work	26	
27. Begin or end school	26	
28. Change in living conditions	25	
29. Revision of personal habits	24	
30. Trouble with boss	23	
31. Change in work hours or conditions	20	
32. Change in residence	20	
33. Change in schools	20	
34. Change in recreation	19	
35. Change in church activities	19	
36. Change in social activities	18	
37. Mortgage or loan less than $10,000	17	
38. Change in sleeping habits	16	
39. Change in number of family get-togethers	15	
40. Change in eating habits	15	
41. Vacation	13	
42. Christmas	12	
43. Minor violations of the law	11	
TOTAL		

Reprinted with permission from *Journal of Psychosomatic Research,* 11:213–218, T. H. Holmes and R. H. Rahe, "A Social Adjustment Scale," Pub. 1967, Elsevier Science Ltd., Pergamon Imprint, Oxford, England.

Figure 14.2

Comparison of stimulus reduction and optimum drive theories

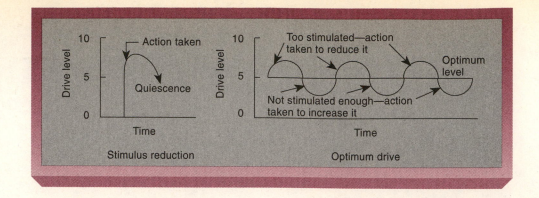

Novelty

Toffler's term for the dissimilarity of new situations in our lives.

Diversity

According to Toffler, stress is increased by what percentage of our lives is in a state of change at any one time.

- **Novelty.** Some changes are more novel than others. New situations in our lives are more dissimilar from old situations than they used to be, and therefore far more stressful.

- **Diversity.** What percentage of our lives is in a state of change at any one time also matters. People used to maintain stability in most of their lives, allowing only a few aspects to change at any particular point. This stable proportion is now much smaller for most of us.

Although the escalating rate of change in our lives has increased the amount of pressure we are under, research is increasing our understanding of it and so helping us deal with it better.

Stimulus Reduction versus Optimum Drive Level

■ **Many a gifted person has been done in by a promotion. (Cassem, 1975)**

Practically everything we do or attempt to do involves overcoming some type of obstacle. Therefore, to be alive is to be under stress. According to Canadian physiologist Hans Selye (1982), the most successful researcher and theorist in this field, "Crossing a busy intersection, exposure to a draught, or even sheer joy are often enough to activate the body's stress mechanism to some extent" (p. 5).

Stimulus reduction

Freud's notion that human beings try to avoid stimulation whenever possible.

Quiescence

A condition in which an individual has no needs at all.

Freud was the first to espouse the notion that human beings try to avoid stimulation whenever possible. He referred to this tendency as **stimulus reduction.** According to this idea, all our activities are attempts to eliminate stimulation from our lives. Drinking when we are thirsty, sleeping when we are tired, the pursuit of sex—all are efforts to reduce some drive. Thus, Freud believed that the natural state of human beings is **quiescence,** a condition in which we have no needs at all. Some Eastern philosophers have this condition as their main goal in life, a goal they call nirvana.

Most psychologists today believe that Freud's view of stress was wrong. The results of a considerable amount of research (reviewed in Dacey, 1982) indicate that individuals have a level of stimulation that is optimum for them. This is referred to as the **optimum drive level** of stimulation. Figure 14.2 compares stimulus reduction theory with optimum drive level theory.

Optimum drive level

The level of optimum stimulation for an individual.

According to the concept of optimum drive, when individuals have too much stimulation, they may seek to reduce the stimulation by satisfying the need causing it. This is Freud's position. But at other times, too little stimulation, as in boredom, may occur. Under these circumstances, people seek new types of stimulation. Thus the goal is not to reduce stimulation to zero but to maintain it at some optimum level.

What level is optimum differs from individual to individual and from situation to situation. For example, some people enjoy a high level of stimulation in the morning and become less excitable as the day goes on. Others, who call themselves

Figure 14.3

The general adaptation syndrome

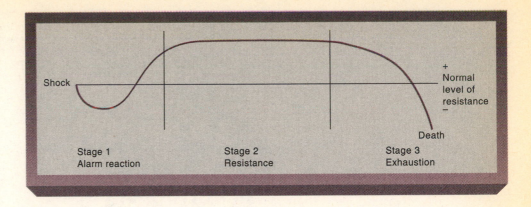

The General Adaptation Syndrome

In 1936 Hans Selye (the father of stress research) was studying a little-known ovarian hormone, which led to the discovery of the **general adaptation syndrome** (Selye, 1956, 1975). In one of the experiments, hormones from cattle ovaries were injected into rats to see what changes would occur. Selye was surprised to find that the rats had a broad range of reactions:

General adaptation syndrome

Selye's theory about the three stages of reaction to stress.

- The cortex became enlarged and hyperactive.

- A number of glands shrank.

- Deep bleeding ulcers occurred in both the stomach and upper intestines.

Further experiments showed that these reactions occurred in response to all toxic substances, regardless of their source. Later experiments also showed them occurring, although to a lesser degree, in response to a wide range of noxious stimuli, such as infections, hemorrhage, and nervous irritation.

Alarm reaction

Selye's term for a generalized "call to arms" of the body's defensive forces.

Selye called the entire syndrome an **alarm reaction.** He referred to it as a generalized "call to arms" of the body's defensive forces. Seeking to gain a fuller understanding of the syndrome, he wondered how the reaction would be affected if stress were present for a longer period of time. He found that a rather amazing thing happens. If the organism survives the initial alarm, it enters a **stage of resistance.** In this second stage, an almost complete reversal of the alarm reaction occurs. Swelling and shrinkages are reversed; the adrenal cortex, which lost its secretions during the alarm stage, becomes unusually rich in these secretions; and a number of other shock-resisting forces are marshalled. During this stage, the organism appears to gain strength and to have adapted successfully to the stressor.

Stage of resistance

The second stage in Selye's theory of stress. During this stage, the organism appears to gain strength and to have adapted successfully to the stressor.

However, if the stressor continues, a gradual depletion of the organism's adaptational energy occurs (Selye, 1982). Eventually this leads to a **stage of exhaustion.** Now the physiological responses revert to their condition during the stage of alarm. The ability to handle the stress decreases, the level of resistance is lost, and the organism dies. Figure 14.3 portrays these three stages. Table 14.2 lists the physical and psychological manifestations of the three stages, and table 14.3 details these reactions.

Stage of exhaustion

The third stage in Selye's theory of stress, caused by a gradual depletion of the organism's adaptational energy.

As you grow older, your ability to remain in the resistance stage decreases. Activity over the years gradually wears out your "machine," and the chances of sustaining life are reduced. As we discuss in chapter 21, no one dies of old age. Rather, they succumb to some stressor because their ability to resist it has become weakened through aging.

Table 14.2	Selye's Stress Adaptation Syndrome		
Stage	**Function**	**Physical Manifestations**	**Psychological Manifestations**
Stage I: Alarm reaction	Mobilization of the body defensive forces.	Marked loss of body weight. Increase in hormone levels. Enlargement of the adrenal cortex and lymph glands.	Person is alerted to stress. Level of anxiety increases. Task-oriented and defense-oriented behavior. Symptoms of maladjustment, such as anxiety and inefficient behavior, may appear.
Stage II: Stage of resistance	Optimal adaptation to stress.	Weight returns to normal. Lymph glands return to normal size. Reduction in size of adrenal cortex. Constant hormonal levels.	Intensified use of coping mechanisms. Person tends to use habitual defenses rather than problem-solving behavior. Psychosomatic symptoms may appear.
Stage III: Stage of exhaustion	Body resources are depleted and organism loses ability to resist stress.	Weight loss. Enlargement and depletion of adrenal glands. Enlargement of lymph glands and dysfunction of lymphatic system. Increase in hormone levels and subsequent hormonal depletion. If excessive stress continues, person may die.	Personality disorganization and a tendency toward exaggerated and inappropriate use of defense mechanisms. Increased disorganization of thoughts and perceptions. Person may lose contact with reality, and delusions and hallucinations may appear. Further exposure to stress may result in complete psychological disintegration (involving violence or stupor).

Source: Adapted from *Adult Health Nursing* by Carol Ren Kneisl and SueAnn Wooster Ames, Addison-Wesley, Menlo Park, Calif., 1986.

Table 14.3	Reactions to Stress		
Thoughts	**Feelings**	**Bodily Responses**	**Actions**
Initially			
Attentiveness, increased alertness, focus, discrimination, problem-solving, mental coping devices	Surge of energy, tension, and/or excitement, elation, anxiety, fright, frustration, anger, fulfillment, happiness.	Tachycardia, hypertension, shallow respiration, dry mouth, paleness, perspiring hands, difficulty voiding/defecating, insomnia, fatigue, tremors, diarrhea, nervousness.	Increased activity level: restlessness, irritability, increased sensitivity and responsiveness, cooperation, alternative plans, compromise.
Later			
Continued or diminished clarity, focus, discrimination, problem-solving skills, and mental coping devices	Any emotion is possible: ambivalence, loneliness, sadness, helplessness, or hopelessness.	Hypotension, bradycardia, slow respiration, faintness and dizziness, blurred vision, and incontinence.	Problem solving; work, play, exercise; diversification; withdrawal; overuse of drugs, alcohol, and food; excessive sleeping; regression; daydreaming.
With overwhelming stress			
Impaired perception and cognition; disorganized thinking; minimal focus and discrimination; reality distortions	Panic, detachment.	Fixed, dilated pupils; exhaustion; death.	Disorganization, immobilization.

Source: From S. Jasmin and L. N. Trygstad, *Behavioral Concepts and the Nursing Process*, C. V. Mosby, St. Louis, Mo., 1979.

Selye (1975) compared his general adaptation stages with the three major stages of life. Childhood, he said, is characteristic of the alarm stage: Children respond excessively to any kind of stimulus and have not yet learned the basic ways to resist shock. In early adulthood, a great deal of learning has occurred, and the organism knows better how to handle the difficulties of life. In middle and old age, however, adaptability is gradually lost, and eventually the adaptation syndrome is exhausted, leading ultimately to death.

Selye suggested that all resistance to stress inevitably causes irreversible chemical scars that build up in the system. These scars are signs of aging. Thus, he said, the old adage that you shouldn't "burn the candle at both ends" is supported by the body's biology and chemistry. Selye's work with the general adaptation syndrome has also helped us to discover the relationship between disease and stress.

> The nature of the family in Western countries has changed dramatically in the past century. How have these changes altered the nature of stress in adulthood?

Disease as a Result of Stress

■ A merry heart doeth good like a medicine.
(Proverbs 17:22)

We are all aware of short-term physical upsets such as fainting, rapid heartbeat, and nausea, caused by the strains of living (see table 14.3). You can easily see how many reactions are impairing. Only recently have we come to understand more about the relationship between long-term emotional stress and illness.

International studies have shown how widespread this relationship is. For example, it is estimated that in Western industrialized countries, up to 70 percent of all patients whom family doctors treat suffer from conditions whose origins lie in unrelieved stress (Blythe, 1973). The World Health Organization (WHO) has listed a large number of illnesses, such as coronary disease, diabetes mellitus, and bronchial asthma, as being caused almost entirely by stress. Stress can also cause skin disease, ulcers, nervous tension, dizziness, sore throat, impotence, angina, tachycardia, itchiness, and even accident-proneness.

Stress may not be a main cause of cancer, but little doubt exists that it can be a precipitating factor in those who are prone to it. The big question is how. Japanese researchers are investigating how anxiety may be linked to cancer through oxidative damage to cellular DNA (Science News, 1993). In other words, a fight-or-flight response diverts blood to the heart, brain, and muscles; after a fight-or-flight response has subsided, oxygen-rich blood rushes back into internal organs. At this point, free radicals are produced, which may be the cause of DNA lesions. At the same time, stress weakens the immune system, thereby increasing the chances that a damaged cell might remain and later become malignant.

What makes one person handle difficult life stress better than another person? One answer is practice. Success with similar situations leaves a person with some experience and confidence to draw on in coping with a new stressful situation. The person is less rattled and able to think more clearly and make more realistic responses to the situation.

Social support has also been found to be an important factor in a person's ability to remain composed and to adapt successfully to stressful situations. According to Bowlby (1980), these social supports are created during infancy when a person learns the essential base of security that will carry him or her throughout life. Erikson, you may recall, described this process in his first stage, trust versus mistrust. One study (Nuckolls & others, 1972) looked at the social supports of a group of pregnant women. These social supports were defined as people with whom the women were close, from whom they could obtain affection, and on whom they could rely. The researchers found that women who had many social supports had significantly fewer pregnancy complications than women who had relatively little support. The lack of social support was even more damaging to those women who had high levels of life change. Close family and friends seem to provide a cushioning effect during the stressful times in our lives.

Dave Mack, an urban youth worker in Chicago, observes that a variety of differences exist among Asian people living in America, and these differences can cause intense stress (cited in Borgman, 1986). Referring to someone as an "Asian" may be misleading. The Chinese are proud of their vast history and the cultures it has spawned. Koreans also possess a rich, though separate, history. Filipinos, Burmese, and Vietnamese, though possibly educated in Chinese schools, nevertheless associate with some Asians while dissociating with others. For instance, among Southeast Asian people, a great deal of animosity exists between Cambodians and the Hmong.

These attitudes of cultural pride provoke endless problems, especially in our large cities. Mack tells of a group of Vietnamese students waiting for a bus in the rain after a basketball game. These students got on the bus when it arrived, just as some Chinese students appeared at the bus stop. Since another bus was not immediately available to transport all of the students, the Vietnamese bus driver ordered his students off of the bus and into the rain so that the Chinese students could get onto the bus first.

Assimilation into urban American culture, itself a smorgasbord of ethnicities all within a few square miles, often proves immensely stressful for all involved. The tension also involves how far one should go in regard to becoming "American." Is there such a thing as an "ethnic American"? Should people who immigrate into America be expected to set aside cultural conflicts for the sake of their new home? At what cost?

Much of the research looking at the relationship between stress and disease has been completed with adults. Some studies have been completed with adolescents, and the results are similar to the adult findings. Compos and Willams (1990) found that the stressful life events are related to psychological and behavioral problems in adolescents. Not surprisingly, behavioral and psychological problems of adolescence are also related to parents' stress. When parents experience a lot of stress, their children are more likely to have emotional difficulties as well (Compos & Williams, 1990). For African American adolescent females, a greater number of negative life events was found to be linked to depression, conduct disorder, posttraumatic stress symptoms, and physical illness (Brown & others, 1989).

Other researchers (Daniels & Moos, 1990) found that depressed youths reported more major stressors and daily hassles than healthy youths. Youths with behavioral problems reported more parent and school stressors than healthy youths. At school, highly stressed adolescents are more likely to get into fights, talk back to teachers, play the class clown, and get headaches and stomachaches (Finian & Blanton, 1987).

We now know that being angry a lot of the time, a typical reaction to stress, is highly related to heart attack. A growing body of research links stress with a number of forms of cancer (Cooper, 1984). As a result of the research of Selye and associates, we are beginning to get a much better understanding of this interaction.

Measuring the Relationship between Stress and Physical Illness

Psychologists and psychiatrists have long attempted to measure accurately the relationship between stress and disease. In the early 1900s Adolph Meyer introduced the concept of *psychobiology,* which emphasized the importance of biographical study in understanding the whole person. He attempted to relate the biology of the person to the likelihood of their getting a variety of diseases. The most successful attempt in this area was by Holmes and Rahe (1967). They developed the *Social Readjustment Rating Scale,* which measures the relationship between events in one's life that require considerable adjustment and the likelihood of getting sick as a result of these crises. The scale is composed of life events that require coping, adaptation, or adjustment. The adult version of this scale was presented at the beginning of this section on stress. Preschool, elementary, and high school versions also exist.

Life change unit (LCU)
Changes in life (e.g., divorce) that are rated in units according to the degree that they tend to cause stress.

Why are some people so much more resilient than others?

Resilience
A term used to describe individuals who deal well with stress and who have few psychological, behavioral, or learning problems because of it.

Risk factors
Characteristics of individuals who are prone to suffer serious problems when under stress.

Protective factors
Characteristics of resilient persons that protect them from the problems related to stress.

The events in the scale are ranked according to the relative degree of adjustment required by the average individual. A numerical weight, called the **life change unit (LCU),** is assigned to each of the events. The greater the degree of the life change, the higher the unit number.

Holmes and Rahe designed the original adult scale by developing a list of events that could affect psychological well-being. The list was submitted to a sample of adults who rated each item according to the relative amount of adjustment required. The results of this study were then mathematically interpreted and a numerical value (LCU) assigned to each event. To find out what your score is, look again at table 14.1. For each life event that you checked as having happened to you within the last year, give yourself the number of points indicated. Then total your score.

Holmes and Rahe's studies show that a score of 200 or more makes some kind of illness likely. Colligan (1975) reported that 86 percent of those who experienced more than 300 LCUs in a year developed some serious health problem.

Of course this does not mean that every person who has a high number of LCUs in one year will definitely get sick. It only means that the odds of getting sick are considerably increased. One caution is necessary here: There is the danger of a self-fulfilling prophecy. That is, persons who know they have a higher number of LCUs in a year may believe they are going to become sick, and therefore they do. Nevertheless, it is clear that people under a high level of stress should take especially good care of their bodies and should be ready to check with their doctors quickly if they do develop symptoms of illness.

Risk and Resilience

Individuals who deal well with stress and who have few psychological, behavioral, or learning problems as a result of it are said to have **resilience** (see chapter 10). In recent years, researchers have become interested in studying the characteristics of resilient individuals. The stressors that individuals experience are called **risk factors.** Risk factors include poverty, chronic illness, parental mental illness and drug abuse, exposure to violence through war or some of the tragedies in the inner cities, and the family experiences of divorce and teenage motherhood. Researchers have been interested in identifying **protective factors** (characteristics of resilient individuals that protect them from stress). Three kinds of protective factors have been found so far: family environments, support networks, and personality characteristics (Hauser & Bowlds, 1990).

An Applied View

How Young Cancer Patients Feel When They Learn They Have Cancer

What It Is That I Have, Don't Want, Didn't Ask For, Can't Give Back and How I Feel About It (Ohio Cancer Information Service, undated) is a wonderful book of quotes from cancer patients. Here are some quotes reflecting how these young people felt when they first learned they had cancer:

- I kept some of my feelings to myself. I knew that my parents were upset, so I tried to be sorry for them.—Kathy
- Mom cried and Dad got mad and I just felt numb inside.—Marsha
- My doctor told me I had cancer, I didn't know what to think. I told him that someone had mixed up the report and had made a mistake. I wish they had.—Dan
- I was very angry. I thought "Why me?" Everybody reassured me it wasn't my fault.—Joyce
- I panicked. I didn't understand. I didn't know who to go to or what to do. Fortunately, my parents were there to help me.—David
- I couldn't believe it! I thought I would wake up in the morning and everything would be just as it was before I got sick.—Kay

- I had my future all planned and it didn't include getting sick. Guess I need to change my plans a little, or postpone them a few years.—Michelle

If you read these quotes carefully, you will get a picture of how people often react to severe stress of all kinds. How could you help a person who is undergoing a period of extreme distress such as learning they have cancer to be resilient? The introduction to this book offers a good suggestion:

> Your experiences and the feelings you have about your illness are unique to you. No one has ever felt exactly the way you feel. Sometimes it can be hard for you and others to understand what is happening to you. Other patients have gone through similar experiences. Some of them have shared their feelings in this book. Remember, since no two people are alike, their experiences, treatments and feelings might be different than yours. (p. 1)

Book available from: Ohio Cancer Information Service, 101A Hamilton Hall, 1645 Neil Avenue, Columbus, OH 43210.

Guided Review

16. The Social _____ Rating Scale shows the relationship between stress and illness by use of a numerical scale.

17. One of the causes of stress is _____ change, which Alvin Toffler called future shock.

18. Toffler stated that the rate of change has three major aspects: _____ , novelty, and diversity.

19. The stimulus reduction theory (the person seeks quiescence or a state with no needs at all) and the _____ drive level (the person seeks stimuli that are most useful for him or her) are two theories that attempt to explain the response to stimuli.

20. Hans Selye outlined three stages of a general adaptation syndrome. These include: alarm reaction; a stage of _____ , and a stage of exhaustion.

21. Each of Selye's stages can be understood in terms of its _____ , physical manifestations, and _____ manifestations.

22. The stressors that people feel are called risk factors, while the characteristics that increase resilience are called _____ factors.

Answers

16. Readjustment 17. accelerated 18. transience 19. optimum 20. resistance 21. function, psychological 22. protective

🌳 CONCLUSION

We began this chapter by comparing how youths are inducted into adulthood in preindustrial tribes and in the modern United States. We concluded that our situation is much more complex than that of the tribes and that although several good suggestions have been made for initiation activities in postindustrial societies, the absence of clear initiation rites still causes problems for us.

Next we looked at definitions of sexual identities and gender roles, and at specific aspects of each. We examined Erikson's studies and looked into the concept of androgyny. We considered Ronald Slaby's ideas about the young adolescent's rigid view of gender.

We then considered the concept of stress and reviewed Alvin Toffler's concept of "future shock" and Hans Selye's "general adaptation syndrome." The general adaptation syndrome has three stages: alarm reaction, resistance, and exhaustion. We discussed the major warning that comes out of this research: When one is unable to relieve stress over a prolonged period, disease is likely to result. The mature person is one who learns the many skills that help avoid this dire consequence. Finally, we looked at the relationship between risk and resilience.

Is there any way to sum up the concept of maturity? We believe that Erikson's term, integrity, probably comes closest. The mature person is one who has achieved an integrated life. But integration of what? That will be the subject of the rest of this book. In the next chapter, we tackle the developmental processes of early adulthood.

🌳 CHAPTER HIGHLIGHTS

Initiation Rites

- Initiation rites in other cultures offer a formal ceremony marking the transition from child to adult.
- Our own culture provides no such universal and formal way for taking leave of adolescence and being accepted into the adult community.
- Some researchers have suggested parallels to the initiation process in the crimes juveniles are often required to commit in order to become a member of a gang, and in the sequence of experiences that so often lead to drug addiction.

Analysis of an Initiation Rite

- The purpose of initiation rites in preindustrial societies is to cushion the emotional disruption arising from the transition from one life status to another.
- For the male, these rites also formally end dependence on his mother and other women and bring him into the group of male adults.
- Initiation rites also serve as an introduction of both genders to the sexual life of an adult.

The Passage to Adulthood in Western Countries

- In our industrial past, the transition to adulthood was fairly clear.
- Entry into adulthood is far more complex for adolescents today, largely due to the increase of sophisticated technologies and the need for many more years of formal education.
- No specific rituals exist in present Western societies to aid youths through this difficult change.
- Five types of activities signal the passage to maturity in America today: religious, sexual, social, educational, and economic.
- The adolescent moratorium, or "time out," allows teens to explore possibilities and extend education. The moratorium comes about because of our advanced economic system.
- Some have suggested that the moratorium is ineffective, and this causes teens to try to create their own initiation rites, which may be dangerous.
- Organized sports, the adolescent counterculture, and delinquency all provide some sort of trials that must be passed for acceptance into adulthood.
- The Australian aborigines require all 16-year-old males to spend six months alone surviving in the wilderness. This ritual, called the walkabout, confers adulthood on the youth who completes it. An American form of the walkabout, incorporating varied work in real-world settings, has been suggested.
- The Outward Bound program, with its emphasis on various forms of wilderness survival, serves as a rite of passage for many youth.

Sexual Identity and Gender Roles

- Sexual identity results from those physical characteristics and behaviors that are part of our biological inheritance.
- Gender role, on the other hand, results partly from genetic makeup and partly from the specific traits in fashion at any one time and in any one culture.
- Views of acceptable gender-role behaviors have changed considerably during the past 20 years. Androgyny is now considered an acceptable alternative to masculine and feminine gender roles.

Dealing with the Stresses of Adulthood

- Change, especially that caused by future shock, is the major factor in stressful situations.
- Many life events, including major events and daily hassles, contribute to stress in our lives.
- Selye's concept of the general adaptation syndrome includes the stages of alarm reaction, resistance, and exhaustion.
- It is not unusual for disease to result from long-term and varied stressors.
- People who are exposed to many risk factors but develop few behavioral or psychological problems are called resilient.

🌳 KEY TERMS

🌳 WHAT DO YOU THINK?

1. Do you remember any experiences from your own youth that were particularly helpful in your transition to adulthood?
2. The adolescent moratorium seems to be getting longer and longer. Do you think this is a good thing? Why or why not?
3. Can you think of a third plan for initiation along the lines of the walkabout and Outward Bound?
4. What aspects of traditional male and female gender roles do you think we should try to keep?
5. What is your attitude toward androgyny? Would you describe yourself as androgynous? If not, do you wish you were?
6. How high is your Social Readjustment Rating in total LCUs (life change units)? Do you believe you have anything to worry about? What should you do?
7. Can you name five productive ways of dealing with everyday stress?

🌳 SUGGESTED READINGS

Angelou, M. (1970). *I know why the caged bird sings.* New York: Random House. Ms. Angelou recounts her childhood in rural Arkansas. Her strength and resilience model the building of a strong personal and cultural identity.

Benson, H. & Proctor, W. (1985). *Beyond the relaxation response.* New York: Berkeley. A stress reduction program that has helped millions of people live healthier lives. Includes Benson's concept of the "faith factor."

Blume, J. (1987). *Letters to Judy: What your kids wish they could tell you.* New York: G. P. Putnam's Sons. Judy Blume offers letters from young adults who confide their concerns over the stresses of friendships, families, abuse, illness, suicide, drugs, sexuality, and other problems. In return, the author shares similar moments from her own life, both as a child and as a parent. She does not hesitate to reveal her own embarrassing situations to help us feel less alone. A special "Resources" section lists books for additional reading and addresses of special-interest organizations.

Bly, R. (1990). *Iron John.* Reading, MA: Addison-Wesley. An intriguingly different way to look at male development told in the form of a Grimm brothers fairy tale.

Csikszentmihalyi, M. (1990). *Flow.* New York: Harper & Row. "This book summarizes, for a general audience, decades of research on the positive aspects of human experience." A fine example of optimal drive.

Erikson, E. (ed.) (1978). *Adulthood.* New York: Norton. A collection of essays on what it means to become an adult. Written by experts from a wide variety of fields.

CHAPTER REVIEW TEST

1. A bar mitzvah or bas mitzvah is an example of a(n) _____ rite of passage.
   a. religious
   b. sexual
   c. social
   d. educational

2. Which of the following statements regarding the adolescent moratorium is true?
   a. It has become obsolete in today's technological society.
   b. It has remained a constant as society has evolved.
   c. It was a useful period during preindustrial society.
   d. It comes about because of our advanced economic system.

3. David's interest in news reporting during high school led to work on the school newspaper, freelance writing, and an internship during the summer for the local city paper. David's early commitment to reporting paid off, because he got a job right out of college. David has an
   a. achieved identity.
   b. ascribed identity.
   c. approach-approach conflict.
   d. approach-avoidance conflict.

4. During which phase of the walkabout do adolescents study personal, consumer, citizenship, career, and lifelong learning skills?
   a. pre-walkabout
   b. walkabout
   c. post-walkabout
   d. All of the answers are correct.

5. Gender-role orientation is defined by
   a. a desire that either society or one's gender could be changed so that one's sex role would be different.
   b. whether other people judge individual behavior as masculine or feminine.
   c. how confident individuals feel about their sexual identity.
   d. physical characteristics that are part of our biological inheritance.

6. The three aspects of gender role are orientation, preference, and
   a. androgyny.
   b. adaptation.
   c. conflict.
   d. stereotype.

7. According to gender-role researcher Sandra Bem, men who have better psychological adjustment during adolescence than most other males is characteristic of
   a. androgynous males.
   b. highly masculine adult males.
   c. men who have close relationships with their mothers.
   d. men who have close relationships with their fathers.

8. According to Erikson, the roomlike structures built by girls represent _____ , and the towers built by the boys represent _____ .
   a. inferiority, superiority
   b. the womb, the penis
   c. fear, aggression
   d. aggression, fear

9. Androgyny refers to
   a. persons who are more likely to behave in a way appropriate to a situation, regardless of their sex.
   b. women who have higher than average male elements in their personalities.
   c. men who have higher than average female elements in their personalities.
   d. the midpoint between the two poles of masculinity and femininity.

10. If someone forced his way into a line at a football game, an androgynous female
    a. would accept the fact that he probably had good reason to cut in line.
    b. would be angry, but not let her feelings show.
    c. would look disapproving.
    d. would tell the offender to go to the end of the line.

11. Ted attended six different schools by the time he reached high school because of his father's job transfers. This relates to which aspect of future shock?
    a. novelty
    b. diversity
    c. transience
    d. replacement

12. When an individual seeks to maintain stimulation at some optimum level, it is an example of
    a. drive reduction.
    b. maintenance.
    c. optimum drive.
    d. goal attainment.

13. What is Freud's view of stress?
    a. Individuals try to avoid stimulation whenever possible.
    b. Achieving quiescence is the main goal of life.
    c. Individuals seek to maintain stimulation at some optimum level.
    d. Individuals seek to increase stimulation whenever possible.

14. If a person is alerted to stress, the level of anxiety increases, and task-oriented and defense-oriented behavior takes place, the person is experiencing the psychological manifestations of
    a. alarm reaction.
    b. an anxiety attack.
    c. defense mechanisms.
    d. denial.

15. According to Selye, your ability to remain in the resistance stage decreases when you are
    a. experiencing optimum drive.
    b. experiencing an alarm reaction.
    c. an adolescent.
    d. growing older.

16. What scale measures the relationship between events in one's life that require considerable adjustment and the likelihood of getting sick as a result of these crises?
    a. Identity Adjustment Scale
    b. Stress Management Scale
    c. Social Readjustment Rating Scale
    d. Adult Health and Wellness Scale

Answers

1.a 2.d 3.a 4.a 5.c 6.b 7.b 8.b 9.a 10.d 11.c 12.c 13.a 14.a 15.d 16.c

Chapter Outline

s I see it, there are four definitions of "adult." First, the biological definition: we become adult biologically when we reach the age at which we can reproduce. . . . Second, the legal definition: we become adult legally when we reach the age at which the law says we can vote, get a driver's license, marry without consent. . . . Third, the social definition: we become adult socially when we start performing adult roles. . . . Finally, the psychological definition: we become adult psychologically when we arrive at a self-concept of being responsible for our own lives, of being self-directing. From the viewpoint of learning, it is the psychological definition that is most crucial. But it seems to me that the process of gaining a self-concept of self-directedness starts early in life, . . . and grows cumulatively as we become biologically mature, start performing adult-like roles, . . . and take increasing responsibility for making our own decisions. So we become adult by degree as we move through childhood and adolescence, and the rate of increase by degree is probably accelerated if we live in homes, study in schools, and participate in youth organizations that foster our taking increasing responsibilities. But most of us probably do not have full-fledged self-concepts of self-directedness until we leave school or college, get a full-time job, marry, and start a family.

Malcolm Knowles, *The Adult Learner,* 1989

Although most adults probably believe that they know what *adulthood* is, the term is really somewhat difficult to define, as we saw in the preceding chapter. The four definitions mentioned in this quote from Malcolm Knowles are useful, but three others are also essential to an understanding of young adulthood: physical, cognitive, and sexual. In this chapter, we will concentrate on these three.

After reading chapter 15, you should be able to

- Discuss how early adulthood signifies the peak in physical development.

- Define what is meant by "organ reserve."

- Suggest ways in which lifestyle choices, such as food, tobacco, and alcohol use and marriage, affect health.

- Discuss Gagnon and Simon's notion of "sexual scripts."

- Explain Wilson's sociobiological view of the objective of sex.

- Describe young adults' premarital and marital sexual practices.

- List Perry's nine stages of intellectual/ethical development.

- Contrast women's and men's "ways of knowing."

- Identify Sternberg's seven forms of love.

- Define Fromm's notion of "validation" as it relates to love.

Table 15.1	**Summary of Physical Development in Early Adulthood**

Height

Female: maximum height reached at age 18.
Male: maximum height reached at age 20.

Weight (age 20–30)

Female: 14-pound weight gain and increase in body fat.
Male: 15-pound weight gain.[a]

Muscle structure and internal organs

From 19–26: Internal organs attain greatest physical potential. The young adult is in prime condition as far as speed and strength are concerned.

After 26: Body slowing process begins.
Spinal disks settle, causing decrease in height.
Fatty tissue increases, causing increase in weight.
Muscle strength decreases.
Reaction times level off and stabilize.
Cardiac output declines.[b]

Sensory function changes

The process of losing eye lens flexibility begins as early as age 10 and continues until age 30. This loss results in difficulty focusing on close objects.

During early adulthood, women can detect higher-pitched sounds than men.

Nervous system

The brain continues to increase in weight and reaches its maximum potential by the adult years.[c]

Sources: (a) *Statistical Abstract of the United States, 1986,* U.S. Bureau of the Census, Washington, D.C., 1986; (b) H. A. deVries, "Physiology of Exercise and Aging" in *Aging: Scientific Perspectives and Social Issues,* edited by D. F. Woodruff and J. E. Birren, Van Nostrand Reinhold, New York, 1981, pages 464–465; (c) Wang & Busse, 1974.

Physical Development

We address three main questions about physical development in this section: When is peak development reached? What is organ reserve? and What are the effects of lifestyle?

The Peak Is Reached

Early adulthood is the period during which physical changes slow down or stop. Table 15.1 provides some basic examples of physical development in early adulthood.

In sports, young adults are in their prime condition as far as speed and strength are concerned. A healthy individual can continue to partake in less strenuous sports for years. As the aging process continues, however, the individual will realize a loss of the energy and strength felt in adolescence.

Early adulthood is also the time when the efficiency of most body functions begins to decline. For example, cardiac output and vital capacity start to decrease (DeVries, 1981). As table 15.2 clearly shows, these declines are quite steady right through old age. It is important to remember that this chart gives the average changes; considerable differences will occur from individual to individual.

Organ Reserve

Organ reserve

Refers to that part of the total capacity of our body's organs that we do not normally need to use.

Although table 15.2 makes it look all downhill from what is probably your present age, the actual experience of most people is not that bad. This is because of a human capacity called organ reserve. **Organ reserve** refers to that part of the total capacity of our body's organs that we do not normally need to use. Our body is

Table 15.2	Approximate Declines in Various Human Functional Capacities with Age		
	Percent of Function Remaining		
	30 Years	*60 Years*	*80 Years*
Nerve conduction velocity	100	96	88
Basal metabolic rate	100	96	84
Standard cell water	100	94	81
Cardiac index	100	82	70
Glomerular filtration rate	100	96	61
Vital capacity	100	80	58
Renal plasma flow	100	89	51
Maximal breathing capacity	100	80	42

From Alexander P. Spence, *Biology of Human Aging,* © 1989, p. 8. Adapted by permission of Prentice-Hall, Inc., Englewood Cliffs, NJ. Based on data from *The Biology of Aging,* edited by B. L. Strehler et al., American Institute of Biological Sciences, Washington, D.C., 1960.

designed to do much more than it is usually called upon to do. Much of our capacity is held on reserve. As we get older, these reserves grow smaller. The peak performance that each of our organs (and muscles, bone, etc.) is capable of declines. A 50-year-old man can fish all day with his 25-year-old son and can usually take a long walk with him without becoming exhausted, but he has no chance at all of winning a footrace against him.

This is why people are aware of little decline during the early adult years and often do not experience a sharp decline in most of their everyday activities even into middle age. Our organ reserves are diminishing, but we are unaware of it because we call on them so seldom.

Of course, some individuals regularly try to use the total capacity of their organ reserves. Professional athletes are an example. Here again we see the biopsychosocial model in action. Biology sets the limits, but psychological factors (e.g., personal pride) and social factors (e.g., the cheering crowd) determine whether the person "gives it her all."

The Effect of Lifestyle on Health

Young adults are healthier than older adults in just about every way. All of the body's systems reach peak functioning at this age. Less illness occurs, too. For example, young adults have fewer hospitalizations and visits to the doctor's office than later, and those that do occur are caused mainly by injuries. Even catching a cold happens more rarely at this stage than at any other stage of life (U.S. Bureau of the Census, 1992).

Good health is clearly related to factors such as genetics, age, and the medical treatment locally available. But these factors are generally beyond the control of the individual. Increasingly, people are beginning to realize that their style of life plays an enormous role in their own health.

The impact of lifestyle on health is dramatically illustrated by the observations in the book *The Healing Brain* (Ornstein & Sobel, 1987). These researchers determined that the miraculous technological gains in medicine over the last 100 years have not had as great an impact on health as one might think. It is true that at birth, we can expect many more years of life than people could in the last century. However, a person who has reached the age of 45 today has a life expectancy of only a couple years more than the person who had reached the age of 45 a hundred years ago, in spite of all the money and effort now spent on medicine after that age.

As a counterexample, Ornstein and Sobel offer the people of Nevada and Utah, two states and populations that are similar in geography, education, income, and availability of medical treatment. Yet Nevada's death rate is 40 percent higher than Utah's. Utah is largely composed of Mormons who live a relatively quiet and stable lifestyle, including very low incidences of smoking and drinking. In Nevada, people drink and smoke much more heavily, and it shows. The rates of cirrhosis of the liver and lung cancer are 100 to 600 percent higher in Nevada than in Utah. A man who reaches the age of 45 in Utah can expect to live 11 years more than the man who reaches age 45 in Nevada. The point is that simple, cost-free choices under the control of the individual are much more effective at improving health than all the expensive, time-consuming medical advances of the last century. Perhaps our priorities are misplaced.

Based on this information, we could conclude that a simple difference in style of life can have more of an effect on health than medical advances. Let's look at the influence on health of some specific lifestyle choices.

Choices of Foods

Nutrition plays an important role throughout human development, from the neonate to the elderly. By the time we reach middle adulthood, however, increasing evidence demonstrates the influence of nutrition on two major health concerns, heart disease and cancer. Medical science has recently established a link between heart disease and a substance in the blood, **cholesterol.** Cholesterol has been found to leave deposits along the walls of blood vessels, blocking the flow of blood to the heart and resulting in a heart attack. The main culprit in high levels of cholesterol has been found to be diets high in fat. Typically Americans consume 40 percent of their total calories as fat. The American Heart Association (1984) recommends changes in diet, such as eating fish and poultry instead of red meat, yogurt and cottage cheese instead of cheese, margarine instead of butter, fewer eggs, and drinking skim milk instead of whole milk, as ways of lowering cholesterol in the body. Exercise is also very helpful.

A similar link has been found between diet and certain types of cancer, such as cancer of the breast, stomach, intestines, and the esophagus. The American Cancer Society has also come out with a set of recommendations for an improved, healthy diet. They too recommend lowering fat intake to no more than 30 percent of the daily caloric total and following a diet that is high in fiber, a substance that helps the digestive process. High-fiber foods include leafy vegetables such as cauliflower, broccoli, and brussels sprouts, as well as whole-grain cereals and breads. The proliferation of new products that feature lower levels of fat and higher levels of fiber indicates that the American public is taking this new knowledge to heart (no pun intended).

Anyone who is 10 percent over the normal weight for their height and build is considered overweight. Anyone who is 20 percent over the normal weight is considered obese. Obesity has been a very serious health concern and is rapidly getting worse. The percentage of our population that is obese has gone from one-fourth to one-third over the past 10 years! The problem is especially crucial for African American women (National Institute for Health Statistics, 1994).

What are the main causes of obesity? According to obesity expert F. X. Pi-Sunyer (1994), lack of exercise and snacking are the culprits. As he puts it, "We drive everywhere. Nobody wants to walk anywhere. And we use a lot of other labor-saving devices. For example, if people cut lawns, they're sitting on the lawn mowers. They don't push them around" (p. 238).

The impact on health is significant and widespread. Obesity increases the risk of such diseases as heart disease, diabetes, arthritis, and cancer. In addition, our society places great importance on physical appearance. Overweight persons are likely to suffer from low self-esteem or even depression because of the way they are treated by others.

Cholesterol

A substance in the blood that adheres to the walls of the blood vessels, restricting the flow of blood and causing strokes and heart attacks.

Young adults today are probably more health conscious than at any other time in history.

At the other extreme, some disagreement exists over what is considered to be too thin. Some researchers suggest that it is better to be a little overweight than it is to be underweight. Recent research on animals indicates that a restricted diet that leaves the animal lean and thin might be healthiest (Campbell & Gaddy, 1987; Masoro, 1984). A severely restricted diet leads to some of the complications associated with eating disorders such as anorexia nervosa (see chapter 13). Once again, moderation is the safest course to follow.

Use of Alcohol

Although alcohol is the most abused and most dangerous drug used, why does its use continue to be considered a "rite of passage" by many young adults?

The consumption of alcohol is another great health concern to our society. Alcohol abuse is estimated to cost our economy more than $100 billion annually (Holden, 1987). This figure includes medical treatment for cirrhosis of the liver, osteoporosis, ulcers, heart disease, nervous system damage, and certain types of cancer such as breast cancer; the insurance and medical costs incurred by automobile accidents resulting from drinking and driving; the drug treatment necessary to help people control their addiction; and the enormous cost of labor that is lost when heavy drinkers are unable to come in to work.

Ingalls (1983) conducted a survey among college students and reported that 82 percent consumed alcohol and 21 percent were heavy users. Eight percent admitted to having an alcohol problem. Alcohol consumption was found to be directly related to low grade-point average. White males consume more alcohol than women or African Americans. Most people consume alcohol to attain the relaxed, uninhibited feeling that alcohol tends to produce. The fact is, alcohol dulls the senses. Specifically, it decreases reaction times in the brain and nervous system. Continued drinking may affect the sex life of males, by making it difficult for them to attain and keep an erection.

Alcohol leads to a variety of problems in the family, with the law, and with one's health. Physical problems associated with alcoholism include cirrhosis of the liver, increased changes of cardiomyopathy, a weakening of the heart muscles, stomach and intestinal ailments, as well as cancer of the mouth, liver, and esophagus (Schemeck, 1983).

White males consume more alcohol than either white females or African Americans, according to one study. Can you think of any reasons why this might be so?

AN APPLIED VIEW

Dealing with Adult Children of Alcoholics (ACoA)

According to Woititz (1990), clear agreement exists on three aspects of alcoholism: Alcoholism runs in families; children of alcoholics run a higher risk of developing alcoholism than other children; children of alcoholics tend to marry alcoholics. She also found that adult children of alcoholics usually manifest 13 characteristics. They

- are often not clear on what normal behavior is,
- have difficulty following a project through from beginning to end,
- lie when it would be just as easy to tell the truth,
- judge themselves without mercy,
- have difficulty having fun,
- take themselves very seriously,
- have difficulty with intimate relationships,
- overreact to changes over which they have no control,
- constantly seek approval and affirmation,
- usually feel that they are different from other people,
- are overly responsible or irresponsible,
- are extremely loyal, even in the face of evidence that the loyalty is undeserved, and

- are impulsive. They tend to lock themselves into a course of action without giving serious consideration to alternative behaviors or possible consequences.

Woititz suggested that although these traits can make life difficult, it is important that the adult children of an alcoholic recognize that they are likely to possess most of them. "They could decide to work on changing aspects of themselves that cause them difficulty, or they could choose not to do so. In either event they have greater self-knowledge, which leads to greater self-understanding, which helps in the development of a sense of self. It is a win-win situation" (p. 98). She urged that: "Being the adult child of an alcoholic is not a disease. It is a fact of your history. Because of the nature of this illness and the family response to it, certain things occur that influence your feelings, attitudes and behaviors in ways that cause you pain and concern. The object of ACoA recovery is to overcome those aspects of your history that cause you difficulty today and learn a better way. The process of recovery for adult children is very disruptive. It means changing the way you have perceived yourself and your world up until now." (p. 101)

Ironically, some research has indicated that a daily, moderate intake of alcohol may be beneficial (although not for those over the age of 50—see chapter 17). Such small amounts of alcohol seem to produce a protein in the blood that helps lower cholesterol. Unfortunately, the addictive qualities of alcohol make it impossible for many people to drink in only moderate amounts. This is why treatment programs such as the very successful Alcoholics Anonymous ask their clients to abstain totally from alcohol rather than try to control their drinking.

WHAT'S YOUR VIEW?

CAN DRINKING ALCOHOL HAVE POSITIVE EFFECTS?

In most articles you may have read about alcohol consumption, it has been associated with a variety of negative biological and psychological effects. Earlier research seemed to indicate that alcohol had no redeeming qualities. More recently, studies have indicated that alcohol may have some beneficial effects, such as a decreased risk of heart attack. According to Criqui (1990), "The consistency of results across studies and the biological plausibility of alcohol's beneficial impact through high-density lipoprotein cholesterol and blood pressure suggest a potential benefit of several drinks per week" (p. 857).

Light social drinking may also encourage cross-cultural interactions. For example, vanWilkinson (1989) attempted to investigate the possible lifestyle influences on alcohol use among south Texas Mexican Americans. He surveyed 247 respondents who were classified into six subgroups: working class, urban middle class, farmworkers, farmer/ranchers, migrants, and upper-class Mexican Americans. All subgroups drank at home and at parties. "Almost all pachangas (parties) are held at someone's home and transcend any social class structure. Important for the rich as well as the poor, these events tend to make equals of those who might be unequals."

Do you think the consumption of alcohol can have positive physiological and social effects? What advice would you give to young adults about their drinking habits?

Although the dangers of "passive smoke"—smoke inhaled by those in the vicinity of a smoker—are well established, many people still disregard the no-smoking signs that seem to be springing up everywhere.

Use of Tobacco

The use of tobacco has been falling rapidly, at about 1 percent per year since 1987. About 28 percent of American men are smokers, as compared with 23 percent of American women ("Cigarette Smoking among Adults," June 15, 1992).

As with immoderate use of alcohol, tobacco use is also linked to a variety of health problems. The most common way to use tobacco is to smoke cigarettes. Most people are now aware that heavy cigarette smoking greatly increases the risk of lung cancer. They are perhaps less aware of the links between smoking and cancer of the kidney and stomach, along with the links to other diseases such as heart disease and emphysema (Engstrom, 1986).

The main culprit in tobacco is nicotine. Nicotine is a stimulating drug that the Surgeon General of the United States has concluded is as addictive as heroin or cocaine. Individuals can be affected by nicotine in ways other than by smoking cigarettes. Recent attention has focused on the dramatic increase in the use of smokeless chewing tobacco, primarily in young men. This type of tobacco use leads to a higher risk of cancer of the larynx, mouth, esophagus, and stomach. Awareness of this type of health risk is quickly spreading, as people see news photos of teenage boys who have had to have entire portions of their face removed due to cancer. Smokers are 14 times more likely to die from cancer of the lungs, and twice as likely to die of a heart attack as nonsmokers. Other diseases linked to smoking are bronchitis, emphysema, and increased blood pressure.

The Department of Health and Human Services has outlined the personality types of smokers versus nonsmokers (Brody, 1984). Adult smokers tend to be risk-takers, impulsive, defiant, and extroverted. Blue-collar workers tend to be the heaviest smokers among men. For females, white-collar workers are the heaviest smokers, and homemakers tend to smoke more than women who work.

Peer pressure from friends is the major reason that young adults smoke. As in adulthood, young people who smoke tend to be extroverted and more disobedient toward authority than nonsmokers. Some young adults see smoking as a way of appearing older and more mature. Young adults who go on to college smoke less than those who do not continue their education. Among young women, smokers are less athletic, more social, study less, get lower grades, and generally dislike school more than nonsmoking females.

You may also involuntarily be exposed to the dangers of tobacco use. A growing body of research is documenting the deleterious effects of passive smoking. Passive smoking is the breathing in of the smoke around you that others produce. For example, a nonsmoker who is married to a heavy smoker has a 30 percent greater risk of lung cancer than someone who is married to a nonsmoker (National

Institute for Health Statistics, 1986). (The role of smoke in the environment is also covered in chapter 4.) Evidence also indicates that children can be affected when their mothers smoke. This mounting evidence has led to a flurry of legislation prohibiting smoking in certain public areas such as elevators, airplanes, and restaurants and the designation of smoking areas in workplaces.

The message does seem to be reaching the public. Overall, fewer people smoke now than at any time in the past 25 years (with the exception of teenage females). Numerous stop-smoking programs spring up all the time. These programs run the gamut from classic behavioral techniques to hypnosis. But perhaps the most telling evidence that smoking is on the decline in the United States is the reaction of the giant tobacco companies. In recent years these companies have increasingly targeted foreign markets (a growing ethical controversy, since these markets are typically Third World countries) while diversifying their domestic market with different and healthier products.

Physical Fitness

There was a time when only males did calisthenics. Now exercise classes are becoming very popular with female adolescents.

One of the most popular trends of recent years has been the so-called fitness craze. Health benefits are the obvious reason for this enthusiasm for exercise. Regular, strenuous exercise can increase heart and lung capacity, lower blood pressure, decrease cholesterol in the blood, keep weight at normal levels, enhance cognitive functioning, relieve anxiety and depression, and increase self-esteem (Elsayed & others, 1980; Lee & others, 1981; McCann & Holmes, 1984). Failure to get regular exercise is twice as great a risk factor (56%) as other causes—smoking (25%), obesity (22%), hypertension (17%), and diabetes (5%) ("Coronary Disease Attributable to Sedentary Lifestyle," September 19, 1990).

During a physical workout, oxygen travels more deeply into the lungs, and the heart pumps harder to carry more blood into the muscles. Healthy lungs and heart are vital for a long life. Persons who do not exercise and have inactive jobs are at twice the risk for a heart attack compared with persons who do exercise. Individuals who exercise report other health benefits, including better concentration at work and better sleep patterns (VanderZanden, 1989).

Johns Hopkins Hospital in Baltimore reported that a family medical history of heart attacks increases a person's chances of having a heart attack (Findlay, 1983). Among individuals under age 50 from at-risk families, 42 percent have significantly high blood pressure, compared with 20 percent of the general population. Of the same group, 28 percent have dangerously high cholesterol levels, compared with 5 to 10 percent of the general population. Nearly 25 percent show evidence of "silent" coronary artery disease—double the rate of the general population.

Studies at Harvard show that at-risk individuals do not properly metabolize cholesterol, which collects in the arteries and eventually leads to a heart attack (Bishop, 1983). Carey (1983) explains that young adults who gain a large amount of weight after adolescence are more at risk for heart disease. Scientists feel that with greater public awareness of the dangers of cholesterol, and early detection and treatment, they can decrease heart disease among at-risk individuals.

One study (Ossip-Klein & others, 1989) assigned a number of clinically depressed women to one of three groups: a group that did regular running, a group that lifted weights regularly, or a control group that did nothing special. The women in both exercise groups showed increased self-concept over the women in the control group. The two types of exercise worked equally well.

Many corporations are now providing the time and facilities for employees to build regular exercise into their workday. The reasoning is that work time lost in this way is more than made up for by more productive employees, who end up losing less time due to illness. In one new trend, some health insurance programs are offering free access to exercise facilities, again looking at the long-term gain of having healthier members.

Marital Status

Another lifestyle factor that appears to affect health is marital status. Despite comedians' jokes, married people seem to be healthier than single, divorced, or widowed people (Verbrugge, 1979). They tend to have less frequent and shorter stays in hospitals. They tend to have fewer chronic conditions and fewer disabilities. Never-married and widowed people are the next healthiest. Divorced and separated people show the most health-related problems. A number of possible explanations could account for this, but clearly one must consider the emotional and economic support that an intact family can provide.

Based on the preceding information, we could conclude that a healthy lifestyle consists of a diet with reasonable caloric intake that is low in fat and high in fiber, moderate or no consumption of alcohol, no tobacco use, plenty of regular, strenuous exercise, and a supportive spouse. In fact, this accurately describes the Mormon lifestyle in Utah, which allows the average resident of Utah to live years longer than the average resident of Nevada. This, of course, is no reason to go out and change your religious preference, but it is reason to examine your current lifestyle and consider some prudent changes.

As you can see, health is also an aspect of life in which all three factors of the biopsychosocial model are clearly evident. Now let us turn to another complex area, sexuality.

Guided Review

1. Early adulthood is the time when the efficiency of most body functions begins to _____.

2. Although physical ability has peaked, bodily responses in adulthood are supplemented by _____ _____ ; that is, the part of the total capacity of our body's organs that we do not normally need to use.

3. Our lifestyle affects our health, mainly through our choices of foods, use of alcohol, use of tobacco, _____ _____ , and marital status.

4. Cholesterol, a substance in the blood related to heart attack, can be controlled by _____.

5. Alcohol not only affects the person who drinks it. _____ children of alcoholics often have problems, including difficulty finishing projects, having fun, and constantly seeking the _____ of others.

6. Regular exercise that brings _____ deep into the lungs and enables the heart to take more blood to the muscles contributes to overall health.

7. Research indicates that married people tend to be _____ than single people.

Sexuality

Sexuality has important physical and cognitive roles in our lives. Most people who disregard or repress their sexuality suffer for it. Of course, the sex drive, unlike other instinctual drives such as hunger and thirst, can be thwarted without causing death. Some people are able to practice complete chastity without apparent harm to their personalities. The great majority of us, however, become highly irritable when our sexual needs are not met in some way. There is also reason to believe that our personalities do not develop in healthy directions if we are unable to meet sexual needs in adulthood. Why is sexuality so important to us? Although the answer may seem obvious, in fact a number of sexual motivations exist.

Most people seem to find a strong need to develop a sexual and romantic relationship with another person.

Answers

1. decline 2. organ reserve 3. physical fitness 4. diet 5. Adult, approval 6. oxygen 7. healthier

Psychologist John Gagnon argues that humans learn to behave sexually according to scripts established by the culture in which they live. For most people, this learning takes place during adolescence and young adulthood.

For Freud, human sexuality is the underlying basis for all behavior (see chapter 2). He held that *genitality* (the ability to have a successful adult sex life) is the highest stage of development. He believed that those people who do not have adequate adult sex lives fail to do so because they have become fixated at some earlier and less mature level. Today psychologists view sexuality rather differently.

Sexual Scripts: Gagnon and Simon

Psychologists John Gagnon and William Simon (1987) see sexual behavior as "scripted" behavior. They believed that children begin to learn scripts for sexual attitudes and behavior from the other people in their society. They view sexuality, therefore, as a cultural phenomenon rather than a spontaneously emerging behavior. They believed that

> in any given society, [children] acquire and assemble meanings, skills, and values from the people around them. Their critical choices are often made by going along and drifting. (1987, p. 2)

Learning sexual scripts occurs in a rather haphazard fashion throughout childhood, but this changes abruptly as children enter adolescence. Here much more specific scripts are learned: in classrooms, from parents, from the media, and most specifically, from slightly older adolescents. This process continues throughout early adulthood, through a process of listening to and imitating older adults whom the individual admires. For these researchers, then, the roles sexuality plays in a society come about largely through transmission of the culture by idealized adults.

The Sociobiological View: Wilson

Whatever we see as our reasons for seeking sex, this complicated behavior has obviously evolved through a number of complex stages over which we have had no control. What genetic purposes has the evolution served? E. O. Wilson (1978) and his fellow sociobiologists have a number of unorthodox suggestions:

- Sex is not designed for reproduction. Sociobiologists argue that the primary motivation of all human behavior is the reproduction of the genes of each person. Wilson, however, believed that if reproduction were the primary goal of the human species, many other techniques would have been far more effective:

  > Bacteria simply divide in two (in many species, every twenty minutes), fungi shed immense numbers of spores, and hybrids bud offspring directly from their trunks. Each fragment of a shattered sponge grows into an entire new organism. If multiplication were the only purpose of reproductive behavior, our mammalian ancestors could have evolved without sex. Every human being might be asexual and sprout new offspring from the surface cells of a neutered womb. (p. 121)

- Sex is not designed for giving and receiving pleasure. Wilson pointed out that many animal species perform intercourse quite mechanically with virtually no foreplay. Furthermore, lower forms achieve sex without benefit even of a nervous system. Thus, he suggests that pleasure is only one of the means of getting complex creatures to "make the heavy investment of time and energy required for courtship, sexual intercourse and parenting" (p. 122).

- Sex is not designed for efficiency. The very complexity of human genital systems makes them subject to a variety of disorders and diseases, such as ectopic pregnancy and venereal disease. The genetic balance brought about by sex is easily disturbed, and if the human being has one sex chromosome too many or too few, abnormalities in behavior and in physiology often result.

- Sex is not designed to benefit the individual's drives. If an individual's drive is to reproduce himself or herself, sex is actually an impairment. When sexual reproduction is employed, the organism must accept partnership with an individual whose genes are different. Only with asexual reproduction is multiplication of self totally possible.

- Sex does create diversity. Wilson concluded that the only possible reason that evolution brought about the human sexual system is to create a greater diversity of individuals. The purpose of this diversity is to increase the chances of the survival of the species. As conditions have changed throughout history (e.g., during an ice age), some individuals have had a greater chance to survive than others. If only one type of human being with only one set of genes had existed, and that inheritance had not been suited to the changing environment, the species would have become extinct.

Wilson pointed out that when two different individuals mate, there is the possibility of offspring like individual A, offspring like individual B, and offspring with the characteristics of both. As these individuals mate with others, the possible variations increase exponentially. Diversity, brought about through sex, leads to adaptability of the species, and therefore its greater survival rate.

WHAT'S YOUR VIEW?

IS SEXUALITY MAINLY THE RESULT OF GENETIC INFLUENCES?

As you might imagine, the whole theory of sociobiology (which is also covered in other sections of this book) is not without its critics. Obviously, genes do affect our behavior, but not nearly as much as they do in the other species of the animal kingdom. Many experts say that sociobiology has made a valuable contribution to the theory of human sexuality but that it overemphasizes the role of genes.

We find that many of our students reject sociobiology completely. "Wilson treats people as though we are no better than animals," they say. What do you think? Is there a place for sociobiology in your understanding of human sexuality? If so, what is it?

Why are there not hundreds of sexes instead of just two? Wilson argued that two sexes are enough to create tremendous diversity while keeping the system as simple as possible. Diversity may not only be responsible for variation in the offspring but may contribute to the wide range of values people place on sexuality.

In a recent article, Weinrich (1987) extended the sociobiological theory to explained homosexuality. He suggests that homosexual behavior is the result of a "reproductively altruistic trait." That is, homosexuals give up their right to reproduce their genes. The theory, Weinrich qualified, is applicable only in societies like ours that do not strictly require marriage and reproductivity.

Practices of Young Adults

Two options are covered in this section: premarital experiences and marital practices.

Premarital Experiences

A number of findings of the new Janus Report (Janus & Janus, 1993; see chapter 13) are relevant to the premarital behavior and attitudes of young adults. Here are some of the most important findings:

- More than 80 percent of respondents were seriously concerned about sexually transmitted diseases, but most respondents reported increased rather than decreased sex activity in the past three years.

- Although many singles are exercising more caution, more men than women reported they had become more cautious about sex in the past three years.

- Nineteen percent of the single men and 23 percent of the single women surveyed reported using no contraception.

- The majority of singles do not find their lifestyle gratifying, but only one in three would prefer being married.

- Thirty-eight percent of single men and 45 percent of single women would like to become parents even if they do not marry.

- Middle-income women had had less premarital sexual experience than either low- or high-income women.

- For both men and women, premarital sex experience has increased: from 48 percent to 55 percent for men, and from 37 percent to 47 percent for women.

- Abortion has become more acceptable in the intervening years between phase 1 (1985) and phase 2 (1992)—from 36 percent to 30 percent agreement that abortion is murder, and from 29 percent to 53 percent disagreement.

We have considered evidence that sexual experience has increased among college students. For example, in their study of 793 undergraduates, Earle and Perricone (1986) found "significant increases in rates of premarital intercourse, significant decreases in age at first experience, and significant increases in number of partners" (p. 304).

Kinnaird and Gerrard (1986) examined the premarital sexual activity of unmarried female undergraduates. Young women from divorced and reconstituted families reported significantly more sexual behavior than those from intact families. Family conflict, disruption, and father-abuse were also related to such behavior.

Many studies of the premarital experiences of college students have been conducted, but few studies of persons who have not gone to college have been undertaken. We know from the classic studies that the noncollege educated are almost always more conservative (i.e., less experienced) than those who go to college (Kinsey & others, 1948, 1953; Masters & Johnson, 1966, 1970) but that they are subject to the same kinds of societal influence. Therefore we can expect that although noncollege populations have a lower experience rate, theirs, too, is considerably higher than it used to be.

A study of university students by Story (1982) sought a comparison of various sexual outlets (such as masturbation, premarital intercourse with other than future marriage partner, group sex, and sexual experience with person of same sex) over a six-year span. Fifty single males and 50 single females were tested in 1974, and another group of the same size was tested in 1980. Results showed that both males and females in the group tested in 1980 appeared to adhere more to society's conservative or traditional sexual behavior than the group tested in 1974.

With increased public awareness about sexually transmitted diseases and AIDS, why is it that sex education programs seem to increase awareness but do not translate into behavior change? Do you agree with this statement?

A MULTICULTURAL VIEW

Pregnant, Poor, and Alone in the Inner City

■ Hera is a 22-year-old African American woman who lives in Los Angeles. She describes a situation that is tragically not so unusual for poor women who live in large urban areas (Otteson, 1993).

I went to visit my boyfriend to tell him I was pregnant. When I arrived he was painting his room, so I decided to put it off until later that evening. When I got home, I felt empty, my heart began to beat very fast and my mind traveled beyond unhappiness for some reason. So I decided to call my boyfriend for comfort.

I recognized his voice on the answering machine but I just hung up the phone. Then I went to his home where I found the lights on but no one was there. I sat in my car waiting for his return. A half hour went by and he didn't come. So I went home.

The next day I received a phone call. It was his sister and she said, "Bernard was killed the same day you came to visit him. Two gang members tried to take his car at the hamburger stand and they shot him in the back." I did not believe it to be true. I hung up the phone, reached for his picture, held it tight to my heart and began to cry. I thought someone would call and say it was a joke. I waited an hour and no one called so I called his mother to ask her if it was true and she said it was.

In four years of being with Bernard, every quiet moment we shared together he always asked, "When can we have a baby?" Now I was angry and hurt. How could they kill an innocent person over a car? And not only did they take one life but they scarred our lives forever. My child would never have the opportunity to know its father. But I knew I had to stay strong for my baby's sake. I knew that in spirit he would always be with us. The gang members were arrested and thrown into jail. I thought of going to see them. I wanted to let them know the pain they had caused by taking that one life.

I did go to the trial of one of the gang members, to support Bernard's mother. I stared at this man who killed my baby's father. The anger was there but my thoughts were only, why? I listened closely as they repeatedly told the story. The gang member always looked around to see who was in the room. No one came to support him except his younger sister who testified of his abusive childhood. I felt sorry for her because she really loved her brother, but he let her down when he chose gangs over her. The lawyer gave her no sympathy and tortured her with questions. When she cried, the gang member showed some feelings for her and I realized this guy still had some deep feelings inside of him. This changed my heart from anger to crying out for God to help him.

After all the arguments, the jury decided he was guilty of murder. His sentence was the gas chamber. The gang member was shocked and his lawyer comforted him. As he looked over his shoulder, I looked him in the eyes.

The gang member's face is in my mind everyday. The incident travels with me daily, especially when my daughter asks, "Mommy, where is my daddy?" As I try to find the right words to tell her, my mind relives it all. My daughter is only three years old and will still ask questions until she's grown to understand what really happened.

I've been given strength through this tragedy. Learning about God has given me a more positive outlook on the situation. I have forgiven the gang member and I hope he can realize that now God is the one from whom he should ask forgiveness.

Marital Intercourse

Intercourse between a husband and wife is the only type of sexual activity totally approved by American society. Much is expected of it, and when it is unsatisfactory, it usually generates other problems in the marriage (McCary, 1978). Sexual closeness also tends to lessen significantly with the birth of each child, except in cases where the couple has taken specific steps to maintain the quality of their sexual relationship. Two studies (Whitehead & Mathews, 1986) learned that when young couples who are having sexual difficulties regularly attend therapy sessions, they are usually able to resolve their problems. Interestingly, those couples who received placebos (sugar pills) or small doses of testosterone did better than those who did not. This indicates how important the mind is in the area of sexuality.

A number of findings of the Janus Report (Janus & Janus, 1993; see chapter 13) are relevant to the marital behavior and attitudes of young adults. Among the most important findings are:

- Women who lived with their spouses before marriage are more likely to be divorced than women who didn't; men, less likely. Couples still married had lived together, on the average, for a shorter period of time before marriage than those who are now divorced.

- Among the divorced, men cite sexual problems as the primary reason for the divorce three times more frequently than women. Women cite extramarital affairs twice as frequently as men. But both cite emotional problems as the most frequent cause of divorce.

- Among the divorced respondents, 39 percent of the men and 27 percent of the women reported using no contraception.

Keeping pace with the important physical and sexual changes in young adulthood is growth in cognitive functioning. In the next section we turn to an examination of this type of development.

🌳 Guided Review 🌳

8. According to Freud, sexuality was the underlying basis for all behavior. He taught that if people did not have a healthy adult sex life, it was because they had _____ at an earlier stage.

9. Gagnon and Simon see sexual behavior as "scripted." Children learn sexual _____ and _____ much as they would learn a script for a play.

10. Gagnon and Simon argue that the roles sexuality plays in a society come about largely through transmission of the _____ by idealized adults.

11. Wilson suggests an unorthodox rationale for seeking sex. He claims that _____ leads to adaptability of the species and, therefore, its greater survival rate.

12. Research on marital intercourse indicates that sexual closeness between many couples tends to _____ significantly with the birth of each child.

Cognitive Development

As with physical development, there has not been a great deal of research on the cognitive development of young adults. Possibly this is because cognitive functioning appears to peak during this period, and so there is less concern over change. A major emphasis of research has been on the relationship between intellectual and ethical growth.

Intellectual/Ethical Development

Perry (1968a, 1968b, 1981) studied the intellectual/ethical development of several hundred Harvard college students, a group of males ages 17 to 22. These students responded to several checklists on their educational views and were interviewed extensively on the basis of their responses. The results of these studies led Perry to suggest a sequence of intellectual and ethical development that typically occurs during the transition from late adolescence to early adulthood. This sequence consists of nine positions, which indicate progress from belief in the absolute authority of experts to the recognition that one must make commitments and be responsible for one's own beliefs.

Perry's nine stages are divided among three broader categories, as follows:

Dualism

Perry's initial phase of ethical development, in which "things are either absolutely right or absolutely wrong."

I. **Dualism** ("Things are either absolutely right or absolutely wrong.")

- Position 1: The world is viewed in such polar terms as right versus wrong, we versus they, and good versus bad. If an answer is right, it is absolutely right. We get right answers by going to authorities who have absolute knowledge.

Answers

8. fixated   9. attitudes, behaviors   10. culture   11. diversity   12. lessen

- Position 2: The person recognizes that uncertainty exists, but ascribes it to poorly qualified authorities. Sometimes individuals can learn the truth for themselves.
- Position 3: Diversity and uncertainty are now acceptable but considered temporary because the authorities do not know what the answers are yet. The person becomes puzzled as to what the standards should be in these cases.

Relativism

The second phase in Perry's theory. An attitude or philosophy that says anything can be right or wrong depending on the situation; all views are equally right.

II. **Relativism** ("Anything can be right or wrong depending on the situation; all views are equally right.")

- Position 4a: The person realizes that uncertainty and diversity of opinion are often extensive and recognizes that this is a legitimate status. Now he or she believes that "anyone has a right to an opinion." It is now possible for two authorities to disagree with each other without either of them being wrong.
- Position 4b: Sometimes the authorities (such as college professors) are not talking about right answers. Rather, they want students to think for themselves, supporting their opinions with data.
- Position 5: The person recognizes that all knowledge and values (including even those of an authority) exist in some specific context. It is therefore relative to the context. The person also recognizes that simple right and wrong are relatively rare, and even they exist in a specific context.
- Position 6: The person apprehends that because we live in a relativistic world, we must make some sort of personal commitment to an idea or concept, as opposed to looking for an authority to follow.

Commitment (Perry's term)

The third phase in Perry's theory, in which the individual realizes that certainty is impossible but that commitment to a certain position is necessary, even without certainty.

III. **Commitment** ("Because of available evidence and my understanding of my own values, I have come to new beliefs.")

- Position 7: The person begins to choose the commitments that she or he will make in specific areas.
- Position 8: Having begun to make commitments, the person experiences the implications of those commitments and explores the various issues of responsibility involved.
- Position 9: The person's identity is affirmed through the various commitments made. There is a recognition of the necessity for balancing commitments and the understanding that one can have responsibilities that are expressed through a daily lifestyle. Perry (1981) describes this position:

Most college students are making the transition from Perry's category of dualism to relativism and, finally, commitment. What types of behaviors might you observe from a college student at each of these levels of intellectual development?

This is how life will be. I will be whole-hearted while tentative, fight for my values yet respect others, believe my deepest values right yet be ready to learn. I see that I shall be retracing this whole journey over and over—but, I hope, more wisely. (p. 276)

Some students move through these stages in a smooth and regular fashion; others, however, are delayed or deflected in one of three ways:

Temporizing

An aspect of Perry's theory of ethical development, in which some people remain in one position for a year or more, exploring its implications but hesitating to make any further progress.

- **Temporizing.** Some people remain in one position for a year or more, exploring its implications but hesitating to make any further progress.

Escape

Perry's term for refusing responsibility for making any commitments. Since everyone's opinion is "equally right," the person believes that no commitments need be made, and so escapes from the dilemma.

- **Escape.** Some people use opportunities for detachment, especially those offered in positions 4 and 5, to refuse responsibility for making any commitments. Since everyone's opinion is "equally right," the person believes that no commitments need be made and, thus, escapes from the dilemma.

Life is full of situations in which the difference between right and wrong is far from clear.

Retreat
According to Perry's theory of ethical development, when someone retreats to an earlier ethical position.

- **Retreat.** Sometimes, confused by the confrontation and uncertainties of the middle positions, people retreat to earlier positions.

Some have criticized Perry's theory (see Brabeck, 1984; Kitchener & King, 1981). For example, it should be remembered that the subjects of his research were all males. Now let us turn to research on females that Perry's work spurred.

"Women's Ways of Knowing"

In a collaborative study, Belenky and associates (1986) set out to answer the questions, "Do female ways of knowing develop differently from those of males? If so, how do they come to learn and value what they know?" The study was rooted in Perry's work and the work of Carol Gilligan, whose ground-breaking research on the morality of care and responsibility versus the morality of rights and justice was covered in chapter 9.

Belenky and her associates conducted a series of lengthy and intense interviews with 135 women of diverse socioeconomic backgrounds. The researchers found five general categories of ways in which women know and view the world. Though some of the women interviewed clearly demonstrated a progression from one perspective to the next, the researchers contend that they are unable to discern a progression of clear-cut stages, as did Perry and Gilligan. The five perspectives are silence, received knowledge, subjective knowledge, procedural knowledge, and constructed knowledge.

Silence
Belenky's first phase of women's thinking, characterized by concepts of right and wrong.

1. **Silence.** Females in the silence category describe themselves as "deaf and dumb." These women feel passive and dependent. Like players in an authority's game, they feel expected to know rules that don't exist. These women's thinking is characterized by concepts of right and wrong, similar to the men in Perry's first category of dualism. Questions about their growing up revealed family lives filled with violence, abuse, and chaos. The researchers noted that "gaining a voice and developing an awareness of their own minds are the tasks that these women must accomplish if they are to cease being either a perpetrator or victim of family violence" (Belenky & others, 1986, p. 38).

Received knowledge
Belenky's second phase of women's thinking; characterized by being awed by the authorities but far less affiliated with them.

2. **Received knowledge.** Women in the received knowledge category see words as central to the knowing process. They learn by listening and

assume truths come from authorities. These women are intolerant of ambiguities and paradoxes, always coming back to the notion that there are absolute truths. Received knowers seem similar to the men that Perry described as being in the first stage of dualism, but with a difference. The men Perry interviewed felt a great affiliation with the knowing authority. The women of this perspective were awed by the authorities but far less affiliated with them. In contrast to the men of Perry's study, women of received knowledge channel their energies and increased sense of self into the care of others.

Subjective knowledge

Belenky's third phase of women's thinking; characterized by some crisis of male authority that sparked a distrust of outside sources of knowledge, and some experience that confirmed a trust in women thinkers themselves.

3. **Subjective knowledge.** The researchers noted that women in the subjective knowledge category often had experienced two phenomena that pushed them toward this perspective: some crisis of male authority that sparked a distrust of outside sources of knowledge, and some experience that confirmed a trust in themselves. Subjectivists value their "gut" or firsthand experience as their best source of knowledge and see themselves as "conduits through which truth emerges" (p. 69). The researchers note that subjectivists are similar to males in Perry's second category of relativism in that they embrace the notion of multiple truths.

Procedural knowledge

Belenky's fourth phase of women's thinking; characterized by a distrust of both knowledge from authority and the female thinker's own inner authority or "gut."

4. **Procedural knowledge.** The women in the procedural knowledge category have a distrust of both knowledge from authority and their own inner authority or "gut." The perspective of procedural knowledge is characterized by an interest in form over content (how you say something rather than what you say). Women in this category also have a heightened sense of control. This category is similar to Perry's position 4b, where students learn analytic methods that authorities sanction. But analytic thinking emerges differently in women because they are less likely to affiliate with authorities.

The researchers describe women as having two kinds of procedural knowledge: separate knowing and connected knowing. These terms are reminiscent of Gilligan's work. Separate knowers are analytical and try to separate the self, to reveal the truth. Connected knowers learn through empathy with others.

Constructed knowledge

Belenky's fifth phase of women's thinking; characterized by an integration of the subjective and procedural ways of knowing (types 3 and 4).

5. **Constructed knowledge.** Those in the constructed knowledge category have integrated the subjective and procedural ways of knowing (types 3 and 4). Women of this perspective note that "all knowledge is constructed and the knower is an intimate part of the known" (p. 137). They feel responsible for examining and questioning systems of constructing knowledge. Their thinking is characterized by a high tolerance of ambiguity and internal contradiction. Indeed, the women whose ways of knowing are of this perspective often balance many commitments and relationships, as well as ideas.

What are some of the gender differences in cognitive development of young adult women and men?

The work of Perry and Belenky and her associates (as well as that of Piaget, Kohlberg, and Gilligan, discussed earlier in this book) has greatly advanced our knowledge of intellectual and ethical development in the late adolescent and early adult years. It has also produced much controversy. Many questions remain to be answered. For example, does socioeconomic level make any difference? What about cultural background? We hope that the research in this area will provide further insights into how we can help youth progress through this period successfully. We could say the same for the next aspect of development we will review, love in young adulthood.

YOUR VIEW?

How Does Age Affect High School Graduation Rates?

In the following table, you can see that a larger percentage of young adults aged 25 to 29 have a high school diploma and have four or more years of college than do all adults 25 and older. Why do you suppose this is true? Another interesting fact found in this table is that although educational level in general has risen steadily since 1940, there has been a slight decrease in high school graduation among the 25- to 29-year-olds in recent years. To what do you attribute this surprising finding?

Level of School Completed

| Year | % Ages 25 to 29 | | % Ages 25 and over | |
	H.S. or more[1]	4 or more years of college	H.S. or more[1]	4 or more years of college
1940	38.1	5.9	24.5	4.6
1950	52.8	7.7	34.3	6.2
1960	60.7	11.0	41.1	7.7
1970	75.4	16.4	55.2	11.0
1980	85.4	22.5	68.6	17.0
1986	86.1	22.4	74.7	19.4
1987	86.0	22.0	75.6	19.9
1988	85.9	22.7	76.2	20.3
1989	85.5	23.4	76.9	21.1

[1]Includes recipients of high school equivalency certificates

Source: National Center for Education Statistics, *American Education at a Glance*. Office of Educational Research and Improvement, Washington, D.C., 1992, page 8.

Guided Review

13. William Perry examined the intellectual and ethical changes in Harvard males and found them to move through three broad categories of change. These categories include _____ (things are absolutely right or wrong), relativism (all views are equal), and _____ (holding to beliefs based on the best available evidence and values).

14. Perry describes nine stages within these three categories. Some students move through the stages smoothly, others are delayed by _____ , escape, and _____ .

15. Mary Belenky and her colleagues, building on Perry's work and the work of Carol Gilligan, examined the _____ and _____ development of women.

16. Belenky and others found five general categories of ways in which women view the world. The five perspectives include silence, _____ _____ , subjective knowledge, procedural knowledge, and _____ _____ .

Answers

13. dualism, commitment   14. temporizing, retreat   15. ethical, intellectual   16. received knowledge, constructed knowledge

Physical and Cognitive Aspects of Love

The words written about love over the course of human history are uncountable. In this book, we will limit ourselves to describing the developmental aspects of this emotion: the seven forms of love that psychologist Robert Sternberg has suggested, and psychoanalyst Erich Fromm's definition of the essence of love.

The Seven Forms of Love: Sternberg

Sternberg (1986) argued that love is made up of three different components:

- **Passion.** A strong desire for another person, and the expectation that sex with them will prove physiologically rewarding.

- **Intimacy.** The ability to share one's deepest and most secret feelings and thoughts with another.

- **Commitment.** The strongly held conviction that one will stay with another, regardless of the cost.

Each of these components may or may not be involved in a relationship. The extent to which each is involved defines the type of love that is present in the relationship. Sternberg believed that the various combinations actually found in human relations produce seven forms of love (see table 15.3).

Passion

Sternberg's term for a strong sense of desire for another person, and the expectation that sex with them will prove physiologically rewarding.

Intimacy

One of Sternberg's three aspects of love; the ability to share one's deepest and most secret feelings and thoughts.

Commitment

One of Sternberg's three aspects of love; the strongly held conviction that one will stay with another, regardless of the cost.

Table 15.3	**Sternberg's Seven Forms of Love**
Linking	Intimacy, but no passion or commitment
Infatuation	Passion, but no intimacy or commitment
Empty love	Commitment, but no passion or intimacy
Romantic love	Intimacy and passion, but no commitment
Fatuous love	Commitment and passion, but no intimacy
Companionate love	Commitment and intimacy, but no passion
Consummate love	Commitment, intimacy, and passion

From R. J. Sternberg, "The Triangular Theory of Love" in *Psychological Review,* 93:119–135. Copyright © 1986 by the American Psychological Association. Reprinted with permission.

This is not to say that the more of each, the better. A healthy marriage will usually include all three, but the balance among them is likely to change over the life of the marriage. For example, early in the marriage, passion is likely to be high relative to intimacy. The physical aspects of the partnership are new, and therefore exciting, while probably not enough time has passed for intimacy to develop fully. This is a dangerous time in the marriage, because when intimacy is moderate, the couple may misunderstand each other in many situations or may make unpleasant discoveries about each other. Such problems are often much more painful than they are later, when deeper intimacy and commitment have developed.

Passion, Sternberg states, is like an addiction. In the beginning, the smallest gesture can produce intense excitement. As the relationship grows older, however, larger and larger "doses" are needed to evoke the same feelings. Inevitably, passion loses some of its power.

Of course, wide differences exist among couples (Hatfield & others, 1984; Traupmann & others, 1981). Some never feel much passion, whereas others maintain at least moderately passionate feelings into old age. Some appear to have strong commitments from the earliest stage of their association (love at first sight?), whereas others waver for many years.

Sternberg's theory has numerous implications for couples, and for marriage therapists as well. For example, more and more couples are engaging in premarital counseling. In this, they analyze with their counselor the three factors of love, and

For more and more engaged couples, premarital counseling is becoming a part of their plan to marry.

Validation

Fromm's term for the main ingredient of love.

how each person feels about them. This often helps them to avoid later problems and to get their relationship off to a good start. For some, it provides information that makes them realize that although their passion is high, their intimacy and commitment may not be, and they wait until these develop or decide not to get married at all. It is hoped that such counseling will bring about a decrease in our nation's high divorce rate.

Validation: Fromm

In his highly enlightening book on this subject, *The Art of Loving* (1968), Erich Fromm has given us a highly respected understanding of the meaning of love. First, he argues, we must recognize that we are prisoners in our own bodies. Although we assume that we perceive the world around us in much the same way as others, we cannot really be sure. We are the only one who truly knows what our own perceptions are, and we cannot be certain they are the same as other people's. In fact, most of us are aware of times when we have misperceived something: We heard a phrase differently from everyone else; had a hallucination when under the influence of a fever, alcohol, or a drug; and so on.

Thus we must constantly check on the reality our senses give us. We do this thousands, maybe millions, of times every day. Let us give you an example. We assume you are sitting or lying down while you are reading this book. Did you make a conscious check of the surface you are sitting or lying on when you got on it? Probably not. Nevertheless your brain did. You know that if it had been cold, sharp, or wet, you would have noticed. That it is none of these things is something your unconscious mind ascertained without your having to give it a thought.

With some insane people, this is the major problem. Their "reality checker" isn't working right. They cannot tell fact from imagination. They dwell in "castles in the air," out of contact with the real world. We need the feedback from all our senses, doing repeated checks at lightning speeds, to keep in contact with reality.

Fromm's point is this: As important as these "reality checks" on our physical environment are, how much more important are the checks on our innermost state—our deepest and most important feelings and thoughts! To check on the reality of these, we must get the honest reactions of someone we can trust. Such a person tells us, "No, you're not crazy. At least I feel the same way, too!" Even more important, these individuals prove their insight and honesty by sharing with us their own secret thoughts and feelings. In Fromm's words, others give us **validation.**

Validation is essential to our sanity. We are social animals, and we need to know that others approve of us (or, for that matter, when they don't). When someone regularly makes you feel validated, you come to love them. This is the essence of what Erikson calls intimacy, which we will discuss at length in the next chapter. Intimacy fulfills what Maslow calls the need for self-esteem.

It is no accident that the first person outside of our family who validates us is almost always a person of the same gender. It usually happens during adolescence, with your "best girlfriend" if you are female, or "best buddy" if you are male. This first intimate relationship is usually with a person of the same gender because the risk of them misunderstanding you is lower than in a relationship with the opposite gender.

There is, however, great risk in receiving validation. The person who gives it to you is able to do so only because you have let him or her in on your deepest secrets. This gives the person great power, for good or for ill. Because that individual knows you and your insecurities so well, she or he has the capability to hurt you horrendously. This is why many divorces are so acrimonious. No one knows how to get you better than a spouse with whom you have shared so many intimacies. This is why it is said that "There is no such thing as an amicable divorce."

Nevertheless, we truly need love and the validation that leads to it. As studies of mental illness make clear, those who try to live without love risk their mental health.

17. Robert Sternberg examined the nature of love, claiming that love is made up of three different components: passion, _____ , and commitment.

18. A healthy marriage will involve all three components, but the _____ among them is likely to change over time.

19. Erich Fromm's concept of _____ is closely related to what Erikson calls intimacy.

20. Often the first person who validates us is of the same _____ (such as a friend during adolescence).

Answers

17. intimacy   18. balance   19. validation   20. gender

🌳 CONCLUSION

Young adulthood is an exciting period in life, during which many changes are taking place. The peak of physical development is reached, and the decline of certain abilities begins. These declines are almost never apparent, however, because of organ reserve. Our style of life has a powerful effect on this development, including our diet, use of alcohol, drugs and nicotine, and marital status.

There are several quite different explanations of why sexuality develops as it does and a number of important changes in the current sexual practices of young adults. The major change occurring in the area of cognitive development involves the relationship between intellectual and ethical growth. Love, too, may be variously explained, for example with the theories of Sternberg and Fromm.

Physical and mental development form the basis of our interactions with the world around us. These interactions, which we refer to as psychosocial development, are covered in the next chapter.

🌳 CHAPTER HIGHLIGHTS

Physical Development
- Early adulthood is the period during which physical changes slow down or stop.
- The human body is designed to do much more than it is usually called upon to do. Much of its total capacity is held in "organ reserve."
- Lifestyle, food choices, alcohol and tobacco use, physical fitness, and marital status all play an enormous role in the health of a young adult.

Sexuality
- Freud believed that human sexuality is the underlying basis for all behavior.
- Gagnon and Simon see sexual behavior as culturally derived, "scripted" behavior.

- Wilson concludes that the only possible reason that evolution brought about the human sexual system was to create a greater diversity of individuals in a species.
- Sexual experience has increased among college students.
- Intercourse between a husband and wife is the only type of sexual activity totally approved by American society.

Cognitive Development
- Perry suggested three categories of intellectual and ethical development that typify transition from late adolescence to early adulthood: dualism, relativism, and commitment. By avoiding the three obstacles that might impede their progress (temporizing, escape, or retreat), young adults

should be able to achieve commitments that are the hallmark of the mature person.
- Belenky and associates suggest women know and view the world through five perspectives: silence, received knowledge, subjective knowledge, procedural knowledge, and constructed knowledge.

Physical and Cognitive Aspects of Love
- Sternberg argues that love is made up of three different components: passion, intimacy, and commitment.
- Fromm states that people need to have their deepest and most important thoughts and feelings "validated" by others who are significant to them.

🌳 KEY TERMS

Cholesterol 388
Commitment (Perry's term) 399
Commitment (Sternberg's term) 403
Constructed knowledge 401
Dualism 398
Escape 399

Intimacy 403
Organ reserve 386
Passion 403
Procedural knowledge 401
Received knowledge 400

Relativism 399
Retreat 400
Silence 400
Subjective knowledge 401
Temporizing 399
Validation 404

🌳 WHAT DO YOU THINK?

1. What would life be like if we did not reach the peak of our physical abilities in early adulthood?

2. How would you describe your style of life? According to the research you have read about in this chapter, would you say you are more like or unlike the average American?

3. Are you clear on your sexual values? Could you state your principles with precision?

4. Do you agree with Wilson's sociobiological theory? Why or why not?

5. Make a list of 10 of your best friends. In which of Perry's three categories would you place each of them?

6. Do you agree that major differences exist in the ways males and females view ethical issues? In what ways?

7. How can you tell if you are truly in love?

🌳 SUGGESTED READINGS

Fromm, E. (1968). *The art of loving.* New York: Harper & Row. A highly readable classic in the field. You will never think about love the same way after reading this book.

Geer, J., Heiman, J., & Leitenberg, H. (1984). *Human sexuality.* Englewood Cliffs, NJ: Prentice-Hall. This impressively comprehensive book covers virtually all aspects of sex with a depth of understanding.

Lawrence, D. H. [1920] (1976). *Women in love.* New York: Penguin. This novel probes the relationships between two sisters and their lovers. It offers timeless examination of the many aspects of adult interactions. Another of Lawrence's books, *Sons and Lovers,* is also magnificent on this subject.

May, R. (1975). *The courage to create.* New York: Norton. A remarkably insightful psychoanalyst, May brings to this book his many years of experience helping highly creative people deal with their many stresses.

Peck, Scott M. (1978). *The road less traveled.* New York: Simon & Schuster. "Confronting and solving problems is a painful process, which most of us attempt to avoid. And the very avoidance results in greater pain and the inability to grow both mentally and spiritually." Drawing heavily on his own professional experience, Dr. Peck, a practicing psychiatrist, suggests ways in which confronting and resolving our problems—and suffering through the changes—can enable us to reach a higher level of self-understanding.

Sternberg, R. J. (1986). The triangular theory of love. *Psychological Review, 93,* 129–35. This article, too, offers a penetrating view of this most elusive topic.

Woititz, J. (1990). *Adult children of alcoholics.* Lexington, MA: Health Communications, Inc. Janet Woititz describes the characteristics of the adult children of alcoholics but insists that these are not character defects. "It is my belief that knowledge is freedom and that those who identify can now have new choices. They can decide to work on changing aspects of themselves that cause them difficulty, or they can choose not to do so." This book provides readers with basic tools that will enable them to achieve greater self-knowledge and understanding.

🌳 CHAPTER REVIEW TEST

1. Because we seldom call on its total capacity, people often are not aware of the decline of their

   _____ _____

   during early adulthood.
   a. aerobic capacity
   b. blood pressure
   c. heart rate
   d. organ reserves

2. Based on the death rates of the people of Nevada and Utah, what can be concluded about the impact of lifestyle on health?
   a. Technological gains in medicine have had a remarkable impact on life expectancy.
   b. Lifestyle decisions have little effect on health.
   c. Lifestyle decisions are important to health but rarely affect life expectancy.
   d. Cost-free choices under the individual's control are much more effective at improving health than any medical advances.

3. Research indicates that heart disease and cancer are linked to
   a. nutrition.
   b. other related diseases.
   c. exercise.
   d. none of the above.

4. Lack of exercise, snacking, and use of labor-saving devices are the main causes of
   a. heart disease.
   b. cancer.
   c. obesity.
   d. high blood pressure.

5. A survey among college students on alcohol use showed that alcohol consumption was directly related to
   a. low grade-point average.
   b. poor relations with peers.
   c. memory loss.
   d. length of time needed to earn a college degree.

6. What is the major reason that young adults smoke?
   a. stress
   b. economic reasons
   c. peer pressure
   d. get a fix

7. According to the Department of Health and Human Services, what are some common characteristics of adult smokers?
   a. They are defiant and extroverted.
   b. They are impulsive, risk-takers, and extroverted.
   c. They are risk-takers and obedient to others.
   d. They are introverted, defiant, and stubborn.

8. Which marital status group shows the most health-related problems?
   a. single
   b. married
   c. divorced and separated
   d. widowed

9. According to Freud, human sexuality is the underlying basis for
   a. aggression.
   b. pleasure.
   c. human behavior.
   d. the fear of death.

10. Young adolescents learning sexual scripts are learning
    a. the need for intimacy.
    b. the need for belonging.
    c. the desire for submission.
    d. sexual attitudes and behavior in society.

11. The statement "sex creates diversity" reflects what view of sexuality?
    a. a psychoanalytic view
    b. a sociobiological view
    c. a Darwinian view
    d. a cognitive-affective view

12. Perry's stages of dualism, relativism, and commitment refer to a person's
    a. relationship development.
    b. intellectual and ethical development.
    c. ability to make moral decisions.
    d. interpersonal relationships.

13. In a study of women's perspectives on knowledge (Belenky & others, 1986), received knowledge refers to
    a. the view that words are central to the knowing process.
    b. an experience that resulted in a distrust of outside sources of knowledge.
    c. a distrust of knowledge from authority.
    d. learned passivity and dependency in relationships.

14. Belenky's category of procedural knowledge is most similar to which of Perry's stages?
    a. dualism
    b. commitment
    c. affirmation
    d. relativism

15. In Sternberg's conceptualization of love, when a person is able to share his or her deepest feelings and thoughts with another, they are experiencing
    a. passion.
    b. commitment.
    c. intimacy.
    d. true love.

16. According to Fromm, validation happens when "reality checks" on our innermost state come from
    a. the honest reactions of someone we can trust.
    b. a superior.
    c. our family of origin.
    d. our physical environment.

Answers

1. d   2. d   3. a   4. c   5. a   6. c   7. b   8. c   9. c   10. d   11. b   12. b   13. a   14. d   15. c   16. a

What can today's young adults expect life to be like in the twenty-first century? Research editor Judith Waldrop of *American Demographics* summarizes some of the likely facts and trends:

- As the twentieth century closes, white men will make up less than half of the labor force.
- By 2010 married couples will no longer be a majority of households.
- Asians will outnumber Jews by a margin of two to one, and Latinos will lead African Americans as the nation's largest minority.
- By the year 2000 more than half of all children will spend part of their lives in single-parent homes.
- By 2010 about one in three married couples with children will have a stepchild or an adopted child.
- Most children will never know a time when their mothers did not work outside the home.
- Households that the Census Bureau now defines as "nonfamilies," including unmarried heterosexual couples, homosexual couples, and friends who live together, eventually will receive legal recognition as families in all states.
- If no attempt is made to stop current trends, half of all children born in New York City this year will be on welfare by 2010. Other big cities will face the same problem.
- As the new century begins, more than 80 percent of women aged 25 to 54 will be in the labor force. Most of the rest will be out of work only temporarily.
- Parental leave and flexible working hours will be the rule for all but the smallest businesses.
- Working won't always mean going to the office. With advanced communications equipment, employees on the road or in small satellite offices will be able to work closely with the main office.
- Higher education will be expensive but jobs will be plentiful, so many young people will work before they go to college. By 2000 half of all college students will be aged 25 or older.
- To retire in 2030 on today's equivalent of $1,000 a month, workers will have to save $4,800 a year starting now.
- By the early twenty-first century, the United States will face severe shortages of hospital beds, physicians, and nurses. Staying healthy will become a priority.
- The fastest-growing segment of homemakers will be unmarried men who live alone or head families.
- Before the U.S. population hits 300 million, in 2029, strict national laws will govern recycling, packaging standards, and waste disposal.
- Traffic jams will take to the air. Airlines will serve approximately 800 million passengers in 2000, almost twice as many as in 1990.

Source: Adapted from Waldrop (1990).

As you can conclude from the preceding list, life in the next century will certainly involve a great deal of change. No aspects of life will undergo more change than those dealt with in this chapter: marriage and the family, work and leisure, and stages of personal development.

After reading chapter 16, you should be able to

- Discuss changes that have occurred regarding American marriage and families.

- Define the different types of marriage relationships.

- Appraise Holland's and Super's theories of career selection.

- List the pros and cons of a dual-career family.

- Explain Gould's "transformational" stages of adult development.

- Discuss Levinson's theory of adult development as it relates specifically to men.

- Compare both Levinson's and Gould's theories with Erikson's young adult stage of intimacy and solidarity versus isolation.

- Define what is meant by individuation and discuss how it applies differently to women and men.

Marriage and the Family

■ When two people are under the influence of the most violent, most divisive and most transient of passions, they are required to swear that they will remain in that excited, abnormal, and exhausting condition continuously until death do them part.

—George Bernard Shaw

Changing American Marriages and Families

Finding critics of marriage is not difficult (e.g., Kathrin Perutz's book, *Marriage Is Hell*). Not many Americans are paying attention, though. Almost 95 percent of Americans get married at some point in their lives (U.S. National Center for Health Statistics, 1988). To better understand the present situation, let us take a look at the trends in marriage and family relations.

Today 25 percent of all people who get married for the first time are likely to marry someone who has been married before (Sweet & Bumpass, 1987). In 20 percent of all marriages, both partners were married previously. Trends in the rates of first marriage, divorce, and remarriage since the early twentieth century reflect patterns of change in economic and social conditions in the United States. These changes can be clearly seen in table 16.1. One of the most interesting trends has been the change in the average age at first marriage. At the turn of the century, the average age for females was almost 22 years, and for males almost 26 years. With the exception of the late Depression and war years, the trend has been toward earlier and earlier marriages.

This trend led Duvall (1971) to predict that marriages in 1990 would come even earlier, at about age 20 for both males and females. Several other investigators (e.g., Neugarten & Moore, 1968) said the same thing in the late 1960s. But these miscalculations only demonstrate the difficulty of predicting the behavior of human beings.

The average age at first marriage in the United States has gradually increased since the record lows during the mid-1950s (table 16.1). Small increases in the age at first marriage occurred from 1955 to 1975. However, sharper increases have occurred in the last two decades. One explanation for this trend may be the rising numbers of women who have entered the workforce during this period.

Although women's standard of living typically decreases following divorce, it is often perceived that men get "taken to the cleaners" during divorce proceedings. What is the source of this perception?

The modern American family is quite different from those of the last century. Those families were larger and much more likely to live near each other in the same city or town. What are the advantages and disadvantages of this tendency?

Table 16.1	Median Age at First Marriage, by Sex: 1890 to 1991				
Year	**Men**	**Women**	**Year**	**Men**	**Women**
1991 . . . . 26.3		24.1	1955 . . . . 22.6		20.2
. . . .			1950 . . . . 22.8		20.3
1985 . . . . 25.5		23.3	1940 . . . . 24.3		21.5
1980 . . . . 24.7		22.0	1930 . . . . 24.3		21.3
1975 . . . . 23.5		21.1	1920 . . . . 24.6		21.2
1970 . . . . 23.2		20.8	1910 . . . . 25.1		21.6
1965 . . . . 22.8		20.6	1900 . . . . 25.9		21.9
1960 . . . . 22.8		20.3	1890 . . . . 26.1		22.0

Source: From A. F. Saluter, "Marital Status and Living Arrangements: March 1991" in *Current Population Reports,* P-20 (No. 461), U.S. Bureau of the Census, Washington, D.C., 1991.

Another interesting change has been the nearly triple rise in the proportion of young adults who have not married during the past two decades. Eighty percent of men aged 20 to 24 years had never married in 1991, up from 55 percent in 1970. In this same time period, the rate went from 19 percent to 47 percent for men 25 to 29 years old, and from 9 percent to 27 percent for men aged 30 to 34. As expected, since men marry later, men have higher proportions of the never-married in all age groups. For African Americans, however, the proportions are very similar for both genders (Saluter, 1991). An explanation may be that African American females may view African American males as poor marriage prospects because of their lack of employment opportunities (Chapman, 1988).

The rate of divorce and, as a result, the rate of remarriage are higher. In their study of the responses of thousands of women, Norton and Moorman (1987) discovered several trends: "Currently many young adult women (particularly African Americans) will never marry, remarriage after divorce is becoming less frequent, and data indicate that divorce is leveling [at almost 50 percent]" (p. 3). Interracial marriage represents only one-half of 1 percent of all marriages (Sweet & Bumpass, 1987). However, this number indicates a rapid increase over earlier periods.

The Bureau of the Census suggests that the recent trend in increased divorced rates is probably caused, at least in part, by four factors:

- Liberalization of divorce laws

- Growing societal acceptance of divorce and of remaining single

- The reduction in the cost of divorces, largely through no-fault divorce laws

- The broadening educational and work experience of women that has contributed to increased economic and social independence, a possible factor in marital dissolution

Other factors that affect divorce rates are race, the wife's workforce participation, husband's employment status, and residence status (Buehler & others, 1986; Kalter, 1987; Phillips & Alcebo, 1986; South & Spitze, 1986).

Although early and middle-age adults are certainly concerned about every aspect of their family lives, the crucial part of family life for most of them is how they manage their relationship with their spouse. Their major concern is: "What kind of marriage will I have, and how can I make it a happy marriage?"

Although there are confounding effects of cohorts and age with length of marriage, VanLear and Zietlow (1991) found that high marriage satisfaction was associated with less deference in couples who had been married a short time and with more deference and less equality for long-term couples.

YOUR VIEW?

IS THE INCREASE IN THE NUMBER OF WORKING MOTHERS SERIOUSLY HARMING THE AMERICAN FAMILY?

No doubt you have recently heard at least one politician wringing his or her hands over what serious shape the American family is in. In chapter 13, we reported on many of the changes affecting the relationship between parents and children in today's families—for example, the loss of such family functions as job training, and economic dependence. Some even worry that the family itself is on the way out. They prophesy that professionals will have ever-increasing roles in raising our children, as more and more American women seek careers.

Are other countries as concerned about this as we are? There are countries in which the family has always been of tremendous importance—Asian countries such as Japan and China, and Western countries such as Italy and Spain, for example. Is this becoming a big problem for them? What about Russia, where 50 percent of children 1 to 3 years old, and 90 percent of children 4 to 5 years old, are in day care? Do you think they have solved the problem of how to raise children when both parents work full time? What's your view?

More than 40 percent of marriages are remarriages (Wilson & Clarke, 1992). And many of these remarriages involve children: One in five married couples with children had a stepchild in 1985. Stepparenting may involve considerable strain because of feeling excluded from the family or trapped in the role. High expectations, especially for a stepmother who sees herself as a nurturer and caretaker, may contrast sharply with her feelings about her stepchildren (Whisett & Land, 1992). A third of the stepfathers in one study (Marsiglio, 1992) felt that to some degree they are more like a friend than a parent to their stepchildren; 52 percent disagreed somewhat that it is harder to love a stepchild than your own child. Researchers are continuing their investigation of the special characteristics of stepfamilies.

A MULTICULTURAL VIEW

Ethnic Differences in Expectations about Marriage

A national survey of 2,000, unmarried, noncohabiting 19- to 35-year-olds from the National Survey of Families and Households was used to explore marital aspirations and perceived costs and benefits of marriage among African Americans, Hispanics, and whites (South, 1993). A larger percentage of Hispanic men was found to be more desiring of marriage than African American or white men, although Hispanic women are less desiring of marriage than white women. South suggests that this may be due, in part, to the importance of family to Hispanic men as an indication of personal achievement and adult responsibility. There is an emphasis on male dominance and superiority, a paternal authoritarianism that fosters dependence and submission among wives. On the other hand, Hispanic women did not differ from non-Hispanics in the anticipated impact of marriage on their economic and emotional well-being.

Both African American men and women were less desiring of marriage than their white and Hispanic counterparts. It is suggested that the limited educational and economic opportunities available to African American men may contribute to the perception of a wife and child as an economic burden. It also appeared from these findings that lower marriage rates among African Americans may be more a function of African American men's (than of African American women's) reluctance to marry. African American men anticipate less improvement from marriage in their sex lives and personal relationships.

Types of Marriage

Monogamy

The standard marriage form in the United States and most other nations, in which there is one husband and one wife.

Polygamy

A marriage in which there is one husband but two or more wives.

Attitudes toward marriage, and therefore types of marriage, vary greatly throughout the world. Despite many variations in the ways humans begin their married lives, there are basically four kinds of marriage throughout the world: monogamy, polygamy, polyandry, and group marriage.

Monogamy is the standard marriage form in the United States and most other nations, in which there is one husband and one wife. In **polygamy,** there is one husband but two or more wives. In earlier times in this country, this form of marriage was practiced by the Mormons of Utah. There are still some places in the

The polygamous family, consisting of one husband and several wives, is almost nonexistent today.

Polyandry
A marriage in which there is one wife but two or more husbands.

Group marriage
A marriage that includes two or more of both husbands and wives, who all exercise common privileges and responsibilities.

Homosexual marriage
Though not accepted legally, the weddings of homosexuals are now accepted by some religions.

world where it exists, but the number is dwindling. **Polyandry** is a type of marriage in which there is one wife but two or more husbands. The rarest type of marriage, it is practiced only in situations where there are very few females. **Group marriage** includes two or more of both husbands and wives, who all exercise common privileges and responsibilities. In the late 1960s this form of marriage received considerable attention, but it accounts for a minuscule percentage of the world's population and has lost considerable popularity in recent years.

Homosexual marriages, although not officially sanctioned in many parts of the world, are beginning to be accepted in some religions. Such marriages, according to Wyers (1987),

> can provide individuals with an intimate, mature relationship. At the same time, though, this type of relationship presents a number of unique challenges to the couple. Aside from prejudice and lack of understanding from society at large, in the United States many social service networks and agencies are unprepared to offer services to gay and lesbian men and women. (p. 148)

Guided Review

1. The sharpest increases in the average age at first marriage have occurred in the last two decades. One reason for this trend may be that higher numbers of women have entered the _____ during this time.

2. Couples married for a longer time _____ their spouses more, but couples married for a shorter time saw their partner as more equal.

3. A stepmother who sees herself as _____ may feel conflicted in her feelings about her stepchildren.

4. Four factors are attributed to a recent trend in increased divorce rates. These factors include liberalization of divorce laws, growing _____ _____ of divorce, reduction in cost of divorces, and the broadening educational and work experience of women.

5. Basically, four types of marriage exist in the world: monogamy, polygamy, _____, and group marriage.

Answers
1. workforce (or job market) 2. respected 3. nurturing 4. social acceptance 5. polyandry

Table 16.2	
Approximate Years	**Primary Role of Work**
Early history	Search for food.
8000 B.C.	Cultivation of cereal grains, domestication of animals.
5000 B.C.	Greater division of labor, surplus production of goods, trade.
500 B.C.	Work seen as degrading and brutalizing by upper classes; done as much as possible by slaves.
A.D. 500	Serfdom (lord of manor system replaces slavery).
A.D. 1350	Black Death makes workers scarce. Move to towns; guilds of craftspersons formed. Cottage industry, capitalism start.
A.D. 1750	Inventions cause "industrial revolution," demise of small business. Factory system takes advantage of cheap labor.
A.D. 1900	Unions, government regulations, electricity and automation, new management policies greatly improve life of workers.
A.D. 1950	Computers, technology create world of highly skilled, white-collar workers.
A.D. 1970	Age of information processing.

Patterns of Work

■ Waste of time is thus the deadliest of sins. Loss of time through sociability, idle talk, luxury, or more sleep than is necessary for health (six hours) is worthy of absolute moral condemnation. Thus inactive contemplation is also valueless, or even reprehensible if it is at the expense of one's daily work.

—Max Weber, *The Protestant Ethic and the Spirit of Capitalism*

Weber, a philosopher and economist, was a leading spokesperson on the role of labor at the turn of the century. How differently we view that role today! Table 16.2 displays a brief summary of the history of work in Western society and indicates how much our attitudes toward work have changed. Changes in the world of work have been coming more rapidly in recent years than ever before. Working in the United States today is complicated. The rest of this section is devoted to explicating the major trends, their causes, and likely results.

Employment Patterns

Most of the total population 16 years old and older who choose to work are working (U.S. National Center for Health Statistics, 1992). The figure is decidedly lower for the African American population—around 89 percent, compared with 93 percent for whites. Not surprisingly, the highest percentage of unemployment is found among persons 16 to 19 years old. For African Americans in that age group, the percentage is a disconcerting 40 percent, as compared with 15 percent for whites.

Another important aspect of employment patterns has to do with the effects of education. The lower the level of education, the more likely a person is to be unemployed. Unfortunately, this is even more true for African Americans than for whites and Latinos. For example, of those with less than four years of high school, 19.9 percent of whites and 15.8 percent of Latinos are unemployed, compared with 35.9 percent of African Americans.

AN APPLIED VIEW

Getting a Job

How many jobs have you held so far in your life? Do you remember how you got them? What do the people who hire workers consider when they are hiring? Do blue-collar jobs have significantly different criteria than white-collar jobs?

To find out, you might interview the managers of a bank and a supermarket and ask what they look for in a new employee. Are there differences in behavioral, attitudinal, cognitive, or appearance criteria? Why or why not?

The "artistic" type of person, according to Holland, has a preference for ambiguous, free, unsystematized activities.

How People Choose Their Careers

Two theories are described here, those of John Holland and of Donald Super. These two theories have achieved the most acceptance in this field.

Holland's Personality Theory

On the basis of research still considered to be highly reliable, Holland (1973) developed an interesting theory on how people choose their careers. He suggested that in our culture, all people can be categorized as one of six personality types: realistic, investigative, artistic, social, enterprising, or conventional. An individual's personality pattern is estimated by figuring out how much a person's attributes resemble each type.

For example, a person might resemble an artistic type most. This type exhibits "a preference for ambiguous, free, unsystematized activities that entail the manipulation of physical, verbal, or human materials to create art forms or products, and an aversion to explicit, systematic, and ordered activities" (p. 120). This kind of person learns to be competent in artistic endeavors such as language, art, music, drama, and writing.

Our hypothetical person may next most resemble the social type. Such an individual is likely to be cooperative, friendly, generous, helpful, idealistic, insightful, responsible, tactful, and understanding. This person is then rated on the remaining four types in descending order. The six-category composite is the person's personality pattern.

The theory also holds that people live in six kinds of environments. These have the same names as the personality types. According to Holland (1973),

> ■ each environment is dominated by a given type of personality, and each environment is typified by physical settings posing special problems and stresses. For example, realistic environments are "dominated" by realistic types of people—that is, the largest percentage of the population in the realistic environment resembles the realistic type. A conventional environment is dominated by conventional types. (p. 22)

People tend to search out environments in which they feel comfortable and competent. Artistic types seek out artistic environments, enterprising types seek out enterprising environments, and so forth. You can take a test—the Strong Vocational Interest Blank—to see which personality type is most like you.

Super's Developmental Theory

Donald Super has been one of the most influential figures in advancing theories of career choice and development during recent years. Super (1957, 1983, 1990) developed a life stage theory of career development to explain how career identity develops over time and to determine a person's readiness to make a career choice. Super described five career stages, which he originally associated with

Exploration stage

According to Super's theory, that period in a person's career, usually from ages 15 to 24, during which a variety of work experiences are chosen.

Dual-career family

A family in which the wife does some sort of paid work and also manages the family's functions.

Many of the changes in the American family have been attributed to the phenomenon of the dual-career couple. Is there any truth to this perception? In what ways do two working parents alter (positively and negatively) the family's operation as a unit?

different developmental periods. In more recent revisions of his theory (Super & Thompson, 1981), Super suggests that we recycle through each of these stages several times during our lives.

The **exploration stage** is associated primarily with early adulthood. Through school, leisure, and part-time work activities, the adolescent or young adult is exposed to a wider variety of experiences. Through these experiences, individuals further define their self-concept and have the opportunity to test out abilities and interests. Early in this stage, initial work-related choices are made by assessing interests, abilities, needs, and values. By the end of this stage, a beginning full-time job is often selected. Super believes that most adolescents are not ready to make definite career choices because they have not yet had the chance to adequately explore available opportunities.

The Phenomenon of the Dual-Career Family

The old family pattern of the husband who goes off to work to provide for his family and the wife who stays home and manages that family is almost extinct. Economic realities and the women's movement have combined to change all that. Now most women do some sort of paid work and contribute 30 percent of the family income. This phenomenon of the **dual-career family** has manifested itself in some unusual ways.

First, women are still considered responsible for the maintenance of the family (Gerson, 1985). Therefore, women are often considered unreliable by employers for the more important, higher-paying jobs. Women in general have better access to low-paying jobs with little opportunity for advancement. Women often choose jobs that fit in well with the needs of their family. Women tend to work shorter hours and change the nature of their work more often than men do (Berk, 1985; Moen, 1985).

As Serakan (1989, p. 116) found, women experience increased self-esteem and feelings of self-worth and self-regard when working, critical variables that moderate the relationship among work factors and job satisfaction. Women who spend more time at work, though, experience less job satisfaction because of guilt over not being home than those who work less.

A recent study (Guelzow & others, 1991) confirmed that multiple roles in dual-career families are not necessarily related to stress but did find that longer working hours were associated with higher role strain for women; and larger family size and inflexible work schedules were associated with stress for men. Flexibility of work for men was related with role sharing in the household. Hertz (1989) found that when a wife's career became as demanding as her husband's, there was no time for a wife to be a wife; hence, the role of wife was the first to change. Sharing housework became inevitable; as one man put it, "If both of us were relying on the other to fix meals, we'd both starve."

Hertz also found that men have had to adjust psychologically to the increased role of their wives as providers for the family. Men have historically derived much of their self-image and personal satisfaction from their work and their ability to "provide" for their family. Women now contribute much more of the family income than in previous times, and in a small but increasing number of cases, women are the primary breadwinners.

The assumption was that the more conservative blue-collar worker would have more trouble dealing with this new division of labor than the better educated and more "enlightened" upper-class and middle-class husbands. Recent research suggests just the opposite. Upper-middle-class men seem to have the most problem sharing their roles as family providers, unless they earn considerably more money than their wives (Fendrich, 1984; Hood, 1983). Other research suggests that these men feel cheated because they have no wife at home full time to support them, as their fathers perhaps had.

Working-class men have adapted better to this change, perhaps because the financial reality gives them little choice. The more dependent a family is on the

On the average, the wife in a family does two to three times as much of the family's work as the husband.

contributions of a wife's income, the more accepting the husband is of the new role of his spouse (Rosen, 1987). All classes of men and women, however, try to continue to portray the husband as the primary provider and the wife as providing secondary support.

According to a recent study by Rosin (1990), "Research indicates, however, that many husbands believe that membership in a dual-career marriage leads to marital satisfaction because of a sense of companionship and partnership with their wives, an increased vitality in the relationship, and a greater feeling of independence" (p. 182).

Although women are entering the workforce in increasing numbers, men are in general not participating more in the family work. Whereas some research suggests that men are doing more housework than ever before (Pleck, 1985), other studies conclude that men do about the same amount of housework as they did in the nineteenth century (Cowan, 1987).

Most wives do about two to three times as much family work as the husbands (Berk, 1985). Women tend to do all the everyday work, including most of the child care, washing of clothes, cooking, and general cleaning. They tend to work alone, during the week and on the weekends, and during all parts of the day.

Men tend to do the less frequent, irregular work, such as household repairs, taking out the trash, mowing the lawn, and so on. They tend to do family work in the company of others, on the weekend, or perhaps during the evening. In the evening, this work may involve child care while the wife does the after-dinner chores. The tasks that men are most willing to share are the very tasks that women find most enjoyable: cooking and child care. During the inevitable argument over who does what around the house, the husband may point out that he helped out in these areas, not recognizing that he left the more onerous jobs for his wife.

We mentioned that men seem to derive their self-image and identity from their work and that this is increasingly threatened by the entrance of women into the workplace. One obvious way men could derive more satisfaction is by taking on a greater role in the care of their children. This change, however, does not appear to be occurring at the same pace as women entering the workforce. It is estimated that mothers are actively involved with their children three to five times as much as fathers (Lamb, 1987). Mothers do all the routine chores such as feeding, bathing, and dressing. Fathers primarily play with their children. Fathers tend to spend their time with the children when the mothers are around, whereas mothers spend much more time alone with the children.

■ It seems that men in a dual career marriage, no longer cushioned by the traditional wife, need to learn to balance competing demands of work and family. Where these men do not have role models, their changing roles may increase stress or change men's relationship to work, the cornerstone of male identity and self-esteem. (Rosin, 1990, p. 175)

Some male participation occurs regardless of whether the mother is employed. However, as economic necessity forces women to spend more time at a paid job, they are demanding that men help out more equitably. Recent research suggests that men who are forced to participate more in child care may form better relationships with their children. At the same time, this results in significantly more marital distress (Crouter & others, 1987). One of the challenges of the family in the 1990s will be to get husbands to take on voluntarily more of the responsibility of child care (not to mention equitable household management).

■ The results may lead to increased communication and interaction between husband and wife, enhancing the marriage, as well as an increase in job satisfaction for the working wife and mother who is able to devote more time to work without feeling stress over family obligations. (Serakan, 1989, p. 115)

🌳 Guided Review 🌳

6. The nature of work has changed, moving from a primary focus on food gathering (early human history) to a factory system (1750–1950) to an emphasis on _____ _____ (1970).

7. Level of education affects employment status, with less education related to higher unemployment rates. African Americans suffer more from less education than do whites or _____.

8. Holland's theory on how people select careers is based on a categorization of six _____ _____.

9. According to Holland, people choose careers that will place them in environments in which they feel _____ and _____.

10. In a dual-career family, men can get more satisfaction in their marriage by taking on an increased responsibility for _____ _____, as well as household duties.

11. Contrary to popular perception, _____-class men seem to adjust more poorly to dual-career families than do _____-class men.

Stages of Personal Development

In this section, we discuss the theories of Roger Gould, Daniel Levinson, and Erik Erikson. We also consider gender differences in individuation.

Transformations: Gould

To better understand how adults try to gain maturity, psychoanalyst Roger Gould and his colleagues at the University of California at Los Angeles combined their findings on a large number of outpatients. They discussed the primary concerns of patients at various age levels. Also at that time, Gould administered a questionnaire

Answers

6. information processing 7. Hispanics 8. personality types 9. comfortable, competent 10. child care 11. middle, working

Table 16.3	**Gould's Four Stages of Adult Development**
Stage One—Age 17 to 22—Leaving Our Parents' World	
Major false assumption: "I'll always belong to my parents and believe in their world."	
Stage Two—Age 22 to 28—I'm Nobody's Baby Now	
Major false assumption: "Doing things my parents' way, with willpower and perseverance, will bring results. But if I become too frustrated, or tired, or am simply unable to cope, they will step in and show me the right way."	
Stage Three—Age 28 to 34—Opening Up to What's Inside	
Major false assumption: "Life is simple and controllable. There are no significant coexisting contradictory forces within me."	
Stage Four—Age 35 to 45—Midlife Decade	
Major false assumption: "There is no evil or death in the world. The sinister has been destroyed."	

Source: Data from R. Gould, *Transformations*, Simon & Schuster, New York, N.Y., 1978.

on this same topic to 524 persons who were not outpatients. Based on the results of these two investigations, Gould generated a theory of adult growth that is reported in his book *Transformations* (1978).

Transformations is not a scientific report of the data, statistics, and research conclusions derived from these studies. Rather, it is a theoretical discussion illustrated by selected case studies, in the manner of Freud (see chapter 2). Gould contended that four developmental periods occur in adult life up through middle age (he did not go into later adulthood). At each of these stages, a **major false assumption** remains from childhood, which each individual must now reexamine and readjust if he or she is to progress in maturity. On the surface, each assumption seems obviously false, but Gould argued that it still controls us subconsciously. A summary of the stages, typical ages, and major false assumptions at each stage is presented in table 16.3. In this chapter, we will look only at the first three stages, the transition from late adolescence up to the midlife decade. The fourth stage is covered in chapter 18.

As Gould (1978) defined adult development, "Growing and reformulating our self-definition becomes a dangerous act. It is the act of transformation" (p. 25). Reexamining one's childhood angers and hatred (he referred to them as demons) is often a painful and difficult task. Many adults avoid it or soon give up on the struggle after they have entered it. This prevents them from reaching true maturity.

Gould recommended seven steps, called an **inner dialogue,** which he believed can help in mastering the demons of one's childhood experiences. These steps are:

1. Recognize your tension and confusion.

2. Understand that people are faced with contradictory realities.

3. Give full intensity to the childhood reality; that is, accept the fact that it is real.

4. Realize that contradictory realities still exist (between childhood and adulthood).

5. Test reality. Pick a risk that discriminates one view from another. For example, write a letter to your mother about your childhood concern (that time she was unexplainably mean to you).

6. Fight off the strong urge to retreat when just on the verge of discovery.

7. Reach an integrated, trustworthy view of reality, unencumbered by the demonic past.

Major false assumptions
Remaining from childhood, these beliefs must be reexamined and readjusted by individuals if they are to progress in maturity.

Inner dialogue
Gould's seven steps, which he believes can help in mastering the demons of one's childhood experiences.

Gould states that "growing and reformulating our self-definition becomes a dangerous act." What is dangerous about making transformations in our lives? Why might this be so?

At every stage, in addition to major false assumptions, several component false assumptions exist. These steps are aimed at helping us recognize false assumptions and eventually reject them in favor of a more realistic view of the world.

Stage One—Age 17 to 22—"Leaving Our Parents' World"

At stage one, youth begin to recognize the difficulties in accepting their major false assumption: "I'll always belong to my parents and believe in their world." As a result of this misunderstanding, five other false assumptions exist, which derive from the first:

- "If I get any more independent, it will be a disaster."

- "I can see the world only through my parents' assumptions."

- "Only my parents can guarantee my safety."

- "My parents must be my only family."

- "I don't own my own body."

For most young adults, society's gender roles determine their careers and the type of relationships they have.

Stage Two—Age 22 to 28—"I'm Nobody's Baby Now"

The major false assumption here: "Doing things my parents' way, with willpower and perseverance, will bring results. But if I become too frustrated, confused, or tired, or am simply unable to cope, they will step in and show me the way." Thus even though the direct dependence on parents is, or should have been, mastered at the previous stage, the strong influence of parents must be dealt with now. (As Gilligan pointed out so well in her book *Making Connections* (1990), interdependence, not dependence, is a more healthy objective.) The following false assumptions need to be recognized and exorcised:

- "Rewards will come automatically if we do what we're supposed to."

- "There is only one right way to do things."

- "My loved ones can do for me what I haven't been able to do for myself."

- "Rationality, commitment, and effort will always prevail over all other forces."

Now one's adult sex role begins to take decisive form. Young adults decide on their careers, their relationships with other persons, and whether to become parents. Their dreams for the rest of their lives now take clear form.

Over nine-tenths of all Americans eventually marry, and the great majority of them marry during this stage. Gould believes that, in part, the motivation for those marriages and the choice of the specific partner result from our inability to deal adequately with our relationship with our parents. As he puts it:

> ■ Each and every one of us pick partners that, in subtle ways at least, recreate a parent-child relationship that has not yet been mastered. Our separateness from our parents in our twenties is really just a fiction. (1978, p. 145)

Stage Three—Age 28 to 34—"Opening Up to What's Inside"

At stage three, the major erroneous belief of most individuals is that "Life is simple and controllable. There are no significant contradictory forces within me." People at this stage begin to realize that life is really quite relativistic and that very few "eternal verities" exist. The dream of the successful salesman or the fulfilled mother now comes to be questioned. Both men and women seem to need to reevaluate their entire lives as they enter the fourth decade of their existence.

According to Gould, this reevaluation forces an examination of four false assumptions:

- "What I know intellectually, I know emotionally."

- "I am not like my parents in ways that I don't want to be."

- "I can see the reality quite clearly of those close to me."

- "Threats to my security aren't real."

The major cause of conflict at this stage of life is parenthood. In explaining to children what their values ought to be, we are often forced to see how unsure we are of our own values. Divorce increases at this time, too, as spouses attempt to adjust to each other's developing values.

All of this conflict, however, has a good side. Gould cited Bertrand Russell's statement that this stage was "intellectually the highest point of my life." Gould believed that the age-30 crisis often forces us to come to know ourselves finally for what we really are. "Our confidence in the world increases as we accept the limitations of our powers and the complexity of reality. . . . In short, we come to see that life is not fair" (1978, p. 61).

AN APPLIED VIEW

Responsibility for Self

One of the clearest indexes of maturity is the ability to be responsible for your own life and behavior. This exercise asks a number of questions involving responsibility for your own behavior.

1. Name two major purchases you have made in the past year by yourself without a strong influence by anyone else.

   _____

   _____

2. Wherever it is that you live, do your parents support you, or do you pay for your own housing?

   _____

3. Are you completely in charge of what time you come home at night, or do you have to answer to someone else? _____

4. Are you the sole person who decides what clothing you wear?

   _____

5. To what extent have your parents influenced your career, that is, whether you have chosen to go to college or work, the acceptability of your grades or pay, and so on?

   _____

6. Are you able to make independent decisions about your sex life? Do you let your parents know what you have decided?

   _____

You might compare your answers with those of some of your friends to get a relative idea of how responsible for your life you are.

The Adult Life Cycle: Levinson

Yale psychologist Daniel Levinson, who died in 1994, was one of the most respected researchers in adult developmental psychology. Working with his colleagues at Yale, he derived a theory of adult development based on intensive interviews with 40 men and 40 women. Rather than depend on questionnaire data from a large number of individuals as Gould did, Levinson decided that intensive interviewing and psychological testing with a small number of representative cases would more likely provide him with the information for a theory of adult development. Because of the number of hours necessary in this study (almost 20 hours were spent on interviews with each subject), Levinson decided to limit the number of cases so that he could get more detailed information.

Life course

Levinson's term. *Life* refers to all aspects of living—everything that has significance in a life; *course* refers to the flow or unfolding of an individual's life.

Life cycle

Levinson's term. The life cycle is a *general* pattern of adult development, while the life course is the unique embodiment of the life cycle by an *individual*.

Biopsychosocial

A term for the idea that development proceeds by the interaction of biological, psychological, and social forces.

Transition

Levinson's concept that each new era begins as an old era is approaching its end. That "in-between" time is a transition.

Life structure

Levinson's term. The underlying pattern or design of a person's life *at a given time*.

Structure building

Levinson's term. During structure-building periods, individuals face the task of building a stable structure around choices they have made.

Structure changing

Levinson's term. A process of reappraising the existing life structure and exploring the possibilities for new life structures characterizes the structure-changing period.

Key to Levinson's (1986, 1990a) theory of adult development is the notion of **life course.** *Life* refers to all aspects of living—everything that has significance in a life. *Course* refers to the flow or unfolding of an individual's life. Life course, therefore, looks at the complexity of life as it evolves over time.

Equally important to Levinson's theory is the notion of **life cycle.** Building on the findings of his research, Levinson proposed that there is "an underlying order in the human life course; although each individual life is unique, everyone goes through the same basic sequence" (1986, p. 4). The life cycle is a general pattern of adult development, whereas the life course is the unique embodiment of the life cycle by an individual.

Through his studies, Levinson further defined parts of the life cycle. He defined the life cycle as a sequence of eras. Each era is **biopsychosocial** in character: It is composed of the interaction of the individual, complete with his or her own biological and psychological makeup, with the social environment. Each era is important in itself and in its contribution to the whole of the life cycle. A new era begins as the previous era approaches its end. That in-between time is characterized as a **transition.**

The intricacies of Levinson's theory of adult life course and life cycle are further elaborated by his concept of the adult **life structure.** Life structure is the underlying pattern or design of a person's life at a given time. Levinson noted that "a theory of life structure is a way of conceptualizing answers to a different question: 'What is my life like now?'" (1986, p. 6). The primary components of a life structure are the relationships that an individual has with significant others. It is through relationships that we "live out" various aspects of ourselves. Levinson regarded relationships as actively and mutually shaped. Life structure may have many components, but generally only one or two components are central in the structure at a given time. The central component(s) is the one that most strongly influences the life structure of the individual.

The evolutionary sequence of the life structure includes an alternating series of **structure-building** and **structure-changing** transitions. During the structure-building periods, individuals face the task of building a stable structure around choices they have made. They seek to enhance the life within that structure. This period of relative stability usually lasts five to seven years. During that time, the stability of the life structure affords individuals the freedom to question their choices and to consider modifying their life.

This process of reappraising the existing life structure and exploring new life structures characterizes the structure-changing period. This period usually lasts around five years. Its end is marked by the making of critical life choices around which the individual will build a new life structure. Levinson noted that the individual decides at this point, "This I will settle for" (1986, p. 7).

In considering the periods of stability and change in the adult life cycle, Levinson noted, "We remain novices in every era until we have had a chance to try out an entry life structure and then to question and modify it in the mid-era transition" (1986, p. 7). Individuals enter into new stages of adult development as they become focused on certain developmental tasks. You will understand these tasks better when we describe each stage in the following pages.

Levinson gave equal weight to periods of stability and transition. This captures the evolution of the focus of an individual and the flowing quality of adult development. Unlike most theories of child development, in which development takes the form of positive growth, Levinson's study of adult development recognized a coexistence of growth and decline.

Seasons of a Man's Life: Levinson

Levinson made two separate studies, one of men (1978) and one of women (1990b) (both to be further described in chapter 18). In his first study, which was solely of

Figure 16.1
Levinson's theory

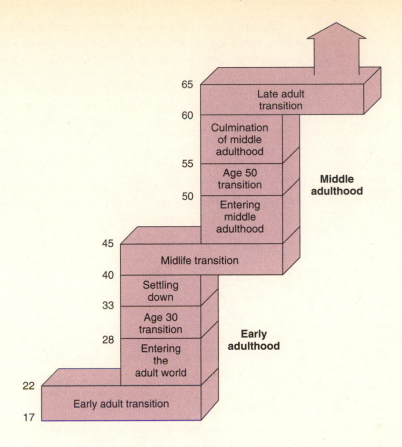

men, 40 male subjects ranging in age from 35 to 45 were selected, representing four categories (10 each): blue-collar workers paid on an hourly basis, middle-level executives, academic biologists, and novelists.

The hourly workers and the executives were employees of an industrial firearms manufacturer or an electronics plant (about half from each). The biologists were employed at two highly rated universities located between Boston and New York. Of the writers, some were highly gifted novelists whose work had already been accepted by critics; others were less well known but were regarded as promising and worthy of serious consideration. Of course, this sample cannot be considered to represent the average male in the United States, but the diversity of the people selected in social class origins, racial, ethnic, and religious backgrounds, education, and marital status does make it typical of a great deal of American society today.

The study concentrates on the choices made by each man during his life and how he has dealt with the consequences of his choices, especially as they affect the main components of living: occupation, marriage, and family. After studying these components, Levinson suggested that there are four main seasons of life: (1) childhood and adolescence—birth to 22 years; (2) early adulthood—17 to 45 years; (3) middle adulthood—40 to 65 years; and (4) older adulthood—60 years and older.

Obviously, considerable overlap occurs between each of his stages. Between these major stages are substages that help to bring about the transitions necessary for development. Figure 16.1 gives a description of various stages and substages. Levinson himself concentrated on the early and middle adult periods, leaving further consideration of the childhood and late adult periods to others.

He believed that "even the most disparate lives are governed by the same underlying order—a sequence of eras and developmental periods" (1978, p. 64). The purpose of these developmental transitions is to cause greater individuation. **Individuation** refers to our becoming more individual; we develop a separate and special personality, derived less and less from our parents and teachers and more from our own behavior.

Individuation
Refers to our becoming more individual; we develop a separate and special personality, derived less and less from our parents and teachers and more from our own behavior.

Although Levinson hypothesized more than 10 substages in the course of life, he chooses to concentrate on three phases in male development. These are the novice phase, the settling-down phase, and the midlife transition (the latter two are discussed in chapter 18).

The Novice Phase

The **novice phase** of human development extends from age 17 to 33 and includes the early adult transition, entering the adult world, and the age-30 transition (see figure 16.1). In this phase of life, four major tasks are to be accomplished. The individual in the novice phase should form

Novice phase
Levinson's initial phase of human development extends from ages 17 to 33 and includes the early adult transition, entering the adult world, and the age-30 transition.

- *The dream.* "Most men construct a vision, an imagined possibility that generates vitality" (p. 91).

- *Mentor relationships.* Each man should find someone who is older, more experienced, and willing to make suggestions at each of the choice points in his early adult life.

- *An occupational decision.* A man should begin to build on his strengths and to choose a vocation that values those strengths.

- *Love relationships.* Each man should make decisions on a marriage partner, the number of children, and the type of relationship that he wants to have with wife and children.

The Mentor

Mentoring
The act of assisting another, usually younger, person with his or her work or life tasks.

The concept of **mentoring** has received considerable attention in recent years (e.g., Frey & Noller, 1983; Moyers & Bly, 1989; Noller, 1983; Rivchun, 1980). Of particular interest are Robert Bly's notions (1990) on the subject (which, by the way, he calls "male mothering").

Bly suggested that two events have wreaked havoc with the modern American male's sense of himself. The first, which began in the first half of the nineteenth century, was the Industrial Revolution. As a result of this, fathers were forced to leave home, where they traditionally worked by the side of their sons, and seek employment in factories. The second, which began in the 1960s with "no-fault" divorce, led to the proliferation of single-parent families, about 90 percent of which are headed by females.

It is suggested that women have more difficulty than men finding mentors for their professional development. Would you expect this to be true? Why or why not?

With each of these events, much of the teaching and appreciation that boys used to get from their ever-present fathers was lost. Mothers have tried to make up for this loss, but because of deep-seated gender differences, only another male can induct a boy into adulthood successfully (see chapter 14). Bly believed that only those young men who achieve a mentor relationship with some other older man are likely to attain a mature personality. This man may be an uncle, one of the father's friends, or some older man at work. Without such a person, the young man will not be brave enough to confront himself, and he will sink into a defensive, self-deluding lifestyle. Bly also suggested that because the typical conflicts that exist between sons and fathers are absent in the mentor relationship, the mentor actually can be more helpful to the young man.

A solid relationship with an older mentor is crucial to the career success of a young adult, according to Levinson. Why is it, do you think, that older males are more likely to take a mentoring attitude toward their younger colleagues than are older females toward their younger colleagues?

Levinson found that after each man selects a dream, mentor relationship, occupation, and love relationship, at around age 30 (plus or minus two years) he comes to reexamine his feelings about the four major tasks. Important decisions are made at this time, such as an alteration of the dream, a change in mentor, a change in occupation, and sometimes a change in marital status. For some, this transitional period proves to be very smooth. In most cases, however, it challenges the very foundations of life itself. Although he often keeps it to himself, the typical male at this stage undergoes a seriously disturbing period of self-doubt. Fortunately, most emerge from these doubts with a clearer understanding of their strengths and weaknesses, and a clearer view of what they wish to make of themselves.

A MULTICULTURAL VIEW

The Gender-Role Training of Western Men

Judith Jordan (cited in Bergman, 1991) stated:

■ "I used to think that what we have here is just Western culture—competitive, individualistic, self-sufficient. But the cross-cultural data suggests that this country is off the scale—that we are so far into the individualistic, competitive ethic, and that, in fact, we continue to socialize males to be soldiers—whether on the battlefield or in industry—and you don't socialize soldiers to be empathic, listening, caring people. I think, ultimately, the individualistic ethic is starting to fail in terms of ecological and economic success in the world, and it will push the system to move into some new paradigms, and I feel some hope about that."

The well-being of young American men has been found to be influenced by closeness to child and wife, adjustment to the husband role, and the number of close friends (Julian & others, 1992). If Jordan is right that men are socialized to be soldiers and dread close relationships, this would indicate that the emotional health of American men is endangered by their gender-role training. If they are not taught to be caretakers of relational processes in the way women are, then they will have difficulty being emotionally close to their wives and children, and thus their personal well-being will suffer. What's your opinion? What new paradigms for men might Ms. Jordan be referring to?

Thus, for both Gould and Levinson, the transition from late adolescence to early adulthood (and also for the years to come) tends to proceed in stages as orderly as those we have seen in the earlier stages of life. More variation occurs as we grow older, because we are controlled less and less by our genetic inheritance and more and more by the environment in which we find ourselves, and by our own individual decisions. This growing independence from our genes and our early experiences is reflected clearly in these two theories. Even if we have had a hard childhood, with alcoholic parents and traumatic accidents, we should be developing the ability to be in charge of our lives. As we grow older, we have the opportunity, and indeed the responsibility, to reinvent ourselves. Of course, how we reinvent ourselves depends on our culture. Some have suggested that both Gould's and Levinson's theories are culturally limited to the United States. What do you think? The next personality theorist we will cover, Erikson, would certainly have agreed.

Intimacy versus Isolation: Erikson

We last talked about Erikson's theory in chapter 11, where we discussed his fifth stage (adolescence), identity and repudiation versus identity confusion. Now we will consider his sixth stage, intimacy and solidarity versus isolation. This stage applies to what he defined as young adulthood, ages 18 to 25.

In his definition of intimacy, Erikson stated that it should include

1. Mutuality of orgasm

2. with a loved partner

3. of the other sex

4. with whom one is able and willing to share a mutual trust

5. and with whom one is able and willing to regulate the cycles of
    a. work
    b. procreation
    c. recreation

6. so as to secure to the offspring, too, all the stages of a satisfactory development (1963, p. 266).

Erikson pointed out, however, that sexual intercourse should not be assumed to be the most important aspect of intimacy between individuals. He was speaking here of far more than sexual intimacy. He was talking about the ability to relate one's deepest hopes and fears to another person and to accept another's need for intimacy in turn.

Intimacy

Erikson's stage that represents the ability to relate one's deepest hopes and fears to another person and to accept another's need for intimacy in turn.

Solidarity

Erikson's term for the personality style of persons who are able to commit themselves in concrete affiliations and partnerships with others and have developed the "ethical strength to abide by such commitments, even though they may call for significant sacrifices and compromises."

Distantiation

The readiness of all of us to distance ourselves from others when we feel threatened by their behavior.

Isolation

The readiness all of us have to isolate ourselves from others when we feel threatened by their behavior.

Those who have achieved the stage of **intimacy** are able to commit themselves to concrete affiliations and partnerships with others and have developed the "ethical strength to abide by such commitments, even though they may call for significant sacrifices and compromises" (1963, p. 262). This leads to **solidarity** between partners.

Erikson was fond of quoting Freud's response when asked what he thought a normal person should be able to do well: *"Lieben und arbeiten"*—"to love and to work." To Freud, then, sharing responsibility for mutual achievements and the loving feelings that result from them are the essence of adulthood. Erikson fully agreed with this. Thus when Freud uses the term *genitality* to describe this same period, he does not merely mean sexual intercourse; he is referring rather to the ability to share one's deeply held values, needs, and secrets with another through the generosity that is so important in intimacy.

It must be admitted, nevertheless, that Freud was far more concerned with the physical aspects of sex than Erikson, who deserves major credit for moving the school of psychoanalysis away from its fascination with genitalia and toward a greater concern for adult intimacy in general.

The counterpart of intimacy is **distantiation.** This is the readiness all of us have to distance ourselves from others when we feel threatened by their behavior. Distantiation is the cause of most prejudices and discrimination. Propaganda efforts mounted by countries at war are examples of attempts to increase distantiation. It is what leads to **isolation.**

Most young adults vacillate between their desires for intimacy and their need for distantiation. They need social distance because they are not sure of their identities. They are always vulnerable to criticism, and since they can't be sure whether the criticisms are true or not, they protect themselves by a "lone wolf" stance.

Although intimacy may be difficult for some males today, Erikson believed that it used to be even more difficult for females. "All this is a little more complicated with women, because women, at least in yesterday's cultures, had to keep their identities incomplete until they knew their man" (1978, p. 49). Now that less emphasis occurs in the female gender role on getting married and pleasing one's husband, and more emphasis is on being true to one's own identity, Erikson believed that both sexes have a better chance of achieving real intimacy.

A growing number of theorists, however, many of them feminist psychologists, argue that females still have a harder time "reinventing" themselves, because of the way our society educates them. In the next section, we present their position.

Male versus Female Identity

■ Identity precedes intimacy for men. . . . For women, intimacy goes with identity, as the female comes to know herself as she is known, through her relationships with others. (Gilligan, 1982, p. 12)

Sigmund Freud would have concurred with this statement by Gilligan, but for reasons that many modern women disagree with. According to feminist Betty Friedan, Freud believed "that women need to accept their own nature, and find fulfillment the only way they can, through 'sexual passivity, male domination, and nurturing maternal love' " (Friedan, 1963, p. 43).

The view of the feminists is that because females are trained to believe in the necessity of their maintaining relationships within the family, and because this role often involves self-sacrifice, women find it harder to individuate—that is, to develop a healthy adult personality of their own. They argue that for the young adult male, identity formation "involves separating himself from dependency on his family and

In what ways do you think a person's environment influences identity development? In what ways do biological processes influence identity development?

The 1960s were a time when many grass-roots action groups, such as Students for a Democratic Society, came into being. They were anxious to promote "justice, peace, equality, and personal freedom."

taking his place in the adult world as an autonomous, independent being, competent, with a clear sense of career and confidence in his ability to succeed" (Wolfson, 1989, p. 11).

For the young adult female, career and self-assurance are not so emphasized. Winning the attention and then the commitment of a man are more important aspects of her identity, and intimacy is the major goal. This is seen as unhealthy. As Wolfson (1989) puts it, "It is difficult to have a sense of yourself that is internally consistent and congruent if your identity is dependent on the identity of someone else. 'I am who you are' is very different from 'I am who I am'" (p. 12).

This new point of view arose in the 1960s, primarily with the publication of Betty Friedan's book, *The Feminine Mystique* (1963). The affluent 1950s had "created a generation of teenagers who could forgo work to stay in school. Inhabiting a gilded limbo between childhood and adult responsibility, these kids had money, leisure, and unprecedented opportunity to test taboos" (Matusow, 1984, p. 306). At this time many youths, particularly those of the newly affluent middle class, "wanted to live out the commitments to justice, peace, equality and personal freedom which their parents professed" (Gitlin, 1987, p. 12) but, the young people felt, failed to live up to. Groups such as the Students for a Democratic Society sprang up. Programs such as Rennie Davis's Economic Research and Action Project, whose goal was to "change life for the grassroots poor," developed (Matusow, 1984, p. 315). This movement worked for justice and equality not only for the poor and racial minorities but also for women.

The movement fostered a new commitment to women's issues and to studies of women themselves. For example, as a result of her research on the female perspective (see chapter 9), Harvard psychologist Carol Gilligan has come to believe that

■ for girls and women, issues of femininity or feminine identity do not depend on the achievement of separation from the mother or on the progress of individuation. Since masculinity is defined through separation while femininity is defined through attachment, male gender identity is threatened by intimacy while female gender is threatened by separation. (1982, p. 9)

Research has also pointed to two other concerns about women's identity formation. One has been the tendency of society to "objectify" women, which means seeing them as a particular type of creature or object rather than as individuals. Psychoanalyst Erich Fromm (1955) suggested that "To be considered an object can lead to a deep inner sense that there must be something wrong and bad about oneself" (p. 323).

The second concern involves the ability to admit vulnerability. "Men are taught to avoid, at all costs, showing any signs of vulnerability, weakness, or helplessness, while women are taught to cultivate these qualities" (Wolfson, 1989, p. 44). Psychologist Jean Baker Miller writes that a "necessary part of all experience is a recognition of one's weakness and limitations. The process of growth involves admitting feelings, and experiencing them so one can develop new strengths" (1976, p. 31).

Miller sums up the feminist indictment of Erikson's position. His theory is flawed, she argues, because of his belief that

■ women's reality is rooted in the encouragement to "form" themselves into the person who will be of benefit to others. . . .This selfhood is supposed to hinge ultimately on the other person's perceptions and evaluations, rather than one's own. (1976, p. 72)

Obviously more work is needed to resolve this question of the role of gender in the development of the adult personality. Erikson (1963) himself appears to have endorsed this point of view, by stating that

■ there will be many difficulties in a new joint adjustment of the sexes to changing conditions, but they do not justify prejudices which keep half of mankind from participating in planning and decision-making, especially at a time when the other half [men], by its competitive escalation and acceleration of technological progress, has brought us and our children to the gigantic brink on which we live, with all our affluence. (p. 293)

In each of the theories described in this section on personality, the role of psychological and social forces is evident. Do you believe that biology also plays a part? For example, might hormones make a difference?

Guided Review

12. Roger Gould defines transition as growth and _____ by challenging false assumptions of our childhood through inner dialogue.

13. The steps of an inner dialogue begin with recognition of tension and confusion and, through a series of steps including _____ _____ and fighting off the urge to retreat, ending with an integrated and _____ view of reality.

14. Gould's three stages of early adulthood include: Leaving our parents' world; I'm nobody's baby now; and _____ _____ _____ _____ _____.

15. Daniel Levinson's theory looks at adult development by examining life _____ (the unique development of the individual) and the life _____ (the general pattern of adult development).

16. Life structure is the underlying pattern or design of a person's life at a given time. It is _____ in character, with a primary component being the _____ that an individual has with significant others.

17. Erik Erikson's sixth stage of psychosocial development, intimacy versus isolation, focuses on building a _____ as opposed to Levinson's more career-oriented approach.

18. Women's sense of identity is seen by Miller and Gilligan as developing within _____.

Answers

12. reformulation 13. reality testing, trustworthy 14. opening up to what's inside 15. course, cycle 16. biopsychosocial, relationships 17. relationship 18. relationships

How's Your Individuation Index?

A number of theorists have stressed that maturity involves becoming more and more of an individual as one goes through life's stages; that is, one becomes less dependent on the opinions of one's parents, other relatives, teachers, and friends. The person is better able to determine her or his own personality, using these other influences only as guides. Thus one index of maturity level is the extent to which one is "individuating." Fill in the blanks below to get an idea of your own individuation.

1. Can you think of any occasion within the last month when your friends asked you to do something with them and you refused?

_____

_____

2. Can you think of three important decisions you have made within the past year that were definitely not influenced by your parents?

_____

_____

_____

3. Can you name at least two things about yourself that you used to hate but that you now feel are not all that bad?

_____

_____

4. Can you name at least two people who used to have a big influence on your life but who are no longer able to influence you very much?

_____

_____

5. Can you name two things that you now like to do by yourself that you previously didn't like to do?

_____

_____

6. Can you name two beliefs or values you hold with which your friends would disagree?

_____

_____

7. Can you name three things you do of which your parents would disapprove? Three things of which they would approve?

_____

_____

_____

8. Do you think you organize your time differently from most of your friends? Name three ways in which you do things differently from them.

_____

_____

_____

9. Are you an "individual"? Suggest five ways in which you are different from everybody else.

_____

_____

_____

_____

_____

The answers to these questions do not prove or disprove that you are fully mature. They should help you gain some insight into yourself. Do you like your answers?

🌳 CONCLUSION

By now you can see that the study of human development is mainly the study of change. Few chapters in this book, however, have described a more changing scene than this one.

Americans are getting married later for a larger variety of reasons. They are staying married for shorter periods, having fewer children, and are more reluctant to remarry if they become divorced or widowed. As we discussed in chapter 11, the functions of the family itself have changed tremendously in this century, and some have even predicted the family's demise.

The nation's workers experience a very different environment than their predecessors of 50 years ago, as we leave the industrial age and enter the age of "information processing." Many problems still must be solved—especially the treatment of persons of color and women.

Perhaps the liveliest area in developmental study in recent years has been the field of personality research. More and more we are realizing that, just as in childhood and adolescence, adulthood has predictable stages. Distinct life cycles apparently exist, the goals of which are individuation and maturity. And differences between male and female development are becoming apparent.

In the next chapter, we return to the topics of physical and mental development, because they are worth understanding for their own sake, and so that you can see the foundations of psychosocial development in the middle adult years.

🌳 CHAPTER HIGHLIGHTS

Marriage and the Family

- Almost 95 percent of Americans get married at some point in their lives.
- Basically four kinds of marriage exist throughout the world: monogamy (one husband, one wife), polygamy (two or more wives), polyandry (two or more husbands), and group marriage (two or more of both husbands and wives). Homosexual marriages are also beginning to win acceptance.

Patterns of Work

- Most of the total population 16 years old and older who choose to work are working.

- Holland suggested that, in our culture, all people can be categorized in one of six vocational interest types as to career choice: realistic, investigative, artistic, social, enterprising, or conventional.
- Economic realities and the feminist movement have given rise to dual-career families in which both husband and wife work outside of the home.

Stages of Personal Development

- Gould theorizes four developmental periods, each characterized by a major false assumption, through which adults pass as they mature.

- Levinson suggested that adults develop according to a general pattern known as the life cycle. Each individual's own personal embodiment of the life cycle is known as his or her life course.
- Levinson also described stages of development unique to men.
- According to Erikson's theory, early adulthood is defined in terms of intimacy and solidarity versus isolation.
- Individuation, the ability to develop a healthy adult personality apart from others, is necessary and occurs differently for men and women.

🌳 KEY TERMS

Biopsychosocial 422
Distantiation 426
Dual-career family 416
Exploration stage 416
Group marriage 413
Homosexual marriage 413
Individuation 423
Inner dialogue 419

Intimacy 426
Isolation 426
Life course 422
Life cycle 422
Life structure 422
Major false assumptions 419
Mentoring 424
Monogamy 412

Novice phase 424
Polyandry 413
Polygamy 412
Solidarity 426
Structure building 422
Structure changing 422
Transition 422

🌳 WHAT DO YOU THINK?

1. Which of the four types of marriage described in this chapter do your parents have? Your grandparents?
2. Which of the types of marriages described in this chapter are likely to exist 100 years from now?
3. What are some ways of helping the dual-career family meet its responsibilities?
4. How well do Gould's major false assumptions fit the early and middle adult periods?
5. Gould suggests seven steps in what he calls an "inner dialogue." What is your opinion of this approach?
6. Levinson believed that forming a mentor relationship is an essential part of the novice phase. Have you

formed such a relationship? What are its characteristics?
7. To be intimate, you must know your own identity. But to achieve an identity, you need the feedback you get from being intimate with at least one other person. How can this catch-22 be resolved?

🌳 SUGGESTED READINGS

Bly, Robert. (1990). *Iron John*. Reading, MA: Addison-Wesley. A teacher of both poetry and philosophy, Bly combines the two in this fascinating tale of a journey into the self. Among other insights, he explores the modern young man's grief over his inability to become close to his father.

Fowles, J. (1977). *The magus* (revised edition). Boston: Little, Brown. This is surely one of the best psychological mystery stories ever written. It concerns a young man who is unable to keep commitments. A secret society decides to try and help him to become more mature.

Friedland, R. & C. Kort. (Eds.). (1981). *The mother's book: Shared experiences*. Boston: Houghton-Mifflin. A moving and realistic collection of essays by mothers about motherhood.

Gordon, M. (1978). *Final payments*. New York: Random House. The heroine of this marvelously revealing novel struggles with numerous obstacles, from within and without, to gain her independence as a responsible adult.

Kilpatrick, W. K. (1975). *Identity and intimacy*. New York: Delacorte. This highly readable examination of Erikson's fifth and sixth stages is brilliant. We guarantee you will see

yourself in a new light after reading this book.

Miller, J. Baker. (1976). *Toward a new psychology of women*. Boston: Beacon. A classic in the field of feminist psychology.

Updike, J. (1960). *Rabbit, run*. New York: Knopf. This is the first of four books that chronicles the development of an ordinary man whose nickname is "Rabbit." (He got that name because of his speed as a high school basketball player.) In the book, we follow his efforts to leave behind his exciting life as a sports star and become a responsible family man. It is not an easy trip.

🌳 CHAPTER REVIEW TEST

1. The average age at first marriage in the United States has
   a. increased for males and decreased for females.
   b. increased for females and decreased for males.
   c. increased for both males and females.
   d. decreased for both males and females.

2. A group marriage can be defined as
   a. when there is one husband and two or more wives.
   b. when there is one wife and two or more husbands.
   c. when one husband marries two or more sisters.
   d. when there are two or more of both husbands and wives, who all exercise common privileges and responsibilities.

3. The lower the level of education, the more likely a person is to be unemployed. Which cultural group is affected the most?
   a. Caucasians
   b. African Americans
   c. Latinos
   d. Japanese

4. The theory on how people choose their careers that suggests that in our culture, all people can be categorized into six personality types was developed by whom?
   a. Super
   b. Holland
   c. Gould
   d. Miller

5. Holland's theory claims that there are six different types of _____ that are dominated by a given type of personality.
   a. environments in which people live
   b. work settings
   c. organizational structures
   d. structured learning environments

6. Donald Super has been one of the most influential figures in developing a life stage theory of _____ to explain how career identity develops over time.
   a. vocational training
   b. career development
   c. educational experiences
   d. human development

7. A recent study by Guelzow and others indicates that long working hours can lead to _____ for women in a dual-career family.
   a. stress
   b. decreased self-esteem
   c. feelings of guilt
   d. higher role strain

8. According to Serakan (1989), women who spend more time at work experience less job satisfaction than those women who work less because of
   a. a lack of female coworkers.
   b. relatively low pay.
   c. a lack of role models.
   d. guilt over not being home.

9. Recent studies found that the men who had the most problem sharing the role of family provider with their wives were:
   a. upper-class men.
   b. blue-collar workers.
   c. upper-middle-class men.
   d. men from all socioeconomic levels.

10. According to Gould, people need to work through major false assumptions during each of four developmental periods in adult life. This process needs to happen so that the person can achieve
    a. individuation.
    b. self-actualization.
    c. the next stage in his/her personal development.
    d. maturity.

11. The major false assumption "Life is simple and controllable. There are no significant contradictory forces within me" occurs during
    a. stage one.
    b. stage two.
    c. stage three.
    d. stage four.

12. According to Levinson, the purpose of the developmental periods in our lives is to cause greater individuation, which refers to
    a. our developing separate and special personalities, derived less and less from our parents and teachers and more from our own behavior.
    b. the realization that one does not need to be in a relationship to attain happiness.
    c. the recognition of our distinct interests.
    d. the inability for peers to have great influence on major life decisions.

13. Erikson used the term distantiation to describe
    a. the distance we keep between ourselves and others during personal conversation.
    b. our ability to distance ourselves from our families of origin.
    c. the time we need to progress between one developmental stage to the next.
    d. the readiness all of us have to distance ourselves from others when we feel threatened by their behavior.

14. Who finds fault with Erikson because of his belief that women are judged through their relationships with others?
    a. Baker Miller
    b. Gilligan
    c. Friedan
    d. Gould

15. According to Jean Baker Miller, the process of growth involves _____ so that we can develop new strengths.
    a. dealing with difficult childhood experiences
    b. discovering our strengths in personality
    c. admitting and experiencing our feelings
    d. forming strong relationships with others

16. Researcher Carol Gilligan states that since femininity is defined through attachment, female gender is most threatened by
    a. divorce.
    b. personal loss.
    c. separation.
    d. dispassionate males.

Answers

1.c 2.d 3.b 4.b 5.a 6.b 7.d 8.d 9.c 10.d 11.c 12.a 13.d 14.a 15.c 16.c

PART VIII

Middle Adulthood

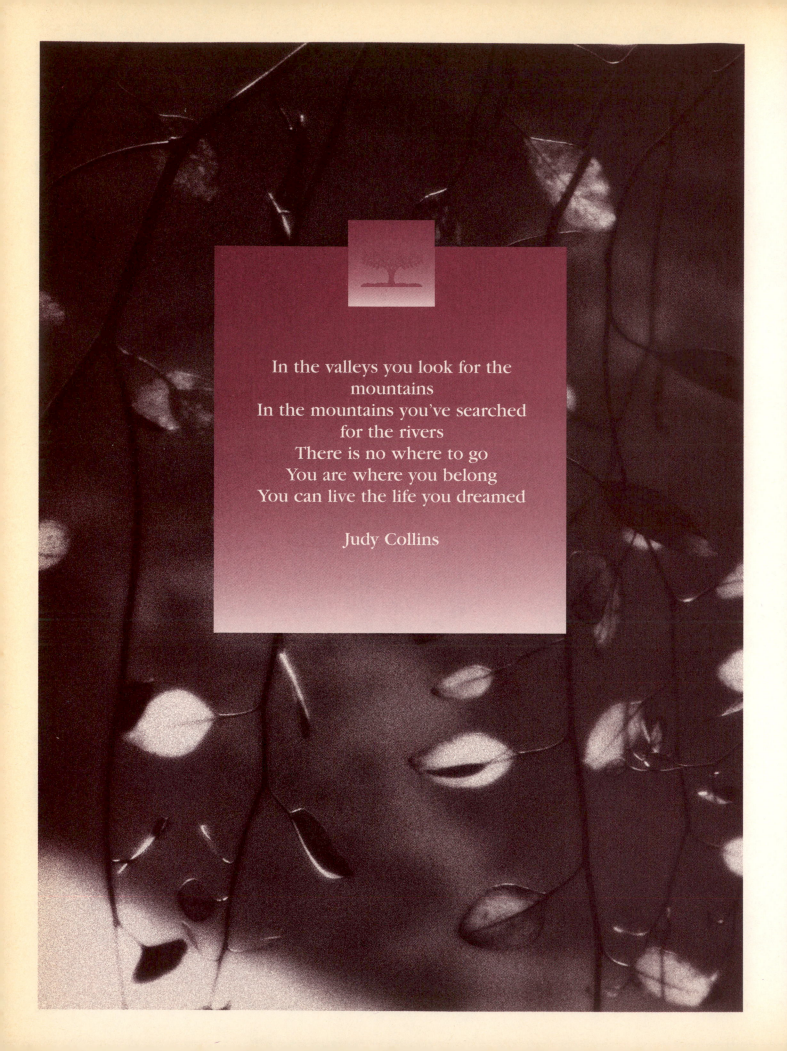

In the valleys you look for the
mountains
In the mountains you've searched
for the rivers
There is no where to go
You are where you belong
You can live the life you dreamed

Judy Collins

CHAPTER 17

Physical and Cognitive Development in Middle Adulthood

The idea that there is a "middle" phase in adult life is a rather modern idea. Most non-Western and preindustrial cultures recognize only a mature stage of adulthood, from about 25 to about 60 years old, followed by a stage of old age decline. Many Western scientists (including the authors of this book) now recognize four stages of adult life: young adulthood (approximate age range from 19 to 34); middle adulthood (approximate age range from 35 to 64); young elderly (approximate age range from 65 to 79), and old elderly (80+).

One non-Western country that does recognize middle adulthood is Japan. The Japanese word for middle age, *sonen,* refers to the "prime of life," the period between early adulthood and senility. Another quite positive word often used for the middle adult years in Japan is *hataraki-zakari,* meaning the "full bloom of one's working ability."

Not all Japanese words for middle adulthood are quite so joyful. The word *kanroku* means "weightiness" or "fullness," both as in bearing a heavy load of authority, and in being overweight.

Why do you suppose industrialized cultures like North America and Japan have several words for middle adulthood, and other cultures have no words at all? 🌳

After reading chapter 17, you should be able to

- Identify health concerns of particular importance to middle-aged adults.

- Discuss how muscular and sensory abilities change in middle adulthood.

- Explain the role of hormone treatments in dealing with the climacteric and other aspects of aging.

- Discuss the sexual practices of adults in middle age.

- Contrast the various positions presented regarding the nature of intelligence as people pass through middle age.

- Describe creative individuals and suggest ways in which creativity develops in middle adulthood.

- Decide whether you believe that learning ability declines as people age.

Physical Development

■ "You're not getting older, you're getting better!"

You may hear middle-aged people saying this to each other. They hope that the changes they are experiencing are minor and not too negative, but let's face it, physical systems do decline with age. As you will see, biological forces greatly influence physical development, but be on the lookout for ways that psychological and social forces are at work as well. Now let us take a closer look at some of these functions.

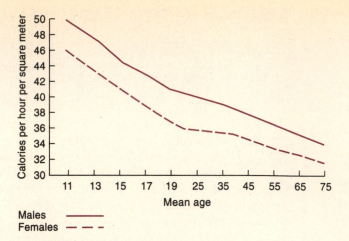

Figure 17.1
The decline of basal metabolism rate through the life cycle. BMR varies with age and sex. Rates are usually higher for males and decline proportionally with age for both sexes.

Basal metabolism rate (BMR)

The minimum amount of energy an individual tends to use when in a resting state.

Self-fulfilling prophecy

Making an idea come true simply by believing it will.

The media present us with countless programs to help us stay younger looking, lose weight, and so on. Can you think of ways the money spent on such advertisements and programs might be better spent to enhance the physical health of adults in Western society?

Health

Weight and Metabolism

As one moves into middle adulthood, weight gain becomes a matter of concern. For example, about one-half of the United States adult population weighs over the upper limit of the "normal" weight range. For some, this is the result of genetic inheritance—about 40 percent of the people with one obese parent become obese, as compared with only 10 percent of those whose parents are not obese (U.S. National Center for Health Statistics, 1986). Others become overweight simply because they do not compensate for their lowering **basal metabolism rate (BMR).**

BMR is the minimum amount of energy an individual tends to use when in a resting state. As you can see from figure 17.1, this rate varies with age and gender. Males have a slightly higher rate than females. The rate drops most quickly during adolescence, and then more slowly during adulthood. This is caused by a drop in the ratio of lean body mass to fat, which "results in a lower BMR, since the metabolic needs of fat tissue are less than those of lean. Even for those who exercise regularly, fewer calories need to be consumed" (Kart & others, 1988, p. 171).

Thus if you continue to eat at the same rate throughout your life, you will definitely gain weight. If you add to this a decreased rate of exercise, the weight gain (sometimes called "middle-age spread," referring to wider hips, thicker thighs, a "spare tire" around the waist, and a "beer belly") will be even greater. If you expect this to happen, it probably will (another **self-fulfilling prophecy**).

Many people think that weight gain in middle age is natural, but in fact a number of recent studies (Beneke & Timson, 1987; Clifford & others, 1991; Troumbley & others, 1990) have clearly demonstrated that increased levels of health problems and risk of death do result from being overweight.

On the other hand, the warnings against "crash diets" should be heeded, especially by middle-aged people. Probably the most popular diet these days includes the use of dietary supplements, and the most popular ingredient in them is an amino acid known as L-tryptophan. This acid has been linked to a blood disorder in which white blood cells increase to abnormally high numbers (American Association of Retired Persons, 1990a). This can result in swelling of extremities, severe pain in muscles and joints, fever, and skin rash. To date there have been almost 300 cases in 37 states, and one known death.

Effects of Alcohol

Anyone over the age of 50 should "go on the wagon" and stay there, according to Teri Manolio of the National Heart, Lung and Blood Institute (cited in AARP, 1990b, p. 7). Even one or two drinks each day can be dangerous, because they can cause enlargement of the left ventricle of the heart. Such enlargement causes the heart to

Many men in their 30s find it hard to accept that their muscular ability is slowly declining. Unfortunately, this sometimes causes them to overexert themselves, leading to such dire results as serious injury and heart attack.

work harder and often can cause irregular heartbeats. If a person's heart is already enlarged, the danger is even greater. These data come from the Framingham (Massachusetts) Heart Study, which has also furnished the following findings:

- The older the person and the larger the number of drinks per day, the greater the risk.

- The risk is smaller for women.

- Men who are obese or have high blood pressure are at the greatest risk.

Muscular Ability

Muscle growth is complete in the average person by age 17, but improvements in speed, strength, and skill can occur throughout the early adult years. In fact, most people reach their peak around age 25—females somewhat earlier than that and males somewhat later. Variations in peak muscular ability depend very much on the type of activity. Consider, for example, the 20-year-old female Olympic gymnast who is thought of as an "old lady" because peak ability in this area tends to come at around age 16.

Between the ages of 30 and 60, loss of strength is gradual—about 10 percent on the average (Gimby & Saltin, 1983; Spence, 1989):

- Most loss occurs in the back and legs.

- Muscle tone and flexibility decrease.

- Injuries take longer to heal.

- Muscle is gradually replaced by fat.

A 175-pound man has 70 pounds of muscle at age 30 but typically loses 10 pounds of that muscle to fat by the time he reaches old age (Schulz & Ewen, 1988). However, the current popularity of aerobic activities may be reversing this trend (Buskirk, 1985). Aerobic activity such as swimming and brisk walking appears to help maintain general health because it demands that the heart pump a great deal of blood to the large muscles of the legs.

In the middle period of adulthood (35 to 64) there is a common but unnecessary decline in muscular ability. Unfortunately, the majority of people in this stage of life do not get much exercise. Both males and females may undergo a marked change in lifestyle. Growing success in one's chosen field often leads to greater leisure and indulgence in the so-called finer things of life.

Sensory Abilities

The five physical senses—vision, hearing, smell, taste, and touch—are responsible for gathering information about the world around us. Although the stereotyped image of an older person losing hearing or vision is sometimes made fun of, the gradual loss of function of one of the senses is a serious concern for all of us. We often take everyday experiences such as reading a good book, watching television, driving a car to the grocery store, tasting or even smelling a good meal, or just holding a child in our arms for granted. Yet all these experiences depend on one or more of the five senses. What changes in sensory ability can we expect as we pass through middle adulthood? The following trends are only general and vary widely from one individual to another.

Vision

Vision is the sense that we most depend on for information about what's going on around us. The eye begins to change physically at about age 40. The lens becomes less elastic and more yellow. The cornea begins to lose its luster. By age 50 the cornea is increasing in curvature and thickness. At 50, the iris begins to respond less well to light (Eifrig & Simons, 1983; Schulz & Ewen, 1988).

What do these physical changes mean for our vision? In general, our eyes don't adapt to sudden intense light or darkness as effectively as they once did. The ability to focus on nearby objects decreases, leading to a diagnosis of farsightedness and possibly a prescription for bifocals. The ability to detect certain colors can also be hampered by age-related changes in the eye. As the lens yellows, shades of blue and green become more difficult to discern. The ability to detect moving objects may also decrease as we grow older (Leigh, 1982; Warabi & others, 1984). For most people, these changes in visual ability pose a problem only when lighting is reduced, such as in night driving.

Eye disease is a more serious matter. Increasing age often brings a heightened risk for such diseases. **Glaucoma** results from a buildup of pressure inside the eye due to excessive fluid. The resulting damage can destroy one's vision. Glaucoma is increasingly common after the age of 40 and is the leading cause of blindness by age 70. About 60,000 people in the United States are blind because of it (Johnson & Goldfinger, 1981). Routine eye examinations, however, now usually include a glaucoma test and blindness is often prevented.

Less well known but more dangerous is **senile macular degeneration.** This disease of the retina is also a cause of blindness. It begins as blurred vision and a dark spot in the center of the field of vision. Advances in laser surgery have shown promise in treating diseases of the retina such as this.

Hearing

Hearing also seems to be susceptible to decline at about age 40. This is when we begin to lose the ability to detect certain tones. As you progress from middle to old age, certain frequencies, the higher ones in particular, may need to be much louder for you to hear them (Schulz & Ewen, 1988). Our ability to understand human speech also appears to decrease as we grow older. The most likely result is an inability to hear certain consonants, especially *f, g, s, t, z, th,* and *sh* (Marshall, 1981). Cognitive capacity may play a role in the fact that the ability to listen to speech in a crowded environment (e.g., a party) declines faster than the ability to listen to someone alone with no background noise (Bergman & others, 1976; Bergman, 1980).

Our visual system is a more reliable sense than our auditory system. In fact, in contrast to the success that medical science has made in fighting blindness, deafness in the United States appears to be increasing. In 1940 you could expect to find deafness in 200 out of every 10,000 people in this country. By 1980 you could expect to find it in 300 (Hunt & Lindley, 1989). Bear in mind, however, that these

Because of changes in the eye that occur when we reach our 40s, glasses are often necessary.

Glaucoma

Results from a buildup of pressure inside the eye due to excessive fluid. The resulting damage can destroy one's vision.

Senile macular degeneration

This disease of the retina is a leading cause of blindness, beginning as blurred vision and a dark spot in the center of the field of vision.

effects are partly a result of choice. Cross-cultural studies have shown that our relatively loud, high-tech culture contributes to our society's general loss of hearing (Bergman, 1980).

One curious aspect of the age-related decline in hearing is that, of the five senses, hearing is easily the most stigmatized loss. People who wouldn't think twice about getting prescription eyeglasses will refuse to get a hearing aid or even admit they are suffering a hearing loss.

Smell

Olfactory sense
The sense of smell, which uses the olfactory nerves in the nose and tongue.

Although not as important a sense as vision or hearing, the **olfactory sense** does a little more than just tell us when dinner is about ready. First, the olfactory sense works closely with our taste buds to produce what we think of as the "taste" of a given food. In fact, it is difficult in studies to separate which sense—taste or smell—is actually contributing to the decline in performance on a certain task. Besides bringing us pleasurable smells, this sense warns us against spoiled foods, smoke or fire, and leaking gas (Stevens & Cain, 1987).

Various studies suggest that our sense of smell decreases as we grow older (Murphy, 1983; Schiffman & Pasternak, 1979; Stevens & Cain, 1987). The decline seems to begin slowly around age 50 and increases rapidly after age 70.

Taste

As we mentioned, our sense of taste is closely tied to our sense of smell, which makes studying age-related effects on taste very difficult. One estimate is that 95 percent of taste derives from the olfactory nerves. Not coincidentally, taste seems to begin to decline around the age of 50 (Cooper & others, 1959; Schiffman, 1977).

Recent studies have suggested that older adults may experience a decline in the ability to detect weak tastes but retain their ability to discriminate among those foods that have a strong taste, such as a spicy chicken curry (Spence, 1989). The decline in the ability to taste (and smell) may account in part for the decrease in weight that many elderly persons experience.

In general, we can say that although our senses do decline somewhat throughout middle age, we are finding more and more ways to compensate for the losses, so they cause only slight changes in lifestyle. Another physical concern in our middle years is the climacteric.

The Climacteric

Climacteric
Refers to a relatively abrupt change in the body, brought about by changes in hormonal balances.

Menopause
The cessation of menstruation.

Male change of life
Change in hormonal balance and sexual potency.

Climacterium
Refers to the loss of reproductive ability.

The word **climacteric** refers to a relatively abrupt change in the body, brought about by changes in hormonal balances. In women, this change is called **menopause.** It normally occurs over a four-year period at some time during a woman's 40s or early 50s (Masters & Johnson, 1966). The climacteric also refers to the **male change of life,** whereas the menopause refers only to the cessation of menstruation, most often between the ages of 48 and 52. The term **climacterium** refers to the loss of reproductive ability. This occurs at menopause for women, but men tend to be quite old when they are no longer able to produce fertile sperm.

The main physical change in menopause is that the ovaries cease to produce the hormones estrogen and progesterone, although the adrenal glands continue to produce some estrogen. Does this decline in hormonal output always cause significant changes in female behavior? The question is difficult to answer. In the first place, women seem to react to menopause in many different ways. As Neugarten (1968) discovered in her extensive study of white mothers, there is not much agreement as to what menopause means or how it feels. Only 4 percent of the women interviewed thought that menopause was the worst thing about middle age, and many found it much less difficult than they had expected. On the other hand, half the women thought that menopause caused a negative change in their appearance, and a third experienced negative changes in their physical and emotional health. The great majority thought that menopause had no effect on their sexual relationships.

Many other things are happening in a woman's life at the same time as her menopause, so it is difficult to sort out what is causing what. Undoubtedly a lack of understanding of menopause, coupled with normal fears of growing old, accounts for at least some of the negative feelings about menopause. It should be noted that many women have positive feelings. For example, they no longer have to be concerned about becoming pregnant.

A recent study found no negative mental health consequences from menopause for the majority of middle-aged women sampled (Matthews & others, 1990). Also on the positive side, Sheehy (1992) found that menopause is a time of "coalescence," a time of integration, balance, liberation, confidence, and action. A menopausal woman no longer worries about pregnancy; many feel relief when their children leave the nest.

The menopausal woman moves from the old age of youth to the youth of old age or, in other terms, she moves into a second adulthood. Many women in their fifties may find themselves in the prime of their lives (Fodor & Franks, 1990). They have good health, autonomy, security in their major relationship, freedom, higher income, status, and confidence. Brown (1982) found that many postmenopausal women in a variety of cultures experience greater powers, freedoms, and higher-level responsibilities when their children become adults; but as one study cautions, it may be that only women of higher status feel this increase in power (Todd & others, 1990).

Estrogen replacement therapy (ERT)

A process in which estrogen is given in low levels to a woman experiencing severe problems with menopause.

For those women who experience serious problems with menopause, **estrogen replacement therapy (ERT)** can offer considerable relief. When estrogen was first instituted, ERT was found to increase the risk of cancer. Today, however, it is given in quite low levels and is combined with progesterone, which greatly reduces the risk. In addition, a recent study (Myers & Morokoff, 1986) found that postmenopausal women who are receiving ERT demonstrate a higher level of arousal when watching an erotic movie than those who are not receiving ERT.

Estrogen, which eliminates the symptoms of menopause, also stems the deterioration of the cardiovascular, urinary, genital, and nervous systems; slows the aging of the bones and skin; and cuts the death rate from heart disease for women in half. Recent Veterans Administration research, using human growth hormone, initially found that 60 men aged 60 to 80 may have regained the vitality of men 15 to 20 years younger. A study by the National Institute on Aging has begun testing two other hormones, DHEA and testosterone, suspected of retarding age-related symptoms such as loss of strength and vitality and the diminishing size of internal organs in frail, elderly men. Perhaps in the future, doctors may routinely prescribe hormone therapy for both men and women to slow the aging process (Rudman, 1992).

At one time, it was thought that the male hormone balance parallels that of the female. According to a well-designed study conducted by the National Institute on Aging (1979), however, the level of testosterone declines only very gradually with age. Dr. Mitchell Hermann, who conducted the study on men from age 25 to 89, says that his findings contradict earlier results because most of those previous studies were of men in hospitals and in nursing homes who were afflicted with obesity, alcoholism, or chronic illness. All of his subjects were healthy, vigorous men.

Hermann suggests the decrease in sexual potency that men experience in later years is probably not the result of hormone changes, but rather slowing down in the central nervous system, together with a self-fulfilling prophecy (men expect to become impotent, so they do). The effects of hormonal changes on the appearance and emotional state of men are unclear at the present.

It seems likely that as we better understand precisely how hormone balances change and how the different changes interact with each other, the impairments that have been attributed to these changes will decrease (Rowland & others, 1987).

Although middle-aged people are generally healthier than the elderly, chronic health problems are especially prevalent for poor African American middle-aged women. African Americans also sustain 39 percent more work-related injuries and diseases than whites and thus are more likely to drop out of the labor force before

Menopause can be a positive life change for many women, yet a number of women find it to be a time of great emotional upheaval. What factors contribute to this difference among women?

retirement (Jackson & Gibson, 1985). These socioeconomic and racial differences are a good place to see how the biopsychosocial model operates. What role would you say each of these three major forces play in causing these differences?

Health also plays an important role in the sexual feelings and behavior of middle-aged adults. In the next section, we examine this and other aspects of sexuality.

Guided Review

1. Adulthood has recently been thought of as having four stages: young adulthood (19 to 34 years of age), _____ _____ (35 to 64 years of age), _____ _____ (65 to 79 years of age) and old-elderly (80+ years of age).

2. Basal metabolic rate is the _____ amount of energy an individual uses when in a resting state.

3. Our basic metabolism rate decreases with age, meaning that if we eat the same amount all our lives we will _____ weight.

4. According to recent research people over the age of 50 should be concerned about the effects of alcohol as its use can result in enlargement of the _____ , causing it to work harder.

5. On the average, there is a _____ percent gradual loss of strength between the ages of 30 and 60.

6. All five senses decline during middle adulthood, but _____ loss has the greatest social stigma attached to it.

7. "Climacteric" is the term used for the abrupt change that occurs in the body due to changes in _____ balances.

8. The term "menopause" refers to the _____ change of life, which includes the cessation of menstruation.

9. A number of women experience positive consequences from menopause, including a time of coalescence, of integration, and _____.

10. _____ _____ therapy can be used to offer relief to women who are experiencing problems with regard to menopause.

Sex in Middle Adulthood

At midlife, minor physiological changes occur in both male and female sexual systems. For the male, there may be lower levels of testosterone, fewer viable sperm, a decrease in sex steroids affecting muscle tone and the cardiovascular system, slight changes in the testes and prostate gland, and a change in the viscosity and volume of ejaculate (Hunter & Sundel, 1989). There is usually a need to spend more time and to give more direct stimulation to the penis to attain erection. None of these changes is sufficient to alter significantly the man's interest and pleasure in a sexual and sensual life.

For the female, the reduction in estrogen occurring during and after menopause may cause changes, such as less vaginal lubrication and possible vaginal irritation at penetration, that can eventually affect the ease and comfort of sexual intercourse. Sexual arousal may be somewhat slower after the fifth decade, but orgasmic response is not impaired. As with the males, females may need more time and appropriate stimulation for vaginal lubrication and orgasmic responsivity. Some studies have found a reduction of female interest and desire, whereas others have

Answers

1. middle adulthood, young elderly 2. minimum 3. gain 4. heart 5. 10 6. hearing 7. hormonal 8. female 9. liberation 10. Estrogen replacement

Table 17.1	Frequency of Sexual Intercourse by Age									
	Ages (Years)									
	18 to 26		27 to 38		39 to 50		51 to 64		65+	
	M	*F*	*M*	*F*	*M*	*F*	*M*	*F*	*M*	*F*
N =	*254*	*268*	*353*	*380*	*282*	*295*	*227*	*230*	*212*	*221*
a. Daily	15%	13%	16%	8%	15%	10%	12%	4%	14%	1%
b. A few times weekly	38	33	44	41	39	29	51	28	39	40
c. Weekly	19	22	23	27	29	29	18	33	16	33
d. Monthly	15	15	8	12	9	11	11	8	20	4
e. Rarely	13	17	9	12	8	21	8	27	11	22
Active = lines a + b	53%	46%	60%	49%	54%	39%	63%	32%	53%	41%
At Least Weekly = lines a through c	72%	68%	83%	76%	83%	68%	81%	65%	69%	74%

From S. Janus and C. Janus, *The Janus Report on Sexual Behavior.* Copyright © 1993 Wiley & Sons, New York. Reprinted by permission of John Wiley & Sons, Inc.

Why is it that some couples keep joy in their marriages and sexual relationships over many decades, whereas other couples barely remain cordial? What keeps the vitality in long-term relationships?

found a decrease in frequency of intercourse (Cutler & others, 1987). Bretschneider and McCoy (1988) argued that low estrogen levels are associated with decreased sexual interest in women. Hysterectomies can catapult a woman into premature menopause and can cause her to experience postoperative sexual problems that may require estrogen replacement therapy (Leiblum, 1990).

A study of lesbian women at menopause (Cole & Rothblum, 1990) found very few sexual problems. The 10 percent who did list one or more symptoms qualified their responses to say there were differences, not problems. Masters and associates (1986) found that lesbians make smooth transitions into the middle years, usually in lasting relationships. Peplau (1981) found a similar pattern for gay men.

As you can see, by the time people reach middle adulthood, sexual preferences are clearly a very individual matter. Some couples engage in sexuality a lot right into their old age, and some have a fine marriage without making love very much at all.

The most recent report on frequency of sexual activity among the adults of all ages, the Janus Report (see chapter 13), gives a picture that weakens the stereotype that as we grow older, we become more inactive sexually. As table 17.1 illustrates, there is a small increase in sexual activity in the middle years, as compared with early adulthood. For men, middle age is the peak sexual time but there is little drop with age, and for women, age makes little difference across the adult lifespan.

The experts pretty well agree on the nature of physical alterations that occur through the middle years of adulthood. Much less agreement exists, however, on the course of cognitive development in these years.

Many couples find that when they reach middle age, their relationship becomes more romantic.

Guided Review

11. Bretschneider and McCoy claimed that low _____ levels are associated with decreased sexual interest for women.

12. The Janus Report indicates that the stereotype that people become less _____ sexually as they age is not supported by the Januses' research.

13. The Janus Report found that middle age is the _____ sexual time for men with little change with age. For women, age makes little difference across the adult _____ .

Answers

11. estrogen 12. active 13. peak, lifespan

Cognitive Development

> ■ I am all I ever was and much more, but an enemy has bound me and twisted me, so now I can plan and think as I never could, but no longer achieve all I plan and think.
>
> —William Butler Yeats at age 57

Of course, the "enemy" Yeats refers to is age. Was he right in believing he could think as well as ever or was he just kidding himself? The question of declining intelligence across adulthood has long concerned humans.

Theories about Intelligence

Indeed, no aspect of adult functioning has received more research than intelligence (e.g., Cooney & others, 1988; Nesselroade & others, 1988). Despite this considerable research, investigators still do not agree on whether we lose intellectual ability as we grow old. In fact, three basic positions exist: yes, it does decline; no, it does not decline; and yes, it does in some ways, but no, it doesn't in others. Let's look at the evidence for these positions.

Wechsler's Answer: Yes

Undoubtedly the strongest proponent of the hypothesis that intelligence declines with age is psychologist David Wechsler, who said:

> ■ Beginning with the investigation by Galton in 1883 . . . nearly all studies dealing with the age factor in adult performance have shown that most human abilities . . . decline progressively, after reaching a peak somewhere between ages 18 and 25. (1958, p. 135)

The most widely used test of adult intelligence was designed by Wechsler himself (1955).

Terman's Answer: No

Lewis Terman began his study of the development of intelligence in the 1920s.

The classic Terman study (1925) is an excellent longitudinal study that found an increase in intelligence with age. That study was started in 1924 and used the Stanford-Binet Intelligence Test for children. The subjects were tested 10 years later, in 1941, and then retested in 1956 with the Wechsler Adult Intelligence Scale (WAIS), which is highly correlated with the Stanford-Binet. At the end of the second 15-year interval, when the subjects were in their twenties, there was an average increase of scores (Bradway & others, 1958).

The subjects were retested in 1969 by Kangas and Bradway (1971). The average subject was then 40 years old. Their scores were found to have increased to an average of nearly 130! Another study supporting the no-decline hypothesis is reported by Owens (1953). In 1919 a group of 363 students entering Ohio State College had their intelligence tested. Thirty years later Owens retested 127 of them, and all but one of the subjects showed an increase over the 30 years. In 1966, when the individuals were approximately 61 years old, 97 of the subjects were retested and none of the scores had changed significantly.

Canestrari (1963) found that adults in middle age do more poorly on speed tests than do younger subjects. However, when they were given more time, for example, to memorize digits, they did as well as the younger subjects.

Figure 17.2

Horn's three types of intelligence

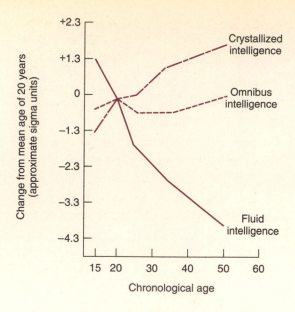

Horn's Answer: Yes and No

J. L. Horn believes that intelligence does decline in some ways, but in other ways it does not. The picture is probably more complicated than either of the first two positions reveals. Evidence indicates that

- one type of intelligence declines, whereas another does not.

- some individuals decline while others do not.

- although decline does eventually occur, it happens only late in life.

Horn has described two dimensions of intelligence: fluid and crystallized. The two can be distinguished as follows: **fluid intelligence** depends on the proper functioning of the nervous system. It is measured by tasks that show age-related declines (speeded tasks, tests of reaction time). **Crystallized intelligence** demonstrates the cumulative effect of culture and learning of task performance and is measured by tests of verbal ability and cultural knowledge (Labouvie-Vief & Lawrence, 1985).

Horn (1975, 1978) hypothesized that whereas crystallized intelligence does not decline and may even increase, fluid intelligence probably does deteriorate, at least to some extent (see figure 17.2). Horn and his colleagues (1981) found that this decline in fluid intelligence averages three to seven IQ points per decade for the three decades spanning the period from 30 to 60 years of age.

Some research has suggested that some kinds of achievement may rely more on one type of intelligence than on the other (Lehman, 1964). For example, in fields such as mathematics, music, chemistry, and poetry, the best work is usually produced at a relatively young age and therefore may rely most on fluid intelligence. Other major achievements, such as in history, astronomy, philosophy, writing, and psychology, usually occur later in life, which may indicate greater reliance on crystallized intelligence (more on this later).

Earlier work on mental abilities was flawed because the studies were cross-sectional rather than longitudinal. A cross-sectional study looks at different groups of people at different ages and then makes inferences about age-related changes (see chapter 2). The problem is that people of different ages, having grown up at different periods, have necessarily had different life experiences. Therefore the results may be more due to this cohort effect than to aging.

A longitudinal study avoids this weakness because it looks at the same group of people over an interval of time. Schaie and Hertzog (1983) conducted a longitudinal study on cognitive abilities and found evidence that they decline as one ages. The evidence for a decline after the age of 60 was strong. They also found evidence that this process starts after the age of 50, although it is probably not observable in

Fluid intelligence

Involves perceiving relationships, educing correlates, maintaining span of immediate awareness in reasoning, abstracting, concept formation, and problem solving, as measured in unspeeded as well as speeded tasks involving figural, symbolic, or semantic content.

Crystallized intelligence

Involves perceiving relationships, educing correlates, reasoning, abstracting, concept of attainment, and problem solving, as measured primarily in unspeeded tasks involving various kinds of content (semantic, figural, symbolic).

everyday life. Making the situation even more complex, Hertzog's latest research suggests that a decline in speed of performance makes declines in intelligence look worse than they are. "It may be the case that a substantial proportion of the age changes actually observed by Schaie in his longitudinal studies is not loss of thinking capacity per se but, rather, slowing in rate of intelligent thought" (Hertzog, 1989, p. 650). Perhaps you simply need more time to think and respond when you get older.

New Views of Intelligence

Part of the debate is a matter of definition. What, exactly, is intelligence? How is it measured? It is certainly composed of several different cognitive abilities, such as memory, language, reasoning, and the ability to manipulate numbers. Each of these mental processes can, in turn, be divided into various subprocesses.

Different definitions of intelligence lead to different measures of it. Each measure emphasizes different mental abilities. For example, if you define intelligence as rank in class or school achievement, then cognitive abilities such as verbal comprehension and general information may be much more important than rote memory and perceptual tasks (for a review, see Horn & Donaldson, 1980). In fact, most of the commonly used IQ tests measure only a few of the cognitive abilities that could be measured. Under these circumstances, the question of whether intelligence declines with age becomes unanswerable. Clearly, more specific questions must be asked.

Increasingly, general intelligence is being abandoned as a scientific concept and subject of study. More and more, researchers are proposing several quite distinct cognitive abilities. Horn has now added supporting abilities to the concepts of fluid and crystallized intelligence. These include short-term memory, long-term memory, visual processing, and auditory processing (Horn, 1985; Horn & Donaldson, 1980). Howard Gardner (1983) contends there are seven different cognitive abilities. His list includes linguistic, musical, logical-mathematical, spatial, bodily-kinesthetic, self-understanding, and social understanding abilities. Other researchers have generated other lists (e.g., Sternberg, 1990).

Certainly intelligence cannot be separated from memory. Your mind can process information like lightning, but if you cannot recall the proper information, processing abilities are useless. Does memory decline with age? The stereotype is of the doddering old person who can't quite seem to remember the names of his grandchildren. But the research does not always confirm the existence of a decline.

We mentioned earlier in this chapter that memory itself can be separated into different types of memory. Horn and his colleagues make a distinction between short-term acquisition and retrieval factors (SAR) and the tertiary storage and retrieval dimension (TSR). Simply put, SAR refers to short-term memory and TSR refers to long-term memory. Short-term memory allows the individual to keep the details of a reasoning problem in awareness so that it can be processed. Long-term memory allows the individual to recall information from the relatively distant past and use it to solve a current problem. Horn and colleagues found that SAR declined with age in much the same way as fluid intelligence, and TSR either did not decline or improved, just as crystallized intelligence did (Horn & Donaldson, 1980).

Baltes and his associates (Baltes & others, 1977; Baltes & Schaie, 1976) have suggested a resolution to the question of how intelligence develops with age. They have proposed a **dual-process model** of intelligence. There is likely to be a decline in the mechanics of intelligence, such as classification skills and logical reasoning, but the pragmatics are likely to increase. Pragmatics include social wisdom, which is defined as "good judgment about important but uncertain matters of life" (Baltes & others, 1977, p. 66).

This seems the most reasonable position. There are just too many famous people whose thinking obviously got better as they got older. To name a few: George Burns, Coco Chanel, Benjamin Franklin, Albert Einstein, Mahatma Gandhi, Helen

Dual-process model
A model of intelligence that says there may be a decline in the *mechanics* of intelligence, such as classification skills and logical reasoning, but that the pragmatics are likely to increase.

A MULTICULTURAL VIEW

Cultural Bias and Cognitive Decline

Schaie (1994) has further pinpointed some of the most salient variables that reduce the risk of cognitive decline in old age. Some of these variables are particularly pertinent to the middle adult and are related to economic level, culture, and lifestyle. Two of the most important are rating one's self as being satisfied with one's life accomplishments and reporting a flexible personality style at midlife. These in turn tend to be related to having a high socioeconomic level, a complex and intellectually stimulating environment, being married to a spouse with high cognitive status, maintaining high levels of perceptual processing speed, and the absence of chronic diseases, especially cardiovascular disease. In summary, the richer you are and the higher your social class, the less your cognitive abilities decline.

These findings are strong evidence for a class bias in cognitive decline. What reasons can you give to explain the results?

Hayes, Michelangelo, Grandma Moses, Georgia O'Keeffe, Pope John XXIII, Eleanor Roosevelt, Bertrand Russell, George Bernard Shaw, Sophocles, Frank Lloyd Wright, and so on and so on. It is no coincidence that these people also maintained their creative abilities well into old age.

The Development of Creativity

As the world changes more and more rapidly, the role of creativity becomes more crucial. In this section, we explore the development of creative ability in the adult years. But first, here is a description of creative individuals.

Traits of the Highly Creative Adult

A number of studies (reviewed in Dacey, 1989a and 1989c; Dacey & Packer, 1992) have compared highly creative and average adults in a number of important traits. In general, highly creative adults

The "grande dame" of modern dance, Martha Graham's contributions to choreography make her one of the most creative adults in the twentieth century.

- like to do their own planning, make their own decisions, and need the least training and experience in self-guidance.

- do not like to work with others and prefer their own judgment of their work to the judgment of others. They therefore seldom ask others for opinions.

- take a hopeful outlook when presented with complex, difficult tasks.

- have the most ideas when a chance to express individual opinion is presented. These ideas frequently invoke the ridicule of others.

- are most likely to stand their ground in the face of criticism.

- are the most resourceful when unusual circumstances arise.

- can tolerate uncertainty and ambiguity better than others.

- are not necessarily the "smartest" or "best" in competitions.

In their compositions, creative adults typically

- show an imaginative use of many different words.

- are more flexible; for example, in a narrative they use more situations, characters, and settings. Rather than taking one clearly defined train of thought and pursuing it to its logical conclusion, creative adults tend to switch the main focus quickly and easily and often go off on tangents.

- tend to elaborate on the topic assigned, taking a much broader connotation of it to begin with, and then proceeding to embellish even that.

Figure 17.3
Graph of Lehman's findings

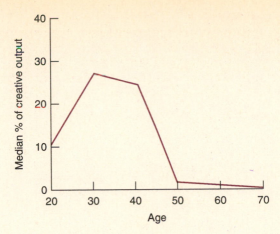

- are more original. (This is the most important characteristic. The others need not be evidenced, but this one must be.) Their ideas are qualitatively different from the average person's. Employers frequently react to the creative person's work in this way: "I know what most of my people will do in a particular situation, but I never know what to expect from this one!"

Now let us turn to the research on the development of creativity.

Psychohistorical Studies of Creative Achievement

Lehman (1953) examined biographical accounts of the work of several thousand individuals born since 1774. He studied the ages at which these persons made their creative contributions. He compared the contributions of deceased persons with those still living. On the basis of his study, he concluded that

> on the whole it seems clear that both past and present generation scientists have produced more than their proportionate share of high-quality research not later than at ages 30 to 39, and it is useless to bemoan this fact or to deny it. (p. 26)

Figure 17.3 portrays Lehman's general results.

In his report of his own research on this subject, Dennis (1966) criticized Lehman's work, stating that it included many individuals who died before they reached old age. Dennis points out that this biased the study statistically, because we cannot know what proportion of creative contributions these deceased people would have made had they lived longer.

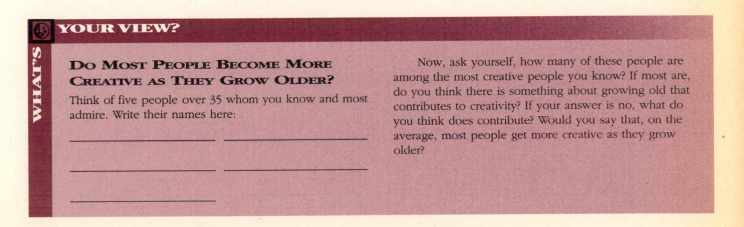

YOUR VIEW?

WHAT'S

DO MOST PEOPLE BECOME MORE CREATIVE AS THEY GROW OLDER?

Think of five people over 35 whom you know and most admire. Write their names here:

_____   _____

_____   _____

_____

Now, ask yourself, how many of these people are among the most creative people you know? If most are, do you think there is something about growing old that contributes to creativity? If your answer is no, what do you think does contribute? Would you say that, on the average, most people get more creative as they grow older?

Figure 17.4
Graph of Dennis's findings

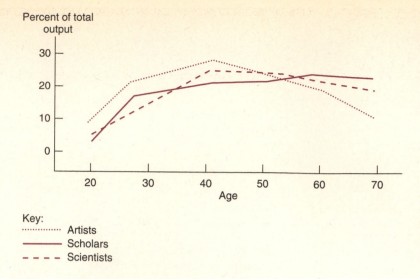

Key:
.... Artists
———— Scholars
— — — Scientists

Dennis himself studied the biographies of 738 creative persons, all of whom lived to age 79 or beyond, and whose contributions were considered valuable enough to have been reported in biographical histories. He did this because he believed "that no valid statements can be made concerning age and productivity except from longitudinal data involving no dropouts due to death" (1966, p. 8).

He looked at the percentage of works done by these persons in each of the decades between the ages of 20 and 80. When creative productivity is evaluated in this way, the results are quite different. Dennis found that scholars and scientists (with the exception of mathematicians and chemists) usually have little creative output in their 20s. For most of them, the peak period is between their 40s and 60s, and most produce almost as much in their 70s as they did in their earlier years. The peak period for artists tended to be their 40s, but they were almost as productive in their 60s and 70s as they were in their 20s. Figure 17.4 depicts these relationships.

Dennis offers an interesting hypothesis to explain the difference in creative productivity between the three groups. The output curve of the arts rises earlier and declines earlier and more severely because productivity in the arts is primarily a matter of individual creativity. Scholars and scientists require a greater period of training and a greater accumulation of data than do others. The use of accumulated data and the possibility of receiving assistance from others causes the scholars and scientists to make more contributions in later years than do people in art, music, and literature.

Most of the productive persons in Dennis's study were males. It would be interesting to investigate the patterns of productivity among a comparable all-female group.

More recent studies by Simonton (1975, 1976, 1977a, 1977b) have attempted to resolve the differences between the Lehman and Dennis research. In general, Simonton found evidence that quantity declines with age, which favors Lehman, but that quality does not, which favors Dennis. Unfortunately, because of differences in design and criteria (e.g., differing data sources, differing criteria for inclusion in the studies), it cannot be said that this issue is fully resolved at this time.

We started this section on cognitive development by looking at the measurement of changes in intelligence over the adult years. Next we reviewed what we know about creative development. Now we will consider a third aspect, one that attempts to pull together a variety of intellectual factors.

Schools and industry are, at times, criticized for not fostering the creative potential of students and employees. What are some ways that schools, colleges, and businesses could enhance the creative abilities of their students and employees?

Obstacles and Aids to Creativity

We may agree that creativity is a valuable trait and should be fostered, but how? A number of theorists have offered excellent suggestions (e.g., Adams, 1986; Treffinger & others, 1983), but educator Ralph Hallman's suggestions (1967) on the obstacles and aids to creativity are still classic. According to him, creativity has several persistent obstacles:

- Pressures to conform. The pressure on the individual to follow standardized routines and inflexible rules is probably the major inhibitor. Authoritarian parents, teachers, and managers who demand order are responsible for destroying a great deal of creative talent.
- Ridicule of unusual ideas. This destroys one's feelings of worth and makes one defensive and compulsive.
- An excessive quest for success and the rewards it brings. An overconcern with material success is often the result of trying to meet the standards and demands of others to obtain the rewards they have to give. In the long run, this distorts one's view of reality and robs one of the strength of character to be creative (Amabile, Hennessey, & Grossman, 1986).
- Intolerance of a playful attitude. Innovation calls for playing around with ideas, a willingness to fantasize and make believe, and a healthy disrespect for accepted concepts. Creative persons often are seen as childlike and silly and their activity wasteful, but these are only appearances. As Hallman remarks, "Creativity is profound fun."

In addition to recommending that we avoid these obstacles, Hallman urges that we promote the following aids in ourselves and others:

- Engage in self-initiated learning. Most people who are in charge of others (managers, teachers, parents) find it hard to encourage others to initiate and direct their own learning. After all, this is certainly not the way most people were taught. They fear that if their subordinates are given greater freedom to explore reality on their own, they will learn wrong things or will not learn the right things in the proper sequence. We must put less emphasis on learning "the right facts," and more on learning how to learn. Even if we do temporarily mislearn a few things, in the long run the practice in experimentation and imagination will be greatly to our benefit.
- Become deeply knowledgeable about your subject. Only when people make themselves fully familiar with a particular situation can they detach themselves enough to get an original view of it.
- Defer judgment. It is important to make wild guesses, to juggle improbable relationships, to take intellectual risks, to take a chance on appearing ridiculous. Refrain from making judgments too early.
- Be flexible. Shift your point of view; to dream up new ideas for things, imagine as many possible solutions to a particular problem as possible.
- Be self-evaluative. When a person comes up with a creative idea, he or she is always a minority of one. History is replete with examples of ideas that were rejected for years before people began to realize their worth. Therefore, the creative person must be one who knows his or her own mind and is relatively independent of the judgment of others. To become a good judge of their own thinking, people must practice making many judgments.
- Ask yourself lots of open-ended questions. One extensive study showed that 90 percent of the time the average teacher asks questions to which there can be only one right answer, which the teacher already knows. Questions that pique curiosity and allow many possible right answers were asked only 10 percent of the time. Realize that you were probably taught that way, and take steps to rectify the tendency.
- Learn to cope with frustration and failure. Thomas Edison tried more than 2,000 combinations of metal before he found just the right kind for the electric element in his first light bulb.

Learning Ability

Is there a serious drop from early to late adulthood in the ability to learn? Despite some classic studies (e.g., Eisdorfer & Wilkie, 1973; Hulicka, 1967; Knowles, 1989; Taub, 1975), considerable disagreement over this matter still exists.

For example, many studies have shown a marked decline in paired associate learning (the ability to remember associations between two lists of words) (Kimmel, 1974). Obviously, memorizing pairs of words is itself of no great importance, but much essential learning is based on this skill. In most of these studies, however, the

Does the apparent drop in learning ability from early to late adulthood occur strictly because of ability, or because of factors such as motivation and dexterity?

Pedagogy
The science of teaching children.

Androgogy
The science of teaching adults.

measure of how well the associations have been learned is speed of response. Do older persons perform poorly because they are slower to learn, or only because they take longer to show what they have learned? As Botwinick (1977) reports:

> ■ The research strategy has been to vary both the amount of time the stimulus is available for study and the amount of time that is available for response. A general finding is that elderly people need more time for responding than typically is provided; they are at a disadvantage when this time is not available. When sufficient time for response is available, the performance of elderly people is only slightly inferior, or not inferior at all, to that of young people. (p. 278)

Another factor in learning ability that has been studied is motivation to learn (Botwinick, 1977). It has been suggested that persons in middle and late adulthood are less motivated to learn than younger people. Further, it appears that often they are aroused and anxious when placed in a laboratory situation for testing their learning ability. To the extent that this is true, their ability to learn is underestimated.

It has also been found in laboratory experiences that older adults are more likely than younger adults to make the "omission error." That is, when they suspect they may be wrong, they are more likely to refrain from responding at all, and therefore are scored as having not learned the task. But when asked what they think the answer is, they are often right.

Also, the meaningfulness of the task affects motivation. It is clear that the motivation for middle-aged and elderly adults is different from that of younger adults, and many experiments have not taken this into consideration in studying learning ability.

Decline in cognitive ability due to aging can often be offset through motivation and new learning experiences. This is shown by the growing number of adults who return to formal education in middle adulthood.

AN APPLIED VIEW

The Lifelong Learning Resource System

As work environments undergo more and faster changes, there is a growing emphasis on learning how to learn, rather than on mastering a specific skill that may become obsolete. Secondary education or even a college education may no longer suffice for an entire career. Workers require "regular booster shots of education and training" (Abeshouse, 1987, p. 23). We need a system for "lifelong learning." Corporations and policymakers are grappling with the issues of retraining technologically displaced workers, especially older workers (Wallace, 1989).

Knowles (1984) makes a marked distinction between teaching aimed at children and youths **(pedagogy)** and the teaching of adults **(androgogy).** Adults differ from younger persons in the following ways:

- The need to know. Adults need to know why they need to learn something before undertaking it.
- The learners' self-concept. Adults have a self-concept of being responsible for their own decisions, for their own lives.

- The role of the learners' experience. Adults come into an educational activity with both a greater volume and a different quality of experience than youths.
- Readiness to learn. Adults become ready to learn those things they need to know and be able to do in order to cope effectively with their real-life situations.
- Orientation to learning. In contrast to children's and youths' subject-centered orientation to learning (at least in school), adults are life-centered (or task-centered or problem-centered) in their orientation to learning.
- Motivation. While adults are responsive to some external motivators (better jobs, promotions, higher salaries, and the like), the most potent motivators are internal pressures (the desire for increased job satisfaction, self-esteem, quality of life, and the like).

In some situations older, more seasoned workers may feel threatened by new, younger workers. What recommendations do you have for dealing with these feelings?

Why are more and more adults going back to school? In the past, children could be educated to deal with a society and workplace that would remain essentially unchanged for their entire lives. Today the rate of change and innovation is too rapid. Fifty-year-old men and women who were born before the computer was being invented, and certainly didn't learn about computers in school as children, are now routinely asked to use them at work. It is now commonplace for people to return to school in order to advance or even maintain their present career. Also, sometimes an adult returns to school in order to learn a new skill or hobby that will be enjoyable during retirement.

Women in particular are going back to school in large numbers. Middle-aged women of today were not encouraged to pursue higher education when they were young. Some women are trying to catch up to be competitive with their male counterparts. Other women may return to school, not to study accounting or computer science, but to study literature or history, just to broaden their knowledge and for their own personal enjoyment. Many need occupational training to support themselves and their families after a divorce.

The education system is having to adapt to this change. Most adults cannot afford to quit their current jobs to go back to school. More schools are now offering evening and part-time programs. Many schools offer courses that can be taken at home, in some cases taking advantage of technology such as TV or computers.

Not all new learning by middle-aged adults takes place in a formal school setting. Employees in many different types of work settings are asked to keep abreast of new innovations. Other social experiences, such as practicing a religion, going to a library, watching television, and serving as a volunteer, involve new learning. Learning is now more than ever a lifelong task.

Guided Review

14. Despite extensive research on intelligence during adulthood, investigators do not agree on the state of intellectual ability. For instance, Terman's longitudinal study showed an increase in IQ scores with age among his gifted population. Horn's studies, however, show decline in _____ intelligence, with an increase in _____ intelligence.

15. According to Horn, fluid intelligence depends on the proper functioning of the nervous system. Crystallized intelligence indicates the cumulative effects of _____ and _____ of task performance.

16. Memory is closely related to intelligence. Short-term memory (SAR—the ability to hold things in your mind while processing them) _____ with age, whereas long-term memory (TSR—tertiary storage and retrieval dimension) appears to _____ with age.

17. The dual-process model for intelligence described by Baltes and associates describes _____ (classification skills and logical reasoning) and _____ (social wisdom).

18. Highly creative people like to do their own planning, are the most _____ when unusual circumstances arise, and can tolerate uncertainty and _____ better than others.

19. Dennis researched the accomplishments of people in each of the decades between the ages of 20 and 80. One of his findings is that scholars and scientists (except mathematicians and chemists) are most productive between _____ and _____ years of age.

20. In studying learning ability in adulthood, it remains to be shown if older persons perform poorly because they are learning slower, or because they take longer to show _____ _____ _____ _____ .

21. Motivation affects learning and is in turn affected by the _____ of the task.

Guided Review—Continued

22. Decline in cognitive ability due to aging can often be offset through _____ and new learning experiences.

23. Today more adults are going back to school because the rate of change and _____ in our society is so rapid.

Answers

14. fluid, crystallized   15. culture, learning   16. decreases, increase   17. mechanics, pragmatics   18. resourceful, ambiguity   19. 40, 60   20. what they have learned   21. meaningfulness   22. motivation   23. innovation

CONCLUSION

What is true of personality and social development appears to be true, though probably to a lesser extent, of physical and mental development: What you expect is what you get. If you expect

- your weight to go up,
- your muscles to grow flabby and weak,
- your senses to dull,

- your climacteric to be disruptive,
- your intelligence to drop,
- your creativity to plummet, and
- your sexual interest and ability to decline,

they probably will. This is called the self-fulfilling prophecy. People who take a positive outlook, who enthusiastically try to maintain their bodies and minds, have a much better chance at success. They

are also better able to deal with the stresses that life naturally imposes on us all.

This is not to say that we can completely overcome the effects of aging. It means that through our attitudes, we can learn to deal with them more effectively. In the next chapter we look at the psychosocial features of middle age, which depend so much, as we have said before, on physical and cognitive development.

CHAPTER HIGHLIGHTS

Physical Development

- Health concerns in middle adulthood include increasing weight and lower metabolism.
- In the middle period of adulthood there is a common but often unnecessary decline in muscular ability, due in part to a decrease in exercise.
- Sensory abilities—vision, hearing, smell, and taste—begin to show slight declines in middle adulthood.
- The climacterium, the loss of reproductive ability, occurs at menopause for women but at much older ages for most men.

Sex in Middle Adulthood

- Frequency of sexual intercourse as well as marital satisfaction appear to increase over the middle years.
- Some minor changes in sexual physiology occur for both sexes, but usually these need not hamper sexual satisfaction.

Cognitive Development

- Horn suggests that while fluid intelligence deteriorates with age, crystallized intelligence does not.
- Baltes has proposed a dual-process model of intelligence,

which suggests a decline in the mechanics of intelligence (classification skills, logical reasoning), yet an increase in the pragmatics of intelligence (social wisdom).

- Creativity, important in a rapidly changing world, manifests itself at different peak periods throughout adulthood.
- Learning in middle adulthood can be enhanced through motivation, new learning experiences, and changes in education systems.

KEY TERMS

Androgogy   450
Basal metabolism rate (BMR)   436
Climacteric   439
Climacterium   439
Crystallized intelligence   444
Dual-process model   445

Estrogen replacement therapy (ERT)   440
Fluid intelligence   444
Glaucoma   438
Male change of life   439

Menopause   439
Olfactory sense   439
Pedagogy   450
Self-fulfilling prophecy   436
Senile macular degeneration   438

✿ WHAT DO YOU THINK?

1. When you look at the physical shape your parents and grandparents are in, and their attitudes toward the subject, do you see evidence of the self-fulfilling prophecy?

2. If you are a female and have not yet gone through menopause, what do you anticipate your feelings will be about it?

3. If you are a male, can you imagine what women facing menopause must be feeling?

4. What are some ways that our society might foster the cognitive abilities of its adult citizens?

5. What are some ways that our society might foster the creative abilities of its adult citizens?

6. What are some ways that our society might foster the learning of its adult citizens?

7. What is your attitude toward your parent's sexuality?

✿ SUGGESTED READINGS

The Boston Women's Book Collaborative. (1984). *Our bodies, growing older*. Boston: Author. An excellent update of the popular *Our bodies, our selves*. This book is for middle-aged and elderly women.

Gardner, H. (1983). *Frames of mind: The theory of multiple intelligences*. New York: Basic Books. Offers a comprehensive view of the numerous faces of intelligence.

The Journal of Creative Behavior. Pick up any volume of this fascinating journal at your library and browse through it. A wide variety of interesting topics are covered, and more often than not the articles are written creatively.

Nilsson, L. & J. Lindberg. (1974). *Behold man: A photographic journey of discovery inside the body*. New York: Delacorte. A book of photographs, many of them pictures enlarged thousands of times. This is a magnificent description of the human body.

Wolfe, T. (1987). *The bonfire of the vanities*. New York: Farrar, Straus & Giroux. With his customary verve, Wolfe looks inside the heads of five men and two women, all New Yorkers in early middle age, and shows us how they think.

✿ CHAPTER REVIEW TEST

1. **Basal metabolism rate refers to**
   a. the minimum amount of energy an individual tends to use after exercising.
   b. the minimum amount of energy an individual tends to use when in a resting state.
   c. the maximum amount of energy an individual tends to use after exercising.
   d. the maximum amount of energy an individual tends to use when in a resting state.

2. **For persons over age 50, even one or two drinks each day can be dangerous, because they can cause**
   a. permanent liver damage.
   b. irreversible kidney damage.
   c. clogged arteries.
   d. enlargement of the left ventricle of the heart.

3. **During middle adulthood, how does one's vision change?**
   a. The lens becomes more elastic.
   b. The cornea decreases in curvature and thickness.
   c. The iris responds less well to light.
   d. The ability to focus on nearby objects increases.

4. **Due to physical changes in middle adulthood, our vision can be affected in what ways?**
   a. Eyes do not adapt to sudden intense light or darkness as effectively.
   b. Detection of certain colors can be more difficult.
   c. There is a heightened risk of eye diseases.
   d. All of the answers are correct.

5. **During middle adulthood, how does hearing ability change?**
   a. Higher frequencies need to be louder to be heard.
   b. Lower frequencies need to be louder to be heard.
   c. The ability to hear human speech remains constant.
   d. The ability to listen to speech in a crowded environment declines, while the ability to listen to someone alone without background noise increases.

6. **Estrogen replacement therapy has offered relief for women who experience serious problems with**
   a. midlife crises.
   b. menopause.
   c. weight loss.
   d. fertility.

7. **Women who experience decreased sexual interest probably have**
   a. a chronic illness.
   b. experienced a midlife crisis.
   c. high estrogen levels.
   d. low estrogen levels.

8. **According to Hermann, the decrease in sexual potency that men experience in later years is probably the result of**
   a. hormonal changes.
   b. a slowing down in the central nervous system.
   c. impotence.
   d. a result of a midlife crisis.

9. **What type of intelligence deteriorates with age, to some extent?**
   a. learned
   b. natural
   c. crystallized
   d. fluid

10. **What is an example of crystallized intelligence?**
    a. arithmetical reasoning
    b. letter grouping
    c. recalling paired associates
    d. dominoes

11. People who like to do their own planning, make their own decisions, are flexible, and are able to stand their ground in the face of criticism demonstrate traits of a
    a. highly creative person.
    b. career-oriented person.
    c. person with strong cognitive abilities.
    d. person who has successfully individuated him/herself from significant others.

12. An aid to creativity is
    a. self-initiated learning.
    b. deferring judgment and being flexible.
    c. self-evaluation.
    d. All of the answers are correct.

13. While being tested on paired associate learning tasks the group most at a disadvantage if the amount of time available for response is not sufficient is
    a. the group in early adulthood.
    b. the group in middle adulthood.
    c. the group in late adulthood.
    d. All groups would be at a disadvantage.

14. Groups of middle-aged and elderly subjects are tested on their ability to remember associations between two lists of words. How are they most likely to respond when they suspect they may be wrong?
    a. take an educated guess
    b. refrain from responding
    c. confer with other group members
    d. state that they do not know the answer

15. Research indicates that adults need to know why they need to learn something before undertaking it, that they have a self-concept of being responsible for their own decisions, and that they are life-centered in their orientation to learning. These findings highlight the difference between children and adults in
    a. cognitive abilities.
    b. level of individuation.
    c. self-fulfillment.
    d. the learning process.

16. A factor in learning ability during middle adulthood is motivation to learn. It is important for researchers to keep in mind that
    _____ affects an adult's level of motivation.
    a. level of education
    b. meaningfulness of the task
    c. interest
    d. external distractions

Answers

1.b 2.d 3.c 4.d 5.a 6.b 7.d 8.b 9.d 10.a 11.a 12.d 13.c 14.b 15.d 16.b

CHAPTER 18

Psychosocial Development in Middle Adulthood

R ecently, a middle-aged woman friend shared some reflections with me: I remember walking to school one day in the second grade, chatting with my girlfriend's mother as she escorted us. I told her that I had noticed how much more quickly the day seemed to pass than it used to. Seven seemed a very advanced age to me then, so I was sure this phenomenon was related to being finally grown-up. Later that year we moved into a new house in a new community. Moving day was very exciting. The real grown-ups were very busy, so the most entertaining thing I had to do was to sit around and think about my life. Moving seemed to have wrapped up the first part of my life into a discrete little package. And it came to me that there I was, almost 8 years old, and I didn't have a feeling for all that time. I promised myself, as I sat in our old, soft maroon chair, holding some of my accumulated possessions dislocated by their recent journey, that five years later to the day I would sit again in the same spot, in the same position, holding the same objects. Then, I figured, with all the awareness born of old age, I would really know what five years would feel like. And five years later I did just that.

I am still trying to comprehend or capture a sense of time passing. Now only the units have changed. Every once in a while I hold very still and try to catch 20 years. Twenty years feel like those five did long ago. Twenty from now, if I'm lucky, I'll be staring my death in the face. It's all so odd. Somewhere inside I was all grown-up when I was 7. That "me" hasn't really aged or changed much, and it's still watching as the world wrinkles on the outside. Days are minutes, months are weeks, and years are months. I'll probably be menopausal in the morning!

Quoted by Lila Kalinich, MD, in "The Biological Clock," 1992

After reading chapter 18, you should be able to

- Explain what is meant by "emotional divorce" and the "empty nest syndrome."

- List some components of a happy marriage.

- Discover how relationships with parents and siblings change in middle adulthood.

- Discuss the positive and negative effects of divorce on middle-aged adults and their families.

- Determine your position on whether personality development is continuous or changing.

- List Levinson's three major developmental tasks for middle-aged men, along with the four polarities men must confront.

- Describe the differences between Levinson's research with men and his more recent research with women.

- Explain and compare Gould's Stage IV transformation, Vaillant's concept of "adaptive mechanisms," and Erikson's stage, "generativity versus stagnation."

- Define the NEO model of personality.

- Highlight particular employment concerns among middle-aged adults.

- Describe the five major problem areas for working women.

- Discuss what is meant by a "midcareer crisis," as well as ways of dealing with it.

Marriage and Family Relations

In this section, we consider four important aspects of middle-aged life today: relationships in marriage, relationships with aging parents, relationships with brothers and sisters, and divorce. Although not all would agree, we define this part of life as going from 35 to 64 years of age.

Marriage at Middle Age

Middle age is often a time when husbands and wives reappraise their marriage. The **midlife transition** (a period during which people seriously reevaluate their lives up to that time) often causes a person to simultaneously examine current relationships and consider changes for the future. Often, whatever tension that exists in a marriage is suppressed while the children still live at home. As they leave to go off to college or to start families of their own, these tensions are openly expressed.

Sometimes couples learn to "withstand" each other rather than live with each other. The only activities and interests they share are ones that revolved around the children. When the children leave, they are forced to recognize how far apart they have drifted. In effect, they engage in **emotional divorce** (Fitzpatrick, 1984).

But most couples whose marriages have lasted this long have built the type of relationship that can withstand reappraisal, and they continue for the rest of their lives. Census data suggest that the highest rates for separation and divorce occur about five years after the beginning of the marriage (Sweet & Bumpass, 1987).

In fact, some studies suggest that this period after the children leave home is like a second honeymoon (e.g., Rhyne, 1981). After the initial period of negative emotions that follow this disruption of the family, often called the **empty nest syndrome,** married couples can evaluate the job they have done with their children. They can pat themselves on the back for a job well done and then relax now that a major life goal has been accomplished. They then realize that they have more freedom and privacy and fewer worries. They usually have more money to spend on themselves. And this period after the children leave home is now much longer than it used to be. Husbands and wives now can look forward to spending 20 or 30 years together as a couple rather than as a large family.

The Happy Marriage

What does research have to say about the components of a happy, or at least a lasting, marriage? Gottman and Krokoff (1989) conducted a longitudinal study looking at the types of interactions between husband and wife and the effect on marital satisfaction. Earlier research suggested that there was always more negative interaction in unhappy marriages than in happy marriages.

Gottman and Krokoff decided to look at the effect of different types of negative interactions rather than one global category. They found that certain types of conflict may in fact be positive factors in a happy, lasting marriage. They also found that certain types of conflict, particularly defensiveness, stubbornness, and withdrawal on the part of the husband, indicated that a marriage was in trouble.

Gottman and Krokoff assign to the wife the role of manager of marital disagreements and suggest she get her husband to "confront areas of disagreement and to openly vent disagreement and anger" (p. 50). Most husbands tend to try to avoid relational confrontations (Moyers & Bly, 1990). Therefore, overcoming this reluctance can have extremely beneficial long-term effects on the marriage.

Midlife transition

Levinson's term for the phase that usually lasts for five years and generally extends from age 40 to 45.

The period in a marriage after which there is no longer a need to care for children is often a time for pursuing dreams that were previously impractical.

Emotional divorce

Sometimes a couple learns to "withstand" each other, rather than live with each other. The only activities and interests that they shared were ones that revolved around the children. When the children leave, they are forced to recognize how far apart they have drifted; in effect, they are emotionally divorced.

Empty nest syndrome

Refers to the feelings parents may have as a result of their last child leaving home.

The Unmarried

About 1 in 20 people in middle age have never been married (Sweet & Bumpass, 1987). In general, a person who has never married by middle age will not get married. Such people tend either to have very low or very high education levels. At the low extreme, of those who have less than five years of school, one person in seven has never married. The factors that kept these people from completing school, such as mental illness or other handicaps, are probably the same ones that make them less likely to get married. At the other extreme, 13 percent of middle-aged women with 17 or more years of education have never been married.

A number of possible explanations could account for this. These women may choose higher education and a career over marriage. They may believe marriage will hold them back. A cultural factor may be at work, since some men feel threatened by women with more education than they have. Perhaps women who delay marriage to pursue an education end up having a smaller pool of available men to choose from.

Relationships with Aging Parents

Middle age is also a time when most people develop improved relationships with their parents. Middle-aged children, most of them parents themselves, gain a new perspective on parenthood and so reevaluate the actions taken by their own parents (Farrell & Rosenberg, 1981). Also, grandchildren can strengthen bonds that may have weakened when people left their parents' home during early adulthood.

In many cases, however, the relationship begins to reverse itself: As elderly parents grow older, they sometimes become as dependent on their middle-aged children as those children once were on them. Most people fail to anticipate the costs and emotional strains that the aging of their parents can precipitate. This can lead ultimately to new sources of tension and rancor in the relationship.

It is not uncommon for people in middle adulthood to care for elderly parents while still raising their own teenage children. How does this situation enhance and detract from familial relationships?

The most frequently cited problem of middle-adult women is not menopause or aging, but caring for their aging parents and parents-in-law (James, 1990). This is not so surprising when we realize that it is virtually always the daughter(s) in the family who is responsible for the care of the elderly parents (Brody & Schoonover, 1986; Kendig & others, 1992; Matthews, 1987). Brody and associates (1986) found that the daughter who is the primary caretaker relies on siblings, especially her sisters if she has them, for emotional support. These sisters typically feel guilty about not doing enough. On the average, brothers provide less help and feel less guilty about it. It seems that the demands on women to fulfill the role of family nurturer are deeply rooted and powerful. Of course, as more women enter the workplace, and as more of them become assertive about equitable family responsibilities, this pattern may well change, with males assuming more of the burden.

Relationships and roles among the generations are always changing.

We will deal here with two other features of family life in middle adulthood: relationships with siblings and the problems of divorce.

Relationships with Siblings

Developmental psychology has, for some time now, recognized the importance of sibling relationships for a child's cognitive and social growth. But do these special relationships stop contributing to a person's development after adolescence? Does the relationship slowly decline in importance as one ages? Are the characteristics of the relationship the same in middle adulthood as they were in childhood? Psychological research has recently begun to focus on some of these questions.

Sibling relationships have the potential to be the most enduring that a person can have. You don't usually meet your spouse until young adulthood or at least adolescence. Your parents usually pass away before you do. You usually pass away before your children do. But most siblings are born within a few years of each other, and such a relationship can last 60, 80, or even 100 years!

Nevertheless, sibling relationships do change. As Cicirelli (1980), a prominent researcher on adult sibling relationships, notes:

> At the beginning it is one of intimate daily contact and sharing of most experiences, including the socializing influence of the same parents. Throughout the school years, siblings may have different teachers and different friends and peer groups, but they still have their home experiences in common. Later, when they leave their parents' home to pursue a career or to marry and establish families of their own, they tend to separate from each other as well. They may live in different cities or even different countries. Contact becomes voluntary except on certain ritual occasions, and most life experiences are no longer shared. Still later, they may share the obligations of caring for their parents during their declining years. With the death of the parents, sibling contact returns to a more voluntary level until the end of life. (p. 455)

What then are some of the characteristics and effects of such a long and evolving relationship? Although the research on adulthood sibling relationships is considerably less abundant than that on childhood and adolescent sibling relationships, this question has some partial answers. Some researchers have measured change of the relationship with age by looking at how close siblings live to one another and how often they see one another. They reason that such contact is necessary for a relationship to exist. This research indicates that sibling relationships do decline with

A MULTICULTURAL VIEW

Sibling Relationships in Industrial and Nonindustrial Societies

In industrial societies, close relationships among siblings tend to be optional, based on the siblings' desires to be friendly toward one another or not. In nonindustrial societies, sibling relationships are based on the constraints that cultural norms impose. Such norms demand that siblings should behave in certain ways toward each other. These differences, in large part, are due to differences in economic structure.

Nonindustrial societies tend to be agrarian, village-centered, and relatively poor. Because resources are limited in such societies, sibling cooperation is necessary to accomplish tasks, to maintain family functioning, and to attain economic goals. In these societies, a greater

number of siblings exists and they are expected to fulfill certain responsibilities. Siblings share caretaking and act as educational and socializing agents for each other's children. Parents usually have this role in industrial societies. In these societies, sibling relationships are secondary to spouse-spouse and parent-child relationships.

In nonindustrial societies, sister-brother and brother-brother relationships are closest, whereas sister-sister relationships are closest in industrial societies. Control mechanisms exist in nonindustrial societies to deal with tension and conflicts, such as an emphasis on the authority of older children over younger siblings.

age. However, other researchers (e.g., Cicirelli, 1979) suggest that measures of feelings of closeness and affection are better indicators of a relationship than proximity and frequency of contact. This research supports the notion of strong sibling relationships even in old age. One consistent finding is that the relationship between sisters tends to be stronger than the relationship between brothers.

What is the nature of adult sibling relationships? As in childhood, there is often rivalry, in addition to closeness. Some researchers have found this rivalry to be very common, especially among adult brothers (Adams, 1968). Other researchers suggest that childhood rivalry dissipates in adulthood (Allan, 1977), largely because the siblings have less contact with each other as they grow older. On the other hand, a study of adult sibling support (White & Reidmann, 1992) found 29 percent of those studied would call on a sibling first in an emergency, despite low levels of interaction with siblings normally. Sibling support was highest for those with sisters and without adult children. African Americans and persons with lower income and education are less likely to count on sibling support.

One would hope that a growing maturity would also lessen rivalry. Certainly adult siblings are faced with more serious and important tasks than are childhood siblings. For example, most middle-aged siblings must make mutual decisions concerning the care of their elderly parents and eventually deal with the aftermath of their death.

Another consideration is the effect of changing family patterns on sibling relationships. Couples now are having fewer or even no children. Children will therefore be less available to parents for companionship and psychological support. On the other hand, parents and their siblings will be living longer, more active lives. The obvious conclusion is that sibling relationships will become more and more important in the future.

Friendships

Middle age is a time when friendships become fewer and more precious. Actually, the findings of Carstensen (1992) suggest that individuals begin narrowing their range of social partners long before middle age. The most dramatic decline occurs between the ages of 18 and 30. In early adulthood, interaction frequency with acquaintances and close friends begins to decline while at the same time it increases with spouses and siblings. It would seem that at about age 30, individuals choose a select few relationships with which to derive support, self-definition, and a sense of stability. Emotional closeness, however, increases throughout adulthood in relationships with relatives and close friends. These relationships with a select few, then, become increasingly close and satisfying during the middle adult years. Further, the idea that face-to-face contact is necessary for closeness cannot be supported. In fact, many parents report feeling closest to their adult children when they see them the least.

The Middle-Aged Divorced Person

Because divorce rates have been increasing for those over 40, midlife divorce will become an important focus in the future (Uhlenberg & others, 1990). The divorce rates are higher for second or subsequent marriages, for African Americans, and for those who are less educated and who have lower earning ability. Although midlife is a time when a divorce is less likely to occur (see figure 18.1), the proportion of divorced persons in midlife is relatively high, since many who divorced earlier have never remarried. Men and women over 40 experience significantly more turmoil and unhappiness than younger people at the same stage of divorce (Chiriboga, 1989). The reasons are clear: length of time of marriage, complex economic and property linkages, a web of social relationships, and a generally higher standard of living.

Figure 18.1

The chart of divorces in the United States shows that most divorces occur within the first five years of marriage, with the peak at three years. Interestingly, the same pattern is found in most other societies, ranging from contemporary Sweden to the hunting and gathering groups of southwest Africa.

Duration of marriages that ended in divorce

In respect to the last point, it should be noted that women, especially at midlife, are often hard hit economically by divorce. The National Longitudinal Survey found they experience significant declines in income, increased rates of poverty, and dramatic lifestyle changes upon separation, divorce, or widowhood; they do not recover unless they remarry (Arendell, 1987; Hoffman & Duncan, 1988). Furthermore, since most women who divorce at midlife are already working, they have little room to maneuver for more income after divorce. This is especially true for African American women, since the only notable increase in workforce participation after divorce is for white women (Morgan, 1991).

More and more children are living in homes without fathers. More than half of single-parent mothers are not receiving full child support, and half of those are not receiving any. Whereas 68 percent of white women were awarded child support, only 35 percent of African American women and 41 percent of Latina women received such awards (Crohan & others, 1989).

A discomforting finding of White (1992) is that children of divorce, even after they have left home and their parents enter middle age, receive significantly less support (child care, advice, transportation, loans, and so forth) than do children whose parents have remained married. Remarriage does not seem to increase or decrease this support deficit.

In general, new divorce laws were considered to have a liberating effect on women. Until the liberalization of divorce laws and attitudes, women usually had no choice but to endure a difficult and sometimes even abusive marriage. Cultural norms allowed men much more moral latitude, the so-called double standard. Women basically just had to put up with it.

Before liberalization, it was necessary to establish "reasonable grounds" for divorce, such as adultery or physical abuse. Women who were granted divorces were almost always awarded larger alimony settlements than they receive today, to make up for the loss of income. This was necessary because women lagged far behind men in their earning potential, and often women stayed at home to raise the children and run the household while the husband advanced a career. A woman could not survive a divorce if it left her and her family destitute.

No-fault divorce

The law that lets people get divorced without proving some atrocious act by one of the spouses. In legal language, this is known as an irretrievable breakdown of a marriage.

In 1970 the divorce laws were liberalized in California, a change soon followed across the country. This was the introduction of a **no-fault divorce.** Weitzman (1985) contends that the new divorce laws have impoverished divorced women and their children. A major facet of the new laws is supposed to be their gender neutrality. Men and women are treated equally under the divorce law, and this includes the division of property and alimony.

But perhaps these laws were premature. Men and women did not in 1970, and still do not today, live in an economically equitable system. Men still possess a competitive advantage in earning potential, and the culture still holds women responsible for raising the children and running the household. When a divorce judge divides up the property equally, grants little or no alimony, and provides inadequate child support, it is the woman and children who suffer.

This is particularly true of the middle-aged homemaker. The courts seldom give much recognition to the years spent running the household while the husband invested time in advancing a career. Such a woman cannot reasonably be expected to compete with others who have been gaining experience in the marketplace while she stayed at home.

In the year following a divorce, a woman and her children can expect a 73 percent decline in their standard of living, according to Weitzman's research. The former husband can expect a 42 percent increase. After five years, the woman's standard of living will likely be 30 percent lower than what it was during the marriage, whereas the husband's will be 14 percent higher.

Another effect is that no-fault divorce laws mandate an even division of property. This often means that the family house must be sold. Before these laws, the house was almost always given to the woman and her children. Besides being an economic burden, the loss of the house has psychological consequences for the development of the children. The dislocation often requires that the children leave their school, neighborhood, and friends. And this usually comes just after the divorce, a period of tremendous stress for any child.

Some indications show that reform is on the way. In California the rules for division of property and spousal support are being revised. More things are now being considered family assets, to be divided equally, such as the major wage earner's salary, pension, medical insurance, and future earning power. In addition, some states have now become aggressive at pursuing husbands who are delinquent on child support payments. Their names are being published and a part of their wages is being withheld and given to the ex-wife. Massachusetts is even considering paying spouses the money lost through delinquent payments and reimbursing itself through taxes and garnishments of the other spouse.

Divorce will probably never be the "civilized" process that the early proponents of no-fault divorce laws hoped it would become. At best, we can expect the suffering of spouses to become more equal, and the suffering of the children to be reduced.

Marriage and family life are but two of the factors that have a marked effect on personality development, to which we now turn.

Guided Review

1. During middle age, marriage is sometimes affected by emotional _____ (which means drifting apart while still married).

2. After the initial period of negative emotions that follow after the children leave home, called the "_____ _____ syndrome," couples can evaluate the job they have done in raising their family.

3. Certain types of conflict in a marriage can be positive and are particularly beneficial if the _____ is willing to confront areas of disagreement.

4. It is unlikely that a middle-aged person who has never married will marry. Such people tend to have either very high or very low levels of _____ .

5. One of the most challenging problems facing middle-adult women is that their parents or parents-in-law are now _____ on them.

6. New divorce laws were considered to have a _____ effect on women. These laws, however, have had the result of impoverishing many women.

Personality Development: Continuous or Changing?

In earlier chapters, we have examined the controversy over whether personality is stable or changing. This debate is concerned with middle adulthood, too.

Continuity versus Change

All of us have heard someone say, "Oh, he's been like that ever since he was a baby!" Such a comment doesn't sound like a philosophical statement, but think about what it implies. It implies that individuals can remain basically the same throughout their lifespan. This is the fundamental question that the issue of change versus continuity of development addresses. Do human beings ever really change, or do we all stay pretty much the same? It is the focus of great debate by child-development and lifespan psychologists alike because of its implications.

If we assume that people remain the same regardless of what happens to them as their life continues, then the period of early childhood takes on great meaning (Brim & Kagan, 1980; Kagan, 1984; Rubin, 1981). Several of the developmental theorists we have discussed (e.g., Freud and Piaget—see chapter 2) have focused much energy on the early years of childhood in the belief that what happens to a person during childhood determines much of what will happen to him or her in the future.

Conversely, others (e.g., Erikson and other adult development theorists) believe that because people are constantly changing and developing, all life experiences must be considered important. In that case, early childhood becomes a somewhat less significant period in the whole of development, and adolescence and adulthood come more into focus. It also implies that getting children "off on the right foot" is not enough to ensure positive development. These are just some of the implications of the debate about personality continuity versus change.

In the study of adulthood, the issue of continuity versus change gets even more complex. In general, two distinct theoretical positions influence the study of adult personality. Some theorists feel that adults remain basically the same—that the adult personality is stable. This is continuity in adult development. Other theorists view the adult as constantly in a process of change and evolution. That is what the position of change refers to.

Answers

1. divorce 2. empty nest 3. husband 4. education 5. dependent 6. liberating

Trait theorists

Researchers who look at pieces of the personality (personality traits), as measured by detailed questionnaires.

Stage theorists

Researchers who believe that research based on personality traits is too narrow in focus and that we must also look at the stages of change each person goes through.

Do our personalities remain stable throughout adulthood or do we experience a series of changes in personality? Which theory do you support?

The study of continuity versus change in adulthood is complicated by the many ways that the issue is studied. Some researchers look at pieces of the personality (personality traits) as measured by detailed questionnaires. They think that the answers to such questionnaires assess adult personality. These researchers are known as **trait theorists.**

Others note that such questionnaires measure only parts of the personality. They argue that adult personality is much more complicated than any list of personality traits. What is interesting to them is how those traits fit with the whole of the person. Beyond that, they are also interested in how an adult's personality interacts with the world around him or her. They believe that research based on personality traits is too narrow in focus and that we must also look at the stages of change each person goes through. These researchers are known as **stage theorists.** The old saying, "you can't see the forest for the trees," sums up their position—the parts prevent you from seeing the whole.

The differences in how to go about measuring adult personality complicate the study of continuity and change in adulthood. Researchers use extremely different methods of measuring adult personality and then relate their findings to support either the position of continuity or change. In general, trait theorists have found that the adult personality remains the same: Their work supports continuity (McCrae & Costa, 1984). McCrae and Costa summed up their research in the title of an article: "Still Stable after All These Years." Researchers looking at the whole of the adult personality through extensive interviews have found support for the notion of change in adulthood (Erikson, 1963, 1975; Gould, 1978; Levinson, 1978, 1986, 1990a, 1990b; Vaillant, 1977).

The study of continuity versus change in adult psychology has important implications, just as it does in childhood psychology. The findings of personality studies add to our knowledge of what "normal" adult development means. Yet as we have seen, the studies vary in their definitions of what adult personality is and how it should be measured. Not surprisingly, studies also differ in what they tell us about normal adult development. Theorists have different answers to the question: "If nothing very unusual happens (like a catastrophe), how will the adult personality develop?"

Trait theorists like McCrae and Costa might say, "If nothing unusual happens, then the adult personality will stay relatively the same. Normal adult personality development is really the maintenance of personality." Gould, Levinson, Vaillant, and Erikson, looking at the whole of the adult, would respond differently (see also chapter 16). They might say, "The adult personality naturally and normally develops through change. Normal adult personality development is a continual process of growth and change."

Who is right? We suggest you read our summary of the studies that each camp provides, and try to make up your own mind. We begin with Roger Gould's theory, as it applies to middle age.

Transformations: Gould

The part of Roger Gould's theory of personality development that deals with middle adulthood is labeled Stage IV. Let us remind you that the basis of his theory is the concept that all of us unconsciously learn assumptions about the nature of life. In his study of adult women and men, he found that healthy personality development depends on rejecting these "major false assumptions."

The midlife decade (ages 35 to 45) is often a time in life when one's parents, other relatives, and some close friends go through serious illness and death. It is also the time when our self-deceptions and the lies of others can have repercussions far more serious than ever before, because of the greater power that middle-aged persons usually have. Therefore, the major false assumption that tends to be rejected at this time of life is "There is no evil or death in the world. Everything sinister has been destroyed."

Five false assumptions accompany this erroneous belief, all of which should now be abandoned:

- "The illusions of safety can last forever."

- "Death can't happen to me or to my loved ones."

- "It is impossible to live without a protector" (a substitute "mother" or "father" who is usually the person's spouse).

- "There is no life beyond this family."

- "I am innocent."

Even if one's parents are still living and well at this time, most adults experience a role reversal with them. Parents who are in their sixties and seventies often become dependent on their middle-aged children, thus bringing the cycle full circle. There is a growing sense of vulnerability, of the passage of time, and a realization of what is truly important. Men at this time say that they no longer fear their bosses or idealize their mentors. Women begin to realize that male protectors really are not all that necessary. Those who come to this realization, both male and female, have a feeling of freedom never before experienced.

Gould realizes, of course, that developments in life occur after the midlife transition, but his research ends at this period.

Seasons of a Man's Life: Levinson

This section continues a discussion of Levinson's (1978) theory that was begun in chapter 16. Figure 18.2 reproduces that part of his theory that applies to middle adulthood.

Settling Down

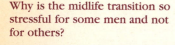

Why is the midlife transition so stressful for some men and not for others?

The settling-down phase usually extends from age 33 to 40. At this time, most men have pretty well decided what occupation they choose to pursue. During this period, most men attempt to achieve two tasks: (1) establish a niche in society, and (2) advance up the ladder of the occupational group. During this phase, the male attempts to overcome his dependency on his mentor and slowly is able to "become his own man." This is a step in the direction of greater individuation, in that the man thinks less and less as others want him to, and more and more as his own views dictate. He is now ready to go into the third phase of his adulthood, the midlife transition.

Figure 18.2

Levinson's theory—middle age

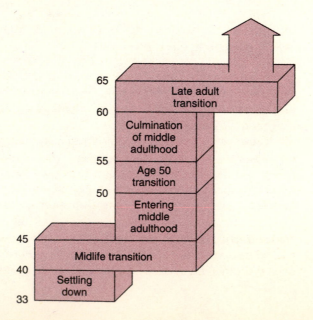

The so-called midlife crisis—do you think most middle-aged men go through one?

The Midlife Transition

The *midlife transition,* which usually lasts for five years, generally extends from age 40 to 45. It involves three major developmental tasks:

- The review, reappraisal, and termination of the early adult period

- Decisions as to how the period of middle adulthood should be conducted

- Dealing with the polarities that are the source of deep division in the man's life at this stage. These polarities, which represent the continual struggle toward greater individuation, are (1) young/old (2) destruction/creation, (3) masculinity/femininity, and (4) attachment/separation

Young/Old.   Young/old is the major polarity to be dealt with during the midlife transition. Levinson referred to Freud's disciple, Carl Jung (1966), who suggested that the experience of thousands of generations of human beings has gradually produced deep-seated ideas that each of us must learn to deal with. The major one is that although we begin to grow old even at birth, we are also interested in maintaining our youth, if only to avoid the ultimate consequence of our mortality: death.

In tribal symbolism, the word *young* represents fertility, growth, energy, potential, birth, and spring. *Old,* on the other hand, encompasses termination, death, completion, ending, fruition, and winter. Until the age of 40, the man has been able to maintain his youthful self-image. Through producing and raising children, and in some cases through a creative product such as a book, invention, or painting, he has been able to see himself as part of a new and youthful recycling of life. Subconsciously, at least, he has been able to maintain the myth of immortality.

At about the time of his 40th birthday, he is confronted with evidence of his own declining powers. He is no longer able to run, play tennis, or shoot basketballs as effectively as he could in his twenties. He sometimes forgets things, and his eyesight may not be as good. Even more damaging to his hope for immortality is the illness of his friends. Heart attacks, strokes, and other serious illnesses are more frequent among people of his age. In many cases, his parents suffer serious illnesses, or even die. These events lead to one inevitable realization: He is going to die, and perhaps in the not-too-distant future. Even the 32 years left him (on the average) do not seem like much, because over half of life is now already past.

A sense of wanting to leave a legacy now emerges. Most individuals want to feel that their life has made some difference, and they want to leave something behind them that can be remembered. Therefore, it is typical at this time that the individual becomes more creative and often works harder than he has in the past to make a contribution considered worthwhile by those who follow him.

Destruction/Creation.   The male going through a midlife transition realizes not only the potential of the world to destroy but also his own capacity to be *destructive.* He recognizes the evil within himself and his own power to hurt, damage, and injure himself and others. He knows, if he is honest with himself, that he has not only hurt others inadvertently but sometimes with clear purpose. He sees himself as both victim and villain in the "continuing tale of man's inhumanity to man" (Levinson, 1978, p. 224).

The more honest he is with himself, the more he realizes how tremendous is his capacity to destroy. This honesty, has a bonus, however: In recognizing his power to be destructive, he begins to realize how truly powerful he can be in *creating* new and useful forms of life. As with the young/old polarity, he now attempts to strike a new balance between his destructive and creative sides.

Masculinity/Femininity.   Levinson again borrowed from Jung, using his concept that all persons have a *masculine* and *feminine* side and that they emphasize one over the other because of the demands of society. This emphasis often costs us greatly. A rich adulthood can be achieved only by compensating for that part of us that was denied during our childhood. In most males, the feminine side has typically been undernourished and now must come to the fore if they are to be all they are capable of being.

According to Levinson, in early adulthood, femininity has a number of undesirable connotations for the male. To the young man, masculinity connotes bodily prowess and toughness, achievement and ambition, power, and intellectuality. Also to the young man, the feminine role represents physical ineptness, incompetence and lack of ambition, personal weakness, and emotionality. Now is the time when the polarity between these self-concepts must be seen and reconciled.

The male who is to achieve greater individuation now recognizes that these dichotomies are false and that he does indeed have a feminine side that must also be nourished. The mature male is able to allow himself to indulge in what he before has disparaged as feminine aspects of his personality. Such a male feels secure enough in his masculinity to enjoy his ability to feel, to nurture, to be dependent. Levinson suggests such men are now freer to assume more independent relationships with their mothers, to develop more intimate love relationships with peer women, and to become mentors to younger men and women alike.

Attachment/Separation.   By the *attachment/separation* process, Levinson meant that each of us needs to be attached to our fellow members of society but also to be separate from them. As the human being develops, a fascinating vacillation occurs between each of these needs. In childhood, a clear-cut attachment to mother and later to family exists. Children need support because of their incompetence in dealing with the complexity of the world around them. Nevertheless, children do begin the separation process by forming attachments to their peers.

During adolescence, this need switches toward an emphasis on separateness from family, as the individual proceeds through the identity moratorium. During this time, most adolescents need to separate themselves not only from their parents but also from the entire society around them in order to try out new ways of being. This need vacillates back toward attachment during early adulthood. The ultimate goal, of course, is interdependence (see chapter 6).

Throughout their twenties and thirties, most men are involved in entering the world of work and in family and have a strong attachment to others who can help them be successful in these goals. Now, in the midlife transition, a new separateness, perhaps a second adolescence, takes place. The man, especially the successful man, begins to look inside and to gain greater awareness of his sensual and aesthetic feelings. He becomes more in touch with himself by being temporarily less in touch with the others around him.

Because the men interviewed so extensively by Levinson and his colleagues were between the ages of 35 and 45, their study of adult development ends at the midlife transition. Levinson recognized, however, that a great deal is still to be learned about development after this stage. He ends his book by encouraging those who are attempting to develop theory and research on the periods following this stage of life.

Farrell and Rosenberg's Findings

Contrary to Levinson's position, some researchers feel that although midlife crises do occur in some individuals, they are not a universal part of adult development (Costa & McCrae, 1980). Further, they believe that because middle-aged adults have such a strong tendency to deny the experience of crises of any kind, it is difficult to confirm or deny the existence of a midlife crisis simply by taking adults' responses at face value. When interviewed or when completing questionnaires, adults may consciously or unconsciously give the socially desirable responses. To get a true understanding of adult development, it may be necessary to look beyond the answers and narratives adults give.

Figure 18.3
Typology of responses to middle-age stress.

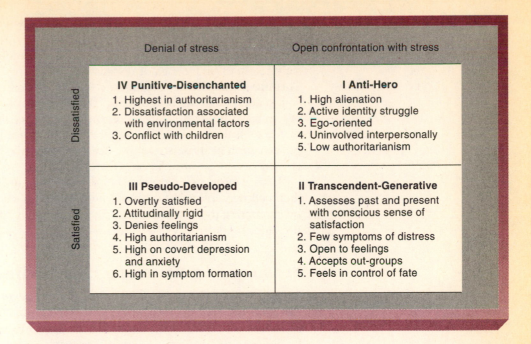

	Denial of stress	Open confrontation with stress
Dissatisfied	**IV Punitive-Disenchanted** 1. Highest in authoritarianism 2. Dissatisfaction associated with environmental factors 3. Conflict with children	**I Anti-Hero** 1. High alienation 2. Active identity struggle 3. Ego-oriented 4. Uninvolved interpersonally 5. Low authoritarianism
Satisfied	**III Pseudo-Developed** 1. Overtly satisfied 2. Attitudinally rigid 3. Denies feelings 4. High authoritarianism 5. High on covert depression and anxiety 6. High in symptom formation	**II Transcendent-Generative** 1. Assesses past and present with conscious sense of satisfaction 2. Few symptoms of distress 3. Open to feelings 4. Accepts out-groups 5. Feels in control of fate

The work of Farrell and Rosenberg (1981) is a good example. They interviewed and gave a battery of personality tests to two groups of men: those between the ages of 25 and 30 and those between the ages of 38 and 48. Included in that battery was a midlife crisis scale developed for the purpose. They asked the participants about tasks central to midlife development, such as:

- Assuming the role of "patron" of the family

- Becoming a source of financial/emotional stability for younger and older generations

- Learning to live with changing physical abilities and accepting unfulfilled dreams of youth

These tasks probably sound familiar, since they are similar to some in Levinson's theory.

Farrell and Rosenberg analyzed the responses of the men in their study in a manner radically different from Levinson. They listened to the responses and then assessed the responses on two dimensions: ability to confront stress and amount of life satisfaction. Figure 18.3 is a summary of the four personality types that result from their findings.

The researchers confirmed the idea that many middle-aged men work hard at denying feelings of weakness or distress. Glaring differences across socioeconomic lines were also found: Those who typically confronted their stressful feelings (types I and II) were much more likely to be affluent than those who had not (types III and IV).

Men who deny stress showed manifestations of coping with it in different ways. Those whose responses were grouped in the category of Pseudo-Developed (III) represented themselves as being similar to the Transcendent-Generative, with "cheery self-confidence," when really they were not. Responses of this type were interpreted to be "masks" of true feelings. "We call the men's reports of their experiences 'masks' to emphasize our suspicion that the subjective experience of the men and their presentations of self are not necessarily congruent with each other" (Farrell & Rosenberg, 1981, p. 31). The researchers hypothesize that these men create a highly structured life, one that leaves little room for self-exploration or expression.

The fourth type of response, termed Punitive Disenchanted (IV), was also one that avoided confronting the stress of midlife. Responses of this type reflect a faulty interpretation of feelings. Men in this category interpreted personal feelings of dissatisfaction to be feelings of dissatisfaction with others and the world around them. This transformation of feelings is called *projection* (see chapter 2).

In contrast to the findings of other theorists, Farrell and Rosenberg's findings do not suggest the existence of a universal midlife crisis per se. They suggest, instead, that universal stresses occur at midlife and thus each man must create a buffer from or resolution of those stressors. "For most men, then, the movement toward midlife is a process of self-insulation" (Farrell & Rosenberg, 1981, p. 212).

Either most men experience a distinct crisis during their early forties that alters their self-perceptions and behavior (as Levinson says), or most react to middle age by attempting to "insulate" themselves from reality (as Farrell and Rosenberg argue). It cannot be both ways. What do you think?

Seasons of a Woman's Life: Levinson

In recent years, Levinson (1990b) turned his attention to female progress toward maturity. For his research, he selected three groups of women between the ages of 35 and 45. One-third are homemakers whose lives have followed the traditional family-centered pattern, one-third are teachers at the college level, and one-third are businesswomen. He saw these women as representing a continuum from the domestic orientation to the public orientation, with the college teachers being somewhere in between. Each of the 45 women has been interviewed eight to ten times by the research staff (half of whom are female) for a total of 15 to 20 hours.

Of greatest importance is the finding that females go through a sequence of stages very similar to the stages experienced by the males who were studied. Each gender may be seen as going through an alternating series of structure-building and structure-changing stages. Levinson found, for example, that men in their late thirties want to "become their own man." He also found that at just this time, women desire to "become their own woman"; that is, they want greater affirmation both from the people in their world and from themselves.

Although male and female growth toward maturity may be in similar stages, Levinson and his associates also believed that major differences exist between the genders within these similar stages. Sociohistorical differences are important. For women, the central themes are gender splitting, the traditional marriage enterprise, and the emerging gender revolution.

Gender Splitting

All societies support the idea that a clear difference should exist between what is considered appropriate for males and for females: **Gender splitting** appears to be universal. Women's lives have traditionally been devoted to the domestic sphere; men's to the public sphere. Human societies have seen a need for females to stay at home to protect the small number of offspring (compared with other species) while the male goes about being the "provisioner" (getting the resources the family needs outside of the home).

The Traditional Marriage Enterprise

In the final analysis, everyone gets married because they believe they can have a better life by doing so. Some exceptions may occur, but they are probably rare. At any rate, the main goal of the **traditional marriage enterprise** is to form and maintain a family. Gender splitting is seen as contributing to this goal.

Being supportive of the husband's "public" role—that is, getting resources for the family—is seen by the woman as a significant part of her role. When she goes

In what ways would you expect midlife transitions to differ for men and women?

Gender splitting

Levinson's term; all societies support the idea that there should be a clear difference between what is considered appropriate for males and for females; gender splitting appears to be universal.

Traditional marriage enterprise

Levinson's term. The main goal of this type of marriage is to form and maintain a family.

to work, this goal is not largely different. Levinson reported that it is still a source of conflict when a female does get to be the boss. Women pay a heavy price for the security this role affords. Many find it dangerous to develop a strong sense of self.

The Gender Revolution

But the meanings of gender are changing and becoming more similar. This is because young and middle-aged adults have so much more work to do. The increase in life expectancy has created a large group, the elderly, who consume more than they produce. This, together with the decrease in birth rate, has brought many more women out of the home and into the workplace. Two other factors have also been at work in creating the **gender revolution:** the divorce rate, which has reached 50 percent, and the increase in the educational levels of women.

In his study of women, Levinson found support for the existence of the same stages and a similar midlife crisis as for men (Levinson, 1986). A major study of women's development (Reinke & others, 1985) used a methodology similar to Levinson's and found important transitions in the lives of women, but not exclusively clustered around the midlife period (ages 40 to 45). Instead, women described important transitions in their lives at ages 30, 40, and 60.

Interestingly, Reinke found a universal turning point for women to occur between the ages of 27 and 30. Among women in their twenties and thirties, 80 percent of those with preschool children experienced a major transition, and of these, 50 percent were between the ages of 27 and 30. Women who manifested the transition were more likely to have been employed outside their home in their midtwenties (63%) than women who did not manifest the transition. The 27- to 30-year-old transition period was characterized by personal disruption, reassessment, and reorientation. The transition lasted an average of 2.7 years and generally ended in increased life satisfaction. Many women in their early forties also manifested a transition that included decreases in marital satisfaction and increases in assertiveness. The transition was not as widespread as the transition occurring at age 30 and seemed to be tied to children growing up.

Their data led Reinke and associates to conclude that transitions in a woman's life may be integrally tied to family life cycle. "My research on women suggests that the course of relationships exerts a greater press on women's development than does chronological age" (Reinke & others, 1985, p. 275).

Gender revolution
Levinson's term; the meanings of gender are changing and becoming more similar.

For women, an important transition appears to occur at about 30 years of age. The transition involves a period of self-evaluation that usually leads to greater satisfaction with life.

We are, in Levinson's opinion, at a cultural crossroads. The old division of female homemakers and male providers is breaking down, but no clear new direction has yet appeared. Researchers will be watching this dramatic change closely.

A MULTICULTURAL VIEW

Does Having a "Midlife Crisis" Depend on Your Ethnic Background?

Over the years, a number of researchers have noticed that people of color are less likely to report having had a "midlife crisis" than are whites. A number of hypotheses have been proposed as to why this might be so (can you guess what might be?). In her extensive review of the literature, however, Gallagher (1994) refuted this conclusion. She believed that encountering a midlife crisis depends mainly on one's socioeconomic status, and the higher that is, the more likely is the individual to feel that she or he has been through such an experience. Since persons of color are more likely to be in the lower socioeconomic level, they are less likely to report the experience:

■ Midlife crises are an affliction of the relatively affluent: rosy illusions are easier to maintain when a person is already somewhat shielded from reality.

Just as childhood is often constricted among the poor, who early in life face adult realities and burdens, so middle age may be eclipsed by a premature old age brought on by poverty and poor health. Among working-class people, for whom strength and stamina may mean earning power, middle age may begin at thirty-five rather than the forty-five often cited by respondents drawn from the sedentary middle class.

In Gallagher's view, then, just as "the moratorium of youth" we considered in chapter 11 is mainly experienced by middle- and upper-class adolescents, the so-called midlife crisis is primarily a problem for those who have the time and money to afford it. Can you think of any other life crises that may pertain only to one socioeconomic group? How about one ethnic group?

Both Gould and Levinson operated from the viewpoint of psychology. The next theory is that of a psychiatrist, most of whom are trained in the Freudian tradition. As we shall see, that makes for a rather different view of adult personality development.

Adaptations to Life: Vaillant

The subtitle of George Vaillant's book *Adaptation to Life* (1977) is "How the Best and the Brightest Came of Age." Vaillant's claim that the subjects of his study were among the smartest young men of their time seems to be justified. He has investigated mountains of data collected on a carefully selected group of students from Harvard University's classes of 1939 through 1944. The investigation included 260 white males.

The young men were selected because of the superiority of their bodies, minds, and personalities. A major consideration was that each subject be highly success oriented. Although their intelligence was not greatly higher than that of other students at Harvard, almost two-thirds of them graduated with honors (as compared with one-fourth of their classmates), and three-fourths went on to graduate school.

Almost all had solid, muscular builds and were in excellent health. Their average height was 70 inches, and their average weight was 160 pounds. Interestingly, 98 percent were right-handed. If the current theory is correct (Dacey, 1989a), persons dominated by the left side of the brain (which is indicated by right-handedness) tend to be intelligent but not very imaginative. Left-handed people are thought to be more creative. It would be interesting to know how creatively productive this group of men has been, but because he was interested only in their mental health, Vaillant has not addressed this question.

Almost 20 hours of physical, mental, and psychological tests were administered to the men. Their brain waves were recorded, and anthropologists measured each man to determine his body type, although these last two measurements had little bearing on the results of the study. Finally, the family history of each of the subjects was carefully recorded. Using this voluminous data, Vaillant set out to describe the personal development of these special people.

As in the theories of Sigmund Freud and Erik Erikson, defense mechanisms are important in Vaillant's explanation of the mental health of these subjects. He believes that everyone uses defense mechanisms regularly. Thus defense mechanisms can range all the way from serious psychopathology to perfectly reasonable "adaptations to life." As he puts it:

> ■ These intrapsychic styles of adaptation have been given individual names by psychiatrists (projection, repression, and sublimation are some well-known examples). . . . In this book, the so-called mechanisms of psychoanalytic theory will often be referred to as coping or adaptive mechanisms. This is to underscore the fact that defenses are healthy more often than they are psychopathological. (1977, p. 7)

On the basis of his data, Vaillant concluded that adaptive mechanisms, as he calls them, are as important to the quality of life as any other factor. Nevertheless, he does not challenge Freud's definition; that is, these mechanisms are subconscious defenses of the ego (see chapter 2). Vaillant makes a number of generalizations about these mechanisms on the basis of his observations. He believes that they

- are not inherited;
- do not run in families;
- are not related to mental illness in the family;
- cannot be taught;
- are discrete from one another; and
- are dynamic and reversible.

Vaillant believes that four other generalizations also emerge from the data:

- Life is shaped more by good relationships than by traumatic occurrences during childhood.
- The constantly changing nature of human life may qualify a behavior as mentally ill at one time and adaptive at another.
- To understand the healthiness or psychopathology of the individual, it is necessary to understand what part these adaptive mechanisms play in the healing process. Furthermore, most people have a natural tendency to progress to higher-level mechanisms as they grow toward maturity.
- Since human development continues into adulthood, it is necessary to have a longitudinal study such as this to understand that development.

Generativity versus Stagnation: Erikson

Let us turn now to a theory that is considered a classic. In this final section, we will put forth Erikson's explanation of personality development in middle adulthood: generativity versus stagnation.

Generativity means the ability to be useful to ourselves and to society. As in the industry stage, the goal here is to be productive and creative. However, productivity in the industry stage is a means of obtaining recognition and material reward. In the generativity stage, which takes place during middle adulthood, one's productivity is aimed at being helpful to others. The act of being productive is itself rewarding, regardless of recognition or reward. Erikson added that generativity is

> ■ that middle period of the life cycle when existence permits you and demands you to consider death as peripheral and to balance its certainty with the only happiness that is lasting: to increase, by whatever is yours to give, the good will and the higher order in your sector of the world. (1978, p. 124)

Generativity
Erikson's term for the ability to be useful to ourselves and to society.

Generativity, Erikson's term for the major goal of the middle years of adulthood, includes coming to understand those who are different from you and desiring to make a lasting contribution to their welfare.

Although Erikson certainly approved of the procreation of children as an important part of generativity for many people, he did not believe that everyone needs to become a parent in order to be generative. For example, some people, who from misfortune or because of special and genuine gifts in other directions, cannot apply this drive to offspring of their own and instead apply it to other forms of altruistic concern and creativity (Erikson, 1968).

At this stage of adulthood some people become bored, self-indulgent, and unable to contribute to society's welfare; they fall prey to **stagnation.** Such adults act as though they were their own only child. People who have given birth to children may fail to be generative in their parenthood and come to resent the neediness of their offspring.

Stagnation

According to Erikson, the seventh stage of life (middle-aged adulthood) tends to be marked either by generativity or by stagnation—boredom, self-indulgence, and the inability to contribute to society.

Although generativity can provide great satisfaction to those who reach it, several theorists (e.g., Roazen, 1976) have suggested that the majority of adults never do. Many males appear to become fixed in the industry stage, doing their work merely to obtain the social symbols of success—a big car, a fancy house, a huge television. Many women, these theorists suggest, may become fixed in the identity stage, confused and conflicted about their proper role in life. They rarely achieve intimacy and therefore rarely reach the stage of generativity.

Becoming generative is not easy. It depends on the successful resolution of the six preceding Eriksonian crises we have described in this book. People who are able to achieve generativity have a chance to reach the highest level of personhood in Erikson's hierarchy: integrity. We will examine that stage in chapter 20.

As you can see, all of the theories described thus far hold that as we age we go through many important changes. Let us turn now to the other side of the coin: the position that the adult personality is made up of traits that remain continuously stable, in most cases, throughout adulthood.

Continuous Traits Theory

In their extensive study of men at midlife, McCrae and Costa (1984) found no evidence of personality change over the adult years, nor any evidence for the existence of any midlife crisis. The research measured the stability of several different personality traits over a period of six years (longitudinal study) and also looked at those same personality traits in a cross-age population (cross-sectional analysis).

At the first testing, McCrae and Costa administered several personality inventories to men ranging in age from 17 to 97. When they combined the data they gathered from the inventories, they defined three major personality traits that they feel govern the adult personality: neuroticism, extroversion, and openness to experience. Each of those three traits is supported by six subtraits or 'facets' (see figure 18.4). The three major traits together are termed the **NEO model of personality.** The researchers found relative stability of those traits throughout male adulthood.

NEO model of personality

McCrae and Costa's theory that there are three major personality traits, which they feel govern the adult personality.

Neuroticism is described as an index of instability or a predisposition for some kind of breakdown under stress. Behaviors associated with this trait include the following:

- A tendency to have more physical and psychiatric problems (without medical problems)

- Greater tendencies to smoke and drink

- More general unhappiness and dissatisfaction with life

Extroversion, the tendency to be outgoing and social, is the second global trait found by McCrae and Costa. Extroversion seems to spill over into almost all aspects of the personality, since it implies an overriding interest in people and social connections.

Openness to experience, the third general trait, is exactly that: an openness to new ideas, fantasies, actions, feelings, and values. Overall, a lack of rigidity in regard to the unfamiliar characterizes openness to experience.

Figure 18.4

Schematic representation of the three-dimensional, 18-facet NEO (neuroticism, extroversion, openness) model.

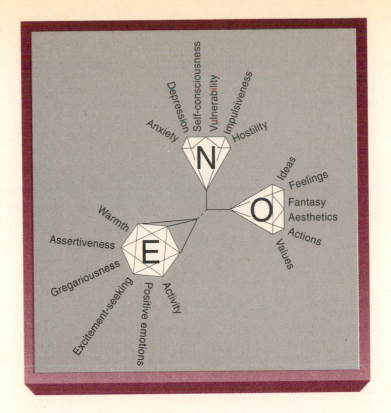

The researchers note that although habits, life events, opinions, and relationships may change over the lifespan, the basic personality of an individual does not (McCrae & Costa, 1984). They feel that people who experience a midlife crisis probably have the personality makeup that biases them toward that behavior. The Costa and McCrae research, however, lacks consideration of the reciprocal nature of influence of a person with his or her environment. Even so, the rigor of McCrae and Costa's work warrants careful consideration from those interested in personality development across the lifespan.

WHAT'S YOUR VIEW?

TRAITS VERSUS STAGES

As you can see, a clear conflict exists between the trait researchers and the positions of the four stage theorists. It appears that they cannot both be correct, although the truth may lie somewhere in between. We have devoted much more space to the stage theories. In part this is because they have received so much attention in the popular press, as well as by scholars. It is also because

we are biased toward them. (It is certainly obvious throughout this book that we have a great deal of admiration for the ideas of Erikson.)

Whatever the case may be, the important thing is that, through discussion, further reading, and observation, you try to come to your own opinion. What do you think?

Another recent study that has looked at stability of traits across adult periods has been conducted by Dorothy Eichorn and her associates at Berkeley (1981; see also Sears & Sears, 1982). These researchers examined stability by looking at the relationship between traits in adolescence and in middle age. They found that middle-age blood pressure, goodness of health, IQ, IQ gain, political ideology, and drinking problems can be predicted fairly well in adolescence. Other traits, however, such as the status of marriage and psychological health, are less stable.

⚜ Guided Review ⚜

7. Two theoretical positions influence the study of personality: Trait theorists believe that adults remain basically the same, and _____ theorists believe that the adult is constantly changing and evolving.

8. Roger Gould, a stage theorist, found through his research that healthy personality development depends on the rejection of major _____ _____ .

9. In his discussion on midlife transition, Daniel Levinson identifies four polarities that are a source of division in the life of a middle-adult man. These polarities are young/old, destruction/creation, masculinity/femininity, and _____ .

10. From his studies on women, Levinson stated that the stages of women's development are similar to the stages for men, but he found three women's themes: _____ _____ , the traditional marriage enterprise, and the emerging gender revolution.

11. Farrell and Rosenberg's research on adult men suggests that a universal midlife crisis does not exist. Instead, they describe midlife _____ that men need to deal with.

12. As a result of his study on a group of Harvard men, Vaillant suggests that life is shaped by good relationships and that the changing nature of life means that a behavior might be considered indicative of a mental illness at one time and _____ at other times.

13. Erikson saw generativity (the ability to be useful to ourselves and society) versus _____ as the challenge for middle adulthood.

14. According to McCrae and Costa, _____ , extroversion, and openness to experience are the three traits they found to be stable in middle-age adult males.

Patterns of Work

As the "baby boom" generation enters middle age, many changes are beginning to occur in the workplace. Fewer and fewer new young workers will be available to enter the workforce. Employers will find themselves with a larger number of older workers. This shrinking labor pool is leading many employers to pay more attention than ever to the welfare of their employees. Some of the new issues of the 1990s are child care, elderly care, home-based work, nontraditional work schedules, and the spiraling cost of health-care benefits.

Employers are also attempting more creative approaches to development and training. In the past, employers have tended to spend the majority of their training and development resources on younger employees. Perhaps this is just a matter of employers being unaware of the problems and concerns of their older employees. Or perhaps money and time invested in younger employees were considered better spent than that on older employees.

But in recent years, a trend has emerged among employers to recognize some of the concerns of middle-aged employees. Among them are the following:

- Awareness of advancing age and awareness of death

- Awareness of body changes related to aging

- Knowing how many career goals have been or will be attained

- Search for new life goals

- Marked change in family relationships

- Change in work relationships

Answers

7. stage   8. false assumptions   9. attachment/separation   10. gender splitting   11. stressors   12. adaptive   13. stagnation   14. neuroticism

- Sense of skills and abilities becoming outdated

- Feeling of decreased job mobility and increased concern for job security

Businesses have responded to these issues with continuing education, seminars, workshops, degree programs, and other forms of retraining. As the labor pool shrinks, the welfare of the older, established workforce becomes more valuable. Another concern is the midcareer crisis.

A MULTICULTURAL VIEW

Work in the Lives of African American and White Women

What does a career contribute to a woman's identity? "The power to earn one's way has a profound effect on one's inner landscape" (Baruch & others, 1983, p. 152). For both African American and white women, occupational status was positively associated with perceived control. African American women with higher than average personal earnings reported greater feelings of control, and white women with higher than average earnings reported greater life satisfaction (Crohan & others, 1989). The self-esteem and personal worth of middle-aged African American women has been found to be determined by their ability to be good providers

(Coleman & others, 1987). This is because few African American women are solely homemakers. Furthermore, an even higher percentage of African Americans are single parents.

This does not mean that African American women are more eager to work than white women (Crohan & others, 1989). It is the degree of control they feel over their jobs that contributes to the well-being of both groups of women (Adelman, 1987). The major concern of the educated midlife women interviewed by Grossman and Chester (1990) was their economic vulnerability, despite the fact that most were working.

Special Problems of the Working Woman

It is probably not news to you that the problems facing women in the workplace are different from those of men. But what actual difference does being a woman make? Some recent research has been unable to establish clear differences (Northcott & Lowe, 1987), but many more reveal important differences. The difficulties working women face have been studied intensively in recent years (Amato, 1987; Galambos & Lerner, 1987; Smart & Ethington, 1987). A review of this literature reveals the following four major problem areas.

Sexual Harassment on the Job

Sexual harassment can take many forms (Garvey, 1986), such as verbal sexual suggestions or jokes; leering; "accidentally" brushing against your body; a "friendly" pat, squeeze, or pinch, or arm around you; catching you alone for a quick kiss; explicit propositions backed by the threat of losing your job; and forced sexual relations (Faier, 1979).

Although harassment of professional women has received considerable media attention in recent years (e.g., Justice Thomas's nomination hearings), blue-collar women have even more difficulty with this problem. Many women who work in the trades report that their marriages are strained by their jobs; not only do their husbands not like their nontraditional occupation, but they are unwilling to support them against the sex discrimination and harassment they suffer (Dinnerstein, 1992; Grossman & Chester, 1990).

Most blue-collar women have been verbally harassed (88%), and many have been pinched, fondled, and otherwise physically assaulted (28%). They have little support from their supervisors; in fact, 20 percent of the perpetrators are the supervisors. These women also suffer discrimination: Their competence is questioned, the job requirements are stiffer, they are denied advancement, and necessary job information is withheld. They have little support for their complaints (Schroedel, 1990).

What are some of the obstacles faced by women entering non-traditional jobs and careers (e.g., engineering)?

Equal Pay and Promotion Criteria

The Equal Pay Act was passed in 1963 and states that men and women in substantially similar jobs in the same company should get the same pay. Under this act, the complainant may remain anonymous while the complaint is being investigated.

In spite of these legal protections, women make less money on the average than men and are less often promoted to management-level jobs. Why? Male prejudice is one reason, no doubt, but there are probably others. Among the several explanations that have been offered (but for which little current research evidence exists) are: Women may be absent more from work due to illness of children and are much more likely to take parenthood leave; many women seem to have greater anxiety about using computers than males; and women take less math in school.

Career and/or Family

The research reported on the dual-career family in Chapter 16 applies here as well.

Travel Safety

Working women are exposed to a considerable number of hazards to which the average housewife and mother is not subjected. Crimes against women are no longer limited to the inner city but now occur in suburban and even rural areas with a high frequency.

These four problems are gradually being recognized in the workplace, and there is hope that they will be alleviated.

The Midcareer Crisis

Considerable attention is now being given to the crisis many people undergo in the middle of their careers. For some it is a problem of increasing anxiety, which is troublesome but no serious problem. For others the difficulty is truly threatening.

A number of changes in the middle years are not caused by work: the awareness of advancing age, the death of parents and other relatives, striking changes in family relationships, and a decrease in physical ability. Other changes are entirely work related.

Coming to Terms with Attainable Career Goals

By the time a person reaches the age of 40 in a professional or managerial career, it is pretty clear whether she or he will make it to the top of the field. If individuals haven't reached their goals by this time, most adjust their level of aspirations and, in some cases, start over in a new career. Many, however, are unable to recognize that they have unrealistic aspirations and thus suffer from considerable stress.

Even people whose career patterns are stable, such as Catholic priests, often have a midcareer letdown. Nor is this crisis restricted to white-collar workers. Many blue-collar workers, realizing that they have gone about as far as they are going to go on their jobs, suffer from depression.

This is also the time when family expenses, such as college education for teenage children, become great. If family income does not rise, this obviously creates a conflict, especially if the husband is the sole provider for the family. If the wife goes back to work, other types of stress often occur.

The Change in Work Relationships

Relationships with fellow employees obviously change when one has come to the top of one's career. Some middle-aged adults take a mentoring attitude toward younger employees, but others feel resentful toward the young because they still

Often employers are unwilling to spend money on the training of older workers.

have a chance to progress. When people reach their forties and fifties, they often try to establish new relationships with fellow workers, and this contributes to the sense of conflict.

A Growing Sense of Outdatedness

In many cases, an individual has to work so hard just to stay in a job that it is impossible to keep up-to-date. Sometimes a younger person, fresh from an extensive education, will join the firm and will know more about modern techniques than the middle-aged person does. These circumstances usually cause feelings of anxiety and resentment in the older employee because he or she is afraid of being considered incompetent.

Inability to Change Jobs

Age discrimination in employment starts as early as age 35 in some industries and becomes pronounced by age 45. A federal law against age discrimination in employment was passed in 1968 to ease the burden on the older worker, but to date the law has been poorly enforced on both the federal and state levels. Many employers get around the law simply by telling older applicants that they are "overqualified" for the available position.

The Generativity Crisis

Erikson suggests that people in the middle years ought to be in the generativity stage (discussed earlier in this chapter). This is a time when they should be producing something of lasting value, making a gift to future generations. In fact, this is definitely a concern for middle-aged workers. The realization that the time left to make such a contribution is limited can come with shocking force.

The generativity crisis is similar to the identity crisis of late adolescence in many ways. Both often produce psychosomatic symptoms such as indigestion and extreme tiredness. Middle-aged persons often get chest pains at this time. These symptoms are rarely caused by organic diseases in people younger than 50 and usually are due to a depressed state associated with career problems.

The resolution of this crisis, and of other types of crises that occur during early and middle adulthood, depends on how the person's personality has developed during this period. In the following section, we continue our examination of this topic, which began in chapter 16.

Some Suggestions for Dealing with the Midlife Crisis

Levinson and others have found that a fair number of workers experience a stressful midlife transition. One major way of dealing with it is for the middle-aged worker to help younger employees make significant contributions. Furthermore, companies are taking a greater responsibility for fostering continuing education of their employees. More equitable patterns of responsibilities in the home are also developing among dual-career middle-aged couples, although there are many exceptions (Coltrane & Ishii-Kuntz, 1992; Dancer & Gilbert, 1993).

We should continue the type of job transfer programs for middle-aged people that we now have for newer employees. Although sometimes the changes can be threatening, the move to a new type of job and the requisite new learning experiences can bring back a zest for work.

Perhaps the federal government should consider starting midcareer clinics. Such clinics could help workers reexamine their goals, consider job changes, and provide information and guidance. Another solution might be the establishment of "portable pension plans" that would move with workers from one company to another so they would not lose all they have built up when they change jobs.

Can you imagine any other remedies?

Guided Review

15. A number of concerns face middle-aged employees. These concerns include knowing how many career goals have been or will be reached, changes in family relationships, change in work relationships, feelings of decreased job _____ and concern for job _____ .

16. Some middle-aged workers may experience a _____ crisis upon the realization that there may be limited time remaining for them to make contributions for future generations.

17. Some of the problems facing women in the workplace are _____ _____ , equal pay, and travel safety.

18. Some women in the workplace experience _____ , resulting in a questioning of competence, tougher job requirements, and blocks to career advancement.

Answers

15. mobility, security 16. midlife 17. sexual harassment 18. discrimination

🌳 CONCLUSION

Dealing with change is as serious a challenge in midlife as at any other time. Learning new ways to get along with one's spouse, parents, siblings, and children is necessary at this time of life. Considerable debate occurs over whether personality changes much during this period. Some think it goes through a series of predictable changes; others view it as continuous with earlier life. Workers often experience a "midlife crisis" at this time, and women workers have an additional set of burdens to handle.

Yet with any luck, we make it safely through middle age and move on to late adulthood. In the next two chapters, we investigate the pluses and minuses of this development.

CHAPTER HIGHLIGHTS

Marriage and Family Relations

- Middle age offers a time for marriage reappraisal, which proves positive for most couples.
- Middle age is also a time when most people develop improved relationships with their parents, though in some cases the relationship begins to reverse itself when those parents become dependent on their middle-aged children.
- Sibling relationships have the potential to be the most enduring that a person can have, with the relationship between sisters being strongest. It is usually one of these sisters who cares for the elderly parents.
- Reducing the number of one's friends begins in early adulthood. A deepening of the friendships that remain begins in middle age and goes on throughout the rest of life.
- Liberalization of divorce laws has improved the position of women following divorce; however, Weitzman argues that serious inequity still exists.

Personality Development: Continuous or Changing?

- Research by trait theorists such as Kagan, and McCrae and Costa, generally supports the notion that human beings remain fairly stable throughout life.
- By contrast, theorists such as Erikson, Gould, Levinson, and Vaillant argue that human beings are best described as constantly changing and developing throughout life.
- According to Roger Gould, the major false assumption to be rejected during middle adulthood is that "there is no evil or death in the world. Everything sinister has been destroyed."
- Levinson suggested that most men go through a midlife transition in which they must deal with the polarities between young and old, masculinity and femininity, destruction and creation, and attachment and separation.
- Levinson also suggested that females go through a similar experience to that of males, with some notably different influences.
- Vaillant, in his study of the "smartest" young men of their time, concluded that adaptive mechanisms are very important to quality of life.

- Erikson's theory placed middle adulthood within the stage labeled "generativity versus stagnation." Generativity means the ability to be useful to ourselves and to society without concern for material reward.
- McCrae and Costa defined three major personality traits that they feel govern the adult personality: neuroticism, extroversion, and openness to experience.

Patterns of Work

- In recent years, a trend has emerged among employers to recognize some of the concerns of middle-aged employees.
- Four major problem areas are related to working women: sexual harassment on the job, equal pay and promotion criteria, career and/or family, and travel safety.
- Considerable attention is now being given to the crisis many people undergo in the middle of their careers.
- One major way of dealing with the midlife crisis is for the middle-aged worker to help younger employees make significant contributions.

KEY TERMS

WHAT DO YOU THINK?

1. What is the best way for middle-aged people to take care of their ailing, elderly parents?
2. What changes would you make in our divorce laws?
3. Would you agree that almost everyone has a midlife crisis, but they just deny it?
4. What are the main differences between male and female personality development?
5. Who's right, the stage theorists or the trait theorists?
6. What laws would you make to improve the workplace for women?

🌳 SUGGESTED READINGS

Breslin, J. (1986). *Table money*. New York: Ticknor & Fields. An empathetic tale of matrimony, alcoholism, and the struggle to attain maturity, focusing on a poor middle-aged Irish American couple.

Guest, J. (1976). *Ordinary people*. New York: Ballantine. The evocative story of the relationships among a middle-aged couple, their teenage son, and his psychiatrist.

Hansberry, L. (1959). *A raisin in the sun*. A moving drama portraying the inner lives of an African American family.

Updike, J. (1981). *Rabbit is rich*. New York: Knopf. The third in Updike's series about an ordinary American male. In this volume, Rabbit reaches middle age.

🌳 CHAPTER REVIEW TEST

1. Francis and Joan have drifted apart over the years but remain married to each other because of their children. Their relationship illustrates the
   a. functional marriage.
   b. practical marriage.
   c. functional divorce.
   d. emotional divorce.

2. According to Gottman and Krokoff's longitudinal research on marital interactions, those who tend most to avoid relational confrontations are
   a. divorcing couples.
   b. couples married for more than 25 years.
   c. husbands.
   d. wives.

3. What is the most frequently cited problem of middle-aged adult women?
   a. aging
   b. menopause
   c. caring for their children
   d. caring for their aging parents

4. Research suggests that the best indicator of a sibling relationship is
   a. proximity.
   b. frequency of contact.
   c. mutual caring for elderly parents.
   d. feelings of closeness.

5. Because the no-fault divorce laws do not account for an inequitable economic system, who suffers most financially by divorce?
   a. the middle-aged homemaker
   b. the career oriented woman
   c. the middle-aged father
   d. the adult children

6. The notion that adult personality changes over time is supported by
   a. stage theorists.
   b. transition theorists.
   c. trait theorists.
   d. lifespan theorists.

7. Trait theory is to _____ as stage theory is to _____ .
   a. lifespan development; stair step transition
   b. continuity in adult development; change in adult development
   c. change in adult development; continuity in adult development
   d. stair step transition; lifespan development

8. When Ahmad's law firm was destroyed by arson, he realized that, like it or not, there do exist people who commit evil acts of destruction. According to Roger Gould, Ahmad has
   a. faced an unpleasant reality.
   b. confronted a mistaken belief.
   c. rejected the major false assumption of midlife.
   d. adopted a major false assumption.

9. The _____ that occur during Levinson's midlife transition represent the continual struggle toward greater individuation.
   a. attachments
   b. separations
   c. level of intimacy
   d. polarities

10. Jim is dissatisfied with the world around him, although he is actually experiencing feelings of personal dissatisfaction. According to Farrell and Rosenberg, what is Jim's personality type?
    a. Anti-hero
    b. Pseudo-developed
    c. Transcendent-generative
    d. Punitive-disenchanted

11. The idea that a clear difference exists between what is appropriate for males and for females is referred to as
    a. gender splitting.
    b. the gender revolution.
    c. role strain.
    d. the traditional marriage.

12. In Vaillant's research on adaptations to life, he concluded that adaptive mechanisms are an important factor to
    a. a person's reactive mechanisms.
    b. a person's defense mechanisms.
    c. the quality of a person's life.
    d. a person's coping mechanisms.

13. According to Erikson, during the generativity stage one's productivity is aimed at
    a. career advancement.
    b. material rewards.
    c. being helpful to others.
    d. recognition.

14. McCrae and Costa defined three major personality types as neuroticism, extroversion, and
    a. introversion.
    b. openness to experience.
    c. outdatedness.
    d. None of the above.

15. Consequences of discrimination against women in the workplace include
    a. stiffer job requirements.
    b. inability to advance in their career.
    c. questioning of a woman's competence.
    d. All of the answers are correct.

16. When an accountant 20 years younger than Dan joined his marketing firm, Dan felt resentful and anxious because he feared he would be considered incompetent. Dan has a growing sense of
    a. job distress.
    b. outdatedness.
    c. the "gold watch" syndrome.
    d. job reluctance.

Answers

1.d 2.c 3.d 4.d 5.a 6.a 7.b 8.c 9.d 10.d 11.a 12.c 13.c 14.b 15.d 16.b

PART IX

Late Adulthood

As a white candle
In a holy place
So is the beauty
Of an aged face.

Joseph Campbell

Even when he was very old and ill, Winston Churchill's fabled sense of humor never left him. In addition, it was only in his later years that he found time to sharpen his artistic skills, which brought him world renown in that realm. He was an excellent example of how fruitful the last third of life can be.

A nd just as young people are all different, and middle-aged people are all different, so too are old people. We don't all have to be exactly alike. . . . There are all kinds of old people coping with a common condition, just as kids in puberty when their voices start cracking. . . . Every one of them is different. We old folks get arthritis, rheumatism, our teeth fall out, our feet hurt, our hair gets thin, we creak and groan. These are the physical changes, but all of us are different. And I personally feel that you follow pretty much the pattern of your younger years. I think that some people are born young and some people are born old and tired and gray and dull. . . . You're either a nasty little boy turned old man or a mean little old witch turned old or an outgoing, free-loving person turned old.

As for myself, I feel very excited about life and about people and color and books, and there is an excitement to everything that I guess some people never feel. . . . I have a lot of friends who are thirty-year-old clods. They were born that way and they'll die that way. . . . But me, I'm happy, I'm alive, and I want to live with as much enjoyment and dignity and decency as I can, and do it gracefully and my way if possible, as long as possible.

> Author M. F. K. Fisher, who died recently at 82
> Quoted in Berman and Goldman (1992)

■ A special session of the British House of Lords was being held to honor Winston Churchill on his ninetieth birthday. As he descended the stairs of the amphitheater, one member turned to another and said, "They say he's really getting senile." Churchill stopped, and leaning toward them, said in a stage whisper loud enough for many to hear, "They also say he's deaf!" ♣

Figure 19.1
Age distribution of United States
population, selected years

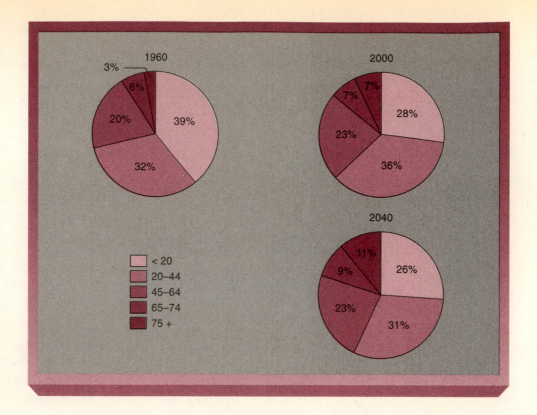

Although positive, these vignettes remind us of the stereotypes of old age as being a rather negative stage of life. Must growing old mean decline? Must the teeth and hair fall out, the eyes grow dim, the skin wrinkle and sag? Must intelligence, memory, and creativity falter? Must old age be so awful?

Or is there actually only a relatively slight decline in capacity, a decline greatly exaggerated by our values and presumptions? Many elderly people seem to be having the time of their lives! Could it be that the negative aspects of aging are largely the result of a self-fulfilling prophecy (people expect to deteriorate, so they stop trying to be fit, and then they do deteriorate)? Could most of us in our later years be as capable as those famous few who seem to have overcome age and remained vigorous into their nineties and beyond?

These questions concern most of the 23 million men and women over 65 who constitute 10 percent of our population today. In 1900 the over-65 population was 3 million, only 3 percent of the total. By the year 2040 it will have reached 20 percent (see figure 19.1). Such questions should also concern those of us who hope to join their ranks some day. In the next section we look at the answers to these questions, as revealed by considerable new research.

After reading chapter 19, you should be able to

- Compare the major physiological theories of aging.

- Determine the contribution of genetics and the environment to aging.

- Explain changes that occur in late adulthood related to reaction time and sensory abilities.

- Describe the ways in which the skeletal system, skin, teeth, and hair alter in appearance as people age.

- Evaluate the nature of the relationship of hormone balance to physical ability.

- Define Alzheimer's disease and identify several theories about its cause.

- List Gerson and associates' findings regarding the relationship between mental and physical health.

- Explain other factors in the relationship between cognition and aging.

- Appraise the theory known as terminal drop.

- Discuss Dacey's theory of creativity and list critical periods of life during which creative ability can be cultivated most effectively.

Must We Age and Die?

"Nothing is inevitable except death and taxes," the old saying goes. But is death inevitable? True, no one so far has attained immortality; the oldest known person in the United States, as certified by the Social Security Administration, is 114 years old. And, of course, the vast majority of the people who have ever lived are dead.

But not all organisms die. Some trees alive today are known to be more than 2,500 years old; they have aged but show no sign of dying. Bacteria apparently are able to live indefinitely, as long as they have the requirements for their existence. The fact is, we are not sure why we age, and until we are, we cannot be certain that aging and death are absolutely inevitable. If fact, recent cover stories in the popular press (e.g., Darrack, 1992) have trumpeted as yet unpublished research that offers hope that aging can be slowed, stopped, or even reversed! Let's look now at the three types of explanations of aging that have been documented (Spence, 1989): physiological, genetic, and environmental aspects of aging.

Physiological Theories of Aging

It is apparent that organisms inherit a tendency to live for a certain length of time. An animal's durability depends on the species it belongs to. The average human lifespan of approximately 70 years is the longest of any mammal. Elephants, horses, hippopotamuses, and asses are known to live as long as 50 years, but most mammals die much sooner.

Some doctors are fond of stating that "no one ever died of old age." This is true. People die of some physiological failure that is more likely to occur the older one gets. One likely explanation of aging, then, is that the various life-support systems gradually weaken. Illness and death come about as a cumulative result of these various weaknesses. Seven different physiological factors have been suggested as accounting for this process.

Wear and Tear Theory

The **wear and tear theory** seems the most obvious explanation for aging, but there is actually little evidence for it. To date, no research has clearly linked early deterioration of organs with either hard work or increased stress alone.

A complex interaction, however, may be involved. It is known that lower rates of metabolism are linked to longer life and that certain conditions, such as absence of rich foods, cause a lower metabolism. Therefore, the lack of the "good life" may prolong life. On the other hand, it is also known that poor people who seldom get to eat rich foods tend to die at an earlier age than middle-class or wealthy people. Therefore, the evidence on this theory is at best conflicting.

Aging by Program

According to the **aging by program** theory, we age because it is programmed into us. It is hard to understand what evolutionary processes govern longevity (if any). For example, the vast majority of animals die at or before the end of their reproductive period, but human females live 20 to 30 years beyond the end of their reproductive cycles. This may be related to the capacities of the human

This olive tree found in Greece is more than 2,500 years old. Do you think it's possible that it might live forever?

Wear and tear theory
The theory that aging is due to the cumulative effects of hard work and lifelong stress.

Aging by program
The theory that all animals seem to die when their "program" dictates.

brain. Mead (1972) argued that this extra period beyond the reproductive years has had the evolutionary value of helping to keep the children and grandchildren alive. For example, in times when food is scarce, older people may remember where it was obtained during the last period of scarcity. On the other hand, it may be that we humans have outwitted the evolutionary process and, due to our medical achievements and improvements in lifestyle, are able to live on past our reproductive usefulness.

Another enduring hypothesis, proposed by Birren (1960), is known as the "counterpart" theory. According to this concept, factors in human existence that are useful in the earlier years become counterproductive in later years. An example is the nonreplaceability of most cells in the nervous system. The fact that brain cells are not constantly changing enhances memory and learning abilities in the earlier years, but it also allows the nervous system to weaken because dead cells are not replaced.

Spence (1989) suggested that the hypothalamus may well be an "aging chronometer" (p. 17), a "timer" that keeps track of the age of cells and determines how long they should keep reproducing. Although research on aging by program is in its infancy, some findings indicate that older cells may act differently from younger cells. Although cells in the nervous system and muscles do not reproduce themselves, all the other cells in the body do reproduce, at least to some extent. But these cells are able to reproduce only a limited number of times, and they are more likely to reproduce imperfectly as they get older. There is also reason to believe that reproduced older cells do not pass on information accurately through the DNA. This weakens the ability of older cells to continue high-level functioning.

Homeostatic Imbalance

Homeostatic imbalance
The theory that aging is due to a failure in the systems that regulate the proper interaction of the organs.

It may be a failure in the systems that regulate the proper interaction of the organs, rather than wear of the organs themselves, that causes aging and ultimately death. These homeostatic (feedback) systems are responsible, for example, for the regulation of the sugar and adrenalin levels in the blood. Apparently there is not a great deal of difference in the systems of the young and the old when they are in a quiet state. It is when stress is put on the systems (death of a spouse, loss of a job, a frightening experience) that we see the effects of the elderly **homeostatic imbalance.** The older body simply isn't as effective, qualitatively or quantitatively, in reacting to these stresses. Figure 19.2 shows graphically the relationship between problems with the homeostatic systems and the competence of the organism to react effectively to dangers in the environment.

Collagen
The major connective tissue in the body; it provides the elasticity in our skin and blood vessels.

Cross-Linkage Theory

Cross-linkage theory
A theory of aging stating that the proteins that make up a large part of cells are themselves composed of peptides. When cross-links are formed between peptides (a natural process of the body), the proteins are altered, often for the worse.

The proteins that make up a large part of cells are themselves composed of peptides. When cross-links are formed between peptides (a natural process of the body), the proteins are altered, often for the worse. For example, **collagen** is the major connective tissue in the body; it provides, for instance, the elasticity in our skin and blood vessels. When its proteins are altered, skin and vessels are adversely affected. This is known as the **cross-linkage theory.**

Accumulation of Metabolic Waste

Accumulation of metabolic waste
Waste products resulting from metabolism build up in various parts of the body, contributing greatly to the decreasing competence of those parts.

Although the connection has not been clearly established as yet, it may be that waste products resulting from metabolism build up in various parts of the body and contribute to the decrease in competence of those parts. Examples of this effect of the **accumulation of metabolic waste** are cataracts on the eye, cholesterol in the arteries, and brittleness of bones.

Figure 19.2

Homeostasis and health. Progressive stages of homeostasis from adjustment (health) to failure (death). In the healthy adult, homeostatic processes ensure adequate adjustment in response to stress, and even for a period beyond this stage compensatory processes are capable of maintaining overall function without serious disability. When stress is exerted beyond compensatory capacities of the organism, disability ensues in rapidly increasing increments to severe illness, permanent disability, and death. When this model is viewed in terms of homeostatic responses to stress imposed on the aged and to aging itself, a period when the body can be regarded as at the "limit of compensatory processes," it is evident that even minor stresses are not tolerable, and the individual moves rapidly into stages of breakdown and failure.

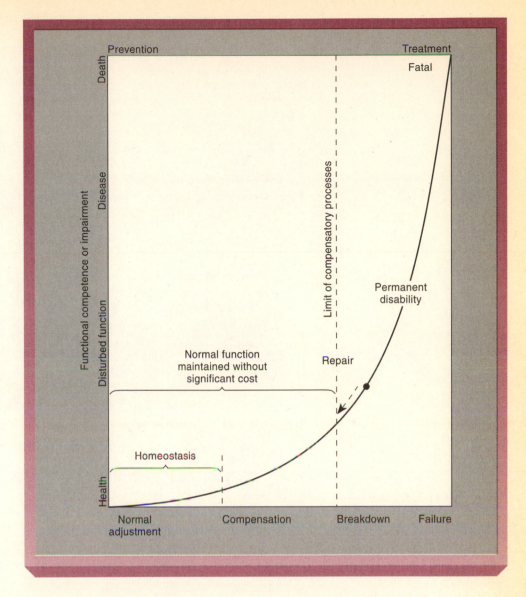

Autoimmunity

The process by which the immune system in the body rejects the body's own tissue.

Antigens

The substances in the blood that fight to kill foreign bodies.

Accumulation-of-errors theory

As cells die, they must synthesize new proteins to make new cells. As this is done, occasionally an error occurs. Over time, these errors mount up and may finally grow serious enough to cause organ failure.

Autoimmunity

With increasing age, there is increasing **autoimmunity,** the process by which the immune system in the body rejects the body's own tissue. Examples of this are rheumatoid arthritis, diabetes, vascular diseases, and hypertension. It may be that, with age, the body's tissues become more and more self-rejecting.

This may be the result of the production of new **antigens,** the substances in the blood that fight to kill foreign bodies. These new antigens may come about for one of two reasons:

- Mutations cause the formation of altered RNA or DNA.

- Some cells may be "hidden" in the body during the early part of life. When these cells appear later, the body does not recognize them as its own, and forms new antigens to kill them. This in turn may cause organ malfunction.

Accumulation of Errors

As cells die, they must synthesize new proteins to make new cells. As this is done, occasionally an error occurs. Over time, these errors mount up. This **accumulation of errors** may finally grow serious enough to cause organ failure.

Genetic Theories of Aging

Gene theory
The theory that aging is due to certain harmful genes.

Gene theory also suggests that aging is programmed but says that the program exists in certain harmful genes. As Spence (1989) explained it,

 perhaps there are genes which direct many cellular activities during the early years of life that become altered in later years, thus altering their function. In their altered state, the genes may be responsible for the functional decline and structural changes associated with aging. (p. 19)

Which of the explanations of why we age and die do you find most persuasive?

Whatever the reason, little doubt exists that genes affect how long we live. Kallman and Jarvik's (1959) research into identical twins still offers strong evidence of this. They found that monozygotic twins (those born from the same egg) have more similar lengths of life than do dizygotic twins (those born from two eggs). This effect is illustrated in figures 19.3 and 19.4.

Figure 19.3
One-egg twins at the ages of 12, 17, 67, and 91 years (note the long separation of these twins between the ages of 18 and 66).

Figure 19.4
One-egg twins at the ages of 5, 20, 55, and 86 years

Effects of the Natural Environment on Aging

Our genes and the physiology of our organs greatly affect the length of our lives. This may be seen in the extreme accuracy with which insurance companies are able to predict the average number of deaths at a particular age. A mathematical formula to predict the number of deaths within a population was produced as early as 1825 by Gomertz. The formula is still quite accurate except for the early years of life.

Today many fewer deaths occur in early childhood, since vaccines have eliminated much of the danger of diseases at this age. This shows that the natural environment is also an important factor in the mortality rate. Many of today's elderly would have died in childhood had they been born in the early part of the nineteenth century.

Considering mortality rates for specific cultures rather than world population shows the effects of the environment more specifically. Starvation in Africa and earthquakes in Guatemala obviously had a tragic effect on the mortality rates of those two countries. A number of authors have reported on the effects of radiation (Demoise & Conrad, 1972; Spence, 1989). Some evidence indicates that the nuclear testing in the Pacific in the 1950s is affecting the aging process of some of the residents there. Little or no evidence exists, however, to suggest that the radiation we are all exposed to every day is having any impact on aging. It remains to be seen if events such as the nuclear accident at Three Mile Island will have adverse effects.

Other Modifiers of Ability

In addition to genetic, physiological, and natural environmental factors that indirectly affect the individual's rate of aging, other factors can modify a person's level of ability more directly. Many of these modifiers interact with one another in complex ways. Some of the major modifiers are training, practice, motivation, nutrition, organic malfunction, illness, injury, stress level, educational level, occupation, personality type, and socioeconomic status.

For example, although it appears that social networks (the number and extent of friendships a person has) do not directly affect the survival of elderly people, they are related to their quality of life. Within nursing homes, those who tend to be aggressive and verbally agitated have poor social networks and generally lack intimacy with their fellow patients. It is less clear whether the behavior causes the poor quality of network, or vice versa (Cohen-Mansfield & Marx, 1992). Socioeconomic factors such as amount of income and quality of housing do promote superior networks, however (Shahtahmasebi & others, 1992).

Figure 19.5 summarizes the relationships between the hypothesized factors that affect aging of physical and mental systems. These include two genetic, five physiological, and five environmental factors, as well as twelve other modifiers of human abilities. You could find no clearer example of the biopsychosocial model at work!

Figure 19.5

Influences on adult mental and
physical systems

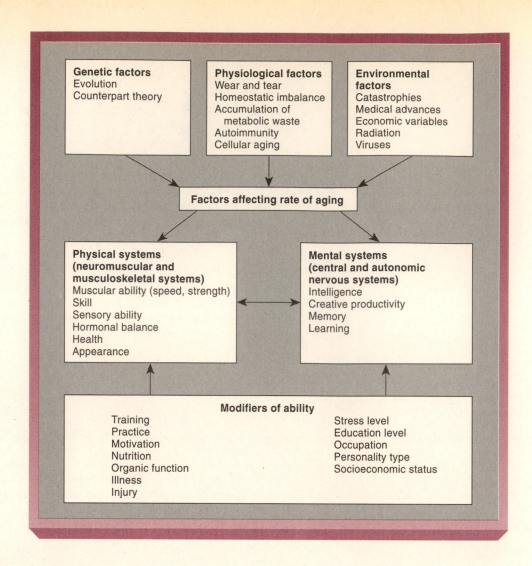

A MULTICULTURAL VIEW

The Role of Relatives in the Health of Persons of Color

A number of studies have indicated that although African American and Latino elderly are more susceptible than whites to health problems, if their relatives are involved in their lifestyle choices, this difference is greatly lessened. For example, persons of color are more susceptible to diabetes and hypertension, in part because they often have inadequate diets (too much sugar and fat, not enough fresh vegetables, etc.). Relatives can make sure that appropriate foods are purchased and properly prepared. They can also provide informal health care and intervene with health services to ensure that help is provided to the elderly when needed.

More recent research (Krause & Wray, 1991) indicates, however, that when these relatives themselves are not knowledgeable about appropriate health procedures such as dietary concerns, they can do more harm than good. What is needed is a concerted effort to teach relatives and others on whom the elderly depend for health assistance the information they need to do the job well.

Guided Review

1. Theorists have proposed three generic explanations for aging and death: physiological aspects, _____ aspects, and environmental aspects.

2. Within the physiological aspects one of the explanations is called the _____ and _____ theory, meaning that hard work and stress gradually destroy body parts.

3. The other physiological aspects are: aging by program, homeostatic imbalance, _____ theory, accumulation of metabolic waste, autoimmunity, and accumulation of errors.

4. The impact of the environment on aging and death helps us understand that our genes and the _____ of our organs affects the length of our lives.

5. According to Spence, a follower of the aging by program theory, the _____ may serve as a timer that keeps track of the age of cells and determines how long our cells should keep reproducing.

Before reading the next section, try your hand at the true–false test on the topic of aging in the following box.

AN APPLIED VIEW

The Facts on Aging Quiz

Mark the items *T* for true or *F* for false.

1. A person's height tends to decline in old age.

2. More older persons (over 65) have chronic illnesses that limit their activity than younger persons.

3. Older persons have more acute (short-term) illnesses than persons under 65.

4. Older persons have more injuries in the home than persons under 65.

5. Older workers have less absenteeism than younger workers.

6. The life expectancy of African Americans at age 65 is about the same as whites'.

7. The life expectancy of men at age 65 is about the same as women's.

8. Medicare pays over half of the medical expenses for the aged.

9. Social Security benefits automatically increase with inflation.

10. Supplemental Security Income guarantees a minimum income for needy aged.

11. The aged do not get their proportionate share (about 11%) of the nation's income.

12. The aged have higher rates of criminal victimization than persons under 65.

13. The aged are more fearful of crime than are persons under 65.

14. The aged are the most law abiding of all adult groups, according to official statistics.

15. There are two widows for each widower among the aged.

16. More of the aged vote than any other age group.

17. There are proportionately more older persons in public office than in the total population.

18. The proportion of African Americans among the aged is growing.

19. Participation in voluntary organizations (churches and clubs) tends to decline among the healthy aged.

20. The majority of the aged live alone.

21. About 3 percent less of the aged have incomes below the official poverty level than the rest of the population.

22. The rate of poverty among aged African Americans is about three times as high as among aged whites.

23. Older persons who reduce their activity tend to be happier than those who remain active.

24. When the last child leaves home, the majority of parents have serious problems adjusting to their "empty nest."

25. The proportion widowed is decreasing among the aged.

The key to the correct answers is simple: Alternating pairs of items are true or false (i.e., 1 and 2 are true, 3 and 4 are false, 5 and 6 are true, etc.; and 25 is true).

Answers

1. genetic 2. wear, tear 3. cross-linkage 4. physiology 5. hypothalamus

Physical Development

In this section, we consider development from the standpoints of reaction time, sensory abilities, other body systems, health, and appearance.

Reaction Time

It is obvious that physical skills decline as people grow older. This appears to be especially true of manual dexterity (Ringel & Simon, 1983). As one psychologist (Troll, 1975) puts it, "After about 33, hand and finger movements are progressively more clumsy" (p. 20). Although older people are able to perform short, coordinated manual tasks, a long series of tasks such as playing a stringed instrument becomes increasingly difficult for them. Famed Spanish guitarist Andrés Segovia and pianist Vladimir Horowitz are notable exceptions.

Seniors usually find that their coordination declines with the years, and so they often quit playing sports. Now there is a strong movement to reverse this trend.

Is this because the human nervous system is deteriorating through aging? To answer this question, psychologists have completed numerous studies of "reaction time," the time between the onset of a stimulus and the actual muscle activity that indicates a reaction to it. Studying reaction time is a scientific way of separating the effects of the central nervous system from the ability of the rest of the body to perform manual tasks.

In their classic review of this research, Elias and associates (1977) presented a decidedly positive picture. They reported that in simple discrimination tasks, where the subject is asked to respond to a sensory cue, essentially no decrease in reaction time occurs with age. Even when tasks are made more complicated, such as when a series of responses are called for or a number of stimuli must be matched, increases in reaction time with age are not great.

We can conclude that variables other than sheer neural or motor activities account for most change in physical skills over time. One example of an alternative factor is **ageism.** It has been shown that young people process and respond to the speech of older people in stereotypical ways such as "baby talk" or pandering (Giles & others, 1992). This type of prejudice is known as ageism. Several studies (e.g., Dellman-Jenkins & others, 1986; Harris & Fiedler, 1988) have found that ageism is as serious a problem today as it was several decades ago.

Ageism
The prejudice that the elderly are inferior to those who are younger.

Because they are often treated in a condescending way, elderly persons sometimes behave in a less competent manner than they are capable of. Ageism can be a prejudice that can seriously affect the elderly, lowering the quality of their lives. Furthermore, it robs our society of the diverse contributions that might otherwise be made by elderly persons, if their feelings of self-esteem and competence were not undermined by this prejudice.

What are some things you could do to fight this unfair attitude? For example, how might you help change the stereotype that senility is normal in the elderly?

Other factors that influence the reaction time of the elderly are motivation, depression, anxiety, response strategies, and response style. Older adults can improve their ability in any of these areas if they desire.

Sensory Abilities

Each of the five senses undergoes change in late adulthood. We look at some of those changes in the following paragraphs.

Vision

A number of problems may affect the eye as the adult ages (Eifrig & Simons, 1983). The lenses may become less transparent, thicker, and less elastic. This tends to result in farsightedness (Corso, 1971). The illumination required to perceive a stimulus also increases with age. Timiras (1972) stated that retina changes almost never occur before the age of 60, but Elias and associates (1977) argued that conditions that affect the retina, such as glaucoma, are often not detected, so problems may occur without causing noticeable changes in the eye.

Cataracts are the result of cloudy formations on the lens of the eye. They form very gradually and inhibit the passage of light through the eye. Cataracts are most common after the age of 60. If they become large enough, they can be removed, usually by laser surgery. At any rate, with the improvements in recent years in ophthalmology and optical surgery (Kornzweig, 1980), the declining ability of the human eye need not greatly affect vision in older age (with the single exception of poor night vision, which hampers driving).

WHAT'S YOUR VIEW?

WHAT SHOULD HAPPEN WHEN THE ELDERLY LOSE THEIR LICENSE?

By 2020, up to one out of every five Americans will be 65 or older, and the vast majority will possess a driver's license. This is of concern because statistics show that accidents caused by drivers over the age of 75 equal or surpass those of teenagers, considered the most dangerous group of drivers. A number of states are moving to monitor older drivers more aggressively.

However, in those cases where a license is denied or revoked, the drivers may find themselves stranded without crucial transportation (Harvard Health Letter, 1991).

Does society have the responsibility to provide transportation for people when it takes away their licenses? If not, does government have any responsibility to help such people? What's your view?

Hearing

Decline in hearing ability may be a more serious problem than decline in vision. However, we seem to be much less willing to wear hearing aids than we are to wear glasses, perhaps because we rely on vision more.

Most people hear fairly well until late adulthood, but men seem to lose some of their acuity for higher pitches during their middle years (Marshall, 1981). This difference may occur mostly in men who are exposed to greater amounts of noise in their occupations and in traveling to and from their jobs.

Smell

Some atrophy of olfactory fibers in the nose occurs with age. When artificial amplifiers are added, however, the ability of the older people to recognize foods by smell is greatly improved.

Taste

Studying the effects of aging on the sense of taste is difficult because taste itself is so dependent on smell. About 95 percent of taste derives from the olfactory nerves. It is clear, however, that there is decline in tasting ability among the elderly (Grzegorczyk & others, 1979). Rogers (1979) reported that whereas young adults have an average of 250 taste buds, 70-year-olds have an average of no more than 100.

Touch

The tactile sense also declines somewhat after the age of 65 (Turner & Helms, 1989), but the evidence for this comes strictly from the reports of the elderly. Until scientific studies are performed, this finding must be accepted with caution.

Other Body Systems

Included in the category of body systems are the skeletal system, skin, teeth, hair, and locomotion (ability to move about).

A number of factors can cause the body to become shorter and stiffer with age.

Skeletal System

Although the skeleton is fully formed by age 24, changes in stature can occur because of the shrinking of the discs between spinal vertebrae (Mazess, 1982). As was mentioned earlier, collagen changes. Frequently this causes bone tissue to shrink (Hall, 1976; Twomey & others, 1983). Thus the bones become more brittle. Because the entire skeletal system becomes tighter and stiffer, the aged frequently have a small loss of height. Diseases of the bone system such as arthritis are probably the result of changes in the collagen in the bones with age. Diseases such as osteoporosis and arthritis can be very crippling.

Skin

Collagen is also a major factor in changes in the skin. Because continuous stretching of collagen causes it to lengthen, the skin begins to lose its elasticity with age. Other changes are a greater dryness and the appearance of spots due to changes in pigmentation (Dotz & German, 1983; Robinson, 1983; Walther & Harber, 1984). The skin becomes coarser and darker, and wrinkles begin to appear. Darkness forms under the eyes, more because of a growing paleness of the skin in the rest of the face than because of any change in the under-eye pigmentation. Years of exposure to the sun also contribute to these effects.

Another important cause of the change in skin texture has to do with the typical weight loss among the elderly. They have a tendency to lose fat cells, which decreases the pressure against the skin itself. This tends to cause sagging, folds, and wrinkles in the skin. Older persons not only need less nourishment, but they also lose the social motivation of eating at meetings and parties that younger persons have (Carnevali & Patrick, 1986). As the elderly eat less, their skin becomes less tight and wrinkles appear.

Teeth

The loss of teeth is certainly one physical aspect that makes a person look older (Pizer, 1983). Even when corrective measures are taken, the surgery involved and the adjustment to dentures have a major impact on the person's self-image. In most cases, the loss of teeth is more the result of gum disease than decay of the teeth themselves. Education, the use of fluorides, the use of new brushing techniques, and daily flossing likely will make this aspect of aging far less of a problem in the future.

Hair

Probably the most significant signature of old age is change of the hair. Thinness, baldness, grayness, stiffness, and a growing amount of facial hair in women are all indications of growing old. Hormonal changes are undoubtedly the main culprit here. Improvements in hair coloring techniques and hair implants may make it possible to avoid having "old-looking" hair (for those to whom this is important).

Locomotion

Johnny Kelly of Boston ran the Boston Marathon every year until he was well into his eighties. Why do some people seem to age so much better than others?

It is generally assumed that the decrease in locomotion by older adults is due to aging. However, a recent study suggests that although older people do indeed walk more slowly, the pattern of coordination between their limbs remains essentially the same as for younger adults. Thus if people maintain good health and an active lifestyle, there is reason to believe that this locomotive decline can be kept to a minimum (Williams & Bird, 1992).

Table 19.1	Death Rates, by Age, Sex, and Race: 1960 to 1989 [Number of deaths per 100,000 population in specified group.]

Sex, Year, and Race	All ages	Under 1 yr. old	1–4 yr. old	5–14 yr. old	15–24 yr. old	25–34 yr. old	35–44 yr. old	45–54 yr. old	55–64 yr. old	65–74 yr. old	75–84 yr. old	85 yr. old and older
Male												
1960	1,105	3,059	120	56	152	188	373	992	2,310	4,914	10,178	21,186
1989	922	1,077	47	32	152	203	302	628	1,570	3,415	7,950	17,695
Female												
1960	809	2,321	98	37	61	107	229	527	1,196	2,872	7,633	19,008
1989	817	891	41	21	54	76	142	338	888	1,997	5,083	14,070

Source: From *Vital Statistics of the United States,* U.S. National Center for Health Statistics, 1992.

Table 19.2	Chronic Conditions among Elderly Persons

Type of Chronic Condition and Year: Prevalence per 1,000 Population									
Age, Sex and Family Income	Arthritis	Asthma	Chronic Bronchitis	Diabetes	Heart Conditions	Hypertensive Disease	Impairments of Back or Spine (except paralysis)	Hearing Impairments	Vision Impairments
Average	380.3	35.8	41.2	78.5	198.7	199.4	67.1	294.3	204.6
Sex									
Male	287.0	42.3	47.3	60.3	199.3	141.2	54.6	338.2	183.1
Female	450.1	31.1	36.6	91.3	198.3	240.9	76.3	262.1	220.4
Family Income									
Less than $5,000	411.7	41.4	45.4	82.0	219.0	216.1	78.7	232.0	232.0
$5,000–$9,999	353.3	32.6	37.2	76.1	190.0	179.5	57.3	271.6	163.2
$10,000–$14,999	310.9	•	27.4	81.1	158.9	192.6	39.3	247.3	181.3
$15,000 or more	300.8	•	40.7	62.7	174.8	161.4	48.5	259.2	169.2

Data based on household interviews of samples of the civilian noninstitutionalized population. Source: Division on Health Interview Statistics, National Center for Health Statistics. Selected reports from the Health Interview Survey, 1969–1973, Vital and Health Statistics, Series 10, and unpublished data from the Health Interview Survey.

Health

It is well known that health declines when one reaches the older years. This decline, however, usually does not occur until quite late in life (Kart & others, 1988). Table 19.1 shows rates of death per 100,000 people. (A number of interesting comparisons can be found in this table—can you spot them?)

Illness is not a major cause of death until one reaches the thirties, and only then among African American females. This is probably because they receive fewer preventive health services, and because medical treatment is frequently delayed until the later stages of disease. Not until adults reach the age of 40 does ill health, as opposed to accidents, homicide, and suicide, become the major cause of death. Arteriosclerotic heart disease is the major killer after the age of 40 in all age, sex, and race groups. Table 19.2 details chronic conditions among the elderly.

Alzheimer's Disease

Probably the single greatest scourge of the elderly, and in many ways the most debilitating, is Alzheimer's disease. The German neurologist Alois Alzheimer discovered the disease in 1906, but it did not gain much attention until the 1970s.

Researchers recently announced that they have found a gene that is implicated in the cause. This does not, however, mean they have found a cure for it. Alzheimer's is difficult to diagnose and even more difficult to treat. Relatively few of its symptoms respond to any type of treatment, and then only in the earliest stages. The single exception is that the depression that normally accompanies the disease can be treated effectively (Gierz & others, 1989). Alzheimer's disease usually follows a 6- to 20-year course.

The normal brain consists of billions of nerve cells (neurons), which convey messages to one another chemically by way of branchlike structures called dendrites and axons. Neuron groups generate specific chemical transmitters that travel between cells at the synapses. Although Alzheimer's victims look normal externally, their brains are undergoing severe changes. One particular trait of Alzheimer's is the breakdown of the system in the brain that produces the chemical transmitter acetylcholine. A decrease in the enzyme that tells the system to produce acetylcholine is directly related to insanity. Brain autopsies unmask severe damage, abnormalities, and even death of neurons. Often as little as 10 percent of the normal amount of acetylcholine exists, and the degree of its loss corresponds closely to the severity of the disease (Gelman, 1989).

Several theories have been put forth to explain the causes of Alzheimer's. Some theorists feel that a virus causes the disease, whereas others feel that environmental factors are involved. A popular theory is that an overabundance of metal accumulation in the neurons, mainly aluminum, causes it. Some dispute this theory, since although we all ingest aluminum, our bodies reject it by refusing to digest it.

It now appears that Alzheimer's may be transmitted genetically, since we know that a sibling of an Alzheimer's patient has a 50 percent chance of contracting the disorder. Almost all persons with Down syndrome, a genetic disorder, will develop Alzheimer's disease if they live long enough. It may be that a defective gene makes a person likely to get it if environmental conditions are present.

Much of the economic burden of adult care facilities and nursing homes rests with the person's family. Does society in general have an obligation to relieve some of this expense?

The president of the Alzheimer's Association reports that the cost of caring for an Alzheimer's patient in the home is $18,000 to $20,000 per year, whereas nursing home care may reach as high as $36,000 per year (Cowley, 1989; Kantrowitz, 1989). The financial burden is usually placed on the patient's family, since Medicare does not cover the cost and Medicaid covers only families who are in poverty. Sadly, a family must exhaust all its resources before becoming eligible for Medicaid.

Another alternative to chronic care is the adult-care facility. These programs provide help with daily tasks such as feeding, washing, toileting, and exercising. The average cost of adult-care centers is $27 per day, including meals. One drawback to many of the adult-care facilities is that the staff often does not include medical personnel.

At this time the outlook is bleak for patients and families suffering with Alzheimer's. If you desire further information on what is known about the disease, write to the Alzheimer's Association, 70 East Lake Street, Suite 600, Chicago, Illinois, 60601.

AN APPLIED VIEW

Facts about Alzheimer's

- Approximately 10 percent of the 65-and-over population may have Alzheimer's. Forty-seven percent over 85 already have the disease.
- The National Institute of Health allocated $5.1 million for Alzheimer's research in 1978, and $123.4 million for research in 1989. Though the dollar amount allocated for research has increased each year, more money is needed.
- Heredity is the cause in 10 to 30 percent of all Alzheimer's cases.
- There are always at least two victims of Alzheimer's: the afflicted person and the primary caregiver. The stress of caring for Alzheimer's patients makes the primary caregiver much more vulnerable to infectious disease, as well as vulnerable to all the problems that go with dealing with high levels of stress.
- Although caring for the Alzheimer's patient may often seem to be a thankless task, evidence indicates that sensitive listening and attempts to enter the patient's reality may help prevent antisocial behavior and anxiety-related outbursts (Bohling, 1991).

The Relationship between Physical and Mental Health

In their study of the general health of 1,139 elderly persons living in an urban community, Gerson and associates (1987) made a number of interesting findings that another study (Lohr & others, 1988) has supported:

- A strong relationship exists between physical and mental health.

- Married men have better health than unmarried men (married women are not healthier than unmarried women). This may be because their wives take care of them, or because they feel responsible to their families to maintain their health.

- Social resources are strongly associated with mental health for women, but less so for men. Probably women are more likely than men to use their social resources to help them maintain their mental health. Many men hate to admit to their friends that they are having a mental disturbance, because it is not considered "manly."

- Economic resources are clearly related to mental health. As was pointed out, this is especially true for African American women.

A stereotype exists that the older people get, the less health-conscious they become. The picture is usually more complex than this. For example, compared with those in their sixties and eighties, centenarians (those over 100) ate breakfast more regularly, avoided diets, ate more vegetables, and relied on their doctor more than on the news media for nutrition information (Johnson & others, 1991). They also were found to be more dominant and imaginative (Martin & others, 1992). On the other hand, they did not tend to avoid fats or comply with nutritional guidelines designed to reduce the risk of chronic disease (Johnson & others, 1991). Here again we see the complex interaction of biopsychosocial factors as they affect health and the aging process.

Health and Retirement

Muller and Boaz (1988) stated: "Many studies of the retirement decision have found that poor health increases the probability of retirement. Yet doubts have been expressed whether self-reported deterioration of health is a genuine cause of retirement, rather than a socially acceptable excuse" (p. 52). These researchers studied the actual health status of retirees and found support for the idea that the majority of those who say they are retiring for health reasons are telling the truth.

A MULTICULTURAL VIEW

Gateball and the Japanese Elderly

Gateball, developed in post–World War II Japan, is a team sport combining elements of golf and croquet. It employs strategies that exercise both mind and body. While the object is to score the most points, a great deal of emphasis is placed on the individual's contributions to the team as opposed to individual achievement.

In addition to these benefits, gateball also provides a social outlet, building relationships around a common interest. Gateball has become immensely popular among "silver agers," as older people are called by the Japanese. In a modern, crowded, industrial country like Japan, with early retirement and the highest life expectancy in the world, gateball provides a way for seniors to continue their lifelong pattern of group participation in something worthwhile.

Observations of gateball players in action found people who share information, laughter, and a relaxed sense of belonging. When a player who hadn't been there for some time reappeared, he or she was warmly welcomed back. Exchange of food occurs routinely on the break, and people often encourage others to take some home with them.

In America, this kind of community spirit among seniors is evidenced in some sports (such as golf and bowling), but the stereotype of the elderly person in the rocking chair remains pervasive. Sports provide a means by which older people can remain healthy as well as connected to other people. It is another important lesson we might glean from Japanese culture.

Health unquestionably affects the physical abilities of adults across the age range. Yet it is also clear that social circumstances are the main factor in health in the older years. Thus, the healthiness of adults appears to be more a result of the cultural conditions in which they find themselves than of their age.

Appearance

All of the physical factors treated earlier have an effect on the person's self-concept, but none has a stronger impact than physical appearance. Appearance is of great importance in the United States. A youthful appearance matters a great deal, and to women more than to men. Because women are affected by the "double standard" of aging, they are more likely to use diet, exercise, clothing, and cosmetics to maintain their youthful appearance. Nevertheless, significant changes in physical appearance occur with age that cannot be avoided.

As you can see from the data presented in this chapter, a certain amount of physical decline happens in later life, but it does not occur until most people are quite advanced in age. And with the new medical technologies and marked trend toward adopting more healthy living styles, you can expect to see a much more capable elderly population. Will this happy news also be true for cognitive development?

Do you believe elderly people are more or less concerned about appearance than those of other age groups? Why?

Sales of products that promote youth and beauty are booming.

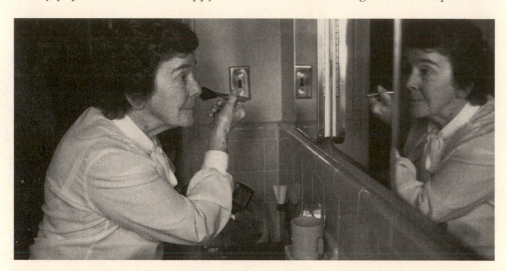

Guided Review

6. Physical abilities such as reaction time are not only affected by the aging process but also by motivations, depression, anxiety, _____ _____ , response style, and ageism.

7. All five senses decline with age but hearing ability may be a more serious problem than _____ because people are less likely to wear a hearing aid than they are _____ .

8. Because of continuous stretching of _____ , the skin begins to lengthen and lose its elasticity with age.

9. Alzheimer's disease, a serious mental loss in some elderly persons, is caused by the inability of the _____ to produce acetylcholine.

10. Research indicates that Alzheimer's disease may be transmitted _____ , since we know that a _____ of an Alzheimer's patient has a 50 percent chance of contracting the disorder.

11. When it comes to appearance in aging, there is a _____ _____ for men and for women.

Answers

6. response strategies   7. vision, glasses   8. collagen   9. brain   10. genetically, sibling   11. double standard

A Comparison of Physical Abilities

One of the best ways of comprehending adult development is to do a miniseries of experiments of your own. In this activity, you can compare the physical development of friends and relatives with just a few simple pieces of equipment. Pick at least three people in at least two age groups. The·results might surprise you.

You may find that you need to alter the instructions of the following experiments to make it more convenient for you to do the study. This is perfectly all right, as long as you make sure that each test is the same for every person who takes it. The greater the variety of the adults you enlist in the study, in factors such as age, sex, and religion, the more interesting your results will be.

A. *Muscular strength*. Several of the following tests require a heavy table. Simply have each subject grasp a leg of the table with one hand and raise the leg off the ground 3 inches. Subjects who can hold it up 3 inches for 30 seconds have succeeded in step 1. Now have them try to hold it up another 3 inches, and if they succeed they get credit for step 2 (each step must be done for 30 seconds). In step 3 they must hold it at a height of 1 foot, in step 4 they must hold it at a height of 1 1/2 feet, and in step 5 at a height of 2 feet. Record one point for each step successfully completed.

B. *Vision*. The subject should be seated at the table with chin resting on forearms and forearms resting on the table. Set a magazine at a distance of 2 feet and ask the subject to read two lines. Next 3 feet, then 4 feet, then 5 feet, and finally at 6 feet. One point is given for each step.

C. *Hearing*. The subject is seated with his or her back to the table. You will need some instrument that makes the same level of noise for the same period of time. For example, a portable radio might be turned on a brief moment and turned back off, each time at the same volume. A clicker might be used. Whatever you use, make the standard noise at 2 feet behind the subject and have him or her raise a hand when the sound is heard. Then make the sound at 4 feet, 6 feet, 10 feet, and 20 feet. You may need to vary these distances, depending on the volume of the instrument you are using. Be sure to vary the intervals between the noises that you make, so that you can be sure the subject is really hearing the noise when you make it. Give points for each appropriate response.

D. *Smell,* E. *Taste,* and F. *Touch*. For these three tests, you will need five cups of equal size. The cups should hold milk, cola, soft ice cream, yogurt, and applesauce. Each food should be chilled to approximately the same temperature. Blindfold subjects and ask them to tell you what the five substances are.

G. *Reaction Time—I*. For this test you will need three squares, three circles, three triangles; one of each is 1 inch high, 2 inches high, and 3 inches high. Make them of cardboard, plastic, or wood. Arrange the nine figures in random order in front of the subject. Tell the subject that when you call out the name of one of the figures (e.g., a large square), he or she is to put a finger on it as quickly as possible. Call out the name of one of the figures, and time the response. Repeat this test five times, calling out a different figure each time, and compute the total time required for the five trials.

H. *Reaction Time—II*. Again arrange the nine pieces randomly in front of the subject. You will call out either the shape ("circle") or a size ("middle-size"). The subject puts the three circles or the three middle-size pieces in a pile as quickly as possible. Repeat this experiment five times, using a different designator each time, and compute the total time the task requires.

I. *Health—I*. Ask subjects to carefully count the number of times they have been in the hospital. Give them one point if they have been hospitalized 10 times or more, two points for 5 through 9 times, three points for 3 times, four points for no more than 1 time, five points if they have never been hospitalized for any reason (pregnancy should not be counted).

J. *Health—II*. Ask subjects to carefully remember how many times they have visited a doctor within the past year. Give one point for four or more times, two points for three times, three points for two times, four points for one time, five points for no visits at all.

Compare the scores for each test for persons within the age groups you have chosen. Do you see any patterns? Are the results of aging evident? What other conclusions can you draw?

Cognitive Development

In chapter 17, we described the changes in intelligence that develop across the adult lifespan, focusing on middle age. In this chapter we take a closer look at old age. The major question is whether a significant decline in cognitive competence tends to occur as we become elderly. A review of the research on this question reveals a serious conflict. Salthouse (1990) stated it well:

> ■ Results from psychometric tests and experimental tasks designed to assess cognitive ability frequently reveal rather substantial age-related declines in the range from 20 to 70 years of age. . . . On the other hand, adults in their 60s and 70s are seldom perceived to be less cognitively competent than adults in their 20s and 30s, and in fact, many of the most responsible and demanding leadership positions in society are routinely held by late middle-aged or older adults. (p. 310)

Cognitive Ability in the Elderly: Tests versus Observations

So wherein lies the truth—in the results of tests, or in our observations of actual performance? As we said, the answer is not simple. What factors could account for this discrepancy? Currently there are four hypotheses, each of which play a part (Salthouse, 1990):

- *Differences in type of cognition*. Intelligence tests tend to measure specific bands of cognitive ability, whereas assessments of real-life activities probably also include noncognitive capacities, such as personality traits. Thus some aspects of IQ may decline without causing lowered performance on the job, for example.

- *Differences in the representativeness of the individuals or observations*. Many examples exist of elderly persons who can perform admirably even into their nineties, but do these individuals really represent the average elderly person? Probably not. It is also probable that only the most competent individuals are able to survive in such demanding situations. Those who are less competent will have dropped out of the competition at an earlier age. Therefore, when we examine the abilities of successful older persons, we may be studying only the "cream of the crop." Finally, it seems likely that observed competence represents only one type of cognitive ability (balancing the company's books, reading music), whereas intelligence testing involves several (verbal, math, reasoning, and other abilities).

- *Different standards of evaluation*. Most cognitive tests tend to push individuals to their limits of ability. Assessments of real-life tasks, those with which people are quite familiar (such as reading the newspaper), may require a lower standard of testing.

- *Different amounts of experience*. Doing well on an intelligence test requires one to employ traits that are not used every day, such as assembling blocks so that they resemble certain patterns. The skills assessed in real-life situations are more likely to be those the individual has practiced for years. For example, driving ability may remain high if the person continues to drive regularly as she ages.

Each of these hypotheses seeks to explain the discrepancy between tested ability and actual performance as being the result of faulty research techniques. Many other writers have suggested that perhaps the elderly really are inferior in cognitive competence to younger persons but that they find ways to compensate for their lost cognitive abilities. Thus older persons are able to maintain performance levels even as ability is waning. Unfortunately, no one has suggested how such compensation might be achieved, so this hypothesis is doubtful.

Another question about the decline of cognitive ability in the elderly is, Can lowered capacity be recovered through training? Here there is good news. Numerous methods have been successful in improving elderly cognitive skills. For example, important improvements have been demonstrated in:

- Spatial orientation and inductive reasoning (Willis & Schaie, 1986)

- The flexibility of fluid intelligence and problem-solving strategies (Baltes & others, 1989)

- Cognitive plasticity of memory skills (Kliegl & others, 1989, 1990)

- Long-term effects of fluid ability (in the old-old) (Willis & Nessleroade, 1990)

It seems likely that, through the use of new training techniques and possibly through new drugs, the decline in cognitive ability in old age (whatever it may actually be) will submit to reductions and even reversals in the years to come.

Another aspect of cognitive decline has proven of great interest to psychologists. It is referred to as terminal drop.

Terminal Drop

Terminal drop
The period of from a few weeks up to two years prior to a person's death, during which his or her intelligence is presumed to decline rapidly.

Birren was the first to discuss **terminal drop** (1964). He defined it as the period preceding the person's death, from a few weeks up to two years prior. This research looks at the relationship, not between intelligence and age (which is the number of years from birth till the time of testing), but between intelligence and survivorship (which is the number of years from the time of testing until death). The hypothesis is that the person's perception, consciously or unconsciously, of impending death may cause the decline in intelligence. This perception causes the person to begin withdrawing from the world. Consequently, performance on an intelligence test drops markedly.

According to Birren,

> the individual himself may or may not be aware in himself of diffuse changes in mood, in mental functioning, or in the way his body responds. Terminal [drop] may be paced by a disease initially remote from the nervous system, such as a cancer of the stomach. Thereafter, over a series of months, a rapid sequence of changes might be observed in overt behavior or in measured psychological characteristics of the individual. It is as though at this point the physiology of the individual had started on a new phase, that the organism is unable to stop. (p. 280)

Researchers have come to several different conclusions concerning the effect of age on intelligence level.

The terminal drop hypothesis has had considerable support. Siegler (1975) reviewed eight studies of the phenomenon and discovered a strong positive relationship between the length of survivorship and high level of intellectual ability. That is, the higher the intelligence, the longer the person is likely to live after the time of testing.

Some researchers have questioned whether terminal drop pervades all cognitive abilities or is restricted to specific ones. In a study designed to answer this question, White and Cunningham (1988) found terminal drop to apply to a shorter period than five years and to be more restricted than was previously thought. They reached the following conclusions:

> ■ Only vocabulary scores for those who died at age 70 or less and within two years of testing were affected by terminal drop. . . . Thus the terminal drop phenomenon may be limited to abilities that typically are relatively unaffected by age, such as vocabulary or other verbal abilities. Furthermore, the effects may be restricted to a time period much closer to death than had been originally proposed. (p. 141)

One final warning: Although virtually all studies described here use IQ tests to measure intelligence, the two are not identical. IQ involves school-related abilities, whereas intelligence is made up of these and many other abilities (e.g., spatial ability and "street smarts"). It is not possible at present to discern how much this discrepancy affects the research. Another mental trait that is hard to study, but is even more vital to understand and cultivate, is creativity.

Creativity

In chapter 17, we concluded that quantity of creative production probably drops in old age but that quality of production may not. This is based on studies of actual productivity. But what about potential for production? Might it be that the elderly are capable of great creativity but that, as with IQ, factors like motivation and opportunity prevent them from fulfilling this ability? That is the question addressed by the next set of studies we'll discuss.

Cross-Sectional Studies of Creative Productivity

The first large-scale study to look at the creative productivity of typical people at various ages who are still alive was completed by Alpaugh and associates (1976; also Alpaugh & Birren, 1977). They administered two batteries of creativity tests to 111 schoolteachers aged 20 to 83. Their findings support the idea that creativity does decline with age. One major criticism of their research is that the tests they used are probably not equally valid for all age groups. The younger subjects are more likely to have had practice with these types of materials than the older ones. For example, the study of creativity is relatively new, so the tests used to measure it have been designed recently. Thus those who attended school more recently are more likely to have encountered such tests than those who graduated many years ago. Such familiarity would provide an advantage to the younger subjects in the study.

Jaquish and Ripple (1980) attempted to evaluate the effects of aging while avoiding the problem of using age-related materials. These researchers gathered data on six age groups across the lifespan: 10 to 12 years (61 people); 13 to 17 years (71 people); 18 to 25 years (70 people); 26 to 39 years (58 people); 40 to 60 years (51 people); and 61 to 84 years (39 people). The study had a total of 350 subjects.

The definition of creativity in this study was restricted to the concepts of fluency, flexibility, and originality; these are collectively known as divergent thinking abilities. These three traits were measured through the use of an auditory exercise, which was recorded on cassette. Known as the Sounds and Images Test, it elicits responses to the "weird" sounds presented on the tape. Responses are then scored according to the three traits of divergent thinking. The researchers believe that this test is so unusual that no age group is likely to have had more experience with it than any other.

A number of interesting findings have resulted from this study, as you can see in table 19.3. On all three measures of divergent thinking, the scores generally increased slightly across the first five age groups. Scores for the 40- to 60-year-old group increased significantly, whereas scores for the 61- to 84-year-old group

Table 19.3	Means for Divergent Thinking and Self-Esteem Scores			
Age Group	Fluency	Flexibility	Originality	Self-Esteem
	Mean	*Mean*	*Mean*	*Mean*
18–25	31	19	19	34
26–39	30	18	19	37
40–60	36	21	20	38
61–84	22	15	15	32

From G. Jaquish and R. E. Ripple, "Cognitive Creative Abilities Across the Adult Life Span" in *Human Development*. Copyright © 1980 S. Karger AG, Basel, Switzerland. Reprinted by permission of the publisher.

decreased significantly below the scores of any of the younger age groups. Furthermore, when decline in divergent thinking did occur, it was more pronounced in quantity than in quality. That is, greater age differences occurred in fluency (a measure of quantity) than in originality (a measure of quality). Finally, it is not known to what extent the oldest subjects were affected by hearing loss, particularly of high and low tones. Obviously, this could be an alternative explanation of the findings for this oldest group.

Probably the most important finding of the study had to do with the relationship between divergent thinking and self-esteem, which was measured by the Coopersmith Self-Esteem Inventory. Table 19.3 indicates that self-esteem follows a pattern quite similar to the other three traits.

Of special interest is the relationship between self-esteem and divergent thinking for the oldest group: The correlations were moderately high in every case. This indicates that self-esteem may have a positive effect on creative abilities over the years, or that creativity may enhance self-esteem, or both. Jaquish and Ripple (1980) concluded that

> there is much more plasticity in adult development than has been traditionally assumed. Such an interpretation should find a hospitable audience among those people concerned with educational intervention. If the creative abilities of older adults were to be realized in productivity, it would be difficult to overestimate the importance of the formation of new attitudes of society, teachers in continuing adult education programs, and in the older adults themselves. (p. 152)

Programs in which young people meet regularly with elderly adults seem to have rewards for all involved. By what other means might we better tap the knowledge and creativity of the elderly?

The Stages of Life during Which Creativity May Best Be Cultivated

In this final section we present Dacey's theory (1989b) that there are certain critical periods in life during which creative ability can be cultivated most effectively. Its relevance to the study of late adulthood will be obvious. Table 19.4 presents a list of these periods for males and females.

The basic premise of this theory is that a person's inherent creativity can blossom best during a period of crisis and change. The six periods chosen in table 19.4 are ages at which most people experience stress due to life changes.

The table presents a new theory, and thus it must be considered speculative. Nevertheless some direct evidence supports it. Some excellent research from the fields of personality and cognitive development also indicates that these periods are more volatile than any others.

Included in the theory is the concept that major gains in creative performance are less likely with each succeeding period. That is, what happens to the person in the early years is far more influential than what happens in the later years. The older people become, the less likely they are to have a sudden burst of highly creative production.

Table 19.4	**Peak Periods of Life during Which Creativity May Most Readily Be Cultivated**	
For Males	**For Females**	
1. 0–5 years old	0–5 years old	
2. 11–14 years old	10–13 years old	
3. 18–20 years old	18–20 years old	
4. 29–31 years old	29–31 years old	
5. 40–45 years old	40 (37?)–45 years old	
6. 60–65 years old	60–65 years old	

Reprinted with the permission of Lexington Books, an imprint of The Free Press, a Division of Simon & Schuster, Inc., from *Fundamentals of Creative Thinking* by John S. Dacey. Copyright © 1989 by Lexington Books.

Research indicates that the time right after retirement can be a period of creative growth, as the individual turns from the demands of a work schedule to the opportunities offered by an artistic endeavor.

The Sixth Peak Period

Evidence for the first five peak periods has been presented earlier in this book. The first period is mentioned in chapter 7 (although not called creativity per se), the second and third in chapter 12, the fourth in chapter 16, and the fifth in chapter 18. The rationale for the sixth period, from 60 to 65, is reviewed here.

For most men and for a growing number of women, this is the period in which retirement occurs. Even if a woman has not been in the labor force, she has many adjustments to make because of her husband's retirement. Thus most adults are faced with a major adjustment of self-concept at this time in their lives.

Although some do not adjust well and begin withdrawing from society, others take advantage of the change to pursue creative goals that had previously been impossible for them. Obviously a majority of the "young old" (the new term for those who are 60 to 70) do not suddenly become creative, but a substantial number do. Of the several thousand highly productive people he studied, Lehman (1953, 1962) found more than 100, or almost 5 percent, whose major productivity began in the years after 60.

In addition to highly visible contributions, many of the elderly become creative in less newsworthy ways. Gerontologist Jack Botwinick, who presents an excellent analysis of this topic in his book *Aging and Behavior* (1984), suggests that many elderly persons exercise a newfound creativity by mentoring younger people. Though largely unheralded, such guidance and encouragement of younger creators unquestionably has invaluable benefits for society.

Table 19.5	Summary, Simplified Comparison among Wisdom, Intelligence, and Creativity		
	Construct		
Aspect	*Wisdom*	*Intelliegence*	*Creativity*
Knowledge	Understanding of its presuppositions and meanings as well as its limitations	Recall, analysis, and use	Going beyond what is available
Processes	Understanding of what is automatic and why	Automatization of procedures	Applied to novel tasks
Primary intellectual style	Judicial	Executive	Legislative
Personality	Understanding of ambiguity and obstacles	Eliminating ambiguity and overcoming obstacles within conventional framework	Tolerance of ambiguity and redefinition of obstacles
Motivation	To understand what is known and what it means	To know and to use what is known	To go beyond what is known
Environmental context	Appreciation in environment of depth of understanding	Appreciation in environment of extent and breadth of understanding	Appreciation in environment of going beyond what is currently understood

From R. J. Sternberg, *Wisdom*. Copyright © 1990, Cambridge University Press, New York. Reprinted with the permission of Cambridge University Press.

This is not to say that maintaining or increasing creative performance in one's later years is easy. There are inherent problems that are not readily overcome. Psychologist B. F. Skinner (1983), who had a 60-year-long career of highly creative achievement, stated that productivity is difficult for the elderly because they tend to lose interest in work, find it hard to start working, and work more slowly:

> ■ It is easy to attribute this change to them, but we should not overlook a change in their world. For motivation, read reinforcement. In old age, behavior is not so strongly reinforced. Biological aging weakens reinforcing consequences. Behavior is more and more likely to be followed by aches and pains and quick fatigue. Things tend to become "not worth doing" in the sense that the aversive consequences exact too high a price. Positive reinforcers become less common and less powerful. Poor vision closes off the world of art, faulty hearing the enjoyment of highly fidelitous music. Foods do not taste as good, and erogenous tissues grow less sensitive. Social reinforcers are attenuated. Interests and tastes are shared with a smaller number of people. (p. 28)

It is increasingly clear that creativity may blossom at any age. This theory of "the peak periods of creative growth" is not meant to disparage that fact. Solid evidence indicates, however, that the best opportunities lie in the six periods identified by the theory. Are there also periods in the development of gender roles in later life that have special importance? of sexuality? of family relations? of work and retirement? We'll examine these questions in the next chapter.

One final point: What is the relationship between intelligence and creativity, and how do they relate to the highest level of human cognition, wisdom? In table 19.5, Robert Sternberg's (1990) comparison of the three is presented.

12. Discrepancies between the results of tests and our observations of cognitive abilities may be due to differences in type of cognition, differences in the representation of the individuals or observations, different standards of _____ , and different amounts of experience.

13. Training can increase abilities in older adults. However, about two years before death, a _____ _____ in mental functioning often occurs.

14. It is suggested that a decline in intelligence in the later years may be caused by the person's _____ of impending death.

15. Jaquish and Ripple found in their studies on creativity that there is a correlation between _____ and creativity.

16. Dacey sees creativity as blossoming during periods of _____ and _____ .

17. Wisdom is different from both creativity and intelligence, in that it has a focus on _____ .

Answers

12. evaluation (or testing)   13. terminal drop   14. perception   15. self-esteem   16. crisis, change   17. understanding

🌳 CONCLUSION

At the beginning of this chapter we asked, "Must growing old mean decline?" The answer is that some decline is inevitable, but the picture is much less gloomy than we have been led to believe. The loss of mental and physical abilities is, on the average, relatively slight; some individuals experience only moderate physical loss and no cognitive loss at all. For many older adults, compensatory skills and abilities may replace lost capacities. The same is true for personal and social development.

Here once again we run into the bugaboo of all human development: the self-fulfilling prophecy. Because American society has been changing rapidly for many decades, older adults are frequently viewed as incompetent—their experience appears to have little relevance in "modern times." Yet carefully controlled laboratory measurements of their abilities make clear that their losses may be relatively slight.

Perhaps as we learn to understand the aging process, and as the process is better understood by the public in general, the majority of adults will not assume that their abilities must undergo severe decline. In such a situation, the quality of life of the elderly will surely improve greatly, and because we could reasonably expect an increase in the productive contributions of seniors, all of society would benefit! As you'll see in the next chapter, such improvements are already taking place in the social and personal lives of the elderly.

🌳 CHAPTER HIGHLIGHTS

Must We Age and Die?

- A variety of physiological theories regarding aging and death exist. These include aging by program, homeostatic imbalance, and cross-linkage theories.
- Gene theory also suggests that aging is programmed but says that the program exists in certain harmful genes.
- The natural environment is also an important factor in mortality (e.g., now fewer elderly mortalities are due to the spread of influenza).

- Major modifiers of ability such as training, nutrition, illness, stress level, and personality type also affect one's rate of aging.

Physical Development

- While reaction time appears to decline with age, Elias and others have pointed to several reasons for this decline.
- We may conclude that variables other than sheer neural or motor activities account for most change in physical skills over time. These include ageism, motivation, depression, anxiety, response strategies, and response style.

- Changes in sensory abilities, the skeletal system, skin, teeth, hair, and locomotion are noticeable in late adulthood.
- Even though hormone production slows down during late adulthood, a detriment in one area is often compensated for by some other gland.
- Probably the single greatest scourge of the elderly, and in many ways the most debilitating, is Alzheimer's disease.
- A strong relationship exists between physical and mental health.

Cognitive Development

- A number of factors have been suggested as explaining the difference between tested and observed changes in elderly cognition. These include differences in type of cognition, the representativeness of the individuals or observations, standards of evaluation, and amounts of experience.
- The person's perception, consciously or unconsciously, of impending death may cause a decline in intelligence in the later years. This is called terminal drop.
- Creativity is evidenced in late adulthood and in some cases may be strongest during this time. Although quantity of creative production probably drops in old age, the quality of creative production and potential ability probably do not.

KEY TERMS

Accumulation of errors   487
Accumulation of metabolic waste   486
Ageism   492
Aging by program   485

Antigens   487
Autoimmunity   487
Collagen   486
Cross-linkage theory   486

Gene theory   488
Homeostatic imbalance   486
Terminal drop   501
Wear and tear theory   485

WHAT DO YOU THINK?

1. Must we grow old and die?
2. Which factors do you believe most strongly affect aging: physiological, genetic, environmental, or some others?
3. Regarding the decline of physical systems, which has the greatest impact on the person's life: reaction time, sensory abilities, other body systems, hormonal balance, health, or appearance? Why?
4. Regarding the decline of cognitive systems, which has the greatest impact on the person's life: intelligence, creativity, memory, or learning? Why?
5. What is the nature of wisdom?

SUGGESTED READINGS

Cunningham, W. & Brookbank, J. (1988). *Gerontology*. New York: Harper & Row. An up-to-date general reference on the psychological, biological, and sociological factors in aging.

Olsen, T. (1961). *Tell me a riddle*. New York: Dell. The superb title story details the difficulties of old age and terminal illness as they occurred to a working-class woman during the Great Depression.

Sarton, M. (1973). *As we are now*. New York: Norton. A novel in the form of the diary of a retired schoolteacher, this is a powerful portrayal of her experiences when she is put in a nursing home by her relatives.

Skinner, B. F. & Vaughan, M. E. (1983). *Enjoy old age: A program of self-management*. New York: Norton. In this book, the grandfather of behaviorism explains how to use behavior modification to better handle the problems of aging. A good read, whether you are elderly or plan to help someone who is.

Spence, A. (1989). *Biology of human aging*. Englewood Cliffs, NJ: Prentice-Hall. A highly detailed look at the systems of the body and how they are affected by aging.

CHAPTER REVIEW TEST

1. The counterpart theory holds that
   a. the aging process is programmed.
   b. factors in human existence useful in earlier years become counterproductive in later years.
   c. early deterioration is due to hard work and a stressful lifestyle.
   d. the aging process is due to alterations in cell proteins.

2. One explanation of aging is that the various life-support systems gradually weaken and that death comes about as a cumulative result of these various weaknesses. This refers to which aspect of aging?
   a. genetic
   b. environmental
   c. physiological
   d. human abilities

3. According to the cross-linkage theory, what happens to collagen, the major connective tissue in the body that provides elasticity in our skin, as we grow older?
   a. It becomes a waste product as a result of a metabolism build up in the body.
   b. It causes early aging.
   c. It contributes to our body's tissues becoming more self-rejecting.
   d. Our skin wrinkles because the proteins of collagen are altered.

4. A failure in the body's systems to regulate the proper interaction of organs is known as
   a. cross-linkage theory.
   b. autoimmunity.
   c. homeostatic imbalance.
   d. counterpart theory.

5. Studies of monozygotic twins showing that they have more similar lengths of life than do dizygotic twins are evidence of which aspect of aging?
   a. human ability
   b. environmental
   c. physiological
   d. genetic

6. In examining the effects of the environment on aging, one factor that has contributed to lower mortality rates in Western culture is
   a. better diet.
   b. changes in the evolutionary process.
   c. the increased use of vaccines in early childhood.
   d. None of the above.

7. Stress level, educational level, motivation, and personality type are examples of
   a. genetic factors.
   b. physiological factors.
   c. environmental factors.
   d. modifiers of ability.

8. Ageism can be defined as
   a. the study of late adulthood.
   b. the study of human development as one ages.
   c. a type of prejudice toward older adults.
   d. physical changes from middle to older adulthood.

9. A breakdown in the system in the brain that produces acetylcholine results in
   a. Huntington's chorea.
   b. Alzheimer's disease.
   c. terminal drop.
   d. lowered intelligence.

10. Relatively few symptoms of Alzheimer's respond to any treatment, with the exception of
    a. anxiety.
    b. long-term memory loss.
    c. short-term memory loss.
    d. depression.

11. Research indicating that there is a strong positive relationship between the length of survivorship and high level of intellectual ability is known as the
    a. terminal drop theory.
    b. cross-linkage theory.
    c. homeostasis theory.
    d. the aging by program theory.

12. According to terminal drop theory, a person's perception of _____ causes the person to begin withdrawing from the world and, consequently, performance on an IQ test drops markedly.
    a. personal health
    b. impending death
    c. intellectual abilities
    d. interpersonal abilities

13. Jaquish and Ripple (1980) found a positive relationship between self-esteem and _____ for the oldest group of subjects.
    a. divergent thinking
    b. originality
    c. flexibility
    d. fluency

14. Jaquish and Ripple defined creativity using the concepts of fluency, flexibility, and originality—collectively known as
    a. divergent thinking.
    b. congruent thinking.
    c. a measure of intelligence.
    d. None of the above.

15. Dacey proposed that there are certain _____ in life during which creative ability can be cultivated most effectively.
    a. work-related experiences
    b. critical periods
    c. ages
    d. educational experiences

16. During the sixth peak period, many people exercise a newfound creativity by
    a. relieving themselves from the stresses of life.
    b. retiring.
    c. increasing their cognitive abilities.
    d. mentoring younger people.

Answers

1. b 2. c 3. d 4. c 5. d 6. c 7. d 8. c 9. b 10. d 11. a 12. b 13. a 14. a 15. b 16. d

Chapter Outline

G etting married in 1948 I married into a world that had a very definite definition of marriage. I married into a man-oriented society, where the man was the provider, the center, the whatnot, and the woman circled around the man. But I married Ruby Dee; Ruby had some other ideas about marriage. [Laughs.] There were one or two other extra things on her agenda that I didn't know about, but when they came up I saw no reason to challenge her. For example, after our first baby was born and we moved down to Mount Vernon, New York, I remember Ruby standing washing dishes one day and saying to me, quite confidently, "You know, I'm not going to do this the rest of my life." I said, "No? What are you going to do?" She said, "Well, I'm going to be an actor. I'm still going to act." I said, "Yes." She said, "I'm going to go to acting school." And I said, "Well, okay." And at that time we didn't have much money, so we decided that Ruby would go to acting school and I would stay home and sometimes wash the dishes and take care of the baby. And when Ruby came home she would teach me what she learned at the acting class.

Now, when I stepped into the marriage I didn't think of that, but that happened. And over the years I think the central thing that I've learned is how to more easily open my life and let Ruby in. I think women are much more generous in letting people into their lives than men—although I might be wrong. I think that men come with a sense that they are the complete embodiment of what God intended should represent value, virtue, power, and all that sort of thing, and that women, to some degree, are there to service and serve them—that's how women fulfill themselves. Gradually my wife and the circumstances of the time led me to a different understanding, and I'm glad for that, because it made me a broader and a deeper and a much richer person. It has enriched my spirit, my spirituality. It means also—and this is the best part of it all—that I learned a lesson a long time ago, and the lesson is, "The way to make a man rich is to decrease his wants." I learn more and more every day what not to want and how not to want it. To me that is the regimen of the spirit.

Actor and biographer Ossie Davis, age 75
Quoted in Berman and Goldman (1992)

After reading chapter 20, you should be able to

- Define what is meant by "crossover" regarding gender roles in late adulthood.

- Contrast the social, emotional, and physical aspects of sexuality for men and women in late adulthood.

- Analyze White's summary comments regarding sexuality in late adulthood.

- Identify the four basic phases through which most adults pass in relation to their families.

- Describe characteristics of the older worker.

- Assess the relationship between retirement and leisure.

- Evaluate Williamson and associates' seven phases of retirement.

- Summarize Neugarten's findings regarding the effects of aging on personal development.

- Contrast activity theory with disengagement theory.

- Appraise Erikson's final stage of human development: integrity versus despair.

Social Development

This section is devoted to five aspects of social development: gender roles, sexuality, families, the older worker, and retirement.

Gender Roles

Role discontinuity

Abrupt and disruptive change caused by conflicts among one's various roles in life.

Crossover

Older men become more like women, and older women become more like men.

■ When people enter their sixties, they enter a new and final stage in the life cycle. At this point they confront the loss of many highly valued roles, the need to establish a new life structure for the remaining years, and the undeniable fact of life's termination. Widowhood and retirement are the central role transitions likely to occur at this time, but the death of friends and relatives also diminishes one's social network. Although people are aware of the inevitability of these role losses as they enter old age, their often abrupt reality may result in severe role discontinuity. (Sales, 1978, p. 185)

To sum up, the major concern for gender roles among the elderly is **role discontinuity.** See the accompanying box for several questions you should keep in mind as you read the theories and research summaries that follow.

WHAT'S YOUR VIEW?

IS ROLE DISCONTINUITY INHERENT IN GROWING OLD?

Role discontinuity occurs when people experience an abrupt change in their style of life and their role in it. Is this a natural part of growing old? Should we expect our world to shrink and our power to erode? Or is this just a stereotype of old age?

Is role discontinuity a problem only for the poor, who have less control over their lives than the wealthy? Does high intelligence make a difference? How about gender? What's your view?

The "crossover effect" concerns the tendency of men to do more things that are considered feminine, such as washing the dishes, and for women to do more things that are considered masculine, such as taking charge of repairs to the home.

A number of gerontologists have noted that people in late adulthood experience a **crossover** in gender roles. Older men become more like women, and older women become more like men. They do not actually cross over—they just become more like each other. This is what Neugarten (1968) found in her studies of aging men and women. She states that "women, as they age, seem to become more tolerant of their own aggressive, egocentric impulses; whereas men, as they age, [become more tolerant] of their own nurturative and affiliative impulses" (p. 71). In Gutman's terms (1973), men pass from "active to passive mastery," and women do just the opposite.

The differences between men and women, so many of which seem to be based on sexuality, are no longer as important. With the barriers breaking down, older men and women seem to have more in common with each other, and thus may be more of a solace to each other as they deal with the disruptive changes of growing old. This is not to say that men and women reverse gender roles. Rather, they move toward androgyny (see chapter 14), accepting whatever role, male or female, is appropriate in the situation.

On the basis of data obtained by University of California at Berkeley, Norma Haan (1976, 1981, 1989) concluded that the gender-role changes that result from aging generally lead toward greater candor with others and comfort with one's self. For the most part, she said, "people change, but slowly, while maintaining some continuity" (1989, p. 25).

Sexuality

Until the 1980s, most reports on sex among the elderly agreed that sexual practices drop off sharply in old age. For example, Pearlman (1972) reported that only 20 percent of elderly males have sex two times or more per month. Serious doubts exist, however, about the reliability of these reports. Society disapproves of the idea of sex among the elderly, so it may be that many do not report what actually goes on.

A study at Duke University centered primarily on the social and emotional aspects of sexuality in later adulthood but included the physical component as well (Williamson & others, 1980). Since 1960, when the study began, researchers at Duke University have interviewed and medically evaluated 270 people over age 60. Their main goal was to define interest in sex and amount of sexual activity as people age. Here are the study's main conclusions:

- At age 68, about 70 percent of males engage in intercourse, and one out of five are sexually active in their eighties.

- For women, activity does not decrease with age as it does for men.

- Older men are more sexually active and more interested in sex than older women.

- Interest decreases for both genders, but not as much as sexual activity does.

- Sexual interest is positively linked to health for males. Healthier individuals are more interested in sex.

- For women, interest depends on the enjoyment and quality of sex in the past.

The Janus Report

The most recent report on frequency of sexual activity among the elderly, the Janus Report (see chapter 13), gives a picture that weakens the stereotype of the sexually inactive elder even more. As table 17.1 makes clear (see chapter 17), in the last decade of this century, there is little difference in the practices of young adults and elderly adults! In fact, this study found rather minor differences among any of its four age groups. Either the adults in the Janus study were more honest in reporting what they actually do, or some great changes in sexual attitudes among older Americans have occurred in recent years.

Widowhood and Sexuality

A number of factors account for gender differences in attitudes and interest in sex. For example, women outlive men by approximately seven years. Most married women will become widows because they marry men nearly four years older than themselves. In contrast, most men in society will not become widowers unless they reach age 85 (National Center for Health Statistics, 1992). Due to this imbalance of elderly males and females, it is more difficult for women to find sexual partners in their aging years.

Whether or not a woman is sexually active depends mainly on her marital status. In contrast, single men in the Duke study were just as sexually active as their married counterparts. Men have generally had more opportunity for extramarital sexual relations than women, due to the **differential opportunity structure.** This

Traditionally in Western society, elderly men marrying young women has been more accepted than elderly women marrying young men. Why do you believe these attitudinal differences arose?

Differential opportunity structure
Due to social disapproval and more rigid rules enforced by parents, peers, and the legal system, women have not had the same access to sex that men have had.

means that due to social disapproval and more rigid rules enforced by parents, peers, and the legal system, women have not had the same access to sex as men have had.

Impotency

Impotency
The inability to engage in the sexual act.

One of the biggest fears in males of increasing age is **impotency.** Physical changes, nonsupportive partners and peers, and internal fears may be enough to inhibit or terminate sexual activity in males. It may become a self-fulfilling prophecy.

Sleep laboratory experiments have shown that many men in their sixties to eighties who have labeled themselves as impotent regularly experience erections in their sleep. In many cases a man is capable of having intercourse, but a physical condition such as diabetes impedes it. New types of prosthetic devices can remedy a variety of psychological and physical problems.

One pervading myth is that surgery of the prostate gland inevitably leads to impotency. Many elderly men experience pain and swelling of this small gland, and a **prostatectomy** (removal of all or a part of this gland) is necessary. Most impotency that results from the removal of this gland is psychological rather than physical.

Prostatectomy
The removal of all or part of the male prostate gland.

Most sexual problems that women experience are due to hormonal changes. The vaginal walls begin to thin, and intercourse may become painful, with itching and burning sensations. Estrogen pills and hormone creams relieve many of these symptoms. Further, if women believe that sexual activity ceases with menopause and aging, it probably will. Although women have fewer concerns about sex, they are often worried about losing their attractiveness, which can also have a negative effect on their sex lives (McCary, 1978).

Starr and Weiner (1981) surveyed 800 adults between the ages of 60 and 91, drawn from all parts of the country and representing all ethnic and racial groups. Fifty percent were married, 30 percent were widowed, 11 percent were divorced, and 4 percent had never married. The group responded to 50 open-ended questions about their sexual lives and then mailed back the questionnaire anonymously. Table 20.1 presents their surprising findings.

Table 20.1	**Findings of the Starr-Weiner Study of Sexual Activity in Later Life**

Frequency of intercourse is 1.4 times per week. (Kinsey had reported a frequency of once every two weeks for 60-year-olds.)

- The ideal or fantasized lover for most, particularly women, is close to their own age.
- Most see their sex lives remaining pretty much the same as they grow even older.
- Most have a strong continuing interest in sex.
- They believe that sex is important for physical and mental well-being.
- The perception of most of the respondents is that sex is as good as when they were younger.
- For a large number, both male and female, sex is *better* in the later years.
- Orgasm is considered an essential part of the sexual experience.
- Most of the women are orgasmic and always have been.
- The orgasm for many is stronger now than when they were younger.
- Masturbation is an acceptable outlet for sexual needs.
- For a majority, living together without marriage is acceptable.
- An overwhelming number of respondents, including widows, widowers, divorcees, and singles, are sexually active.
- Most are satisfied with their sex lives.
- Many vary their sexual practices to achieve satisfaction.
- For a surprising number of older people, oral sex is considered the most exciting sexual experience.
- Respondents typically show little embarrassment or anxiety about sex.
- Most enjoy nudity with their partners.

Source: Data from B. Starr and M. Weiner, *The Starr-Weiner Report on Sex and Sexuality in the Mature Years,* 1981, p. 241.

The question of whether to allow residents of nursing homes to engage in sex has been a growing problem as elders' attitudes toward sex change.

A decline in sexual activity among elderly men may be due to concern about ability to consummate intercourse. What would you say are some of the concerns of elderly women?

Sex in Nursing Homes

In their study of the sexual behavior of 63 residents in nursing homes, Wasow and Loeb (1979) reported the following findings:

> The aged interviewees believed that sexual activity was appropriate for other elderly people in the homes; they personally were not involved, chiefly because of lack of opportunity. Most of them admitted having sexual thoughts and feelings. Medical and behavioral personnel showed great reluctance to discuss the subject. It would seem that, if the quality of life in old age is to be improved, there should be some provision in nursing homes for those who desire appropriate sexual activity. (p. 73)

Sex and the "Old-Old"

In a fascinating study restricted to people 80 to 102 years old by Bretschneider and McCoy (1988), we get a look at the sexual activities of those elderly who used to be thought totally inactive. Table 20.2 gives us some surprises! In their past lives, the men claim to have engaged in intercourse more than the women, but no difference occurred in enjoyment. In their present lives, 63 percent of the men and 30 percent of the women say they have intercourse at least sometimes, and 76 percent of the men and 39 percent of the women say they enjoy it at least mildly. Another interesting finding of this study is that the men reported having their first intercourse at an average age of 22 and women at age 25. What a difference from today's figures (see chapter 13)!

Nevertheless, it is quite likely a real decline in sexual activity occurs among the elderly. Men are often concerned about their ability to consummate intercourse. They also worry about their loss of masculinity, in terms of looks and strength.

Table 20.2	Reported Frequency and Enjoyment of Sexual Intercourse by 80- to 102-Year-Old Men and Women in the Past (Younger Years) and in the Present									

	Frequency									
	Entire Sample		**Never (1)**		**Sometimes (2–3)**		**Often (4–5)**		**Very often (6–7)**	
	N	%	n	%	n	%	n	%	n	%	x^2
Past										
Men	92	92	3	3	3	3	60	65	26	28	
Women	90	88	2	2	10	11	70	78	8	9	14.2
Present										
Men	80	80	30	38	27	34	21	26	2	3	
Women	80	78	56	70	16	20	8	10	0	0	18.5

	Enjoyment								
	Entire Sample		**None (1)**		**Mild (2–3)**		**Moderate (4–5)**		**Great (6–7)**	
	N	%	n	%	n	%	n	%	n	%
Past									
Men	91	91	3	3	5	6	23	25	60	66
Women	92	90	5	5	9	10	34	37	44	48
Present									
Men	79	79	19	24	11	14	21	27	28	35
Women	82	80	50	61	10	12	13	16	9	11

From J. G. Bretschneider and N. L. McCoy, "Sexual Interest and Behavior in Healthy 80- to 102-Year-Olds" in *Archives of Sexual Behavior,* 17(2):117. Copyright © 1988 Plenum Press, New York, NY. Reprinted by permission.

Generative love

Most characteristic of parenthood, a time during which sacrifices are gladly made for the sake of the children.

Existential love

The capacity to cherish the present moment, perhaps first learned when we confront the certainty of our own personal death.

However, the literature on sex among the elderly shows a new attitude emerging. Datan and colleagues (1987) described very well a difference between **generative love** and **existential love:**

> ■ We believe that existential love, the capacity to cherish the present moment, is one of the greatest gifts of maturity. Perhaps we first learn this love when we first confront the certainty of our own personal death, most often in middle adulthood. Generative love is most characteristic of parenthood, a time during which sacrifices are gladly made for the sake of the children. However, it is existential love, we feel, that creates the unique patience and tenderness so often seen in grandparents, who know how brief the period of childhood is, since they have seen their own children leave childhood behind them.
>
> We have not yet awakened to the potential for existential love between old women and old men, just as we are not yet prepared to recognize the pleasures of sexuality as natural to the life span, particularly to the postparental period.
>
> Those old people who have had the misfortune of spending their last days in nursing homes may learn that love can be lethal. We have been told of an old woman and an old man who fell in love. The old man's children thought this late flowering was "cute"; however, the old woman's children thought it was disgraceful, and over her protests, they removed her from the nursing home. One month later she registered her final protest: she died. (p. 287)

Out of all the hundreds and hundreds of studies of monkeys, one finding applies to every type: From the largest gorilla to the tiniest spider monkey, they all spend about four hours a day in "grooming." Grooming refers to their different ways of touching—stroking, removing bugs, hugging, sex. It is obviously genetic. It seems likely that we humans have something in common with them. We all need to be touched, too. The elderly get less touching than the rest of us, perhaps because they are not seen as being attractive. But they need physical contact just as much as everyone else. It is hoped that a new attitude will spread and make their lives that much happier.

The Elderly and Their Families

The familial relationship undergoes changes in membership, organization, and role during the aging process. Due to improved health care, individuals can expect to live longer, which means that married couples will have more years together after their children leave home. Though exceptions (those who are divorced, childless, or who never married) occur, most middle-aged couples go through similar stages in the life cycle (Williamson & others, 1980). Following are the four basic phases:

1. The child-launching phase

2. The childless preretirement period

3. The retirement phase

4. Widowhood

The duration of each stage in the life cycle, and the ages of the family members for each stage, vary from family to family. Childbearing patterns have a lot to do with life in the late stages of life. Couples who complete their families in their early years will have a different lifestyle when their last child leaves home than couples with "change of life" babies, who may have a dependent child at home when they are ready to retire. This can pose serious economic problems for those retirees on fixed incomes, trying to meet the staggering costs of education. In addition, with children in the home, saving for retirement is difficult.

AN APPLIED VIEW

Decisions Most Older Couples Must Make

Most older couples need to make a number of decisions that will be vital to their family lives (Cox, 1988), including whether or not to

- remain in their current home with its history and memories, or move to a new home or apartment.

- remain in the same community or move to a different one, or perhaps move to a retirement community.

- remain active in current organizations, join new ones, or simply not be bothered with organizational affiliations.

- try to locate near children and close friends or move to a different section of the country.

- seek activities satisfying to both husband and wife, or participate independently.

Obviously the decisions they make can have a major impact on their families and themselves. Each of these decisions has the capacity to cause considerable stress for all the family's members. Being aware of them, and confronting them openly, perhaps with a counselor, can greatly reduce the stress.

Retirement may bring about changes for both spouses, but wives who have not properly prepared themselves emotionally and financially for retirement may find it particularly stressful. Retirement generally signifies a decrease in income and a lowering of the standard of living, but it may take a while before some of these problems are noticed. Household duties may change, with the husband generally helping more.

Widowhood

Older women, who are more likely to be widowed than men because the men die earlier, often turn to activities with other widows for enjoyment.

With women outliving men by large margins, the wife is most often the survivor. Only half of women over 65 are living with a partner. Lopata's (1973) study of Chicago-area widows sought to find what changes occur with the death of a spouse. She found that "widowhood means the loss, reorganization, and acquisition of social roles" (p. 6). A widow forfeits the role of her partner's "nurse, confidant, sex partner and housekeeper."

Many widows have to take on additional duties, including managing household finances and janitorial tasks, and some will have to seek employment. Widowhood affects social relationships with family and friends. Often a widow is the "fifth wheel" in social settings, and former relationships may dissipate. Fortunately, new social activities and friends emerge and replace the old ones. Many of Lopata's widows came to realize some compensations in widowhood, including increased independence and a decline in their work load.

Children may play an integral part in their mother's adjustment to widowhood in three ways: by taking over some of the father's responsibilities; by supplanting the father as the mother's center of attention; and by being supportive and maintaining relationships (Lopata, 1973).

Remarriage is an alternative to the loneliness that most widows and widowers feel after losing their spouse. However, remarriage rates for senior citizens are low, and it is not an option for most. The reasons for not remarrying include the following:

- Many of the elderly view it as improper.

- Children may oppose remarriage.

- Social Security laws penalize widows who remarry.

- There are three single women for every single man over age 65.

Seniors who choose to remarry, however, enjoy much success if the ingredients of love, companionship, financial security, and offspring consent are present.

An important aspect of happiness in the elderly person's family life is whether he or she is living with a spouse, with children, or with another relative. The first has been more common in recent years (Turner & Helms, 1989), probably as a result of better health among the elderly, and better support systems for them. In most cases, living with one's spouse is preferred, so this is probably contributing to an increase in happiness in our senior citizens.

Care of Elderly Parents

Elderly people identify their adult children, when they have them, as the primary helpers in their lives. When these people have both an adult son and an adult daughter, elderly people most often name the son as the primary helper (Stoller & others, 1992). This is surprising, because as we pointed out in chapter 18, care of elderly parents is almost always undertaken by daughters, if the elderly persons have any.

In the past, elder care was most often done by unmarried daughters, if there were any. They were expected to do this because it was assumed that the work would be easier for them, since they had no responsibilities for husband or children. In fact, married women report that their married status makes caregiving for their elderly parents easier. They have less depression, higher incomes, and other forms of socioeconomic support than unmarried women (Brody & others, 1992).

What about the situation in which the elders have no children, or at least none who are willing or able to care for them? Research indicates that elderly individuals who have no kin tend to substitute a close friend whom they persuade to take the place of the absent relative. Nearly 40 percent of a group of elders surveyed could actually identify such a person who filled this role (MacRae, 1992).

A MULTICULTURAL VIEW

Caregiving for Elderly in Swarthmore, Pennsylvania, and Botswana, Africa

Draper and Keith (1992) were perplexed by the question, "Why is care for the elderly such a problem for Americans?" Draper had recently returned from studying the lifestyle of the !Kung people of Botswana and decided to do a comparison study with Keith of elder care in Swarthmore, a Philadelphia suburb.

Older residents of Swarthmore are extremely worried about their care, especially with regard to loss of health, which generates feelings of fear. The researchers learned that for many of the elders, need for care is a primary reason for moving into Swarthmore. They do so to be near a child or relative who could supervise their eventual move into a retirement home should professional care prove necessary. The problem is that whether they moved into Swarthmore (to be near relatives), or moved out

of Swarthmore (to enter a retirement community), the costs to the older person usually involve loss of ties to their communities.

In contrast, elders of the !Kung villages "age in place." They do not retire, relocate, or enter age-graded elder care institutions. Indeed, they have no other place to go. The !Kung were asked, "For an old person, what makes a good life?" One-third responded, "If you have a child to take care of you, you have a good life." Care is almost always provided by one's children and community.

For the people of Swarthmore, technologically superb care is available, but its benefits must be weighed against the loss of community ties and personal autonomy. For the !Kung, social needs and physical care are compatible.

Clearly, most family and close friends still feel that they ought to take care of the elderly in their own homes if possible. In their study of the outcome of several types of elder care, however, Strawbridge and Wallhagen (1992) concluded: "While important, family care for frail elders is not always appropriate and should be but one option in long-term care" (p. 92).

The Changing Role of the Grandparent

In today's world, with increased life expectancy, grandparenthood has become a unique experience within the family system (Smith, 1989). Grandparenthood is positively linked to the mental health and morale of elderly persons. Kornhaber and Woodward (1981) suggested that a "vital connection" exists between grandparent and grandchild.

In a classic study, Neugarten and Weinstein (1964) examined styles of grandparenting and created categories for five general styles: "formal," "the fun seeker," "the surrogate parent," "the reservoir of family wisdom," and "the distant figure." An interesting finding was that the fun seeker and the distant figure emerged as the most popular styles of grandparenting. Both exclude an emphasis on authority. Many grandparents preferred a grandparent-grandchild relationship in which their role was simply to enjoy being with their grandchildren rather than feeling responsible as coparents with their adult children.

In the American culture of today, the importance of grandparents is intensified, due to the many roles they feel they must play: providing emotional support and financial assistance to their children and grandchildren in divorce and substance abuse situations (Smith, 1989) and acting as gender-role socialization agents (Thomas & Datan, 1983). Bengston and Robertson (1985) included some "symbolic functions" of the grandparent role in today's culture: acting as the "family watchdog"; behaving as arbitrators; and merely "being there."

With the changing nature of American families in recent decades, the role of the grandparent has changed. Are these changes positive, or should we attempt to return to past family patterns?

AN APPLIED VIEW

Do You Know Your Grandparents?

Are your grandparents still alive? Even though you have probably known them for many years, you may not know them very well. Try answering the questions below for one set of your grandparents, and if possible, check your answers with them to get your GKQ (Grandparent Knowledge Quotient).

1. What's your grandmother's favorite activity?
2. In total, how many rings do your grandparents wear?
3. What color are your grandfather's eyes?
4. Where does your grandfather eat lunch?
5. What is your grandmother's favorite TV show?
6. In what year did your grandparents meet?

7. For whom did your grandmother vote for president in 1992?
8. Does your grandfather know how to prepare asparagus?
9. Who is your grandfather's favorite relative?
10. Name some of either of your grandparents' favorite movie stars.

You might try making up a test like this about yourself and asking your grandparents, parents, siblings, and friends to respond to it. It should be interesting to see which of them knows you best.

Erikson (1963) explained, in his stage of generativity, the significance of grandchildren to grandparents. Erikson believed that generativity referred to providing a better life for future generations and that not having reached the stage of generativity would cause stagnation and self-absorption in the individual (see chapter 18). Thomas and Datan (1983) highlight the reciprocal nature of generativity by arguing that the personal development of grandparents is furthered by their close rapport with younger generations and vice versa.

A MULTICULTURAL VIEW

Grandfather-Grandchild Relations among White and African American Men

What causes grandfathers to be close to their grandchildren? Kivett (1991) found that a number of factors make important differences. For both whites and African Americans, relationship with the grandchild is more warm and loving when: they live near each other (most lived within 10 minutes of each other); the grandchild is a grandson; both grandfather and grandchildren are younger (most grandchildren were 15 years or younger); and health of the grandfather is good. The closeness of the relationship also increases with the number of grandchildren and the educational and income levels of the grandfather. Both groups rated the grandfather role as third in importance to other roles (spouse first, then father).

The grandfather role assumed more importance among African American than white men, however. African American grandfathers had more levels of kin in their households, more associations with grandchildren, and greater expectations for assistance. They also reported getting along better with grandchildren and felt closer to them than white grandfathers. Differences appear to be a function of ethnic background rather than economic factors. Kivett observed that African American grandfathers see children as holding the key to the future, whereas white grandfathers seemed to emphasize the past and hold themselves up as models, seeing their role as passing on customs to the young.

The Older Worker

Only a small percentage of all older adults are in the labor force—about 11 percent. Much of this is due to forced retirement (Sommerstein, 1986). However, even with the extension of the mandatory age of retirement from 65 to 70 by Congress in 1978, not many people want to continue working past 65. For example, a large steel corporation that has never had mandatory retirement finds that less than 1 percent of their 40,000 workers stay on past 65. The average age of retirement at this company is below 62.

Interest in Work

Older people clearly care less about working than younger people. For example, Cohn (1979) reported: "Toward the end of the period of labor force participation, the satisfactions men derive from work are transferred from the actual experience of work to its consequences" (p. 264). These percentages likely are even lower today. That is, no more than half of older workers may be willing to work for its own sake. Of course, many younger workers do it only for the pay, too. The social value of the work itself is probably the most significant differential.

Discrimination

Discrimination against the older worker can be subtle and hard to detect (Findley, 1979). For example, one 61-year-old female designer was told by the company she worked for that they were going out of business and that she would not be able to collect her company pension. Also losing their jobs were two other persons who had the same job as her, ages 32 and 29. After the company folded, the older woman learned that the owners had formed a new company and had reemployed the two younger designers. She complained to the U.S. government, which took the case to court and won $125,000 in benefits for her.

Performance

As this society ages through greater longevity, the aging of the baby boom generation, and decreased birth rates, some of the stereotypes about aging are coming under closer scrutiny. One stereotype is that work performance necessarily declines with age (Rhodes, 1983). An excellent series of longitudinal studies performed by Erdman Palmore and his colleagues (1985), which yielded a sample of more than 7,000 subjects, has provided an in-depth look at this and other aspects of the relationships between old age and work. The stereotype that age equals declining performance is getting more research attention because the number of workers in the last two decades of their careers will grow 41 percent while the number of workers 16 to 35 years old will decline slightly (Johnston, 1987).

The stereotype is bolstered by research on aging that demonstrates a decline in abilities such as dexterity, speed of response, agility, hearing, and vision. If all these abilities decline, then surely job performance must decline with age. However, McEvoy and Cascio (1989) recently conducted an extensive meta-analysis (a study that compiles the results of many other studies) of 96 studies and found no relationship between age and job performance. It made no difference whether the performance measure was ratings or productivity measures, nor whether the type of job was professional or nonprofessional.

What explanation is there for these results? How does the older worker deal with the mild decline of physical abilities that affects most elderly persons? Experience is one answer. There is said to be no substitute for it, and it is certainly valued by employers. Other reasons cited are that older workers have lower absenteeism, turnover, illness, and accident rates (Kacmar & Ferris, 1989; Martocchio, 1989). They also tend to have higher job satisfaction and more positive work values than younger workers (Rhodes, 1983). These qualifications seem to offset any decreases in physical ability that increasing age causes.

A number of new programs are being set up to help more older workers achieve as much as they can on the job (Brady & Gray, 1988). When older workers are adequately advised, they can remain a useful and satisfied part of the workforce (Bornstein, 1986; Cahill & Salomone, 1987). More and more, we find that counselors in this field employ the biopsychosocial model in their work. Can you see how?

Retirement

■ "I just don't want to retire," said Charlie, a 65-year-old shipping clerk. "But you've worked hard, and you should get the fruits of your labor," said his boss. "Fruits of my labor, my backside! I know lots of guys, as soon as they retire, they get sick or something and then they die. I know if I retire I'm gonna die. I'm gonna die!" Despite his protestations, Charlie was retired. Three months later he was dead.

For many people, retirement is a welcome relief from a frustrating and boring job. For others, it is just as difficult as being unemployed. Retirement requires changing the habits of an adult lifetime. This probably explains why more than 11 percent of those 65 and over are employed.

Nevertheless, the great majority of the elderly do not choose to work. Money is probably not the major factor in that decision (Hayward, 1986). The decision is a complicated one, but most people now feel they have enough financial security so that they need not work. Health may be the biggest factor. Crowley (1986) found that the well-being of 1,200 retirees was highly dependent on the state of their health at the time of retirement.

Retirement seems to be harder on males than females. Many feel that they have nothing to do, while their wives still have a job. The home still must be taken care of, the meals cooked, the clothes cleaned. Most older wives have already adjusted to a reduction in their roles because their children have left home. For men, the change usually comes all at once.

Retirement and Leisure

How you view retirement depends on the work and leisure experiences you have had up to the point of retirement. The leisure activities pursued throughout life play a crucial role in your social adjustment later on. The relationships among work, retirement, and leisure can be seen in figure 20.1.

Figure 20.1

The interrelatedness of work, leisure, and retirement. Solid lines denote the direct influence of (1) work on leisure, and (2) work and leisure upon retirement. Broken lines suggest a possible feedback influence whereby preferences for uses of leisure time may affect choice of jobs, and the availability of more time in retirement may affect content of leisure activities.

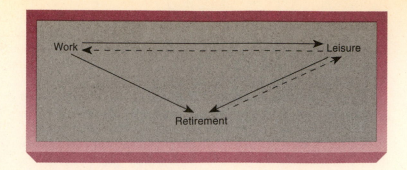

The type of work you do directly affects how you spend leisure time, in two ways. The scheduling of work affects when leisure time is available. A person who works second or third shift might be unable to take part in activities that are often thought of as evening activities, such as dining and dancing. Second, the content of work may influence how much time will be left over for leisure activities. Persons with physically draining positions may be too tired to do anything but nap after work. On the other hand, a person with a desk job may choose physically challenging activities during leisure hours.

When leisure is no more than an extension of work experiences and attitudes, it performs what leisure theorists call a *spillover function*. For example, some people try to relax by performing some of their easier tasks at home—the "stuffed briefcase" syndrome. Conversely, when leisure time is engaged in to make up for disappointment and stress at work, it is described as a *compensatory function*. An example would be excessive partying at the end of the workday or week. An overabundance of compensatory leisure will leave one as unprepared to face retirement as an overabundance of work-related activities.

Making Retirement More Enjoyable

What are some ways that the experience of older workers facing mandatory retirement could best be used in our society?

The belief is growing that retired persons are an important resource to the community. Numerous efforts have been made in recent years to tap this powerful resource. A number of national programs now make an effort to involve retired persons in volunteer and paid work of service to society.

AN APPLIED VIEW

Pet Ownership by Elderly People

Most pets are important to their families, and they have proven especially important to older people. Pets play a role in the lives of elderly people who find retirement boring or are lonely because of the death of family and friends. In a recent study, a sample of older people indicated that their pets were a factor in their choice of housing (Smith & others, 1992). Unfortunately, past practices often discriminated against pet owners, who often were forced either to give up their pet or seek alternative housing. Younger people usually have more housing options, but those options for older people are often limited, due to reduced incomes or health concerns.

Fortunately, things are changing. In 1983 President Reagan signed a law prohibiting discrimination against elderly and handicapped pet owners in federally assisted housing (Public Law 98–181). This law has been enforced unequally because of clumsy state guidelines. Nevertheless, several private housing facilities for semi-independent elderly people in the Chicago area have recently changed their policies to permit pet ownership. This, along with other similar actions across the country, is encouraging.

Since pets are often vital companions for older people, can you think of other things that might be done to help the elderly obtain pets, and to help make ownership easier?

Recent surveys seem to indicate that the "golden years" are not so golden for many retired persons. But with improving health conditions (see chapter 17), improved understanding of the nature of life after 65, and a considerable increase in government involvement, the lives of retirees have a far better chance of being fruitful.

Contrary to the stereotype, getting old need not, and usually does not, mean being lonely. In fact, the elderly, most of whom have a good deal of free time, often use it to develop their social lives. We now move to a consideration of their personal development.

A MULTICULTURAL VIEW

Western and Eastern Views of Retirement

According to Thomas Cole (1991), the Western view of life divides it into three stages: becoming educated, working, and retiring. Those who get a good education and who rise to the upper ranks in their career path can afford to have many choices in their retired years. Those who are not so successful, and they are by far the majority, will have meager retired financial status or will depend on public funds for their sustenance. In either case, they will lose power, respect, and options in their elder years because Westerners see them as weak.

As a result, Cole asserts, many seek to alter, reverse, or somehow control the biological process of aging. In so doing, they fail to appreciate being old as part of human existence. In the view of many Easterners, as physical strength is lost, the wisdom of age takes its place. The elderly grow in respect and thus their role is changed but not diminished. Perhaps we in the West need to become more aware of and rethink our life course perspective.

Guided Review

1. Many changes occur in late adulthood, including role _____ (an abrupt and disruptive change in role) and "crossover" of sex roles.

2. In late adulthood, the gender role of older men becomes _____ like that of women, and women's role becomes _____ like that of men.

3. The child-launching phase, the childless preretirement period, the retirement phase, and _____ are stages most middle-aged and aged couples can anticipate.

4. Five general styles of grandparenting have been identified by Neugarten and Weinstein (1964): formal, fun seeking, _____ _____ , reservoir of family wisdom, and distant figure.

5. Although some decline in dexterity, speed, and agility occurs in older workers, _____ may be one of the reasons that job performance does not generally decline among these workers.

6. Leisure theorists write about two functions for leisure: a spillover function and a _____ function.

7. Retirement is _____ difficult for females than for males.

Personal Development

Two points of view have received most interest in the field of personality development in the elderly: those of the Committee on Human Development and those of Erik Erikson.

Answers

1. discontinuity 2. more, more 3. widowhood 4. surrogate parent 5. experience 6. compensatory 7. less

Personal Development: Committee on Human Development

What are the effects of aging on personal development? The Committee on Human Development, consisting of gerontologist Bernice Neugarten and her associates at the University of Chicago have been responsible for some of the most highly respected research on this topic (e.g., Havighurst & others, 1968; Neugarten, 1968).

Adults between the ages of 54 and 94 who were residents of Kansas City were asked to participate in a study of change across the adult lifespan. The sample is somewhat biased in that it represents only white persons who were living on their own (i.e., not institutionalized) at the time of the study. They were somewhat better educated and of a higher socioeconomic group than is typical for this age group. Nevertheless, the sample is reasonably well balanced, and because of the thoroughness with which these persons were studied, this research has become a classic in the field of adult psychology. Neugarten summarizes the findings:

- In the middle years (especially the fifties), a change occurs in the perception of time and death and the relationship of the self to them. Introspection, contemplation, reflection, and self-evaluation become important aspects of life. People at this age become more interested in their "inner selves."

- Perception of how well one can control the environment undergoes a marked change:

> ■ Forty-year-olds, for example, seem to see the environment as one that rewards boldness and risk-taking, and to see themselves as possessing energy congruent with the opportunities perceived in the outer world. Sixty-year-olds, however, perceive the world as complex and dangerous, no longer to be reformed in line with one's wishes, and the individual as conforming and accommodating to outer-world demands. (1968, p. 140)

- **Emotional energy** declines with age. Tests showed that intensity of emotion invested in tasks undergoes a definite decline in the later years.

- **Gender-role reversals** also occur with age (discussed earlier in this chapter).

- **Age-status** becomes more rigid with development. Age-status refers to society's expectations about what is normal at various ages. These expectations change not only with advancing years, but according to the particular society and to the historical context. For example, in 1940 a woman who was not married by age 22 was not considered unusual, but if she had not married by the time she was 27, people began to worry. In the late 1980s, the expected age of marriage is much less rigid. This holds only for the United States; in Samoa, for example, concern arises if a person is not married by age 15.

What is the optimum pattern of aging in terms of our relationships with other people? The Committee on Human Development has also investigated this question. For many years, there have been two different positions on this question, known as the activity theory and the disengagement theory.

According to the **activity theory,** human beings flourish through interaction with other people and through keeping physically active. They are unhappy when, as they reach the older years, their contacts with others shrink as a result of death, illness, and societal limitations. Those who are able to keep up the social activity of their middle years are considered the most successful.

Disengagement theory contradicts this idea. According to this position, the belief that activity is better than passivity is a bias of the Western world. This was

---

Emotional energy

The emotional feelings invested in various life tasks.

Gender-role reversals

Older men see themselves and other males as becoming submissive and less authoritative with advancing years. Conversely, older women see themselves and other women as becoming more dominant and self-assured as they grow older.

Age-status

Refers to society's expectations about what is normal at various ages.

Activity theory

Human beings flourish through interaction with other people. They are unhappy when, as they reach the older years, their contacts with others shrink as a result of death, illness, and societal limitations. Those who are able to keep up the social activity of their middle years are considered the most successful.

Disengagement theory

According to this position, the *most mature* adults are likely to gradually disengage themselves from their fellow human beings in preparation for death. They become less interested in their interactions with others, and more concerned with internal concerns.

Clearly the group on the left is enjoying itself more than the woman on the right, but does that mean that the disengagement theory is wrong? Isn't it only natural for people to slowly disengage from society as they approach death?

not always so; the Greeks, for example, valued their warriors and athletes but reserved the highest distinction for such contemplative philosophers as Sophocles, Plato, and Aristotle (Bellah, 1978). Many people in the countries of the Eastern Hemisphere also hold this view. According to disengagement theory, the most mature adults are likely to gradually disengage themselves from their fellow human beings in preparation for death. They become less interested in their interactions with others and more absorbed in internal concerns. They accept the decreasing attention of a society that views them as losing power.

In a second aspect of the study by the Committee (Havighurst & others, 1968), a distinction is made between social and psychological disengagement. *Social disengagement* refers to restricting interactions with other human beings; *psychological disengagement* has to do more with concentrating one's attention within oneself. In a sense, they are opposite sides of the same coin. The results were quite clear: Both social and psychological disengagement increase with age. The investigators found that psychological disengagement is more prevalent in a person's fifties, apparently as a precursor to social disengagement, which becomes more apparent in 60- and 70-year-olds.

Does this mean that the tendency toward disengagement is more normal than the tendency toward activity? Not necessarily. Researchers found that as disengagement increases, the individual's feelings of happiness also usually decrease. This seems to indicate that activity is more desired by the elderly, but they simply cannot achieve it. On the other hand, the unhappiness that results from disengagement is really quite moderate, which may support the disengagement theory.

Havighurst and associates (1968) found that, in terms of "successful aging," a person who stays at home and pursues a hobby can be just as happy and adjusted as one who joins many postretirement activities and work. The different personality types have their unique ways of adjusting to life stresses and changing life occurrences.

In summary, neither the activity theory nor the disengagement theory of optimal aging is totally supported by the Committee. The authors conclude that some older persons

■ accept this drop in activity as an inevitable accompaniment of growing old; and they succeed in maintaining a sense of self-worth and a sense of satisfaction with past and present life as a whole. Other older persons are less successful. (Havighurst & others, 1968, p. 171)

What are some behaviors that our society expects from the elderly? How do we respond to elderly adults who do not fit "the mold"?

Neugarten (1968) concluded that most elderly persons are conflicted. They wish to remain active in order to maintain their sense of self-worth, but they also wish to withdraw from social commitments to protect themselves from the pain of loss, caused by the deaths of people they care about and by thoughts of their own death. She suggested that this conflict is resolved in different ways by people of different personality types; therefore, neither the activity theory nor the disengagement theory can completely explain the process of aging.

Nevertheless, it is unfortunate that some administrators of retirement programs and nursing homes have used the disengagement theory to justify restricting the activities of some elderly. Cath (1975) believed that because some of these individuals have "unconscious gerontophobic [fear of the elderly] attitudes . . . , they interpreted [disengagement] according to their personal motivation and limitation— often colored by financial considerations" (p. 212).

Without question, the research reported in this section is now dated. However, the theoretical conclusions that have resulted from this work are still respected throughout the field.

AN APPLIED VIEW   *Getting Perspective on Your Thinking*

If you hope to be the kind of person who ends his or her life with a sense of integrity, the time to begin is right now. You don't get to be a happy elderly person unless you plan and work for it. You can do this in many ways, but we have some suggestions to pass along to you.

Whenever you are about to make an important decision, follow these four steps:

1. Come to some tentative conclusion about what you should do.
2. Close your eyes and picture yourself as a 75-year-old woman or man.

3. Imagine yourself explaining your decision to that old person, and try to picture her or him telling you what she or he thinks of what you have decided.
4. If you don't like what you hear, rethink the decision and go through this process again.

Use this technique to get a better perspective on your thinking; you will be surprised by how much wisdom you already have.

Personal Development: Erikson

Integrity
The resolution of each of the first seven crises in Erikson's theory should lead us to achieve a sense of personal integrity. Older adults who have a sense of integrity feel their lives have been well spent. The decisions and actions they have taken seem to them to fit together.

Erikson believed that resolution of each of the first seven crises in his theory should lead us to achieve a sense of personal **integrity.** Older adults who have a sense of integrity feel their lives have been well spent. The decisions and actions they have taken seem to them to fit together—their lives are integrated. They are saddened by the sense that time is running out and that they will not get many more chances to make an impact, but they feel reasonably well satisfied with their achievements. They usually have a sense of having helped to achieve a more dignified life for humankind.

The acceptance of human progress, including one's own, is essential for this final sense of integrity. This is the path to wisdom, which Erikson defined as "the detached and yet active concern with life itself in the face of death itself" (1978, p. 26).

Despair
The counterpart to integrity in the last stage of Erikson's theory. When people look back over their lives and feel that they have made many wrong decisions, or more commonly, that they have not made any decisions at all.

When people look back over their lives and feel that they have made many wrong decisions, or more commonly, that they have frequently not made any decisions at all, they tend to see life as lacking integrity. They feel **despair,** which is the second half of this last stage of crisis. They are angry that there can never be another chance to make their lives make sense. They often hide their fear of death by appearing contemptuous of humanity in general, and those of other religions and races in particular. As Erikson put it, "Such despair is often hidden behind a show of disgust" (1968, p. 140).

Erikson believes that the character of the old Swedish doctor in Ingmar Bergman's famous film, *Wild Strawberries,* excellently reflects the eight stages he proposes.

Erikson (1978) provided a panoramic view of his life-cycle theory in an analysis of Swedish film director Ingmar Bergman's famous film *Wild Strawberries.* In this picture, an elderly Swedish doctor goes from his hometown to a large city, where he is to be honored for 50 years of service to the medical profession. On the way, he stops by his childhood home and, resting in an old strawberry patch, begins an imaginary journey through his entire life, starting with his earliest memories. In the ruminations of this old man, Erikson saw clear and specific reflections of the eight stages he proposed.

Erikson demonstrated through Bergman's words that, like his other seven stages, this last stage involves a life crisis. Poignantly, the old doctor struggles to make sense out of the events of his life. He is ultimately successful in achieving a sense of integrity. The film is well worth seeing, and Erikson's analysis makes it an even more meaningful experience.

🌳 Guided Review 🌳

8. Researchers with the Committee on Human Development found that adults between the ages of 54 and 94 changed their perception of how well they could control the environment and that there was a marked decline in the _____ _____ they invested in tasks as they aged.

9. _____ theory and _____ theory offer explanations of ways in which people cope with aging.

10. According to the disengagement theory, most adults will disengage themselves from their fellow human beings in preparation for _____ .

11. According to Neugarten, many elderly people are in conflict as to whether to remain active so as to maintain their sense of _____ or to withdraw from social commitments to protect themselves from the pain of loss.

12. Erikson suggests that as we look back over our lives, if we see our lives as _____ , we have achieved the goal of his final stage of life.

Answers

8. emotional energy 9. Activity, disengagement 10. death 11. self-worth 12. integrated

CONCLUSION

Many changes happen during later adulthood. A "crossover" effect in gender roles occurs, sexual activity changes, and the nature of family relationships undergoes several alterations.

As we leave the industrial age and enter the age of information processing, the nation's older workers experience an incredibly different environment from that of their predecessors of 50 years ago. Even retirement is a much-changed adventure. As in each of the preceding chapters, life appears as never-ending change but change with discernible patterns. Perhaps more stress takes place in old age than before, but more effective techniques are also available for dealing with it.

In the next, final chapter, we examine the final experience of life, one that is itself often a very significant stressor—dying. We also review research on the principal method of dealing with both stress and death, and a vital part of life for most Americans: spirituality.

 ## CHAPTER HIGHLIGHTS

Social Development

- A number of gerontologists have noted that people in late adulthood experience a "crossover" in gender roles: Older men become more like women, and older women become more like men.
- White summarizes that in late adulthood males are generally more sexually active than females but that declining activity in the female is usually attributable to declining interest or illness in the male partner.

- Research suggests four basic phases through which most middle-aged and aged couples pass: child-launching, childless preretirement, retirement, and widowhood.
- Although older people show less interest in working than younger people, discrimination and stereotypes about older workers underestimate their desire to help.
- Men usually find retirement more difficult than do women.

Personal Development

- Neugarten's work on the effects of aging on personal development reveals that elderly people become more interested in their "inner selves," perceptions of the environment change, psychic energy declines, gender-role reversals occur, and age-status becomes more rigid.
- The Committee on Human Development investigated patterns of aging, including activity theory and disengagement theory.
- For Erikson, resolution of each of the first seven stages in his eight-stage theory should lead people to achieve a sense of integrity in the last stage. If not, they experience despair.

 ## KEY TERMS

Activity theory 522
Age-status 522
Crossover 510
Despair 524
Differential opportunity structure 511

Disengagement theory 522
Emotional energy 522
Existential love 514
Gender-role reversals 522
Generative love 514

Impotency 512
Integrity 524
Prostatectomy 512
Role discontinuity 510

 ## WHAT DO YOU THINK?

1. Which would you rather be, an old man or an old woman? Why?
2. What is your position on sex in old-age institutions? Should there be any restrictions at all?

3. Which aspect of your family life do you most fear change in as you get old?
4. Which do you favor, the activity theory or the disengagement theory?
5. Some have said that whereas Erikson's first seven stages describe crises in which action should be taken, the last stage, integrity versus despair, is merely reactive. All he has the elderly doing is sitting in a rocking chair and looking back over their lives. Do you believe that this criticism is valid?

🌳 SUGGESTED READINGS

Cowley, M. (1980). *The view from 80*. New York: Penguin. Critic Donald Hall describes this book as "Eloquent on the felt disparity between an unchanged self and the costume of altered flesh." Cowley wrote this intensely personal book when he himself was 82.

de Beauvoir, S. (1971). *Coming of age*. This magnificent psychological study gives one an intense look at what it means rather than how it feels to become old.

Publications of the American Association of Retired Persons (AARP). With about 30 million members, the powerful AARP is a rich source of information on the elderly. Write to them at National Headquarters, 601 E Street NW, Washington, DC 20049.

Roff, L. & Atherton, C. (1989). *Promoting successful aging*. Chicago: Nelson-Hall. This readable book is half about theory and research and half about the specific strategies for dealing with the needs of the elderly. It is a bible for those who want to work with older adults.

🌳 CHAPTER REVIEW TEST

1. In late adulthood, crossover in sex roles means that
   a. older men and women identify with each other more.
   b. older men become more like women, and older women become more like men.
   c. older men take on roles most often associated with women.
   d. older women take on roles most often associated with men.

2. Whether or not an older woman is sexually active depends mainly on her
   a. level of interest.
   b. marital status.
   c. perception of her children's attitudes.
   d. number of interpersonal relationships.

3. Examples of experiences that may inhibit or terminate sexual activity in adult men include
   a. physical changes.
   b. nonsupportive partners and peers.
   c. internal fears.
   d. All of the answers are correct.

4. What is the first phase of the life cycle most middle-aged couples go through?
   a. widowhood
   b. the retirement phase
   c. the child-launching phase
   d. the childless preretirement period

5. John and Sarah are the parents of three children and provide an example of generative love. They
   a. gladly make many sacrifices for the sake of the children.
   b. cherish the time they have with their children at present.
   c. expose their children to the culture and traditions of their ancestry.
   d. are committed to spending all their time with the children.

6. In Helena Lopata's study of changes that occur with the death of a spouse, many widows reported that a compensation of widowhood is
   a. managing household finances.
   b. employment.
   c. increased independence.
   d. increased economic well-being.

7. When children supplant the deceased father as the mother's center of attention, they are
   a. preventing their mother from becoming independent.
   b. prolonging their mother's grief.
   c. helping their mother adjust to widowhood.
   d. not allowing their mother to remarry.

8. Older workers make valued employees for all of the following reasons, *except*
   a. lower absenteeism.
   b. lower turnover.
   c. lower accident rates.
   d. lower health-care costs.

9. From research on 1,200 retirees, Crowley (1986) found that a person's state of health was highly dependent upon
   a. whether they were still married.
   b. their financial stability.
   c. their well-being.
   d. their level of education.

10. Retirement may be most stressful for wives who have not properly prepared themselves for retirement financially and
    a. physically.
    b. emotionally.
    c. spiritually.
    d. legally.

11. According to leisure theorists, a spillover function refers to
    a. when leisure is no more than an extension of work experiences and attitudes.
    b. when leisure time is engaged in to make up for disappointment and stress at work.
    c. when leisure time is spent worrying about stressful events at work.
    d. when leisure time takes away from time to be spent at work.

12. The idea that there are societal expectations about what is normal at various stages refers to
    a. gender roles.
    b. socialization.
    c. age-status.
    d. role continuity.

According to Havighurst and others (1968), concentrating on one's inner self refers to

a. psychological engagement.
b. psychological disengagement.
c. reflection.
d. existential love.

14. When adults distance themselves from other human beings in preparation for death and become less interested in their interactions with others, it is referred to as

a. disengagement theory.
b. separation theory.
c. distantiation.
d. personal engagement theory.

15. For Erikson (1978), what leads us to a sense of personal integrity?

a. personal well-being
b. a sense of self-worth
c. achievement
d. a sense that life has been well spent

16. According to Erikson, people who are contemptuous of humanity

a. have psychologically disengaged.
b. have socially disengaged.
c. are preparing for death.
d. are looking back over their lives and hiding their fear of death.

Answers

1. b 2. b 3. d 4. c 5. a 6. c 7. c 8. d 9. c 10. b 11. a 12. c 13. b 14. a 15. d 16. d

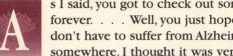

21   Dying and Spirituality

Chapter Outline

A s I said, you got to check out some time; you can't stay here forever. . . . Well, you just hope you go with a little dignity, that you don't have to suffer from Alzheimer's or die slowly in a rest home alone somewhere. I thought it was very interesting when I was in Bora Bora for six months. I was down there making a movie. . . . I did not live with the company, but found a house by myself up a road. There was a family next door—Polynesian natives—and the old lady of the house was there and she was dying. She suddenly said, "I'm going to die," and went to bed for three days and died. I remember at her funeral that everybody was dressed in white; it was like a wedding almost. And I was talking to them about it and they said, "Oh, yes, the fathers and the mothers are the most respected. They just go and die when they're ready." I said, "Geez, does that really go on like this all the time?" They said, "That's the way this society works." There are no old age homes, no old people wandering around, you know, suffering to death. Isn't it a strange thing, I thought to myself. What a respect for age that we don't have. . . . Like I say, life is like a hotel. We all check in and we all check out. Seems to me that the Polynesian approach to checking out is a great deal better than ours.

Actor Jason Robards, age 69
Quoted in Berman and Goldman (1992)

The Role of Death in Life

Americans, who have long been accused of abhorring the subject of death, are now giving it considerable attention. From the ways we teach the young about death (Lansdown & Benjamin, 1985; Speece & Brent, 1984; Stambrook & Parker, 1987) to the ways in which we bury our dead (Marshall & Levy, 1990; Schneider, 1984; Swanson & Bennett, 1983), we seem to have switched to an eager confrontation of the problem.

In this section, we review research and theory from the social and physical sciences to examine three major concerns: What is death? How do we deal with the death of others? How do we deal with our own death?

After reading chapter 21, you should be able to

- Explain the four types of death.

- Give the legal definition of death.

- Explain what is meant by grief work and its place in Lindemann's stages.

- Explain what is meant by "pathological grieving" and how it prevents successful conclusion of a life crisis.

- Discuss the positive effects of grief and the funeral on dealing with another's death.

- Discuss suicide among the elderly along with the influence of race, residence, and gender.

- Evaluate information on alternative ways of dying "successfully."

- Present reasons for the growth in religious participation among adults.

Since the first historian, Homer, began recording the lives of the Greeks, the meaning of death has been a central issue.

- Compare the theories of spirituality presented by Frankl, Jung, and Wilson.
- List and describe Fowler's six stages of faith development.

What Is Death?

> The matter of my friend rests heavy upon me.
> How can I be salved?
> How can I be stilled?
> My friend, who I loved, has turned to clay.
> Must I, too, lie me down
> Not to rise again for ever and ever?
>
> Gilgamesh, c. 2000 B.C.

In the movies, death is almost invariably portrayed in the same sequence: Dying people make a final statement, close their eyes, fall back on the pillow or into the arms of a loved one, and are pronounced dead. In fact, death rarely occurs that way (Veatch, 1981, 1984). In most cases, the person dies gradually. Death, then, is a process, not a moment.

Ascertaining when people are truly and finally dead has been a medical problem for centuries. For example, in the early 1900s, Franz Hartmann claimed to have collected approximately 700 cases of premature burial or "close calls" (Hardt, 1979). In 1896 the "Society for the Prevention of Premature Burial" was founded. Fear of premature burial was so strong that in 1897 in Berlin, a patent was granted for a life signal device that sent up a warning flag and turned on a light if movement was detected inside the coffin.

We no longer have any serious problem in determining whether a person is dead. But determining exactly when death occurred has come to be of even greater importance because of organ donations. All the body's systems do not cease simultaneously, so disagreements exist over which system is most significant in judging whether a person is dead.

Four Types of Death

Today, four types of death are recognized: clinical death, brain death, biological or cellular death, and social death.

Clinical Death

In one sense, the individual is dead when his or her respiration and heartbeat have stopped. This is the aspect of dying referred to in the movies when the doctor turns and sadly announces, "I'm sorry, but he's gone." Actually, **clinical death** is the least useful to the medical profession and to society at large because it is unreliable.

Since the advent of **cardiopulmonary resuscitation (CPR)** many individuals whose lungs and heart had ceased to function have been saved. In other cases, spontaneous restarting of the heart and lungs has occurred after failure.

Brain Death

Death of the brain occurs when it fails to receive a sufficient supply of oxygen for a short period of time (usually 8 to 10 minutes). The cessation of brain function occurs in three stages: First the cortex stops, then the midbrain fails, and finally the brain stem ceases to function. When the cortex and midbrain stop operating, **brain death** has occurred, and the person enters an irreversible coma. The body can remain alive in this condition for a long time, because the autonomic processes are governed by the brain stem. Consciousness and alertness, however, will never be regained (Kammerman, 1988).

Biological Death

The cells and the organs of the body can remain in a functioning condition long after the failure of the heart and lungs. **Biological death** occurs when it is no longer possible to discern an electrical charge in the tissues of the heart and lungs.

Social Death

Sudnow (1967) was the first to suggest the concept of **social death,** which, "within the hospital setting, is marked at that point at which a patient is treated essentially as a corpse although perhaps still 'clinically' or 'biologically' alive" (p. 74). He cites cases in which body preparation (e.g., closing the eyes, binding the feet) were started while the patient was still alive, to make things easier for the staff. Also, in some cases, family members have signed autopsy permissions while the patient was still alive.

So when is a person really dead? If a person has suffered brain death, but the heart is still beating, should the heart be removed and used for a transplant operation?

One complex case (Goldsmith, 1988) involved the Loma Linda University Medical Center, famous for its work in the area of organ transplants. They attempted to initiate a program that would provide scarce organs for transplants. In this program, healthy hearts and other organs would be taken from babies born with *anencephaly,* a condition in which part or all of the brain is missing at birth. Ninety-five percent of these babies die within one week. When the anencephalic infants were born, they were flown to Loma Linda and given traditional "comfort care" (warmth, nutrition, and hydration). In addition, they were put on artificial breathing support for a maximum of seven days. The hospital maintained that they were put on respirators until a technical definition of brain death could be ascertained. But critics contended that this was done because the organs needed the time to mature for a successful transplant to occur. A storm of controversy ended the program before any donations could be made. Critics accused the hospital of "organ farming." The hospital argued that it was not only trying to increase the number of organ donors for infants but also giving the families of anencephalic babies an opportunity to "turn their tragedy into something good." With the advent of more advanced technology, the distinction between life and death becomes blurred, and the ethical considerations grow increasingly complex.

Clinical death

The individual is dead when his or her respiration and heartbeat have stopped.

Cardiopulmonary resuscitation (CPR)

A technique for reviving an individual's lungs and/or heart that have ceased to function.

Brain death

Death of the brain occurs when it fails to receive a sufficient supply of oxygen for a short period of time (usually eight to ten minutes).

Biological death

Death occurs when it is no longer possible to discern an electrical charge in the tissues of the heart and lungs.

Social death

The point at which a patient is treated essentially as a corpse, although perhaps still "clinically" or "biologically" alive.

The decision to remove life-support systems from a person who is brain-dead—does it belong in the judicial system, or is this decision a personal one to be made by family members only?

It is possible to ensure that all or part of your body will be donated for use after your death, usually by a designation on your driver's license. Have you done this? If not, what are your reasons for refraining?

Legal death

Condition defined as "unreceptivity and unresponsivity, no movements or breathing, no reflexes, and a flat electroencephalogram (EEG) reading that remains flat for 24 hours."

Electroencephalogram (EEG)

A graphic record of the electrical activity of the brain.

The Legal Definition of Death

In 1968 the Harvard Ad Hoc Committee to Examine the Criteria of Brain Death suggested the following criteria for **legal death:** "Unreceptivity and unresponsivity, no movements or breathing, no reflexes, and a flat **electroencephalogram (EEG)** reading that remains flat for 24 hours."

Such criteria preclude the donation of organs in most cases, because the organs would probably suffer irreparable damage in the 24 hours needed to check the EEG. Others have suggested that the time at which the cerebral cortex has been irreparably damaged should be accepted as the time when organs can be removed from the body (Jefko, 1980).

Organ donation is not the only difficulty involved. An increasing number of cases illustrate the ethical problem created by maintaining the life of comatose individuals with the support of technical equipment. A number of medical personnel, philosophers, and theorists have suggested that maintaining life under these conditions is wrong. What do you think?

Although scientists may disagree on the exact nature of death itself, we have been learning a great deal about how people deal, and how they should deal, with the death of their loved ones. We turn to that subject now.

Dealing Successfully with the Death of Others

■ Representative Bryan had the true passion of a runner. It's a shame he's gone, but I can't help feeling that he might not have regretted the manner of his death. Outdoors on a brisk autumn afternoon, in the company of a friend, with a feeling of life in all of the nerve ends that a long life excites. (McCarthy, 1979, p. 120)

In modern Western societies, death comes mostly to the old. For example, 55 percent of all males are 65 or over when they die, and almost a third are past 75. The mortality rate has declined in our country from 17 per 1,000 population in 1900 to slightly less than 9 per 1,000 today. For the first time in history, a family may expect to live 20 years (on the average) without one of its members dying.

The causes of this lower mortality are clear: virtual elimination of infant and child mortality, and increasing control over the diseases of youth and middle age. For this reason, the subject of death became more and more taboo in the first half of this century. Probably as a result, social scientists spent little time studying our reactions to it or trying to find better ways to help us deal with it. Fortunately, in recent decades, this has changed.

Grief Work

■ No one ever told me that grief felt so like fear. I am not afraid, but the sensation is like being afraid. The same fluttering in the stomach, the same restlessness, the yawning. I keep on swallowing. (Lewis, 1963, p. 7)

It has been suggested that people in Western society typically are more fearful of death than are members of Eastern cultures. If so, what factors contribute to our more frightened attitude?

Grief has a great deal in common with fear, and most grieving people really are afraid, at least unconsciously. They are frightened by the strength of their feelings, and they often fear that they are losing their sanity. They feel that they cannot go on, that their loss is so great that their own lives are in danger.

In fact, in some cases they are. Seligman (1975) notes documented cases in which persons have died as a direct cause of grief. Most people who have experienced a loss of a loved one have felt that they never want to love that deeply again. Fortunately, when the grieving is over at last, most people find a renewed desire to love, together with a deepened capacity to do so. As Kübler-Ross (1975) puts it, "If we choose to love, we must also have the courage to grieve" (p. 96).

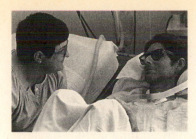

Anticipatory grief, which precedes the sick person's death, is usually very difficult. It often provides a number of benefits to the grieving, however.

Grief not only follows death; when there is advance warning, it frequently precedes it. Fulton (1977) finds that *anticipatory grief* has four phases: depression, a heightened concern for the ill person, rehearsal of death, and finally an attempt to adjust to the consequences that are likely to occur after the death.

The topic of anticipatory grief has received increasing attention lately. Major debates have occurred about its exact nature. For example, Hill and associates (1988) found that those widows who had anticipated their husband's death reported a higher level of mental health than those who had not. Most researchers agree that a forewarning of the impending death of a loved one can have therapeutic consequences (Parke & Weiss, 1983):

- Avoiding the shock and fear that often accompanies sudden death

- Being able to make plans for the future that won't be regarded as betrayals

- Expressing thoughts and feelings to the dying loved ones, thereby avoiding a sense of lost opportunity

- A time to prepare for the changes ahead

But researchers disagree over whether an actual grief process is experienced before the death. Some say that true grief and an actual confrontation of the realities of the death of a loved one can come only after the death has occurred (Parke & Weiss, 1983). Other scientists contend that some type of grieving process is at work when a person is forewarned of an impending death. One need only look at the anguish of a parent or spouse to recognize it. This process should not be expected to take the same form as postdeath grieving and surely won't fully reconcile those who grieve to the realities ahead (Rando, 1986).

Rando and others have begun to devise therapeutic intervention techniques to facilitate the unique aspects of anticipatory grief. As medical technology increasingly makes it possible to stall death, such work will continue to grow in importance.

Pathological Grieving

The process of grieving, painful as it is, is experienced and resolved by most individuals. In some cases, however, morbid grief reactions occur that prevent the successful conclusion of this life crisis. Three types of these grief reactions are: delayed reaction, distorted reaction, and pathological mourning.

Delayed Reaction

In some cases, the intense reaction of the first stage is postponed for days, months, and in some cases years. In these cases, it is common for some seemingly unrelated incident to bring to the surface an intense grieving, which the individual does not even recognize as grief.

Lindemann (1944) gave the example of a 42-year-old man who underwent therapy to deal with an unaccountable depression. It was soon discovered that when he was 22, his 42-year-old mother committed suicide. Apparently, the occurrence of his own 42nd birthday brought to the surface all the feelings that he had managed to repress since that time.

Distorted Reactions

In most cases, distorted reactions are normal symptoms carried to an extreme degree. They include adopting the behavior traits of the deceased, such as aspects of the deceased's fatal illness and other types of psychosomatic ailments, particularly colitis, arthritis, and asthma.

An example we know of is a young man whose mother died of lymphomic cancer. At her death, she had large boils on her neck. Some weeks after she died, her son discovered lumps on his neck that quickly developed into boils. On examination, they were found to be benign. In fact, it was determined that they were entirely psychosomatic. That is, the doctors decided that the only explanation of their existence was the great stress in the young man's mind over the loss of his mother.

Pathological Mourning

In pathological mourning the process is not skipped but is prolonged and intensified to an abnormal degree (disabling distress is experienced for a period of years). Frequently, the person suffering from pathological mourning tries to preserve every object of the deceased in perpetual memory.

An example of this illness is the man who worked hard with his wife to renovate an old cottage they had bought in order to live by a lake not far from their home. A few days before they were going to move in, she died of a heart attack. Many months later, friends noticed that he would disappear for several days at a time. One friend followed him to the cottage and found that he had created a shrine to her memory in it. Her clothes and other possessions were laid out in all the rooms, and her picture was on all the walls. Only after extensive therapy was he able to go through a more normal grief, give up the shrine, and move on with his life.

AN APPLIED VIEW — A Personal Experience of One of the Authors

I am stepping out of my role as an author to relate an experience of mine that is relevant to this discussion of the function of grief. In April 1957 I joined the U.S. Navy and sailed to the Mediterranean for a six-month tour of duty on an oil supply ship. In early November I returned home to a joyful reunion with my family. After this wonderful weekend at home, I returned to my ship. Two days later I received a telegram informing me of a tragedy: My mother, two younger brothers, and two younger sisters had been killed in a fire that had destroyed our house. My father and three younger brothers and a sister had escaped with serious burns.

On the long train ride home from the naval port, I recall thinking that, as the oldest, I should be especially helpful to my father in the terrible time ahead. I was also aware of a curious absence of dismay in myself.

In our medium-sized upstate New York town, the catastrophe was unprecedented, and expressions of grief and condolences were myriad. People kept saying to me, "Don't try to be so brave. It's good for you to let yourself cry." And I tried to, but tears just wouldn't come.

At the funeral, the caskets were closed, and I can remember thinking that maybe, just maybe, this was all just a horrible dream. I distinctly remember one fantasy about my brother Mike. He was born on my first birthday and in the several years before the fire, I had become especially close to him. I imagined that he had actually hit his head trying to escape and had wandered off to Chicago with a case of amnesia and that no one was

willing to admit that they didn't know where he was. I knew this wasn't true, but yet I secretly clung to the possibility. After a very difficult period of time, our family gradually began a new life. Many people generously helped us, and eventually the memories faded.

Several times in the years that followed, I went to doctors because of a stomachache, a painful stiff neck, or some other malady that couldn't be diagnosed physically. One doctor suggested that I might be suffering from an unresolved subconscious problem, but I doubted it.

Then one night in 1972, 15 years after the fire, I was watching "The Walton's Christmas," a television show in which the father of a close family is lost and feared dead. Although dissimilar from my own experience, this tragedy triggered an incredible response in me. Suddenly and finally it occurred to me: "My God, half my family is really gone forever!" I began sobbing and could not stop for more than three hours. When I finally stopped, I felt weak and empty, relieved of an awful burden. In the days that followed I believe I went through a clear-cut "delayed grief" reaction.

Therefore, the answer to the question, at least in my experience, is clear: Grief work really is essential, and we avoid it only at the cost of even greater pain. My father died some years ago, and my grief was immediate and intense. I cannot help but feel that my emotional response this time was considerably more appropriate and healthy.

John Dacey

The Role of Grief

Most psychologists who have examined the role of grief have concluded that it is an essential aspect of a healthy encounter with the crisis of death. They believe that open confrontation with the loss of a loved one is essential to accepting the reality of a world in which the deceased is no longer present. Attempts to repress or avoid thoughts about the loss are only going to push them into the subconscious, where they will continue to cause problems until they are dragged out and accepted fully.

And yet, dealing with grief is also costly. For example, Fulton (1977) found that the mortality rate among grieving persons is seven times higher than a matched sample of nongrieving persons. The first five items on Holmes and Rahe's Social Readjustment Rating Scale (see chapter 14) all involve separation and loss from loved ones. These five most stressful events, in descending order, are death of a spouse, divorce, marital separation, going to jail, and death of a close family member. These events and the grief attached to them are most likely to cause illness.

On the other hand, anthropologist Norman Klein (1978) has suggested that psychologists may be too insistent that our grief be public and deep:

> ■ In our own society, faddish therapies stress the idea that expressing sorrow, anger, or pain is a good thing, and the only means for "dealing with one's feelings" honestly . . . yet it is surely conceivable that some Americans can work through grief internally and privately, without psychological cost. It is even more conceivable that whole cultural subgroups may have different ways of conceding and responding to such experience. (p. 122)

Klein goes on to cite the Japanese, who are most reticent about public grief and yet seem to suffer no ill effects from this reticence. The Balinese frequently laugh at the time of death, because, they say, they are trying to avoid crying; yet they seem to be psychologically healthy. Some cultures employ "keeners" who wail loudly so that the bereaved will not have to do so themselves.

Is the expression of grief essential? At this time, the studies of social and medical scientists do not offer us a conclusive answer.

The Role of the Funeral

In your opinion, what are the appropriate arrangements for a funeral? Are you in favor of formal religious services? Why or why not?

One of the hardest aspects of dealing with the death of a loved one is deciding how the funeral (if there is to be one) is to be conducted. Funerals have always been an important part of American life, whether the elaborate burial rituals practiced by Native Americans, or the simple funerals of our colonial forbearers. Some research indicates that the rituals surrounding funerals have a therapeutic benefit that facilitates the grieving process (Bolton & Camp, 1989; Kraeer, 1981; Marshall & Levy, 1990; Rando, 1986).

Once the intimate responsibility of each family, care for the dead in the United States has been transferred to a paid service industry. The need for this new service was brought about by changes in society during the first part of this century. The more mobile, urbanized workforce had less family support and less time to devote to the task of caring for the dead. In a relatively short time, funeral homes and funeral directors became the accepted form of care for one's dead relatives (Fulton & Owen, 1988).

This commercialization of care for the dead has had mixed results. During the 1950s and 1960s, funeral homes came under stinging criticism for their expense and their lack of sensitivity to the needs of the surviving family members (Mitford, 1963). The bereaved often felt that the funeral directors were more interested in dramatic and expensive presentations of the body than in what might be best for the family members.

A MULTICULTURAL VIEW

The Funeral in Other Times and Countries

Looking at the funeral practices of former cultures shows us not only how they buried their dead but also something about their values.

Ancient Egypt

Upon the death of the head of the house in ancient Egypt, women would rush frantically through the streets, beating their breasts from time to time and clutching their hair. The body of the deceased was removed as soon as possible to the embalming chambers, where a priest, a surgeon, and a team of assistants proceeded with the embalming operation. (The Egyptians believed in the life beyond; embalming was intended to protect the body for this journey.) While the body was being embalmed arrangements for the final entombment began. When the mummified corpse was ready for the funeral procession and installation in its final resting place, it was placed on a sledge drawn by oxen or men and accompanied by wailing servants, professional mourners simulating anguished grief, and relatives. It was believed that when the body was placed in an elaborate tomb (family wealth and prestige exerted an obvious influence on tomb size), its spirits would depart and later return through a series of ritualistic actions.

Ancient Greece

Reverence for the dead permeated burial customs during all phases of ancient Greek civilization. Within a day after death the body was washed, anointed, dressed in white, and laid out in state for one to seven days, depending on the social prestige of the deceased. Family and friends could view the corpse during this time. For the funeral procession, the body was placed on a bier carried by friends and relatives and followed by female mourners, fraternity members, and hired dirge singers. Inside the tomb were artistic ornaments, jewels, vases, and articles of play and war. Like the Egyptians, the ancient Greeks prepared their tombs and arranged for subsequent care while they were still alive. About 1000 B.C. the Greeks began to cremate their dead. Although earth burial was never entirely superseded, the belief in the power of the flame to free the soul acted as a strong impetus to the practice of cremation. A choice of burial or cremation was available during all the late Greek periods.

The Roman Empire

Generally speaking, the Romans envisioned some type of afterlife and, like the Greeks, practiced both cremation and earth burial. When a wealthy person died, the body was dressed in a white toga and placed on a funeral couch, feet to the door, to lie in state for several days. For reasons of sanitation, burial within the walls of Rome was prohibited; consequently, great roads outside the city were lined with elaborate tombs erected for the well-to-do. For the poor, there was no such magnificence; for slaves and aliens, there was a common burial pit outside the city walls.

Anglo-Saxon England

In Anglo-Saxon England (approximately the time when invading Low German tribes conquered the country in the fifth century), the body of the deceased was placed on a bier or in a hearse. On the corpse was laid the book of the Gospels as a symbol of faith and the cross as a symbol of hope. For the journey to the grave, a pall of silk or linen was placed over the corpse. The funeral procession included priests bearing lighted candles and chanting psalms, friends who had been summoned, relatives, and strangers who deemed it their duty as a corporal work of mercy to join the party. Mass was then sung for the dead, the body was solemnly laid in the grave (generally without a coffin), the mortuary fee was paid from the estate of the deceased, and liberal alms were given to the poor.

Colonial New England

Burials and funeral practices were models of simplicity and quiet dignity in eighteenth-century New England. Upon death, neighbors (or possibly a nurse if the family was well-to-do) would wash and lay out the body. The local carpenter or cabinetmaker would build the coffin, selecting a quality of wood to fit the social position of the deceased. In special cases, metal decorations imported from England were used on the coffin. In church, funeral services consisted of prayers and sermons said over the pall-covered bier. Funeral sermons often were printed (with skull and crossbones prominently displayed) and circulated among the public. The funeral service at the grave was simple, primarily a brief prayer followed by the ritual commitment of the body to the earth. The filling of the grave, with neighbors frequently supplying the necessary labor because there were no professional gravediggers, marked the formal end of the early-colonial funeral ceremony.

Let's hope it won't happen, but what would you do if you were called upon to organize a funeral tomorrow? Would you know whom to notify? How would you arrange for the preparation and disposition of the body? What kind of ceremony, religious or otherwise, would you ask for? What would you do about a funeral home, a cemetery plot, and the will and death benefits of the deceased?

Perhaps you could discuss this with some of your friends or classmates, to see how they would feel. Notice how you feel about opinions that differ from yours.

Source: Turner & Helms (1989, pp. 492–93).

A more current survey has revealed that only about 42 percent of funeral directors have had any formal education in the physical and psychological effects of the death of a loved one, and most of those who had some education felt it was inadequate (Weeks, 1989). Recent trends such as cremations and memorial services without the body (often because some body parts have been donated for transplants or science research) have relieved people of the more unpleasant and expensive aspects of funeral services (Marshall & Levy, 1990). Some families are now involving a professional grief counselor in the process.

Dealing Successfully with One's Own Death

Having nearly died, I've found death like that sweet feeling that people have that let themselves slide into sleep. I believe that this is the same feeling that people find themselves in whom we see fainting in the agony of death, and I maintain that we pity them without cause. If you know not how to die, never trouble yourself. Nature will in a moment fully and sufficiently instruct you; she will exactly do that business for you; take you no care for it. (Michel de Montaigne, "Of Physiognomy," 1585–88)

Why is the acceptance of death so painful to so many of us? Why does it come up in every developmental stage, only to be partially resolved and partially denied?

Many people find dying a much harder experience than Montaigne would have us believe it is. Many dying patients feel seriously depressed before their deaths, and a large number have suicidal feelings. Among the reasons for these depressions are the following:

- Medication-induced mood alterations

- Awareness of how little time is left

- Feelings of isolation from relatives and friends who are withdrawing

- Feelings of grief for the losses that are close at hand

- Feelings of disillusion and resentment over injustice

The increased feeling of depression was the greatest difference between a group of terminal and nonterminal cancer patients (Schulz, 1978). This depression is sometimes described as cognitive withdrawal, because many patients have a decreasing ability and motivation to process stimuli as death nears (see terminal drop, chapter 19). Also common is a strong sense of fear and a deep sense of sorrow (Sanders, 1989).

Must dying, then, always be such an unhappy experience? European psychiatrist Elisabeth Kübler-Ross is the most famous student of the process of death. Her three books on the subject have all been best sellers: *On Death and Dying* (1969), *Death—The Final Stage of Growth* (1975), and *To Live Until We Say Goodbye* (1978).

Kübler-Ross discovered that, far from wanting to avoid the topic of death, many dying patients have a strong urge to discuss it. She interviewed hundreds of terminally ill persons. On the basis of these interviews, she developed a five-stage theory, describing the emotions that underlie the process of dying. The stages in her theory are flexible, in that people can move through them quickly, slowly, or not at all. Some fluctuation occurs between the stages, but by and large people tend to move through them in sequential order. They are portrayed in figure 21.1.

Kübler-Ross's stage theory was the first to counter the common assumption that it is abnormal to have strong emotions during the dying process. However, no empirical confirmation that this particular sequence of stages is universal exists. Her theory overlooks the effects of personality, ethnic, or religious factors. It also does not take into account the influence of the specific illness and treatment, nor the availability of social support (Kastenbaum & Kastenbaum, 1989). So, should we accept Kübler-Ross's model or not? The biological, psychological, and social aspects

Figure 21.1
Kübler-Ross's stages of dying

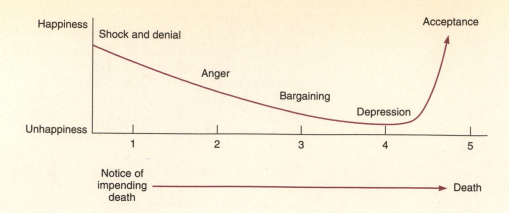

of the process of dying are obviously very complex. We will need to know much more—knowledge gained through careful research—before we can answer this question. We can say that her theory, like all good theories, has at least provided us with five constructs (the five stages) to help guide that research.

A more recent theory, also based on observation and also describing five stages, is that of Saunders (1989). Her suggested stages are shock, awareness of loss, withdrawal, healing and renewal. The similarities with Kübler-Ross's stages are noteworthy. Wortman & Silver (1989) agree with the themes presented by Kübler-Ross and Saunders but urge that they do not occur in set stages in all individuals. Rather, these studies find that the themes are intermingled, ending with some people on a positive note while others react finally with anger and/or depression. As to the latter, some have urged that it is the right reaction. We are reminded of Dylan Thomas's famous lines of poetry, addressed to his father:

> Do not go gentle into that good night—
> Rage, rage, against the dying of the light.

No matter how well prepared we are, death is always sad and stressful. Most of the time, though, we know that we can do nothing about it, and so we must accept the inevitable. How different it is when the death was not inevitable but was chosen by the person because life had become no longer worth living.

Guided Review

1. Currently four different definitions of death exist: clinical death (stoppage of respiration and heart), brain death (cessation of cortex and midbrain activity), _____ death (not possible to discern electrical changes in tissues of heart and lungs), and _____ death (person treated essentially as dead).

2. The criteria for legal death is unreceptivity, no movements or breathing, no reflexes, and a flat _____ reading that remains flat for 24 hours.

3. The causes in Western society for lower mortality rates are the reduction of infant and child mortality and increasing control over the _____ of youth and middle age.

4. In addition to normal grief, there are three types of morbid grief reactions: _____ grief, distorted reactions, and _____ mourning.

5. Anticipatory grief is characterized by four phases: _____ , a heightened concern for the ill person, _____ of death, and an attempt to adjust to the consequences that will occur after death.

6. Most psychologists believe that grief is essential as a part of a _____ encounter with death, but the forms that healthy grief might take have not yet been studied well empirically.

Suicide: The Rejection of Life

As you will see, we are beginning to learn more about how and why suicides happen. This information will surely help us in our efforts to prevent such unfortunate deaths.

The Overall Picture

Suicide and attempted suicide among adolescents are growing national problems (Holinger & others, 1987) and an increasingly common response to stress and depression among young persons (Kienhorst & others, 1987). Suicide now ranks as the second leading cause of death among persons age 15 to 19, and many experts believe that if no suicides were "covered up," it would be the leading cause. Teenagers have become not only more suicidal but apparently more reckless and self-destructive in general. As the suicide rate has risen steadily over the past 20 years, so too has the rate for motor vehicle accidents (the leading cause of death), accidents of other types, and homicides (Bem, 1987; U.S. Bureau of the Census, 1992).

Although suicide rates for teenagers have risen 72 percent since 1988, the rate for most other age groups has decreased. It would be safe to say that although the United States as a whole has become slightly less suicidal, teenagers and young people in general (age 30 and under) have become dramatically more suicidal. The increase has risen most steadily and most consistently among teenagers. It should be noted, however, that teen suicidal deaths rank high because teens have a relatively low rate of death from other causes (Swedo & others, 1991).

Two other groups are much more prone to suicide, however: the so-called middle-old and old-old groups. Although the suicide rate for 15- to 24-year-olds is high—12.5 per 100,000—the rate for those 75 and older is almost double that, with males accounting for almost all the difference (U.S. National Center for Health Statistics, 1986) (also see table 21.1). In fact, the older single white male is by far the person most likely to die of suicide. Woodruff-Pak (1988) states that adolescent suicides are paid more attention to because those individuals are usually in good health. For the elderly, poor health is often both a cause of suicide and a way of covering it up. Loneliness is a second major factor.

Woodruff-Pak relates the story of an elderly retiree from the police force who had made an excellent adjustment to leaving the force. When he discovered that he had a large brain tumor, however, he became very depressed at the thought of leaving his wife, children, and nine grandchildren, to all of whom he was deeply attached. One day, after asking his wife to go to the store for his favorite candy, he shot himself. His wife discovered him and threw away his pistol. She told the paramedics she saw a man fleeing from her house. The "case" remained unsolved, and she was able to bury her husband in a Catholic cemetery.

Soon after the suicide of a famous person, "copycat" suicides often occur. How can we best prevent them from happening?

Answers

5. depression, rehearsal   6. healthy   7. resentment   8. bargaining

1. biological, social   2. electroencephalogram (EEG)   3. diseases   4. delayed, pathological

Table 21.1	Suicide Rates, by Sex, Race, and Age Group: 1970 to 1988 (Lives lost per 100,000)																	
	Total			Male						Female							
Age				White			African American			White			African American				
	1970	1980	1988	1970	1980	1988	1970	1980	1988	1970	1980	1988	1970	1980	1988		
All ages	11.6	11.9	12.4	18.0	19.9	21.7	8.0	10.3	11.5	7.1	5.9	5.5	2.6	2.2	2.4		
10–14 years old	0.6	0.8	1.4	1.1	1.4	2.1	0.3	0.5	1.3	0.3	0.3	0.8	0.4	0.1	0.9		
15–19 years old	5.9	8.5	11.3	9.4	15.0	19.6	4.7	5.6	9.7	2.9	3.3	4.8	2.9	1.6	2.2		
20–24 years old	12.2	16.1	15.0	19.3	27.8	27.0	18.7	20.0	19.8	5.7	5.9	4.4	4.9	3.1	2.9		
25–34 years old	14.1	16.0	15.4	19.9	25.6	25.7	19.2	21.8	22.1	9.0	7.5	6.1	5.7	4.1	3.8		
35–44 years old	16.9	15.4	14.8	23.3	23.5	24.1	12.6	15.6	16.4	13.0	9.1	7.4	3.7	4.6	3.5		
45–54 years old	20.0	15.9	14.6	29.5	24.2	23.2	13.8	12.0	11.7	13.5	10.2	8.6	3.7	2.8	3.8		
55–64 years old	21.4	15.9	15.6	35.0	25.8	27.0	10.6	11.7	10.6	12.3	9.1	7.9	2.0	2.3	2.5		
65 years and over	20.8	17.8	21.0	41.1	37.5	45.0	8.7	11.4	14.0	8.5	6.5	7.1	2.6	1.4	1.6		
65–74 years and over	20.8	16.9	18.4	38.7	32.5	35.4	8.7	11.1	12.9	9.6	7.0	7.3	2.9	1.7	2.0		
75–84 years and over	21.2	19.1	25.9	45.5	45.5	61.5	8.9	10.5	17.6	7.2	5.7	7.4	1.7	1.4	1.3		
85 years and over	19.0	19.2	20.5	45.8	52.8	65.8	8.7	18.9	10.0	5.8	5.8	5.3	2.8	—	—		

Source: From *Vital Statistics,* U.S. Bureau of the Census, Washington, D.C., 1992.

The Influence of Race and Place of Residence on Suicide

Suicidal behavior remains, as it has consistently for decades, a behavior in which whites (U.S. Bureau of the Census, 1992) and the middle class (Jacobziner, 1965; Tishler, 1981; Weisman, 1974) are overrepresented. A comparative chart for white versus African American suicide rates is presented in table 21.1.

In regard to place of residence, since the late 1960s persons from rural areas have had a higher rate of suicide than those from urban areas (Wilkinson & Isreal, 1984).

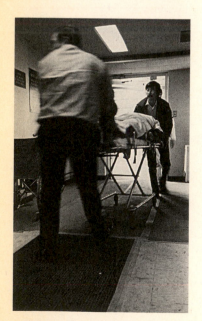

Males are three to four times more likely to die of suicide attempts than are females.

The Influence of Gender on Suicide

Table 21.1 also presents the suicide rates by gender. As you can see by looking at this table, major gender differences exist. The rate for males is much higher because of the type of suicidal behavior engaged in, the methods used, the lethality of the attempt, and the degree of psychiatric disturbance present. Males and females are two very different suicidal types. Universally, males are about four times more likely to die of suicide than females (U.S. Bureau of the Census, 1992).

Attempt rates show even more dramatic gender differences, but in the opposite direction. Failed attempts at suicide among females are much higher than for males (Woodruff-Pak, 1988). The literature consistently has cited female-to-male ratios of at least 3 to 1. Weiner (1970) and White (1974) reported ratios of 4 to 1. More recent studies show a far greater number of females among teenage suicide attempters: 5 to 1 (Curran, 1984), 9 to 1 (Hawton, 1982b, 1982c, 1986; McIntire, 1980), 9.5 to 1 (Birtchnell & Alarcon, 1971), and 10 to 1 (Toolan, 1975).

A major reason for the high survival rate among females is the method used. Whereas males often resort to such violent and effective means as firearms and hanging, females tend to choose less violent and less deadly means, such as pills. Male suicidals are considered significantly more disturbed than female (Blum & others, 1992; Hawton, 1982a, 1982b, 1982c). Males are usually more committed to dying and therefore succeed far more often.

AN APPLIED VIEW

My Attempts at Suicide (Anonymous)

My first psychiatrist told my parents that my psychological tests indicated that I was potentially suicidal. I was 14 then. At 22, I had made five suicide attempts and had been in six mental institutions, which add up to 29 months as a mental patient and five years of intensive therapy. My diagnosis was borderline schizophrenia, chronic depression, and sadomasochism. Why? How had I become so obsessed with suicide?

When I flash back on my adolescent days, I remember feeling ugly, socially awkward, stuck away in an all-girls' boarding school reading Camus and Hesse, unpopular, and stupid! In fact, I was not quite as dreadful as all that, but in my mind I was. I felt different. I once wrote, "I'm at the bottom of an upside-down garbage can and it's so ugly." The world was horrible, but I was the worst part of it.

Suicide was my escape. Unsuccessful suicide attempts put me in the care of others who delicately forced me to confront my feelings of sadness and anger. I had to learn to share with others and sometimes that was what I secretly wanted. Two of my attempts, however, were calculated, purposeful acts. Despite what shrinks may say, I wanted to be dead, not taken care of.

What did death mean to me? One of my earliest memories is sitting on moss-covered ground in a grove of pines, reading *The Prayer for the Dead* with my basset hound curled up beside me. Suicide meant escape from hell on earth. No other purgatory could be worse than this one. Even if I were reincarnated, I would end up being some "lowly animal" with the kind of mind that could not plague me with frightening, lonely, depressing thoughts. I clung to my friends and family, but it only increased my anger and self-contempt. I treated those people as my keepers who temporarily saved me from being left alone with my tormenting mind.

The final blow hit in Boston. I gradually withdrew from the few friends I had as well as my family. Death had grown so close that I no longer felt that I had much time. It was impossible to commit myself to anyone or anything. I was reserved, yet few people could sense how obsessed I was with death. Signs of affection terrified me because I knew I could not let anyone count on me. I needed death if life became too unbearable.

It finally did. I had become so passive that I no longer made contact with people. They had to call me. So much time had elapsed since I had felt close to someone that it seemed my "disappearance" would not really upset anyone. In addition to this, I was convinced that I was too stupid to handle academics or even a menial job (even though I had two jobs at the time). On a day when I knew no one would try and reach me, I took three times the lethal dosage of Seconal.

I was found 24 hours later and came out of a coma after 48 more. My arm was paralyzed. This time, I was placed in a long-term hospital. Another try at life began. With the help of an excellent therapist and the patient love of those whom I had thus far rejected, I have started once more. It has been two years since I took the pills. I think I know why people bother to live now.

Guided Review

9. Suicide and attempted suicide is an increasingly common response to _____ and depression among young people.

10. The suicide rate for men and women over _____ years of age is almost twice as high as for men and women between the ages of 15 and 24 years.

11. The African American suicide rate is about the same as whites until age 24, then African American rates are generally _____ than those of whites.

12. In recent decades, suicidal behavior remains a behavior in which whites and the _____ _____ are overrepresented.

"Successful" Dying

Thus far, this chapter has been pretty depressing, we know. Death and dying, by whatever means, are not one of our favorite topics, but they do have an important place in our study of life. In the next section of this chapter, however, we will be talking about two of the ways we humans have to deal with death in a mature and satisfying way.

The "Death with Dignity" Law

On 30 September 1976, Governor Edmund Brown, Jr., of California signed the "Natural Death Act," the first death with dignity law in the nation. The statute states the right of an adult to sign a written directive instructing her or his physician to withhold or withdraw life-sustaining procedures in the event of a terminal condition. The law contains specific definitions for "terminal condition," "life-sustaining procedure," and "qualified patient." The directive must be drawn up in the form set forth by the statute. It must be signed and dated by an adult of sound mind and witnessed by two persons not related by blood or entitled to the estate of the declarant.

Since then all but 10 states have established such procedures. In June 1990 the Supreme Court ruled that because the desires of a Missouri woman who has been lying in a coma since 1983 had not been made explicit (through a signed document), she could not be allowed to die despite her parents' wishes. However, the Court has ruled that when procedures established within each state are followed, the "right to die" would be constitutional.

Almost 80 percent of Americans die in hospitals, and 70 percent of those deaths involve some aspect of medical technology such as breathing, feeding, and waste elimination equipment. Hence it is essential that those who do not want to be maintained on life-support systems if they become terminal put their wishes in writing according to their state's laws.

WHAT'S YOUR VIEW?

IS THE "DEATH WITH DIGNITY" CONCEPT FAIR TO ALL?

Many things spread in popularity even if they are not always good for people. Although the "death with dignity" concept does appear to grant greater control over life to the person whose life it is, it has been argued that many individuals will invoke the law only when they believe they are dying. It won't occur to most people to think about it before then.

When people know they are likely to die, they are frequently in a depressed state. They may feel that now they are becoming worthless and so should not be a burden on those around them. They may feel that they "just want to get it over with." Opponents of the law say that this is no time for a person to be making judgments about what should happen if death appears imminent. Their judgment is impaired by the depression. As Attorney Thomas Marzen has remarked, "People who are not dying are being denied treatment. The family doesn't object, the doctor doesn't object, and no one seems to care" (Gest, 1989, p. 36). What do you think?

The Hospice: "A Better Way of Dying"

The "death ward" in most hospitals is not a nice place to be. The atmosphere is one of hushed whispers and fake smiles. No children below the age of 12 are allowed. Medications to control the pain are usually given on a schedule rather than as needed. Machines are used to continue life at all costs, though the patient may desire death. Viewing a typical American death ward made British historian Toynbee conclude that "Death is un-American."

In reaction to this, some have reached back to the Middle Ages, when religious orders set up havens where dying pilgrims could come to spend their last days (Stoddard, 1977). The modern **hospice** was established to provide for a more

Hospice
A facility and/or program dedicated to assisting those who have accepted the fact that they are dying and desire a "death with dignity." Provides pain control and counseling but does not attempt to cure anyone.

The modern hospice is organized to afford a more "natural death" to the dying. Although this woman knows she does not have long to live she is able to maintain a positive attitude with the help of the hospice staff.

"natural" death for those who are terminally ill. The first U.S. hospice opened in New Haven, Connecticut, in 1971. Since then the National Hospice Organization has been formed to help promulgate this movement.

The hospice is not a new type of facility; it is a new philosophy of patient care in the United States (although not new in Europe). "What people need most when they are dying is relief from the distressing symptoms of their disease, security of a caring environment, sustained expert care, and the assurance that they and their families won't be abandoned" (Craven & Wald, 1975, p. 1816).

Hospices do pioneering work in such neglected areas as the easing of pain and psychological counseling of patients and their families. Even before patients begin to suffer pain, which in diseases such as cancer can be excruciating, they are given a mixture of morphine, cocaine, alcohol, and syrup so that they come to realize that pain can be controlled. Known as "Brompton's Mixture," this concoction is used only when the patient's need is severe; it is very effective in alleviating both pain and the fear accompanying it. A major goal of the hospice is to keep the person's mind as clear as possible at all times (Greer & Castro, 1986; Morris & others, 1985).

Whenever advisable, the hospice allows the patient to remain at home and provides daily visits by staff nurses and volunteers. Jane Murdock, a California schoolteacher,

> ▇ recalls how her dying mother at first refused to see her grandchildren after she was brought home from the hospital. But when the visiting hospice team began reducing her pain and reassuring her and her family in other ways, a new tranquility set in. Finally the woman even let the youngsters give her medication, and assist her about the house. Says Murdock: "I felt when she died that it was a victory for all of us. None of us had any guilt." ("A Better Way of Dying," Alban, 1978, p. 66)

The hospice program movement has now grown to the point that it supports its own journal. Articles in the *Hospice Journal* often provide supplementary information about special issues concerning the terminally ill. For example, one recent article on hospice care for patients with AIDS (Schofferman, 1987) delved into additional issues of concern: irrational fear of contagion, homophobia (fear of homosexuals) by friends and relatives, and special difficulties in caring for substance abusers.

One of the major questions now being considered is whether the hospice should continue as a separate facility run solely for that purpose or become a standard part of all major hospitals. Currently, hospice programs in the United States are primarily home-based care, with the sponsorship of such programs evenly divided between hospitals and community agencies (Torrens, 1985). Many insurance programs now cover hospice care (Bulkin & Lukashok, 1988).

Whatever the case, it seems clear that this movement will continue to grow considerably. This is because hospices have already proved that they are better places to die. As Cronin and Wald (1979) put it, they are places "where we can finally come to terms with the self—knowing it, loving it reasonably well, and being ready to give it up" (p. 53); in short, they are places where we have an opportunity for successful dying.

For most of us, though, dying is frightening and, ultimately, very hard to understand. To come to terms with it, we almost always rely on our spiritual rather than our cognitive powers.

Guided Review

13. A law was passed in California in 1976 that allows death with dignity, which means that adults have the right to legally state their rejection of _____ procedures when they are in a terminal condition.

14. The hospice was established to provide a more _____ death for people who are terminally ill.

15. The hospice movement contributes to the death with dignity movement by providing relief from distressing symptoms and providing a _____ _____ for the terminal patient.

16. One of the major goals of the hospice is to keep the patient's _____ as clear as possible.

Spirituality

■ There is but one true philosophical problem, and this is suicide: Judging whether life is or is not worth living amounts to answering the fundamental question of philosophy.

Albert Camus, 1955

■ Religion is for those who are afraid to go to Hell. Spirituality is for those who have already been there.

A recovering alcoholic

Spirituality is concerned not only with whether life is worth living but why it is worth living. It may involve the attempt to better understand the reasons for living, through striving to know the intentions of a Supreme Being. An example is reading inspired books such as the Bible. Another is trying to discern the purposes and goals of some universal life force by, for example, examining historical trends in biological changes of species. In any case, spirituality includes all of our efforts to gain insight into the underlying, overriding forces of life. For many, it is the only justification for morality.

How important a role does spirituality play in the lives of typical American adults? One way this question has been investigated is through looking at religious participation and at religious attitudes. These factors are sometimes misleading, but together they offer one fairly reliable answer to the question.

Answers
13. life-sustaining   14. natural   15. caring environment   16. mind

AN APPLIED VIEW

If You Had Your Life to Live Over Again, What Would You Do Differently?

This question was recently asked of 122 retired persons by DeGenova (1992). She discovered that her sample chose the pursuit of education more than any other area. This emphasis on education among retirees may be because they feel their lack of education led to missed or limited opportunities. While these people indicated they would have spent more time doing a variety of things, they said that they would have spent less time worrying about work.

This poem describes the feelings of one 81-year-old (Nadine Stair) on the topic.

If I Had My Life To Live Over

I'd like to make more mistakes next time. I'd relax, I would limber up. I would be sillier than I have been this trip. I would take fewer things seriously. I would take more chances. I would climb more mountains and swim more rivers. I would eat more ice cream and less beans. I would perhaps have more actual troubles, but I'd have fewer imaginary ones.

You see, I'm one of those people who live sensibly and sanely hour after hour, day after day. Oh, I've had my moments, and if I had it to do over again, I'd have more of them. In fact, I'd try to have nothing else. Just moments, one after another, instead of living so many years ahead of each day. I've been one of those persons who never goes anywhere without a thermometer, a hot water bottle, a raincoat, and a parachute. If I had to do it again, I would travel lighter than I have.

If I had my life to live over, I would start barefoot earlier in the spring and stay that way later in the fall. I would go to more dances. I would ride more merry-go-rounds. I would pick more daisies!

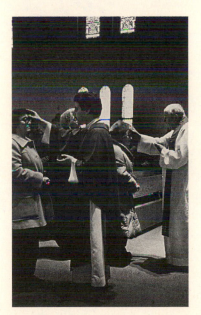

Religious life is of great importance to many of the elderly.

Religious Participation

Americans have always been highly religious. This statement is supported by numerous Gallup polls (Gallup, 1988). A majority of the elderly consider religious practice to be of major importance in their lives. According to surveys, 96 percent of those over 65 believe in God, and 82 percent report that religion plays a significant role in their lives (Koenig & others, 1988).

Religious values become stronger with age. For example, the percentage of people who express strong religious beliefs increases from 35 percent among young adults to 47 percent in middle age to 66 percent among the elderly. Attending services once or more each month grows among these three age groups from 50 percent to 67 percent to nearly 75 percent (Russell, 1989).

Furthermore, the influence of religion appears to be highly related to a sense of well-being in elderly persons. Studies of the relationship, however, may be criticized. It is known that those who attend services regularly are healthier than those who do not, so perhaps it is good health rather than religion that is causing the good feelings (George & Landerman, 1984; Lawton, 1984; Levin & Markides, 1986).

In their study of 836 elderly persons, Koenig and associates (1988) attempted to clear this up. They looked at nonorganizational practices (prayer, Bible reading, etc.) and subjective religious feelings, as well as organized religious practices. They found moderately strong correlations between morale and all three religious measures. The relationships were especially strong for women and for those over 75.

Spirituality does appear to develop with age. A number of theories have been offered as to how and why this is so. Among them, four views have come to receive highest regard: those of Viennese psychoanalysts Viktor Frankl and Carl Jung, sociobiologist E. O. Wilson, and theologian James Fowler.

SOME QUESTIONS ABOUT RELIGIOUS PREFERENCE

Religious Preference, Church Membership, and Attendance: 1957 to 1989 (in percent)

The following chart lists a number of facts about American religious practices.

Year	Religious Preference					Church/ synagogue members	Persons attending church/ synagogue	Age and Region	Church/ synagogue members, 1989
	Protestant	Catholic	Jewish	Other	None				
1957	66	26	3	1	3	73	47	18–29 years old	61
1967	67	25	3	3	2	73	43	30–49 years old	66
1975	62	27	2	4	6	71	41	50 years and over	76
1980	61	28	2	2	7	69	40	East	69
1985	57	28	2	4	9	71	42	Midwest	72
1988	56	28	2	2	9	65	42	South	74
1989	56	28	2	4	10	69	43	West	55

Source: Bureau of the Census (1992).

These facts suggest a number of interesting questions. For example:

- The percentage of our population who belong to Protestant religions has been dropping, and the number who say they have no religious preference has been growing. Is this a real change, or are people becoming more honest? If the latter, why?

- Church/synagogue membership was dropping but has recently rebounded. Why?
- Older people participate more in religious services than younger people. Why?
- The West has the least religious participation, the South the most. Why?

What are your opinions on these questions?

Frankl's Theory of Spirituality

Dr. Victor Frankl, survivor of six years in a Nazi concentration camp, has made many contributions to the field of psychology and spirituality.

Frankl (1967) described human life as developing in three interdependent stages according to the predominant dimension of each stage.

1. The **somatic** (physical) **dimension.** According to the somatic dimension, all persons are motivated by the struggle to keep themselves alive and to help the species survive. This intention is motivated entirely by instincts. It exists at birth and continues throughout life.

2. The **psychological dimension.** Personality begins to form at birth and develops as a result of instincts, drives, capacities, and interactions with the environment. The psychological dimension and the somatic dimension are highly developed by the time the individual reaches early adulthood.

3. The **noetic dimension.** The noetic dimension has roots in childhood but primarily develops in late adolescence. It is spiritual not only in the religious sense but also in the totality of the search for the meaningfulness of life. This aspect distinguishes humans from all other species. The freedom to make choices is the basis of responsibility. Reason exists in the noetic realm. Conscience, which greatly affects the meaningfulness that we discover in life, resides in the noetic.

Frankl believed that development in the physical and personality dimensions results from the total sum of the influences bearing upon an individual. The noetic, on the other hand, is greater than the sum of its parts. This means that we as adults

Somatic dimension

The first stage of Frankl's theory of human development, in which all persons are motivated by the struggle to keep themselves alive and to help the species survive.

Psychological dimension

The second stage of Frankl's theory of human development, in which personality begins to form at birth and develops as a result of instincts, drives, capacities, and interactions with the environment.

Noetic dimension

Frankl's third stage of human development has roots in childhood but primarily develops in late adolescence. It is spiritual, not only in the religious sense but in the totality of the search for the meaningfulness of life.

are responsible for inventing (or reinventing) ourselves! Whatever weaknesses our parents may have given us, we can and should try to overcome them. They need not govern our lives.

It is in the noetic dimension that the person is able to transcend training and to aspire to the higher levels of spiritual thought and behavior. For example, Teilhard de Chardin (1959) urges that if a person uses this noetic capacity to perceive the "Omega" or final point toward which human life is moving, frailties and foolishness can be overcome, and a high level of morality becomes natural.

Jung's Theory of Spirituality

Jung (1933, 1971), a student of Freud's, agreed to a large extent with his mentor's description of development in the first half of the human life. But he felt that Freud's ideas were inadequate to describe development during adulthood. Jung saw spiritual development as occurring in two stages.

The First Half of Life

In each of the Jungian functions of thinking, feeling, sensing, and intuiting, the personality develops toward individuation (see chapter 16). Most people are well individuated by the middle of life, at approximately age 35; that is, we are most different from each other at this age.

Dr. Carl Jung, a student of Freud's, introduced many concepts into psychology, including the anima and animus.

The Second Half of Life

The goal of human development in the second half of life is just the opposite. Here a movement toward wholeness or unity of personality is the goal. Somewhere around midlife, the individual should begin to assess the various systems of his or her personality and come to acknowledge the disorganized state of these systems. There should be a turning inward or self-inspection that marks the beginning of true adult spirituality. The goals of this introspection are

How might a person with no spiritual beliefs deal with death?

Anima

The female side of the personality. Males tend to repress it until later in life.

Animus

The male side of the personality. Females tend to repress it until later in life.

- discovering a meaning and purpose in life;

- gaining a perspective on others, determining values and activities in which one is willing to invest energy and creativity; and

- preparing for the final stage of life—death.

Spirituality in the second half of life develops as a complement to the first half of life. By nourishing one's undeveloped side of life, one comes to a recognition of the spiritual and supernatural aspects of existence. For men, this means developing the **anima,** and for females the **animus.**

In contrast to the self-determination of spirituality seen in Frankl's and Jung's psychological points of view, sociobiology sees spirituality as determined almost entirely by instinct, that is, as a function of the genes.

Wilson's Theory of Spirituality

███ The predisposition to religious belief is the most complex and powerful force in the human mind and in all probability an ineradicable part of human nature. (Wilson, 1978, p. 169)

Harvard sociobiologist Edward O. Wilson, the leading spokesperson for the sociobiological point of view (see chapter 15), argued that religion and spirituality are inseparable. Together they grant essential benefits to believers. He argued that all societies, from hunter-gatherer bands to socialist republics, have religious practices with roots that go back at least as far as the Neanderthal period.

For example, he argued that even modern Russian society, which is still largely anticlergy, pro-socialism, is as much a religious society as any other. Wilson (1978) cited one of Lenin's closest disciples, Grefori Pyatakov, who describes what it is to be "a real Communist"—one who

███ will readily cast out from his mind fears in which he has believed for years. A true Bolshevik has submerged his personality in the collectivity, the "Party," to such an extent that he can make the necessary effort to break away from his opinions and convictions and can honestly agree with the "Party"—that is the test of a true Bolshevik. (p. 184)

Wilson said that in this statement we see the essence of religious spirituality. Humans, he argued, have a need to develop simple rules for handling complex problems. We also have a strong need for an unconscious sense of order in our daily lives. We strongly resist attempts to disrupt this order, which religion almost always protects.

Religion is one of the few uniquely human behaviors. Rituals and beliefs that make up religious life are not seen among any other animals. Some scientists, notably Lorenz and Tinbergen (Hinde, 1970), argued that animal displays, dances, and rituals are similar to human religious ceremonies. Wilson believed this comparison was wrong; animal displays are for the purpose of communicating (sexual desire, etc.), but religious ceremonies intend far more than mere communication.

Their goal is to "reaffirm and rejuvenate the moral values of the community" (Wilson, 1978, p. 179). Furthermore, religious learning is almost entirely unconscious. Most religious tenets are taught and deeply internalized early in life. Early teaching is a necessity if children are to learn to subvert their natural self-interests to the interest of society.

The sociobiological explanation of spirituality, then, is that through religious practice, the survival of practitioners is enhanced. Those who practice religion are more likely to stay alive (or at least they were in the past) than those who do not practice religion.

Wilson believed that even a person's willingness to be controlled may be genetic. Although all societies need some rebels, they also require that the vast majority of people be controllable, typically through religious and political beliefs. Therefore, Wilson believed that over the long run genes that favor willingness to be controlled have been favored by natural selection.

The potential for self-sacrifice can be strengthened in this manner, because the willingness of individuals to relinquish rewards or even surrender their own lives will favor group survival. The Jonestown mass suicide, for example, appears to have occurred because of the group's hope to remain united in afterlife. This concept of self-sacrifice is also the basis for Weinrich's (1987) assertion that homosexuality is an altruistic behavior (see chapter 15).

Religions usually favor survival of their believers. This is not always true, though, and is true to differing degrees. It has been estimated that there have been more than 100,000 different religious faiths since humankind began. Obviously most have failed.

Some religions are even contrary to the survival needs of their believers. The Shaker religion, which disallows sexual intercourse to any of its participants, is an example. Shakerism lasted in this country for no more than two centuries. It flourished in the nineteenth century, but only a very few believers exist today. With no new recruits, it seems doomed to extinction. This, Wilson argued, is always the case for those religions that do not somehow enhance the vitality and hardiness of the groups that support them. The constant pursuit of a better chance for survival is why new ones are started.

Religions, according to the sociobiological point of view, develop through three steps:

1. **Objectification.** First, a perception of reality is described. Objectification occurs, which includes images and definitions that are easy to understand. Examples are good versus evil, heaven versus hell, and the control of the forces of nature by a god or gods.

2. **Commitment.** People devote their lives to these objectified ideas. Out of this commitment, they are willing under any circumstances to help those who have done the same.

3. **Mythification.** In mythification, stories are developed that tell why the members of the religion have a special place in the world. These stories are rational and enhance the person's understanding of the physical as well as spiritual world. The stories include explanations of how and why the world, as well as the religion, came to be. In earlier, less sophisticated religions, the faith is said to have been founded at the same time as the beginning of the race. These rarely include all-powerful or all-knowing gods. In less than one-third of the known religions is there a highly placed god, and in even fewer is there a notion of a moral god who has created the world. In the later religions, God is always seen as male, and almost always as the shepherd of a flock.

Not surprisingly, Wilson saw science as taking the place of theology today, because science has explained natural forces more effectively than theology. In fact, he asserted that science has explained theology itself. Although he saw theology as being phased out, he argued that the demise of religion is not at all likely. As long as religions make people more likely to survive and propagate themselves, Wilson suggested, they will enjoy worldwide popularity.

Wilson's theory attempted to explain spiritual development within societies. Theologian James Fowler has offered a description of the development of faith throughout the life cycle of individuals, without regard to the culture in which faith forms.

Fowler's Theory of Spirituality

James Fowler (1974, 1975a, 1975b) offered a theoretical framework built on the ideas of Piaget, Erikson, and Kohlberg. He believed strongly that cognitive and emotional needs are inseparable in the development of spirituality. Spirituality cannot develop faster than intellectual ability, and also depends on the development of personality. Thus Fowler's theory of faith development integrates the role of the unconscious, of needs, of personal strivings, and of cognitive growth.

Fowler saw faith developing in six steps. He said that the stages in faith development can be delayed indefinitely, but the person must have reached at least a certain minimal age at each stage in order to move on to a succeeding stage. His six stages are as follows:

1. **Intuitive-projective faith.** For intuitive-projective faith, minimal age is 4 years. In this stage, the individual focuses on surface qualities, as portrayed by adult models. This stage depends to a great extent on fantasy. Conceptions of God or a supreme being reflect a belief in magic.

Objectification

Fowler's term for the first step in the birth of a religion in which a perception of reality is described.

Commitment

For Fowler, the third step in the birth of a religion, in which people devote their lives to objectified ideas. They are willing under any circumstances to help those who have done the same.

Mythification

Stories are developed that tell why members of a religion have a special place in the world. These stories are rational and enhance the person's understanding of the physical as well as the spiritual world.

Intuitive-projective faith

The first developmental step of Fowler's theory of faith. In this stage, the individual focuses on surface qualities, as portrayed by adult models.

Mythical-literal faith

The second developmental step of Fowler's theory of faith. Fantasy ceases to be a primary source of knowledge at this stage, and verification of facts becomes necessary.

Poetic-conventional faith

The third developmental step of Fowler's theory of faith. Faith is still conventional and depends on a consensus of opinion of other, more authoritative persons.

Individuating-reflective faith

The fourth developmental step of Fowler's theory of faith. Individuals in stage four begin to assume responsibility for their own beliefs, attitudes, commitments, and lifestyle.

Paradoxical-consolidation faith

The fifth developmental step of Fowler's theory of faith. In this stage, such elements of faith as symbols, rituals, and beliefs start to become understood and consolidated.

Universalizing faith

The final developmental step of Fowler's theory of faith. Here the individual lives in the real world but is not of it. Such persons do not merely recognize the mutuality of existence; they act on the basis of it.

Fowler states that there is a certain minimal age for each of his stages of spiritual development. What kinds of experience do you think would move a person from one stage to the next?

2. **Mythical-literal faith.** For mythical-literal faith, minimal age is 5 to 6 years. Fantasy ceases to be a primary source of knowledge at this stage, and verification of facts becomes necessary. Verification of truth comes not from actual experience but from such authorities as teachers, parents, books, and tradition. Faith in this stage is mainly concrete, and depends heavily on stories told by highly credible storytellers. For example, the traditional story of Adam and Eve is taken quite literally.

3. **Poetic-conventional faith.** For poetic-conventional faith, minimal age is 12 to 13 years. The child is entering Piaget's codification stage. Faith is still conventional and depends on a consensus of opinion of other, more authoritative persons. Now the person moves away from family influence and into new relationships. Faith begins to provide a coherent and meaningful synthesis of these relationships.

    Individuals become aware of symbolism and realize that there is more than one way of knowing truth. Learned facts are still taken as the main source of information, but individuals in stage 3 begin to trust their own judgment and the quality of selected authorities. Nevertheless, they do not yet place full confidence in their own judgment.

4. **Individuating-reflective faith.** For individuating-reflective faith, minimal age is 18 to 19 years. Youths in stage 3 are unable to synthesize new areas of experience, because depending on others in the community does not always solve problems. Individuals in stage 4 begin to assume responsibility for their own beliefs, attitudes, commitments, and lifestyle. The faith learned in earlier stages is now disregarded, and greater attention is paid to one's own experience. Those individuals who still need authority figures have a tendency to join and become completely devoted to clubs and cults.

5. **Paradoxical-consolidation faith.** For paradoxical-consolidation faith, minimal age is 30. In this stage such elements of faith as symbols, rituals, and beliefs start to become understood and consolidated. The person begins to realize that other approaches to dealing with such complex questions as the supernatural and supreme being can be as valid as her or his own. The individual at this stage considers all people to belong to the same universal community and has a true regard for the kinship of all people.

6. **Universalizing faith.** For universalizing faith, minimal age is 40 years. As with Kohlberg's final stage, very few people ever reach this level. Here the individual lives in the real world but is not of it. Such persons do not merely recognize the mutuality of existence; they act on the basis of it. People at this stage appear to be truly genuine and lack the need to "save face" that exists at the lower stages.

Stage 6, as described by Fowler, compares closely with a hypothetical stage 7 of morality proposed by Kohlberg (1973). Although he never found anyone at a stage 7 level of morality, Kohlberg believed that theoretically there should be a stage for those few persons who rise above the purely cognitive and achieve a place where they transcend logic. These individuals, who are rare indeed, come to understand why one should be just and ethical in a world that is unjust. A burning love of universal humankind presses them always to act in truly moral ways.

The development of spirituality and morality appears to be parallel all along the sequence, especially in the Kohlberg and Fowler models. At the early levels, the orientation is basically selfish; ethical thinking and behavior are virtually nonexistent. The child is "good" only to please more powerful persons.

At the second two levels, concern for the opinion of the community in general takes over. "What will people think!" is uppermost in religion as well as in moral decisions. Only if and when the highest levels are reached do true spirituality and morality emerge. And for a few individuals at the highest level, the distinction between the moral and the spiritual no longer exists.

In a recent extension of this view of spirituality too complex to be covered here, Eugene and associates (1993) discussed Wilbur's nine-stage developmental model of consciousness. This theory draws equally from Western and Eastern approaches and expands on Piaget's work. The last three stages deal with transpersonal development, in which perceptual power arises from inner sight rather than from thought. Cross-cultural similarities at the higher levels of spiritual development reported in the study support the claim that there is deep mystical unity of the world's spiritual traditions.

Why do people vary so much in level of spirituality? Can the biopsychosocial model help us answer this question? Do you believe that Fowler's ideas would apply to Eastern cultures? What's your opinion?

Guided Review

17. _____ is concerned with whether life is worth living and why it is worth living.

18. For many Americans religion is connected to spirituality. The influence of religion appears to be highly related to a sense of _____ in elderly persons.

19. Victor Frankl looks at spirituality, and especially the third or _____ dimension, as directed toward transcending training and aspiring to higher levels of thought and behavior.

20. Carl Jung sees life in two halves, with the _____ second half of life directed toward finding meaning and _____ , and preparing for death.

21. Wilson argues that the evolutionary or survival value of spirituality develops in three stages. These stages are objectification, commitment, and _____ .

22. Fowler, like Piaget, Erikson, and Kohlberg, includes stages of development and a _____ age for each stage in his theory of faith development.

23. Fowler sees faith developing in six stages: intuitive-projective, _____ , poetic-conventional, individuating-reflective, paradoxical-consolidation, and _____ .

Answers

17. Spirituality 18. well-being 19. noetic 20. spiritual, purpose 21. mythification 22. minimal 23. mythical-literal, universalizing

CONCLUSION

"The distinction between the moral and the spiritual no longer exists." What a wonderful goal to choose as a means of living the good life. It is probably also the best way to ensure a successful death. We sincerely hope that having read this book will contribute in some small way to your achievement of those two preeminent goals.

CHAPTER HIGHLIGHTS

The Role of Death in Life

- Today, four types of death are recognized: clinical death, brain death, biological or cellular death, and social death.
- In modern Western societies, death comes mostly to the old.
- Grief both follows and can precede the death of a loved one.
- In some cases, morbid grief reactions occur that prevent the successful conclusion of the life crisis. These are known as delayed reactions, distorted reactions, and pathological reactions.
- Most psychologists who have examined the role of grief have concluded that it is a healthy aspect of the crisis of death.

- Funerals have always been an important part of American life. Research has indicated that the rituals surrounding funerals have therapeutic benefit that facilitates the grieving process.
- Kübler-Ross has offered five stages of dying: shock and denial, anger, bargaining, depression, and acceptance.

Suicide: The Rejection of Life

- Suicide rates for those over 75 is double that of adolescents, with the older white male most likely to take his life.
- Males and females are very different regarding suicide, with men being more likely to die than women.

"Successful" Dying

- The hospice movement and "death with dignity" legislation have provided people with more control over their own death, making it a bit easier to accept.

Spirituality

- In recent decades, participation in religious activities has been changing in a number of ways.
- The elderly practice their religions to a greater degree than other adults.
- Theories of spirituality have been presented by Frankl, Jung, Wilson, and Fowler.
- Fowler has incorporated the work of Erikson, Piaget, and Kohlberg in his theory of the development of faith, which proceeds through six stages.

KEY TERMS

Anima   547
Animus   547
Biological death   531
Brain death   531
Cardiopulmonary resuscitation (CPR)   531
Clinical death   531
Commitment   549

Electroencephalogram (EEG)   532
Hospice   542
Individuating-reflective faith   550
Intuitive-projective faith   549
Legal death   532
Mythical-literal faith   550
Mythification   549
Noetic dimension   546

Objectification   549
Paradoxical-consolidation faith   550
Poetic-conventional faith   550
Psychological dimension   546
Social death   531
Somatic dimension   546
Universalizing faith   550

WHAT DO YOU THINK?

1. What do you think is the best way to define death?
2. Most of us think of grief as something that happens to us. Do you think it makes sense to describe it as "work"?
3. How do you feel about the idea of "successful death"?
4. Are there some old people—those who have lost their spouse and all their friends, or those who are undeniably terminal—who should be allowed to take their own lives? Should these people be helped to have a "ceremony of death"?
5. In this chapter we have suggested two ways of making death more dignified. Can you think of any others?
6. Are you satisfied with your own level of religious participation? What do you think you should do differently?
7. How would you define your own spirituality?
8. How does Fowler's use of the term "commitment" compare with Sternberg's and Perry's (chapter 15)?

🌳 SUGGESTED READINGS

Agee, J. [1957] (1971). *A death in the family*. New York: Bantam. This Pulitzer Prize–winning novel focuses on the effect of a man's death on his young son.

Becker, E. (1973). *The denial of death*. New York: Free Press. This is a brilliant analysis of the human failure to acknowledge death. Looks into the theories of Freud, Rank, Jung, Fromm, and others. Becker was awarded the Pulitzer Prize for this work.

Caine, L. (1987). *Widow*. New York: Bantam. Describes the feelings of a woman about her husband's death and the ways she finds to deal with her grief.

Freud, S. (1950). *Totem and taboo*. New York: Norton. One of Freud's most famous works, it explains how psychoanalysis looks at death and dying.

Kübler-Ross, E. (1969). *On death and dying*. New York: Macmillan. Briefly described in this chapter, this is a classic in the field.

Tolstoy, L. [1886] (1981). *The death of Ivan Illich*. New York: Bantam. Upon learning that he has terminal cancer, a man starts a lonely journey into understanding the meaning of life and the ability to accept his own death.

🌳 CHAPTER REVIEW TEST

1. If brain death occurs, a person still remains alive in this condition because
   a. autoplasia stimulates the autonomic processes.
   b. neuroplasia stimulates the autonomic processes.
   c. the autonomic processes are governed by the brain stem.
   d. the autonomic processes are governed by the cortex.

2. Legal death occurs when
   a. respiration and heartbeat have stopped.
   b. the brain fails to receive sufficient amount of oxygen.
   c. there is an unreceptivity and unresponsivity, no movements or breathing, no reflexes, and a flat electroencephalogram reading that remains flat for 24 hours.
   d. it is no longer possible to discern an electrical charge in the tissues of the heart and lung.

3. The phases of anticipatory grief are
   a. depression, a heightened concern for the ill person, rehearsal of death, and an attempt to adjust to the consequences that are likely to occur after the death.
   b. depression and rehearsal of death.
   c. a heightened concern for the ill person, rehearsal of death, and an attempt to adjust to the consequences that are likely to occur after the death.
   d. depression, a heightened concern for the ill person, and rehearsal of death.

4. Knowledge of the impending death of a loved one can have which therapeutic consequences?
   a. avoidance of shock
   b. ability to plan for the future
   c. time to prepare for impending changes
   d. All of the answers are correct.

5. According to Kübler-Ross, many dying people want to discuss
   a. plans for the family.
   b. burial arrangements.
   c. feelings and emotions about their death.
   d. anything but their death.

6. A young man, whose father died from lung cancer, is displaying grief known as distorted reaction. He has
   a. experienced grieving stages that are prolonged and intensified to an abnormal degree.
   b. developed some of the same symptoms his father had, which his doctor determined were entirely psychosomatic.
   c. created a shrine in memory of his father.
   d. experienced anticipatory grief.

7. Why do many dying patients feel depressed before their deaths?
   a. medication-induced mood alterations
   b. feelings of isolation from relatives and friends who are withdrawing
   c. awareness of how little time is left
   d. All of the answers are correct.

8. Older single white males are most likely to die of
   a. cancer.
   b. heart disease.
   c. accident.
   d. suicide.

9. The law that grants an adult the right to instruct his or her physician to withhold or withdraw life-sustaining procedures in the event of a terminal condition is known as the
   a. "right to life" law.
   b. "living will" law.
   c. "death with dignity" law.
   d. None of the answers are correct.

10. Home-based care for the dying is known as the
    a. Visiting Nurses Program.
    b. Hospice program.
    c. Behavioral Medicine program.
    d. Home-Health Program.

11. Whether life is worth living and why it is worth living is the major premise of
    a. spirituality.
    b. religion.
    c. separation anxiety.
    d. None of the answers are correct.

12. In what stage in Frankl's theory of spirituality are persons motivated by the struggle to keep themselves alive and to help the species survive?
    a. somatic dimension
    b. psychological dimension
    c. noetic dimension
    d. None of the answers are correct.

13. In Fowler's theory of spirituality, stages in _____ can be delayed indefinitely, but the person must have reached a certain minimal age at each stage to move on to a succeeding stage.
   a. psychological growth
   b. spiritual belief
   c. faith development
   d. commitment

14. According to Fowler, what is the minimal age at which a person can gain universalizing faith?
   a. 12 to 13 years old
   b. 18 to 19 years old
   c. 30 years old
   d. 40 years old

15. According to Jung, by the age of 35, most people are well
   a. established.
   b. prepared for life's work.
   c. individuated.
   d. on their way to developing a wholeness of personality.

16. The sociobiological point of view states that we develop religion through what steps?
   a. objectification, commitment, mythification
   b. commitment and mythification
   c. objectification and mythification
   d. objection and commitment

Glossary

A

Absorbent Mind: Montessori's term for a child's ability to absorb experiences from the environment (0 to 6 years) (Ch. 7).

Accommodation: Piaget's term that refers to a change in cognitive structures that produces corresponding behavioral changes (Ch. 2).

Accumulation-of-Errors Theory: As cells die, they must synthesize new proteins to make new cells. As this is done, occasionally an error occurs. Over time, these errors mount up and may finally grow serious enough to cause organ failure (Ch. 19).

Accumulation of Metabolic Waste: Waste products resulting from metabolism build up in various parts of the body, contributing greatly to the decreasing competence of those parts. Some examples of this effect are cataracts on the eye, calcification in the arteries, and brittleness of bones (Ch. 19).

Action Theory: A belief that proposes people influence the paths of their own development throughout the lifespan (Ch. 1).

Activity Theory: Human beings flourish through interaction with other people. They are unhappy when, as they reach the older years, their contacts with others shrink as a result of death, illness, and societal limitations. Those who are able to keep up the social activity of their middle years are considered the most successful (Ch. 20).

Adaptation: Piaget's term for one of the two psychological mechanisms that enable us to adjust to our environments (Ch. 2). Piaget states that all human beings tend to adapt to the environment. Adaptation consists of two complementary processes: **assimilation** and **accommodation**

(Ch. 2). Also refers to how an individual, child or adult, adjusts to his or her environment (Ch. 9).

Adhesion: The time during which the prepared surface of the uterus and the outer surface of the fertilized egg, now called the trophoblast, touch and actually "stick together" (Ch. 4).

Adolescent Egocentrism: The reversion to the self-centered thinking patterns of childhood that sometimes occurs in the teen years (Ch. 12).

Adolescent Moratorium: A "time-out" period during which the adolescent experiments with a variety of identities, without having to assume the responsibility for the consequences of any particular one (Ch. 14).

Afterbirth: The period following birth in which the **placenta** and other membranes are discharged (Ch. 4).

Ageism: The prejudice that the elderly are inferior to those who are younger (Ch. 19).

Age-Status: Refers to society's expectations about what is normal at various ages. These expectations change not only with advancing years, but according to the particular society and to the historical context (Ch. 20).

Aging by Program: The vast majority of animals die at or before the end of their reproductive period, but human females live 20 to 30 years beyond the end of their reproductive cycles. Nevertheless, all animals seem to die when their "program" dictates (Ch. 19).

AID: An acronym for "Artificial Insemination by Donor" (Ch. 3).

AIDS (Acquired Immune Deficiency Syndrome): A condition caused by a virus that invades the body's immune system, making it vulnerable to infections and life-threatening illnesses (Ch. 4, 13).

Alarm Reaction: Selye's term for a generalized "call to arms" of the body's defensive forces (Ch. 14).

Amniocentesis: Entails inserting a needle through the mother's abdomen, piercing the **amniotic sac,** and withdrawing a sample of the amniotic fluid (Ch. 4).

Amniotic Sac: The sac that is filled with amniotic fluid and in which the embryo and fetus develop (Ch. 4).

Anal Stage: Freud's belief that the anus is the main source of pleasure during the ages 1½ to 3 years (Ch. 2).

Androgogy: The science of teaching adults (Ch. 17).

Anima: The female side of the personality. Males tend to repress it until later in life (Ch. 21).

Animism: Children consider a large number of objects as alive and conscious that adults consider inert (Ch. 7).

Animus: The male side of the personality. Females tend to repress it until later in life (Ch. 21).

Anorexia Nervosa: A syndrome of self-starvation that mainly affects adolescent and young adult females. It is characterized by an "intense fear of becoming obese, disturbance of body image, significant weight loss, refusal to maintain a minimal normal body weight, and amenorrhea. The disturbance cannot be accounted for by a known physical disorder" (Ch. 12).

Anoxia (lack of oxygen): If something during the birth process should cut the flow of oxygen to the fetus, there is the possibility of brain damage or death (Ch. 4).

Anticipatory Images: Piaget's term for images (which include movements and transformation) that enable the child to anticipate change (Ch. 6).

Antigens: The substances in the blood that fight to kill foreign bodies (Ch. 19).

Apgar: A scale to evaluate a newborn's basic life signs; administered one minute after birth and repeated at three-, five-, and ten-minute intervals; it uses five life signs: heart rate, respiratory effort, muscle tone, reflex irritability, and skin color (Ch. 5).

Apnea: Brief periods when breathing is suspended (Ch. 5).

Apposition: The fertilized **egg,** now called a **blastocyst,** comes to rest against the uterine wall (Ch. 4).

Artificialism: Consists in attributing everything to human creation (Ch. 7).

Assimilation: Piaget's term for incorporating information from the environment; we change the information to fit our cognitive structures (Ch. 2).

Attachment: Behavior intended to keep a child (or adult) in close proximity to a significant other (Ch. 6).

Authoritarian Parenting Style: The parents strive for complete control over their children's behavior by establishing complex sets of rules. They enforce the rules through the use of rewards and, more often, strong discipline (Ch. 11).

Authoritarian Parents: Baumrind's term for parents who demand complete obedience from their children (Ch. 8).

Authoritative Parenting Style: In this, the most common style, parents are sometimes authoritarian and sometimes permissive, depending to some extent on the mood they happen to be in. They believe that both parents and children have rights, but that parental authority must predominate (Ch. 11).

Authoritative Parents: Baumrind's term for parents who respond to their children's needs and wishes; believing in parental control, they attempt to explain the reasons for it to their children (Ch. 8).

Autoimmunity: The process by which the immune system in the body rejects the body's own tissue. Examples are rheumatoid arthritis, diabetes, vascular diseases, and hypertension (Ch. 19).

Autonomy: Infants realize that they have a share in controlling their interactions with others (Ch. 6).

Autosexuality: The love of oneself; the stage at which the child becomes aware of himself or herself as a source of sexual pleasure, and consciously experiments with masturbation (Ch. 13).

B

Babbling: Infant produces sounds approximating speech at about five or six months (Ch. 5).

Basal Metabolism Rate (BMR): The minimum amount of energy an individual tends to use when in a resting state (Ch. 17).

Binocular Coordination: Three-dimensional vision; appears around age 4 months (Ch. 5).

Biological Death: Death occurs when it is no longer possible to discern an electrical charge in the tissues of the heart and lungs (Ch. 21).

Biopsychosocial: A term meaning that development proceeds by the interaction of biological, psychological, and social forces (Ch. 1, 16).

Blastocyst: Name of the fertilized egg after initial divisions (Ch. 3).

Brain Death: Death of the brain occurs when it fails to receive a sufficient supply of oxygen for a short period of time (usually eight to ten minutes). The cessation of brain function occurs in three stages: first the cortex stops, then the midbrain fails, and finally the brain stem ceases to function (Ch. 21).

Brazelton Neonatal Behavioral Assessment Scale: An assessment tool that emphasizes how an infant interacts with its environment (Ch. 5).

Breech Birth: About four out of every hundred babies are born feet first, or buttocks first, while one out of a hundred are in a cross-wise position (transverse presentation) (Ch. 4).

Bulimia Nervosa: This disorder is characterized by "episodic binge-eating accompanied by an awareness that the eating pattern is abnormal, fear of not being able to stop eating voluntarily, and depressed mood and self-deprecating thoughts following the eating binges. The bulimic episodes are

not due to **anorexia nervosa** or any known physical disorder" (Ch. 12).

C

Cardiopulmonary Resuscitation (CPR): A technique for reviving an individual's lungs and/or heart that have ceased to function (Ch. 21).

Centration: A feature of preoperational thought—the centering of attention on one aspect of an object and the neglecting of any other features (Ch. 7).

Cesarean Section: Surgery to deliver the baby through the abdomen when a vaginal delivery is impossible (Ch. 4).

Chlamydia: Now the most common **STD,** with about 5 to 7 million new cases each year. There often are no symptoms; it is diagnosed only when complications develop (Ch. 13).

Cholesterol: A substance in the blood that comes to adhere to the walls of the blood vessels, restricting the flow of blood and causing strokes and heart attacks (Ch. 15).

Chorionic Villi Sampling (CVS): A catheter (small tube) is inserted through the vagina to the villi, and a small section of the villi is suctioned into the tube (Ch. 4).

Chromosome Failure: A genetic abnormality such as gynecomastia (breast growth in the male) or hirsutism (abnormal female body hair) (Ch. 14).

Classification: Concrete operational children can group objects with some similarities within a larger category (e.g., brown wooden beads and white wooden beads are all beads) (Ch. 7, 9).

Climacteric: Refers to a relatively abrupt change in the body, brought about by changes in hormonal balances (Ch. 17).

Climacterium: Refers to the loss of reproductive ability (Ch. 17).

Clinical Death: The individual is dead when his or her respiration and heartbeat have stopped (Ch. 21).

Cognitive Structures: Piaget's term to describe the basic tools of cognitive development (Ch. 2).

Collagen: The major connective tissue in the body; it provides the elasticity in our skin and blood vessels (Ch. 19).

Color Blindness: A condition affecting the ability to detect some colors; caused by a defective **gene** on the X **chromosome** (Ch. 3).

Commitment (Fowler's term): For Fowler, the third step in the birth of a religion, in which people devote their lives to objectified ideas. They are willing under any circumstances to help those who have done the same (Ch. 21).

Commitment (Perry's term): The third phase in Perry's theory. The individual realizes that certainty is impossible, but that commitment to a certain position is necessary, even without certainty (Ch. 15).

Commitment (Sternberg's term): One of Sternberg's three aspects of love; the strongly held conviction that one will stay with another, regardless of the cost (Ch. 15).

Concrete Operational Period: Piaget's third stage of cognitive development during which children begin to employ logical thought processes with concrete material (Ch. 9).

Conservation: Concrete operational children gradually master the idea that something may remain the same even though its surface features change (Ch. 7, 9).

Constructed Knowledge: Belenky's fifth phase of women's thinking; characterized by an integration of the **subjective** and **procedural** ways of knowing (types 3 and 4) (Ch. 15).

Contingency: The effects of a parent's behavior on the infant's state (Ch. 6).

Continuity: The lasting quality of experiences; development proceeds steadily and sequentially (Ch. 1).

Controlled Scribbling: Drawing in which children carefully watch what they are doing, whereas before they looked away; they have better control of the crayon and hold it now like an adult (Ch. 7).

Convergent Thinking: Thinking used to find one correct answer (Ch. 12).

Cooing: Early language sounds that resemble vowels (Ch. 5).

Coordination of Secondary Schemes: Infants combine secondary schemes to obtain a goal (Ch. 5).

Crawling: Locomotion in which the infant's abdomen touches the floor and the weight of the head and shoulders rests on the elbows (Ch. 5).

Creeping: Movement in which a child is on hands and knees and the trunk does not touch the ground; most youngsters creep at about 9 months of age (Ch. 5).

Critical Thinking: Those mental processes that help us to solve problems and make decisions (Ch. 9).

Cross-Linkage Theory: A theory of aging stating that the proteins that make up a large part of cells are themselves composed of peptides. When cross-links are formed between peptides (a natural process of the body), the proteins are altered, often for the worse (Ch. 19).

Crossover: Older men become more like women, and older women become more like men. They do not actually cross over—they just become more like each other (Ch. 20).

Cross-Sectional Studies: Research method comparing groups of individuals of various ages at the same time in order to investigate the effects of aging (Ch. 1).

Crowds: Adolescent peer groups with a reputation for certain values, attitudes, or activities (Ch. 11).

Crystallized Intelligence: Involves perceiving relationships, educing correlates, reasoning, abstracting, concept of attainment, and problem solving, as measured primarily in unspeeded tasks involving various kinds of content (semantic, figural, symbolic) (Ch. 17).

Culture: Those values, beliefs, and behaviors characteristic of a large group of people, for example, those of Hispanic origin (Ch. 1).

Cystic Fibrosis: A chromosomal disorder that produces a malfunction of the exocrine glands (Ch. 3).

Cytogenetics: The study of chromosomes (Ch. 3).

Cytomegalovirus (CMV): A virus that can cause damage such as mental retardation, blindness, deafness, and even death. A major difficulty in combating this disease is that is remains unrecognized in pregnant women (Ch. 4).

D

Day Care: Locations providing services and care for children (Ch. 8).

Decentering: Concrete operational children can concentrate on more than one aspect of a situation (Ch. 9).

Deferred Imitation: Imitation that continues after the disappearance of the model to be imitated (Ch. 7).

Delayed Puberty: The stages of pubertal change do not begin until a significant time after the normal onset (Ch. 12).

DES (Diethylstilbestrol): In the late 1940s and 1950s, DES (a synthetic hormone) was administered to pregnant women, supposedly to prevent miscarriage. It was later found that the daughters of the women who had received this treatment were more susceptible to vaginal and cervical cancer (Ch. 4).

Descriptive Studies: Information is gathered on subjects without manipulating them in any way (Ch. 1).

Despair: The counterpart to **integrity** in the last stage of Erikson's theory. When people look back over their lives and feel that they have made many wrong decisions, or more commonly, that they have frequently not made any decisions at all, they tend to see life as lacking integrity. They are angry that there can never be another chance to make their lives make sense (Ch. 20).

Developmental Biodynamics: A new method of studying motor development; stresses the relationship between perception and action (Ch. 5).

Developmental Risk: A term used to describe those children whose well-being is in jeopardy due to a range of biological and environmental conditions (Ch. 4).

Developmental Tasks: Havighurst suggests these specific tasks at each stage of life, which lie midway between the needs of the individual and the ends of society. These tasks, such as skills, knowledge, functions, and attitudes, are needed by an individual in order to succeed in life (Ch. 11).

Developmentally Delayed: Children who experience a developmental lag because of either physical or psychological causes; if the condition is corrected, these children usually "catch up" (Ch. 7).

Differential Opportunity Structure: Due to social disapproval and more rigid rules enforced by parents, peers, and the legal system, women have not had the same access to sex that men have had (Ch. 20).

Difficult Children: Children whose temperament causes conflicts with those around them (Ch. 6).

Dilation: Stage one of the birth process during which the cervix dilates to about 4 inches in diameter (Ch. 4).

Discontinuity: Behaviors that are apparently unrelated to earlier aspects of development (Ch. 1).

Disengagement Theory: According to this position, the belief that activity is better than passivity is a bias of the Western world. In disengagement theory, the *most mature* adults are likely to gradually disengage themselves from their fellow human beings in preparation for death. They become less interested in their interactions with others, and more concerned with internal concerns (Ch. 20).

Distantiation: The readiness of all of us to distance ourselves from others when we feel threatened by their behavior. Distantiation is the cause of most prejudices and discrimination (Ch. 16).

Divergent Thinking: Thinking used when a problem to be solved has many possible answers (Ch. 12).

Diversity: According to Toffler, stress is increased by what percentage of our lives is in a state of change at any one time (Ch. 14).

Dizygotic Twins: Twins that result from two ripened **eggs** being fertilized by separate **sperm**. Their **genes** are no more alike than those of siblings born of the same parents but at different times (Ch. 3).

DNA (Deoxyribonucleic acid): Often referred to as the structure of life (Ch. 3).

Dominant: The **gene** that tends to be expressed in a trait (Ch. 3).

Down Syndrome: Genetic abnormality caused by a deviation on the twenty-first pair of **chromosomes** (Ch. 3).

Drawing: The ability to form lines into objects that reflect the world; a physical activity that often reveals cognitive and emotional development (Ch. 7).

Drive-by Shootings: Shootings committed by someone riding in a car past the victim (Ch. 13).

Dual-Career Family: A family in which the wife does some sort of paid work and also manages the family's functions (Ch. 16).

Dual-Process Model: A model of intelligence that says there may be a decline in the *mechanics* of intelligence, such as **classification** skills and logical reasoning, but that the **pragmatics** are likely to increase (Ch. 17).

Dualism: Perry's initial phase of ethical development, in which "things are either absolutely right or absolutely wrong" (Ch. 15).

DUPE: Problem-solving model (Determine a problem exists, Understand its nature, Plan for its solution, and Evaluate the solution) (Ch. 9).

E

Easy Children: Children whose temperament enables them to adjust well and to get along with others (Ch. 6).

Ectoderm: The outer layer of the embryo that will give rise to the nervous system, among other developmental features (Ch. 4).

Ectopic Pregnancy: The fertilized **egg** attempts to develop in one of the **fallopian tubes;** sometimes referred to as a *tubal pregnancy* (Ch. 4).

Ego: One of the three structures of the psyche, according to Freud; it is in contact with reality, and mediates between the **id** and **superego** (Ch. 2).

Egocentric Speech: Piaget's term to describe children's speech when they do not care to whom they speak (Ch. 5).

Egocentrism: Refers to Piaget's belief that children think that everything centers on them (Ch. 5, 7).

Electroencephalogram (EEG): A graphic record of the electrical activity of the brain (Ch. 21).

Embryonic Period: Third through the eighth week following **fertilization** (Ch. 4).

Emotional Divorce: Sometimes a couple learns to "withstand" each other, rather than live with each other. The only activities and interests that they shared were ones that revolved around the children. When the children leave, they are forced to recognize how far apart they have drifted; in effect, they are emotionally divorced (Ch. 18).

Empiricism: The process of making careful observations (Ch. 11).

Empty Nest Syndrome: Refers to the feelings parents may have as a result of their last child leaving home (Ch. 18).

Encoding: Translating objects and events into language (Ch. 9).

Endoderm: The inner layer of the embryo that will give rise to the lungs and liver, among other developmental features (Ch. 4).

Endometriosis: A condition in which tissue normally found in the uterus grows in other areas, such as the **fallopian tubes** (Ch. 3).

Entrainment: Term used to describe the rhythm that is established between a parent and an infant's behavior (Ch. 7).

Equal Potential: Experiences have the same capacity to be meaningful at all times in our lives (Ch. 1).

Equilibration: Piaget's term to describe the balance between assimilation and accommodation (Ch. 2).

Escape: Perry's term for refusing responsibility for making any commitments. Since everyone's opinion is "equally right," the person believes that no commitments need be made, and so escapes from the dilemma (Ch. 15).

Esteem Needs: Refers to the need for positive reactions of others to us as individuals and also to the need for a positive opinion of ourselves. One level of Maslow's need hierarchy (Ch. 2).

Estrogen Replacement Therapy (ERT): A process in which estrogen is given in low levels to a woman experiencing severe problems with **menopause** (Ch. 17).

Ethnic: Refers to national or linguistic backgrounds included within the larger culture, for example, Mexican Americans (Ch. 1).

Existential Love: The capacity to cherish the present moment, perhaps first learned when we confront the certainty of our own personal death (Ch. 20).

Explicit Memory: Those events that we consciously remember (Ch. 5).

Exploration Stage: According to Super's theory, that period in a person's career, usually from ages 15 to 24, during which a variety of work experiences are chosen (Ch. 16).

Expressive Language: Children move from purely receptive speech to expressing their own ideas and needs through language (Ch. 7).

Expulsion: Stage two of the birth process during which the baby passes through the birth canal (Ch. 4).

External Fertilization: Fertilization that occurs outside of the woman's body (Ch. 3).

Extinction: According to behavioral theory, refraining from **reinforcing** behavior is the best way to extinguish it; extinction differs from **punishment** in that no action is taken (Ch. 2).

F

Failure-to-Thrive (FTT): The weight and height of FTT infants consistently remain far below normal (the bottom 3% of height and weight measures); there are two types of FTT cases: organic and nonorganic (Ch. 5).

Fallopian Tubes: Passageway for the **egg** once it is discharged from the ovary's surface (Ch. 3).

Fast Mapping: Techniques to help children detect word meanings (Ch. 7).

Fertilization: Union of **sperm** and **egg** (Ch. 3).

Fetal Alcohol Syndrome (FAS): Refers to babies affected when their mothers drink alcohol during pregnancy; they manifest four clusters of symptoms: physiological functioning, growth factors, physical features, and structural effects (Ch. 4).

Fetal Period: The period extending from the beginning of the third gestational month to birth (Ch. 4).

Fetoscopy: A tiny instrument called a fetoscope is inserted into the amniotic cavity, making it possible to see the fetus (Ch. 4).

Fiscal Fitness: The idea that many women lack experience in managing money, and need to become "fiscally fit" (Ch. 19).

Fluid Intelligence: Involves perceiving relationships, educing correlates, maintaining span of immediate awareness in reasoning, abstracting, concept formation, and problem solving, as measured in unspeeded as well as speeded tasks involving figural, symbolic, or semantic content (Ch. 17).

Forceps Delivery: Occasionally, for safety, the physician withdraws the baby with forceps during the first phase of birth (Ch. 4).

Fragile X Syndrome: A sex-linked inheritance disorder in which the bottom half of the X **chromosome** looks as if it is ready to fall off; causes mental retardation in 80% of the cases (Ch. 3).

Friend: A nonfamilial relationship that offers feelings of warmth and support (Ch. 10).

Functional Invariants: In Piaget's theory, the psychological mechanisms of adaptation and organization (Ch. 2).

Future Shock: The illness that results from having to deal with too much change in too short a time (Ch. 14).

G

Gamete Intrafallopian Transfer (GIFT): The **sperm** and the **egg** are placed in the **fallopian tube** with the intent of achieving fertilization in a more natural environment (Ch. 3).

Gender Identity: The conviction that one belongs to the sex of birth (Ch. 1).

Gender Revolution: Levinson's term; the meanings of gender are changing and becoming more similar (Ch. 18).

Gender Role: Culturally acceptable sexual behavior (Ch. 1, 14).

Gender-Role Adaptation: Defined by whether the individual's behavior may be seen as in accordance with her or his gender (Ch. 14).

Gender-Role Orientation: Individuals differ in how *confident* they feel about their sexual identity. Those with low confidence have a weak orientation toward their gender role (Ch. 14).

Gender-Role Preference: Some individuals feel unhappy about their gender role, and wish either society or their gender could be changed, so that their gender role would be different (Ch. 14).

Gender-Role Reversals: Older men see themselves and other males as becoming submissive and less authoritative with advancing years. Conversely, older women see themselves and other women as becoming more dominant and self-assured as they grow older (Ch. 20).

Gender-Role Stereotypes: Beliefs about the characteristics associated with male or female behavior (Ch. 1, 14).

Gender Splitting: Levinson's term; all societies support the idea that there should be a clear difference between what is considered appropriate for males and for females; gender splitting appears to be universal (Ch. 18).

General Adaptation Syndrome: Selye's theory about the three stages of reaction to **stress** (Ch. 14).

Generative Love: Most characteristic of parenthood, a time during which sacrifices are gladly made for the sake of the children (Ch. 20).

Generativity: Erikson's term for the ability to be useful to ourselves and to society. As in the industry stage, the goal is to be productive and creative, but in the generativity stage, which takes place during middle adulthood, one's productivity is aimed at being helpful to others (Ch. 18).

Gene Theory: The theory that aging is due to certain harmful genes (Ch. 19).

Genetic Theory of Homosexuality: The theory that homosexuality is caused by some factor in a person's DNA (Ch. 13).

Genital Herpes: An incurable sexually transmitted disease, with about

500,000 new cases every year. With no cure, about 30 million people in this country now experience the recurring pain of this infection (Ch. 13).

Genital Stage: Freud's belief in a resurgence of a strong sex drive from 12 years and beyond (Ch. 2).

Genotype: An individual's genetic composition (Ch. 3).

German Measles (Rubella):   A typically mild childhood disease caused by a virus; pregnant women who contract this disease may give birth to a baby with a defect: congenital heart disorder, cataracts, deafness, or mental retardation. The risk is especially high if the disease appears early in the pregnancy (Ch. 4).

Germinal Period: The first two weeks following **fertilization** (Ch. 4).

Glaucoma: Results from a buildup of pressure inside the eye due to excessive fluid. The resulting damage can destroy one's vision (Ch. 17).

Gonorrhea: Well-known venereal disease accounting for between one and a half and two million cases per year. One quarter of those were reported among adolescents. The most common symptoms are painful urination and a discharge from the penis or the vagina (Ch. 13).

Goodness of Fit: Compatibility between parental and child behavior; how well parents and their children get along (Ch. 6).

Group Marriage: A marriage that includes two or more of both husbands and wives, who all exercise common privileges and responsibilities (Ch. 16).

H

Habituation: A process in which stimuli that are presented frequently cause a decrease in an infant's attention (Ch. 5).

Handedness: Children's preference for using one hand over the other (Ch. 7).

Hazing Practices: The often dangerous practices used by some fraternities to initiate new members (Ch. 14).

Head Start: Early intervention program intended to provide

educational and developmental services to disadvantaged children (Ch. 7).

Hemophilia: A genetic condition causing incorrect blood clotting; called the "bleeder's disease" (Ch. 3).

Hepatitis B: A viral disease transmitted through sex or shared needles (Ch. 13).

Herpes Simplex: An infection that usually occurs during birth; a child can develop the symptoms during the first week following the birth. The eyes and nervous system are most susceptible to this disease (Ch. 4).

Heterosexuality: Love of members of the opposite sex (Ch. 13).

Holophrases: Children's first words; they usually carry multiple meanings (Ch. 5).

Holophrastic Speech: The use of one word to communicate many meanings and ideas (Ch. 5).

Homeostatic Imbalance: The theory that aging is due to a failure in the systems that regulate the proper interaction of the organs (Ch. 19).

Homosexuality: Love of members of one's own sex (Ch. 13).

Homosexual Marriage: Though not accepted legally, the weddings of homosexuals are now accepted by some religions (Ch. 16).

Hormonal Balance: One of the triggering mechanisms of puberty that may be used to indicate the onset of adolescence (Ch. 12).

Hospice: A facility and/or program dedicated to assisting those who have accepted the fact that they are dying and desire a "death with dignity." Provides pain control and counseling, but does not attempt to cure anyone (Ch. 21).

Human Genome Project: The attempt to identify and map the 50,000 to 100,000 **genes** that constitute the human genetic endowment (Ch. 3).

I

Id: One of the three structures of the psyche, according to Freud. Present at birth, it is the source of our instinctive desires (Ch. 2).

Identical Twins: Twins whose **genes** are identical; they share the same **genotype** (Ch. 3).

Identity Achievement: Marcia's final status, in which numerous crises have been experienced and resolved, and relatively permanent commitments have been made (Ch. 11).

Identity Confusion: Marcia's initial status, in which no crisis has been experienced and no commitments have been made (Ch. 11).

Identity Crisis: Erikson's term for the situation, usually in adolescence, that causes us to make major decisions about our identity (Ch. 11).

Identity Foreclosure: One of Marcia's statuses, in which no crisis has been experienced, but commitments have been made, usually forced on the person by the parent (Ch. 11).

Identity Moratorium: One of Marcia's statuses of adolescence, in which considerable crisis is being experienced but no commitments are yet made (Ch. 11).

Identity Status: Refers to Marcia's four types of identity formation (Ch. 11).

Imaginary Audience: Adolescents' perception that the world is constantly scrutinizing their behavior and physical appearance (Ch. 12).

Imitative Behavior: The tendency of infants to mimic the behavior of others (Ch. 5).

Implantation: When a fertilized egg becomes embedded in the uterine wall (Ch. 3, 4).

Implicit Memory: Memory that affects our behavior without our being aware of it (Ch. 5).

Impotency: The inability to engage in the sexual act (Ch. 20).

Individuating-Reflective Faith: The fourth developmental step of Fowler's theory of faith. Individuals in stage four begin to assume responsibility for their own beliefs, attitudes, commitments, and life-style. The faith learned in earlier stages is now disregarded, and greater attention is paid to one's own experience (Ch. 21).

Individuation: Refers to our becoming more individual; we develop a separate and special personality, derived less and less from our parents and teachers and more from our own behavior (Ch. 8, 16).

Infantile Amnesia: Our inability to recall events from early in life (Ch. 5).

Infertility: An inability to achieve pregnancy after two years (Ch. 3).

Initiation Rites: A cultural and sometimes ceremonial task that signals the entrance to some new developmental stage. Such rites can indicate the passage from adolescence to adulthood (Ch. 14).

Inner Dialogue: Gould's seven steps, which he believes can help in mastering the demons of one's childhood experiences (Ch. 16).

Insecure Parents: Those parents who believe everything they do inevitably influences their child's destiny; they feel overwhelmed by the difficulties of parenting (Ch. 8).

Instrumental Conditioning: Skinner's form of conditioning in which a reinforcement follows the desired response; also known as **operant conditioning.**

Integrity: The resolution of each of the first seven crises in Erikson's theory should lead us to achieve a sense of personal integrity. Older adults who have a sense of integrity feel their lives have been well spent. The decisions and actions they have taken seem to them to fit together (Ch. 20).

Interaction: Behaviors involving two or more people (Ch. 6).

Interactive Errors: Interactions between a mother and child that result in a miscoordination (Ch. 6).

Interactive Repair: Correcting negative interactions and returning them to a positive state (Ch. 6).

Intergenerational Continuity: Appearance of identical behavior in different generations; for example, child abusers have often been abused themselves as children (Ch. 6).

Internal Fertilization: A natural process in which fertilization occurs within the woman (Ch. 3).

Intimacy (Erikson's term): Erikson's stage that represents the ability to relate one's deepest hopes and fears to another person and to accept another's need for intimacy in turn (Ch. 16).

Intimacy (Sternberg's term): One of Sternberg's three aspects of love; the ability to share one's deepest and most secret feelings and thoughts (Ch. 15).

Intimidated Parents: Those parents who lack the ability to be firm with their child (Ch. 8).

Intra-Propositional Thinking: The ability to think of a number of possible outcomes that would result from a *single* choice (Ch. 12).

Intrauterine Devices (IUDs): Usually a plastic loop inserted into the uterus as a contraceptive device (Ch. 3).

Intuitive-Projective Faith: The first developmental step of Fowler's theory of faith. In this stage, the individual focuses on surface qualities, as portrayed by adult models. This stage depends to a great extent on fantasy. Conceptions of God or a supreme being reflect a belief in magic (Ch. 21).

Invasion: Period in which the **trophoblast** "digs in" and begins to bury itself in the uterine lining (Ch. 4).

In Vitro Fertilization: Fertilization that occurs "in the tube" or "in the glass"; an external fertilization technique (Ch. 3).

Irreversibility: A child's inability to reverse thinking; a cognitive act is reversible if it can utilize stages of reasoning to solve a problem and then proceed in reverse, tracing its steps back to the original question or premise (Ch. 7).

Isolation: The readiness all of us have to isolate ourselves from others when we feel threatened by their behavior (Ch. 16).

IUGR: Intrauterine growth retardation; a condition that can occur when the mother's nutrient supply during pregnancy is too low (Ch. 4).

K

Klinefelter Syndrome: A chromosomal disorder in which males possess an XXY chromosomal pattern (Ch. 3).

Knowledge-Acquisition Components: Sternberg's term for those components that help us to learn how to solve problems in the first place (Ch. 9).

L

Language Acquisition Device (LAD): Chomsky's term for the biological predisposition to acquire language (Ch. 5).

Language Acquisition Support System (LASS): Bruner's term for the support children get in acquiring their language (Ch. 5).

Language Explosion: Rapid acquisition of words beginning at 18 months (Ch. 5).

Latency: Freud's belief that the sex drive becomes dormant 5 to 12 years (Ch. 2).

Lateralization: There is a preferred side of the brain for a particular activity (if you are right-handed in writing, you are left-lateralized for writing) (Ch. 7).

Learning Theory of Homosexuality: The belief that homosexuality is the result of learned experiences from significant others (Ch. 13).

Legal Death: Condition defined as "unreceptivity and unresponsivity, no movements or breathing, no reflexes, and a flat **electroencephalogram** (EEG) reading that remains flat for 24 hours" (Ch. 21).

Life Change Unit (LCA): Changes in life (e.g., divorce) that are rated in units according to the degree that they tend to cause stress. The higher the life change is rated, the more stress, and possible disease, the change is likely to cause (Ch. 14).

Life Course: Levinson's term. *Life* refers to all aspects of living—everything that has significance in a life; *course* refers to the flow or unfolding of an individual's life (Ch. 16).

Life Cycle: Levinson's term. The life cycle is a *general* pattern of adult development, while the life course is the unique embodiment of the life cycle by an *individual* (Ch. 16).

Life Structure: Levinson's term. The underlying pattern or design of a person's life *at a given time* (Ch. 16).

Longitudinal Studies: The experimenter makes several observations of the same individuals at two or more times in their lives. Examples are determining the long-term effects of learning on behavior; the stability of habits and intelligence; and the factors involved in memory (Ch. 1).

Love and Belongingness Needs:
Refers to the need for family and friends. One level of Maslow's need hierarchy (Ch. 2).

M

Major False Assumptions:
Remaining from childhood, these beliefs must be reexamined and readjusted by each individual if he or she is to progress in maturity (Ch. 16).

Male Change of Life: Change in hormonal balance and sexual potency (Ch. 17).

Manipulative Experiments: The experimenter attempts to keep all variables (all the factors that can affect a particular outcome) constant except one, which is carefully manipulated (Ch. 1).

Maturation: The process of physical and mental development due to physiology (Ch. 12).

Maximum Growth Spurt: The period of adolescence when physical growth is at its fastest (Ch. 12).

Meiosis: Division of the germ cells, in which the number of chromosomes is halved (Ch. 3).

Menarche: The onset of **menstruation** (Ch. 12).

Menopause: The cessation of **menstruation** (Ch. 17).

Mentoring: The act of assisting another, usually younger, person with his work or life tasks (Ch. 16).

Mesoderm: The middle layer of the embryo that gives rise to muscles, the skeleton, and the circulatory and excretory systems (Ch. 4).

Metacognition: The theory of mind that refers to children's ability to construct their own ideas of how their minds work (Ch. 7).

Metacognitive Experience:
Responses to cognitive stimuli (Ch. 7).

Metacognitive Knowledge: A child's knowledge and beliefs, gained from experience about cognitive matters (Ch. 7).

Metacomponents: Sternberg's term for those components that help us to plan, monitor, and evaluate our problem-solving strategies (Ch. 9).

Metalinguistic Awareness: A capacity to think about and talk about language (Ch. 7, 9).

Midlife Transition: Levinson's term for the phase that usually lasts for five years and generally extends from age 40 to 45. It involves three major developmental tasks (Ch. 18).

Miscarriage: When a pregnancy ends spontaneously before the twentieth week (Ch. 4).

Mitosis: Cell division in which the number of chromosomes remains the same (Ch. 3).

Modeling: Bandura's term for observational learning (Ch. 2).

Monogamy: The standard marriage form in the United States and most other nations, in which there is one husband and one wife (Ch. 16).

Monozygotic Twins: Identical twins (Ch. 3).

Moral Dilemma: A modified clinical technique used by Kohlberg to discover the structures of moral reasoning and the stages of moral development; a conflict leads subjects to justify the morality of their choices (Ch. 9).

Moratorium of Youth: A "time-out" period during which the adolescent experiments with a variety of identities, without having to assume the responsibility for the consequences of any particular one (Ch. 11).

Motherese: Using simple words when talking to children (Ch. 5).

Multiple Intelligences: Gardner's theory that attributes seven types of intelligence to humans (Ch. 9).

Mythical-Literal Faith: The second developmental step of Fowler's theory of faith. Fantasy ceases to be a primary source of knowledge at this stage, and verification of facts becomes necessary. Verification comes not from actual experience, but from such authorities as teachers, parents, books, and traditions (Ch. 21).

Mythification: Stories are developed that tell why members of a religion have a special place in the world. These stories are rational and enhance the person's understanding of the physical as well as the spiritual world (Ch. 21).

N

Nativist Theory: A biological explanation of language development (Ch. 5).

Naturalistic Experiments: In these experiments, the researcher acts solely as an observer and does as little as possible to disturb the environment. "Nature" performs the experiment, and the researcher acts as a recorder of the results (Ch. 1).

Negative Identity: Persons with a negative identity adopt one pattern of behavior because they are rebelling against demands that they do the opposite (Ch. 11).

Negative Reinforcement: Any event that, when it *ceases to occur* after a response, makes that response more likely to happen in the future (Ch. 2).

NEO (neuroticism, extrovertism, openness) Model of Personality:
McCrae and Costa's theory that there are three major personality traits, which they feel govern the adult personality. Each of those three traits is supported by six subtraits or "facets" (Ch. 18).

Neonate: Term for an infant in the days immediately following birth (Ch. 5).

Neurological Assessment: Identifies any neurological problem, suggests means of monitoring the problem, and offers a prognosis about the problem (Ch. 5).

New York Longitudinal Study:
Long-term study by Chess and Thomas of the personality characteristics of children (Ch. 6).

Noetic Dimension: Frankl's third stage of human development has roots in childhood, but primarily develops in late adolescence. It is spiritual, not only in the religious sense but in the totality of the search for the meaningfulness of life. This aspect makes humans specifically different from all other species (Ch. 21).

No-Fault Divorce: The law that lets people get divorced without proving some atrocious act by one of the spouses. This new law recognized that people could, in the course of their lives, simply grow apart from each other to the point that they no longer made good marriage partners. In legal language, this is known as an irretrievable breakdown of a marriage (Ch. 18).

Normal Range of Development: The stages of pubertal change occur at times that are within the normal range of occurrence (Ch. 12).

Novelty: Toffler's term for the dissimilarity of new situations in our lives (Ch. 14).

Novice Phase: Levinson's initial phase of human development extends from ages 17 to 33, and includes the early adult transition, entering the adult world, and the age-30 transition (Ch. 16).

Numeration: Concrete operational children grasp the meaning of numbers, the oneness of one (Ch. 9).

Nurturing Parenting Style: The style of parenting in which parents use indirect methods such as discussion and modeling rather than punishment to influence their child's behavior. Rules are kept to a minimum (Ch. 11).

O

Objectification: Fowler's term for the first step in the birth of a religion in which a perception of reality is described. This includes images and definitions that are easy to understand. Examples are good versus evil, heaven versus hell, and the control by a god or gods of the forces of nature (Ch. 21).

Object Permanence: Refers to children gradually realizing that there are permanent objects around them, even when these objects are out of sight (Ch. 5).

Observational Learning: A term associated with Bandura, meaning that we learn from watching others. Also called **social learning** (Ch. 2, 10).

Olfactory Sense: The sense of smell, which uses the olfactory nerves in the nose and tongue (Ch. 17).

One-Time, One-Group Studies: Studies that are carried out only once on only one group of subjects (Ch. 1).

Operant Conditioning: Skinner's form of conditioning in which a reinforcement follows the desired response (Ch. 2).

Optimum Drive Level: The level of optimum stimulation for an individual (Ch. 14).

Oral Stage: Freud's belief that the mouth is the main source of pleasure from 0 to 1½ years (Ch. 2).

Organization: Our innate tendency to organize causes us to combine our **schemes** more efficiently. The schemes of the infant are continuously reorganized to produce a coordinated system of higher-order structures (Ch. 2).

Organogenesis: The formation of organs during the embryonic period (Ch. 4).

Organ Reserve: Refers to that part of the total capacity of our body's organs that we do not normally need to use. For example, when you walk up the stairs, you probably use less than half of your total lung capacity (Ch. 15).

Outward Bound: A program in which people learn to deal with their fears by participating in a series of increasingly threatening experiences. As a result, their sense of self-worth increases and they feel more able to rely on themselves. The program uses such potentially threatening experiences as mountain climbing and rappeling, moving about in high, shaky rope riggings, and living alone on an island for several days (Ch. 14).

Overextensions: Children's tendency to apply a word too widely (Ch. 7).

Overinterpretive Parents: Those parents who feel they must explore in depth the complex psychological meanings behind their child's behavior (Ch. 8).

Overregulation: At a certain point in their language development, children inappropriately use the language rules they have learned—for example, "I comed home" (Ch. 7).

P

Paradoxical-Consolidation Faith: The fifth developmental step of Fowler's theory of faith. In this stage, such elements of faith as symbols, rituals, and beliefs start to become understood and consolidated. The person begins to realize that others' approaches to dealing with such complex questions as the supernatural and supreme being can be as valid as her or his own (Ch. 21).

Passion: Sternberg's term for a strong sense of desire for another person, and the expectation that sex with them will

prove physiologically rewarding (Ch. 15).

Pathological Parents: Those parents who actually suffer from a form of mental illness, which does not necessarily mean that their child will be subject to psychological disturbances (Ch. 8).

Pedagogy: The science of teaching children (Ch. 17).

Peers: Refers to youngsters who are similar in age to other children, usually within 12 months of one another (Ch. 10).

Pelvic Inflammatory Disease (PID): Disease that often results from **chlamydia** or **gonorrhea,** and frequently causes prolonged problems, including infertility. Symptoms include lower abdominal pain and a fever (Ch. 3, 13).

Performance Components: Sternberg's term for those components that help us to execute the instructions of the **metacomponents** (Ch. 9).

Permissive Parenting Style: The parents have little or no control over their children, and refrain from disciplinary measures (Ch. 11).

Permissive Parents: Baumrind's term for parents who take a tolerant, accepting view of their children's behavior, including both aggressive and sexual urges; they rarely use **punishment** or make demands of their children (Ch. 8).

Personal Fable: Adolescents' tendency to think of themselves in heroic or mythical terms (Ch. 12).

Phallic Stage: Freud's belief that the sex organs become the main source of pleasure from 3 to 5 years (Ch. 2).

Phenotype: The observable expression of gene action (Ch. 3).

Phenylketonuria: Chromosomal disorder resulting in failure to break down the amino acid phenylalanine (Ch. 3).

Phonology: Describes how to put sounds together to form words (Ch. 7).

Physiological Needs: Refers to those dominant needs (hunger, thirst) that must be satisfied if higher levels of motivation are to become active. One level of Maslow's need hierarchy (Ch. 2).

Placenta: The placenta supplies the embryo with all its needs, carries off all its wastes, and protects it from danger (Ch. 4).

Play: An activity that children engage in because they enjoy it for its own sake (Ch. 8).

Poetic-Conventional Faith: The third developmental step of Fowler's theory of faith. Faith is still conventional and depends on a consensus of opinions of other, more authoritative persons. Now the person moves away from family influence and into new relationships. Faith begins to provide a coherent and meaningful synthesis of these relationships (Ch. 21).

Polyandry: A marriage in which there is one wife but two or more husbands (Ch. 16).

Polygamy: A marriage in which there is one husband but two or more wives (Ch. 16).

Positive Reinforcement: Any event that, when it *occurs after* a response, makes that response more likely to happen in the future (Ch. 2).

Postnatal Depression: Many women feel "down" a few days after giving birth; this is fairly common and is now thought to be a normal part of pregnancy and birth for some women (Ch. 4).

Pragmatics: The rules of pragmatics describe how to take part in a conversation (Ch. 7).

Precociousness: The ability to do what others are able to do, but at a younger age (Ch. 12).

Premature Foreclosure: A situation in which a teenager chooses an identity too early, usually because of external pressure (Ch. 11).

Prematurity: About 7 out of every 100 births are premature, occurring less than 37 weeks after conception; prematurity is defined by low birth weight and immaturity (Ch. 4).

Preoperational Period: Piaget's second stage of cognitive development, extending from about 2 to 7 years of age (Ch. 7).

Prepared Childbirth: A combination of relaxation techniques and information about the birth process; sometimes called the *Lamaze method,* after its founder (Ch. 4).

Prepared Environment: Use of age-appropriate materials to further cognitive development (Ch. 7).

Primary Circular Reactions: Infants repeat some act involving their bodies (Ch. 5).

Procedural Knowledge: Belenky's fourth phase of women's thinking; characterized by a distrust of both knowledge from authority and the female thinker's own inner authority or "gut" (Ch. 15).

Prodigiousness: The ability to do *qualitatively* better than the rest of us are able to do; such a person is referred to as a prodigy (Ch. 12).

Prosocial Behavior: Refers to behaviors such as friendliness, self-control, and being helpful (Ch. 10).

Prostatectomy: The removal of all or part of the male prostate gland (Ch. 20).

Protective Factors: Characteristics of **resilient** persons that protect them from the problems related to stress (Ch. 14).

Psychoanalytic Theory: Freud's theory of the development of the personality (Ch. 2).

Psychoanalytic Theory of Homosexuality: Freud's theory suggests that if the child's first sexual feelings about the parent of the opposite sex are strongly punished, the child may identify with the same-sex parent and develop a permanent homosexual orientation (Ch. 13).

Psycholinguistic Theory: Language theory that attempts to identify the psychological mechanisms by which individuals learn their native language (Ch. 5).

Psychological Dimension: The second stage of Frankl's theory of human development, in which personality begins to form at birth and develops as a result of instincts, drives, capacities, and interactions with the environment. This and the **somatic dimension** are highly developed by the time the individual reaches early adulthood (Ch. 21).

Puberty: A relatively abrupt and qualitatively different set of physical changes that normally occur at the beginning of the teen years (Ch. 12).

Puberty Rites: An initiation ceremony often scheduled to coincide with the peak in adolescent physiological maturation (Ch. 14).

Punishment: Any action that makes a behavior less likely to happen (Ch. 2).

Q

Quiescence: A condition in which an individual has no needs at all (Ch. 14).

R

Race: Usually identification by blood type (Ch. 1).

Random Scribbling: Drawing in which children use dots and lines with simple arm movements (Ch. 7).

Realism: Children learn to distinguish and accept the real world (Ch. 7).

Recapitulation Theory: G. Stanley Hall's psychological theory of teenage development (Ch. 11).

Received Knowledge: Belenky's second phase of women's thinking; characterized by being awed by the authorities, but far less affiliated with them (Ch. 15).

Receptive Language: Language that children use to show an understanding of words without necessarily producing them (Ch. 7).

Recessive: A **gene** whose trait is not expressed unless paired with another recessive gene; for example, both parents contribute genes for blue eyes (Ch. 3).

Recidivism Rates: The percentage of convicted persons who commit another crime once they are released from prison (Ch. 14).

Reciprocal Interactions: A term intended to explain a child's active role in its development; I do something to the child, the child changes; as a result of the changes in the child, I change (Ch. 5).

Reconciliation Fantasies: When children wish their parents could get together again following divorce (Ch. 8).

Reflective Listening: A method of talking to others; you rephrase the person's comments to show you understand (Ch. 13).

Reflex: When a stimulus repeatedly elicits the same response (Ch. 5).

Reinforcement: Increasing the probability that a response will recur under similar conditions (Ch. 2).

Relativism: The second phase in Perry's theory. An attitude or philosophy that says anything can be right or wrong depending on the situation; all views are equally right (Ch. 15).

Representation: Child's growing ability to engage in abstract thinking (Ch. 7).

Reproductive Images: Mental images that are faithful to the original object or event being represented; Piaget's term for images that are restricted to those sights previously perceived (Ch. 7).

Repudiation: Choosing an identity involves rejecting other alternatives (Ch. 11).

Resiliency: The ability to recover from either physiological or psychological trauma and return to a normal developmental path (Ch. 1, 14).

Resilient Children: Children who sustain some type of physical or psychological trauma yet remain on a normal developmental path (Ch. 10).

Respiratory Distress Syndrome (RDS): This problem is most common with prematures, but it may strike full-term infants whose lungs are particularly immature; RDS is caused by the lack of a substance called *surfactant,* which keeps the air sacs in the lungs open (Ch. 5).

Retreat: According to Perry's theory of ethical development, when someone retreats to an earlier ethical position (Ch. 15).

Rh Factor: Term describing Rh incompatibility, an incompatibility between the blood types of mother and child; if the mother is Rh-negative and the child Rh-positive, miscarriage or even infant death can result (Ch. 4).

Risk Factors: Characteristics of individuals who are prone to suffer serious problems when under stress (Ch. 14).

Role Discontinuity: Abrupt and disruptive change caused by conflicts among one's various roles in life (Ch. 20).

S

Safety Needs: Refers to the importance of security, protection, stability, freedom from fear and anxiety, and the need for structure and limits. One level of Maslow's need hierarchy (Ch. 2).

Scaffolding: Developing a support system to help children acquire their language (Ch. 5).

Schemes: Patterns of behavior that we use to interact with the environment (Ch. 2).

Secondary Circular Reactions: Infants direct their activities toward objects and events outside themselves (Ch. 5).

Secular Trend: The phenomenon (in recent centuries) of adolescents entering puberty sooner and growing taller and heavier (Ch. 12).

Secure Parents: Those parents who are confident of their techniques; they assume they will cope successfully and look on parenting as an exciting challenge (Ch. 8).

Self-Actualization Needs: Refers to the tendency to feel restless unless we are doing what we think we are capable of doing. One level of Maslow's need hierarchy (Ch. 2).

Self-Fulfilling Prophecy: Making an idea come true simply by believing it will (Ch. 17).

Semantics: The rules of semantics describe how to interpret the meaning of words (Ch. 7).

Senile Macular Degeneration: This disease of the retina is a leading cause of blindness, beginning as blurred vision and a dark spot in the center of the field of vision. Advances in laser surgery have shown promise in treating diseases like this (Ch. 17).

Sensitive Periods: Certain times in the lifespan when a particular experience has a greater and more lasting impact than at another time (Ch. 1).

Sensitive Responsiveness: Refers to the ability to recognize the meaning of a child's behavior (Ch. 6).

Sensorimotor Period: Piaget's term for the first of his cognitive stages of development (0 to 2 years) (Ch. 5).

Sequential Studies: A cross-sectional study done at several times with the same groups of individuals (Ch. 1).

Seriation: Concrete operational children can arrange objects by increasing or decreasing size (Ch. 9).

Sex Cleavage: The custom that youngsters of the same sex tend to play together (Ch. 8).

Sex-Linked Inheritance: Sex-linked inheritance is explained by the fact that the female carries more **genes** on the 23rd **chromosome** (Ch. 3).

Sexual Identity: Sexual identity results from those *physical characteristics* and *behaviors* that are part of our biological inheritance. They are the traits that make us males or females. Examples of sex-linked physical characteristics are the penis and testes of the male. A corresponding behavior is the erection of the penis when stimulated (Ch. 14).

Sexual Revolution: The extraordinary change in human sexual behavior that occurred in the 1960s and 1970s (Ch. 13).

Sexually Transmitted Diseases (STDs): A class of diseases, such as **AIDS, gonorrhea, herpes,** and **chlamydia,** that are transmitted through sexual behavior (Ch. 3, 13).

Sibling: A brother or sister (Ch. 10).

Sickle-Cell Anemia: A chromosomal disorder resulting in abnormal hemoglobin (Ch. 3).

Silence: Belenky's first phase of women's thinking, characterized by concepts of right and wrong; similar to the thinking of men in Perry's first stage (Ch. 15).

Skeletal Growth: The development of the bone structure in the body (Ch. 12).

Slow-to-Warm-Up Children: Children whose reactions are initially mildly negative but then show slow adaptation (Ch. 6).

Social Death: That point at which a patient is treated essentially as a corpse, although perhaps still "clinically" or "biologically" alive (Ch. 21).

Socialization: The need to establish and maintain relations with others and to regulate behavior according to society's demands (Ch. 8).

Socialized Speech: Piaget's term for the time when children begin to exchange ideas with each other (Ch. 5).

Social (Cognitive) Learning Theory: Bandura's theory that refers to the process whereby the information we glean from observing others influences our behavior (Ch. 2).

Social Learning: Another name for **observational** learning; children (and all of us) learn from watching others. The term is associated with Albert Bandura (Ch. 2, 10).

Social Perspective Taking: Children's views on how to relate to others emerge from their personal theories about the traits of others (Ch. 10).

Solidarity: Erikson's term for the personality style of persons who are able to commit themselves in concrete affiliations and partnerships with others, and have developed the "ethical strength to abide by such commitments, even though they may call for significant sacrifices and compromises" (Ch. 16).

Somatic Dimension: The first stage of Frankl's theory of human development, in which all persons are motivated by the struggle to keep themselves alive and to help the species survive. This intention is motivated entirely by instincts. It exists at birth and continues throughout life (Ch. 21).

Spina Bifida: A genetic disorder resulting in the failure of the neural tube to close (Ch. 3).

Stability: A belief that children's early experiences affect them for life (Ch. 1).

Stage of Exhaustion: The third stage in Selye's theory of **stress,** caused by a gradual depletion of the organism's adaptational energy. The physiological responses revert to this condition during the stage of alarm. The ability to handle the stress decreases, the level of resistance is lost, and the organism dies (Ch. 14).

Stage of Resistance: The second stage in Selye's theory of **stress.** If the organism survives the initial alarm, an almost complete reversal of the alarm reaction occurs. Swelling and shrinking are reversed, the adrenal cortex that lost its secretions during the alarm stage becomes unusually rich in these

secretions, and a number of other shock-resisting forces are marshalled. During this stage, the organism appears to gain strength and to have adapted successfully to the stressor (Ch. 14).

Stage Theorists: Researchers who believe that research based on personality traits is too narrow in focus, and that we must also look at the stages of change each person goes through (Ch. 18).

Stagnation: According to Erikson, the seventh stage of life (middle-aged adulthood) tends to be marked either by **generativity** or by stagnation—boredom, self-indulgence, and the inability to contribute to society (Ch. 18).

State of Identity: According to Erikson, the main goal of adolescence (Ch. 11).

Stillbirth: After the twentieth week, the spontaneous end of a pregnancy is called a *stillbirth* if the baby is born dead (Ch. 4).

Stimulus Reduction: Freud's notion that human beings try to avoid stimulation whenever possible. According to this idea, all our activities are attempts to eliminate stimulation from our lives (Ch. 14).

Storm and Stress: Hall's description of the rebirth that takes place during adolescence (Ch. 11).

Stress: Anything that upsets our equilibrium—both psychological and physiological (Ch. 10).

Structure Building: Levinson's term. During structure-building periods, individuals face the task of building a stable structure around choices they have made. They seek to enhance the life within that structure. This period of relative stability usually lasts five to seven years (Ch. 16).

Structure Changing: Levinson's term. A process of reappraising the existing life structure and exploring the possibilities for new life structures characterizes the structure-changing period. This period usually lasts for around five years. Its end is marked by the making of critical life choices around which the individual will build a new life structure (Ch. 16).

Subculture: A group of people who have social, economic, ethnic, or age characteristics distinctive enough to

distinguish them from others within the same culture or society (Ch. 11).

Subjective Knowledge: Belenky's third phase of women's thinking; characterized by some crisis of male authority that sparked a distrust of outside sources of knowledge, and some experience that confirmed a trust in women thinkers themselves (Ch. 15).

Sudden Infant Death Syndrome (SIDS): About 10,000 2- to 4-month-old infants die each year from this syndrome; thought to be brain-related (Ch. 5).

Symbolic Play: The game of pretending; one of five preoperational behavior patterns (Ch. 7).

Symmetry: An infant's capacity for attention and style of responding influence any interactions (Ch. 6).

Synchrony: The ability of parents to adjust their behavior to that of an infant (Ch. 6).

Suggestibility: Adolescent behavior resulting from the perceived wishes of others. Some adolescents may attempt suicide out of the perception, true or not, that their parents wish them dead (Ch. 13).

Superego: One of the three structures of the psyche, according to Freud (Ch. 2).

Syntax: The rules of syntax describe how to put words together to form sentences (Ch. 7).

Syphilis: A **sexually transmitted disease,** which presents a great danger in that in its early stage there are no symptoms. Its first sign is a chancre ("shanker"), a painless open sore that usually shows up on the tip of the penis and around or in the vagina. After a while this sore disappears, and if no treatment follows, the disease enters its third stage, which is usually deadly (Ch. 4, 13).

T

Tay-Sachs Disease: A fatal disease in which a **gene** fails to produce proper enzyme action (Ch. 3).

Telegraphic Speech: Initial multiple-word utterances, usually two or three words (Ch. 5).

Temperament: A child's basic personality, which is now thought to be discernible soon after birth (Ch. 6).

Temporizing: An aspect of Perry's theory of ethical development, in which some people remain in one position for a year or more, exploring its implications but hesitating to make any further progress (Ch. 15).

Teratogens: Any agents that can cause abnormalities, including drugs, chemicals, infections, pollutants, and the mother's physical state (Ch. 4).

Terminal Drop: The period of from a few weeks up to two years prior to a person's death, during which his or her intelligence is presumed to decline rapidly (Ch. 19).

Tertiary Circular Reaction: Repetition with variation; the infant is exploring the world's possibilities (Ch. 5).

Thalidomide: During the early 1960s, thalidomide was a drug popular in West Germany as a sleeping pill and an anti-nausea measure that produced no adverse reactions in pregnant women. In 1962, physicians noticed a sizeable increase in children born with either partial or no limbs. Feet and hands were directly attached to the body. Other outcomes were deafness, blindness, and occasionally mental retardation. Investigators discovered that the mothers of these children had taken thalidomide early in their pregnancy (Ch. 4).

Total Quality Management (TQM): A concept to improve the quality of leaning in our schools (Ch. 10).

Toxoplasmosis: A disease caused by a protozoan that may cause damage to the nervous system; transmitted by animals, especially cats (Ch. 4).

Traditional Marriage Enterprise: Levinson's term. The main goal of this type of marriage is to form and maintain a family (Ch. 18).

Trait Theorists: Researchers who look at pieces of the personality (personality traits), as measured by detailed questionnaires (Ch. 18).

Transience: Toffler's term for the lack of permanence of things in our lives that leads to increased **stress** (Ch. 14).

Transition: Levinson's concept that each new era begins as an old era is approaching its end. That "in-between" time is a transition (Ch. 16).

Transsexual Operation: An operation that changes the physical characteristics of an individual to those of the opposite sex (Ch. 14).

Treatment: The variable that the experimenter manipulates (Ch. 1).

Triarchic Model: A three-tier explanation of intelligence proposed by Robert Sternberg (Ch. 9).

Trophoblast: The outer surface of the fertilized egg (Ch. 4).

Turner Syndrome: A chromosomal disorder in which females possess an XO chromosomal pattern (Ch. 3).

U

Umbilical Cord: A cord that connects the mother and fetus. Contains arteries and veins that supply the fetus with blood (Ch. 4).

Uniform Growth: Montessori's term to describe the developmental period in which children show considerable stability (Ch. 7).

Universalizing Faith: The final developmental step of Fowler's theory of faith. Here the individual lives in the real world, but is not of it. Such persons do not merely recognize the mutuality of existence; they act on the basis of it (Ch. 21).

Use of Metaphor: The ability to think of a word or phrase that by comparison or analogy can be used to stand for another word or phrase (Ch. 12).

V

Validation: Fromm's term for the main ingredient of love (Ch. 15).

Variable Accommodation: Focusing on objects at various distances; appears at about 2 months (Ch. 5).

Victimized Parents: Those parents who believe it just isn't fair if their child has any sign of a problem after all *they* have done for the child (Ch. 8).

Vocables: Consistent sound patterns to refer to objects and events (Ch. 5).

W

Walkabout: Originally an Aborigine initiation rite, the American version attempts to focus the activities of secondary school by demonstrating to the student the relationship between education and action (Ch. 14).

Wear and Tear Theory: The theory that aging is due to the cumulative effects of hard work and lifelong **stress** (Ch. 19).

Whole Language: Students learn to read by obtaining the meaning of words from context, with phonics being introduced when needed (Ch. 7).

Z

Zone of proximal development: The distance between a child's actual developmental level and a higher level of potential development that can be attained with adult guidance (what children can do independently and what they can do with help) (Ch. 2).

Zygote: The fertilized egg (Ch. 3).

Zygote Intrafallopian Transfer (ZIFT): The fertilized **egg** (the zygote) is transferred to the **fallopian tube** (Ch. 3).

References

Abeshouse, R. P. (1987). *Lifelong learning, Part I: Education for a competitive economy*. Washington, DC: Roosevelt Center for American Policy Studies.

Ackerman, J. W. (1958). *The psychodynamics of family life*. New York: Basic Books.

Adalbjarnardottir, S. & Selman, R. (1989). How children propose to deal with the criticisms of their teachers and classmates: Developmental and stylistic variations. *Child Development, 60,* 539–550.

Adams, B. N. (1968). *Kinship in an urban setting*. Chicago: Markham.

Adams, J. (1986). *Conceptual blockbusting* (3rd ed.). Reading, MA: Addison-Wesley.

Adelman, P. (1987). Occupational complexity, control, and personal income: Their relation to psychological well-being in men and women. *Journal of Applied Psychology, 72,* 529–537.

Ainsworth, M. (1973). The development of infant-mother attachment. In B. Caldwell & H. Riccuti (Eds.), *Review of child development research*. Chicago: Univ. of Chicago Press.

Ainsworth, M. (1979). Infant-mother attachment. *American Psychologist, 34,* 932–937.

Ainsworth, M. & Bowlby, J. (1991). An ethological approach to personality. *American Psychologist, 46,* 333–341.

Alban, D. F. (1978, June 5). A better way of dying. *Time,* 66.

Alexander, A. & Kempe, R. S. (1982). The role of the lay therapist in long-term treatment. *Child Abuse and Neglect, 6*(30), 329–334.

Alexander, T. (1987). *Make room for twins*. New York: Bantam.

Allan, G. (1977). Sibling solidarity. *Journal of Marriage and the Family, 39,* 177–184.

Alpaugh, P. & Birren, J. (1977). Variables affecting creative contributions across the adult life-span. *Human Development, 20,* 240–248.

Alpaugh, P., Renner, V., & Birren, J. (1976). Age and creativity. *Educational Gerontology,* 1, 17–40.

Altman, L. (1994). High H.I.V. levels raise risks to newborns. *New York Times,* August 17.

Amabile, T. M., Hennessey, B. A., & Grossman, B. S. (1986). Social influences on creativity. *Journal of Personality and Social Psychology, 50,* 14–24.

Amato, P. R. (1987). Maternal employment: Effects on children's family relationships and development. *Australian Journal of Sex, Marriage and Family, 8*(1), 5–16.

American Association of Retired Persons. (1990a, January). FDA warns against dietary supplement. *A.A.R.P., 31*(1), 7.

American Association of Retired Persons. (1990b, January). Study links alcohol to heart damage. *A.A.R.P., 31*(1), 7.

American Heart Association. (1984). *Eating for a healthy heart: Dietary treatment of hyperlipidemia*. Dallas: American Heart Association.

American Psychiatric Association. (1985). *Diagnostic and statistical manual of mental disorders* (3rd ed.). Washington, DC: Author.

Anderson, A. M. & Noesjirwan, J. A. (1980). Agricultural college initiations and the affirmation of rural ideology. *Mankind, 12*(4), 341–347.

Anderson, J., Crawford, C., Nadeau, J., & Lindberg, T. (1992). Was the Duchess of Windsor right? A cross cultural review of the socioecology of ideals of female body shape. *Ethology and Sociobiology, 13*(3), 197–227.

Angier, N. (1993). Map of all chromosomes to guide genetic hunters. *The New York Times,* December 16.

Anselmo, S. (1987). *Early childhood development*. Columbus, OH: Merrill.

Apgar, V. (1953). A proposal for a new method of evaluation of the newborn infant. *Anesthesia and Analgesia, 32,* 260–267.

Arendell, T. J. (1987). Women and the economics of divorce in the contemporary United States. *Signs, 13,* 121–135.

Aslin, R. (1987). Visual and auditory development in infancy. In J. Osofsky (Ed.), *Handbook of infant development*. New York: Wiley.

Avery, M. E. & Litwack, G. (1983). *Born early*. New York: Little, Brown.

Azar, B. (July, 1994a). Hypocrisy influences teens condom use. *APA Monitor,* 34–35.

Azar, B. (July, 1994b). Efforts to eroticize use of condoms fail to change behavior. *APA Monitor,* 35.

Baier, J. L. & Williams, P. S. (1983, July). Fraternity hazing revisited: Current alumni and active member attitudes toward hazing. *Journal of College Student Personnel, 24*(4), 300–305.

Baillargeon, R. (1987). Object permanence in 3 1/2 and 4 month old infants. *Developmental Psychology, 23,* 655–664.

Baker, B. (1994). Outsmarting Alzheimer's. *AARP Bulletin, 35*(9), 1.

Baker, S. W. (1980, Autumn). Biological influence on human sex and gender. *Signs, 17,* 80–96.

Baltes, P. B., Reese, H. W., & Nesselroade, J. R. (1977). *Life-span developmental psychology: Introduction to research methods*. Monterey, CA: Brooks/Cole.

Baltes, P. B. & Schaie, K. W. (1976). On the plasticity of intelligence in adulthood and old-age—Where Horn and Donaldson fail. *American Psychologist, 31,* 720–725.

Baltes, P. B., Sowarka, D., & Kliegl, R. (1989). Cognitive training research on fluid intelligence in old age: What can older adults achieve by themselves. *Psychology and Aging, 4*(2), 217–221.

Bandura, A. (1986). *Social foundations of thought and action*. Englewood Cliffs, NJ: Prentice-Hall.

Bandura, A., Ross, D., & Ross, S. (1963). Imitation of film-mediated aggressive models. *Journal of Abnormal and Social Psychology, 66,* 3–11.

Bandura, A. & Walters, R. (1963). *Social learning and personality development*. New York: Holt, Rinehart and Winston.

Banks, S. & Kahn, M. (1982). *The sibling bond*. New York: Basic.

Barchers, S. (1994). *Teaching language arts*. New York: West.

Barnicle, M. (August 3, 1992). The spread of gangs. *The Boston Globe,* 34.

Baruch, G., Barnett, R., & Rivers, C. (1983). *Lifeprints: New patterns of love and work of today's women*. New York: McGraw-Hill.

Baumrind, D. (1967). Child-care practices anteceding three patterns of preschool behavior. *Genetic Psychology Monographs, 75,* 43–88.

Baumrind, D. (1971). Current patterns of parental authority. *Developmental Psychology Monographs, 4,* 1–103.

Baumrind, D. (1986). *Familial antecedents of social competence in middle childhood*. Unpublished manuscript.

Baumrind, D. (1991). To nurture nature. *Behavioral and Brain Sciences, 14,* 386.

Baumrind, D. (1993). The average expectable environment is not good enough: A response to Scarr. *Child Development, 64*(5), 1299–1317.

Beaconsfield, P., Birdwood, G., & Beaconsfield, R. (1983). The placenta. *Scientific American, 34,* 94–102.

Beckwith, L., Sigman, M., Cohen, S., & Parmelee, A. (1990). A longitudinal study of preterm infants from birth to twelve years. *Ab Initio, 2*(2), 4–5.

Belenky, M., Clinchy, B., Goldberger, N., & Tarule, J. (1986). *Women's ways of knowing*. New York: Basic Books.

Bellah, R. (1978). To kill and survive or to die and become. In E. Erikson (Ed.), *Adulthood* (pp. 61–80). New York: W. W. Norton.

Belsky, J. & Braungart, J. (1991). Are insecure-avoidant infants with extensive daycare experience less stressed by and more independent in the strange situation? *Child Development, 62,* 567–571.

Belsky, J. & Rovine, M. (1988). Nonmaternal care in the first years of life and the security of infant-parent attachment. *Child Development, 59,* 157–167.

Bem, A. (1987). Youth suicide. *Adolescence, 22*(86), 271–290.

Bem, S. L. (1975). Androgyny vs. the light little lives of fluffy women and chesty men. *Psychology Today, 9*(4), 58–59, 61–62.

Bendiet, J. (1988). Institution dying. In H. Wass & others. *Dying* (2nd ed.). Washington, DC: Hemisphere.

Beneke, W. & Timson, B. (1987). Some health risk benefits of behavioral weight-loss treatments. *Psychological Reports, 61*(1), 199–206.

Bengston, V. L. & Robertson, J. L. (Eds.). (1985). *Grandparenthood*. Beverly Hills, CA: Sage.

Berg, W. K. & Berg, K. (1987). Psychophysiological development in infancy: State, startle, and attention. In J. Osofsky (Ed.), *Handbook of infant development*. New York: Wiley.

Bergman, M. (1980). *Aging and the perception of speech*. Baltimore, MD: University of Baltimore Press.

Bergman, M., Blumenfield, V. G., Cascardo, D., Dash, B., Levitt, H., & Margulios, M. K. (1976). Age-related decrements in hearing for speech: Sampling and longitudinal studies. *Journal of Gerontology, 31,* 533–538.

Bergman, S. (1991). *Men's psychological development: A relational perspective, Work in Progress: No. 48*. Wellesley, MA: The Stone Center, Wellesley College.

Berk, L. (1994). *Child development*. Boston: Allyn & Bacon.

Berk, S. F. (1985). *The gender factory: The apportionment of work in American households*. New York: Plenum Press.

Berman, A. L. & Jobes, D. A. (1991). *Adolescent suicide: Assessment and intervention*. Washington, DC: American Psychological Association.

Berman, M. (1975, March 30). Review of life history and the historical movement by E. Erikson. *New York Times Magazine,* 2.

Berman, P. L. & Goldman, C. (1992). *The ageless spirit*. New York: Ballantine Books.

Berndt, T. (1992). *Child development*. New York: Harcourt Brace Jovanovich.

Bettelheim, B. (1976). *The uses of enchantment*. New York: Knopf.

Billingsley, A. (1992). *Climbing Jacob's ladder: The enduring legacy of African American families*. New York: Simon & Schuster.

Bing, L. (1991). *Do or die*. New York: Harper/Collins.

Birren, J. (1960). Behavioral theories of aging. In N. Shock (Ed.), *Aging*. Washington, DC: American Association for the Advancement of Science.

Birren, J. (1964). *The psychology of aging*. Englewood Cliffs, NJ: Prentice-Hall.

Birtchnell, J. & Alarcon, J. (1971). The motivation and emotional state of 91 cases of attempted suicide. *British Journal of Medical Psychology, 44,* 45–52.

Bishop, J. E. (1983, December 23). New gene probes may permit early predictions of disease. *Wall Street Journal,* 11.

Bishop, J. E. & Waldholz, M. (1990). *Genome*. New York: Simon & Schuster.

Black, A. (1974). *Without burnt offerings*. New York: Viking.

Blackman, J. (1984). *Medical aspects of developmental disabilities in children birth to three*. Rockville, MD: Aspen Publications.

Blass, E. & Ciaramitaro, V. (1994). A new look at some old mechanisms in human newborns. *Monographs of the Society for Research in Child Development, 59*(1), Serial No. 239.

Block, J. (1983). Differential premises arising from differential socialization of the sexes: Some conjectures. *Child Development, 54,* 1335–1354.

Block, J. H., Block, J., & Gjerde, P. (1986). The personality of children prior to divorce: A prospective study. *Child Development, 57,* 827–840.

Bloom, B. (1964). *Stability and change in human characteristics*. New York: Wiley.

Bloom, B. (1985). *Developing talent in young people*. New York: McGraw-Hill.

Blum, R. W., Harmon, B., Harris, L., Bergeisen, L., & Resnick, M. (1992). American-Indian-Alaska native youth health. *Journal of the American Medical Association, 267,* 1637–1644.

Bly, Robert. (1990). *Iron John.* Reading, MA: Addison-Wesley.

Blythe, P. (1973). *Stress and disease.* London: Barker.

Boas, F. (1911). Growth. In H. Kiddle (Ed.), *A cyclopedia of education.* New York: Steiger.

Bock, R. (1993). *Understanding Klinefelter syndrome.* Washington, DC: National Institute of Health.

Bohling, H. R. (1991). Communication with Alzheimer's patients: An analysis of caregiver listening patterns. *International Journal of Aging and Human Development, 33*(4), 249–267.

Boivin, M. & Begin, G. (1989). Peer status and self-perception among early elementary school children: The case of the rejected children. *Child Development, 60,* 591–596.

Bolton, C. & Camp, D. J. (1989). The post-funeral ritual in bereavement counseling and grief work. *Journal of Gerontological Social Work, 13,* 49–59.

Booth, D. (1994). *Classroom voices: Language-based learning in the elementary school.* New York: Harcourt Brace.

Borgman, R. (1986). "Don't come home again:" Parental banishment of delinquent youths. *Child Welfare, 65*(3), 295–304.

Bornstein, J. M. (1986). Retraining the older worker: Michigan's experience with senior employment services. Special issue: Career counseling of older adults. *Journal of Career Development, 13*(2), 14–22.

Boston Women's Health Book Collective. (1984). Our bodies, ourselves (3rd ed.). New York: Simon & Schuster.

Botwinick, J. (1977). Intellectual abilities. In J. E. Birren & K. W. Schaie (Eds.), *Handbook of the psychology of aging.* New York: Van Nostrand Reinhold.

Bourne, R. (1913). *Youth and life.* Boston: Little, Brown.

Bowe, E. (1988). The pregnant body. In D. Tapley & W. Todd (Eds.), *Complete guide to pregnancy.* New York: Crown.

Bowlby, J. (1969). *Attachment.* New York: Basic Books.

Bowlby, J. (1980). *Attachment and loss, Vol. 3.* New York: Basic Books.

Bowlby, J. (1982). Attachment and loss: Retrospect and prospect. *American Journal of Orthopsychiatry, 52,* 664–678.

Bowlby, J. (1988). *A secure base.* New York: Basic Books.

Brabeck, M. (1983). Moral judgment: Theory and research on differences between males and females. *Developmental Review, 3,* 274–291.

Brabeck, M. (1984). Longitudinal studies of intellectual development during adulthood. *Journal of Research and Development in Education, 17*(3), 12–25.

Bradway, K., Thompson, C., & Graven, S. (1958). Preschool IQs after 25 years. *Journal of Educational Psychology, 49,* 278–281.

Brady, B. A. & Gray, D. D. (1988). Employment services for older job seekers. *The Gerontologist, 27,* 565–568.

Brandt, R. (1992). On Deming and school quality: A conversation with Enid Brown. *Educational Leadership, 50*(3), 28–31.

Bransford, J. & Stein, B. (1992). *The IDEAL problem solver.* New York: W. H. Freeman.

Brazelton, T. B. (1981). *On becoming a family: The growth of attachment.* New York: Delacorte.

Brazelton, T. B. (1984). *Neonatal behavioral assessment scale.* London: Heinemann.

Brazelton, T. B. (1987). *Working and caring.* Reading, MA: Addison-Wesley.

Brazelton, T. B. (1990). Saving the bathwater. *Child Development, 61,* 1661–1671.

Brazelton, T. B. & Cramer, B. (1990). *The earliest relationship.* Reading, MA: Addison-Wesley.

Brazelton, T. B., Nugent, J. K., & Lester, B. (1981). Neonatal behavioral assessment scale. In J. Osofsky (Ed.), *Handbook of infant development.* New York: Wiley.

Brenner, A. (1984). *Helping children cope with stress.* San Diego, CA: Lexington Books.

Bretherton, I. (1992). The origins of attachment theory: John Bowlby and Mary Ainsworth. *Developmental Psychology, 28*(5), 759–775.

Bretschneider, J. G. & McCoy, N. L. (1988). Sexual interest and behavior in healthy 80 to 102 year olds. *Archives of Sexual Behavior, 17*(2), 109–129. New York: Plenum Press.

Bridges, K. (1930). A genetic theory of the emotions. *Journal of Genetic Psychology, 37,* 514–527.

Brim, O. G. & Kagan, J. (Eds.) (1980). *Constancy and change in human development.* Cambridge, MA: Harvard University Press.

Brislin, R. (1990). Applied cross-cultural psychology: An introduction. In R. Brislin (Ed.), *Applied cross-cultural psychology.* Newbury Park, CA: Sage.

Brody, E. M., Hoffman, C., Kleban, M. H. & Schoonover, C. B. (1986). Caregiving daughters and their local siblings: Perceptions, strains, and interactions. *The Gerontologist, 29*(4), 529–538.

Brody, E. M., Litvin, S. J., & Hoffman, C. (1992). Differential effects of daughters' marital status on their parent care experiences. *The Gerontologist, 32,* 58–67.

Brody, E. M. & Schoonover, C. B. (1986). Patterns of parent-care when adult daughters work and when they do not. *The Gerontologist, 26,* 372–381.

Brody, G., Stoneman, Z., McCoy, J., & Forehand, R. (1992). Contemporaneous and longitudinal associations of sibling conflict with family relationship assessments and family discussions about sibling problems. *Child Development, 63,* 391–400.

Brody, J. E. (1984, January 15). The growing militance of the nation's nonsmokers. *New York Times,* 31.

Bronfenbrenner, U. (1977). Nobody home: The erosion of the American family. *Psychology Today, 10*(12), 40.

Bronfenbrenner, U. (1978). *The ecology of human development.* Cambridge, MA: Harvard Univ. Press.

Bronfenbrenner, U. (1989). Ecological systems theory. *Annals of Child Development, 6,* 187–249.

Bronfenbrenner, U. & Crouter, M. (1983). The evolution of environmental models in developmental research. In P. Mussen (Ed.), *Handbook of child psychology.* New York: Wiley.

Bronson, M., Pierson, D., & Tivnan, T. (1984). The effects of early education on children's competence in elementary school. *Evaluation Review, 8*(5), 615–627.

Brooks, B. & Kann, M. (1993). What makes character education programs work? *Educational Leadership, 51*(3), 19–21.

Brooks, J. & Lewis, M. (1976). Midget, adult and child: Infants' responses to strangers. *Child Development, 47,* 323–332.

Brooks-Gunn, J. (1987). Pubertal processes. In V. B. Van Hasselt & M. Hersen (Eds.), *Handbook of adolescent psychology*. New York: Pergamon.

Brooks-Gunn, J., Peterson, A., & Eichorn, D. (1985). The study of maturational timing effects in adolescence. *Journal of Youth and Adolescence, 14*(3), 149–161.

Brown, B. B. (1990). Peer groups and peer cultures. In S. Feldman & G. Elliot (Eds.), *At the threshold: The developing adolescent*. Cambridge, MA: Harvard University Press.

Brown, G. W., Bhrolchain, M. N., & Harris, R. (1975). Social class and psychiatric disturbance among women in an urban population. *Sociology, 9,* 225–254.

Brown, J. K. (1982). Cross-cultural perspectives on middle-aged women. *Current Anthropology, 23*(2), 143–156.

Browne, A. & Finkelhor, D. (1986). Impact of child sexual abuse: A review of the research. *Psychological Bulletin, 99,* 66–77.

Bruch, H. (1981). *Eating disorders*. Canada: Basic Books.

Bruner, J. (1990). *Acts of meaning*. Cambridge, MA: Harvard Univ. Press.

Buchanan, C., Maccoby, E., & Dornbusch, S. (1991). Caught between parents: Adolescents' experience in divorced homes. *Child Development, 62,* 1008–1029.

Buehler, C. A., Hogan, M. J., Robinson, B. E., & Levy, R. J. (1985–86). The parental divorce transition: Divorce-related stressors and well-being. *Journal of Divorce, 9*(2), 61–81.

Bulkin, W. & Lukashok, H. (1988). Rx for dying. *New England Journal of Medicine, 318,* 376–378.

Bullinger, A. & Chatillen, J. (1983). Recent theory and research of the Genevan school. In Paul Mussen (Ed.), *Handbook of child psychology*. New York: Wiley.

Burke, T. (1990). Home invaders: Gangs of the future. *The Police Chief, 57,* 23.

Burnham, W. (1911). Hygiene and adolescence. In H. Kiddle (Ed.), *A cyclopedia of education*. New York: Steiger.

Burros, M. (1994). Eating well. *New York Times,* Wednesday, July 13, C6.

Burton, C. A. (1978). *Juvenile street gangs: Predators and children*. Unpublished manuscript, Boston College.

Bushnell, E. & Boudreau, J. (1993). Motor development and the mind: The potential role of motor abilities as a determinant of aspects of perceptual development. *Child Development, 64,* 1005–1021.

Buskirk, E. R. (1985). Health maintenance and longevity: Exercise. In C. E. Finch & E. L. Schneider (Eds.), *Handbook of the biology of aging* (2nd ed.). New York: Van Nostrand Reinhold.

Buunk, B. & van Driel, B. (1989). *Variant lifestyles and relationships*. Newbury Park, CA: Sage.

Cahill, M. & Salomone, P. R. (1987). Career counseling for work life extension: Integrating the older worker into the labor force. *Career Development Quarterly, 35*(3), 188–196.

Campbell, B. & Gaddy, J. (1987). Rates of aging and dietary restrictions: Sensory and motor function in the Fischer 344 rat. *Journal of Gerontology, 42*(2), 154–159.

Campos, J. (1976). Heart rate: A sensitive tool for the study of emotional development in the infant. In L. Lipsitt (Ed.), *Developmental psychology*. New York: Erlbaum.

Caplan, T. & Caplan, F. (1984). *The early childhood years*. New York: Bantam.

Carey, J. (1983, December 16). Weight gained later in life is more risky for the heart. *USA Today,* 3.

Carnevali, D. L. & Patrick, M. (Eds.). (1986). *Nursing management for the elderly* (2nd ed.). Philadelphia: J. B. Lippincott.

Carstensen, L. (1992). Social and emotional patterns: Support for socioemotional selectivity theory. *Psychology and Aging, 7*(3), 331–338.

Cassidy, J. & Asher, S. (1992). Loneliness and peer relations in young children. *Child Development, 63,* 350–365.

Cassidy, J., Parke, R., Butkovsky, L., & Braungart, J. (1992). Family-peer connections: The role of emotional expressiveness within the family and children's understanding of emotions. *Child Development, 63,* 603–618.

Catania, J. A., Turner, H., Kegeles, S. M., Stall, R., Pollack, L., & Coates, T. J. (1989). Older Americans and AIDS: Transmission risks and primary prevention research needs. *The Gerontologist, 29,* 373–381.

Cath, S. H. (1975). The orchestration of disengagement. *International Journal of Aging and Human Development, 6,* 199–213.

Centers for Disease Control. (1989b). First 100,000 cases of Acquired Immunodeficiency Syndrome—United States. *Morbidity and Mortality Weekly Report, 38,* 561–562.

Centers for Disease Control. (1989c). Update: Heterosexual transmission of Acquired Immunodeficiency Syndrome and Human Immunodeficiency virus infection—United States. *Morbidity and Mortality Weekly Report, 38,* 36–40.

Chall, J. (1992). *Stages of reading development*. New York: McGraw Hill.

Chapman, A. B. (1988). Male-female relations: How the past affects the present. In H. P. McAdoo (Ed.), *Black families* (2nd ed., p. 200). Newbury Park, CA: Sage.

Charlesworth, R. (1987). *Understanding child development*. Albany, NY: Delmar.

Cheal, D. (1989). Women together: Bridal showers and gender membership. In B. Risman & P. Schwartz (Eds.), *Gender in intimate relationships* (pp. 87–93). Belmont, CA: Wadsworth.

Cherry, S. (1992). *Understanding pregnancy and childbirth*. New York: Collier.

Chess, S. & Thomas, A. (1987). *Know your child*. New York: Basic Books.

Children's Defense Fund (1989). *A day in the lives of some teens*. Washington, DC: Children's Defense Fund.

Chiriboga, D. A. (1989). Mental health at the midpoint. In S. Hunter & M. Sundel (Eds.), *Midlife myths*. Newbury Park, CA: Sage.

Chisholm, J. S. (1983). *Navajo infancy*. New York: Aldine.

Choi, S. (1991). Children's answers to yes-no questions: A developmental study in English, French, and Korean. *Developmental Psychology, 27*(3), 407–420.

Chomsky, N. (1965). *The development of syntax in children 5 to 10 years.* Cambridge, MA: MIT Press.

Cicirelli, V. G. (1979). *Social services for elderly in relation to the kin network.* Report to the NRTA-AARP Andrus Foundation, Washington, DC.

Cicirelli, V. G. (1980). Sibling relationships in adulthood: A lifespan perspective. In L. W. Poon (Ed.), *Aging in the 1980s: Psychological issues* (pp. 455–462). Washington, DC: American Psychological Association.

Cicirelli, V. G. (1994). Sibling relationships in cross-cultural perspective. *Journal of Marriage and the Family, 56,* 7–20.

Cigarette smoking among adults. (June 15, 1992). *Journal of the American Medical Association, 267*(3), 3133.

Clarke-Stewart, A. (1993). *Daycare.* Harvard Univ. Press.

Clay, M. (1993). *Reading recovery: A guidebook for teachers in training.* New York: Heinemann.

Clifford, P., Tan, S., & Gorsuch, R. (1991). Efficacy of a self-directed behavioral health change program: Weight, body, composition, cardiovascular fitness, blood pressure, health risk and psychological mediating variables. *Journal of Behavioral Medicine, 14*(3), 303–323.

Clifton, R., Perris, E., & Bullinger, A. (1991). Infants' perception of auditory space. *Developmental Psychology, 27,* 187–197.

Cohen-Mansfield, J. & Marx, M. S. (1992). The social network of the agitated nursing home resident. *Research on Aging, 14*(1), 110–123.

Cohn, R. (1979). Age and the satisfactions from work. *Journal of Gerontology, 34,* 264–272.

Cole, E. & Rothblum, E. (1990). Commentary on "Sexuality and the midlife woman." *Psychology of Women Quarterly, 14*(4), 509–512.

Cole, T. (1991). The specter of old age: History, politics, and culture in an aging America. In B. Hess and E. Markson (Eds.), *Growing old in America* (pp. 23–38). New Brunswick, NJ: Transaction.

Coleman, J. S. (1961). *The adolescent society.* Glencoe, IL: The Free Press.

Coleman, L. M., Antonucci, T. C., & Adelman, P. K. (1987). Social roles in the lives of middle-aged and older black women. *Journal of Marriage and the Family, 49,* 761–771.

Coll, C. T. G. (1990). Developmental outcome of minority infants: A process-oriented look into our beginnings. *Child Development, 61*(2), 270–289.

Colletta, N. (1982). How adolescents cope with problems of early motherhood. *Adolescence, 16*(63), 499–512.

Colligan, J. (1975). Achievement and personality characteristics as predictors of observed tutor behavior. *Dissertation Abstracts International, 35,* 4293–4294.

Colten, M. E., & Gore, S. (1991). *Adolescent stress: Causes and consequences.* New York: Aldine deGruyter.

Coltrane, S. & Ishii-Kuntz, M. (1992). Men's housework: A life course perspective. *Journal of Marriage & Family, 54,* 43–57.

Compos, B. E. & Williams, R. A. (1990). Stress, coping and adjustment in mother and young adolescents in single- and two-parent families. *American Journal of Community Psychology, 19*(4), 525–545.

Comstock, G. & Paik, H. (1991). *Television and the American child.* New York: Academic.

Cooney, T. M., Schaie, K. W., & Willis, S. L. (1988). The relationship between prior functioning on cognitive and personality dimensions and subject attrition in longitudinal research. *Journal of Gerontology: Psychological Sciences, 43*(1), 12–17.

Cooper, C. L. (Ed.), (1984). *Psychosocial stress and cancer.* New York: Wiley & Sons.

Cooper, C. R. & Grotevant, H. D. (1987). Gender issues in the interface of family experience and adolescents' friendship and dating identity. *Journal of Youth and Adolescence, 16*(3), 247–265.

Cooper, H. (1989, November). Synthesis of research on homework. *Educational Leadership,* 85–91.

Cooper, R. M., Bilash, I., & Zubek, J. P. (1959). The effect of age on taste sensitivity. *Journal of Gerontology, 14,* 56–58.

Coopersmith, S. (1967). *The antecedents of self-esteem.* San Francisco: Freeman.

Coronary disease attributable to sedentary lifestyle. (September 19, 1990). *Journal of the American Medical Association, 328*(8), 574–578.

Corso, J. (1971). Sensory processes and age effects in normal adults. *Journal of Gerontology, 26,* 90.

Costa, P. T., Jr. & McCrae, R. (1980). Still stable after all these years: Personality as a key to some issues in adulthood and old age. In P. B. Baltes (Ed.), *Life-span development and behavior* (Vol. 3, pp. 65–102). New York: Academic Press.

Cote, J. E. & Levine, C. (1988). The relationship between ego identity status and Erikson's notions of institutionalized moratoria, value orientation stage, and ego dominance. *Journal of Youth and Adolescence, 17*(1), 81–100.

Cowan, C. P. & Cowan, P. A. (1994). Is there love after baby? In F. Fenson & J. Fenson (Eds.), *Human development, 94/95* (22 Ed.). Guilford, CN: Dushkin.

Cowan, R. S. (1987). Women's work, housework, and history: The historical roots of inequality in work-force participation. In N. Gerstel & H. E. Gross (Eds.), *Families and work* (pp. 164–177). Philadelphia: Temple University Press.

Cowley, G. (1989, December 18). Medical mystery tour. *Newsweek,* 59.

Cox, H. (1988). *Later life.* Englewood Cliffs, NJ: Prentice-Hall.

Cox, M., Owen, M., Henderson, V. K., & Margand, N. (1992). Prediction of infant-father and infant-mother attachment. *Developmental Psychology, 28,* 474–483.

Craig-Bray, L., Adams, G. R., & Dobson, W. R. (1988). Identity formation and social relations during late adolescence. *Journal of Youth and Adolescence, 17*(2), 173–188.

Cratty, B. (1986). *Perceptual and motor development in infants and children.* Englewood Cliffs, NJ: Prentice-Hall.

Craven, J. & Wald, F. (1975, October). Hospice care for dying patients. *American Journal of Nursing,* 1816–1822.

Criqui, M. H. (1990). Comment on Shaper's "Alcohol and mortality." *British Journal of Addiction, 85*(7), 854–857.

Crockenberg, S. (1981). Irritability, mother responsiveness, and social support influences on the security of infant-mother attachment. *Child Development, 52,* 857–865.

Crockett, L., Losaff, M., & Petersen, A. (1986). Perceptions of the peer group and friendship in early adolescence. *Journal of Early Adolescence, 4*(2), 155–181.

Crohan, S. E., Antonucci, T. C., Adelman, P. K., & Coleman, L. M. (1989). Job characteristics and well-being at mid-life: Ethnic and gender comparisons. *Psychology of Women Quarterly, 13,* 223–235.

Cronin, K. & Wald, K. (1979). *Successful dying.* Unpublished manuscript, Boston College, Chestnut Hill, MA.

Crouter, A. C., Perry-Jenkins, M., Huston, T. L., & McHale, S. M. (1987). Processes underlying father involvement in dual-earner and single-earner families. *Developmental Psychology, 23,* 431–440.

Crowell, D. (1987). Childhood aggression and violence. In D. Crowell, I. Evans, & C. O'Donnel (Eds.), *Childhood aggression and violence.* New York: Plenum.

Crowley, J. E. (1986). Longitudinal effects of retirement on men's well-being & health. *Journal of Business and Psychology, 1*(2), 95–113.

Csikszentmihalyi, M. (1990). *Flow.* New York: Harper & Row.

Curran, D. (1984). Peer attitudes toward attempted suicide in midadolescents. *Dissertation Abstracts International, 44*(12), 3927B.

Curtiss, S. (1977). *Genie: A psycholinguistic study of a modern-day "wild child."* New York: Academic.

Cutler, W., Schleidt, W., & Friedmann, E. (1987). Lunar influences on the reproductive cycle in women. *Human Biology, 59,* 959–972.

Dacey, J. (1993). Reducing dropout rate in inner city middle school students through instruction in self-control. *Journal of Research in Middle Level Education,* Fall, 109–116.

Dacey, J. S. (1989a). *Fundamentals of creative thinking.* Lexington, MA: D.C. Heath/Lexington Books.

Dacey, J. S. (1989b). Peak periods of creative growth across the life span. *The Journal of Creative Behavior, 24*(4), 224–247.

Dacey, J. S. (1989c). Discriminating characteristics of the families of highly creative adolescents. *The Journal of Creative Behavior, 24*(4), 263–271.

Dacey, J. S. (1986). *Adolescents today* (3rd ed.). Glenview, IL: Scott, Foresman.

Dacey, J. S. (1982). *Adult development.* Glenview, IL: Scott, Foresman.

Dacey, J. S. & Kenny, M. (1994). *Adolescent development.* Dubuque, IA: Brown & Benchmark.

Dacey, J. S. & Packer, A. (1992). *The nurturing parent: How to raise a creative, loving, responsible child.* New York: Fireside/Simon & Schuster.

Damon, W. (1983). *Social and personality development.* New York: Norton.

Dancer, L. & Gilbert, L. (1993). Spouses' family work participation and its relation to wives' occupational level. *Sex Roles, 28*(3/4), 127–145.

Daniels, D. & Moos, R. (1990). Assessing life stressors and social resources among adolescents. *Journal of Adolescent Research, 5,* 268–289.

Darling-Hammond, L. (1994). Performance-based assessment and educational equity. *Harvard Educational Review, 64*(1), 5–30.

Darrach, B. (1992). The war on aging. *Life, 15*(10), 32–45.

Dash, U. & Mohanty, A. (1992). Relationship of reading comprehension with metalinguistic awareness. *Social Science International, 8*(1), 5–13

Datan, N., Rodeheaver, D., & Hughes, F. (1987). Adult development and aging. *Annual Review of Psychology, 38,* 153–180.

DeCasper, A. & Fifer, W. (1980). Studying learning in the womb. *Science, 208,* 1174.

DeChardin, T. (1959). *The phenomenon of man* (B. Wall, Trans.). New York: Harper & Row.

deCuevas, J. (1990). "No, she holded them loosely." *Harvard Magazine, 93,* 60–67.

DeGenova, M. K. (1992). If you had your life to live over again, What would you do differently? *International Journal of Aging and Human Development, 34*(2), 135–143.

Dekovic, M. & Janssens, J. (1992). Parents' child-rearing style and child's sociometric status. *Developmental Psychology, 28,* 925–932.

Dellas, M. & Jernigan, L. P. (1987). Occupational identity status development, gender comparisons, and internal-external locus of control in first-year Air Force cadets. *Journal of Youth and Adolescence, 16*(6), 587–600.

Dellman-Jenkins, M., Lambert, D., Fruit, D., & Dinero, T. (1986). Old and young together. *Childhood Education,* 206–212.

Demoise, C. & Conrad, R. (1972). Effects of age and radiation exposure on chromosomes in a Marshall Island population. *Journal of Gerontology, 27*(2), 197–201.

Dennis, W. (1966). Creative productivity between 20 and 80 years. *Journal of Gerontology, 21,* 1–8.

deVries, H. A. (1981). Physiology of exercise and aging. In D. F. Woodruff & J. E. Birren (Eds.), *Aging: Scientific perspectives and social issues* (pp. 464–465). New York: Van Nostrand Reinhold.

Diamond, M. (1982). Sexual identity, monozygotic twins reared in discordant sex roles, and a BBC follow-up. *Archives of Sexual Behavior, 11,* 181–185.

DiClemente, R. J., Boyer, C. B., & Mills, S. J. (1987). Prevention of AIDS among adolescents: Strategies for the development of comprehensive risk-reduction health education programs. *Health Education Research, 2*(3), 287–291.

Dinnerstein, M. (1992). *Women between two worlds: Reflections on work and family.* Philadelphia: Temple University Press.

Dornbusch, S., Ritter, P., Leiderman, P., Roberts, D., & Fraleigh, M. (1987). The relation of parenting style to adolescent school performance. *Child Development, 58,* 1244–1257.

Dotz, W. & German, B. (1983). The facts about treatment of dry skin. *Geriatrics, 38,* 93.

Downey, G., Wortman, C., & Silver, R. (1990). Reconsidering the attribution-adjustment relation following a major negative event: Coping with the loss of a child. *Journal of Personality and Social Psychology, 59,* 925–940.

Dranoff, S. M. (1974). Masturbation and the male adolescent. *Adolescence, 9*(34), 16–176.

Draper, P. & Keith, J. (1992). Cultural contexts of care: Family caregiving for elderly in America and Africa.

Journal of Aging Studies, 6(2), 113–134.

Dresher, M. & Zenge, S. (1990). Using metalinguistic awareness in first grade to predict achievement in third and fifth grades. *Journal of Educational Research, 84*(1), 13–21.

Duncan, C. (1979). *A death curriculum*. Unpublished doctoral dissertation, Boston College, Chestnut Hill, MA.

Dunn, J. (1985). Sibling relationships in early childhood. *Child Development, 54,* 787–811.

Dunn, J. (1985). *Sisters and brothers*. Cambridge, MA: Harvard Univ. Press.

Dunn, J. (1988). Connections between relationships: Implications of research on mothers and siblings. In R. Hinde & J. Stevenson-Hinde (Eds.), *Relations between relationships*. Oxford: Clarendon.

Dunn, J. (1990). Rita Dunn answers questions on learning styles. *Educational Leadership, 48,* 15–18.

Dunn, R., Slomkowski, C., & Beardsall, L. (1994). Sibling relationships from the preschool period through middle childhood and early adolescence. *Developmental Psychology, 30*(3), 315–324.

Duvall, E. (1971). Family development. Philadelphia: Lippincott.

Earle, J. R. & Perricone, P. J. (1986). Premarital sexuality: A ten-year study of attitudes and behavior on a small university campus. *Journal of Sex Research, 22*(3), 304–310.

Eichorn, D. H., Clausen, J. A., Haan, N., Honzik, M. P., & Mussen, P. H. (Eds.). (1981). *Past and present in middle life*. New York: Academic Press.

Eifrig, D. E. & Simons, K. B. (1983). An overview of common geriatric ophthalmologic disorders. *Geriatrics, 38,* 55.

Eisdorfer, C. & Wilkie, F. (1973). Intellectual changes and advancing age. In L. Jarvik (Ed.), *Intellectual functioning in adults*. New York: Springer.

Eisenberg, N. (1992). *The caring child*. Cambridge, MA: Harvard Univ. Press.

Elias, M., Elias, P., & Elias, J. (1977). *Basic processes in adult developmental psychology*. St. Louis: Mosby.

Elkind, D. (1978). *The child's reality: Three developmental themes*. Hillsdale, NJ: Erlbaum.

Elkind, D. (1981). *The hurried child*. Reading, MA: Addison-Wesley.

Elkind, D. (1987). *Miseducation: Preschoolers at risk*. New York: Knopf.

Elkind, D. (1989, June 30). Under pressure. *The Boston Globe Magazine,* 24ff.

Elkind, D. & Bowen, R. (1979). Imaginary audience behavior in children and adolescents. *Developmental Psychology, 15,* 38–44.

Elliott, D. S., Huizinga, D., & Menard, S. (1989). *Multiple problem youth*. New York: Springer-Verlag.

Elsayed, M., Ismail, A. H., & Young, J. R. (1980). Intellectual differences of adult men related to age and physical fitness before and after an exercise program. *Journal of Gerontology, 35,* 383–387.

Emde, R., Plomin, R., Robinson, J., Corley, R., DeFries, J., Fulker, D., Reznick, J., Campos, J., Kagan, J. & Zahn-Waxler, C. (1992). Temperament, emotions, and cognition at fourteen months: The MacArthur, Longitudinal Twin Study. *Child Development, 63*(6), 1437–1455.

Engstrom, P. F. (1986). Cancer control objectives for the year 2000. In L. E. Mortenseon, P. F. Engstrom, & P. N. Anderson (Eds.), *Advances in cancer control*. New York: Alan R. Liss.

Enright, R. D., Levy, V. M., Harris, D., & Lapsley, D. K. (1987). Do economic conditions influence how theorists view adolescents? *Journal of Youth and Adolescence, 16*(6), 541–560.

Erikson, E. (1958). *Young man Luther: A study in psychoanalysis and history*. New York: Norton.

Erikson, E. (1959). Growth and crises of the healthy personality. *Psychological Issues, 1,* 17–34.

Erikson, E. (1963). *Childhood and society* (2nd ed.). New York: Norton.

Erikson, E. (1968). *Identity: Youth and crisis*. New York: Norton.

Erikson, E. (1969). *Gandhi's truth: On the origins of militant nonviolence*. New York: Norton.

Erikson, E. (1975). *Life, history and the historical movement*. New York: Norton.

Erikson, E. (1978). *Adulthood*. New York: Norton.

Eugene, S., Brewer, J. & Krause, P. (1993). *Journal of Humanistic Psychology, 33*(3), 66–81.

Ewing, C. (1990). *When children kill: The dynamics of juvenile homicide*. Lexington, MA: Lexington Books/D. C. Heath.

Fagot, B. (1985a). Changes in thinking about early sex role development. *Developmental Review, 5,* 83–98.

Fagot, B. (1985b). Beyond the reinforcement principle: Another step toward understanding sex role development. *Developmental Psychology, 21,* 1097–1104.

Fagot, B. & Hagan, R. (1991). Observations of parent reactions to sex-stereotyped behaviors: Age and sex effects. *Child Development, 62,* 617–628.

Fagot, B. & Kavanagh, K. (1990). The prediction of antisocial behavior from avoidant attachment classifications. *Child Development, 61,* 864–873.

Fagot, B., Leinbach, M., & O'Boyle, C. (1992). Gender labeling, gender stereotyping, and parenting behaviors. *Developmental Psychology, 28,* 225–230.

Faier, J. (1979, August). Sexual harassment on the job. *Harper's Bazaar,* 90–91.

Fantz, R. (1961). The origin of form perception. *Scientific American,* 204, 66–72.

Farber, E. & Egeland, B. (1987). *The invulnerable child*. New York: Guilford.

Farrell, M. P. & Rosenberg, S. D. (1981). *Men at midlife*. Boston: Auburn House.

Feinbloom, R. (1993). *Pregnancy, birth, and the early months* (2nd ed.). Reading, MA: Addison-Wesley.

Feldman, D. (1979). The mysterious case of extreme giftedness. In A. H. Passow (Ed.), *The gifted and the talented: Their education and development*. Chicago: Univ. of Chicago Press (NSSE).

Fendrich, M. (1984). Wives' employment and husbands' distress: A meta-analysis and a replication. *Journal of Marriage and the Family, 46,* 871–879.

Ferber, R. (1985). *Solve your child's sleep problems*. New York: Simon & Schuster.

Field, D. (1987). A review of preschool conservation training: An analysis of analyses. *Developmental Review, 7,* 210–251.

Field, T. (1990). *Infancy.* Cambridge, MA: Harvard Univ. Press.

Findlay, S. (1983, December 6). Study finds family link to heart ills. *USA Today,* 1.

Findley, P. (1979, December 13). This law is for you. *Parade,* 5–6.

Finian, M. J. & Blanton, L. P. (1987). Stress, burnout, and role problems among teacher trainees and first-year teachers. *Journal of Occupational Behavior, 8*(2), 157–165.

Fischbach, G. (1992). Mind and brain. *Scientific American, 267*(3), 48–60.

Fischer, K., Shaver, P., & Carnochan, P. (1990). How emotions develop and how they organize behavior. *Cognition and Emotion, 4,* 81–127.

Fischer, P. & Breakey, W. (1991). The epidemiology of alcohol, drug, and mental disorders among homeless persons. *American Psychologist, 46,* 1115–1128.

Fitzpatrick, M. A. (1984). A typological approach to marital interaction: Recent theory and research. In L. Berkowitz (Ed.), *Advances in experimental social psychology* (Vol. 18). New York: Academic Press.

Flavell, J. (1992). Cognitive development: Past, present, and future. *Developmental Psychology, 28*(6), 998–1005.

Flavell, J. H. (1963). *The developmental psychology of Jean Piaget.* New York: Van Nostrand.

Flavell, J. H. (1985). *Cognitive development.* Englewood Cliffs, NJ: Prentice-Hall.

Fodor, I. & Franks, V. (1990). Women in midlife and beyond: The new prime of life? *Psychology of Women Quarterly, 14,* 445–449.

Fonagy, P., Steele, M., & Steele, M. (1991). Maternal representations of attachment during pregnancy predict the organization of infant-mother attachment at one year of age. *Child Development, 62,* 891–905.

Ford, M. (1992). *Motivating humans.* Newbury Park, CA: Sage.

Fordham, S. & Ogbu, J. U. (1986). Black students' school success: Coping with the burden of "acting white." *Urban Review, 18,* 176–206.

Forste, R. & Heaton, R. (1988). Initiation of sexual activity among female adolescents. *Youth and Society, 19*(3), 250–268.

Forstein, M. (1989, April 7–9). *Sexuality and AIDS.* Paper presented at the Conference on the Psychiatric Treatment of Adolescents and Young Adults, Harvard Medical School, Boston, MA.

Foster, S. (1988). *The one girl in ten: A self portrait of the teenage mother.* Washington, DC: The Child Welfare League of America.

Fowler, J. (1974). Toward a developmental perspective on faith. *Religious Education, 69,* 207–219.

Fowler, J. (1975a). *Stages in faith: The structural developmental approach.* Harvard Divinity School Research Project on Faith and Moral Development.

Fowler, J. (1975b, October). *Faith development theory and the aims of religious socialization.* Paper presented at annual meeting of the Religious Research Association, Milwaukee, WI.

Fox, N., Kimmerly, N., & Schafer, W. (1991). Attachment to mother/attachment to father: A meta-analysis. *Child Development, 62,* 210–225.

Fraiberg, S. (1980). *Clinical studies in infant mental health: The first year of life.* New York: Basic.

Frankl, V. (1967). *Psychotherapy and existentialism.* New York: Simon & Schuster.

Freud, A. (1968). Adolescence. In A. E. Winder & D. L. Angus (Eds.), *Adolescence: Contemporary studies.* New York: American Book.

Freud, S. (1955). Totem and taboo. In J. Strachey (Ed. and Trans.), *The standard edition of the complete psychological works of Sigmund Freud* (Vol. 13). London: Hogarth Press (Original work published 1914).

Freud, S. (1966). *The complete introductory lectures on psychoanalysis.* Translated and edited by James Strachey. New York: Norton.

Frey, B. A. & Noller, R. B. (1983). Mentoring: A legacy of success. *Journal of Creative Behavior, 17*(1), 60–64.

Friedan, B. (1963). *The feminine mystique.* New York: W. W. Norton.

Friedenberg, E. (1959). *The vanishing adolescent.* Boston: Beacon Press.

Fromm, E. (1955). *The sane society.* New York: Holt, Rinehart & Winston.

Fromm, E. (1968). *The art of loving.* New York: Harper & Row.

Fulton, R. (1977). General aspects. In N. Linzer (Ed.), *Understanding bereavement and grief.* New York: Yeshiva University Press.

Fulton, R. & Owen, G. (1988). Death and society in twentieth century America. *Omega, 18,* 379–395.

Furman, W. & Buhrmester, D. (1985). Children's perceptions of the qualities of sibling relationships. *Child Development, 56,* 448–461.

Furstenberg, F. F. (1990). The new extended family. In K. Pasley & M. Ihinger-Tallman (Eds.), *Remarriage and stepparenting.* New York: Guilford.

Gabriel, A. & McAnarney, E. R. (1983). Parenthood in two subcultures: White, middle-class couples and black, low-income adolescents in Rochester, New York. *Adolescence, 18*(71), 595–608.

Gagnon, J. H. & Simon, W. (1969). They're going to learn on the street anyway. *Psychology Today, 3*(2), 46 ff.

Gagnon, J. H. & Simon, W. (1987). The sexual scripting of oral genital contacts. *Archives of Sexual Behavior, 16*(1), 1–25.

Galambos, N. L. & Lerner, J. V. (1987). Child characteristics and the employment of mothers with young children: A longitudinal study. *Journal of Child Psychology and Psychiatry and Allied Disciplines, 28*(1), 87–98.

Gallagher, W. (1994). Midlife myths. In F. Fenson & J. Fenson (Eds.), *Human development, 94/95* (22 Ed.). Guilford, CN: Dushkin.

Gallup, G. (1988). *The Gallup poll.* New York: Random House.

Galton, F. (1870). *Hereditary genius.* New York: Appleton.

Galton, F. (1879). Psychometric experiments. *Brain, 2,* 148–162.

Garapon, A. (1983, August/September). Place de l'initiation dans la délinquance juvenile. (Initiation role in juvenile delinquency.) *Neuropsychiatrie de l'Enfance et de l'adolescence, 31*(8–9), 390–403.

Garbarino, J. (1992). *Children and families in the social environment.* New York: Aldine.

Garbarino, J. & Abramowitz, R. (1992). The family as a social system. In J. Garbarino, *Children and families in the social environment*. New York: Aldine.

Garbarino, J. & Benn, J. (1992). The ecology of childbearing and childrearing. In J. Garbarino, *Children and families in the social environment*. New York: Aldine.

Garcia-Coll, C. (1990). Developmental outcome of minority infants: A process-oriented look into our beginnings. *Child Development, 61,*(2), 270–289.

Garcia-Coll, C., Hoffman, J., & Oh, W. (1987). The social ecology and early parenting of Caucasian adolescent mothers. *Child Development, 58*(4), 955–963.

Gardner, H. (1993a). *Creating minds*. New York: Basic Books.

Gardner, H. (1993b). *Multiple intelligences*. New York: Basic Books.

Gardner, H. (1980). *Artful scribbles*. New York: Basic.

Gardner, H. (1982a). *Art, mind, and brain: A cognitive approach to creativity*. New York: Basic Books.

Gardner, H. (1982b). *Developmental psychology*. Boston: Little, Brown.

Gardner, H. (1983). *Frames of mind: The theory of multiple intelligences*. New York: Basic Books.

Gardner, H. (1985). *The mind's new science: A history of the cognitive revolution*. New York: Basic Books.

Gardner, H. (1991). *The unschooled mind*. New York: Basic Books.

Gardner, H. & Winner, E. (1982). Children's conceptions (and misconceptions) of the arts. In H. Gardner, *Art, mind, and brain*. New York: Basic Books.

Garmezy, N. (1987). Stress, competence, and development: The search for stress-resistant children. *American Journal of Orthopsychiatry, 57,* 159–174.

Garn, S. M. & Petzold, A. (1983). Characteristics of the mother and child in teenage pregnancy. *American Journal of Diseases of Children, 137*(4), 365–368.

Garvey, M. S. (1986). The high cost of sexual harassment suits. *Personnel Journal, 65*(1), 75–78, 80.

Gary, L. & Booker, C. (1992). Empowering African Americans to achieve academic success. *Urban Education,* 51–55.

Gates, D. & Jackson, R. (1990). Gang violence in L.A. *The Police Chief, 57,* 20–21.

Gay, P. (1988). *Freud: A life for our time*. New York: W. W. Norton.

Gelman, D. (1989, December 18). The brain killer. *Newsweek,* 54–83.

Gelman, R. & Baillargeon, R. (1983). A review of some Piagetian concepts. In P. Mussen (Ed.), *Handbook of child psychology* (Vol. 3). New York: Wiley.

George, L. K. & Landerman, R. (1984). Health and subjective well-being. *International Journal of Aging and Human Development, 19,* 133–156.

Gershon, E. & Rieder, R. (1992). Major disorders of mind and brain. *Scientific American, 267*(3), 126–133.

Gerson, J. (1985). Women returning to school: The consequences of multiple roles. *Sex Roles, 13*(1–2), 77–92.

Gerson, L. W., Jarjoura, D., & McCord, G. (1987). Factors related to impaired mental health in urban elderly. *Research on Aging, 9*(3), 356–371.

Gesell, A. (1940). *The first five years of life*. New York: Harper.

Gest, T. (1989, December 1). Is there a right to die? *Time,* 35–37.

Gibbons, M. (1974). Walkabout: Searching for the right passage from childhood and school. *Phi Delta Kappan, 55*(9), 596–602.

Gibson, E. & Walk, R. (1960). The visual cliff. *Scientific American, 202,* 64–71.

Giddings, L. (1992). Literature-based reading instruction: An analysis. *Reading Research and Instruction, 31*(2), 18–30.

Gierz, M., Haris, J., & Lohr, J. B. (1989). Recognition and treatment of depression in Alzheimer's disease. *Geriatrics, 36,* 901–911.

Giles, H., Coupland, N., Coupland, J., Williams, A., & Nussbaum, J. (1992). Intergenerational talk and communication with older people.

Gilligan, C. (1982). *In a different voice*. Cambridge, MA: Harvard Univ. Press.

Gilligan, C., Lyons, N., & Hanmer, T. (1990). *Making connections: The relational worlds of adolescent girls at Emma Willard School*. Cambridge, MA: Harvard Univ. Press.

Gilman, L. (1987). *The adoption resource book*. New York: Harper & Row.

Gimby, G. & Saltin, B. (1983). The aging muscle. *Clinical Physiology, 3,* 209–218.

Gitlin, T. (1987). *Years of hope, days of rage*. New York: Bantam Books, Inc.

Glass, A., Holyoak, K., & Santa, J. (1987). *Cognition*. Reading, MA: Addison-Wesley.

Gleason, J. B. (1985). Studying language development. In J. B. Gleason (Ed.), *The development of language*. Columbus, OH: Merrill.

Goertzel, V. & Goertzel, M. (1962). *Cradles of eminence*. Boston: Little, Brown.

Goethals, G. & Klos, D. (1976). *Experiencing youth*. Boston: Little, Brown.

Goldberg, S. & DiVitto, B. (1983). *Born too soon*. San Francisco: Freeman, Cooper.

Goldsmith, H. H. & Campos, J. (1990). The structure of temperamental fear and pleasure in infants: A psychometric perspective. *Child Development, 61,* 1944–1964.

Goldsmith, M. F. (1988). Anencephalic organ donor program suspended; Loma Linda report expected to detail findings. *Journal of the American Medical Association, 260,* 1671–1672.

Goleman, D. (1987, October 13). Thriving despite hardship: Key childhood traits identified. *New York Times, 82,* 104.

Goosens, F. & van Ijzendoorn, M. (1990). Quality of infants' attachments to professional caregivers: Relation to infant-parent attachment and day-care characteristics. *Child Development, 61,* 832–837.

Gottman, J. M. & Krokoff, L. J. (1989). Marital interaction and satisfaction: A longitudinal view. *Journal of Consulting and Clinical Psychology, 57,* 47–52.

Gould, R. (1978). *Transformations*. New York: Simon & Schuster.

Graham, S. (1994). Motivation in African-Americans. *Review of Educational Research, 64*(1), 55–117.

Grant, C. & Sleeter, C. (1993). Race, class, gender, and disability in the classroom. In J. Banks & C. Banks (Eds.), *Multicultural education: Issues and perspectives*. Boston: Allyn & Bacon, 1993.

Greenspan, S. & Greenspan, N. T. (1985). *First feelings*. New York: Viking.

Greer, C. R. & Castro, M. D. (1986). The relationship between perceived unit effectiveness and occupational stress: The case of purchasing agents. *Journal of Applied Behavioral Science, 22,* 159–175.

Gregory, T. (1978). *Adolescence in literature.* New York: Longman.

Grob, C. & De Rios, M. (1992). Adolescent drug use in cross-cultural perspective. *Journal of Drug Issues, 22*(1), 121–138.

Grobstein, C. (1988). *Science and the unborn.* New York: Basic Books.

Grossman, H. Y. & Chester, N. L. (1990). *The experience and meaning of work in women's lives.* Hillsdale, NJ: Erlbaum.

Grotevant, H. D., Thorbeck, W., & Meyer, M. L. (1982). An extension of Marcia's identity status interview into the interpersonal domain. *Journal of Youth and Adolescence, 11*(1), 33–47.

Gruber, K., Jones, R. J., & Freeman, M. H. (1982). Youth reactions to sexual assault. *Adolescence, 17*(67), 541–551.

Grzegorczyk, P. B., Jones, S. W., & Mistretta, C. M. (1979). Age-related differences in salt taste acuity. *Journal of Gerontology, 34,* 834–840.

Guelzow, M. G., Bird, G. W., & Koball, E. H. (1991). An exploratory path analysis of the stress process for dual career men and women. *Journal of Marriage and the Family, 53,* 151–164.

Guilford, J. P. (1975). Creativity: A quarter century of progress. In I. A. Taylor & J. W. Getzels (Eds.), *Perspectives in creativity.* Chicago: Aldine.

Gutman, D. (1973, December). Men, women and the parental imperative. *Commentary,* 59–64.

Guttmacher, A. & Kaiser, I. (1986). *Pregnancy, birth, and family planning.* New York: Signet.

Haan, N. (1976). ". . . change and sameness . . ." reconsidered. *International Journal of Aging and Human Development, 7,* 59–65.

Haan, N. (1981). Common dimensions of personality development. In D. M. Eichorn (Ed.), *Present and past in middle life.* New York: Academic Press.

Haan, N. (1989). Personality at midlife. In S. Hunter & M. Sundel (Eds.),

Midlife myths. Newbury Park, CA: Sage.

Hajcak, F. & Garwood, P. (1989). Quick-fix sex: Pseudosexuality in adolescents. *Adolescence, 23*(92), 75–76.

Hakim-Larson, J. & Hobart, C. J. (1987). Maternal regulation and adolescent autonomy: Mother-daughter resolution of story conflicts. *Journal of Youth and Adolescence, 16*(2), 153–166.

Hale-Benson, J. (1986). *Black children: Their roots, culture, and learning styles.* Baltimore: Johns Hopkins Univ. Press.

Halford, G. S. (1989). Reflection on 25 years of Piagetian cognitive psychology, 1963–1988. *Human Development, 32,* 325–357.

Hall, D. A. (1976). *Aging of connective tissue.* London: Academic Press.

Hall, G. S. (1904). *Adolescence.* (2 vols.) New York: Appleton-Century-Crofts.

Hallman, R. (1967). Techniques for creative teaching. *Journal of Creative Behavior, 1*(3), 325–330.

Hammond, W. R. & Yung, B. (1993). Psychology's role in the public health response to assaultive violence among young African-American men. Special Issue: Adolescence. *American Psychologist, 48*(2), 142–154.

Hansson, R., O'Connor, M., Jones, W., & Blocker, T. (1981). Maternal employment and adolescent sexual behavior. *Journal of Youth and Adolescence, 10*(1), 55–60.

Hardt, D. (1979). *Death: The final frontier.* Englewood Cliffs, NJ: Prentice-Hall.

Harre, R. & Lamb, R. (1983). *The encyclopedic dictionary of psychology.* Cambridge, MA: MIT Press.

Harris, J. & Fiedler, C. (1988). Preadolescent attitudes toward the elderly. *Adolescence, 23,* 335–340.

Harris, J. R. & Liebert, R. (1992). *Infant & child.* Englewood Cliffs, NJ: Prentice-Hall.

Harrison, H. (1983). *The premature baby book.* New York: St. Martin's.

Harry, J. (1986). Sampling gay men. *Journal of Sex Research, 22,* 21–34.

Harter, S. (1983). Developmental perspectives on the self-system. In Paul Mussen (Ed.), *Handbook of child psychology.* New York: Wiley.

Hartup, W. (1985). Peer relations. In P. Mussen (Ed.), *Handbook of child psychology.* New York: Wiley.

Hartup, W. (1989). Social relationships and their developmental significance. *American Psychologist, 44,* 120–126.

Harvard Health Letter. (1991). *Elderly drivers.* Cambridge, MA: Harvard University Press.

Hatfield, E., Traupmann, J., & Sprecher, S. (1984). Older women's perceptions of their intimate relationships. *Journal of Social and Clinical Psychology, 2*(2), 108–124.

Hauser, S., Book, B., Houlihan, J., & Powers, S. (1987). Sex differences within the family: Studies of adolescent and parent family interactions. Special issue: Sex differences in family relations at adolescence. *Journal of Youth and Adolescence, 16*(3), 199–220.

Hauser, S. T. & Bowlds, M. K. (1990). In S. Feldman & G. Elliot (Eds.), *At the threshold: The developing adolescent.* Cambridge, MA: Harvard University Press.

Hauser-Cram, P., Pierson, D., Klein Walker, D., & Tivnan, T. (1991). *Early education in the public schools.* San Francisco: Jossey-Bass.

Havighurst, R. J. (1951). *Developmental task and education.* New York: Longmans, Green.

Havighurst, R., Neugarten, B., & Tobin, S. (1968). Disengagement and patterns of aging. In B. Neugarten (Ed.), *Middle age and aging.* Chicago: University of Chicago Press.

Hawton, K. (1986). *Suicide and attempted suicide among children and adolescents.* Beverly Hills, CA: Sage.

Hawton, K. (1982a). Motivational aspects of deliberate self-poisoning in adolescents. *British Journal of Psychiatry, 141,* 286–290.

Hawton, K. (1982b). Adolescents who take overdoses: Their characteristics, problems and contacts with helping agencies. *British Journal of Psychiatry, 140,* 118–123.

Hawton, K. (1982c). Classification of adolescents who take overdoses. *British Journal of Psychiatry, 140,* 124–131.

Hayward, M. D. (1986). The influence of occupational characteristics on men's early retirement. *Social Forces, 64*(4), 1032–1045.

Held, L. (1981). Self-esteem and social network of the young pregnant teenager. *Adolescence, 16*(64), 905–912.

Herdt, G. (1993). Rituals of manhood: Male initiation in Papua New Guinea. In C. Brettell & C. Sargent, *Gender: In a cross-cultural perspective* (pp. 111–115). Englewood Cliffs: Prentice-Hall.

Hersch, P. (1991a, April). Teen epidemic. *American Health,* 42–45.

Hersch, P. (1991b, May). Sexually transmitted diseases are ravaging our children. *American Health,* 42–52.

Hertz, R. (1989). Dual-career corporate couples: Shaping marriages through work. In B. Risman & P. Schwartz, (Eds.), *Gender in intimate relationships*. Belmont, CA: Wadsworth.

Hertzog, C. (1989). Influences of cognitive slowing on age differences in intelligence. *Developmental Psychology, 25,* 636–651.

Herz, E. & Reis, J. (1987). Family life education for young inner city teens: Identifying needs. *Journal of Youth and Adolescence, 16*(4), 361–377.

Hetherington, E. M. (1972). Effects of father absence on personality development in adolescent daughters. *Developmental Psychology, 7,* 313–326.

Hetherington, E. M. (1991). The role of individual differences and family relationships in children's coping with divorce and remarriage. In P. Cowan & E. M. Hetherington (Eds.), *Family transitions*. Hillsdale, NJ: Erlbaum.

Hetherington, E. M. & Camara, K. A. (1984). Families in transition. In R. D. Park (Ed.), *Review of child development research, 7.* Chicago: University of Chicago Press.

Hetherington, E. M., Cox, M., & Cox, R. (1985). Long-term effects of divorce and remarriage on the adjustment of children. *Journal of the American Academy of Child Psychiatry, 5,* 518–530.

Hetherington, E. M. & Parke, R. (1993). *Child psychology*. New York: McGraw-Hill.

Hetherington, E. M., Staney-Hagan, M., & Anderson, E. (1989). Marital transitions: A child's perspective. *American Psychologist, 44,* 303–312.

Hill, C. D., Thompson, L. W., & Gallagher, D. (1988). The role of anticipatory bereavement in older women's adjustment to widowhood. *The Gerontologist, 28*(6), 7–12.

Hill, J. P. & Holmbeck, G. N. (1987). Disagreements about rules in families with seventh-grade girls and boys. *Journal of Youth and Adolescence, 16*(3), 221–246.

Hill, P., Jr. (1987, July). *Passage to manhood: Rearing the male African-American child*. Paper presented at the annual conference of the National Black Child Development Institute, Detroit, MI.

Hinde, R. (1970). *Animal behavior* (2nd ed.). New York: McGraw-Hill.

Hinde, R. (1979). *Towards understanding relationships*. New York: Academic Press.

Hinde, R. (1987). *Individuals, relationships and culture*. Cambridge: Cambridge Univ. Press.

Hinde, R. (1992). Developmental psychology in the context of other behavioral sciences. *Developmental Psychology, 28*(6), 1018–1029.

Hirshberg, H. (1990). When infants look to their parents: Twelve-month-olds' response to conflicting parental emotional signals. *Child Development, 61,* 1187–1191.

Hochhauser, M. & Rothenberger, J. (1992). *AIDS education*. Dubuque, IA: Wm. C. Brown.

Hoffman, S. & Duncan, G. (1988). What are the economic consequences of divorce? *Demography, 25,* 641–645.

Holden, C. (1987). Alcoholism and the medical cost crunch. *Science, 235,* 1132–1133.

Holinger, P. C., Offer, D., & Ostrov, E. (1987). Suicide and homicide in the United States: An epidemiologic study of violent death, population changes, and the potential for prediction. *American Journal of Psychiatry, 144*(2), 215–219.

Holland, J. L. (1973). *Making vocational choices: A theory of careers*. Englewood Cliffs, NJ: Prentice-Hall.

Holmes, J. & Rahe, S. (1967). A social adjustment scale. *Journal of Psychosomatic Research, 11,* 213–218.

Honig, A. (1986, May). Stress and coping in children. Part 1. *Young Children,* 50–63.

Hood, J. C. (1983). *Becoming a two-job family*. New York: Praeger.

Horgan, J. (1993, June). Eugenics revisited. *Scientific American, 268*(6), 122–131.

Horn, J. L. (1975). *Psychometric studies of aging and intelligence*. New York: Raven Press.

Horn, J. L. (1978). Human ability systems. In P. B. Baltes (Ed.), *Life-span development and behavior* (Vol. 1). New York: Academic Press.

Horn, J. L. & Donaldson, G. (1980). Cognitive development in adulthood. In O. G. Brim, Jr. & J. Kagan (Eds.), *Constancy and change in human development* (pp. 445–529). Cambridge, MA: Harvard University Press.

Horn, J. L., Donaldson, G., & Engstrom, R. (1981). Apprehension, memory, and fluid intelligence decline in adulthood. *Research on Aging, 3,* 33–84.

Horwitz, A. V. & White, H. R. (1987). Gender role orientations and styles of pathology among adolescents. *Journal of Health and Social Behavior, 28*(2), 158–170.

Hulicka, I. (1967). Short-term learning and memory. *Journal of the American Geriatrics Society, 15,* 285–294.

Hunt, T. & Lindley, C. J. (1989). *Testing older adults*. Washington, DC: Center for Psychological Services.

Hunter, S. & Sundel, M. (1989). *Midlife myths*. Newbury Park, CA: Sage.

Huston, A., McLoyd, V., & Gracia-Coll, C. (1994). Children and poverty: Issues in contemporary research. *Child Development, 65*(2), 275–282.

Huttenlocher, J., Haight, W., Bryk, A., Seltzer, M., & Lyons, T. (1991). Early vocabulary growth: Relation to language input and gender. *Developmental Psychology, 27,* 236–248.

Ingalls, Z. (1983, January 19). Although drinking is widespread, student abuse of alcohol is not rising, new study finds. *The Chronicle of Higher Education,* 9.

Isabella, R. (1993). Origins of attachment: Maternal interactive behavior across the first year. *Child Development, 64*(2), 605–621.

Izard, C. E. (1978). On the ontogenesis of emotions and emotion-cognition relationships in infancy. In M. Lewis & L. Rosenblum (Eds.), *The development of affect*. New York: Plenum.

Izard, C., Haynes, O. H., Chisholm, G., & Baak, K. (1991). Emotional determinants of infant-mother attachment. *Child Development, 62,* 906–917.

Izard, I. & Malatesta, C. (1987). Perspectives on emotional development I: Differential emotions theory of early emotional development. In J. Osofsky (Ed.), *Handbook of infant development.* New York: Wiley.

Jackson, J. S. & Gibson, R. C. (1985). Work and retirement among the black elderly. In Z. S. Blou (Ed.), *Current perspectives on aging and the life cycle: Vol. 1: Work, retirement, and social policy.* Greenwich, CN: JAI Press.

Jacobsen, T., Edelstein, W., & Hofmann, V. (1994). A longitudinal study of the relation between representations of attachment in childhood and cognitive functioning in childhood and adolescence. *Developmental Psychology, 30*(1), 112–124.

Jacobson, S. & Frye, K. (1991). Effect of maternal social support on attachment: Experimental evidence. *Child Development, 62,* 572–582.

Jacobziner, H. (1965). Attempted suicide in adolescence. *Journal of the American Medical Association, 10,* 22–36.

James, M. (1990). Adolescent values clarification: A positive influence on perceived locus of control. *Journal of Alcohol and Drug Education, 35*(2), 75–80.

Janus, S. & Janus, C. (1993). *The Janus report on sexual behavior.* New York: Wiley.

Jaquish, G. & Ripple, R. E. (1980). Cognitive creative abilities across the adult life span. *Human Development, 34,* 143–152.

Jaquish, G. A., Block, J., & Block, J. H. (1984). *The comprehension and production of metaphor in early adolescence: A longitudinal study of cognitive childhood antecedents.* Unpublished manuscript.

Jasmin, S. & Trygstad, L. (1979). *Behavioral concept and the nursing process.* St. Louis: Mosby.

Jaynes, G. & Williams, R. (1989). *A common destiny: Blacks and American society.* Washington, DC: National Academy Press.

Jefko, W. (1980). Redefining death. In E. Schneiderman (Ed.), *Death:*

Current perspectives. Palo Alto, CA: Mayfield.

Johnson, B., Shulman, S., & Collins, W. A. (1991). Systemic patterns of parenting as reported by adolescents: Developmental differences and implications for psychosocial outcomes. *Journal of Adolescent Research, 6*(2), 235–252.

Johnson, T. G. & Goldfinger, S. E. (1981). *The Harvard Medical School health letter book.* Cambridge, MA: Harvard University Press.

Johnston, W. B. (1987). *Workforce 2000: Work and workers for the 21st century.* Indianapolis, IN: Hudson Institute.

Jonaitis, M. A. (1988). Nutrition during pregnancy. In D. Tapley & W. Todd (Eds.), *Complete guide to pregnancy.* New York: Crown.

Julian, T., Mc Kenry, P., & McKelvey, M. (1992). Components of men's well-being at mid-life. *Issues in Mental Health Nursing, 13*(4), 285–299.

Jung, C. G. (1933). *Modern man in search of a soul.* New York: Harcourt, Brace & World.

Jung, C. G. (1966). *The spirit in men, art and literature.* New York: Bollingen Foundations.

Jung, C. G. (1971). *The portable Jung.* (Joseph Campbell, Ed.). New York: Viking Press.

Jurich, A. P., Schumm, W. R., & Bollman, S. R. (1987). The degree of family orientation perceived by mothers, fathers, and adolescents. *Adolescence, 22*(85), 119–128.

Kacmar, K. M. & Ferris, G. R. (1989). Theoretical and methodological considerations in the age-job satisfaction relationship. *Journal of Applied Psychology, 74,* 201–207.

Kagan, J. (1984). *The nature of the child.* New York: Basic Books.

Kagan, J. (1992). Yesterday's premises, tomorrow's promises. *Developmental Psychology, 28*(6), 990–997.

Kagan, J. (1994). *Galen's prophecy.* New York: Basic Books.

Kagan, J. & Moss, H. (1962). *Birth to maturity: A study in psychological development.* New York: Wiley.

Kail, R. (1990). *The development of memory in children.* New York: Freeman.

Kallman, F. & Jarvik, L. (1959). Individual differences in constitution and genetic background. In J. Birren

(Ed.), *Handbook of aging and the individual.* Chicago: Univ. of Chicago Press.

Kalter, N. (1987). Long-term effects of divorce on children: A developmental vulnerability model. *American Journal of Orthopsychiatry, 57*(4), 587–600.

Kammerman, J. B. (1988). *Death in the midst of life.* Englewood Cliffs, NJ: Prentice-Hall.

Kangas, J. & Bradway, K. (1971). Intelligence at midlife: A 38-year follow-up. *Developmental Psychology, 5,* 333–337.

Kantrowicz, B. (1989, December 18). Trapped inside her own world. *Newsweek,* 56–58.

Kart, C. S., Metress, E. K., & Metress, S. P. (1988). *Aging, health and society.* Boston: Jones & Bartlett Publishers, Inc.

Kassebaum, N. (1994). Head Start: Only the best for America's children. *American Psychologist, 49*(2), 123–126.

Kastenbaum, R. & Kastenbaum, B. (1989). *The encyclopedia of death.* Phoenix: Oryx Press.

Kelley, S. (1986). Learned helplessness in the sexually abused child. *Pediatric Nursing, 9,* 193–207.

Kelley-Buchanan, C. (1988). *Peace of mind during pregnancy.* New York: Dell.

Kellog, J. (1988). Forces of change. *Phi Delta Kappan, 70,* 199–204.

Kelly, J. A. & Hansen, D. J. (1987). Social interactions and adjustment. In V. B. Van Hasselt & M. Hersen (Eds.), *Handbook of adolescent psychology* (pp. 131–146). New York: Pergamon Press.

Kendig, H., Hashimoto, A., & Coppard, L. (Eds.). (1992). *Family support for the elderly: The international experience.* Oxford: Oxford University Press.

Kessler, J. (1988). *Psychopathology of childhood.* Englewood Cliffs, NJ: Prentice-Hall.

Kienhorst, C. W., Wolters, W. H., Diekstra, R. F., & Otto, E. (1987). A study of the frequency of suicidal behavior in children aged 5 to 14. *Journal of Child Psychology and Psychiatry and Allied Disciplines, 28*(1), 153–165.

Kilpatrick, W. (1975). *Identity and intimacy.* New York: Delacorte.

Kim, H. (1991). Do you have eyelashes? In C. Gilligan, A. Rogers, &

D. Tolman. *Women, girls & psychotherapy: Reframing resistance*. New York: Harrington Park Press.

Kim, U. (1990). Indigenous psychology: Science and applications. In R. Brislin (Ed.), *Applied cross-cultural psychology*. Newbury Park, CA: Sage.

Kimmel, D. (1974). *Adulthood and aging*. New York: Wiley.

Kimmel, D. C. & Weiner, I. B. (1985). *Adolescence: A developmental transition*. Hillsdale, NJ: Erlbaum.

Kinard, E. & Reinherz, H. (1987). School aptitude and achievement in children of adolescent mothers. *Journal of Youth and Adolescence, 16*(1), 69–87.

King, I. (1914). *The high school age*. Indianapolis: Bobbs-Merrill.

Kinnaird, K. & Gerrard, M. (1986). Premarital sexual behavior and attitudes toward marriage and divorce among young women as a function of their mothers' marital status. *Journal of Marriage and the Family, 48*(4), 757–765.

Kinsey, A., Pomeroy, W., Martin, C., & Gebhard, P. (1948). *Sexual behavior in the human male*. Philadelphia: Saunders.

Kinsey, A., Pomeroy, W., Martin, C., & Gebhard, P. (1953). *Sexual behavior in the human female*. Philadelphia: Saunders.

Kirkland, M. & Ginther, D. (1988). Acquired Immune Deficiency Syndrome in children: Medical, legal, and school related issues. *School Psychology Review, 17*, 304–305.

Kitahara, M. (1983). Female puberty rites: Reconsideration and speculation. *Adolescents, 18*(72), 957–964.

Kitchener, K. & King, P. (1981). Reflective judgment: Concepts of justification and their relationship to age and education. *Journal of Applied Developmental Psychology, 2*, 89–116.

Kivett, V. R. (1991). Centrality of the grandfather role among older rural black and white men. *Journal of Gerontology, 46*(5), 250–258.

Klassen, A. D., Williams, C. J., & Levitt, E. E. (1989). *Sex and morality in the U.S.: An empirical enquiry under the auspices of the Kinsey Institute*. Middletown, CT: Wesleyan University Press.

Klaus, M. & Kennell, J. (1983). *Bonding*. New York: Mosby.

Klein, H. & Cordell, A. (1987). The adolescent as mother: Early risk identification. *Journal of Youth and Adolescence, 16*(1), 47–58.

Klein, N. (1978, October). Is there a right way to die? *Psychology Today, 12*, 122.

Kliegl, R., Smith, J., & Baltes, P. (1989). Testing-the-limits and the study of adult age differences in cognitive plasticity of a mnemonic skill. *Developmental Psychology, 25*(2), 247–256.

Kliegl, R., Smith, J., & Baltes, P. (1990). On the locus and process of magnification of age differences during mnemonic training. *Developmental Psychology, 26*(6), 894–904.

Kneisl, C. R. & Ames, S. W. (1986). *Adult health nursing: A biopsychosocial approach*. New York: Addison-Wesley.

Knowles, M. (1984). *The adult learner: A neglected species*. Houston: Gulf.

Knowles, M. (1989). *The adult learner: A neglected species*. Houston: Gulf.

Koch, H. (1960). The relation of certain formal attributes of siblings to attributes held toward each other and toward their parents. *Monographs of the Society for Research in Child Development, 25*(4), 1–124.

Koenig, H. G., Kvale, J. N., & Ferrell, C. (1988). Religion and well-being in later life. *The Gerontologist, 28*(1), 18–20.

Koff, E., Rierdan, J., & Sheingold, K. (1980, April). *Memories of menarche: Age and preparedness as determinants of subjective experience*. Paper presented at the annual meeting of the Eastern Psychological Association, Hartford, CT.

Kogan, N. (1973). Creativity and cognitive style: A life-span perspective. In P. B. Baltes & K. W. Schaie (Eds.), *Life-span developmental psychology*. New York: Academic Press.

Kogan, N. (1983). Stylistic variation in childhood and adolescence: Creativity, metaphor, cognitive styles. In P. H. Mussen (Ed.), *Handbook of child psychology* (Vol. 3). New York: Wiley.

Kohlberg, L. (1966). A cognitive-developmental analysis of children's sex-role concepts and attitudes. In E. Maccoby (Ed.), *The development of sex differences*. Stanford, CA: Stanford Univ. Press.

Kohlberg, L. (1973). The claim to moral adequacy of a highest stage of moral judgment. *Journal of Philosophy, 60*, 630–646.

Kohlberg, L. (1975). The cognitive-developmental approach to moral education. *Phi Delta Kappan, 56*, 670–677.

Kohlberg, L. (1976). Moral stages and moralization: The cognitive developmental approach. In T. Lickona (Ed.), *Moral development and behavior: Theory, research, and social issues*. New York: Holt, Rinehart, & Winston.

Kohlberg, L. (1981). *The philosophy of moral development*. New York: Harper & Row.

Kohner, M. (1977, October 11). Adolescent pregnancy. *The New York Times, 38*.

Kolata, G. (1990). *The baby doctors*. New York: Dell.

Konner, M. (1991). *Childhood*. Boston: Little, Brown.

Kornhaber, A. & Woodward, K. L. (1991). G*randparents/grandchildren: The vital connection*. Brunswick, NJ: Transaction Press.

Kornzweig, A. L. (1980). New ideas for old eyes. *Journal of the American Geriatrics Society, 28*, 145.

Koyle, P. R., Jensen, L. C., Olsen, J., & Cundick, B. (1989). Comparison of sexual behaviors among adolescents. *Youth and Society, 20*(4), 461–476.

Kozol, J. (1991). *Savage inequalities*. New York: Crown.

Kraeer, R. J. (1981). The therapeutic value of the funeral in post-funeral counseling. In O. S. Margolis & others (Eds.), *Acute grief*. New York: Columbia University Press.

Krause, N. & Wray, L. (1991). Psychosocial correlates of health and illness among minority elders. *Generations, 15*, 25–30.

Kroger, J. & Haslett, S. J. (1988). Separation-individuation and ego identity status in late adolescence. *Journal of Youth and Adolescence, 17*(1), 59–80.

Kübler-Ross, E. (1969). *On death and dying*. New York: Macmillan.

Kübler-Ross, E. (1975). *Death: The final stage of growth*. Englewood Cliffs, NJ: Prentice-Hall.

Kübler-Ross, E. & Warshaw, W. (1978). *To live until we say goodbye*. Englewood Cliffs, NJ: Prentice-Hall.

Labouvie-Vief, G. & Lawrence, R. (1985). Object knowledge, personal knowledge, and processes of equilibration in adult cognition. *Human Development, 28,* 25–39.

Lamb, M. & Campos, J. (1982). *Development in infancy.* New York: Random House.

Lamb, M. & Sternberg, K. (1990). Some thoughts about infant daycare. *Research and Clinical Center for Child Development, 12,* 70–77.

Lamb, M. E. (1987). *The father's role: Cross-cultural perspectives.* Hillsdale, NJ: Erlbaum.

Lancaster, J. B. & Hamburg, B. A. (1986). *School-age pregnancy and parenthood.* New York: Aldine de Gruyter.

Langlois, J., Ritter, J., Rogman, L., & Vaughn, L. (1991). Facial diversity and infant preferences for attractive faces. *Developmental Psychology, 27,* 79–84.

Langone, J. (1991). *AIDS: The facts.* Boston: Little, Brown.

Lansdown, R. & Benjamin, G. (1985). The development of the concept of death in children ages 5–9. *Childcare, Health and Development, 11,* 13–30.

Lansdown, R. & Walker, M. (1991). *Your child's development from birth through adolescence.* New York: Knopf.

Larson, R. & Johnson, C. (1981). Anorexia nervosa in the context of daily experience. *Journal of Youth and Adolescence, 10*(6), 455–471.

Lawton, M. P. (1984). Health and subjective well-being. *International Journal of Aging and Human Development, 19,* 157–166.

Lazar, I. & Darlington, R. (1982). Lasting effects of early education: A report from the consortium for longitudinal studies. *Monographs of the Society for Research in Child Development,* No. 47.

Lease, K. P. & Robbins, S. B. (1994). Relationships between goal attributes and the academic achievement of Southeast Asian adolescent refugees. *Journal of Counseling Psychology, 41*(1), 45–52.

Leboyer, F. (1975). *Birth without violence.* New York: Knopf.

Lee, P. R., Franks, P., Thomas, G. S., & Paffenberger, R. S. (1981). *Exercise and health: The evidence and its implications.* Cambridge, MA: Oelgeschlager, Gunn, & Hain.

Lehman, H. C. (1953). *Age and achievement.* Princeton, NJ: Princeton University Press.

Lehman, H. C. (1962). The creative production rates of present versus past generations of scientists. *Journal of Gerontology, 17,* 409–417.

Lehman, H. C. (1964). The relationship between chronological age and high level research output in physics and chemistry. *Journal of Gerontology, 19,* 157–164.

Leiblum, S. R. (1990). Sexuality and the midlife woman. *Psychology of Women Quarterly, 14*(4), 495–508.

Leigh, R. J. (1982). The impoverishment of ocular motility in the elderly. In R. Sekuler, D. Kline, & K. Dismukes (Eds.), *Aging and human visual function* (pp. 173–180). New York: Alan R. Liss.

Leitman, D., Wortman, C., & Williams, A. (1987). Long-term effects of losing a spouse or child in a motor vehicle crash. *Journal of Personality and Social Psychology, 52,* 216–231.

Lenneberg, E. (1967). *Biological foundations of language.* New York: Wiley.

Levin, J. S. & Markides, K. S. (1986). Religious attendance and subjective health. *Journal for the Scientific Study of Religion, 25,* 31–38.

Levinson, D. (1990a). A theory of life structure development in adulthood. In C. N. Alexander & E. J. Langer (Eds.), *Higher states of human development* (pp. 35–54). New York: Oxford University Press.

Levinson, D. (1990b). *Seasons of a woman's life.* Presented at the 98th annual convention of the American Psychological Association, Boston.

Levinson, D. (1978). *The seasons of a man's life.* New York: Knopf.

Levinson, D. (1986). A conception of adult development. *American Psychologist, 41*(1), 3–13.

Lewis, C. (1963). *A grief observed.* New York: Seabury Press.

Lewis, M. (1989). Emotional development in the preschool child. *Pediatric Annals, 18*(5), 317–326.

Lewis, M. & Brooks-Gunn, J. (1979). *Social cognition and the acquisition of self.* New York: Plenum.

Lickona, T. (1991). *Education for character: How our schools can teach respect and responsibility.* New York: Bantam.

Lickona, T. (1993). The return of character education. *Educational Leadership, 51*(3), 6–11.

Lidz, T. & Lidz, R. W. (1984). Oedipus in the Stone Age. *Journal of the American Psychoanalytic Association, 32*(3), 507–527.

Liebert, R. M., Sprafkin, J. N., & Davidson, E. (1988). *The early window.* New York: Pergamon.

Lifson, A., Hessol, N., & Rutherford, G. W. (1989, June). *The natural history of HIV infection in a cohort of homosexual and bisexual men: Clinical manifestations, 1978–1989.* Paper presented at the Fifth International Conference on AIDS, Montreal.

Lin, C. & Fu, V. (1990). A comparison of child-rearing practices among Chinese, immigrant Chinese, and Caucasian American parents. *Child Development, 61*(2), 429–433.

Lindemann, E. (1944). Symptomology and management of acute grief. *American Journal of Psychiatry, 101,* 141–148.

Lindholm, K. J. (1990). Bilingual immersion education: Educational equity for language minority students. In A. Barona & E. E. Garcia (Eds.), *Children at risk: Poverty, minority status, and other issues in educational equity* (pp. 77–89). Washington, DC: National Association of School Psychologists.

Lips, H. (1993). *Sex and gender.* Mountain View, CA: Mayfield.

Lisina, M. I. (1983). The development of interaction in the first seven years. In W. Hartup (Ed.), *Review of child development research.* Chicago: Univ. of Chicago Press.

Lockman, J. & Thelen, E. (1993). Developmental biodynamics: Brain, body, behavior connections. *Child Development, 64,* 953–959.

Lohr, M. J., Essex, M. J., & Klein, M. H. (1988). The relationships of coping responses to physical health status and life satisfaction among older women. *Journal of Gerontology: Psychological Sciences, 43*(2), 54–60.

Lopata, H. Z. (1973). *Widowhood in an American city.* Cambridge, MA: Schenkman.

Lorand, S. & Schneer, H. I. (Eds.). (1961). *Adolescence: Psychoanalytic approaches to problems and theory.* New York: Hoeber.

Lott, B. (1989). *Women's lives.* Monterey, CA: Brooks/Cole.

Lowenkopf, E. (1982, May/June). Anorexia nervosa: Some nosological considerations. *Comprehensive Psychiatry, 23*(3), 233–239.

Maccoby, E. (1988). Social emotional development and response to stressors. In N. Garmezy & M. Rutter (Eds.), *Stress, coping and development in children*. Baltimore: Johns Hopkins Univ. Press.

Maccoby, E. (1992). The role of parents in the socialization of children: An historical overview. *Developmental Psychology, 28*(6), 1006–1017.

Maccoby, E. & Jacklin, C. (1974). *The psychology of sex differences*. Palo Alto, CA: Stanford Univ. Press.

Maccoby, E. & Martin, J. (1983). Socialization in the context of the family: Parent-Child Interaction. P. Mussen (Ed.), *Handbook of child psychology*. New York: Wiley.

Mack, J. E. & Hickler, H. (1982). *Vivenne: The life and suicide of an adolescent girl*. New York: New American Library.

MacRae, H. (1992). Fictive kin as a component of the social networks of older people. *Research on Aging, 14*(2), 226–247.

Madaus, G. (1994). A technological and historical consideration of equity issues associated with proposals to change the nation's testing policy. *Harvard Educational Review, 64*(1), 76–95.

Magid, K. & McKelvey, C. (1987). *High risk: Children without a conscience*. New York: Bantam.

Main, M. & Goldwyn, R. (1990). Interview-based adult attachment classifications: Related to infant-mother and infant-father attachment. *Developmental Psychology, 26*, 370–375.

Males, M. (1992). Adult liaison in the "epidemic" of "teenage" birth, pregnancy, and venereal disease. *Journal of Sex Research, 29*(4), 525–545.

Malowald, M. (1992). To be or not to be a woman: Anorexia nervosa, normative gender roles, and feminism. *Journal of Medicine and Philosophy, 17*(2), 233–251.

Manchester, W. (1983). *The last lion: Winston Spencer Churchill*. Boston: Little, Brown.

Marcia, J. E. (1966). Development and validation of ego identity status.

Journal of Personality and Social Psychology, 3, 551–558.

Marcia, J. E. (1967). Ego identity status: Relationship to change in self-esteem, general maladjustment and authoritarianism. *Journal of Personality, 35*, 118–133.

Marcia, J. E. (1968). The case history of a construct: Ego identity status. In E. Vinacke (Ed.), *Readings in general psychology*. New York: Van Nostrand Reinhold.

Marcia, J. E. (1980). Identity in adolescence. In J. Adelson (Ed.), *Handbook of adolescent psychology*. New York: Wiley.

Marcia, J. E. (1983). Some directions for the investigation of ego development in early adolescence. *Journal of Early Adolescence, 3*(3), 215–223.

Marshall, L. (1981). Auditory processing in aging listeners. *Journal of Speech and Hearing Disorders, 46*, 226–240.

Marshall, V. & Levy, J. (1990). Aging and dying. In R. Binstock & L. George, (Eds.), *Handbook of aging and the social sciences*. San Diego, CA: Academic Press.

Marsiglio, W. (1992). Stepfathers with minor children living at home. *Journal of Family Issues, 13*(2), 195–214.

Martin, C. & Little, J. (1990). The relation of gender understanding to children's sex-typed preferences and gender stereotypes. *Child Development, 61*, 1427–1439.

Martin, C., Wood, C., & Little, J. (1990). The development of gender stereotype components. *Child Development, 61*, 1891–1904.

Martin, D. H., Mroczkowski, T. F., Dalu, Z. A., McCarty, J., Jones, R. B., & Hopkins, S. J. Azithromycin for Chlamydial Infections Study Group (1992). A controlled trial of a single dose of Azithromycin for the treatment of chlamydial urethritis and cervicitis. *New England Journal of Medicine, 327*(13), 921–925.

Martocchio, J. J. (1989). Age-related differences in employee absenteeism: A meta-analysis. *Psychology and Aging, 4*, 409–414.

Maslow, A. (1987). *Motivation and personality*. (Revised by R. Frager, J. Fadiman, C. McReynolds, & R. Cox.) New York: Harper & Row.

Mason, J. & Au, K. (1990). *Reading instruction for today*. Glenview, IL: Scott, Foresman/Little, Brown.

Masoro, E. J. (1984). Nutrition as a modulator of the aging process. *Physiologist, 27*(2), 98–101.

Massachusetts Department of Public Health (1991). *Adolescents at risk 1991: Sexually transmitted diseases*. Boston, MA: Author.

Masters, W. & Johnson, V. (1966). *Human sexual response*. Boston: Little, Brown.

Masters, W. & Johnson, V. (1970). *Human sexual inadequacy*. Boston: Little, Brown.

Masters, W. H., Johnson, V. E., & Kolodny, R. C. (1986). *Masters and Johnson on sex and human loving*. Boston: Little, Brown.

Matheny, A. P. (1980). Bayley's infant behavior record: Behavioral components and twin analyses. *Child Development, 51*, 466–475.

Matthews, K., Wing, R., Kuller, L., Meilahn, E., Kelsey, S., Costello, E., & Caggiula, A. (1990). Influences of natural menopause on psychological characteristics and symptoms of middle-aged healthy women. *Journal of Consulting and Clinical Psychology, 58*(3), 345–351.

Matthews, S. H. (1987). Provision of care to old parents: Division of responsibility among adult children. *Research on Aging, 9*, 45–60.

Matusow, A. J. (1984). *The unraveling of America*. New York: Harper & Row.

Maurer, D. & Maurer, C. (1988). *The world of the newborn*. New York: Basic Books.

Mazess, R. B. (1982). On aging bone loss. *Clinical Orthopaedics and Related Research, 165*, 239–252.

McCall, P. L. (1991). Adolescent and elderly white male suicide trends. *Journal of Gerontology, 46*, S43–51.

McCann, I. L. & Holmes, D. S. (1984). Influence of aerobic exercise on depression. *Journal of Personality and Social Psychology, 46*(5), 1142–1147.

McCarthy, J. (1979, May 5). Jogging. *Time*, 46.

McCary, J. (1978). *McCary's human sexuality*. New York: Van Nostrand Reinhold.

McCaslin, M. (1989). Theory, instruction, and future implementation. *Elementary School Journal, 90*, 223–229.

McCrae, R. & Costa, P. T., Jr. (1984). *Emerging lives, enduring dispositions: Personality in adulthood.* Boston: Little, Brown.

McDevitt, T., Spivey, N., Sheehan, E., Lennon, R., & Story, R. (1990). Children's beliefs about listening: Is it enough to be still and quiet? *Child Development, 61,* 713–721.

McEvoy, G. M. & Cascio, W. F. (1989). Cumulative evidence of the relationship between employee age and job performance. *Journal of Applied Psychology, 74,* 11–17.

McGhee, P. (1979). *Humor: Its origin and development.* San Francisco: W. H. Freeman.

McGhee, P. (1988). The role of humor in enhancing children's development and adjustment. *Journal of Children in Contemporary Society, 20,* 249–274.

McIntire, J. (1980). Suicide and self-poisoning in pediatrics. *Resident and Staff Physician, 21,* 72–85.

McKenry, P., Walters, L., & Johnson, C. (1979). Adolescent pregnancy: A review of the literature. *Family Coordinator, 33,* 17–29.

McLaughlin, B. (1990). Development of bilingualism: Myth and reality. In A. Barona & E. E. Garcia (Eds.), *Children at risk: Poverty, minority status, and other issues in educational equity* (pp. 77–89). Washington, DC: National Association of School Psychologists.

Mead, M. (1972, April). *Long living in cross-sectional perspective.* Paper presented to the Gerontological Society, San Juan, Puerto Rico.

Medway, F. J. & Rose, J. S. (1986). Grade retention. In T. R. Kratochwill (Ed.), *Advances in school psychology* (Vol. 5, pp. 141–175). Hillsdale, NJ: Erlbaum.

Meilman, P. (1979). Cross-sectional age changes in ego identity status during adolescence. *Developmental Psychology, 15*(2), 230–231.

Meltz, B. F. (1988, November 26). Saving the magic moments. *Boston Globe,* 56.

Mendes, C. F. (1992). Anger and impatience/irritability in patients of low socioeconomic status with acute coronary heart disease. *Journal of Behavioral Medicine, 15*(3), 273–284.

Menyuk, P. (1982). Language development. In C. Kopp & J. Krakow (Eds.), *The child.* Reading, MA: Addison-Wesley.

Miller, J. B. (1976). *Toward a new psychology of women.* Boston: Beacon Press, Inc.

Minde, K. (1990). The long-term impact of prematurity on the family. *Ab Initio, 2*(2). 1–3.

Mintz, B. I. & Betz, N. E. (1988). Prevalence and correlates of eating disordered behaviors among undergraduate women. *Journal of Counseling Psychology, 35,* 463–471.

Minuchin, P. & Shapiro, E. (1983). The school as a context for social development. In P. Mussen (Ed.), *Handbook of child psychology.* New York: Wiley.

Mitford, J. (1963). *The American way of death.* New York: Simon & Schuster.

Moen, P. (1985). Continuities and discontinuities in women's labor force activity. In G. H. Elder (Ed.), *Life course dynamics: Trajectories and transitions, 1968–1980* (pp. 113–155). Ithaca, NY: Cornell Univ. Press.

Molnar, J. & Rubin, D. (1991). *The impact of homelessness on children: Review of prior studies and implications for future research.* Paper presented at the NIMH/NIAA research conference, Cambridge, MA.

Money, J. (1980). *Love and love sickness.* Baltimore: The Johns Hopkins Univ. Press.

Money, J. (1987). Sin, sickness, or status? Homosexual gender identity and psychoneuroendocrinology. *American Psychologist, 42*(4), 384–399.

Montemayor, R. & Brownlee, J. R. (1987). Fathers, mothers, and adolescents: Gender-based differences in parental roles during adolescence. *Journal of Youth and Adolescence, 16*(3), 281–291.

Montessori, M. (1967). *The absorbent mind.* New York: Dell.

Monthly Vital Statistics Report. (1994). Provisional number of deaths and death rates by age, race and sex, and age-adjusted rates by race and sex. *Vital Statistics, 43*(3), 13–15.

Moore, B. N. & Parker, R. (1986). *Critical thinking.* Mountain View, CA: Mayfield Publishing Co.

Moore, E. W., McCann, H., & McCann, J. (1985). *Creative and critical thinking.* Boston, MA: Houghton Mifflin.

Moore, G. (1983). *Developing and evaluating educational research.* Boston: Little, Brown.

Morgan, L. A. (1991). *After marriage ends: Economic consequences for midlife women.* London: Sage.

Morinis, A. (1985). The ritual experience: Pain and the transformation of consciousness in ordeals of initiation. *Ethos, 13*(2), 150–174.

Morison, P. & Masten, A. (1991). Peer reputation in middle childhood as a predictor of adaptation in adolescence: A seven-year followup. *Child Development, 62,* 991–1007.

Morris, J. (1974, July). Conundrum. *Ms.,* 57–64.

Morris, N. M., Rouse, W. B., & Fath, J. L. (1985). The effects of type of knowledge upon human problem solving in a process control task. *IEEE Transactions on Systems, Man and Cybernetics, 15,* 698–707.

Morton, T. (1987). Childhood aggression in the context of family interactions. In D. Crowell, I. Evans, & C. O'Donnell (Eds.), *Childhood aggression and violence.* New York: Plenum Press.

Moskowitz, B. (1979). The acquisition of language. *Scientific American, 239,* 92–108.

Moyers, W. & Bly, R. (1989). *A gathering of men.* New York: N.E.T.

Muehlbauer, G. & Dodder, L. (1983). *The losers: Gang delinquency in an American suburb.* New York: Praeger.

Muller, C. F. & Boaz, R. F. (1988). Health as a reason or a rationalization for being retired? *Research on Aging, 10*(1), 37–55.

Murphy, C. (1983). Age-related effects on the threshold, psychophysical function, and pleasantness of menthol. *Journal of Gerontology, 38,* 217–222.

Myers, L. S. & Morokoff, P. J. (1986). Physiological and subjective sexual arousal in pre- and postmenopausal women and postmenopausal women taking replacement therapy. *Psychophysiology, 23*(3), 283–292.

Nagin, D. & Farrington, D. (1992). The stability of criminal potential from childhood to adulthood. *Criminology, 30,* 235–260.

Nanda, S. (1993). Neither man nor woman: The hijras of India. In C. Brettell & C. Sargent, *Gender: In a cross-cultural perspective* (pp. 175–179). Englewood Cliffs: Prentice-Hall.

National Association for the Education of Young Children. (1986). *How to choose a good early childhood program*. Washington, DC: Author.

National Center for Education Statistics. (1992). *American education at a glance*. Washington, DC: Office of Educational Research and Improvement.

National Center for Health Statistics. (August 1990). Advance Report. *Monthly vital statistics report*. Hyattsville, MD: Public Health Service.

National Commission on Children. (1991). *Beyond rhetoric: A new American agenda for children and families*. Washington, DC: U.S. Government Printing Office.

National Institute for Health Statistics. (1986). *Obesity in the American population*. Washington, DC: U.S. Government Printing Office.

National Institute for Health Statistics. (1994). *Obesity in the American population*. Washington, DC: U.S. Government Printing Office.

National Institute of Allergy and Infectious Diseases. (1987). *STDA*. Atlanta: Centers for Disease Control.

National Institute on Aging. (1979). *Is male menopause a myth?* Washington, DC: U.S. Government Printing Office.

Nesselroade, J. R., Pedersen, N. L., McClearn, G. E., Plomin, R., & Bergeman, C. S. (1988). Factorial and criterion validities of telephone-assessed cognitive ability measures: Age and gender comparisons in adult twins. *Research on Aging, 10*(2), 220–234.

Neugarten, B. (Ed.). (1968). *Middle age and aging*. Chicago: University of Chicago Press.

Neugarten, B. & Moore, J. (1968). The changing age-status system. In B. Neugarten (Ed.), *Middle age and aging*. Chicago: Univ. of Chicago Press.

Neugarten, B. L. & Weinstein, K. K. (1964). The changing American grandparent. *Journal of Marriage and the Family, 26,* 199–206.

Newcombe, N. & Fox, N. (1994). Infantile amnesia: Through a glass darkly. *Child Development, 65,* 31–40.

Newman, J., Roberts, L., & Syre, C. (1993). Concepts of family among children and adolescents: Effect of cognitive level, gender, and family structure. *Developmental Psychology, 29*(6), 951–962.

New voices: Immigrant students in U.S. public schools. (1988). Boston: National Coalition of Advocates for Students.

New York City Youth Board. (1989). Characteristics of gangs. New York City: *New York Times,* p. 12.

Nightingale, E. O. & Goodman, M. (1990). *Before birth*. Cambridge, MA: Harvard Univ. Press.

Nightingale, E. O. & Wolverton, L. (1988). *Adolescent rolelessness in modern society*. Washington, DC: Carnegie Council on Adolescent Development.

Nilsson, L., Furuhjelm, M., Ingleman-Sundberg, A., & Wirsen, C. (1987). *A child is born*. New York: Delacorte.

Noller, R. B. (1983). *Mentoring: An annotated bibliography*. Buffalo, NY: Bearly Limited.

Northcott, H. C. & Lowe, G. S. (1987). Job and gender influences in the subjective experience of work. *Canadian Review of Sociology and Anthropology, 24*(1), 117–131.

Norton, A. J. & Moorman, J. E. (1987). Current trends in marriage and divorce among American women. *Journal of Marriage and the Family, 49*(1), 3–14.

Nuckolls, K. B., Cassell, J., & Kaplan, B. H. (1972). Psychosocial assets, life crisis, and the prognosis of pregnancy. *American Journal of Epidemiology, 95,* 431–441.

Nuttal, R. & Nuttal, E. (1980). *The impact of disaster on coping behaviors of families*. Unpublished manuscript. Boston College, Chestnut Hill, MA.

Office of Technology Assessment (1991). *Adolescent health* (Vol. 1–3). Washington, DC: U.S. Government Printing Office.

Olson, G. & Sherman, T. (1983). Attention, learning and memory in infants. In P. Mussen (Ed.), *Handbook of child psychology*. New York: Wiley.

Ornstein, R. & Sobel, D. (1987). *The healing brain*. New York: Simon & Schuster.

Osofsky, J. (1976). Neonatal characteristics and mother-infant interaction in two observational situations. *Child Development, 47,* 1138–1147.

Osofsky, J. (Ed.) (1987). *Handbook of infant development*. New York: Wiley.

Ossip-Klein, D. J., Doyne, E. J., Bowman, E. D., Osborn, K. M., McDougall-Wilson, I. B., & Neimeyer, R. A. (1989). Effects of running or weight lifting on self-concept in clinically depressed women. *Journal of Consulting and Clinical Psychology, 57,* 158–161.

Ottesen, C. C. (1993). *L. A. Stories*. Yarmouth, ME: Intercultural Press.

Outward Bound, U.S.A. (1988). *Outward bound*. Greenwich, CT: Outward Bound National Office.

Owens, W. (1953). Aging and mental abilities. *Genetic Psychology Monographs, 48,* 3–54.

Palmore, E., Burchett, B., Fillenbaum, C., George, L., & Wallman, M. (1985). *Retirement: Cause and consequences*. New York: Springer.

Parke, C. M. & Weiss, R. S. (1983). *Recovery from bereavement*. New York: Basic Books.

Parke, R. & Slaby, R. (1983). The development of aggression. In P. Mussen (Ed.), *Handbook of child psychology*. New York: Wiley.

Parker, J. & Asher, S. (1993). Friendship and friendship quality in middle childhood: Links with peer group acceptance and feelings of loneliness and social dissatisfaction. *Developmental Psychology, 29*(4), 611–621.

Paul, R. W. (1987). Dialogical thinking. In J. B. Baron & R. J. Sternberg (Eds.), *Teaching thinking skills*. New York: W. H. Freeman.

Paulos, J. (1988). *Innumeracy*. New York: Hill & Wang.

Pearlman, C. (1972, November). Frequency of intercourse in males at different ages. *Medical Aspects of Human Sexuality,* 92–113.

Pedlow, R., Sanson, A., Prior, M., & Oberklaid, F. (1993). Stability of maternally reported temperament from infancy to 8 years. *Developmental Psychology, 29*(6), 998–1007.

Peplau, L. (1981). What homosexuals want. *Psychology Today,* 28–58.

Perkins, U. (1987). *Explosion of Chicago's black street gangs 1900 to the present*. Chicago: Third World Press.

Perris, E., Myers, N., & Clifton, R. (1990). Long-term memory for a single infancy experience. *Child Development, 61,* 1796–1807.

Perry, W. (1968a). *Forms of intellectual and ethical development in the college years*. New York: Holt, Rinehart & Winston.

Perry, W. (1968b, April). *Patterns of development in thought and values of students in a liberal arts college: A validation of a scheme*. Washington, DC: U.S. Department of Health, Education, and Welfare, Office of Education, Bureau of Research. Final report.

Perry, W. (1981). Cognitive and ethical growth. In A. Chickering (Ed.), *The modern American college*. San Francisco: Jossey-Bass.

Petersen, A. (1988). Adolescent development. In M. Rosenzweig & L. Porter (Eds.), *Annual review of psychology*. Palo Alto, CA: Annual Reviews.

Petersen, A. C., Crockett, I., Richards, M., & Boxer, A. (1988). A self-report measure of pubertal status. *Journal of Youth and Adolescence, 17,* 117–134.

Phares, V. (1992). Where's poppa? The relative lack of attention to the role of fathers in child and adolescent psychopathology. *American Psychologist, 47,* 656–664.

Phillips, R. T. & Alcebo, A. M. (1986). The effects of divorce on black children and adolescents. *American Journal of Social Psychiatry, 6*(1), 69–73.

Phinney, J. (1993). Three-stage model of ethnic identity development in adolescence. In M. Bernal and G. Knight. *Ethnic identity: Formation and transmission among Hispanics and other minorities*. Albany: State University of New York Press.

Pi-Sunyer, F. X. (1994). The fattening of America. *The Journal of the American Medical Association, 272*(3), 238.

Piaget, J. (1926). *The language and thought of the child*. New York: Harcourt, Brace, & World.

Piaget, J. (1929). *The child's conception of the world*. New York: Harcourt, Brace & World.

Piaget, J. (1932). *The moral judgment of the child*. New York: Macmillan.

Piaget, J. (1952). *The origins of intelligence in children*. New York: International Universities Press.

Piaget, J. (1966). *Psychology of intelligence*. Totowa, NJ: Littlefield, Adams & Co.

Piaget, J. (1967). *Six psychological studies*. New York: Random House.

Piaget, J. (1973). *The child and reality*. New York: Viking Press.

Piaget, J. & Inhelder, B. (1969). *The psychology of the child*. New York: Basic.

Piccigallo, P. (1988, Fall). Preschool: Head start or hard push? *Social Policy,* 45–48.

Pinker, S. (1994). *The language instinct*. New York: Morrow.

Pinon, M., Huston, A., & Wright, J. (1989). Family ecology and child characteristics that predict young children's educational television viewing. *Child Development, 60,* 846–856.

Pizer, H. (Ed.). (1983). *Over fifty-five, healthy and alive*. New York: Van Nostrand Reinhold.

Pleck, J. H. (1985). *Working wives/Working husbands*. Beverly Hills, CA: Sage.

Plomin, R., DeFries, J., & Fulker, D. (1988). *Nature and nurture during infancy and early childhood*. Cambridge, MA: Cambridge University Press.

Plomin, R., Emde, R., Braungart, J., Campos, J., Corley, R., Fulker, D., Kagan, J., Reznick, J., Robinson, J., Zahn-Waxler, C., & DeFries, J. (1993). Genetic change and continuity from fourteen to twenty months: The MacArthur Longitudinal Twin Study. *Child Development, 64*(5), 1354–1376.

Polit, D. (1985). *A review of the antecedents of adolescent sexuality, contraception, and pregnancy outcomes*. Jefferson City, MO: Humanalysis.

Postman, N. (1982). *The disappearance of childhood*. New York: Dell.

Pullin, D. (1994). Learning to work: The impact of curriculum and assessment standards in educational opportunity. *Harvard Educational Review, 64*(1), 31–54.

Rafferty, M. & Shinn, M. (1991). The impact of homelessness on children. *American Psychologist, 46,* 1170–1179.

Ralph, N., Lochman, J., & Thomas, T. (1984). Psychosocial characteristics of pregnant and multiparous adolescents. *Adolescence, 19,* 283–294.

Ramsey, P. (1987). *Teaching and learning in a diverse world*. New York: Teachers College Press.

Ramsey, P. W. (1982). Do you know where your children are? *Journal of Psychology and Christianity, 1*(4), 7–15.

Rando, T. A. (1986). Creation of rituals in psychotherapy. *Forum Newsletter, 6,* 8–9.

Raphael, D., Feinberg, R., & Bachor, D. (1987). Student teachers' perceptions of the identity formation process. *Journal of Youth and Adolescence, 16*(4), 331–344.

Regoli, R. & Hewitt, J. (1991). *Delinquency in society*. New York: McGraw-Hill.

Reinke, B., Ellicott, A., Harris, R., & Hancock, E. (1985). Timing of psychosocial change in women's lives. *Human Development, 28,* 259–280.

Remafedi, G. (1988). Homosexual youth. *Journal of the American Medical Association, 258*(2), 222–225.

Rest, J. (1983). Morality. In P. Mussen (Ed.), *Handbook of child psychology*. New York: Wiley.

Rhodes, S. (1983). Age-related differences in work attitudes and behavior: A review and conceptual analysis. *Psychological Bulletin, 93,* 328–367.

Rhyne, D. (1981). Basis of marital satisfaction among men and women. *Journal of Marriage and the Family, 43,* 941–955.

Ricks, M. (1985). The social transmission of parental behavior: Attachment across generations. In I. Bretherton & E. Waters (Eds.), *Growing points of attachment: Theory and attachment. Monographs of the Society for Research in Child Development*. Chicago: University of Chicago Press.

Rierdan, J., Koff, E., & Stubbs, M. (1988). *A longitudinal analysis of body image as a predictor of the onset and persistence of adolescent girls' depression*. Working Paper No. 188, Wellesley College Center for Research on Women.

Riese, M. (1990). Neonatal temperament in monozygotic and dizygotic twin pairs. *Child Development, 61,* 1230–1237.

Ringel, S. P. & Simon, D. B. (1983). Practical management of neuromuscular diseases in the elderly. *Geriatrics, 38,* 86.

Ritter, J., Casey, R., & Langlois, J. (1991). Adults' responses to infants varying in appearance of age and attractiveness. *Child Development, 62,* 68–82.

Ritter, J. & Langlois, J. (1988). The role of physical attractiveness in the observation of adult-child interactions: Eye of the beholder or behavioral reality. *Developmental Psychology, 24,* 254–263.

Rivchun, S. B. (1980, August). Be a mentor and leave a lasting legacy. *Association Management, 32*(8), 71–74.

Roazen, P. (1976). *Erik H. Erikson: The power and limits of a vision.* New York: The Free Press.

Robins, L. & Rutter, M. (1990). *Straight and devious pathways from childhood to adulthood.* Cambridge, England: Cambridge University Press.

Robinson, J. K. (1983). Skin problems of aging. *Geriatrics, 38,* 57–65.

Rodman, H. (1989). Controlling adolescent fertility. *Society, 23*(1), 35–37.

Rogers, D. (1979). *Adult psychology.* Englewood Cliffs, NJ: Prentice-Hall.

Rogoff, B. (1990). *Apprenticeship in thinking: Cognitive development in social context.* New York: Oxford University Press.

Rogoff, B. & Morelli, G. (1989). Perspectives and children's development from cultural psychology. *American Psychologist, 44*(2), 343–348.

Rose, S., Feldman, J., Wallace, I., & McCarton, C. (1991). Information processing at 1 year: Relation to birth status and developmental outcome during the first 5 years. *Developmental Psychology, 27,* 723–737.

Rosen, B. M., Bahn, A. K., Shellow, R., & Bower, E. M. (1965). Adolescent patients served in outpatient clinics. *American Journal of Public Health, 55,* 1563–1577.

Rosen, E. I. (1987). *Bitter choices: Blue-collar women in and out of work.* Chicago: Univ. of Chicago Press.

Rosen, J. C., Gross, J., & Vara, L. (1987). Psychological adjustment of adolescents attempting to lose or gain weight. Special issue: Eating disorders. *Journal of Consulting and Clinical Psychology, 55*(5), 742–747.

Rosen, R. (1980). Adolescent pregnancy decision-making: Are parents important? *Adolescence, 15*(57), 43–54.

Rosin, H. M. (1990). The effects of dual career participation on men: Some determinants of variation in career and personal satisfaction. *Human Relations, 43*(2), 169–182.

Rosser, P. & Randolph, S. (1989). Black American infants: The Howard University normative study. In J. K. Nugent (Ed.), *The cultural context of infancy* (Vol. 1). Norwood, NJ: Ablex.

Rotheram-Borus, M. (1993). Biculturalism among adolescents. In M. Bernal & G. Knight, *Ethnic identity: Formation and transmission among Hispanics and other minorities.* Albany: State Univ. of New York Press.

Rowe, I. & Marcia, J. E. (1980). Ego identity status, formal operations, and moral development. *Journal of Youth and Adolescence, 9*(2), 87–99.

Rowland, D. L., Heiman, J. R., Gladue, B. A., & Hatch, J. P. (1987). Endocrine, psychological and genital response to sexual arousal in men. *Psychoneuroendocrinology, 12*(2), 149–158.

Roy, A. (1990). Family rituals: Functions and significance for clergy and psychotherapists. *Group, 14*(1), 59–64.

Rubin, K., Fein, G., & Vandenberg, B. (1983). Play. In P. Mussen (Ed.), *Handbook of child psychology.* New York: Wiley.

Rubin, R. H. (1981). Attitudes about male-female relations among black adolescents. *Adolescence, 16*(61), 159–174.

Rubin, Z. (1980). *Children's friendships.* Cambridge, MA: Harvard Univ. Press.

Ruble, T. (1983). Sex stereotypes. *Sex Roles, 9,* 397–402.

Rudman, D. (1992). The fountain of youth. *Milwaukee Magazine,* pp. 12–13.

Russ-Eft, D., Springer, M., & Beever, A. (1979). Antecedents of adolescent parenthood and consequences at age 30. *Family Coordinator, 16,* 173–178.

Russell, C. H. (1989). *Good news about aging.* New York: Wiley.

Rutter, M. (1979). *Fifteen thousand hours.* Cambridge, MA: Harvard University Press.

Rutter, M. (1980). *Changing youth in a changing society.* Cambridge, MA: Harvard University Press.

Rutter, M. (1981). *Maternal deprivation reassessed.* New York: Penguin.

Rutter, M. (1988). Stress, coping, and development: Some issues and some questions. In N. Garmezy & M. Rutter (Eds.), *Stress, coping and development in children.* Baltimore: Johns Hopkins Univ. Press.

Rutter, M. (1989). Pathways from childhood to adult life. *Journal of Child Psychology and Child Psychiatry, 30,* 23–50.

Rutter, M. & Garmezy, N. (1983). Developmental psychopathology. In P. Mussen (Ed.), *Handbook of child psychology.* New York: Wiley.

Sadker, M. & Sadker, D. (1994). *Failing at fairness: How America's schools cheat girls.* New York: Scribners.

Sadler, T. W. (1985). *Langman's medical embryology.* Baltimore: Williams & Wilkins.

Sales, E. (1978). Women's adult development. In I. Fieze (Ed.), *Women and sex roles.* New York: W. W. Norton.

Salthouse, T. (1990). Cognitive competence and expertise in aging. In *Handbook of the psychology of aging.* New York: Academic Press.

Saluter, A. F. (1991). *Marital status and living arrangements: March 1991.* Current Population Reports, P-20 (No. 461). Washington, DC: Bureau of the Census.

Sameroff, A. (1975). Early influence on development: Fact or fancy. *Merrill-Palmer Quarterly of Behavior and Development, 21*(4), 23–24, 267–294.

Sanders, C. M. (1989). *Grief: The mourning after.* New York: Wiley-Interscience.

Sanders, G. F. & Mullis, R. L. (1988). Family influences on sexual attitudes and knowledge as reported by college students. *Adolescence, 23* (92), 837–846.

Santrock, J. W. (1987). The effects of divorce on adolescents: Needed research perspectives. *Family Therapy, 14*(2), 147–159.

Santrock, J. & Yussen, S. (1992). *Child development*. Madison, WI: Wm. C. Brown.

Sapolsky, R. & Finch, C. E. (1994). On growing old. In F. Fenson & J. Fenson (Eds.), *Human development, 94/95* (22 Ed.). Guilford, CN: Dushkin.

Saudino, K. & Eaton, W. (1991). Infant temperament and genetics: An objective twin study of motor activity level. *Child Development, 62,* 1167–1174.

Saunders, J. B. (1989). The efficacy of treatment for drinking problems. Special issue: Psychiatry and the addictions. *International Review of Psychiatry, 1,* 121–137.

Savin-Williams, R. C. & Berndt, T. J. (1990). Friendship and peer relations. In S. Feldman & G. Elliot (Eds.), *At the threshold: The developing adolescent*. Cambridge, MA: Harvard University Press.

Scarr, S. (1992). Developmental theories for the 1990s: Developmental and individual differences. *Child Development, 63,* 1–19.

Scarr, S., Weinberg, R., & Levine, A. (1986). *Understanding development*. New York: Harcourt Brace Jovanovich.

Schaie, K. W. (1994). The course of adult intellectual development. *American Psychologist, 49*(4), 304–313.

Schaie, K. W. & Hertzog, C. (1983). Fourteen-year cohort-sequential analyses of adult intellectual development. *Developmental Psychology, 19,* 531–543.

Schemeck, H. M. (1983, September 2). Alcoholism tests back disease idea. *New York Times,* A10.

Schiedel, D. S. & Marcia, J. E. (1985). Ego identity, intimacy, sex role orientation, and gender. *Developmental Psychology, 21*(1), 149–160.

Schiffman, S. (1977). Food recognition of the elderly. *Journal of Gerontology, 32,* 586–592.

Schiffman, S. & Pasternak, M. (1979). Decreased discrimination of food odors in the elderly. *Journal of Gerontology, 34,* 73–79.

Schneider, J. (1984). *Stress, loss and grief*. Rockville, MD: Aspen Pubs.

Schoem, D. (1991). *Inside separate worlds: Life stories of young Blacks, Jews, and Latinos*. Ann Arbor: University of Michigan Press.

Schofferman, J. (1987). Hospice care of the patient with AIDS. *The Hospice Journal, 3,* 51–84.

Schroedel, J. R. (1990). Blue-collar women: Paying the price at home on the job. In H. Y. Grossman & N. L. Chester (Eds.), *The experience and meaning of work in women's lives*. Hillsdale, NJ: Erlbaum.

Schulman, M. (1991). *The passionate mind*. New York: Macmillan.

Schulz, R. (1978). *The psychology of death, dying, and bereavement*. Reading, MA: Addison-Wesley.

Schulz, R. & Ewen, R. B. (1988). *Adult development and aging: Myths and emerging realities*. New York: Macmillan.

Science News. Psychological stress linked to cancer. (September 23, 1993). *Science News, 144,* 196.

Scott, D. (Ed.). (1988). *Anorexia and bulimia*. New York: New York University Press.

Scott-Jones, D. & White, A. (1990). Correlates of sexual activity in early adolescence. *Journal of Early Adolescence, 10*(2), 221–238.

Sears, R. R. & Sears, P. S. (1982). Lives in Berkeley. *Contemporary Psychology, 27*(12), 925–927.

Sebald, H. (1977). *Adolescence: A social psychological analysis* (2nd ed.). Englewood Cliffs, NJ: Prentice-Hall.

Seginer, R. & Flum, H. (1987). Israeli adolescents' self-image profile. *Journal of Youth and Adolescence, 16*(5), 455–472.

Seligman, M. (1975). *Helplessness*. San Francisco: W. H. Freeman.

Selman, R. (1980). *The growth of interpersonal understanding*. New York: Academic Press.

Selman, R. L. & Schultz, L. H. (1990). *Making a friend in youth: Developmental theory and pair therapy*. Chicago: University of Chicago Press.

Selye, H. (1956). *The stress of life*. New York: McGraw-Hill.

Selye, H. (1975, October). Implications of stress concept. *New York State Journal of Medicine,* 2139–2145.

Selye, H. (1982). History and present status of the stress concept. In L. Goldberger & S. Breznitz (Eds.), *Handbook of stress: Theoretical and clinical aspects*. New York: The Free Press.

Serakan, U. (1989). Understanding the dynamics of self-concept of

members in dual-career families. *Human Relations, 42*(2), 97–116.

Serbin, L., Powlishta, K., & Gulko, J. (1993). The development of sex typing in middle childhood. *Monographs of the Society for Research in Child Development, 58*(2).

Sessions, W. (1990). Gang violence and organized crime. *The Police Chief, 57,* 17.

Shahtahmasebi, S., Davies, R., & Wenger, G. C. (1992). A longitudinal analysis of factors related to survival in old age. *The Gerontologist, 32*(3), 404–413.

Shatz, C. (1992, September). The developing brain. *Scientific American, 267*(3), 61–67.

Sheehy, G. (1992). *The silent passage: Menopause*. New York: Random House.

Shields, P. & Rovee-Collier, C. (1992). Long-term memory for context-specific category information at six months. *Child Development, 63,* 245–259.

Shirk, S. R. (1987). Self-doubt in late childhood and early adolescence. *Journal of Youth and Adolescence, 16*(1), 59–68.

Shweder, R. (1991). *Thinking through cultures*. Cambridge, MA: Harvard Univ. Press.

Siegler, I. (1975). The terminal drop hypothesis: Fact or artifact? *Experimental Aging Research, 1,* 169.

Silber, T. (1980). Values relating to abortion as expressed by the inner city adolescent girl—Report of a physician's experience. *Adolescence, 15*(57), 183–189.

Silverberg, S. B. & Steinberg, L. (1987). Influences on marital satisfaction during the middle stages of the family life cycle. *Journal of Marriage and the Family, 49*(4), 751–760.

Simonton, D. K. (1975). Age and literary creativity. *Journal of Cross-Cultural Creativity, 6,* 259–277.

Simonton, D. K. (1976). Biographical determinants of achieved eminence. *Journal of Personality and Social Psychology, 33,* 218–276.

Simonton, D. K. (1977a). Creativity, age and stress. *Journal of Personality and Social Psychology, 35,* 791–804.

Simonton, D. K. (1977b). Eminence, creativity and geographical marginality. *Journal of Personality and Social Psychology, 35,* 805–816.

Singer, S. (1985). *Heredity*. San Francisco: Freeman.

Skinner, B. F. (1938). *The behavior of organisms*. New York: Appleton-Century-Crofts.

Skinner, B. F. (1953). *Science and human behavior*. New York: Macmillan.

Skinner, B. F. (1957). *Verbal behavior*. New York: Appleton-Century-Crofts.

Skinner, B. F. (1971). *Beyond freedom and dignity*. New York: Knopf.

Skinner, B. F. (1974). *About behaviorism*. New York: Knopf.

Skinner, B. F. (1983). *A matter of consequences*. New York: Knopf.

Skinner, B. F. (1983, September). Origins of a behaviorist. *Psychology Today, 17*(2), 22–33.

Skinner, B. F. (1984). The shame of American Education. *American Psychologist,* September, 947–954.

Slaby, R. (1990, Spring). Gender concept development legacy. *New Directions for Psychology, 47,* 21–29.

Slugoski, B. R., Marcia, J. E., & Koopman, R. F. (1984). Cognitive and social interactional characteristics of ego identity statuses in college males. *Journal of Personality and Social Psychology, 47*(3), 646–661.

Smart, J. C. & Ethington, C. A. (1987). Occupational sex segregation and job satisfaction of women. *Research in Higher Education, 26*(2), 202–211.

Smith, B. K. (1989). *Grandparenting in today's world*. Austin, TX: Hogg Foundation for Mental Health.

Smith, D. W. E., Seibert, C. S., Jackson, F. W., & Snell, J. (1992). Pet ownership by elderly people: Two new issues. *International Journal of Aging and Human Development, 34*(3), 175–184.

Smith, R. (1990). *A theoretical framework for explaining the abuse of hyperactive children*. Unpublished doctoral dissertation, Boston College, Chestnut Hill, MA.

Sommerstein, J. C. (1986). Assessing the older worker: The career counselor's dilemma. Special issue: Career counseling of older adults. *Journal of Career Development, 13*(2), 52–56.

Sonnenstein, F. L., Pleck, J. H., & Ku, L. C. (1990). Sexual activity, condom use and AIDS awareness among adolescent males. *Family Planning Perspectives, 21*(4), 151–158.

South, S. J. (1993). Racial and ethnic differences in the desire to marry. *Journal of Marriage and the Family, 55,* 357–370.

South, S. J. & Spitze, G. (1986). Determinants of divorce over the marital life course. *American Sociological Review, 51*(4), 583–590.

Speece, M. & Brent, S. (1984). Children's understanding of death. *Child Development, 55,* 1671–1686.

Spence, A. (1989). *Biology of human aging*. Englewood Cliffs, NJ: Prentice-Hall.

Sprafkin, J. N., Liebert, R. M., & Poulos, R. W. (1975). Effects of a prosocial televised example on children's helping. *Journal of Experimental Child Psychology, 20,* 119–126.

Spreen, O., Tuppet, D., Risser, A., Tuokko, H., & Edgell, D. (1984). *Human developmental neuropsychology*. New York: Oxford Univ. Press.

Sroufe, L. A. & Cooper, R. (1992). *Child development*. New York: Knopf.

Sroufe, L. A., Cooper, R., & DeHart, G. (1992). *Child development*. New York: Knopf.

St. Peters, M., Fitch, M., Huston, A., Wright, J., & Eakins, D. (1991). Television and families: What do young children watch with their parents? *Child Development, 62,* 1409–1423.

Stambrook, M. & Parker, K. (1987). The development of the concept of death in childhood. *Merrill-Palmer Quarterly, 33,* 133–157.

Starr, B. & Weiner, M. (1981). *The Starr-Weiner report on sex and sexuality in the mature years*. New York: Stein & Day.

Steinberg, L. (1987). Single parents, step-parents, and the susceptibility of adolescents to antisocial peer pressure. *Child Development, 58*(1), 269–275.

Steinberg, L. (1990). Autonomy, conflict, and harmony in the family relationship. In S. Feldman & G. Elliot (Eds.), *At the threshold: The developing adolescent*. Cambridge, MA: Harvard University.

Steinberg, L., Fegley, S., & Dornbusch, S. (1993). Negative impact of part-time work on adolescent adjustment: Evidence from a longitudinal study. *Developmental Psychology, 29*(2), 171–180.

Stern, D. (1977). *First relationships*. Cambridge, MA: Harvard Univ. Press.

Stern, D. (1985). *The interpersonal world of the child*. New York: Basic.

Stern, D. (1990). *Diary of a baby*. New York: Harper Collins.

Sternberg, R. (1986). *Intelligence applied*. New York: Harcourt Brace Jovanovich.

Sternberg, R. (1988). *The triarchic mind: A new theory of human intelligence*. New York: Viking Press.

Sternberg, R. J. (1986). The triangular theory of love. *Psychological Review, 93,* 129–135.

Sternberg, R. J. (1990). *Wisdom*. New York: Cambridge University Press.

Stevens, J. C. & Cain, W. S. (1987). Old-age deficits in the sense of smell as gauged by thresholds, magnitude matching, and odor identification. *Psychology and Aging, 2,* 36–42.

Stevenson, H. & Lee, S. (1990). Contexts of achievement: A study of American, Chinese, and Japanese children. *Monographs of the Society for Research in Child Development 55,* (1–2, Serial No. 221).

Stiffman, A., Earls, F., Robins, L., & Jung, K. (1987). Adolescent sexual activity and pregnancy: Socioenvironmental problems, physical health, and mental health. *Journal of Youth and Adolescence, 16*(5), 497–569.

Stigler, J., Shweder, R., & Herdt, G. (Eds.). (1990). *Cultural psychology*. New York: Cambridge Univ. Press.

Stimmel, B. (1991). *The facts about drug use*. New York: Consumer Report Books.

Stoddard, S. (1977). *The hospice movement: A better way of caring for the dying*. New York: Stein & Day.

Stoller, E. P., Forster, L. E., & Duniho, T. S. (1992). Systems of parent care within sibling networks. *Research on Aging, 14*(1), 28–49.

Story, M. D. (1982). A comparison of university student experience with various sexual outlets in 1974 and 1980. *Adolescence, 17*(68), 737–747.

Strawbridge, W. & Wallhagen, M. (1992). Is all in the family always best? *Journal of Aging Studies, 6*(1), 81–92.

Strobino, D. (1987). Health and medical consequences. In C. Hayes & S. Hofferth (Eds.), *Risking the future: Adolescent sexuality, pregnancy, and child-bearing* (pp. 107–123). Washington, DC: National Academy Press.

Subcommittee on Health and the Environment. (1987). *Incidence and control of chlamydia*. Washington, DC: U.S. Government Printing Office.

Sudnow, D. (1967). *Passing on.* Englewood Cliffs, NJ: Prentice-Hall.

Sue, S. & Okazaki, S. (1990). Asian-American educational achievements: A phenomenon in search of an explanation. *American Psychologist, 45,* 913–920.

Sugarman, L. (1986). *Lifespan development: Concepts, theories and interventions.* New York: Methuen.

Sullivan, T. & Schneider, M. (1987). Development and identity issues in adolescent homosexuality. *Child and Adolescent Social Work Journal, 4*(1), 13–24.

Super, D. E. (1957). *The psychology of careers.* New York: Harper & Row.

Super, D. E. (1983). Assessment in career guidance: Toward truly developmental counseling. *Personnel and Guidance Journal, 61,* 555–562.

Super, D. E. (1990). A life-span, life-space approach to career development. In D. Brown, L. Brooks, & others (Eds.), *Career choice and development.* San Francisco: Jossey-Bass.

Super, D. E. & Thompson, A. S. (1981). *The adult career concerns inventory.* New York: Teachers College, Columbia University.

Surjan, L., Devald, J., & Palfalvi, J. (1973). Epidemiology of hearing loss. *Audiology, 12,* 396–410.

Sutton-Smith, B. (1988). *Toys as culture.* New York: Gardner Press.

Swanson, E. A. & Bennett, T. F. (1983). Degree of closeness: Does it affect the bereaved's attitudes toward selected funeral practices? *Omega, 13,* 43–50.

Swedo, S., Rettew, D., Kuppenheimer, M., Lum, D., Dolan, S., & Goldberger, E. (1991). Can adolescent suicide-attempters be distinguished from at-risk adolescents? *Pediatrics, 88,* 620–629.

Sweet, J. A. & Bumpass, L. L. (1987). *American families and households.* New York: Sage.

Takata, S. R., Zevitz, R. G., Berger, R. J., Salem, R. G., Gruberg, M., & Moore, J. (1987). Youth gangs in Racine: An examination of community perceptions. *Wisconsin-Sociologist, 24,* 132–141.

Tanner, J. M. (1989). *Fetus into man.* Cambridge, MA: Harvard Univ. Press.

Tapley, D. & Todd, W. D. (Eds.). (1988). *Complete guide to pregnancy.* New York: Crown.

Tashakkori, A. and Thomson, V. D. (1994). Racial differences in self-perception and locus of control during adolescence and early adulthood. *Genetic, Social and Psychological Monographs, 120,* 135–152.

Task Force (1976). *The walkabout.* Bloomington, IN: Phi Delta Kappa.

Taub, D. D. & Blinde, E. M. (1992). Eating disorders among adolescent female athletes: Influence of athletic participation and sport team membership. *Adolescence, 27*(108), 833–848.

Taub, H. (1975). Effects of coding cues upon short-term memory. *Developmental Psychology, 11,* 254.

Taylor, R. D., Casten, R., Flickinger, S. M., Roberts, D., & Fulmore, C. D. (1994). Explaining the school performance of African-American adolescents. *Journal of Research on Adolescence, 4,*(1), 21–44.

Tedesco, L. & Gaier, E. (1988). Friendship bonds in adolescence. *Adolescence, 89,* 127–136.

Terman, L. M. (1925). *Genetic studies of genius.* Stanford, CA: Stanford University Press.

Thomas, A. (1981). Current trends in developmental theory. *American Journal of Orthopsychiatry, 51,* 580–609.

Thomas, A. & Chess, S. (1977). *Temperament.* New York: Brunner/Mazel.

Thomas, A., Chess, S., & Birch, H. (1970). The origin of personality. *Scientific American, 223,* 102–109.

Thomas, J. & Datan, N. (1983). *Change and diversity in grandparenting experience.* Paper presented at the Annual Convention of the American Psychological Association.

Thomas, R. (1992). *Comparing theories of child development.* Belmont, CA: Wadsworth.

Tiedt, P. & Tiedt, I. (1990). *Multicultural teaching.* Boston: Allyn and Bacon.

Timiras, R. S. (1972). *Developmental physiology and aging.* New York: Macmillan.

Tishler, C. (1981). Adolescent suicide attempts: Some significant factors. *Suicide and Life Threatening Behavior, 11*(2), 86–92.

Tobin, J., Wu, D., & Davidson, D. (1989). How three key countries shape their children. *World Monitor,* April, 36–45.

Todd, J., Friedman, A., & Karinki, P. (1990). Women growing stronger with age: The effect of status in the U.S. and Kenya. *Psychology of Women Quarterly, 14,* 567–577.

Toffler, A. (1970). *Future shock.* New York: Bantam Books.

Toffler, A. (1984). *The third wave.* New York: Bantam Books.

Toolan, J. (1975). Depression in adolescents. In J. Howell (Ed.), *Modern perspectives in adolescent psychiatry.* New York: Brunner/Mazel.

Torgersen, A. M. (1982). Genetic factors in temperamental individuality: A longitudinal study of same-sexed twins from two months to six years of age. *Journal of the American Academy of Child Psychiatry, 20,* 702–711.

Torrens, P. R. (1985). Current status of hospice programs. In P. R. Torrens (Ed.), *Hospice programs and public policy* (pp. 35–59). Chicago, IL: American Hospital Publishing.

Traupmann, J., Peterson, R., Utne, M., & Hatfield, E. (1981). Measuring equity in intimate relations. *Applied Psychological Measurement, 5*(4), 467–480.

Travers, J. (1982). *The growing child.* Glenview, IL: Scott, Foresman.

Treffinger, D. J., Isaksen, S. G., & Firestien, R. (1983). Theoretical perspectives on creative learning and its facilitation: An overview. *Journal of Creative Behavior, 17*(1), 9–17.

Triandis, H. (1990). Theoretical concepts that are applicable to the analysis of ethnocentrism. In R. Brislin (Ed.), *Applied cross-cultural psychology.* Newbury Park, CA: Sage.

Troll, L. E. (1975). *Early and middle adulthood.* Monterey, CA: Brooks/Cole.

Tronick, E. (1989). Emotions and emotional communication in infants. *Child Development, 44,* 112–119.

Troumbley, P., Burman, K., Rinke, W., & Lenz, E. (1990). A comparison of the health risk, health status, self motivation, psychological symptomatic distress, and physical fitness of overweight and normal weight soldiers. *Military Medicine, 155*(9), 424–429.

Turner, J. S. & Helms, D. B. (1989). *Contemporary adulthood.* New York: Holt, Rinehart & Winston.

Tversky, A. & Kahneman, D. (1981). The framing of decisions and the psychology of choice. *Science, 211,* 453–458.

Twain, M. (1980). *Adventures of Tom Sawyer.* New York: American Library.

Twain, M. (1979). *Adventures of Huckleberry Finn.* New York: Dodd, Mead.

Twomey, L., Taylor, J., & Furiss, B. (1983). Age changes in the bone density and structure of the lumbar vertebral column. *Journal of Anatomy, 136,* 15–25.

U.S. Bureau of the Census. (1992). *Vital statistics.* Washington, DC: U.S. Government Printing Office.

U.S. Bureau of the Census. (1986). *Statistical abstract of the United States, 1986.* Washington, DC: U.S. Government Printing Office.

U.S. Bureau of the Census. (1991). *Statistical abstract of the United States, 1991.* Washington, DC: U.S. Government Printing Office.

U.S. Department of Health, Education, and Welfare. (1972). Pub. No. (HSM) 72-8134. Atlanta, GA: Centers for Disease Control.

U.S. Department of Health and Human Services. (1982). *Television and behavior: Ten years of scientific progress and implications for the eighties.* Washington, DC: U.S. Government Printing Office.

U.S. Department of Health and Human Services. (1991). Public Health Service, Centers for Disease Control. Premarital sexual intercourse among adolescent women—U.S., 1970–1988. *Morbidity & Mortality Weekly Report, 39*(51/52), 929–932.

U.S. Department of Labor, Bureau of Labor Statistics. (1991). *Child care arrangements for children under 5 years old with employed mothers.* Washington, DC: U.S. Government Printing Office.

U.S. National Center for Health Statistics. (1992). *Aging in the eighties.* Washington, DC: U.S. Government Printing Office.

U.S. National Center for Health Statistics. (1986). *Advance data from vital and health statistics, No. 125.* DHHS Pub. No. (PHS) 86–1250. Hyattsville, MD: Public Health Service.

U.S. National Center for Health Statistics. (1988). *Vital statistics of the United States, 1968–1987. Death rates by age, race, sex—5 and 10 year age groupings.* Washington, DC: U.S. Government Printing Office.

Uhlenberg, P., Cooney, T., & Boyd, R. (1990). Divorce for women after midlife. *Journals of Gerontology, 45,* 3–11.

Unger, R. (1979). Toward a redefinition of sex and gender. *American Psychologist, 34,* 1085–1094.

Vaillant, G. (1977). *Adaptation to life.* Boston: Little, Brown.

VanderMay, B. J. & Neff, R. L. (1982). Adult child incest: A review of research and treatment. *Adolescence, 17*(68), 717–735.

VanderZanden, J. (1989). *Human development* (4th ed.). New York: Knopf.

Van Gennep, A. [1909] (1960). *The rites of passage.* (M. Vizedom & G. Caffee, Trans.) Chicago: The Univ. of Chicago Press.

vanLear, C. & Zietlow, P. H. (1990). Toward a contingency approach to marital interaction: An empirical integration of three approaches. *Communication Monographs, 57*(3), 202–218.

vanWilkinson, W. (1989). The influence of lifestyles on the patterns and practices of alcohol use among South Texas Mexican Americans. *Hispanic Journal of Behavioral Sciences, 11*(4), 354–365.

Vaughan, V. & Litt, I. (1990). *Child and adolescent development: Clinical implications.* Philadelphia, PA: W. B. Saunders.

Vaughn, B., Stevenson-Hinde, J., Waters, E., Kotsaftis, A., Lefever, G., Shouldice, A., Trudel, M., & Belsky, J. (1992). Attachment security and temperament in infancy and early childhood: Some conceptual clarification. *Developmental Psychology, 28,* 463–473.

Veatch, R. M. (1981). *A theory of medical ethics.* New York: Basic Books.

Veatch, R. M. (1984). Brain death. In J. Schneidman (Ed.), *Death: Current perspectives* (3rd ed.). Mountain View, CA: Mayfield.

Verbrugge, L. M. (1979). Marital status and health. *Journal of Marriage and the Family, 41,* 267–285.

Vigil, J. D. (1988). *Barrio gangs: Street life and identity in southern California.* Austin: University of Texas Press.

Vygotsky, L. S. (1962). *Thought and language.* Cambridge, MA: MIT Press.

Vygotsky, L. S. (1978). *Mind in society.* Cambridge, MA: Harvard University Press.

Vygotsky, L. S. (1981). The development of higher forms of attention in childhood. In J. V. Wertsch (Ed.), *The concept of activity in Soviet psychology* (pp. 189–240). Armonk, NY: Sharpe.

Wagner, C. (1980). Sexuality of American adolescents. *Adolescence, 15*(59), 567–580.

Waldholz, M. (1992). Scientists near the end of race to discover a breast-cancer gene. *The Wall Street Journal,* December 11.

Waldrop, J. (1990, December). You'll know it's the 21st century when . . . *American Demographics,* pp. 23–27.

Walker, L. & Taylor, J. (1991). Family interaction and the development of moral reasoning. *Child Development, 62,* 264–283.

Walker, L. S. & Greene, J. W. (1987). Negative life events, psychosocial resources, and psychophysiological symptoms in adolescents. *Journal of Clinical Child Psychology, 16*(1), 29–36.

Wallace, M. (1989). Brave new workplace: Technology and work in the new economy. *Work and Occupations, 16*(4), 363–392.

Wallach, M. A. & Kogan, N. (1965). *Modes of thinking in young children.* New York: Holt, Rinehart & Winston.

Wallerstein, J. & Blakeslee, S. (1989). *Second chances: Men, women and children. Decade after divorce.* New York: Ticknor & Fields.

Walsh, M. (1992). *Moving to nowhere.* New York: Auburn House.

Walsh, R. (1989). Premarital sex among teenagers and young adults. In K. McKinney & S. Sprecher (Eds.), *Human sexuality: The societal and interpersonal context.* Norwood, NJ: Ablex.

Walther, R. R. & Harber, L. C. (1984). Expected skin complaints of the geriatric patient. *Geriatrics, 39,* 67.

Warabi, T., Kase, M., & Kato, T. (1984). Effect of aging on the accuracy of visually guided saccadic eye movement. *Annals of Neurology, 16,* 449–454.

Washington, A. E., Arno, P. S., & Brooks, M. A. (1986). The economic cost of pelvic inflammatory disease. *Journal of the American Medical Association, 225*(13), 1021–1033.

Wasow, M. & Loeb, M. B. (1979). Sexuality in nursing homes. *Journal of the American Geriatric Society, 28*(2), 73–79.

Watson, J. (1924). *Behaviorism.* New York: Norton.

Watson, J. (1968). *The double helix.* New York: Atheneum Press.

Weber, M. (1904). *The protestant ethic and the spirit of capitalism.* New York: Charles Scribner's Sons.

Wechsler, D. (1955). *Manual for the Wechsler adult intelligence test.* New York: Psychological Corp.

Wechsler, D. (1958). *The measurement and appraisal of adult intelligence.* Baltimore: Williams & Wilkins.

Weeks, D. (1989). Death education for aspiring physicians, teachers, and the funeral directors. *Death Studies, 13,* 17–24.

Weiner, B. (1990). History of motivational research in education. *Journal of Educational Psychology, 82,* 616–622.

Weiner, I. B. (1970). *Psychological disturbances in adolescence.* New York: Wiley Interscience.

Weinrich, J. D. (1987). A new sociobiological theory of homosexuality applicable to societies with universal marriage. *Ethology and Sociobiology, 8*(1), 37–47.

Weis, L., Farrar, E., & Petrie, H. (1989). *Dropouts from school: Issues, dilemmas, and solutions.* Albany: State University of New York Press.

Weisman, M. (1974). The epidemiology of suicide attempts, 1960–1971. *Archives of General Psychiatry, 30,* 737–746.

Weitzman, B., Knickman, J., & Shinn, M. (1990). Pathways to homelessness among New York City families. *Journal of Social Issues, 46*(4), 125–140.

Weitzman, L. J. (1985). *The divorce revolution: The unexpected social and economic consequences for women and children in America.* New York: Macmillan.

Werner, E. (1991). Children of the Garden Island. In N. Lauter-Klatell (Ed.), *Readings in child development.* Mountain View, CA: Mayfield.

Wertheimer, M. (1962). Psychomotor coordination of auditory-visual space at birth. *Science,* 134.

Wertsch, J. (1985). *Vygotsky and the growth of mind.* Cambridge, MA: Harvard Univ. Press.

Wertsch, J. V. & Tulviste, P. (1992). L. S. Vygotsky and contemporary developmental psychology. *Developmental Psychology, 28*(4), 548–557.

Westoff, C. F., Calot, G., & Foster, A. D. (1983). Teenage fertility in developed nations. *Family Planning Perspectives, 15,* 105.

Whisett, D. & Land, H. (1992). Role strain, coping and marital satisfaction of stepparents. *Families in Society: The Journal of Contemporary Human Services,* 79–91.

White, H. C. (1974). Self-poisoning in adolescents. *British Journal of Psychiatry, 124,* 24–35.

White, L. (1992). The effect of parental divorce and remarriage on parental support for adult children. *Journal of Family Issues, 13*(2), 234–250.

White, L. & Reidmann, A. (1992). *Social Forces, 71*(1), 85–102.

White, N. & Cunningham, W. R. (1988). Is terminal drop pervasive or specific? *Journals of Gerontology, 43*(6), 141–144.

Whitehead, A. & Mathews, A. (1986). Factors related to successful outcome in the treatment of sexually unresponsive women. *Psychological Medicine, 16*(2), 373–378.

Wilkinson, K. & Isreal, G. (1984). Suicide and rurality in urban society. *Suicide and Life Threatening Behavior, 14*(3), 187–200.

Will, J., Self, P., & Datan, N. (1976). Maternal behavior and perceived sex of infant. *American Journal of Orthopsychiatry, 46,* 135–139.

Williams, K. & Bird, M. (1992). The aging mover: A preliminary report on constraints to action. *International Journal of Aging and Human Development, 34*(4), 271–297.

Williams, L. (1989, July 21). Teens feel having sex is their own right. *The New York Times,* 13.

Williamson, J. B., Munley, A., & Evans, L. (1980). *Aging and society: An introduction to social gerontology.* New York: Holt, Rinehart & Winston.

Willis, S. & Nesselroade, C. (1990). Long-term effects of fluid ability training in old-old age. *Developmental Psychology, 26*(6), 905–910.

Willis, S. & Schaie, K. W. (1986). Training the elderly on the ability factors of spatial orientation and inductive reasoning. *Psychology and Aging, 1*(3), 239–247.

Wilson, B. F. & Clarke, S. C. (1992). Remarriages: A demographic profile. *Journal of Family Issues, 13*(2), 123–141.

Wilson, E. O. (1978). *Sociobiology.* Cambridge, MA: Harvard University Press.

Wilson, H. S. & Kneisl, C. (1979). *Psychiatric nursing.* Menlo Park, CA: Addison-Wesley.

Wilson, J. & Herrnstein, R. (1985). *Crime and human nature.* New York: Simon & Schuster.

Wilson, P. (1987). Psychoanalytic therapy and the young adolescent. *Bulletin of the Anna Freud Centre, 10*(1), 51–79.

Wing, S. (1992). The challenge of multiculturalism. *American Counselor,* 6–14.

Wingerson, L. *Mapping our genes.* (1990). New York: Plume.

Woititz, J. (1990). *Adult children of alcoholics.* Lexington, MA: Health Communications, Inc.

Wolf, M. & Dickinson, D. (1985). From oral to written language: Transitions in the school years. In Jean B. Gleason (Ed.), *The development of language.* Columbus: Merrill.

Wolfson, M. (1989). *A review of the literature on feminist psychology.* Unpublished manuscript, Boston College, Chestnut Hill, MA.

Wolpert, L. (1991). *The triumph of the embryo.* New York: Oxford.

Woodruff-Pak, D. (1988). *Psychology and aging.* Englewood Cliffs, NJ: Prentice-Hall.

Woodward, A., Markman, E., & Fitzsimmons, C. (1994). Rapid word learning in 13- and 18-month-olds. *Developmental Psychology, 30*(4), 553–566.

Wortman, C. & Silver, R. (1989). The myths of coping with loss. *Journal of Consulting and Clinical Psychology, 57,* 349–357.

Wyatt, G. (1989). Reexamining factors predicting Afro-American and White American women's age at first coitus. *Archives of Sexual Behavior, 18*(4), 271–297.

Wyers, N. (1987). Homosexuality in the family: Lesbian and gay spouses. *Social Work, 32,* 143–148.

Wynne, E. (1988, February). Balancing character development and academics in the elementary school. *Phi Delta Kappan,* 424–426.

Yan, W. & Gaier, E. L. (1994). Causal attributions for college success and failure. *Journal of Cross-Cultural Psychology, 25*(1), 146–158.

Yao, E. L. (1988, November). Working effectively with Asian immigrant parents. *Phi Delta Kappan,* 223–225.

Yogman, M. (1982). Development of the father-infant relationship. In H. Fitzgerald, B. Lester, & M. Yogman (Eds.), *Theory and research in behavioral pediatrics.* New York: Plenum.

Youngs, B. (1991). *The 6 vital ingredients of self-esteem and how to develop them in your child.* New York: Rawson Associates.

Youniss, J. & Smollar, J. (1985). Parent-adolescent relations in adolescents whose parents are divorced. *Journal of Early Adolescence, 5*(1), 129–144.

Zepeda, M. (1986). *Early caregiving in a Mexican origin population.* Paper presented at the International Conference on Infant Studies, Los Angeles.

Zigler, E. & Hall, N. (1989). Day care and its effects on children: An overview for pediatric professionals. *Annual Progress in Child Psychiatry and Child Development,* 543–560.

Zigler, E. & Lang, M. (1991). *Child care choices: Balancing the needs of children, family, and society.* New York: The Free Press.

Zigler, E. & Muenchow, S. (1992). *Head Start.* New York: Crown.

Zigler, E. & Styfco, S. (1994). Head Start: Criticisms in a constructive context. *American Psychologist, 49*(2), 127–132.

Zoja, L. (1984). Sucht als unbewusster Versuch zur initiation, Teil I. (Addiction as an unconscious attempt toward initiation: I.) *Analyische Psychologie, 15*(2), 110–115.

Credits

Figures and Tables

Chapter 1

Figures 1.1 and 1.2 From John F. Travers, *The Growing Child.* Scott, Foresman and Company, Glenview, Ill., 1982. Reprinted by permission of the author. **Table 1.1** From John Dacey, *Adolescents Today,* 3d ed. Scott, Foresman and Company, Glenview, Ill., 1986. Reprinted by permission of the author.

Chapter 2

Table 2.1 From John Dacey, *Adolescents Today,* 3d ed. Scott, Foresman and Company, Glenview, Ill., 1986. Reprinted by permission of the author. **Figure 2.1** Source: Data for diagram based on Hierarchy of Needs, in "A Theory of Human Motivation" in *Motivation and Personality,* 2d edition, by Abraham H. Maslow, 1970.

Chapter 3

Tables 3.1, 3.2, and 3.4; Figures 3.1, 3.2, 3.3, and 3.6 From John F. Travers, *The Growing Child.* Scott, Foresman and Company, Glenview, Ill., 1982. Reprinted by permission of the author. **Figure 3.7** From Larue Allen and John W. Santrock, *Psychology, The Contexts of Behavior.* Copyright © 1993 Wm. C. Brown Communications, Inc., Dubuque, Iowa. All Rights Reserved. Reprinted by permission.

Chapter 4

Figure 4.5 Modified from K. L. Moore and T. V. N. Persaud, *The Developing Human: Clinically Oriented Embryology,* 5th ed. Copyright © 1993 W. B. Saunders Company, Philadelphia, PA. Reprinted by permission.

Chapter 5

Tables 5.1, 5.3, and 5.4 From John F. Travers, *The Growing Child.* Scott, Foresman and Company, Glenview, Ill., 1982. Reprinted by permission of the author. **Figure 5.1** From *The Conscious Brain* by Steven Rose. Copyright © 1973 by Steven Rose. Reprinted by permission of Alfred A. Knopf, Inc.

Chapter 7

Table 7.1; Figures 7.1 and 7.3 From John F. Travers, *The Growing Child.* Scott, Foresman and Company, Glenview, Ill.,

1982. Reprinted by permission of the author. **Figure 7.4** From John W. Santrock and Steve R. Yussen, *Child Development: An Introduction,* 4th ed. Copyright © 1989 Wm. C. Brown Communications, Inc., Dubuque, Iowa. All Rights Reserved. Reprinted by permission.

Chapter 9

Table 9.1; Figures 9.1 and 9.2 From John F. Travers, *The Growing Child.* Scott, Foresman and Company, Glenview, Ill., 1982. Reprinted by permission of the author.

Chapter 13

Figure 13.1 Source: From U.S. Department of Health and Human Services, Public Health Service, Centers for Disease Control, Center for Infectious Diseases, Division HIV/AIDS, "HIV/AIDS Surveillance," Atlanta, Ga., September 1990. **Figure 13.2** Reprinted courtesy of *The Boston Globe.* **Figure 13.4** Source: Office of Technology Assessment, 1991, based on U.S. Department of Health and Human Services, Public Health Service, Centers for Disease Control, National Center for Health Statistics, Division of Vital Statistics, *Vital Statistics of the United States, Volume 1: Natality.* U.S. Government Printing Office, Washington, D.C., various years. **Figure 13.5** Source: Youth Indicators, Trends in the Well-Being of American Youth. U.S. Government Printing Office, Washington, D.C., 1993.

Chapter 16

Table 16.2 From John Dacey, *Adult Development.* Scott, Foresman and Company, Glenview, Ill., 1982. Reprinted by permission of the author. **Figure 16.1** From *The Seasons of a Man's Life* by Daniel J. Levinson. Copyright © 1978 by Daniel J. Levinson. Reprinted by permission of Alfred A. Knopf, Inc.

Chapter 17

Figure 17.1 Source: Data from L. L. Langley, *Physiology of Man,* 4th edition. Van Nostrand Reinhold, 1971. **Figure 17.2** Source: From J. L. Horn, "Remodeling Old Models of Intelligence" in *Handbook of Intelligence: Theories, Measurements, and Applications,* edited by B. B. Wolman, Wiley & Sons, New York, 1985. **Figure 17.3** Source: Data from H. C. Lehman, *Age and Achievement,*

Princeton University Press, Princeton, N.J., 1953. **Figure 17.4** Source: Data from W. Dennis, "Creative Productivity Between 20 and 80 Years" in *Journal of Gerontology* 21:1–8, 1966.

Chapter 18

Figure 18.1 Source: U.S. Bureau of the Census. **Figure 18.2** From *The Seasons of a Man's Life* by Daniel J. Levinson. Copyright © 1978 by Daniel J. Levinson. Reprinted by permission of Alfred A. Knopf, Inc. **Figure 18.4** From R. McCrae and P. Costa, Jr., *Emerging Lives, Enduring Disposition: Personality in Adulthood.* Copyright © 1984 Little, Brown and Company, Boston, MA. Reprinted by permission of the authors.

Chapter 19

Figure 19.1 Source: Social Security Administration. **Figure 19.2** Reprinted with the permission of Simon & Schuster, Inc. from *Developmental Physiology and Aging* by Paola S. Timiras. Copyright © 1972 P. S. Timiras.

Chapter 20

Figure 20.1 From Robert Havighurst, "Perceived Life Space" in *Contributions to Human Development* 3:93–112 (1963). Copyright © 1963 S. Karger AG, Basel, Switzerland. Reprinted by permission of the publisher.

Chapter 21

Figure 21.1 Source: From E. Kübler-Ross, *On Death and Dying,* Macmillan, New York, 1969.

Photos

Part Openers

Part I: © H. Armstrong Roberts; **Part II and Part III:** © Laura Dwight; **Part IV:** © H. Armstrong Roberts; **Part V:** © Erika Stone/Photo Researchers, Inc.; **Part VI:** © Cleo/PhotoEdit; **Part VII:** © Erika Stone/ Photo Researchers, Inc.; **Part VIII:** © H. Armstrong Roberts; **Part IX:** © D&I MacDonald/PhotoEdit

Chapter 1

p. 3, p. 5 a–e and p. 9: The Bettmann Archive; **p. 10 top:** © David Hurn/Magnum

Photos; **p. 10 bottom:** © W. Marc Bernsaw/The Image Works; **p. 12:** © Jean-Claude Lejeune

Chapter 2

p. 26: The Bettman Archive; **p. 27:** © Elizabeth Crews/The Image Works; **p. 30:** The Bettmann Archive; **p. 32:** © 1994 Ulrike Welsch; **p. 36:** © Dr. Andrew Schwebel; **p. 41:** © Christopher Johnson/Stock Boston

Chapter 3

p. 50: © Spencer Grant/Picture Cube; **p. 51 top:** © Walter Dawn/Photo Researchers, Inc.; **p. 51 bottom:** © SIU/Photo Researchers Inc.; **p. 61:** The Granger Collection; **p. 64:** © Alan Carey/The Image Works

Chapter 4

p. 73: © Nancy D. McKenna/Photo Researchers, Inc.; **p. 76 top:** © D. W. Fawcett/D. Phillips/Photo Researchers, Inc.; **p. 76 bottom:** © Omikron/Photo Researchers, Inc.; **p. 77 top:** © Dr. C. Reather/Photo Researchers, Inc.; **p. 77 bottom and p. 78:** © Petit Format/Nestle/Science Source/Photo Researchers, Inc.; **p. 83 top:** © Michael J. O'Koniewski/Image Works; **p. 83 middle:** Courtesy of A. P. Streissguth, H. M. Barr, and D. C. Martin (1984); **p. 83 bottom:** © John Griffin/The Image Works; **p. 87:** © Nancy D. McKenna/Photo Researchers, Inc.; **p. 92:** © H. Armstrong Roberts; **p. 94:** © Eric Roth/The Picture Cube

Chapter 5

p. 101: © Tim Davis/Photo Researchers, Inc.; **p. 105:** Courtesy Tiffany Field; **p. 107, p. 109, p. 113, and p. 118:** Author provided; **Figure 5.2:** William Vandivert, *Scientific American,* April 1960; **p. 119:** © Barbara Rios/Photo Researchers, Inc.

Chapter 6

p. 131: © Suzanne Szasz/Photo Researchers, Inc.; **p. 133:** © 1994 Ulrike Welsch; **p. 138:** © Elizabeth Crews/The Image Works; **p. 141:** © Janice Fullman/The Picture Cube; **p. 144:** © Sandra Johnson/The Picture Cube; **p. 145:** © Marjorie Nichols/The Picture Cube; **p. 147:** © Alan Carey/The Image Works; **p. 150:** © Julie O'Neil/The Picture Cube

Chapter 7

p. 159: © Myrleen Ferguson/PhotoEdit; **p. 160:** © Elizabeth Crews/The Image Works; **p. 163:** Author provided; **p. 165:** © Tony Freeman/PhotoEdit; **p. 166:** © Henry Horenstein/The Picture Cube; **p. 167:** © Sharon L. Fox/The Picture Cube; **p. 168:** © Carol Palmer/The Picture Cube; **p. 175:** © Robert Knowles/Black Star; **p. 177:** © Skjold Photographs

Chapter 8

p. 187: © Pedro Coll/The Stock Market;

p. 188: © Carol Palmer/The Picture Cube; **p. 189:** © Steve Takatsuno/The Picture Cube; **p. 197:** © Erika Stone/Photo Researchers, Inc.; **p. 198 left:** © Nancy Lutz/The Picture Cube; **p. 198 right:** © Carol Palmer/The Picture Cube; **p. 202:** © Ulrike Welsch/ Photo Researchers, Inc.; **p. 205 top:** © Linda Benedict-John/The Picture Cube; **p. 205 bottom:** © Erika Stone/Photo Researchers, Inc.; **p. 207:** © Elizabeth Crews/The Image Works; **p. 210:** © Laura Dwight

Chapter 9

p. 217: © Myrleen Ferguson/PhotoEdit; **p. 221:** © Alan Carey/The Image Works; **p. 222:** © Mimi Forsyth/Monkmeyer Press; **p. 226:** © James Carroll; **p. 231 left:** © Michael Siluk; **p. 231 right:** © Myrleen Ferguson/PhotoEdit; **p. 236:** © Roberta Hershenson/Photo Researchers, Inc.; **p. 241:** Author provided

Chapter 10

p. 247: © Robert Brenner/PhotoEdit; **p. 249:** © Felicia Martinez/PhotoEdit; **p. 250:** © 1994 Ulrike Welsch; **p. 254:** Meri Hantschens-Kitchens/The Picture Cube; **p. 256:** © Elizabeth Crews/The Image Works; **p. 258:** © Jack Spratt/The Image Works; **p. 261:** © Michael Siluk; **p. 269:** © Bob Kalman/The Image Works; **p. 270:** © James L. Shaffer

Chapter 11

p. 280: © Elizabeth Crews/The Image Works; **p. 282:** © Giraudon/Art Resource; **p. 283:** Archives of the History of American Psychology, The University of Akron; **p. 286:** University of Chicago; **p. 288:** © Archiv/Photo Researchers, Inc.; **p. 289:** © Mark Antman/The Image Works; **p. 293:** © 1994 Ulrike Welsch; **p. 294:** © Thelma Shumsky/The Image Works; **p. 296:** © Margaret Thompson/The Picture Cube

Chapter 12

p. 307: © Toni Michaels; **p. 311:** © Susan Rosenberg/Photo Researchers, Inc.; **p. 313:** © James Carroll; **p. 315:** © Spencer Grant/Photo Researchers, Inc.; **p. 317:** © Jean-Claude Lejeune; **p. 318:** The Granger Collection

Chapter 13

p. 327: Cleo Freelance Photography; **p. 332:** © Robert Eckert/The Picture Cube; **p. 338:** © Rohn Engh/The Image Works; **p. 339:** © John Griffin/The Image Works; **p. 344:** © Susan Kuklin/Photo Researchers, Inc.; **p. 350:** © Phil McCarten/PhotoEdit

Chapter 14

p. 359: © Martin Etter/Anthro Photo; **p. 362 and 363:** © Ellis Herwig/The Picture Cube; **p. 364:** © Mark Antman/The Image Works; **p. 366:** © Irven DeVore/Anthro Photo; **p. 368:** © Bob Daemmrich/The Image

Works; **p. 369 left:** © AP/Wide World; · **p. 369 right:** © Fayne R. Phillips/The Picture Cube; **p. 370 and p. 371:** © Alan Carey/The Image Works

Chapter 15

p. 388: © Toni Michaels; **p. 389:** © Eric Breitenbach/The Picture Cube; **p. 391:** © Thelma Shumsky/The Image Works; **p. 392:** © Therese Frare/The Picture Cube; **p. 393:** © Bob Kalman/The Image Works; **p. 394:** © Alan Carey/The Image Works; **p. 400:** © Michael Siluk; **p. 404:** © Toni Michaels

Chapter 16

p. 410: © Bobbi Carrey Collection/The Picture Cube; **p. 413:** AP/Wide World; **p. 415:** © Dion Ogust/The Image Works; **p. 417:** © Toni Michaels; **p. 420:** © 1994 Ulrike Welsch; **p. 424:** © Toni Michaels; **p. 427:** © Charles Gatewood/The Image Works

Chapter 17

p. 437: © Ellis Herwig/The Picture Cube; **p. 438:** © Toni Michaels; **p. 442:** © Mikki Ansin/The Picture Cube; **p. 443:** Courtesy News & Publication Service, Stanford University; **p. 446:** The Bettmann Archive; **p. 450:** © Ellis Herwig/The Picture Cube

Chapter 18

p. 456: © 1994 Ulrike Welsch; **p. 457:** © Elizabeth Crews/The Image Works; **p. 465:** © Toni Michaels; **p. 469:** © Toni Michaels/The Image Works; **p. 471:** © Nita Winter/The Image Works; **p. 477:** © Mark Antman/The Image Works

Chapter 19

p. 483: © Topham/The Image Works; **p. 485:** © F. B. Grunzweig/Photo Researchers, Inc.; **Figures 19.3 and 19.4:** University of Chicago Press; **p. 492:** © Toni Michaels; **p. 494:** © Alan Carey/The Image Works; **p. 498, p. 501, and p. 504:** © Toni Michaels

Chapter 20

p. 510: © Toni Michaels; **p. 513:** © Frank Siteman/The Picture Cube; **p. 515:** © Toni Michaels; **p. 523 left:** © Frank Siteman/The Picture Cube; **p. 523 right:** © Toni Michaels; **p. 525:** The Museum of Modern Art Film Stills Archive

Chapter 21

p. 530: The Granger Collection; **p. 531:** © Toni Michaels; **p. 533:** © William Thompson/The Picture Cube; **p. 535:** © Michael J. Okoniewski/The Image Works; **p. 540:** © Alan Carey/The Image Works; **p. 543:** © Toni Michaels/The Image Works; **p. 545:** © Alan Carey/The Image Works; **p. 546 and 547:** © Keystone/The Image Works

Color Plates

1.1: © David Woods/The Stock Market; **1.2:** © David M. Grossman/Photo Researchers, Inc.; **1.3:** © Elizabeth Hathon/The Stock Market; **1.4:** © Laura Dwight; **2.1:** © Suzanne Szasz/Photo Researchers, Inc.; **2.2:** © Michael Newman/PhotoEdit; **2.3:** © Laura Dwight; **2.4:** © Michael Newman/PhotoEdit; **3.1, 3.2, and 3.3:** © Laura Dwight; **3.4:** © Michael Siluk; **4.1:** © Margaret Miller/Photo Researchers, Inc.; **4.2:** © Ariel Skelley/The Stock Market; **4.3:** © Michael Siluk; **4.4:** © Bryan Peterson/The Stock Market; **5.1:** © Tony Freeman/PhotoEdit; **5.2:** © Bill Aron/PhotoEdit; **5.3:** © Jose Carrillo/PhotoEdit; **5.4:** © Mark Richards/PhotoEdit; **6.1:** © Elena Rooraid/PhotoEdit; **6.2:** © Bill Bachman/Photo Researchers, Inc.; **6.3:** © George Holton/Photo Researchers, Inc.; **6.4:** © Paul Conklin/PhotoEdit; **7.1:** © Diane Rawson/Photo Researchers, Inc.; **7.2:** © M. Roessler/H. Armstrong Roberts; **7.3:** © Gary A. Conner/PhotoEdit; **7.4:** © Tony Freeman/PhotoEdit; **8.1:** © Tony Freeman/PhotoEdit; **8.2:** © Ulrike Welsch/PhotoEdit; **8.3:** © Amy C. Etra/PhotoEdit

Name Index

Subject Index